SOCIAL PSYCHOLOGY

SOCIAL PSYCHOLOGY

Second Edition

Sharon S. Brehm

State University of New York
at Binghamton

Saul M. Kassin

Williams College

Houghton Mifflin Company   BOSTON   TORONTO

DALLAS   GENEVA, ILLINOIS   PALO ALTO   PRINCETON, NEW JERSEY

This book is dedicated to those who motivated us to seek knowledge, love ideas, and teach others what we have learned.

Jack W. Brehm	Charles A. Lowe
Philip Costanzo	Arthur S. Reber
Edward E. Jones	Lawrence S. Wrightsman

Education—whether its object be children or adults, individuals or an entire people, or even oneself—consists in creating motives.
Simone Weil

Senior Sponsoring Editor   Michael DeRocco
Senior Development Editor   Susan Granoff
Project Editor   Christina Horn
Electronic Production Specialist   Jeff Zabin
Production/Design Coordinator   Patricia Mahtani/Jill Haber
Senior Manufacturing Coordinator   Marie Barnes
Marketing Manager   Diane McOscar

COVER CREDIT

Artist: Wladyslaw Garnik, Wroclaw, Poland. Porcelain Sculpture, 1991. Courtesy The Clay Studio, Philadelphia, Pa.
Photo: John Carlano.
Design: Len Massiglia.

(Credits continue following the References.)

Printed in the U.S.A.

Library of Congress Catalog Card Number: 92-72369

ISBN
Student text: 0-395-53804-1
Examination text: 0-395-63832-1

23456789-DC-96 95 94 93

Brief Contents

Contents

Preface

Three years ago, with fingers crossed, we launched the first edition of *Social Psychology*. We hoped that its combination of serious scholarship, organizational clarity, and lively writing would appeal to both instructors and students. To our delight, the book was well received. In preparing the second edition, we have reconsidered every sentence, attended to advice from many readers, and incorporated important new information from our remarkably dynamic discipline. The result, we believe, is a textbook that is uniquely informative *and* accessible.

MEETING THE CHALLENGE: FEATURES OF THE SECOND EDITION

The major challenge for any revision is to be up-to-date. But what does "up-to-date" really mean? Obviously, we must describe recent advances in theory and research, and we do—30 percent of our references are new to this edition. More important, current work is not simply cited, but integrated into the conceptual framework of each chapter. Topics new to this edition include:

- meta-analysis (Chapter 1).
- cognitive factors that influence self-reports (Chapter 1).
- alcoholism and suicide as escapes from the self (Chapter 1).
- cognitive heuristics (Chapter 3).
- the overconfidence effect in social perception (Chapter 3).
- jealousy (Chapter 6).
- effects of cohabitation on marital quality (Chapter 6).
- homelessness (Chapter 7).
- testosterone and violence (Chapter 8).
- norm salience and conformity (Chapter 9).
- effects of age, sex, and culture on conformity (Chapter 9).
- the theory of planned behavior (Chapter 10).
- the process of joining a group (Chapter 11).
- the intergroup public goods paradigm (Chapter 11).
- leadership by women and minorities (Chapter 13).
- effects of subliminal self-help tapes (Chapter 13).
- the role of negative affectivity in stress and coping (Chapter 14).
- health effects of talking or writing about a traumatic event (Chapter 14).

Extensive new material is also included in our discussion of:

- nonverbal communication (Chapter 3).
- cultural institutions that foster gender stereotypes (Chapter 4).

- the sociobiology of attraction (Chapter 5), helping (Chapter 7), and aggression (Chapter 8).
- the benefits of physical attractiveness (Chapter 5).
- AIDS (Chapters 6 and 14).
- rape (Chapters 6, 8, and 14).
- altruism (Chapter 7).
- the weapons effect (Chapter 8).
- groupthink (Chapter 11).
- children as witnesses in sex-abuse cases (Chapter 12).
- performance appraisals in the work setting (Chapter 13).
- stressful effects of natural disasters and combat experience (Chapter 14).

As before, we also anchor this text in the issues and events of our time. Since the first edition was published, much has happened, including the Persian Gulf War, the collapse of the Soviet Union and the end of the Cold War, Anita Hill's testimony in the confirmation hearings of Clarence Thomas, the trial of William Kennedy Smith, Magic Johnson's AIDS disclosure, the release of Terry Anderson and other hostages held in Lebanon, the civil war in Yugoslavia, the beating of Rodney King, and the Los Angeles riots. Throughout this text, we use these and other contemporary events to illustrate the value of social psychology for understanding the world in which we live.

A third feature of this new edition is its increased coverage of multicultural issues. Cultural diversity is an important topic in social psychology as well as in our society. Here, we examine the relevant research in a number of areas. Notable examples include multicultural perspectives on the self (Chapter 2); cross-cultural comparisons of friendship (Chapter 6), love (Chapter 6), jealousy (Chapter 6), social responsibility (Chapter 7), and homicide (Chapter 8); and cultural influences on conformity (Chapter 9).

The up-to-date coverage of this edition has been achieved within the context of in-depth, comprehensive coverage of the discipline. We describe the full range of inquiry in social psychology: established "classics" as well as new arrivals, a variety of theoretical perspectives, and an array of methodological approaches. Moreover, as readers of the first edition have come to expect, we have not ducked controversy nor rushed to premature conclusions.

MAPPING THE TERRAIN: ORGANIZATION OF TOPICS

To explore effectively, one needs a good map. Without a clear perspective on the field, one of the great advantages of social psychology—its breadth—becomes a liability. Confronted with so many different topics, students can feel lost and overwhelmed. We seek to avoid this problem by providing a simple, sturdy structure for the book. After an introduction to the field and its research methods, the book is divided into four parts that flow naturally from one to another. We start with an internal focus on the perception of self and others (Part I), build outward to social interaction (Part II) and social influence (Part III), and conclude with applications (Part IV). This four-part structure helps students to see social psychology as a cohesive whole, to locate specific topics within a general framework, and to acquire a sense of cumulative learning.

Part I. Within each part, some of the chapters bear familiar titles; others do not. For example, no single chapter is devoted to social cognition. Instead, recent work on schemas, priming, memory, cognitive heuristics, and social categorization are described throughout Part I in chapters on the social self, perceiving persons, and perceiving groups. This last chapter offers a comprehensive look at stereotypes and prejudice, followed by a detailed discussion of two specific forms of discrimination—sexism and racism.

Part II. Ours was the first textbook to reflect the extraordinary growth of research on interpersonal attraction and intimate relationships by providing two separate chapters on these topics, a practice continued in this edition. These chapters present a uniquely comprehensive discussion that is of great interest to students. Part II also includes chapters on some of the best and worst aspects of human behavior: helping others and aggression.

Part III. The third part brings together various perspectives on social influence. Here are some of the gems of social psychology: an unusually vivid description of Milgram's obedience study in the chapter on conformity, a thorough integration of theory and research in the chapter on attitudes, and—in the chapter on social processes—a wide-ranging survey of phenomena such as mob violence, the exploitation of natural resources, and conflict escalation.

Part IV. Previous textbooks have taken various approaches to covering applied social psychology. Some texts do not devote any chapters to applied areas; others cover applications in one omnibus chapter; still others scatter a number of applied chapters throughout the book. Our approach is to illustrate the principles of social psychology in each and every chapter with vivid examples from history, sports, TV and film, literature, and current events. Then, in Part IV, we focus on three major areas: law, business, and health. This organization accomplishes two important objectives. First, we show how basic principles can be generalized and applied far beyond their research origins. Second, we take applied social psychology seriously as a valuable enterprise in its own right. We believe this two-track approach is particularly useful in expanding students' knowledge and understanding.

MAKING IT CLEAR: SPECIAL FEATURES TO HELP STUDENTS LEARN

This edition retains the "lean, clean" format that was praised in the first edition. Despite strong temptations to the contrary, we have inserted no boxes. All the text is, literally, *in the text*. This no-box format makes the book easier to read, prevents conceptual fragmentation, and keeps high-interest material in the body of each chapter.

We also continue to pay close attention to the process by which students learn. The writing style is clear and engaging, and each chapter provides a coherent, integrated presentation of major themes. Accessibility is further enhanced by various pedagogical devices:

- A *narrative preview* and a *chapter outline* beginning each chapter
- A *review summarizing major points* at the end of each chapter
- *Key terms* highlighted in the text, defined in the margin, and reprinted in an alphabetized *glossary* at the end of the book
- A full program of *tables, figures, photographs, and cartoons* carefully selected to summarize or illustrate material presented in the text
- *Detailed subject and author indexes*, along with an *extensive reference section* to assist in selecting additional materials for reading

PROVIDING HELP: ANCILLARIES

In keeping with this commitment to teaching effectiveness, *Social Psychology* is accompanied by a set of unusually helpful ancillary items.

- **Instructor's Resource Manual**   For each chapter of the text, the *Instructor's Resource Manual* includes an extended chapter outline, a set of learning objectives that are repeated in the *Study Guide* and used in the *Test Bank,* discussion topics, classroom exercises, handouts, and audiovisual resources. More than thirty new demonstrations and activities have been added.
- **Test Bank**   The *Test Bank* includes 125 multiple-choice questions for each chapter of the text. For each question, the corresponding learning objective, text page number, question type, and correct answer are noted.
- **Study Guide**   The *Study Guide* provides a complete review of each chapter in the text through the use of chapter outlines, learning objectives, fill-in-the-blank reviews of key terms, true-false items, and multiple-choice questions. The *Guide* provides an explanation of each incorrect answer to these questions as well as the correct answers.
- **Computerized Test Bank**   This computerized version of the *Test Bank* allows instructors to generate exams and to integrate their own test items with those on a disk.

ACKNOWLEDGMENTS

This textbook reflects the joint effort of a great many people. As always, we are indebted to an outstanding staff and production crew at Houghton Mifflin. We also want to thank Christopher Leone for his thorough revision of the *Instructor's Resource Manual, Test Bank,* and *Study Guide.*

For their comments and suggestions, we are deeply grateful to those individuals who reviewed various drafts of this book for the first or second edition, or both. Their perspective was invaluable in helping us figure out how to separate the vital wheat from the expendable chaff.

Lyn Y. Abramson, *University of Wisconsin, Madison*

Gina Agostinelli, *University of New Mexico*

Craig A. Anderson, *University of Missouri*

Michael L. Atkinson, *University of Western Ontario*

Robert S. Baron, *University of Iowa*

Dan Batson, *University of Kansas*

Jack W. Brehm, *University of Kansas*

Marilyn Brewer, *University of California, Los Angeles*

Jerry M. Burger, *University of Santa Clara*

Arnie Cann, *University of North Carolina*

Kenneth L. Dion, *University of Toronto*

Joan Fimbel DiGiovanni, *Western New England College*

Ed Donnerstein, *University of California, Santa Barbara*

John F. Dovidio, *Colgate University*

Karen Grover Duffy, *State University of New York, Geneseo*

Jacquelynne S. Eccles, *University of Colorado, Boulder*

Julie Felender, *San Diego State University*

Jeffrey D. Fisher, *University of Connecticut, Storrs*

Randy D. Fisher, *University of Central Florida*

Susan T. Fiske, *University of Massachusetts, Amherst*

Solomon M. Fulero, *Sinclair College*

Daniel Gilbert, *University of Texas, Austin*

Peter Glick, *Lawrence University*

Mary Alice Gordon, *Southern Methodist University*

Jeff Greenberg, *University of Arizona*

Martin S. Greenberg, *University of Pittsburgh*

Julia Glover Hall, *Drexel University*

Ruth T. Hannon, *Bridgewater State College*

Valerie P. Hans, *University of Delaware*

Robert B. Hays, *University of California, San Francisco*

Susan S. Hendrick, *Texas Tech University*

Miles Hewstone, *University of Bristol, England*

James L. Hilton, *University of Michigan*

B. Kent Houston, *University of Kansas*

L. Rowell Huesmann, *University of Illinois, Chicago*

Gene Indenbaum, *State University of New York at Farmingdale*

Donn L. Kaiser, *Southwest Missouri State University*

Martin F. Kaplan, *Northern Illinois University*

Christopher Leone, *University of North Florida*

Angela Lipsitz, *Northern Kentucky University*

David Lundgren, *University of Cincinnati*

Diane M. Mackie, *University of California, Santa Barbara*

Neil M. Malamuth, *University of California, Los Angeles*

Alan Marks, *University of Texas of the Permian Basin*

Susan E. Mickler, *Seton Hall University*

Rowland S. Miller, *Sam Houston State University*

Steven L. Neuberg, *Arizona State University*

Richard E. Petty, *Ohio State University*

Steven Prentice-Dunn, *University of Alabama*

Dean G. Pruitt, *State University of New York at Buffalo*

B. Taramanohar Rao, *Ferris State University*

Deborah R. Richardson, *University of Georgia*

Janet Morgan Riggs, *Gettysburg College*

Joan Rollins, *Rhode Island College*

Karen Rook, *University of California, Irvine*

Caryl Rusbult, *University of North Carolina, Chapel Hill*

Mark Schaller, *University of Montana*

Janet Ward Schofield, *University of Pittsburgh*

Robert Seaton, *College of DuPage*

David J. Senn, *Clemson University*

Jerry I. Shaw, *California State University, Northridge*

Steve Slane, *Cleveland State University*

Jeanne Smith, *University of Virginia*

Timothy W. Smith, *University of Utah*

Homer Stavely, *Keene State College*

Mary K. Stevenson, *Purdue University*

William B. Swann, Jr., *University of Texas, Austin*

Sarah Tanford, *Purdue University*

Abraham Tesser, *University of Georgia*

Rhoda Unger, *Montclair State College*
Russell Veitch, *Bowling Green State University*
Ann L. Weber, *University of North Carolina,*
    Asheville
Daniel M. Wegner, *Trinity University*

Russell H. Weigel, *Amherst College*
Gary L. Wells, *Iowa State University*
Ladd Wheeler, *University of Rochester*
David Wilder, *Rutgers University*
Max Zwanziger, *Central Washington University*

Finally, we each have a few words to say about some people who helped keep us reasonably sane during the writing of this revision. Sharon thanks her office staff, especially Anne McCarthy and Eugene Flood. Because they run such a tight ship, it was possible for her to survive having two full-time jobs at once. She also wants to express her appreciation to Carrie Pietrucho, whose skills as a library detective were equal to the chase of even the most obscure reference. Saul thanks his wife, Carol, for her continuing support and his children, Briana and Marc, for graciously donating some of their playtime with Dad. Both of us are especially grateful to our students for their thoughtful feedback on the first edition.

About the Authors

Sharon S. Brehm is Professor of Psychology and Dean of Harpur College of Arts and Sciences at the State University of New York at Binghamton. Born and raised in Roanoke, Virginia, she received her B.A. and Ph.D. from Duke University and completed an internship in clinical psychology at the University of Washington Medical Center in Seattle. Brehm was a faculty member at the University of Kansas for fifteen years. In 1981–1982, she spent her sabbatical in Paris as a Fulbright Senior Research Scholar. She also has been a visiting scholar in Germany and Italy. Her current research interests range from interpersonal attraction to public policy in higher education. In addition to numerous articles and chapters, Brehm has published eight books—including *The Application of Social Psychology to Clinical Practice*, a recognized classic in the field, and *Intimate Relationships*, a popular textbook now in its second edition.

Saul M. Kassin is Professor of Psychology at Williams College, Williamstown, Massachusetts. Born and raised in New York City, he graduated with a B.S. from Brooklyn College. After receiving a Ph.D. in personality and social psychology from the University of Connecticut, he spent one year at the University of Kansas and two years at Purdue University. In 1984–1985, he was awarded a U.S. Supreme Court Judicial Fellowship; in 1985–1986, he received a Research Fellowship in the Psychology-Law Program at Stanford University. Kassin is coauthor of *The American Jury on Trial: Psychological Perspectives* and has edited four other books. The author of numerous articles, he is on the editorial boards of *The Journal of Personality and Social Psychology* and *Law and Human Behavior*. His research interests are in social perception and its applications to evidence, trial procedure, and jury decision making. Kassin often works as a consultant to trial lawyers.

SOCIAL PSYCHOLOGY

Introduction to Social Psychology

1

Outline

Preview

This chapter introduces you to the study of social psychology. We begin by *getting to know it*, considering the definition and history of the field. Next, we provide *an overview of research methods in social psychology:* how social psychologists come up with and test ideas. We then turn to important questions about *ethics and values in social psychology.* The concluding section is *the beginning, not the end* because it offers a brief, guided tour of what awaits you in this textbook.

Human beings are fascinated by each other. Just think about how much time we spend watching people's behavior. We watch people on TV, in the movies, and on stage. We take photographs of friends and family for our own enjoyment and to show to others. Sitting in a cafe or on a park bench, we observe the human scene that passes by in front of us. The extensive live coverage of major events offered by CNN puts the whole world and its peoples on view. Amateur videotapes are shown on TV, making public what the participants thought only they knew. And then, of course, we watch people through the printed page. Novels and biographies, magazines and newspapers, all rely on our curiosity about other people's lives to get our attention. People watching is the world's oldest spectator sport and still the most popular one.

Human behavior is fascinating because it is so complex and diverse. Sometimes, people feel secure and self-confident; at other times, they are worried and ill at ease. Perceptions of other individuals and groups can be based on a careful examination of the evidence, or tailored to fit preconceptions and biases. People fall in and out of love; nations make war and peace. Individuals slavishly conform to others' wishes, yet also rebel against restraints on their freedom. It's not easy to make sense of the social world we live in. Nor is it easy to understand our own behavior. Just as we can be puzzled by what others do, so can we be puzzled by our own actions. Often, we want to know about others so that we can better understand ourselves.

Human beings are fascinated by each other. Like an audience at a play, patrons of a sidewalk cafe watch the real-life human drama taking place before their eyes.

Social psychology speaks to both of these desires. It examines self-perception as well as the perception of others, how we influence others as well as how we are influenced by them. Social psychology also studies social relationships—such as dating and marriage, giving and receiving help, and obedience to an authority. And it explores group processes: how individuals behave within a group and how groups interact with each other. Social psychology covers a lot of ground, all of it filled with issues and questions that people face throughout their lives. We find it fascinating—and believe that you will too.

The purpose of this chapter is to provide you with a broad overview of the field of social psychology. First, we consider the definition of social psychology and review its history. Next, various research methods used in social psychology are described. Then we turn to some of the more general concerns that affect any scientific endeavor: ethical issues and the role of values. The concluding section offers a preview of what awaits you in the rest of this text. By the time you finish this chapter, you should be ready and (we hope) eager for what lies ahead.

SOCIAL PSYCHOLOGY: GETTING TO KNOW IT

We begin by defining the new territory you're about to enter. Then we map out the history of its development, from its origins to contemporary trends and issues.

What is Social Psychology?

social psychology
The scientific study of the way individuals think, feel, and behave in social situations.

Social psychology is the scientific study of the way individuals think, feel, and behave in social situations. There are three key elements in this definition: social psychology's approach to knowledge, its relation to other disciplines in the social sciences, and its distinction from other kinds of psychological inquiry.

The Scientific Study   There are many approaches to understanding how people think, feel, and behave. We can learn about human behavior from novels, films, history, philosophy—just to name a few possibilities. What makes social psychology different from these artistic and humanistic endeavors is that social psychology is a science. It applies the *scientific method* of systematic observation, description, and measurement to the study of the human condition. As we will see when we consider its historical development, social psychology is a very young science. Social psychologists often wish their discipline had the power and precision of older, more established sciences like physics and chemistry, but they find it exciting to be part of a field that is still so open to creativity and innovation.

Of the Way Individuals Think, Feel, and Behave   Many other disciplines also employ scientific techniques to study human behavior: anthropology, economics, political science, and sociology. All of these disciplines, along with social psychology, are called *social sciences*. The social sciences differ in the aspects of human behavior they examine. Some concentrate on relatively limited, specific content areas. For example, economists focus on economic issues and political scientists on politics. Social psychology, like anthropology and sociology, offers a broader perspective, studying a wide range of behaviors that take place in many different settings. Research on attitudes (see Chapter 10) provides a good illustration of this approach. By investigating a whole host of specific attitudes (including those about consumer products and political candidates), social psychologists attempt to establish general principles of attitude formation and change that will apply in various situations. This search for general principles is not limited to the study of attitudes, but extends across a diverse array of human behaviors. In terms of the breadth of its interests, social psychology is one of the most far-reaching and wide ranging of the social sciences.

The level of analysis also sets social psychology apart from other social sciences. Sociology, for instance, classifies people in terms of their nationality, race, socioeconomic class, and other *group* factors. In contrast, social psychology typically focuses on the *individual*. Even when social psychologists study groups of people, they usually emphasize the behavior of the individual in the group context. Research methods provide another important distinction. Far more than other social sciences, social psychology uses experiments to investigate human behavior. Later in this chapter, we describe the basic features of an experiment. Summing up, social psychology is characterized by a broad perspective, a focus on the individual, and the frequent use of an experimental methodology.

In Social Situations   Having disentangled social psychology from other social sciences, we now face the problem of separating the part from the whole. Psychology as a whole can be defined as the scientific study of the way individuals think, feel, and behave. Psychology as a whole has a broad perspective with a focus on the individual, and it often employs experimental techniques. So what makes social psychology a unique branch of psychology? The obvious answer lies in the name itself, *social* psychology's particular concern with human behavior in *social* situations: the ways people perceive each other, interact with one another, and influence one another. There is, however, some debate about just how "social" social psychology is (Carlson, 1984; Kenrick, 1986). And, in fact, the "socialness" of social psychology varies. In investigating general principles of behavior, social psychologists sometimes explore nonsocial factors that affect our thoughts, emotions, and behavior. Although whatever social psychologists study is relevant to social behavior, not everything they examine is itself a social phenomenon.

A Brief History of Social Psychology

Social psychology has a rich and complex heritage. Here, we sketch just a few highlights taken from a much larger canvas. But even this brief review demonstrates the debt that all social psychologists owe to those who established the discipline. For the student of social psychology, to explore the history of the discipline is to take a trip "back to the future." Questions and concerns originating in the past influence today's research and lay the groundwork for tomorrow's insights.

The Gathering Forces: 1880–1935   As is true for most fields, there are many potential nominees for the title of "founder of social psychology," and not everyone agrees on who should receive the honor (Farr, 1991). But if you write a textbook, you have to make the call, and ours is to declare a tie between American psychologist Norman Triplett and a French agricultural engineer named Max Ringelmann. Triplett published the first research article in social psychology at the close of the nineteenth century (1897–1898); Ringelmann's research was conducted in the 1880s but wasn't published until 1913. The questions asked by these two early researchers continue to be of vital interest even today. Will an individual's performance be enhanced by the presence of others? Or will individual performance decline in a group setting? In Chapter 11 on group processes, we consider some of the answers provided by current research.

Despite their pride of place in the history of social psychology, neither Triplett nor Ringelmann actually established social psychology as a distinct subfield of psychology. Credit for this creation goes to the writers of the first three textbooks in social psychology: the English psychologist William McDougall (1908) and Americans Edward Ross (1908) and Floyd Allport (1924). These authors announced the arrival of a new approach to the social aspects of human behavior. Social psychology was born.

The Great Leap Forward: 1936–1945   But in its infancy, social psychology lacked a distinct identity. What exactly was this new discipline? How was it different from other branches of psychology? These issues were soon addressed by some great contributors to social psychology. One of them was Muzafer Sherif, who in 1936 published an innovative study of social influence. As described in more detail in Chapter 9 on conformity, participants in this research observed a visual illusion—a dot of light that was actually stationary but appeared to move. Watching alone, participants differed considerably in their individual estimates of the light's movement. When they watched together in groups, however, their estimates of the light's movement converged. The light itself never budged, but opinions moved toward a common perception. Sherif's research was crucial for the development of social psychology because it demonstrated that it is possible to study the complex human behavior of social influence in a rigorous, scientific manner. As you will see in Part III of this text, social influence continues to be an exciting topic in social psychology.

Another great contributor to social psychology was Kurt Lewin, a bold and creative theorist who established many of the discipline's defining characteristics (Ash, 1992). Lewin's (1935) *field theory* was highly influential. According to this theory, *behavior* is a function of the *interaction* between the *person* and the *environment*: $B = f(PE)$. You can see the significance of Lewin's position by comparing it to other viewpoints that had a major impact during much of the twentieth century. When asking what kinds of factors determine human behavior, psychoanalyst Sigmund Freud focused on internal, psychological processes; political theorist Karl Marx opted for external, societal forces. But Kurt Lewin answered: both, together.

interactionist perspective An emphasis on the combined effects of both the person and the situation on human behavior; serves as common ground for personality and social psychologists.

Lewin's conviction that both internal and external factors influence human behavior was an early version of what today is called the **interactionist perspective** (Blass, 1984). This approach combines personality psychology (which has traditionally stressed internal, psychological differences among *individuals*) with social psychology (which has traditionally emphasized differences among external *situations*). The marriage, or at least serious dating, between these two branches of psychology has produced an important area of research and theory (Kihlstrom, 1987; Snyder & Ickes, 1985). In this book, we examine the effects of both individual differences and situational factors, alone and in combination.

Yet another aspect of Lewin's influence was his strong interest in the application of social psychology. By research on practical issues, such as how to promote more economical and nutritious eating habits (Lewin, 1947), he demonstrated that social psychology could be applied to the analysis of social problems and could help solve them. Built on Lewin's legacy, applied social psychology flourishes today as one of the most rapidly expanding areas in the field. Theory and research are applied in areas such as advertising, business, education, environmental protection, health, law, politics, public policy, religion, and sports. Throughout this text, we draw on the findings of applied social psychology to illustrate the implications of fundamental social psychological principles for our daily lives. In Part IV, three prominent areas of applied social psychology are examined in detail: law, business, and health.

The Classical Period: 1946–1960   During the prosperous years in the United States after World War II, all of psychology received an enormous boost (Benjamin, 1986). Increased government funding was available, and public regard for the profession was greatly enhanced. Social psychology blossomed in this era of rapid economic and intellectual development, as major contributors generated systematic programs of research in topic areas that are still of great significance. Table 1.1 lists a few of the people and topics involved in what could be called social psychology's golden age.

Contributor	Contribution	Discussed in This Text
Gordon Allport	Prejudice and stereotyping	Perceiving Groups (Chap. 4)
Solomon Asch	Conformity Person perception	Conformity (Chap. 9) Perceiving Persons (Chap. 3)
Leon Festinger	Cognitive dissonance Social comparison	Attitudes (Chap. 10) The Social Self (Chap. 2)
Fritz Heider	Attribution theory Balance theory	Perceiving Persons (Chap. 3) Interpersonal Attraction (Chap. 5)
Carl Hovland	Attitudes and persuasion	Attitudes (Chap. 10)
John Thibaut and Harold Kelley	Social exchange	Intimate Relationships (Chap. 6)

Table 1.1   Major Contributions to Social Psychology During the Classical Period (1946-1960)   These major contributors generated systematic programs of research in topic areas that continue to be of great significance in social psychology.

Confidence and Crisis: 1961–1975   With its foundation firmly in place, social psychology entered a period of expansion and enthusiasm. The sheer range of its investigations was staggering. Social psychologists considered how people thought (Kelley, 1967) and felt (Schachter, 1964) about themselves and others. They studied interactions in groups (Moscovici & Zavalloni, 1969) and social problems such as why people fail to help others in distress (Latané & Darley, 1970). They examined aggression (Bandura, 1973), physical attractiveness (Berscheid & Walster, 1974b), and stress (Glass & Singer, 1972). All of these topics are considered in this text. For the field as a whole, it was a time of great productivity.

Ironically, it was also a time of crisis. Social psychologists engaged in heated debate. They argued about the *ethics* of research procedures, the *validity* of findings, and the *generalization* of conclusions across time and space. Many of the strong disagreements during this period can be understood as a reaction to the dominant research method of the day: the laboratory experiment. Those social psychologists who questioned the laboratory method maintained that certain practices were unethical (Kelman, 1967), that experimenters' expectations influenced their subjects' behavior (Orne, 1962; Rosenthal, 1966), and that the theories being tested in the laboratory were historically and culturally limited (Gergen, 1973). Those who favored laboratory experimentation contended that their procedures were ethical, their results valid, and their theoretical principles widely applicable (McGuire, 1967). For a time, social psychology seemed split in two.

An Era of Pluralism: 1976 to the Present   Fortunately for the future of the field, both sides won. The debate on ethics led to more rigorous and uniform standards for research. Careful scrutiny of possible sources of bias produced improved procedures. Concerns about historical and cultural limits on scientific findings led to a more sophisticated understanding of the personal and political values that can underlie scientific activities. But just as important, the baby was not thrown out with the bath water. Laboratory experiments continued. They did, however, get some company. A single-minded attachment to laboratory work evolved into an acceptance of a wide variety of research methods. This pluralistic orientation is based on two conclusions about the nature of research in social psychology (Houts et al., 1986). First, since different topics require different kinds of investigations, a range of research techniques is needed. Second, no research method is perfect; each one has unique advantages and disadvantages. Thus, any single topic will benefit from being investigated by a number of approaches. The various research methods used by today's social psychologists are described later in this chapter.

Pluralism in social psychology is not confined to its methods. Two broad perspectives on the nature of human behavior also contribute to the breadth and diversity of the discipline. One is a "hot" perspective that sees individuals as driven by desires and emotions. According to this view, people are social animals who want and feel before they think (Zajonc, 1984). This approach focuses on *motivation* and *emotion* as determinants of our thoughts and actions. In contrast, a "cold" perspective emphasizes the more rational, analytical aspects of human behavior. With its focus on *cognition*, this viewpoint holds that people's thoughts affect what they want, how they feel, and what they do (Lazarus, 1984).

The balance between these two perspectives has shifted back and forth during the history of social psychology. In the 1950s and 1960s, the hot perspective predominated. Beginning in the 1970s and accelerating in the 1980s, the cold perspective held sway. Indeed, the cold perspective was so powerful in all of psychology during the 1980s that it was hailed as the "cognitive revolution."

social cognition
The study of how people perceive, remember, and interpret information about themselves and others.

Social cognition—the study of how we perceive, remember, and interpret information about ourselves and others—became one of the most creative and exciting areas in social psychology. Part I of this textbook explores the three faces of theory and research in social cognition: perceptions of self, of individual others, and of groups. Now, in the 1990s, motivation and emotion are making a comeback. Increasingly, social psychologists take into account the whole person—who desires, feels, *and* thinks.

Another source of pluralism in contemporary social psychology is found in its international and multicultural scope. British and European influences have always been strong: Ringelmann conducted his research in France; McDougall wrote his 1908 textbook in England; and Kurt Lewin was a prominent psychologist in Germany before seeking asylum in the United States during the Nazi era. Today, there are social psychologists in many different countries—including Australia, Canada, France, Germany, Great Britain, Israel, Italy, Japan, Spain, and Poland.

In this book, you will read about research conducted around the world on such topics as social life in Hong Kong (Wheeler et al., 1989), crowding in India (Evans et al., 1989), and a murder trial in South Africa (Colman, 1991). You will also examine social psychological processes that make it more difficult for people of different races, ethnic backgrounds, and nations to interact in peace and harmony: stereotypes and prejudice (Chapter 4) and intergroup conflict (Chapter 11). In a world that seems composed of cooperative ventures and warring factions, in about equal measure, we all need to better understand the forces that drive people apart and those that bring them together. The study of social psychology can help us gain important insights about these issues.

The value of social psychology for understanding the world we live in has been recognized by psychologists and nonpsychologists alike. Many profession-al schools (for example, those of business, education, and journalism) now recommend or require courses in social psychology for their undergraduate

Social psychological research is conducted around the world. Later in this book, you will read about a study comparing the social life of students in Hong Kong with that of students in the United States.

students. Career opportunities in the field have also expanded. Typically, advanced graduates who hold a Ph.D. in social psychology are employed at colleges or universities in a department of psychology. But they are also on the faculties of sociology departments and schools of business, law, and education. In addition, social psychologists work in business organizations, government agencies, and medical centers. Constantly extending their horizons, social psychologists search for new knowledge and new opportunities to apply what they have learned (Altman, 1987).

We have presented a definition of the field and traced its development across more than a century. But the portrait we have drawn is still incomplete. Social psychology is a lively, dynamic process. People *do* social psychology. How do they do it? In the next section, we take a look at social psychology in action.

AN OVERVIEW OF RESEARCH METHODS IN SOCIAL PSYCHOLOGY

The research process involves generating ideas, testing those ideas, and pursuing various intellectual and societal goals through research activities. Understanding this process is crucial for your study of social psychology. Subsequent chapters in this book emphasize *what* social psychologists have found in their research. This section examines *how* they go about finding these results.

Generating Ideas in Social Psychology

It all begins with an idea, a vision of what might be. Generating ideas in social psychology is not some strange, esoteric enterprise. Like everyone else, social psychologists get ideas about human behavior from events in their own lives, informal observations of others, books they read, or something they see on TV. In addition, social psychologists are stimulated by each other's work. A new idea takes shape in response to those already proposed, enlarging an existing viewpoint or offering a radically different alternative.

Starting with an idea about human behavior—an idea that may be so vague that it amounts to a hunch or an educated guess—social psychologists talk about it with other people. Consultation is a basic feature of all science. On research teams, ideas are proposed, criticized, and refined. At professional conferences, ideas are discussed at formal meetings and during informal gatherings. In books and journals, theoretical developments and research findings are presented in detail. The process of consultation is continuous; it never ends.

Professional conferences are an important part of the consultation process that is a basic feature of all science. At such conferences, ideas are presented at formal meetings and discussed in informal gatherings.

Hypotheses and Theories   At some point, however, an idea becomes clear

hypothesis A test-able prediction about the conditions under which an event will occur.

and firm enough to serve as a **hypothesis**: a precise, testable prediction about the conditions under which an event will occur. Once a hypothesis is formu-lated, research can be planned and carried out. In some ways, research is another form of consultation. Now, the social psychologist obtains the reactions of *subjects,* those individuals whose thoughts, feelings, or behaviors are being studied. (Perhaps you served as a subject when you were enrolled in an in-troductory psychology course.) Usually, research findings don't just confirm or disconfirm a hypothesis. Often they indicate how the hypothesis should be modified or point to a related idea that needs to be investigated.

theory An organized set of principles used to explain observed phenomena.

As ideas and data regarding a specific aspect of human behavior accumulate, the social psychologist may develop a **theory**: an organized set of principles used to explain observed phenomena. Theories are usually evaluated in terms of three major criteria: simplicity, comprehensiveness, and generativity. All else being equal, the best theories are elegant and precise, encompass all of the relevant information, and lead to further research and deeper understanding.

In social psychology, there are many theories. Social psychologists do not attempt the grand theory: the "one simple and sovereign formula [that] holds the key to social behavior" (Allport, 1985, p. 4). Instead, they rely on "mini-theories," which address more limited and specific aspects of the way people behave. These relatively simple minitheories lack the sweep of more comprehensive theories (such as those of Freud or Piaget, which you may have studied in introductory psychology), but they allow a more precise understanding of human behavior.

Most social psychological theories are highly generative. They stimulate systematic programs of research by the theory's advocates. They may also provoke sharp criticism by the theory's opponents. Beginning students of social psychology are often surprised by the fact that so many of its principles are disputed by a number of contenders. In part, this lack of consensus reflects social psychology's status as a young science. At this stage in its development, premature closure is a worse sin than contradiction or even confusion. But debate is an essential feature of even the most mature science. It is the fate of *all* scientific theories to be criticized and, eventually, surpassed.

basic research Research whose goal is to increase the understanding of human behavior, often by testing hypotheses based on a theory.

applied research Research whose goal is to increase the understanding of naturally occurring events or to find solutions to practical problems.

Basic and Applied Research Is testing a theory the purpose of research in social psychology? For some researchers, yes. The goal of **basic research** is to increase the understanding of human behavior. Basic research is often designed to examine a specific hypothesis from a specific theory. **Applied research** has a different purpose: to make use of social psychology's theories or methods to contribute to the understanding of naturally occurring events or to the solution of social problems (Cook et al., 1985; Rodin, 1985). In applied research, the focus is on the event or problem itself; the theory is simply useful. In basic research, the focus is on the theory; the naturally occurring phenomenon simply provides an interesting opportunity to test the theoretical hypotheses.

Although there is an important difference between basic and applied research, much of social psychology blends the two together. Some researchers switch back and forth between these two types of research; some studies test a theory *and* explain a real-world phenomenon simultaneously. However it is accomplished, the integration of basic and applied research makes a valuable contribution to social psychology. In defense of applied social psychology, Kurt Lewin (1951) remarked, "There is nothing so practical as a good theory." We would add that there is nothing so good for a theory as a practical application. Applying a theory can produce the new ideas that make it possible to construct a better theory. And a better theory provides the foundation for more powerful applications.

The generation of ideas is an ongoing process. It occurs in the mind of an individual social psychologist, as he or she tries to find a clear path through what can sometimes seem a maze of theories and findings. It takes place in a social network composed of members of the research team, other investigators, and subjects. It links past conceptions with future innovations, theoretical developments with practical solutions. But in social psychology, ideas are not an end in themselves. Whenever a social psychologist has a good idea, the question

Applied research on problems and issues of everyday life is often conducted in real-world settings. As described in Chapter 12 on law, social psychology can help us understand many aspects of what takes place in a courtroom.

"How do we test it?" is sure to follow. We turn now to some answers to this question.

Testing Ideas Through Correlations: Looking for Associations

correlation An association between two variables. A correlation is positive when both variables increase or decrease together. It is negative when as one variable increases the other decreases.

In all social sciences, one of the most popular ways to test an idea is with a correlation. A **correlation** is an association between two factors that vary in quantity. When a correlation is *positive,* as one variable increases, so does the other; as one decreases, so does the other. When a correlation is *negative,* the two variables go in opposite directions: one up, the other down. And when there is *no correlation,* there is no relationship at all between the two variables. These three types of patterns are illustrated in Figure 1.1.

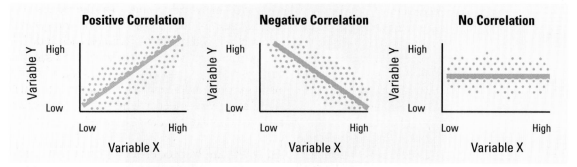

Figure 1.1   Correlations: Positive, Negative, and None.   Correlations reveal a systematic association between two variables. Positive correlations indicate that variables are in sync: increases in one variable are associated with increases in the other, decreases with decreases. Negative correlations indicate that variables go in opposite directions: increases in one variable are associated with decreases in the other. When two variables are not systematically associated, there is no correlation.

Mathematically, correlations are computed in terms of the *correlation coefficient*, which ranges from +1.0 to –1.0. A perfect positive correlation has a correlation coefficient of +1.0; a perfect negative correlation has a correlation coefficient of –1.0; and the total absence of any correlation has a correlation coefficient of 0. Since most correlations are not perfect one way or the other, most correlation coefficients have more moderate values such as +.39, or –.67, or +.05.

Typically, correlations are obtained by comparing the scores of different individuals on the factors of interest. Consider, for example, the idea that "birds of a feather flock together." If the proverb holds for people as well as for our feathered friends, we would expect that similarity and interpersonal attraction would have a positive correlation. And they do. As described in Chapter 5 on interpersonal attraction, similarity on various dimensions is associated with liking and with establishing a relationship:

- College students living in the same dormitory like those with similar attitudes more than they like those with dissimilar attitudes (Newcomb, 1961).
- Couples who are dating, cohabiting, engaged, or married are more similar in their level of physical attractiveness than are randomly paired couples who have no relationship with each other (Feingold, 1988).

Correlations can also be computed for a single individual over a number of repeated measurements. In his study of emotional experience, Seymour Epstein (1983) examined both types of correlations: "between" (different individuals) and "within" (a single individual). Subjects in this research rated their emotional experiences on each of twenty-eight days. Comparing different individuals, the totals for sadness and anger were positively correlated, with a correlation coefficient of .51. People who reported more sad feelings than did others also reported more anger. These findings suggest that people differ on the general tendency to experience negative emotions. But now let's focus on each individual, each day at a time. Here sadness and anger were uncorrelated. For a specific individual, being sad neither increased nor decreased the likelihood of being angry. Thus, between individuals, sadness and anger were packaged together, but within individuals, sadness and anger were independent. Together these two types of correlations give us a more complete picture of emotional experience than does either one alone.

Correlational research is used widely in the social sciences because it is relatively easy to conduct. All you need to do is measure the variables of interest, perform the statistical calculation, and—voilà!—you have your findings. Moreover, you have a great deal of freedom about where and how you measure the variables. You can bring subjects into a *laboratory* where space and equipment are specially constructed for research purposes, or you can conduct research in the *field*—the natural settings of the real world.

For all its advantages, correlational research has one, very serious disadvantage. A correlation indicates an association between two variables, but it cannot demonstrate cause and effect. Just because similar people like each other doesn't necessarily mean that similarity causes liking. It could go the other way. People who like each other could influence each other and thus become more similar. And then there's the "third variable" problem. Perhaps some other factor (such as spending time together) produces both similarity and liking. Whenever you see a correlation, you should think through all three possibilities: X causes Y; Y causes X; Z causes X and Y. The cardinal rule to be remembered is this: **Correlation is not causation.**

Testing Ideas in Experiments: Looking for Cause and Effect

experiment A form of research that can examine cause-and-effect relationships because (1) the experimenter has control over the events that occur and (2) subjects are randomly assigned to conditions.

If you want to examine cause-and-effect relationships, you will need to conduct an **experiment**. Experiments in social psychology range from the very simple to the almost incredibly elaborate. All of them, however, share two essential characteristics. First, the researcher has *control* over the experimental procedures: manipulating the variables of interest and ensuring uniformity elsewhere. All subjects are treated in exactly the same manner—except for the specific differences the experimenter wants to create. By exercising control, the researcher attempts to ensure that differences obtained after the experimental manipulation are produced only by that manipulation and are not affected by other events in the experiment.

The second distinguishing feature of an experiment is that subjects are *randomly* assigned to the different manipulations (called *conditions*) included in the experiment. If there are two conditions, who goes where may be determined by simply flipping a coin. If there are many conditions, a computer program is used. However it's done, random assignment means that subjects are *not* assigned to a condition on the basis of their personal or behavioral characteristics. By randomly assigning subjects to experimental conditions, the experimenter attempts to ensure that conditions begin on a level playing field. On the average, the subjects assigned to one condition are no different from the subjects assigned to another condition. Differences that appear between conditions after an experimental manipulation can, therefore, be attributed to the impact of that manipulation and not to any pre-existing differences between subjects.

Because of experimenter control and random assignment of subjects, an experiment is a powerful technique for examining cause and effect. Both characteristics serve the same goal: to eliminate the influence on subjects' behavior of any factors other than the experimental manipulation. By ruling out alternative explanations for research results, we become more confident that we understand just what has, in fact, caused a certain behavior to occur. As you will see in Chapter 5, experimental evidence indicates that similarity does indeed cause attraction to increase.

The Language of Research   To illustrate some of the terms used to describe experimental procedures, consider an experiment by Kenneth Leonard (1989) on the effects of alcohol on aggression. The subjects were forty-eight male undergraduates who had agreed to participate in a study on "the influence of alcohol on perceptual-motor skills." Only subjects who indicated that they drank alcohol were included. When each subject arrived at the research laboratory, he was randomly assigned to receive either a couple of alcoholic drinks (vodka mixed with ginger ale) or no drink of any kind. All subjects were then informed that they would be competing against another subject on an experimental task and that the loser on each trial would receive an electric shock administered by the winner. Actually, there was no other subject; this person's behavior was simulated through tape-recorded messages and programmed responses during the task. At the beginning of the first trial, half of the subjects (randomly assigned within the alcohol and no-alcohol conditions) were led to believe that their opponent intended to administer the most severe shock available; the other half were led to believe that the opponent intended to use only the mildest possible shock. After the first trial was over, however, all subjects learned that their opponent had set the minimum shock level.

independent variables   The factors manipulated in an experiment to see if they affect the dependent variable.

In an experiment, researchers manipulate an independent variable and examine the effect of this manipulation on the dependent variable. There were two **independent variables** in Leonard's study of alcohol and aggression:

1. Whether the subject drank alcohol: alcohol versus no alcohol
2. The opponent's intentions: aggressive cue versus nonaggressive cue

dependent variables   The factors measured in an experiment to see if they are affected by the independent variable.

The outcome being studied—the **dependent variable**—was the level of shock subjects selected before each trial to be administered to the opponent in the event that the subject was the winner on that trial. Thus, the results in this experiment consist of the level of shock selected on each trial by subjects in each of the four conditions:

Alcohol/Aggressive cue
No alcohol/Aggressive cue
Alcohol/Nonaggressive cue
No alcohol/Nonaggressive cue

Results obtained in an experiment are examined by means of statistical analyses that allow the researcher to determine how likely it is that the results could have occurred by chance. The standard convention is that if a result could have occurred by chance only 5 or fewer times in 100 possible outcomes, then the result is *statistically significant* and should be taken seriously. But significant results are not absolutely certain effects. In essence, statistical significance is an attractive betting proposition. The odds are quite good (at least 95 out of 100) that the effects obtained in the study were due to experimental manipulation of the independent variable. But there is still the possibility (as high as 5 out of 100) that the findings were merely a chance occurrence.

The results of Leonard's study of alcohol and aggression are depicted in Figure 1.2. As you can see, these findings differed on each of the two trials. On the first trial, subjects who believed the opponent had aggressive intentions selected higher levels of shock than did those who believed the opponent had nonaggressive intentions. This result, in which the levels of a single independent variable produce differences in the dependent variable, is called a *main effect*. The other possible main effect in this experiment was not significant: there was no difference in the level of shock selected before the first trial between subjects who had drunk alcohol and those who had not had anything to drink.

On the second trial, however, both independent variables affected the dependent variable. Subjects who initially believed that the opponent had aggressive intentions *and* who had consumed alcohol were more aggressive than subjects in any of the other three conditions. Thus, subjects in the aggressive-cue condition who had not consumed alcohol were able to adjust their behavior after learning that the opponent had, in fact, refrained from selecting a severe shock. But those who had taken two stiff shots of vodka were not so flexible. They kept right on with their aggressive retaliation, even when they learned there was nothing to retaliate against. Statistically, there are two ways in which joint effects of two independent variables can occur. Sometimes, the main effects just add together. But when the joint effect is *greater* than the sum of the main effects, the result is called an *interaction*. In an interaction, the whole of a joint effect is more than the sum of its contributing parts.

Evaluating Research

Although all experiments share certain characteristics (experimenter control, random assignment of subjects, manipulation of the independent variables,

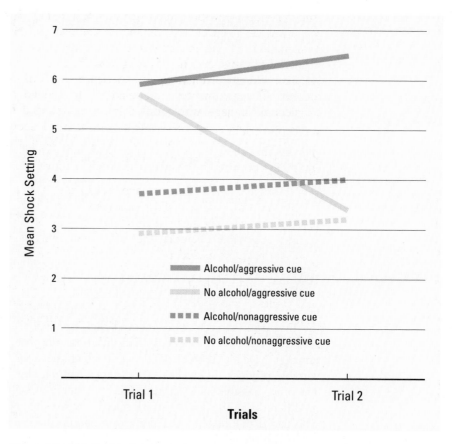

Figure 1.2   Alcohol and Aggression.   In this study, subjects either consumed alcohol or had nothing to drink. They then were led to believe that a supposed opponent had aggressive or nonaggressive intentions. On the first trial, subjects who anticipated an aggressive opponent retaliated. Before the second trial, all subjects learned that the opponent had behaved nonaggressively. On the second trial, only those subjects who had consumed alcohol *and* who had initially expected the opponent to be aggressive continued their own aggressive behavior. [Adapted from Leonard, 1989.]

internal validity
The degree to which there can be reasonable certainty that the independent variable in an experiment caused the effects obtained on the dependent variable.

measurement of the dependent variables), they differ widely in other attributes. This section describes the basic dimensions that researchers use to evaluate the quality and meaning of experiments. We also explore some of the tradeoffs involved in the decision to conduct research in the field or in the laboratory.

Internal Validity: Having Confidence in the Results   When an experiment is properly conducted, it is said to have **internal validity**: there is reasonable certainty that the independent variable did, in fact, cause the effects obtained on the dependent variable (Cook & Campbell, 1979). As described earlier, both experimenter control and random assignment seek to rule out alternative explanations of the research results, thereby strengthening internal validity. Experiments also include *control groups* for this purpose. Typically, a control group consists of subjects who experience all of the experimental procedures except the experimental manipulations. In Leonard's study on alcohol and aggression, subjects who didn't drink alcohol and didn't hear their supposed opponent express aggressive intentions (the no-alcohol/nonaggressive-cue condition) served as a control group. As a sort of "dry run," the control group provides a base line against which to compare the effects of the independent variables.

Although commonplace in laboratory experiments, control groups can be highly controversial in field experiments that examine real-life events. For example, research on new medical treatments for deadly diseases, such as AIDS, creates a horrible dilemma. Individuals randomly assigned to the nontreated control group are excluded for the duration of the study from what could turn out to be a life-saving treatment. Yet without an untreated control group, it is extremely difficult to determine which treatments are effective and which ones are useless. For someone afflicted with a fatal disease, participating in a nontreated control group is a heroic and altruistic act: the knowledge obtained may well benefit others more than oneself.

An experimenter's knowledge and behavior can also affect internal validity. Unwittingly, experimenters sometimes sabotage their own research. Here's how it can happen. Experimenters often have expectations about the effects of various independent variables. If they know what conditions subjects have been assigned to, they may, without realizing it, treat subjects in one condition differently from the way they treat subjects in another condition. Since the experimenter's behavior can influence the subject's behavior, the results could then be produced by the experimenter's actions rather than by the independent variable. The best way to protect an experiment from the influence of experimenters' expectations—called **experimenter expectancy effects** (Rosenthal, 1976)—is to keep them *uninformed* about assignments to conditions. If experimenters do not know the condition to which a subject has been assigned, they cannot treat subjects in different conditions differently.

Leonard's study of alcohol and aggression appears to have been conducted in its entirety by a single experimenter who was aware of subjects' experimental assignments. In an effort to reduce the opportunity for experimenter expectancy effects to occur, the interaction between the experimenter and each subject was minimized by the use of tape-recorded instructions at various points in the experiment. Nevertheless, the experimenter did sometimes interact directly with the subject. These occasions create the possibility of experimenter expectancy effects and thereby weaken the internal validity of this research.

External Validity: Generalizing the Results In addition to guarding the internal validity of their experiments, researchers are concerned about **external**

experimenter expectancy effects The effects produced when an experimenter's expectations about the results of an experiment affect his or her behavior toward a subject and thereby influence the subject's responses.

external validity The degree to which one can be reasonably confident that the same results would be obtained for other people and in other situations.

validity, the extent to which the results obtained under one set of circumstances would also occur in a different set of circumstances (Berkowitz & Donnerstein, 1982). When an experiment has external validity, its findings can be assumed to generalize to other people and to other situations. Let us consider how both the subjects who participate and the setting of the experiment affect external validity.

Because social psychologists often desire to establish universal principles of human behavior, their ideal sample of subjects should be representative of the whole human race. Such an all-inclusive **representative sample** has never been seen and probably never will be. Representative samples of more limited populations do exist. For example, samples representative of all registered voters in the United States are often used in surveys examining preferences for political candidates and opinions on political issues. Using highly sophisticated sampling methods, such surveys can provide a reasonably accurate snapshot of how people think and feel when they respond to the survey (Schuman & Kalton, 1985).

But social psychologists rarely employ representative samples. Usually, they rely on a **convenience sample** drawn from a population that is readily available to the researcher. Consider, in this regard, those male undergraduates who

representative sample A sample that reflects the characteristics of the population of interest.

convenience sample A sample selected because the subjects are readily available.

A representative sample reflects the characteristics of the population of interest. Suppose we're interested in studying people who attend sporting events in a particular city or country. A representative sample of this population would have a similar composition in terms of demographic factors such as gender, race, age, and socioeconomic class.

participated in Leonard's experiment on alcohol and aggression. Strictly speaking, the results of this research can be generalized only to young adult males who currently drink alcohol, attend a particular university, and are willing to participate in a psychology experiment in order to earn some money. Since it seems reasonable to suppose that Leonard wants his results to generalize to, at least, the young adult male population of the United States, the convenience sample weakens the external validity of this research.

The common practice of using convenience samples in social psychological research poses an important question: Is it possible to establish universal principles of human behavior with research on nonrepresentative samples? Those who favor the use of convenience samples point to some very real practical issues. Representative samples are fine for surveys requiring short answers to a short list of questions. But what about complex, time-consuming experiments like Leonard's? The expense of bringing subjects from all over the United States to his lab would be staggering. And since extraneous variables (travel fatigue, disruptions in one's regular routine) could influence the results, increased external validity might be purchased only at the price of decreased internal validity. Advocates of convenience samples also contend that there is no contradiction between universal principles and particular subjects. Indeed, the more basic the principle, the less it matters who participates in the research.

Not everyone agrees with this perspective. Urging social psychologists to study *inconvenient* samples, David Sears (1986) emphasized the advantages of including subjects from a variety of backgrounds and life experiences, even if gaining their participation is difficult. Increasingly, social psychologists have taken Sears' advice to heart. As noted earlier in this chapter, social psychological research is now conducted in many countries, thus ensuring the participation of subjects from different cultures. And, just as important, field research has expanded enormously in social psychology. If the subject won't come to the lab, take the lab to the subject!

Field research, however, raises its own set of issues (Greenberg & Folger, 1988). First, most research conducted in natural settings is correlational and lacks the power of experiments to examine cause-and-effect relationships. Second, even when field research is experimental, it lacks the level of experimenter control found in laboratory experiments. Experiments conducted on the subway, in a parking lot, or along a busy street are vulnerable to a multitude of distractions and interruptions. Thus, internal validity in field experiments is often weaker than in lab experiments.

But what about external validity? Since field research occurs in the real world rather than in the artificial setting of a laboratory, aren't its results more generalizable to real, everyday behavior? Perhaps. It depends on where you stand on the issue of mundane versus experimental realism (Aronson & Carlsmith, 1968). **Mundane realism** refers to the extent to which the research setting resembles the real-world setting of interest. Theodore Newcomb's (1961) research in which he set up an entire college dormitory in order to study interpersonal attraction is a striking example of mundane realism. The logic of

mundane realism
The degree to which the experimental situation resembles places and events that exist in the real world.

mundane realism is that appearances count. If research procedures mimic real-world events, it is more likely that research findings will reveal what goes on in the real world. As a general rule, mundane realism is greater in field research than in lab investigations.

experimental realism   The degree to which experimental procedures are involving to subjects and lead them to behave naturally and spontaneously.

In contrast, **experimental realism** refers to the degree to which the experimental setting and procedures are real and involving *to the subject,* regardless of whether they resemble real life or not. Leonard's research on alcohol and aggression was a far cry from the bars and sporting events where this volatile mixture often occurs. But extensive research conducted with similar procedures indicates that such an apparently artificial setting is usually highly involving to subjects. Because their experiences are real to them, subjects respond naturally and spontaneously.

deception   Research methods that provide false information to subjects.

Notice, however, that in order to strengthen experimental realism, Leonard had to resort to **deception**, providing subjects with false information about an opponent who did not actually exist. Another kind of deception used by social psychologists involves **confederates**, who act as though they are subjects in the experiment but are actually working for the experimenter. Deception is not only used to strengthen experimental realism by creating highly involving experiences for subjects. It also allows the experimenter to manufacture situations in the laboratory that would be difficult to observe in a natural setting; to study potentially harmful behaviors, like aggression, in a regulated, safe manner; and to assess people's spontaneous reactions rather than their carefully controlled, socially acceptable presentations. But the use of deception creates some serious ethical concerns, which we consider later in this chapter.

Measure for Measure

Whether at work in the lab or in the field, conducting an experiment or looking for a correlation, social psychologists use a variety of measures. In this section, we examine two major types: self-reports and observations. Then we describe some ways to integrate the findings from different studies.

Self-Reports: Going Straight to the Source   Perhaps the most widely used measurement technique is to collect *self-reports,* in which subjects report on their own thoughts, feelings, and behaviors. One popular self-report measure, the Rosenberg Self-Esteem Scale, is presented in Table 1.2. This scale measures an individual's assessment of his or her own self-worth.

Self-reports are relatively easy to obtain from people and give the researcher direct access to an individual's beliefs and perceptions. But self-reports are not always accurate and can be misleading. For example, respondents may actively distort their answers in order to make a good impression on others. Suppose that you read the questions on the Rosenberg scale to your friends and asked them to respond out loud. Your friends might reveal their true feelings, or they might try to look more self-confident than they really are. As Shakespeare put

Indicate whether you *strongly agree, agree, disagree,* or *strongly disagree* with each of these statements.

1. I feel that I'm a person of worth, at least on an equal plane with others.
2. On the whole, I am satisfied with myself.
3. I wish I could have more respect for myself.
4. I certainly feel useless at times.
5. At times I think I am no good at all.
6. I feel that I have a number of good qualities.
7. All in all, I am inclined to feel that I am a failure.
8. I am able to do things as well as most other people.
9. I feel that I do not have much to be proud of.
10. I take a positive attitude toward myself.

To score responses on this scale, score items 1, 2, 6, 8, and 10 in a positive direction (*strongly agree* = 4, etc.), and items 3, 4, 5, 7, and 9 in a reversed direction (*strongly agree* = 1, etc.). The highest possible score is 40; the lowest possible is 10. Higher scores indicate higher self-esteem.

Table 1.2   The Rosenberg Self-Esteem Scale.   Self-reports are a widely used measurement technique in social psychology. The Rosenberg Self-Esteem Scale measures an individual's perception of his or her own self-worth. [Morris Rosenberg, *Society and the Adolescent Self-Image.* Copyright © 1965 by Princeton University Press. Self-Esteem Scale reprinted with permission of Princeton University Press.]

it in the play from which we took the title of this section, "It oft falls out, to have what we would have, we speak not what we mean."

But even when people intend to answer honestly, self-reports can still be inaccurate. Norbert Schwarz (1990) describes a number of cognitive factors that can influence people's reports about the events in their lives.:

Cumulative versus particular questions.   When subjects were asked to indicate how many times they had eaten dinner in a restaurant over a three-month period, the average number of trips reported was 20.5. But when asked the same question for each of several different types of restaurants (for example, Chinese, Italian, Mexican), the average total number of trips was 26. Although we don't know for certain which answer is more accurate, it seems reasonable to assume that the more detailed set of questions helped people remember restaurant meals they didn't recall when asked the more general question.

Vivid versus dull events.   Typically, people overestimate the recency and frequency of dramatic, vivid events, while underestimating the recency and frequency of dull, uninspiring events. The former stand out in memory; the latter fade.

Available response alternatives. When people provide self-reports, they are often given a set of response alternatives to choose from. The way these alternatives are structured can influence what people report. Among German adults asked how many hours a day they watched TV, only 16.2 percent said they watched more than 2.5 hours per day when given a low-frequency scale on which "more than 2.5 hours" was the *maximum* response. But when "up to 2.5 hours" was the *minimum* response alternative, 37.5 percent reported they watched TV for more than 2.5 hours. These results are displayed in Table 1.3. Presumably, the low-frequency scale implied that more than 2.5 hours a day was unusual, while the high-frequency scale implied that more than 2.5 hours was fairly common. And, at least when it comes to heavy-duty TV watching, many people seem reluctant to report (or believe) that they are unusual.

Table 1.3   How Many Hours of TV Did They Watch?   When German adults were given the low-frequency scale, only 16.2 percent said they watched more than 2.5 hours of TV each day. But when they were given the high-frequency scale, 37.5 percent said they watched more than 2.5 hours of TV per day. Providing a different set of response alternatives altered people's responses. [Adapted from Schwarz et al., 1985.]

Low-Frequency Scale	Percentage
Up to 0.5 hour	7.4
0.5 to 1 hour	17.7
1 hour to 1.5 hours	26.5
1.5 hours to 2 hours	14.7
2 hours to 2.5 hours	17.7
More than 2.5 hours	**16.2**

High-Frequency Scale	Percentage	
Up to 2.5 hours	62.5	
2.5 hours to 3 hours	23.4	
3 hours to 3.5 hours	7.8	
3.5 hours to 4 hours	4.7	**37.5**
4 hours to 4.5 hours	1.6	
More than 4.5 hours	0	

Sensitive to possible inaccuracies in self-reports, psychologists have developed some improved ways to obtain these responses (Tennen et al., 1991). For example, the Rochester Interaction Record (RIR) is used by subjects to record every social interaction lasting ten minutes or more that occurs during the course of the study, usually a week or two (Reis & Wheeler, 1991). Subjects are instructed to use a special form to record each interaction as soon as possible after it occurs. The RIR typically includes measures of quantitative variables (such as length of the interaction and the number of others present) as well as qualitative variables (such as intimacy, satisfaction, and social influence). The RIR's standardized format and the emphasis on reporting soon after the event has occurred are both designed to increase the accuracy of subjects' reports.

Other methods have a similar goal. In one study, undergraduate students carried a paging device with them for a period of one week (Kernis et al., 1989). Whenever the beeper went off, they were instructed to complete a measure of how they were feeling at the time. If you're having a hard time picturing how these students managed to combine their research participation with attending classes, don't worry. Subjects were not beeped until the afternoon, when most of their classes were over. This method of using beeper prompts to collect information about everyday activities and thoughts is called the Experience Sampling Method (Larsen & Csikszentmihalyi, 1983). Repeated self-reports can also be obtained by asking subjects to complete a daily questionnaire (Bolger et al., 1989). This approach is less intrusive than either the Rochester Interaction Report or the Experience Sampling Method, but may not be as accurate since more time is likely to have elapsed between the event and the person's report of it.

Observations: Looking On   There is an alternative to asking subjects about their thoughts, feelings, and behavior. Instead, researchers can observe their actions. Sometimes these observations are very simple, such as observing which of two items a person selects. Some observations, however, are more elaborate and require that interrater reliability be established (Weick, 1985). **Interrater reliability** refers to the level of agreement among multiple observers of the same scene. Only when different observers agree on what they saw can the data be trusted. In the Dyadic Interaction Paradigm developed by William Ickes and his colleagues (1990), the interaction between two strangers meeting for the first time is videotaped. Two independent observers then work from the videotapes to code the frequency of such behaviors as interpersonal distance, body posture, looking at each other, and smiles. The extent to which the two observers agree upon the frequency of each behavior determines the degree of interrater reliability.

But observations don't require human observers. The time it takes to respond to a stimulus (called *response latency*) can be measured by computer devices (Fazio, 1990). Physiological responses are tracked by various kinds of equip-

interrater reliability
The degree to which different observers agree on their observations.

Observational methods provide a useful alternative to self-reports. For example, studies of young children often rely on observations because their verbal skills are relatively limited. Sometimes actions speak louder, and more clearly, than words.

ment, the most well known of which is the electrocardiogram (EKG), which measures heart rate (Blascovich & Kelsey, 1990; Cacioppo & Tassinary, 1990).

The advantage of observational methods is that they by-pass subjects' recollections and interpretations of their own behavior. Sometimes actions do speak louder than words. But observational methods also have a major disadvantage: subject *reactivity* (Kazdin, 1982). When subjects know that they are being observed, they may have difficulty acting naturally or may even deliberately alter their behavior.

Archival research is another method of tracing the patterns of human behavior. In archival research, records of previous behavior (such as divorce records, sports statistics, and crime rates) are studied rather than on-going actions. For example, one way to examine whether individuals in established relationships tend to have similar levels of physical attractiveness is to use wedding pictures published in the newspaper.

Many archival records are based on *unobtrusive measures* that do not interfere with spontaneous behavior and, therefore, do not produce the self-conscious reactivity of individuals who are aware that they are being studied (Webb et al., 1981). For example, professional athletes may lose their concentration for any number of reasons, but worrying about some social psychologist using their team's record in a research project isn't one of them! However, archival records based on obtrusive measures or on self-reports share the problems of reactivity and inaccuracy discussed earlier. Moreover, all archival research encounters a basic limitation: records are not perfect mirrors of human behavior (Jones, 1985). Not all human behaviors have been recorded, and not all records have survived. Thus, archival researchers, like those who work directly with subjects, have to be concerned about the nature of their sample and whether their results can be generalized.

Literature Reviews: Putting It All Together As the amount of research conducted in social psychology has grown by leaps and bounds over the last few decades, researchers have become increasingly interested in summarizing and integrating the results obtained in different studies. This task is, of course, an essential feature of any textbook. By reading this book, you obtain an overview of important theories and findings in social psychology. The kind of literature review provided in textbooks is called a *narrative review*: the authors read the relevant literature and use their own best judgment about how to put it all together.

It used to be the case that narrative reviews also attempted to declare winners and losers by adding up the "hits" (confirmations) and "misses" (disconfirmations) among studies testing a specific hypothesis. Narrative reviews are no longer used for this purpose. Instead, psychologists rely on a set of statistical procedures called *meta-analysis* to combine the quantitative results from multiple studies (Cooper, 1990; Rosenthal, 1991). Compared with narrative reviews, meta-analysis provides a more reliable and precise conclusion about whether there is adequate support for a particular hypothesis (Miller & Cooper, 1991). Many of the literature reviews cited in this text are based on meta-analyses.

ETHICS AND VALUES IN SOCIAL PSYCHOLOGY

Regardless of where research is conducted (in the lab or in the field), what kind of method is used (correlational or experimental), or what kind of measures are employed (self-reports or observations), ethical issues must always be considered. Although researchers in all fields have a moral and legal responsibility to abide by ethical principles, discussions about ethics have been particularly intense in social psychology (Diener & Crandall, 1978; Greenberg & Folger, 1988; Sieber, 1982). For the most part, this level of intensity is created by those concerns about the use of deception noted earlier in this chapter (Gross & Fleming, 1982). Deceptive techniques have produced considerable controversy (Baumrind, 1985; Kelman, 1967).

This controversy was heightened by the publication of several studies that provoked fierce debates about whether they had gone beyond the bounds of ethical acceptability. Each of these studies addressed a crucial societal concern. Would people obey orders to harm an innocent person? Would people assigned to a role that permitted brutal behavior toward others begin to act brutally? Could some flimsy reference to "authority" and a promise of "immunity" induce people to break the law? No one, then or now, disputes the importance of these questions. What has been debated, however, is whether the significance of the research topic justified exposing subjects to possibly harmful psychological consequences. Table 1.4 describes each of these studies and the debate about their ethicality.

Today, probably none of these studies could be conducted in their original format. But even with current provisions for safeguarding the welfare of human subjects, some research still raises ethical concerns. For example, a study by Dennis Middlemist and his colleagues (1976) used a hidden observer to monitor men's urination in a public lavatory. Was this an acceptable use of a public facility for research purposes or an unacceptable invasion of privacy? More recently, subjects in a study by Robert Croyle and Julie Hunt (1991) were led to believe that they tested positive for a (fictitious) enzyme deficiency. To guard against adverse reactions to this procedure, the seriousness of the supposed disorder was minimized and subjects were deceived for only a short period of time (Croyle & Ditto, 1990). Were these precautions and the importance of studying reactions to medical test results sufficient to justify misleading subjects about a medical diagnosis? Not everyone will agree on the answers to these questions.

But there is agreement about the process investigators must follow in examining the ethical aspects of their research. First, there are government regulations to be adhered to; second, there are professional principles to be followed; and third, there is research on the consequences of deception to be learned from. Let us consider each of these contributions to the development of ethical research practices.

Institutional Review Boards: The Ethical Watchdog

In 1974, the agency then called the United States Department of Health, Education, and Welfare established regulations for the protection of human subjects. These regulations created institutional review boards (IRBs) at all institutions seeking federal funding for research involving human subjects (Gray, 1982; McCarthy, 1981). Charged with the responsibility for reviewing research proposals to ensure that the welfare of subjects was adequately protected, IRBs were to be the "watchdogs" of research. Initially, there was wide-

	Milgram's Research on Obedience (Milgram, 1963; 1974)	Zimbardo's Prison Simulation (Zimbardo et al., 1973)	The "Ubiquitous Watergate" Study (West et al., 1975)
Description	Subjects were instructed to continue delivering electric shocks to a protesting individual as part of a supposed learning study (see Chap. 9).	Under very realistic circumstances, undergraduates were assigned to play the role of a prisoner or a prison guard (see Chap. 12).	Experimenters approached people in a public place and asked them to engage in illegal activities. Some were informed that these activities were sanctioned by authorities, who would protect them from prosecution (see Chap. 3).
Topic	How far will people go when they are told to obey?	How much influence do social roles exert on behavior?	Will people agree to break the law when told that they will not be held responsible for their actions?
Implications	Can this research help us to understand why terrible events, such as the Holocaust of the Jews in World War II, take place in human society?	Can this research help us understand why people in certain societal roles can behave brutally toward others?	Can this research help us understand how people can be induced to break the law when they believe they can get away with it?
Potential Harm	Anxiety experienced during the study as subjects confronted difficult decisions and unusual circumstances; guilt and lowered self-esteem after the study for those who behaved in ways that were discrepant with their moral principles and views of themselves; anger at the researchers for having caused their anxiety and undesirable behavior.		
Sources for Further Reading	Initial critique by Baumrind (1964); initial reply by Milgram (1964); summary by Miller (1986).	Critique by Savin (1973a, 1973b); reply by Zimbardo (1973).	Commentary by Cook (1975).

Table 1.4   Some Controversial Studies in Social Psychology.   Several controversial studies provoked concern about research ethics in social psychology. The three studies described here addressed issues crucial to society but created debate about whether the importance of the topics justified exposing subjects to the possibility of being harmed by research procedures.

spread concern about possible effects on research and, no doubt, numerous complaints from researchers about "more bureaucracy." Since then, researchers have become accustomed to submitting their proposals to IRBs, and revised regulations allow for more efficient and flexible procedures (Applegate, 1984).

Nevertheless, researchers still worry that IRBs might go beyond their watchdog responsibilities and begin to censor research. An investigation of the actions of university IRBs across the United States by Stephen Ceci and his colleagues (1985) was designed to examine this issue. In this study, each IRB received one of nine research proposals to review. These proposals were divided into three levels of ethical violation: clear, questionable, and none. At each level of violation, there were three proposals. Two of the proposals included hypotheses that were socially sensitive, having potential implications for societal groups or policies: one was consistent with conservative political beliefs, the other with liberal political beliefs. The third proposal in each group contained only a neutral hypothesis, unrelated to political beliefs.

The findings from this study were troubling. First, there was considerable variation in judgment. IRBs reviewing the same proposal did not necessarily reach the same conclusion about whether the research should be approved. Second, the judgments of IRBs were affected by the political orientation of the proposals (see Figure 1.3). By a large margin, proposals that were politically neutral were the most likely to be approved. There was also a slight tendency for liberal proposals to be approved more often than conservative ones.

Third, the level of ethical violation in the proposed research procedures did not have a consistent effect on evaluations by the IRBs. For politically neutral proposals, ethics mattered: the ethically responsible proposal was more likely to be approved than were those that were questionable or in clear violation. Among politically sensitive proposals, however, ethics had no effect. The squeaky-clean proposal had no advantage over the ethically unacceptable proposal. Clearly, socially sensitive topics do raise serious ethical questions that require careful scrutiny by investigators and IRBs (Sieber & Stanley, 1988). But better research, not censorship, is the answer. Properly conducted, socially sensitive research can offer vital information needed to address major societal issues, including the needs of disadvantaged groups (Scarr, 1988) and public health concerns such as AIDS (Melton & Gray, 1988; Melton et al., 1988).

Informed Consent: Do You (Really) Want to Participate?

Researchers are not only subject to government-mandated IRBs, they are also required to abide by their profession's code of ethics. The American Psychological Association's (APA) code of ethics, *Ethical Principles of Psychologists* (1990), considers a wide range of ethical issues, including those that affect research procedures and practices. Essentially, the APA code stipulates that researchers

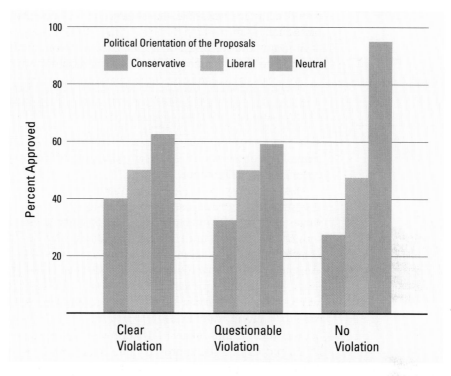

Figure 1.3 Percentages of Research Proposals Approved by Institutional Review Boards. IRBs are supposed to be the watchdogs of research, but sometimes they may act more like censors. In this study, politically neutral research proposals were approved more often than socially sensitive proposals that were consistent with either a liberal or a conservative political position. In addition, politically neutral proposals with no ethical violations were approved more often than were those that were questionable or in clear violation. But socially sensitive proposals were approved at the same rate, regardless of their level of ethical violation. [Data from Ceci et al., 1985.]

---

are obligated to perform a cost-benefit analysis, carefully weighing the benefits of research to knowledge and society against any costs involved for the subjects (Cook, 1976).

informed consent
An individual's deliberate, voluntary decision to participate in research, based on the researcher's description of what will be required during such participation.

To protect the welfare of human subjects, the APA code requires researchers to obtain **informed consent**. Subjects must be asked whether they wish to participate in the research and must be given enough information to make an informed decision. There is considerable debate among psychologists over what information must be provided if a subject's consent is to be truly informed (Macklin, 1982; Sieber, 1984). At a minimum, subjects must be told that they can withdraw from the research at any time. But what about informing subjects about *all* of the procedures to be used in the research? Such complete disclosure would make it impossible to use any kind of deception, even of the mildest nature.

A recent draft (1992) of a proposed revision of the APA code of ethics attempts to clarify when full disclosure is required:

> Psychologists never deceive research participants about significant aspects that would affect their willingness to participate, such as physical risks, discomfort, or unpleasant emotional experiences (pp. 41–42).

It is also recognized that research "involving only anonymous questionnaires, naturalistic observations, or certain kinds of archival research" (p. 41) may not require informed consent.

Most social psychologists believe that the most important factor in protecting the welfare of subjects participating in these kinds of research is to guarantee their anonymity (Aronson et al., 1985; Ruback & Greenberg, 1986). The individual's privacy must be strictly guarded by keeping his or her identity completely hidden in any report on the study. But researchers must also consider whether even anonymous responses could have negative repercussions. Employees, for example, can be reluctant to participate in research on work satisfaction because they fear the consequences if management discovers how their group really feels.

Should informed consent be obtained from people observed in a public place like this shopping mall? Most researchers believe that anonymity is more important. By avoiding the identification of any individual in research reports, the subject's right to privacy is protected.

Debriefing: Telling All

Have *you* ever been a subject in a social psychology study? If so, what was your reaction to this experience? Overall, interviews with subjects have usually found positive attitudes about research (Clark & Word, 1974; Gerdes, 1979; Schwartz & Gottlieb, 1981). But exceptions to this generally favorable response do occur. Compared with subjects who have not been deceived, those who *have* been, tend to perceive psychologists as less trustworthy and are somewhat more likely to report having had a harmful experience (Smith & Richardson, 1983).

Despite these negative effects, deception also has some positive outcomes. Subjects who have been deceived are more positive in their self-evaluations than are those who have not been deceived (Silverman et al., 1970) and sometimes more positive in their evaluation of research activities (Smith & Richardson, 1983). To understand why reactions could be more positive after an experience with deception, we need to consider what happens during debriefing.

Debriefing is a process that occurs after all research data have been collected. At this time, the researcher goes over all procedures, explaining exactly what happened and why. Deceptions are revealed; the purpose of the research is discussed; and the researcher makes every effort to help the subject feel good about having participated. A skillful debriefing takes time and close attention to the individual subject (Cramer et al., 1988; Mills, 1976).

But does it work? Does debriefing *dehoax* the subject, clearing up deceptions and getting the facts straight? Does debriefing *desensitize* the subject, removing any and all distress caused by experimental procedures? From his review of research on debriefing, David Holmes (1976a, 1976b) concluded that if it is done with "care, effort, and vigilance," debriefing can be effective in both getting the facts straight and removing distress. Some reviewers, however, believe that the evidence to date indicates that debriefing is more effective in desensitizing subjects than it is in dehoaxing them (Greenberg & Folger, 1988).

Debriefing done with "care, effort, and vigilance" may account for why subjects who participated in research where they were deceived can have more positive attitudes about themselves and about research activities than do subjects who weren't deceived. When research is deceptive, debriefing is likely to be extensive and thorough. It may be that an especially good experience during debriefing increases the subject's positive attitudes (Smith & Richardson, 1983; Thompson et al., 1980). Subjects usually do respond positively to researchers who act in a serious, professional manner; emphasize the importance of the research they are conducting; and treat their subjects with respect and courtesy (Epstein et al., 1973; Holmes & Appelbaum, 1970). This is exactly the way a researcher behaves during a well-conducted debriefing.

debriefing A disclosure, made to subjects after research proceudres are completed, in which the researcher explains the purpose of the research, attempts to resolve any negative feelings, and emphasizes the scientific contribution made by subjects' participation.

Values and Science: A Matter of Conscience

The ethical issues that have arisen in social psychology all involve a fundamental question of values: Does any scientific advance, no matter how potentially important, ever justify harming—no matter how slightly—any human being? If your answer to this question is *not* an absolute "no," where do you draw the line? How do you weigh the costs and benefits? How do you protect the dignity and welfare of human beings *and* promote the advancement of knowledge? And who should make these judgments—scientists, research subjects, citizens, government, clergy? These are all very difficult questions. Even if we cannot find immediate answers, we need to keep asking them.

We also need to reflect on the fundamental relationship between science and values. Is science value-free? Senator Orrin Hatch thinks it should be: "We in Congress look to social science to provide us unbiased and objective information" (1982, p. 1036). But compare that conception of social science with the one proposed by George S. Howard (1985), who calls on his fellow psychologists to "shift in roles . . . from neutral truth seekers to chroniclers and molders of human action" (p. 263). Senator Hatch's desire for an unbiased, objective social science differs sharply from Professor Howard's advocacy of a more activist psychology.

Senator Hatch and Professor Howard disagree about the goals of science. Underlying their disagreement, however, is a deeper question (Kukla, 1982, 1984). Even if the goal of science is to be unbiased and objective, can this goal ever be fully reached? David Raup (1986), a paleontologist involved in a major scientific controversy about events in Earth's history, is only guardedly optimistic:

> The structure of science, with its rigid procedures and standards for testing of hypotheses, helps to organize our knowledge (and ignorance), and the results of the "scientific method" are probably more objective and dispassionate than in most other fields of human inquiry. But the process still contains strong emotional and sociological elements. (p. 193)

On the basis of his knowledge and experience, Raup is not convinced that science can ever be completely unbiased and objective.

And indeed how could it be? Science is a human enterprise. Scientists choose what to study and how to study it; their choices are influenced by their personal perspectives and values (Gergen, 1985; Rapoport, 1991). To acknowledge the effects of values on science is not to embrace this influence. In fact, it is necessary to acknowledge such influences in order to *reduce* the bias and subjectivity inherent in any human endeavor. As Maureen McHugh and her colleagues (1986) indicate, "Perhaps one of the most difficult tasks of a scientist is to become disengaged from 'everyday' shared assumptions about the nature of reality and to generate alternative, testable conceptualizations of reality" (p. 879).

Good science is the effort to shake oneself free of preconceptions and see reality more clearly, even if never perfectly. An individual's values can promote that clarity of vision or obscure it. Scientific procedures can be ethical and principled or inhumane and barbarous; scientific results can benefit individuals and society or harm them. In other words, science is not a world apart, existing free from moral responsibilities. It is a member of the human tribe, not a lone wolf.

THE BEGINNING, NOT THE END

Your introduction to the field of social psychology is now complete. You have gone step by step through a definition of social psychology, a review of its history and research methods, and a consideration of ethics and values. Before moving on, we'd like to give you a brief, guided tour of how this text is organized.

As you may have already noticed, we've designed a user-friendly format. Each chapter begins with an outline and a short *Preview* of the topics discussed in that chapter. Within the chapters, important terms appear in **boldface type**. These are explained in the text and defined both in the margin and in an alphabetized glossary at the back of the book. At the end of each chapter, a *Review* summarizes the major points that have been covered.

The topics discussed in this text are divided into four major parts. The first three make up the foundations of social psychology—the theories and research that lie at the heart of the discipline. The fourth part applies this knowledge to important issues in law, business, and health. For a sneak preview of what awaits you, consider the following questions:

Part I *Social Perception* The Social Self Perceiving Persons Perceiving Groups	■ When you think about yourself, are you generally satisfied with what you find? Do you see yourself as similar to or different from other people? ■ Why is it that once you form a first impression of someone, that impression often sticks like glue despite all that happens in subsequent meetings? ■ Why is it so difficult to overcome stereotypes and prejudices about various social groups?
Part II *Social Interaction* Interpersonal Attraction Intimate Relationships Helping Others Aggression	■ Why are you immediately attracted to some people but not at all interested in others? ■ How do intimate relationships develop? What problems do intimate partners face? ■ Why do we help others, for their benefit or for our own? ■ Why do people aggress against each other, and how can aggression be reduced?

Part III
Social Influence
Conformity
Attitudes
Group Processes

- Why do so many of us conform in the clothes we wear and the opinions we express?
- What persuasive techniques do politicians use to win votes and advertisers to sell products?
- What accounts for mob violence? Why do groups of highly intelligent individuals sometimes make remarkably bad decisions?

Part IV
Applying Social Psychology
Law
Business
Health

- Have you ever witnessed a crime and tried to remember what you saw? Do you ever wonder what it would be like to sit on a jury?
- Are you intrigued by the stock market—its bullish ups and bearish downs?
- Do you sometimes feel that the stresses of life are getting to you? Are you curious about how people cope with psychological distress and physical illness?

As you study the material presented in the coming chapters, the two of us who wrote this book invite you to share our enthusiasm. You can look forward to information that overturns common sense assumptions, to lively debate and heated controversy, and to a better understanding of yourself and other people. Welcome to the world according to social psychology. We hope you enjoy it!

REVIEW

SOCIAL PSYCHOLOGY: GETTING TO KNOW IT

What Is Social Psychology?

Social psychology is the scientific study of the way individuals think, feel, and behave in social situations. Applying the scientific method in its research, social psychology usually emphasizes the behavior of the individual rather than group factors such as race and socioeconomic class. Seeking to establish general principles of human behavior, social psychologists sometimes examine nonsocial as well as social factors.

A Brief History of Social Psychology

Early research by Triplett and Ringelmann established an enduring topic in social psychology: how the presence of others affects an individual's performance. Sherif's work laid the foundation for later studies of social influence. The legacy of Kurt Lewin is evident today in research guided by the interactionist perspective and in the rapidly expanding area of applied social psychology. After World War II, social psychology prospered and developed systematic programs of research on major topics (see Table 1.1). In the 1960s and early 1970s, there was intense concern about the ethics of research procedures, the validity of research results, and the generalization of conclusions based on research. Today's social psychology is pluralistic in its research methods and perspectives on human behavior. It is international and multicultural in scope.

AN OVERVIEW OF RESEARCH METHODS IN SOCIAL PSYCHOLOGY

Generating Ideas in Social Psychology

The generation of ideas is a continuous, ongoing process that takes place in the mind of the individual social psychologist, in research teams and among colleagues, and in response to research findings. Theories in social psychology are precise rather than comprehensive and generate research by both supporters and opponents. The goal of basic research is to increase understanding, often by testing a specific hypothesis from a specific theory. The goal of applied research is to understand real-world events or to solve practical problems.

Testing Ideas Through Correlations: Looking for Associations

A correlation is an association between two variables. Correlations can be positive or negative. They can be computed between different individuals or within a single individual. Correlation is not causation. A correlation can suggest but not prove a cause-and-effect relationship.

Testing Ideas in Experiments: Looking for Cause and Effect

To examine cause-and-effect relationships, an experiment requires (1) control by the experimenter over events in the experiment and (2) random assignment of subjects to conditions. The effects of the independent variables on the dependent variable are examined. In a main effect, the levels of a single independent variable produce differences in the dependent variable. When two (or more) independent variables affect the dependent variable, the effect can be additive or interactive. In an interaction, the joint effect is greater than the sum of its separate parts.

Evaluating Research

An experiment has internal validity to the extent that changes in the dependent variable can be attributed to the independent variable. Control groups strengthen internal validity; experimenter expectancy effects weaken it. An experiment has external validity to the extent that its results can be generalized to other people and other situations. A representative sample strengths external validity; a convenience sample weakens it. Field research often studies samples that are more representative of the general population than are samples studied in laboratory research. But field research is more often correlational and lacks the control of the laboratory setting. External validity is strengthened by both mundane and experimental realism. Deception is sometimes used to increase experimental realism.

Measure for Measure

In all the social sciences, self-reports are the most popular measure of human behavior. But self-reports can be inaccurate because of efforts to make a good impression and cognitive factors that influence people's responses. To improve accuracy, new techniques obtain self-reports as soon as possible after the event of interest has occurred. Observations can be made by human observers, collected by machines, or derived from existing archival records. Meta-analysis allows researchers to integrate the quantitative results of different studies.

ETHICS AND VALUES IN SOCIAL PSYCHOLOGY

Ethical issues are particularly important in social psychology because of the use of deception in some research. The publication of several controversial studies (see Table 1.4) increased attention to these issues.

Institutional Review Boards: The Ethical Watchdog

Established by the federal government, IRBs are responsible for reviewing research proposals to ensure that the welfare of subjects is adequately protected. Research indicates that IRBs may apply different standards to socially sensitive research than to politically neutral projects.

Informed Consent: Do You (Really) Want to Participate?

The American Psychological Association provides guidelines for research with human subjects. The benefits of research are to be weighed against any physical or psychological costs to subjects. Psychologists are required to secure informed consent from subjects. In some research, anonymity provides the best protection of subjects' welfare.

Debriefing: Telling All

Deceptive research is more likely than nondeceptive research to elicit negative reactions from subjects. When deception is used, a full debriefing is essential. Conducted properly, debriefing is likely to produce positive reactions in subjects.

Values and Science: A Matter of Conscience

Along with other scientists, social psychologists face basic questions of morality and values. Does any scientific advance, no matter how potentially important, ever justify harming—no matter how slightly—any human being? Can science ever be completely unbiased and totally objective? What is good science?

THE BEGINNING, NOT THE END

This text consists of four parts. The first three (on social perception, social interaction, and social influence) describe the foundations of social psychology. The fourth part discusses applications of social psychology in the areas of law, business, and health.

SOCIAL PERCEPTION:
Thinking About Ourselves and Others

I

Preview

Part I of this book examines *social perception,* the ways in which people try to make sense of themselves, other persons, and groups. Chapter 2, on *the social self,* considers how people form a self-concept, maintain self-esteem, and present themselves to others. Chapter 3, on *perceiving persons,* examines how people make snap judgments based on surface appearances, analyze behavior, and form impressions that guide their social interactions. Chapter 4, on *perceiving groups,* describes how people's beliefs about groups are influenced by stereotypes and how their attitudes are tainted by prejudice. As indicated by the theories and research reviewed in these chapters, social perception engages our thoughts and feelings and has profound implications for our daily lives.

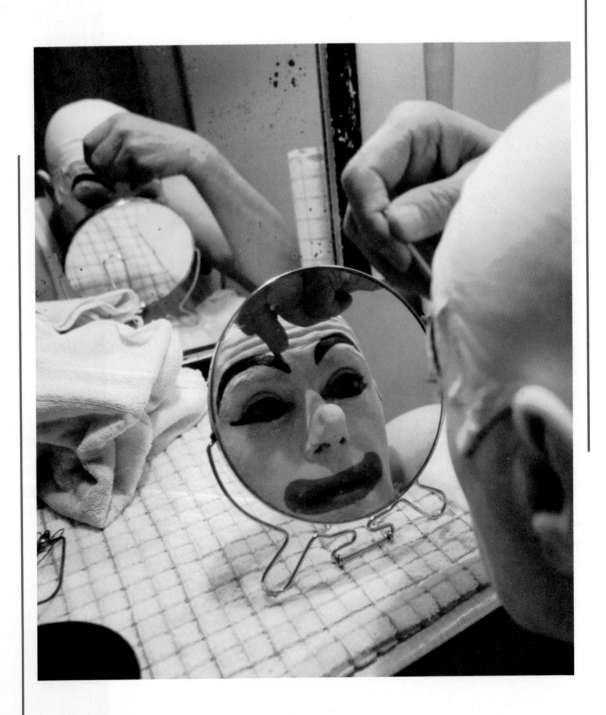

The Social Self

Preview

This chapter examines three interrelated aspects
of the "social self." First, it considers the cognitive *self-concept* and the question of how people
come to understand their own actions, emotions,
and motivations. Second, it considers *self-esteem,*
the affective component, and the question of
how people evaluate themselves and defend
against threats to their self-esteem. Third, it considers *self-presentation,* a behavioral manifestation
of the self, and the question of how people present themselves to others. As we will see, the self
is complex and multifaceted.

Can you imagine living a meaningful or coherent life without a clear sense of who you are? In *The Man Who Mistook His Wife for a Hat,* neurologist Oliver Sacks (1985) described such a person—a patient named William Thompson. According to Sacks, Thompson suffered from an organic brain disorder that impairs a person's memory of recent events. Unable to remember anything for more than a few seconds, Thompson was chronically disoriented and lacked a sense of inner continuity. The effect on his behavior was startling. Trying to grasp a constantly vanishing identity, Thompson would construct one tale after another to account for who he was, where he was, and what he was doing. From one moment to the next, he would improvise new identities—a grocery store clerk, a minister, or a medical patient, to name just a few. In social settings, Thompson's behavior was especially intriguing. As Sacks (1985) observed,

> the presence of others, other people, excite and rattle him, force him into an endless, frenzied, social chatter, a veritable delirium of identity-making and -seeking; the presence of plants, a quiet garden, the nonhuman order, making no social demands upon him, allow this identity-delirium to relax, to subside. (p. 110)

Thompson's plight is unusual, but it highlights two important points—one about the private "inner" self, the other about the "outer" self we show to others. First, the capacity for self-reflection is necessary for people to feel as if they understand their own motives and emotions and the causes of their behavior. Unable to ponder his own actions, Thompson appeared vacant and without feeling—"de-souled," as Sacks put it. Second, the self is heavily influenced by social factors. Thompson himself seemed compelled to put on a face for the sake of others and to improvise characters for the company he kept. We all do, to some extent. We may not create a kaleidoscope of multiple identities as Thompson did, but how we think of and try to present ourselves is influenced by the people around us.

In this chapter, we look at the ABC's of the self: *affect, behavior,* and *cognition,* as depicted in Figure 2.1. First, we ask the cognitive question: How do people come to know themselves, develop a self-concept, and maintain a stable sense of identity? Second, we explore the affective, emotional question: How do people evaluate themselves, enhance their self-images, and defend against threats to their self-esteem? Third, we confront the behavioral question: How do people present themselves to others and regulate their actions according to interpersonal demands?

SELF-CONCEPT: THE COGNITIVE COMPONENT

Have you ever been at a noisy gathering and yet managed to hear someone at the other end of the room mention your name? If so, then you experienced the "cocktail party phenomenon"—the ability to pick a personally relevant stimulus out of a complex environment (Moray, 1959). To cognitive psychologists, this behavior indicates that people are selective in their perceptions of stimuli. To social psychologists, it shows that the self is not just another social stimulus but is the most important object of our attention.

Beginnings of the Self-Concept

When you stand in front of a mirror, what do you see? If you were a dog, a cat, or some other animal, you would not realize that the image you see is your own reflection. Except for human beings, only great apes—chimpanzees, gorillas, and orangutans—seem capable of self-recognition.

How can we know what nonhumans think about mirrors? In a series of studies, Gordon Gallup (1977) placed different species of animals in a room with a large mirror. At first, they greeted their images by vocalizing, gesturing, and making other social responses. After several days, the great apes—but not the other animals—began to use the mirror to pick food out of their teeth, groom themselves, blow bubbles, and make faces for their own entertainment. From all appearances, they recognized themselves. In other studies, Gallup

Figure 2.1   Aspects of the Social Self.   In this chapter, we look at the ABC's of the self: *affect, behavior,* and *cognition.*

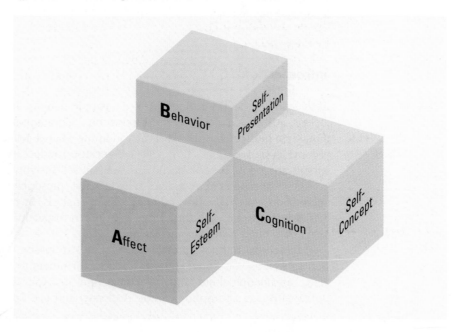

anesthetized the animals, painted an odorless red dye on their brows, and returned them to the mirror. Upon seeing the red spot, only the apes reached for their brows—proof that they perceived the image as their own. By using the same red dye test, developmental researchers have found that most human infants begin to recognize themselves in the mirror when they are between 18 and 24 months old (Lewis & Brooks-Gunn, 1979).

self-concept The sum total of an individual's beliefs about his or her own personal attributes.

Being able to recognize yourself as a distinct entity is a necessary first step in the evolution and development of a **self-concept**, the sum total of beliefs you have about yourself. The second step involves social factors. Many years ago, sociologist Charles Horton Cooley (1902) used the term "looking-glass self" to suggest that other people serve as a mirror in which we see ourselves. Expanding on this idea, George Herbert Mead (1934) added that we often come to know ourselves by imagining what significant others think of us and then incorporating these perceptions into our self-concept. It is interesting that when Gallup tested his apes, those who were reared in isolation—without exposure to their peers—could not recognize themselves in the mirror. Only after such exposure did they begin to show signs of self-recognition. Among human beings, our self-concepts do closely match our *perceptions* of what others think of us, as Cooley and Mead would have predicted. Unfortunately, there's a hitch: our self-concepts often do not match what others *actually* think of us (Felson, 1989; Shrauger & Schoeneman, 1979).

In recent years, social psychologists have broken new ground in their efforts to understand the social self. People are not born thinking of themselves as reckless, likable, or outgoing. So where do their self-concepts come from? In the coming pages, the following sources are considered: introspection, perceptions of one's own behavior, information received from other people, and autobiographical memories.

Introspection

Let's start at the beginning: How do people achieve insight into their own beliefs, attitudes, emotions, and motivations? Common sense makes this question seem ludicrous. After all, don't you know what you think because *you* think it? And don't you know how you feel because *you* feel it? If you look through almost any popular book on how to achieve self-insight, you'll find the answer to these questions to be yes. Whether the prescribed technique involves meditation, psychotherapy, religion, dream analysis, or hypnosis, the advice is basically the same: self-knowledge requires introspection, a looking inward at one's own inner thoughts and feelings.

If these how-to books are correct, it stands to reason that no one can know you as well as you know yourself; indeed, for others to know you at all, they need information about your inner states, not just your overt behavior. Do you agree with this assumption? Susan Andersen and Lee Ross (1984) interviewed college students and asked them to discuss various personal topics: relationships with family and friends, career goals, important decisions and conflicts, and past experiences. Before the interview, subjects were instructed to focus their self-descriptions primarily on their thoughts and feelings, their actual behavior, or a mixture of both. Afterwards, they were asked if they were satisfied that their self-descriptions had communicated a complete and accurate impression. As it turned out, subjects who had described their thoughts and feelings rated the interviews as more informative about themselves than did those who had focused on their behavior. Independent observers—strangers to the speakers themselves—felt the same way.

People assume that to truly know someone—whether it is yourself or somebody else—you must have access to private, subjective experiences. Is this the case? Although people place a good deal of faith in introspection, some social psychologists are not so sure that this faith is justified. Richard Nisbett and Timothy Wilson (1977), for example, claimed that in many studies, including their own, subjects cannot accurately explain the causes or correlates of their own behavior. This argument has attracted a good deal of criticism (Quattrone, 1985; Smith & Miller, 1978), but it has also forced researchers to confront a thorny question: Does introspection improve the *accuracy* of self-knowledge?

Wilson (1985) claims it does not. In fact, he contends that introspection can sometimes impair self-knowledge. In a series of studies, he found that subjects' reported attitudes about different objects corresponded closely with their behavior toward those objects. The more subjects said they enjoyed a particular task, the more time they spent on it; the more attractive they found a scenic landscape, the more pleasure they revealed in their facial expression; the happier they said they were with a dating partner, the longer the relationship ultimately lasted. But after subjects had been told to analyze the reasons for how they felt, their reported attitudes no longer corresponded with their behaviors. Too much introspection can also reduce the quality of our judgments. In a study by Timothy Wilson and Jonathan Schooler (1991), for example, subjects tasted and rated five brands of strawberry jam. Those who were asked to list the reasons for their preferences agreed less with *Consumer Reports* experts than did those who made their ratings without analysis. Apparently, it is possible to think *too* much, only to get confused.

Is this true? Is introspection futile? Not necessarily. According to Murray Millar and Abraham Tesser (1986, 1989), people can reflect on their behavior by listing *reasons* or *feelings*. Whether these reflections provide valuable insight depends on whether the behavior in question is caused more by cognitive or affective factors, thoughts or feelings. For behaviors that are cognitively driven, such as making investment decisions, listing reasons may well increase the accuracy of self-knowledge. But for behaviors that are affectively determined, such as romantic relationships, it may not. To determine why you like a certain puzzle, enjoy a work of art, or love another person, focusing on your feelings may be more helpful than making a list of reasons.

*"I don't sing because I am happy. I am
happy because I sing."*

As suggested by self-perception theory, we sometimes infer how we feel by observing
our own behavior. [Drawing by Frascino; © 1991 The New Yorker Magazine, Inc.]

Perception of Our Own Behavior

**self-perception
theory** The theory
that when internal
cues are difficult to
interpret, people
gain self-insight by
observing their own
behavior.

Regardless of what we learn from introspection, Daryl Bem (1972) believes
people can learn about themselves the same way outside observers do—by
watching their own behavior. Bem's **self-perception theory** is simple yet
profound. To the extent that internal states are weak or difficult to interpret,
people infer what they think or how they feel by observing their own behavior
and the situation in which it takes place. Think about it. Have you ever listened
to yourself argue with someone, only to "realize" with amazement how angry
you were? Or have you ever devoured a sandwich in record time, only then to
conclude that you must have been incredibly hungry? In each of these cases,
you made an inference about yourself by watching your own actions. There are
limits, of course. According to Bem, people do not infer their internal states
from behavior that occurred in the presence of compelling situational pressures
such as reward or punishment. If you argued or wolfed down a sandwich

because you were paid to do so, you probably would *not* assume that you were angry or hungry. In other words, people learn about themselves through self-perception only when the situation alone seems insufficient to have caused their behavior.

A good deal of research supports self-perception theory. When people are gently coaxed into doing something, and when they are not otherwise certain about how they feel, they come to view themselves in ways that are consistent with their behavior (Chaiken & Baldwin, 1981; Fazio, 1987; Schlenker & Trudeau, 1990). Subjects induced to describe themselves in flattering terms thus scored higher on a later test of self-esteem than those who were led to describe themselves more modestly (Jones et al., 1981; Rhodewalt & Agustsdottir, 1986). Similarly, subjects who were maneuvered by leading questions into describing themselves as introverted or extroverted came to define themselves as such later on, unless they were certain of this aspect of their personality (Fazio et al., 1981; Swann & Ely, 1984). British author E. M. Forster anticipated the theory well when he asked, "How can I tell what I think 'til I see what I say?"

action identification theory The theory that our *interpretation* of our own behavior in high-level or low-level terms forms the basis for self-perception.

Action Identification: A Matter of Interpretation The self-perception process is somewhat more complicated than it appears. Bem claimed that people make inferences about themselves by observing their own behavior. But is it behavior per se that matters or how we *interpret* that behavior? The **action identification theory** of Robin Vallacher and Daniel Wegner (1985) suggests that the interpretation is what's important. According to this theory, all actions can be understood or "identified" within a hierarchy of meanings. In this hierarchy, people can view an action in either high-level or low-level terms. Consider, for example, what you're doing at this very moment. Presumably, you're reading this sentence. But there's more to it than that. If asked to identify this behavior, some readers would describe it in low-level, mechanistic terms: you're sitting, moving your eyes across the page, reading words, reflecting on the important concepts, and perhaps even highlighting key sentences as you go along. Yet other readers would focus on the "big picture" and identify this behavior in more general, high-level terms: you're trying to learn social psychology, earn three credits, graduate from college, or prepare for a career. Using the examples presented in Table 2.1, Vallacher and Wegner (1989) find that some people consistently view their actions in either high-level or low-level terms.

Action identification theory is concerned with the causes and effects of conceptualizing behavior at different levels. In terms of self perception, for example, people are more likely to base inferences about themselves on behaviors they identify in high-level terms than on those behaviors identified in low-level terms. If you think of what you're doing right now as simply moving your eyes across the page, your behavior—reading this text—will have little significance for your self-concept. If you think you're trying to prepare for a career in psychology, however, the same behavior implies something more revealing about your self-concept (Wegner et al., 1986). People do make

Behaviors	Responses
1. Making a list	
a. getting organized	73%
b. writing things down	27
2. Paying the rent	
a. maintaining a place to live	65
b. writing a check	35
3. Eating	
a. getting nutrition	59
b. chewing and swallowing	41
4. Painting a room	
a. applying brush strokes	35
b. making the room look fresh	65
5. Locking a door	
a. putting a key in the lock	11
b. securing the house	89

Table 2.1   Levels of Action Identification.   For each behavior, select an identification, *a* or *b*, that best describes what you're doing. Do you prefer to identify actions in mechanistic low-level terms or in high-level terms that have implications for your self-concept? Next to each item is the percentage of people out of 1,400 respondents who selected the two alternatives. [From Vallacher & Wegner, 1989.]

---

self-inferences from their own actions, as Bem suggested—but only when they identify those actions in high-level terms.

Facial Feedback: Effects of a Happy Face   Draw the corners of your mouth back and up and tense your eye muscles. Relax. Now raise your eyebrows, open your eyes wide, and let your mouth drop open slightly. Relax. Now pull your brows down and together and clench your teeth. Relax. If you followed these directions, you would have appeared to others to be feeling first happy, then fearful, and finally angry. The question is, how would you have appeared to yourself?

Social psychologists who study emotion have asked precisely that question. Viewed within the framework of self-perception theory, the **facial feedback hypothesis** states that changes in facial expression can lead to corresponding changes in the subjective experience of emotion. To test this hypothesis, James Laird (1974) told subjects that they were taking part in an experiment on activity of the facial muscles. After attaching electrodes to subjects' faces, he showed them a series of cartoons. Before each one, the subjects were instructed to contract certain facial muscles in ways that created either a smile or a frown.

facial feedback hypothesis The hypothesis that changes in facial expression can lead to corresponding changes in emotion.

As Laird predicted, subjects rated what they saw as funnier, and reported feeling happier, when they were smiling than when they were frowning. In follow-up research, subjects were similarly induced through posed expressions to feel fear, anger, sadness, and disgust (Duclos et al., 1989).

But why? With 80 muscles in the human face that can create more than 7,000 expressions, can people actually manipulate their own emotions by contracting certain muscles and wearing certain expressions? Research suggests they can (Laird, 1984), but the issue is complicated for two reasons. First, not all studies support the facial feedback hypothesis, and the effects are often limited (Matsumoto, 1987; Winton, 1986). Second, it is not clear what the supportive results mean. According to Laird, facial expressions affect emotion through a process of self-perception: "I'm smiling, so I guess I must be happy. If I'm frowning, I must be angry." Others, however, maintain that facial movements spark emotion by producing physiological changes in the brain (Izard, 1990). For example, Robert Zajonc and his colleagues (1989) find that smiling causes facial muscles to increase the flow of air-cooled blood to the brain, which produces a pleasant state by lowering brain temperature. Conversely, frowning decreases blood flow, which produces an unpleasant state by raising temperature. According to this analysis, people need not infer how they feel; rather, facial expressions evoke physiological changes that produce an emotional experience.

Are self-perception processes necessary for facial feedback to work? Probably not. In one study, Fritz Strack and others (1988) had subjects hold a pen with either their front teeth or their lips, supposedly to test their ability to use different parts of the body for various tasks. Try it, and you'll see that holding a pen with the front teeth causes you to smile but holding it with the lips prevents you from smiling. The subjects didn't realize this was occurring. Yet those in the teeth group found a series of cartoons funnier than did those in the lips condition. In another study, Zajonc and others (1989) asked subjects to repeat various vowels 20 times each, including the sounds "ah," "e," "u," and the German vowel "ü." In the meantime, temperature changes in the forehead were measured and subjects were asked to report how they felt. As shown in Figure 2.2, "ah" and "e" (vowel sounds that cause speakers to mimic smiling) lowered forehead temperature and elevated mood, and "u" and "ü" (vowel sounds that cause speakers to mimic frowning) increased temperature and dampened mood. Apparently, movement of the facial muscles can influence emotion even when people are not aware that they are wearing a particular expression. This research teaches a useful lesson: it's possible to alter how you feel by putting on the right face. If you want to feel good, just say "cheese"!

Overjustification: Paradoxical Effects of Reward Without realizing it, Mark Twain was a self-perception theorist. In *The Adventures of Tom Sawyer*, written in the late 1800s, he quipped, "there are wealthy gentlemen in England who drive four-horse passenger coaches twenty or thirty miles on a daily line, in the summer, because the privilege costs them considerable money; but if they were offered wages for the service that would turn it into work then they would resign."

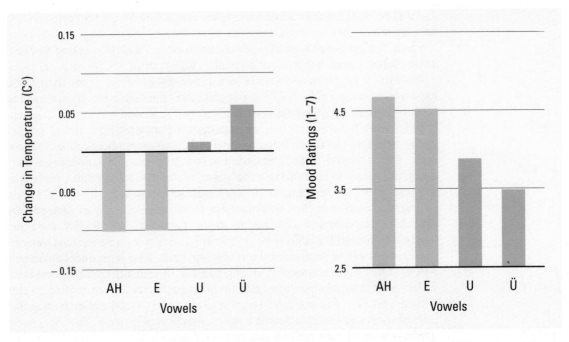

Figure 2.2   Facial Feedback and Emotion.   Subjects were asked to repeat different vowel sounds. As you can see, "ah" and "e"—sounds that cause us to mimic smiling—lowered brain temperature (left) and elevated mood (right). In contrast, "u" and "ü"—vowels that cause us to mimic frowning—raised brain temperature (left) and dampened mood (right). [Zajonc et al., 1989.]

Twain's hypothesis—that rewarding people for an enjoyable activity undermines their interest in that activity—seems to contradict intuition and a good deal of psychological research as well. After all, aren't we all motivated by reward, as declared by the late B. F. Skinner and other behaviorists? The answer depends on how *motivation* is defined. As a keen observer of human behavior, Twain anticipated a key distinction between intrinsic and extrinsic motivation. *Intrinsic motivation* originates in factors within an individual. People are said to be intrinsically motivated when they engage in an activity for its own sake, out of sheer enjoyment, without expecting a tangible payoff for their efforts. Eating a fine meal, listening to music, spending time with friends, and working on a hobby are among the activities you might find intrinsically motivating. In contrast, *extrinsic motivation* originates in factors outside the person. People are said to be extrinsically motivated when they engage in an activity as a means to an end—to obtain money, grades, or recognition; to fulfill obligations; or to avoid punishment. As the behaviorists have claimed, people do strive for reward. But what then happens to their intrinsic motivation once that reward is no longer available?

From the standpoint of self-perception theory, Twain's hypothesis makes sense. When people are rewarded for listening to music, or playing games, or eating tasty food, their behavior becomes *over*justified, or "overrewarded," and can be attributed to extrinsic as well as intrinsic motives. For self-perceivers, such **overjustification** can be dangerous: observing that their efforts have paid off, people begin to wonder if the activity was ever worth pursuing for mere enjoyment. This problem has been demonstrated in numerous experiments (Deci & Ryan, 1985; Lepper & Greene, 1978; Pittman & Heller, 1987).

Mark Lepper and his colleagues (1973), for example, gave children attending a preschool a chance to play with colorful felt-tipped markers—a chance most of them couldn't resist. By observing how much time the children spent on the activity, the researchers were able to measure their intrinsic motivation. Two weeks later, the children were divided into three groups, all about equal in their initial levels of intrinsic motivation. In one, they were simply asked if they would draw some pictures with the markers. In the second, they were told that if they used the markers they would receive a "Good Player Award," a certificate with a gold star and a red ribbon. In the third group, the children were not offered a reward for drawing pictures but then—like those in the second group—received a reward when they were done.

About a week later, the teachers placed the markers and paper on a table in the classroom while the experimenters observed through a one-way mirror. Since no rewards were available, the amount of free time the children spent playing with the markers reflected their intrinsic motivation. The results were as predicted. Children who had previously expected and received a reward for their efforts were no longer as interested in the markers as they had been. Subjects who hadn't received a reward were not adversely affected. Neither were those who had unexpectedly received the reward; having played with the markers without the promise of reward, these children remained intrinsically motivated (see Figure 2.3).

The paradox that reward undermines rather than enhances intrinsic motivation has been observed in numerous settings with children and adults. Deadlines, competition, and other extrinsic factors can have the same detrimental effect. Accept money for a hobby or leisure activity, and before you know it, what used to be "play" comes to feel like "work."

The overjustification effect can have serious implications for how parents socialize their children, for how classroom teachers use reward to improve study habits, and for how business managers use incentives to increase worker productivity. In one study, for example, college students who were paid to help someone felt less morally obligated to offer their assistance "for free" in a later situation (Kunda & Schwartz, 1983). Are we to conclude, then, that rewards should always be avoided? No, not at all. If a person is not intrinsically motivated to start with, then reward cannot hurt because the behavior would not be overjustified. Also, if reward is presented as a special "bonus" for superior

overjustification
The tendency for intrinsic motivation to diminish for activities that have become associated with reward or other extrinsic factors.

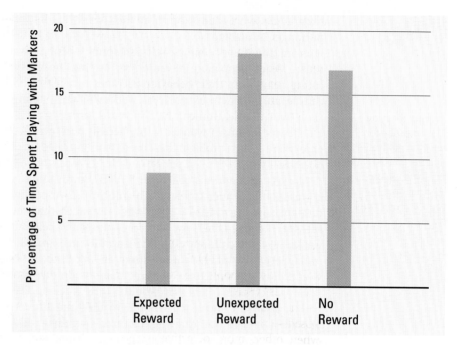

Figure 2.3   Paradoxical Effects of Reward on Intrinsic Motivation.   In this study, an expected reward undermined children's intrinsic motivation to play with felt-tipped markers. Children who received an unexpected reward or no reward did not lose interest. [Data from Lepper et al., 1973.]

performance, rather than as a "bribe" for mere task engagement, then it can *enhance* intrinsic motivation (Enzle & Ross, 1978; Harackiewicz, 1979; Rosenfield et al., 1980). Clearly, the effect of reward depends on how it is perceived.

Influence of Other People

As we noted earlier, Cooley's (1902) theory of the looking-glass self emphasized that other people help us to define ourselves. In this section, we will see the importance of this proposition.

Social Comparison Theory   Suppose a stranger were to ask, "Who are you?" If you had only five minutes to answer, would you mention your ethnic or religious background? What about your hometown? Would you describe your talents and your interests or your likes and dislikes? Faced with the question, people tend to describe themselves in ways that set them apart from others in their immediate environment. Among children, for example, boys are more likely to cite their gender when they grow up in families that are predominantly female; girls do the same when they come from homes that are predominantly male (McGuire et al., 1979). Whether the unique attribute is gender, age, height, or eye color, the pattern is the same (McGuire & McGuire, 1988). This finding has an interesting implication: change someone's social surroundings, and you can change that person's spontaneous self-descriptions.

This reliance on distinguishing features in self-description indicates that the self is a social construct and that we define ourselves in part by making comparisons with others. Indeed, that is what Leon Festinger (1954) proposed in his **social comparison theory**. According to Festinger, when people are uncertain about their abilities or opinions—that is, when objective information is not available—they evaluate themselves by drawing comparisons with similar others. The theory seems reasonable enough, but is it valid? Over the years, social psychologists have put social comparison theory to the test, focusing on two key questions: (1) *When* do we turn to others for comparative information? (2) Of all the people who inhabit the Earth, *to whom* do we choose to compare ourselves? (Suls & Wills, 1991; Wood, 1989).

The answer to the "when" question appears to be—as Festinger had proposed—that people engage in social comparison under states of uncertainty, when other, more objective means of self-evaluation are not available. The answer to the "to whom" question, however, is that to evaluate our taste in music, our value on the job market, or our athletic ability, we look to others who are similar in relevant ways (Goethals & Darley, 1977; C. T. Miller, 1984; Wheeler et al., 1982). If you're curious about your flair for writing, for example, you're more likely to compare yourself to other college students than to high school students or to best-selling authors. There are, as usual, exceptions to the rule. Later in this chapter, we will see that sometimes people cope with personal inadequacies by focusing on others who are *less* able or *less* fortunate than themselves.

Two-Factor Theory of Emotion People seek social comparison information to evaluate their abilities and opinions. But do we also use others to determine something as personal and subjective as our own *emotions*? In a series of experiments on affiliation, Stanley Schachter (1959) found that when subjects were frightened into thinking they would receive painful electric shocks, most sought the company of others who were in the same predicament. Nervous and uncertain about how they should be feeling, subjects wanted to affiliate with similar others for the purposes of comparison. Yet when subjects were not fearful, expecting only mild shocks, or when the alleged "others" were not participants in the same experiment, subjects preferred to be alone. As Schachter put it, "misery doesn't just love any kind of company; it loves only miserable company" (p. 24).

Intrigued by the possibilities, Schachter and his research team took the next step. Could it be, they wondered, that when people are uncertain of how

social comparison theory The theory that people evaluate their own abilities and opinions by comparing themselves to others.

they feel, their emotions are actually determined by the reactions of others around them? In answer to this question, the researchers proposed that two factors are necessary to feel a specific emotion. First, the person must experience *physiological arousal*—a racing heart, perspiration, rapid breathing, a tightening of the stomach. Second, the person must make a *cognitive interpretation* that explains the source of that arousal. And that is where the people around us come in: their reactions help us to interpret our own arousal.

two-factor theory of emotion The theory that the experience of emotion is based on two factors: physiological arousal and a cognitive interpretation of that arousal.

To test this provocative **two-factor theory of emotion**, Schachter and Jerome Singer (1962) injected male subjects with epinephrine, a drug that produces physiological arousal. Although one group was forewarned about the actual side effects, a second group was not. In a third group, subjects were injected with a harmless placebo. Before the drug (which was described as a vitamin supplement) actually took effect, subjects were left alone with a male confederate introduced as another subject who had received the same injection. For some subjects, the confederate behaved in a euphoric manner. For twenty minutes, he bounced around happily, doodling on scratch paper, sinking jump shots into the waste basket, flying paper airplanes across the room, and playing with a Hula-Hoop. For other subjects, the confederate displayed anger, ridiculing a questionnaire they were filling out and, in a fit of rage, ripping it up and hurling it into the waste basket.

Think for a moment about these various situations. Subjects in the *drug-informed* group begin to feel their hearts pound, their hands shake, and their faces flush. Having been told to expect these symptoms, however, they need not search for an explanation. Subjects in the *placebo* group don't become aroused in the first place, so they have no symptoms to explain. But now consider the plight of those subjects in the *drug-uninformed* group who suddenly become aroused without knowing why. Trying to identify the sensations, these subjects, according to the theory, should take their cues from others in the same predicament—namely, the confederate.

In general, the experimental results supported Schachter and Singer's line of reasoning. Drug-uninformed subjects reported feeling relatively happy or angry depending on the confederate's performance. In many instances, they even exhibited similar kinds of behavior. One subject, for example, "threw open the window and, laughing, hurled paper basketballs at passersby." In the drug-informed and placebo groups, however, subjects were, as expected, less influenced by these social cues.

Schachter and Singer's two-factor theory has attracted a good deal of controversy, for some experiments have corroborated their findings but others have not. Overall, however, one limited but important conclusion can safely be drawn: when people are uncertain of their own emotional states, they sometimes interpret how they feel by watching others (Reisenzein, 1983). The "sometimes" part of the conclusion is important. For others to influence your emotion, your level of physiological arousal should not be too intense, or else it will be interpreted in negative, aversive terms—regardless of the situation (Marshall & Zimbardo, 1979; Maslach, 1979). Also, other people must be present as a possible explanation for arousal *before* its onset; once aroused, people turn for an explanation to events that preceded rather than followed their physiological state (Schachter & Singer, 1979). In subsequent chapters, we will see that this two-factor theory has far-reaching implications for passionate love and other diverse experiences.

Autobiographical Memory

Philosopher James Mill once said, "the phenomenon of the Self and that of Memory are merely two sides of the same fact." If the story of patient William Thompson at the start of this chapter is any indication, Mill was right. Without autobiographical memory—recollections of the sequence of events that have touched your life (Rubin, 1986)—you would have no self-concept. After all, who would you be if you could not remember your parents, your childhood friends, the places you lived, the schools you attended, and the experiences you had? Clearly, memories shape the self-concept. In this section, however, we will see that the self-concept shapes our memories as well (Greenwald & Pratkanis, 1984; Ross, 1989; Ross & Conway, 1985).

The self guides our recollections in three important ways—by means of the self-reference effect, egocentric bias, and hindsight bias. First, there is the **self-reference effect**: people are more likely to remember something—a word, a concept, or an event—if they think about it in relation to the self than if they view it in other contexts. In one study, subjects sat in front of a microcomputer and looked at forty trait adjectives (for example, *shy, friendly, ambitious*). For some words, subjects were instructed to consider whether they were self-descriptive; for others, subjects were to judge the word's length, sound, or meaning. When later asked to recall as many of the words as they could, subjects remembered more of the words they had thought about in reference to themselves than the ones they had considered for other purposes (Rogers et al., 1977). Although it is not clear why this difference in recall occurs, it is clear that the self is like a mnemonic device: by viewing new information as *relevant* to our own experiences, we consider that information more fully and organize it around common themes. The net result is an improvement in memory (Greenwald & Banaji, 1989; Klein & Loftus, 1988).

Although self-referencing can facilitate recall, it can also lead to a distortion of the past. Some events, to be sure, are vivid in memory and not easily distorted. Ask people who are old enough to remember November 22, 1963, and the chances are they will be able to describe precisely where they were, what was happening, and with whom, when John F. Kennedy was assassinated. For events of great personal or societal impact, people often have what are called "flashbulb memories"—memories that, like a snapshot, are distinct and vivid (Brown & Kulik, 1977). But what about our recollections of ordinary events?

self-reference effect
The finding that information is recalled better when it is relevant to the self than when it is not.

egocentric bias Bias toward perceiving and recalling oneself as a central actor in past events.

According to Anthony Greenwald (1980), autobiographical memory is often colored by **egocentric bias**, as people tend to overemphasize their own role in past events and the extent to which they were the target of other people's actions. As Greenwald put it, "the past is remembered as if it were a drama in which the self was the leading player" (p. 604). To illustrate egocentricity at its best (or worst), let's turn the clock back to a momentous event in American history: the Senate Watergate hearings of 1973. The witness was John Dean, former counsel to President Richard Nixon. Dean had submitted a 245-page statement in which he recounted word for word the details of many conversations. Dean's memory seemed so impressive that he was called "the human tape recorder." In an ironic twist of fate, Nixon had taped the meetings that Dean recalled. Was Dean accurate? A comparison of his testimony with the actual tapes revealed that although he correctly remembered the gist of his White House meetings, he consistently exaggerated his own role and his own importance in the events. Ulric Neisser (1981), the cognitive psychologist who analyzed Dean's testimony, wondered, "Are we all like this? Is everyone's memory constructed, staged, self-centered?" The answer is yes—there is a bit of John Dean in all of us. Thus, when college basketball players from opposing teams were asked to describe a turning point in the games they played against each other, 80 percent of them referred to plays initiated by their own team (Ross & Sicoly, 1979).

hindsight bias
The tendency, once an event has occurred, to overestimate one's ability to have foreseen the outcome.

Another important feature of autobiographical memory is the **hindsight bias**, our tendency to think after an event that we knew beforehand what was going to happen. Historians are sometimes criticized for making the past seem inevitable in hindsight. Apparently, we all do. After learning a new fact or the outcome of some event—whether it's the outcome of a political election, an earthquake, the invasion of one country by another, or the winner of the last Super Bowl—people tend to say, "I knew it all along" (Fischhoff, 1975; Hawkins & Hastie, 1990; Wood, 1978). In one study, for example, physicians who were told about a case history later overestimated the likelihood that they would have made the correct diagnosis (Arkes et al., 1981).

When it comes to the self, the implications of 20/20 hindsight are intriguing. Do people revise their fading personal histories in light of current information? Michael Ross and his colleagues (1981) addressed this question by changing subjects' attitudes on an issue and then asking those subjects to report on their past behaviors. In one experiment, for example, subjects listened to a medical expert argue convincingly either for or against the wisdom of brushing teeth after every meal. Later, supposedly as part of a different experiment, those who had heard the favorable argument reported that they brushed their teeth more often in the previous two weeks than did those who had heard the unfavorable argument. Having adopted new attitudes on the issue, subjects "updated" their recall of past behaviors. Contemplating the social ramifications, Ross (1989) suggested that our revisionist tendencies could account for why successive generations of parents bemoan how today's children are not as responsible as those who grew up in the good old days. According to Ross, adults do not compare the younger generation to what they themselves were really like at a comparable age. Instead, adults forgetfully assume that they used to be as they are in the present. By comparison, the next generation is bound to appear deficient. After studying adult development, psychiatrist George Vaillant (1977) drew a similar conclusion: "It is all too common for caterpillars to become butterflies and then to maintain that in their youth they had been little butterflies. Maturation makes liars of us all" (p. 197).

Self-Schemas

As we have seen, people can learn about themselves through introspection, by observing their own behavior, by comparing themselves to others, and by organizing their personal memories around existing beliefs about the self. But what, specifically, does the self-concept consist of, and how does it affect our views of the world? Personality, social, and developmental psychologists have been asking these questions for many years but have found no single answer. The study of human cognition, however, provides an important new perspective.

self-schemas Beliefs people hold about themselves that guide the processing of self-relevant information.

According to Hazel Markus (1977), the cognitive molecules of the self-concept are called **self-schemas**: beliefs about oneself that guide the processing of self-relevant information. Self-schemas are to an individual's total self-concept what hypotheses are to a theory, what books are to a library. You can think of yourself as masculine or feminine, independent or dependent, liberal or conservative, introverted or extroverted. Indeed, any specific attribute may have relevance to the self-concept for some people but not for others. The self-schema for body weight is a good example. People who regard themselves as

Sometimes people communicate their self-schemas on the cars they drive.

extremely overweight or underweight, or for whom body image is a conspicuous aspect of the self-concept, are considered *schematic* with respect to their
weight. In contrast, those who do not regard their weight as extreme or as a
central part of their lives are *aschematic* on that attribute (Markus et al., 1987).

Self-schemas are important because they lead us to interpret and recall our
life experiences according to personally relevant themes. For body-weight
schematics, a wide range of otherwise mundane events—a trip to the supermarket, new clothing, dinner at a restaurant, a day at the beach, or a friend's eating
habits—may trigger self-relevant thoughts. When processing information, people (1) make rapid judgments about themselves on matters relevant to their self-
schemas, (2) are quick to recall or reconstruct past events that fit their self-
schemas, and (3) reject information that is inconsistent with their self-schemas
(Kihlstrom & Cantor, 1984). In fact, people often view others through the lens
of their own self-schemas (Carpenter, 1988; Lewicki, 1983; Markus et al.,
1985). Body-weight schematics, for example, always seem to notice whenever
someone *else* eats too much or gains an ounce.

Consisting of many self-schemas, the self is multifaceted. In fact, people think
not only about their current selves but about *possible selves* as well—what they
might become, would like to become, and are afraid of becoming in the future.
Thus, when college students were asked to rate themselves on a list of attributes,
there were marked differences between current views of the self and possible
selves. Most imagined possibilities were in a positive direction, as most students
believed it possible for them to become good parents, happy, physically fit, rich,
well respected, secure, and successful (Markus & Nurius, 1986). Conceptions
of possible selves provide people with an imaginary blueprint for future goals
and plans (Ruvolo & Markus, 1992). Thus, they persist throughout adulthood,
until people reach old age (Ryff, 1991).

Multicultural Perspectives

In America, "the squeaky wheel gets the grease." In Japan, "the nail that stands
out gets pounded down." In America, parents tell their children to be independent, self-reliant, and assertive, a "cut above the rest." In Japan, children are
raised to get along and fit in with others in the community. Impressed by these
cultural differences, social psychologists wonder: Do people in America and
Japan have different conceptions of the self?

According to Hazel Markus and Shonobu Kitayama (1991), different cultures
foster different conceptions of the self. In many Western countries, people have
an *independent* view of themselves as entities that are distinct, autonomous, self-
contained, and endowed with unique dispositions. Yet in much of Asia, Africa,
and Latin America, people hold a collective or *interdependent* view of the self as
part of a larger social network in which harmonious relationships with others
are more important than individual self-expression. People with an independent
view of the self tend to believe that "the only person you can count on is

For people who hold an *interdependent* view of the self, fitting in with others in the group is more important than individual self-expression.

yourself," whereas those with an interdependent view are more likely to think that "I'm partly to blame if one of my family members or coworkers fails" (Triandis, 1989). In what cultures are these differing views the most extreme? In a worldwide study of 116,000 employees of IBM, Geert Hofstede (1980) found that the most fiercely independent people were from the United States, Australia, Great Britain, Canada, and the Netherlands, in that order. In contrast, the most interdependent people were from Venezuela, Colombia, Pakistan, Peru, and Taiwan. These two conceptions are illustrated in Figure 2.4.

How do these cultural differences influence the way we perceive, evaluate, and present ourselves in relation to others? Markus and Kitayama (1991) found three interesting differences. First, American college students perceive themselves as less similar to others than do Asian Indian students, reinforcing the idea that people with independent conceptions of the self believe they are unique. Second, Americans are quick to express jealousy, anger, pride, and other "ego-focused" emotions that affirm the self as an autonomous entity; but non-Westerners often feel "other-focused" emotions that promote interpersonal harmony rather than conflict. In Japan, for instance, people often report feeling "oime" (indebtedness to someone), "fureai" (connection with someone), and "shitashimi" (familiarity to someone). Third, people in independent cultures

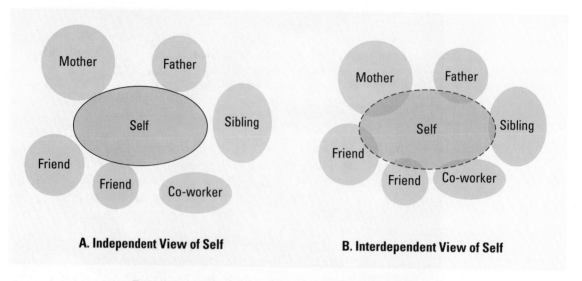

Figure 2.4   Cultural Conceptions of Self.   As depicted here, different cultures foster different conceptions of the self. Many Westerners have an *independent* view of the self as an entity that is distinct, autonomous, and self-contained. Yet many Asians, Africans, and Latin Americans hold an *interdependent* view of the self that encompasses others in a larger social network. [Markus & Kitayama, 1991.]

strive for personal achievement, but those in interdependent cultures derive much of their self-esteem by fitting in with the group. Thus, while Americans overestimate their contribution to joint efforts, take credit for success, and blame others for failure, Japanese people tend to underestimate their role and portray themselves in more modest, humble terms. In one study, American and Chinese college students were asked to complete twenty sentences beginning with "I am." The Americans were more likely to fill in the blanks with individualistic statements, while the Chinese were more likely to describe themselves by their group affiliations (Trafimow, et al. 1991). How deep are these differences? Do they trigger conflict between individuals with opposing self-conceptions? Social psychologists may have answers to these questions in the years to come.

SELF-ESTEEM: THE AFFECTIVE COMPONENT

How do you feel about yourself? Are you generally satisfied with your appearance, your personality, your abilities, and your friendships? Do you ever feel useless? Are you optimistic or pessimistic about your future? In this section, we will see that when it comes to the self, people are not cool, objective, and dispassionate. In fact, quite the opposite: we are highly judgmental, emotional, and self-protective. Thus, we move from the relatively cognitive self-concept to **self-esteem**—an affectively charged component of the self.

The word *esteem* comes from the Latin *aestimare,* which means "to estimate or appraise." Self-esteem thus refers to our positive and negative evaluations of ourselves (Coopersmith, 1967). It is important to keep in mind that self-esteem is not a single trait etched in stone. Although most people think highly of themselves, we all suffer through occasional periods of self-doubt, feelings of inadequacy, incompetence, and worthlessness. Also, since the self-concept consists of numerous self-schemas, people evaluate some parts of the self more favorably, or more clearly, than they evaluate other parts of the self (Fleming & Courtney, 1984; Pelham & Swann, 1989). Interestingly, the clearer people are about their self concept, the higher is their self-esteem (Campbell, 1990).

Self-esteem is linked in important ways to how people approach their daily lives. Those who feel good about themselves tend to be happy, healthy, successful, and adaptable. In contrast, those who evaluate themselves in negative terms are relatively anxious, unhealthy, depressed, pessimistic about the future, and prone to failure. Part of the problem is that people who lack self-esteem have a self-defeating attitude that can trap them in a vicious cycle (see Figure 2.5). Expecting to fail, they get anxious, exert little effort, and "tune out" on life's important challenges. Then when they do fail, people with low self-esteem

self-esteem An affective component of the self, consisting of a person's positive and negative self-evaluations.

Figure 2.5   The Vicious Cycle of Low Self-Esteem.   Low self-esteem triggers a self-defeating cycle in which negative expectations impair performance and, in turn, reinforce low self-esteem.

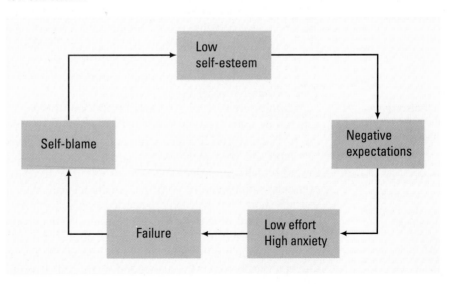

Discrepancy	Emotional State	Disorder
Own oughts	Agitation from self-criticism (guilt)	Anxiety
Others' oughts	Agitation from fear and threat (shame)	Anxiety
Own ideals	Dejection from perceived lack of self-fulfillment (disappointment)	Depression
Others' ideals	Dejection from anticipated loss of social affection (lack of pride)	Depression

Table 2.2   Effects of Discrepancies with the Self-Concept.   The emotions and possible disorders associated with four types of self-discrepancies. [Based on Higgins, 1989.]

blame themselves, leading them to feel more and more incompetent (Brockner, 1983).

Self-Discrepancies

Are you smart? Easygoing? Sexy? Excitable? On a blank sheet of paper, list up to ten traits that describe the kind of person *you* think you *actually* are. Next, list ten traits that describe the kind of person you think you *ought* to be, traits that you feel are needed to meet your sense of duty, obligation, and responsibility. Then make a list of traits that describe an *ideal* of what you would like to be, an ideal that embodies your hopes, wishes, and dreams. Now think of some-one—your mother, father, sibling, best friend, or lover—whose opinion of you matters the most. What traits would that *significant other person* list to describe how you ought to be and how he or she would like you to be? By following these instructions, you should now have five lists—your actual self, two *ought* selves (from your own and another's standpoint), and two *ideal* selves (also from your own and another's standpoint).

self-discrepancy theory The theory linking the perception of discrepancies between a person's self-concept and various self-guides to specific, negative emotional states.

According to E. Tory Higgins's (1989) **self-discrepancy theory**, these trait lists can be used to predict your self-esteem and emotional well-being. According to Higgins, the first list represents your self-concept. The four remaining lists represent your personal standards, or *self-guides*—these are the standards toward which you strive. Different people may have different self-guides, but everyone is motivated by some personally relevant standards. To the extent that you fall short, you will experience lowered self-esteem, unpleasant emotional symptoms, and in extreme cases a serious affective disorder.

As summarized in Table 2.2, research shows that the specific consequences depend on which self-guide you fail to achieve. First, there is the possibility for discrepancies between the actual and ought self. If your self-concept is incompatible with (a) your own feelings of obligation or (b) the "oughts" held for you by a significant other, you will feel guilty, shameful, and resentful. In extreme cases, you might suffer from excessive fear and anxiety-related disorders. Second, there is the possibility for discrepancies between your actual and ideal self. If your first list doesn't match (a) your own ideals, hopes, wishes, and aspirations or (b) those held for you by a significant other, you will feel disappointed, frustrated, sad, and unfulfilled. In extreme cases, you might even suffer from depression (Higgins et al., 1986; Strauman, 1989, 1992).

Every one of us must live with some degree of discrepancy between our self-concept and self-guides. Nobody is perfect. Yet we do not all suffer from the symptoms of anxiety-related disorders and depression. Why? According to Higgins (1989), the emotional consequences of self-discrepancy depend on two factors. The first is simply the *amount* of discrepancy: the more of it there is, the more intense is the emotional discomfort. The second factor is *accessibility:* the more aware of a discrepancy you are, then, again, the more intense is the discomfort. The second factor raises an important question: If self-discrepancies exist in all people, what influences their accessibility? In other words, what makes us self-conscious about our personal shortcomings? For an answer, we turn to self-awareness theory.

Self-Awareness

If you carefully review your daily routine—classes, work, chores at home, leisure activities, social interactions, and meals—you will probably be surprised at how little time you actually spend thinking about yourself. An interesting study makes the point. More than 100 people, ranging in age from 19 to 63, were equipped with an electronic beeper that sounded every two hours or so between 7:30 A.M. and 10:30 P.M. for a full week. Each time the beeper went off, subjects interrupted whatever they were doing, wrote down what they were thinking at that moment, and filled out a brief questionnaire. Out of a total of 4,700 observations, only 8 percent of all recorded thoughts were about the self. For the most part, attention was focused on work and the other specific activities that consume one's time. Even more interesting is that while subjects thought about themselves, they reported feeling relatively unhappy and wished they were doing something else (Csikszentmihalyi & Figurski, 1982).

self-awareness theory
The theory that self-focused attention leads people to notice self-discrepancies, thereby motivating either an escape from self-awareness or a change in behavior.

Self-Focusing Situations: Mirrors, Cameras, and Audiences Is self-reflection unpleasant? If so, is it unpleasant because it makes us acutely aware of our self-discrepancies? Robert Wicklund and his colleagues think the answer is yes (Duval & Wicklund, 1972; Wicklund, 1975; Wicklund & Frey, 1980). According to their **self-awareness theory**, we are not usually self-focused, but certain situations predictably force us to turn inward and become the objects of our own attention. When we talk about ourselves, glance into a mirror, stand in front of an audience or a camera, watch ourselves on videotape, or occupy a conspicuous position within a group, we enter a state of self-awareness that leads us naturally to compare our behavior to internal standards. This comparison often results in an unpleasant negative discrepancy and a temporary reduction in self-esteem as we discover that we fall short of our ideal and ought selves. Thus, when people are put in front of a mirror, they experience a negative mood state (Hass & Eisenstadt, 1990). In fact, research shows that the more self-absorbed people are in general, the more likely they are to suffer from alcohol abuse, depression, anxiety, and other clinical disorders (Ingram, 1990).

Is there a solution? Self-awareness theory suggests there are two ways to cope with the discomfort: (1) "shape up" by behaving in ways that reduce one's self-discrepancies, or (2) "ship out" by withdrawing from self-awareness. According to Charles Carver and Michael Scheier (1981a), the solution chosen depends on whether people expect that they can successfully reduce their self-discrepancy —and whether they're pleased with the progress they are making once they try (Duval et al., 1992). If so, they match their behavior to the standard; if not, they tune out, search for distractions, and turn their attention away from the self. This process is depicted in Figure 2.6.

In general, research supports these predictions (Gibbons, 1990). When people are self-focused, they are more likely to behave in ways that are consistent either with their own personal values or with socially accepted ideals.

Figure 2.6   The Causes and Effects of Self-Awareness. Self-awareness pressures people to reduce self-discrepancies by matching their behavior to personal or societal standards, or by withdrawing from self-awareness.

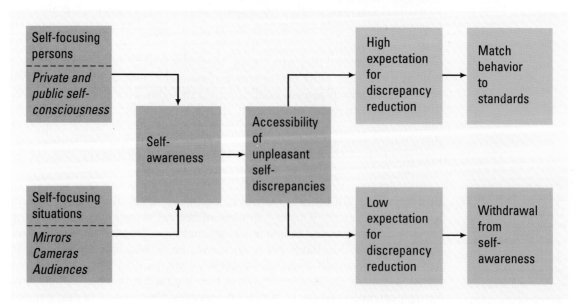

In an interesting field study, for example, Halloween trick-or-treaters—children fully dressed in costumes, masks, and painted faces—were greeted at a researcher's door and left alone to help themselves from a bowl of candy. Although the children were asked not to take more than one piece, 34 percent violated the request. When a full-length mirror was placed right behind the candy bowl, however, the number of violators dropped to only 12 percent. Apparently, the mirror forced children to become self-focused, leading them to behave in ways that are consistent with public standards of desirable conduct (Beaman et al., 1979).

The specific standard that serves as a self-guide may also depend on which significant others in one's life come to mind at a given moment. In a study of "private audiences," Mark Baldwin and John Holmes (1987) asked one group of female college students to visualize campus friends and another group to think about their parents. Minutes later, ostensibly as part of another experiment, they read a sexually permissive article and rated how much they enjoyed it. Half of the subjects were seated in front of a mirror for this task and half were not. Results supported self-awareness theory: subjects who were self-focused by the mirror behaved in ways that would please their private audience. As if they were being observed, these subjects reported liking the sexual article more after thinking about their friends than after thinking about their parents.

When the prospects for self-discrepancy reduction seem grim, individuals take the second route: escape from self-awareness (Baumeister, 1991). This coping strategy has some disturbing implications. One concerns the use of alcohol. According to Jay Hull, people often drown their sorrows in a bottle as a way to escape from the negative implications of self-awareness. To test this hypothesis, Hull and Richard Young (1983) administered what was supposed to be an IQ test to male subjects and gave false feedback suggesting that they had either succeeded or failed. Supposedly as part of a separate study, subjects were then asked to taste and evaluate different wines. As they did, experimenters kept track of how much they drank during a fifteen-minute tasting period. As predicted, subjects who were prone to self-awareness drank more wine after failure than after success, presumably to escape the negative implications for their self-esteem. Among subjects not prone to self-awareness, there was no difference in alcohol consumption. Similar results were obtained in a study of men who were hospitalized for alcoholism and released. After three months, those who were both self-aware and under stress were the most likely to relapse into heavy drinking (Hull et al., 1986).

According to Claude Steele and Robert Josephs (1990), alcoholic intoxication provides more than just a means of tuning out on the self. By causing people to lose touch with reality and shed their inhibitions, it also evokes a state of "drunken self-inflation." In one study, for example, subjects rated their actual and ideal selves on thirty-five traits—some important to their self-esteem, others not important. After drinking either an 80-proof vodka cocktail or a harmless placebo, subjects re-rated themselves on the same traits. As measured by the perceived discrepancy between actual and ideal selves, subjects who were

"More wine! Less truth!"

People often drown their sorrows in a bottle to escape from the negative implications of self-awareness. [Drawing by Cline; © 1991 The New Yorker Magazine, Inc.]

drinking expressed inflated views of themselves on traits they considered important (Banaji & Steele, 1989).

Taken to the extreme, attempted suicide may be the ultimate escape from self-awareness. This provocative implication was suggested by Roy Baumeister (1990), who has argued that people contemplate suicide when they (1) come to realize they're falling short of personal standards, (2) blame themselves for the failure, (3) focus too much attention on the self, (4) suffer negative affect, such as depression, (5) think in rigid, short-sighted terms to cope mentally with their anguish, and thus (6) shed the inhibitions that normally prevent people from harming themselves. This theory cannot be tested directly, but Baumeister presents an impressive array of suicide statistics and research findings compatible with his propositions. Consistent with the hypothesis that suicide is most likely when high expectations are followed by disappointment, for example, is the finding that suicide rates are highest among people newly separated or divorced, on the days right after weekends and holidays, and when the economy begins to take a downward turn. And consistent with the hypothesis that suicide victims are highly self-focused is the finding that suicide notes—compared to notes written by people who face death by illness—contain more first-person pronouns ("I" and "me"). In short, says Baumeister, suicide is a desperate act of last resort whose main purpose is "oblivion"—a complete loss of self-consciousness.

Self-Focusing Persons: Private and Public Self-Consciousness Just as *situations* can evoke self-awareness, certain *individuals* are characteristically more self-focused in their attention than others. Research has revealed an important distinction between **private self-consciousness**—the tendency to introspect on our *inner* thoughts and feelings—and **public self-consciousness**—the tendency to be aware of our *outer* public image (Buss, 1980; Fenigstein et al., 1975). Table 2.3 presents a sample of items used to measure these traits.

There is some controversy over whether private and public self-consciousness should be considered distinct traits (Wicklund & Gollwitzer, 1987). The distinction has proved useful, however, in predicting behavior (Carver & Scheier, 1987; Fenigstein, 1987). For example, people who score high rather than low on a test of *private* self-consciousness tend to fill in incomplete sentences by using first-person pronouns, are quick to make self-descriptive statements, and are acutely aware of changes in their internal bodily states (Mueller, 1982; Scheier et al., 1979). In contrast, those who score high rather than low on a measure of *public* self-consciousness are sensitive to how they are viewed from an outsider's perspective. Thus, when people were asked to draw

private self-consciousness A personality characteristic of individuals who are introspective, often attending to their own inner states.

public self-consciousness A personality characteristic of individuals who focus on themselves as social objects, as seen by others.

Table 2.3 How Self-Conscious Are You? These sample items appear in the Self-Consciousness Scale. How would you describe yourself on both the public and the private aspects of self-consciousness? [From Fenigstein et al., 1975.]

Items That Measure Private Self-Consciousness

- I'm always trying to figure myself out.
- I'm constantly examining my motives.
- I'm often the subject of my fantasies.
- I'm alert to changes in my mood.
- I'm aware of the way my mind works when I work on a problem.

Items That Measure Public Self-Consciousness

- I'm concerned about what other people think of me.
- I'm self-conscious about the way I look.
- I'm concerned about the way I present myself.
- I usually worry about making a good impression.
- One of the last things I do before leaving my house is look in the mirror.

a capital letter *E* on their foreheads, 43 percent of those who were high in public self-consciousness, compared to only 6 percent of the lows, oriented the *E* so it was backward from their own standpoint but correct for an outside observer (Hass, 1984).

The distinction between private and public self-awareness also has implications for how people reduce self-discrepancies. According to Higgins (1989), people are motivated to meet either their own standards or the standards held for them by significant others. Perhaps self-awareness theorists who draw the public-private distinction can tell us which of these discrepancies is likely to cause trouble at a particular time for a particular individual. When you're privately self-conscious, you listen to an inner voice and try to reduce discrepancies with your own personal standards; when you're publicly self-conscious, however, you try instead to match your behavior to socially accepted norms. As illustrated in Figure 2.7, there are "two sides of the self: one for you and one for me" (Scheier & Carver, 1983, p. 123).

Standing before a mirror or an audience, we become the object of our own attention. Whereas mirrors are likely to bring out private self-consciousness, audiences provoke public self-consciousness.

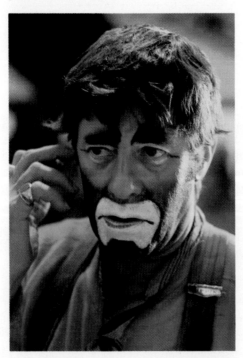

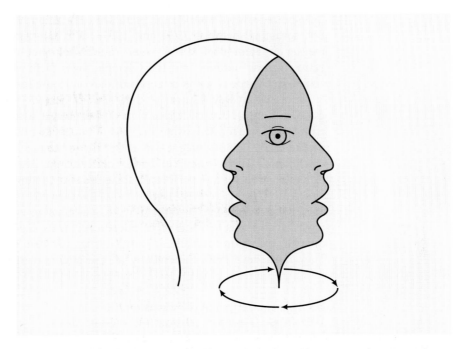

Figure 2.7   Revolving Images of Self.   According to self-awareness theory, people try to meet either their own standards or those standards held for them by others—depending, perhaps, on whether they are in a state of private or public self-consciousness. As Scheier & Carver (1983, p. 123) put it, there are "two sides of the self: one for you and one for me." [C. R. Snyder et al., 1983.]

"Choking" Under Pressure   Entering the 1992 Winter Olympics, Canadian figure skater Kurt Browning and American speed skater Dan Jansen were favored to win gold medals. In their moments of truth, however, Browning faltered on jumps he had landed all year, and Jansen crossed the finish line in his slowest time. Neither skater won a medal. What happened? Did all the media hype cause these champions, like so many other athletes, to "choke" under all the pressure?

Up to this point, we have seen that self-focused attention leads people to strive toward personally and socially desirable standards or to "escape" through various self-defeating behaviors. There's another downside. Consider the so-called home-field advantage in sports. Look at the record books, and you'll find that this advantage turns to disadvantage precisely when it is needed most. In NBA playoff games between 1967 and 1982, for example, home teams won 70 percent of the time during the first four games of each series but then won only 38.5 percent of the decisive seventh games—even though that final home "advantage" always went to the team with the better overall record! In World Series baseball between 1924 and 1982, there is a very similar pattern (Baumeister & Steinhilber, 1984). One cannot help but notice the resemblance between these findings and the Olympic sagas of Browning and Jansen. Can achieving a favored status in competition contribute to failure?

According to Roy Baumeister and Carolin Showers (1986), playing a key game in front of a vocal hometown crowd creates such intense pressure that athletes become too self-aware and pay too much attention to every step of what they're doing. Unfortunately, concentrating on the mechanics of what is otherwise an automatic process can disrupt performance. Although any audience can have this effect on any performer, there are two circumstances that are important. First, people are more likely to choke if they are low in self-consciousness and, therefore, not accustomed to the self-focusing experience. Second, the most harm seems to result from audiences having high expectations that are difficult to live up to. This last result brings us back to our Olympic heroes. They must have been flattered by all the attention they received before the

U.S. Figure skater Paul Wylie was an underdog in the 1992 Winter Olympics. Lacking the pressure that builds with high audience expectations, Wylie skated the finest performance of his career—and won a silver medal.

competition. In retrospect, however, all the pressure may have set them up for their bitter disappointments.

Self-Enhancement

We have seen that self-awareness can create discomfort and lower self-esteem by focusing attention on discrepancies. People may avoid focusing on themselves, but such avoidance is not always possible. How, then, does the average person cope with his or her faults, inadequacies, and uncertain future?

Let's begin with a stark fact about human behavior. Most often, most people think quite highly of themselves. Time and again, social psychologists find that research subjects view positive traits as more descriptive of themselves than negative traits (Alicke, 1985). Compared to others, people view themselves as better (Allison et al., 1989), overestimate their contribution to a team effort (Ross & Sicoly, 1979), exaggerate their control over life events (Wright et al., 1985), predict that they have a brighter future (Weinstein, 1980), and seek more information about their strengths than about their weaknesses (Brown, 1990). Illustrating the "mere ownership effect," people even rate the letters in their name more favorably than the other letters of the alphabet (Nuttin, 1987) and rate consumer products that they own more favorably than comparable products they do not own (Beggan, 1992). It's not that we consciously and deliberately flatter ourselves, either. The response is more like a reflex action. Thus, when subjects are busy or distracted as they make self-ratings, their judgments are quicker and even more favorable (Paulhus et al., 1989; Paulhus & Levitt, 1987). We can't all be perfect; nor can we *all* be better than average. So what supports this illusion?

In the 1982 movie *The Big Chill,* there was a dialogue that provides at least one answer:

SAM: Why is it what you just said strikes me as a massive rationalization?

MICHAEL: Don't knock rationalization. Where would we be without it? I don't know anyone who could get through the day without two or three juicy rationalizations. They're more important than sex.

SAM: Ah, come on. Nothing's more important than sex .

MICHAEL: Oh yeah? You ever gone a week without a rationalization?

In this section, we examine four methods used to rationalize or in other ways enhance self-esteem: self-serving cognitions, self-handicapping, basking in reflected glory, and downward social comparisons.

Biased, Self-Serving Cognitions   When students receive their exam grades, those who do well take credit for the success; those who do poorly complain about the instructor and the questions (Whitley & Frieze, 1985). When college professors have articles accepted for publication, they assume that the acceptance reflects on the quality of their work; when articles are rejected, these same professors blame the editor, reviewers, and the lack of journal space (Wiley et al., 1979). When gamblers win their bets, they view themselves as skillful; after losing, they moan and groan about random, fluke events that transformed near victory into defeat (Gilovich, 1983). When professional athletes win, they fill the sports pages with self-congratulatory quotes; when they lose, they complain about officials, weather conditions, and opposing players (Lau, 1984). Whether people are high or low in their self-esteem, explain their behavior publicly or in private, and try to be honest or make a good impression, there is bias: people take credit for success and distance themselves from failure (Schlenker et al., 1990).

People are also unrealistically optimistic. Students who were asked to predict their own future compared to that of the average person believed they would graduate at the top of their class, get a better job, earn a higher salary, have a happier marriage, and give birth to a gifted child. They also believed they were less likely to get fired or divorced, have a drinking problem, become depressed, or suffer from a heart attack (Weinstein, 1980). Other examples are plentiful. In polls taken between 1952 and 1980, American voters—regardless of whether they supported the ultimate winner or the loser—expected their candidate to prevail by a 4-to-1 ratio (Granberg & Brent, 1983). Similarly, sports fans let their team preferences interfere with the bets they place, even when they are trying to be "objective" (Babad & Katz, 1991). In one study, college students estimated that there was only a 20 percent chance that they will get divorced, despite knowing that the divorce rate for today's marriages is 50 percent (Kunda, 1987). Once again, you have to wonder: the future is not always bright, so what supports this unwavering optimism? Ziva Kunda finds that people bolster their rosy outlook by holding elaborate theories that link their own personal attributes with desirable outcomes. In one study, for example, subjects who had been involved in a serious high school relationship believed that such an experience promotes a stable marriage; yet those who had not been romantically involved believed that a *lack* of experience promotes a happy-ever-after ending.

Unfortunately, we can't always think of ourselves in ways that let us feel good. Sometimes reality sets in, and we have to concede that a goal is out of reach, that a job is too hard, or that someone we like is not interested in a friendship. Are there situations in which bias overwhelms reality? And if so, do we rationalize our shortcomings privately, or is the purpose of our rationalizing to save face in front of others? Studies show that people are most likely to exhibit self-serving biases when an event has meaning for self-esteem. Moreover, although most of us care about how we come across to others—as when we openly react to victory with false modesty or to defeat with self-criticism—sometimes we genuinely believe our own biased cognitions. Thus, after subjects in one study learned that they got high or low scores on an intelligence test, they took credit for success but denied blame for failure even though the experimenter was fully aware of their performance (Greenberg et al., 1982). Subjects in other studies showed the same pattern even when they were wired to a machine believed to be a lie-detector test (Reiss et al., 1981) or were urged to respond honestly (Schlenker et al., 1990).

Self-Handicapping: Sabotaging One's Own Performance C. R. Snyder and his colleagues (1983) tell a story about inventor Mason Zelazny, who built a pay-telephone device called "What's Your Excuse." For the price of a dollar, callers could select one of a dozen recordings of sound effects to corroborate excuses they wanted to make over the phone. For example, the noise of roaring engines and other machinery could be used to support the excuse that "My car broke down and I'm at the shop." Other tapes included the sounds of airplanes flying overhead, pouring rain, and a hospital waiting room.

When it comes to failure, all of us have made excuses for past performance. Of course, we don't really need a machine to do this. Researchers find that when people are afraid of failing an important task, they use shyness, anxiety, depression, medical ailments, traumas, and other disclaimers in anticipation of a negative outcome (Baumgardner, 1991; DeGree & Snyder, 1985; Mayerson & Rhodewalt, 1988; Snyder et al., 1985). By admitting to a physical or mental weakness, we can shield ourselves from what could be the most painful attribution of all—a lack of ability.

Making verbal excuses is one way to handle the threatening implications of failure. Under certain conditions, this strategy is taken one step further: people actually *sabotage* their own performance. It may seem paradoxical, but many people purposely set themselves up for failure. First described by Stephen Berglas and Edward Jones (1978), **self-handicapping** refers to actions people take to handicap their own performance in order to build an excuse for anticipated failure.

self-handicapping
Behaviors designed to sabotage one's own performance in order to provide a subsequent excuse for failure.

To demonstrate, Berglas and Jones recruited college students for an experiment supposedly on the effects of drugs on intellectual performance. All subjects worked on a 20-item test of analogies and were told that they had done well, after which they expected to work on a second, similar test. For one group, the problems were relatively easy, leading subjects to expect more success; for a second group, the problems were insoluble, leaving subjects confused about their initial success and worried about possible failure. Before taking the second test, subjects were given a choice of two drugs: Actavil, which was supposed to improve performance, or Pandocrin, which was supposed to impair it. Although no drugs were actually administered, most subjects who were confident about the upcoming test selected the Actavil; in contrast, male subjects—but not the females—who feared the outcome of the second test chose the Pandocrin. By handicapping themselves, these men set up a convenient excuse for failure—an excuse, we should add, that may have been intended more for the experimenter's benefit than for the subjects themselves. A follow-up study showed that although self-handicapping occurs when the experimenter witnesses the subjects' drug choice, it is reduced when the experimenter is not present while that choice is made (Kolditz & Arkin, 1982).

Some people more than others use self-handicapping as a defense (Rhodewalt et al., 1984), and there are different ways to do so. For example, men often handicap themselves by taking drugs (Berglas & Jones, 1978; Higgins & Harris, 1988) or neglecting to practice (Hirt et al., 1991). Women tend to report stress and physical symptoms instead (Hirt et al., 1991; Smith et al., 1983). People even differ in the reasons for self-handicapping. Specifically, the strategy offers two distinct benefits: a defensive excuse in case you fail (it's not your fault) and enhanced credit if you succeed (you must be amazing).

Which of those two benefits do we seek most? According to Dianne Tice (1991), it depends. People who are low in self-esteem seek to protect their fragile image by avoiding failure at all costs. Those high in self-esteem seek to enhance their image through bold, against-the-odds success. To test this hypothesis, Tice asked subjects varying in self-esteem to work on a task that measures nonverbal intelligence. Half were told that the task identifies people who are intellectually deficient, thus highlighting the motive to avoid failure. The other half were told that the task identifies people who are extraordinarily gifted, highlighting the motive for success. All subjects were then allowed to practice as long as they wished. As predicted, low–self-esteem subjects practiced less when they tried to protect themselves from possible failure, and high–self-esteem subjects practiced less in order to boost themselves by success (as you might expect, these strategies were used only when the task was important to the self-concept). Other researchers have also seen a difference (Rhodewalt et al., 1991). For people who are low in self-esteem, self-handicapping offers a face-saving defense against failure. For those high in self-esteem, it is used to enhance the self through success (see Figure 2.8).

Whatever the specific goal, self-handicapping seems like an ingenious strategy: with the odds stacked against us, the self is insulated from failure and enhanced by success. Unfortunately, this strategy is not without considerable cost. Sure, it may ease the pressure to succeed, but sabotaging yourself—by not studying or practicing, by drinking too much, by taking drugs, or by faking an illness—also increases the likelihood of failure. Sometimes you just have to take risks in order to forge ahead in life.

Reflection: Basking in the Glory of Others   To some extent, our self-esteem is influenced by individuals and groups with whom we identify. According to Robert Cialdini and his colleagues (1976), people often **bask in reflected glory** (or **BIRG**) by showing off their connections to successful others. The Cialdini team first observed BIRGing on the university campuses of Arizona State, Louisiana State, Notre Dame, Michigan, Pittsburgh, Ohio State, and Southern California. On the Monday mornings after a football game, they counted the number of school sweat shirts worn on campus and found that more of them were worn if the team had won its game on the previous Saturday. In fact, the larger the margin of victory, the more school shirts were counted. To evaluate the effects of self-esteem on BIRGing, Cialdini gave students a general-knowledge test and rigged the results so half would succeed and half would fail. Students were then asked to describe in their own words the outcome of a recent school football game. In these descriptions, students who thought they

basking in reflected glory (BIRGing) Increasing self-esteem by associating with others who are successful.

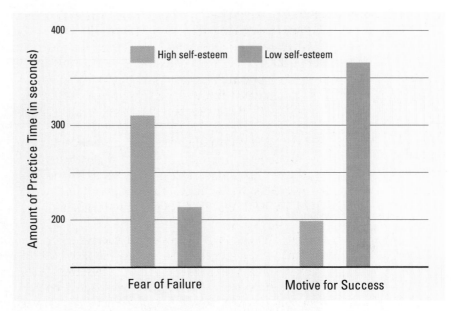

Figure 2.8 Self-Handicapping: To Protect or Enhance Self-Esteem? Subjects worked on a task that supposedly measured intelligence. When the success motive was prominent, high–self-esteem subjects practiced less. When the fear of failure was prominent, low–self-esteem subjects practiced less. This pattern suggests that self-handicapping is a face-saving defense against failure for people low in self-esteem and an opportunity for enhancement through success for those high in self-esteem. [Data from Tice, 1991.]

had just failed a test were more likely than those who had succeeded to share in their team's victory by exclaiming that "*we* won" and to distance themselves from the shadow of defeat by lamenting how "*they* lost." In another study, subjects coming off a recent failure were quick to point out that they had the same birth date as someone known to be successful—thus BIRGing by a merely coincidental association (Cialdini & De Nicholas, 1989).

If self-esteem is influenced by association with others, how do people cope with friends, family members, teammates, and coworkers of low status? Consider sports fans again, an interesting breed. As loudly as they cheer their teams in victory, they often turn and jeer these teams in defeat. This behavior may seem fickle, but it is consistent with the idea that people derive part of their self-esteem from associations with others. In one study, subjects took part in a problem-solving team that succeeded, failed, or received no feedback about its performance. Subjects were later offered a chance to take home a team badge. In the successful and no-feedback groups, 68 and 50 percent took badges; in the failure group, only 9 percent did (Snyder et al., 1986). In a second study,

When Operation Desert Storm troops returned from the Middle East in 1991, Americans welcomed them home with open arms (above). When Vietnam veterans (right) had returned in defeat some twenty years earlier, they were neglected, even scorned. It seems that the tendency to bask in reflected glory is matched by an equally powerful need to cut off reflected failure.

students who were committed to a career in psychology but insecure about their potential were quick to reject a fellow psychology student who was an embarrassment to their major (Wagner et al., 1990). It appears that the tendency to bask in reflected glory is matched by an equally powerful tendency to "cut off reflected failure."

Downward Comparison: Benefiting from the Misfortune of Others
Earlier in this chapter, we discussed Festinger's (1954) theory that people evaluate themselves through social comparison with similar others. But let's contemplate the possible implications. If the people around us achieve *more* than we do, what does that do to our self-esteem? Perhaps the many adults who shy away from class reunions to avoid having to compare themselves with their former classmates are acting out an answer to that question.

downward social comparison Defensive tendency to compare ourselves to others who are worse off than we are.

Festinger realized that people don't always seek objective information from similar others and that social comparisons are sometimes made in self-defense. Indeed, research shows that when a person's self-esteem is at stake, he or she may benefit from making **downward social comparisons**—comparisons with others who are inferior, less successful, less happy, or less fortunate (Hakmiller, 1966; Wills, 1981). To illustrate, educators used to be puzzled by the finding that disadvantaged elementary school children often score higher on measures of academic self-esteem than do children from more affluent, academically rigorous schools. Why? Students feel better about themselves when they are surrounded by classmates who are lower rather than higher in their average levels of achievement. Apparently, it's better to be a big fish in a small pond than the other way around (Marsh & Parker, 1984).

There are also striking implications for health-related issues. When victimized by tragic life events—a crime, an accident, disease, or the death of a loved one—people often cope in two ways: they affiliate with others who are adjusting well, role models who offer hope and guidance, yet they also compare themselves with others who are worse off, a form of downward social comparison

For successful alumni, for whom social comparison increases self-esteem, class re-unions must be an enjoyable experience.

(Taylor & Lobel, 1989). Apparently, it helps to know that life could be worse, which is why most cancer patients compare themselves to others who are *not* adjusting well (J. V. Wood et al., 1985) and why the vast majority believe they are in better shape than their peers (Taylor et al., 1986). Interviews with breast cancer patients tell the story. One woman who had only a lump removed wondered "how awful it must be for women who have had a full mastectomy." An older woman who had a mastectomy said: "The people I really feel sorry for are these young gals. To lose a breast when you're so young must be awful." Yet a young mastectomy patient derived comfort from the fact that "If I hadn't been married, this thing would have really gotten to me" (Taylor, 1989, p. 171). As these quotes so poignantly illustrate, there's always someone with whom we can favorably compare ourselves for the sake of coping. In the words of a dying patient who appeared on the CBS documentary *A Time to Die*, "It's not the worst thing that could happen."

Sometimes it just isn't possible to defend the self through downward comparison. To echo what we asked earlier, when a sibling, spouse, or close friend has more success than you do, what happens to your self-esteem? Abraham Tesser's (1988) theory of **self-evaluation maintenance** predicts two possible reactions. On the one hand, you could feel proud of your close association with this successful other, as in the process of basking in reflected glory. Indeed, if you've ever bragged about the achievements of a loved one as if they were your own, you know fully well how "reflection" can bolster self-esteem. On the other hand, you may feel overshadowed by the success of others and experience social comparison jealousy—a mixture of emotions that include envy, resentment, and a drop in self-esteem (Salovey & Rodin, 1984).

According to Tesser, the key to whether one experiences the pleasure of reflection or the pain of jealousy is the self-relevance of the other person's success. When close friends surpass us in ways that are important to our self-concept, we feel jealous and distance ourselves from them in order to keep up our own self-esteem. When intimate others surpass us in ways that are not vital

self-evaluation maintenance
A theory predicting the conditions under which people react to the success of signifi-cant others with either pride or jealousy.

to the self-concept, however, we feel good and take pride in their triumphs through a process of reflection (Tesser & Collins, 1988; Tesser et al., 1989). Applying the model to family dynamics, for example, Tesser (1980) found that college students were most likely to report friction with their brothers or sisters when the two were close in age and when there was a disparity in their levels of ability.

Realities, Illusions, and Mental Health

> I refuse to be intimidated by reality anymore. . . . Reality is the leading cause of stress amongst those in touch with it. . . . Now, since I put reality on a back burner, my days are jam-packed and fun-filled. (Lily Tomlin as Trudy, the Bag Lady; Wagner, 1986)

Psychologists used to think that an accurate perception of reality is vital to mental health. More and more, however, this view is challenged by research on the mechanisms of self-defense. Consistently, people delude themselves and others with biased cognitions, self-handicapping, reflection, and downward social comparison. Are these illusions a sign of health and well-being, or are they symptoms of a disorder?

When Shelley Taylor and Jonathon Brown (1988) reviewed all the relevant research, they found that individuals who are depressed or low in self-esteem have more realistic views of themselves than most others who are better adjusted. Their self-appraisals are more likely to match appraisals of them made by neutral observers; they make fewer self-serving attributions to account for success and failure; they are less likely to exaggerate their control over uncontrollable events; and they make more balanced predictions about their future. Accordingly, Taylor and Brown reached the provocative conclusion that when it comes to the self, positive illusions promote happiness, the desire to care about others, and the ability to engage in productive and creative work—hallmark characteristics of mental health. In the authors' words, "these illusions help make each individual's world a warmer and more active and beneficent place in which to live" (1988, p. 205).

Taylor and Brown are not alone in their conclusion. Indeed, many psychologists now believe that the mechanisms of "self-deception" are adaptive not only for the lives of individuals but for the evolution of the human species (Lockard & Paulhus, 1988). Again, research indicates that the higher a person's self-esteem, the more likely the person is to employ mechanisms of self-defense. But is this illusional pattern truly adaptive? Are *you* better off overestimating your abilities or the degree of control you can exert over the events in your life? Are you better off being the eternal optimist, or a hard realist? Roy Baumeister and Steven Scher (1988) are not so sure. Their analysis of self-defeating behavior points out that illusions can give rise to chronic patterns of self-destruction. People escape from self-awareness through drug abuse and suicide, self-handicap themselves into underachievement and failure, deny health-related problems until it's too late, and rely on the illusion of control to protect them from the tender mercies of the gambling casino. Research also shows that people who blame others for their own misfortunes—such as having a miscarriage, giving birth to a handicapped child, getting hurt in an automobile accident, or suffering from cancer, a heart attack, or arthritis—are emotionally more impaired than those who do not externalize the blame (Tennen & Affleck, 1990). Reality or illusion: which is more adaptive? In Chapter 14, we address this thorny debate in further detail.

SELF-PRESENTATION: THE BEHAVIORAL COMPONENT

The human quest for self-knowledge and self-esteem tells us about the cognitive and affective components of the inner self. The portrait is not complete, however, until we paint in the outer layer, the behavioral expression of the social self. Most people are concerned, at least to some extent, about the images they present to others. The fashion industry, cosmetic counters, diet centers, plastic surgery advertisements, and the endless search for miracle drugs that grow hair, remove hair, and smooth out wrinkles exploit our preoccupation with physical appearance. Of course, people are just as concerned about the impressions they convey through their public *behavior*. What, as they say, will the neighbors think?

In *As You Like It*, William Shakespeare wrote, "All the world's a stage, / And all the men and women merely players." This insight was first put into social science terms by sociologist Erving Goffman (1959), who argued that life is like a theater in which each of us acts out certain *lines,* as if from a script. Most important, said Goffman, is that each of us assumes a certain *face,* or social identity, that others help us to maintain. Inspired by Goffman's theory, social psychologists now study **self-presentation**: the process by which we try to shape what others think of us, and even what we think of ourselves (Leary & Kowalski, 1990; Schlenker & Weigold, 1992; Tedeschi, 1981). An act of self-presentation may take on many different forms. It may be conscious or unconscious, accurate or misleading, and intended for an audience or for ourselves. In this section, we look at the goals of self-presentation and the ways in which people try to achieve these goals.

self-presentation
Strategies people use to shape what others think of them.

The Two Faces of Self-Presentation

There are basically two motives for self-presentation: strategic self-presentation and self-verification. *Strategic self-presentation* consists of our efforts to shape others' impressions in specific ways in order to gain influence, power, sympathy,

"My not wearing a hairpiece indicates to others that I'm comfortable with myself."

People use their appearance as well as their behavior to cast themselves in a particular light. [Drawing by Weber; © 1987 The New Yorker Magazine, Inc.]

or approval. You don't have to search long and hard for prominent examples: personal ads, political campaign promises, and a defendant's appeal to the jury are a few. The specific goals vary from one person and situation to another and include the desire to be perceived as likable, competent, moral, dangerous, and helpless. Whatever the goal, people often try to control their self-presentations through the use of nonverbal behaviors (DePaulo, 1992). Research shows, for example, that women sometimes eat less in front of men in order to appear appropriately feminine (Mori et al., 1987; Pliner & Chaiken, 1990).

Two strategic self-presentation goals are particularly common. The first is *ingratiation,* a term used to describe acts that are motivated by the desire to "get along" and be *liked.* The second goal is *self-promotion,* a term used to describe acts that are motivated by a desire to "get ahead" and be *respected* for one's competence (Arkin, 1981; Jones & Pittman, 1982). On the surface, it seems easy to achieve these goals. When people want to be liked, they put their best foot forward, smile a lot, give eye contact, nod their heads, express agreement with what is said, and if necessary resort to favors, compliments and apple-polishing flattery. When people want to be respected for their competence, they try to impress others by talking about themselves and immodestly showing off their knowledge, status, and exploits. In both cases, there are tradeoffs. As the term "brown-nosing" all-too-graphically suggests, ingratiation tactics need to be subtle or else they will backfire (Jones, 1964). Similarly, the tactics of self-promotion are not without cost. People who spend too much time trumpeting their own achievements are seen as self-absorbed and boastful and are disliked as a result (Godfrey et al., 1986).

The second self-presentation motive is *self-verification*: the desire to have others perceive us as we genuinely perceive ourselves. According to William Swann (1987), people are highly motivated to verify their existing self-concept in the eyes of others. Swann and his colleagues have gathered a good deal of evidence for this hypothesis—finding, for example, that people selectively elicit, recall, and accept personality feedback that confirms their self-conceptions. In fact, subjects bend over backward to correct others whose impressions are positive but mistaken. In one study, for example, subjects interacted with a confederate who then said they seemed dominant or submissive. When the comment was consistent with the subject's self-concept, it was accepted. When it was inconsistent, however, subjects went out of their way to prove the confederate wrong: those who viewed themselves as dominant but were labeled submissive later behaved more assertively than usual; those who viewed them-selves as submissive but were labeled dominant subsequently became even more docile (Swann & Hill, 1982).

Self-verification seems desirable, but wait—when people view themselves unfavorably, do they want others to do the same? Nobody is perfect, and everyone has some faults. But do we really want to verify these faults? Do those of us who feel painfully shy, socially awkward, or insecure about our abilities want others to see these weaknesses, or would we rather present ourselves as bold, graceful, and competent? What happens when the desire for self-verification clashes with the need for self-enhancement? To answer this question, Swann and his colleagues (1992b) had subjects fill out a self-concept questionnaire and then choose an interaction partner from two subjects—one who had evaluated them favorably, the other unfavorably. The result? Although subjects with a positive self-concept wanted someone who viewed them favor-ably, nearly 80 percent of those with a negative self-concept preferred an evaluator whose impression was unfavorable (see Figure 2.9).

If people seek self-verification from their partners in a laboratory experiment, it stands to reason that they want the same from their close relationships. In a study of married couples, husbands and wives separately answered questions about their self-concept, evaluations of their spouse, and commitment to the marriage. As predicted, people who had a positive self-concept expressed more commitment to partners who appraised them favorably, and those with a negative self-concept felt more committed to partners who appraised them *un*favorably (Swann et al., 1992a). It appears that the desire for self-verification is so powerful that it can overwhelm the need for self-enhancement. We may want to make a good impression, but we also want others to have an *accurate* impression, one that is consistent with our own self-concept.

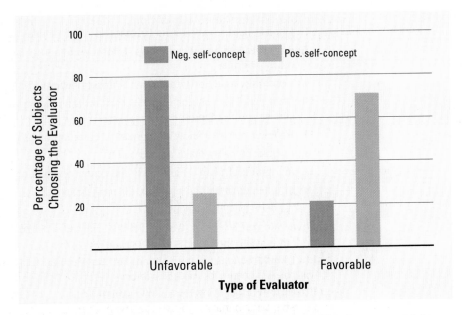

Figure 2.9   What's More Important: Self-Verification or Self-Enhancement? Subjects filled out a self-concept scale and were then asked to choose an interaction partner from two subjects—one who had evaluated them favorably, the other unfavorably. As you can see, subjects with a positive self-concept wanted a partner who saw them favorably (right), but those with a negative self-concept preferred someone who saw them unfavorably (left). In this situation, the desire for self-verification overpowered the need for self-enhancement. [Swann et al., 1992b.]

Self-Monitoring: Personality Differences in Self-Presentation

self-monitoring
The tendency to change behavior in response to the self-presentation concerns of the situation.

Although self-presentation is a way of life for all of us, it differs considerably among individuals. Some people are generally more conscious of their public image than others. Also, some people are more likely to engage in strategic self-presentation, while others seem to prefer self-verification. According to Mark Snyder (1987), these differences are related to a personality trait called **self-monitoring**: the tendency to regulate our behavior to meet the demands of social situations.

Individuals who are high in self-monitoring seem to have a repertoire of selves from which to draw. They are sensitive to strategic self-presentation concerns, poised, ready, and able to modify their behavior as they move from one situation to another. As measured by the Self-Monitoring Scale (Snyder, 1974; Snyder & Gangestad, 1986; see Table 2.4), they are likely to agree with

1. I find it hard to imitate the behavior of other people.
2. At parties and social gatherings, I do not attempt to do or say things that others will like.
3. I can only argue for ideas which I already believe.
4. I can make impromptu speeches even on topics about which I have almost no information.
5. I guess I put on a show to impress or entertain others.
6. I would probably make a good actor.
7. In a group of people I am rarely the center of attention.
8. In different situations and with different people, I often act like very different persons.
9. I am not particularly good at making other people like me.
10. I'm not always the person I appear to be.
11. I would not change my opinions (or the way I do things) in order to please someone or win their favor.
12. I have considered being an entertainer.
13. I have never been good at games like charades or improvisational acting.
14. I have trouble changing my behavior to suit different people and different situations.
15. At a party I let others keep the jokes and stories going.
16. I feel a bit awkward in company and do not show up quite as well as I should.
17. I can look anyone in the eye and tell a lie with a straight face (if for a right end).
18. I may deceive people by being friendly when I really dislike them.

Table 2.4   Self-Monitoring Scale.   Are you a high or low self-monitor? For each statement, answer *True* or *False*. When you are done, give yourself one point if you answered *T* to items 4, 5, 6, 8, 10, 12, 17, and 18. Then give yourself one point if you answered *F* to items 1, 2, 3, 7, 9, 11, 13, 14, 15, and 16. Count your total number of points. This total represents your Self-Monitoring Score. Among North American college students, the average score is about 10 or 11. [From Snyder & Gangestad, 1986.]

statements such as "I would probably make a good actor" and "In different situations and with different people, I often act like very different persons." In contrast, low self-monitors are self-verifiers by nature, appearing less concerned about the social propriety of their behavior. Like character actors always cast into the same role, they express themselves in a consistent manner from one situation to the next, exhibiting what they regard as their true and honest self.

On the Self-Monitoring Scale, low self-monitors say that "I can only argue for ideas that I already believe" and "I have never been good at games like charades or improvisational acting."

Social psychologists disagree on (1) whether the Self-Monitoring Scale measures one global trait or a combination of two or more specific traits (Briggs & Cheek, 1988; Lennox, 1988) and (2) whether high and low self-monitors represent two discrete types of people or points along a continuum (Gangestad & Snyder, 1985, 1991; Miller & Thayer, 1989). Either way, scores on the Self-Monitoring Scale can be used to predict important social behaviors. Preoccupied with public image, high self-monitors—not only adults but children too (Graziano et al., 1987)—go out of their way to learn about others with whom they might interact and about the rules for appropriate action. Then once they have the situation sized up, they modify their behavior (Danheiser & Graziano, 1982; Shaffer et al., 1982). If a situation calls for conformity, high self-monitors conform; if the same situation calls for autonomy, they refuse to conform (Snyder & Monson, 1975). Low self-monitors, in contrast, maintain a relatively consistent posture from one situation to the next.

In the coming chapters, we will see that because so much of our behavior is influenced by social norms, self-monitoring is relevant to many aspects of social psychology. It may also have interesting developmental implications. Indeed, a survey of 18- to 73-year-olds revealed that self-monitoring scores tend to drop with age—presumably because people become more settled and secure about their personal identities as they get older (Reifman et al., 1989). For now, however, ask yourself this question: Is it better to be a high or low self-monitor? Is one orientation inherently more adaptive than the other?

The research does not enable us to make this kind of value judgment. Consider high self-monitors. Quite accurately, they regard themselves as *pragmatic,* flexible, and adaptive and as able to cope with the diversity of life's roles. But wait—we could also describe them as fickle, or as phony opportunists, more concerned with appearances than with reality and willing to change colors like a chameleon just to fit in. Now think about low self-monitors. They describe themselves as *principled* and forthright; they are without pretense, always speaking their mind so others know where they stand. Of course, they could also be viewed as rigid and stubborn, insensitive to their surroundings, and unwilling to compromise just to get along. On the relative value of these two orientations, then, it is safe to conclude that neither high nor low self-monitoring is necessarily undesirable—unless carried to the extreme. Goffman (1955) made this same point many years ago, when he wrote,

> Too little perceptiveness, too little *savoir faire,* too little pride and considerateness, and the person ceases to be someone who can be trusted to take a hint about himself or give a hint that will save others embarrassment. . . . Too much *savoir faire* or too much considerateness and he becomes someone who is too socialized, who leaves others with the feeling that they do not know how they really stand with him, nor what they should do to make an effective long term adjustment. (p. 227)

EPILOGUE: THE MULTIFACETED SELF

Throughout history, writers, poets, philosophers, and personality theorists have portrayed the self as an enduring aspect of the human personality, an invisible "inner core" that is stable over time and slow to change. The struggle to "find yourself" or "be true to yourself" is based on this portrait. Yet social psychologists have discovered that at least part of the self is malleable—molded by life experiences and different from one situation to the next. In this perspective, the self is multifaceted and has many different faces.

When you look into the mirror, what do *you* see, one self or many? Do you see a person whose self-concept is enduring or one whose identity seems to change from time to time? Do you see a person who evaluates his or her strengths and weaknesses with an objective eye or one who is insulated from unpleasant truths by the mechanisms of self-defense? And do you see a person who has an inner, hidden self that is different from the face shown to others?

From the material presented in this chapter, the answer to these questions seems always to be the same: the self has all these characteristics. Over one hundred years ago, William James (1890) said that the self is not simple but complex and multifaceted. Based on current theories and research, we can now appreciate just how right James was. Sure, there's an aspect of the self-concept that seems accessible only by introspection and that is stable over time. But there's also an aspect that changes according to the company we keep and the information we obtain from other people. When it comes to self-esteem, there are times when we are self-focused enough to become acutely aware of our shortcomings; yet there are also times when we guard ourselves with the help of motivationally biased cognitions, self-handicapping, and downward social comparisons. Then there is the matter of self-presentation. It is clear that each of us has a private self consisting of our innermost thoughts and feelings, memories, and self-schemas; but it is equally clear that we also have an outer self, portrayed by the roles we play and the masks we wear in public. As you read through the pages of this text, you will see that these cognitive, affective, and behavioral components of the self are not separate and distinct, but interrelated. They are also of great significance for the rest of social psychology.

REVIEW

SELF-CONCEPT: THE COGNITIVE COMPONENT

The self-concept is the sum total of a person's various beliefs about her or his own personal attributes. It is the cognitive component of the self.

Beginnings of the Self-Concept

Recognizing oneself as a distinct entity is the first step in the development of a self-concept. Except for human beings and apes, other animals do not recognize their mirror-image reflections as their own. As Cooley's "looking-glass self" suggests, social factors are a necessary second step.

Introspection

People believe that introspection is the key to understanding the true self. Yet research suggests that it often diminishes the accuracy of self-reports. Self-knowledge is increased when people analyze the reasons for cognitively driven behaviors and the feelings behind affectively driven behaviors.

Perception of Our Own Behavior

Bem's self-perception theory states that when internal states are weak or difficult to interpret, people infer their inner states by observing their behavior and the surrounding situation. Action identification theory adds that inferences about the self may be made only when behavior is identified in high-level terms.

Self-perception theory has generated two hypotheses. First, the facial feedback hypothesis states that facial expressions can produce an emotional experience (for example, smiling causes people to feel happy). It's unclear, however, whether the emotional response occurs because of self-perception or because the facial expression triggers physiological changes that produce the emotion. Second, the overjustification hypothesis states that people sometimes lose their intrinsic motivation toward activities for which they have been previously rewarded.

Influence of Other People

According to social comparison theory, people who are uncertain of their own opinions and abilities often evaluate themselves by comparisons with similar others. Schachter and Singer proposed that the experience of emotion is based on two factors: physiological arousal and a cognitive interpretation of that arousal. When people are uncertain of their emotional states, they may interpret their arousal by watching others in the same situation.

Autobiographical Memory

Memory of one's life events is critical to a self-concept. There are three ways in which the self guides our recollections. First, there is the self-reference effect—the finding that people are more likely to remember something if it relates to the self than if they encounter it in other contexts. Second, autobiographical memory is shaped by egocentric bias; people overemphasize their own roles in past events. Third, the hindsight bias leads people to revise their personal histories in light of new information about themselves.

Self-Schemas

A self-schema is a belief about oneself that guides the processing of information. On matters relevant to self-schemas, people make rapid judgments about themselves and are quick to recall past actions or predict future actions.

Multicultural Perspectives

Cultures foster different conceptions of self. Many Westerners have an independent view of themselves as entities that are distinct and autonomous. In most of Asia, Africa, and Latin America, people hold a collective or interdependent view of the self that encompasses their network of social relationships. These differences may influence the way we perceive, evaluate, and present ourselves in relation to others.

SELF-ESTEEM: THE AFFECTIVE COMPONENT

Self-esteem is a person's positive and negative evaluations of self. People with low self-esteem can get caught in a vicious cycle of self-defeating behavior.

Self-Discrepancies

According to self-discrepancy theory, large discrepancies between one's actual self and self-guides produce lowered self-esteem and affective disorders. Discrepancies between the actual and the ideal selves are related to feelings of disappointment and depression; discrepancies between the actual and the ought selves are related to feelings of shame, guilt, and anxiety. The emotional consequences depend on the amount of discrepancy and whether it is accessible to awareness.

Self-Awareness

Although people generally spend little time thinking about themselves, certain situations (mirrors, cameras, audiences) produce self-focusing. Self-awareness often forces attention on self-discrepancies and can result in a temporary reduction in self-esteem. To cope, we adjust our behavior to meet standards or we withdraw from the self-focusing situation. Heavy drinking and suicide can be viewed as ways of escaping from self-awareness.

Certain individuals are generally more self-focused than others. People may be high or low in their private and public self-consciousness. "Choking" under pressure is a negative consequence of self-awareness. People often "choke" when they are not accustomed to the self-focusing experience and are in front of audiences having high expectations that are difficult to meet.

Self-Enhancement

Most people think highly of themselves and protect their self-esteem in four ways. First, people's cognitions are often motivationally biased (we take credit for success but deny the blame for failure). Second, people make excuses and even, at times, handicap themselves (for example, through drug use or reduced effort) to excuse anticipated failure. Third, people bask in reflected glory, boosting self-esteem from associations with successful others. Fourth, people compare themselves to others who are less successful, less happy, or less fortunate than they. When others surpass us in ways important to our self-concept, we feel jealous and distance ourselves from them. When surpassed in ways that are not self-relevant, we feel pride and seek closeness.

Realities, Illusions, and Mental Health

A review of self-defense mechanisms suggests that those illusions may foster mental health. An alternative view is that in the long run they promote self-defeating behavior patterns.

SELF-PRESENTATION: THE BEHAVIORAL COMPONENT

Self-presentation is the process by which we try to shape what others think of us and even what we think of ourselves.

The Two Faces of Self-Presentation

There are basically two motives for self-presentation. The first is strategic, consisting of efforts to shape others' impressions in order to be liked or respected. The second motive is self-verification, getting others to perceive us as we genuinely perceive ourselves.

Self-Monitoring: Personality Differences in Self-Presentation

Individuals differ in the tendency to regulate their behavior to meet the demands of social situations. High self-monitors strategically modify their behavior from one situation to the next. Low self-monitors express themselves in a consistent manner, exhibiting what they regard as their true self.

EPILOGUE: THE MULTIFACETED SELF

As this chapter has shown, the self is not simple but complex and multifaceted.

Perceiving Persons

3

Preview

This chapter examines how people come to know, or think they know, other persons. First, we introduce the *elements* of social perception—those aspects of persons, situations, and behavior that guide initial observations. Next, we examine how people make explanations, or *attributions,* for the behavior of others and how they form integrated *impressions* based on initial perceptions and attributions. We then consider *confirmation biases,* the subtle ways in which initial impressions lead people to distort later information, setting in motion a self-fulfilling prophecy.

As the American economy faltered in the 1990s, resulting in the worst recession in years, business leaders disagreed on whom to blame: Were the Japanese at fault, or had Americans lost their competitive edge? When Mikhail Gorbachev, who turned out to be the last president of the Soviet Union, first talked of peace, Americans were suspicious: Was he carrying an olive branch, or was he armed with ulterior motives? When William Kennedy Smith and boxer Mike Tyson were tried for rape, juries had to decide: Did they force women to have sex against their will, or had their accusers been consenting partners? And when couples divorce after years of marriage, friends and relatives wonder: Whose fault was it?

Whatever the topic—economics, international politics, crime and punishment, or events closer to home—we are all active and interested participants in **social perception**, the processes by which people come to understand one another. This chapter is divided into four sections. First, we look at the "raw data" of social perception—persons, situations, and behavior. Second, we examine how perceivers explain and analyze behavior. Third, we consider how people integrate their explanations into a coherent impression of other persons. Fourth, we discuss the subtle ways in which our impressions create a distorted picture of reality, often setting in motion a self-fulfilling prophecy. As you read this chapter, you will notice that the various processes are considered from a perceiver's vantage point. Keep in mind, however, that in the events of life, you are both a *perceiver* and the *target* of others' perceptions.

social perception
A general term for the processes by which people come to understand one another.

OBSERVATION: THE ELEMENTS OF SOCIAL PERCEPTION

As our opening examples suggest, understanding others may be difficult, but it's a vital part of everyday life. How do we do it? What kinds of evidence do we use? One cannot actually "see" someone's economic projections, political motives, or sexual intentions, any more than a detective can see crimes that have already been committed. So, like a detective who reconstructs crimes by turning up witnesses, fingerprints, and blood samples, the social perceiver forms impressions of others by relying on indirect clues—the elements of social perception. What are these elements? This section considers clues from three sources: persons, situations, and behavior.

Persons: Judging a Book by Its Cover

Have you ever had the experience of meeting someone for the first time and immediately forming an impression based only on a quick "snapshot" of information? As children, we were told that you can't judge a book by its cover, that things are not always what they seem, that appearances are deceptive, and that all that glitters is not gold. As adults, however, we can't seem to help ourselves. In 500 B.C., the mathematician Pythagoras looked into the eyes of prospective students to determine if they were truly gifted. At about the same time, Hippocrates—the founder of modern medicine—used facial features to make diagnoses of life and death. In the nineteenth century, Viennese physician Franz Gall introduced a carnival-like science called "phrenology" and claimed to assess people's character by examining the shape of their skull. And in 1954, psychologist William Sheldon mistakenly concluded from flawed studies of adult men that there is a strong link between physique and personality.

People may not measure each other by bumps on the head, as phrenologists used to do, but first impressions are influenced in subtle ways by a person's height, weight, skin color, hair color, eyeglasses, and other aspects of appearance. Among Americans, for example, blonde women are considered fun loving and sociable, while brunettes are thought to be smart and dependable; men who are overweight are considered weak, lazy, and dependent; those who are thin are assumed to be tense, stubborn, and suspicious. In one study, men who were bald were viewed as less successful than similar others who had heads full of hair (Cash, 1990). Clearly, people perceive many links between the body and the mind (Alley, 1988; Bull & Rumsey, 1988; Herman et al., 1986).

The human face in particular attracts more than its share of attention. In a survey of college students, 90 percent said they thought that the face reveals one's inner character (Liggett, 1974). Indeed, Diane Berry and Leslie Zebrowitz-McArthur (1986) find that adults who have baby-faced features—a combination of large round eyes, high eyebrows, round cheeks, a large forehead, smooth skin, and a rounded chin—are perceived as warm, kind, naive, weak, honest, and submissive. In contrast, adults with mature features—small eyes, low brows and a small forehead, wrinkled skin, and an angular chin—are perceived as stronger, more dominant, and less naive. Thus, at home, parents view their baby-faced children as less responsible and punish them less for misbehavior than they punish their more mature-looking sons and daughters (Zebrowitz et al., 1991a). In small claims court, judges are more likely to favor baby-faced defendants accused of intentional wrongdoing, but they tend to rule against baby-faced defendants who are accused of negligence (Zebrowitz & McDonald, 1991). And in the workplace, baby-faced applicants are more likely to be recommended for employment as daycare teachers, while mature-faced adults are considered to be better suited for work as bankers (Zebrowitz et al., 1991b).

What accounts for these findings? And why, in general, are people so quick to judge others by appearances? There are three possible explanations. One is that human beings are genetically programmed to respond gently to infantile features so that real babies are treated with tender loving care. Another possibility is that we simply learn to associate infantile features with helplessness and then generalize this expectation to baby-faced adults. Third, maybe there is an actual link between appearance and behavior—a possibility suggested by the

In 1989, Richard Singleton was arrested and charged with the shooting murder of a seventeen-year-old boy in Sacramento. When his baby-faced picture appeared in the newspapers, people were shocked.

fact that subjects exposed only to photographs or brief videotapes of strangers formed impressions that correlated with the self-descriptions provided by these same strangers (Berry, 1990; Kenny et al., 1992). Whatever the explanation, the perceived link between appearance and behavior may account for the shock we often experience when our expectations are disconfirmed (see above photo).

Situations: The Scripts of Life

When George Bush sent half a million troops to Saudi Arabia in 1990, he drew parallels between the United States's involvement in the Middle East and its intervention in World War II. Saddam Hussein sought control over his Arab neighbors the way Hitler terrorized Europe, Bush said, and needed to be stopped. Following this World War II script, Bush led Americans to expect that allied forces would triumph. Meanwhile, Iraq's Hussein repeatedly compared U.S. presence in his region to the disastrous war in Vietnam. According to this script, the United States would lose its will to fight on foreign soil as casualties began to mount.

script A preconception about a sequence of events likely to occur in a particular kind of situation.

     In the Middle East crisis, two scripts were written for the same impending conflict, each designed to convince the world that a particular outcome would prevail. In fact, all of us have preconceived notions about various situations—**scripts** that enable us to anticipate the goals, behaviors, and outcomes likely to occur in a particular setting (Abelson, 1981; Read, 1987). Based on past experience, for example, people find it easy to imagine the sequence of events likely to unfold in a typical job interview, picnic, or beer party. The more experience you have in a situation, the more detail your scripts should contain.

In a study of the "first date" script, John Pryor and Thomas Merluzzi (1985) asked college students to list the sequence of events that take place in this situation. From these lists, a picture of a typical first date emerged. Among the sixteen steps identified were the following: (1) male arrives; (2) female greets male at door; (3) female introduces date to parents or roommate; (4) male and female discuss plans and make small talk; (5) they go to a movie; (6) they get something to eat or drink; (7) male takes female home; (8) if interested, he remarks about a future date; (9) they kiss; and (10) they say good night. Sound familiar? Pryor and Merluzzi then randomized the list of events and asked a group of subjects to arrange them into the appropriate order. They found that subjects who had extensive dating experience were able to organize the statements more quickly than those who had less dating experience. When people are familiar with a type of situation, the events fall into place like the pieces of a puzzle. When presented with incomplete scripts, people insert the expected

The first date script has remained predictable for generations. This depiction appeared on the cover of the *Saturday Evening Post* in 1953. Familiarity with situations like this provides us with expectations about our own and others' behavior. [Reprinted from the *Saturday Evening Post*. Copyright 1953, The Curtis Publishing Co.]

missing pieces into their subsequent "memory" of the events in question (Bower et al., 1979).

Knowledge about social settings provides an important context for understanding other people's verbal and nonverbal behavior. This knowledge, for example, leads us to expect someone to be polite at a job interview, playful at a picnic, and rowdy at a beer party. Scripts influence social perceptions in two important ways. First, we sometimes see what we expect to see in a given situation. In one study, for example, subjects looked at photographs of human faces with a neutral expression. When subjects were told that the person in the photograph was being threatened by a vicious dog, they perceived the person's facial expression as fearful; when subjects were told the person had just won money in a TV game show, they interpreted the *same* expression as a sign of happiness (Trope, 1986; Trope et al., 1988). Even young children use situational cues to determine how someone else is feeling (Hoffner & Badzinski, 1989). Second, people use a knowledge of situations to explain the causes of human behavior. As we see later in this chapter, an action seems to offer more information about a person when it departs from the norm than when it is common within a situation. To illustrate the point, consider how much more you would learn about someone who is rowdy in a job interview or polite at a beer party, instead of the other way around.

Behavioral Evidence

An essential first step in social perception is to recognize what someone is doing at a particular moment. Identifying the behaviors produced by human movement is relatively simple. Even when actors dressed in black clothing move about in a totally dark room with lights attached only to the joints of their body, people have little trouble recognizing such acts as walking, running, jumping, exercising, falling, and dancing (Johansson et al., 1980).

More interesting, perhaps, is that people derive *meaning* from their observations by dividing the continuous stream of human behavior into discrete units. By having subjects observe someone on videotape and press a button whenever they detect a meaningful action, Darren Newtson and his colleagues (1987) have found that some perceivers break the behavior stream into a large number of fine units, while others break it into a small number of gross units. While watching a baseball game, for example, you might press the button after each pitch, after each batter, after every inning, or only after runs are scored.

Several factors influence whether behaviors are divided into a small or large number of units. Perhaps the most important factor is the perceiver's familiarity with the script of an event. When subjects begin to watch a behavior, they typically divide the opening moments into many fine units. Then as the sequence of events becomes more and more predictable, they gravitate toward fewer, larger chunks. If the actor departs from the routine by doing something peculiar, perceivers shift into high gear and revert to a pattern of many fine units. Perceivers who are familiar with a particular script (for example, those who know the rituals of a baseball game) thus break their perceptions into a few large chunks right from the start. The more you already know about someone and the situation he or she is in, the less closely you need to attend to the fine points of behavior.

The manner in which people divide a stream of behavior can influence perceptions in important ways. Subjects who are told to break an event into fine rather than gross units attend more closely, detect more meaningful actions, and remember more details about the actor's behavior than do gross-unit subjects (Lassiter et al., 1988). Also, fine-unit subjects become more familiar with the actor they've observed, so they also come to view that person in more positive terms (Lassiter, 1988). As we will see in Chapter 5, familiarity often enhances attraction.

The Silent Language of Nonverbal Behavior   Behavioral evidence is used not only to identify someone's actions but to determine his or her inner states as well. Sometimes, people tell us how they feel. At other times, however, either they do not tell us, they are themselves uncertain, or they actively try to conceal their intentions and true feelings. Thus, we tune into a silent language, the language of **nonverbal behavior**.

nonverbal behavior
Behavior that communicates a person's feelings without words—through facial expressions, body language, and vocal cues.

In *The Expression of the Emotions in Man and Animals,* Charles Darwin (1872) proposed that the *face* expresses emotion in ways that are innate and understood by people all over the world. Contemporary research supports this notion. Numerous studies have shown that when presented with photographs similar to those on page 102, people can quite reliably identify at least six primary emotions: happiness, fear, sadness, anger, surprise, and disgust (Ekman et al., 1972). Indeed, subjects from ten different countries—Estonia, Germany, Greece, Hong Kong, Italy, Japan, Scotland, Sumatra, Turkey, and the United States—had high levels of agreement in their recognition of these emotions (Ekman et al., 1987).

Darwin believed that the ability to recognize emotion in others has survival value for all members of a species. This hypothesis suggests that not all emotions are equally important. It may be more adaptive, for example, to know when someone else is angry—and hence, prone to act aggressively—than to know when someone is happy, a nonthreatening emotion. Are people more sensitive to signs of anger than to signs of happiness? In a series of experiments, Christine and Ranald Hansen (1988) asked subjects to find discrepant facial expressions in photographs of crowds, each consisting of happy, neutral, or angry faces. In some pictures, all individuals wore the same expression; in others, there was one discrepant expression. As Darwin would have predicted, the subjects exhibited what the Hansens called the "face-in-the-crowd effect": they made fewer errors and took less time to locate discrepant angry faces than they did to locate discrepant faces that were happy or neutral. Other research has shown that people are similarly sensitive to facial expressions of fear, an emotion that may also signal danger (Lanzetta & Orr, 1986).

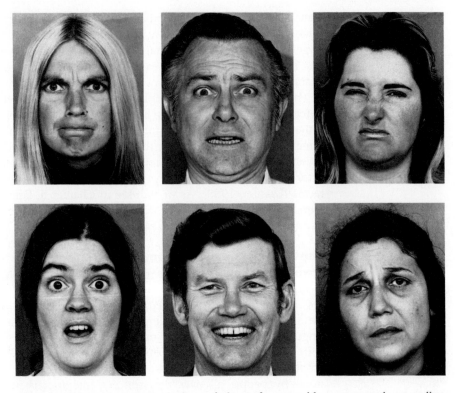

Can you tell how these individuals are feeling? If you are like most people, regardless of your culture, you will have little trouble recognizing the emotions portrayed. [Copyright Paul Ekman 1975.]

Other nonverbal expressive behaviors also influence social perceptions, enabling us to make quick, sometimes accurate judgments of others (Ambady & Rosenthal, 1992). For example, people are fluent readers of *body language*—the ways people stand, sit, walk, and express themselves through various gestures. Thus, men and women who have a relatively youthful walking style—who sway their hips, bend their knees, pick up their feet, and swing their arms in a bouncy rhythm—are seen as happier and more powerful than those who walk more slowly, take shorter steps, and stiffly drag their feet (Montepare & McArthur, 1988). Eye contact is also a common form of communication. Eyes have been called "windows of the soul." In many cultures, people tend to assume that someone who avoids eye contact is evasive, cold, fearful, shy, or indifferent; that frequent gazing signals intimacy, sincerity, self-confidence, and respect; and that the person who stares is tense, angry, and unfriendly. Typically, however, eye contact is interpreted in light of a pre-existing relationship. If a relationship is friendly, frequent eye contact elicits a positive impression. If a relationship is not friendly, eye contact is seen in negative terms. Thus, it has been said that if two people lock eyes for more than a few seconds, they are either going to make love or kill each other (Kleinke, 1986; Patterson, 1983).

Another powerful, primitive form of nonverbal behavior is *touch*—a congratulatory high-five, a sympathetic pat on the back, a joking elbow in the ribs, and a loving embrace are just a few familiar examples. Physical touching has long been regarded an expression of friendship, nurturance, sexual interest, and the like. However, it may also serve other functions. Several years ago, Nancy Henley (1977) observed that men, older persons, and those of high socioeconomic status were more likely to touch women, younger persons, and others of lower status than the other way around. Henley's interpretation was that touching is an expression not only of intimacy but of dominance and control. Researchers are particularly intrigued by the sex differences. In one study, Brenda Major and her colleagues (1990) watched people in city streets, parks, shopping malls, college campuses, beaches, airports, bus stations, and other public settings. Sure enough, men were more likely to touch women than women were to touch men. A difference did not exist among children or in places where friends ritually greet or say good-bye to each other. In another study, Judith Hall and Ellen Veccia (1990) observed 4,500 pairs and found in mixed-sex situations that although men were more likely to initiate contact with

Gait is an aspect of body language that may give rise to specific impressions of a person. [Drawing by W. B. Park; © 1987 The New Yorker Magazine, Inc.]

The Man with the Purposeful Stride

the hand, the differences were complicated for other kinds of touching. For example, men are more likely to put their arms around women, while women are more likely to link arms with men.

Distinguishing Truth from Deception   Social perception can be tricky because people sometimes try to hide or stretch the truth about themselves. Poker players bluff to win; witnesses lie to protect themselves; and political candidates make campaign promises they don't intend to keep. On occasion, nearly everyone tells something less than "the truth, the whole truth, and nothing but the truth." We make excuses, present ourselves in a particular light, or pretend for the sake of being polite. Can social perceivers tell the difference? Can *you* tell when someone is lying?

Sigmund Freud, the founder of psychoanalysis, once said that "no mortal can keep a secret. If his lips are silent, he chatters with his fingertips; betrayal oozes out of him at every pore" (1905, p. 94). Paul Ekman and Wallace Friesen (1974) revised Freud's observation by pointing out that some pores "ooze" more than others. Ekman and Friesen proposed that some channels of communication are relatively difficult for deceivers to control, while others are relatively easy. To test this hypothesis, they showed a series of films—some pleasant, others disgusting—to a group of female nurses. While watching, subjects were instructed either to report their honest impressions of these films or to conceal their true feelings. Through the use of hidden cameras, the subjects were videotaped. Others acting as observers then viewed the tapes and judged whether subjects had been truthful or deceptive. The results showed that the judgment accuracy of observers was influenced by which types of nonverbal cues they were exposed to. Observers who watched tapes that focused on the body were better at detecting deception than were those who watched tapes focused on the face. The face can communicate emotions effectively, but, unlike nervous movements of the hands and feet, it is relatively easy for deceivers to control.

This study was the first of many. In other studies as well, one group of subjects made truthful or deceptive statements while another group read the transcripts, listened to audiotapes or watched videotapes, and then tried to evaluate the statements. This research has shown that people frequently make mistakes in their judgments of truth and deception, too often accepting what is said at face value and giving speakers the benefit of the doubt. Even people who make these kinds of judgments for a living—police investigators, judges, psychiatrists, and polygraphers (who administer lie-detector tests) for the CIA, FBI, and the military—are prone to error (Ekman & O'Sullivan, 1991; see Table 3.1). But why? What seems to be the problem?

After a review of over thirty experiments, Miron Zuckerman and his colleagues (1981) concluded that there is a *mismatch* between the behaviors actually associated with deception and those used by perceivers to detect that deception. There are four channels of communication that provide relevant information: words, the face, the body, and the voice. When people have a

Observer Groups	Accuracy Rates
College students	52.82
CIA, FBI, and military	55.67
Police investigators	55.79
Trial judges	56.73
Psychiatrists	57.61
U.S. Secret Service agents	64.12

Table 3.1   Can the "Experts" Catch a Liar?   In this study, lie-detection experts with experience at making judgments of truth and deception were shown brief videotapes of ten women—half of them telling the truth, half of them lying about their feelings. Considering that there was a fifty-fifty chance of guessing correctly, the accuracy rates were remarkably low. Only a sample of U.S. Secret Service agents posted a better-than-chance performance. [Based on Ekman & O'Sullivan, 1991.]

reason to lie, *words* alone cannot be trusted. The *face* is also controllable. We tend to think that people do not smile when they lie, but it is common for deceivers to mask their real feelings with false smiles that do not involve movement of the eye muscles (Ekman et al., 1990). The *body* is somewhat more revealing than the face, as deception is often accompanied by fidgety movements of the hands and feet and by restless shifts in posture (Ekman & Friesen, 1974). Finally, the *voice* is the leakiest, most revealing cue. When people lie, especially when they are highly motivated to do so, their voice rises in pitch and there is an increase in speech hesitations (DePaulo et al., 1983; Streeter et al., 1977).

In light of these findings, it appears that perceivers tune into the wrong channels of communication. Too easily seduced by the silver tongue and the smiling face, we often fail to notice the restless body and the quivering voice. Ironically, subjects are more accurate in their judgments of truth and deception when they are too busy to attend closely to what a speaker says (Gilbert & Krull, 1988) or when the speaker is highly motivated to succeed in the attempted deception (DePaulo et al., 1991). Also, when subjects are instructed to pay more attention to the telltale body or voice than to the face, then again they become more accurate in their judgments (DePaulo et al., 1982).

Every now and then, the targets of social perception face an awkward communication dilemma. Being observed by more than one audience, they sometimes find it necessary to send mixed messages—one truthful, the other deceptive. You may recall, for example, that American pilots captured in the war with Iraq were videotaped as they confessed to war crimes and denounced U.S. policy. Forced to make these statements, these pilots had to convince their captors that their performance would be believed yet simultaneously communicate to viewers back home that they were being coerced. A similar dilemma confronts teenagers who confide in a close friend within earshot of a parent, or politicians who address audiences consisting of opposing special interest groups. Can people communicate the truth to one audience while concealing it from another? What strategies are used? As perceivers, are we sensitive to "hidden" messages?

Referring to this predicament as the *multiple audience problem,* John Fleming and his colleagues (1990) are seeking answers to these questions. In one study, Fleming and John Darley (1991) asked a group of high school students to make videotapes in which they communicate the location of a secret meeting to an audience of peers while concealing it from an audience of parents and other adults. As it turned out, the students were able to achieve their objectives, as peers who saw the videotapes were more likely than adult observers to guess the correct location of the meeting. The students were able to send their covert message by using private hand signals and slang expressions known only by their teenaged peers. As Fleming and Scott (1991) pointed out, this same strategy was evident in a videotape made by an American hostage in Beirut. Forced to claim he was a CIA agent, the hostage communicated a lack of sincerity by speaking in broken English and crossing his fingers. He even managed to signal that he was in south Beirut by speaking in a southern accent.

ATTRIBUTION: FROM ELEMENTS TO DISPOSITIONS

To interact effectively with others, it is useful to know how they feel and when they can be trusted. But to understand people well enough to predict their future behavior, we must also try to identify their *dispositions*—stable characteristics such as personality traits, attitudes, and abilities. Since we cannot actually see dispositions, we can only infer them from what a person says and does. In this section, we look at the processes that lead us to make these inferences.

The Logic of Attribution

Do you ever think about the influence you have on other people? What about the roles of heredity, childhood experiences, and social forces? Do you wonder why some people succeed while others fail? Some of us more than others try hard to explain the events of human behavior. Among college students, for example, psychology majors seem more curious about such matters than do natural science majors (Fletcher et al., 1986). Although there are individual differences, most people ask "Why?" about important events that are negative or unexpected (Hastie, 1984; Weiner, 1985).

To make sense of our social world, we try to understand the causes of our own and other people's behavior. But what kinds of explanations do we make, and how do we go about making them? In his book *The Psychology of Interpersonal Relations*, Fritz Heider (1958) took the first step toward answering these questions. To Heider, we are all scientists of a sort. Motivated to understand others well enough to manage our social environment, we observe, analyze, and explain their behavior. The explanations we come up with are called *attributions*, and the theory that describes the process is called **attribution theory**. The questions posed at the beginning of this chapter—regarding the economy, Gorbachev, the trials of William Kennedy Smith and Mike Tyson, and couples that divorce—are all questions of attribution.

Although people come up with different kinds of explanations for the events of human behavior (Weiner, 1986), Heider found it useful to group these explanations into two major categories: personal and situational. When the economy fails, business and political leaders can blame themselves (a **personal attribution**), or the losses can be blamed on foreign nations and other outside forces (a **situational attribution**). The leader who makes great concessions at the negotiating table may have had a penchant for peace or may have been under outside pressure. The man charged with rape may have forced himself on his victim, or the woman may have offered consent. And when competitors or lovers clash, we blame one party, both parties, or the circumstances. To the attribution theorist, the task is not to determine the *true* causes of these events but to discern people's *perceptions* of the causes. For now, two major attribution theories are described.

Jones's Correspondent Inference Theory

According to Edward Jones and Keith Davis (1965), each of us tries to understand other people by analyzing their behavior. Jones and Davis's **correspondent inference theory** predicts that people try to infer from an action whether the action itself corresponds to an enduring personal characteristic of the actor. Is the person who commits an act of aggression a beast? Is the person who donates money to charity an altruist? To answer these kinds of questions, people make inferences on the basis of three factors.

The first factor is a person's degree of *choice*. Behavior that is freely chosen is more informative about a person than behavior that is coerced. In one study, subjects read a speech, presumably written by a college student, that either favored or opposed Fidel Castro, the communist leader of Cuba. Some subjects were told that the student had freely chosen to take this position, and others were told that the student was assigned the position by a professor. When asked to estimate the student's true attitude, subjects were more likely to assume that there was a correspondence between his or her essay (behavior) and attitude (disposition) when the student had a choice than when he or she was assigned to the role (Jones & Harris, 1967; see Figure 3.1). Keep this study in mind. It supports correspondent inference theory, but, as we will see later, it also demonstrates one of the most tenacious biases of social perception.

---

attribution theory A generic term for a group of theories that describe how people explain the causes of behavior.

personal attribution Attribution to *internal* characteristics of an actor, such as ability, personality, mood, or effort.

situational attribution Attribution to factors *external* to an actor, such as the task, other people, or luck.

correspondent inference theory The theory that we make inferences about someone whose actions are freely chosen and unexpected and result in a small number of desirable effects.

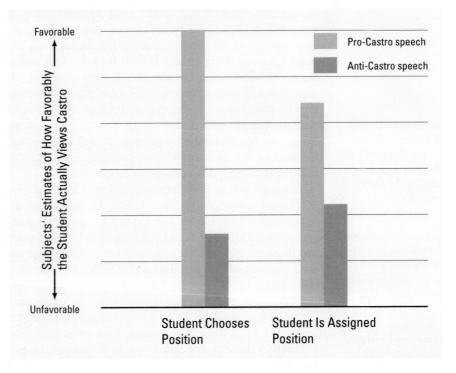

Figure 3.1 What Does This Speechwriter Really Believe? As predicted by correspondent inference theory, subjects who read a student's speech (behavior) were more likely to assume that it reflected the student's true attitude (disposition) when the position taken was freely chosen (left) rather than assigned (right). But also note the evidence for a fundamental attribution error (see page 113): even subjects who thought the student had been assigned a position inferred the student's attitude from the speech. [Data from Jones & Harris, 1967.]

The second factor that leads us to make dispositional inferences is the *expectedness* of behavior. Actions tell us more about a person when they depart from the norm than when they are typical, part of a social role, or otherwise expected under the circumstances (Jones et al., 1961). Thus, people think they know more about the personality of a student who wears three-piece suits to class or of a citizen who openly refuses to pay taxes than about a student who wears blue jeans to class or a citizen who files tax returns on April 15.

Third, people consider the intended *effects* or consequences of someone's behavior. Acts that produce many desirable outcomes do not reveal a person's specific motives as clearly as acts that produce only a single desirable outcome (Newtson, 1974). For example, you are likely to be uncertain about why a person stays on a job that is enjoyable, high paying, and in an attractive location—three desirable outcomes, each sufficient to explain the behavior. In contrast, you may feel more certain about why a person stays on a job that is tedious and low paying but is in an attractive location—only one desirable outcome.

Kelley's Covariation Theory   Correspondent inference theory describes how people try to determine someone's personal characteristics from a slice of behavioral evidence. However, behavior can be attributed not only to personal factors but to situational factors as well. How is this distinction made? In Chapter 1, we noted that the causes of human behavior can be derived only by conducting *experiments;* that is, one has to make more than a single observation and compare behavior in two or more settings in which everything stays the same except for the independent variables. Like Heider, Harold Kelley (1967) believes that people are like scientists in this regard. They may not observe others in a laboratory, but they too make comparisons and think in terms of "experiments." According to Kelley, people make attributions by using the **covariation principle**—that for something to be the cause of a behavior, it must be present when the behavior occurs and absent when it does not. Three kinds of covariation information are particularly useful: consensus, distinctiveness, and consistency.

To illustrate these concepts, imagine you are standing on a street corner one hot, steamy evening minding your own business, when all of a sudden a stranger bursts out of an air-conditioned movie theater and blurts out, "Great flick!" Looking up, you don't recognize the movie title, so you wonder what to make of this candid recommendation. Was the behavior (the rave review) caused by something about the person (the stranger), the stimulus (the film), or the circumstances (say, the air-conditioned theater)? Possibly interested in spending an evening at the movies, how would you proceed to explain what happened? What kinds of information would you seek?

Thinking like a scientist, you might try to collect *consensus information* to see how different persons react to the same exact stimulus. In other words, how do other moviegoers feel about this film? If others also rave about the film, the stranger's behavior is high in consensus and is attributed to the stimulus. If others are critical of the same film, the behavior is low in consensus and is attributed to the person. Still thinking like a scientist, you might also seek *distinctiveness information* to see how the same person reacts to different stimuli. In other words, how does this moviegoer react to other films? If the stranger is critical of other films, the target behavior is high in distinctiveness and is attributed to the stimulus. If the stranger raves about everything, however, the behavior is low in distinctiveness and is attributed to the person.

Finally, you might seek *consistency information* to see what happens to the behavior at another time when the person and the stimulus both remain the same. How does this moviegoer feel about this film on other occasions? If

covariation principle A principle of attribution theory that people attribute behavior to factors that are present when the behavior occurs and absent when it does not.

the stranger raves about the film on video as well as in the theater, the behavior is high in consistency. If the stranger does not always enjoy the film, the behavior is low in consistency. According to Kelley, behavior that is consistent is attributed to the stimulus when consensus and distinctiveness are also high, and to the person when they are low. In contrast, behavior that is low in consistency is attributed to transient circumstances, such as the temperature of the movie theater.

Kelley's theory and the predictions it makes are represented in Figure 3.2. Does this model describe the kinds of information *you* seek when you try to determine what causes people to behave as they do? Research shows that subjects who are instructed to make attributions for various events do, in general, follow the logic of covariation (Cheng & Novick, 1990; Fosterling, 1989; Hewstone & Jaspars, 1987; McArthur, 1972).

Figure 3.2   Kelley's Covariation Theory of Attribution.   For behaviors that are high in consistency, people make personal attributions when there is low consensus and low distinctiveness (top row) and stimulus attributions when there is high consensus and high distinctiveness (bottom row). Behaviors that are low in consistency (not shown) are attributed to passing circumstances. [Based on Kelley, 1967.]

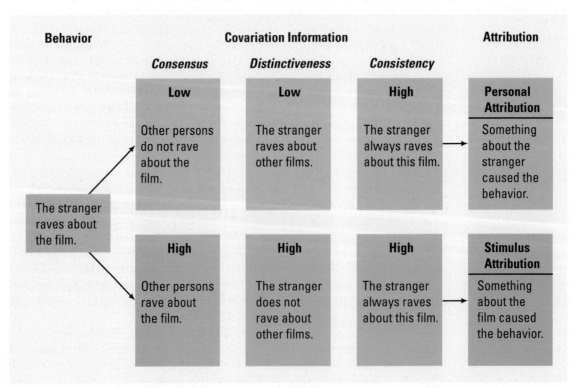

Attribution Biases

When the major theories of attribution were first proposed, they were represented by such complicated flow charts, cubes, arrows, formulas, and diagrams that many social psychologists began to wonder: Do people really analyze behavior as one might expect of computers? Do social perceivers have the time, the motivation, or the cognitive capacity for such elaborate, mindful processes? The answer is sometimes yes, sometimes no. As social perceivers, we may be limited in our ability to process all relevant information, or we may lack the kinds of training needed to employ fully the principles of attribution theory (Allen et al., 1987; Fong et al., 1986). More importantly, we often don't make an effort to think that carefully about our attributions. With so much to explain and not enough time in the day, people take mental short cuts, cross their fingers, hope for the best, and get on with life (Fiske & Taylor, 1991). The problem is that with speed comes bias and perhaps even a loss of accuracy. In this section, we examine some of the short cuts and their consequences—the biases of attribution.

cognitive heuristics
Information-processing short cuts that enable us to make judgments that are quick but often in error.

Cognitive Heuristics   Attribution theory assumes that people base their social perceptions on an objective reading of behavioral facts and figures. For example, it is assumed that to draw firm conclusions about an individual, we compare his or her behavior to social *norms*. Actions that are atypical, or low in consensus, are attributed to the person; those that are typical, or high in consensus, are attributed to the situation. The theory is logical, even intuitive. Yet researchers find that the average person, unlike the scientist, often fails to make adequate use of normative information (Borgida & Brekke, 1981; Kassin, 1979). Why is this the case? According to Daniel Kahneman, Amos Tversky, and others, the problem can be traced to the use of **cognitive heuristics**—information-processing "rules of thumb" that enable us to make judgments that are quick and easy but often in error (Kahneman et al., 1982; Gilovich, 1991; Nisbett & Ross, 1980).

Many cognitive heuristics lead people to make judgments that defy logic (see Table 3.2). One that has particularly troublesome consequences for the attribution process is the *availability heuristic*, the tendency to estimate the likelihood of an event on the basis of how easily instances of that event come to mind. To demonstrate this, Tversky and Kahneman (1973) asked subjects the following question: Which is more common, words that start with the letter *r* or words that contain *r* as the third letter? It turns out that although the English language contains far more words with *r* as the third letter rather than the first, most subjects incorrectly guess that more words begin with the letter *r*. The reason for this disparity is that it's easier to bring to mind words in which *r* appears first rather than third. In short, our likelihood estimates are heavily influenced by events that are readily available in memory.

false-consensus effect   The tendency to overestimate the consensus for our own opinions, attributes, and behavior.

The availability heuristic can lead us astray in two ways. First, it gives rise to the **false-consensus effect**, the tendency for people to overestimate the extent

Heuristics	Descriptions	Examples
Representativeness	The tendency to assume, despite compelling odds to the contrary, that someone belongs to a particular group because he or she resembles or "represents" a typical member of that group.	When people read about a conservative man who enjoys mathematical puzzles and has no interest in social or political issues, they guess that he is an engineer rather than a lawyer—even though he was said to be randomly selected from a group containing seventy lawyers and thirty engineers (Kahneman & Tversky, 1973).
Availability	The tendency to estimate the likelihood of an event from the ease with which instances of that event come to mind and are "available" in memory.	When asked to guess the major causes of death, people tend to overestimate the number of those who die in shootings, fires, floods, tornadoes, accidents, and other dramatic events and underestimate the number of deaths caused by strokes, heart attacks, and other mundane events (Slovic et al., 1982).
Framing	The tendency to be influenced by the way an issue is presented, or "framed."	People are more likely to recommend a new medical treatment if it is described as having a 50 percent "success rate" rather than a 50 percent "failure rate" (Levin et al., 1988).
Anchoring	The tendency for numerical estimates to be biased by an initial, even arbitrary starting point, or "anchor."	People who were initially asked if the chances of nuclear war were more or less than 1 percent later estimated a likelihood of 11 percent. Those initially asked if the chances of a nuclear war were more or less than 90 percent subsequently gave estimates of 26 percent (Plous, 1989).
Simulation	The tendency to predict and explain the outcome of an event on the basis of how easy it is to imagine alternative scripts or "simulations" of that event.	When people hear that a passenger was killed in an airline crash, they find the death more tragic if the person had just switched from another flight ("if only . . .") than if they think that the person scheduled for weeks to take the fatal trip (D. T. Miller et al., 1990).

Table 3.2 Cognitive Heuristics. Note the names, descriptions, and examples of five heuristics that bias our social perceptions.

to which others share their opinions, attributes, and behaviors (Ross et al., 1977b; Marks & Miller, 1987). A few years ago, one of us conducted a government-sponsored study of 292 federal judges. After reading cases in which plaintiffs sued defendants, the judges made hypothetical decisions and then predicted how their peers would vote. Although opinions varied widely, the judges believed that others would make the same decisions they had made. Those who favored the plaintiff estimated that 63 percent of other judges would also favor the plaintiff; among those who ruled against the plaintiff, that estimate was only 15 percent (Kassin, 1985). This bias is pervasive. Whether people are asked to predict how others feel about the defense budget, abortion, Dan Rather, Jane Fonda, or Campbell's soup, they consistently exaggerate the percentage of others who agree with their views (Mullen et al., 1985; Nisbett & Kunda, 1985). The problem? Since we tend to associate with others who are like us in important ways, we are more likely to notice and later recall instances of similar rather than dissimilar behavior (Deutsch, 1989).

A second consequence of the availability heuristic is that social perceptions are influenced more by a single, vivid life story than by hard statistical facts. Have you ever wondered why so many people buy lottery tickets despite the astonishingly low odds, or why so many travelers are afraid to fly even though they are more likely to perish in a car accident? These behaviors are sympto-

base-rate fallacy
The finding that people are relatively insensitive to consensus information presented in the form of numerical base rates.

matic of the **base-rate fallacy**—that people are relatively insensitive to numerical base rates, or probabilities, and are influenced instead by graphic, dramatic events such as the sight of a million-dollar lottery winner rejoicing on TV or a photograph of bodies being pulled from the wreckage of a plane crash (Bar-Hillel, 1980).

Every day, we are besieged by both types of information: we read about the unemployment rate, and we watch interviews with frustrated job seekers; we read the casualty figures of war, and we witness the agony of a parent who has lost a child in combat. Logically speaking, statistics that summarize the experiences of many people are more informative than a single, perhaps even atypical case, but perceivers march to a different drummer. In one study, for example, college students were asked to fill out a tentative course schedule for their upcoming semesters. Before doing so, some heard firsthand comments about various courses from two or three more experienced students. Others received the results of a comprehensive survey, numerical evaluations that summarized the opinions of a large number of students. Lo and behold, subjects were swayed more by the personal recommendations than by the survey results (Borgida & Nisbett, 1977). As long as the personal information is perceived to be relevant (Schwarz et al., 1991b) and from a source that is credible (Hinsz et al., 1988), it seems that one memorable anecdote is worth a thousand numbers.

The Fundamental Attribution Error   By the time you complete this textbook, you will have learned the cardinal lesson of social psychology: people are influenced in profound ways by the *situational* context of behavior. This point

Lotteries rely on the base-rate fallacy. People disregard the low odds that they will win in favor of the remote chance that their dreams will come true.

is not as obvious as it may seem. That is why parents are often surprised to hear that their mischievous child, the family monster, is a perfect angel in the classroom. And that is why students are often surprised when they see that their favorite professor, who is so eloquent in the lecture hall, stumbles over words in less formal surroundings. These reactions are symptomatic of a well-documented part of social perception. When people explain the behavior of others, they overlook the impact of situations and overestimate the role of personal factors. Because this bias is so pervasive, and sometimes so misleading, it is called the **fundamental attribution error** (Ross, 1977).

fundamental attribution error The tendency to underestimate the impact of situations on other people's behavior and to focus on the role of personal causes.

Evidence of the fundamental attribution error was first provided by the Jones and Harris (1967) experiment described earlier in the chapter, in which subjects read a speech presumably written by a student. In that study, subjects were more likely to infer the student's true attitude when the position taken was freely chosen than when they thought the student had been assigned to it. But take another look at Figure 3.1, and you'll see that even when subjects thought the student had no choice but to assert a position, they still used the speech to infer his or her attitude. This finding has been repeated many times. Whether the essay topic is nuclear power, abortion, drug laws, or the death penalty, the results are essentially the same (Jones, 1990).

People fall prey to the fundamental attribution error even when they are fully aware of the situation's impact on behavior. In one study, the subjects themselves were assigned to take a position, whereupon they swapped essays and rated each other. Remarkably, they still jumped to conclusions about each other's attitudes (Miller et al., 1981). In another study, subjects inferred attitudes from a speech even when they were the ones who assigned the position to be taken (Gilbert & Jones, 1986). People seem to correct themselves only when the assigned essay is perceived to be brief, half-heartedly written, and not very convincing (A. G. Miller et al., 1990) or when they are suspicious that the target has ulterior motives for the position taken (Fein et al., 1990). This last point is important. In a series of experiments, Steven Fein (1991) found that suspicion—a state of mind that leads us to think critically about the behavior of others—can eliminate the problem.

A fascinating experiment by Lee Ross and others (1977a) demonstrates the fundamental attribution error in a more familiar setting, the TV quiz show. By

On TV, children's entertainer Pee Wee Herman played a goofy, clean-cut young man (left). Yet in the summer of 1991, the real Pee Wee, Paul Reubens (right), was arrested in an X-rated movie theater for indecent exposure. A few months later, Reubens pleaded no contest and was sentenced to pay a small fine and do community service. Despite realizing that Pee Wee's on-screen character was fixed by the role he played, his adult fans were shocked. This reaction is symptomatic of the fundamental attribution error—the tendency to assume that what you see (behavior in one situation) is what you get (a personal disposition).

a flip of the coin, subjects were randomly assigned to play the role of either the questioner or the contestant in a quiz game, while spectators looked on. In front of the contestant and spectators, the experimenter instructed the questioner to write ten challenging questions from his or her own store of general knowledge. If you are a trivia buff, you can imagine how esoteric these questions could be: Who was the first governor of Idaho? What team won the NHL Stanley Cup in 1968? It is no wonder that contestants correctly answered only about 40 percent of the questions asked. When the game was over, all participants rated the questioner's and contestant's general knowledge on a scale of 0 to 100.

Picture the events that transpired. The questioners appeared more knowledgeable than the contestants. After all, they knew more of the answers. But a moment's reflection should remind us that the situation put the questioner at a distinct advantage (there were no differences between the two groups on an objective test of general knowledge). Did subjects take the questioner's advantage into account, or did they assume that the questioners actually had greater knowledge? The results were startling. Spectators rated the questioners as above average in their general knowledge and the contestants as below average. The contestants even rated themselves as inferior to their partner. Like the spectators, they too were fooled by the loaded situation (see Figure 3.3).

What's going on here? Why do social perceivers consistently make assumptions about persons and fail to appreciate the impact of situations? According to Daniel Gilbert (1989), the problem stems from *how* we make attributions. Attribution theorists used to assume that people survey all the evidence and then decide on a personal or situational attribution. Instead, claims Gilbert, social perception is a two-step process: first we identify the behavior and make a quick personal attribution; then we correct or adjust that inference to account for situational influences. The first step is simple and automatic, like a reflex; the second requires attention, thought, and effort (see Figure 3.4).

Research findings support this hypothesis. First, people tend to form quick impressions of persons, without realizing it, based on a brief sample of behavior (Lupfer et al., 1990; Newman & Uleman, 1989). Second, when perceivers are active, cognitively busy, or distracted as they observe someone, or when they have to attend closely to the observed behavior, they become *more* likely to commit the fundamental attribution error (Gilbert & Osborne, 1989; Gilbert et al., 1992). Third, when perceivers take time before making their attributions for someone's behavior, they become *less* likely to commit the fundamental attribution error (Burger, 1991). Since the model predicts that personal attributions are relatively automatic but that adjustments for the situation require conscious thought, it makes sense that when a perceiver's attention is divided, or the attribution made quickly, the second step suffers more than the first. As Gilbert and his colleagues (1988) put it, "the first step is a snap, but the second one's a doozy" (p. 738).

But why is the first step such a snap, and why does it seem so natural for people to assume a link between acts and personal dispositions? There are three possible explanations. The first is that human beings in general have an

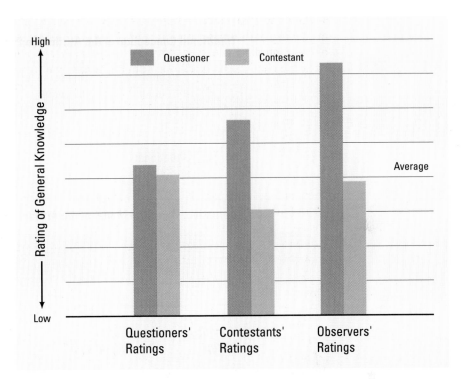

Figure 3.3 Fundamental Attribution Error and the TV Quiz Show. Even though the simulated quiz show situation placed questioners in an obvious position of advantage over contestants, observers rated the questioners as more knowledgeable (right). Questioners did not overrate their general knowledge (left), but contestants, like the observers, rated themselves as inferior (middle). These results illustrate the fundamental attribution error. [Data from Ross et al., 1977a.]

impulsive tendency to accept what they encounter as true, and that additional time is needed to think critically and to correct or reject these observations. To demonstrate, Gilbert and others (1990) presented subjects with bogus foreign language propositions ("a suffa is a cloud"), each followed by a signal indicating that it was true or false. Normally, subjects were able later to identify true and false propositions about equally. When subjects were distracted during the task, however, they subsequently identified many of the false propositions as true. In short, we are quick to assume that an act accurately reflects an actor's disposition just as we assume that all observations are true—unless otherwise suggested by the evidence.

A second explanation is that perhaps culture teaches us to commit the fundamental attribution error. Westerners believe that individuals are autonomous, motivated by internal forces, and responsible for their own actions. Yet

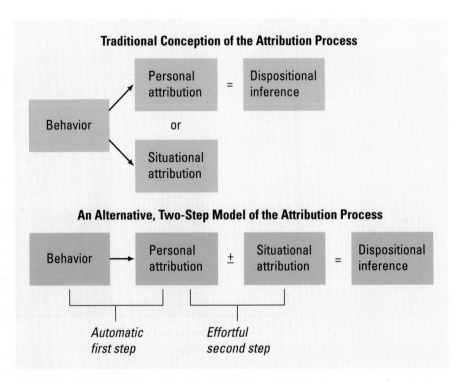

Figure 3.4 Alternative Conceptions of the Attribution Process. Traditional attribution theories assumed that people analyze behavior by searching for a personal or situational cause (top). A more recent, two-step model suggests that people make personal attributions *automatically* and later make conscious adjustments to that inference in order to account for situational factors (bottom).

many non-Western cultures take a holistic view that emphasizes the relationship between individuals and their social roles. To see if these differing world views are related to attributions, Joan Miller (1984) asked American subjects and Asian Indian subjects of varying ages to describe the causes of positive and negative behaviors they had observed in their lives. Among the youngest children, there were no differences between the cultures. With increasing age, however, American subjects made more personal attributions, while the Indian subjects made more situational attributions (see Figure 3.5). Coupled with the fact that Indians place more emphasis on social rules and obligations (Miller & Bersoff, 1992), these findings raise a provocative question: Is the fundamental attribution error merely a Western attribution error? At this point, there is not enough cross-cultural research to draw a firm conclusion.

A third explanation for the fundamental attribution error is based on Heider's (1958) insight that people see dispositions in behavior because of a perceptual bias, something like an optical illusion. When you listen to a speech or watch

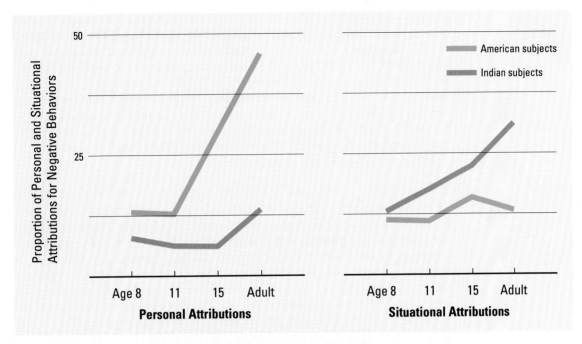

Figure 3.5 Fundamental Attribution Error: A Western Bias? American and Asian Indian subjects of varying ages described the causes of negative behaviors they had observed in their lives. Among young children, there were no differences between the cultures. With increasing age, however, Americans made more dispositional attributions, and Indian subjects made more situational attributions. A similar pattern emerged when subjects made attributions for positive behaviors. This finding raises a provocative question: Is the fundamental attribution error a strictly Western phenomenon? [Data from Miller, 1984.]

a quiz show, the actor is the conspicuous *figure* of your attention; the situation fades into the *background* ("out of sight, out of mind," as they say). According to Heider, people attribute events to factors that are perceptually conspicuous, or *salient*. To test this hypothesis, Shelley Taylor and Susan Fiske (1975) varied the seating arrangements of subjects who observed two actors having a carefully staged conversation. In each session, subjects were seated so they faced actor A, actor B, or both. When later questioned about their observations, subjects rated the actor they faced as the more dominant member of the pair, the one who set the tone and direction. Similarly, when people watch others interacting, they attribute what occurs to the actor who draws more visual attention—by sitting under a bright light, wearing a boldly patterned shirt, or rocking back and forth in a rocking chair (McArthur & Post, 1977).

Whatever the factors at work, the fundamental attribution error may have important implications for how news gets transmitted. If perceivers emphasize persons over situations, they are likely to communicate that emphasis when they describe one person's actions to another. A study by Thomas Gilovich (1987) demonstrates the point. Subjects whose impression of a person was based solely on secondhand information made stronger personal attributions than the firsthand perceivers themselves had made. From one generation to the next, persons seem to grow in prominence, while situations fade further and further into the background. What might this tell us about conceptions of history? Is there, perhaps, a tendency for historians to overplay the role of individual men and women and overlook the guiding hand of political, economic, environmental, and social forces?

The Actor-Observer Effect   People may be prone to commit the fundamental attribution error when they explain the behavior of others, but do we exhibit the same bias in explaining our own behavior? Think about it. Are you shy or outgoing, or does your behavior depend on the situation? Are you calm or intense, quiet or talkative, lenient or firm? Or again—does your behavior depend on the situation? Now pick a friend and answer the same questions. Do you notice a difference? Chances are, you do. Research shows that people are more likely to say "It depends on the situation" to describe themselves than to describe others. When Lewis Goldberg (1978) administered 2,800 English trait words to 14 groups, each containing 100 subjects, he found that 85 percent checked off more traits for other persons than for themselves.

actor-observer effect
The tendency to attribute our own behavior to situational causes and the behavior of others to personal factors.

The tendency to make personal attributions for the behavior of others and situational attributions for ourselves is called the **actor-observer effect** and has been widely demonstrated (Jones & Nisbett, 1972; Watson, 1982). In a study patterned after the 1970s Watergate break-in, college students were urged to commit a real burglary. Whether they agreed or refused, these subjects later attributed their decisions to compelling factors within the situation. Yet observers who read about the request attributed their decisions to aspects of the subjects' character (West et al., 1975). In another study, sixty prison inmates and their counselors were asked to explain why the inmates had committed their offenses. Again, the counselors cited enduring personal characteristics, and the prisoners referred to transient situational factors (Saulnier & Perlman, 1981). Even in letters to "Dear Abby," those seeking advice explained the behavior of others in more dispositional terms than they used to explain their own actions (Schoeneman & Rubanowitz, 1985).

There are two reasons for the difference between actors and observers. First, people have more privileged *information* about themselves than about others—enough to know that their behavior changes dramatically from one situation to the next (Prentice, 1990; White & Younger, 1988). Second, observers focus *attention* on the actor whose behavior they are trying to explain, but actors must attend to the situation that guides their behavior. Absorbed in a conversation, you gaze at your partner; playing tennis, you keep your eye on the ball; taking an exam, you concentrate on the questions. The result is that actors find it easier to make judgments about situations, and observers find it easier to make judgments about persons (Bassili & Racine, 1990). Indeed, the effect is reversed when actors and observers review the actor's behavior on videotape from each other's visual perspective (Storms, 1973).

Motivational Biases   As we saw in Chapter 2, people naturally make favorable, one-sided attributions for their own behavior. Research conducted with students, teachers, parents, workers, athletes, sports fans, and others shows that we take more responsibility for success than for failure—a bias that is found in many cultures of the world (Fletcher & Ward, 1988). Other self-serving biases are evident too, as people seek more information about their strengths than about their weaknesses, overestimate their contribution to group efforts, exaggerate their control over life events, and predict a rosy personal future. The false-consensus effect described earlier also has a self-serving aspect to it. We overestimate the extent to which others behave as we do in order to reassure ourselves that our own actions are correct, normal, and socially appropriate (Sherman et al., 1984).

When it comes to the perception of others, people are not similarly motivated. In *The Devil in the Shape of a Woman*, Carol Karlsen (1987) found that many of the women accused of witchcraft in colonial New England were branded as such not because they were witches but because they were too independent, too smart, or too attractive or had too much money. Refusing to accept these qualities as natural, the accusers—who were often jealous neighbors, peers, and rejected lovers—made attributions to the devil.

This historical example suggests that jealousy may lead us to deny people the credit they deserve. Other motives may also influence our attributions for someone else's behavior. In one study, for example, William Klein and Ziva Kunda (1992) showed subjects the performance on a practice quiz of another subject, a male target, who was later expected to become either their partner or their opponent in a competition. In all cases, the target answered the practice questions correctly. The reason for his success? Hoping he was not too competent, subjects who thought that the target was to be their opponent perceived him as less able than those who thought he was their prospective partner. To justify their wishful thinking, these subjects reasoned that the task was easy and that luck was a contributing factor.

Sometimes, defensive motives lead us to blame others for their misfortunes. Consider the following classic experiment. Subjects thought they were taking part in an emotion-perception study. One subject, actually a confederate, was selected randomly to take a memory test while the others looked on. Each time the confederate made a mistake on the test, she was jolted by a painful electric shock (actually, there was no shock; what subjects saw was a staged videotape). Since subjects knew that only the luck of the draw had kept them off the "hot seat," you might think they would react with sympathy and compassion. Not so. As it turned out, subjects belittled the hapless confederate (Lerner & Simmons, 1966).

belief in a just world
The belief that individuals get what they deserve in life; used to explain why people disparage victims.

Melvin Lerner (1980) argues that the tendency to be critical of victims stems from our deep-seated **belief in a just world**. According to Lerner, people need to view the world as a just place in which we "get what we deserve" and "deserve what we get"—a world where hard work and a clean life always pay off and where laziness and a sinful life are punished. To believe otherwise is to concede that we too are vulnerable to the cruel twists and turns of fate. So how do people defend themselves from this realization? If people cannot assist or compensate the victims of misfortune, they turn on them. Thus, it is often assumed that poor people are lazy (Furnham & Gunter, 1984), that rape victims are careless (Carli & Leonard, 1990), that battered wives provoke their abusive husbands (Summers & Feldman, 1984), and that people infected with AIDS lack moral integrity (Hunter & Ross, 1991).

The tendency to disparage victims may seem like just another symptom of the fundamental attribution error: too much focus on the person and not enough

Some people openly disparage gay men with AIDS and blame these victims for their fate. This reaction may stem from the need to believe that the world is just, and that tragedy strikes only those who are sinful or careless—not us.

on the situation. But the conditions that influence this tendency suggest there is more to it than that. Studies of *defensive attribution* show that accident victims are held more responsible for their fate when the consequences of the accident are severe rather than mild (Walster, 1966), when the victim is in a situation similar to the perceiver's (Burger, 1981; Shaver, 1970), or when the perceiver is emotionally aroused by the event (Thornton et al., 1986) and characteristically anxious about possible threats to the self (Thornton, 1992). In other words, the more personally threatened people feel by an apparent injustice, the greater is their need to protect themselves from the implication that *it* could happen to *them*. One means of defending their shaken belief in a just world is to distance themselves psychologically from the victim through disparagement. Fortunately, people do not resort to derogation when they can restore justice by helping the victim (Lerner & Simmons, 1966; see Chapter 7) or when they are encouraged to take the victim's perspective (Aderman et al., 1974).

INTEGRATION: FROM DISPOSITIONS TO IMPRESSIONS

When behavior is attributed to situational factors, we generally do not make inferences about the actor. Nevertheless, personal attributions often lead us to infer that the actor has a certain trait, or disposition—that the leader of a failing business is incompetent or that a former enemy who extends the olive branch is peaceful. Human beings are not one-dimensional, however, and one trait does not a person make. Before we have a complete picture of someone, we must assemble the various bits and pieces into a unified impression.

Information Integration: The Arithmetic

impression formation The process of integrating information about a person to form a coherent impression.

Once personal attributions are made, how are they combined into a single, coherent picture of a person? How do we approach the process of **impression formation**? Do we simply add up all of a person's traits, do we calculate a mental average, or do we combine the information in more complicated ways? Anyone who has written or received letters of recommendation will appreciate the practical implications. Suppose you're told that an applicant is intelligent and friendly, two highly favorable qualities. Would you be more or less impressed if you learned that the same applicant was also prudent and even-tempered, two moderately favorable qualities? If you are more impressed, you are intuitively following a *summation* model of impression formation: the more positive traits there are, the better. If you are less impressed, you are using an *averaging* model: the higher the average value of all the various traits, the better.

To quantify the formation of impressions, Norman Anderson (1968) had subjects rate the desirability of 555 trait adjectives on a 7-point scale. By calculating the average ratings, he obtained a *scale value* for each trait (*sincere* had the highest scale value; *liar* had the lowest). In an earlier study, Anderson (1965) used similar values and compared the additive and averaging models. Specifically, he asked a group of subjects to rate how much they liked a person described by two traits with extremely high scale values (H, H). A second group received a list of four traits, including two that were high and two that were moderately high in their scale values (H, H, M+, M+). In a third group, subjects received two extremely low, negative traits (L, L). In a fourth group, they received a list of four traits, including two that were low and two that were moderately low (L, L, M–, M–). What effect did the moderate traits have on subjects' impressions? As predicted by the averaging model, the moderate traits diluted rather than added to the impact of the extremely positive and negative traits. The implications for those who write letters of recommendation are clear. Applicants are better off if their letters include only the most glowing comments and omit favorable remarks that are somewhat more guarded in nature.

After extensive amounts of research, it now appears that although people combine traits by averaging, the process is somewhat more complicated. According to Anderson's (1981) **information integration theory**, impressions formed of others are based on an integration of (1) personal dispositions of the perceiver and (2) a *weighted* average, not a simple average, of the target person's characteristics. Let's look more closely at these two factors.

information integration theory The theory that impressions are based on (1) perceiver dispositions and (2) a weighted average of a target person's traits.

Perceiver Dispositions

Like other aspects of social perception, impression formation does not follow the rules of cold logic. Weighted averaging may describe the way most people combine different traits, but keep in mind that the whole process begins with a warm-blooded human perceiver, not a computer. Thus, certain deviations from the "arithmetic" are inevitable.

One example of the limitations of arithmetic is the *person positivity bias*, which is the tendency to rate individual human beings more favorably than groups or impersonal objects (Sears, 1983). Individual politicians are liked more than politicians in general, and individual professors are rated more highly than the courses they teach. An analysis of 300,000 teacher evaluations at UCLA, for example, revealed that students rated 97 percent of their instructors as "above average." Why? According to Sears, person positivity reflects the fact that people are more similar to individual human beings than to groups or impersonal objects, and that similarity heightens attraction (see Chapter 5).

Although the person positivity bias is common, perceivers differ considerably in the kinds of impressions they form of others. Some people seem to measure everyone with an intellectual yardstick; others look for physical beauty, a friendly smile, a sense of humor, or a firm handshake. Whatever the characteristic, each of us is more likely to notice and recall certain traits more than others (Higgins et al., 1982; Bargh et al., 1988). Thus, when subjects are asked to describe a group of target persons, there is often more overlap between the various descriptions provided *by* the same *perceiver* than between the descriptions provided *for* the same *target* (Dornbusch et al., 1965; Park, 1986).

Which characteristics we tend to notice in others may also change from time to time, depending on recent experiences. Have you ever noticed that once a novel word slips into conversation, it gets repeated over and over again? If so, you have observed **priming**, the tendency for frequently or recently used concepts to come to mind easily and influence the interpretation of new information. The effects of priming on impression formation were first demonstrated in a study by E. Tory Higgins and his colleagues (1977). Subjects were presented with a list of trait words, ostensibly as part of a memory experiment. In fact, the task was used as a priming device to plant certain ideas in their minds. Some subjects read words that evoked a positive image: *brave, independent, adventurous*. Others read words that evoked a negative image: *reckless, foolish, careless*. Later, in what they thought was an unrelated experiment, subjects read about a man who climbed mountains, drove in a demolition derby, and crossed the Atlantic in a sailboat. As predicted, subjects' impressions were shaped by the trait words they earlier memorized. Those exposed to positive words formed more flattering impressions of the character than those exposed to negative words. Even though all subjects read the same description, they formed different impressions depending on what was already on their mind. Priming even works when the prime words are presented so rapidly that subjects are not aware of the exposure (Bargh & Pietromonaco, 1982; Erdley & D'Agostino, 1988).

Just as recent experiences can prime people to view others in a certain light, *mood* also influences impression formation. In one study, Joseph Forgas and Gordon Bower (1987) told subjects that they had performed very well or poorly on a test of social adjustment. As expected, this feedback altered the subjects' moods; it also affected their outlook on others. When presented with behavioral information about various characters, subjects spent more time attending to positive facts and formed more favorable impressions when they were happy than when they were sad. Follow-up research shows that the biasing effects of mood are particularly pronounced when we form impressions of others who are atypical, requiring more thought and effort in order to be understood (Forgas, 1992). To summarize, the combined effects of individual differences, recent experiences, and fluctuating mood point to an important conclusion: to some extent, impression formation is in the eyes of the beholder.

Target Characteristics

Just as all perceivers are not created equal, all traits are not created equal either. Whether a particular attribute weighs heavily in our overall judgments depends

priming The tendency for recently used words or ideas to come to mind easily and influence the interpretation of new information.

on several factors. We now consider two of these: implicit personality theories and the power of first impressions.

Implicit Personality Theories   When Jeffrey MacDonald was convicted of brutally murdering his pregnant wife and two young daughters, those who knew him were shocked. MacDonald—the subject of Joe McGinniss's 1983 bestseller, *Fatal Vision*—was young, attractive, intelligent, charming, and successful. Quarterback of his high school football team, he was voted the most popular student of his class and the most likely to succeed. He graduated from Princeton, married his childhood sweetheart, went on to medical school, and then served as a doctor in the Green Berets. As McGinniss put it, "He was almost too good to be true" (p. 6). Yet a North Carolina jury concluded that the evidence against MacDonald was overwhelming.

It is easy to understand why so many people reacted to the guilty verdict with disbelief. MacDonald just didn't seem like *the kind of person* who would commit murder. That reaction is based on an **implicit personality theory**—a network of assumptions each of us makes about the relationships among various traits and behaviors. Knowing that a person has one trait leads people to infer other traits as well (Bruner & Tagiuri, 1954; Cantor & Mischel, 1979; Schneider, 1973). You might assume, for example, that someone who is unpredictable is also dangerous or that someone who talks slowly is also slow-witted. You might also assume that certain traits are linked to certain behaviors (Reeder & Brewer, 1979)—that a man as attractive and successful as Jeff MacDonald, for example, could not possibly massacre his family.

Solomon Asch (1946) was the first to discover that the presence of one trait often implies the presence of others. Asch told one group of subjects that an individual was "intelligent, skillful, industrious, warm, determined, practical and cautious." Another group read an identical list of traits, except the word *warm* was replaced by *cold*. Although only one term was changed, the two groups formed different impressions. Subjects inferred that the warm person was also happier and more generous, humorous, and good-natured than the cold person. When two other words were varied (*polite* and *blunt*), however, the differences were far less pronounced. Asch concluded that *warm* and *cold* are **central traits**, meaning that they suggest the presence of certain other traits and exert a powerful influence on final impressions. The impact of central traits is not limited to studies using trait lists either. When college students in different classes were led to believe that a guest lecturer was either a warm or a cold person, their impressions after the lecture were consistent with these beliefs, even though he gave the same lecture to everyone (Kelley, 1950; Widmeyer & Loy, 1988).

There is another factor that influences the impact of a trait on impressions. It seems paradoxical, but precisely because we tend to perceive others in positive terms, we fall prey to a *trait negativity bias*, the tendency for negative information to weigh more heavily than positive information (Coovert & Reeder, 1990; Fiske, 1980; Skowronski & Carlston, 1989). This means that we

---

implicit personality theory   A network of assumptions people make about the relationships among traits and behaviors.

central traits   Traits that exert a powerful influence on overall impressions, causing us to assume the presence of other traits as well.

form more extreme impressions of a person who is said to be untrustworthy or obnoxious than of one who is said to be kind, honest, or nice. We tend to view others favorably and assume they are similar to us. So when we learn that someone has negative attributes, we sit up, take notice, and pay careful attention (Pratto & John, 1991). In other words, one bad trait may be enough to destroy a person's reputation—regardless of other qualities. Research on American political campaigns confirms this point: public opinion is shaped more by negative information about candidates than by positive information (Lau, 1985; Klein, 1991).

The Power of First Impressions   The order in which a trait is discovered also influences how heavily it weighs in our judgment. It is often said that first impressions are critical, and social psychologists are quick to agree. Studies show that information has a greater impact when it is presented early in a sequence rather than late—a finding known as the **primacy effect**.

primacy effect   The finding that information presented early in a sequence has more impact on impressions than information presented later.

In one of Asch's (1946) experiments, a group of subjects learned that a person was "intelligent, industrious, impulsive, critical, stubborn, and envious." A second group received exactly the same list but in the reverse order. Rationally, the two groups should have felt the same way about the person. But instead, subjects who heard the first list—in which the more positive traits came first—formed more favorable impressions than those who heard the second list. Similar findings were obtained among subjects who watched a videotape of a woman taking an SAT-like test. In all cases, she correctly answered fifteen out of thirty multiple-choice questions. However, subjects who observed a pattern of initial success followed by failure perceived the woman as more intelligent than did those who observed the opposite pattern of failure followed by success (Jones et al., 1968). Although there are exceptions, people are heavily influenced by the "early returns."

Why is the primacy effect so powerful? There are two major reasons. The first is that once perceivers think they have formed an accurate impression, they become less attentive to subsequent contradictory information. Thus, when subjects read a series of statements about a person, the amount of time they spend reading declines steadily as they proceed through the list (Belmore, 1987). Does this mean we are doomed to a life of primacy? Not necessarily. Unstimulated, attention may wane. But if perceivers are motivated to keep from tuning out, primacy is diminished (Anderson & Hubert, 1963; Benassi, 1982; Kruglanski & Freund, 1983).

The second reason for primacy, known as the change-of-meaning hypothesis, is more unsettling. Once people form an initial impression, they interpret subsequent inconsistent information in light of that impression. Asch's research shows just how malleable the meaning of a trait can be. When people are told that a kind person is *calm,* they assume that he or she is gentle, peaceful, and serene. When a cruel person is said to be *calm,* however, the same word is interpreted to mean cool, shrewd, and calculating. Numerous examples illustrate the point. Based on your first impression, the word *proud* can mean self-respecting or conceited; *critical* can mean astute or picky; *impulsive* can mean spontaneous or reckless (Hamilton & Zanna, 1974; Watkins & Peynircio-glu, 1984; Wyer, 1974).

It is remarkable how creative we can be in our effort to transform a bundle of contradictions into an integrated, coherent impression. For example, the person who is said to be "good" but is also "a thief" can be viewed as a character like Robin Hood (Burnstein & Schul, 1982). Or that person could be perceived to have changed over time (Silka, 1989). When Asch and Zukier (1984) presented subjects with these kinds of inconsistent pairs of traits, they identified several strategies that were used to reconcile the conflicts en route to forming impressions (see Table 3.3).

Table 3.3   Forming Coherent Impressions in the Face of Contradiction.   Is it possible to be both brilliant and foolish? Sociable and lonely? When subjects were given inconsistent pairs of traits, they used several different strategies to reconcile the apparent contradictions and form a coherent impression. Six common strategies are described here. [Based on Asch & Zukier, 1984.]

Contradictions	Resolution Modes	Impressions
Brilliant-Foolish	*Segregation* Traits are segregated by assigning each to a different aspect of the person.	"Probably very bright about abstract matters, but silly about day-to-day practical tasks."
Sociable-Lonely	*Depth Dimension* A distinction is drawn between inner and outer layers of the person.	"Has many superficial ties but is unable to form deep relations, and so feels lonely."
Dependent-Hostile	*Cause-Effect* One trait is seen as having caused the other.	"This person is dependent but is resentful of that dependence, and consequently becomes hostile."
Cheerful-Gloomy	*Common Source* The traits are seen as stemming from the same underlying sources.	"They are both common characteristics of a *moody* person."
Strict-Kind	*Means-End* An undesirable trait is seen as a necessary means to a desirable end.	"Setting some limits for someone who is not capable is indeed a kindness—a protective measure."
Intelligent-Unambitious	*Interpolation* New information is introduced as a bridge between the traits.	"The person's efforts have in the past met with disappointment, and this caused him or her to become unambitious."

CONFIRMATION BIAS: FROM IMPRESSIONS TO REALITY

"Please your majesty," said the knave, "I didn't write it and they can't prove I did; there's no name signed at the end." "If you didn't sign it," said the King, "that only makes the matter worse. You must have meant some mischief, or else you'd have signed your name like an honest man."

This exchange, taken from Lewis Carroll's *Alice's Adventures in Wonderland,* illustrates the power of existing impressions. It is striking but often true: once people make up their minds about something—even if they have incomplete information—they become more and more unlikely to change their minds when confronted with evidence. Political leaders refuse to withdraw their support for government programs that don't work, and scientists stubbornly defend their theories in the face of conflicting research data. These instances are easy to explain. Politicians and scientists have a personal investment in their opinions, for pride, funding, and reputation may be at stake. But what about people who more innocently fail to revise their opinions, to their own detriment? What about the baseball manager who clings to strategies that are ineffective or the trial lawyer who repeatedly selects juries according to false stereotypes? Why are such people often so slow to face the facts? As we will see, people are subject to various types of **confirmation bias**—the tendency to *interpret, seek,* and *create* information in ways that verify existing beliefs.

confirmation bias
The tendency to seek, interpret, and create information that verifies existing beliefs.

Perseverance of Beliefs

Imagine you are looking at a slide that is completely out of focus. Gradually, it is focused enough so that the image becomes less blurry. At this point, the experimenter wants to know if you can recognize the picture. The response you're likely to make is interesting. Subjects have more trouble making an identification if they watch the gradual focusing procedure than if they simply view the final, blurry image. In the mechanics of the perceptual process, people apparently form early impressions that interfere with their subsequent ability to "see straight" once presented with improved evidence (Bruner & Potter, 1964). In this section, we will see that social perception is subject to this same kind of interference—yet another reason why first impressions often stick like glue even after we are forced to confront information that discredits our existing beliefs.

Consider what happens when you're led to expect something that does not materialize. In one study, subjects were asked to evaluate the academic potential of a nine-year-old white girl named Hannah. One group was led to believe Hannah came from an upper-middle-class environment in which both parents were well-educated professionals (high expectations). A second group thought she was from a run-down urban neighborhood and that both parents were uneducated blue-collar workers (low expectations). As one might predict, subjects in the first group were slightly more optimistic in their ratings of Hannah's potential than were those in the second group. In each of these groups, however, half of the subjects watched a videotape of Hannah taking an achievement test. Her performance on the tape seemed average. She correctly answered some difficult questions but missed others that were relatively easy. Even though all subjects saw the same tape, Hannah now received much lower ratings of ability from subjects who thought she was poor and higher ratings from those who thought she was affluent. Presenting an identical body of mixed evidence did not extinguish the biasing effects of beliefs; it *fueled* these effects (Darley & Gross, 1983).

Unfortunately, people are similarly biased in matters of life and death. What happens, for example, when advocates and opponents of nuclear technology are confronted with evidence of a near-fatal accident? If a nuclear power plant breaks down but the system's safeguards prevent a disaster, how do people react? If we assume that advocates will feel humbled by the breakdown and opponents will feel comforted by the effectiveness of the safeguards, we might expect the two sides to converge somewhat in their opinions. But, that's not what happens. After subjects with strongly pro or anti points of view read a story about a nuclear power plant accident that was not catastrophic, most became more certain, not less certain, of their initial positions (see Figure 3.6). Advocates focused on the safeguards, and opponents focused on the breakdown—thus magnifying their initial differences of opinion (Plous, 1991).

Events that are ambiguous enough to support contrasting interpretations are like inkblots: perceivers see in them what they expect or want to see. But what about information that plainly disconfirms beliefs? What happens to our first impressions under those circumstances? Craig Anderson and his colleagues (1980) addressed this question by supplying subjects with false information. After the subjects had enough time to think about the information, they were told that it was untrue. In one experiment, half of the subjects read case studies suggesting that individuals who take risks make better firefighters than do those who are cautious. The other half read cases suggesting the opposite conclusion. Next, subjects were asked to come up with a theory for the suggested correlation. The possibilities are easy to imagine: "He who hesitates is lost" supports risk taking, and "You have to look before you leap" supports caution. Finally, subjects were led to believe the experiment was over and were told that the information they received was fictitious, manufactured for the sake of the experiment. Subjects, however, did not abandon their firefighter theories. Instead, they exhibited **belief perseverance**, sticking to initial beliefs even after they are discredited. Apparently, it's easier to get people to build a theory than to convince them to tear it down. Even social psychologists may be slow to change their theories in light of inconsistent research data (Greenwald et al., 1986).

belief perseverance
The tendency to maintain beliefs even after they have been discredited.

Why do beliefs outlive the evidence on which they are supposed to be based? The problem is that when we conjure up explanations that make sense, those explanations take on a life of their own. In fact, once people form an opinion, that opinion is strengthened by merely *thinking* about the topic—even without

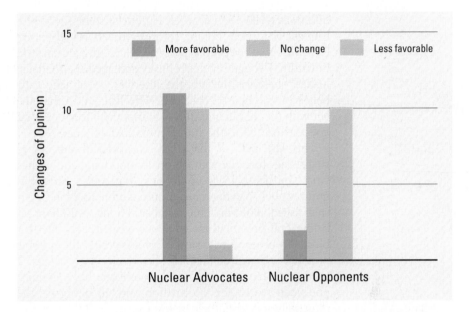

Figure 3.6   Mixed Evidence: Does It Extinguish or Fuel Our First Impressions?   In this study, subjects with pro or anti points of view reported their opinions before and after reading about a noncatastrophic nuclear power plant accident. Although both sides were exposed to the same evidence, proponents became more favorable (left), and opponents became less favorable (right), thus magnifying their initial differences of opinion. [Data from Plous, 1991.]

articulating the reasons for the opinion (Tesser, 1978). And therein lies the solution. By asking people to consider why an *alternative* theory might be true, belief perseverance can be reduced or eliminated (Anderson & Sechler, 1986).

Confirmatory Hypothesis Testing

Social perceivers are not passive recipients of information. Like detectives, we ask questions and actively search for clues. But do we seek information objectively, or are we inclined to confirm the suspicions we already hold? Mark Snyder and William Swann (1978) addressed this question by having pairs of subjects who were strangers to one another take part in an interview. In each pair, one subject was asked to interview the other. But first, that subject was falsely led to believe that the person to be interviewed was either introverted or extroverted (actually, subjects were assigned on a random basis to these conditions) and was then told to select questions from a prepared list. Those who thought they were talking to an introvert chose mostly introvert-oriented questions ("Have you ever felt left out of some social group?"), while those who thought they were talking to an extrovert asked extrovert-oriented questions ("How do you liven up a party?"). Expecting a certain kind of person, subjects unwittingly sought evidence that confirmed their expectations. By asking these loaded questions, in fact, the interviewers actually gathered support for their beliefs. Thus, neutral observers who listened to the tapes afterwards were also left with the mistaken impression that the interviewees really were as introverted and extroverted as the interviewers had assumed.

This last part of the study is powerful but, in retrospect, not all that surprising. Imagine yourself on the receiving end of an interview. Asked about what you do to liven up parties, you would probably talk about organizing group games, playing dance music, and telling jokes. On the other hand, if you were asked about difficult social situations, you might talk about being nervous before oral presentations or about what it feels like to be the new kid on the block. In other words, simply by answering the questions that are asked, you provide evidence confirming the interviewer's beliefs. Thus, perceivers set in motion a vicious cycle: thinking someone has a certain trait, they engage in a one-sided search for information and, in doing so, they create a reality that ultimately supports their beliefs (Snyder, 1984).

Are people so blinded by their existing beliefs that they can't manage an objective search for evidence? It depends on the situation. In the situation devised by Snyder and Swann, people conduct a biased, confirmatory search for information. Even experienced psychotherapists—professionals trained in diagnosis—select questions that are likely to confirm initial beliefs (Dallas & Baron, 1985). Thankfully, however, different circumstances produce less biasing results. When subjects are not certain of their beliefs and are concerned about the accuracy of their impressions (Kruglanski & Mayseless, 1988), when they are allowed to prepare their own interviews (Trope et al., 1984), or when the available nonconfirmatory questions are better than the confirmatory questions (Skov & Sherman, 1986), then a more neutral search for information is pursued.

Self-Fulfilling Prophecies

self-fulfilling prophecy The process by which a perceiver's expectations about a person eventually lead that person to behave in ways that confirm those expectations.

In 1948, sociologist Robert Merton told a story about Cartwright Millingville, president of the Last National Bank during the Depression. Although the bank was solvent, a rumor began to spread that it was floundering. Within hours, hundreds of depositors were lined up to withdraw their savings before no money was left to withdraw. The rumor was false, but the bank eventually failed. Using stories such as this, Merton proposed what seemed like an outrageous hypothesis: that a perceiver's expectation can actually lead to the fulfillment of that expectation, a **self-fulfilling prophecy**.

Merton's hypothesis lay dormant within psychology until Robert Rosenthal and Lenore Jacobson (1968) published the results of a study entitled *Pygmalion in the Classroom*. Noticing that teachers had higher expectations for better students, they wondered if teacher expectations *influenced* student performance rather than the other way around. To address the question, they told teachers in a San Francisco elementary school that certain pupils were on the verge of an intellectual growth spurt. The results of an IQ test were cited but, in fact, the pupils were randomly selected. Eight months later, when real tests were administered, the "late bloomers"—but not children assigned to a control group—improved their IQ scores by as much as 30 points. They were also evaluated more favorably by their classroom teachers.

When the Pygmalion study was first published, it was greeted with chagrin. If positive teacher expectations can increase student performance, can negative expectations have the opposite effect? And what about the social implications? Could wealthy children be destined for success and disadvantaged children doomed to failure because educators hold different expectations for them? Many researchers were critical of the study and skeptical about the generality of the results.

Unfortunately, the findings cannot be swept under the proverbial rug. Teachers form expectations early in the school year based on a student's background, reputation, physical appearance, initial performance, and standardized-test scores. Teachers then alter their behavior toward the student accordingly. If expectations are high rather than low, students receive more attention, emotional support, challenging homework, and praise. To some extent, teacher expectations are predictive of academic performance because teachers are often accurate in their initial assessments of ability (Jussim, 1989). Still, it's important to recognize that teacher expectations—even when they were totally fabricated by researchers—significantly *influenced* student performance in 36 percent of 400 experiments designed to test the hypothesis (Rosenthal, 1985). In fact, student expectations of a teacher can have similar effects. When two high school classes were led to believe that their new English teacher was highly regarded, they became noticeably more attentive in class and achieved higher final grades as a result (Jamieson et al., 1987).

Self-fulfilling prophecies are at work in noneducational settings as well, including business organizations and the military. For example, in a study of twenty-nine platoons that consisted of a thousand men in the Israeli Defense Forces, Dov Eden (1990) led some but not all platoon leaders to expect that the group of trainees they were about to receive had unusually high potential (in fact, these groups were of average ability). After ten weeks, those trainees who were assigned to the high-expectation platoons obtained higher scores than the others on written exams and on the ability to operate a weapon.

How does the Pygmalion effect work? How do social perceivers transform expectations into reality? Research indicates that it is helpful to view the self-fulfilling prophecy as a three-step process (see Figure 3.7). First, the perceiver forms an impression of the target person. This impression may be based on initial interactions with the target or on hearsay. Second, the perceiver behaves in a manner that is consistent with that first impression. Third, the target unwittingly adjusts his or her behavior to the perceiver's actions. Both inside and outside the classroom, the self-fulfilling prophecy is a powerful

"DO PEOPLE HATE US BECAUSE WE DRESS THIS WAY OR DO WE DRESS THIS WAY BECAUSE PEOPLE HATE US?"

In the vicious cycle of a self-fulfilling prophecy, it's hard to pinpoint the problem: Is the perceiver's expectation based on the target's behavior, or was the target's behavior conditioned by the perceiver's expectation? [Sidney Harris.]

phenomenon (Cooper & Good, 1983; Darley & Fazio, 1980; Harris & Rosenthal, 1985).

Now, let's straighten out this picture of human nature. It would be a sad commentary, indeed, if each of us could be so easily molded by others' perceptions into appearing brilliant or stupid, introverted or extroverted, competitive or cooperative, warm or cold. The effects are well established, but thankfully there are limits. By viewing the self-fulfilling prophecy as a three-step process, it is possible to identify two links in the chain that can be broken to prevent an often vicious cycle.

Consider the first step, the link between one's expectations and behavior toward the target. In many studies, perceivers interact with the target on only a casual basis and are not necessarily driven by the goal of forming an accurate impression. But when perceivers are highly motivated to seek the truth (as when they are considering the target as a possible teammate or opponent), they start to probe for an accurate assessment and, in so doing, they often fail to confirm expectations (Darley et al., 1988; Hilton & Darley, 1991). Forewarned that someone is unfriendly, for example, perceivers may go out of their way to be nice in an effort to *disconfirm* an unwelcome expectation (Ickes et al., 1982).

Next is the second step, the link between a perceiver's behavior and the target's response. In much of the research, as in much of life, target persons are not aware of others' false impressions. Thus, it is unlikely that Rosenthal and Jacobson's "late bloomers" knew of their teachers' high expectations or that Snyder and Swann's "introverts" and "extroverts" knew of their interviewers' misconceptions. But what if they did know? How would you react if *you* found yourself cast in a particular light? When it happened to subjects in one experiment, they managed to overcome the self-fulfilling prophecy by behaving in ways that led perceivers to abandon their initial expectations (Hilton & Darley, 1985). As you may recall from the discussion of self-verification in Chapter 2, this result is most likely to occur when our expectations clash with a target person's self-concept. Thus, when targets who think of themselves as extroverted were interviewed by perceivers who believed they were introverted (and vice versa), what changed as a result of the interaction were the

---

Figure 3.7 Self-Fulfilling Prophecy as a Three-Step Process. How do people transform their expectations into reality? (1) A perceiver has expectations of a target person. (2) The perceiver then behaves in a manner consistent with those expectations. (3) The target unwittingly adjusts his or her behavior according to the perceiver's actions.

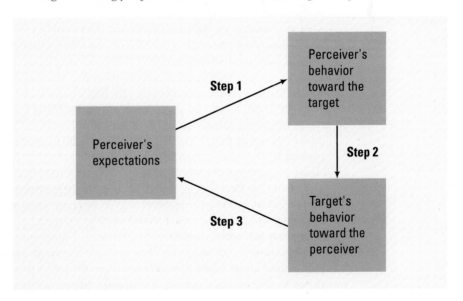

perceivers' beliefs—not the targets' behavior (Swann & Ely, 1984). It's important to keep in mind that the persons we perceive have their own prophecies to fulfill.

SOCIAL PERCEPTION: THE BOTTOM LINE

Trying to understand people—business and world leaders, criminal defendants and their accusers, or loved ones closer to home—is no easy task. As you reflect on the material in this chapter, you will notice that there are two radically different views of social perception. One view suggests the process is quick and relatively automatic. Without much thought, effort, or awareness, people make rapid-fire snap judgments about others based on physical appearance, preconceived notions, or just a hint of behavioral evidence. According to the second view, however, the process is relatively mindful. People observe others carefully and reserve judgment until their analysis of the person, behavior, and situation is complete. As suggested by theories of attribution and information integration, the process is eminently logical.

It is safe to conclude that both views of social perception are correct. Sometimes judgments are made with the snap of a finger; at other times they are based on a painstaking analysis of behavior (Brewer, 1988; Fiske & Neuberg, 1990). Either way, we often steer our interactions with others along a path that is narrowed by our initial impressions, a process that can set in motion a self-fulfilling prophecy. The various processes of social perception as described in this chapter are summarized in Figure 3.8.

At this point, we must confront an important question: How *accurate* are people's impressions of each other? For years, this question has proved provocative but hard to answer (Cronbach, 1955; Kenny & Albright, 1987; Kruglanski, 1989). Granted, people often depart from the ideals of logic and exhibit many biases in their social perceptions. In this chapter alone, we have seen that perceivers tend to rely on cognitive heuristics without regard for numerical base rates; overlook situational influences on behavior; disparage victims whose misfortunes threaten their sense of justice; form premature first impressions primed by recent experiences and mood fluctuations; and interpret, seek, and create evidence in ways that support these impressions.

To make matters worse, we seem to have little awareness of our limitations, leading us to feel *overconfident* in our judgments. In a series of studies, David Dunning and others (1990) asked college students to predict how a target person would react in different situations. Some subjects made predictions about a fellow student whom they had just met and interviewed; others made predictions about their roommates. In both cases, they reported their confidence in the accuracy of each prediction, and accuracy was determined by the

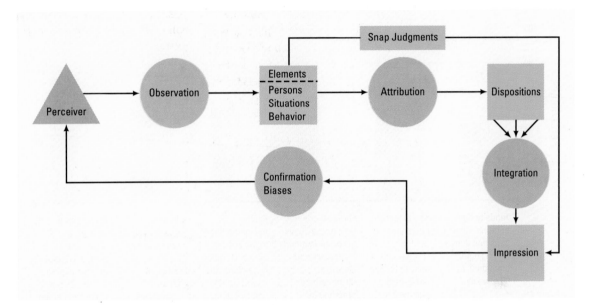

Figure 3.8 Processes of Social Perception.   Summarizing Chapter 3, this diagram depicts the various processes of social perception. As you can see, social perception begins with the observation of persons, behavior, and situations. Sometimes, we make snap judgments from these cues. At other times, we form impressions only after making attributions and then integrating these attributions. Either way, our impressions are subject to confirmation biases and the risk of a self-fulfilling prophecy.

responses of the target persons themselves. The results were clear: regardless of whether they had judged a stranger or their roommate, subjects consistently overestimated the accuracy of their predictions (see Figure 3.9). Even subjects who are depressed and prone to view themselves negatively exhibit overconfidence (Dunning & Story, 1991). In addition, people overestimate their ability to predict their own future behavior. When 98 freshmen made 3,800 self-predictions about the upcoming academic year, predictions that were later verified (for example, "Will you decide on a major?" "Will you have a steady boy/girlfriend?" "Will you call your parents more than twice a month?"), they estimated they would be accurate 82 percent of the time but had an accuracy rate of only 68 percent (Vallone et al., 1990).

When you stand back from the material presented in this chapter, the list of shortcomings, punctuated by the problem of overconfidence, is long and depressing. But how can we reconcile this list with the triumphs of civilization? "If we're so dumb, how come we made it to the moon?" (Nisbett & Ross, 1980, p. 249). Part of the answer comes with realizing that *bias*—that is, a deviation from the rules of logic—does not necessarily produce *error*—defined as real-life judgments that are incorrect (Funder, 1987). The fundamental attribution

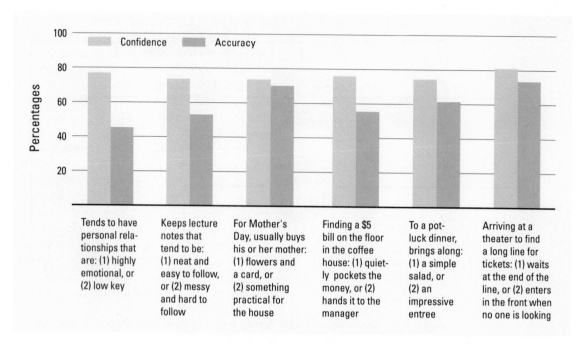

Figure 3.9   The Overconfidence Effect in Social Perception.   As this sample of items indicates, people overestimate their ability to predict how others behave in various situations. [Data from Dunning et al., 1990.]

"error" is a good example: we may make personal attributions to the neglect of situations, but sometimes behavior really *is* caused by personal factors (Funder, 1982; Harvey et al., 1981).

It is true that people fall prey to the biases identified by social psychologists and probably even to some biases that have not yet been noticed. It is also true that we sometimes get fooled by con artists, misjudge our partners in marriage, and hire the wrong job applicants. As Thomas Gilovich (1991) points out in his book *How We Know What Isn't So*, more Americans today believe in ESP than in evolution, and there are twenty times as many astrologers as astronomers. The problem is, these biases can have harmful consequences—giving rise to racial stereotypes, prejudice, and discrimination (see Chapter 4) and causing people to sink into debt through gambling and poor investments (see Chapter 13).

Despite the imperfections, there are five reasons to be guardedly optimistic about our competence as social perceivers. First, the more experience people have with each other, the more accurate they become in their judgments. Research shows, for example, that although subjects cannot accurately assess the personality of strangers they meet in the laboratory, they can accurately judge the personality of their own friends and acquaintances (Colvin & Funder,

1991; Malloy & Albright, 1990; Paunonen, 1989). Second, although we are not proficient at making global judgments about others (that is, at knowing what others are like across a range of settings), we can make modest, more circumscribed predictions of how others will behave in our own presence. You may have a mistaken impression of the personality of your roommate or a coworker, but to the extent that you can predict your roommate's behavior at home or your coworker's on the job, the mistakes may not matter (Swann, 1984). Third, people are more sensitive to others on judgments that have adaptive significance (Baron, 1988). Thus, counselors in charge of a group of socially maladjusted boys were able to judge how aggressive the boys were more accurately than they could evaluate other, less pressing characteristics (Wright & Dawson, 1988). Fourth, people are less biased and less overconfident when they feel that they need to be accurate (Kunda, 1990). Fifth, social perception skills can be enhanced by teaching people the rules of probability and logic (Nisbett et al., 1987). Thus, graduate students in psychology—because they take courses in statistics—improve in their ability to reason about everyday social events (Lehman et al., 1988). This last result may have valuable implications: perhaps awareness of the kinds of problems described in this chapter is a necessary first step toward a better understanding of others.

REVIEW

OBSERVATION: THE ELEMENTS OF SOCIAL PERCEPTION
To understand other people's emotions, motives, and personal dispositions, social perceivers rely on indirect clues—the elements of social perception.

Persons: Judging a Book by Its Cover
Snap judgments of others are often based on physical appearances. Adults with baby-faced features, for example, are perceived to have childlike qualities.

Situations: The Scripts of Life
People have preconceptions about various types of situations. These scripts lead them to interpret ambiguous behaviors in ways that fit expectations and influence their interpretations of behavior.

Behavioral Evidence
Perceivers derive meaning from behavior by breaking it into discrete, meaningful units. Nonverbal behaviors are used to determine how others are feeling. From expressions of the face, for example, people throughout the world can identify the emotions of happiness, fear, sadness, surprise, anger, and disgust. Body language and touch are also important forms of nonverbal communication.

People use nonverbal cues to detect deception but are often not accurate in these judgments. The problem is that perceivers pay too much attention to words and facial expressions, communication channels that are under the deceiver's control, while neglecting body movements and tone of voice, leaky channels that are revealing.

ATTRIBUTION: FROM ELEMENTS TO DISPOSITIONS

Attribution is the process by which we explain other people's behavior.

The Logic of Attribution

People try to understand others by making personal or situational attributions for their behavior. According to correspondent inference theory, people infer a person's characteristics from a behavior to the extent that the behavior was freely chosen, was unexpected, and produced a small number of desirable outcomes. From multiple behaviors, people base their attributions on three kinds of covariation information: consensus (how other persons react to the stimulus under consideration), distinctiveness (how the person involved reacts to other stimuli), and consistency (how the person reacts to a stimulus on other occasions).

Attribution Biases

People depart from the logic of attribution theory in several ways. First, we tend to rely on cognitive heuristics—"rules of thumb" that enable us to make judgments that are quick and easy but often in error. Due to the availability heuristic, for example, people overestimate the consensus of their own behavior and are relatively insensitive to the information provided by numerical base rates.

Second, people commit the fundamental attribution error when they explain the behavior of others, underestimating the impact of situations and overestimating the role of personal factors. This occurs because we tend to accept our observations at face value, because personal attributions fit the Western belief that persons are responsible for their own actions, and because actors are salient against situational backgrounds.

Third, although people tend to make personal attributions for others, they tend to make situational attributions for their own behavior. This actor-observer difference appears because people have more information about how their own behavior changes across situations, and they focus their attention on these situations.

Fourth, people are often motivated to make biased attributions for the behavior of others. Needing to believe in a just world, for example, we often criticize victims, holding them responsible for their own misfortune.

INTEGRATION: FROM DISPOSITIONS TO IMPRESSIONS

Information Integration: The Arithmetic

Initial research indicated that impressions are based on an averaging of individual traits, not a summation. Information integration theory adds that impressions are based on (1) a perceiver's predispositions and (2) a weighted average of individual traits.

Perceiver Dispositions

People tend to rate individuals more favorably than they rate groups or objects. This difference is evidence of a person positivity bias. Perceivers also differ in terms of their sensitivity to certain traits and their predisposition to form favorable or unfavorable impressions. These differences are the result of perceiver characteristics, recent experiences, and current mood.

Target Characteristics

Some information weighs more heavily than other information in overall impressions. Two factors are particularly important. First, some traits are more central than others. On the basis of implicit personality theories, people who know that a person has a central trait, such as warmth or coldness, will assume that the person has certain other characteristics as well.

Second, information has a greater impact when it unfolds early in a sequence rather than late. This primacy effect occurs because once we form a first impression, we become less attentive to subsequent information and interpret that information in light of the initial impression. Faced with conflicting descriptions of someone, people manage to form coherent impressions through a variety of reconciling strategies.

CONFIRMATION BIAS: FROM IMPRESSIONS TO REALITY

Once an impression is formed, people become less likely to change their minds when confronted with nonsupportive evidence. Rather, they tend to interpret, seek, and create information in ways that confirm existing beliefs.

Perseverance of Beliefs

First impressions may stick after people are forced to confront information that fails to support or even discredits existing beliefs. Ambiguous evidence is interpreted in ways that bolster first impressions. The effect of evidence later discredited perseveres because people formulate theories to support their initial impressions, theories that outlive the evidence on which they are based.

Confirmatory Hypothesis Testing

Once perceivers have beliefs about someone, they often but not always seek additional information in ways that confirm those beliefs.

Self-Fulfilling Prophecies

As demonstrated by the effects of teacher expectancies on student achievement, first impressions set in motion a self-fulfilling prophecy. This self-fulfilling prophecy is based on a three-step interpersonal process: (1) the perceiver develops an expectation concerning a target; (2) the perceiver behaves in a manner that is consistent with that expectation; and (3) the target adjusts to the perceiver's actions. This effect is powerful, but there are limits. When perceivers are motivated to seek the truth about a target, they probe more objectively for information. Also, when targets are aware of a perceiver's expectations and believe them to be false, they actively seek to disconfirm them.

SOCIAL PERCEPTION: THE BOTTOM LINE

Sometimes we make snap judgments; at other times we evaluate others by carefully analyzing their behavior. Research suggests that our judgments are biased and that people are overconfident. Still, there are reasons to be optimistic about our everyday competence as social perceivers.

Perceiving Groups

4

Preview

This chapter considers how people think, feel, and behave in response to social groups. We begin by examining *stereotypes,* beliefs about groups that bias our evaluations of specific persons. Next, we examine *prejudice,* negative feelings toward others based on their group membership. To illustrate these processes, we focus on *sexism,* a form of discrimination based on gender, and *racism,* a form of discrimination based on skin color or ethnic heritage. Possible ways to reduce stereotyping and prejudice are discussed throughout the chapter.

Ann Hopkins was hoping to become a partner in one of the largest accounting firms in the country. On paper, her record was impeccable. In just a few years, Hopkins had single-handedly brought in more than $25 million in contracts, tops among her peers. Yet she was denied a partnership even though several less productive men were promoted. Why? According to Hopkins, it was because she was a woman.

As in most disputes, there are two sides to the story. The firm claimed that Hopkins was abrasive, overbearing, and difficult to work with. Some partners complained that she used profanity and was insensitive to coworkers. One member of the firm was said to have quit and sought employment elsewhere, presumably because he could not tolerate working with her.

Was Ann Hopkins rejected because of her personality, her gender, or a combination of the two? Would a man have been promoted under the same circumstances? Hopkins took the case to court and claimed she was described by partners as a "macho" "lady partner candidate" who needed to take a course at "charm school." One partner even advised her to "wear make-up, have my hair styled, and wear jewelry." What do these comments prove? To answer the question, Hopkins called on social psychologist Susan Fiske to testify as an expert on

Despite an exceptional record of productivity, Ann Hopkins was denied partnership in a large accounting firm. Was it because she was a woman perceived to be too much like a man?

The beating of black motorist Rodney King by four white police officers was captured on videotape and played repeatedly on television. Were these officers motivated by racism, or did they use necessary force to make an arrest? The tape seems clear. Yet on April 29, 1992, a California jury announced its controversial verdict: not guilty.

stereotypes. Citing much of the research presented in this chapter, Fiske concluded that Hopkins was a likely victim of sex discrimination. The trial judge agreed. Then by a 6 to 3 vote, so did the U.S. Supreme Court (Fiske et al., 1991).

Sex discrimination claims raise difficult questions about biases in social perception. Equally troubling questions are raised by claims of racial discrimination, as in the highly publicized beating of black motorist Rodney King by white Los Angeles police officers. The incident took place in the spring of 1991, after police cars chased King through the night, stopped his car, and cornered the unarmed man on the street. After King resisted arrest, one officer fired a 50,000-volt "stun gun" at his chest, knocking him to the ground. Three others took turns kicking and clubbing him with their nightsticks while eleven officers looked on. The result: King suffered a fractured skull, a crushed cheekbone, burn marks on his chest, a broken ankle, and assorted internal injuries (Lacayo, 1991; Prud'Homme, 1991).

To members of the black community, this horrifying incident was like an old-fashioned lynching—an act of pure racism. What's worse, they say, it's just the tip of an iceberg. Indeed, the only reason this case received attention was that a bystander just happened to capture two minutes of the beating with his home video camera, making a tape that was played over and over again on national television. While expressing regret, then Los Angeles police chief Daryl Gates dismissed the incident as a mere "aberration" and insisted that it was not racially motivated. Then on April 29, 1992, a jury sent shock waves across the United States, triggering riots in Los Angeles. In the trial of the four police officers charged with King's assault, the jury returned a verdict of not guilty. Was the beating of Rodney King racially motivated? Would King have been beaten if he were white, or if the police officers who stopped him were black? How can we know for sure when behavior stems from prejudice?

discrimination   Any behavior directed against persons because of their identification with a particular group.

The term **discrimination** is used to describe *behaviors* that are directed against persons because of their identification with a particular group. It would be nice to think of discrimination as a sin of the past. Unfortunately, recent incidents suggest that it still exists and that its victims are avoided, excluded, rejected, belittled, and attacked because of the groups to which they belong. What do we mean by "group"? Actually, there are many kinds of groups—families, political parties, nations, religious affiliations, ethnic subcultures, and so on—which is why social psychologists have defined the term in various ways.

group   Two or more persons perceived as related because of their direct interactions, membership in the same social category, or common fate.

For the purposes of this chapter, a **group** is defined as two or more people perceived as having at least one of the following characteristics: (1) direct interactions with each other; (2) joint membership in a social category based on sex, race, or other attributes; (3) a shared, common fate.

This chapter is divided into four parts. First, we consider the causes and effects of *stereotypes*—beliefs people have about individuals based on their membership in a social group. Second, we examine *prejudice*, which consists of negative feelings about others because of their connection to a social group. To put these problems in concrete terms, we then focus on *sexism* and *racism*, two common forms of discrimination. For the most part, stereotypes and prejudice are discussed separately. Note, however, that these beliefs and feelings influence each other, that both give rise to discrimination, and that discriminatory behavior, in turn, fuels stereotypes and prejudices (see Figure 4.1). It is also important to note that although we focus on sexism and racism, victims of discrimination include homosexuals, AIDS sufferers, the handicapped, senior citizens, and people from foreign cultures.

STEREOTYPES

stereotypes   Beliefs that associate groups of people with certain traits.

Stereotypes are beliefs that associate groups of people with certain types of characteristics. When you stop to think about it, the list of well-known stereotypes seems virtually endless. Consider some examples: the Japanese are sneaky, jocks are brainless, librarians are serious, Italians are emotional, the British are reserved, Jews are materialistic, accountants are dull, and used-car salesmen can't be trusted as far as you can throw them. How many of these images ring a bell? In this section, we raise three questions: (1) How do stereotypes form? (2) What keeps them alive when so often they prove to be wrong? (3) How are they used to evaluate individuals?

How Stereotypes Form: Cognitive Foundations

The origins of stereotypes can be traced in a number of different ways (Allport, 1954). From a historical perspective, stereotypes spring from past events. Thus, it can be argued that slavery in America gave rise to the portrayal of blacks as inferior, just as the sneak attack on Pearl Harbor in World War II fostered the belief that the Japanese cannot be trusted. From a political perspective, stereotypes are viewed as a means by which groups in power rationalize war, religious intolerance, and economic oppression. And from a sociocultural perspective, it is argued that real differences between social groups contribute to the birth of perceived differences. Each of these perspectives has something unique to offer. Social psychologists, however, pose a different question: Regardless of how a stereotype is born within a culture, how does it grow and operate in the minds of individuals?

The formation of stereotypes involves two related processes. The first is *categorization*. As perceivers, people naturally sort single objects into groups rather than think of each one as perfectly unique. Biologists classify animals into families; archaeologists divide time into eras; and geographers split the Earth into regions. Likewise, people sort each other on the basis of gender, race, and other common attributes—a process called **social categorization** (Taylor, 1981; Wilder, 1986). Social categorization can be an adaptive feature of social perception. By grouping people the way we group foods, animals, and other objects, we form impressions quickly and use past experience to guide new interactions. Stereotypes thus provide us with rich, vivid expectations about individuals we do not know (Andersen & Klatzky, 1987; Bond & Brockett, 1987). Of course,

social categorization
The classification of persons into groups on the basis of common attributes.

Figure 4.1 Perceiving Groups: Three Reactions.   There are two paths to discrimination: one based on stereotypes, the other on prejudice. There are other mutual links among these variables. Discriminatory practices may support stereotypes and prejudice; stereotypes may cause people to become prejudiced; and prejudiced people may use stereotypes to justify their feelings.

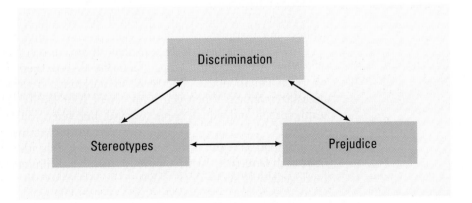

there is a major drawback. Like lumping apples and oranges because both are fruit, categorizing people leads us to overestimate differences *between* groups and underestimate the differences *within* groups (Allen & Wilder, 1975; Wilder, 1978).

The second process that promotes stereotyping follows from the first. Although grouping human beings is much like grouping objects, there is a vital difference. When it comes to social categorization, perceivers themselves are members or nonmembers of the categories they employ. Groups that we identify with are called *ingroups*; those that we do not identify with are our *outgroups*. This distinction is important because people tend to assume that there is greater similarity among the members of outgroups than among the members of our ingroups, an assumption known as the **outgroup homogeneity bias**. In other words, we're generally quite aware of the fine, subtle differences between "us," the individuals in our own groups; but when we look at outgroups, "they" all seem to be alike (Linville & Jones, 1980). And the greater the perceived homogeneity in an outgroup, the more likely we are to overestimate the number of its members who fit the stereotype (Judd et al., 1991b). Thus, while the natives of New York City proclaim their ethnic diversity, elsewhere there is talk of the typical New Yorker.

As a consequence of the outgroup homogeneity bias, people are quick to generalize from one individual to a whole group. In one study, for example, male students from Rutgers and Princeton—rival universities in the state of New Jersey—looked at a videotape of another subject taking part in a decision-making experiment. After being led to believe that the experiment took place at either Rutgers or Princeton, subjects watched the target person choose between classical or rock music and between verbal or math problems. When later asked to predict the percentage of other subjects who made the same choices, students assumed that similarity between the target person and other subjects was greater at the rival university than at their own (Quattrone & Jones, 1980). It's important to note that the reverse is also true: people often generalize from the group to specific individuals. For example, outsiders tend to assume that a group's decision reflects the views of all members—as if they all speak with one voice (Allison & Messick, 1985b; Worth et al., 1987).

Research has shown that the outgroup homogeneity bias occurs in the mutual perceptions of young and old, political liberals and conservatives, blacks and whites, and members of different campus-wide clubs. For groups other than their own, people tend to believe that "If you've seen one, you've seen them all." Why? According to George Quattrone (1986), there are two reasons. First, we often fail to notice differences in outgroups because we don't have the necessary contact. When you think about your family or your favorite sports team, specific individuals come to mind. But when you think about unfamiliar outgroups, you're likely to think in more abstract terms about the group as a whole (Judd & Park, 1988). Consistent with this idea, research shows that increased familiarity with outgroup members eliminates the perception of homogeneity (Linville et al., 1989).

outgroup homogeneity bias   The tendency to assume that there is greater similarity among members of outgroups than of ingroups.

SAN FRANCISCO
A VIEW OF THE WORLD

Stereotypes can spring from the outgroup homogeneity bias. People think of ingroup members as distinct, but they're quick to generalize about members of outgroups.

The second problem, says Quattrone, is that contacts with outgroups are often limited by two *sampling biases*. The first is that groups usually interact in only certain situations. The Princetonian who sees Rutgers students only when they cruise into town for a football game, waving pennants and screaming at the top of their lungs, will not see the diversity of their behavior. The second sampling bias is that people usually interact only with certain members of an outgroup, not with all members. Thus, the Rutgers student who meets only the most avid Princeton fans will not have encountered a representative sample of that outgroup.

How Stereotypes Survive: Self-Perpetuating Biases

Social categorization and the outgroup homogeneity bias supply fertile ground for stereotyping. As generalized beliefs, stereotypes offer quick, convenient summaries of social groups. As *overgeneralized* beliefs, however, they cause us to overlook the diversity within categories and to form mistaken impressions of specific individuals. Is convenience worth the risk of error? Why do stereotypes endure?

illusory correlations
Overestimates of the association between variables that are only slightly correlated or not correlated at all.

Illusory Correlations   One answer can be found in **illusory correlations**: a tendency for people to overestimate the link between variables that are only slightly or not at all correlated. Illusory correlation was first discovered by Loren Chapman (1967), who presented subjects with lists of paired words such as *lion-tiger, lion-eggs, bacon-tiger,* and *bacon-eggs.* Subjects then estimated how often each word was paired with every other word. Two biases were found. First, although all words were paired an equal number of times, subjects overestimated the number of times distinctive, conspicuous words were paired—words, for example, that were noticeably longer than others on the list (*blossoms-note-book*). Second, subjects overestimated the frequency of word pairs that were meaningfully associated in their own minds (*lion-tiger, bacon-eggs*).

Is it possible that these same two biases lead people to perceive false support for existing stereotypes? David Hamilton and his colleagues believe so. In one study, Hamilton and Robert Gifford (1976) tested the hypothesis that distinctive persons and actions—those that capture attention because they are novel or deviant—produce illusory correlations. Subjects read a series of sentences, each describing a desirable or an undesirable behavior on the part of someone who belonged to one of two groups, A or B. Overall, two-thirds of the behaviors were desirable ("visited a sick friend in the hospital") rather than undesirable ("was late to work"), and two-thirds involved members of hypothetical group A (the majority) rather than group B (the minority). The ratio of desirable to undesirable acts was the same for the two groups, so objectively subjects should not have formed an impression more favorable toward one group than toward the other. But they did. As shown in Figure 4.2, subjects overestimated the number of times that the two relatively infrequent variables—undesirable behavior and group B members—were paired together. Unless otherwise motivated, people overestimate the joint occurrence of distinct variables such as minority groups and deviant behaviors (Hamilton et al., 1985; Schaller, 1991).

Next, Hamilton and Terrence Rose (1980) reasoned that stereotypes would lead people to expect real groups and traits to fit together like bacon and eggs. In their study, subjects read twenty-four sentences, each linking someone from a familiar occupational category (accountant, doctor, salesman, stewardess, librarian, and waitress) to a trait (perfectionist, wealthy, thoughtful, timid, enthusiastic, talkative, productive, serious, attractive, comforting, busy, and loud). Each occupation was paired equally often with each trait. Yet subjects later overestimated the number of times they had read about timid accountants, wealthy doctors, talkative salesmen, attractive stewardesses, serious librarians, and loud waitresses. Jaded by preconceived notions, subjects saw correlations that were expected but did not exist.

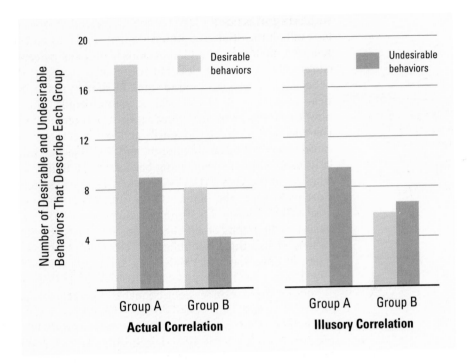

Figure 4.2 The Illusory Correlation. Subjects read sentences, each pairing a person from group A or group B with either a desirable or an undesirable behavior. Notice the actual correlation on the left side: (1) two-thirds of the persons were from group A; (2) two-thirds of the behaviors were desirable; and (3) the ratio of desirable to undesirable behaviors was exactly the same for the two groups. The illusory correlation on the right side, however, shows that subjects overestimated how often the two infrequent variables (group B members and undesirable acts) appeared together. People tend to see an illusory correlation between variables that stand out because they are unusual or deviant. [Hamilton & Gifford, 1976.]

Research on illusory correlations helps to explain the formation and stubborn persistence of stereotypes. First, members of minority groups—precisely because they are distinctive in the population—are under the spotlight, so everything they do gets blown out of numerical proportion. Second, pre-existing stereotypes may be sustained by false support. The person who thinks politicians are dishonest will overestimate the number of corruption scandals that occur in government compared to other settings. Likewise, the person who believes that the mentally ill are dangerous will overestimate the number of murders committed by deranged mental patients compared to those committed by other violent criminals. In other words, once a stereotype is in place, we tend to notice only the supporting evidence.

Subcategorizations   Have you ever noticed that people can hold negative views about a social group even though they like individual members of that group? One of the unnerving paradoxes of social perception is that stereotypes stubbornly survive one disconfirmation after the next. Why?

Social psychologists used to think of stereotypes as broad, sweeping categories—men, women, blacks, whites, young people, old people, and so on. We now know that many stereotypes consist of more limited, specific *subcategories*. For example, people distinguish at least five types of women: housewives, career women, athletes, feminists, and sex objects (Deaux et al., 1985). Similarly, people differentiate among black athletes, middle-class blacks, and blacks who live in the ghetto (Devine & Baker, 1991). Research on conceptions of the elderly illustrates the point. College students automatically associate the term "old" with negative traits (Perdue & Gurtman, 1990). Yet when they were asked to sort photographs of elderly persons into piles and then rate the pictures on various traits, three subcategories emerged: family-oriented grandmotherly types, distinguished elder statesmen, and inactive senior citizens (Brewer et al., 1981).

Subcategories seem less objectionable than general stereotypes because they are more precise. But now consider the implications. Confronted with Ann Hopkins, or with any woman who is not overly warm and nurturant, people can either develop a more diversified image of females or toss the mismatch into a special subtype, "career women." To the extent that people create this subcategory, their existing image of women-in-general will remain relatively intact. Similarly, to the extent that white Americans dismiss their amiable black neighbors as atypical "middle-class blacks," less flattering images of blacks-in-general will also resist change. This problem was enacted in the 1989 movie *Do the Right Thing*, in which a white bigot is asked to reconcile his racist views with the fact that Magic Johnson is his favorite basketball player and Eddie Murphy his favorite actor. "Let me explain myself," he replies. "They're black, but they're not really black. . . . It's different."

Donna Desforges and her colleagues (1991) note that exposure to a member of a group may force a revision of beliefs about the group as a whole by means of a three-step chain of events. First, through social categorization, we initially *expect* the individual to fit some stereotypical mold. Second, after exposure or personal contact, we *adjust* our impressions of that individual, making his or her social categories less relevant. Third, confronted with a mismatch between our stereotype and observations, we *generalize* from the individual to the group as a whole. The last step is the key.

Does disconfirming evidence about a single member lead people to revise their beliefs, or are groups destined to remain trapped in the shadow of their stereotypes? According to Renée Weber and Jennifer Crocker (1983), there are certain conditions under which generalization takes place. These investigators reasoned that target persons who disconfirm a stereotype *can* force a revision of that stereotype if they are otherwise viewed as representative members of the group. To test this hypothesis, they had subjects read about corporate lawyers who did not fit the usual image: they wore ill-fitting clothes and could not analyze problems and draw logical conclusions. For some subjects, the sample lawyers came from the demographic group typically expected (white, married, and rich). For others, the lawyers were atypical (black, single, and poor). Later, when subjects were asked to report on their beliefs about corporate lawyers in general, atypical members were dismissed as flukes, leaving the overall stereotype relatively untarnished. When typical members disconfirmed the stereotype, however, subjects revised their beliefs about the group as a whole.

These results suggest a general rule. Whether people judge human beings or inanimate objects, their beliefs about a whole category change more after exposure to cases that are viewed as *typical,* rather than as atypical, of the stereotyped group (Rothbart & Lewis, 1988). For members of stereotyped groups, the process creates a difficult dilemma. To overcome negative expectations, they may try to present themselves as *atypical* members of their group, as exceptions to the rule. Yet to foster a change in the stereotype, these same people should appear *typical,* inviting perceivers to generalize to the group as a whole. This conflict of interest explains why one of this book's authors reacted with mixed feelings the day a friend said, "You're pretty normal for a psychologist!"

How Stereotypes Distort Perceptions of Individuals

Illusory correlations and subcategorization help to explain why beliefs about *groups* are so durable. Now, let's consider how these beliefs influence the perception of *individuals.* Remember Ann Hopkins, the productive but abrasive accountant? In her court case, Hopkins claimed that her aggressive manner proved offensive only because it clashed with traditional conceptions of women. Is her claim justified? Is the same tough-mindedness more acceptable in a man?

As a general rule, judgments of a stimulus are influenced by the discrepancy between that stimulus and one's expectations (Eiser & Stroebe, 1972; Sherif & Hovland, 1961). When something differs only slightly from expectations, the difference is barely noticed, if at all. When a new stimulus varies considerably from expectations, however, the perceived difference is magnified as the result of a **contrast effect**. To illustrate, imagine that you've been presented with three buckets of water—one cold, one hot, and the third at room temperature. After placing your right hand into the cold water and your left hand into the hot water, you place both hands simultaneously into the third bucket. You can probably predict the amusing result: even though both hands are in the same water, your right hand now feels warm and your left hand feels cool. The temperature you now feel depends on the sensation that preceded it.

Like this influence on physical sensations, contrast effects can also affect *social* perceptions (Herr, 1986; Manis et al., 1986). In a study by Melvin Manis and others (1988), subjects read sentences ostensibly written by mental patients at two hospitals and were led to believe that one group of patients was seriously

contrast effect The tendency to perceive stimuli that differ from expectations as being even more different than they really are.

disturbed but the other was not. Subjects then evaluated new sentences that depicted a *moderate* level of psychopathology. The results paralleled the water temperature test. When the material was supposedly written by patients from the disturbed group, the sentences seemed normal. When the same sentences were thought to emanate from the more normal group, however, they seemed relatively disturbed. These results support Ann Hopkins's analysis of her situation in the workplace. As we will see, gender stereotypes lead people to expect warm, gentle women and assertive, forceful men. Since those who break the mold are subject to contrast effects, it is conceivable that Ann Hopkins seemed tougher and more abrasive than a man would be under the same circumstances. Similarly, a warm, gentle man would seem more passive and weak than a woman would be under the same circumstances.

Stereotyping: A Necessary Evil?

If we assume that stereotypes are born of the human tendency to categorize people and other objects, it's easy to justify them as a necessary evil, an innocent by-product of the way we think. In other words, "Don't blame me; it can't be helped." Not so. Sure, some degree of social categorization is inevitable and so, probably, is the formation of stereotypes. But none of us needs to be trapped into evaluating specific persons in light of social categories. Three factors lead people to ignore stereotypes and judge others on an individualized basis (Fiske & Neuberg, 1990).

The first factor is the *personal information* we have about someone. Once such information is available, stereotypes and other preconceptions lose relevance and impact. Thus, when subjects read about a man or woman who consistently reacted to difficult situations by behaving assertively or passively, their impressions of that person were influenced more by his or her actions than by gender (Locksley et al., 1980). In fact, people will often set aside their stereotypes even when the personal information they have is not clearly relevant to the judgment they have to make (Hilton & Fein, 1989). As we learn more and more about an individual, social categories fade farther and farther into the background (Krueger & Rothbart, 1988).

The second factor is a perceiver's cognitive *ability* to focus on unique aspects of an individual member of a stereotyped group. Research shows that people are most likely to form an impression that is based on existing stereotypes when they're busy (Gilbert & Hixon, 1991) or pressed for time (Pratto & Bargh, 1991)—and unable to think carefully about the unique attributes of a single person. A perceiver's state of mind can also influence the extent to which he or she forms quick, stereotyped impressions. In an intriguing test of this hypothesis, Galen Bodenhausen (1990) classified subjects by their circadian arousal patterns, or "biorhythms," into two types: "morning people," who describe themselves as most alert early in the morning, and "night people," who say they peak much later, in the evening. By random assignment, subjects took part in a study of human judgment that was scheduled at either 9 A.M. or 8 P.M. The result? Morning people were more likely to use stereotypes when they were tested at night; night owls were more likely to do so early in the morning. When people are tired and lack the mental energy to individualize their judgments, they fall back on simple-minded rules of thumb.

The third factor is a perceiver's *motivation*. When people are sufficiently motivated to form an accurate impression of someone—say, if they're in an interdependent relationship or if they need to compete against the person—they manage to set aside their pre-existing beliefs (Neuberg, 1989; Ruscher & Fiske, 1990). In one study, subjects expected to interact with a former mental patient who had supposedly been treated for schizophrenia. Ordinarily, people would pre-judge this individual on the basis of their beliefs about mental illness. But when subjects were told that they would be working with the former patient and would earn money based on their joint performance, they paid more attention to the patient's personal characteristics and formed impressions on a more individualized basis (Neuberg & Fiske, 1987). To summarize: we *can* stop ourselves from making hasty, stereotypic judgments—when we have personalized information and when we are both able and willing to use that information.

PREJUDICE

Stereotypes may form and endure by the way we categorize people and distinguish between ingroups and outgroups. This cognitive perspective—in which stereotypes are considered a cool by-product of the way human beings think—suggests that if people could be prevented from viewing each other in categorical terms or could be enlightened by accurate information, discrimination throughout the world would be eliminated. But would it, really? Is the way we *think* about groups all that matters? If you look back at Figure 4.1, you'll see that there's another potent factor to consider: how people *feel* about the social groups they encounter. In this section, we trace this second path to discrimination, one based on motivations and emotions.

prejudice Negative feelings toward persons based solely on their membership in certain groups.

Prejudice—a term used to describe negative feelings toward persons based solely on their membership in a group—is one of the most tenacious social problems of modern times. In South Africa, the white ruling class discriminates against a black majority. In Germany, neo-Nazi skinheads terrorize Turkish immigrants. In the Middle East, Israelis and Arabs fight what seems like an eternal war. And in what used to be the Soviet Union, raging ethnic conflicts are too numerous to mention. The streets of America are also witness to bigotry—and the ivory tower is no exception. At one university, members of a fraternity painted their faces black and held a mock slave auction. At another, the Jewish student union building was spray-painted with large swastikas. On a third campus, rocks and bottles were thrown at gay men and women in a parade. Stories like these make news on a regular basis and bring to life a very important point: people's attitudes—toward whites, blacks, Jews, homosexuals, and other groups—may be based more on emotions than on beliefs (Stangor et al., 1991).

Incidents like these also leave no doubt that prejudice brings out the worst in human behavior. It's worth noting, however, that our perceptions of prejudice are influenced not only by objective actions but by social context. Specifically, Miriam Rodin and others (1990) suggested that an act of discrimination is more likely to prompt charges of prejudice when it singles out members of historically victimized groups rather than members of more empowered groups. In a series of studies, subjects read about an incident in which a group was excluded, derogated, or unequally treated—all forms of discrimination. In each case, the race, gender, age, or sexual preference of the actor and targets was varied. As illustrated by the sample behavior shown in Figure 4.3, subjects thought there was more prejudice when acts discriminated against blacks, women, old people, and homosexuals than when these acts targeted whites, men, young people, and heterosexuals. This kind of asymmetry is pervasive, which is why white student associations and all-male groups often provoke charges of racism and sexism but black student unions and women's groups do not. Apparently, people perceive that discriminatory acts by historically victimized groups can be motivated by a need for self-protection or solidarity, not prejudice.

The Prejudiced Personality

Hatred, resentment, and hostility are universal human reactions to outgroups and always have been. But why? Why are people so hateful of groups that often are barely different from their own? One approach is to treat prejudice as the problem of *individuals*. After all, some of us are more clearly prejudiced than others. In a study conducted in the 1940s, college students evaluated thirty-five groups of nationalities—including some that did not exist. Results indicated that subjects who showed contempt for one outgroup held a generalized hostility toward others as well (Hartley, 1946). More recent research backs up this basic point. Prejudices against women, homosexuals, blacks, old people, and ethnic minorities tend to coexist in the same individuals (Bierly, 1985; Weigel & Howes, 1985). The question is, who are these individuals?

authoritarian personality
A personality trait characterized by rigid thinking, submissiveness to authority, and prejudice toward others who are different.

After World War II, researchers from the University of California at Berkeley studied people who were anti-Semitic and prone to other forms of prejudice (Adorno et al., 1950). Through extensive questionnaires, case studies, and interviews, they identified what they called the **authoritarian personality**. Authoritarians are conventional, rigid in their thinking, sexually inhibited, submissive to authority figures, and intolerant of those who are different. Developmental studies revealed that as children they had domineering parents who used harsh disciplinary measures. It seems that prejudice finds a home in

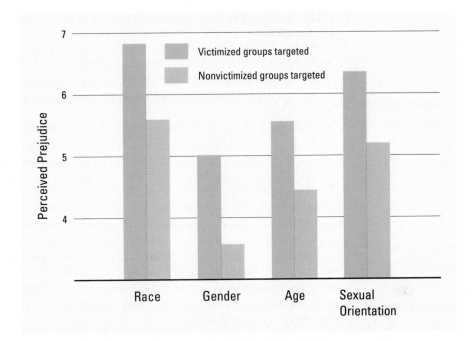

Figure 4.3   Asymmetries in the Attribution of Prejudice. Subjects read about J.D., who wanted to form employee softball teams at work. In recruiting players, J.D. says that the teams are only for whites (or for blacks, men, women, people over forty, people under forty, gays, or straights). How prejudiced do you think J.D. is about the excluded group? As you can see, subjects attributed the most prejudice to acts that excluded members of victimized groups (blacks, women, older people, and homosexuals) rather than nonvictimized groups (whites, men, younger people, and heterosexuals). This asymmetry shows that the perception of prejudice is influenced not only by behavior but by social context. [From Rodin et al., 1990.]

persons who think in simple, categorical terms and who need an outlet for their personal frustrations.

Robbers Cave: Setting the Stage

Although some people are generally more prejudiced than others, the problem is so pervasive and so widespread that it seems nobody is immune. Social psychologists have thus sought to identify common situational factors that give rise to prejudice. In this section, we describe a classic study of intergroup conflict that sets the stage for theories that focus on the role of social situations.

We begin our analysis in an unlikely place: Robbers Cave State Park, Oklahoma. In the summer of 1954, a small group of eleven-year-old boys—all white, healthy, middle-class youngsters, all strangers to one another—arrived at a 200-acre camp located in a densely wooded area of the park. The boys spent the first week or so hiking, swimming, boating, and camping out. After a while, they gave themselves a group name and printed it on their caps and T-shirts. At first, the boys thought they were the only ones at the camp. Soon, however, they discovered that there was a second group and that tournaments had been arranged between the two groups.

What these boys didn't know was that they were subjects in an elaborate study conducted by Muzafer Sherif and his colleagues (1961). Parents had given permission for their sons to take part in an experiment for a study of competitiveness and cooperation. The two groups were brought in separately, and only after each had formed its own culture was the other's presence revealed. Now, the "Rattlers" and the "Eagles" were ready to meet. They did so under tense circumstances, competing against each other in football, a treasure hunt, tug-of-war, and other events. The winning team of each event was awarded points; the tournament winner was promised a trophy, medals, and other prizes. Almost overnight the groups turned into hostile antagonists, and their rivalry escalated into a full-scale war. Group flags were burned; cabins were ransacked; and a food fight that resembled a riot exploded in the mess hall. Keep in mind that the subjects in this study were well-adjusted boys, not street-gang members. Yet as Sherif (1966) noted, a naive observer would have thought the boys were "wicked, disturbed, and vicious" (p. 85).

superordinate goals
Shared goals that can be achieved only through cooperation among individuals or groups.

Creating a monster through competition was easy. Restoring the peace, however, was not. First the experimenters tried saying nice things to the Rattlers about the Eagles and vice versa, but the propaganda campaign did not work. Then the two groups were brought together under noncompetitive and relaxed circumstances, but that didn't help either. What did eventually work was the introduction of **superordinate goals**, mutual goals that could be achieved only through cooperation between groups. For example, the experimenters arranged for the camp truck to break down, and both groups were needed to pull it up a steep hill. These activities worked like a charm. By the end of camp, the two groups were so friendly that they insisted on traveling home on the same bus. In just three weeks, the Rattlers and Eagles experienced the kinds of changes that usually take generations to unfold: they formed close-knit groups, went to war, and made peace.

Realistic Conflict Theory

The events of Robbers Cave mimicked the kinds of conflict that plague people all over the world (Taylor & Moghaddam, 1987). The simplest explanation for it is *competition*. Assign strangers to groups, throw the groups into contention, stir the pot, and soon there's conflict. This recipe is not limited to boys at camp, either. Intense animosity was aroused, for example, among a thousand corporate executives who were placed in competing groups as part of a management

According to realistic conflict theory, people become resentful of groups that threaten their economic well-being. Frustrated by a sluggish economy, this American worker took to smashing a car imported from Japan.

realistic conflict theory The theory that hostility between groups is caused by direct competition for limited resources.

training program (Blake & Mouton, 1984). The view that direct competition for valuable but limited resources breeds hostility between groups is called **realistic conflict theory** (Levine & Campbell, 1972). As a simple matter of economics, one group may fare better in the struggle for land, jobs, or power than another group. The loser becomes frustrated and resentful; the winner feels threatened and protective; and before long conflict heats to a rapid boil. Chances are, a good deal of prejudice in the world is driven by the realities of competition (Olzak & Nagel, 1986).

If realistic conflict theory is correct, then prejudice is likely to be found only among those who fear that the quality of their lives is being threatened by an outgroup. Not so. White Americans who are personally affected by desegregated schools and low-income housing are no more prejudiced against blacks than are those who are untouched by these policies (Kinder & Sears, 1981; Sears & Kinder, 1985). Could it be that realistic conflict is *unrelated* to prejudice? As more and more white Americans complain bitterly about affirmative action policies that give preference to certain minorities, it's hard to believe that competition for resources does *not* fuel prejudice. It's been suggested, for example, that racial tensions often spring from resentment among those who feel that affirmative action gains are achieved at their expense (D'Souza, 1991).

relative deprivation Feelings of discontent aroused by the belief that one fares poorly compared to others.

To reconcile matters, an important distinction must be made. Research suggests that people become resentful not because of what they have but because of their **relative deprivation**—the belief that they fare poorly compared to others (Crosby, 1976; Olson et al., 1986). What matters to the pro-verbial Smiths is not the size of their house but whether it is larger than the Jones's house next door. There are two potential sources of discontent: "egoistic" deprivation, a concern for one's *self*-interest, and "fraternal" deprivation, a concern for the interest of one's *group* (Runciman, 1966). This distinction is crucial to the theory that competition breeds prejudice. Among white Ameri-cans, for example, antiblack feelings are related not to personal gains or losses but to a fear that whites as a group are falling behind (Bobo, 1988). The same result—that people resent those who threaten the ingroup—has character-ized the negative feelings of black Americans for whites (Abeles, 1976), French-speaking Canadians for their English neighbors (Guimond & Dubé-Simard, 1983), and Muslims for the Hindus in India (Triparthi & Sriva-stava, 1981).

Why are people so sensitive about the status of ingroups relative to rival outgroups, even when personal interests are not directly at stake? Is it possible that personal interests really *are* at stake, that our protectiveness of ingroups is nourished by a concern for the self? If so, could that explain why people all over the world think their own nation, culture, language, and religion are better and more deserving than those of others? And could it explain why people often sacrifice their lives in order to preserve the integrity of their group?

Social Identity Theory

Those questions were raised in a study of high school boys in Bristol, England (Tajfel et al., 1971). The boys were shown a series of dotted slides and asked to estimate the number of dots on each. The slides were presented in rapid-fire succession, so the dots could not be counted. Afterwards, the experimenter told subjects that some people are chronic "overestimators" and others are "underes-timators." As part of a second, entirely separate task, subjects were supposedly divided for the sake of convenience into groups of overestimators and underes-timators (in fact, they were divided randomly). Knowing who was in their group, subjects allocated points to each other, points that could be cashed in for money.

This procedure was designed to create *minimal groups*—persons categorized according to arbitrary, minimally important similarities. Overestimators and underestimators were trivial, stripped-down groups. They were not long-term rivals, did not have a history of antagonism, were not frustrated, did not compete for a limited resource, and were not acquainted with each other. Still, subjects consistently allocated more points to members of their own group than to the other group. This pattern of discrimination, called **ingroup favoritism**, is observed in studies conducted in many countries. Even in groups that are constructed arbitrarily—for example, by the flip of a coin—subjects still favor others with whom they are aligned (Brewer, 1979; Messick & Mackie, 1989).

Our preference for ingroups is so powerful that its effects can be measured by the language we use. According to Charles Perdue and others (1990), "ingroup"

ingroup favoritism
The tendency to discriminate in favor of ingroups over outgroups.

pronouns such as *we*, *us*, and *ours* trigger positive emotions, and "outgroup" pronouns such as *they*, *them*, and *theirs* elicit negative emotions. To test this hypothesis, the investigators presented subjects with numerous pairs of letter strings on a computer—each pair containing a pronoun and a nonsense syllable ("we-xeh," "they-yof," "his-giw"). For subjects, the task was to decide as fast as possible which letter string in each pair was a real word. They didn't realize it, but one nonsense syllable was consistently paired with ingroup pronouns, another with outgroup pronouns. Afterwards, subjects were asked for their reactions to each of the nonsense syllables. The result: those that were previously paired with ingroup words were considered more pleasant than those paired with outgroup words. The ingroup-outgroup distinction has such emotional meaning for people that it can bias their impressions of an unfamiliar string of letters . . . or person.

social identity theory The theory that people favor ingroups over outgroups in order to enhance their self-esteem.

To explain ingroup favoritism, Henri Tajfel (1982) and John Turner (1987) proposed **social identity theory**. According to this theory, each of us strives to enhance our self-esteem, which has two components: a *personal* identity and various *social* identities that derive from the groups to which we belong. In other words, we can boost self-esteem through our own achievements and by affiliating with groups that are relatively successful. What's nice about the need for social identity is that it leads people to derive pride from their connections with others. What's tragic, however, is that sometimes we feel the need to belittle "them" in order to raise our own self-image. Religious fervor, racial and ethnic pride, and patriotism may all serve to fulfill this darker side of social identity. The theory is illustrated in Figure 4.4.

Social identity theory makes two basic predictions: (1) threats to a person's self-esteem should heighten the need for ingroup favoritism, and (2) expressions of ingroup favoritism should, in turn, enhance a person's self-esteem. Research tends to support these predictions, but it also suggests that the theory needs to be more precise (Hogg & Abrams, 1990). One important factor to consider is the relative size of the ingroup. Noting that people want to belong in categories that are small enough for them to feel distinctive, Marilyn Brewer (1991) notes that ingroup loyalty—and the favoritism that results—is more intense for those in minority groups than for those in a large, overly inclusive majority. A second key factor is the nature of discrimination. Research shows that although people are quick to allocate more rewards to ingroupers than to outgroupers, they will not allocate punishment in a discriminatory manner unless they're desperate for a positive social identity (Mummendey et al., 1992).

Finally, social identity theory poses another interesting question: If self-esteem is tied to the status of our ingroups relative to outgroups, how do people cope with ingroups of low status or with weak ingroup members? How do *you* cope with associations that you find embarrassing? The theory predicts two possible reactions: risk a loss of self-esteem, or distance yourself from those in question. So which is it?

To examine the question, José Marques (1990) and his colleagues conducted studies in which subjects had to evaluate ingroup and outgroup members who behaved in positive or negative ways. In one study, subjects listened to two

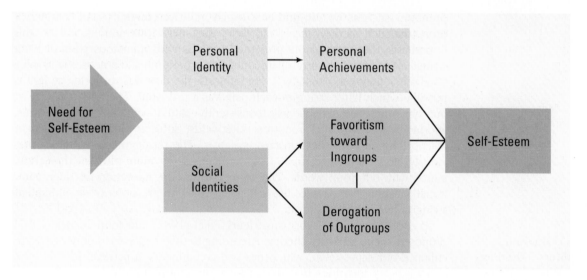

Figure 4.4   Social Identity Theory.   Tajfel and Turner claim that people strive to enhance self-esteem, which has two components: a personal identity and various social identities that derive from the groups to which people belong. Thus, people may boost their self-esteem by viewing their ingroups more favorably than outgroups. Threats to the self trigger ingroup favoritism, which, in turn, restores self-esteem.

---

taped speeches, one of high quality and one of low quality, one made by a fellow law student, the other by a philosophy student. Which of the two made the better speech varied. As it turned out, subjects overrated the ingroup speaker who performed well but they also underrated the ingroup speaker who performed poorly. To preserve the integrity of an important ingroup, people may be excessively harsh in their treatment of less able fellow members.

So far, we have seen that stereotypes are distorted but enduring images of social groups that lead people to overlook the diversity within outgroups and rush to judgment about specific individuals. We have also seen that prejudice, which involves negative feelings toward certain groups, stems from deep-seated personality factors, competition for resources, and the need to favor ingroups in the service of self-esteem. We now put these problems into concrete terms by focusing on sexism and racism, two common forms of discrimination.

SEXISM

When a baby is born, the first words uttered ring loud and clear: "It's a boy (girl)!" Immediately, the newborn receives a gender-appropriate name and is showered with gender-appropriate gifts. Over the next few years, the typical boy is supplied with toy trucks, baseball bats, hammers, guns, and chemistry sets; the typical girl is furnished with dolls, stuffed animals, toy make-up kits, sewing machines, and tea sets. As they enter school, the boy is expected to earn money by delivering newspapers and to enjoy computers, math, and sports; the girl is expected to baby-sit and to enjoy crafts, music, and social activities. The distinctions then persist in college, as male students major in economics and the sciences and participate in competitive athletics while female students thrive in the arts, languages, and humanities. In the work force, men become doctors, construction workers, airplane pilots, engineers, and investment bankers; women become secretaries, nurses, schoolteachers, flight attendants, bank tellers, and housewives. Back on the home front, the life cycle begins again when a man and woman have their first baby and realize that "It's a girl (boy)!"

Growing up in the same New England home, these children learned at a young age how to skate on ice. Fitting traditional sex-role stereotypes, however, *he* went on to play hockey, while *she* became a figure skater.

Gender Stereotypes: Blue for Boys, Pink for Girls

sexism
Discrimination based on a person's gender.

The traditional pinks and blues are not as distinct today as they used to be. To some extent, gender barriers of the past have broken down, and the colors have somewhat blended together. Nevertheless, **sexism**—discrimination based on a person's gender—still exists. It begins with the fact that sex is probably the most conspicuous social category we use to identify ourselves and others (Stangor et al., 1992; Zarate & Smith, 1990).

Whenever people are asked for characteristics of the typical man and woman, males are described as adventurous, assertive, aggressive, independent, and task oriented; females as sensitive, gentle, dependent, emotional, and people oriented. These beliefs are so universal that they were consistently reported by subjects from thirty countries of North and South America, Europe, Africa, Asia, and Australia (Williams & Best, 1982). They're especially salient to young children—who identify themselves and others as boys or girls by three years of age, form stereotypic beliefs about toys and other objects soon after that, and then use their simplified stereotypes in the judgment of others (Biernat, 1991; Fagot et al., 1992; Martin et al., 1990).

gender-role orientation The extent to which people report having characteristics ordinarily associated with males and females.

Two additional features of gender stereotypes are worth noting. First, many people assume that certain traits belong only to males and others only to females and that no one person can be both masculine and feminine (Deaux & Lewis, 1984). Research on gender-role orientation, however, shows that these assumptions are incorrect. **Gender-role orientation** refers to the judgments people make about whether they have traditionally male or female characteristics (Spence, 1985). Those who report having male attributes are considered *masculine* in their orientation. Those who report having female attributes are considered *feminine*. On average, men tend to view themselves as primarily masculine, and women see themselves as primarily feminine. However, some men are feminine in their gender orientation, and some women are masculine. Moreover, many people report having both orientations. These individuals—who may be competitive and independent yet sensitive and supportive—are labeled *androgynous* (Bem, 1974). A fourth orientation, *undifferentiated*, refers to individuals who say they have few of the attributes typically associated with either male or female behavior (Spence & Helmreich, 1978).

Second, beliefs about males and females are so deeply ingrained that they influence the behavior of adults literally the moment a baby is born. In a fascinating study, first-time parents of fifteen girls and fifteen boys were interviewed within twenty-four hours of the baby's birth. There were no differences between the male and female newborns in height, weight, or other aspects of physical appearance. Yet the parents of girls rated their babies as softer, smaller, and more finely featured, and the fathers of boys described their sons as stronger, larger, more alert, and better coordinated (Rubin et al., 1974). Could it be there really were differences that only the parents were able to discern? Doubtful. In a second study, men and women were shown a videotape of a nine-month-old baby. Half were told they were watching a boy, the other half a girl. Although all subjects saw the same tape, their perceptions were influenced by gender beliefs. At one point, for example, the baby burst into tears over a jack-in-the-box. How did the subjects interpret this reaction? *He* was *angry,* and *she* was *frightened* (Condry & Condry, 1976). These gender beliefs do not take a lifetime to learn, either. Even five-year-olds perceive infants through gender-curved lenses (Vogel et al., 1991).

People all over the world make profound distinctions between boys and girls, men and women. The question is not *whether* these stereotypes exist but (1) when do they influence our social perceptions, (2) are they accurate, and (3) why do they endure. Let's begin with the first question: When do stereotypic beliefs influence our perceptions of men and women?

What Activates Gender Stereotypes?

According to Kay Deaux and Brenda Major (1987), three factors determine if gender stereotypes are activated: the perceiver, target, and situation. To begin with, *perceivers* differ in the extent to which gender considerations bias their perceptions. Sandra Bem (1981) calls people who have masculine or feminine gender-role orientations "gender schematics" and claims that they consistently divide the world into masculine and feminine terms. In contrast, people who are more balanced in their orientations are "gender *a*schematic" perceivers for whom sex is not a dominant social category. Although there is some debate about the differences between schematics and aschematics (Bem, 1981; Edwards & Spence, 1987), many studies support the notion that individuals vary in the extent to which gender influences their social judgments. Thus, gender schematics are more likely to pay attention to the sex of a job applicant, to assume that someone referred to by the generic "he" is male rather than female, and to form negative impressions of others who violate cultural norms for acceptable male and female behavior (Frable, 1989). In one experiment, subjects listened to a group discussion and then tried to recall who said what. More than others, gender schematics confused the different members of the opposite sex—a symptom, perhaps, of an outgroup homogeneity bias. For these subjects, "they" all looked and sounded alike (Frable & Bem, 1985).

Deaux and Major (1987) note that characteristics of the *target person* also activate gender stereotypes. People who are highly masculine or feminine in their physical appearance elicit the perception that they are masculine or feminine in other ways as well (Deaux & Lewis, 1984). Even a simple title can activate a stereotype. In a study by Kenneth Dion (1987), subjects read a description of a woman, varying only her preferred title. When she used the title *Ms.* rather than *Miss* or *Mrs.*, she was assumed to be more assertive, achievement oriented, and dynamic, but also cold, unpopular, and unlikely to achieve a happy marriage. These perceptions are triggered not by the *Ms.* title itself but by the woman who states a preference for that title (Dion & Cota, 1991).

One of the most noticeable differences between men and women is in the way they dress. Certain kinds of clothing are likely to heighten attention to one's gender. Consider an unusual incident that took place recently. Brenda Taylor, a Florida attorney, was fired because she dressed for work in designer blouses, tight-fitting skirts, and ornate jewelry, rather than in conservative attire. Her supervisor later said that her appearance in court "created the impression that she was a bimbo interested only in meeting men" (Associated Press, 1988). Did Taylor's clothing undermine her credibility by activating the stereotype of "bimbo" rather than "career woman"? Studies show that clothing can have this effect. When banking and marketing administrators viewed videotaped interviews of female applicants for a management position, the women received more positive recommendations when they were dressed in a "masculine" navy suit with a blazer jacket than when they wore a softer and more "feminine" light-colored dress (Forsythe, 1990). The question confronting Brenda Taylor and other working women is whether "dress for success" rules are fair. Taylor says professional women should not have to dress like men. What do you think?

Finally, certain *situations* are more likely than others to make gender considerations salient. Deaux and Major (1987) point out that a nursery school, an auto mechanic's shop, and a singles bar are the kinds of settings that naturally prompt perceivers to make gender distinctions. Especially important is the

To gender-schematic perceivers, even food may be categorized as masculine or feminine. [Drawing by M. Stevens; © The New Yorker Magazine, Inc.]

prominence of a target person relative to others in the situation. Picture a man in an all-female discussion group or a woman in an all-male group. Research shows they draw a disproportionate amount of attention (Lord & Saenz, 1985). As a result, they are likely to be evaluated in gender-stereotypic terms: the token male seems more masculine (a "father figure, leader, or macho type"), and the token female seems more feminine (a "motherly type, a bitch, or the group secretary"), than when these same individuals are judged in more balanced, mixed-sex groups (Fiske et al., 1991; Taylor, 1981). Again, we're reminded of Ann Hopkins and others who have minority status in an organization. In the limelight, everything they do is noticed, scrutinized, and blown out of proportion.

Are Gender Stereotypes Accurate?

Gender stereotypes are so widespread that one has to wonder if they are accurate. Enlightened by years of research on the biological, psychological, and social differences between the sexes, two conclusions can now be drawn: (1) conventional wisdom concerning the sexes contains a kernel of truth (Eagly & Wood, 1991; Maccoby & Jacklin, 1974), but (2) it oversimplifies and exaggerates that truth (Spence et al., 1985; Tavris & Wade, 1984; Unger, 1979). Yes, most men are somewhat more competitive, aggressive, and task focused than most women. And yes, most women are more socially sensitive, cooperative, and people focused than most men. But our stereotypes about male-female differences are stronger and more numerous than the differences themselves.

A study by Carol Lynn Martin (1987) illustrates the point. Male and female adults received a list of thirty traits that were stereotypically masculine, feminine, or neutral. They were asked to circle those traits that accurately described themselves. A separate group of subjects received the same list and estimated the percentage of men and women in general for whom each trait was an accurate description. By comparing the percentage of male and female subjects who *actually* found the traits self-descriptive with the *estimated* percentages, Martin found that expectations outstripped reality: in actuality, the "masculine" traits were just slightly more self-descriptive of men, and the "feminine" traits of women, yet the estimated differences were substantial. Like the cartoonist who draws caricatures, social perceivers seem to stretch, expand, and enlarge the ways in which men and women differ.

Why Do Gender Stereotypes Endure?

If men and women are more similar than most people think, why do exaggerated perceptions of difference endure? And why, despite considerable social changes that have marked the past thirty or so years, have gender stereotypes remained relatively constant (Werner & LaRussa, 1985)? Earlier in this chapter, we cited two phenomena to help explain why stereotypes, like cats, have nine lives. These same mechanisms apply to perceptions of gender as well. Expecting male-female differences, people are prone to (1) perceive illusory correlations, overestimating the percentage of masculine men and feminine women, and (2) dismiss individuals who don't match the stereotype as mere exceptions to the rule or representatives of a subcategory. Additional explanations have been proposed to account for why gender stereotypes in particular are so stubborn.

Cultural Institutions Cultural institutions foster gender distinctions. Studies have shown, for example, that children's "Dick and Jane" readers, TV shows, cartoons, movies, and magazines consistently portray male and female characters in traditional roles (Ruble & Ruble, 1982). These media have reflected social changes since the days when women were depicted as housewives who frantically cooked, polished, and ironed everything in sight. Still, some gender stereotyping persists—for example, in TV commercials (Lovdal, 1989) and in children's books (Purcell & Stewart, 1990). Even recently produced rock music videos, as played on MTV, often portray men and women in sex-stereotyped ways (Hansen, 1989).

More to the point is that media depictions can influence viewers. In a series of studies, Florence Geis and her colleagues created two sets of TV commercials (1984; Jennings et al., 1980). In one, male and female characters were portrayed in stereotypic fashion: a woman served her working man his dinner or behaved in a coy, alluring manner. In the other, these roles were reversed, with the man playing the domestic and seductive roles. Female college students watched one of the two sets. Those who saw the stereotypical ads later expressed lower self-confidence, less independence, and fewer career aspirations in experimental tasks than did those who viewed counter-stereotypical ads. Whether or not consumers purchase the products explicitly advertised on television, they seem to buy the implicit messages about gender.

Media images of men and women may differ in other ways almost too subtle to notice. In any visual representation of a person—whether a photograph, drawing, or painting—you can measure the relative prominence of the face by calculating the percentage of the vertical dimension occupied by the model's head. When Dane Archer and his colleagues (1983) inspected 1,750 photographs from *Time, Newsweek,* and other periodicals, they found what they called "face-ism," a bias toward greater facial prominence in pictures of men than of women. This phenomenon is so prevalent that it also appeared in analyses of 3,500 photographs published in eleven countries, classic portraits painted in the seventeenth century, and the amateur drawings of college students. It even showed up in the women's magazines *Ms.* and *Good Housekeeping* (Nigro et al., 1988).

Why is the face more prominent in pictures of men than of women? At this point, we can only speculate. One possibility is that face-ism reflects historical conceptions about the sexes. The face and head symbolize the mind and intellect—which are traditionally associated with men. For women, more importance is attached to the heart, emotions, or perhaps just the body. This interpretation can be questioned. But when people are asked to evaluate strangers from photographs, those pictured with high facial prominence are perceived to be smarter and more active, assertive, and ambitious—regardless of their gender (Archer et al., 1983; Schwarz & Kurz, 1989). So photographers and artists, beware: gender stereotypes may be perpetuated by the subtleties of the human portrait.

Social Roles Theory   There is another reason for the durability of gender stereotypes. Imagine a secretary typing a letter for a corporate vice president. Now, admit it: Didn't you visualize a *female* secretary working for a *male* executive?

social roles theory
The theory that small gender differences are magnified in perception by the contrasting social roles occupied by men and women.

Alice Eagly's (1987) **social roles theory** states that the perception of sex differences may be based on actual differences, but then it is magnified by the unequal social roles occupied by men and women. The process involves three steps. First, through a combination of biological and social factors, a division of labor between the sexes has emerged over time—at home and in the work setting. Men are more likely to work in construction or business; women are more likely to care for children and take lower-status jobs. Second, since people behave in ways that fit the roles they play, men are more likely than women to wield physical, social, and economic power. Third, these behavioral differences provide a continuing basis for social perception, leading us to perceive men as dominant "by nature" and women as domestic "by nature," when in fact the differences reflect the roles they play. In short, sex stereotypes are shaped by—and often confused with—the unequal distribution of men and women into different social roles (see Figure 4.5). An alternative possibility is that sex

Figure 4.5   Eagly's Social Roles Theory of Gender Stereotypes.   According to social roles theory, stereotypes of men as dominant and women as subordinate persist because men occupy higher-status positions in society. This division of labor, a product of many factors, leads men and women to behave in ways that fit their social roles. But rather than attribute the differences to these roles, people attribute the differences to gender.

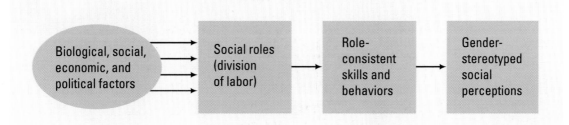

stereotypes arise to help us rationalize the fact that men and women occupy such different social roles (Hoffman & Hurst, 1990).

If Eagly's theory is correct, then perceived differences between men and women are based on real behavioral differences mistakenly assumed to arise from gender rather than from social roles. To test this hypothesis, Eagly and Valerie Steffen (1984) asked subjects for their impressions of fictitious men or women who had a full-time job or worked as a homemaker. Persons employed outside the home were viewed in relatively masculine terms—regardless of their sex. In contrast, those who worked inside the home were seen in relatively feminine terms—again, regardless of whether they were male or female. Social roles, not gender, gave rise to stereotypic perceptions. When the roles were reversed, gender stereotypes disappeared (Eagly & Wood, 1982).

Carrying the theory one step further, Eagly and Mary Kite (1987) raised an intriguing possibility. If our perceptions of foreign nations are influenced by news images, and if newsworthy events are dominated by men in prominent positions, then our stereotypes of nations should be based primarily on our images of the *men* in those nations. Think about it. When Iraqi soldiers stormed into Kuwait in 1990, Iraqis were regarded as impassioned, belligerent people. But did the image apply to the inconspicuous Iraqi women, many of whom cover their faces in public? Eagly and Kite asked subjects for their impressions of fourteen nationalities, their men and women. As predicted, the stereotypical

The Bureau of Labor statistics reports that only 2 percent of all construction workers are women. Shown on a building site in downtown Chicago, these female workers are noticeable exceptions to that rule. According to social roles theory, images like this one should help break down existing gender stereotypes.

Cuban, Egyptian, or Chinese person closely matched perceptions of the men in those countries but not the women.

By suggesting that estimates of the norm are based primarily on our perceptions of men, this finding could help to explain the way news media interpret gender gaps. It seems that whenever pollsters discover a sex difference—for example, that female voters in recent elections have favored the Democrats and male voters the Republicans—they try to explain the difference by focusing on why the women, not the men, voted as they did. Why? Dale Miller and others (1991) believe that the so-called norms are based on men, which means that females are the "deviants" who need to be understood. To test this hypothesis, Miller and his colleagues asked college students to imagine the typical American voter. Seventy-two percent described this person as male. When other subjects were asked about the gender gap in the 1988 presidential election, they were five times more likely to attribute that split to aspects of the female voters ("women see Dukakis as better on childcare and pro-choice") than to the male voters ("men are more military oriented"). The gender gap is not only a "woman's issue." As implied by social roles theory, however, the behavior of men seems to set the standard against which both men and women are judged.

Sex Discrimination: A Double Standard?

It could be argued that variety is the spice of life and that there's nothing inherently wrong with gender stereotypes as long as men and women are portrayed as different but equal. But are masculine and feminine attributes equally valued? Are men and women judged by the same standard, or is there—as Ann Hopkins maintained—a "double standard" (see Table 4.1)?

Many years ago, Philip Goldberg (1968) asked students at a women's college to evaluate the content and writing style of some articles. When the material was supposedly written by "John McKay" rather than "Joan McKay," it received higher ratings, leading Goldberg to wonder about prejudice against women. A few more studies showed that people often devalue the performance of women who take on tasks usually reserved for men (Lott, 1985) and attribute their achievements to luck rather than ability (Deaux & Emswiller, 1974; Nieva & Gutek, 1981). It now appears, however, that the devaluation of women is an exception, not the rule. More than a hundred studies modeled after Goldberg's now show that people are *not* generally biased by gender in the evaluation of performance (Swim et al., 1989; Top, 1991).

In other subtle ways, however, sex discrimination still exists in the home, the classroom, and the workplace. Earlier we saw that parents view their newborn sons and daughters through different eyes. Educators unwittingly make distinctions between boys and girls as well (Tittle, 1986). Take computers, for example. As we confront the challenges of high technology, computer literacy has become an essential skill and a top-dollar commodity. Yet it's also clear that computers—from the bells, whistles, and space wars of the video arcade to more serious applications of computer programming—are fast becoming a male

A businessman is aggressive; a businesswoman is pushy.

A businessman is good with details; a businesswoman is picky.

He loses his temper because he's so involved in his job; she's a bitch.

When he's depressed or hungover, everyone tiptoes past his office. If she's moody, it must be her time of the month.

He follows through; she doesn't know when to quit.

He's confident; she's conceited.

He stands firm; she's hard.

His judgments are her prejudices.

He is a man of the world; she's been around.

If he drinks it's because of job pressure; she's a lush.

He's never afraid to say what he thinks; she's always shooting off her mouth.

He exercises authority diligently; she's power mad.

He's close-mouthed; she's secretive.

He's a stern taskmaster; she's hard to work for.

He climbed the ladder of success; she slept her way to the top.

Table 4.1   How to Tell a Businessman from a Businesswoman.   Are men and women judged by a double standard? This table is exaggerated for effect, but it makes you wonder about evaluations in the classroom and on the job. And what about double standards that work against men? People are rigid in their definitions of maleness (Hort et al., 1990). Thus, compared to the classic image of the strong and silent type, men who are expressive, gentle, or emotional are sometimes called "wimps." [From Doyle, 1983.]

enterprise. A survey of twenty-three summer computer camps that serve some 5,000 students revealed that boys outnumber girls by a 3-to-1 margin—a difference that increases with the cost, grade level, and difficulty level of the camp (Hess & Miura, 1985).

There are at least two reasons for this gender difference. First, computer programming in the school is often introduced as part of math, a subject in which males receive more support from adults than do females (Chipman et al., 1985; Jacobs, 1991). Second, research suggests that educational software is designed primarily with boys in mind. Thus, when forty-three educators (thirty-four of whom were female) were asked to invent a grammar game for seventh-grade students-in-general, their new programs resembled those they had otherwise designed for boys rather than for girls (Huff & Cooper, 1987). Expecting users to be male, software developers flood the market with male-oriented products—a situation that can set in motion a self-fulfilling prophecy and help to *create* differences between the sexes. Studying the development of math skills in children from hundreds of families, Jacquelynne Eccles and her colleagues (1990) find that parents who accept the idea that girls are weaker than boys at math view their daughters as less competent, set lower expectations, attach less importance to math, and guide their daughters in other directions. As a result, girls lose interest and self-confidence and avoid future math-related pursuits.

What about today? Clearly, employment patterns are different for men and women. After all, how many female airline pilots have you encountered? And how many male secretaries have you met lately? Gender discrimination in the early school years paves the way for diverging career paths and occupational segregation in adulthood. But the problem does not end there. When equally qualified men and women compete for a job, gender considerations can enter the picture once again.

Does sex discrimination in the workplace still exist in the 1990s? If it does, under what conditions? Are the victims ever male? A study by Peter Glick and others (1988) brings us a few steps closer to the answers. Assuming that personal information about individual applicants would overcome an employer's gender stereotypes, these researchers predicted that women with masculine traits could compete with men for the so-called masculine jobs and that men with feminine traits could compete with women for so-called feminine jobs.

[Drawing by Richter; © 1973 The New Yorker, Inc.]

"Welcome aboard. This is your captain, *Margaret Williamson, speaking."*

Sex discrimination can take many forms. Lisa Olson, pictured here, was a sports reporter for the *Boston Herald.* According to Olson, one Sunday afternoon in 1990, several New England Patriots football players exposed themselves and made lewd remarks while Olson was in the locker room trying to conduct a postgame interview.

To test this hypothesis, Glick and his colleagues sent fictitious résumés to 212 real business professionals. The applicant was a recent college graduate named either Ken or Kate Norris. In one version of the résumé, Ken or Kate had worked in a sporting goods store and on a grounds-maintenance crew and had led the varsity basketball team (a masculine profile). In a second version, Ken or Kate had worked in a jewelry store, taught aerobics, and was captain of the pep squad (a feminine profile). After reading the résumés, subjects indicated their impressions of the applicant's personality and rated the chance that they would interview the applicant for three jobs: sales manager for a machinery company (masculine job), administrative bank assistant (gender-neutral job), and dental receptionist (feminine job). What mattered, an applicant's gender or background?

Figure 4.6 shows that although individual characteristics had an influence on hiring decisions, men were still favored for the so-called masculine job and

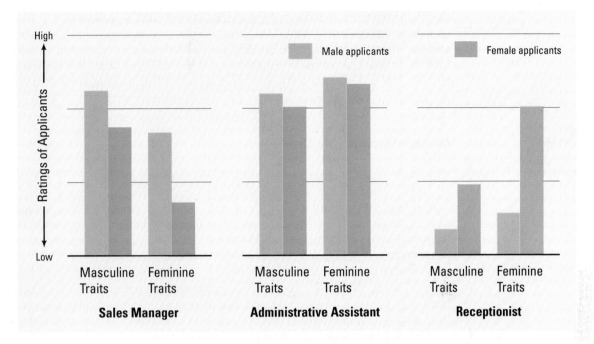

Figure 4.6 Sex Discrimination: Matching Gender to Occupation. Business professionals rated résumés of applicants for jobs considered masculine, feminine, or gender-neutral. The applicants were male or female and had masculine or feminine attributes. You can see that personal information was taken into account (people with masculine traits were rated higher for a sales manager job, those with feminine traits for a receptionist job). But there was also sex discrimination: men fared better for the sales manager job and women for the receptionist job even though half of the men had feminine traits and half of the women had masculine traits. Only for the neutral administrative assistant role were men and women similarly evaluated. [Data from Glick et al., 1988.]

women for the so-called feminine job. When Glick (1991) later assessed people's perceptions of different occupations, he found that some were easily identified as men's jobs (the most exclusive being auto mechanic, construction worker, and real estate developer) and others as women's jobs (the most exclusive being daycare worker, secretary, and receptionist). Once an occupation is typecast as male or female, it becomes difficult to write a new gender-free script.

RACISM

While broadcasting a National Football League game in 1983, Howard Cosell referred to a black player as a "little monkey." Criticized for his choice of words,

Cosell apologized and explained that it was not intended as a racial slur. A few years later, sportscaster Jimmy "the Greek" Snyder said that black athletes were bred for their size and strength. Snyder, too, said he meant no harm, but he was fired. Did these comments reflect deep-seated prejudice, or were they innocent remarks taken out of context? And what about **racism** in general, is it more subtle than it used to be?

Modern Racism: The Disease

In a classic study of ethnic stereotypes, Daniel Katz and Kenneth Braly (1933) found that white college students viewed the average white American as smart, industrious, and ambitious. Yet these same students perceived the average African American to be superstitious, lazy, happy-go-lucky, and ignorant. In follow-up surveys conducted in 1951, 1967, and 1982, however, the negative images of blacks had faded considerably (Dovidio & Gaertner, 1986).

According to public opinion polls, racial prejudice in the United States has dropped since World War II. In 1942, most white Americans felt that black families of equivalent income should live in separate neighborhoods and that their children should attend separate schools. Challenged by the civil rights movement, these views had become less popular by 1963. Today, very few Americans express these kinds of sentiments (Schuman et al., 1985). But can the polls be trusted, or is racism still alive?

People tend to associate antiblack prejudice with the images of old-fashioned racism characterized by slavery, lynch mobs, the Ku Klux Klan, segregation of public facilities, and the position that African Americans are inferior. These overt signs of bigotry may be on the decline, but some social psychologists believe they have simply been replaced by **modern racism**, a subtle form of prejudice that surfaces in less direct ways when it is safe, socially acceptable, and easy to rationalize. In modern racism, the overt symptoms have changed but the underlying disease remains (Gaertner & Dovidio, 1986; Katz et al., 1986; McConahay, 1986).

According to theories of modern racism, most people really want to believe that they are fair and nondiscriminatory, but they still harbor negative feelings toward other races. Torn between their egalitarian and prejudiced impulses, these people try but fail to be open-minded and relaxed about racial matters—which is why stereotyping, prejudice, and discrimination persist, but in ways that are disguised and easy to rationalize. Thus, many white Americans pay lip service to the *principles* of racial equality, but in *practice* they oppose mixed marriages, black candidates for political office, affirmative action, welfare, and other racially symbolic policies (Sears & Allen, 1984). These opinions expose the raw nerve of modern racism. So do the explanations people give for the inequalities that exist in housing, education, and employment. Sociologist James Kluegel (1990) notes that white Americans no longer attribute the racial gap in economic status to a lack of inborn ability among blacks, but they do still make attributions that are personal ("most blacks just don't have the motivation

racism
Discrimination based on a person's skin color or ethnic heritage.

modern racism
A form of prejudice that surfaces in subtle ways when it is safe, socially acceptable, and easy to rationalize.

The burning cross stands as a terrifying symbol of the
Ku Klux Klan and its old-fashioned racism. Incidents
like this may be less common today than in the past,
but more subtle forms of modern racism persist.

or will power to pull themselves out of poverty") rather than situational ("most
blacks don't have the chance for education that it takes to rise out of poverty").

If people will not admit to prejudice, how can we ever know if it lingers?
What symptoms are there to suggest that the disease still exists? Several
methods have been used (Crosby et al., 1980). One is the *bogus pipeline,* a
phony lie-detector test in which subjects are attached with electrodes to a
machine that supposedly records their true feelings. Since people don't want to
get caught lying, this method elicits more honest answers to sensitive questions.
Indeed, white college students rated blacks in more negative terms when the
bogus pipeline was used than when it was not (Sigall & Page, 1971).

Modern racism can also be detected without asking direct questions. Samuel
Gaertner, John Dovidio, and others find that *reaction-time*—the speed in which
a question is answered—can be used to uncover hidden prejudices. In one
study, for example, white subjects read word pairs and pressed a button
whenever they thought the words fit together. In each case, the word *blacks* or

whites was paired with either a positive trait (such as clean or ambitious) or a negative trait (such as stupid or lazy). The results were revealing. Subjects did not openly associate blacks with negative terms or whites with positive terms, and they were equally quick to reject the negative terms in both cases. However, subjects were *quicker* to respond to the positive words when paired with whites than with blacks. Since it takes less time to react to stimuli that fit already existing attitudes, this suggests that subjects were more predisposed to associate positive traits with whites than with blacks (Dovidio et al., 1986; Gaertner & McLaughlin, 1983).

Results like these may seem subtle, but the research message is clear: racial prejudice is so deeply ingrained in our culture that negative stereotypes of blacks are as difficult to break as a bad habit (Devine, 1989). In fact, many whites with egalitarian personal standards admit that they often do not react to blacks as they should, a self-discrepancy that causes these nonprejudiced individuals to feel embarrassed, guilty, and ashamed of themselves (Devine et al., 1991).

Cognitive Symptoms   No matter how well hidden they are, negative stereotypes bias social perceptions. Interested in how rumors spread, Gordon Allport and Leo Postman (1947) showed subjects a picture of a subway train filled with passengers. In the picture were a black man dressed in a three-piece suit and a white man holding a razor blade (see Figure 4.7). One subject viewed the scene briefly and described it to a second subject who had not seen it. The second subject communicated the description to a third subject and so on, through six rounds of communication. In more than half of the sessions, the final subject's report indicated that the black man, not the white man, held the razor. Some subjects even reported that he was brandishing it in a threatening manner. "Whether this ominous distortion reflects hatred and fear of Negroes we cannot definitely say. . . . Yet the distortion may occur even in subjects who have no anti-Negro bias. It is an unthinking cultural stereotype that the Negro is hot tempered and addicted to the use of razors and weapons" (Allport & Postman, 1947, p. 63).

More recent research suggests that the *interpretation* of an event may also be biased by racial stereotypes. In one study, white subjects watched on a TV screen what they thought was a live interaction involving two men (Duncan, 1976). A discussion developed into a heated argument, and one man seemed to shove the other. When the protagonist was white and the victim black, only 17 percent of the subjects interpreted the shove as an act of violence, and most perceived it to be "horseplay." Yet when the protagonist was black and the victim was white, the number of "violent act" interpretations rose to 75 percent. A similar result was obtained in a study of sixth-grade children (Sagar & Schofield, 1980). It even appeared among first-graders who evaluated cartoon characters—but, interestingly, only when the children were tested by white, not black, experimenters (Lawrence, 1991).

Figure 4.7 How Racial Stereotypes Distort Social Perceptions. After briefly viewing this picture, one subject described it to a second subject, who described it to a third, and so on. After six rounds of communication, the final report often placed the razor blade held by the white man into the black man's hand. This study illustrates how racial stereotypes can distort social perception. [From Buckhout, 1974.]

Behavioral Symptoms Theories of modern racism claim that overt prejudice against minorities surfaces when it is safe, socially acceptable, and easy to rationalize. Three studies illustrate the point.

In a study of aggression, Ronald Rogers and Steven Prentice-Dunn (1981) had white subjects administer electric shocks to another subject, supposedly as part of a biofeedback experiment. Although all subjects were instructed to deliver the same number of shocks, they could adjust the intensity as they saw fit. In fact, no shocks were received, and the second subject was really a black or white confederate trained to treat the subject in either a friendly or an insulting manner. As shown in Figure 4.8, the results are consistent with the portrait of modern racism. Subjects administered *less* intense shocks to the friendly confederate when he was black than when he was white—a pattern of *reverse discrimination* indicating that subjects bent over backward to appear nonracist. In response to the insulting confederate, however, subjects delivered

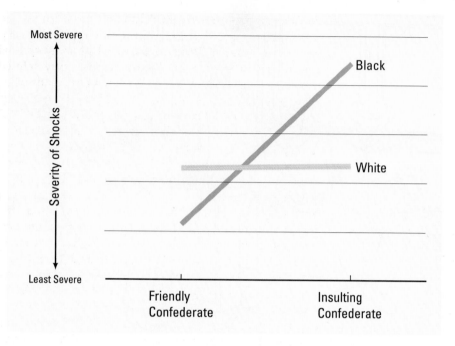

Figure 4.8   Interracial Aggression in the Laboratory.   In a study of aggression, subjects delivered the mildest shocks to a friendly black confederate and the most intense shocks to an insulting black confederate. This pattern suggests that people go out of their way to appear nonprejudiced (left), but then they act on hostile prejudicial feelings when they have a socially acceptable excuse (right). [From Rogers & Prentice-Dunn, 1981.]

---

more intense shocks if he was black than if he was white—a pattern of *modern racism* in which people act on their hostile feelings whenever doing so can be justified in nonracial terms.

In another study, sixty-two therapists, some of whom had extensive experience, watched a videotape of a staged interaction between a therapist and female client. The "client" was either black or white and behaved in a manner that was either normal or depressed, negative, and pessimistic. How did trained therapists perceive the woman? In the normal condition, evaluations were generally favorable and unaffected by race. In the depressed condition, however, subjects evaluated the client more negatively when she was black than when she was white. Apparently, the client's psychological disorder provided enough cover for latent prejudices to surface (Jenkins-Hall & Sacco, 1991).

A third study revealed that modern racism is also evident when people refuse to help others because of their race. In this case, white female subjects participated in work groups in which either a black or white confederate needed assistance to complete the task. When subjects were led to believe that the confederate had exerted sufficient effort, or when the request was made by a third party, subjects were uniformly willing to offer help. But when subjects were led to believe that the confederate had not worked hard enough and there was no pressure of a third-party request, they refused to help the black confederate more often than they refused to help the white one. Once again, as soon as circumstances allowed subjects to excuse a negative response, they discriminated on the basis of race (Frey & Gaertner, 1986).

Perhaps the most troubling aspect of modern racism is that although it adversely affects its victims, it can be invisible to its perpetrators. Thus, in the context of a job interview, Carl Word and others (1974) found that when white subjects questioned an applicant who was black rather than white, they sat farther away, made more speech errors, and held shorter interviews—a distant interpersonal style that causes interviewees to behave in a more nervous and awkward manner. For black men and women on the job market, the implications are sobering. And there's more. Thomas Pettigrew and Joanne Martin (1987) note that when blacks enter the workplace, they confront three biases. First, negative racial stereotypes lead white employers and coworkers to hold low expectations for performance that may be difficult to overcome. Second, in organizations that hire few minorities, black employees draw more than their fair share of attention, leading perceivers to exaggerate both the positive and the negative. Third, it is often believed that blacks are hired as "tokens," and this belief raises more doubts about their competence. Together, these biases subject black employees to what Pettigrew and Martin call "triple jeopardy."

The Victim's Plight   Bryant Gumbel, co-host of TV's "Today Show," tried to explain it:

> It's very hard for any white person to appreciate the depth of what it means to be black in America. . . . Racism isn't only being called a nigger and spit on. It's being flipped the bird when you're driving, or walking into a store and being asked to check your bag, or being ignored at a checkout counter, or entering a fine restaurant and being stared at. (Plaskin, 1988, p. 31)

Modern racism may seem invisible, but its impact is real and is felt by the targets of prejudice. Public opinion polls show that although white Americans believe that racial discrimination is on the decline in housing, education, employment, and wages, black Americans are skeptical (Sigelman & Welch, 1991). The trial of the L.A. police officers who beat motorist Rodney King illustrates the point. After the jury's surprising acquittal, 45 percent of blacks who were surveyed, compared to only 12 percent of whites, attributed the verdict to racism (Lacayo, 1992).

There are even sharp differences of opinion among highly paid professional athletes. In 1991, *Sports Illustrated* surveyed three hundred athletes who play for teams in the NFL, NBA, and Major League Baseball (Johnson, 1991). The results were crystal clear: 63 percent of black respondents, compared to only 2

Survey Topics	Black Athletes Who Agree			White Athletes Who Agree		
	Blacks Better Off Than Whites	Blacks the Same as Whites	Blacks Worse Off Than Whites	Blacks Better Off Than Whites	Blacks the Same as Whites	Blacks Worse Off Than Whites
Overall treatment	5%	28%	63%	17%	79%	2%
Salaries/contracts	3	28	61	11	84	3
Support of fans	6	59	27	5	79	13
Treatment by coaches	2	52	37	17	77	4
Opportunities for management	2	12	77	5	49	43
Commercial endorsements	4	16	73	14	62	20

Table 4.2 Racial Discrimination in Professional Sports? Three hundred athletes playing in the NFL, NBA, and Major League Baseball were questioned about the status of blacks in their own sport. As you can see, blacks were far more likely than their white teammates to say they were victims of discrimination on a range of specific issues. [Data from Johnson, 1991.]

percent of their white teammates, thought that blacks were victims of discrimination in their own sports. Disparities like this were found in response to specific questions concerning salaries, fan support, treatment by coaches, management opportunities, and commercial endorsements (see Table 4.2). One black football player wrote, "Black players who make too much, talk too much, or don't play three times better than whites get cut." Yet a white player from the same league protested that "there are more instances of discrimination against white athletes" (Johnson, p. 45).

Perhaps the truth lies somewhere in between. Shelby Steele (1990), a black English professor, says that "the heaviest weight that oppression leaves on the shoulders of its former victims is the memory of itself" (p. 150). For Steele, painful emotions are aroused by the sight of a Confederate flag, pickup trucks with gun racks, black lawn jockeys, and the patronizing phrase "He is a credit to his race." Then there's the pressure felt by minority professionals who often feel as if the reputation of their group is riding on their performance (White, 1991). It is no wonder, says Steele, that victims are so sensitive that they may see prejudice where it does not exist and use it to protect their self-esteem when they're anxious about failing.

Jennifer Crocker and Brenda Major (1989) agree that victims of discrimination may cope with life's challenges by attributing outcomes to prejudice, but they find that this strategy has both benefits and drawbacks. In a study reported by Crocker and her colleagues (1991), black subjects described themselves on a questionnaire, supposedly to be evaluated by an unknown white student who sat in an adjacent room. Subjects were told that they were either liked or disliked by this unknown student; then they completed a self-esteem questionnaire. As shown in Figure 4.9, self-esteem scores predictably rose after positive feedback and declined after negative feedback. But when subjects thought the evaluating student had seen them through a one-way mirror, negative feedback did *not* lower their self-esteem. In this situation, subjects coped by blaming the unfavorable evaluations on racial prejudice. However, there was a drawback: one-way mirror subjects who received positive feedback actually showed a

Figure 4.9   Attributing Success and Failure to Prejudice: Benefits and Drawbacks. Black subjects received a positive or negative evaluation from a white student in a nearby room. They thought the white student had or had not seen them through a one-way mirror. In the unseen condition, self-esteem increased after positive feedback and decreased after negative feedback. For subjects who thought the evaluator saw they were black, negative feedback did not lower self-esteem (the benefit), but positive feedback did (the drawback). Thinking the evaluator knew they were black, subjects attributed the feedback to racial factors; thus, they denied both the blame for failure and the credit for success. [Data from Crocker et al., 1991.]

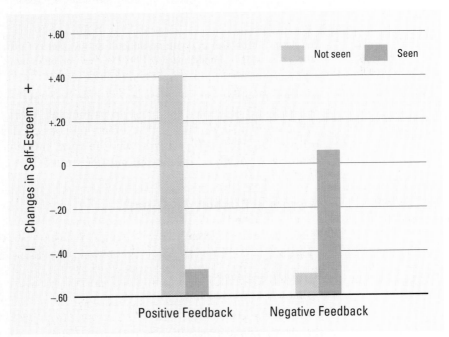

"I like you, Jim, not because you're black but because you have excellent qualifications."

For victims of prejudice, it can be difficult to interpret even the positive evaluations of others. [Drawing by Handelsman; © 1991 The New Yorker Magazine, Inc.]

decrease in self-esteem. The reason? Rather than take credit for their success, these subjects attributed the praise to patronizing, reverse discrimination.

Racism is a social disease that afflicts millions. It distorts perceptions and behavior and harms its victims, who, in turn, misperceive others to protect themselves. Somehow, the disease must be treated. The question is, how?

Intergroup Contact: The Cure?

See that man over there?

Yes.

Well, I hate him.

But you don't know him.

That's why I hate him.

(Allport, 1954, p. 253)

Modern racism is difficult to overcome because it lurks like a wolf in sheep's clothing and manifests itself in indirect ways. Is there a solution to the problem? Can stereotypes and prejudice against blacks be wiped out by a mass media blitz designed to inform whites that their expectations and fears are unfounded? Social psychologists used to believe that such efforts would prove effective, but they do not. Indeed, when you consider the many sources of stereotypes and prejudice, the prospects seem dim, though there is reason for hope.

School Desegregation: The Great Experiment   In the historic 1954 case of *Brown v. Board of Education of Topeka,* the U.S. Supreme Court ruled that racially separate schools were inherently unequal, in violation of the Constitution. In part, the decision was informed by empirical evidence supplied by thirty-two eminent social scientists on the harmful effects of segregation on the self-esteem and academic achievement of black students and on race relations (Allport et al., 1953). The Supreme Court's decision propelled the nation into a large-scale social experiment. One question remained: What would be the effect?

contact hypothesis
The theory that direct contact between hostile groups will reduce prejudice under certain conditions.

At the time, the *Brown* decision was controversial. Many Americans opposed school desegregation, arguing that morality cannot be legislated and that forcing interracial contact would escalate the conflict. Meanwhile, others advanced the **contact hypothesis**: under certain conditions, direct contact between members

Trying to combat racism, artist Mark Heckman put this billboard up on a highway near Chicago. His objective was to give white Americans a taste of discrimination. Did it work? It's hard to tell. After a day, vandals painted swastikas and the letters KKK on the poster. After two days, it was taken down in response to a flurry of protest calls.

of hostile groups will reduce stereotyping, prejudice, and discrimination (Allport, 1954; Amir, 1969; Stephan, 1985).

Despite the Court's ruling, desegregation proceeded slowly. There were stalling tactics, lawsuits, and vocal opposition to busing. Many schools remained untouched until the early 1970s. Then, as the dust began to settle, research brought the grave realization that little had changed, that contact between black and white schoolchildren was not working. When Walter Stephan (1986) reviewed studies conducted both during and after desegregation, he found that 13 percent of the studies reported a decrease in white prejudice, 34 percent no change, and 53 percent an *increase* in white prejudice. Desegregation had no negative academic effects, but it seemed to have a positive impact on black students in only a few schools. These findings forced social psychologists to challenge the wisdom of their testimony to the Supreme Court and re-examine the contact hypothesis that guided that advice in the first place (Cook, 1984; Gerard, 1983; Miller & Brewer, 1984).

Is the original contact hypothesis wrong? No. It now appears that although desegregation did not produce the desired changes, the resulting pessimism was premature for two reasons. First, the conditions necessary for effective intergroup contact had not existed within the public schools. Second, the possible long-term benefits of desegregation had not yet had time to materialize. In the following sections, we examine these two issues.

The Contact Hypothesis: A Re-Examination   Nobody ever said that prejudice rooted in generations can be erased just by throwing groups together. According to the contact hypothesis, certain conditions must exist for contact to succeed—conditions that did not exist in the public schools.

First, the two groups should be of *equal status*, at least in the contact situation. Blacks and whites had interacted long before 1954, but too often in situations where blacks worked at a clear disadvantage in lower-status jobs or in outright servitude. If anything, these unequal-status contacts only perpetuate existing negative stereotypes. You may recall Eagly's (1987) theory that gender stereotypes are sustained by the different social roles played by men and women. The same logic applies to the perception of blacks and whites. Situations that did promote equal-status contact—desegregation in the army or in public housing projects—were successful (Pettigrew, 1969). When public schools were desegregated, however, white children were coming from more affluent families, were better prepared, and thus were favored more in class than their black peers (Cohen, 1984).

Second, successful contact requires *personal interactions* between individuals from the two groups. As we saw, when people are divided into social categories, ingroups tend to assume that outgroup members are all alike. Through intimate, one-on-one interactions, however, categories should break down, and outgroup members should be perceived in more individualized terms (Brewer & Miller, 1984; Wilder, 1986). Unfortunately, interracial contact among individual schoolchildren is often difficult to achieve. Studies show that the school is not a melting pot. After the bus arrives, students gravitate toward members of their own race on the playground, in the cafeteria, and in the classroom. Teachers then compound the problem by tracking students on the basis of academic achievement, a policy that further separates advantaged white students from disadvantaged blacks (Epstein, 1985; Schofield, 1982). Voluntary racial separation can even be seen on today's college campuses. The point is, for personal contacts to occur, it's not enough simply to get blacks and whites under the same roof. School *desegregation* does not ensure *integration*.

The third condition for successful contact is that the opposing groups engage in *cooperative activities* to achieve superordinate goals. This strategy was effective in the Robbers Cave study. By creating conditions that led the Rattlers and Eagles to take part in a joint venture, Sherif and his team (1961) transformed bitter enemies into allies. Yet the typical classroom is a setting filled with competition—exactly the wrong ingredient. Picture the scene. The teacher stands in front of the class and asks a question. Several children wave their hands, straining to catch the teacher's eye. Then as soon as one student is called on, the others groan in frustration. In the contest for the teacher's approval, they feel like losers—hardly a scenario that seems fit for positive intergroup contact (Aronson, 1988).

Why is the introduction of superordinate goals so important? One possibility is that cooperation breaks down the psychological barrier between groups, leading members to re-categorize the two groups into one—and reducing ingroup favoritism (Bettencourt et al., 1992). To test this hypothesis, Gaertner and others (1990) brought six subjects into the laboratory and divided them into two three-person groups. Each group wore color-coded ID tags, gave itself a name, and worked on a decision-making task. Next, the two groups were brought together and either listened to others discussing a problem (a neutral interaction) or joined forces to solve the problem themselves (a cooperative encounter). The re-categorization hypothesis was supported in two ways. First, despite their initial allegiances, 58 percent of the subjects in the cooperative condition said they felt like one large group rather than two separate groups, an increase compared to only 28 percent in the neutral condition. Second, when subjects evaluated each other, those in the cooperative condition did not exhibit the usual ingroup favoritism bias. Instead of derogating former outgroup members, they evaluated them as more likable, honest, and similar to the self. Thanks to cooperation, "they" became part of "us" (see Figure 4.10).

Finally, intergroup contact can work only if it is supported by *social norms*. If these norms—which are determined in part by figures of authority—promote intergroup contact, interactions should be more positive. If not, then stereotypes and prejudice will continue unchecked. As we'll see in later chapters, people are influenced heavily by the behavior and attitudes of others. In one study, subjects expressed more prejudice after they first overheard a confederate uttering a racial slur (Greenberg & Pyszczynski, 1985). In a second study, college students who were interviewed about a highly publicized racial incident

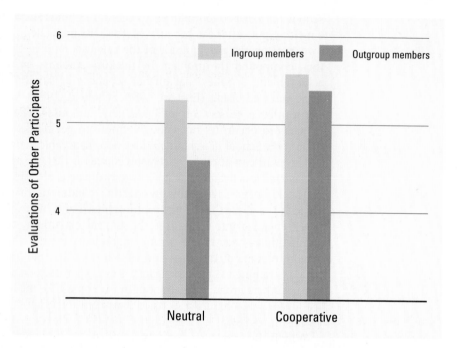

Figure 4.10   Intergroup Cooperation: Re-categorizing "Them" as Part of "Us." After working in separate three-person groups, six subjects were assembled for a neutral or cooperative interaction; then they reported their impressions of each other. In the neutral condition, subjects rated former ingroup members more favorably than they rated former outgroup members (left). In the cooperative condition, however, their evaluations of the outgroup were more favorable (right). [Data from Gaertner et al., 1990.]

on campus communicated more racist sentiment after they heard a fellow student do the same (Blanchard et al., 1991). And in a third study, subjects were more likely to rate an outgroup member as "typical" when they were with fellow ingroup members, presumably a partisan audience, than when they were alone (Wilder & Shapiro, 1991). Norms have a powerful impact on us. Yet in the case of school desegregation, the social climate was not supportive. Many principals, teachers, and political officials objected, and many parents boycotted busing. The necessary conditions of the contact hypothesis are summarized in Table 4.3.

The Jigsaw Classroom   Although problems have plagued school desegregation efforts, research shows that racial prejudice can be reduced in situations that satisfy the chief requirements of the contact hypothesis: intimate, equal-status contact, supported by local authorities and necessary for the achievement of a superordinate goal (Cook, 1985).

1. *Equal status:* The contact should occur in circumstances that place the two groups at equal status.

2. *Personal interaction:* The contact should involve one-on-one interactions among individual members of the two groups.

3. *Cooperative activities:* Members of the two groups should join together in an effort to achieve superordinate goals.

4. *Social norms:* The social norms, defined in part by relevant authorities, should favor intergroup contact.

Table 4.3   The Contact Hypothesis: Necessary Conditions.   Several conditions are deemed necessary for intergroup contact to serve as a treatment for racism. However, many desegregated schools have failed to create a setting that meets these conditions.

jigsaw classroom
A cooperative learning method used to reduce racial prejudice through interaction in group efforts.

In the classroom, Elliot Aronson and his colleagues (1978) developed a cooperative learning method they called the **jigsaw classroom**. In newly desegregated elementary schools in Texas and California, they assigned fifthgraders to small, racially and academically mixed groups. The material to be learned within each group was divided into subtopics, much the way a jigsaw puzzle is broken into pieces. Each student was responsible for learning one piece of the group's puzzle; then all members took turns teaching their material to each other. Under the system, everyone—regardless of race, ability, or self-confidence—needs everyone else if the group as a whole is to succeed. The method produced impressive results. Compared to children in traditional classes, those in jigsaw classrooms grew to like each other more, were less prejudiced, liked school more, and had higher self-esteem. In addition, academic test scores improved for minority students and remained the same for white students.

The jigsaw classroom—like an interracial sports team—offers a promising way to create a truly integrated educational setting. For widespread use, however, certain details may need to be ironed out. For example, how much school time should be devoted to cooperative learning? Is it better in some age groups than in others? And what happens in groups that fail? This last question is important, because just as successful cooperation reduces conflict between alienated groups, cooperative failure can backfire and intensify the conflict (Worchel, 1986).

Outlook: Toward a Colorblind Society?   Another reason for hope comes from the long-term benefits of desegregation that are just now beginning to materialize. In a comprehensive review of research evidence for the U.S. Department of Education, a group of experts concluded that desegregation has increased the reading levels of black students (Cook et al., 1984). It also appears that blacks from desegregated schools, especially in the North, have more success in college and on the job market. And later in life, blacks and whites who attended desegregated schools are more likely to live in an integrated community and want their own children to attend an integrated school (Braddock, 1985). Although 36 percent of white Americans overall favor the use of busing to achieve desegregation, among those who were bused as children, that figure is 54 percent (Sussman, 1988).

Consistent with the contact hypothesis, interracial interactions under the right circumstances can break new ground in the fight against racism. But what, specifically, should be the goal? Should the differences between groups be ignored or acknowledged? One view is that we should strive to become *colorblind*, a state in which race and ethnic heritage have no bearing whatsoever on the way individuals are treated. In a colorblind society, healthy race relations require that the categories be dissolved and that individuals be perceived on a strictly personal basis (Brewer & Miller, 1984; Wilder, 1986). But is this goal possible, or even desirable?

One possible implication of social identity theory is that social categories should *not* be erased because people derive pride and self-esteem from desirable ingroup characteristics (Hewstone & Brown, 1986). In other words, even though we should strive to reduce inequalities among blacks, whites, and other minorities, racial and ethnic diversity should be celebrated, not ignored. The same argument is made from another perspective. Based on a four-year study of an integrated middle school, Janet Schofield (1986) observed that in an effort to treat all students equally and without discrimination, teachers bent over backward to create a colorblind environment in which racial differences were never discussed. The problem is that because modern racism surfaces when it can be justified in socially acceptable terms, a supposed *lack* of racial awareness provides a comfortable setting for discrimination. At one point, Schofield discovered that a white teacher purposely miscounted the votes of a student-held election because the girl who really won was "unstable." That girl also happened to be black.

PROBLEMS AND PROSPECTS

The sex discrimination case of Ann Hopkins and the merciless beating of Rodney King invite us to think carefully about stereotypes and prejudice: their origins, effects on social perception and behavior, and possible solutions. Now let's review briefly what we know and what we can expect from the future.

Stereotypes are false or exaggerated beliefs that ultimately lead people to overlook the diversity within outgroups and jump to conclusions about specific persons. Once formed, stereotypes—regardless of whether they are based on gender, race, or other social categories—are hard to erase. Indeed, even if individual perceivers are not biased, many stereotypes are preserved by the forces of culture and slow to change. The problems stemming from prejudice and intergroup conflict are equally daunting. Negative feelings toward outgroups arise from stable personality factors, competition for limited resources, and the need to favor ingroups over outgroups in order to boost self-esteem. Modern racism in America is a particularly acute problem, one that is poised and ready to strike at the first provocation.

Sexism and racism are similar in some respects, different in others. Both women and racial minorities occupy low-status social roles, and both are known victims of discrimination. But sexism rests heavily on caricatures of men and women, and racism is further inflamed by negative emotions toward racial outgroups. It is interesting that despite the differences, there may be a single solution to both problems: change behavior, and hearts and minds will follow. Hire men for "feminine" jobs, and hire women for "masculine" jobs, and gender stereotypes should begin to fade. Likewise, bring whites, blacks, and other minorities together as intimate, cooperative equals in schools and other settings, and racial prejudice should also diminish. We cannot expect these changes overnight, and we may even have to conclude that some degree of discrimination is inevitable among human beings. But there is much room, and much hope, for improvement.

REVIEW

Discrimination is influenced by both beliefs and feelings about social groups.

STEREOTYPES

Stereotypes are cognitive beliefs that associate groups of people with certain types of characteristics.

How Stereotypes Form: Cognitive Foundations

The formation of stereotypes begins with the tendency for people to group themselves and others into social categories and assume that similarity among members of outgroups is greater than similarity among members of ingroups. This outgroup homogeneity bias leads us to generalize from individuals to whole groups and vice versa.

How Stereotypes Survive: Self-Perpetuating Biases

Stereotypes may provide convenient generalizations, but they are overgeneralized and misleading. Two processes perpetuate existing stereotypes. First, people perceive illusory correlations between groups and traits when the groups and traits are distinctive and when the correlation fits preconceived notions. Second, group members who do not fit the mold may be subcategorized, leaving the overall stereotype intact. Individuals who do not match the stereotype elicit a revision of beliefs only when they are, in other ways, typical members of the stereotyped group.

How Stereotypes Distort Perceptions of Individuals

Stereotypes may influence how behavior is interpreted. Behaviors that differ markedly from expectations are judged as even more discrepant than they really are, the result of a contrast effect.

Stereotyping: A Necessary Evil?

Social categorization is inevitable, but perceivers can overcome stereotypes and form individualized impressions of others when they have personal information as well as the cognitive ability and motivation to use that information.

PREJUDICE

Prejudice refers to negative feelings toward persons based solely on their membership in certain groups.

The Prejudiced Personality

Some people are generally more prejudiced against outgroups than others. Research shows that individuals who have an authoritarian personality exhibit high levels of prejudice.

Robbers Cave: Setting the Stage

In the Robbers Cave study, boys were divided into two groups, which competed in a tournament and developed into bitter rivals. Many efforts to restore peace failed, but the groups came together after the experimenters introduced tasks that required intergroup cooperation.

Realistic Conflict Theory

Realistic conflict theory maintains that direct competition for resources gives rise to prejudice. It now appears that prejudice is aroused by a perceived threat not to personal interests but to the interests of the ingroup. The question is why are people so sensitive about the status of their ingroups even when personal interests are not at stake.

Social Identity Theory

In studies of minimal groups, subjects categorized arbitrarily into one of two groups discriminate in favor of the ingroup. To explain this result, social identity theory maintains that self-esteem is influenced by the fate of the social groups with which we identify. Threats to the self trigger ingroup favoritism, which, in turn, increases self-esteem. People also distance themselves from ingroups, or from members of ingroups, that fail.

SEXISM

Sexism is a form of discrimination based on a person's gender.

Gender Stereotypes: Blue for Boys, Pink for Girls

Across the world, men are described as assertive, independent, and task oriented; women as sensitive, dependent, and people oriented. Masculinity and femininity are seen as opposites but, in fact, many individuals have both "masculine" and "feminine" characteristics. Gender stereotypes are so deeply ingrained that they bias perceptions of baby boys and girls.

What Activates Gender Stereotypes?

Gender stereotypes are most likely to bias social perceptions (1) for some perceivers (gender schematics) more than others, (2) for target persons who are unusually masculine or feminine in their appearance, and (3) in situations that increase the visibility of gender characteristics.

Are Gender Stereotypes Accurate?

Although there are differences between men and women, stereotypes are stronger and more numerous than the actual differences.

What Do Gender Stereotypes Endure?

These stereotypes persist for two reasons. First, cultural institutions foster gender distinctions in the way males and females are portrayed. Second, men and women occupy different social roles. Their role-consistent behaviors serve to confirm existing portrayals.

Sex Discrimination: A Double Standard?

Occupational segregation may begin early in life. Among schoolchildren, boys are supported more than girls in math and computer skills. Later on, men and women are judged more favorably when they apply for jobs that are consistent with gender stereotypes.

RACISM

Racism is a form of discrimination based on a person's skin color or ethnic heritage.

Modern Racism: The Disease

Over the years, surveys have recorded a decline in negative views of black Americans. Blatant, old-fashioned racism may have faded, but research has uncovered a subtle, modern form of racism that surfaces when people can rationalize racist behavior. Cognitively, people recall and interpret ambiguous actions in negative terms if the actor is black. Among the behavioral symptoms is that white subjects are more aggressive, more unflattering, and less helpful to black confederates when such actions are safe, socially acceptable, and easy to rationalize.

Intergroup Contact: The Cure?

The 1954 U.S. Supreme Court decision *Brown v. Board of Education* ordered public schools to desegregate. According to the contact hypothesis, this policy should reduce negative stereotypes and prejudice. Desegregation did not provide an overnight cure, but the necessary conditions—equal-status contact, personal interactions, cooperation, and social norms—did not exist. When they do, as in the jigsaw classroom, positive changes take place. Also, possible long-term benefits are now beginning to materialize.

PROBLEMS AND PROSPECTS

Despite the differences between sexism and racism, the same solution may serve both problems. Once behavior is changed, hearts and minds will follow.

SOCIAL INTERACTION:
Relating to Others

II

Preview

In Part II we move from people's thoughts and perceptions of themselves and others to *social interaction,* the ways in which people relate to one another. The four chapters included here cover a wide range of social interactions—from initial encounters to enduring partnerships, from helpfulness to violence. *Interpersonal attraction,* the desire to approach and get to know someone, is described in Chapter 5. Some attractive encounters result in the *intimate relationships* discussed in Chapter 6: close attachments between friends, lovers, and spouses. Chapter 7, on *helping others,* considers why people help others and how people react to receiving help. In Chapter 8, possible causes and consequences of *aggression* are examined. The research and theory reviewed in these chapters enlarge our understanding of those patterns of behavior that create the complex fabric of our interactions with others.

Interpersonal Attraction

5

Preview

This chapter examines how people become attracted to each other. First, we describe *theories of attraction* proposing that attraction is based on rewarding interactions. Then we consider four factors that affect whether social encounters will be rewarding: *characteristics of the individual* who is attracted, *characteristics of others* who are perceived as attractive, *the fit between people* attracted to each other, and *situational influences* on social interactions. Overall, attraction is *a rewarding experience.*

Daisy Buchanan is an attractive person. As seen through the eyes of her cousin Nick in F. Scott Fitzgerald's novel *The Great Gatsby*, Daisy makes a vivid and compelling impression:

I looked back at my cousin, who began to ask me questions in her low, thrilling voice. It was the kind of voice that the ear follows up and down, as if each speech is an arrangement of notes that will never be played again. Her face was sad and lovely with bright things in it, bright eyes and a bright passionate mouth, but there was an excitement in her voice that men who had cared for her found difficult to forget: a singing compulsion, a whispered, "Listen," a promise that she had done gay, exciting things just a while since and that there were gay, exciting things hovering in the next hour.

But what makes Daisy so very attractive to Nick's neighbor—the thoroughly infatuated Jay Gatsby? Does Gatsby adore Daisy because of *his* own personal needs or because of *her* appeal? Was there just the right fit between them when they first met—the nice young woman who lived in a beautiful house, the male stranger who came to town in a military uniform? Or were they simply thrown together, in their youth as well as later, in situations that made it easy for attraction to take hold?

The causes of attraction have been pondered throughout human history, and not just by novelists. Have you ever been surprised by your own reactions to people you've just met? Why did you have such a positive reaction to some but a negative reaction to others? In studying interpersonal attraction, social psychologists examine the forces that bring us together and those that keep us apart (Berscheid, 1985).

Attraction refers to a motivational state: the desire to approach. It is the opposite of repulsion—the desire to avoid—and is distinct from indifference. Since people are attracted to things as well as to human beings, the term **interpersonal attraction** is used to refer specifically to a person's desire to approach another individual. In this chapter, we discuss some theoretical perspectives on attraction and then consider various factors that influence reactions to initial social encounters. You should note, however, that social psychological research on attraction (as well as on the topic of intimate relationships discussed in Chapter 6) has focused primarily on heterosexuals. Thus, it is not known how well the findings we describe apply to homosexual relationships. This uncertainty is a serious limitation on our understanding. Nevertheless, it seems likely that the basic social psychological processes addressed in this and the next chapter are relevant for a great many individuals and couples, regardless of their sexual orientation (Kurdek, 1991b).

interpersonal attraction A person's desire to approach another person.

THEORIES OF ATTRACTION: THE ROLE OF REWARDS

According to most theories of attraction, we are attracted to individuals whose presence is rewarding to us (Lott & Lott, 1974). A person's presence can be rewarding in two different ways: directly and through association. Direct rewards encompass all the various positive consequences we obtain from being with someone. Perhaps an individual showers us with attention, support, understanding, and other rewarding behaviors. We also respond to beauty, intelligence, a sense of humor, and other rewarding characteristics. And then there are external rewards to be considered. Some people give us access to valuable commodities (such as money, status, or information) that we coud not have secured on our own. The more of these various types of rewards that someone provides us, the more we should be attracted to that person.

But what about just being with an individual under enjoyable circumstances? Suppose you meet someone at a victory celebration for your favorite basketball team. Are you more likely to be attracted at that time and place than you would be if you met the same person on another, less euphoric occasion? It's a distinct possibility. We can become attracted to people we happen to associate with a positive, rewarding experience—even though they are not responsible for that experience.

reinforcement-affect model The theory that positive feelings in someone's presence increase attraction to that person, while negative feelings decrease attraction.

Donn Byrne and his colleagues believe that both direct and associated rewards influence attraction by means of a single factor (Byrne & Murnen, 1988; Clore & Byrne, 1974). Their **reinforcement-affect model** views attraction as determined by "affect" (that is, emotion). Whether produced directly by the person or simply by association, positive emotional experiences reinforce the desire to be with that person. In contrast, negative emotional experiences in someone's presence motivate us to avoid the person, thereby decreasing attraction. The reinforcement-affect model, illustrated in Figure 5.1, views our own emotional reactions as the fundamental cause of attraction to others.

balance theory The theory that people desire consistency in their thoughts, feelings, and social relationships.

reciprocity A quid-pro-quo mutual exchange—for example, liking those who like us.

Fritz Heider's (1958) **balance theory** points to another factor that contributes to attraction: the psychological balance created by consistency in our thoughts, feelings, and social relationships. Balanced relationships, says the theory, should be rewarding; imbalance should be unpleasant. Between two people, balance is created by **reciprocity**: a mutual, quid-pro-quo exchange between what we give and what we receive. And, indeed, we are attracted to those we believe are attracted to us (Backman & Secord, 1959; Curtis & Miller, 1986). In groups of three or more individuals, a balanced social constellation involves liking someone whose relationships with others are similar to ours. If you've ever found yourself attracted to someone your best friend thought was a total disaster, you've had a personal experience with the awkwardness and discomfort of *im*balanced relationships. Usually, we like those who are friends of our friends *and* enemies of our enemies (Aronson & Cope, 1968).

Influenced by direct rewards, rewards by association, and rewarding social arrangements, attraction is highly variable. When it comes to the specific case, we have to examine those four factors we noted as possible causes for Jay Gatsby's attraction to Daisy Buchanan: personal needs, the characteristics of the other person, the relationship between the two individuals, and the situational context. Although we consider each of these factors one by one in this chapter, the relationship among them is dynamic and interactive (Gifford & Gallagher, 1985; T. L. Wright et al., 1985). Characteristics of the individual, for example,

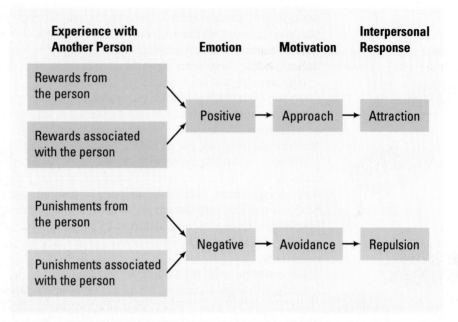

Figure 5.1   The Reinforcement-Affect Model of Attraction.   The reinforcement-affect model of attraction holds that our emotional response in someone's presence is the ultimate cause of whether attraction occurs. Positive emotions, produced directly by or associated with someone, reinforce the desire to be with that person and so increase attraction. Negative emotions produce the desire to avoid that person, thus decreasing attraction. [Based on Clore & Byrne, 1974.]

can modify the effect of a given situation. A particular situation can intensify or dampen the effect of individual characteristics. Examining these factors separately is like removing the pieces from a mosaic and sorting them into piles of different colors. The general principles we discover help us understand the process of attraction, but they do not reduce it to a routine formula. In both the mosaic and the human encounter, the pattern these pieces create is always unique—and sometimes astonishingly beautiful.

CHARACTERISTICS OF THE INDIVIDUAL

Do some people make friends under almost any circumstances? Do some people respond eagerly to almost anyone's opening lines? In other words, are some people more likely than others to become attracted? To answer this question, we

Interpersonal attraction is like a mosaic. We can analyze them in terms of their separate parts. But in both the mosaic and the human encounter, the pattern these pieces create is always unique and sometimes quite beautiful.

examine four personal characteristics that influence a person's readiness to approach other people: self-esteem, social motives, social difficulties, and interpersonal expectations.

Self-Esteem: Confidence Versus Insecurity

The notion that *self-esteem,* a person's evaluation of his or her own worth, affects attraction to others has a long history in psychology. Sigmund Freud (1922), the founder of psychoanalysis, and Theodore Reik (1944), who developed his own school of psychotherapy, both traced the source of interpersonal attraction back to dissatisfaction with oneself. Other prominent psychotherapists, such as Karen Horney (1939) and Harry Stack Sullivan (1947), disagreed. They believed that genuine and spontaneous attraction to others requires feeling secure and confident about oneself. So which is it? Does attraction flow from weakness or from strength?

At first, research in social psychology seemed to support the role of dissatisfaction with the self. In a 1965 study by Elaine Walster (now Hatfield), female subjects received bogus feedback rigged by the experimenter. Those whose self-esteem was lowered by being told that they had a poor personality liked a friendly male confederate more than did subjects whose self-esteem was bolstered by positive feedback about their personality. Subsequent studies, however, failed to confirm these initial results, finding no evidence of a direct relationship between self-esteem and attraction to others (Sprecher & Hatfield, 1982). Does self-esteem, then, have no effect on how eagerly people will respond to the kindness of strangers? Were Freud, Reik, Horney, and Sullivan all wrong?

Actually, they were all right, but they failed to realize that high and low self-esteem have different effects on different aspects of the attraction process (Dion & Dion, 1988). High self-esteem allows people to pursue potential social rewards despite the risk of failure. But since their need for these rewards is less, they may be less motivated to approach those to whom they are attracted. In contrast, people low in self-esteem feel a greater need for positive regard from others and may be especially grateful when they receive it. However, their concerns about appearing foolish or being rejected can prevent them from acting on their feelings of attraction. Thus, those who *lack* a strong need for social rewards feel self-assured in going after them, while those who *have* a strong need lack the confidence necessary for pursuit. Because need and confidence tend to cancel each other out, self-esteem ends up having little overall effect on attraction. In the following sections, we examine some needs that do influence attraction, along with some social difficulties that can reduce a person's confidence in interactions with others.

Social Motives: Affiliation and Intimacy

Building on the pioneering work of Henry Murray (1938) and David McClelland (1951), Dan McAdams (1982) distinguished between two positive social motives that prompt people to seek out social contact:

- *The need for affiliation (NAff):* The desire to establish and maintain many rewarding interpersonal relationships
- *The need for intimacy (NInt):* The preference for warm, close, communicative relationships

The need for affiliation inspires active, controlling social behavior with an emphasis on the breadth and quantity of social contacts. Compared with people whose NAff is weak, individuals with a strong NAff communicate more with other people, find social activities more enjoyable, and react more positively to the company of others (McClelland, 1985). In contrast, the need for intimacy gives rise to more passive, less controlling social behavior with an emphasis on the depth and quality of social relations (McAdams, 1988). Compared with those whose NInt is relatively low, individuals with a strong NInt are more

The need for affiliation motivates people to engage in active social behavior with an emphasis on the quantity of social interactions. Events such as big parties and community festivals provide an opportunity for people to satisfy their need for affiliation by enjoying a large number of social contacts within a short period of time.

trusting and confiding in their relationships and experience a greater sense of well-being (McAdams & Bryant, 1987; McAdams et al., 1984).

In the long run, the need for intimacy may be a better predictor of an individual's overall psychosocial adjustment than is the need for affiliation. Consider the results of a longitudinal study that examined the relationship between the social motives of a group of male college graduates at age thirty and their adjustment status some seventeen years later (McAdams & Vaillant, 1982). The strength of these men's need for affiliation as young adults did not predict their middle-aged adjustment, measured by such factors as job enjoyment and marital satisfaction. But their youthful need for intimacy did foretell their future.

Those who had been high in NInt were better adjusted than those whose NInt had been low. It seems that, as time goes by, attraction based on the quality of relationships may yield greater benefits than attraction based on the quantity of social rewards.

Social Difficulties: Anxiety and Loneliness

NAff and NInt are positive social motives; they stimulate people to seek the rewards of social interactions despite possible failure and rejection. But there is also a troubling side of attraction: wanting to approach someone but being too afraid to do so. It's a common, often painful, experience. Here, we examine two social difficulties that deprive people of the rewarding social interactions they desire.

social anxiety A feeling of discomfort in the presence of others, often accompanied by the social awkwardness and inhibition characteristic of shyness.

Social Anxiety: Fearing Social Failure   **Social anxiety** is the emotion we experience when we are uncomfortable in the presence of others (Leary, 1983). It is often accompanied by *shyness*—social awkwardness, inhibition, and a tendency to avoid social interaction (Bruch et al., 1989; Zimbardo, 1977). People suffering from social anxiety find it hard to make small talk before class, call someone on the phone for a date, enter a room full of strangers, or meet people at parties. Worst of all, their anxiety can trap them into increasingly unpleasant social interactions (DePaulo et al., 1990; Jones & Carpenter, 1986; Langston & Cantor, 1989). Shy and socially anxious individuals tend to reject other people, perhaps because they fear being rejected themselves. They are also withdrawn and ineffective in social interactions, perhaps because they perceive negative reactions even where there are none (Pozo et al., 1991). Not surprisingly, however, other people often do react negatively to interactions with socially anxious individuals. Each of these behaviors strengthens the others, creating the self-perpetuating vicious circle illustrated in Figure 5.2. Caught in a trap, the person can't get out.

For many people, interactions with the opposite sex may be particularly likely to set this trap. Two studies on shyness make the point. In one, shy women were less likely than nonshy women to ask a man for assistance on a task (DePaulo et al., 1989). In another, shy men felt uncomfortable and self-conscious, and their behavior was awkward and inhibited, when they were unexpectedly left alone in a waiting room with a woman (Garcia et al., 1991). Taken together, these results suggest that people who are shy find different types of interactions with the opposite sex to be problematic. Shy women are most likely to withdraw from encounters that require them to be assertive about their needs; shy men find informal, unstructured interactions especially difficult.

Feelings of social discomfort can arise from a number of sources (Leary, 1987). They can be a learned reaction to unpleasant social encounters, as social problems in the past contribute to social anxiety about the future. Social anxiety may also have a significant cognitive component. Socially anxious individuals

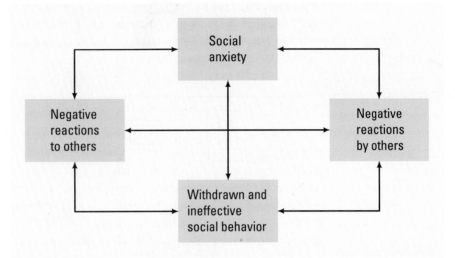

Figure 5.2   Social Anxiety: A Vicious Circle.   Individuals who are socially anxious often experience unsatisfying social interactions. Social anxiety is associated with negative reactions to others, withdrawn and ineffective social behavior, and negative reactions by others. These components can interact and trap the person into an ever-worsening state of social anxiety and dissatisfaction. People who are lonely or depressed can experience similar vicious circles.

often believe that they lack the skills necessary for social success (Maddux et al., 1988). Even if the person actually has such skills, the belief that they are lacking affects feelings and behavior in social situations. When an individual wants to impress others but is convinced that the chances for success are low, social anxiety springs up like a weed in the gap between desire and confidence (Schlenker & Leary, 1982).

Because of the influence of people's thoughts and beliefs on social anxiety, research on ways to reduce it has often focused on cognitive factors. One such approach targets the *attributions* we use to explain what caused our own and others' behavior (see Chapter 3). Consider, for instance, speech anxiety—or, as it's commonly called, stage fright. For countless numbers of people, having to say something in front of an audience is pure agony. The symptoms are distinctly unpleasant: pulse racing, palms sweaty, throat dry, breathing labored, body sometimes shivering or shaking. As the time for participation draws near, people become intensely aware of how anxious they are and wonder if they will be able to exert enough control to get through it all. Getting anxious about being anxious makes the ordeal much worse (Storms & McCaul, 1976).

If you've ever suffered from speech anxiety, this dreadful scenario may be all too familiar. But what if you had an alternative explanation for your distress? When James Olson (1988) led subjects to believe they were hearing a "subliminal noise" that would make them feel tense and anxious, these individuals were

"Hope you don't mind, Charlene—I've always been more comfortable with a script in front of me."

Individuals who are shy may find interactions with the opposite sex particularly difficult. Shy men, for example, feel uncomfortable during informal, unstructured interactions with women. [Drawing by Maslin; © 1992 The New Yorker Magazine, Inc.]

able to give a smoother, more fluent speech than were subjects who had been told that the noise would not have any side effects. At first glance, this seems a very strange result: those who thought the noise would make them anxious performed calmly. What's going on?

misattribution An inaccurate explanation that shifts the cause for arousal from the true source to another one.

The technique that Olson used is called **misattribution**: the explanation of the physiological symptoms of arousal is switched from the true source (such as a person's own anxiety) to a different source (such as noise). This switch helps the individual avoid the cycle of ever-escalating arousal produced by anxiety-provoking explanations: "I'm so anxious; I know I'm just going to fall apart when they call on me." Instead, the subjects in Olson's experiment who were told that the noise would make them tense and anxious could say to themselves, "What, me anxious about having to give a speech? No way. It's just this noise that has me a little rattled."

Under certain conditions, misattribution can improve performance and the ability to cope. However, there are limits to its effectiveness (Olson & Ross, 1988; Reisenzein, 1983). One of the most important is the level of arousal. For misattribution to work, the true cause of arousal must be unclear so that the person can accept a calming alternative explanation. But such ambiguity is possible only when arousal is relatively low. When arousal is intense, people usually know why they feel it and won't believe another explanation (Conger et al., 1976; Nisbett & Schachter, 1966). For this reason, efforts to misattribute the source of *severe* cases of anxiety are unlikely to have much effect.

The misattribution treatment of social anxiety attempts to remove anxiety-producing explanations for a person's emotional state. In their approach to social anxiety, Robert Montgomery and Frances Haemmerlie (1986, 1987) developed a procedure to provide anxiety-reducing explanations for the person's social outcomes. This approach, the *biased interaction technique,* has been used primarily with individuals suffering from "dating anxiety"—social anxiety about interacting with potential romantic partners. Let's see how it works.

Participants in this research were heterosexual male and female undergraduates who reported high levels of dating anxiety. Unknown to them, the experimenters had enlisted opposite-sex confederates who were instructed to act in a friendly and positive fashion with the subjects. Each subject met each confederate twice over the course of several days, thus engaging in two successful social encounters with each of five different people. This procedure confronted subjects with a positive outcome for which all *un*favorable attributions were blocked. Could they attribute their social success to something peculiar about a particular interaction partner? No, they met a number of people and were successful with all of them. Could they conclude that they just happened to encounter some people who were temporarily in an extra-friendly mood? No, their success was consistent over time. The only plausible explanation was that they succeeded because of their own social skills and attractive personal characteristics. This attribution was expected to increase self-confidence and reduce anxiety.

And it did. After their social successes, subjects experienced less dating anxiety. In one study, anxiety was still low six months later, and actual dating had increased. You might wonder, however, what happened when subjects were debriefed and informed that their successful encounters were rigged by the experimenters. According to Montgomery and Haemmerlie, they didn't care! "What seemed of most interest was the fact that they had enjoyed the interactions and felt good about having done well in them" (1987, p. 142).

Despite this reluctance to look a gift horse in the mouth, the biased interaction technique isn't likely to be applied on a widespread basis. It takes a lot of personnel, and therapists and counselors don't like to dupe their clients, even for a noble purpose. Fortunately, though, the general principle behind the biased interaction technique doesn't require elaborate stage management. The critical ingredient is for people to take credit for a success by attributing the cause to their own efforts and characteristics (Brehm & Smith, 1986; Forsterling, 1985). Usually, such attributions do not have to be engineered and manufactured. But they can and should be encouraged.

Loneliness: Feeling Isolated Of all social difficulties, loneliness may be the most common. Loneliness can occur during any time of transition and disrup-

loneliness   A feeling
of deprivation pro-
duced by dissatisfac-
tion with existing
social relations.

tion: during the first year at college, on a new job, after a romantic breakup, when the children leave home. Loneliness is not the same as physical isolation. Almost everyone has at some time felt lonely in a crowd and happy as a clam in complete solitude. Instead, **loneliness** is a feeling of deprivation produced by existing social relations. The individual wants something more, or something different, than what is currently available (Perlman & Peplau, 1981). According to Robert Weiss (1973), there are two kinds of loneliness. In *social isolation,* a person wants but doesn't have a network of friends or relatives; in *emotional isolation,* a person wants but doesn't have a single, intense relationship. Since these two kinds of loneliness share a common emotional core, there is some debate about how clearly they can be distinguished (Russell et al., 1984; Vaux, 1988a).

Contrary to the stereotype of the lonely old person, the loneliest people in American society are adolescents and young adults (Peplau et al., 1982; Rubenstein & Shaver, 1982). In fact, loneliness declines with age, at least up to a point where age-related difficulties such as poor health may interfere with social activities (Schultz & Moore, 1984). Regardless of age, however, the loss of a close relationship increases loneliness. Widowed, divorced, and separated individuals are lonelier than those who are married or have never been married (Perlman & Peplau, 1981).

Loneliness is associated with social anxiety and with depression (Jones & Carpenter, 1986). Indeed, all three of these conditions are characterized by the

Loneliness appears to reach its peak during adolescence and young adulthood. Realizing that many of their peers are lonely, too, may help young people to avoid blaming themselves for their predicament.

debilitating pattern of social interaction described earlier and illustrated in Figure 5.2. Compared with those who are not lonely, lonely people hold more negative opinions about others (Wittenberg & Reis, 1986). They also lack social skills in their interactions with others and are less socially responsive (Jones et al., 1982; Solano & Koester, 1989). And, at least under some circumstances, lonely people elicit negative reactions from others (Jones & Carver, 1991; Rook, 1988).

Depressed individuals exhibit the same general pattern: rejection of others, awkward or inadequate social skills, and negative evaluations from others (Burchill & Stile, 1988; Hokanson et al., 1986). In addition, those suffering social anxiety, loneliness, or depression are socially cautious (Pietromonaco & Rook, 1987; Vaux, 1988b). They tend to avoid interpersonal situations that pose the risk of rejection. Although this caution may reduce social failures, it also cuts down on opportunities for social success. As the saying goes, "Nothing ventured, nothing gained." Overall, there is a strong family resemblance among social anxiety, loneliness, and depression (Anderson & Harvey, 1988). Each one involves personal distress and social dissatisfaction. In Chapter 14, on health, we examine the causes and consequences of depression in more detail.

We have seen how a favorable attribution for social success can build confidence among people who suffer from dating anxiety. Causal attributions also appear to have important effects on loneliness. When Carolyn Cutrona (1982) examined the duration of loneliness among first-year college students, she found that it lasted longer among those who initially blamed aspects of themselves—their shyness, their personality, their fear of rejection, or their lack of social skills—for their lonely feelings.

These explanations are based on an *internal, stable attribution* for loneliness. Internal attributions locate the cause of a condition or event in the person rather than in external circumstances; stable attributions focus on enduring causes rather than on temporary, changeable ones. Blaming themselves by making an internal, stable attribution for loneliness may discourage people from trying to meet others and make friends (Peplau et al., 1979). In contrast, explanations involving attributions that are external, unstable, or both offer some hope that things can be changed for the better (see Figure 5.3). With a hopeful attitude, the lonely person may be able to take a few more social risks and gain more opportunities for social satisfaction. Hope lets us dare to be attracted.

Expectations and Reality

People's expectations and beliefs can often come true by setting in motion a *self-fulfilling prophecy* (discussed in Chapter 3). When a teacher has high expectations for a student, for example, the student performs better; when an interviewer thinks an interviewee is extroverted, the interviewee behaves in an extroverted manner. Is it possible that the same process applies to interpersonal attraction? The answer is yes. A classic study by Mark Snyder and his colleagues

(1977) demonstrates that the power of self-fulfilling prophecies makes its mark on initial encounters as well as in the classroom and during an interview.

Subjects in this experiment were pairs of unacquainted male and female subjects who had no opportunity to see each other before they were assigned to separate rooms. All subjects were given some background information about their partner, and the men also received a photograph of their supposed partner. In fact, however, the photographs had been prepared before the experiment began and were of women who never participated in the study. Half of the male subjects received a photo of a physically attractive woman, while the other half received one of a physically unattractive woman. After seeing the photograph and reading over some demographic information, men rated their impressions of their female partner. All subjects then engaged in a brief audio-only conversation over headphones. Independent judges later rated these conversations. One set of judges listened only to what the men said, and another set listened only to the women.

When Snyder and his colleagues examined the men's initial impressions, they found that those who expected to interact with a physically attractive woman expected her to have more socially desirable personality characteristics as well. Furthermore, analysis of the male portions of the audiotapes indicated that men who believed their partner was attractive were themselves more sociable and outgoing in their conversational behavior. But how did the female subjects

---

Figure 5.3   Causal Attributions for Loneliness.   The explanations that people give for why they are lonely may influence how long they stay lonely. An internal, stable attribution is associated with prolonged loneliness. [Based on Shaver & Rubenstein, 1980.]

	Locus of Causality	
	Internal	*External*
Stability		
Stable	I'm lonely because I'm unlovable. I'll never be worth loving.	The people here are cold and impersonal; none of them share my interests. I think I'll move.
Unstable	I'm lonely now, but I won't be for long. I'll stop working so much and go out and meet some new people.	The first semester in college is always the worst. I'm sure things will get better.

behave during their portions of the conversation? Compared with women interacting with men who received unattractive photographs, those thought to be attractive were, in fact, warmer, more confident, and more animated. Fulfilling their own prophecies, men who expected an attractive partner created one. As in the Greek myth, Pygmalion fell in love with the statue he had carved and brought it to life.

It's easy for fully informed outside observers to see through a self-fulfilling prophecy. A person's expectations influence his or her behavior toward others who, in turn, respond to the way they are being treated. But our own self-fulfilling prophecies may be much more difficult to discern. In those gray areas of social life where reality is not hard and fixed, what we expect may determine what we get. Sometimes, the characteristics of "others" that affect attraction reside in us, not in them.

CHARACTERISTICS OF OTHERS

Although our own needs and expectations certainly influence attraction, the other person isn't just a blank screen on which we project whatever picture we want to see. That person has distinct characteristics that will affect our response. Some characteristics are not apparent until after we get to know someone reasonably well. But there's one that shows up right away: physical appearance. In this section, we examine the effects of physical appearance on interpersonal attraction. We also discuss how an individual's evaluation *of* others can influence that person's attractiveness *to* others. Is it better to be a "liker" or to play hard to get? We'll see.

Physical Attractiveness

Considerable evidence indicates that people are attracted to and react more favorably toward individuals who are physically attractive (Hatfield & Sprecher, 1986). This preferential response to good-looking individuals is particularly strong when we consider *perceptions* of another's appearance. If we perceive someone to be highly attractive physically, our attraction to that individual is greater than to someone we perceive as less attractive. Similar findings, though not quite as strong, have been obtained when physical attractiveness is rated by independent judges. Why is there a bias for beauty?

What Creates the Bias for Beauty?   Four possible reasons have been proposed to account for the bias for beauty. One is *aesthetic appeal*. People, as much as objects, are more rewarding to be with when we find their appearance pleasing. However, what makes a person's looks pleasing to us is not well understood. Some researchers believe that people respond favorably to characteristics that satisfy various interpersonal motives. For example, perhaps smiling increases perceived attractiveness because those who smile are viewed as more likely to meet the perceiver's need for a friendly social interaction (Reis et al., 1990). Or take the fact that women seem to be attracted to men whose facial characteristics combine childlike (big eyes) and mature (prominent cheekbones) features (Cunningham et al., 1990a). For a woman who wants both to nurture someone and to have a mature sexual partner, this combination might be especially rewarding.

On the other hand, aesthetic appeal could be simply a matter of averages. According to research conducted by Judith Langlois and Lori Roggman (1990), a composite of many faces is the most attractive. When undergraduate subjects rated pictures of other undergraduates, they gave more positive ratings to computer-generated composites averaged across sixteen and thirty-two faces than to the individual pictures used in the composites. Ratings of composites based on fewer faces did not differ from those given to individual pictures. Some of the composites used in this study are reprinted on page 213.

Langlois and Roggman maintain that averaged faces are more attractive because, by definition, they are more prototypically facelike. They set the norm from which more unusual faces differ. But is this norm constant across time and place? Would the face that launched a thousand ships off to the Trojan War get more than a passing glance today? Langlois and Roggman believe that it would. They cite previous research indicating substantial consistency in judgments of facial attractiveness among raters of varying ages and different ethnic backgrounds. Still, one wonders. The accepted standard of bodily attractiveness for females has clearly changed a great deal from the ample proportions considered ideal in former times to the thin, athletic form currently in vogue (Ryckman et al., 1989). As for faces, take a look at two other computer-generated composites displayed on page 214. One combines the features of the famous beauties of the 1950s; the other is based on the faces considered beautiful in the 1980s. If you find the latter more attractive than the former, your reaction suggests that the standard of facial attractiveness is subject to change. Of course, if the standard changes, the actual average may not be far behind—as the rest of us do our best to look just like the top of the line.

Despite the importance of aesthetic appeal, it is unlikely that the bias for beauty is simply a matter of sheer viewing pleasure. Another possible explanation is that people overgeneralize from appearance, assuming that those who are attractive on the outside also have attractive personal characteristics. Initial research on this **what-is-beautiful-is-good stereotype** suggested that it included a wide range of assumed characteristics (Dion et al., 1972). However, a recent comprehensive review of the research revealed that the what-is-beautiful-is-good stereotype is more limited in scope (Eagly et al., 1991). Physically attractive individuals *are* seen as more socially competent than those who are less attractive. They are also regarded as more intellectually competent, better adjusted, and more self-assertive. In contrast, physical attractiveness has little

what-is-beautiful-is-good stereotype
The belief that physically attractive individuals also possess desirable personality characteristics.

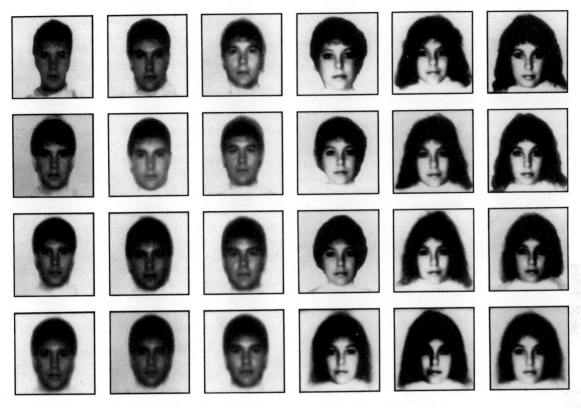

Computer-generated composites were created in order to study people's reactions to averaged faces. The faces here, from left to right, represent six different composite sets. From top to bottom, these sets were based on 4, 8, 16, and 32 faces. Subjects rated the 16- and 32-face composites as more attractive than the individual faces on which they were based. [From Langlois & Roggman, 1990.]

effect on judgments of integrity or of concern for others. And, on one characteristic, what is beautiful is perceived as bad. Physically attractive individuals are viewed as less modest (and more vain) than those who are less attractive.

Despite these limitations, the what-is-beautiful-is-good stereotype still covers a lot of territory. There are two ways in which it could influence attraction. First, believing that someone is good as well as beautiful doubles the pleasure of being with that person. The reward of being in the presence of personal superiority is added to that of being in the presence of a pleasing appearance. Second, the what-is-beautiful-is-good stereotype could produce a self-fulfilling prophecy (Langlois, 1986). Believing that beauty is associated with desirable traits, people may be especially friendly and supportive in their behavior toward a physically attractive person, who may respond by developing the expected characteristics.

The videographic composite on the left combines the beautiful faces of the 1950s: Bette Davis, Audrey Hepburn, Grace Kelly, Sophia Loren, and Marilyn Monroe. The one on the right is based on the beauties of the 1980s: Jane Fonda, Jacqueline Bisset, Diane Keaton, Brooke Shields, and Meryl Streep. Which one do you find more attractive? [From Burson et al., 1986.]

Is this what happens? Are the beautiful, in fact, better? In general, the answer is no. Physical attractiveness (as rated by judges) has little if any association with self-esteem, mental health, personality traits, and intelligence (Feingold, 1992). But what about a more specific advantage? Perhaps the positive social experiences of physically attractive people help them develop good *social skills*. After all, the strongest stereotype held about good-looking individuals is that they are socially competent. Is this part of the stereotype accurate? It seems so. Physical attractiveness (as rated by judges) is associated with being more socially skilled (Feingold, 1992). These skills could explain why beautiful people elicit more positive responses from others. Interactions with the socially adept are usually more rewarding than those with the socially inept.

Still another possible explanation for the social bias in favor of physically attractive people involves the *social profit* that may come from associating with good-looking people. Are we hoping that the glitter will rub off? Research on this possibility indicates that both gender and timing determine profits, and losses, from this association.

When two individuals are observed together, *assimilation* is the rule. People of average attractiveness are judged as more attractive when they are with someone who is very good-looking and as less attractive in the presence of someone who is relatively unattractive. Assimilation occurs with same-sex pairs of individuals, both male and female (Geiselman et al., 1984; Kernis & Wheeler, 1981). Among opposite-sex pairs, the rule stays the same for men, who benefit from being paired with a highly attractive woman (Sigall & Landy, 1973). Evaluations of women, however, are not affected by the looks of a male partner (Bar-Tal & Saxe, 1976).

Now, think about a situation in which individuals are observed separately, one after the other. Concentrating on same-sex comparisons, research on sequential appearances has usually found a *contrast* effect (Cramer et al., 1985; Wedell et al., 1987). The perceived attractiveness of an average person gains from comparison with a less attractive individual, but loses from comparison with someone who is very good-looking. Consider, for example, what happens when people take a look at highly attractive nude photographs (Kenrick et al., 1989). Compared with subjects who viewed abstract art slides or pictures of average-looking nude women, both male and female subjects who had examined very attractive female centerfolds from *Playboy* and *Penthouse* magazines were more negative in their later evaluations of a female nude of average attractiveness. A second study, however, suggested that looking at nature's perfect forms may have a stronger influence on men than on women. Here, only men gave lower ratings of the sexual attractiveness of and love for their own sexual partner after viewing attractive female nudes. Women's ratings were not affected by having seen photos of attractive male nudes.

We have now examined four possible causes for the social bias in favor of physically attractive individuals:

- The joy of looking at them
- The beautiful-is-good stereotype
- Their better social skills
- The desire to benefit from associating with attractive individuals

No single one of these factors completely explains the bias, although they may all make some contribution. But what about the eye of the beholder? Do some people have a stronger bias for beauty than others? In the next section, we examine some possible individual differences in how people respond to the good looks of others.

Is Beauty More Important to Some Beholders?   When you think about people you would like to date, what characteristics come to mind? What do you look for in a potential romantic partner? When researchers asked men and women such questions, men were more likely than women to emphasize the importance of their partner's physical appearance (Berscheid et al., 1971; Buss & Barnes, 1986). And, as we have seen, only men's evaluations of their real-life sexual partners were influenced by viewing photos of extremely attractive female nudes. So are men particularly susceptible to a bias for beauty? Not necessarily. After having actually gone out together, women were at least as responsive as men to the physical appearance of their opposite-sex dates (Byrne et al., 1970). Fortunately, Alan Feingold's (1990) review of the relevant research helps us sort through these apparently contradictory findings. On the one hand, physical attractiveness affects men's romantic attraction more than women's. On the other hand, this gender difference is substantially stronger when people estimate the importance of physical appearance than when they actually interact with someone. Overall, men's estimates are consistent with their behavior, while women tend to underestimate the impact of physical attractiveness.

According to research on the personality trait of self-monitoring, some men are more concerned than others about their partner's appearance (Snyder & Simpson, 1987). As described in Chapter 2, high self-monitors carefully observe their own behavior in social situations; they seek to impress other people. In contrast, low self-monitors are guided by their personal desires and preferences; they usually won't modify their behavior just to make a positive impression. Since men can profit socially from being paired with an attractive woman, Mark Snyder and his colleagues (1985) predicted that the physical appearance of a female dating partner would be more important to men who are high in self-monitoring.

And it is. When male subjects were presented with dating choices that pitted good looks against a good personality, 69 percent of the high self-monitors preferred to date the woman who was physically attractive but difficult to get along with. Among low self-monitors, 81 percent preferred the woman who was relatively unattractive physically but had an engaging and outgoing personality. High self-monitoring men are also less cautious than low self-monitors about getting into romantic situations (Glick, 1985). Thus, it seems that what people are attracted to in a partner affects their romantic pursuits. Those interested in a person's personality need time to get to know the person before deciding to begin a romance. Those who care mainly about external appearance can move in much more quickly—but they may also move on to someone else much sooner (Snyder & Simpson, 1984).

The Real Gains and Losses of Beauty   Although its strength may vary among different individuals, the bias for beauty is real. Beautiful people have a significant social advantage. They are less lonely, less socially anxious (especially about interactions with the opposite sex), more popular, and more sexually experienced (Feingold, 1992). Given such benefits, it's surprising that, as indicated earlier, physical attractiveness and psychological well-being are not strongly correlated. The life of Marilyn Monroe offers a classic example. Still considered one of the most beautiful women of all time, Monroe was chronically anxious and insecure. How could so much praise and popularity have so little effect?

One possible reason is that *actual* physical attractiveness, as perceived by others, may be less psychologically important than *self-perceived* physical attractiveness. People who think they are physically attractive do report higher self-esteem and better mental health than those who think they are less attractive (Feingold, 1992). But judges' ratings of physical attractiveness are only modestly correlated with self-perceived attractiveness. Individuals who do not see the beauty that is so visible to others are less likely to profit psychologically from their appearance.

The life of Marilyn Monroe is a sad illustration of the fact that great physical beauty does not guarantee personal happiness.

Even self-perceived attractiveness may have its drawbacks. People don't just accept social rewards without question; they interpret the meaning of such positive enounters. And individuals who regard themselves as physically attractive may not believe the flattery they receive. Research by Brenda Major and her colleagues investigated this possibility. Do those who think they are attractive trust praise from others? Or do they discount it?

Subjects in this study were men and women who saw themselves as either very attractive physically or quite unattractive. Each subject wrote an essay and was told that the essay would be judged by another subject of the opposite sex, who was described as interested in potential dating relationships. Half of the subjects were informed that this person would be watching them through a one-way mirror while they wrote the essay; the other half were led to believe that their evaluator could not see them. Actually, there was no evaluator, and all subjects received an identical, highly positive evaluation of their work. Subjects were then asked why they thought their essay had been so well reviewed.

As Major and her colleagues expected, subjects' willingness to attribute their positive evaluations to the quality of their work was affected by their physical attractiveness and by whether they thought they were observed while writing their essay (see Figure 5.4). Unattractive subjects felt better about the quality of their work after getting a glowing evaluation from someone who could see them. But attractive subjects felt more confident about their work when the favorable evaluation was from someone who could *not* see them. For the physically attractive, being seen can sometimes promote disbelieving.

Physically attractive individuals may also fail to benefit from the social bias for beauty because of pressures they experience to maintain their appearance. In contemporary American society, such pressures are particularly strong in regard to the body. Although both facial and bodily appearance contribute to perceived attractiveness, an unattractive body appears to be a greater liability than an unattractive face (Alicke et al., 1986). Such a "body bias" can produce a healthy emphasis on nutrition and exercise. It can, however, sometimes lead to distinctly unhealthy consequences. Men, for example, may pop steroids in order to build up impressive muscles. Among women, the desire for a body beautiful often takes a different form.

Women are more likely than men to suffer from what Janet Polivy and her colleagues (1986) call the "modern mania for slenderness." This zeal for thinness is promoted by the mass media. Rosanne Arnold aside, popular female characters in TV shows are more likely than popular male characters to be exceedingly thin; women's magazines stress the need to maintain a slender body more than do men's magazines (Silverstein et al., 1986b). Given the unrealistic

---

Figure 5.4   When Being Seen Leads to Disbelief: Physical Attractiveness and the Discounting of Praise.   Subjects who believed they were physically unattractive were more likely to cite the quality of their work as the reason for receiving a positive evaluation on their essay when they thought they were seen by the evaluator. However, subjects who believed they were attractive were more likely to credit the quality of their work when they thought they were *not* seen. [Data from Major et al., 1984.]

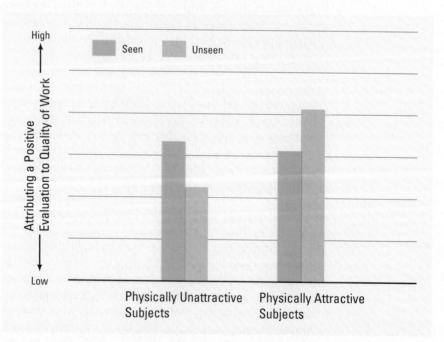

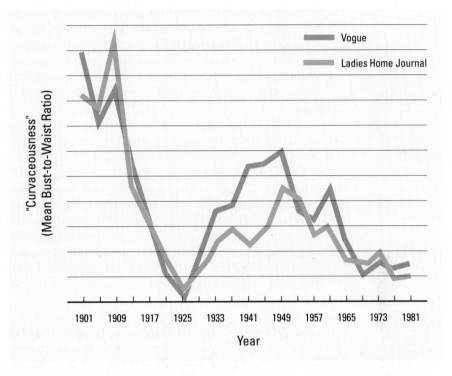

Figure 5.5 **"Curvaceousness" of Models Appearing in Women's Magazines During the Twentieth Century.** Models pictured in *Vogue* and *Ladies Home Journal* were particularly flat-chested in the 1920s and the 1970s. During these decades, boyish figures were seen as the ideal for women. The excessively thin standard for female beauty is still widely promoted in the United States. [From Silverstein et al., 1986a.]

standards set by the mass media, it's not surprising that women more than men are critical of their bodies and worry about their appearance (Pliner et al., 1990; Tiggemann & Rothblum, 1988). In the extreme, an obsession with thinness can contribute to serious disorders such as *bulimia* (food binges that alternate with purging by means of vomiting, laxatives, excessive exercise, or fasting) and *anorexia nervosa* (self-imposed starvation, which can be fatal). Both bulimia and anorexia nervosa are far more common among women than among men (Polivy et al., 1986; Striegel-Moore et al., 1986).

We noted earlier in this chapter that the thin standard of bodily attractiveness is a modern invention. And during recent years, it has grown more stringent. From 1959 to 1978, *Playboy* magazine centerfolds and Miss America Pageant contestants became increasingly thinner (Garner et al., 1980). But when Brett Silverstein and his colleagues (1986a) examined the "curvaceousness" of models appearing in two popular women's magazines from 1901 through 1981 (see Figure 5.5), they found *two* periods during which the bodies of these models were particularly streamlined: the 1920s and the 1970s. Interestingly, both eras were also characterized by greater opportunities for women in education and employment. This correlation cannot prove causation, but it does raise some provocative questions. Is the promotion of a standard of thinness that most women cannot achieve part of a "backlash against feminism" as Naomi Wolf (1991) contends? Is a boyish appearance the price of admission into "a man's world"?

Overall, being beautiful appears to be a mixed blessing. There are some real gains, but there also seem to be some serious losses. This tradeoff between benefits and costs raises the question of long-term effects. In the long run, are beautiful people happier? To answer this question, Ellen Berscheid and her colleagues (1972) compared the physical attractiveness of college students (based on their college yearbook pictures) with their life adjustment when they reached middle age. There was little relationship between youthful appearance and later happiness. Those who had been especially good-looking during college were more likely to have married, but physical attractiveness in college failed to predict later reports of marital satisfaction and contentment with life. This study suggests that, over time, beauty is *not* destiny.

Liking "Likers" Versus Pursuing the Hard-to-Get

Research on physical attractiveness demonstrates that appearance can influence attraction. But the behavior of others is also important, as indicated by the following imaginary exchange in a newspaper advice column:

> Dear Eddy,
>
> I've just read in my social psychology textbook that people like people who are good-looking. Did I really need a textbook to tell me that? I've known it all my life. The problem is that I'm not good-looking. So what can I do? How can I get people to like me? (Surgery is out of the question.)
>
> Yours truly,
> Desperately Seeking Social Survival

Suppose Eddy wrote back:

> Dear Desperate,
>
> You'll be glad to know that things aren't as bad as you think. There's an easy way to get people to like you—without surgery. Just like *them*. In fact, like everyone and everything. People like to be liked, and they like likers.
>
> Best wishes,
> Eddy

Eddy's advice to Desperate is certainly worth considering. As noted in our earlier discussion of balance theory, people do like those who like them. They also like someone who says nice things about them (Sachs, 1976). Moreover,

Eddy is right about "likers." We are more attracted to people who express positive opinions than to those who make negative judgments (Folkes & Sears, 1977; Lynn & Bates, 1985). But Eddy's advice has to be taken with two grains of social psychological salt.

First, likers may pay a price for their upbeat response to life. Others may take their praise for granted and find them less rewarding to be with than people whose compliments have to be earned (Aronson & Linder, 1965). Likers may also be at a disadvantage when it comes to judgments of intellectual ability. Based on her research, Teresa Amabile (1983a) concluded that highly critical "dislikers" are perceived as "brilliant but cruel" while bubbly likers are seen as nice but a bit dim.

hard-to-get effect
The tendency to prefer people who are highly selective in their social choices over those who are more readily available.

Second, even though people like likers, they may be inclined to pursue the hard-to-get. The tendency to prefer people who are selective in their social choices is called the **hard-to-get effect**. This effect is alive and well in many a novel, movie, and TV show. The script is a familiar one. In social psychology, however, the hard-to-get effect turned out to be harder to get than was originally anticipated (Walster et al., 1973).

According to Rex Wright and Richard Contrada (1986), the problem is that being hard to get can *decrease* attraction under certain circumstances. People can say no because they have absolutely no interest in the person approaching them or are involved with someone else. These turndowns are usually turnoffs. In their research, Wright and Contrada eliminated personal rejection and commitment to someone else. Subjects evaluated available dating partners who were presented as being nonselective (said yes to virtually anyone who asked for a date), moderately selective (usually said no, but sometimes said yes), or extremely selective (almost always said no). Since people who are extremely hard to get may be perceived as conceited and arrogant, it was predicted that attraction should be greatest toward the moderately hard-to-get individual. It was. The moderately selective individual was consistently preferred over the nonselective person and was usually preferred over the extremely selective one. A careful approach to selection was more attractive than either indiscriminate liking or universal rejection. It appears that Desperate should temper Eddy's advice with a little moderation.

THE FIT BETWEEN US

In a mosaic, the relationship among the pieces is often more important than the pieces themselves. In attraction, the fit between two people may matter more than their specific, individual characteristics in isolation. As we will see in this section, social psychologists studying the attraction process have found that some arrangements fit better than others.

Complementarity: Is It a Good Fit?

Proverbial wisdom says that "opposites attract," a phenomenon known as *complementarity*. Most of the research on complementarity has examined the effects of opposite needs and personalities on attraction. Don't people who need to dominate others get along best with those who need to be submissive? That sounds like a reasonable, even obvious proposition. Yet research evidence does not indicate that personality complementarity influences attraction (O'Leary & Smith, 1991). On this point, proverbial wisdom seems to have missed the boat.

Resource Exchange: Mix and Match

Another way differences can fit together involves the *resources* people possess. The traditional mix and match between resources pairs the beauty of women with the wealth of men (Elder, 1969). Such an arrangment sounds old-fashioned and out-of-date in this day of more equal opportunity, but is it? Research on the "dating marketplace" (personals ads in newspapers and magazines; information supplied by commercial dating services) suggests that the heterosexual looks-for-money exchange may still flourish (Green et al., 1984; Harrison & Saeed, 1977; Koestner & Wheeler, 1988). Among these advertisers, women offered physical attractiveness and sought economic status; men offered economic status and sought a physically attractive partner. In the words of one investigator, such ads feature "men as success objects and women as sex objects" (Davis, 1990).

These preferences are not restricted to the United States. In a cross-cultural study, David Buss (1989) found evidence for this basic pattern among respondents from thirty-three different countries (including Nigeria, China, Poland, Australia, and Brazil, as well as North America and Western Europe). Men in most countries rated "good looks" in a mate as more important than did women, a result we've seen before. Women rated "good financial prospect" and "ambition and industriousness" as more important than did men. In all the countries included in this study, men preferred to be older than their spouse, while women preferred to be younger.

But having found a pattern, the more interesting—and difficult—task is to account for it. *Why* are these gender differences in mate preferences so widespread? According to **sociobiology**, the application of the principles of evolutionary biology to the understanding of social behavior, this particular heterosexual fit is a product of natural selection (Buss, 1988a; Kenrick et al., 1990). Since reproductive success is crucial for the survival of a species, natural selection should favor the mating patterns that promote the conception, birth, and survival of offspring.

Among humans, female fertility declines after young adulthood. In addition, a woman in good health is more likely to be fertile, to carry a pregnancy to term, and to nurse effectively. Thus, reproductive success should be increased

sociobiology The application of the principles of evolutionary biology to the understanding of social behavior.

for men who mate with a younger, healthy adult woman. In the absence of more direct evidence, men may rely on (attractive) physical appearance to estimate (young) age and (good) health. Women, say the sociobiologists, have different requirements for reproductive success. Because of the length of pregnancy and nursing, mother and child are deemed to benefit from being associated with a powerful man who can provide them with the resources necessary for their well-being. If human ancestors who chose their mates according to these principles did enjoy greater reproductive success than those who chose on other grounds, the genes underlying these mating preferences could have become part of our evolutionary heritage. For sociobiologists, the voice we hear in those personals ads ("DWM seeks expansion of horizons") is that of gender-specific, genetically wired, culture-free desire.

Perhaps. Or maybe it's just a good story. Starting with the status quo and looking back to the evolutionary past, sociobiology has all of the advantages of hindsight. Without more explicit rules for determining which accounts will be accepted and which ones rejected, it's difficult to separate plausible explanations from fanciful inventions (Gould, 1978; Travis & Yeager, 1991). Just because certain behaviors are common does not necessarily imply that they are universal evolutionary products built into our genes. As R. C. Lewontin and his colleagues (1984) remark, "This argument confuses the observation with the explanation. If its circularity is not evident, one might consider the claim that, since 99 percent of Finns are Lutherans, they must have a gene for it" (p. 255).

An alternative to the sociobiological explanation isn't hard to find. Women may have been forced to obtain desirable resources through men because they were denied direct access to political and economic power (Howard et al., 1987). But, today, things have changed; dual-earner couples are the norm. We get a glimpse of this moving socioeconomic picture in research by Scott South (1991). Subjects in this study were a national sample of unmarried and noncohabiting men and women, ages nineteen to thirty-five, who completed questionnaires in 1987–1988. In some respects, their answers were consistent with past indications of the beauty-for-money exchange. Men were less willing than women to marry someone who was not good-looking; women were less willing than men to marry someone earning less than they were; men preferred younger partners while women preferred older ones. But when asked how willing they were to marry someone not likely to hold a steady job, men were not at all enthusiastic. And both men and women said they were more willing to marry someone earning much more than they did as opposed to someone earning much less. Higher educational attainment by a spouse was also evaluated favorably by both men and women. These findings are displayed in Table 5.1. On the whole, men *and* women appear to be looking for someone who can bring home those resources.

Furthermore, there are a number of psychological characteristics that people of both genders prefer to have in a mate (Goodwin, 1990). In Buss's cross-cultural study, for example, both men and women rated "kind-understanding" and "intelligent" as more important than earning power and attractiveness. This

	Responses by					
Willingness to Marry Someone Who Was . . .	Black Males	Black Females	Hispanic Males	Hispanic Females	White Males	White Females
Not good-looking	**3.40**	4.06	**3.87**	3.96	**3.41**	4.53
Earning much less than you	4.18	**3.44**	4.88	**2.99**	4.70	**3.75**
5+ years older	**4.13**	5.20	3.52	4.56	**4.13**	5.40
5+ years younger	4.32	**2.52**	5.01	**2.73**	4.61	**3.03**
Unlikely to hold a job	**2.39**	1.99	**3.29**	1.90	**2.79**	1.47
Earning much more than you	5.23	5.87	5.06	5.59	5.19	5.97
With more education than you	5.09	5.48	5.12	5.51	5.24	5.93

Note: **Bold data** = Relatively unwilling to marry.

Table 5.1   Would You Be Willing to Marry Someone Who Was . . . ?   A national sample of U.S. unmarried adults answered this question by rating a number of factors on a scale from 1 ("not at all willing") to 7 ("very willing"). Their responses to items listed in the top half of the table reflected the traditional heterosexual exchange of beauty/youth for money/status. But on the items in the bottom half of the table, men and women agreed on the importance of economic and educational resources in mate selection. [From South, 1991.]

consistency in mate preferences was also demonstrated when undergraduates were asked to judge 101 acts on how effective they would be in attracting members of the opposite sex (Buss, 1988b). Although some acts were judged differentially effective for men and women, the clear majority were viewed as equally effective for both sexes. Being good-humored, sympathetic, and considerate came highly recommended—for everyone.

Similarity: Liking Those Just Like Us

One of the problems with proverbial wisdom is that it contradicts itself. The same folklore that brought us "opposites attract" also tells us that "birds of a

"I like walks in the rain, old barns, and Edna St. Vincent Millay. Does that ring any bells?"

Since similarity increases attraction, it's a smart move to try to get the other person interested in you by finding some things you have in common. [Drawing by Weber; © 1991 The New Yorker Magazine, Inc.]

feather flock together." But this time, proverbial wisdom is on the right track. Similarity plays a powerful role in interpersonal attraction. This section considers several types of similarity and concludes with a discussion of possible reasons for its influence on the attraction process.

Demographic Similarity   Just name a demographic characteristic (such as age, education, religion, or physical health) and you can find a study indicating that those who go together (such as friends, dates, or spouses) resemble each other in that characteristic (Warren, 1966). But these correlations cannot prove a causal relationship. Though still correlational, a more powerful case would be made if we could measure people's demographic characteristics *before* they meet, and then see if those who are similar like each other more than do those who are dissimilar. This is exactly what Theodore Newcomb (1961) did when he set up an entire college dormitory for the study of interpersonal attraction. Newcomb found that among the residents of the experimental dormitory, those who were similar in demographic characteristics (such as age, college major, and urban versus rural background) liked each other more than did those who were dissimilar.

Similarity in Personality and Mood Like demographics, similarity in personality is associated with interpersonal attraction (Barry, 1970; Boyden et al., 1984). Having similar personalities may also contribute to the maintenance of long-term, enduring relationships. For example, husbands and wives whose personalities are similar report greater marital happiness than spouses who have differing personalities (Caspi & Harbener, 1990). There has been relatively little research on the effects of mood similarity on attraction. However, a recent study by Kenneth Locke and Leonard Horowitz (1990) suggests that such effects could be quite powerful. These investigators found that partners similar in depressive mood (both feeling depressed; neither feeling depressed) were more satisfied with their interaction than were mixed pairs. Perhaps, then, the social rejection of depressed individuals, described earlier in this chapter, is primarily a response of *non*depressed individuals to those whose mood differs from theirs. People in similar moods, even bad ones, seem to experience a rewarding sense of being *simpático*.

Similarity in Physical Attractiveness Have you ever noticed how people react to couples in which one partner is gorgeous and the other quite plain? Their comments can be questioning, sometimes even cruel. Such reactions suggest that individuals are expected to prefer partners whose level of good looks is similar to their own. Social psychologists shared this expectation. But the trouble they ran into offers a good illustration of how results obtained in the laboratory may not always agree with those found in the real world. In laboratory experiments, the evidence for the **matching hypothesis**—the proposition that individuals prefer others who are similar to them in level of physical attractiveness—has been mixed. The matching hypothesis was confirmed in some studies (Berscheid et al., 1971; Stroebe et al., 1971), but not in others (Huston, 1973; Walster et al., 1966).

matching hypothesis
The proposition that people are attracted to and form relationships with those who are similar to them in particular characteristics, such as physical attractiveness.

Research outside the laboratory provided an entirely different picture (Feingold, 1988). Repeatedly, there was evidence of a match in physical attractiveness among romantic couples, including those who were dating, engaged, cohabiting, or married. Similar levels of physical attractiveness are also associated with progress in the relationship. Clients of a professional dating service were more likely to begin and continue dating when they were similar in physical attractiveness (Folkes, 1982). Dating couples who were similarly attractive were more likely than dissimilar couples to grow closer and more in love over time (Murstein, 1972; White, 1980). But married couples are an exception. Research has not typically found an association between marital quality and similarity in physical attractiveness (Murstein & Christy, 1976; White, 1980).

This pattern of findings suggests that similarity in physical attractiveness may be a more important factor early in a relationship. But what if similarity declines? What if one partner becomes more or less attractive than the other as they grow older? Could *changes* in appearance so rekindle the power of a physical mismatch that it could damage even a long-term, committed relationship? A study on sexual problems in marriage raises this possibility (Margolin & White, 1987). These investigators found that husbands who perceived their wife to be losing her looks while their own attractiveness was well preserved reported the greatest incidence of sexual difficulties (such as lack of interest, unhappiness, and unfaithfulness). Perceived discrepancies in physical attractiveness were not related to wives' reports of sexual difficulties.

Just as similarity in physical attractiveness may sometimes matter more to men than to women, it can also be of greater concern to the more attractive member of a partnership. Among college roommates, similarity in physical attractiveness was associated with greater satisfaction with the relationship and greater intention to room together the following year *only* for the more attractive of the two roommates (Carli et al., 1991). Though less attractive individuals reported being envious of a more attractive roommate, they were also well aware of the social advantages: "My roommate helps me to meet other people." As far as they were concerned, the glitter did rub off. Not so for the more attractive individuals. Sensitive to the disadvantages in being associated with someone less physically attractive ("My roommate interferes with my social life"), they were more satisfied with a roommate whose appearance was as attractive as theirs.

At this point, we need to step back and reconsider that sharp discrepancy between the results obtained in the laboratory and those found among actual couples. Why is similarity in physical attractiveness so weak in creating attraction in the laboratory and yet so strongly associated with real-world attachments? The exact reasons for this difference are not known, but there are a number of possible explanations (Aron, 1988). First, laboratory subjects may simply take advantage of the artificial nature of being in an experiment and indulge in "fantasy" choices of the most attractive alternative rather than make the more realistic choices they would make in their daily lives.

Second, since the real-world findings are correlational, they are susceptible to various alternative explanations. Perhaps being attracted to someone produces similarity in physical attractiveness. People who like each other may influence each other on their choice of makeup, clothes, and hairstyle—resulting in a more similar level of physical attractiveness. Or, perhaps, the effect is more subtle. It has been suggested that people who spend time together grow to look alike because they unconsciously mimic each other's facial expressions, which cut the same wrinkles in the same places (Zajonc et al., 1987). This last possibility has sparked a spirited rejoinder (Hinsz, 1989), ensuring us of continuing debate on this topic.

Attitudinal Similarity   So far, we have discussed three types of similarity associated with interpersonal attraction: demographic, personality, and physical attractiveness. A fourth type is attitudinal: sharing similar opinions, beliefs, and values. There are two kinds of attitudinal similarity. *Perceived similarity* refers to

"I read somewhere that when two people live together for a long time they start to look like each other."

[Drawing by S. Gross; © 1988 The New Yorker Magazine, Inc.]

people's beliefs that others share their attitudes, although this may or may not be true. In *actual similarity,* there is an objective match between people's attitudes.

These two kinds of attitudinal similarity differ in how their effects on attraction come about. Again, Newcomb's (1961) experimental dormitory provides a particularly useful setting for understanding the process of attraction. When Newcomb traced attraction across the school year, he found that perceived similarity in attitudes was associated immediately and continuously with liking among the college students in his dorm. Since this association occurred before students knew each other's true attitudes, attraction was the active ingredient. When we are attracted to people, we believe they share our attitudes (Marks & Miller, 1982). In turn, perceived attitudinal similarity enhances liking even further.

But what about the effects of actual attitude similarity on attraction? Here, the time course is much slower, as people get to know each other and find out about each other's attitudes. In Newcomb's research, the strength of the association between actual attitudinal similarity and liking increased gradually

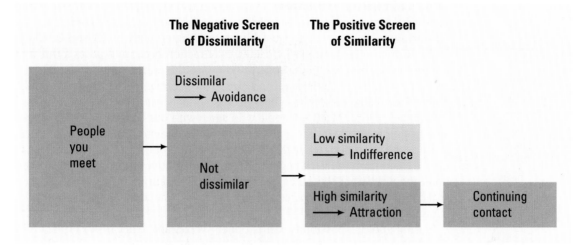

**The Negative Screen
of Dissimilarity**   **The Positive Screen
of Similarity**

Figure 5.6   What Comes First? A Two-Stage Model of the Attraction Process.   Proposed by Donn Byrne and his colleagues (1986), the two-stage model of attraction holds that we first avoid dissimilar others and then approach similar others.

throughout the school year. Actual attitudinal similarity can also be manipulated experimentally. Subjects presented with an attitude survey supposedly filled out by another subject (but actually rigged by the experimenter) like the other person more when that individual's attitudes agree with their own (Byrne, 1971).

Most social psychologists regard attitudinal similarity as a pervasive factor in interpersonal attraction, but Milton Rosenbaum (1986) believes that its effects have been greatly exaggerated. Instead of similarity creating attraction, he maintains that attitudinal *dissimilarity* produces **interpersonal repulsion**—the desire to avoid someone. Similarity, he argues, is expected and often not even noticed, but dissimilarity is surprising and grabs our attention. According to Rosenbaum, we sort out our reactions to strangers on the basis of the unpleasant shock of attitudinal *dissimilarity* rather than the calm reward of similarity.

In reply, Donn Byrne and his colleagues contend that Rosenbaum has greatly underestimated the effects of attitudinal similarity (Byrne et al., 1986; Smeaton et al., 1989). However, they also offer an interesting resolution to the clash between these different points of view. Perhaps, they suggest, two steps are involved in interpersonal attraction. First, people avoid associating with those who are dissimilar. Then, among those who are still left in the social picture, people are attracted to those who are most similar. This two-stage model, shown in Figure 5.6, can be applied to various types of interpersonal similarity, not just attitudinal. For example, perhaps avoiding those who are *dissimilar* in appearance is the first step in the formation of couples similar in physical attractiveness.

**interpersonal
repulsion**   A person's
desire to avoid an-
other person.

Why is Similarity Attractive?   The reason usually offered for why similarity increases attraction is that similarity increases our own self-confidence by reassuring us that others are just like us and agree with us (Byrne & Clore, 1970). Conversely, dissimilarity decreases attraction because it poses a threat to our self-evaluation and our understanding of the world around us. But not everyone would subscribe to this account. For example, perhaps we like similar others and dislike dissimilar others because of *anticipatory reciprocity* (Aronson & Worchel, 1966). Meeting people who agree with our beliefs and opinions, we anticipate that they will like us. Therefore, we like them in (anticipated) return. With people who disagree with us, the anticipation of being disliked leads us to dislike them from the very beginning. In a comparative study, people's expectations about whether the other person would like them had a stronger effect on attraction than did the perceived similarity of the other person's attitudes (Condon & Crano, 1988).

Raising another possibility, Christopher Wetzel and Chet Insko (1982) proposed that the apparent effect of similarity on attraction actually reflects a search for someone who will live up to our ideals. Usually, our ideals are quite close to the way we see ourselves—only better. Based on an elaborate series of studies in which the effects of similarity and idealism were separated, Wetzel and Insko concluded that meeting ideal standards had a greater influence on attraction than did similarity. In a related line of reasoning, some researchers have suggested that the match between partners on physical attractiveness occurs automatically in the interpersonal "marketplace," as people seek the *very* best but have to settle for what's available (Kalick & Hamilton, 1986, 1988). The fact that people end up with partners of similar physical attractiveness would, then, be an accidental by-product of supply and demand rather than a deliberately sought outcome.

These various explanations for the "birds of a feather" phenomenon illustrate an important general point: the demonstration of a phenomenon is not the same as understanding its causes. Much of the progress in social psychology, as in other sciences, comes from subjecting established phenomena to new and more penetrating analyses.

SITUATIONAL INFLUENCES

The attraction mosaic is nearly complete. We have gathered up the individual pieces and carefully considered the way they fit together. But what do they fit *into?* Mosaics are not created in a void, nor is attraction. The development of attraction often requires the right time and the right place. In this section, we consider situational influences that help determine whether individuals experience a close encounter or a near miss.

Proximity

Ironically, we often overlook the single most important factor in attraction. Since almost all initial encounters take place between people who happen to be in the same place at the same time, sheer physical *proximity* is a prerequisite for the vast majority of our social interactions, positive or negative. Being there doesn't guarantee attraction, but attraction usually requires being there. For example, where we live can determine what friends we make. When Leon Festinger and his colleagues studied married-student housing at the Massachusetts Institute of Technology, they found that friendship patterns were strongly influenced by the location of apartments (Festinger, 1951; Festinger et al., 1950). People were more likely to become friends with residents of nearby apartments than with those who lived farther away. Even the alphabet can affect a person's social life. Police academy trainees who were assigned classroom seats in alphabetical order made friends with those adjacent to them (Segal, 1974).

The effects of proximity are not, however, always positive. You don't always love the one you're with. Neighbors can be the best of friends, or the worst of enemies. An investigation of a condominium complex in California found that residents established most of their friendships with people who lived in the

Proximity provides the opportunity for social interactions, but it does not determine their quality. Neighbors can be the best of friends or the worst of enemies.

same housing cluster; most of the people they *dis*liked also lived in the same cluster (Ebbesen et al., 1976). Proximity provides the opportunity for social interactions; it does not determine their quality.

Personal Space: Very Close Encounters   Another spatial factor that can influence interpersonal attraction is **personal space**, that "area individual humans actively maintain about themselves into which others cannot intrude without arousing discomfort" (Hayduk, 1978, p. 118). There are strong individual, situational, and cultural differences in people's preferred distance from one another (Hall, 1966; Hayduk, 1983). But when someone violates our personal space by coming closer than we expect or desire, our reactions to that individual intensify. People we like, we like more when they get close; people we don't like, we like even less up close (Storms & Thomas, 1977). Like proximity, violations of personal space don't create a specific emotional response. Instead, they increase arousal, which magnifies the delights of a positive reaction or the discomfort of a negative one (Knowles, 1980).

personal space The physical distance people like to maintain between themselves and others.

Familiarity: Once Is Not Enough

Both proximity and personal space are spatial concepts—the location of another person relative to us. Another situational factor that affects attraction is *familiarity*, the frequency of actual contact. Folk wisdom takes a dim view of familiarity, which, it says "breeds contempt." But research contradicts the proverb. In most cases familiarity breeds attraction. According to Robert Zajonc (1968), **mere exposure**—simple repeated contact with something or someone—is sufficient to increase attraction.

Imagine, for example, that you had a photograph of yourself developed into two pictures—one that showed you as you actually appear and another that showed your reverse, mirror image. Which picture do you think your friends would prefer? Which one would you prefer? Based on the results of an experiment that compared these two kinds of images, we can confidently predict that your friends would like the regular print and that you'd prefer the reversed photo. Why? The answer is frequency of exposure. Your friends are used to your actual appearance, but you've grown accustomed to your face as it appears in the mirror (Mita et al., 1977). Indeed, the variety of ways in which familiarity can influence attraction is amazing. We like words that occur frequently in our native language more than we like rare words (Zajonc, 1968). Known politicans are preferred to unfamiliar ones (Grush, 1980). Even rats get in on the act. Rats raised on the music of Mozart later preferred new selections from Mozart rather than works by Schoenberg (Cross et al., 1967).

The interpersonal effects of frequent exposure were particularly dramatic in a study conducted by Susan Saegert and her colleagues (1973). In this research, subjects were asked to evaluate a variety of liquids, some of them pleasant (various flavors of Kool-Aid) and some of them unpleasant (weak solutions of

mere exposure The phenomenon in which the more often people are exposed to a stimulus, the more positively they evaluate that stimulus.

vinegar, quinine, and citric acid). While tasting the liquids, subjects were sometimes alone and sometimes in the presence of others. More frequent exposure to others increased attraction regardless of whether subjects were having a pleasant or unpleasant tasting experience when the interactions took place. Even when these interactions were severely constrained, with no talking and only thirty-five seconds of face-to-face contact during each encounter, subjects liked the people they had seen often more than those they had seen less frequently.

The psychological processes responsible for the effects of mere exposure are not precisely understood. Current thinking, however, views habituation and boredom as major factors (Bornstein, 1989). As we get used to people or objects, any concerns that they might pose a threat to our safety or comfort diminish, and positive feelings increase. But what about repeated exposures that continue even after we're very familiar with a person or object? At this point, boredom sets in. Gains in attraction become smaller, and eventually attraction declines (Bornstein et al., 1991). Remember that song on the radio that you couldn't get enough of at first but later couldn't stand to hear again?

Boredom limits the power of familiarity to increase attractiveness. So, it appears, does hostility. If you strongly dislike someone or something to begin with, repeated exposure can increase your *un*favorable opinions (Perlman & Oskamp, 1971). For example, research on student exchange programs indicates that for many students, the stresses and strains of adjusting to a foreign culture create negative attitudes toward the host country (Stroebe et al., 1988). The longer the students who participated in this study stayed in a foreign country, the more negative their attitudes became. Sometimes, despite everyone's good intentions, familiarity does breed contempt.

Affiliation, Attributions, and Overcoming Obstacles

Earlier in this chapter, we described various characteristics and behaviors of individuals that affect attraction. Among them were the need for affiliation, the role of attributions, and the increase in attraction toward someone who is selectively hard to get. Each of these individual factors has a situational parallel. In this section, we examine the situational context of attraction in terms of affiliation, attributions, and overcoming obstacles.

Stressful Situations: Is Togetherness Useful?   In his systematic study of the origins of situationally induced affiliation, described in Chapter 2, Stanley Schachter (1959) compared individuals anticipating a physically painful event with others anticipating a more neutral experience. He found that those expecting to receive electric shocks were more likely to want to wait with others (specifically, others in the same predicament). On the other hand, when Irving Sarnoff and Philip Zimbardo (1961) placed their subjects in the awkward situation of expecting to engage in the embarrassing behavior of sucking on large nipples and pacifiers, the desire to wait with others fell off drastically. How can these divergent findings be reconciled? Why do those in fearful misery love company, whereas those in embarrassed misery seek solitude?

According to Yacov Rofé (1984), there is a simple solution: utility. Rofé proposes that stress will increase the desire to affiliate only when being with other people is perceived to be useful in reducing the negative impact of the stressful situation. And the utility of affiliation depends, in part, on the type of stress. Schachter's subjects had good reason to believe that affiliation would be useful. They would have the opportunity to compare their emotional reactions with those of others to help judge whether they really needed to feel so afraid. For the subjects in the study by Sarnoff and Zimbardo, however, affiliation had little to offer. Embarrassment is a form of *social* anxiety, and being with others is more likely to increase this type of stress rather than reduce it.

Personal characteristics also influence affiliation in stressful circumstances. Some individuals—females and those who are first-born in their family—are more likely than others to affiliate. Perhaps their life experiences (such as social approval for dependent behavior and strong doses of parental attention) have led them to believe that other people can help them adjust to stress. Furthermore, the characteristics of others contribute to whether we want to be with them in a stressful situation. For example, those who can help us cope are more desirable affiliates than those who can't offer any assistance (Kulik & Mahler, 1989). Table 5.2 summarizes the circumstances in which affiliation under stress is most, and least, likely to occur.

Attribute Ambiguity: Undercover Operations Many movies and TV shows comically highlight a common anxiety-provoking experience: calling a potential date for the first time. The nervous caller hopes that attraction is mutual but fears rejection. This risky business of attraction is much less threatening when you operate under the cover of **attribute ambiguity**, circumstances in which the exact causes of a person's behavior are hard to pinpoint (Snyder & Wicklund, 1981).

attribute ambiguity
Circumstances in which the causes of behavior are unclear.

A study by William Bernstein and his colleagues (1983) investigated the effects of attribute ambiguity on people's willingness to approach an attractive member of the opposite sex. Each of the male college students who participated in this research walked into an experimental room arranged as illustrated in Figure 5.7. Directly in front of the door through which the subject entered was a partition dividing the far end of the room into two cubicles. In each cubicle stood two chairs facing a table with a video monitor on it. An attractive young woman was seated in one of the cubicles watching the monitor. The subject was told that the young woman was another research subject (although she was actually a confederate) and that she had been given the same information he was about to receive. Half of the subjects were then informed that a different movie would play on each monitor; the other half were told that because of a

	Factors That Increase Affiliation Under Stress	Factors That Decrease Affiliation Under Stress
Type of Stress	■ Manageable fear	■ Unmanageable fear ■ Embarrassment
Characteristics of the Person Experiencing the Stress	■ First-born ■ Female	■ Later-born ■ Male
Characteristics of the Potential Affiliate	■ Similar to the person experiencing stress ■ Able to handle the stressful situation	■ Dissimilar to the person experiencing stress ■ Unable to handle the stressful situation

Table 5.2 Factors That Determine When People Will Affiliate Under Stress. According to Rofé (1984), stress increases the desire to affiliate with others only when the person under stress believes that the presence of others will reduce that stress. The perception of others' utility for stress reduction is influenced by three major factors.

broken VCR the same movie had to be played on both monitors. At this point, the subject was allowed to choose where he wanted to sit.

Most of the subjects in the same-movie condition probably wanted to enjoy the company of an attractive woman while watching the film, but they faced a difficult dilemma. It takes some nerve for a man to boldly take the seat next to an attractive woman when *he* knows that *she* knows that both monitors will show exactly the same material. What excuse does he have? A subject in the different-movie condition had a much easier time of it. He could always say (and perhaps even believe) that he just happened to like the movie playing on her monitor better than the other movie. With excuse in hand, the guys were free to move in. And they did. Among subjects in the different-movie condition, a whopping 75 percent joined the young woman in her cubicle, compared with only 25 percent in the same-movie condition. An ambiguous situation reduces the personal risks of approaching someone to whom we are attracted.

psychological reactance The theory that people react against threats to specific behavioral freedoms by perceiving a threatened freedom as more attractive and trying to re-establish it.

Psychological Reactance: Barriers to Romance   The final situational context that we will explore in this chapter concerns the circumstances under which opposition creates attraction. The role of opposition as a motivational force is the focus of the theory of **psychological reactance**. According to this

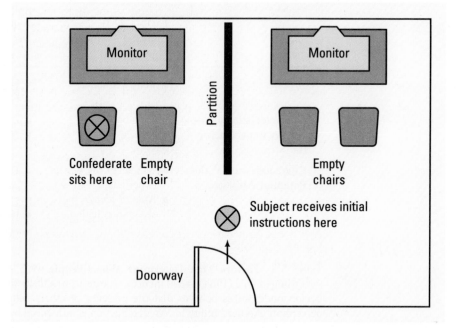

Figure 5.7   Watching a Film With or Without You: The Experimental Room. When male subjects entered the room in this study on attribute ambiguity, they encountered two cubicles, each containing a TV monitor. In one, there was also an attractive female confederate. Some subjects were told that the two monitors would play different movies; others were told that the same film would play on both monitors. Only in the different-movie condition could subjects claim the desire to see a particular film as a good excuse to sit next to the attractive woman.

---

theory, individuals have a set of specific behavioral freedoms—actions, thoughts, and feelings that they feel free to engage in (Brehm, 1966; Brehm & Brehm, 1981). When a specific freedom is threatened or eliminated, the individual will evaluate that freedom more favorably and be motivated to re-establish it.

Sometimes reactance arousal reduces interpersonal attraction (Wright et al., 1992). For example, have you ever played the matchmaker by insisting that your unattached, single friends just *have* to get together? Be forewarned: this tactic can backfire. Motivated to preserve the freedom to make their own romantic choices, your friends may become *less* attracted to each other than they would have without your encouragement. But reactance arousal can also increase interpersonal attraction. The hard-to-get effect described earlier in this chapter could be produced by reactance, with the potential dating partner's selectivity acting as a threat to the freedom to date that person. In this section, we discuss some other barriers to romance that can enhance attraction.

Calling their research "a country and western application to psychology," James Pennebaker and his colleagues (1979) examined the relationship between the passage of time and the attractiveness of potential dating partners. They wondered if Mickey Gilley's song was true to life: Do "the girls all get prettier at closing time"? Interviews with the men and women in three bars in Austin, Texas, indicated that they did—and so did the boys. Members of the opposite sex were seen as more physically attractive as the night wore on. As reactance theory would predict, patrons about to lose their chance to get a date that evening found those still available more desirable.

Although some studies have obtained mixed results, recent research by Brian Gladue and Jean Delaney (1990) succeeded in replicating the closing-time effect. These investigators, however, were not able to identify the psychological process involved. On the one hand, increased attractiveness of the opposite sex did not appear to be created by the blurred vision of a drunken haze. Alcohol consumption was not correlated with attractiveness ratings. On the other hand, the lack of a strong correlation between attractiveness ratings and patrons' reported desire to meet someone of the opposite sex raises some doubts about the reactance theory explanation. But stay tuned. Research on this topic tends to be a favorite for students working on class projects, and we can expect to learn more about it.

If time can be a barrier to romance, it certainly isn't the only one. For example, parents sometimes try to stop what they regard as unsuitable romantic relationships for their children. Long before reactance theory was formulated, William Shakespeare considered how parents' prohibitions affect young love. In *Romeo and Juliet*, parental attempts to block the romantic attachment between Romeo and Juliet don't just fail; they actually increase the couple's love for each other. Was Shakespeare right?

Maybe. In one study, reports by married and unmarried couples revealed a clear association between their romantic love for each other and their perceptions of how much their parents had interfered in their relationship (Driscoll et al., 1972). Those most in love reported the most parental interference. But not all research on parents' reactions to their children's romantic involvements has followed Shakespeare's script. Sometimes children appear to conform to their parents' wishes, getting more involved in relationships their parents support and less involved when they object (Parks et al., 1983). At other times, parental approval or disapproval seems to have little impact on the progress of children's relationships (Leslie et al., 1986). This range of findings indicates the need for further research in order to specify the relationship between parental reactions and children's attractions.

ATTRACTION: A REWARDING EXPERIENCE

Throughout this chapter, we have emphasized the role of rewards. It is rewarding to be with others when they meet our needs for affiliation or intimacy or when they reduce our anxiety or loneliness. For a variety of reasons, being with physically attractive individuals may be particularly rewarding. The rewarding confirmation of our own characteristics and beliefs provides one explanation for the influence of similarity on attraction. And in reactance effects on interpersonal attraction, that which is forbidden or difficult becomes more rewarding to secure. From the initial encounters examined here, we turn in the next chapter to more enduring relationships. Is love, too, a matter of rewards? As you will see, this question has some interesting answers.

REVIEW

THEORIES OF ATTRACTION: THE ROLE OF REWARDS

Attraction is based on rewarding experiences. Being with someone can be rewarding directly or by association. The reinforcement-affect model holds that rewarding experiences in another's presence produce a positive emotional response that creates attraction. Balanced relationships, such as liking those who like us, are also rewarding.

CHARACTERISTICS OF THE INDIVIDUAL

Self-Esteem: Confidence Versus Insecurity

Both high and low self-esteem can increase attraction to others. Those with high self-esteem have the confidence to pursue potential social rewards, but don't particularly need to do so. Those with low self-esteem have a greater need for social rewards, yet may be more reluctant to pursue them.

Social Motives: Affiliation and Intimacy

The need for affiliation produces active, controlling social behavior with an emphasis on the quantity of social contacts. The need for intimacy produces more passive, less controlling social behavior with an emphasis on the quality of social interactions.

Social Difficulties: Anxiety and Loneliness

Social anxiety and loneliness are both associated with unrewarding social interactions, and both are influenced in important ways by attributions. Misattribution, switching the explanation for arousal from the true source to a more neutral one, can reduce anxiety and improve performance. Taking credit for social successes also reduces anxiety and encourages more active social behavior. For people who attribute loneliness to their own personal characteristics (an internal, stable attribution), loneliness lasts longer.

Expectations and Reality

By means of a self-fulfilling prophecy, how attractive we expect others to be can determine how attractive they actually become.

CHARACTERISTICS OF OTHERS

Physical Attractiveness

People respond more favorably to physically attractive individuals. Possible reasons for this bias for beauty include aesthetic appeal, the what-is-beautiful-is-good stereotype, more skillful social behavior by physically attractive individuals, and the desire to increase one's own perceived attractiveness through association with attractive others. The physical attractiveness of a potential romantic partner influences men's attraction more than women's. Among men, the physical appearance of a dating partner is more important if a man is a high rather than a low self-monitor. Individuals judged by others to be physically attractive enjoy greater social success than those who are less attractive, but they are not particularly likely to experience greater psychological well-being. On the other hand, people who judge themselves as being attractive *are* more likely to experience greater psychological well-being, but they also tend to discount the praise they receive for nonsocial endeavors. Social pressure to maintain the very slender body currently regarded as attractive may contribute to serious eating disorders, especially among women. In the long run, physical attractiveness does not predict happiness.

Liking "Likers" Versus Pursuing the Hard-to-Get

People like those who like them and are more attracted to those who express positive attitudes. But indiscriminate likers can be taken for granted and seen as less intelligent than dislikers. In addition, people prefer those who are selectively hard to get over those who are nonselective and, usually, over those who are extremely selective.

THE FIT BETWEEN US

Complementarity: Is It a Good Fit?

The available evidence indicates that complementarity in needs or personality does *not* affect attraction.

Resource Exchange: Mix and Match

Just as men regard physical attractiveness as particularly important in an opposite-sex mate, so do women regard economic success. These differential preferences could reflect evolutionary processes or may be due to traditional social restrictions on women's political and economic power. Today, both men and women value earning power in a spouse.

Similarity: Liking Those Just Like Us

Four types of similarity are associated with greater attraction: demographic, personality and mood, physical attractiveness, and attitudinal. For physical attractiveness, the matching hypothesis—the proposition that people pair up with others whose level of attractiveness is similar to their own—has received greater support in investigations of actual couples than in laboratory experiments. It has been argued that instead of similarity producing attraction, *dissimilarity* produces repulsion. Alternatively, people may react first to dissimilarity and then later to similarity. Similarity may increase attractiveness because it is reassuring, implies that the other person will like us, or is simply the best choice available.

SITUATIONAL INFLUENCES

Proximity

Proximity sets the stage for social interactions but does not determine their quality. A person's enemies as well as friends will typically be those who are located nearby.

Violations of personal space increase arousal, which can make a positive interaction even better or a negative interaction even worse.

Familiarity: Once Is Not Enough

In general, more frequent contact with someone is associated with greater attraction, at least until boredom sets in. However, repeated contact with someone who is strongly disliked can increase hostility.

Affiliation, Attributions, and Overcoming Obstacles

The desire to affiliate with others will increase in stressful situations when being with others is perceived to be useful in reducing stress. This perception is influenced by the type of stress, by our own characteristics, and by characteristics of the other people. An ambiguous situation allows people to reduce the personal risk of rejection in approaching those to whom they are attracted. Situational barriers making it harder to be with someone (such as closing time at a bar or parental interference) can increase attraction.

ATTRACTION: A REWARDING EXPERIENCE

The factors described in this chapter influence attraction by affecting the level of rewards available in an initial encounter.

Intimate Relationships

6

Preview

This chapter begins by *defining intimate relationships*. Among the ways to get *from attraction to love*, two are considered in detail: *building a relationship* through the gradual accumulation of rewards and experiencing different *types of relationships*. Next, *relationship issues* of sexuality, jealousy, and social power are discussed, followed by an analysis of *conflict in relationships*. The concluding section describes some important factors involved in *coping after a relationship ends*.

What is the most important aspect of your life? What matters more to you than anything else? Although each of us has different desires and aspirations, there are some major life goals that many people have in common:

1. A satisfying and enduring relationship with a romantic partner
2. A good education
3. A successful career
4. Contributing to a better society
5. Financial security
6. Physical fitness

Now, force yourself to make some choices. Compare the goal of having a good relationship with *each* of the other goals in turn. If you could reach only one goal from each pair, which would it be?

When researchers administered a similar questionnaire to 300 college students, they found that 73 percent of their respondents said they would sacrifice a majority of their other life goals rather than give up a satisfying relationship (Hammersla & Frease-McMahan, 1990). For most people, having a strong and enduring relationship with a loving partner is very important.

But what, in fact, are the chances of having such a relationship? Not very good, if marriage is any indicator. It is now estimated that some 50 percent of first marriages taking place in the United States today will end in divorce (Norton & Moorman, 1987). If both divorce and separation are included, the lifetime rate of marital disruption among today's young adults may be as high as 64 percent (Castro Martin & Bumpass, 1989).

This dramatic discrepancy between the kind of relationship that most of us want and the kind many of us are likely to get is a hallmark of our time and our society. Although divorce rates have increased in all Western countries, the United States has the dubious distinction of leading the pack (Phillips, 1988). And in some countries, divorce is still an uncommon occurrence. In Japan, for example, the divorce rate is less than 25 percent of that in the United States (Cornell, 1989).

The extraordinarily high level of marital dissolution in American society has given a new sense of urgency to the study of relationships. There is, of course, no magic formula for a satisfying relationship. But bringing to bear your own beliefs, values, and personal experiences on the information presented in this chapter can be a useful endeavor. If we are to improve our relationships in the future, there is no better way to begin than by increasing our understanding of those we have at present.

DEFINING INTIMATE RELATIONSHIPS

Although there are many significant relationships in people's lives, most research in social psychology has concentrated on adult relationships between friends,

intimate relationships Close relationships between two adults involving at least one of the following: emotional attachment, fulfillment of psychological needs, and interdependence.

dating partners, lovers, and spouses (Brehm, 1992; Duck, 1988; Hendrick, 1989). These **intimate relationships** involve at least one of three basic components:

- Emotional attachment, feelings of affection and love
- Fulfillment of psychological needs of the partners, such as sharing feelings and gaining reassurance (Weiss, 1969)
- Interdependence between the individuals, each of whom has a meaningful and enduring influence on the other (Berscheid & Peplau, 1983)

Ideally, an intimate relationship provides all three elements: love, fulfillment, and interdependence. In some relationships, however, only one or two are present. For example, a summer romance usually involves an intense emotional attachment, but once the summer is over people often resume their own independent lives. In contrast, an "empty shell" marriage can involve considerable mutual dependence as spouses coordinate daily activities and future plans, but emotional attachment is weak and psychological needs are not met. Different combinations of love, fulfillment, and interdependence create an immense variety of intimate relationships.

Indeed, intimate relationships come in all shapes and sizes. Some are sexual; some are not. Sexual orientation also varies: heterosexual, homosexual, bisexual. Some partners make a strong commitment to a long-lasting relationship; others are merely dropping by for a brief stay. Feelings about relationships run the gamut from joyful to painful; from loving to hateful. And the intensity of those feelings ranges all the way from mild to megawatt. Thus, each intimate relationship is a unique partnership between two unique individuals. It is still possible, however, to sort out some of the basic factors that affect the development, quality, and endurance of a relationship. We start by tracing the road that runs from attraction to love.

FROM ATTRACTION TO LOVE

Psychologically speaking, there's quite a distance from the attractive initial encounters described in Chapter 5 to the intimate relationships discussed in this chapter. How do we get from one to the other? Although various maps are drawn (Surra, 1990), three basic forms of locomotion have received the most attention: (1) in stages, (2) step by step, (3) by leaps and bounds.

Stages of Relationship Development

stage theories Theories reflecting the view that relationships develop through a specific set of stages in a specific order.

Stage theories of relationship development propose that relationships go through a specific set of stages in a specific order. One perspective divides the path from attraction to love into immediate versus delayed effects (Berg, 1984; Neimeyer & Neimeyer, 1983). In this two-stage model, one set of characteristics produces initial repulsion or attraction, and then a different set determines whether an established relationship remains casual or grows into a close and meaningful attachment (Davis & Oathout, 1987; Duck, 1977).

Bernard Murstein's (1986, 1987) *stimulus-value-role (SVR) theory* ups the number of stages to three. According to SVR theory, intimate relationships proceed from a stimulus stage, where attraction is based on external attributes such as physical appearance, to a value stage where attachment is based on similarity of values and beliefs. The final transition is to a role stage, in which commitment is based on successful performance of relationship roles, such as husband and wife. Although all three factors are supposed to have some influence throughout a relationship, each one is said to be prominent during only one stage (see Figure 6.1).

In evaluating any stage theory, the critical question concerns *sequence*. For example, does the value stage always precede the role stage? Or might a couple work out roles before exploring whether their values are compatible? Some investigators have concluded that evidence for a fixed sequence of stages in intimate relationships is weak (Leigh et al., 1987; Stephen, 1987). The difficulty in coming up with a standard sequence for all relationships is illustrated by a series of studies on newlywed couples (Surra & Huston, 1987). Based on subjects' retrospective reports of how their relationship developed, this research indicates that a couple's progress toward marriage takes a number of different paths. Significant shifts in relationship development do not occur in the same order for all couples, nor do all couples go through the same shifts. Instead, the course of relationship development appears to vary widely.

Quantitative and Qualitative Differences in Relationships

If intimate relationships don't all follow the same script, what does account for how they change? Every relationship has some sort of developmental history: the ups, the downs, the stalls, the accelerations. What pushes a relationship up, pulls it down, or keeps it steady? To answer this question, we could go back to the attraction hat and pull out the same rabbit: rewards. Love, we might say, is just like attraction, only more so. Both depend on experiencing positive emotions in the presence of another person, but love requires more rewarding experiences than does attraction. Step by step, as rewards pile up, love develops. Or, step by step, as rewards diminish, love erodes.

But some would view this emphasis on quantity as misplaced. It's easy to see their objection. Just think about your own experience. Are your feelings toward someone you love simply a more intense version of your feelings toward someone you like? Is the love of a close friend the same as the love of a romantic partner? If your answer to either of these questions is no, you can appreciate the argument that there are qualitative differences between various kinds of affection. According to this perspective, a great leap is required to take us from liking to loving, and love itself comes in different forms.

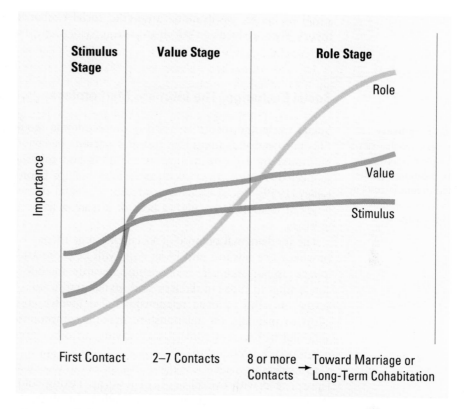

Figure 6.1 Stages of Courtship in SVR Theory. According to Murstein's stimulus-value-role theory, each stage in a relationship is characterized by one dominant factor. The theory maintains that these stages occur in a fixed sequence: stimulus first, then value, and then role. [From Murstein, 1987.]

Each of these versions of how we get from attraction to love has something to offer. As relationships develop and change, *both* step-by-step quantitative factors and leaps-and-bounds qualitative factors are likely to be involved (Sternberg, 1987). Progress on the road from attraction to love depends on the quantity of fuel in the tank *and* on the kind of engine providing the power. The next section takes a closer look at the quantitative, cost-accounting approach to building a relationship. Qualitative differences between various types of relationships are considered later in the chapter.

BUILDING A RELATIONSHIP

Social exchange is, by far, the most widely employed framework for analyzing quantitative factors in relationships. After describing the basic components of social exchange, we examine a specific social exchange model called equity theory. Then we focus on self-disclosure, a particularly intimate social exchange.

Social Exchange: The Intimate Marketplace

social exchange A perspective that views people as motivated to maximize benefits and minimize costs in their relationships with others.

Social exchange theory is based on an economic model of human behavior. This perspective assumes that just as a person's behavior in the marketplace is motivated by a desire to maximize profits and minimize losses, these same motives determine behavior in social relationships (Homans, 1961; Thibaut & Kelley, 1959). Social exchange provides a general framework for analyzing all kinds of relationships—with a boss or a teacher as well as with a friend or a lover.

The fundamental premise of social exchange theory is that relationships that provide more rewards and fewer costs will be more satisfying and will endure longer. In an intimate relationship, rewards include companionship, love, consolation in times of distress, and sexual gratification if the relationship is a sexual one. But intimate relationships also involve costs: spending time and effort to maintain the relationship, making compromises to keep the peace, suffering in times of conflict, and giving up other opportunities in order to continue the relationship.

Considerable evidence suggests that the endurance of an intimate relationship is associated with overall levels of rewards. Dating couples who initially have many rewarding interactions are less likely to break up than those who start out with relatively few rewards (Lloyd et al., 1984). Dating couples who experience greater increases in rewards as their relationship continues are more likely to stay together than are those who experience only small increases or suffer declines (Berg & McQuinn, 1986; Rusbult, 1983).

But what about costs? Early in a relationship—during the "honeymoon" period—costs may be relatively unimportant (Hays, 1985). Honeymoons can't last forever, though. In her study of dating couples, Caryl Rusbult (1983) found that costs first entered into the equation at about three months. Before that, costs were not related to satisfaction; after that, reports of increasing costs were accompanied by diminished satisfaction with the relationship. In established relationships, both rewards and costs enter into the equation. Married couples (Margolin & Wampold, 1981) and cohabiting gay and lesbian couples (Kurdek, 1991a) who perceive rewards to be high and costs low are more satisfied with their relationship.

comparison level (CL) The average, general outcome an individual expects in a relationship.

Rewards and costs do not, however, occur in a psychological vacuum. Each partner brings to a relationship certain expectations about the balance sheet to which he or she is entitled. John Thibaut and Harold Kelley (1959) coined the term **comparison level (CL)** to refer to this average, expected outcome in relationships. A person with a high CL expects to have rewarding relationships; a person with a low CL expects to have unrewarding relationships. Relationships that meet or exceed a person's expectations are more satisfying than those that fall below expectations (Michaels et al., 1984).

Outcome expectations provide an anchor by which to judge satisfaction. Another kind of expectations, those about alternatives to the relationship, create a context for commitment. Here, too, Thibaut and Kelley (1959) coined the term. **Comparison level for alternatives (CLalt)** refers to people's expectations about what they would receive in an alternative relationship or lifestyle. If the rewards available in such alternatives are believed to be high, a person will be less committed to staying in the present relationship (Drigotas & Rusbult, 1992; Rusbult et al., 1991). But when people have few alternatives (a low CLalt), they tend to remain—even in an unsatisfying relationship that fails to meet their general expectations (CL). Not only do alternatives influence commitment; commitment also influences alternatives. Committed individuals are less interested in alternative partners, perceiving them as less attractive (Johnson & Rusbult, 1989; Simpson et al., 1990).

The final factor in the basic model of social exchange is investment. An **investment** is something an individual puts into a relationship that he or she cannot recover if that relationship ends (Kelley, 1983). If you don't like the way a relationship is working out, you can pack your clothes, grab your stereo, and take your cat. But what about all the time and effort you put into trying to make it last, and all those other romantic possibilities and career opportunities you gave up? Investments increase commitment (Rusbult, 1980a, 1980b). Because of those things we can't take with us, we're more likely to stay.

The social exchange framework of rewards, costs, CL, CLalt, and investments is diagrammed in Figure 6.2. This perspective allows us to make sense of many puzzling aspects of our own and others' personal lives. Why is Sarah always content with her relationships, while Rebecca never seems satisfied? Perhaps because Rebecca has much higher expectations about relationships—a higher CL—than Sarah does. Why does Michael hang out with Peter, whom everyone else avoids? Perhaps because Michael has fewer alternatives—a lower CLalt than others have. And why do people sometimes stay in extremely unpleasant, even abusive relationships? Perhaps because they fear that efforts to leave will incur the very high cost of greater violence; perhaps because they lack the economic alternatives to make a decent life on their own (Dutton, 1987).

Investments may also influence a person's response to an abusive relationship (Strube, 1988). In one study, abused women were more likely to remain in the relationship if (1) it had lasted more than four years, and (2) they spontaneously cited "love" as a reason for not leaving (Strube & Barbour, 1983). Sadly, the more time and affection these women had invested, the harder it was for them to cut their losses and protect themselves by leaving.

Perceptions of Rewards and Costs   The language of social exchange comes straight from a certified public accountant. Rewards, costs, investments—it all sounds so cold and objective. But it isn't. The entries in the social exchange

---

comparison level for alternatives (CLalt) The average, general outcome an individual expects from alternative relationships or lifestyles.

investment Resources put into a relationship that cannot be retrieved if that relationship ends.

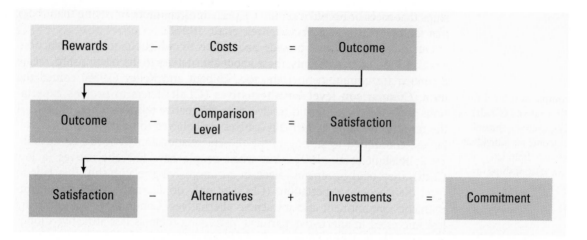

Figure 6.2   Relational Building Blocks: Factors That Influence Satisfaction and Commitment in a Relationship. The building blocks of social exchange are rewards, costs, comparison level, comparison level for alternatives, and investments. These factors produce the overall outcome of a relationship and influence satisfaction and commitment.

ledger are based on some very slippery psychological arithmetic. Rewards and costs, for instance, are not necessarily perceived in the same way by different people. Have you ever given a present that you thought was wonderful to someone who obviously was *not* thrilled to get it? People tend to assume that whatever they find rewarding, others will too (Wills et al., 1974). When this assumption is wrong, the giver who genuinely tries to be rewarding may be met by an indifferent or even suspicious reaction: "Who's this for, anyway—me or you?"

Perceptions of costs can also differ. In their research, Michael Ross and Fiore Sicoly (1979) asked married partners to rate independently how they divided up the responsibility for twenty mutually beneficial activities—such as cleaning house, caring for children, and planning leisure activities. Since taking responsibility for such activities is a cost of living with another person, each spouse was indicating how much he or she had to "pay" for the benefits received. The results were striking. In the vast majority of couples, at least one of the spouses overestimated his or her own costs. As described in Chapter 2, people often display an *egocentric bias,* exaggerating their own role in events. Accordingly, people are more sensitive to what they contribute to a relationship than to the partner's contributions. But the egocentric bias can be overcome, and individuals who are more generous in recognizing their partner's efforts report greater relationship satisfaction (Fincham & Bradbury, 1989).

Rewards and costs aren't unique in having a large psychological component. The other factors in the social exchange model are also influenced by subjective evaluations that may not correspond to reality as others would see it. General expectations for the relationship (CL) can be inappropriate; expectations for alternatives (CLalt) can be vastly overrated or underestimated; and memories about just what investments were made can be faulty. Social exchange provides a useful framework for understanding why some relationships thrive and others fade. It cannot, however, turn the psychological complexities of human behavior into simple cost accounting.

equity theory The theory that people are most satisfied with a relationship when the ratio between benefits and contributions is similar for both partners.

Equity: A Balanced Arrangment **Equity theory** is a specific type of social exchange model (Messick & Cook, 1983; Walster et al., 1978a). This theory maintains that people are most satisfied with a relationship when the ratio between the benefits derived and the contributions made is similar for both partners. Benefits from a relationship are positive when your rewards exceed costs, negative when your costs exceed rewards. As you can see from Table 6.1, contributions can also be positive or negative. Though more precise mathematical models are available (Farkas & Anderson, 1979), the basic equity equation is simply put:

$$\frac{\text{Your Benefits}}{\text{Your Contributions}} = \frac{\text{Your Partner's Benefits}}{\text{Your Partner's Contributions}}$$

Equity is different from equality between partners. From the viewpoint of equity theory, it's the balance that counts. If one partner obtains more benefits from the relationship but also makes a greater contribution to it, the relationship is still equitable. In an inequitable relationship, the balance is disturbed. One of the partners (called the *overbenefited*) receives more benefits than are deserved on the basis of contributions made, while the other partner (called the *underbenefited*) receives fewer benefits than are deserved.

Originally, equity theorists proposed that both overbenefit and underbenefit were unhappy states. Individuals who are underbenefited should feel angry because they are working harder than the partner for their rewards. The overbenefited should feel guilty because they are benefiting unfairly. Both kinds of inequity have been shown to produce negative emotions among college-age dating couples (Walster et al., 1978b), married couples (Schafer & Keith, 1980), and the friendships of elderly widows (Rook, 1987).

In terms of satisfaction with a relationship, however, being underbenefited appears to have a much greater negative effect than does being overbenefited (Austin & Walster, 1974). An extensive program of research by Elaine Hatfield (formerly Walster) and her colleagues indicates that the underbenefited are dissatisfied and discontented (Hatfield et al., 1982; Utne et al., 1984). In sharp contrast, overbenefited individuals resemble those who perceive their relationship as equitable; both report high levels of satisfaction and contentment. Apparently people prefer to receive too much rather than too little—even if they feel guilty about it.

Determining whether a relationship is equitable is a complicated cognitive process. You have to tally up your own benefits and contributions, compute

Benefits	Rewards	Costs
Personal	Having a partner who is socially skilled	Having a partner who is socially inept
Emotional	Being loved by the partner	Not being loved by the partner
Day-to-day	Having a partner who provides satisfying companionship	Having a partner who does not provide satisfying companionship
Opportunities	The positive life experiences that depend on being in a relationship	Giving up certain opportunities in order to maintain the relationship
Contributions	**Positive**	**Negative**
Personal	Being socially skilled	Not being socially skilled
Emotional	Loving your partner	Not loving your partner
Day-to-day	Providing satisfying companionship to your partner	Not providing satisfying companionship to your partner

Table 6.1   Assessing Equity: Benefits and Contributions.   In an equitable relationship, your ratio of benefits to contributions is similar to your partner's. Benefits from the relationship are calculated by subtracting costs from rewards; contributions are calculated by subtracting negatives from positives. [Based on Hatfield (Walster), 1978.]

your partner's benefits and contributions, and compare the two. Rodney Cate and Sally Lloyd (1988) have their doubts about whether people go to all this trouble when much simpler calculations might suffice. In a series of studies, these researchers found that the absolute level of rewarding outcomes was a better predictor of relationship satisfaction and endurance than was either equity or equality of rewards (Cate et al., 1988). The more good things people said they received from the relationship, the better they felt about it.

Differences among individuals may be one reason why equity theory has an uneven track record in predicting relationship satisfaction. Some people expect and prefer immediate, quid-pro-quo reciprocity in their relationships. Whenever they give, they want to receive as soon as possible. Others are more giving and forgiving, having less of an *exchange orientation* (Murstein et al., 1977). Perceived equity in the relationship is more closely associated with relationship satisfaction for those who have a strong exchange orientation (Buunk & Van Yperen, 1991). Not surprisingly, people who regard relationships as exercises in cost accounting are more sensitive to equity considerations.

Exchange orientation is a relatively stable difference between individuals; people who have it now usually have it later too. But what about situational

"We had the usual exchange of gifts—she gave me this diamond collar, and I ate all my dinner."

Overbenefited individuals are often satisfied and content with their inequitable relationship. [Drawing by Lorenz; © 1991 The New Yorker Magazine, Inc.]

factors that might induce the tendency to count one's blessings or the lack of them? Is it possible, for example, that *dissatisfaction* with a relationship creates the perception of inequity, especially underbenefit? It's an interesting hypothesis, directly opposite to the fundamental premise of equity theory that inequity creates dissatisfaction. The evidence at hand, however, supports the original recipe. For women especially, perceived equity predicts relationship satisfaction better than satisfaction predicts perceived equity (Van Yperen & Buunk, 1990). Although this correlational study cannot prove causation, its results are consistent with the notion that, at least among some individuals, equity is a cause of relational satisfaction.

Self-Disclosure: Growing Closer

Think for a moment about your most embarrassing moment, your most cherished ambitions, and your sex life. Would you bare your soul on these private

self-disclosure Revelations about the self that a person makes to other people.

theory of social penetration A theory about the development of close relationships that emphasizes the gradual increase in the breadth and depth of exchanges between partners.

matters to a stranger? How about to a casual acquaintance, a friend, or a lover? The willingness to reveal intimate facts and feelings to someone else, called **self-disclosure**, plays a major role in intimate relationships (Derlega & Berg, 1987; Jourard, 1964). According to Irving Altman and Dalmas Taylor (1973), self-disclosure is a fundamental social exchange that occurs as relationships develop. Their **theory of social penetration** holds that relationships progress from superficial exchanges to more intimate ones. At first, people give relatively little of themselves to another person and receive relatively little in return. When initial encounters are rewarding, however, the two individuals begin to give more. Their exchanges become *broader,* involving more areas of their lives, and *deeper,* involving more important and sensitive areas. As depicted in Figure 6.3, the social interaction between them grows from a narrow, shallow sliver to a wider, more penetrating wedge.

A variety of activities may be involved in the social penetration process, such as sharing possessions and engaging in physical expressions of affection, but self-disclosure has been the most clearly documented. In their research, Altman and Taylor (1973) found that the longer people interacted with one another, the more topics they were willing to discuss (increased breadth of self-disclosure) and the more personally revealing they became (increased depth of self-disclosure). More extensive and intimate self-disclosure is also associated with the quality of a relationship. Partners who self-disclose more to each other report greater emotional involvement in dating relationships (Rubin et al., 1980) and greater satisfaction in marriage (Hansen & Schuldt, 1984).

In addition to the general association between self-disclosure and relationship development, specific phases in a relationship are characterized by specific patterns of self-disclosure. During an initial encounter between strangers, *self-disclosure reciprocity* is the rule. It is polite to match the level of self-disclosure offered by new acquaintances, disclosing more if they do so and drawing back if their self-disclosure declines (Cunningham et al., 1986). Once a relationship is well established, however, strict self-disclosure reciprocity occurs much less frequently (Altman, 1973; Derlega et al., 1976).

Among couples whose relationship is in trouble, the pattern of self-disclosure varies. For some, both breadth and depth decrease as partners withdraw from their relationship (Baxter, 1987). For others, breadth of self-disclosure contracts as satisfaction declines, but depth of self-disclosure actually increases—as the distressed partners bombard each other with cruel and angry statements (Tolstedt & Stokes, 1984). In this case, the social *de*penetration process resembles neither the sliver of a superficial relationship nor the wedge of a satisfying intimate relationship—but rather a long, thin dagger aimed straight at the heart.

Gender Differences in Self-Disclosure and Friendship   On average, women tend to self-disclose more than men do, particularly when highly personal and emotional material is involved (Cozby, 1973; Morton, 1978). But this

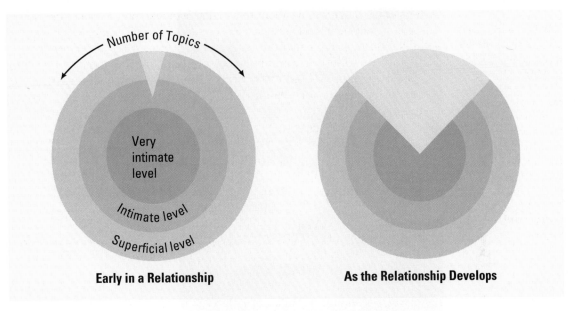

Figure 6.3 From a Sliver to a Wedge: The Theory of Social Penetration. According to the theory of social penetration, as a relationship becomes closer, partners increase the breadth of their exchanges (covering a wider range of topics) and also the depth (revealing more intimate information).

gender difference is by no means uniform. Cultural norms and situational factors have a strong impact on self disclosure (Hill & Stull, 1987). Consider, for example, a study by Ladd Wheeler and his colleagues (1989) that compared the everyday social behavior of American students with that of Chinese students in Hong Kong. Overall disclosure (self and other combined) was higher among the Chinese than among the Americans. When subjects were engaged in interactions with the opposite sex, no gender differences were found. In same-sex interactions, however, American women reported more disclosure than did American men, while Chinese men and women did not differ.

Since subjects in this cross-cultural study recorded only interactions that lasted ten minutes or more, we can assume that they knew most of the people they were interacting with reasonably well. But what happens when strangers meet? Studies conducted in the United States indicate that the gender difference during initial encounters lies in the recipient of the disclosure, not its source. Both men and women are more willing to disclose *to* a woman than to a man (Derlega et al., 1985; Rubin, 1974).

The general tendency for women to either initiate or elicit greater self-disclosure suggests that women's friendships might be more intimate than men's. And that seems to be the case. Women's friendships tend to be based more on

Women's friendships tend to be "face-to-face," based
on self-disclosure and emotional sharing.

emotional sharing; men's are based more on engaging in common activities
(Hays, 1988; Sherrod, 1989). Face-to-face versus side-by-side, as Paul Wright
(1982) put it. Women also regard their same-sex friendships more favorably
than do men (Rose, 1985; Wheeler et al., 1983). This more positive evaluation
occurs for adolescents as well as adults, and in New Zealand and Hong Kong as
well as in the United States (Aukett et al., 1988; Wheeler et al., 1989; Wright
& Keple, 1981).

Consistent with these gender differences in friendship, there are also general
differences between all-male and all-female interactions. Female interactions are
characterized by more agreement and less overt conflict; male interactions
typically involve more disagreement and confrontational behaviors. These
contrasting styles of same-sex interactions have been observed among both
children and adults (Carli, 1989; Maccoby, 1990). Judging by the recent success
of books on male relationships and friendships, such as Robert Bly's *Iron John*
and Sam Keen's *Fire in the Belly,* men are not entirely happy with the present
state of affairs. Over the past generation, the woman's movement has helped

Men's friendships tend to be "side-by-side," based on
engaging in common activities.

women gain access to the public arena of careers and positions of authority.
Now, there seems to be a man's movement seeking access for men to the private
sphere of close, confiding relationships with other men. Fair enough.

TYPES OF RELATIONSHIPS

As we have seen, social exchange models of relationship development are
essentially quantitative: *more* (rewards, equity, self-disclosure) is associated with
better (satisfaction, endurance, and intimacy). Other theories of relationship
development, however, emphasize *qualitative differences* between various types
of relationships. According to this perspective, no matter how many positive
experiences occur within one type of relationship, the result won't necessarily

be a more intimate type of relationship. It's like eating ice cream: no matter how much French Vanilla you consume, you still won't end up with Rocky Road.

Liking Versus Loving: The Great Divide?

Take a look at the six questions listed in Table 6.2. Now, on a scale from 1 ("not at all") to 10 ("totally"), answer all six questions based on your feelings toward a *friend*. Next, answer the same questions based on your feelings toward a current or past *romantic partner*. Then follow the scoring procedure described at the bottom of the table.

When Zick Rubin (1973) asked a large number of college students to respond to items similar to those in Table 6.2, they gave high ratings to their friends on items like those listed in section A and high ratings to their romantic partners on items like those listed in section B. On the basis of their responses, Rubin developed a Liking Scale and a Loving Scale to measure these two types of involvements with others. Did your responses conform to Rubin's distinction? Do you like your friends (high scores in section A) and love your romantic partners (high scores in section B)?

Table 6.2   Liking and Loving.   Some items from the two scales used by Rubin to distinguish between liking and loving. [From Rubin, 1973.]

Answer each of the following questions on a scale from 1 = *not at all* to 10 = *totally*. Answer them first with a good friend in mind, and then thinking of a romantic partner.

	Friend	Partner
1. This person is one of the most likable people I know.	_____	_____
2. I feel I can confide in this person about virtually anything.	_____	_____
3. This person is the sort of person I would like to be.	_____	_____
4. I would forgive this person for practically anything.	_____	_____
5. I have great confidence in this person's good judgment.	_____	_____
6. I would do almost anything for this person.	_____	_____
A. Sum of your responses to questions 1 + 3 + 5 =	_____	_____
B. Sum of your responses to questions 2 + 4 + 6 =	_____	_____
Which is greater? A or B?	_____	_____

From Rubin's perspective, liking and loving are two distinct and, to some extent, mutually exclusive reactions to an intimate relationship. There is some question, however, about just how sharp a distinction can be drawn. For example, Kenneth and Karen Dion (1976) gave Rubin's two scales to casual daters, people dating each other exclusively, engaged couples, and married couples. Although casual daters reported more liking than loving, liking and loving did not differ among those in more committed relationships. In another study, subjects rated some items on the Loving Scale as highly characteristic of loving *and* liking (Steck et al., 1982). Perhaps one reason for the overlap between these two scales is that Rubin took a rather mild view of loving. Later in this chapter, we describe a much more intense type of loving that differs more clearly from liking.

Exchange Versus Communal Relationships   Margaret Clark and her colleagues take another approach to distinguishing between different types of relationships (Berg & Clark, 1986; Clark & Mills, 1979). Clark's work is based on a reconsideration of the principles of social exchange, outlined earlier in this chapter. According to Clark, people operate on a strict cost-accounting basis only in **exchange relationships**. In these relationships, people prefer immediate quid-pro-quo, tit-for-tat repayment for benefits given to each other. Costs are quickly offset by compensating rewards, and the overall balance remains at zero. Exchange relationships have the same characteristics as the exchange orientation described earlier, but here the focus is on the type of relationship rather than on the type of individual.

exchange relationships Relationships in which the participants expect and desire strict reciprocity in their interactions.

Communal relationships operate differently. In these relationships, people prefer to respond to each other's needs over the course of the relationship. The exact amounts of rewards and costs are not carefully monitored. Clark considers both close friendships and meaningful romantic attachments as communal in nature. Thus, exchange relationships are essentially superficial and unemotional, while communal relationships are more intimate, emotional, and committed (Clark & Taraban, 1990).

communal relationships Relationships in which the participants expect and desire mutual responsiveness to each other's needs.

In their research, Clark and her associates have found a number of differences in the way people behave in exchange and communal relationships. As summarized in Table 6.3, people in exchange relationships stick to immediate reciprocity. They expect benefits given or received to be repaid immediately; perceive each other's contributions as separate and keep track of them; and monitor the other person's needs only when they doing think this might lead to an opportunity for personal gain. Moreover, helping the other person doesn't improve their own mood and self-evaluation. But individuals involved in, or desiring the development of, communal relationships manage to avoid strict cost accounting. They do not respond favorably to immediate repayment; do not make a clear distinction between their work and that of the other person; and monitor the other person's needs even when they see no opportunity for personal gain.

Situation	Exchange Relationships	Communal Relationships
When we help the other person	We like the other person who pays us back immediately. Our mood may become less positive. Our self-evaluation does not change.	Our liking for the person who pays us back immediately may decrease. Our mood becomes more positive, as does our self-evaluation.
When the other person does us a favor	We don't like the person who does not ask for immediate repayment.	We like the person who does not ask for immediate repayment.
When we are working with the other person on a joint task	We want to make sure that our contribution can be distinguished from the other person's contribution.	We don't make any clear distinction between the work of the other person and our own work.
When the other person may need some help	We keep track of the other person's needs only when we expect that person to have an opportunity in the near future to take care of our needs.	We keep track of the other person's needs even when that person will not have an opportunity in the near future to take care of our needs.

Table 6.3 Differences Between Exchange and Communal Relationships. Exchange relationships require strict cost accounting; communal relationships are based on responsiveness to each other's needs. The research summarized here indicates how people behave differently in these two types of relationships. [Based on Clark, 1984; Clark & Mills, 1979; Clark et al., 1989; Clark et al., 1986; Clark & Waddell, 1985; Williamson & Clark, 1989, 1992.]

When they help the other person, both their mood and self-evaluation get a boost.

Perhaps the most interesting issue raised by Clark's work concerns the basic principle underlying behavior in communal relationships. Are communal relationships free of any social exchange considerations whatsoever; do those involved give without any desire to receive? Or do partners in a communal relationship rely on an extended version of social exchange, assuming that in the long run rewards and costs will balance out? In short, can people give selflessly, or is there always a self-centered bottom line? Chapter 7, on helping others, takes a close look at this basic issue concerning human nature. For now, you should note that the dichotomy itself may not necessarily apply to communal relationships. Arthur Aron and his colleagues (1991) maintain that when people are strongly attached to each other, the boundaries between self and other become blurred; the distinction between "mine" and "yours" is no longer clear. If *we* are *one*, then selfishness and selflessness are the same.

Different Types of Love: How Do I Love Thee?

Both Rubin and Clark see an important difference between a relationship that is *not* love (liking, exchange relationships) and one that *is* (loving, communal relationships). But love itself is not some simple, unitary, psychological state. The poet Elizabeth Barrett Browning asked, "How do I love thee?" and then went on to "count the ways." Apparently, the count can be quite high. *Love* has more entries in *Bartlett's Familiar Quotations* than any other word except *man* (Levinger, 1988). When subjects in one study (Fehr & Russell, 1991) were asked to list all the types of love they could come up with, they produced 216 items! In this section, we examine varieties of loving experiences as they have been defined and counted by social psychologists (Shaver & Hazan, 1988; Sternberg & Beall, 1991).

companionate love A secure, trusting attachment.

The most common approach in social psychology divides love into two types: companionate and passionate (Hatfield, 1988). **Companionate love** is a secure, trusting, stable partnership—similar in many ways to what Rubin called liking. **Passionate love** is state of high arousal: being loved by the partner is ecstasy; being rejected is agony. If you examine the Passionate Love Scale in Table 6.4, you can see that it describes a much more emotionally intense state of affairs than does Rubin's Loving Scale. The basic contrast between companionate and passionate love runs throughout several more elaborate classifications.

passionate love Romantic love characterized by high arousal, intense attraction, and fear of rejection.

attachment style The way a person typically interacts with significant others.

In their perspective on love, Phillip Shaver and his colleagues (1988) propose that the way in which a person interacts with significant others, called **attachment style**, may be relatively constant across the life span. Thus, a person's attachment to a romantic partner will resemble the sort of attachment the person experienced as a child in relation to parents. Basing their approach on research examining parent-child relationships (Ainsworth et al., 1978), Cindy Hazan and Shaver (1987) asked adult subjects which of three attachment styles best described their experiences and feelings. The three alternatives that subjects chose from are listed in Table 6.5. Subjects also responded to a variety of questions about their childhood relations with their parents and about the nature of their adult romantic relationships.

Among subjects who participated in this research, 56 percent indicated that the *secure* style of attachment best described their experiences and feelings. Around 24 percent of subjects chose the *avoidant* description, and about 20 percent selected the *anxious/ambivalent* characterization. Similar percentages have been obtained for other samples of adults in the United States (Pistole, 1989) and in Israel (Mikulincer et al., 1990). Both insecure styles, however, may be less prevalent among married couples than among young singles (Kobak & Hazan, 1991).

Answer each of the following items in terms of this scale:

1	2	3	4	5	6	7	8	9
Not at all true				Moderately true				Definitely true

1. I would feel deep despair if _____ left me.

2. Sometimes I feel I can't control my thoughts; they are obsessively on _____.

3. I feel happy when I am doing something to make _____ happy.

4. I would rather be with _____ than anyone else.

5. I'd get jealous if I thought _____ were falling in love with someone else.

6. I yearn to know all about _____.

7. I want _____—physically, emotionally, mentally.

8. I have an endless appetite for affection from _____.

9. For me, _____ is the perfect romantic partner.

10. I sense my body responding when _____ touches me.

11. _____ always seems to be on my mind.

12. I want _____ to know me—my thoughts, my fears, and my hopes.

13. I eagerly look for signs indicating _____'s desire for me.

14. I possess a powerful attraction for _____.

15. I get extremely depressed when things don't go right in my relationship with _____.

Table 6.4   The Passionate Love Scale.   This questionnaire asks you to describe how you feel when you are passionately in love. Think of the person whom you love most passionately *right now*. If you are not in love right now, think of someone you loved before. The person you choose should be of the opposite sex if you are heterosexual or of the same sex if you are homosexual. Respond according to how you felt at the time your feelings were most intense. Higher scores indicate greater passionate love. [Based on Hatfield & Rapson, 1987.]

According to their retrospective reports in the study conducted by Hazan and Shaver, secure subjects had a warmer relationship with their parents than did insecure subjects. Avoidant subjects said they felt rejected by their mother; anxious/ambivalent subjects reported difficulties in their relationship with their father. In terms of their romantic relationships, secure subjects described highly positive interactions, characterized by happiness, friendship, and trust. Those with the avoidant style indicated a fear of closeness. Anxious/ambivalent subjects reported a love life full of emotional extremes, obsessive preoccupation,

Question: Which of the following best describes your feelings?

A. I find it relatively easy to get close to others and am comfortable depending on them and having them depend on me. I don't often worry about being abandoned or about someone getting close to me.

B. I am somewhat uncomfortable being close to others; I find it difficult to trust them completely, difficult to allow myself to depend on them. I am nervous when anyone gets too close, and often, love partners want me to be more intimate than I feel comfortable being.

C. I find that others are reluctant to get as close as I would like. I often worry that my partner doesn't really love me or won't want to stay with me. I want to merge completely with another person, and this desire sometimes scares people away.

The first type of attachment style is described as "secure," the second as "avoidant," and the third as "anxious/ambivalent."

Table 6.5 Attachment Styles.   The way we typically interact with significant others is called an attachment style. Which of these descriptions best characterizes your adult attachments? Be sure not to look at the labels provided at the bottom of the table until *after* you've made your selection. [From Shaver et al., 1988.]

---

sexual attraction, desire for union with the partner, desire for reciprocation from the partner, and love at first sight. Overall, then, there are clear similarities between the secure attachment style and companionate love, as well as between the anxious/ambivalent attachment style and passionate love. Individuals with an avoidant style seem reluctant to commit to a love relationship at all. Perhaps because of that low level of commitment, avoidant men report distinctly low levels of distress after the breakup of a romance (Simpson, 1990).

For John Lee (1977), love is truly a "many splendored thing," with the emphasis on *many*. Lee uses color as a metaphor for love. Three love styles (which he calls eros, ludus, and storge) are like primary colors; they form the basis for other combinations. Lee also describes three secondary styles (called mania, agape, and pragma), although the potential number runs much higher (Lee, 1988). Lee's six major styles of love are described in Table 6.6. As you can see, they differ in the intensity of the loving experience, commitment to the beloved, desired characteristics of the beloved, and expectations about being loved in return.

When the love styles of French and American undergraduates were compared, a number of cultural differences appeared (Murstein et al., 1991):

Storge: American students reported more extensive engagement in these friendship-like romantic relationships than did French students.

Eros	The Erotic lover is eager for an intense relationship with intimacy and strong physical attraction.
Ludus	The Ludic lover is playful in love and likes to play the field.
Storge	The Storgic lover prefers slowly developing attachments that lead to lasting commitment.
Mania	The Manic lover is demanding and possessive toward the beloved, and has a feeling of being "out of control."
Agape	The Agapic lover is altruistic, loving without concern for receiving anything in return.
Pragma	The Pragmatic lover searches for a person with the proper vital statistics: job, age, religion, etc.

Table 6.6 Styles of Loving. According to Lee, eros, ludus, and storge are the three primary "colors" of love, from which all other types are derived. Mania, agape, and pragma are three of the major secondary types. [Based on Lee, 1977, 1988.]

Mania: American men reported having more of these extremely intense relationships than did French men.
Agape: French women reported having more of these altruistic, self-sacrificing relationships than did American women.

Research conducted in the United States suggests that storge is similar to companionate love; mania, to passionate love (Hendrick et al., 1988). Eros seems to partake of the best of both: a passionate yet secure style of loving.

triangular theory of love The theory that the basic components of love are intimacy, passion, and decision/commitment.

Robert Sternberg's **triangular theory of love** also focuses on three primary types, which can combine to produce a range of ways of loving. According to Sternberg (1986), love consists of

Intimacy: The emotional component, which involves feelings of closeness
Passion: The motivational component, which reflects romantic, sexual attraction
Decision/Commitment: The cognitive component, which includes the decisions people make about being in love and the degree of their commitment to the partner

These three components are the building blocks of love, and various combinations create eight major types of relationships. As you can see from Table 6.7, companionate love is included in Sternberg's classification scheme. Passionate love has two representatives: the pure passion of infatuation and the intimate passion of romantic love.

Given all of these different ways to divide up love, how many types are there? It's hard to tell. Efforts to integrate these various typologies and come up with

Type of Relationship	Intimacy	Passion	Decision and Commitment
Nonlove	Low	Low	Low
Liking	High	Low	Low
Infatuated love	Low	High	Low
Empty love	Low	Low	High
Romantic love	High	High	Low
Companionate love	High	Low	High
Fatuous love	Low	High	High
Consummate love	High	High	High

Table 6.7 The Triangular Theory of Love: All the Possible Combinations. According to Sternberg's triangular theory of love, three basic components of love combine in varying degrees to produce eight different types of relationships. [Based on Sternberg, 1986.]

one set of categories have produced somewhat inconsistent results (Hendrick & Hendrick, 1989; Levy & Davis, 1988). Although there is growing support for the usefulness of the tripartite division of adult attachment styles (Collins & Read, 1990; Feeney & Noller, 1990), the contrast between companionate and passionate love appears to be the most fundamental distinction among those who are willing to be attached. Let's look at these two types more closely.

Passionate Love: The Thrill of It   Because of its intensity, passionate love is the stuff of great drama. What would novelists, playwrights, and scriptwriters do without it? Passionate love also seems to be the stuff of marriage—American style (Simpson et al., 1986). Consider this question: If a man or woman had all the other qualities you desired, would you marry this person if you were *not* in love? When young men and women were asked this question in 1967, 65 percent of the men said no, compared to only 24 percent of the women. By 1976 and continuing into the 1980s, over 80 percent of both sexes stated that they would not marry someone with whom they were not in love. The phrasing "in love" strongly suggests that it is the bliss of passionate love these young adults require, rather than the calmer rewards of companionate love.

Were we not so accustomed to it, in fictional accounts and perhaps in our own lives, we would regard passionate love as a very odd creature. Recall those social exchange theories described earlier that picture love and attachment as increasing with rewarding experiences and decreasing with accelerating costs. But in passionate love, costs don't seem to put out the fire. Indeed, the more difficulties the passionate lover encounters, the more in love he or she may become (Hindy et al., 1989). How can unpleasant, even painful experiences increase love?

According to Elaine Hatfield and Ellen Berscheid, the answer lies in arousal (Berscheid & Walster, 1974a; Walster, 1971). Love, they contend, can be analyzed like any other emotion. Drawing on Schachter's (1964) two-factor theory of emotion, described in Chapter 2, Hatfield and Berscheid propose that passionate love consists of (1) diffuse physiological arousal and (2) the belief that this arousal is caused by a reaction to the beloved.

Sometimes, the connection between arousal and love is obvious. In the presence of the romantic partner of our dreams, we feel a sudden and unmistakable surge of sexual desire. We know we are aroused, and we know why. But the two-factor analysis of passionate love goes beyond the obvious. Arousal can be attributed to the wrong source—*misattributed*. One kind of misattribution was discussed in Chapter 5. There, we saw how attributing feelings of arousal to a nonthreatening cause (noise) rather than the actual, disturbing cause (fear of speaking in public) could reduce anxiety.

In passionate love, say Hatfield and Berscheid, another kind of switch occurs. People explain their feelings of arousal in someone's presence by inferring that they are romantically or sexually attracted to that person. The role of other influences is ignored. This kind of misattribution should increase attraction between strangers and passion between lovers. Dolf Zillmann (1978, 1984) calls the process **excitation transfer**. Arousal caused by one stimulus is transferred and added to arousal elicited by a second stimulus. The combined arousal is then perceived as caused only by the second stimulus.

excitation transfer
The process whereby arousal caused by one stimulus is added to arousal from a second stimulus, and the combined arousal is attributed to the second stimulus.

To illustrate, let's consider Dan, a fearful flyer. Dan's fear isn't terribly severe and he doesn't like to admit it to himself. But as the plane takes off, he experiences all those awful symptoms of anxiety—heart racing, palms sweating, shortness of breath. He's just beginning to calm down a bit when he notices Judy, sitting in the adjacent seat. A conversation gets going, and he realizes that he finds Judy very attractive. He just hopes he can figure out a way to see her when they arrive at their destination. What accounts for Dan's sudden surge of interest in Judy? Is she really that appealing, or has he taken the physiological arousal of fear and mislabeled it as passionate desire?

The possibility that fear might be mislabeled as sexual attraction was first put to the test by Donald Dutton and Arthur Aron (1974). Their study took place on two bridges located in a scenic tourist spot. One of the bridges, the Capilano Canyon Suspension Bridge in North Vancouver, British Columbia, is a nightmare for anyone the least bit afraid of heights: a 450-foot-long, 5-foot-wide passageway that twists in the wind 230 feet above a rocky gorge. Nearby, the other bridge used in the study is more conventional—stable and close to the ground. Whenever an unaccompanied young male walked across one of these bridges, he was met by a male or female research assistant. The research assistant asked him to participate in a brief experiment in which he answered a few questions. Before parting, the research assistant mentioned that if the subject wanted more information about the study, he could give the assistant a call at home. You can probably guess who was most likely to pick up the phone: subjects met by a female research assistant on the suspension bridge. Fear had sparked attraction.

Or had it? Critics have argued that we needn't rely on complicated psychological processes like misattribution and excitation transfer to explain why romance intensifies when a person is afraid (Kenrick & Cialdini, 1977; Riordan & Tedeschi, 1983). Instead, they propose, fondness for those who are with us in a time of distress is based on the comfort we take from their presence. Because it reduces distress, the presence of others is rewarding, and rewards associated with another person increase that person's attractiveness. This analysis brought passionate love right back to basics.

Is the infatuated lover in this cartoon a victim of "excitation transfer"? He thinks that what he likes about New York is Claudia. But perhaps the arousal produced by being in the "Big Apple" fuels his attraction and he only likes Claudia because they're in New York. [Drawing by Weber; © 1984 The New Yorker Magazine, Inc.]

"The thing I like about New York, Claudia, is you."

But it didn't stay there. Research by Gregory White and his colleagues (1981) provided a compelling demonstration of excitation transfer in the service of romantic attraction. The male subjects in this experiment ran in place for either two minutes or fifteen seconds. Then they watched a videotape of a woman they expected to meet later in the experiment. The woman, an experimental confederate, had been made up to look either physically attractive or unattractive. After watching the video, subjects rated the woman's attractiveness.

The men who participated in this study did not experience any physical or emotional discomfort, and so there was no distress to be reduced by the woman's videotaped presence. Nevertheless, arousal enhanced their emotional response. Men who had exercised for two minutes rated the physically attractive woman as more attractive and the unattractive woman as less attractive than did those who had exercised for fifteen seconds. Exercise-produced arousal intensified subjects' initial emotional reaction, positive *or* negative, to a member of the opposite sex.

The implications of this research are mind-boggling. Is passionate love totally at the mercy of airplanes, bridges, exercise, and other irrelevant factors? Fortunately for our peace of mind, the answer is no. Misattribution and excitation transfer have their limits. One limit is imposed by the passing of time. After the stimulus is gone, arousal declines over time, leaving nothing to be transferred (Zillmann et al., 1974). If Dan met Judy after he got off the plane, his interest would be less intense.

Another limit may be set by attributional clarity (White & Kight, 1984). If excitation transfer depends on *mis*attribution, knowing the real reason for our initial arousal will short-circuit the process. When Dan thinks, "Oh gosh, here I go again, afraid of flying," he won't be able to mistake his fear as falling in love with Judy. Some researchers, however, question whether misattribution is necessary for one source of arousal to fuel another (Allen et al., 1989). Instead, they propose that what may be involved is a simple process of response facilitation. Whenever arousal is present, no matter what its source or the degree to which we are aware of that source, our response will be energized. Will Dan get turned on by Judy if he knows full well that his heart is racing from fear? The debate isn't settled. It does seem possible, though, that at least on some occasions we may be aware that some other source of arousal contributes to our passionate response, but we just don't care. If it feels good, go for it.

Unfortunately, passionate love doesn't always feel good; sometimes it feels awful. If any kind of arousal (from pain as well as pleasure) increases it, does this mean that we're caught forever, never to be released? Perhaps. Consider this excerpt from an interview with a man who was passionately in love for a very long time:

> I lived in constant fear of divorce. . . . I would do everything I could think of to try and win her affection. . . . She was unpredictable. I could never be sure of how she'd react. . . . From the day I met her until the day she died, she was the most beautiful woman on earth. . . . She was a real queen and she ruled my emotions for a quarter of a century. (Tennov, 1979, pp. 53–54).

This man's experience suggests the possibility that the ultimate limit on passionate love is *certainty* (Brehm, 1988). If hope is utterly lost, passion dies; if love is secure, passion fades. But if the beloved's commitment remains uncertain, neither lost nor gained, arousal is constantly recharged. In such circumstances, both the agony and the ecstasy of passionate love can last a lifetime.

Companionate Love: The Trust in It   For most people, however, companionate love has a good deal more endurance than passionate attachments. Less emotionally intense than passionate love, companionate love is more stable and, some would contend, deeper. Companionate love exists between friends as well as lovers. It is similar in many respects to the notion of communal relationships, in which partners respond to each other's needs without concern for immediate repayment.

Companionate love rests on a foundation of respect, admiration, and trust. Of these, trust may be the most important (Holmes & Rempel, 1989). Two kinds of interpersonal trust have been described: *reliability* and *emotional trust* (Johnson-George & Swap, 1982). We trust in other people's reliability when we believe they will do what they have promised to do. We trust others emotionally when we believe that they are concerned about how we feel and will act to protect our welfare. Married couples who are more comfortable

Companionate love rests on a foundation of respect, admiration, and trust.

relying on each other are more satisfied with their marriage and are able to work together more cooperatively on solving problems (Kobak & Hazan, 1991). Indeed, trust may be the crucial factor in creating that merger between self and other that we described earlier. And being able to take great joy in our partner's delight gives companionate love its zest and helps ensure its longevity.

RELATIONSHIP ISSUES

In an intimate relationship, the quality of the love partners feel for each other can't be separated from the way they deal with a variety of basic relationship issues. A trusting, generous love helps them cope better with these issues, just as sensitive and sensible coping increases trust and affection. Relationship issues thus offer an opportunity to strengthen a relationship. But they also pose the danger of angry, unresolved disagreements. This section considers three of the most intimate, and potentially explosive, issues couples face: sex, jealousy, and power.

Sexuality

Is the revolution over, or is it still going on? It's not entirely clear. We know when it started. Beginning in the 1960s, the rate of premarital sexual activity in the United States increased dramatically, especially among women and teenagers. According to most investigators, the proportion of unmarried young adults engaging in premarital sex leveled off and stabilized during the more conservative 1980s (I. Robinson et al., 1991). But a recent report by the Centers for Disease Control (1991) questions that conclusion.

In a survey conducted in 1988, the CDC asked 8,450 women between 15 and 44 years old when they had first had sex. (Research on rates of sexual activity usually focuses on women because their sexual behavior varies more across time and place than does men's.) Based on this information, rates of first intercourse were calculated for ages 15 to 19 during the years between 1970 and 1988. For each age, rates of sexual activity increased steadily from 1970 on. Among 15-year-olds, the 1988 rate (25.6 percent) was more than five times the 1970 rate (4.6 percent); for 19-year-olds, the 1988 rate (75.3 percent) was more than 50 percent greater than the 1970 rate (48.2 percent).

These data are by no means foolproof; some subjects were asked to remember eighteen years back. Still, first intercourse is a memorable event for most women, and the findings for 1988 only required subjects to remember if they had had sex, not when. From a practical standpoint, it may not matter all that much whether rates of sexual activity have stabilized or are still increasing. The plain fact is that by their late teens, the vast majority of young women and men (probably about 10 to 20 percent higher than the 75 percent rate for women) are sexually active.

Sex and Satisfaction   The sexual revolution has raised a number of important issues about the relationship between sex and satisfaction. Is having sex like adding butter to a sauce, does it make a crucial difference in satisfaction with the relationship? Or is sex more like the raisin on a cake? When the relationship as a whole is good, sex can top it off. But if the cake is a flop, no little raisin is going to rescue it.

To answer these questions, we can compare relationships that last with those that don't. It does appear that dating relationships with sex may continue longer than those without sex. In one study, college students who were having sex with their dating partner were more likely three months later to still be dating the same person than were those who were not having sex at the time they were first contacted (Simpson, 1987). This association remained even after various other factors (such as satisfaction with the relationship, length of the relationship, and sexual attitudes) were taken into account. Presumably, sexual activity provided these couples with rewarding experiences that contributed to the endurance of their relationship.

But three months is a very short period. What about more long-term effects? Here, comparisons of married couples who lived together before marriage with those who did not cohabit provide especially interesting information. Both sorts of couples may have engaged in premarital sex, but on the average those who cohabited before marriage should have had more of it. Although research in this area has been beset with all kinds of complications, a general consensus is beginning to emerge (DeMaris & Rao, 1992; Glenn, 1990). Cohabitation, it appears, is associated with marital problems. The marriages of couples who cohabited before marriage are less satisfying and more likely to end in divorce than are the marriages of those who did not cohabit. Explanations for this association differ, but reduced commitment to the relationship may be a factor (Booth & Johnson, 1988; Kurdek & Schmitt, 1986). In any event, the greater access to regular sexual activity gained by cohabiting couples does not give them an advantage if they decide to marry.

Rather than viewing sex as the prime mover in determining the quality and endurance of a relationship, we might be better advised to regard it as a part of the larger relational whole. Typically, sexual satisfaction is correlated with overall satisfaction in the relationship for both heterosexual and homosexual couples (Kurdek, 1991c). In turn, sexual and relationship satisfaction are associated with good communication about sexual desires and preferences (Cupach & Comstock, 1990). Talking about sex, however, may be more difficult for some couples than for others. According to William Masters and Virginia Johnson (1979), the two most famous sexologists of our time, homosexual couples are much better at communicating about sex than are heterosexual couples. In the next section, we consider some gender differences in sexual attitudes and roles that might make it more difficult for heterosexual men and women to talk to each other.

Gender Differences in Sexual Attitudes and Roles   Just as men typically have more extensive sexual experiences than do women, so are men more permissive in their sexual values and attitudes (Hendrick et al., 1985). Men are also more likely than women to enjoy sex without intimacy, while women prefer sexual activities to be part of a psychologically intimate relationship (DeLamater, 1987). Recently, Jeffry Simpson and Steven Gangestad (1991) developed the Sociosexual Orientation Inventory (SOI) to measure individuals' willingness to engage in uncommitted sexual interactions (see Table 6.8). Men score higher on this scale than do women, reflecting their more unrestricted sexual behavior and more permissive sexual attitudes.

Women's sociosexuality, however, appears to be a better indicator of the onset of sexual activity in a heterosexual relationship. Women with high SOI scores engaged in sex earlier in their current relationship than did women with low SOI scores; there was no association between men's SOI scores and how early the couple had sex. At first blush, this finding may seem puzzling, but actually it makes perfectly good sense. On any *joint* activity, the more restrictive partner will tend to call the shots. If he always wants to tango and she only sometimes wants to, her degree of enthusiasm will determine if and when the dance begins.

This analysis has some important implications for male and female roles in intimate relationships. It has often been observed that heterosexual men and women differ in the sexual roles that they enact (Grauerholz & Serpe, 1985; Griffitt, 1987). Men are more likely than women to try to initiate sexual activity; women are more likely to be reactive—accepting or refusing the other's proposal. This division of the sexual labor has been summarized in the phrase "men as go-getters and women as gate-keepers" (Zillman & Weaver, 1989, p. 95). As we have seen, the more restrictive, "gate-keeper" role sets the pace of sexual activities in a relationship. Thus, although this role may appear relatively passive, it is actually quite influential.

It can also be dangerous. In the classic date-rape scenario, the "go-getter" male uses physical force to overcome the "gate-keeper" female's refusal to have sex. He won't take her "no" for an answer. Coercive sexual behavior in general follows a similar pattern (Muehlenhard et al., 1991). Both men's and women's reports indicate that men are more likely to engage in coercive behavior—psychological as well as physical—in order to obtain sex (Poppen & Segal, 1988). Date rape is an extremely serious problem on many college campuses today. To combat it, men and women need to join together in rewriting the traditional sexual script (Lundberg-Love & Geffner, 1989; Shotland, 1989). Assigned roles discourage communication because all participants assume they know their lines. When people are free to be either a "go-getter" or a "gate-keeper," depending on their feelings at that moment, they should be more

For the questions dealing with behavior, write your answers in the blank spaces provided. For the questions dealing with thoughts and attitudes, circle the appropriate number on the scales provided.

1. With how many different partners have you had sex (sexual intercourse) within the past year? _____

2. With how many different partners do you foresee yourself having sex during the next five years? (Please give a *specific, realistic* estimate.) _____

3. With how many different partners have you had sex on *one and only one* occasion?

   _____

4. How often do you fantasize about having sex with someone other than your current dating partner? (Circle one).

   1. never
   2. once every two or three months
   3. once a month
   4. once every two weeks
   5. once a week
   6. a few times each week
   7. nearly every day
   8. at least once a day

5. Sex without love is OK

   1   2   3   4   5   6   7   8   9

   I strongly disagree   I strongly agree

6. I can imagine myself being comfortable and enjoying "casual" sex with different partners.

   1   2   3   4   5   6   7   8   9

   I strongly disagree   I strongly agree

7. I would have to be closely attached to someone (both emotionally and psychologically) before I could feel comfortable and fully enjoy having sex with him or her.

   1   2   3   4   5   6   7   8   9

   I strongly disagree   I strongly agree

Scoring: Reverse the values in Item 7 so that 1 = 9, 2 = 8, etc. Items then receive the following weights:

   Item 1 x 5 = _____

   Item 2 x 1 = _____

   Item 3 x 5 = _____

   Item 4 x 4 = _____

   (Total of items 5, 6, & 7) x 2 = _____

   Total = _____

Table 6.8 The Sociosexual Orientation Inventory. The Sociosexual Orientation Inventory measures individuals' willingness to engage in uncommitted sexual interactions. The average score for men is about 68; for women, around 39. [Based on Simpson & Gangestad, 1991.]

inclined to try harder to communicate clearly with each other and, one hopes, less likely to try to get their way by force.

The AIDS Crisis There's another extremely serious problem on college campuses today: sexually transmitted disease (STD). The incidence of STDs such as chlamydia, gonorrhea, and genital herpes is a major public health concern. But these diseases, painful and frightening as they are, pale in comparison with the devastating effects of AIDS (acquired immune deficiency syndrome). Chlamydia and gonorrhea can be cured; you can live with herpes. But AIDS kills.

AIDS is one of the deadliest diseases in human history. By 1992, over 215,000 cases had been reported in the United States. Of these people with AIDS, nearly 65 percent have died. Current estimates by the Public Health Service indicate that some 1 to 1.5 million Americans are infected with HIV, the human immunodeficiency virus that causes AIDS. Worldwide, the number of HIV-infected individuals is expected to be as high as 120 million by the year 2000. Although significant progress has been made in medical research, there is no known cure for AIDS. Some basic facts about AIDS are summarized in Table 6.9.

To date, there have been two major waves in the AIDS epidemic. The victims of the first wave were gay men, who still account for slightly over 50 percent of new cases (Elmer-Dewitt, 1991). Most of these individuals, however, were infected many years ago. The incidence of new HIV infections among gay men has declined dramatically (Watkins, 1988), although there is concern that younger men may not have adopted safe-sex practices as thoroughly as have older individuals (Griggs, 1990). The victims of the second wave are intravenous-drug

In the fight against AIDS, education plays a key role. Here, students participate in an AIDS information workshop.

1. *Can you get AIDS from casual contact?* There is no documented case of the transmission of AIDS from casual contact, even among families of AIDS patients.

2. *Are dental and medical personnel at greater risk for HIV infection?* Because HIV can be transmitted from direct contact of blood with an open sore, dental and medical personnel must take special precautions to protect themselves. As of 1991, forty healthcare workers had been infected on the job. Only five people are known to have been infected by healthcare personnel (Dolan & West, 1991).

3. *Can a person be infected with HIV and still test negative?* Yes, there is a "window" of at least a few weeks between becoming infected and producing enough antibodies to be detected by a test for HIV.

4. *Can a person be infected with HIV and not have any symptoms of AIDS?* Although the average length of time between infection and developing the disease is about 8 years, this interval varies greatly among individuals. Lui et al. (1988) report a range of 4 to 15 years prior to the onset of the disease.

5. *Can a person be infected with HIV and never develop AIDS?* Most scientists believe that, in the absence of treatment, any person who is infected with HIV will eventually develop AIDS.

6. *If a person thinks that he or she might be infected, should this person get tested?* Absolutely. It is important to know whether you are infected in order not to infect others. In addition, taking AZT (currently the most effective treatment for AIDS) is now recommended for individuals who are HIV-infected but have not shown any symptoms of AIDS. This treatment can delay the onset of the disease.

7. *Are all babies who test positive for HIV at birth actually infected with HIV?* No. For reasons that are not now understood, some babies who test positive will later be found not to be infected. For both babies and adults, it is crucial to have more than one test to establish a firm diagnosis.

8. *Is AIDS always fatal?* Up to now, it has been assumed that AIDS is a fatal disease. But new treatments are being rapidly developed, and there is the possibility that AIDS will become a chronic disease, like diabetes or high blood pressure, that can be managed. Although this possibility has not yet been realized, it is seen as a reasonable hope for the future by many of those involved in the research and treatment of AIDS.

Table 6.9 Some Facts About AIDS. Because rumor feeds on fear, inaccurate information about AIDS gets passed around. Here are some of the basic facts, as best we know them in the light of current research.

users (most of whom are heterosexual), their sexual partners, and their children. The spread of HIV infection among this population is increasing rapidly.

Up until November 7, 1991, most heterosexuals who were not intravenous-drug users probably thought they were pretty safe. Then basketball superstar Magic Johnson stepped up to the microphone and announced that he had contracted the virus from heterosexual sex. For many people, their false sense of security vanished that afternoon.

Although Johnson is the most prominent individual to publicly acknowledge having become HIV infected from heterosexual intercourse, statistically he is part of a rising tide. Worldwide, 75 percent of HIV infections are estimated to result from heterosexual intercourse. In the United States, the percentage of new AIDS cases occurring among heterosexuals has risen from 1 percent in 1983 to about 7 percent in 1991. A recent review of research indicates that women are twelve times more likely than men to be infected during heterosexual intercourse, and they survive for a shorter time after diagnosis (Ickovics & Rodin, 1992). No large "third wave" of AIDS among heterosexuals has yet appeared in the United States, but there is every reason to be concerned. High levels of unprotected sex, particularly among young people, may be creating an "underground epidemic" that will be fully visible only in the years to come.

The only 100 percent–guaranteed, foolproof method of avoiding a sexually transmitted disease is abstinence. For individuals who are sexually active, the use of condoms is the principal safe-sex method for reducing the risk of HIV infection. It appears, however, that the majority of sexually active college students use condoms only occasionally, if at all (Biemiller, 1991). Awareness of the risks involved in unprotected sex produced significant changes in sexual behavior among gay men (Stall et al., 1988). What sort of prevention campaigns are needed to encourage similar changes among intravenous-drug users and heterosexuals? In Chapter 14, on health, we consider a number of factors that can increase the effectiveness of efforts to convince people to practice good health habits.

Jealousy

The Song of Solomon describes jealousy as "cruel as the grave," and Shakespeare called it "the green-eyed monster." Such harsh words seem well deserved. Being jealous can be tormenting; being the target of jealousy can be frightening. And sometimes jealousy is fatal. Jean Harris, headmistress of a prestigious private school, murdered her lover, who had been paying attention to another woman. Douglas Hawley of Eudora, Kansas, murdered his former wife and her friend Donald Harris, and then killed himself. Love triangles can be dangerous to the health of all the parties involved. But sometimes the triangle is only in the mind of the beholder. In Shakespeare's great tragedy *Othello*, Desdemona is a faithful, loving wife, but Othello is too blinded by jealousy to notice. **Jealousy**, the reaction to a *perceived* threat to an existing relationship, is not always constrained by reality.

jealousy The reaction to a perceived threat to an existing relationship.

Causes of Jealousy   Typically, jealousy is created by the perception that one's partner is attracted to someone else (Buunk & Bringle, 1987). But the threat doesn't have to be a social one. Female college students, for example, report feeling jealous about their boyfriend's time involvement with family and hobbies (Hansen, 1985). Still, jealousy is usually more intense when a romance breaks up because of the partner's attraction to another person (Mathes et al., 1985).

In general, jealousy is related to feelings of inadequacy and inequity in a relationship (White, 1981a, 1981b). Since short-term relationships (like dating) provide less security than long-term relationships (like marriage), individuals with chronic doubts about their own self-worth may be especially prone to jealousy in the early stages of a relationship (Melamed, 1991). People who are highly dependent on a relationship are also more likely to experience jealousy (Buunk, 1991). But the strongest, and potentially most destructive, feelings of jealousy seem to arise when a threat to *sexual* exclusivity is experienced (Reiss, 1986). Individuals differ in how much importance they place on sexual exclusivity, and there are major cross-cultural differences in the sorts of behaviors that elicit sexual jealousy.

Research by Bram Buunk and Ralph Hupka (1987) documents some of these differences among university students in seven countries: Hungary, Ireland, Mexico, the Netherlands, the (then) Soviet Union, the United States, and (what was then) Yugoslavia. Relative to responses from other national groups, kissing elicited high levels of sexual jealousy from the Hungarians, dancing and sexual relations from the Soviets, flirting from the Yugoslavs, and sexual fantasies from the Dutch. Students from the other countries (Ireland, Mexico, and the United States) reported lower levels of sexual jealousy in response to these behaviors.

Experiencing Jealousy According to Gregory White, the experience of jealousy has four major phases (White, 1981a; White & Mullen, 1989). During *primary appraisal*, the individual perceives that there is a threat to an existing relationship. As we have seen, a person who is insecure about and dependent on the relationship may be especially likely to perceive such a threat. And even a relatively mild threat to sexual exclusivity may trigger a reaction more quickly than would threats to a friendship. In the next phase, *secondary appraisal*, people try to understand the situation better and begin to think of ways to cope with it. Although some people are able to think clearly at this point, some may leap to irrational conclusions: "I bet *everyone* knows she's cheating on me"; "I'll *never* be happy without him."

The third aspect of the jealousy experience is the individual's *emotional reaction*. Jealousy can produce a large and varied range of emotional reactions. Though these feelings are usually negative (distress, embarrassment, suspiciousness, hostility, hurt), some positive reactions (excitement, love, feeling alive) can also occur (Pines & Aronson, 1983; Smith et al., 1988). Finally, the person's perceptions, thoughts, and feelings about jealousy will influence how that person attempts to *cope with jealousy*. Coping also varies tremendously, from constructive actions to destructive rampages.

Cross-cultural research by Jeff Bryson (1991) provides a perspective on how culture, gender, and coping response can all interact in jealousy. Subjects in this research were university students in the United States and four European countries (France, Germany, Italy, and the Netherlands). Asked about their feelings and actions when they were jealous, subjects' responses were scored in terms of nine different coping factors. Table 6.10 lists these factors and indicates which national groups scored very high or very low on each one. Bryson's own (tongue-in-cheek) summary of the results is worth quoting:

> It appears that, when jealous, the French get mad, the Dutch get sad, the Germans would rather not fight about it, the Italians don't want to talk about it, and the Americans are concerned about what their friends think! (p. 191)

In addition to these cross-cultural patterns, there were some striking gender differences in the responses of U.S. students. As you can see from Table 6.10, American men said that when they were jealous, they became aggressive and were interested in other people. American women said they attempted to feign indifference and wanted to talk to friends about their feelings. Americans were the only subjects to show such strong gender differences. Among European subjects, men's and women's responses were usually quite similar.

Given the pain and suffering that it can create in people's lives, most of us would like to be able to cope constructively with jealousy. Psychiatrists and clinical psychologists often try to help their clients deal better with their jealous feelings (Clanton & Smith, 1977). Clinical approaches focus on the need to reduce irrational beliefs, enhance self-esteem, improve communication skills, and increase equity in the relationship (White & Mullen, 1989). Although there has been little research on coping with jealousy, the results of a study by Peter Salovey and Judith Rodin (1988) suggest that a sense of independence and self-worth may be crucial. Those who can avoid the pitfalls of endless recrimination and forge ahead with their own lives should have a much better chance of escaping the destructive effects of the green-eyed monster.

Social Power

Whatever else they may be, both sex and jealousy are related to power. As described earlier, refusing a sexual offer is an exercise of power in the relationship, against which physical force is sometimes used to regain power. Jealousy is a state of perceived powerlessness, as the jealous individual fears that he or she has lost the power to attract the partner. Whether it is used for good, evil, or trivial purposes, power is a ubiquitous feature of social life. It affects all relationships—between friends as well as lovers, among coworkers as well as family members, in superficial as well as close encounters. This section describes some of the basic factors involved in social power as it operates in intimate relationships.

social power The ability to influence others and to resist their influence on us.

Power and Resources   **Social power** is the ability to influence the behavior of others and to resist their influence on us (Huston, 1983). There are many different ways to analyze social power, but the social exchange perspective described earlier in this chapter is one of the most widely adopted. In terms of social exchange, power is based on the control of valuable resources (Blood &

Coping Responses (with sample item from each factor)	National Groups with Highest Scores	National Groups with Lowest Scores
Reaction to Betrayal ("Feel betrayed")	France	Netherlands
Emotional Devastation ("Feel less able to cope with other aspects of my life")	Netherlands	United States (men only)
Aggression ("Threaten the other person")	France United States (men only)	Germany United States (women only)
Impression Management ("Try to make my partner think I don't care")	United States (women only)	All four European countries
Reactive Retribution ("Flirt or go out with other people")	United States (men only)	Netherlands
Relationship Improvement ("Become more sexually active with my partner")	United States France	Italy
Monitoring ("Question my partner about his/her activities")	Netherlands United States	Italy
Intropunitiveness ("Feel guilty about being jealous")	France United States	Italy
Social Support Seeking ("Talk to close friends about my feelings")	United States (women only) Netherlands	Italy

Table 6.10   Coping with Jealousy in Five Countries.   University students from the United States and four European countries responded to a questionnaire asking them how they react when jealous. Their answers indicated strong cultural differences in coping with jealousy, but gender differences were strong only in the United States. [Data from Bryson, 1991.]

Wolfe, 1960). If a person has control over something you want, that person has power over you.

Different resources produce different types of power (French & Raven, 1959; Frost & Stahelski, 1988). For example, our friends have *referent power* over us because we identify with them and want them to like us. Employers have both *reward power* (promotions, raises) and *coercive power* (demotions, firing) over their employees. Regardless of the type of resource involved, two factors affect the amount of power it provides.

First, resource-based power can only exist when the resource is valued. If someone controls a resource that you don't care about, that person has no power over you. Although people differ considerably in how much they value various resources, some basic resources—such as money, love, and prestige—are valued by most (Foa & Foa, 1980). The value of the relationship itself can also affect the power that intimate partners have over each other. In general, if the relationship is more important to one partner than to the other, the one who values the relationship less has more power (Caldwell & Peplau, 1984; Sprecher, 1985). As stated in the *principle of least interest*, "That person is able to dictate the conditions of association whose interest in the continuation of the affair is least" (Waller & Hill, 1951, p. 191). If you care and your partner doesn't, your partner is in the driver's seat.

Alternatives are the second factor affecting resource-based power. When a resource you value is controlled by a large number of people, then no single person has ultimate power over you. People who have attentive admirers waiting in the wings (a sky-high CLalt) will have more power in their existing relationship than those who have no other offers (a low CLalt). Marcia Guttentag and Paul Secord examined relationship alternatives by considering the overall sex ratio in a society (Guttentag & Secord, 1983; Secord, 1983). The **sex ratio** is the number of men per 100 women in a given population. A high ratio means that there are more men than women; a low ratio means fewer men than women. When the sex ratio is 100, the sexes are at parity. Sex ratios have varied dramatically in different historical periods. During the early years of the United States, the sex ratio was high: women were scarce in the colonies and on the frontier. In Europe after World War I, the sex ratio was low: millions of young men had died on the battlefields.

During the 1970s and 1980s, sex ratios created a "marriage squeeze." When the number of unmarried women over eighteen in the United States was compared with the number of unmarried men who were two years older, sex ratios were low: fewer men than women. (Younger women are compared with older men because women tend, on average, to marry men who are two to three years older.) The cause of low sex ratios during this period is no mystery; it's a baby-boom phenomenon. Throughout the post–World War II baby boom (1945–1957), more babies were born each year than in the preceding year: more in 1949 than in 1948; more in 1955 than in 1954. Therefore, the number of baby-boomer females is larger than the number of slightly older males.

But what about those born after the baby boom was over? Take, for example, people born in the 1970s who are now college age (Glick, 1988; Kennedy, 1989). Among this age group, the sex ratio for marriage is high: more men than women. This reversal over the baby-boom pattern reflects the relatively stable birthrates since 1958. Given a stable birthrate, the tendency for men to marry at an older age than do women increases the excess of unmarried young men. In general, the twenty-four-year-old woman in 1995 who is interested in getting married will have more alternatives than will her male peers.

sex ratio The number of men per 100 women in a given population. When men outnumber women, the sex ratio is high. When women outnumber men, the sex ratio is low.

Among students at West Point and the other U.S. military academies, the sex ratio is high, with more men than women. At most other coeducational colleges and universities, there are approximately equal numbers of men and women enrolled.

It should be noted, however, that two groups of women are likely to encounter low sex ratios in the United States regardless of whether they are baby-boomers or not: white women over forty, and black women of all ages (Guttentag & Secord, 1983; Tucker & Mitchell-Kernan, 1990). Factors that affect the sex ratios for these groups include the following:

- Men over forty who remarry tend to marry women who are five to six years younger rather than two to three years younger, thus shrinking the pool of older men available for older women.
- The mortality rate for men is greater than that for women, and the difference increases with age.
- Black men have particularly high mortality rates, regardless of age.
- Black men marry white women more often than black women marry white men.

From a social psychologist's perspective, sex ratios are important because they affect the balance of power between the genders. Since it limits alternatives, scarcity can increase the power of whatever or whoever is in short supply (Brock, 1968). Presumably, sex ratios affect behavior in a subtle and indirect fashion. People don't check out the census data to calculate their social power before going out on a date. Nor do many people think to themselves: "Hey, my gender's got the better market!" But most of us do have some general sense of what relational alternatives are available. Sex ratios that deviate greatly from parity are likely to affect this general assessment and may, then, influence the feelings and choices of individual men and women (Jemmott et al., 1989).

The Process of Power   Resources create the basis of power, but the process by which it is expressed involves behavior. The use of language may be one of the most subtle yet pervasive processes of power; how we talk to another person can be strongly influenced by the balance of power between us. Interrupting someone is usually associated with having greater social power (Kollock et al., 1985). And, on average, men interrupt women more than vice versa (West & Zimmerman, 1983). Men are more likely to dominate discussions of neutral topics as well as traditionally masculine topics, while women are conversationally dominant only on traditionally feminine subjects (Brown et al., 1990).

The relationship between power and touch is a good bit murkier. In her influential book, *Body Politics*, Nancy Henley (1977) maintained that men touch women more often than vice versa and that this difference reflects the use of touch as an expression of higher status and greater social power. Subsequent research confirmed Henley's observation that intentional touches with the hand are greater from male to female than from female to male (Hall & Veccia, 1990; Major et al., 1990). But the meaning of this phenomenon in terms of social power remains uncertain. Touch can be intrusive and demeaning, used to impose dominance over the person being touched. Alternatively, it can function as a gesture of solidarity, indicating warmth and concern. For example, touching each other in public may serve as a signal that a couple is making the transition from a superficial relationship to a more meaningful one. Couples who are seriously dating engage in more public touching than do casual daters or married couples (Guerrero & Andersen, 1991). An adequate understanding of the meaning of touch requires a careful consideration of the specific circumstances in which it occurs.

Possible gender differences in the ways that people get their way, called power strategies, have also been examined. The stereotype is that women employ indirect power strategies such as manipulating, hinting, pleading, and withdrawing, while men adopt more direct strategies such as asking, persuading, and bargaining. Research indicates, however, that the relationship between power strategies and gender is considerably more complicated (Aida & Falbo, 1991). But even if men and women don't always behave in accordance with their stereotypical style, the stereotypes themselves are widely believed (Gruber & White, 1986). What, then, are the social consequences of stepping out of line?

The rather astonishing results of one study suggest that the consequences can be severe (Filsinger & Thoma, 1988). These investigators first observed the verbal interaction of 31 dating couples and then were able to keep in touch with 21 of them over a five-year period. Whether or not the woman interrupted the man during the initial laboratory session was recorded as a measure of female dominance. Five years after this conversation took place, an amazing 80 percent of the couples in which the woman had interrupted the man had broken up! This is, of course, a very small sample of subjects, and it may not be appropriate to generalize these findings to other couples. Nevertheless, the basic point has been amply documented. Both women and men report less satisfaction with female-dominated relationships than with those that are either egalitarian or male dominated. This negative view of female dominance is found in both the United States (Gray-Little & Burks, 1983) as well as in more traditional societies such as India (Shukla & Kapoor, 1990).

Besides examining the responses of actual partners, social psychologists have also studied the social consequences of dominance by presenting subjects with experimentally created stimulus materials (written descriptions, audiotapes, or videotapes). The results of this research are decidedly mixed, particularly for male stimulus persons. Sometimes, dominant men are rated as more sexually attractive and desirable as a date than are nondominant men (Sadalla et al., 1987), but not always (Rainville & Gallagher, 1990). Sometimes dominant men are disliked (Sadalla et al., 1987), but not always (Carli, 1990). Reactions to female stimulus persons are more consistent. Although dominance is not always a social disadvantage for the women portrayed in these studies, it is extremely rare for a dominant woman to be evaluated more positively than a nondominant woman. Overall, then, women who behave in a powerful, assertive, and authoritative manner run a greater risk of experiencing negative social consequences than do men.

CONFLICT IN RELATIONSHIPS

Disagreements over sex, jealousy, and power can create serious conflict in intimate relationships. Whatever the cause, some degree of stress and conflict is inevitable when people have strong emotional ties to each other and, perhaps especially, when they live together. Judging by the extremely high divorce rate for new marriages in the United States that we cited at the beginning of this chapter, couples today have considerable difficulty coping with conflict and creating an enduring relationship.

Is this just a passing phase? Probably not. A high divorce rate may be self-perpetuating: divorce breeds divorce across generations. Children of divorce are themselves more likely to divorce, an effect that is strongest for white women (Glenn & Kramer, 1987). A self-fulfilling prophecy could be involved in this phenomenon. If people have lowered expectations for marital permanance, they may devote less effort to making the marriage work, thereby decreasing its endurance (Glenn, 1991).

There may be relatively little we can do about such lowered expectations. The high divorce rate is a fact that cannot be denied, nor does it seem likely that there would be much support for outlawing divorce or making it very hard to obtain. What we can do, however, is try to understand the process of conflict better so that we can become more skillful in managing it. Good performance, in marriage as elsewhere, depends on a reasonable combination of effort *and* skill.

Negative Affect Reciprocity and "Genderlects"

One of the major sources of conflict in an intimate relationship is the difficulty couples have in talking over their disagreements. Both heterosexual and homosexual couples cite commmunication problems as the most common factor contributing to their breakup (Cleek & Pearson, 1985; Kurdek, 1991b). But how does "bad communication" differ from "good communication"? What makes communication a problem? Studies comparing happy and distressed couples have discovered two communication patterns that often occur in troubled relationships.

negative affect reciprocity The quid-pro-quo exchange of behaviors, often non-verbal in nature, expressing negative feelings.

The first pattern involves **negative affect reciprocity**, the quid-pro-quo, tit-for-tat exchange of expressions of negative feelings (Gottman & Levenson, 1988; Noller & Fitzpatrick, 1990). Among both distressed and happy couples, expressions of negative affect tend to elicit more in-kind responses than expressions of positive affect. But negative affect reciprocity, especially in nonverbal behavior, is greater among distressed couples than among happy ones. These unhappy partners seem locked into a duel. Smiles pass by unnoticed, but every glare, every disgusted look, provokes a sharp response. The inability to terminate unpleasant nonverbal interactions has been found among distressed couples in Germany and Australia as well as in the United States (Halford et al., 1990).

The second pattern that characterizes communication in an unhappy relationship is gender specific. Earlier in this chapter, we described gender differences in same-sex friendships: women's greater emotional closeness, men's greater emphasis on sharing activities. But what happens when a conflict arises between a face-to-face woman and a side-by-side man? What tends to happen is that they don't communicate very well. She wants to talk about feelings; he wants to solve the problem. They both end up feeling like the title of Deborah Tannen's (1990) book on gender differences in communication: "You just don't understand."

These different styles and the lack of understanding they create can have long-term consequences. In a longitudinal study by Robert Levenson and John Gottman (1985), thirty married couples participated in an initial session in which their levels of positive and negative affect reciprocity were assessed, as well as their marital satisfaction. Three years later, nineteen couples who could be located and were still married indicated their current satisfaction. When change across the three-year period was examined, it was found that a decline in marital satisfaction was predicted by *more* reciprocity of the husband's negative affect by the wife in the initial session and by *less* reciprocity of the wife's negative affect by the husband. Thus, the traditional gender roles of the highly emotionally responsive woman and the highly emotionally *unresponsive*

Distressed couples often get locked into negative affect reciprocity, a tit-for-tat exchange in the expression of negative emotions. Such couples have particular difficulty terminating unpleasant *non*verbal interactions.

man appear to pose a risk for heterosexual couples in conflict. She keeps saying "Warm up" while he keeps urging "Calm down." Operating on different wavelengths, they never seem to hear each other.

Tannen (1990) views these gender differences in communication styles as akin to dialects of a language—"genderlects"—and urges men and women to learn to translate. Being sensitive and understanding about the partner's point of view is clearly important for couples' satisfaction with their relationship (Long & Andrews, 1990). But what motivates individuals in the heat of a quarrel to make that effort to understand, to develop a translation? Presumably, it helps to believe that there is, in fact, a communication problem. For this reason, intimate relationships between people with different native languages may have a certain advantage. When difficulties arise in intercultural relationships, the partners are likely to assume that they need to work harder on communicating (Fontaine, 1990). But what if the cause of trouble in the relationship is perceived to lie elsewhere?

The Attributional Trap

As it turns out, identifying the cause of relationship problems is closely associated with the quality of that relationship (Bradbury & Fincham, 1990;

Holtzworth-Munroe & Jacobson, 1987). Happy couples make *relationship-enhancing* attributions. Negative, undesirable behavior by the partner is brushed off: discounted as a reflection of situational influences ("A bad day"), temporary in nature ("It'll pass"), and viewed as unlikely to extend to other areas of the relationship ("That's just a sore spot"). But positive, pleasant behavior by the partner is taken much more seriously: viewed as characteristic of that person, stable across time, and likely to be repeated in other areas of the relationship. Thus, happy couples make external, unstable, and specific attributions for negative behavior by the partner. For positive behavior, they make internal, stable, and global attributions. In short, satisfied partners minimize the bad and exaggerate the good.

On the other hand, unhappy couples flip the attributional coin: they make *distress-maintaining* attributions. Whereas happy partners give each other the benefit of the doubt, distressed couples don't give an inch. For them, negative behaviors of the partner are characteristic of the person ("That's *so* typical"), long lasting ("It's always like this"), and extensive ("Everything turns out this way"). In contrast, positive behaviors get discounted as situational, temporary, and limited. Distressed partners exaggerate the bad and minimize the good. Figure 6.4 outlines the different types of attributions made by happy and unhappy couples.

The tunnel vision produced by these different interpretations of the partner's behavior would seem to act as a screen, latching on to behaviors consistent with the overall state of the relationship and filtering out discrepant behaviors. Over time, the happy should get happier and the miserable more miserable. But do they? Do attributions for the partner's behavior *lead* to differences in satisfaction, or do they simply *reflect* how people already feel? Frank Fincham and his colleagues attempted to answer this question. In one study, wives who initially made more distress-maintaining attributions reported less marital satisfaction a year later (Fincham & Bradbury, 1987). In another study, however, early attributions predicted marital satisfaction a year later only for husbands (Fincham et al., 1990). Although the reasons for the gender differences are not clear, these two studies do suggest that causal attributions for the partner's behavior can have an influence on subsequent satisfaction with the relationship.

The possible role of attributions in affecting the quality of a relationship indicates that trying to understand the other person's point of view during conflict is not sufficient. It is also necessary to consider whether our own point of view is distorted and biased. Distress-maintaining attributions can be traps of our own making. If so, we should be able to dismantle them.

COPING AFTER A RELATIONSHIP ENDS

Conflict does not always lead to the dissolution of a relationship. Indeed, handled skillfully with genuine concern for the partner, conflict can strengthen

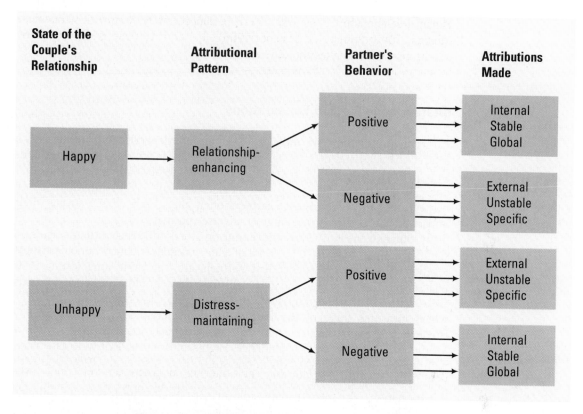

Figure 6.4 Patterns of Attributions Made by Happy and Unhappy Couples. The pattern of attributions made for a partner's behavior varies with the state of the relationship. Happy couples accent the positive and discount the negative; unhappy couples accent the negative and discount the positive.

an intimate attachment. But, sometimes, partners are unable to respond constructively to conflict. Instead, they may become passive—hoping things will get better but fearing they will get worse. Although a passive response to conflict may be adequate in some circumstances, often it isn't. The omission of a positive response can, at times, be as damaging to a relationship as angry, hostile behavior (Rusbult et al., 1986). If conflict continues, one or both of the partners may decide it's time to leave. These four basic responses have been summarized as follows (Rusbult et al., 1982):

Voice: Actively trying to improve the relationship
Loyalty: Passively waiting for things to get better
Neglect: Passively allowing things to get worse
Exit: Leaving the relationship

When a relationship does end, the experience can be traumatic (Kitson & Morgan, 1990; Stroebe & Stroebe, 1986). But not everyone is devastated by such a loss. What makes the difference?

Interdependence and Expectations

Earlier in this chapter, we indicated that the interdependence of partners is a central characteristic of intimate relationships. In an interdependent relationship, partners' lives are intertwined. What each one does affects what the other one can do and wants to do (Berscheid & Peplau, 1983). Interdependence between intimates is frequent (partners often affect each other), strong (their impact on each other is meaningful), diverse (partners influence each other in many different areas of life), and enduring (their influence extends across a significant time period). Like a social glue, interdependence bonds partners together. The more interdependent partners are, the more long lasting their relationship should be and the greater distress they should experience if it ends (Berscheid, 1983). Research using the Relationship Closeness Inventory (RCI), which measures three of the four major characteristics of interdependency (frequency, strength, and diversity of partner impact), provides some support for the importance of interdependence. High scores on the RCI were associated with longer-lasting relationships in one study (Berscheid et al., 1989) and with more post-breakup distress in another (Simpson, 1987).

Expectations also play a major role in reactions to the loss of an intimate relationship. Coping is often more difficult for both heterosexual and homosexual individuals if the partner's desire for separation was not anticipated (Brehm, 1992; Kurdek, 1991b) or if the partner dies unexpectedly (Hansson et al., 1988). But research on the reactions of widows suggests that mere anticipation of the loss of a partner is not the key factor in improving adjustment (Remondet et al., 1987). Instead, anticipation will be helpful to the extent that it allows the individual to engage in coping behaviors before the loss has actually occurred. Those women who began to do things on their own and planned for the future before their husband's death experienced less emotional disruption afterwards. By actively beginning to cope, people create the positive expectation that they will be able to manage their own emotional distress. And, indeed, such expectations are associated with better adjustment after the loss of a relationship (Mearns, 1991).

Social Networks

Confronted with the loss of an intimate relationship, people often seek out others: friends, family, professional help, new romantic relationships (Chiriboga et al., 1979). There is ample evidence that having a social network is associated

"Oh, I've had a few failures, followed by a string of successful marriages."

In the United States, most divorced individuals, around 80 percent, remarry. Remarriages run about the same risk of marital disruption as do first marriages. [Drawing by Bernard Schoenbaum; © 1991 The New Yorker Magazine, Inc.]

with better adjustment to the loss of a relationship. Divorced parents who participate in more social activities outside the home report less stress (Raschke, 1977). Similarly, widows involved with neighbors and friends feel better about their lives (Arling, 1976).

But not all social contacts provide the same type of assistance, and what an individual needs from others may be influenced by what was formerly obtained in the relationship. For example, because close friendships between males are not encouraged in our society, most American husbands have a confiding relationship only with their wife (Veroff et al., 1981). If their marriage ends, they need emotional support. On the other hand, because women earn less than men in our society, many divorced and widowed women suffer considerable financial hardship (Duncan & Hoffman, 1985). They need economic assistance and employment opportunities. Thus, simply having people around is not enough. Individuals who are coping with the loss of an intimate relationship have specific needs for specific kinds of assistance (Gerstel, 1988). How well what they receive matches what they need will have a major influence on their success in rebuilding their lives.

Beginning Again

Among divorced individuals, the preferred method of rebuilding one's life is to marry again. Half of all recent marriages involve at least one previously married individual (Bumpass et al., 1990). Overall, around 80 percent of divorced individuals remarry (Norton, 1987). Men, however, are more likely to remarry than women. The rate of remarriage for men is about 83 percent, while the rate for women may be as low as 70 percent (Norton & Moorman, 1987). Remarried men also report greater marital satisfaction than do remarried women (Vemer et al., 1989). Although most research has indicated that second marriages fail sooner and at a faster rate than do first ones, these findings may reflect the increased likelihood of remarriage for individuals who have an especially high divorce rate: those who first married at a very young age and those with little education. When these factors are taken into account, remarriages appear to have no greater risk of disruption than first marriages (Castro Martin & Bumpass, 1989).

Divorce and remarriage, along with the increasing number of children born to unmarried women, have radically altered the face of family life in the United States. In 1960, 73 percent of American children under the age of 18 lived with both their biological parents. In the 1990s, only a little over 50 percent are expected to be part of a traditional nuclear family (Jacobson, 1987). Most of the rest will live with one parent, usually their mother, or in a stepfamily. This chapter has concentrated on intimate relationships between adults and, as we have seen, these relationships do not always last a lifetime. But some of them produce a child, a living link to the future. As individuals and as a society, it is our most urgent task to ensure that the children in *all* types of families have a decent chance to pursue the important life goals listed at the beginning of this chapter.

REVIEW

College students place a high priority on having a satisfying and enduring relationship with a romantic partner. But 50 percent, or more, of the marriages that take place today will end in divorce. This discrepancy makes the study of intimate relationships particularly important.

DEFINING INTIMATE RELATIONSHIPS

Adult intimate relationships include at least one of three components: emotional attachment, fulfillment of psychological needs, and interdependence. They vary in sexuality, sexual orientation, commitment, and type and intensity of feelings.

FROM ATTRACTION TO LOVE

Stages of Relationship Development

Stage theories, such as the stimulus-value-role theory, propose that intimate relationships go through a specific sequence of stages. But evidence for a fixed sequence is weak.

Quantitative and Qualitative Differences in Relationships

Two other views of relationship development emphasize either the step-by-step accumulation of rewards or the sharp distinction between different types of relationships.

BUILDING A RELATIONSHIP

Social Exchange: The Intimate Marketplace

According to social exchange theory, people seek to maximize gains and minimize costs in relationships. Higher rewards and lower costs are associated with greater satisfaction with the relationship. An outcome that meets or exceeds a person's general expectations for relationships (CL) is associated with greater satisfaction. When expectations about alternatives to the relationship (CLalt) are low, people are more committed. Greater investments in the relationship are also associated with greater commitment. Perceptions of rewards, costs, CL, CLalt, and investments involve subjective judgments. Equity theory, a specific type of social exchange theory, predicts that relationship satisfaction will be greatest when the ratio between benefits and contributions is similar for both partners. Although both overbenefited and underbenefited partners experience negative emotions, the overbenefited are more satisfied. Absolute level of rewards obtained is sometimes a better predictor of relationship satisfaction than is equity, though equity is a good predictor for individuals with an exchange orientation.

Self-Disclosure: Growing Closer

As predicted by the theory of social penetration, self-disclosure between partners becomes broader and deeper as a relationship develops. Some troubled relationships are characterized by self-disclosure that is narrow in topics discussed but deep in negative feelings revealed. In general, women tend to initiate or elicit more self-disclosure than do men. Women's friendships are based more on emotional sharing, men's on engaging in common activities.

TYPES OF RELATIONSHIPS

Liking Versus Loving: The Great Divide?

Liking and loving may be two distinct kinds of intimate relationships, but not all couples distinguish between the two. People in communal relationships are more considerate of and giving to the partner, whereas people in exchange relationships are more self-interested.

Different Types of Love: How Do I Love Thee?

The most common approach to distinguishing among different types of love divides love into two categories: passionate and companionate. Alternative categorizations include attachment styles, "colors" of love, and components of love. By means of excitation transfer, arousal caused by an impersonal experience can be added to arousal elicited by the beloved, thereby increasing sexual attraction and passionate love. Passionate love may endure for long periods of time if an individual is uncertain about the beloved's commitment to the relationship. In contrast, companionate love is based on trust and a concern for the partner as well as for oneself.

RELATIONSHIP ISSUES

Sexuality

By their late teens, the vast majority of young women and men in the United States are sexually active. There is some evidence that dating relationships with sex last longer than those without it. But the greater access to regular sexual activity enjoyed by cohabiting couples does not increase their chances of marital success. Heterosexual couples appear to have more difficulty communicating about sex than do homosexual couples, perhaps because of gender differences in sexual attitudes and roles. Men are more permissive than women in their sexual behavior and values. Women's traditional role as the sexual "gate-keeper" gives them the power to control the pace of sexual activities in the relationship, but exposes them to the risk of being forced to engage in sex. The AIDS epidemic has taken an enormous toll in human lives and suffering. Although new cases of HIV infection have dramatically declined among gay men in the United States, they are increasing among intravenous-drug users and heterosexuals.

Jealousy

Jealousy is created by a perceived threat to an existing relationship, regardless of the actual reality. The strongest feelings of jealousy are produced by a threat to sexual exclusivity. Jealous individuals can develop irrational beliefs about their situation; emotional reactions involved in jealousy are mostly, but not entirely, negative. There are marked cross-cultural differences in coping with jealousy and, at least in the United States, some striking gender differences. A sense of independence and self-worth may be crucial in coping constructively with jealousy.

Social Power

Control over different types of resources produces different types of social power. The partner who values a relationship least has the most power, and people who have more relational alternatives have more power in their relationships. Sex ratios—the number of men compared with the number of women—affect how many alternative partners are available. Interrupting someone is associated with having greater social power. Both men and women report less satisfaction in female-dominated relationships than in either egalitarian or male-dominated relationships.

CONFLICT IN RELATIONSHIPS

Negative Affect Reciprocity and "Genderlects"

Unhappy partners exchange negative nonverbal behaviors more often than do happy partners. During conflict, women tend to become highly emotional and men extremely practical, almost as though they were speaking different languages. Communication can be improved by trying to understand the other person's point of view.

The Attributional Trap

Happy couples make relationship-enhancing attributions. They attribute the partner's positive behavior to internal, stable, and global causes. Negative behavior is attributed to external, unstable, and specific causes. Unhappy couples make distress-maintaining attributions, the mirror image of the pattern shown by happy couples. These attributional patterns may influence subsequent satisfaction with the relationship.

COPING AFTER A RELATIONSHIP ENDS

Four basic responses to relational conflict have been identified: voice, loyalty, neglect, and exit.

Interdependence and Expectations

Partners who are more interdependent (having a frequent, strong, and diverse impact on one another) have longer-lasting relationships or experience more distress if the relationship ends. An unexpected loss creates more distress than one that has been anticipated.

Social Networks

Having a social network is associated with better adjustment to the loss of a relationship. What people need from others may depend on what they previously obtained in the relationship. Typically, men have a greater need for emotional support after the end of a relationship; women, for economic assistance.

Beginning Again

The vast majority of divorced individuals remarry. Divorce and remarriage, along with children born to single mothers, have changed the face of the American family.

Helping Others

7

Outline

Preview

This chapter describes the social psychology of giving and receiving help. First, we examine *personal, situational,* and *interpersonal influences* that affect whether a potential helper will provide assistance to a person in need. Then, people's *reactions to receiving help* are considered. In the concluding section we discuss the important social issue of *helping the homeless.*

S ometimes helping makes the news. On one busy summer day, two New York City police officers delivered a baby and then, before they even had time to write up their report on the first incident, rushed off to pull a would-be suicide from the subway tracks. Their exploits were widely publicized. But most helping never receives any media attention: giving a friend a ride, donating food and clothing for disaster relief, baby-sitting for a relative, working as a volunteer on a literacy project. Helping others is so commonplace, so much a part of the fabric of everyday life, that it usually isn't newsworthy. Yet we know that just because help is needed doesn't mean that it will be given. The homeless wander through city streets; children starve; victims of vicious assaults cry out and are ignored. It seems awfully confusing. Are people helpful or not?

Social psychologists would suggest that we need to rephrase the question. To ask *whether* people are helpful is like asking whether people dance. All of them, all of the time, no. But some of them, some of the time, yes. The real issues are more precise. *Why* do people help? *When* do they help? *Whom* do they help? This chapter seeks to answer these questions, looking first at personal and situational influences on helping and then considering interpersonal factors that affect the help people give. Turning to the other side of helping, we examine how people react to the help they receive. In the final section, we summarize a major theme in this chapter and apply it to the important social issue of helping the homeless.

PERSONAL INFLUENCES: WHY DO PEOPLE HELP?

In his novel *Foundation and Earth,* science fiction writer Isaac Asimov described some imaginary planets whose inhabitants differ markedly in helping behavior. On Gaia, life is a unified whole. Because everyone is interconnected, there is no distinction between helping someone else and helping oneself. What's good for one is good for all. On Solaria, residents live strictly apart, each served by multitudes of robots. Cooperation is kept to a bare minimum and offered only for bare necessities. These planets represent two extremes in helping. Inhabitants of Gaia always help, automatically; inhabitants of Solaria never help unless they have to do so in order to get their own needs met.

There is, however, a third possibility, represented by the character Pelorat, a descendant and seeker of planet Earth. Bliss, who lives on Gaia, finds Pelorat amazing: he "is not selfless because he is part of a greater whole. He is selfless because he is selfless. . . . He has all to lose and nothing to gain" (p. 166). In other words, Pelorat helps others because he puts their welfare above his own. Although the planets Gaia and Solaria and the characters Bliss and Pelorat are fictional creations, they raise some basic questions about real-life helping right here on planet Earth. Do people help automatically because of innate characteristics? Do people help only for personal gain? Do people help in order to benefit the other person? As we will see, social psychologists have considered each of these issues in their examination of personal influences on helping.

Genetic Factors in Helping

We begin at the very beginning: the evolution of the human species. As described in Chapter 5, the application of the principles of evolutionary biology to the understanding of social behavior is known as *sociobiology*. After discussing some sociobiological theories of helping, we examine whether an innate tendency to help might be stronger for some individuals than for others.

Individual and Genetic Survival From the perspective of sociobiology, human social behavior is best understood in terms of its relationship to reproductive success: the conception, birth, and survival of offspring. Genetically based social behaviors that enhance reproductive success have a lock on the future. Passed on to the next generation—and successive generations after that—these behaviors could become part of the common inheritance of the species. In order to reproduce, of course, the individual must survive. Being helped *by* others should increase the chances of survival. But what about being helpful *to* others? Since helping others can be costly in terms of time and effort and, sometimes, even dangerous to the helper, being helpful would seem to decrease one's chances of survival. Any genetically based propensities for helping should have dropped out of the gene pool long ago.

But maybe not. Sociobiologists have identified two types of helping that seem compatible with evolutionary theory. The first is *reciprocal helping*, in which people help those who help them (Krebs, 1987). So long as everyone abides by this golden rule, everyone benefits. But what if some people cheat—taking help from others but not providing it in return? Once cheating enters the picture, the possible evolutionary path of helping becomes a great deal more complicated (Alexander, 1974; Trivers, 1971). On the one hand, ways to prevent or reduce cheating might evolve: the ability to detect cheaters so as to avoid helping them; the desire to punish those who take but don't give back. On the other hand, since cheating provides a survival benefit to the cheater, the tendency to cheat might also pass the test of natural selection. One could imagine a sort of internal War of the Roses as these conflicting innate tendencies—to give, to withhold, to cheat—compete to influence an individual's actual behavior.

The notion of reciprocal helping focuses on the survival of the individual in order to transmit adaptive characteristics to subsequent generations. In fact, however, natural selection operates at the genetic level. Most of the time, genetic and individual survival are identical. Individuals preserve their genes in the gene pool by staying alive long enough to produce offspring. But there is an alternative. You can also preserve your genes by promoting the survival of those who share your genetic make-up, even if you perish in the effort to help them. By means of this indirect route to genetic survival, a second type of helping,

kinship selection
Preferential helping of
blood relatives, which
increases the odds
that genes held in
common will be
transmitted to subse-
quent generations.

called **kinship selection**, could become an innate characteristic (Hamilton, 1964; Ridley & Dawkins, 1981). From the outside, the individual helping a relative looks self-sacrificing. But on the inside, the "selfish gene" plots its immortality (Dawkins, 1976).

The Social Context   Reciprocal helping and kinship selection are the most common sociobiological explanations for how helping could become innate. More recent proposals take a broader view of the social context in which helping occurs. Herbert Simon (1990), for example, maintains that helping others, even at a cost to the helper, occurs as an unintended consequence of "docility." Those who are docile, says Simon, learn from others how to cope with their physical and social environments. For the most part, what is learned is personally advantageous, but docile individuals also adopt individually costly behaviors encouraged by society—such as being helpful to those in need. As long as the costs of helping do not often exceed the benefits of other aspects of social learning, being docile should, on the average, enhance individual survival and reproductive success. Thus, from Simon's perspective, being helpful is just a cost of doing a usually profitable business.

Ross Buck and Benson Ginsburg (1991) also believe that helping others is a consequence of more general innate characteristics. These investigators stress

Do siblings take care of each other in order to preserve their own genes? According to the sociobiological concept of kinship selection, helping a relative survive is an innate, universal tendency that evolved because relatives who reproduce transmit some of the *helper's* genes to future generations.

the importance of the spontaneous communication of feelings and desires—cries of delight, whimpers of fear, gasps of surprise. Buck and Ginsburg regard this type of communication as genetically hard-wired into the organism and see in it the basis for social bonds developed early in life. In turn, social bonds create the capacity to have a sympathetic and helpful response to individuals in need.

The proposed roles of docility and social communication are particularly interesting because they offer an alternative to the view that helping is a direct result of natural selection. Instead, helping is presented as a by-product of other social tendencies that are themselves adaptive. This approach avoids one of the major criticisms lodged against many sociobiological explanations. Sociobiology, its critics contend, frequently makes the mistake of assuming that any existing characteristic must have adaptive benefits (Archer, 1991; Gould, 1991). Actually, natural selection is not that precise. Favorable genes with a reproductive advantage can drop out of the gene pool; multiple adaptive outcomes may be possible, with the choice between them determined by chance events; and the adaptive consequences of natural selection can have by-products that are or are not favorable for reproductive success. By emphasizing such by-products as a possible source for an innate tendency to help others, models focusing on the broader social context remind us of the complex effects of natural selection on social behavior.

Personality   Up to this point, we have considered whether helping could be a genetically transmitted, universal tendency. But perhaps helping runs in families rather than through the whole human race. According to J. Philippe Rushton and his colleagues (1984), some individuals have a stronger genetically based propensity to help than do others. Rushton examines a wide range of actions and feelings in his research on helping, including spontaneous helping not based on anticipated reciprocity, helpful behavior to people who are not blood relatives, and positive social emotions such as kindness and sympathy.

The self-reported characteristics of twins offer some support for Rushton's argument. Genetically identical (monozygotic) twins are more similar in the helpful behavioral tendencies and positive social emotions they report than are fraternal (dizygotic) twins, who share only a portion of their genetic make-up (Matthews et al., 1981; Rushton et al., 1986). Taken at face value, these findings indicate that helpfulness is an inherited trait, especially pronounced in some families and some individuals. But this conclusion should be taken with a grain of skeptical salt. Twin studies using self-report questionnaires provide relatively weak evidence of heritability (Plomin & Fulker, 1987).

altruistic personality
A trait or combination of traits said to produce helping across a wide variety of situations, even where there are no external rewards for helping.

Rushton (1981), however, believes that the evidence for the heritability of helpfulness is sufficient to indicate a genetic basis for what he calls the **altruistic personality**. A person with such a personality is said to engage in many different kinds of helpful behaviors across a wide variety of situations, even where there are no external rewards to be gained by the helper. The notion of an altruistic personality has generated a good deal of controversy (Batson et al.,

1986; Carlo et al., 1991). What does seem clear is that no single personality characteristic, or set of characteristics, has yet been identified that is associated with being helpful in all situations. Personality is relatively constant, but helping appears remarkably varied.

Emotional Factors in Helping

Perhaps because of this variability, many researchers have focused on emotional influences on helping behavior (Salovey et al., 1991). Moods are notoriously changeable, affected by both internal and external factors. How we feel might well contribute to what we do in response to another person's need for assistance. And if our mood changes, so would our willingness to help.

Good Mood: A Spirit of Generosity   Consider, for example, sunshine in Minneapolis. Over the course of a year, some pedestrians in this city were stopped and asked to participate in a survey of social opinions. When Michael Cunningham (1979) tabulated their responses according to the weather conditions, he discovered that people answered more questions on sunny days than on cloudy ones. Moving his investigation indoors, Cunningham found that restaurant customers left more generous tips when there was more sunshine. Sunshine sets the stage for helpful acts, but how?

The most likely explanation is that a sunny day cheers us up. Indeed, all kinds of pleasant, mood-lifting experiences can increase helping: being successful on a task (Isen, 1970); reading pleasant positive statements (Aderman, 1972); being offered a cookie (Isen & Levin, 1972); imagining a Hawaiian vacation (Rosenhan et al., 1981); listening to a comedy routine by Steve Martin (Wilson, 1981). Across many different circumstances, the **good mood effect** has been clearly demonstrated. What makes us happy also tends to make us helpful.

good mood effect
The effect whereby a good mood increases helping behavior.

Despite strong evidence of the effect itself, there is debate about the process by which it occurs (Carlson et al., 1988). On the one hand, the *mood maintenance hypothesis* proposes that happy people help in order to stay happy. Helping others, particularly those with whom we desire a closer relationship, can enhance our own mood (Williamson & Clark, 1992). By helping them when we're happy, we stay happy. On the other hand, perhaps people in a good mood are more helpful because they have more happy *thoughts*. Various kinds of positive thoughts could influence helping. When we feel good, we are more aware of the rewards of helping and expect helping to be a more pleasant experience (Isen et al., 1978). A good mood also increases positive thoughts about other people (Forgas & Bower, 1987), and the more we like someone the more we should be willing to help that person. Combining reward expectations with social sensitivity, Cunningham and his colleagues (1990b) propose that good moods increase helping by means of positive thoughts about the rewarding nature of social activities in general. These possible relationships between feeling good and doing good are diagrammed in Figure 7.1.

Being in a good mood increases helping, and helping others increases good feelings and positive thoughts.

Whatever its exact cause, the good mood effect has two striking features. First, it doesn't last very long. Typically, the increase in helping produced by a good mood is of short duration (Isen et al., 1976). Second, it appears to be a relatively automatic phenomenon. Unlike some other influences on helping, the good mood effect is found across the life span. Even young children help more when they feel happy and cheerful (Moore et al., 1973).

Negative Emotions: Seeking Relief   Since a good mood increases helping, does a bad mood decrease it? Not necessarily. Under some circumstances, being in a bad mood can actually increase helping (Carlson & Miller, 1987). This section examines three instances in which negative emotions could produce helpful consequences: feeling guilty after a transgression, becoming self-aware, and seeking relief from sadness.

When we think about how guilt could increase helping, what usually come to mind are those situations in which the same person triggers our guilt and receives our help. Feeling guilty about getting too worked up during a trivial

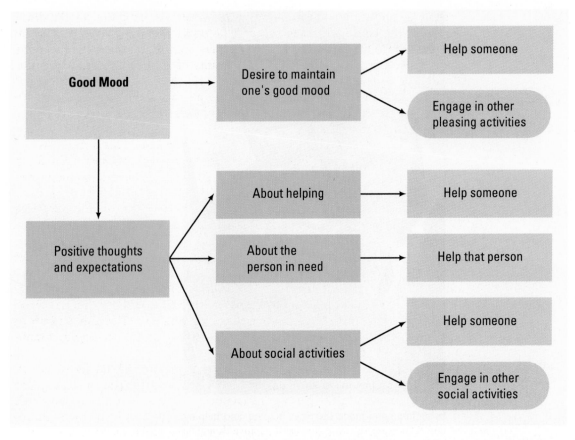

Figure 7.1   Effects of a Good Mood on Helping: Alternative Paths.   Although the positive influence of a good mood on helping behavior has been clearly demonstrated, there is still debate about the process involved. One possibility is that the desire to maintain a good mood leads to helping because helping makes people (continue to) feel good. Alternatively, positive thoughts generated by being in a good mood may lead people to help in order to obtain the rewards they expect from being helpful. You should note that a good mood can also energize actions other than helping.

disagreement with a friend, we may gratefully seize the next available opportunity to help that individual. Here, being helpful restores a good relationship. As social psychologists have demonstrated, however, the effects of guilt on helping can be much more widespread (J. W. Regan, 1971).

Imagine yourself in the following situation. A stranger approaches you on the street and asks you to use his camera to take his picture for a school project. You get ready, aim, and . . . nothing. The camera doesn't seem to work. Looking concerned, the stranger says the camera is rather delicate, asks you if you touched any of the dials, and informs you that now it will have to be fixed. You continue on your way down the street. As you pass a young woman, she drops a file folder containing some papers. Now, here's the question: Are you more likely to help the woman pick up her papers because you think you broke the other person's camera? Based on the results of a study that employed this "broken-equipment" scenario, the answer is clearly yes. In this experiment, 80 percent of subjects who were led to believe that they had broken the male stranger's camera helped the female stranger pick up her papers; only 40 percent of subjects who had no broken-camera experience stopped to help (Cunningham et al., 1980). Feeling guilty about our behavior with one person, we are more helpful to the next person. Indeed, people are sometimes *more* helpful to an uninvolved bystander who witnessed their transgression than to the person they actually harmed (Carlsmith & Gross, 1969).

Guilt is produced by violating the dictates of conscience, our own internal guidelines for what we think we ought to do. In Chapter 2, we described a theory that speaks to the power of conscience. *Self-awareness theory* holds that attention to self usually brings with it a sensitivity to existing discrepancies between our values and our actions (Duval & Wicklund, 1972; Wicklund, 1975). Since such discrepancies are unpleasant, self-aware individuals are strongly motivated to live up to their own internal standards. Think about it. Does becoming more aware of yourself (seeing yourself reflected in a mirror or store window, or hearing your name) increase your helpful actions toward others?

According to Frederick Gibbons and Robert Wicklund (1982), it depends on whether you pay more attention to self-concerns or to the value of helping. The self-aware individual who is preoccupied with various self-concerns pays little attention to the needs of others and is, in fact, unlikely to help others (Berkowitz, 1970). Thinking about our own needs ("Why didn't they like me?" "Why didn't I get a better grade?") takes our mind off the needs of others. But when the value of helping is particularly important for an individual or particularly conspicuous in a specific situation, then self-awareness increases helping as the individual is motivated to behave in accordance with this value. For example, becoming self-aware during the Christmas season, when values of love and charity are prominent in people's minds, should increase helping behavior, but not among those worried about getting all their Christmas shopping done in time.

Self-awareness may also provide a bridge between people's feelings and their helpful behaviors. When people are in a good mood, anxious self-concerns are reduced (Berkowitz, 1987). With fewer self-concerns to distract from the desire to live up to helpful standards, the self-aware individual in a good mood should be more willing to lend a hand. But what about a bad mood? Here, the key is whether people accept responsibility for their feelings. When an individual takes personal responsibility for a bad mood, self-awareness is enhanced, and—as long as the value of helping is important—helpful behaviors increase (Rogers et al., 1982). If, however, the responsibility for being in a bad mood is placed elsewhere, self-awareness is not enhanced, nor is helping increased. On your way home after a bad day, you're more likely to help someone in need if you take responsibility for your own bad mood ("I shouldn't let myself get so upset about these things") than if you blame your mood on others ("Those people can't get anything right! They're driving me crazy!"). Assuming the responsibility for our own distress allows us to respond to the plight of others. Figure 7.2 depicts the relationship among mood, self-awareness, and helping.

Guilt and self-awareness can promote helpful behavior because people want to avoid feeling bad about failing to do the right thing. In their **negative state relief model**, Robert Cialdini and his colleagues stress that people also want to avoid feeling sad (Cialdini et al., 1973; Manucia et al., 1984). As noted earlier, helping can make us feel good. And people know it. Responding to a questionnaire in *Better Homes and Gardens*, readers said that helping others gave them a "helper's high," a sense of well-being and self-worth that could be recaptured by remembering the helping experience (Luks, 1988). Thus, says Cialdini, if people are feeling the blues or the blahs, they will help in order to feel better.

negative state relief model   The proposition that people help others in order to counteract their own feelings of sadness or depression.

Figure 7.2   Effects of Self-Awareness on Helping: Self-Concerns Versus the Value of Helping.   The effect of self-awareness on helping depends on the balance between self-concerns and the value of helping. Increased self-awareness will increase helping when self-concerns are weak and the value of helping is strong. Self-awareness also serves as a bridge between people's feelings and their helpful behavior. Taking responsibility for a negative mood enhances self-awareness and, as long as the value of helping is strong, increases helping. A good mood decreases self-concerns, thereby increasing helping among self-aware individuals.

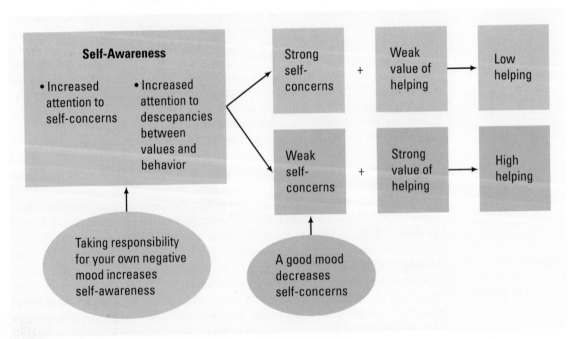

Although the pros (Cialdini & Fultz, 1990) and the cons (Miller & Carlson, 1990) of the negative state relief model are currently the subject of a lively disagreement, even its proponents have emphasized the limits of its application. First, the model specifies that only mild negative feelings such as discomfort, sadness, and temporary depression will increase helping. Hostile negative emotions such as anger and resentment reduce helping. Second, negative state relief appears to work only for adults, not children (Cialdini & Kenrick, 1976). It takes time and experience to learn the connection between helping others and feeling better (Kenrick et al., 1979). The third limitation on the negative state relief model involves the costs and rewards of helping (Weyant, 1978). People in a bad mood help more than those in a neutral mood only when the costs for helping are low (it can be easily provided) and the rewards for helping are high (it is clearly beneficial to those in need). Cost-effective helping may spell relief for the person who is "down" and seeking to be "up." But help that is hard to provide and uncertain in its effects is just another headache.

We have now considered three possible explanations for how negative emotional states might increase helping:

- *Guilt:* People who feel guilty help in order to feel better about themselves.
- *Self-awareness:* Taking personal responsibility for negative emotions increases self-awareness. Heightened self-awareness can motivate individuals to conform to personal standards that emphasize the virtue of helping others.
- *Negative state relief:* People who feel sad or depressed help in order to improve their mood.

Notice that all three of these explanations assume a self-centered bottom line. The ultimate beneficiary is the *helper*, who feels less guilty, more virtuous, or less depressed. Even the good mood effect may be based on a selfish motive—the desire to engage in what is expected to be a rewarding experience. In short, most perspectives on the relationship between emotions and helping reach the same conclusion: helping is **egoistic**, motivated by the desire to increase one's own welfare. People help others in order to help themselves. But wait. Is that the end of the matter?

egoistic Motivated by the desire to increase one's own welfare.

Does Altruism Exist?

Although most psychological theories assume an egoistic, self-interested bottom line (Wallach & Wallach, 1983), not everyone is content with this account of the motives for human behavior. In an impressive series of studies, C. Daniel Batson (1991) has developed a different point of view: some helpful actions are **altruistic**, motivated by the desire to increase another's welfare. You should note that Batson's definition of altruism differs from others' use of the term. On the one hand, he is less inclusive than Rushton, whose notion of an altruistic personality implies that all helpful actions in the absence of a clear external reward are altruistic. On the other hand, Batson is more inclusive than those

altruistic Motivated by the desire to increase another's welfare.

who restrict altruism to helpful actions requiring personal sacrifice by the helper. For Batson, the nature of the helping act is determined by the nature of the helper's motive. Regardless of whether you win the gold or lose your shirt, so long as your motive is to help the other person, your behavior is altruistic. In this section, we consider Batson's model of how altruistic motives develop, and then take a look at some egoistic alternatives seeking to explain the same behavior.

The Empathy-Altruism Hypothesis   Empathy has long been considered an important factor in promoting positive behavior toward others (Eisenberg & Miller, 1987). Although its definition has been much debated (Eisenberg & Fabes, 1991), most researchers regard empathy as a multidimensional phenomenon with both emotional and cognitive components (Davis, 1983). One of the emotional components of empathy is *personal distress:* self-oriented reactions—such as being alarmed, troubled, upset—to a person in need. In contrast, *empathic concern* involves other-oriented feelings such as sympathy, compassion, and tenderness. Research using various behavioral measures (physiological and nonverbal as well as verbal responses) has supported the distinction between these two types of emotional experience (Eisenberg et al., 1989; Tangney, 1991).

The major cognitive component of empathy is *perspective-taking*, using the power of imagination to try to see the world through someone else's eyes. According to Batson's **empathy-altruism hypothesis**, perspective-taking is the beginning of altruism. Perceiving someone in need and imagining how that person feels create other-oriented feelings of empathic concern, which in turn produce the altruistic motive to reduce the other person's distress. Without perspective-taking, the perception of a person in need creates self-oriented feelings of personal distress, which in turn produce the egoistic motive to reduce one's own distress. Thus, says the empathy-altruism hypothesis, altruistic motives require a double dose of empathy, cognitive as well as emotional. The basic features of the empathy-altruism hypothesis are outlined in Figure 7.3.

Describing these connections is just the first step. Now comes the hard part. How can we tell the difference between egoistic and altruistic motives? In both cases, the person helps, but for different reasons. Confronted with this puzzle, Batson came up with an elegant solution based on how easy it is to escape from a helping situation. When empathic concern is low, people can satisfy their motive to reduce their own distress through helping the person in need *or* through escaping from the scene of the victim's suffering. Out of sight, out of mind—so long, personal distress. But when empathic concern is high, people have no such choice. Only by helping the victim can the motive to reduce the victim's distress be satisfied. This logic allowed Batson to separate the sheep from the goats. When a person's motive is egoistic, helping should decline if it's easy for the individual to escape from the situation. When a person's motive is altruistic, however, help will be given regardless of the ease of escape.

empathy-altruism hypothesis The proposition that empathic concern for a person in need produces an altruistic motive for helping.

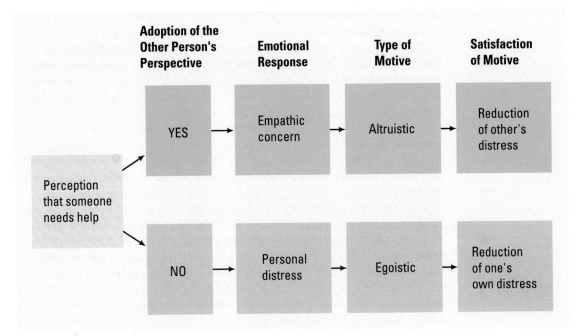

Figure 7.3   The Empathy-Altruism Hypothesis.   According to the empathy-altruism hypothesis, taking the perspective of a person in need creates feelings of empathic concern, which produce the altruistic motive to reduce the other person's distress. When, however, people do *not* take the other's perspective, they experience feelings of personal distress, which produce the egoistic motive to reduce their own discomfort. [Based on Batson, 1991.]

Batson and his colleagues have tested these predictions in a number of studies. To see how you might respond, put yourself in the position of a subject in one of their experiments (Batson et al., 1981). Arriving at the research laboratory, you are told that a second subject, Elaine, is a few minutes late but you should start reading the procedures of the upcoming experiment. Handed an information sheet, you discover that the study will investigate task performance under unpleasant conditions. One of the participants will perform a task while receiving random electric shocks; the other participant will observe. Drawing lots, you're relieved to be assigned to the observer role. You are then escorted to the observation room. Over closed-circuit TV, you see that Elaine has arrived. Hooked up to some scary-looking equipment, she takes a few shocks and appears increasingly uncomfortable. After asking for a glass of water, she tells the experimenter about a frightening childhood experience when she was thrown from a horse against an electric fence. Though she finds the shocks she is now receiving very unpleasant, Elaine says she still wants to go on. The experimenter hesitates; perhaps Elaine should stop at this point. And then the experimenter has a bright idea. Would *you* be willing to trade places?

Actually, as you may have guessed, Elaine was a confederate of the experimenter and never got shocked. But the experimental procedures created a compelling dilemma for subjects. Would they suffer for someone else? Batson and his colleagues expected the answer to depend on the combinations of empathic concern and difficulty of escape manipulated in the experiment. To vary empathic concern for Elaine, half of the subjects were told that her personal values and interests were very similar to their own; the other half were told that her values and interests were quite different. Those who were informed that Elaine was like them should experience greater empathic concern, since similarity increases empathic thoughts and feelings (Houston, 1990).

The ease with which subjects could escape from having to witness Elaine's plight was also manipulated. Subjects in the easy-escape condition were told that they could leave after witnessing two of the ten trials during which Elaine would receive random shocks. Those in the difficult-escape condition were told that they would have to witness all ten trials. Since the experimenter's invitation to trade places came at the end of two trials, easy-escape subjects could refuse to help Elaine without having to stay and watch the consequences. Difficult-escape subjects, however, had to either volunteer to take some shocks themselves or continue to watch Elaine suffer.

The results of this experiment closely matched the pattern predicted by the empathy-altruism hypothesis. Overall, the vast majority of subjects agreed to help Elaine. As Figure 7.4 shows, only in the condition of low empathic concern *and* easy escape did most subjects decline to offer assistance. When the

---

Figure 7.4   When Empathy Helps.   These results supported the predictions made by the empathy-altruism hypothesis. Among subjects with low levels of empathic concern, the proportion who helped was less when escape from the helping situation was easy than when it was difficult. But when empathic concern was high, most people helped regardless of whether escape was easy or difficult. [Based on Batson et al., 1981.]

Difficulty of Escape	Empathic Concern	
	Low	*High*
Easy	18%	91%
Difficult	64%	82%

escape hatch was wide open, subjects with little empathic concern chose to walk away. Those with high empathic concern stayed to help.

Egoistic Alternatives Can we conclude, then, that altruism really does exist? Batson and his colleagues certainly think there's a very good possibility that it does. Others are not so sure and offer egoistic alternatives. The ensuing debate between these different perspectives has been as intense as a championship match at Wimbledon.

The first egoistic contender is empathy-specific punishment for not helping. Perhaps people learn from experience that an empathic response *should* increase helping. If so, they could anticipate feeling guilty whenever they respond empathically but fail to help the person in need. By this reasoning, people whose empathic concern is high will help in order to avoid feeling guilty. This explanation, however, does not seem to hold. Neither external sources of guilt feelings (such as social disapproval for not helping) nor internal sources (when the decision of whether to help is completely private) can account for the helpful inclinations produced by empathic concern (Batson et al., 1988; Fultz et al., 1986).

Second, there is the possibility of empathy-specific rewards for helping. Negative state relief, described earlier in this chapter, is one such reward. Perhaps empathic concern for a person in need increases the potential helper's feelings of sadness, which in turn increase the need for mood enhancement. From this perspective, people whose empathic concern is high will help when escape is easy only if they believe that helping will improve their mood *and* that no other source of relief is readily available. Why help if doing so won't make you feel better? Why help if something else is going to make you feel better anyway? During a flurry of volleys back and forth across the net, evidence was secured in favor of the negative-state-relief explanation (Cialdini et al., 1987; Schaller & Cialdini, 1988) and against it (Batson et al., 1989). But the empathy-altruism hypothesis gained an important advantage when its position was supported by a team of "neutral" investigators without any previous commitment to either side (Schroeder et al., 1988).

Another egoistic alternative involving empathy-specific rewards emphasizes positive well-being rather than negative relief. Kyle Smith and his colleagues (1989) maintain that empathic concern enhances the helper's sensitivity to the joy and relief experienced by the person receiving help. But there's a snake in this paradise of "empathic joy." You can't share the help recipient's joy unless you know that the person was actually helped. And what if there's no way for you to find out whether your effort to help was successful? According to Smith and his colleagues, empathic concern will *not* increase helping under these circumstances.

In order to test this proposition, subjects watched a videotape of an interview with a young woman who said she was having some difficulty coping with the stresses and strains of her first year in college. Half of the subjects were told that if they provided suggestions and advice to help this person, they would see another videotaped interview with her later in the semester, during which she would describe the effects of their advice on her adjustment to college. The other subjects were told that, regardless of whether they offered advice, they would not have any further contact with the person they had seen in the videotape. On the basis of their self-reported responses to the video, subjects were categorized as high versus low in empathic concern.

As you can see in Figure 7.5, subjects high in empathic concern who expected to be able to find out about the effectiveness of their helpful behavior were more likely to offer advice to the stressed-out college student than were subjects in the other three conditions. Contrary to what would be predicted by the empathy-altruism hypothesis, subjects high in empathic concern who *not* expect feedback were similar to low-empathy subjects in their helpful behavior. The empathic joy formulation seems to have scored a significant point against the empathy-altruism hypothesis.

But team Batson came back with a clever question: When do you want to know? If individuals experiencing strong feelings of empathic concern help in order to secure the delights of empathic joy, they should be eager to hear about successful outcomes and uninterested in failures. In fact, however, this preference for "the good news only, please" is characteristics of individuals *low* in empathic concern (Batson et al., 1991). Those high in empathic concern want to know the outcome of their efforts regardless of whether successful helping is likely or improbable. They seem genuinely interested in the other's well-being— which, of course, is exactly what the empathy-altruism hypothesis predicts.

Figure 7.5 Joyful Helping and the Need to Know.   These results supported the predictions made by the empathic joy hypothesis. Among subjects who believed they could obtain feedback about the effects of their helpful behavior, a greater proportion of those high in empathic concern helped compared with those low in empathic concern. But when feedback was not available, high empathic concern did *not* increase the proportion of subjects who provided assistance. [Based on K. D. Smith et al., 1989.]

Feedback Condition	Relative Empathy (Empathic Concern Minus Personal Distress)	
	Low	*High*
No Feedback	53%	53%
Feedback	62%	93%

Altruism: Limits and Importance   Despite the questions that continue to be raised by egoistic perspectives, the evidence for the empathy-altruism hypothesis is very strong. As Batson and his colleagues (1989) put it, "plausible alternative explanations for the growing support for the empathy-altruism hypothesis are increasingly hard to find" (p. 932). Nevertheless, two important issues remain. The first one concerns the multiple motives for helping. Batson has never claimed that *all* helping is altruistically motivated. No doubt, many helpful acts are best explained in terms of the processes we considered earlier—anticipated reciprocity, kinship selection, the good mood effect, guilt-avoidance, self-awareness, and negative state relief. Moreover, any single helpful action can be the result of a mixture of egoistic and altruistic motives.

The second issue focuses on the relationship between motives and behavior. Empathic concern does not always increase helping, as shown by studies in which the needy individual is disliked by the potential helper (Otten et al., 1991), the person needs help on a problem that differs from the problem that initially aroused empathic concern (Dovidio et al., 1990), or the potential helper expects to have to endure significant suffering in order to help (Batson et al., 1983). Are these failures of the empathy-altruism hypothesis? Or do they reflect limits on altruism itself? In Batson's view, such findings indicate that altruism does not exist in a cost-free psychological universe. When the egoistic costs of providing help are greater than the altruistic motive can bear, the other-oriented impulse flickers but lacks the energy to burst into action.

The possibility of such limitations on altruism should not obscure the fact that the empathy-altruism hypothesis has raised the stakes in the scientific enterprise to understand human nature (Kohn, 1990). So many researchers have tried so hard to find plausible, egoistic alternatives to this hypothesis because its confirmation would force all of us to reconsider what, until now, have been some rather easy assumptions. Is self-interest the only engine that drives human behavior? Perhaps not. Is it possible to construct a social environment that promotes empathic concern and altruistic helping? Perhaps so. The answer we give to the question "Does altruism exist?" can have profound implications for our view of self and our hopes for humanity.

SITUATIONAL INFLUENCES: WHEN DO PEOPLE HELP?

But personal factors alone do not a helper make. The effects of genetic factors, personality traits, emotions, and motives are all influenced by the particular situation in which help is needed. As we shall see, a wide range of situational factors, including both social and environmental circumstances, affect helping.

Models: Following Others

Consider these opportunities to help:

- You see someone at the side of the highway struggling to change a flat tire.
- You approach a table where volunteers are collecting money for famine-relief efforts.
- You hear the announcement of a blood-donation drive.

Now, think about your own behavior. Would you be more likely to help—change the tire; contribute money; donate blood—if you observed someone else help first? Probably. The odds are very good that having witnessed others who helped, you'd help out too. Observing helpful others, who serve as *models,* usually does increase helping (Bryan & Test, 1967; Macaulay, 1970; Sarason et al., 1991).

Helpful models have a number of effects. First, they provide an example of behavior for us to imitate directly. Second, when they are rewarded for their helpful behavior, models teach us that helping is valuable and strengthen our own inclination to be helpful. For example, musicians participating in the "benefit beat" (see Table 7.1) serve as models of helping behavior for their fans. The musicians show us what to do: support the cause. And the public acclaim they receive for their charitable efforts highlights the social rewards that helping can bring.

Social Norms: A Helpful Standard

social norms General rules of conduct reflecting standards of social approval and disapproval.

The behavior of helpful models also informs us about **social norms**, general rules of conduct established by society. Social norms embody standards of socially approved and disapproved behavior. They are learned from the deeds of others as well as from their words (Rice & Grusec, 1975). In modern society, mass media presentations convey a great deal of information about normative expectations, and TV is an especially powerful influence (Hearold, 1986; Oskamp, 1988). In fact, you don't have to watch TV to be affected by it. The publicity for special programs can be so intense that it reaches viewers and nonviewers alike. After the 1983 TV movie on nuclear war, *The Day After,* was shown, the estimated probability of nuclear war by the year 2000 increased among those who had watched the film *and* among those who hadn't (Schofield & Pavelchak, 1989).

Two types of social norms bear directly on helping. The first consists of norms based on fairness. As you know from earlier discussions in this and other chapters, reciprocity refers to quid-pro-quo transactions. The *norm of reciprocity* establishes this type of exchange as a socially approved standard: People should be paid back for whatever they give us (Schopler, 1970). This norm makes us feel uncomfortable if we are unable to give back to those from whom we have received (Bar-Tal, 1976). Accordingly, people usually help those who have helped them, especially when the initial assistance was given voluntarily (Gross & Latané, 1974). Equity, described in Chapter 6, on intimate relationships, is the basis of another norm calling for fairness in our treatment of others (Walster et al., 1978a). The *norm of equity* prescribes that people who are overbenefited (receiving more benefits than earned) should help those who are underbene-fited (receiving fewer benefits than earned). Such help restores an equitable balance.

Table 7.1 *Time* **Magazine Reviews the "Benefit Beat."** Celebrity albums dedicated to various social causes have become so popular and so numerous that *Time* magazine selected its top picks for its readers. ["Benefit Beat," 1991.]

Benefit Beat

Ever since George Harrison gathered with Ringo Starr, Eric Clapton, Bob Dylan and Ravi Shankar at Madison Square Garden for the 1971 benefit concert for Bangladesh, philanthropic pop has been a booming business. And in the caring, sharing '90s, a new formula has emerged: the compilation album. Among the best:

	FOR OUR CHILDREN	DEADICATED	RED HOT + BLUE	TAME YOURSELF
For:	Pediatric AIDS	Rainforest Action Network	AIDS research and relief	People for the Ethical Treatment of Animals
Theme:	Children's songs	Songs by the Grateful Dead	Songs by Cole Porter	Songs by animal lovers
Stars:	Bob Dylan, Bruce Springsteen, Paul McCartney, Elton John, Sting, Ziggy Marley, Bette Midler	Elvis Costello, Bruce Hornsby & the Range, Suzanne Vega, Cowboy Junkies, Midnight Oil, Jane's Addiction	The Neville Brothers, David Byrne, Tom Waits, Lisa Stansfield, Annie Lennox, Debbie Harry and Iggy Pop	The Pretenders Howard Jones, k.d. lang, the B-52s, Belinda Carlisle, Exene Cervenka
Best Cuts:	Dylan's quirky *This Old Man,* Little Richard's sassy *Itsy Bitsy Spider,* Elton's jazzy *The Pacifier*	Los Lobos' exultant *Bertha,* Lyle Lovett's *Friend of the Devil,* Costello's *Ship of Fools*	U2's galvanizing *Night and Day,* k.d. lang's torchy *So in Love,* Fine Young Cannibals' silky *Love for Sale*	A live version of B-52's *Quiche Lorraine,* lang's *Damned Old Dog,* Cervenka's *Do What I Have to Do*

norm of social responsibility A moral standard emphasizing people's obligation and duty to help those in need.

Other social norms related to helping go beyond an immediate sense of fairness to a larger sense of what is right. The **norm of social responsibility** dictates that people should help those who are dependent on them (Berkowitz, 1972). This norm creates a sense of duty and obligation (Fellner & Marshall, 1981). The **norm of justice**, however, requires people to help because others deserve their assistance (Lerner & Meindl, 1981). This norm creates a standard of what is morally correct. Although these two norms often coincide and can be hard to tell apart, they differ in terms of the principles they express. The norm of social responsibility is person based, calling on us to be responsive to people's needs regardless of how these needs came about. In contrast, the norm of justice is rule based, calling on us to meet the needs of those who merit our assistance. From one perspective, justice is a higher moral standard than social responsibility (Kohlberg, 1981). From another viewpoint, however, social responsibility has an equally valid claim on moral superiority (Gilligan, 1982).

norm of justice A moral standard requiring people to help those who they believe deserve assistance.

Reciprocity, equity, social responsibility, and justice are powerful norms that can strongly influence people's feelings and actions. But they are not all-powerful. Despite their awareness of these norms, people don't always help those in need. Why do social norms sometimes fail to produce the helpful behavior they prescribe? One reason is that social norms are so general that it is not clear when they apply. People differ considerably in what they regard as unfair or immoral and in the remedies they propose in different situations.

The meaning of a social norm also depends, at least in part, on the society in which we live. In research conducted by Joan Miller and her colleagues (1990), children and adults in the United States were less likely than children and adults in India to believe that people have an obligation to help strangers. American subjects were also less likely than Indian subjects to believe that people are obligated to provide assistance to their children or friends whose need for help is not a life-or-death matter. Figure 7.6 summarizes these results. Overall, the Hindu Indians who participated in this study appeared to regard social responsibilities as an absolute moral obligation. American subjects applied the norm of social responsibility more selectively.

Personal Norms and Heroic Helpers Because social norms are so general and leave so much room for interpretation, Shalom Schwartz doubts their usefulness for understanding when helping will occur. Instead, Schwartz believes that we should focus on **personal norms**: an individual's feelings of moral obligation to provide help to *specific* others in *specific* situations (Schwartz, 1977; Schwartz & Howard, 1982). Personal norms may serve to sustain the courageous actions of "heroic helpers," those who risk their lives to help others (Meindl & Lerner, 1983). Heroic helpers often deviate radically from the norms of their society, yet their behavior is not random or unprincipled. It conforms to the standards embodied in their own personal norms. But how do these individualized norms develop?

personal norms An individual's feelings of moral obligation to provide help to specific others in specific situations.

Parental behavior seems to make an important contribution. In one study, for example, empathic concern for others at age thirty-one was greater for those

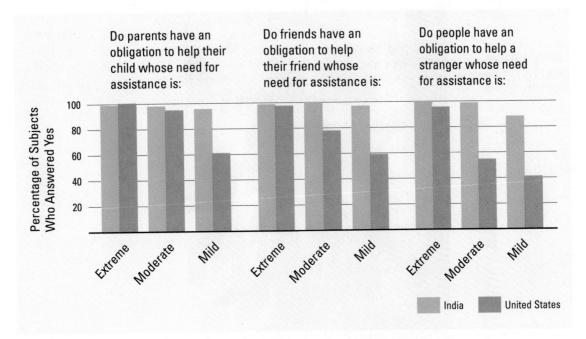

Figure 7.6   Applying the Norm of Social Responsibility in India and the United States.   These results compare the proportion of children and adults in India with the proportion of children and adults in the United States who said that people in different social situations have an obligation to help. As you can see, most Indian subjects perceived this obligation to exist regardless of the extent of need or the type of relationship. In contrast, American subjects indicated that the obligation to help was reduced when the need for assistance was less extreme and when the person in need was a stranger. [Data from J. G. Miller et al., 1990.]

---

subjects whose family life at age five was characterized by higher scores on four factors: father's involvement in child care; mother's tolerance of the child's dependent behavior, her inhibition of the child's aggression, and her satisfaction with the maternal role (Koestner et al., 1990). The child's own behavior seemed to have little long-term significance, although more disobedience in the home was associated with lower levels of empathic concern in adulthood. Heroic helpers themselves also emphasize parental influence. Christians who helped Jews escape from the Nazis during World War II describe an intense identification with at least one parent who was a model of high moral standards (London, 1970; Oliner & Oliner, 1988). Committed civil rights activists, interviewed in the mid-1960s, report a similar pattern of strong parental identification (Rosenhan, 1970). It appears that parents who are nurturing, confident, and principled enable their children to become caring, helpful adults. The good that parents do can live after them.

This is a recent picture of Johtje and Aart Vos, who fifty years ago risked their lives to help dozens of Jews escape from the Nazis in Holland. Heroic helpers like these often describe an intense identification with a parent who provided a living example of strong moral principles.

Self-Perception and Helping Under Pressure

Based on important beliefs and values, personal norms are a significant part of the self-concept. And self-concept influences helping behavior: labeling someone as a helpful person increases that individual's helpful behavior (Kraut, 1973; Strenta & DeJong, 1981). Indeed, because individuals with high self-esteem compensate for failure by increasing their positive view of themselves as kind, considerate, and sensitive, they help more after failure than after success (Brown & Smart, 1991).

External rewards, however, reduce self-perceptions of being a helpful person (Batson et al., 1978), suggesting that helping might be vulnerable to the overjustification effect. In this effect, described in Chapter 2, people rewarded for engaging in an intrinsically enjoyable activity are subsequently less likely to engage in that activity when rewards are not provided (Deci & Ryan, 1985). Although there are a number of possible explanations for the overjustification effect, it has often been regarded as a consequence of self-perception. Once people have expected and received a reward for engaging in an activity, they come to perceive that the reward—rather than their enjoyment—is what motivates them. And when no reward is provided, their involvement declines. Could the same be true of helping?

Research by Richard Fabes and his colleagues (1989) indicates that helping too can be overjustified. In this study, elementary school children who had previously been rewarded for helping "poor, sick children in the hospital" were less likely to continue to help in the absence of rewards for doing so. Even children who had simply seen another child rewarded for helping were less helpful in the later, free-choice situation. Interestingly, this decline in helping among those who associated rewards with helpful behavior was found only for children whose mothers reported a favorable attitude toward using rewards to influence their children's behavior (see Figure 7.7). Perhaps the child-rearing practices favored by these mothers weakened their children's self-concept of being a helpful person, thereby making them more susceptible to the overjustification effect.

But what about internal pressures: those self-administered pats on the back for being helpful, those guilt pangs for failing to help? These too can affect our self-perceptions. In one study, just thinking about why they helped others in circumstances where no external rewards were expected increased subjects' perceptions of their own *selfish* motives for helping (Batson et al., 1987). Presumably such reflections reminded these individuals of internal pressures to help, making them feel less altruistically motivated.

Believing that our motives are altruistic appears to be a factor in long-term helping. Among volunteers at a crisis center, those who placed more importance on altruistic reasons for helping were more likely to complete their term of service (one four-hour shift each week for a nine-month period) than were those who placed more importance on egoistic reasons for helping (Clary & Orenstein, 1991). The altruistic reasons were strictly other oriented: a chance to help others, to express concern to people in need, to give of myself without expecting some sort of "payoff." Some of the egoistic motives referred to external rewards and pressures: to build my résumé, other people want me to do volunteer work. But a number of the egoistic motives involved internal satisfactions: personal growth, self-understanding. This variation between the crass and the admirable didn't seem to matter. When egoistic motives were perceived to be more important, help was less enduring.

Taken as a whole, the research described in this section suggests a close connection among pressures on people to be helpful (rewards and punishments, internal as well as external), self-perceptions, and helping others. Pressuring people to help may be effective in the short run. But such pressures run the risk of diminishing those self-perceptions of character and motives that may be necessary if helping others is to be more than a passing fancy.

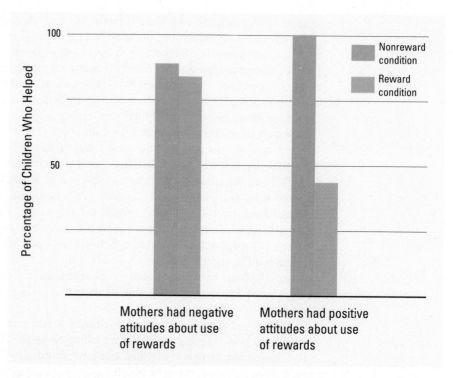

Figure 7.7   Overjustification: Rewards for Helping Can Decrease Helpfulness. Among children whose mothers had negative attitudes toward the use of rewards to influence their children's behavior, associating helping with a reward did not influence helping behavior. In contrast, for children whose mothers had positive attitudes toward the use of rewards, associating helping with an external reward decreased the proportion who helped. External rewards appear to have undermined the intrinsic motivation of these children to help. [Based on Fabes et al., 1989.]

The Place Where We Live

Heroic helpers are quite rare. Few people actually put their lives on the line for others. Less heroic but persistent helpers, like those committed volunteers at the crisis center, also seem a cut above the ordinary. There are, however, some circumstances in which we expect most people to help—and are shocked when they don't. The classic example is the tragedy of Kitty Genovese. Returning home from work at 3 A.M. on the morning of March 13, 1964, the 28-year-old Genovese was stalked, stabbed, and raped just thirty-five yards from her own apartment building. Thirty-eight of her neighbors witnessed her ordeal. Lights went on, windows went up, but no one called the police. After a half an hour of terror, Genovese was dead.

How could this happen? Were these bystanders abnormally cruel and indifferent? It seems unlikely that all thirty-eight of them could have been moral monsters. Perhaps the place was to blame. Genovese was murdered in Queens, New York, and the New York City metropolitan area, like most large cities in the United States, has a high rate of homicides. In the midst of the hectic, sometimes frantic pace of a big city, are pleas for help doomed to go unanswered?

Compared to life in a small town or rural area, life in a large city does have a number of characteristics that might reduce the inclination to help. Stanley Milgram (1970), for example, suggested that cities produce *stimulus overload* for their inhabitants. Bombarded by sights and sounds, city residents may wear a coat of unresponsive armor to protect themselves from being overwhelmed by stimulation. Claude Fischer (1976) noted that the residents of large urban areas are a heterogeneous group—composed of diverse nationalities, races, and ethnic backgrounds. Such diversity could diminish the sense of similarity with others. As we saw earlier, perceived dissimilarity reduces empathic concern and can result in less helping.

Whatever the exact causes, people are less likely to give spontaneous, informal help to strangers in densely populated urban areas than in smaller communities (Steblay, 1987). If you're new in town and need directions, or if you're struck with a sudden illness, you'll receive more help if the town is a small one. But that's only part of the picture. Some kinds of helping are more likely in *larger* communities. For example, residents of large cities are more responsive to requests from societal institutions, such as the Census Bureau, for their assistance on a project (Amato, 1983). And when it comes to help from close friends and romantic partners, where you live is irrelevant. The place of residence doesn't affect how much those with close ties help each other (Franck, 1980; Korte, 1980). In short, the odds of getting help in a big city depend on the kind of help you need.

The Unhelpful Crowd

Clearly, then, Kitty Genovese was at a serious disadvantage in needing spontaneous emergency help in an urban environment. Even so, Bibb Latané and John Darley (1970) were not convinced that the stresses and strains of city life fully explained why she didn't get the help she needed. To test an alternative explanation, the two researchers set out to see if they could produce unresponsive bystanders in the calm and quiet haven of a psychology laboratory. Let's take a close look at one of their studies.

When a subject arrived, he or she was taken to one of a series of small rooms located along a corridor. Speaking over an intercom, the experimenter explained that he wanted subjects to discuss personal problems often faced by college students. Subjects were told that to protect confidentiality the group discussion would take place over the intercom system and the experimenter would not be listening. Participants were required to speak one at a time, taking turns. Some subjects were assigned to two-person dyads, others to larger groups of three or six people.

Although one participant did mention in passing that he suffered from a seizure disorder that was sometimes triggered by study pressures, the opening moments of the conversation were uneventful. But soon an unexpected problem developed. When it came his turn to speak again, the person with a seizure disorder stuttered badly, had a hard time speaking clearly, and sounded as if he were in very serious trouble:

> I could really-er-use some help so if somebody would-er-give me a little h-help-uh-er-er-er-er c-could somebody-er-er-help-er-uh-uh-uh (choking sounds). . . . I'm gonna die-er-er-I'm . . . gonna die-er-help-er-er-seizure-er (chokes, then quiet).

Confronted with this situation, what would *you* do? Would you interrupt the experiment, dash out of your cubicle, and try to find the experimenter? Or, would you sit there—concerned, but unsure about what you should do?

As it turns out, subjects' responses to this emergency were strongly influenced by the size of their group. Actually, all subjects were participating alone, but tape-recorded material led them to believe that others were present and that there was a crisis. *All* the subjects who thought they were involved in a two-person discussion left the room quickly to try to get help. In the larger groups, however, subjects were less likely and slower to intervene. Thirty-eight percent of the subjects in the six-person groups never even left the room, and those who did go for help took longer to get out the door than did subjects in smaller groups. This research led Latané and Darley to a chilling conclusion: the more bystanders there are, the *less* likely the victim will be helped. In the **bystander effect**, the presence of others inhibits helping.

Before the pioneering work of Latané and Darley, most people would have assumed just the opposite. Isn't there safety in numbers? Don't we feel more secure rushing in to help when others are around to lend their support? Latané and Darley overturned this common-sense assumption and provided a careful, step-by-step analysis of the decision-making process involved in emergency interventions (see Figure 7.8).

bystander effect
The effect whereby the presence of others inhibits helping.

Noticing The first step toward being a helpful bystander is to notice that someone needs help or, at least, that something out of the ordinary is happening. Subjects in the seizure study could not help but notice the emergency. In many situations, however, the problem isn't always perceived. The presence of others can be distracting and divert attention away from indications of a victim's plight. As noted earlier, people may also fail to notice that someone needs help when they are caught up in their own self-concerns.

The Biblical parable of the Good Samaritan (Luke 10:25–37) provides a telling example. On the road from Jerusalem to Jericho, three people passed a man lying half-dead by the roadside: a priest, a Levite, and a Samaritan. The only one who helped was the Samaritan, a social and religious outcast in Jewish

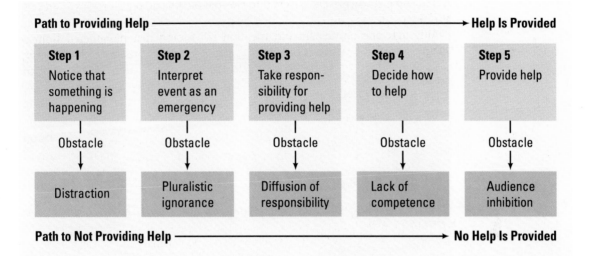

Figure 7.8 The Five Steps in Providing Assistance in an Emergency. On the basis of their analysis of the decision-making process in emergency interventions, Latané and Darley outlined five steps that lead to helping and showed how missing a step can deprive a victim of needed assistance.

society of that time. The moral of the story is that people with low status are sometimes more virtuous than those enjoying high status and prestige. Why? Perhaps in part because high-status individuals tend to be busy people, preoccupied with their own concerns and rushing around to important engagements. Such characteristics may prevent them from noticing a victim in need of assistance.

In an ingenious test of this parable, John Darley and C. Daniel Batson (1973) asked seminary students to think about what they wanted to say in an upcoming talk. For half of these subjects, the talk was to be based on the parable of the Good Samaritan; the other half expected to discuss the jobs seminary students like best. All subjects were then instructed to walk over to a nearby building where the speech would be recorded. At this point, subjects were told either that they were running ahead of schedule, that they were right on time, or that they were already a few minutes behind schedule. On the way to the other building, all subjects passed a research confederate slumped in a doorway, coughing and groaning. Which of these future ministers stopped to lend a helping hand?

Surprisingly, the topic of the upcoming speech had little effect on helping. The pressure of time, however, made a real difference. Of those who thought they were ahead of schedule, 63 percent offered help—compared with 45 percent of those who believed they were on schedule and only 10 percent of those who had been told they were late. In describing the events that took place

The first step toward providing help in an emergency is to notice that someone needs assistance. People can fail to notice another's need because they are distracted or are concentrating on something else. Sometimes, however, they notice a victim's plight but deliberately choose to look away.

in their study, Darley and Batson noted that "on several occasions a seminary student going to give his talk on the parable of the Good Samaritan literally stepped over the victim as he hurried on his way!"

Interpreting   Noticing the victim is a necessary first step toward helping, but it is not enough. People must also interpret the meaning of what they notice. Cries of pain can be mistaken for shrieks of laughter; heart attack victims can appear to be drunk. So observers wonder: Does that person really need help? In general, the more ambiguous the situation, the less likely it is that bystanders will intervene (Clark & Word, 1972). People may even be biased to interpret real emergencies in innocuous ways. If bystanders are reluctant to help in the first place, they may be especially attuned to information that bolsters the conviction that there's nothing to be concerned about (Wilson & Petruska, 1984).

Some of the most powerful information available during an emergency is the behavior of other people. Startled by a sudden, unexpected, possibly dangerous event, a person looks quickly to see what others are doing. But others do the same thing. As everyone looks at everyone else for clues about how to behave,

pluralistic ignorance The phenomenon in which each person in a group assumes that the reason for his or her own behavior is different from the reason other group members are acting in the same way.

the entire group is paralyzed by indecision. When this happens, the person needing help is a victim of **pluralistic ignorance**. In this state of ignorance, members of a group attribute actions of other members that are identical to their own to a different cause (Miller & McFarland, 1987). Each bystander thinks that other people aren't acting because there really isn't an emergency. Actually, everyone is confused and hesitant; but, imputing wisdom to others, each observer concludes that help is not required.

Pluralistic ignorance is not restricted to emergency situations. Have you ever sat through a class feeling totally at sea? You want to ask a question, but you're too embarrassed. No one else is saying anything, so you assume they all find the material a snap. Finally, you dare to ask a question. And, suddenly, hands shoot up in the air all over the classroom. No one understood the material, yet everyone assumed that everyone else was breezing along. Pluralistic ignorance in the classroom interferes with learning. In an emergency situation, it can lead to disaster—unless someone breaks out of the pack and dares to help. Then others are likely to follow.

Taking Responsibility Noticing a victim and then interpreting his or her problem as a real emergency are crucial steps, but by themselves they won't ensure that a bystander will come to the rescue. The issue of responsibility remains. When help is needed, who is responsible for providing it? If a person knows that others are around, it's all too easy to place the responsibility on *them*. People often fail to help because of the **diffusion of responsibility**, the belief that others will or should intervene. Presumably, each of those thirty-eight people who watched and listened to Kitty Genovese's murder honestly believed that someone else would intervene. But no one did.

diffusion of responsibility The belief that others will or should take the responsibility for providing assistance to a person in need.

Diffusion of responsibility cannot occur if an individual believes that only he or she is aware of the victim's need. Remember those subjects in the seizure study who believed that they alone heard the other person's cry for help; all of them helped. When more than two people are involved, diffusion of responsibility becomes a mathematical proposition. Personal responsibility diminishes most when there are few victims and many potential helpers, as in the 1-to-38 ratio involved in the Genovese murder. As the number of victims increases, or the number of potential helpers decreases, help is more likely to occur (Wegner & Schaefer, 1978).

Diffusion of responsibility usually takes place under conditions of anonymity. Bystanders who do not know the victim personally are more likely to see others as responsible for providing help. Accordingly, less psychological distance between a bystander and the victim translates into less diffusion of responsibility. In one study, the mere *anticipation* of meeting someone, who then needed help before the meeting actually took place, was sufficient to eliminate diffusion of responsibility (Gottlieb & Carver, 1980). Reducing the psychological distance among bystanders can also counteract the diffusion of responsibility. Highly cohesive groups in which members know and feel attached to each other are more helpful than groups of unrelated individuals (Rutkowski et al., 1983).

A person's role in the group matters as well. A group leader, even if only recently assigned to that position, is more likely than other group members to take action in an emergency (Baumeister et al., 1988).

Deciding How To Help   Having assumed the responsibility to help, the person must now decide how to help. A decision to offer *direct* help will depend on how competent the person feels to engage in such actions (Shotland & Heinold, 1985). Indeed, as demonstrated in research by Robert Cramer and his colleagues (1988), there is no bystander effect for those who feel competent to intervene directly. The women who participated in this study were either registered nurses or general education students. As each subject was escorted to the experimental laboratory, she passed a workman (actually, an experimental confederate) who was standing on a ladder while repairing a light fixture. Once inside the laboratory, the subject worked alone on an experimental task or was joined by a second subject (another confederate). Suddenly there was a loud crash in the hallway, followed by a thud and moans of pain. Now what?

The results of this research should make nurses extremely popular people to have around. Regardless of whether they were alone or with someone, the vast majority of registered nurses opened the door to see what had happened. Most of the general education students who were working alone were similarly quick to see if their assistance was needed. In stark contrast, however, most general education students in the presence of another bystander (who had been carefully trained to remain unresponsive when the supposed emergency occurred) did not make any effort to check on the workman's condition (see Figure 7.9).

It isn't surprising that helping-relevant training and competency can override the passivity produced by the bystander effect. But people who do not possess the skills that would make them feel competent to intervene directly do have an option available. They can decide to help *indirectly* by calling for assistance from others (Penner et al., 1973). And, in some situations, indirect helping can be by far the wiser course of action. Physical injuries are best treated by medical personnel; dangerous situations are best handled by police officers; and that friendly looking individual standing by the side of a stalled car on a lonely road is best picked up by the highway patrol. Calling others in to help is a helpful thing to do.

Helping   The final step in the intervention process is to take action. Here too the presence of others can have an effect. Latané and Darley point out that people sometimes feel too socially awkward and embarrassed to act helpfully in a public setting. When observers do not act in a recognized emergency because they fear making a bad impression on other observers, they are under the influence of **audience inhibition**. Worrying about how others will view us will not, however, always reduce helping. When people think they will be scorned by others for failing to help, the presence of an audience increases their helpful actions (Schwartz & Gottlieb, 1976, 1980).

audience inhibition
A person's reluctance to help for fear of making a bad impression on observers.

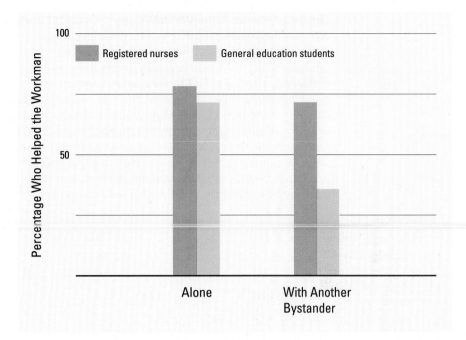

Figure 7.9   Competence and Helping: Nurses to the Rescue.   When subjects who were alone overheard the crash of a workman falling off a ladder, the vast majority quickly checked to see if he needed assistance. If there was another person present, however, most of the general education students were unresponsive. Registered nurses, competent to handle an emergency, were not subject to the bystander effect; being with someone else did not significantly reduce the proportion who helped. [Based on Cramer et al., 1988.]

arousal: cost-reward model   The proposition that people react to emergency situations by acting in the most cost-effective way to reduce the arousal of shock and alarm.

Letting your estimate of how others will respond influence whether you help has a distasteful ring to it. It makes a potential helper sound like a calculating, conniving sort of person. But, according to Jane Piliavin and her colleagues (1981), potential helpers do take potential rewards and costs into account when deciding whether to respond to an emergency. The **arousal: cost-reward model** of helping stipulates that both emotional and cognitive factors influence whether bystanders to an emergency will intervene. Emotionally, bystanders experience the shock and alarm of personal distress; this unpleasant state of arousal motivates them to do something to reduce it. What they do, however, depends on the "bystander calculus," their computation of the costs and rewards associated with helping. When potential rewards (to self and victim) outweigh potential costs (to self and victim), bystanders will help (Dovidio et al., 1991). But raise those costs and lower those rewards, and victims stand a good chance of having to do without.

Getting Helped: One Versus Many   Overall, the evidence for Latané and Darley's analysis is compelling. Distraction, pluralistic ignorance, diffusion of responsibility, feelings of incompetence, and costs of helping such as audience inhibition can converge to make individuals less likely to intervene in an emergency when they are in the company of others than when they are alone. But what about the probability that the victim will actually receive help? Although each person in a group of bystanders is less likely to help than if he or she were alone, won't the greater number of potential helpers compensate for each individual's hesitation? Won't *someone* step forward? Isn't there, after all, safety in numbers? Not when it comes to getting help. Although the difference is relatively small, victims are more likely to receive help if the full weight of their plight rests on the shoulders of only one potential helper (Latané & Nida, 1981).

INTERPERSONAL INFLUENCES: WHOM DO PEOPLE HELP?

We have examined personal and situational influences on a potential helper. But think about those who need help: the student who needs assistance in a class, the newcomer who needs a word of welcome, the family that needs food. Are some people more likely than others to receive help? Are some helpers particularly responsive to certain kinds of individuals who need assistance? This section examines a number of interpersonal influences on helping.

Perceived Characteristics of the Person in Need

As described earlier, the social norm of justice requires that we help those who deserve assistance. But how do we judge who's deserving? One factor that affects these judgments is our perception of the reasons why someone needs help. Consider, for example, research by Richard Barnes and his colleagues (1979). In this study, subjects received a call from another student (actually an experimental confederate), who asked to borrow their class notes to prepare for an upcoming exam. The reason for this request varied. To some subjects, the caller said, "I just don't seem to have the ability to take good notes. I really try to take good notes, but sometimes I just can't do it." Other students were told that help was needed because "I just don't seem to have the motivation to take good notes. I really can take good notes, but sometimes I just don't try." You probably won't be surprised to learn that the caller received much more help from those who learned he had tried yet failed than from those who were told he hadn't tried at all.

This study indicates that people's *attributions* about the needy individual's responsibility affect how much assistance they will give. When people attribute difficulties to controllable factors, they are usually less willing to help than when they attribute difficulties to factors beyond the individual's control (Schmidt & Weiner, 1988). It appears that when we perceive people as not trying to help themselves, we feel they don't deserve our assistance. We may also experience less empathic concern about their predicament (Betancourt, 1990). But how can we be sure that a person hasn't tried hard enough? Can attributing responsibility to someone in need sometimes serve to justify our own reluctance to take on the responsibility of helping? The next time you walk past a homeless person on the street or edge away from a poorly dressed individual in a line at the grocery store, stop and think about your reactions. Do you assume that such people are lazy, haven't made enough of an effort to get a job, could help themselves if they really tried? Such reactions are not uncommon. It seems that all too often we jump to conclusions that make us comfortable with leaving the down-and-out exactly where they are.

Another question about whom we help also has potentially troubling implications. Will a physically attractive individual receive more help than one who is less attractive? Peter Benson and his colleagues (1976) addressed this question in a study of 442 men and 162 women. Going into a phone booth in a large metropolitan airport, each subject discovered a completed graduate school application form, a photograph of the applicant, and a stamped, addressed envelope. For some subjects, the photo depicted a physically attractive individual; for others, the person was relatively unattractive. When the researchers checked their mail, they found that people were more likely to send off the materials in behalf of good-looking applicants. Since those most in need of help may not always have the most attractive appearance, this aspect of the bias for beauty could prevent those who need help from getting it.

The Relationship Between Giver and Receiver

As we have seen, perceived characteristics of people in need, such as their control over the reasons for needing help and their physical attractiveness, have direct effects on helping. Other characteristics of the receiver, however, affect helping in the context of the potential helper's own attributes. Here, we examine whether certain kinds of givers tend to help certain kinds of receivers.

Similarity: Helping Those Just Like Us
Perceiving that a person in need is similar to us increases our willingness to help (Dovidio, 1984). All kinds of similarity (dress, attitudes, nationality) have this effect. But why? There are a number of possible reasons. For example, people find similar people more attractive and empathize more with them (Byrne, 1971; Houston, 1990). As we have seen, both attraction and empathy increase helping. The influence

of similarity on helping could even be a case of mistaken (biological) identity. If, as sociobiologists contend, people are more likely to help a relative who shares their genes, they may help a similar—though biologically unrelated—individual, because they unwittingly associate similarity with genetic closeness (Krebs, 1987).

The strong, multiply determined effect of similarity on helping suggests that members of the same race would help each other more than members of different races. Actually, however, research on black-white helping in the United States indicates that the effects of racial similarity on helping are highly variable. In their review of the research, Faye Crosby and her colleagues (1980) found a same-race helping bias in 44 percent of the studies they examined. Sometimes whites were more biased, sometimes blacks. In the other 56 percent of the studies reviewed, there was either no discrimination or reverse discrimination in which people helped those of a different race *more* than they helped members of their own race.

There's no simple way to fit all these puzzling pieces together, but it is possible to raise some questions about what they mean. First, although helping can be a compassionate response to another, it can also be considered a sign of superiority over the person who needs help (Rosen et al., 1986). Thus, cross-racial helping isn't always a sign of egalitarian attitudes. Second, public displays of racial prejudice risk social disapproval, and even prejudiced individuals may bend over backward, in public at least, to avoid revealing their attitudes. In keeping with the modern racism discussed in Chapter 4, however, more subtle forms of discrimination still occur. For example, if people are provided with an excuse *not* to help, racial discrimination in helping is more likely (Frey & Gaertner, 1986). And then there are those little signs of consideration (picking up something a person has dropped, bringing someone a cup of coffee) that may be withheld from minorities or women whose presence is resented (Dovidio & Gaertner, 1981, 1983). For newcomers on the job or in the neighborhood, these little things can mean a lot, making them feel welcomed—or shut out.

Closeness: A Little Help for Our Friends   Not surprisingly, people are usually more helpful toward those they know and care about than toward strangers or superficial acquaintances (Clark et al., 1987; Schoenrade et al., 1986). But there may be an exception to this general rule: What if a person's ego is threatened? In Chapter 2, we described the *self-evaluation maintenance model* developed by Abraham Tesser (1988). This model maintains that superior performance by a significant other in an area *not* relevant to someone's own ego is a cause for the delight of BIRGing, basking in reflected glory. In contrast, superior performance by a significant other in an area relevant to someone's own ego can be a cause of envious discomfort.

Tesser's model has some important implications for helping. Suppose you have just finished working on a task and are told that you performed "a little below average." Then two other people take their turns at the same task; one of them is a stranger and the other a close friend. You are asked to give some clues to each individual. The clues vary greatly in their level of difficulty. Some are easy and will boost the person's performance; others are so difficult that they will actually hinder performance. What will you do? Will you give your friend easier, more helpful clues than you give to the stranger?

In research presenting subjects with this choice, friends did not always receive more help (Tesser & Smith, 1980). As the self-evaluation maintenance model would predict, it depended on the task. When subjects believed that the task was a trivial game, they gave their friend the easier, more helpful clues. But when the task was important and relevant to their own self-esteem, subjects gave slightly *less* helpful clues to their friend. As Figure 7.10 illustrates, in a conflict between someone's own ego and the welfare of a friend, the need to protect self-esteem can sometimes overcome a person's helpful inclinations.

Figure 7.10   The Self-Evaluation Maintenance Model: When Do Friends Get More Help Than Strangers?   People usually help their friends more than they help strangers, but not always. In this study, subjects who thought they had performed poorly on a task gave clues on the same task to a friend and a stranger. When the task was not ego-relevant for the subjects, they gave more helpful clues to their friend than to the stranger. When the task was ego-relevant, they gave slightly less helpful clues to their friend than to the stranger. [Data from Tesser & Smith, 1980.]

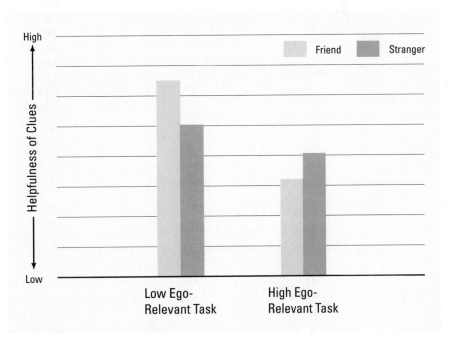

Gender and Ways of Helping Others   The nature of the relationship between helper and receiver may also affect whether men or women are more likely to provide assistance. Consider the following situation:

> Two strangers pass on the street. Suddenly, one of them needs help that might be dangerous to give. Other people are watching. The person in need is female.

Who would help more under these circumstances, a man or a woman? As you probably figured out, a man would. Men are more likely than women to help when the person who needs help is a female stranger, when there is an element of danger, and when helpful actions would be observed by others. Here, the helper is a "knight in shining armor"—physically brave and chivalrous to a lady in distress. Because social psychologists have tended to focus on these kinds of emergency situations, their research has found that, on the average, men are more helpful than women and women receive more help than do men (Eagly & Crowley, 1986). But what if we changed the script?

> Two individuals have a close relationship. Every so often one of them needs assistance that takes time and energy to provide but is not physically dangerous. No one else is around to notice whether help is given. The person who needs help is either male or female.

This is, of course, the sort of help that every day millions of women—mothers, sisters, wives, and female friends—provide for their loved ones (Berg, 1984; Otten et al., 1988). Though it lacks the high drama of an emergency intervention, such tender loving care plays a crucial role in the quality of our lives. In Chapter 14, we examine the effects of this type of helping, called "social support," on coping with stress.

Helping in a Just World   As indicated in Chapter 3, the *belief in a just world* rests on the assumption that people get what they deserve—that good people will secure life's blessings and only bad people will suffer (Lerner, 1980). Presumably this belief is so compelling, despite its obvious inaccuracy, because it has such a comforting implication: if *we* are good, *we* will be rewarded. Although believing in a just world may be common, there are marked individual differences in the strength of this belief (Rubin & Peplau, 1975). And, by definition, a strong believer in a just world is relatively unsympathetic to victims of misfortune.

But will a strong just-world believer refuse to help? It depends on the kind of need for assistance this person encounters. In one study, college students were given a chance to donate their earnings from research participation to needy families (Miller, 1977). The research was conducted between November 15 and December 15, just before Christmas. Some subjects were told that the department of psychology was raising money for families who needed help at Christmas time. Others were informed that the psychology department's fund-raising activities for needy families were a year-long effort; no mention was made of the special needs of families at Christmas. Among those whose belief

Awareness of the suffering of innocent people undermines the belief in a just world where people get
what they deserve.

in a just world was strong, temporary need at Christmas time produced
considerable generosity, but continuous need was met with Scrooge-like stingi-
ness. Subjects whose belief in a just world was relatively weak donated at
moderate levels to both temporarily and continuously needy families (see
Figure 7.11).

   This research indicates again that the characteristics of both the potential
giver and the potential receiver can combine to affect the help that is provided.
When injustice can be easily and quickly rectified, believers in a just world are
more likely to help (Bierhoff et al., 1991). By aiding someone who needs just a
little help to set things right, the just-world believer confirms that, yes indeed,
things work out and life is fair. But what about suffering that is widespread and
enduring? Here, the help provided by any one individual is but a drop in a very
large bucket, and the firm believer is less likely to contribute. Enduring needs
for help pose a threat to the belief in a just world because they convey an
unwanted message: things don't always work out and life isn't always fair.

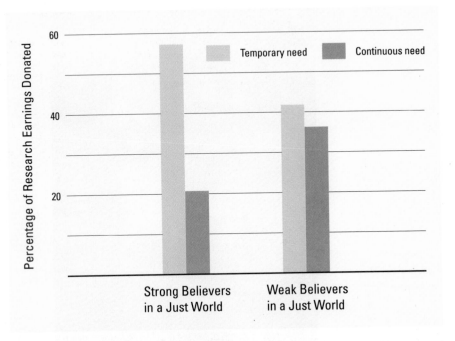

Figure 7.11   Donations to Needy Families: Belief in a Just World and Duration of Need.   On the basis of questionnaire responses, subjects were divided into strong and weak believers in a just world. Asked to donate money to needy families, strong believers gave more to temporarily needy families than to those whose need was of longer duration. Weak believers gave similar amounts regardless of the duration of need. [Data from Miller, 1977.]

The Perceived Relationship Between Attacker and Victim

Just as the relationship between potential helpers and those who need help influences whether help is given, the perceived relationship between an attacker and a victim can affect whether someone will intervene. Here's a true story to think about.

   One summer night in 1951, a young child was riding home with her parents after attending a local production of the musical *Kiss Me Kate*. It had been a great performance, and the family was still laughing. Suddenly, two figures were silhouetted against the glare from the headlights. In the middle of the street, a man was hitting a woman; arms raised to protect her face, she was screaming. Mr. Stephens slammed on the brakes. After a quick glance at his wife, he got out of the car. Walking toward the people in the street, he called out to the man to stop. Startled, the man and woman looked at Mr. Stephens, and then all three began to talk together. In the car, Mrs. Stephens smiled reassuringly at her

Those who want a quick fix, such as strong believers in a just world, are unlikely to commit themselves to a long struggle. [Copyright Bob Haverluck 1988.]

daughter. Then she gasped. Lit up as though on a stage, the fight had resumed, but now Mr. Stephens was being punched and slapped. *Both* the man and woman had turned on him. Running back to the car, Mr. Stephens jumped in, slammed the door, and started the car without a word to his wife or daughter. Only when they were home did he speak, "Well, that's it. I'm never getting involved again in somebody's marital fight. They can beat each other to death for all I care!" The family went to bed. No one called the police.

Years later when the child had become an adult and was busy writing a social psychology textbook, she still remembered that midsummer night's incident. In *Kiss Me Kate,* a musical version of Shakespeare's *The Taming of the Shrew,* the husband's "taming" of his wife had seemed so amusing. But there was nothing humorous about that woman as she stood in the middle of the street, crying and screaming. Nor was there anything funny about Mr. Stephens' anger when his helpfulness was "rewarded" by curses and blows. And the final, lingering question was certainly no joke: What happened between that man and woman when Sharon and her parents were safely asleep?

That question can never be answered. However, research by Lance Shotland and Margaret Straw (1976) can help us understand those factors that influence the response of bystanders when they see a man attack a woman. These investigators staged an attack by a man on a woman—actually, both were confederates—that was overheard by subjects in the study. Half of the attacks were presented as stranger assaults ("I don't know you"); in the other half, the pair was presented as being married ("I don't know why I ever married you"). Among the male and female bystanders in this study, 65 percent tried to stop the attack by a stranger, but only 19 percent attempted to intervene in an attack by the woman's husband.

In other studies by Shotland and Straw, subjects viewed films in which the male attacker was identified as a stranger to or as the husband of the victim. They were then asked what they thought would happen as a result of the attack and what would happen if they intervened. According to their responses, subjects believed that a woman attacked by a stranger was more likely than a wife attacked by her husband to be injured, to want help from a bystander, and to join her helper in fighting off the attacker. Wives attacked by a husband were perceived as more likely to be embarrassed by bystander intervention, and husbands were thought to be more likely than strangers to turn on the helper.

Mr. Stephens' experience was, then, just what many people believe will happen if they intervene in a domestic quarrel. They expect that no one, including the victim, will be grateful and that the one who helps may end up being harmed. These beliefs are not unfounded. Even police officers require special training in how to intervene safely in a violent marital dispute (Bard, 1971). Unfortunately, however, reluctance to intervene directly often spills over into failure to provide safe, indirect help. It usually isn't dangerous to pick up a phone.

Bystanders' reluctance to interfere in domestic quarrels may also place the victims of attacks by strangers in jeopardy. When Shotland and Straw showed subjects a *silent* film of a staged attack, over two-thirds of the observers assumed that the attacker and victim had a close relationship with each other as dates, lovers, or spouses. In fact, the film provided no information about the relationship between the two actors. The assumption observers made was not warranted by the evidence at hand. This bias toward transforming the fact "man attacks woman" into the perception "husband attacks wife" means that anyone reluctant to intervene in marital disputes is also unlikely to take action against assaults by a stranger. Although Sharon's father deliberately decided to become an unresponsive bystander only in domestic altercations, his vow could have had more extensive effects than he intended. But as far as his daughter knows, Mr. Stephens was never again put to the test.

REACTIONS TO RECEIVING HELP

Thus far, we've examined those factors that influence whether helping will occur. Now, we turn to what happens *after* helping. The last time someone helped you, how did you feel? Grateful, relieved, comforted—anything else? Embarrassed, obligated, inferior? Receiving help is often a positive experience, but sometimes it has drawbacks for the recipient. There are costs of providing help, and there can be costs of receiving it.

Help That Supports Versus Help That Threatens

threat-to-self-esteem model The theory that reactions to receiving assistance depend on whether help is perceived as supportive or threatening.

The most extensive examination of reactions to receiving help has been conducted by Jeffrey Fisher and Arie Nadler (Fisher et al., 1982; Nadler & Fisher, 1986). According to their **threat-to-self-esteem model**, receiving help is *self-supportive* when the recipient feels appreciated and cared for, but *self-threatening* when the recipient feels inferior and overly dependent. If recipients feel supported by the help they receive, they respond positively: feeling good, accepting the help, and being grateful to the donor. If, however, recipients feel threatened, they have a negative emotional reaction and evaluate both the help and the helper unfavorably.

Fisher and Nadler pay particular attention to three conditions under which receiving help is threatening. First, individuals with high self-esteem tend to react more negatively to receiving help than do those with low self-esteem. Presumably, people who regard themselves as highly competent are especially sensitive to the implication that they are unable to take care of themselves. Second, being helped by a similar other highlights concerns about personal

According to the threat-to-self-esteem model of recipient reactions, receiving help can have positive or negative effects. If the recipient feels appreciated and cared for, receiving help is a positive experience. If, however, the recipient feels inferior or overly dependent, receiving help is threatening and disturbing.

inadequacy and increases the recipient's negative reactions. Having received help from someone similar, recipients are likely to engage in social comparison and evaluate themselves in terms of the donor's characteristics. The contrast between their need for assistance and the generosity of the donor may imply an inferior status on their part. The third condition under which receiving help is experienced as threatening involves the type of relationship the recipient has with the donor and the area in which help has been received. As would be expected from Tesser's self-evaluation maintenance model, receiving help from a significant other on an ego-relevant task is threatening to an individual's self-esteem.

But not all help from those who are close to us will be seen as threatening. Help on a task that is *not* ego-relevant will not threaten self-esteem. And, when each individual depends on the other, positive reactions to receiving help are particularly likely (Clark, 1983a; Cook & Pelfrey, 1985). In interdependent relationships, the help we receive from a spouse, close friend, or colleague is just one event in a whole series of helpful exchanges. Sometimes we help them; at other times they help us. Even the negative effects of similarity may be limited to superficial relationships between people who do not know each other well. Because similarity is expected and desired in a close relationship, it should not be threatening when help is given by one intimate to another (Nadler, 1991). The basic meaning of both giving and receiving help depends on the nature of the relationship between the two individuals (Wills, 1991).

Factors That Influence Help-Seeking

The threat-to-self-esteem model, as summarized in Figure 7.12, also describes when recipients are most likely to seek subsequent help from others. Help-seeking is encouraged by a positive reaction to the help initially received. When the reaction to help is negative, however, subsequent efforts to obtain assistance will depend on the individual's *perceived control* over future events. An individual who has experienced threatening help and is pessimistic about the likelihood of future control may feel helplessly dependent on the kindness of others (Coates et al., 1983). Help will again be sought, but at a high price to self-esteem. In contrast, an individual who has experienced threatening help but is optimistic about the likelihood of future control may shun seeking help from others and rely instead on self-help efforts (Nadler & Fisher, 1986). Because receiving help has threatened self-esteem in the past, self-reliance is preferred in the future.

Receiving help from others is but one way that concerns about self-esteem can arise. Indeed, any factor that decreases a person's tendency to regard help-seeking as an indication of personal inferiority should increase that person's willingness to seek help (Rosen, 1983). For example, people usually feel more secure in close relationships, which may account for why it's often easier to seek help from significant others than from strangers (Clark, 1983b). Gender also influences the willingness to seek help. Remember that time you and a

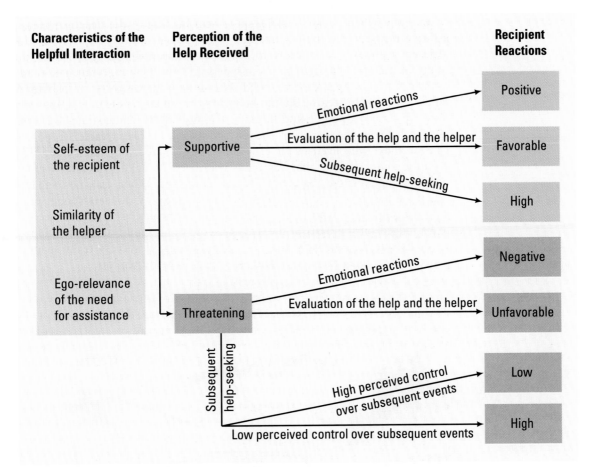

Figure 7.12   The Threat-to-Self-Esteem Model of Recipient Reactions to Aid.   The threat-to-self-esteem model describes how people react when they receive help from others. Being helped in a way that makes the person feel appreciated and cared for is supportive and leads to positive responses. Being helped in a way that makes the person feel inferior and overly dependent is threatening and creates negative responses. The model also describes the circumstances under which people will seek assistance in the future. [Based on Nadler & Fisher, 1986.]

member of the opposite sex got lost while driving in unfamiliar territory? Who wanted to stop early on and ask for directions? Who kept insisting that help wasn't necessary until you almost ran out of gas? For relatively minor problems at least, women ask for help more than do men (McMullen & Gross, 1983). Because help-seeking is less socially acceptable for men, it is more threatening to their self-esteem (Wills & DePaulo, 1991).

Ironically, when people avoid seeking help because of the desire to protect self-esteem, they risk damaging their sense of self-worth. The key to this apparent paradox is what Howard Weiss and Patrick Knight (1980) call "the utility of humility." If personal success depends on obtaining information and assistance from others, then to avoid seeking help increases the probability of failure. Thus, help-seeking should be greatest when success is most important. Research on city-dwelling and kibbutz-residing Israelis demonstrates this connection between the desire for success and asking for help (Nadler, 1986). In general, those who lived in the city valued individual achievement more than group accomplishment, whereas those who lived on a kibbutz valued group accomplishment more than individual achievement. When task performance was to be judged on the basis of individual scores, city dwellers sought more help than did those who lived on kibbutzim. But when task performance was to be judged on the basis of the average score of all group members, kibbutz residents sought more help than did city dwellers. If success really matters, people can swallow their pride and ask others to help them out.

[Drawing by D. Reilly; © 1991 The New Yorker Magazine, Inc.]

"Because my genetic programming prevents me from stopping to ask directions—that's why!"

HELPING THE HOMELESS

Homelessness is one of the great social tragedies of our time and one of the great failures to give help to those who need it (Jones et al., 1991). Nobody knows for sure how many people are homeless today in the United States (Breakey & Fischer, 1990). But exact numbers may not be all that important. According to Peter Rossi (1990),

> No available study suggests a national total of homeless on any given night of less than several hundred thousand, and perhaps it is enough to know that the nation's homeless are at least numerous enough to populate a medium-sized city. Although the "numbers" issue has been quite contentious, in a very real sense, it does not matter which estimate is closest to the truth. By any standard, all estimates point to a national disgrace. (pp. 956–957)

Now, compare that national disgrace with an anthropologist's description of life among the Moose (pronounced "MOH-say") in West Africa:

> Moose welcome anyone who wishes to join the community and move into the village. New arrivals have only to say where they wish to build their homes, and the user of the land in question gives it up for the newcomer's residence. I experienced this myself when I moved into the village and arranged to build huts and a living compound for my family: No one expected any compensation, and indeed, we were gradually assimilated into the family of our hosts. . . . Water is even scarcer than land. It does not rain at all for six months of the year, and, during three months or more, the rains are sparse and unpredictable. . . . Each of the two years that I lived there, the well ran dry and villagers had to walk miles to get water for themselves and their stock from other villages, carrying it home on their heads. Each of these other villages shared their water until their wells were nearly dry, without expecting any reciprocation for the water. Even in these circumstances, any stranger who comes into the village may ask for a drink, and any visitor is offered water. (Fiske, 1991, pp. 190–191)

How can we account for this extraordinary difference in helping those in need? In one of the richest countries in the world, people sleep on the street, transport their belongings in grocery carts, and rummage through piles of garbage to find food. Among some of the poorest people in the world, no one goes without shelter or goes thirsty as long as anyone has water. Homelessness is, of course, a complex phenomenon that is affected by many specific economic and political factors. But it may also be a symptom of a profound loss of social connection in American society (Wuthnow, 1991). Among the Moose, no such loss has occurred. Their sense of being intimately connected to others binds them to those who live in their village *and* to strangers who arrive in their midst.

The relationship between helping and interpersonal connection has been noted repeatedly in this chapter. Consider these examples:

- Traditional sociobiology emphasizes the practical connection of reciprocity and the genetic connection of kinship selection.

Homelessness is affected by many economic and political factors, but it may also be a symptom of a profound loss of social connection in American society.

- Some more recent perspectives on a possible genetic foundation for helping behavior focus on the larger social context in which an individual learns from others and bonds with them.
- Two kinds of connections lie at the heart of the empathy-altruism hypothesis: the cognitive connection of perspective-taking and the emotional connection of empathic concern.
- In an emergency, bystanders who know a victim personally, or who simply expect to get to know this person at some time, are less likely to pass their responsibility to intervene on to others.
- Similarity increases helping, as does a close relationship.

Taken as a whole, these theories and research findings suggest that helping the homeless requires the recognition of individual human beings with whom we can have a meaningful connection. Sometimes language makes that connection (Batson, 1983). Terms like "the human family" and "sisters and brothers" extend a sense of kinship beyond biological boundaries. The mass media can also play a useful role in helping us be more helpful (Johnston & Ettema, 1986). The book or television show that lets homeless individuals tell their life stories evokes our sympathy and reminds us of our common humanity. And perhaps reading this textbook will make a contribution. In one study, students who learned about the decision-making process involved in bystander intervention were more likely than uninformed students to try to help when, two weeks later, they encountered a research confederate sprawled in a hallway (Beaman et al.,

1978). Having studied the social psychology of helping isn't going to turn you into Mother Teresa. But as you think about the homeless and other people in need of a helping hand, you might want to reflect on the theme of interpersonal connection that characterizes so much of the material presented in this chapter. Almost four hundred years ago, the poet John Donne put it this way:

> No Man is an *Iland,* intire of it selfe; every man is a peece of the *Continent,* a part of the *maine;* if a *Clod* bee washed away by the *Sea, Europe* is the lesse, as well as if a *Promontorie* were, as well as if a *Mannor* of thy *friends,* or of *thine owne* were; Any Mans *death* diminishes *me,* because I am involved in *Mankinde;* And therefore never send to know for whom the *bell* tolls; It tolls for *thee.*

REVIEW

PERSONAL INFLUENCES: WHY DO PEOPLE HELP?

Genetic Factors in Helping

The two kinds of helping most commonly proposed by sociobiology are reciprocal helping, in which those who receive also give, and kinship selection, in which people promote their own genes by helping close relatives. Other theories of helpfulness as an innate, universal human characteristic emphasize the consequences of more general social tendencies. Some research suggests that individual differences in helping may be inherited, creating a genetic basis for the altruistic personality. However, no one personality characteristic, or set of characteristics, has been shown to be associated with helping in all situations.

Emotional Factors in Helping

People in a good mood tend to be helpful. Two major explanations for the good mood effect have been offered. According to the mood maintenance hypothesis, people in a good mood help in order to maintain their positive mood. Alternatively, people may help because being in a good mood generates positive thoughts and expectations regarding helpful behavior, the person in need, or social activities in general. Being in a negative mood can also increase helping. Feeling guilty about your behavior in one situation can increase your helpful behavior even in a different situation. Taking personal responsibility for a negative mood increases self-awareness, which can increase helping if self-concerns are low and awareness of the value of helping is high. Finally, the negative state relief model proposes that people who feel sad or depressed help in order to improve their mood. From all of these perspectives, helping is viewed as essentially egoistic—motivated by a desire to benefit oneself.

Does Altruism Exist?

According to the empathy-altruism hypothesis, taking the perspective of a person perceived to be in need creates the other-oriented emotion of empathic concern, which in turn produces the altruistic motive to increase the other's welfare. Egoistic motives are produced by feelings of personal distress in reaction to a person in need. When people are altruistically motivated, they will help even when escaping from the helping situation is easy. Alternatives to the empathy-altruism hypothesis include empathy-specific punishments for not helping and empathy-specific rewards for helping. But at this point, the evidence supporting the empathy-altruism hypothesis is very strong. This hypothesis is the subject of so much scrutiny because it raises basic issues about human nature.

SITUATIONAL INFLUENCES: WHEN DO PEOPLE HELP?

Models: Following Others

Observing a helpful model increases helping. Models elicit direct imitation and, when rewarded, inform us about the potential egoistic benefits of helping others.

Social Norms: A Helpful Standard

Models also provide information about social norms. Social norms that promote helping are based on a sense of fairness or on standards about what is right. Personal norms are individualized and specific standards of conduct, perhaps derived from parental models.

Self-Perception and Helping Under Pressure

People who perceive themselves as helpful individuals with altruistic motives are usually more helpful. However, external rewards for helping diminish these self-perceptions and decrease helpful behavior when rewards are no longer available. Similarly, awareness of internal rewards and punishments for helping increases self-perceived selfishness.

The Place Where We Live

For a number of possible reasons, city residents are less likely to give spontaneous, informal help to strangers than are those who live in smaller communities. But where they live does not affect the amount of help that close friends and intimates give each other.

The Unhelpful Crowd

Research on the bystander effect, in which the presence of others inhibits helping in an emergency, indicates that five steps are involved in the delivery of assistance. Each step is subject to inhibiting conditions. The distractions of others and our own self-concerns may impair our ability to notice that someone needs help. Because of pluralistic ignorance, each member of a crowd of bystanders may infer from the inaction of others that there is no emergency. In the diffusion of responsibility, people avoid taking responsibility because they assume that others will do so. People are more likely to offer direct aid if they feel competent to provide assistance. Even if people intend to help, they may not do so if they fear that behaving in a helpful fashion will make them look foolish—a case of audience inhibition. According to the arousal: cost-reward model of helping, people feel shocked and alarmed at the sight of an emergency, and they help in order to reduce this unpleasant arousal. If there are other, less costly ways to reduce arousal, help will not be provided. Overall, victims are more likely to be helped if there is only one person present at the emergency than if there is a crowd.

INTERPERSONAL INFLUENCES: WHOM DO PEOPLE HELP?

Perceived Characteristics of the Person in Need

People are more willing to help when they attribute a person's need for assistance to uncontrollable causes than when they attribute the need to events under the person's control. Physically attractive individuals are more likely to receive help than are those who are less attractive.

The Relationship Between Giver and Receiver

Perceived similarity to a person in need increases the willingness to help that person. Although the effects of racial similarity on helping are quite varied, subtle forms of discriminatory helping may still occur. In general, people help someone with whom they have a close relationship more than they help a stranger, unless helping a significant other threatens their own ego. Men help more than women do in situations involving a female stranger in need of assistance, possible physical danger, and observation by others. But women are more likely to be helpful in providing tender loving care to significant others. Individuals who have a strong belief in a just world are more willing to provide assistance when a need is temporary than when it is continuous.

The Perceived Relationship Between Attacker and Victim

Bystanders are more likely to intervene in an attack by a stranger than in an attack by a husband on a wife. When no information is provided about the relationship between a male attacker and a female victim, most observers assume that the two have a close relationship.

REACTIONS TO RECEIVING HELP

Help That Supports Versus Help That Threatens

The threat-to-self-esteem model distinguishes between supportive help, where the recipient feels appreciated and cared for, and threatening help, where the recipient feels inferior and overly dependent. Help is most likely to be perceived as threatening by a recipient with high self-esteem who receives help on an ego-relevant task from a similar provider. In close, interdependent relationships, receiving help is usually a positive experience.

Factors That Influence Help-Seeking

Receiving supportive help encourages the recipient to seek assistance again when needed. Individuals who receive threatening help will seek further help if they are pessimistic about their ability to control future events but not if they have a greater sense of control. People are usually more willing to seek help from a person they are close to than from a stranger. Women seek help more often than do men, at least for minor problems. The desire to succeed also influences help-seeking. A greater desire for success increases willingness to seek the help necessary to succeed.

HELPING THE HOMELESS

Homelessness in the United States has been called a "national disgrace" and may reflect, at least in part, a loss of social connection in American society. Consistent with theory and research in this chapter, helping the homeless would appear to require the recognition of individuals with whom we can have a meaningful connection. Possible ways to increase a sense of connection with others include applying kinship language to those who are not biologically related to us, responding sympathetically to mass media presentations, and developing a better understanding of why people help those in need.

Aggression

8

Preview

In this chapter, we examine a disturbing aspect of human behavior, aggression. First, we ask *"What is aggression?"* and consider its definition. After describing possible *origins of aggression,* we explore a variety of *social and situational influences.* Finally, specific *scenes of violence,* each of which may serve to induce further aggression, are discussed. Throughout the chapter, we emphasize ways to prevent or reduce aggressive actions.

During thirty years of studying chimpanzees in their natural environment, Jane Goodall encountered many difficult situations at her field station in Tanzania. But the mid-1970s were the worst: Zairean rebels kidnapped four of the students working with her; the male chimpanzees in her study annihilated another group of chimps living nearby; and a mother-daughter team of chimps cannibalized some eleven chimpanzee infants from their own group. Looking back on this period, Goodall (1990) has no doubt about what caused her the most distress.

> The kidnapping, despite the shock and misery, did little to change my view of human nature. History is peppered with accounts of kidnap and ransom. . . . The intercommunity violence and the cannibalism that took place at Gombe, however, were newly recorded and those events changed forever my view of chimpanzee nature. For so many years I had believed that chimpanzees, while showing uncanny similarities to humans in many ways were, by and large, rather "nicer" than us. Suddenly, I found that under certain circumstances they could be just as brutal. . . . And it hurt. (pp. 108–109)

Goodall's account of her "struggle to come to terms with this new knowledge" reflects the intensity of her admiration for the animals she has studied so carefully. After reading her vivid descriptions or watching one of her TV specials, it would take a very hardhearted person indeed not to share her affection for these creatures. Yet Goodall herself seems a bit hardhearted in her apparent assumption that kidnapping is just a natural part of human nature—unfortunate, to be sure, but not surprising.

It seems entirely possible, however, that she has plenty of company in this assumption about the aggressive inclinations of human beings. Even if our own lives are quiet and peaceful, the mass media provide daily lessons on everything we ever wanted to know, and more, about the extent of human brutality and violence. Compared with war, murder, rape, child abuse, gang shoot-outs, torture, and terrorist attacks, it's understandable that a kidnapping from which all the victims are rescued could appear to be a relatively low-level item on the scale of human aggression. The problem, of course, is that if we accept aggressive behavior as inevitable, we may miss the opportunity to reduce it.

But how did Goodall react to the aggression that she didn't expect, and didn't take for granted? Although she was stunned and dismayed when violence broke out among the chimps at Gombe, she did not simply pack up her bags and run away from this new, disturbing knowledge. Instead, she stayed to learn more about the whole range of behaviors of which chimpanzees are capable. This is our approach to human aggression in this chapter. We examine it thoroughly because the more we know about what increases aggression, the better equipped we will be to develop ways to decrease it in our own lives and throughout society.

PINNING IT DOWN: WHAT IS AGGRESSION?

As both scientists and philosophers have discovered, aggression is a rather slippery concept. Everytime you think you have its definition pinned down, a new riddle springs up. Consider, for example, the following actions. Which ones would you classify as aggressive?

- Accidentally injuring someone
- Shooting to kill but missing
- Hurling insults at someone
- Deliberately failing to prevent harm
- Murdering for money
- Striking out in a rage

For a good many years, social psychologists engaged in a lively debate about exactly how aggression is best defined (Baron, 1977; Berkowitz, 1969; Buss, 1961; Zillmann, 1979). Although some difference of opinion remains, there is reasonably widespread agreement on defining **aggression** as *behavior* that is *intended* to *injure* another person.

aggression Behavior intended to injure another person.

Using this definition, we can rule out the first example in our list. Accidentally injuring someone is *not* an aggressive act because there is no intent to harm. Similarly, actions that produce harm as an unintended by-product are not aggressive. The physician who administers a painful treatment does not act aggressively. Here, the intent is to improve the patient's health, and the pain caused by the treatment is an undesirable side effect. In contrast, intentional efforts to injure that do not succeed *are* aggressive. Shooting to kill is an aggressive act, even if the bullet misses.

But any definition that relies on an individual's intentions has a serious drawback. We can't see another person's intentions, so how do we know what they are? And whose view do we accept when people disagree about someone's intentions? When defined in terms of intent, aggression becomes a matter of subjective judgment. Like beauty, aggression lies ultimately in the eye of the beholder.

Behaviorally, aggressive actions cover the waterfront. Words as well as deeds can be aggressive. Quarreling couples who intend their spiteful remarks to hurt are behaving aggressively. And acts are not required. Inaction, too, can be aggressive. If someone's goal is to get a coworker into trouble, failing to warn that person not to disturb an ill-tempered boss is aggressive.

Violence also refers to behavior, in this case extreme or unwarranted acts of aggression. Some other terms in the language of aggression refer to feelings and attitudes. *Anger* consists of strong feelings of displeasure in response to a perceived injury; *hostility* is a negative, antagonistic attitude toward another person or group. Although we tend to think of them as closely connected, neither anger nor hostility necessarily leads to aggression. People can be angry at others and regard them with great hostility without ever trying to harm them. And aggression can occur without a trace of anger or hostility, as when a contract killer murders a perfect stranger in order to "make a killing" financially.

instrumental aggression Behavior intended to injure another person in order to obtain something of value.

The aggression of a hired gun is an example of **instrumental aggression**: harm is inflicted in order to obtain something of value. The goal of instrumental aggression may be to secure material rewards, such as the contract killer's payment for services rendered. But psychological benefits can also be sought. For example, among individuals with high self-esteem, those whose self-esteem fluctuates from day to day experience more angry feelings than do those whose self-esteem is stable over time (Kernis et al., 1989). The "positive but fragile self-view" of people with high but unstable self-esteem appears to make them particularly vulnerable to feeling insecure and threatened. Getting angry in such situations helps them restore self-esteem by reasserting their own righteousness and placing the blame on others. Aggressive behavior could serve the same purpose, protecting self-esteem by acting strong and brave despite feeling weak and frightened.

angry aggression Impulsive, emotional behavior intended solely to injure another person.

But harm is not always a means to some other desired end; it can also be inflicted for its own sake. Harmful acts carried out in the heat of the moment for the sole purpose of hurting someone are called **angry aggression**. The jealous lover strikes out in rage; fans of rival soccer teams go at each other with fists and clubs. In angry aggression, the desire to harm the other person is both necessary and sufficient for action to occur.

The definitions we have discussed are the crucial first steps in the study of aggression. They provide the framework for the theories and research findings we examine in the following pages. But aggression, of course, raises moral questions that go beyond theory and research in social psychology. Is *all* aggression morally wrong? If not, what kinds of threats justify what kinds of aggression? To answer such questions, each of us needs to carefully consider our own values and principles. Where do *you* draw the line?

ORIGINS OF AGGRESSION

Given the subject matter, it's not surprising that people have strong differences of opinion about the origins of aggression. Beliefs about the root causes of aggression lie at the heart of understanding human nature. Is aggression an innate characteristic of human beings, or is it learned through experience? In scientific circles, this either/or way of phrasing the question is called the "nature-nurture debate." This section takes a look at both sides.

An allied tank column in Saudi Arabia during the 1991 war against Iraq. Like all wars, Operation Desert Storm raised questions about the circumstances, if any, under which aggressive behavior is morally justified.

Is Aggression Innate?

There are various approaches to the question of whether aggression is innate. Here, we examine four of them: instinct theories, sociobiology, behavior genetics, and gender differences.

Instinct Theories On November 11, 1918, a human catastrophe finally ended. Covered in mud, lungs blasted by gas, millions of soldiers had died to gain a few miles of contested territory. For an Austrian physician named Sigmund Freud, the slaughter on the battlefields of Europe during World War I marked a turning point. Rejecting his prewar version of psychoanalysis, Freud (1920) proposed a grim new concept: the *death instinct*, a profound, unconscious desire to escape the tensions of living by becoming still, inanimate, dead. This impulse toward self-destruction does not, according to Freud, exist unchallenged. There is also a life instinct, which motivates human beings to preserve and reproduce themselves. Paradoxically, Freud considered aggression toward others to be a momentary victory for the life instinct. In aggression, the force of the death instinct is deflected, aimed outward at others rather than inward toward the original target—oneself.

Like Freud, Konrad Lorenz (1966) regarded aggression as an innate, built-in instinct. Unlike Freud, who believed that the life and death instincts are antagonistic forces, Lorenz saw the will to live and the will to aggress as perfectly compatible. Based on his observations of animals in their natural habitat, Lorenz argued that aggression is necessary for survival. The individual who successfully aggresses against others gains access to valuable resources such as food, territory, and desirable mates. Thus, said Lorenz, aggression secures an advantage in the struggle to survive, and natural selection favors the development of an aggressive instinct in humans as well as in animals.

Despite the widespread attention that these theories received when they were formulated, they no longer have much influence on scientific research. The primary reason for their fall from favor is their reliance on circular reasoning. Why do people aggress? Because they have an aggressive instinct. How do we know that aggression is instinctive? Because people aggress. Such reasoning endlessly circles in on itself, going nowhere and shutting out the possibility of alternative explanations.

Sociobiology   There are clear similarities between Lorenz's instinct theory and sociobiology, the application of evolutionary biology to the development of social behavior. Sociobiology, too, looks for human universals and, when found, attributes them to innate characteristics favored by natural selection. Indeed, the sociobiological perspective on aggression starts by picking up the Lorenzian thread: aggression has become innate among humans because, on the average, it increases the likelihood of an individual's reproductive success.

In contrast to Lorenz, however, sociobiology emphasizes genetic survival rather than survival of the individual. Since at least some of a person's genes can be transmitted through the reproductive success of one's relatives, genes underlying behaviors that harm relatives should tend to drop out of the gene pool during the course of evolution. This analysis led Edward Wilson (1975) to propose that there is an inevitable limitation on aggression, by both animals and humans. The limit occurs, says Wilson, because indiscriminate aggression would endanger an aggressor's relatives, thereby reducing the probability of the aggressor's genes being transmitted.

As indicated in Chapters 5 and 7, sociobiology is a controversial approach to human social behavior, and the sociobiological perspective on aggression has received its fair share of criticism. For example, an innate tendency *not* to aggress against one's relatives seems distinctly at odds with the high levels of family violence that we describe later in this chapter. But perhaps the most fundamental problem faced by sociobiological accounts is historical and cultural diversity (Lewontin et al., 1984). The year 1991 set a record in the United States, of the sort we can do without. More murders—some 25,000—were committed in 1991 than in any other year for which records are available (Ellis, 1992). In city after city (Anchorage, Dallas, Phoenix, Washington), homicide rates reached an all-time high. The U.S. homicide rate now averages almost 10 murders for every 100,000 citizens. The comparable rate in Great Britain is 5.5 and in Japan 1.3. As illustrated in Figure 8.1, murder rates vary dramatically from country to country. Such historical and cross-cultural differences in aggression challenge any effort to explain it in terms of direct natural selection.

Figure 8.1 International Murder Rates. The murder rate (number of murders per 100,000 people) varies widely among different countries. Since these figures were reported in the late 1980s, murder rates have increased in many of these countries, sometimes dramatically. [Data from United Nations, 1989.]

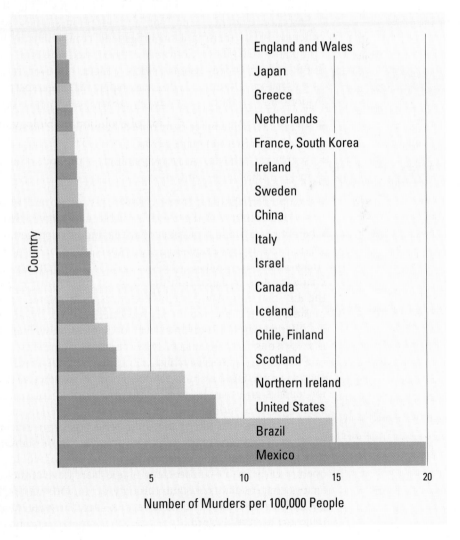

If aggression is an innate, universal human characteristic, how could people differ so much in when and where they display it?

Behavior Genetics   Sociobiology attempts the difficult task of tying together evolution, genetic transmission, and social behavior. Behavior genetics settles for the complexities of connecting the last two. And here, variation is a blessing rather than a curse. To trace a line of genetic transmission (heritability), scientists examine differences among individuals and groups. As described in Chapter 7, monozygotic twins (who are identical in their genetic make-up) will exhibit more similarity on any inherited trait than will dizygotic twins (who share only part of their genes). Similarly, adopted children will resemble their biological parents on any inherited trait more than they resemble their adoptive parents.

Based on evidence from twin and adoption studies, some researchers have concluded that there is a major genetic component in human aggression or criminality (DiLalla & Gottesman, 1991; Mednick et al., 1984; Tellegen et al., 1988; Wilson & Herrnstein, 1985). Others, however, regard such conclusions as premature (Kamin, 1986; Lagerspetz & Lagerspetz, 1983; Scott, 1983; Widom, 1991). Participants in this debate usually take one of two positions:

- Aggressive behavior is determined by an interaction between genetic inheritance and environmental factors.
- Aggressive behavior is overwhelmingly a product of experience, and genetic make-up has little if any effect.

Except perhaps in extreme cases of persistent and unprovoked aggression, few would argue for the third available alternative: that aggression is overwhelmingly a product of genetic factors and environment has little if any effect. Thus, there is agreement that aggressive behavior is, at least to some extent, "made." The question is whether it is, to any significant degree, "born." Two characteristics of aggression that bear on this controversy are its stability over the life span and male-female differences in its expression.

Although the amount of aggression displayed by an individual may vary at different ages, a person's level of aggression is highly stable throughout that person's life. Teenagers may be more aggressive than young children, but the most aggressive child in nursery school tends to become the most aggressive teenager in high school. Such consistency is greater for males than for females and may be particularly pronounced for males who are extremely aggressive as children (Huesmann et al., 1984; Loeber, 1982). The fact of stability across the life span could reflect genetic inheritance but does not prove it. There are many other feasible causes of stability: (1) physiological processes that are not genetically controlled; (2) environmental factors that operate early in life and thereby shape later development; (3) environmental factors that remain constant throughout an individual's lifetime. The list of possibilities is a long one, and various factors could interact with each other (Huesmann et al., 1987).

Gender Differences The difference between males and females in aggressive behavior also raises the possibility of genetic effects. This difference is striking, although limited. On the one hand, males are clearly more *physically* aggressive than are females (Eagly & Steffen, 1986). On the other hand, males and females do not differ in all forms of aggression. Differences in *verbal* aggression are small or nonexistent (Reinisch & Sanders, 1986). And there are few differences in men's and women's feelings of anger (Averill, 1982). Despite these limitations, there has been considerable interest in whether the male-female difference in physical aggression might be genetic in nature.

Such a genetic pathway would start with sex chromosomes and their effect on male and female sex hormones. Though the male sex hormone is present in both sexes, males typically have higher levels of testosterone than do females. If testosterone is a major influence on aggressive behavior, then it could be the connecting link between gender and aggression. Research by James Dabbs and his colleagues makes the case for the role of testosterone in fueling aggression. In their studies of prison inmates (both male and female), those who had committed an unprovoked violent crime had higher testosterone levels than did those who had committed a nonviolent crime (Dabbs et al., 1987; Dabbs et al., 1988). Intriguing as they are, such correlational findings cannot prove that testosterone causes aggression. There are other possible explanations. For example, Dabbs and his colleagues have repeatedly found that testosterone levels are better predictors of antisocial behavior for subjects low in socioeconomic status than for those with greater income and education (Dabbs & Morris, 1990; Dabbs et al., 1990). And higher levels of testosterone are also associated with stress (Thompson et al., 1990). Perhaps, then, people who are poor and badly educated are more vulnerable to the higher levels of stress required to elevate both testosterone and aggression. In any event, the interconnections among physiology, experience, and behavior make it extremely difficult to pinpoint the influence of testosterone on human aggression.

Testosterone levels can be identified only by laboratory analysis. Another approach to a possible genetic foundation for gender differences in physical aggression emphasizes a more visible aspect of the physiological consequences of sex chromosomes: physique. Most men have more bulk and more muscle than most women. If more women were built like Arnold Schwarzenegger, would they be more physically aggressive?

Many reseachers regard chromosome-based explanations of gender differences in physical aggression as fatally flawed. They contend that the most telling difference occurs during childhood when parents teach girls more than boys to feel guilty and anxious about aggressive behavior (Eron, 1980; Perry et al., 1986). As we will see in the next section, learning plays an important role in aggressive behavior. However, the extent to which boys and girls are actually taught different lessons about aggression is not so clear. A recent review of research suggests that North American parents rely on similar methods of socialization for sons and daughters (Lytton & Romney, 1991). But in other Western countries, boys are physically punished more than girls. To understand

When children get a toy they want by hitting, shoving, and tearing it away from another child, their aggression is rewarded. Having learned that aggression pays, they are more likely to aggress again in the future.

the possible effects of physical punishment on aggression, we need to consider the relationship between learning and aggression in more detail.

Is Aggression Learned?

Regardless of the precise role of genetic factors, aggressive behavior is influenced by learning (Bandura, 1973). Rewards obtained by aggression increase its use in the future. Children who get the toy they want by hitting the toy's owner have learned that aggression pays. They are likely to hit again. To an extremely angry person, even the sight of a victim's pain can be rewarding and incite further aggression (Baron, 1983a).

The effects of punishment on aggressive behavior are more complex (Bandura, 1973; Zillmann, 1979). Fear of being punished can decrease aggressive actions when the individual

- has alternative ways to obtain whatever he or she hopes to gain from being aggressive.
- expects that punishment for aggression will be quick and certain.
- is not extremely angry.

■ believes that the person who would deliver the punishment has a legitimate right to do so.

In fact, such stringent conditions are seldom met. People frequently believe that aggression is their only way out of an intolerable situation, know that punishment will not be quick or certain, are very angry, or question the right of the punisher to punish. Under these circumstances, the threat of punishment will probably not reduce aggression. The effects of being punished are even more problematic. If it's strong and swift enough, punishment can stop aggression in its tracks. But there may be a long-term price to pay. Punishment perceived as unfair or arbitrary can provoke later retaliation. And punishment delivered in a hostile or aggressive manner provides a model to imitate, aggressively.

social learning theory The view that behavior is learned through the observation of others as well as through the direct experience of rewards and punishments.

The power of models to affect behavior is a central tenet of Albert Bandura's (1977b) **social learning theory**. Social learning theory emphasizes that learning does not require direct experience with rewards and punishments. We also learn from the example of others. As described in Chapter 7, models can influence prosocial, helpful behavior. They also affect antisocial, aggressive behavior (Bandura, 1983). In an early study, Bandura and his associates (1961) observed the behavior of mildly frustrated children. Those who had previously watched an adult throw around, punch, and kick an inflatable Bobo doll were more aggressive when they later played with the doll than were those who had watched a quiet, subdued adult.

Models are most likely to increase aggression when their behavior is successful. Soon after Dr. Thomas Graves murdered a wealthy Rhode Island widow with a bottle of poisoned whiskey, copycat killers sprang up on both coasts. That was in 1898. Almost a century later, the 1982 Tylenol murders in Illinois triggered at least a hundred copycat poisonings across the country (Levin & Fox, 1985). But what about aggressive models who are punished? Here we have to distinguish between learning and performance. Whenever people watch an aggressive model's behavior, even the far-fetched exploits of ridiculously hyperaggressive movie characters, they *learn* something about how to behave aggressively. If that model is punished, however, they are unlikely to *perform* the aggressive acts they've learned, at least for the moment. But if the situation changes and the fear of punishment diminishes, what was learned before can sometimes burst into action.

Some investigators believe that the pervasive effects of aggressive models can account for large societal trends—such as postwar increases in homicide rates (Archer & Gartner, 1984). Although these increases are greater in victorious countries, even the citizens of defeated nations aggress more after the war than before. According to Murray Straus (1990b), parents and school authorities who physically punish children are particularly powerful models of aggression. In his view, not only do such individuals model specific aggressive behaviors, they also legitimize the general option of resorting to force. Though his research is correlational and cannot prove a cause-and-effect relationship, Straus is firmly convinced that the individual who is physically punished as a child is more likely to engage in aggressive behavior as an adult.

Fortunately, modeling also has positive consequences: *non*aggressive models can *decrease* aggressive behavior (Baron & Kepner, 1970; Donnerstein & Donnerstein, 1976). Observing a nonaggressive response to a provoking situation teaches a peaceful alternative for imitation and strengthens existing restraints against aggression. In addition, observing someone who is calm and reasonable may help an angry person settle down rather than strike out (Baron, 1983a). Aggression can spread like wildfire. But nonviolence too can be contagious.

Nature Versus Nurture: A False Dichotomy

In considering the role of innate and learned factors in aggression, we should avoid oversimplifying human behavior and shoving it into little boxes labeled "nature" and "nurture." Biology is certainly a force to be reckoned with. Hormonal and neurological processes may well influence the acquisition and expression of aggressive tendencies (Flannelly et al., 1984; Simmel et al., 1983). It is, however, highly improbable that human aggression stems from some rigid, fixed, continuously operating instinct. Human beings have survived as a species thanks in large part to the behavioral flexibility that allows us to learn from experience and cope with changing environmental demands. In the next section, we explore those aspects of the social and physical environment that affect aggression.

SOCIAL AND SITUATIONAL INFLUENCES ON AGGRESSION

Mark Twain's novel *The Prince and the Pauper* is a tale of two characters who exchange social roles with each other. The plot of an early Eddie Murphy film *Trading Places* hinges on a similar device. Both the novel and the film reflect an enduring fascination with how behavior changes in response to a new environment. Despite these changes, however, the individual is not completely at the mercy of outside forces. Between the external event and the behavioral response lie a person's thoughts. As we will see, both environmental circumstances and cognitive mediators help determine whether aggressive behavior will occur.

Frustration: Aggression as a Drive

Frustration and Aggression, by John Dollard and his colleagues (1939), is one of the most influential books on aggression ever written. The book sets forth two

frustration-aggression hypothesis The dual proposition that frustration always elicits the motive to aggress and that all aggression is caused by frustration.

major propositions, which taken together are called the **frustration-aggression hypothesis**. The first proposition states that the frustration produced by interrupting a person's progress toward an expected goal will *always* elicit the motive to aggress. The second maintains that aggression has *only one* ultimate cause: frustration. In the classic film *On the Waterfront,* the character played by Marlon Brando insisted, "I want what I want when I want it." The frustration-aggression hypothesis predicts that if he can't have it, he'll aggress.

Dollard and his colleagues claimed that the motive to aggress is a psychological drive that resembles physiological drives like hunger. Hunger is caused by food deprivation; aggression, they said, is caused by frustration. The hunger drive prompts the search for food; the aggressive drive, they argued, prompts the attempt to inflict injury. But the drive to aggress does not always produce aggressive behavior, which can be inhibited by fear of punishment or the inability to get at the source of frustration. Inhibition, though, was not viewed by Dollard and his colleagues as a permanent barrier against aggression. Instead, they believed that inhibition creates **displacement**, in which the inclination to aggress is deflected from the real target only to land on a substitute. After a bad day at work or at school, do you come home and yell at the first available target—be it man, woman, or beast?

displacement Aggressing against a substitute target because aggressive acts against the source of the frustration are inhibited by fear or lack of access.

Now go a step further. Would yelling at the homefolks reduce your inclination to take revenge on the person who gave you a hard time? Dollard and his colleagues thought it would. Just as hunger can be satisfied by hamburgers as well as by caviar, so should "the occurrence of any act of aggression . . . reduce the instigation to aggression" (p. 50). The notion that any aggressive act can reduce a person's inclination to engage in other aggressive behaviors is called **catharsis**. Since the Dollard group defined acts of aggression quite broadly—to include making hostile jokes, telling violent stories, cursing, and observing the aggression of others, real or fictional—their concept of catharsis held out the hope that engaging in some relatively harmless pursuit could drain away energy from more violent tendencies.

catharsis The reduction of the motive to aggress that is said to result from engaging in or witnessing any aggressive act.

The Sequel: Problems and Limitations   Controversial from the beginning, the frustration-aggression hypothesis has been repeatedly revised and modified. Obviously, there is a connection between frustration and aggression. Break into a line of shoppers at the supermarket, interrupt a student cramming for an important exam, or take away a sports fan's hard-won ticket to a championship game, and you can observe the connection for yourself. But does frustration *always* produce the desire to aggress? Is *all* aggression the product of frustration? Critics were quick to point out that the Dollard group had overstated their case. Early on, Neal Miller (1941), one of the originators of the frustration-aggression hypothesis, acknowledged that frustration does not always produce aggressive inclinations. Subsequent research indicated that frustration is most likely to produce an aggressive response when people are thwarted from reaching a particularly important goal to which they feel entitled (Blanchard & Blanchard, 1984; Worchel, 1974). The other absolute decree of the frustration-aggression hypothesis, that all aggression is caused by frustration, was soon overturned as well. Frustration is only one of the many potential causes of aggression discussed in this chapter.

Another aspect of the frustration-aggression hypothesis, the concept of displacement, was also subjected to close scrutiny. In 1940, Carl Hovland and Robert Sears reported an association between racial violence and economic hard times. Reviewing information on fourteen southern states from 1882 to 1930, these investigators found strong negative correlations between the number of lynchings of black men and economic indicators such as the acre value of cotton. As the price of cotton fell, more lynchings occurred. Hovland and Sears suggested that by aggressing against blacks, whites displaced aggressive tendencies caused by economic frustration.

Subsequent studies have confirmed the relationship between economic distress and racial violence (Beck & Tolnay, 1990; Hepworth & West, 1988). The strength of the finding, however, does not prove the validity of concept. Actually, the requirements for a convincing demonstration of displacement are stringent (Berkowitz, 1962) and, overall, the evidence for its role in channeling aggressive behavior is inconclusive (Zillmann, 1979). To illustrate the problem, think back to that bad day at work or school. You might be quite nasty to the innocents at home, but not necessarily because of displacement. As we will see later in this chapter, other processes (such as level of arousal and an individual's thoughts) could account for why it's possible to be provoked by one person but aggress against someone else.

Perhaps because it seemed to offer a way to control aggression, the concept of catharsis received particular attention. Dollard and his colleagues described catharsis as a two-step sequence. First, aggression reduces the level of physiological arousal. Second, because arousal is reduced, people are less angry and less likely to aggress further. It sounds logical and lots of people believe it:

> People's emotions are similar to steam locomotives. If you build a fire in the boiler of a locomotive, keep raising the steam pressure and let it sit on the track, sooner or later something will blow. However, if you take it and spin the wheels and toot the whistle, the steam pressure can be kept at a safe level. Spectator sports give John Q. Citizen a socially acceptable way to lower his steam pressure by allowing him to spin his wheels and toot his whistle. (Proctor & Eckerd, 1976, p. 83)

Surprisingly, though, the evidence for the beneficial effects of catharsis is not at all encouraging (Baron, 1977; Geen & Quanty, 1977). Even the spinning wheels and tooting whistles of spectator sports don't seem to suffice (Russell, 1983). Under some circumstances, aggressing or watching others aggress can decrease arousal. But reduced physiological arousal doesn't guarantee reduced aggression. When anger is gone, aggressive intent can still remain.

Even more troubling for the idea of cathartic release, engaging in or witnessing aggression can *increase* subsequent aggression. As described earlier, people often imitate aggressive models. A person's own aggressive actions can also stimulate further aggression. If yelling at someone makes you feel better by

Does watching or participating in violent sports, such as the hockey game pictured here, reduce aggression elsewhere? Will the catharsis of letting off steam through spectator sports reduce the pressure to aggress in real life? Though many people find the idea appealing, the evidence is not encouraging. Instead, it's more likely that watching or participating in one kind of aggressive behavior will *increase* other kinds of aggression.

reducing your arousal, yelling is reinforced and more likely to occur again. In addition, getting away with a little bit of aggression can chip away at restraints against more violent behavior. Just "horsing around" with friends—a playful pinch here, a playful shove there—is correlated with engaging in more serious aggressive behaviors (Gergen, 1990).

The Reformulation: Frustration as an Unpleasant Experience In his reformulation of the frustration-aggression hypothesis, Leonard Berkowitz (1989) proposed that the key point about frustration is that it is an unpleasant experience. According to Berkowitz, any event that creates negative, uncomfortable feelings will stimulate the inclination to aggress. Thus, whatever makes frustration more unpleasant (for example, a very important goal; an unexpected interruption; an arbitrary, unjustified interference) increases its tendency to produce aggression. By drawing frustration into the fold of negative affect, Berkowitz connects the work by Dollard and his colleagues with more recent theory and research on aggression.

Negative Affect: The Temperature's Rising

A number of other investigators have also emphasized the role of negative affect in producing aggression. Besides frustrating experiences, all sorts of unpleasant experiences and environmental conditions can create negative affect and increase aggression: crowding (Fisher et al., 1984); physical pain (Berkowitz & Heimer, 1989); bad odors (Rotton & Frey, 1985); and cigarette smoke (Zillmann et al., 1981). The effect on aggression of one very common unpleasant condition, high temperature, is especially intriguing. Many people assume that temperature and tempers rise together. Are they right?

negative affect escape model The view that increasing levels of negative affect increase aggression up to a point, beyond which the person tries to escape, becomes passive, or collapses.

Robert Baron (1977) would reply, "Yes, up to a point." From Baron's perspective, the effects of temperature and other noxious stimuli on aggression can best be understood in terms of the **negative affect escape model**. This model holds that noxious stimuli increase aggression up to a point, beyond which the person tries to escape, becomes passive, or collapses. Three steps are involved. First, noxious stimuli elicit a negative emotional response, which increases the likelihood of aggressive behavior. Then, as the intensity of the noxious stimulus increases, so does the intensity of the negative emotional response and so do aggressive tendencies. At some point, however, the tide turns. After this point has been reached, increasing the intensity of the noxious stimulus continues to produce an increasingly negative emotional response, but nonaggressive responses such as escape or fatigue take over and aggression declines.

An initial examination of the relationship between hot weather and urban riots obtained results consistent with the negative affect escape model (Baron & Ransberger, 1978). As Figure 8.2A illustrates, the number of summer riots initially increased as the temperature rose, peaking during those days when the temperature was around 81 to 85 degrees Fahrenheit. At still higher temperatures, the number of riots declined. Subsequent research, however, has not found a turning point. Instead, it has documented a continuing, upward spiral. As the temperature increases, so does the incidence of aggressive behaviors such as murder, rape, assault, and wife-battering (Anderson, 1989).

These conflicting research findings create a puzzle. Here's a clue to its solution. If we plot the number of baseball games that take place in a season according to the temperature on the day they were played, the greatest number of games occurs during those days when the temperature is . . . what? You got it: in that same range of 81 to 85 degrees (Carlsmith & Anderson, 1979; see Figure 8.2B). What's going on? Nobody questions that behavior can get out of hand on the baseball field: pitchers throw at batters; batters charge the mound, sometimes with bat in hand; and the benches clear for the ensuing brawl. But baseball *schedules* are developed well in advance of any riotous behavior on the field. Why would the outbreak of riots and the number of baseball games peak in the same temperature range?

Normal temperature variation solves the puzzle. Days with temperatures of 81 to 85 degrees are simply more frequent in the summer than are days with other temperatures. Thus, there is more opportunity for both baseball games and aggression to occur at these moderate temperatures, yielding the

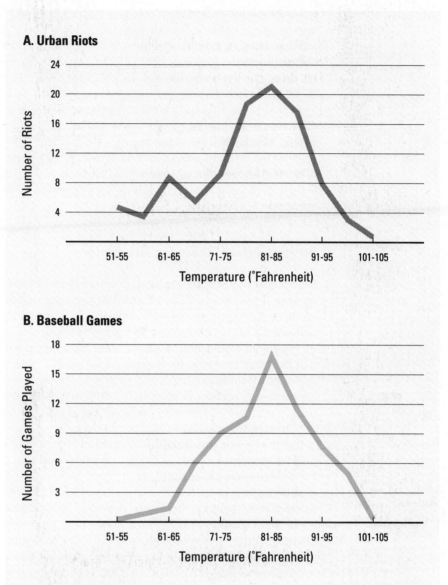

Figure 8.2 The Relationship Between Temperature and Behavior. Section A displays the relationship between temperature and the number of urban riots. Section B displays the relationship between temperature and the number of baseball games played. Notice the remarkable similarity of the two curves: each peaks between 81 and 85 degrees. What could account for this similarity? As explained in the text, the answer is temperature frequency. [A: From Baron & Ransberger, 1978. B: From Carlsmith & Anderson, 1979.]

81-to-85-degree peak. When results are adjusted to take temperature frequency into account, there is no turning point. Aggressive behavior continues to increase as the temperature climbs. And baseball players get a double-dose of this phenomenon (Reifman et al., 1991). Not only do they play more games on hot days, but the hotter the day on which they play, the more likely they are to be hit by a pitch.

Of course, the upward spiral of aggressive behavior as the temperature rises can't continue indefinitely. At some point, aggression *must* decline because people sicken and even die during extreme heat. It's possible that carefully constructed research will be able to find a turning point even within the range of normal temperatures (Anderson & De Neve, 1992; Bell, 1992). Still, across a variety of geographical locations and types of violence, temperature and aggression rise together.

Positive Affect: Reducing Retaliation

Frustration and noxious stimuli are certainly unpleasant. It's annoying to have another driver cut in front of you just as you're about to pull into that last available parking space. It's uncomfortable to have to sit in a hot, crowded room with clouds of cigarette smoke billowing into your eyes and lungs. A third type of unpleasant experience also has a close relationship with aggression: provocation by attack or insult. It's distinctly unsettling to have someone tear into you, calling you names and criticizing your behavior. And, by and large, people who are provoked, retaliate (Dengerink et al., 1978; Geen, 1968). Does provocation trigger retaliatory aggression because, like frustration and noxious stimuli, it creates negative affect?

incompatible responses Responses that are mutually exclusive, so that experiencing one precludes experiencing the other.

Baron's work on **incompatible responses** helps us answer this question. Since positive emotional reactions (such as humor, empathy, or mild sexual arousal) are deemed to be incompatible with the negative emotion of anger, experiencing positive feelings should reduce angry aggression (Baron, 1983b). And they do. In one study, subjects were first provoked and angered by an experimental confederate (Baron & Ball, 1974). They were then shown funny cartoons or neutral pictures. Presented with an opportunity to retaliate by delivering electric shocks as part of a supposedly unrelated learning experiment, those who had seen cartoons delivered fewer shocks. The results of this study suggest that negative affect is a major ingredient in aggressive retaliation to provocation. When humor shoved anger off center stage, aggression declined. Research on empathy has obtained similar effects. An empathic response to another person reduces aggression against that individual (Miller & Eisenberg, 1988).

Arousal: "Wired" for Action

Research on both negative affect and incompatible responses focuses on the *type of emotion* produced by a stimulus. The *intensity of arousal* is also important. As we saw in Chapter 6, arousal created by one stimulus can increase an individual's emotional response to another stimulus through the process of *excitation transfer* (Zillmann, 1979, 1984). For example, men who initially engaged in vigorous exercise were later more attracted to an attractive female than were those who had barely moved (White et al., 1981). Physical exercise is a highly arousing but emotionally neutral experience. If it can increase attraction, could it increase aggression?

Research by Dolf Zillmann and his colleagues demonstrates that it can. In one study, male subjects were angered or not by an experimental confederate, and then either did or did not perform strenuous physical exercise (Zillmann et al., 1972). Subjects were then given the chance to shock the confederate in the context of a supposed learning experiment. As the researchers had predicted, angered subjects who had exercised delivered shocks of greater intensity than did subjects who had not been angered or who had not exercised. You should note that the scope of excitation transfer is not limited to physical exercise. Noise, violent motion pictures, arousing music—all have been shown to increase aggression (Zillmann, 1983). Later in this chapter, we will describe the effects of another arousing stimulus—pornography—on the inclination to aggress.

Thus far, we have considered the type of emotion and the intensity of physiological arousal separately. The **arousal-affect model** combines them (Sapolsky, 1984; Zillmann & Bryant, 1984). Integrating the work of Robert Baron and Dolf Zillmann, this model summarizes a wide range of research findings. For the most part, the arousal-affect model addresses the effects of various emotional experiences on a person who has been angered and then has a chance to retaliate. Such an individual is already experiencing the negative affect created by a personal attack. But what kinds of additional experiences could push the person toward a towering rage or pour oil on troubled waters?

As you can see in Figure 8.3, low arousal creates the world according to Baron. Negative emotions increase aggression; positive emotions decrease it; and a neutral emotional state has no effect at all. But high arousal is Zillmann territory. Stimuli that produce negative emotions *and* high arousal strongly increase aggression. Even neutral stimuli, if highly arousing, can enhance aggressive behavior among individuals who have been provoked. Theories collide, however, when positive emotions *and* high arousal occur simultaneously. Will aggression decrease because a positive emotional experience is incompatible with unpleasant angry feelings? Or will aggression increase because a lot of arousal is available for transfer? It's a tough call and could go either way, depending on the individual, the situation, and the thoughts that come to mind.

arousal-affect model
The proposal that aggression is influenced by the intensity of arousal and by the type of emotion produced by a stimulus.

Thought: Automatic and Considered

Step by step, we have been making our way toward a comprehensive theory of social and situational influences on aggression. We've examined three kinds of

Physiological Arousal

Type of Emotion	Low	High
Negative	Aggression ↑	Aggression ↑↑
Neutral	No effect	Aggression ↑
Positive	Aggression ↓	Aggression ↑ or Aggression ↓

Figure 8.3 The Arousal-Affect Model. According to the arousal-affect model, aggression is influenced by both the intensity of physiological arousal and the type of emotion produced by a stimulus. This model integrates Zillmann's model of excitation transfer with Baron's work on negative affect and incompatible responses.

unpleasant experiences (frustration, noxious stimuli, and provocation) that create negative affect. When positive emotional experiences reduce negative affect, aggression decreases. When highly arousing experiences intensify negative affect, aggression increases. Negative affect, it seems, is the key to aggression. But, now, it's time to add cognition. People don't just feel; they also think. What is the role of thought in aggressive behavior?

According to Leonard Berkowitz, it has a star part. For almost two decades, Berkowitz (1990) has been developing and refining a **cognitive-neoassociation analysis** of anger and aggression. This analysis proposes that the negative affect produced by unpleasant experiences automatically stimulates various thoughts, memories, expressive motor reactions, and physiological responses associated with both fight and flight tendencies. These associations give rise to rudimentary emotional experiences of anger and fear. Subsequently, higher order cognitive processes come into play. People think about how they feel, make causal attributions for what led them to feel this way, and consider the consequences of acting on their feelings. This more deliberate consideration produces more clearly differentiated feelings of anger, fear, or both. It can also suppress or enhance the action-tendencies associated with these feelings. Berkowitz's analysis is diagrammed in Figure 8.4. Let us now take a closer look at two major aspects of this view of aggression: situational cues and higher-order cognitive processing.

cognitive-neoassociation analysis The view that unpleasant experiences create negative affect, which in turn stimulates associations connected with anger and fear. Emotional and behavioral outcomes then depend, at least in part, on higher-order cognitive processing.

Situational Cues: The Weapons Effect   The deadliest aggression in the United States comes from the barrel of a gun. Over 60 percent of all murders in the United States are committed with guns (FBI, 1989). In 1990, more people in Texas died from gunshots than from traffic accidents. And in schools across the nation, guns threaten to turn playgrounds into killing fields. From September 1986 to June 1990, 65 students and 6 employees were shot to death, 201 individuals were severely wounded, and 242 people were taken hostage by armed assailants (Center to Prevent Handgun Violence, 1991). Faced with such gruesome statistics, the National Rifle Association (NRA) responds that guns should not be blamed. People, the NRA says, pull the trigger. Guns are simply neutral tools.

> **weapons effect** The tendency of weapons to increase the likelihood of aggression by their mere presence.

But are they? Or does the presence of a weapon act as a situational cue that increases the likelihood of aggression? In the classic study of the **weapons effect**, subjects who had been provoked by an experimental confederate delivered more shocks to him when a revolver and rifle were present than when badminton racquets and shuttlecocks were scattered about (Berkowitz & Le Page, 1967). Although subsequent research produced mixed results, a thorough review by Michael Carlson and his colleagues (1990) sets the record straight. Among subjects who are not suspicious about what the experimenter is trying to prove, the presence of weapons increases aggression. Among subjects who have figured out the experimental hypothesis, however, the presence of weapons *decreases* aggression. Presumably, these subjects are trying to make a good impression by acting in a socially approved, nonaggressive manner.

Figure 8.4   A Cognitive-Neoassociation Analysis.   Berkowitz's model of aggression holds that unpleasant experiences create negative affect, which in turn stimulates automatic associations connected with fear and anger. Emotional and behavioral outcomes then depend, at least in part, on higher-order cognitive processing.

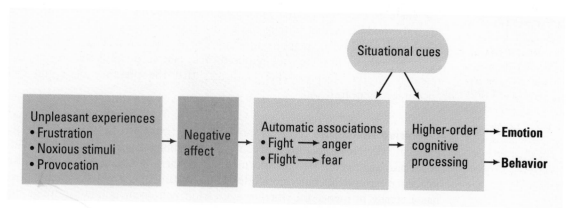

Guns in school teach a deadly lesson as homicides and injuries have increased dramatically. Here, sixteen-year-old Tyrone Sinkler is wheeled out of a Brooklyn high school after he and seventeen-year-old Ian Moore were shot by another student. Both teenagers died from their wounds. Research on the weapons effect indicates that the presence of aggressive situational cues like guns increases aggression.

Both of these findings have implications for real life outside the laboratory. Concerns about conforming to social norms or personal values emphasizing *non*aggressive behavior can turn an aggressive cue into a peacemaker (Josephson, 1987). In the absence of such concerns, however, the presence of weapons increases aggressive inclinations. More troubling still, the harmful effects of situational cues are *not* restricted to retaliatory aggression. An aggressive cue such as a weapon can increase aggression among people who are in a neutral mood, as well as among those who have been angered by provocation (Carlson et al., 1990). Weapons, it seems, can set their own stage for aggressive behavior; other props are not required. Yes, people do pull the trigger, but research on the weapons effect indicates that the presence of a gun can encourage them to do so.

Cognitive Mediators   The weapons effect is presumed to operate relatively automatically by stimulating a network of thoughts and feelings associated with anger and aggression. But the information provided by situational cues can also influence more deliberate, thoughtful considerations. One of the thoughts that has a strong influence on whether aggression will occur is how we judge the intent of those who aggress against us. Compared to harmful actions perceived as *un*intentional, those perceived as intended are more likely to be judged as hostile and to elicit anger and aggression in return (Ferguson & Rule, 1983; Ohbuchi & Kambara, 1985). Chronically aggressive individuals are especially likely to perceive hostile intent on the part of another person (Dodge & Coie, 1987), they also have particularly strong expectations that they will obtain a positive outcome from being aggressive (Dodge & Crick, 1990). Both of these beliefs may contribute to maintaining high levels of aggression among these individuals.

mitigating information Information about a person's situation indicating that he or she should not be held personally responsible for aggressive actions.

Perhaps because it reduces the perception of intent, apologizing for having hurt someone reduces the victim's tendency to retaliate (Ohbuchi et al., 1989). **Mitigating information** indicating that an individual should not be held responsible for aggressive acts should also diminish perceived intent to harm. In criminal law, defendants are excused for aggression that is thought to result from insanity, coercion, ignorance, or self-defense. In our own lives, we too find room for forgiveness. The friend whose love affair just broke up, the coworker whose job is in danger—we don't hold them fully responsible for their actions. Whether we also refrain from retaliating against them, however, may depend on when we learn about their stressful situation. In one study, subjects who were aware of mitigating information *before* being attacked by another person stayed calm and were unaggressive (Zillmann & Cantor, 1976). Those who learned about the other person's stressful situation only *after* being provoked also experienced decreased physiological arousal but still retaliated. If mitigating information is "too little, too late," plans hatched in the heat of anger can still be carried out with cool deliberation.

Some conditions make it more difficult to engage in higher-order processing of cues and information. High arousal, for example, impairs the cognitive control of aggression (Zillmann et al., 1975). So does alcohol. Alcohol consumption is implicated in the majority of violent crimes, suicides, and automobile fatalities. And carefully controlled experiments demonstrate that it increases aggression (Bushman & Cooper, 1990). But how? According to Claude Steele and Robert Josephs (1990), the problem lies in "alcohol myopia"—the tendency for alcohol to restrict the range of cues perceived in a given situation and to reduce the ability to process those cues that are perceived. As Steele and Josephs put it, intoxicated people "see the tree, albeit more dimly, but miss the forest altogether" (p. 923).

Alcohol myopia creates problems in handling mixed messages. Drunken excess occurs because salient, motivating cues are heeded but less salient, inhibiting cues are not processed. A study on alcohol and aggression described in detail in Chapter 1 illustrates the point (Leonard, 1989). Subjects who were told that an opponent intended to aggress against them were aggressive in return, regardless of whether they had consumed alcohol. But then they discovered that their opponent had passed up his original opportunity to be aggressive. Although subjects who had not consumed alcohol quickly reduced their aggressive behavior, intoxicated subjects kept right on zapping their opponent. Similar effects have been obtained in research on helping (Steele et al., 1985). Intoxicated subjects complied with a strong request to help the experimenter by continuing to work on the experimental task; they seemed to forget how dull and boring the task was. Not so easily swept away, sober subjects were less helpful. No matter what the direction, when drunks get going, they're hard to stop.

Multiple Causes, Multiple Cures

As we have seen, the causes of aggression are many and complicated. Human beings come into the world with a set of biologically based capacities and propensities that may influence behavioral tendencies. Beginning in childhood, people learn about aggression from the rewards and punishments they receive and from their observation of others. Interacting with the social and physical environment, individuals have unpleasant experiences with frustration, noxious stimuli, and provocation. High arousal can intensify the negative affect produced by these experiences, but positive emotions can counteract it. Situational cues can increase aggression by stimulating automatic associations connected with anger and aggression. Higher-order processing of information can put the brakes on the inclination to aggress or push the accelerator. Since all these factors have an impact on aggression, it would be pointless to hope for a single cure.

That's the bad news. The good news is that multiple causes create the potential for multiple ways to reduce aggression. Based on the research we've reviewed in this chapter, here's a list of some possible steps that could be taken:

- Teach and reward people to be nonaggressive.
- Provide attractive models of peaceful behavior.
- Reduce all forms of aggression in our society, including physical punishment of children, capital punishment of criminals, and war.
- Reduce frustration by improving the quality of life (health care, employment, child care).
- Provide fans and air-conditioned shelters when it's hot.
- Reduce access to and the display of weapons.
- Apologize when you've angered someone and regard apologies as a sign of strength, not weakness. Encourage others to do likewise.
- Stop and think when you feel your temper rising. Control it instead of letting it control you.
- Discourage drinking and support efforts to provide treatment for alcohol abuse.

Personally, you may not agree that all of these actions are desirable—and that's your choice. What's important is to realize that each of us can do something to reduce aggression. There are many paths to take toward this common goal.

SCENES OF VIOLENCE

So far, we have examined aggression under a microscope, looking at specific factors that can contribute to it. Now we focus on a bigger picture. To gain a better understanding of the causes and consequences of aggressive behavior, we explore three contexts in which the display of aggression may elicit more of it. Two of these displays come from the mass media: depictions of nonsexual violence and pornography. The third strikes at the heart of what most people rely on for peace and security. As we will see, all too often aggression begins at home.

Media Effects: Depictions of Nonsexual Violence

"Have we become violence junkies?" read the cover on a recent *USA Weekend* Sunday magazine. Reviewing the most recent batch of violent action films, the magazine wondered whether all that murder and mayhem on the screen might have some real-life consequences. It's a good question. Sometimes fact does seem to imitate fiction. Following an episode of the TV series "MacGyver" that featured the making of a bomb, eight youths were injured by their own amateur bombs in separate incidents across the United States. Just months later, the opening of the critically acclaimed film *Boyz N the Hood* in United States theaters was accompanied by shootings that left one dead and dozens injured. These events intensified an already heated debate on the relationship between filmed violence and aggressive behavior. Here, we consider the research evidence bearing on this issue. We describe the effects of TV and other media presentations of violence on children and adults, on attitudes as well as on behaviors. Then we discuss some ways to reduce possible negative consequences of these presentations.

Violence on TV and in the News   On average, children in the United States watch around thirty hours of TV each week (Tangney & Feshbach, 1988). And much of what they watch is aggressive. From cartoons to car chases, children are fed a steady diet of violent images. The possibility that youngsters might act out the aggression they observe was raised by a Surgeon General's report in 1972 and by a follow-up report from the National Institutes of Mental Health (Huesmann, 1982; Pearl et al., 1982). Despite massive research on this topic, however, researchers still disagree on the conclusion that should be drawn (Freedman, 1986; Friedrich-Cofer & Huston, 1986; Houts et al., 1986).

There is no dispute about the results of laboratory research, which has clearly demonstrated that aggressive models, live or on film, increase aggressive behavior among children and adults (Geen & Thomas, 1986; Liebert & Sprafkin, 1988). The laboratory, though, is a tightly controlled environment, and some researchers question whether what is found in the lab will also occur in the real world (Freedman, 1988b). Field experiments conducted in a real-world setting such as a school are one way to loosen the reins without losing control. When Wendy Wood and her colleagues (1991) examined both laboratory and field experiments conducted with children and adolescents, they found that exposure to aggressive films increased aggressive behavior in the laboratory, the classroom, the lunchroom, the playground, and the athletic field. There was, however, a tendency for experiments conducted in laboratory settings to yield stronger results than those conducted in natural environments.

Whether conducted in the lab or in a schoolroom, experiments present all subjects in a given condition with the same amount of aggressive materials. We all know, however, that people differ enormously in how much filmed aggression they watch. Will those who watch more be more aggressive? Research on children's naturally occurring TV viewing and aggressive behavior has attempted to answer this question.

When exposure to violent TV is measured at the same time as aggressive behavior, most research finds a positive correlation: children who watch more violent TV are more aggressive. But this correlation can't tell us whether viewing TV violence causes aggressive behavior. One way to examine possible causal

Parents, government officials, and social scientists have been greatly concerned that the violence shown on TV might increase aggression, especially among children. On average, children watch around thirty hours of TV each week and many of the images they see are aggressive.

relationships is to conduct **longitudinal research**, studying the same subjects over a period of time to observe changes in behavior. Is viewing TV violence *at an early age* correlated with aggressive behavior *at a later age?* Although such a correlation can't prove conclusively that early viewing of TV violence causes later aggression, it would clearly support this possibility.

Longitudinal research, however, has obtained conflicting findings. The results of a twenty-two-year study, known as the Rip Van Winkle project, indicated that early exposure to TV violence was related to later aggression, but only among males (Eron & Huesmann, 1984; Eron et al., 1972; Lefkowitz et al., 1977). A more limited, three-year study came to a very different conclusion: that early exposure to TV violence had no association with later aggressive behavior for either boys or girls (Milavsky et al., 1982).

In an extensive cross-cultural study, Rowell Huesmann and Leonard Eron (1986) collaborated with researchers around the world to examine the relationship between TV violence and aggression among children in five different countries: Australia, Finland, Israel, Poland, and the United States. Their findings highlighted the importance of three major factors. One is gender. Contrary to previous indications that exposure to TV violence had a greater impact on boys than on girls, no consensus regarding the role of gender emerged from these studies. Indeed, in the United States, early exposure to TV violence was a clear predictor of later aggression only among girls.

Second, it appears that the relationship between watching violent TV shows and being aggressive may sometimes be a two-way street, with exposure to TV violence increasing aggressiveness *and* aggressive children seeking out violence on TV. Evidence suggesting such a bidirectional pattern was found for girls in the United States. A third factor is identification with aggressive TV characters. Among boys in the United States and Finland, those who at a young age viewed a substantial amount of violent TV *and* identified with aggressive TV characters were most likely to become highly aggressive later in life. Taking these factors into account, researchers found evidence of a connection between early viewing of TV violence and later aggression for children in Finland, Poland, the United States, and urban areas in Israel. However, as you can see from Figure 8.5, no such connection was established for children living in Australia and on kibbutzim in Israel.

Most of the concern about media depictions of violence has concentrated on fictional presentations on TV and in the movies. But what about news coverage of violent real-life events? Does increased exposure to this kind of violence increase aggressive behavior? David Phillips (1983, 1986) thinks it does. Drawing primarily on newspaper stories and TV coverage, Phillips found correlations between a wide variety of media reports and an equally wide variety of aggressive behaviors. For example, after the media blitz surrounding heavyweight championship prizefights, homicides in the general population increased. In the wake of heavily publicized suicides, the suicide rate went up (Stack, 1990). Although provocative, this approach to the effects of media violence has been criticized on methodological grounds (Baron & Reiss, 1985a, 1985b).

Country	Early TV Violence → Later Aggression		Early TV Violence → Later Aggression *and* Early Aggression → Later TV Violence	Importance of Identification with Aggressive TV Characters
	Boys	Girls		
Australia				
Finland				✔
Israel: City Residents	✔	✔		
Israel: Kibbutz Residents				
Poland	✔	✔		
United States		✔	✔	✔

Figure 8.5   TV Violence and Children's Aggression in Five Countries.   Studies carried out in five countries suggest that the relationship between children's aggressive behavior and exposure to TV violence is influenced by a variety of factors. Three of the most important are the gender of the child; the tendency for children who watch TV violence to be more aggressive *and* for aggressive children to seek out violent TV shows; and the child's identification with aggressive TV characters. In studies conducted in Australia and with kibbutz children in Israel, early exposure to TV violence was *not* associated with later aggression. [Based on Huesmann & Eron, 1986.]

Overall, the research discussed in this section suggests that the strength of the relationship between media depictions of violence and aggressive behavior is a matter of focus. In the stripped-down environment of the laboratory, the effect is clearly visible. In the midst of the hurley-burley of real life, it's fuzzier. Similarly, the relationship between watching aggression and doing it is much stronger when we take a one-time snapshot than when we try to map a connection stretched over months, years, or decades. As we open the shutter to let in more light, we inevitably find more complexity. After all, the media do not operate in a vacuum (Cook et al., 1983). Around the individual are family members, peers, social values, and opportunities for education and employment. Nor are all individuals the same; individual differences in personality may heat up or tone down the impact of aggressive displays (Bushman & Geen, 1990). Nevertheless, what we see in media presentations of violence is not a pretty picture. The combination of aggressive models (often very attractive ones), highly arousing action sequences, and aggressive cues galore is a dangerous recipe.

Beyond Imitation: Attitudes and Social Reality   Now add another ingredient to that recipe: thought. As described earlier in this chapter, aggressive behavior can be influenced by relatively automatic associations and by more deliberate reflection. Told to "record only those ideas that you were thinking about," subjects reported many more aggressive thoughts after watching ten minutes of violent action films like *The Vigilante* and *48 Hours* than after observing a peaceful episode of "Dallas" (Bushman & Geen, 1990). But, like the direct imitation of behavior, automatic associations are usually of brief duration and fade over time. Could media violence have more long-term effects?

cultivation   The process by which the mass media (particularly television) construct a version of social reality for the viewing public.

According to George Gerbner, TV viewing can have powerful, long-lasting consequences. Gerbner and his colleagues (1980, 1986) claim that TV creates shared concepts of social reality, a process they call **cultivation**. Cultivation operates by homogenizing attitudes and values throughout the viewing public. When what people see on TV is consistent with what they already believe, their initial attitudes will be strengthened. When what they see disagrees with their opinions, they may change their position. Thus, the cultural mainstream is defined by what is allowed to appear on the screen. If that mainstream glorifies or trivializes violence, aggression may gain acceptance in the hearts and minds of the viewing public. Inhibitions will be weakened and the likelihood of aggression increased.

Recently, concerns about the effects of TV violence on society's values and attitudes have been heightened by an extraordinary possibility: showing actual executions on TV. The effort, ultimately unsuccessful, by a California public television station to get permission to videotape an execution sparked a fierce debate about the possible consequences of reinstating public executions in the United States (Angelo, 1991). Would the horror of the punishment deter potential criminals or increase violence by modeling aggression as an acceptable way to solve problems? Would public executions create a backlash against the death penalty? Or, would viewers just get used to one more form of media violence and find the death penalty more acceptable? As we will see later in this chapter, research on pornography provides some support for the notion that familiarity with violent displays can sometimes breed callous attitudes that could reduce inhibitions against aggression.

Censorship Versus Education   Thinking about whether executions should be public forces us to explore our own, personal beliefs about censorship. The issue here, as in so many other areas of public policy, is how to balance free speech against safety. Even if it can't be proved beyond a shadow of a doubt that exposing children and adults to media presentations of violence increases aggressive behavior, is the potential for harmful effects sufficient grounds on which to ban such displays? And, if so, which ones? Media violence is not limited to gory movies, bruising sports, cops-and-robbers on TV, and sensation-

This 1930s hanging in Missouri was one of the last public executions in the United States. In 1990, however, a public television station went to court to obtain permission to videotape a scheduled execution in California. Although station KQED lost its case, the debate about the potential effects of televised executions continues.

alistic journalism. Recent research suggests that commercials (Caprara et al., 1987), videogames (Cooper & Mackie, 1986; Schutte et al., 1988), and rock music videos (Hansen & Hansen, 1990) may also contribute to making aggressive behavior more likely or at least more acceptable. The pervasiveness of violent materials poses some real practical problems for censorship. There is also a psychological problem. Censorship can boomerang and make whatever is forbidden seem that much more desirable (Worchel et al., 1975).

Because of the political, practical, and psychological issues surrounding censorship, many social scientists believe that educational approaches are preferable. For example, programs have been developed to curb children's undesirable reactions to TV (Eron, 1986, 1987; Singer & Singer, 1983). These programs recommend that parents select shows that provide compelling, vivid prosocial models for their children. An extensive review by Susan Hearold (1986) is encouraging in this regard. Her analysis indicated that *pro*social TV programs produce stronger effects on behavior than do *anti*social TV programs.

Parents have also been advised to watch television with their children—engaging them in active, give-and-take discussions of how TV differs from real life, how imitating TV characters can have negative consequences, and how children might be harmed from watching TV (Huesmann et al., 1983). Parental intervention takes time and effort. But given the extent of media depictions of violence in our society, innoculating people against the disease may be more effective than trying to ban every possible germ.

Media Effects: Pornographic Materials

Just as citizens, scientists, and government officials have been concerned about the possibly harmful effects of mass media presentations of nonsexual violence, so too have they been troubled by mass media displays of sexual material. Such displays are highly visible and widely available. Books and magazines cater to all sorts of specialized sexual tastes. Video stores rent out films that exhibit every inch of human anatomy engaged in virtually every imaginable sexual activity. Comedian Andrew Dice Clay builds a career out of making jokes about sexual assaults on women. Heavy metal and rap groups rely on obscenities to get their fans' attention. Dial-a-porn lines rake in millions for the phone company and a tidy profit for themselves. Sexually explicit computer subscription services provide conference calls, e-mail, and bulletin boards. Sexually oriented computer games come in both hard-core and soft-core versions.

Opposition to the floodtide of pornography is equally prominent. Parents, religious leaders, consumer groups, and feminist activists lobby politicians and go to court to obtain greater legal constraints on the availability of sexually explicit materials. Their efforts have substantial support. Among individuals surveyed in 1986, 41 percent of men and 72 percent of women said that U.S. laws on pornography were not strict enough (Sussman, 1988). In response to public concern, the effects of sexually explicit material were studied by the 1970 Commission on Obscenity and Pornography; the 1986 Attorney General's Commission on Pornography; and the 1986 Surgeon General's Workshop (Koop, 1987; Mulvey & Hauggard, 1986).

Attempts to ban specific works, such as James Joyce's novel *Ulysses* and Robert Mapplethorpe's photos, indicate that the definition of terms like obscenity, erotica, and pornography is often a matter of personal opinion. One person's smut is another person's masterpiece. Given the weight of subjective judgment in such definitions, the term **pornography** is used here to refer to explicit sexual material, regardless of its moral or aesthetic qualities. We do, however, distinguish between nonviolent and violent pornography in describing research on the relationship between pornographic displays and aggression.

pornography
Explicit sexual material.

Rape and Pornography   For over a decade, rape has been increasing in the United States. For example, the National Crime Survey conducted by the Justice Department found that violent crimes (assault, robbery, and attempted and completed rapes) increased 8 percent from 1990 to 1991. Considered separately, however, rapes and attempted rapes increased 59 percent. But these figures may underestimate the incidence of rape in the United States. Another survey, funded by the National Institute of Drug Abuse, indicates that the number of rapes in 1990 was over five times greater than had previously been estimated and that some twelve million women have been raped at least once (Kilpatrick et al., 1992). Contrary to popular stereotypes, rape is not primarily committed by strangers. Instead, as many as 80 percent of rape victims are raped by someone they know. On college and university campuses, acquaintance rape (also called "date rape") is a serious problem. Over 25 percent of a national sample of female college students reported having experienced either an attempted (12 percent) or completed (15 percent) rape (Koss, 1989). In 1991 the trial and subsequent acquittal of William Kennedy Smith sparked a national debate about acquaintance rape and its prosecution. Looking back over the last decade, you can't help but notice the connection: as pornography became more available in the United States, more rapes occurred. Is this just a coincidence?

As it turns out, this is a difficult question to answer. Much of the evidence bearing on the relationship between pornography and sex crimes is difficult to

Concern about rapes on college and university campuses has led many schools to develop rape-prevention programs. Educational workshops, such as the one pictured here, inform students about the legal definition of and penalties for rape, increase their understanding of the trauma suffered by rape victims, and help them develop strategies to reduce rape on their own campuses.

interpret (Marshall, 1989). Studies of retrospective reports by rapists about their experiences with pornography have yielded conflicting results and suffer from various methodological problems (Malamuth & Billings, 1986). Research examining the correlation between violent crime and consumption of pornography has produced contradictory conclusions (Baron & Straus, 1984; Court, 1984; Kutchinsky, 1978). Cross-cultural comparisons are also inconsistent. Extremely violent pornography is widely available in Japan, but the incidence of rape is very low. India, in contrast, bans explicit sex (and even kissing) from commercial films but has a high incidence of rape (Pratap, 1990).

To avoid the ambiguities of self-reports and large-scale correlational data, Neil Malamuth (1988) has attempted to identify and study individuals in the general population who are most likely to commit a rape. The rapist profile developed by Malamuth includes two factors: (1) relatively high levels of sexual arousal in response to violent pornography and (2) attitudes and opinions indicating acceptance of violence toward women (see Table 8.1). In one study, male college students were given an opportunity to retaliate against a female confederate who had angered them (Malamuth, 1983). Those who fit the rapist's profile were more aggressive. Similarly, Malamuth found that the two factors of

---

Table 8.1   Attitudes About Sex and Aggression: Selected Items from Two Scales. Widely used in research on pornography, these two scales assess attitudes about violence toward women and beliefs about the nature of rape. [From Burt, 1980.]

Acceptance of Interpersonal Violence (Toward Women): AIV Scale

1. Being roughed up is sexually stimulating to many women.

2. Many times a woman will pretend she doesn't want to have intercourse because she doesn't want to seem loose, but she's really hoping the man will force her.

3. A man is never justified in hitting his wife.

Scoring: Persons scoring high in acceptance of violence toward women agree with items 1 and 2 and disagree with item 3.

Rape Myth Acceptance: RMA Scale

1. If a woman engages in necking or petting and she lets things get out of hand, it is her own fault if her partner forces sex on her.

2. Any female can get raped.

3. Many women have an unconscious wish to be raped, and may then unconsciously set up a situation in which they are likely to be attacked.

4. In the majority of rapes, the victim is promiscuous or has a bad reputation.

Scoring: Persons scoring high in acceptance of rape myths agree with items 1, 3, and 4 and disagree with item 2.

arousal and attitude correlated with men's self-reports about their past and future behaviors (Malamuth, 1986; Malamuth et al., 1986). Those who fit the rapist's profile said they had more frequently engaged in sexually coercive activities, were more likely to commit rape if they were assured of not getting caught, and foresaw a greater possibility of aggressing against women in the future.

By including men's responses to violent pornography in the rapist's profile, Malamuth's research suggests a possible connection between pornography and aggression against women. His approach, however, does not directly examine the effects of pornography. In the following sections, we consider some of the experimental work that has.

Nonviolent Pornography   Earlier in this chapter, we described the *arousal-affect model,* which proposes that the type of emotion and the intensity of arousal produced by a stimulus influence aggression (see page 364). The results of research on nonviolent pornography confirm the importance of both factors (Donnerstein et al., 1987). For many people, viewing soft-focus attractive nudes elicits a pleasant emotional response and low levels of sexual arousal. Such materials usually reduce retaliatory aggression against a same-sex confederate. However, most people are shocked and disgusted by crude displays of sexual activities. Their emotional response is negative, and their arousal is heightened by alarm, sexual feelings, or both. These kinds of pornographic materials usually increase aggression toward a same-sex confederate.

But what about aggression toward the opposite sex? Since the vast majority of pornography is designed to appeal to heterosexual males, investigators have been especially interested in whether pornographic materials have a specific effect on men's aggression against women (Donnerstein, 1984). In an early study, male subjects were provoked and angered by a male or female confederate and then shown a short film (Donnerstein & Barrett, 1978). Subjects who saw an arousing "stag" film were subsequently more aggressive against the confederate than were those who saw a neutral film. It didn't matter whether the confederate was male or female. The researchers wondered, however, whether subjects might be refraining from even more aggression against the female confederate because of social norms prohibiting male-to-female physical aggression. What would happen if normative restraints were weakened?

Reasoning that repeated opportunities to aggress might reduce restraints against expressing aggressive impulses, Edward Donnerstein and John Hallam (1978) allowed male subjects two chances to retaliate against a confederate who had angered them. On the first opportunity to retaliate, subjects who had watched an arousing but nonviolent pornographic film were more aggressive than those who had not watched any film at all. The amount of aggression against the male and female confederate didn't differ. On their second opportunity, however, subjects who had watched the sexually explicit stag film aggressed more against the female confederate than against the male confederate (see Figure 8.6).

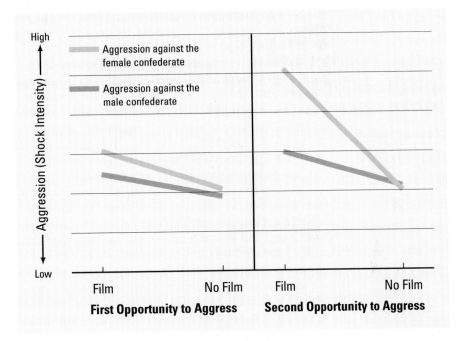

Figure 8.6 The Second Time Around. In this study, male subjects were given two chances to retaliate against a male or female confederate who had provoked them. On both occasions, those who had watched an arousing erotic film aggressed more than did those who had not seen a film. Levels of aggression against the male and female confederate were similar on the first opportunity to retaliate. On the second opportunity, however, subjects who had watched the erotic film aggressed more against the female confederate than against the male confederate. [Based on Donnerstein & Hallam, 1978.]

These findings highlight two important points. First, contact with an arousing stimulus enhanced angry aggression against both men and women. As indicated earlier in this chapter, this effect is not specific to pornography but can be produced by many types of arousing experiences. Second, when normative restraints against male-to-female aggression were reduced by the repeated opportunity to aggress, the effect of pornography was more specific. Male-to-female aggression increased more than male-to-male aggression. Other forms of arousing material do *not* produce this gender-specific increase.

The research described so far exposed subjects to only one "dose" of pornography. What about viewing many pornographic images over an extended period of time? To investigate this issue, Dolf Zillmann and Jennings Bryant (1984) showed either eighteen or thirty-six pornographic films to male and female college students over the course of six weeks. The films involved were X-rated but nonviolent. After the exposure period, experimental subjects and control subjects (who had seen neutral films or no films at all) returned to the laboratory. During follow-up sessions, several factors were assessed—including physiological arousal in response to unfamiliar pornography, aggressiveness toward a same-sex confederate, and attitudes.

habituation Adaptation to something familiar, so that both physiological and psychological responses are reduced.

This research obtained a clear **habituation** effect: repeated exposure to pornography diminished physiological arousal in response to it, especially among those who had been exposed to the greater number of pornographic films. As arousal subsided, so did the power of pornography to intensify aroused behaviors such as angry aggression. After all subjects viewed the new pornographic materials, those who had previously been exposed to a large number of pornographic films were *less* aggressive than control subjects in response to provocation by a same-sex confederate. But before concluding that the best way to guard against the risk of pornography is to show more of it, we have to look at the effects of these images on attitudes.

Three weeks after they had seen the last film, subjects in the study conducted by Zillmann and Bryant read about a rape trial; they also indicated their opinion of the women's liberation movement. Those exposed to pornography recommended a lighter sentence for the rapist and expressed less support for the women's liberation movement than did control subjects. These effects occurred for *both* male and female subjects. Only male subjects were asked at the final follow-up to respond to a series of questions that measured callousness toward women; exposure to a large number of pornographic films produced more negative attitudes toward women. Overall, then, there is both good news and bad about the effects of repeated exposure to nonviolent pornography. On the one hand, habituation reduces arousal, which can decrease aggression in the immediate situation. On the other hand, familiarity also seems to breed indifference and callous attitudes, which could lower restraints against violent behavior in the future (Geen, 1981; Thomas, 1982).

Recent research suggests that *dehumanizing* nonviolent pornography is particularly likely to produce attitudes that trivialize rape and depersonalize women as objects for sexual gratification (Zillmann, 1989; Zillmann & Weaver, 1989). In the words of James Check and Ted Guloien (1989), this type of nonviolent pornography depicts "sexual interactions in which the woman [is] portrayed as hysterically responsive to male sexual demands, [is] verbally abused, dominated, and degraded, and in general [is] treated as a plaything with no human qualities other than her physical attributes" (p. 163). Compared with male subjects in their study who did not see any pornography, those who viewed dehumanizing pornography reported a greater likelihood that they would force a woman to do something sexual against her will and that they would commit rape if they were assured of not getting caught. By demeaning and degrading women, dehumanizing pornography appears to give men permission to think more freely about sexually aggressing against women. The danger is that the thought might be father to the act.

Violent Pornography   The combination of sex and violence raises particularly serious concerns. Depictions of violent sexual behavior, such as rape, produce a range of reactions. Most people experience intense negative emotions such as shock, alarm, and fear; some become sexually aroused. The images shown in violent pornography also prompt cognitive associations consistent with aggression toward women (Berkowitz, 1986; Berkowitz & Rogers, 1986). Thus, violent pornography is a triple threat—bringing together negative emotions, high arousal (whether sexual or not), and aggressive thoughts. There is substantial evidence that this threat is gender-specific (Donnerstein et al., 1987; Linz et al., 1987; Malamuth & Donnerstein, 1982). Male-to-male aggression is no greater after exposure to violent pornography than after exposure to highly arousing but nonviolent pornography. Male-to-female aggression, however, is markedly increased—even among subjects who have *not* been angered by a previous provocation.

The latter effect is startling. Like most experiences that intensify arousal (such as physical exercise) or reduce restraints (such as alcohol consumption), non-violent pornography increases aggression only among subjects who have been provoked. But violent pornography does not require a foundation of anger to build on. What it does seem to require is that women be portrayed as willing participants in their own victimization, that they be seen to "enjoy it." Pornographic films depicting this sort of outcome to acts of sexual violence increase aggression among both provoked and unprovoked male subjects (Donnerstein & Berkowitz, 1981). In contrast, films that emphasize the victim's suffering increase aggression only among men who have been provoked (see Figure 8.7). Like the presence of a gun, pornography that depicts women as enjoying sexual assault provides a situational cue that can trigger aggressive behavior even in the absence of anger. This type of "weapons effect," however, is aimed specifically at women.

In light of these findings, we might like to think that violent pornographic images are found only in the most extreme varieties of hard-core porn, catering to a small number of maladjusted individuals. That does not seem to be the case. In one survey of male college students, over a third stated they had viewed violent pornography during the past year (Demaré et al., 1988). An examination of video pornography revealed that soft-core "adult" films available over the counter contained *more* sexually violent material than hard-core films available under the counter (Palys, 1986). Violent sexual imagery is alive and making money in the local movie theater and on many a home-owned VCR.

The effects of "adult," R-rated sexually violent material on sexually related attitudes and beliefs were investigated in a field study that arranged for 115 college students to attend movies at campus theaters (Malamuth & Check, 1981). Half of these students saw the commercially successful movies *Swept Away* and *The Getaway*, both of which depict women who become sexually aroused by a sexual assault and romantically attracted to their assailant. The other half watched feature-length movies without sexually aggressive content. Several days later, all subjects filled out a questionnaire in class along with the rest of their classmates. They were not aware of any connection between the movies they had seen and the questionnaire they completed.

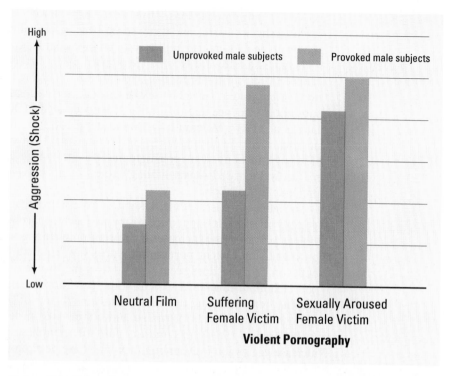

Figure 8.7   When Provocation Isn't Necessary.   Arousing stimuli usually increase aggression only after someone is angry because of a previous provocation. Accordingly, violent pornography depicting a suffering female victim increased aggression significantly only among provoked male subjects in this study. As you can see, however, violent pornographic films depicting a sexually aroused female victim increased aggression even among unprovoked men. [Data from Donnerstein & Berkowitz, 1981. Figure based on Donnerstein et al., 1987.]

Compared with those who had not seen the movies depicting sexual assault, male subjects who had viewed sexually violent films reported greater acceptance of interpersonal violence against women and somewhat greater acceptance of rape myths (see page 377). In contrast, women's acceptance of interpersonal violence against women and of rape myths tended to decline after viewing depictions of male-to-female sexual aggression. Figure 8.8 displays the findings for both men and women.

Assessing and Reducing the Possible Danger   Does, then, the availability of pornography increase the possibility of rape? The developing chain of evidence is certainly suggestive. But, impressive as it is, this chain has a number of missing links. For example, only *non*sexual aggression has been studied in

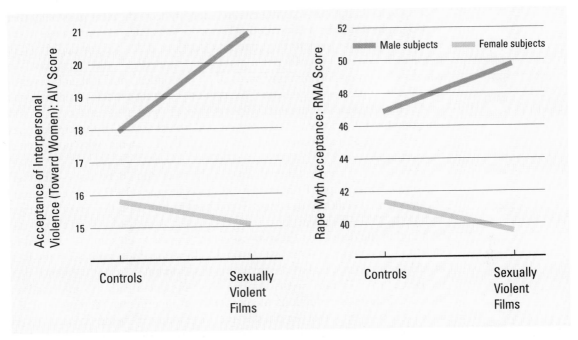

Figure 8.8   Attitudinal Effects of Exposure to Sexually Violent Films.   Compared with control subjects, men who had seen sexually violent films reported greater acceptance of interpersonal violence against women and somewhat greater acceptance of rape myths. In contrast, women's acceptance of interpersonal violence against women and of rape myths declined slightly after viewing the sexually violent films. [Based on Malamuth & Check, 1981.]

laboratory experiments. It is probably impossible to construct ethically acceptable experiments on sexual aggression. Also, although pornography does increase *nonsexual* aggression in the laboratory, it is not certain that these findings generalize to the real world (Freedman, 1988a). As described earlier, the capacity of aggressive TV models to increase aggressive behavior has been consistently demonstrated in the laboratory, yet the evidence for such an effect in the real world is less clear-cut.

Because of ethical constraints, research on *sexual* aggression measures attitudes and self-reports of future intentions, not behavior. In both laboratory and field experiments, there is considerable evidence that pornography increases negative attitudes toward women and sexually aggressive intentions. Such cognitions could play a crucial role in sexual aggression (Linz et al., 1984, 1988; Malamuth & Briere, 1986; McKenzie-Mohr & Zanna, 1990). Although any increase in aggressive behavior due directly to violent pornography should be of brief duration (Malamuth & Ceniti, 1986), attitudes and intentions could last longer and create a more enduring danger.

Despite its limitations, existing research does indicate the clear possibility that pornography could be a contributing factor in sexual aggression against women. This possibility leads to the same set of options described for depictions of nonsexual violence. Should pornography be banned? Should consumers be educated? Banning pornography raises all of the political, practical, and psychological difficulties discussed before. In addition, banning explicit sexual material would not prevent dehumanizing portrayals of women as sex objects and titillating but fully clothed scenes of rape and sexual assault. If the problem lies in the message about women that is promoted by the media, why not go after the message?

Many social scientists think that's exactly what should be done—through education. For example, Donnerstein and his colleagues (1987) urge educational campaigns specifically designed to combat harmful attitudes toward women and myths about their reactions to aggressive sex. A model for such efforts can be found in the debriefing these investigators provide to all subjects exposed to violent pornography in their own research. This debriefing emphasizes the lack of realism in pornographic presentations that combine sex with violence and the lack of truth in rape myths. Among those presented with this information, there are long-term reductions in acceptance of rape myths. More general sex education programs that emphasize the desirability of being respectful and considerate toward one's sexual partner also appear promising. In one study, a general sex education program conducted before subjects were exposed to pornography reduced acceptance of rape myths and increased sympathy for rape victims (Intons-Peterson et al., 1989). According to William Fisher and Azy Barak (1989), sex education programs designed to immunize children against the potential dangers of pornography should be offered in the public schools in order to provide "decent, countervailing sexual information at developmentally critical stages to the largest possible audience" (p. 306). Education, and the public commitment required to implement it, may be the best defense against sexual violence.

Intimate Violence: "The Ultimate Betrayal"

When Assistant U.S. Attorney General Lois Herrington (1985) called family violence "the ultimate betrayal," she expressed the shock many people feel about this form of aggression. A person's home is supposed to be safe. In fact, home is often a dangerous place. Herrington points out that 20 percent of all homicide victims in the United States are killed by a family member. Living at close quarters, protected from public scrutiny, the family can be a peaceful haven—or a battlefield.

Spouse Abuse   Because so much of family life occurs in private, it is difficult to obtain accurate statistics on the extent of family violence. Some of the best estimates come from two national surveys conducted in 1975 and 1985 by

Murray Straus and his colleagues (Hampton et al., 1989; Straus & Gelles, 1986; Straus et al., 1980). In these surveys, respondents were asked to think over situations during the past year when they had a disagreement or were angry with a specific family member and to indicate how frequently they engaged in each of the eight types of physical aggression included in the Conflict Tactics Scale (Straus, 1990a). These types are listed in Figure 8.9. Between 1975 and 1985, spouse abuse remained relatively constant. And high. The 1985 rate of *severe* violence among couples translates into violent interactions in the lives of over 3 million couples.

One of the most surprising aspects of these results is the high level of wife-to-husband abuse, which in terms of *severe* violence was consistently higher than the level of husband-to-wife abuse. Longitudinal research on aggression during the first years of marriage also found higher rates of wife-to-husband abuse (Malone et al., 1989; O'Leary et al., 1989). Because the Conflict Tactics Scale does not assess the offensive or defensive nature of physical violence, or the degree of injury that results, the meaning of such findings has been a subject of considerable controversy (Steinmetz & Lucca, 1988; Walker, 1989). In one study that examined both of these issues, wives were found to initiate physical aggression at least as often as men did (Stets & Straus, 1990). But abused wives reported more serious physical injury and greater psychological distress than did abused husbands.

Figure 8.9   Conflict Tactics Scale: Physical Violence.   The Conflict Tactics Scale measuring physical violence asks respondents to indicate how frequently they have engaged in each of these eight types of violence. These types cover a range of severity, from relatively low to extremely violent. The Conflict Tactics Scale is used in many studies of family violence. [From Straus, 1979.]

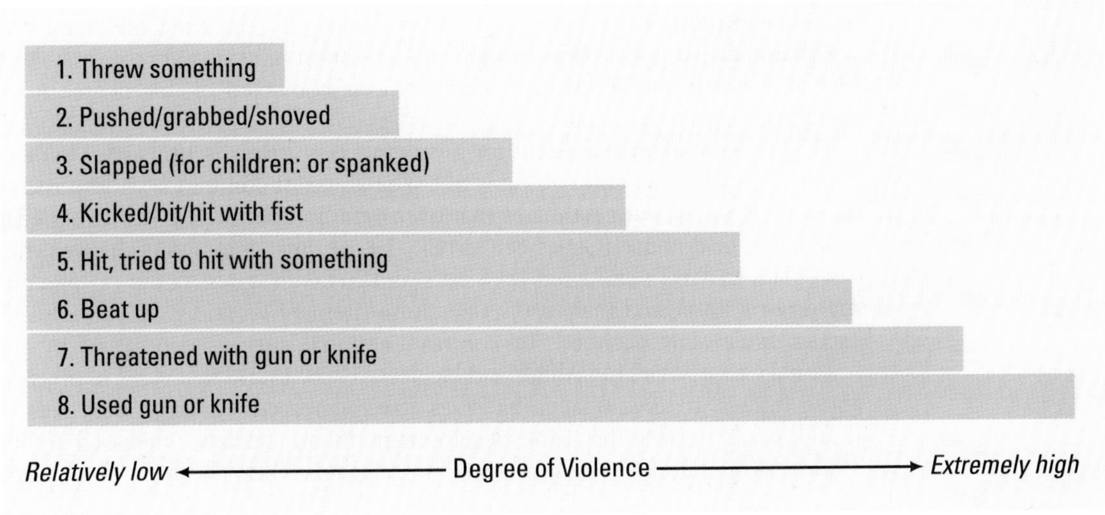

1. Threw something
2. Pushed/grabbed/shoved
3. Slapped (for children: or spanked)
4. Kicked/bit/hit with fist
5. Hit, tried to hit with something
6. Beat up
7. Threatened with gun or knife
8. Used gun or knife

Relatively low ◄─────────────── Degree of Violence ───────────────► *Extremely high*

Similar findings have been obtained in studies of *premarital* violence. A greater proportion of women than men report having been physically aggressive with a dating partner, but more women than men indicate having sustained an injury inflicted during a date (Sugarman & Hotaling, 1989a). The overall level of violence, however, differs according to the type of intimate relationship involved (Makepeace, 1989; Stets & Straus, 1989). Dating couples have the lowest average level of physical violence; married couples are intermediate; and violence is greatest in cohabiting relationships. Although the exact causes for the association between cohabitation and physical abuse are not known, cohabiting partners often face a distinct set of problems. Living together will usually create more stresses and strains than dating couples experience, but commitment to the partner is often weaker than in marriage (Stets, 1991).

A number of factors are associated with increased rates of both premarital and marital violence: stressful events such as unemployment and unplanned pregnancy; low socioeconomic status including low income and lack of education; and family background characteristics such as having grown up in a violent family (Gelles & Straus, 1988; Sugarman & Hotaling, 1989b). Stressful events and low socioeconomic status increase the frustrations people experience, the noxious and arousing stimuli that flood in on them, and the insults and humiliations they have to bear. The influence of family background reflects some combination of genetic and physiological endowment along with learned behaviors and attitudes. Sometimes what a child learns about aggression comes from being abused.

Child Abuse   When six-year-old Lisa Steinberg died in the fall of 1987, the whole country reacted with outrage. Illegally adopted by Joel Steinberg, a disbarred attorney, Lisa lived with Steinberg and Hedda Nussbaum, a former editor of children's books. According to Nussbaum, Steinberg terrorized both her and Lisa by repeated beatings. After one vicious attack, Lisa was left lying on the bathroom floor for nearly twelve hours. By the time Steinberg and Nussbaum called for medical assistance, Lisa's brain injuries were irreversible. A year and a half after Lisa died, Steinberg was convicted of first-degree manslaughter.

The amount of media attention given to Lisa's death is unusual. Unfortunately, the tragedy of child abuse is not. The abuse of children is widespread in the United States, with estimates that over a million children a year experience acts of physical abuse (Gelles & Cornell, 1990). But what about changes over time? The surveys conducted by Straus and his colleagues, based on parental self-reports, indicated that *very severe* abuse (items 4, 6, and 8 on the Conflict Tactics Scale) has declined. In contrast, national surveys conducted by the National Center on Child Abuse and Neglect (1988) found that cases of physical abuse known to investigative agencies have increased. Actually, both sets of results could reflect the same development in our society: increased public awareness of child abuse. As the social norm against child abuse grows stronger,

After a tollbooth collector reported that a child appeared to be in distress, police stopped the car driven by Joel Steinberg. Brought to the police barracks, where this photo of Lisa was taken, Steinberg was questioned and then released. Lisa was allowed to go with him. Less than two weeks later, she died from injuries inflicted by Steinberg during a vicious beating.

abusing parents become more reluctant to admit what they have done, but others (such as family members, neighbors, physicians, and teachers) become more willing to report suspected cases of abuse. The hope, of course, is that eventually there will be much less child abuse committed and, therefore, less to report.

The Conflict Tactics Scale used in Straus's surveys examines only a limited number of abusive behaviors toward children. It does not, for example, ask about sexual abuse. There are some important differences between physical and sexual abuse. Mothers are more likely than fathers to physically abuse their children, and most victims are boys (Straus et al., 1980). But fathers are more likely than mothers to sexually abuse their children, and most of these victims are girls (Russell, 1984). Despite these differences, certain factors are associated with both types of abuse: stress, social isolation, marital conflict, and having been abused as a child (Wolfe, 1985).

cycle of family violence The transmission of aggressive behavior across generations.

The Cycle of Family Violence   At this point, you should begin to see a pattern emerging: the connection between violence in childhood and violence as an adult. This connection is called the **cycle of family violence.** Children who witness parental violence or who are abused are more likely as adults to abuse their spouse or, perhaps, be a victim of spouse abuse (O'Leary, 1988; Rosenbaum & O'Leary, 1986; Widom, 1989). They are also more likely to abuse their own children. In turn, their children are more likely to interact violently with each other (Patterson, 1984) and to aggress against their parents (Peek et al., 1985). The cycle of family violence is illustrated in Figure 8.10.

The intergenerational transmission of violence is by no means inevitable (Zigler et al., 1988). Most people who witness or experience abuse in their families of origin are not abusive or abused in their families of procreation (Emery, 1989). The cycle of family violence refers to an average tendency, not an absolute certainty. But the capacity of family violence to spread throughout all the branches of the family tree is certainly one of its most disturbing characteristics.

Various approaches have been taken to reduce family violence (Gelles & Conte, 1990; Gelles & Cornell, 1990). Reporting laws require certain individ-

---

Figure 8.10   The Cycle of Family Violence.   In the cycle of family violence, aggression breeds further aggression. An adult who was abused as a child is more likely to be a perpetrator or, perhaps, a victim of spouse abuse. Abusing spouses are more likely to abuse their children, who are more likely to abuse each other and their parents. This cycle is not, however, inevitable and most abused children escape it.

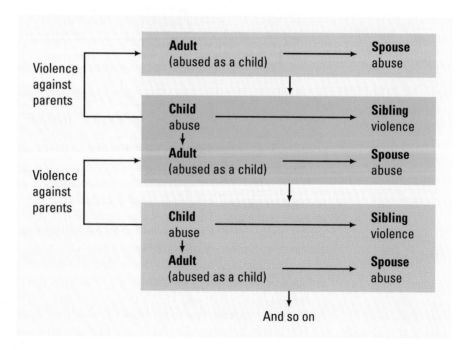

uals—such as physicians—to report suspected cases of child abuse, and some localities list a toll-free number for calls from the general public. Shelters for battered women and their children provide protection and, often, various social services such as legal referrals, psychological counseling, and employment assistance. In some localities, police follow a mandatory arrest policy in regard to domestic assault. Families in which a child has been abused may be required by court order to participate in family therapy; if necessary, an abused child can be removed from the home. Either by court order or voluntarily, many abusing men and women participate in group therapy sessions. Convicted abusers receive varying sentences depending on the crime and the judge's assessment of relevant personal and situational circumstances.

Obviously, specific programs to protect victims of abuse and reduce the likelihood of continued violence by abusers are vitally important. They save lives. But family violence takes place in a societal context. If society legitimizes and glorifies violence, family life is unlikely to be immune from it. Moreover, some of the stress experienced by abusing families involves events beyond their immediate control, such as a lack of educational and employment opportunities. Social programs that enlarge these opportunities may help to prevent family violence and avoid the possibility of its damaging legacy.

REVIEW

PINNING IT DOWN: WHAT IS AGGRESSION?

Aggression is behavior intended to injure another person. Instrumental aggression occurs as a means to obtain desired material or psychological goals. Aggression just for the sake of hurting someone is called angry aggression. Anger is an emotional response to perceived injury; hostility is an antagonistic attitude.

ORIGINS OF AGGRESSION

Is Aggression Innate?

Both Freud and Lorenz regarded aggression as an innate instinct, but the circular reasoning of their instinct theories is unscientific. Sociobiology views aggression as a universal, innate characteristic favored by natural selection but limited by the need to protect the reproductive success of one's relatives. There is considerable debate about the extent to which aggression is an inherited trait, differing among individuals and groups. The stability of aggression over the life span and the difference between men and women in physical aggression are both of consistent with a genetic contribution. But both phenomena have other plausible explanations.

Is Aggression Learned?

Aggression is increased by rewards. It is decreased by the fear of punishment only under specific conditions. Social learning theory emphasizes the influence of models on the behavior of observers. Successful models are more likely than unsuccessful ones to be imitated. But even when models are punished, their behavior can be learned for use on a later, safer occasion.

Nature Versus Nurture: A False Dichotomy

Human aggression is the product of the interaction between biology and experience as that interaction takes place in a specific situation.

SOCIAL AND SITUATIONAL INFLUENCES ON AGGRESSION

Frustration: Aggression as a Drive

The frustration-aggression hypothesis proposes that frustration will always produce the motive to aggress and that all aggression is caused by frustration. In fact, however, frustration produces many motives, and aggression is caused by many factors. According to the frustration-aggression hypothesis, displacement will occur if aggression against the source of frustration is inhibited. Research has yet to offer convincing support for this notion. The frustration-aggression hypothesis also holds that aggressive acts or exposure to aggression by others produces catharsis—a reduction in the motive to engage in further aggression. But research indicates that engaging in aggression or watching others do so is more likely to increase than to decrease aggression. Frustration is one of a number of unpleasant experiences that produce negative affect, which increases the inclination to aggress.

Negative Affect: The Temperature's Rising

Various noxious stimuli also create negative affect. The negative affect escape model predicts that greater amounts of noxious stimuli increase aggressive responses only up to a point. After this, nonaggressive responses, such as escape or collapse, predominate. Although the predicted turning point did appear in early research, this finding resulted from the greater frequency of days with moderately high temperatures. Research controlling for temperature frequency indicates that aggression continues to increase as the temperature rises.

Positive Affect: Reducing Retaliation

Being attacked or insulted by someone also produces negative affect, and retaliation to provocation is a major source of aggressive behavior. But positive emotional responses are incompatible with the negative emotion of anger. Thus, positive feelings, such as humor or empathy, reduce retaliatory aggression.

Arousal: "Wired" for Action

Highly arousing stimuli, neutral as well as negatiave, increase retaliatory aggression. The arousal-affect model holds that both the type of emotion and the intensity of arousal affect aggression, which is greatest in response to stimuli that produce both negative affect and high arousal.

Thought: Automatic and Considered

Berkowitz's cognitive-neoassociation analysis of aggression proposes that unpleasant experiences create negative affect, which, in turn, stimulates automatic associations connected with anger and fear. Behavioral and emotional outcomes then depend, at least in part, on higher-order cognitive processing. Research on the weapons effect indicates that the presence of a gun increases aggression among naive, unaware subjects. Situational cues, such as a weapon, can trigger aggressive behavior even among individuals who have not been provoked to anger. More deliberate thoughts that influence aggression include the perception of intent, which is reduced by information that a person was not fully responsible for harmful acts. To reduce retaliation, however, mitigating information must be received before provocation occurs. Alcohol impairs a person's ability to perceive and process information. Drunken excess, aggressive or helpful, occurs because less salient cues fail to inhibit behavior that has been motivated by more salient cues.

Multiple Causes, Multiple Cures

Since aggression is determined by many factors, there is no one way to end it, but there are many ways to reduce it.

SCENES OF VIOLENCE

Media Effects: Depictions of Nonsexual Violence

In the laboratory, exposure to aggressive models increases aggressive behavior among adults and children. But the results of longitudinal research indicate that the association between TV violence and aggression is modified by such factors as culture, gender, identification with aggressive TV characters, and the seeking out of violent shows by already aggressive children. Intense news coverage of violent events is correlated with subsequent increases in violent behavior by adults. It appears that media presentations can influence attitudes and values concerning aggression. Educational efforts may be more successful than censorship in guarding against the potential risk posed by media depictions of nonsexual violence.

Media Effects: Pornographic Materials

Men who are higher in sexual arousal in response to depictions of violent sex and more accepting of violence toward women report that they engage in more sexually coercive behaviors. Experimental research on nonviolent pornography supports the arosual-affect model of aggression: both the type of emotion and the intensity of arousal influence aggression. When normative restraints against male-to-female aggression are reduced, nonviolent but highly arousing pornography can specifically increase male-to-female aggression. Massive exposure to pornography produces habituation, which may decrease aggression because arousal is reduced *or* increase aggression because inhibitions are weakened. Exposure to dehumanizing nonviolent pornography makes aggression against women more acceptable. In laboratory experiments, violent pornography increases male-to-female aggression. When a female is portrayed as enjoying violent sex, even unprovoked men become more aggressive. Negative attitudes toward women may be a major factor in aggression toward women. It appears that educational programs can change these attitudes.

Intimate Violence: "The Ultimate Betrayal"

Over a ten-year period, spouse abuse in the United States remained relatively constant and high. Some studies of marital and dating violence have found that women engage in more violent behavior than men, but abused women are more likely to be seriously injured. Physical violence is highest in cohabiting relationships. Spouse abuse is associated with stress, low socioeconomic status, and having grown up in a violent family. Child abuse also is widespread in the United States. Although parental self-reports of child abuse have decreased, cases reported to investigative agencies have increased. Child abuse is associated with stress, isolation, marital conflict, and having been abused as a child. In the cycle of family violence, aggression spreads within and across generations. Various approaches have been taken to protecting the victims of family violence and preventing its recurrence.

SOCIAL INFLUENCE:
Changing Attitudes and Behavior

III

Preview

Part III of this book examines *social influence,* the effects people have on the attitudes and behaviors of others. Chapter 9, on *conformity,* considers the reasons we conform to group norms, comply with direct requests, and obey the commands of authority. Chapter 10 focuses on *attitudes* and the ways they are changed by communications from others and by our own actions. Chapter 11 describes the impact of *group processes* on task performance, decision making, cooperation, and conflict. Considered together, these chapters shed light on the ways in which we exert influence on others and react to their influence on us.

Conformity

9

Preview

This chapter examines three ways in which behavior is influenced by others. First, we consider the reasons why people exhibit *conformity* to group norms. Second, we describe the kinds of strategies used to elicit *compliance* with direct requests. Third, we analyze the causes and effects of *obedience* to the commands of authority. The chapter concludes with a discussion of the *continuum of social influence.*

Some say it triggered the eventual breakup of the Soviet Union. On Sunday evening, August 25, 1991, security guards stormed the vacation home of Mikhail Gorbachev, cut his phone lines, blocked local airport runways, and placed the president under house arrest. The next morning, Soviet news agency TASS reported that Gorbachev was ill, to be replaced by his vice president and a committee of hard-line communists. The group had staged a coup. Before long, the streets of Moscow were lined with tanks and armored trucks.

What next? Would Gorbachev yield under pressure or defy his captors? What about the Soviet people, who were prohibited from assembling? And how would world leaders react to the news? The next seventy-two hours were critical. The first reaction was shock, despair, and resignation. But then the tide began to turn. Gorbachev told his captors to "Go to hell." And Boris Yeltsin, president of the Russian Republic, climbed on top of an armored truck and gave a fiery speech condemning the coup. Only 200 Muscovites were there for Yeltsin's performance, but as word spread, the crowd grew to over 150,000. People blocked the tanks, stuffed flowers into the gun barrels, shouted at troops, and built barricades around Yeltsin's headquarters. Sensing the coup might unravel, Western leaders declared that normal relations with the Soviet Union would be suspended until Gorbachev was restored to power. By Wednesday, the plotters were on the run, and Gorbachev was on a plane back to Moscow. The coup had collapsed with astonishing speed (Church, 1991).

What caused this remarkable turn of events? What sparked defiance in a country where people had grown accustomed to passive obedience? That historic week—and the months to follow, culminating in the breakup of the former, once powerful Soviet Union—offered a lesson in the psychology of social influence. On the one hand, those who took to the streets exhibited a fierce independence, refusing to follow the commands of an illegitimate authority. On the other hand, the vast majority of citizens stayed home, and those who joined the resistance did so only after they saw others do the same. As the tension mounted, so did the social influences on behavior.

You don't need to be a social psychologist to realize that people have an impact on each other's behavior. But how, and with what effect? When we use the term *social influence,* we refer to the ways in which people are affected by real and imagined pressures from others (Kiesler & Kiesler, 1969). The kinds of social influences brought to bear on an individual come in different shapes and sizes. In this chapter, we consider three that vary in the degree of pressure brought to bear on a person—*conformity, compliance,* and *obedience.*

As depicted in Figure 9.1, conformity, compliance, and obedience are not distinct, qualitatively different "types" of influence. In all cases, the influence may emanate from a person, a group, or an institution. And in all cases, the behavior in question may be constructive (helping others), destructive (hurting others), or neutral. It is useful to note, however, that social influence varies, as points along a continuum, according to the degree of pressure exerted on the individual. It is also useful to note that people do not always succumb under

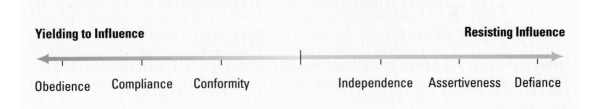

Figure 9.1   Continuum of Social Influence.   The three kinds of social influence vary in the degree of pressure each brings to bear on an individual. People may (1) *conform* to group norms or maintain their independence, (2) *comply* with requests or refuse to comply by being assertive, and (3) *obey* or defy the commands of authority.

pressure. Thus, we may conform or maintain our independence from others; we may comply with direct requests or react with assertiveness; we may obey the commands of authority or oppose that authority in an act of defiance. In this chapter, we consider the factors that lead people to yield to or resist social influence.

CONFORMITY

It is hard to find behaviors that are *not* in some way affected by exposure to the actions of others. As social animals, we are vulnerable to a host of subtle, almost reflex-like influences. We often yawn when we see others yawning and laugh when we hear others laughing. To demonstrate the point, research confederates stopped on a busy street in New York City, looked up, and gawked at the sixth-floor window of a nearby building. Films shot from behind the window indicated that about 80 percent of passersby stopped and gazed up when they saw these confederates (Milgram et al., 1969).

The principle that people are influenced by the behavior of others is one that is frequently exploited. For example, the TV industry fills many situation comedies with canned laughter in order to increase viewer responsiveness. Research shows that the addition of laugh tracks to humorous tapes often leads viewers to rate the material as funnier and to laugh more (Porterfield et al., 1988). And entertainers are not the only ones who appreciate the opportunity to use models to their advantage. Knowing that voters are attracted to a front-runner, politicians often release favorable results from their own public opinion polls. Likewise, bartenders, waiters, waitresses, and musicians put dollar bills into their tip jars at the start of an evening to encourage their customers to do the same. As these examples illustrate, people often imitate others automatically and without conflict. "Monkey see, monkey do," as the saying goes.

conformity The tendency to change perceptions, opinions, or behavior in ways that are consistent with group norms.

When social psychologists talk of **conformity**, they refer to the tendency for people to change their perceptions, opinions, and behavior in ways that are consistent with group norms. With this definition in mind, would you call yourself a conformist or a nonconformist? Do you ever feel pressured to follow what others are doing? At first, you may want to deny the tendency to conform and, instead, declare your individuality (Wolosin et al., 1975). Think about it, though. When was the last time you appeared at a formal wedding dressed in blue jeans? And when was the last time you remained seated during the national anthem at a sports event? People find it remarkably difficult to breach social norms. In an interesting illustration, social psychology research assistants were supposed to ask subway passengers to give up their seats—a conspicuous violation of the norm for acceptable conduct (Milgram & Sabini, 1978). In the end, however, many of the assistants were unable to carry out their assignment. In fact, some of those who tried it became so anxious that they pretended to be ill just to make their request appear justified.

Even though conformity is widespread, people are ambivalent about how desirable it is. In some situations, conformity is essential if individuals are to

When we see that others have left tips, we're more likely to do so ourselves. That is why waiters and waitresses often display their own money to encourage contributions.

coexist peacefully, as when we assume our rightful place in a waiting line. Yet at other times, conformity can have harmful consequences, as when we drink too heavily at parties or tell offensive ethnic jokes because others are doing the same. For social psychologists, the goal is to understand the conditions in which people follow along and the reasons for that behavior.

The Early Classics

In 1936, Muzafer Sherif published a classic laboratory study of how norms develop in small groups. His method, described in Chapter 1, was ingenious. Male students, who believed they were participating in a visual perception experiment, sat in a totally darkened room. Fifteen feet in front of them, a small dot of light appeared for two seconds, after which subjects were asked to estimate how far it had moved. This procedure was repeated several times. Although subjects didn't realize it, the dot of light always remained motionless. The movement they thought they saw was, in reality, an optical illusion known as the *autokinetic effect*: in darkness, a stationary point of light appears to move, sometimes erratically, in various directions.

At first, subjects sat alone and reported their judgments to the experimenter. After several trials, Sherif found that subjects settled in on their own stable perceptions of movement, with most estimates ranging from 1 to 10 inches (although one subject gave an estimate of 80 feet!). During the next three days, subjects returned to participate in three-person groups. As before, lights were flashed and subjects, one by one, announced their estimates. As shown in Figure 9.2, initial estimates varied considerably, but subjects later converged on a common perception. Eventually, each group established its own set of norms.

Some fifteen years after Sherif's demonstration, Solomon Asch (1951) constructed a very different scenario for testing how people's beliefs affect each other. To appreciate what Asch did, imagine yourself in the following situation. You sign up for a psychology experiment; and when you arrive, you find six other subjects waiting around a table. Soon after you take an empty seat, the experimenter explains that he is interested in the ability to make visual discriminations. As an example, he asks you and the others to indicate which of three comparison lines is identical in length to a standard line.

That seems easy enough. The experimenter then says that after each set of lines is shown, you and the others should take turns announcing your judgments out loud in the order of your seating position. Beginning on his left, the experimenter asks the first person for his judgment. Seeing that you are in the next-to-last position, you patiently await your turn. The opening moments pass uneventfully. The discriminations are clear, and everyone agrees on the answers. On the third set of lines, however, the first subject selects what is quite clearly the wrong line. Huh? What happened? Did he suddenly lose his mind, his eyesight, or both? Before you have the chance to figure this one out, the next four subjects choose the same wrong line. Now what? Feeling as if you have entered the Twilight Zone, you wonder if you misunderstood the task. And you

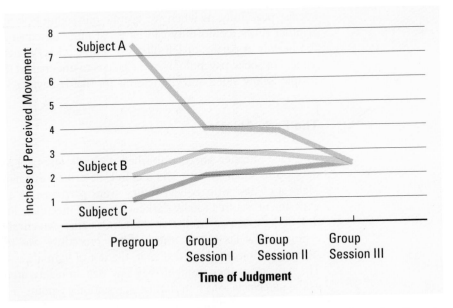

Figure 9.2   A Classic Case of Suggestibility.   This group taken from Sherif's study shows how three subjects' estimates of the apparent movement of light gradually converged. Before the subjects came together, their perceptions varied considerably. Once in groups, however, subjects conformed to the norm that had developed. [From Sherif, 1936.]

wonder what the others will think if you have the nerve to disagree. It's your turn now. You rub your eyes and take another look. What do you see? Better yet, what do you do?

Figure 9.3 gives an idea of the bind in which Asch's subjects found them-selves—caught between the need to be right and the desire to be liked (Insko et al., 1982; Ross et al., 1976). As you may suspect by now, the other "subjects" were confederates who were trained to make incorrect judgments on twelve out of eighteen presentations. There seems little doubt that the real subjects knew the correct answers. In a control group, where they made judgments in isolation, they made almost no errors. Yet Asch's subjects went along with the incorrect majority about 37 percent of the time—far more often than most of us would ever predict. Not everyone conformed, of course. About 25 percent of the subjects refused to agree on any of the incorrect judgments. Yet 50 percent went along on at least half of the critical presentations. The rest of the subjects conformed on an occasional basis. Similarly high levels of conformity were found when Asch's study was repeated nearly thirty years later (Larsen, 1990).

Looking at Sherif's and Asch's research, let's compare these classic studies of social influence. Obviously, both demonstrate that our perceptions can be heavily influenced by others. But how similar are they really? Did Sherif's and

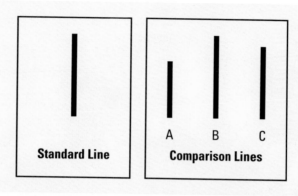

Figure 9.3 Line Judgment Task Used in Asch's Conformity Studies. Which comparison line—A, B, or C—is the same in length as the standard line? What would you say if you found yourself in a unanimous majority that answered A or C? The subjects in Asch's experiments conformed to the majority about a third of the time. [From "Opinions and Social Pressure" by Solomon E. Asch, November 1955. Illustration by Sara Love. Copyright © 1955 by Scientific American, Inc. All rights reserved.]

Asch's subjects exhibit the same kind of conformity, and for the same reasons, or is the resemblance in their behavior more apparent than real?

Right from the start, it was clear that these studies differed in some important ways. In Sherif's research, subjects were quite literally "in the dark," so they naturally turned to others for guidance. When physical reality is ambiguous and we are uncertain of our own judgments, as in the autokinetic situation, others can provide a valuable source of information (Festinger, 1954). Yet Asch's subjects found themselves in a much more awkward position. Their task was relatively simple, and they could see with their own eyes what answers were correct. Still, they often followed the incorrect majority. In interviews, many of Asch's subjects reported afterwards that they went along with the group even though they were not convinced by it. Those who did not conform said they felt "conspicuous" and "crazy," like a "misfit" (Asch, 1956, p. 31).

Why Do People Conform?

informational influence Influence that produces conformity because a person believes others are correct in their judgments.

normative influence Influence that produces conformity because a person fears the negative social consequences of appearing deviant.

These two studies demonstrate that people conform for two very different reasons: informational and normative (Crutchfield, 1955; Deutsch & Gerard, 1955). Through **informational influence**, people conform because they want to be correct in their judgments and they assume that others who agree on something must be right. In Sherif's autokinetic task, as in other ambiguous situations, it is thus natural to assume that four eyes are better than two. **Normative influence**, however, leads people to conform because they fear the

After two uneventful rounds in Asch's study on conformity, the subject (number 6) faces
a dilemma. The answer he had to give in the third test of visual discrimination differs
from that of the first five confederates, who are all in agreement. Should he give his
own answer, or conform to theirs?

private conformity
The change of beliefs
that occurs when a
person privately ac-
cepts the position
taken by others.

public conformity
A superficial change
in overt behavior,
without a correspond-
ing change of opinion,
produced by real or
imagined group pres-
sure.

negative consequences of appearing deviant. Wanting to be accepted, we often
avoid behaving in ways that make us stick out like a sore thumb. Sure, we like
to think of ourselves as unique (Goethals, 1986; Snyder & Fromkin, 1980), but
disagreement and interpersonal conflict can be stressful. It's easy to see why.
Individuals who stray from the group's norm are often disliked, rejected, and
laughed at (Asch, 1951; Levine, 1989; Schachter, 1951)—especially when the
group is trying to reach a consensus (Kruglanski & Webster, 1991). The saying
"To get along, go along" may seem distasteful, but it refers to a real fact of social
life.

Usually, informational and normative influences operate jointly (Insko et al.,
1983). Even some of Asch's subjects admitted that they came to agree with their
group's erroneous judgments. Still, the distinction between the two types of
social influence is important not just for understanding why people conform
but because they produce different types of conformity: private and public
(Allen, 1965; Kelman, 1961). Like beauty, conformity may be skin deep, or it
may penetrate beneath the surface. **Private conformity**, also called true acceptance or conversion, describes those instances in which others cause us to
change not only our overt behavior but our minds as well. To conform at this
level is to be persuaded that others are correct. In contrast, **public conformity**
(sometimes called compliance, a term that is used later in this chapter to

describe a different form of influence) refers to a superficial change in behavior. People often respond to normative pressures by pretending to agree even when privately they do not. This often happens when we want to curry favor with others. The politician who tells constituents what they want to hear is a case in point.

How, you might be wondering, can social psychologists ever tell the difference between the private and public conformist? After all, both exhibit the same change in their observable behavior. The difference is that compared to the individual who merely acquiesces in public, the person who is truly persuaded maintains that change even when others are out of the picture. When this distinction is applied to Sherif's and Asch's research, the results come out as expected. At the end of his study, Sherif (1936) retested subjects alone and found that their estimates continued to reflect the norm previously established in their group—even among subjects who were retested a full year after the experiment (Rohrer et al., 1954). In contrast, when Asch (1956) had subjects write down their answers privately, the level of conformity dropped sharply (Deutsch & Gerard, 1955; Mouton et al., 1956).

Table 9.1 summarizes the comparison of the Sherif and Asch studies and the depths of social influence they demonstrate. Looking at this table, you can see that the difficulty of the task is crucial. When reality can't easily be validated by physical evidence, as in the autokinetic situation, people turn to others for information and conform because they are truly persuaded by that information. When reality is clear, however, the cost of dissent becomes the major issue. As Asch found, it can be difficult to depart too much from others even when you know that they—not you—are wrong. So you play along. Privately, you don't change your mind. But you nod your head in agreement nevertheless.

Table 9.1 Two Types of Conformity. A comparison of the Sherif and Asch studies suggests different kinds of conformity for different reasons. Sherif used an ambiguous task, so others provided a valuable source of information and influenced the subjects' true opinions. Asch used a task that required simple judgments of a clear stimulus, so most subjects exhibited an occasional public conformity in response to normative pressure but privately did not accept the group's judgments.

Experimental Task	Primary Effect of Group	Depth of Conformity Produced
Sherif's Ambiguous Autokinetic Effect	Informational influence	Private acceptance
Asch's Simple Line Judgments	Normative influence	Public conformity

Majority Influence

Realizing that people often succumb to peer pressure is only the first step in understanding the process of social influence. The next step is to identify some of the situational and personal characteristics that make us more or less likely to conform. We know that people tend to conform when the social pressure is intense and they are insecure about how to behave (Campbell & Fairey, 1989; Campbell et al., 1986; Santee & Maslach, 1982). But what factors create this pressure and insecurity? Here, we look at four: the size of the group, the salience of the norms, the presence of an ally, and the personal characteristics of the subject.

Group Size: The Power in Numbers   Common sense would suggest that as the number of people in a majority increases, so should their impact. Actually, it is not that simple. Asch (1956) varied the size of groups, using 1, 2, 3, 4, 8, or 15 confederates, and found that conformity increased with group size—but only up to a point. Once there were three or four confederates, the amount of *additional* influence exerted by the rest was negligible. Other researchers have obtained similar results (Gerard et al., 1968).

Beyond the presence of three or four others, additions to a group are subject to the law of diminishing returns (Knowles, 1983; Mullen, 1983; Tanford & Penrod, 1984). As we will see later, Bibb Latané (1981) likens the influence of people on an individual to the way light bulbs illuminate a surface. When a second bulb is added to a room, the effect is dramatic. When the tenth bulb is added, however, its impact is barely felt, if at all. Economists say the same about the perception of money. An additional dollar seems greater to the person who has only three dollars than to the one who has three hundred.

Another possible explanation is that as increasing numbers of people express the same opinion, an individual is likely to suspect that they are acting either in "collusion" or as "spineless sheep." According to David Wilder (1977), what matters is not the actual number of others per se but our perceptions of how many distinct others, thinking independently, there are. Supporting this hypothesis, Wilder found that subjects were more influenced by two groups of two than by one 4-person group, and by two 3-person groups than by one 6-person group. Conformity increased even further when subjects were exposed to three 2-person groups. Thus, when faced with a majority opinion, we do more than just count the number of warm bodies—we count the number of independent minds.

Salience of the Norms   The size of a majority may influence the amount of pressure that is felt, but social norms lead to conformity only when they are salient. This was demonstrated in research on littering. In one study, confederates passed out handbills to amusement park visitors, varied the amount of litter in one section of the park, and found that the more litter there was, the more likely visitors were to toss their handbills to the ground (Cialdini et al., 1990). A second study, however, indicated that people are influenced by others only when their attention is drawn to the relevant norms. In this case, subjects were observed in a parking garage that was either clean or cluttered with cigarette butts, candy wrappers, paper cups, and other trash. In half of the cases, whichever norm was in place—clean or cluttered—was brought to the subject's attention by a confederate who threw a handbill to the ground as he walked by. In the other half, the confederate passed by without carrying a handbill. As subjects reached their cars, they found a "Please Drive Safely" handbill tucked under the windshield wiper. Did they toss the paper to the ground or take it with them? As shown in Figure 9.4, subjects conformed—in other words, they littered more when the garage was cluttered than when it was clean—only when the confederate had littered, drawing attention to the existing norm. For social norms to influence behavior, they must be "activated," or brought to mind (Cialdini et al., 1991).

Figure 9.4 Conformity to Social Norms That Are Salient.   In a parking garage that was either clean or littered with trash, subjects saw a confederate either throw a handbill on the ground (high norm salience) or not throw a handbill on the ground (low norm salience). From the percentage of subjects who littered moments later, you can see that there was greater conformity—that is, more littering when the garage was messy rather than clean—after the confederate had littered, thus drawing attention to the social norms that existed. [Cialdini et al., 1990.]

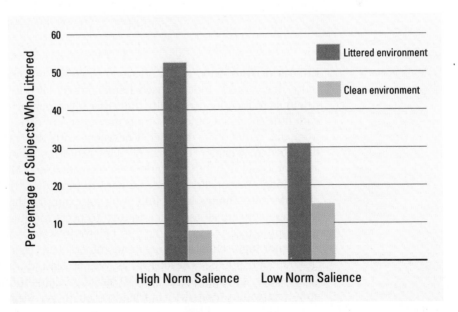

An Ally in Dissent: Getting By with a Little Help   In Asch's (1951) initial experiment, subjects found themselves pitted against unanimous majorities. But what if they had an ally, a partner in dissent? Investigating this issue, Asch found that the presence of a single confederate who agreed with the subject reduced conformity by almost 80 percent. This finding, however, does not tell us why the presence of an ally was so effective. Was it because he or she *agreed* with the subject or because he or she *disagreed* with the majority? In other words, were the views of the subjects strengthened because a dissenting confederate offered validating *information* or because dissent per se reduced *normative* pressures?

A series of experiments explored these two possibilities. In one, Vernon Allen and John Levine (1969) led subjects to believe they were working together with four others who were actually confederates. Three of these others consistently agreed on the wrong judgment. The fourth either followed the majority, agreed with the subject, or made a third, also incorrect judgment. This last variation was particularly interesting: even when the confederate did not validate the subject's own judgment, subjects conformed less often to the majority. In another study, Allen and Levine (1971) varied the competence of the ally. Some subjects received support from an average person. In contrast, others found themselves supported by someone who wore very thick glasses and complained that he could not see the visual displays. Not a particularly reassuring ally, right? Wrong. Even though subjects derived less comfort from this supporter than from one who seemed more competent at the task, his presence still reduced their level of conformity.

Two important conclusions follow from this research. First, it is substantially more difficult for people to stand alone for their convictions than to be part of even a tiny minority. Second, *any* dissent—whether it validates an individual's opinion or not—can break the spell cast by a unanimous majority and reduce the normative pressures to conform.

Effects of Age, Sex, and Culture   We all know some people who conform more than others. Indeed, Asch found individual differences in his research. Attempts to identify personality traits that breed conformity, however, have met with little success. Conformist traits may exist, but their effects on behavior vary from one situation to another. Consistent with the interactionist perspective described in Chapter 1, someone who conforms in one setting may behave autonomously in another (Marlowe & Gergen, 1969; Moscovici, 1985).

Although personality factors are hard to pin down, there are age differences in conformity. Parents know fully well, for example, that their adolescent sons and daughters are all too quick to turn to peers for guidance on how to dress, what music to listen to, and how to behave in ways that are "cool." Are junior and senior high school students more vulnerable to peer pressure than younger children and adults? The answer is yes, at least during the early stages of adolescence. Thomas Berndt (1979) asked students in grades 3, 6, 9, and 12 how they would react if their friends tried to get them to see a movie, help a new kid on the block, cheat on a test, soap windows on Halloween, or participate in other activities. As shown in Figure 9.5, conformity rose steadily, peaked in the ninth grade, and declined in the twelfth. The tendency to conform is weak for actions that are immoral or illegal, but young adolescents in particular are at risk, wanting desperately to "fit in" (Brown et al., 1986; Gavin & Furman, 1989).

Are there also gender differences in conformity? Based on Asch's initial studies, social psychologists used to think that women, once considered the "weaker" sex, conform more than men. In light of more recent research, however, it appears that two additional factors have to be considered. First, sex differences depend on how comfortable subjects are with the experimental task. Frank Sistrunk and John McDavid (1971) had male and female subjects answer questions on stereotypically masculine, feminine, and gender-neutral topics. Along with each question, subjects were told the percentage of others who agreed or disagreed. Although females conformed to the contrived majority more on the masculine items, males conformed more on the feminine items (there were no sex differences on the neutral questions). One's familiarity with the issue at hand, not gender, is what affects conformity. Ask about football or video war games, and women acquiesce more than men. Ask about family planning and fashion design, and the pattern is reversed (Eagly & Carli, 1981).

Figure 9.5 Conformity in Childhood and Adolescence.   Students in grades 3, 6, 9, and 12 reported on how they would react if pressured by peers to participate in certain activities. As you can see, conformity rose steadily, peaked in the ninth grade, and declined. Particularly for young adolescents who want desperately to fit in, it's very difficult to "just say no." [Berndt, 1979.]

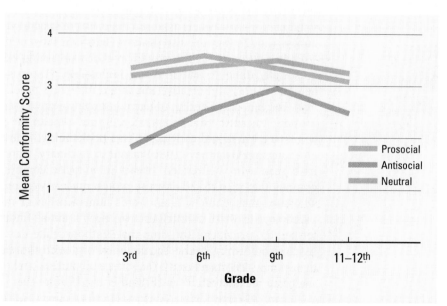

The second factor is the type of social pressure people face. As a general rule, sex differences are weak and unreliable. But there's an important exception: in face-to-face encounters, where individuals must openly disagree with others, small differences do emerge. In fact, when subjects think they are being observed, women conform more and men conform less than they do in a more private situation (Eagly & Chravala, 1986; Eagly et al., 1981b). Why does being "in public" create such a divergence in behavior? Alice Eagly (1987) believes that in front of others, people are concerned about how they are coming across and feel pressured to perform in ways that are "acceptable" within stereotypical gender-role constraints. At least in public, men make it a point to behave with independence and autonomy, and women play a gentler, more docile role.

As you might expect, cultural factors also play an important role. In many Western cultures, like the United States, Canada, Australia, France, and Great Britain, autonomy and independence are highly valued. In contrast, many cultures of Asia, Africa, and Latin America value interpersonal harmony and conformity—fitting in for the sake of the community (Triandis et al., 1988). Among the Bantu of Zimbabwe, for example, an African tribe in which acts of nonconformity are punished, 51 percent of the subjects placed in an Asch-like situation conformed—more than the 30 or so percent usually obtained in the West (Whittaker & Meade, 1967).

Minority Influence

It is not easy for individuals who express unpopular views to enlist support from others. Philosopher Bertrand Russell once said that "Conventional people are roused to frenzy by departure from convention, largely because they regard such departure as criticism of themselves." He may have been right. People who stand tall for their beliefs against a majority are generally seen as competent and honest, though they are also disliked (Bassili & Provencal, 1988; Levine, 1989).

Resisting the pressure to conform and maintaining one's independence may be socially difficult, but it is not impossible. History's famous trend setters, heroes, villains, and creative minds are the living proof: Joan of Arc, Muhammad, Darwin, and Gandhi, to name just a few, were dissenters of their time who continue to capture the imagination. So are some of the people of everyday life who make waves and rock boats. In a book entitled *The Dissenters,* anthropologist Langston Gwaltney (1986) talked to "ordinary" nonconformists such as an Irish man who befriended blacks in a racist community, a New England grandmother who risked arrest to protest nuclear weapons, and a group of nuns who sued their church. Then there's human behavior in the laboratory. Social psychologists were so intrigued by Asch's initial finding that subjects conformed 37 percent of the time that textbooks like this one routinely refer to "Asch's conformity study." Yet the often neglected flip side of the same coin is that Asch's subjects refused to acquiesce 63 percent of the time—thus indicating the power of independence (Friend et al., 1990).

Twelve Angry Men, a classic film starring Henry Fonda, provides a good illustration of how a lone dissenter can not only resist the pressure to conform but convince others to follow. Almost as soon as the deliberation-room door closes, the jury in this film takes a show-of-hands vote. The result is an eleven-to-one majority in favor of conviction, with Fonda the lone holdout. Through ninety minutes of heated deliberation, Fonda works relentlessly to plant a seed of doubt in the minds of his trigger-happy peers. In the end, the jury reaches a unanimous verdict: *not* guilty.

Sometimes art imitates life; sometimes it does not. In this instance, Henry Fonda's heroics are highly atypical. When it comes to jury decision making, the majority almost always wins (see Chapter 12). Yet in juries, as in other small groups, there are occasional exceptions. Thanks to Serge Moscovici, Edwin Hollander, and others, we now know quite a bit about the ways in which nonconformists act as agents of social change (Hollander, 1985; Maass & Clark, 1984; Moscovici, 1980; Mugny, 1982).

The Power of Style According to Moscovici, majorities are powerful by virtue of their sheer *numbers,* but nonconformists derive power from the *style* of their behavior. It is not just what they say that matters, but how they say it. Specifically, Moscovici says that to exert influence, minorities must be forceful, persistent, and unwavering in support of their own positions. At the same time, however, they must appear flexible and open-minded. Confronted with a consistent, evenhanded opposition, those in the majority will sit up, take notice, and rethink their own positions.

Moscovici's model draws on concepts from attribution theory, which accounts for how people explain the causes of each other's behavior (see Chapter 3). Imagine for a moment what you would think of someone who takes an unpopular stand and refuses to back down. In the language of Harold Kelley's (1967) attribution theory, you would have observed a pattern of behavior that is both low in consensus (the person disagrees with most others) and high in consistency (the person holds the same opinion over time). In this case, you are likely to attribute the dissenter's actions to his or her personal qualities rather than to the situation. But what personal characteristics, specifically, would you focus on? One possibility is to assume that anyone who is so self-confident and dedicated might very well be right, and to re-examine your own position in light of that information. A second possibility is to conclude that the dissenter is biased, obstinate, or just plain crazy, in which case you will dismiss the individual and think no further about his or her opinion.

Although not all aspects of Moscovici's model have been tested, research supports the main hypothesis. In one study, Moscovici and his colleagues (1969) turned Asch's procedure on its head by confronting real subjects with a *minority* of confederates who made incorrect judgments. Subjects, in groups of six, took part in what was supposed to be a study of color perception. They viewed a series of slides—all blue, but differing in intensity. For each slide, subjects took turns naming the color. Although the task was simple, two confederates announced that the slides were green. When the confederates were *consistent*—that is, when both made incorrect green judgments for all slides—they had a surprising influence. About a third of all subjects incorrectly reported seeing at least one green slide, and 8 percent of all responses were incorrect. Subsequent research confirmed that consistency is a key factor. As one might expect from Moscovici's attribution model, however, minority influence does not occur if dissenters are perceived to be biased, narrow-minded, or psychologically imbalanced (Nemeth et al., 1974; Papastamou, 1986). Nor does it occur if they are members of a social outgroup and argue in favor of their own self-interests (Clark & Maass, 1988).

Based on the fact that dissent often breeds hostility, Edwin Hollander (1958) recommends a different approach. Hollander warns that people who seek positions of leadership or challenge a group without first becoming accepted, full-fledged members of that group run the risk of having their opinions fall on deaf ears. As an alternative to Moscovici's consistency strategy, Hollander suggests that to influence the majority, people should first conform in order to establish their credentials as competent insiders. By becoming members of the majority, they accumulate **idiosyncrasy credits**, or "brownie points." Once enough good will has been collected within the group, a certain amount of deviance will be tolerated. Several studies have shown that this "first conform, then dissent" strategy, like Moscovici's "consistent dissent" approach, is effective (Bray et al., 1982; Lortie-Lussier, 1987).

idiosyncrasy credits Interpersonal "credits" that a person earns by following group norms.

A Chip Off the Old Block?   Regardless of which strategy is used, minority influence is a force to be reckoned with. But does it work just like the process of conformity, or is there something different about the way minorities and majorities effect change? There are two opposing views. Some theorists believe that a *single process* accounts for both directions of social influence—that minority influence is just a "chip off the old block" (Latané & Wolf, 1981; Tanford & Penrod, 1984; Wolf, 1985). Others take a *dual-process* approach (Moscovici, 1980; Nemeth, 1986). According to this second view, majorities and minorities both exert influence, but in very different ways. Majorities, because they are in control, produce a public conformity by bringing stressful normative pressures to bear on the individual. In contrast, minorities—because they are perceived to be seriously committed to their views—produce a deeper and more lasting private conformity, or *conversion,* by encouraging others to rethink their own positions.

To test these competing single- and dual-process theories, researchers have compared the effects of majority and minority viewpoints on subjects who are otherwise neutral on an issue in dispute. At this point, the following conclusions can be drawn. On direct public measures of conformity, majorities have a clear upper hand over minorities. On indirect and private measures of conformity, however, minorities tend to exert a strong impact (Clark & Maass, 1990; Moscovici & Personnaz, 1991)—at least when the position they take is not an issue of great personal relevance, a situation that leads subjects to resist influence (Trost et al., 1992). As Moscovici so cogently argued, people are changed in a meaningful but subtle way by minority opinion. Because of social pressures, they may be too intimidated to publicly admit it. In fact, they might not even be aware of it themselves (Personnaz, 1981). But the impact is there.

According to Charlan Nemeth (1986), dissenters serve a valuable purpose. Sometimes their views are correct; at other times they are not. But simply by their willingness to maintain independence, minorities can force other group members to think more carefully, more openly, and more creatively about a problem, thus enhancing the quality of a group's decisions. In one study, for example, subjects exposed to a minority viewpoint on how to solve anagram problems later found more novel solutions themselves (Nemeth & Kwan, 1987). In another study, those exposed to a consistent minority view on how to recall information later recalled more words from a list they were trying to memorize (Nemeth et al., 1990).

Earlier, we saw that people are more willing to express their opposition to incorrect majorities when the group as a whole lacks unanimity. But what about opposition to unanimous incorrect majorities? Can people muster enough courage to resist conformity pressure when they truly believe they are right? To examine this possibility, Nemeth and Cynthia Chiles (1988) placed subjects into color-perception groups in which one confederate consistently or inconsistently dissented—by judging blue slides to be green all or some of the time—or voiced no dissent whatsoever. Later, subjects participated in a new group in which all other members judged a series of red slides as orange—the Asch script all over again. The reaction? Like Asch's line judgments, the task was simple and straightforward. On their own, subjects were incorrect in less than 1 percent of their responses. Up against a unanimous group, subjects without prior exposure to dissent made conformity errors 70 percent of the time. But subjects who had witnessed dissent in an earlier experiment had the courage to step forward and oppose the incorrect majority. Indeed, as illustrated in Table 9.2, the more consistent the observed dissent, the more independent subjects later became.

COMPLIANCE

compliance
Changes in behavior that are elicited by direct requests.

In conformity situations, people follow implicit group norms. But another common form of social influence occurs when people make direct *explicit* requests of us in the hope that we will comply. Situations calling for **compliance** take many forms. They include a good friend's request for help, sheepishly prefaced by the question "Can you do me a favor?" They also include the salesperson's pitch for business, prefaced by those dangerous words "Have I got a deal for you!" Sometimes, the request itself is up front and direct; what you see is what you get. At other times, it is part of a subtle and more elaborate manipulation.

	Control (Subjects Alone)	No Prior Dissent	Inconsistent Prior Dissent	Consistent Prior Dissent
Percentage of Conformity Errors	00.85	70.40	33.75	14.15

Table 9.2   **Effects of Exposure to Models of Courage.**   Subjects participated in groups where one confederate consistently or inconsistently dissented by making incorrect judgments, or voiced no dissent. Later, they joined a second, Asch-like group involving an incorrect unanimous majority. This second task was simple, so subjects who participated alone made virtually no errors (far left column). Faced with a unanimous group, however, those without prior exposure to dissent made conformity errors 70 percent of the time. Subjects who had earlier observed dissent made considerably fewer errors, especially when that dissent was consistent. [Data from Nemeth & Chiles, 1988.]

How do people get others to comply with their self-serving requests? How do the police get crime suspects to confess? How do TV evangelists elicit millions of dollars in contributions for their ministries? How do *you* influence others? Do you use threats, promises, deceit, politeness, or reason? Do you hint, coax, sulk, negotiate, throw tantrums, or pull rank whenever you can? The compliance strategies we use depend on how well we know a person, our status in a relationship, our personality, culture, and the nature of the request (Bisanz & Rule, 1989; Buss et al., 1987; Holtgraves & Yang, 1992).

By observing the masters of influence—advertisers, fund raisers, politicians, and business leaders—social psychologists have learned a great deal about the subtle but very effective strategies commonly used. What we see is that people often get others to comply with their requests by setting traps. Once caught in one of these traps, it becomes difficult for the unwary victim to escape.

The Discourse of Making Requests

There is a memorable scene in the film *Beverly Hills Cop II* in which comedian Eddie Murphy, speaking at a rate far too fast for anyone to comprehend, manages to convince a team of builders to abandon their work on a house that he wants to use for the weekend. This scene illustrates the rapid-fire sales pitch at its best. The other guys never had a chance. Murphy capitalized on the fact that fast talkers are perceived to be intelligent and well informed (Apple et al., 1979). He also benefited from the element of surprise. Caught off guard, we tend to capitulate rather quickly. Stanley Milgram and John Sabini (1978), for example, found that when New York City subway passengers were forewarned that someone might ask for their seat, only 28 percent of them said yes when later approached. When the request took passengers by surprise, however, their level of compliance doubled to 56 percent.

People can also be disarmed by the phrasing of a request. As illustrated by Eddie Murphy's masterful use of doubletalk, *how* you ask for something can be more important than *what* you ask for. Consider, for example, requests that sound reasonable but offer no real reason for compliance. Ellen Langer and her colleagues (1978) found that words alone can sometimes trick us into submission. In their research, an experimenter approached people who were using a library copying machine and asked to cut in. Three different versions of the same request were used. In one, subjects were simply asked, "Excuse me. I have five pages. May I use the Xerox machine?" In a second version, the request was justified by the added phrase "because I'm in a rush." As you would expect, more subjects stepped aside when the request was justified (94 percent) than when it was not (60 percent). A third version of the request, however, suggests that the reason offered had little to do with the increase in compliance. In this case, subjects heard the following: "Excuse me. I have five pages. May I use the Xerox machine because I have to make some copies?" If you look closely at this request, you'll see that it really offered no reason at all. Yet 93 percent of the subjects in this condition complied! It was as if the appearance of reason, triggered by the word *because,* was all that was necessary. Although there is some disagreement about how to interpret these results (Folkes, 1985; Langer et al., 1985), Langer (1989) finds that people are often on automatic pilot, responding *mindlessly* to words without fully processing the information they are supposed to convey. At least for requests that are relatively small, "sweet little nothings" may be enough to elicit compliance.

The Norm of Reciprocity

In earlier chapters we describe a simple but very powerful social norm. Known as the *norm of reciprocity,* it dictates that we should treat others as they have treated us (Gouldner, 1960). On the negative side, this norm can be used to sanction retaliation against those who cause us harm: "An eye for an eye." On the positive side, the same norm leads people to feel obligated to repay others for acts of kindness. Thus, when we receive gifts, invitations, free samples, and the like, we usually go out of our way to return the favor.

The reciprocity norm contributes to the predictability and fairness of social interaction. However, it can also be exploited as a means of influence. Dennis Regan (1971) examined this possibility in the following situation. Individual subjects were brought together with a confederate—who was trained to act in either a likable or an unlikable manner—for an experiment on "aesthetics." In one condition, the confederate did the subject an unsolicited favor. He left during a break and returned with two bottles of Coca-Cola, one for himself and the other for the subject. In a second condition, the confederate returned from the break empty-handed. In a third condition, subjects were treated to a Coke—but by the experimenter, not the confederate. The confederate then told subjects in all conditions that he was selling raffle tickets at 25 cents apiece and asked if they would be willing to buy any.

On the average, subjects bought more raffle tickets when the confederate had earlier brought them the soft drink than when he had not. The norm of reciprocity was so strong that subjects returned the favor even when the confederate was not otherwise a likable character. In fact, subjects in this condition spent an average of 43 cents on raffle tickets. At a time when soft drinks cost less than a quarter, the confederate made a handsome quick profit on his investment! Apparently, the norm of reciprocity can be used to trap us into compliance.

Some people are more likely than others to exploit the reciprocity norm in this manner. According to Martin Greenberg and David Westcott (1983), individuals who use reciprocity to elicit compliance can be called "creditors"

Exploiting the powerful norm of reciprocity, people often bear gifts in order to gain compliance with a later request.

"If it please the Court, may I point out that I requested to approach the Bench before learned counsel requested to approach the Bench."

who try to keep others in their debt so they can cash in when necessary. On a questionnaire that measures *reciprocation ideology,* people are identified as creditors rather than noncreditors if they agree with statements such as "If someone does you a favor, it's a good idea to repay that person with a greater favor" (Eisenberger et al., 1987). On the receiving end, some people more than others try not to accept favors that might later set them up for exploitation. On a scale that measures *reciprocation wariness,* people are said to be wary if they are suspicious, for example, that "Asking for another's help gives them power over your life" (Eisenberger et al., 1987).

Setting Traps: Sequential Request Strategies

People who raise money or sell for a living know that it often takes more than a single plea to win over a potential donor or customer. Social psychologists share this knowledge and have studied several compliance techniques that are based on making two or more related requests. *Click!* The first request sets the trap. *Snap!* The second captures its prey. In a fascinating book entitled *Influence,* Robert Cialdini (1988) describes sequential request methods in vivid detail. These are presented in this section.

The Foot in the Door   Folk wisdom has it that one way to get a person to comply with a sizable request is to start small. First devised by traveling salespeople peddling vacuum cleaners, hair brushes, cosmetics, magazine subscriptions, and encyclopedias, the trick is to somehow get your "foot in the door." The expression need not be taken literally, of course. The point of the **foot-in-the-door technique** is to break the ice with a small initial request that the customer can't refuse. Once a first commitment is elicited, the chances are increased that another, larger request will succeed.

foot-in-the-door technique   A two-step compliance technique in which an influencer prefaces the real request by first getting a person to comply with a much smaller request.

Jonathan Freedman and Scott Fraser (1966) tested the impact of this technique in a series of field experiments. In one, an experimenter pretending to be employed by a consumer organization telephoned a group of female homemakers in Palo Alto, California, and asked if they would be willing to answer some questions about household products. Those who consented were then asked a few innocuous questions and thanked for their assistance. Three days later, the experimenter called back and made a considerable, almost outrageous, request. He asked subjects if they would allow a handful of men into their home for two hours to rummage through their drawers and cupboards so they could take an inventory of household products.

The foot-in-the-door technique proved to be very effective. When subjects were confronted with only the very intrusive request, 22 percent consented. Yet among those surveyed earlier, the rate of agreement more than doubled, to 53 percent. This basic result has now been repeated over and over again. People are more likely to donate time, money, blood, the use of their home, and other resources once they have been induced to go along with a small initial request. Although the effect is often not as dramatic as that obtained by Freedman and Fraser, it does appear in a variety of circumstances (Beaman et al., 1983; Dillard, 1991).

The practical implications of the foot-in-the-door effect are obvious. But *why* does it work? Although several explanations have been suggested, the one that seems the most plausible is based on self-perception theory—that people often infer their attitudes by observing their own behavior. As adapted by Freedman and Fraser (1966), this explanation suggests that a two-step process is activated (DeJong, 1979). First, by observing your behavior in the initial, small compliance situation, you adopt an image of yourself as the kind of person who is generally cooperative when approached with that kind of request. Second, having made that attribution, and being confronted with the more burdensome request, you seek to respond in ways that maintain this self-image. In short, the foot-in-the-door effect should occur only when you attribute an initial act of compliance to your own personal characteristics.

Research evidence generally supports this explanation. If the first request is too trivial or if subjects are paid for their first act of compliance, they won't view themselves as inherently cooperative. Under these conditions, the technique does *not* work (Seligman et al., 1976; Zuckerman et al., 1979). Likewise, the effect occurs only when people are motivated to be consistent with their self-image. If subjects are unhappy about what their initial behavior implies about them, if they are too young to appreciate the implications, or if they don't care about behaving in ways that are personally consistent, then again the technique does *not* work (Eisenberg et al., 1987; Kraut, 1973).

Knowing that a foot in the door increases compliance is both exciting and troubling—exciting for the owner of the foot, but troubling for the owner of the door. As Cialdini (1988) put it, "You can use small commitments to manipulate a person's self-image; you can use them to turn citizens into 'public servants,' prospects into 'customers,' prisoners into 'collaborators.' And once you've got a person's self-image where you want it, he or she should comply naturally with a whole range of requests that are consistent with this new self-view" (p. 64).

low-balling A two-step compliance technique in which the influencer secures agreement with a request but then increases the size of that request by revealing hidden costs.

Low-Balling Another two-step trap, perhaps the most unscrupulous of all compliance techniques, is also based on the "start small" idea. Imagine yourself in the following situation. You're at a local automobile dealership and, after some negotiation, you receive from the salesperson a great price on the car of your choice. You cast aside other considerations, shake hands on the deal, and as the salesperson goes off to "write it up," you begin to feel the thrill of owning the car of your dreams. Absorbed in fantasy, you are interrupted by the sudden return of your salesperson. "I'm sorry," he says. "The manager would not approve the sale. We have to increase the price by another $450. Otherwise, we lose money. I'm afraid that's the best we can do." As the victim of an all-too-common trick known as **low-balling**, you are now faced with a difficult decision. On the one hand, you are really wild about the car. You've already

On a car lot, low-balling works when an acceptable
offer makes you feel committed to a particular car, and
you start to imagine all the benefits of ownership. If the
salesperson then raises the price, your attachment may
be too strong to back down from the purchase.

enjoyed the pleasure of thinking it's yours; and the more you think about it, the
better it looks. On the other hand, you don't want to pay more money, and you
have an uneasy feeling in the pit of your stomach that you're being duped. What
do you do?

Salespeople who use this tactic are betting that you'll go ahead with the
purchase despite the added cost. If the behavior of research subjects is any
indication, they are often right. In one study, for example, experimenters
phoned introductory psychology students and asked if they would be willing to
participate in an experiment for extra credit. Some subjects were told up front
that the session would begin at the uncivilized hour of 7 A.M. Knowing that, only
31 percent volunteered. But other subjects were low-balled. Only *after* they
agreed to participate did the experimenter inform them of the 7 A.M. starting
time. Would that be okay? Whether or not it was, the procedure achieved its
objective—the sign-up rate increased to 56 percent (Cialdini et al., 1978).

Low-balling is an interesting technique. Surely, once the low ball has been
thrown, most recipients suspect they were misled. Yet they go along. Why? The
reason appears to be based on the psychology of commitment (Kiesler, 1971).

Once people make a particular decision, they justify it to themselves by thinking of all its positive aspects. As they become increasingly committed to a course of action, people grow more resistant to changing their mind, even if the initial reasons for their action have been changed or withdrawn entirely. In the automobile dealership scenario, you might very well have decided to purchase the car because of the price. But then you would have thought about its sleek new appearance, the leather interior, the sun roof, and the sound quality on the CD player. By the time you learned that the price would be more than you bargained for, it was too late—you were already hooked.

Low-balling also produces another form of commitment. When people do not suspect duplicity, they feel a nagging sense of unfulfilled obligation to the person with whom they negotiated. Thus, even though the salesperson was unable to complete the original deal, you might feel obligated to buy anyway, having already agreed to make the purchase. This commitment to the other person may account for why low-balling works better when the second request is made by the same person than by someone else (Burger & Petty, 1981).

Door in the Face Although shifting from an initial small request to a larger one can be effective, as the foot-in-the-door and low-ball techniques suggest, oddly enough so is its opposite. In his book, Cialdini (1988) describes a time he was approached by a Boy Scout and asked to buy two five-dollar tickets to an upcoming circus. Having better things to do with his time and money, he declined. Then the boy asked if he would be interested in buying chocolate bars at a dollar apiece. Even though he doesn't like chocolate, Cialdini—an expert on social influence—bought two of them! After a moment's reflection, he realized what had happened. Whether the Boy Scout planned it that way or not, Cialdini himself fell for what is known as the **door-in-the-face technique**.

door-in-the-face technique A two-step compliance technique in which an influencer prefaces the real request with a request so large that it is rejected.

The technique is as simple as it sounds. An individual makes an initial request so large that it is sure to be rejected and then comes back with a second, more reasonable request. The assumption is that the second request will stand a better chance after the first one has been declined. Plagued by the sight of uneaten chocolate bars, Cialdini and his colleagues (1975) evaluated the effectiveness of the door-in-the-face technique. They stopped college students on campus and asked if they would volunteer to work without pay at a youth counseling program for juvenile delinquents. The commitment of time would be forbidding: roughly two hours a week for the next two years. Not surprisingly, everyone who was approached politely slammed the proverbial door in the experimenter's face. But then the experimenter followed up with a more modest proposal, asking subjects if they would be willing to take a group of delinquents on a two-hour trip to the zoo. The strategy worked like a charm. Only 17 percent of the students confronted with *only* the second request agreed. But of those who initially declined the first request, 50 percent said yes to the zoo trip. You should note that the door-in-the-face technique does not elicit only empty promises. Most subjects who comply subsequently do what they've agreed to do (Cialdini & Ascani, 1976).

Why is the door-in-the-face technique such an effective trap? One possibility involves the principle of *perceptual contrast*: after exposure to a very large request, the second request "looks smaller." Two dollars' worth of candy bars is not bad compared to ten dollars for circus tickets. Likewise, taking a group of kids to the zoo seems trivial compared to two years of volunteer work. As intuitively sensible as this explanation seems, Cialdini and his colleagues (1975) concluded that perceptual contrast is only partly responsible for the effect. When subjects heard the large request without actually having to reject it, their compliance rate increased only slightly (25 percent) relative to the 17 percent who complied after only the small request.

A second, more compelling explanation for the effect is that of *reciprocal concessions*. A close cousin of the reciprocity norm, this refers to the pressure to respond to changes in a bargaining position. When an individual backs down from a large request to a much smaller one, we view that move as a concession that should be matched by our own compliance. Thus, the door-in-the-face technique does not work if the second request is made by a different person (Cialdini et al., 1975). Nor does it work if the first request is *so* extreme that it comes across as an insincere "first offer" (Schwarzwald et al., 1979).

That's Not All, Folks!   If the notion of reciprocal concessions is correct, then a subject shouldn't actually have to refuse the initial offer for the shift to a smaller request to work. Indeed, another familiar sales strategy manages to use concession without first eliciting refusal. In this strategy, a product is offered at a particular price, but then, before the buyer has a chance to respond, the seller adds, "And that's not all!" At that point, either the original price is reduced or a bonus is offered to sweeten the pot. The seller, of course, intends all along to make the so-called concession.

This ploy, known as the **that's-not-all technique**, seems awfully transparent, right? Surely, no one falls for it, right? Jerry Burger (1986) was not so sure, and predicted that people are more likely to make a purchase when a deal seems to have improved than when that same deal is offered right from the start. To test this hypothesis, Burger set up a booth at a campus fair and sold cupcakes. Some customers who approached the table were told that the cupcakes cost 75 cents each. Others were told that they cost a dollar, but then, before they could respond, the price was reduced to 75 cents. Rationally speaking, Burger's manipulation did not affect the ultimate price, so it should not have affected sales. But it did. When customers were led to believe that the final price was reduced, sales increased from 44 to 73 percent.

At this point, let's step back and look at the various compliance techniques described in this section. All of them are based on a two-step process that involves a shift from a request of one size to another. What differs is whether the small or large request comes first and how the transition between steps is made (see Table 9.3). Moreover, all these strategies work in subtle ways by manipulating the target person's self-image, commitment to the product, feelings of obligation to the seller, or perceptions of the real request. It is even possible to

that's-not-all technique   A two-step compliance technique in which the influencer begins with an inflated request, then decreases the apparent size of that request by offering a discount or bonus.

Request Shifts	Technique	Description
From Small to Large	Foot in the door	Begin with a very small request; secure agreement; then make a separate larger request.
	Low-balling	Secure agreement with a request, and then increase the size of that request by revealing hidden costs.
From Large to Small	Door in the face	Begin with a very large request that will be rejected; then follow that up with a more modest request.
	That's not all	Begin with a somewhat inflated request; then immediately decrease the apparent size of that request by offering a discount or bonus.

Table 9.3 Sequential Request Strategies. Various compliance techniques are based on a sequence of two or more related requests. *Click!* The first request sets the trap. *Snap!* The second captures the prey. Research has shown that the four sequential request strategies summarized in this table are all effective.

---

increase compliance by making a chain of requests that use a combination of techniques (Goldman, 1986) or by prefacing the request by asking "How are you feeling?"—a question that typically elicits a favorable first response from strangers (Howard, 1990a). When you consider the various traps, it makes you wonder whether it's ever possible to escape.

Assertiveness: When People Say No

Robert Cialdini (1988) opened his book with a confession: "I can admit it freely now. All my life I've been a patsy." As a past victim of compliance traps, Cialdini is not alone. Many people find it difficult to be assertive in interpersonal situations. Faced with an unreasonable request from a friend, spouse, or stranger, they become anxious at the mere thought of putting a foot down and refusing to comply. Indeed, there are times when it is uncomfortable for anyone to say no. However, just as we can maintain our autonomy in the face of conformity pressures, we can also refuse direct requests—even clever ones. The trap may be set, but you don't always have to get caught.

"Bernie's problem is his technique draws attention to itself."

Compliance techniques are powerful only if they are not transparent. When people suspect that they are being manipulated, they react with anger, reactance, and stubborn noncompliance. [Drawing by Weber; © 1987 The New Yorker Magazine, Inc.]

According to Cialdini, the ability to resist the pressures of compliance rests, first and foremost, on vigilance. If a stranger hands you a gift and then launches into a sales pitch, you should recognize the tactic for what it is and not feel indebted by the norm of reciprocity. And if you strike a deal with a salesperson who later reneges on the terms, you should be aware that you're being thrown a low ball. Indeed, that is exactly what happened to one of the authors of this book. After a full Saturday afternoon of careful negotiation at the local Nissan dealer, Mr. and Mrs. Kassin finally came to terms on an acceptable price. Minutes later, the salesman returned with the news that the manager would not approve the deal. The cost of an air conditioner, which was to be included in the price, would now have to be added on. Familiar with the research, Saul turned to his wife and exclaimed, "Carol, it's a trick; they're low-balling us!" Realizing what happened, Carol was furious. She went straight to the manager and made such a scene in front of other customers that he backed down and honored the original deal.

What happened in this instance? Why did recognizing the attempted manipulation produce such anger and resistance? As this story illustrates, compliance techniques work smoothly only if they are hidden from view. The problem is not only that they are attempts to influence us but that they are based on deception.

Flattery, gifts, and other ploys often elicit compliance, but not if they are perceived as insincere (Jones, 1964) and not if the target has a high level of reciprocity wariness (Eisenberger et al., 1987). Likewise, the sequential-request traps are powerful to the extent that they are subtle and cannot be seen for what they are (Schwarzwald et al., 1979). People don't like to be deceived. In fact, just feeling manipulated leads us to react with anger, psychological reactance, and stubborn noncompliance—unless the request is a command and the requester is a figure of authority.

OBEDIENCE

Allen Funt, the creator and producer of the original TV program "Candid Camera," spends as much time observing human behavior in the real world as most psychologists do. When asked what he has learned from his people watching, he replied, "The worst thing, and I see it over and over, is how easily people can be led by any kind of authority figure, or even the most minimal signs of authority." He went on to cite the time he put up a road sign that read "Delaware Closed Today." The reaction? "Motorists didn't question it. Instead they asked, 'Is Jersey open?'" (Zimbardo, 1985, p. 47).

Funt is right about the way people react to authority. Taught from birth that it's important to respect legitimate forms of leadership, people think twice before challenging parents, teachers, employers, coaches, and government officials. But often the mere symbols of authority—titles, uniforms, badges, and the trappings of success, even without the credentials—can turn ordinary people into docile servants.

Leonard Bickman (1974) demonstrated this phenomenon in a series of studies in which a male research assistant stopped passersby on the streets of Brooklyn and ordered them to do something unusual. Sometimes, he pointed to a paper bag on the ground and said, "Pick up this bag for me!" At other times, he pointed to an individual standing beside a parked car and said, "This fellow is over-parked at the meter but doesn't have any change. Give him a dime!" Would anyone really take this guy seriously? When he was dressed in street clothes, only a third of the subjects followed his orders. But when he wore a security guard's uniform, nearly nine out of every ten subjects obeyed! Even when the uniformed assistant turned the corner and walked away after issuing his command, the vast majority of passersby followed his orders. Clearly, uniforms signify the power of authority (Bushman, 1984, 1988). This must be what Allen Funt had in mind. Unfortunately, blind **obedience** is not always that funny.

obedience Behavior change produced by the commands of authority.

If people are willing to take inappropriate orders from a complete stranger, how far will they go when it really matters? The pages of history lead us to believe the worst. In World War II, Nazi soldiers and officials participated in the slaughter of millions of Jews, as well as Poles, Russians, gypsies, political opponents, and homosexuals. Yet, when tried for these crimes, the Nazi defense was always the same: "I was just following orders."

Surely, you must be thinking, those events were highly unusual. They say more about the Nazis as individuals—their hatreds, prejudices, and sick minds—than they do about obedience to authority. But two lines of evidence suggest otherwise. First, interviews with Nazi war criminals have failed to uncover signs of an inherently evil character. Indeed, many otherwise reputable physicians participated in the war crimes (Lifton, 1986). Adolf Eichmann, one of the most notorious of the Nazi war criminals, was described by his interrogator as "utterly ordinary" (Arendt, 1963; Von Lang & Sibyll, 1983). Second, the monstrous events of World War II do not stand alone in modern history. American Lieutenant Colonel Oliver North also used the defense of obedience when he defended his illegal actions in the Iran-contra scandal by claiming that "I was a pawn in a chess game being played by giants." So did Ingo Heinrich and other East German border guards who, in 1989, shot people trying to escape in the weeks before the Berlin Wall came tumbling down. Today, crimes of obedience are committed routinely in the service of totalitarian regimes around the world (Kelman & Hamilton, 1989). On one extraordinary occasion, obedi-

At the War Crimes Trials in Nuremburg, key Nazi officials testified that they had been only "following orders" when they participated in heinous war activities. Unfortunately, history holds numerous examples of obedience to powerful authority, even when it is corrupt or cruel.

ence was carried to its limit. In 1978, nine hundred members of the People's Temple cult obeyed an order from the Reverend Jim Jones that they commit suicide.

Milgram's Research: Forces of Destructive Obedience

During the time that Eichmann was being tried for his Nazi war crimes, Stanley Milgram (1963, 1965) began a dramatic series of experiments that culminated in his 1974 book, *Obedience to Authority*. For many years, the ethics of this research have been the focus of much debate. Those who believe it was not ethical point to the potential psychological harm to which the subjects were exposed. In contrast, those who believe that Milgram's research met appropriate ethical standards emphasize the contribution it makes to our understanding of an important social problem. They conclude that, on balance, the extreme danger that destructive obedience poses for all humankind justified Milgram's unorthodox methods. Consider both sides of the debate, which were summarized in Chapter 1, and make your own judgment. For now, however, take a more personal look. Imagine yourself as one of the approximately 1,000 subjects who found themselves in the following situation.

The experience begins when you arrive at a Yale University laboratory and meet two men. One is the experimenter, a stern young man dressed in a gray lab coat and carrying a clipboard. The other is a middle-aged gentleman named Mr. Wallace, an accountant who is slightly overweight but average in appearance. You exchange introductions, and then the experimenter explains that you and your co-subject will take part in a study on the effects of punishment on learning. After drawing lots, it is determined that you will serve as the teacher and that Mr. Wallace will be the learner. So far so good.

Soon, however, the situation takes on a more ominous tone. You find out that your job is to test the learner's memory and administer electric shocks of increasing intensity whenever he makes a mistake. You are then escorted into another room where the experimenter straps Mr. Wallace into a chair, rolls up his sleeves, attaches electrodes to his arms, and applies "electrode paste" to prevent blisters and burns. As if that isn't bad enough, you overhear Mr. Wallace telling the experimenter that he has a heart problem. The experimenter responds by conceding that the shocks will be painful but reassures Mr. Wallace that they will not cause "permanent tissue damage." In the meantime, you can personally vouch for the painfulness of the shocks, because the experimenter stings you with one that is supposed to be mild. From there, the experimenter takes you back to the main room, where you are seated in front of a "Shock Generator," a machine with thirty switches that range from 15 volts, labeled "slight shock," to 450 volts, labeled "XXX."

Your role in this experiment is straightforward. First you read a list of word pairs to Mr. Wallace through a microphone. Then you test his memory with a

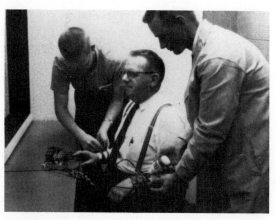

The shock generator used in Milgram's research is similar to the machine used in studies of aggression described in Chapter 8. The subjects in Milgram's study were instructed to administer shocks of increasing intensity to Mr. Wallace, the confederate being strapped into his chair.

series of multiple-choice questions. The learner answers each question by pressing one of four switches that light up signals on the shock generator. If his answer is correct, you move on to the next question. If it is incorrect, you announce the correct answer and shock him. When you press the appropriate shock switch, a red light flashes above it, relay switches click inside the machine, and you hear a loud buzzing sound go off in the learner's room. After each wrong answer, you are told, the intensity of the shock should be increased by 15 volts.

You aren't aware, of course, that the experiment is rigged and that Mr. Wallace—who is actually a confederate—is never really shocked. As far as you know, he gets zapped each time you press one of the switches. As the session proceeds, the learner makes more and more errors, leading you to work your way up the shock scale. As you reach 75, 90, and 105 volts, you hear the learner grunt in pain. At 120 volts, he begins to shout. If you're still in it at 150 volts, you hear the learner cry out, "Experimenter! That's all. Get me out of here. My heart's starting to bother me now. I refuse to go on!" Screams of agony and protest continue. At 300 volts, he says he absolutely refuses to continue. By the time you surpass 330 volts, the learner falls silent and fails to respond—not to be heard from again.

Somewhere along the line, you probably turn to the experimenter for guidance. What should I do? Don't you think I should stop? Shouldn't we at least check on him? You might even confront the experimenter head-on and refuse to continue. Yet in answer to your inquiries, the experimenter—firm in his tone and seemingly unaffected by the learner's distress—prods you along as follows:

- Please continue (or please go on).
- The experiment requires that you continue.
- It is absolutely essential that you continue.
- You have no other choice, you *must* go on.

Do you go on? In a situation that more and more begins to feel like a bad dream, do you follow your conscience or obey the experimenter?

Milgram described this procedure to groups of psychiatrists, college students, and middle-class adults, and he asked them to predict how they would behave. On average, these people estimated that they would call it quits at the 135-volt level. Not a single person thought he or she would go all the way to 450 volts. When asked to predict the percentage of *other* people who would deliver the maximum shock, those interviewed gave similar estimates. The psychiatrists estimated that only one out of a thousand subjects would exhibit that kind of extreme obedience. They were wrong. In Milgram's initial study involving forty men from the surrounding New Haven community, subjects exhibited an alarming degree of obedience, administering an average of twenty-seven out of thirty possible shocks. In fact, twenty-six of the forty subjects—*65 percent*—delivered the ultimate punishment of 450 volts. These grim results are shown in Figure 9.6.

The Obedient Subject   At first glance, it is easy to view these results as a lesson in the psychology of cruelty and conclude that Milgram's subjects were seriously disturbed (Bierbrauer, 1979; Safer, 1980). But research does not support such a simple explanation. To begin with, subjects in a control group, who were not prodded along by an experimenter, refused to continue early in the shock sequence. Moreover, Milgram found that virtually all experimental subjects, including those who administered severe shocks, were tormented by the experience. Many of them pleaded with the experimenter to let them stop. When he refused, they went on. But in the process, they trembled, stuttered, groaned, perspired, bit their lips, and dug their fingernails into their flesh. Some subjects burst into fits of nervous laughter. On one occasion, said Milgram, "we observed a [subject's] seizure so violently convulsive that it was necessary to call a halt to the experiment" (1963, p. 375).

Was Milgram's 65 percent baseline level of obedience attributable to his unique sample of male subjects? Not at all. Forty women who participated in a later study exhibited precisely the same level of obedience: 65 percent threw the 450-volt switch. Before you jump to the conclusion that something was amiss in New Haven, Milgram's basic finding has been obtained in several different countries and with children as well as college students and older adults (Shanab & Yahya, 1977, 1978). Obedience in the Milgram situation is so universal that it led one author to ask, "Are we all Nazis?" (Askenasy, 1978).

The answer, of course, is no. An individual's character can make a difference, and some people, depending on the situation, are more obedient than others (Blass, 1991). In the aftermath of World War II, a group of social scientists,

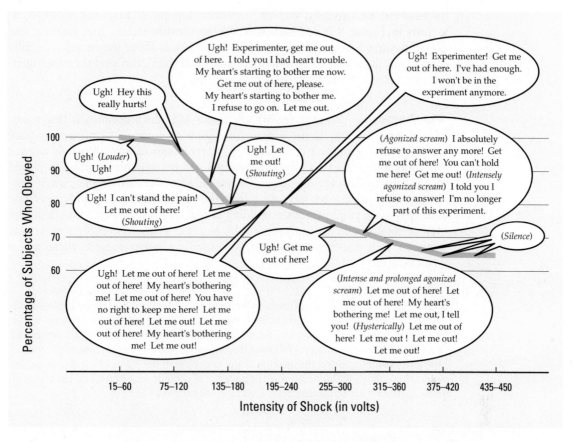

Figure 9.6 Milgram's Basic Results. As Milgram's subjects administered progressively more intense shocks, they heard the learner moan, groan, and protest before falling silent and ceasing to respond. Still, they exhibited a troubling inclination to obey. This graph shows the percentage of male subjects who delivered shocks of maximum intensity in response to the experimenter's commands. [From Milgram, 1974.]

searching for the root causes of prejudice, sought to identify individuals with an *authoritarian personality* and developed a questionnaire known as the F-Scale to measure it (Adorno et al., 1950; see Chapter 4). What they found is that people who get high scores on the F-Scale (F stands for "Fascist") are rigid, dogmatic, sexually repressed, ethnocentric, intolerant of dissent, and punitive. They are submissive toward figures of authority but aggressive toward subordinates. Indeed, subjects with high F scores are also more willing than low scorers to administer high-intensity shocks in Milgram's obedience situation (Elms & Milgram, 1966).

Although personality may make a person vulnerable or resistant to destructive obedience, what seems to matter most is the situation in which people find themselves. By carefully varying particular aspects of his basic scenario, as shown in Figure 9.7, Milgram was able to identify factors that increase and decrease the 65 percent baseline rate of obedience. Three factors are especially important: the authority figure, the proximity of the victim, and the experimental procedure (Miller, 1986).

The Authority   What is remarkable about Milgram's findings is that a lab-coated experimenter is *not* a powerful figure of authority. Unlike a military superior or an employer, a psychology experimenter cannot ultimately enforce his commands. Still, his physical presence and his apparent legitimacy played major roles in drawing obedience. When Milgram diminished the experimenter's status by moving his laboratory from the distinguished surroundings of Yale University to a rundown office building in nearby Bridgeport, Connecticut, the rate of total obedience dropped to 48 percent. When the experimenter was replaced with an ordinary person, supposedly another subject, there was a

---

Figure 9.7   Factors That Influence Obedience.   Milgram varied many factors in his research program. Without commands from an experimenter, less than 3 percent of the subjects exhibited full obedience. Yet in the standard baseline condition, 65 percent of both male and female subjects followed the orders. To identify factors that might reduce this level, Milgram varied the location of the experiment, the status of the authority, the subject's proximity to the victim, and the presence of confederates who rebel. The effects of these variations are illustrated here. [Data from Milgram, 1974.]

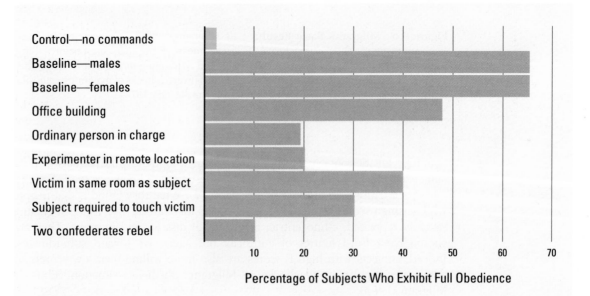

"Nice touch, Jenkins. I like a man who salutes."

People are often obedient in the presence of powerful figures of authority. [Drawing by Woodman; © 1979 The New Yorker Magazine, Inc.]

dramatic reduction to 20 percent. Similarly, Milgram found that when the experimenter was in charge but issued his commands by telephone, only 21 percent of the subjects fully obeyed. In fact, when the experimenter was not watching, many subjects feigned obedience by pressing the 15-volt switch. One conclusion, then, is clear. At least in the Milgram setting, destructive obedience required the physical presence of an authority figure.

If an experimenter can exert such control over research subjects, imagine the control wielded by truly powerful figures of authority—present or not. An intriguing field study examined the extent to which nurses would obey unreasonable orders from a doctor (Hofling et al., 1966). A male physician using a fictitious name called several female nurses on the phone and told them to administer a drug to a specific patient. His order violated hospital regulations: the drug was uncommon; the dosage was too large; and the effects could have been harmful. Yet out of twenty-two nurses contacted, twenty-one of them had to be stopped as they prepared to obey the doctor's orders.

The Victim Situational characteristics of the victim are also important in destructive obedience. Milgram noted that Nazi war criminal Adolf Eichmann felt sick when he toured concentration camps but only had to shuffle papers from behind a desk to fulfill his role in the Holocaust. Similarly, the B-29 pilot who dropped the atom bomb on Hiroshima in World War II said of his mission, "I had no thoughts, except what I'm supposed to do" (Miller, 1986, p. 228). These events suggest that because Milgram's subjects were physically separated from the learner, they were able to distance themselves emotionally from the consequences of their actions.

To examine the effects of a victim's proximity on destructive obedience, the learner in one of Milgram's studies was seated in the same room as the subject. Under these conditions, only 40 percent fully obeyed. When subjects were required to physically grasp the victim's hand and force it onto a metal shock plate, full obedience dropped to 30 percent. These findings represent significant reductions from the 65 percent baseline. Still, three out of ten subjects were willing to use brute force in the name of obedience.

The Procedure   Finally, there is the situation created by Milgram. A close look at the dilemma his subjects experienced reveals two particularly important aspects of the experimental procedure. First, subjects were led to feel relieved of any personal sense of *responsibility* for the victim's welfare. The experimenter said up front that he was accountable. Indeed, when subjects are led to believe that *they* are responsible, their level of obedience drops considerably (Tilker, 1970). The ramifications of this finding are immense. In military and other organizations, individuals often occupy positions in the middle of a hierarchical chain of command. Eichmann, for example, was a middle-level bureaucrat who received orders from Hitler and transmitted them to others for implementation. Caught between individuals who make policy and those who carry it out, how personally responsible do those in the middle feel for their role in the chain of events? Wesley Kilham and Leon Mann (1974) examined this issue in an obedience study that cast subjects into one of two roles: the transmitter (who took orders from the experimenter and passed them on) and the executant (who actually delivered the shocks). As predicted, transmitters were more obedient (54 percent) than executants (28 percent).

The second feature of Milgram's scenario that promotes obedience is gradual escalation. Subjects began the experiment by delivering mild shocks and then, only gradually, escalated to voltage levels of high intensity. After all, what's another 15 volts compared to the current level? By the time subjects realize the frightening implications of what they're doing, it has become more and more difficult for them to escape (Gilbert, 1981). This sequence is like the foot-in-the-door technique. In Milgram's words, people become "integrated into a situation that carries its own momentum. The subject's problem . . . is how to become disengaged from a situation which is moving in an altogether ugly direction" (1965, p. 73). We should point out that obedience by momentum is not restricted to Milgram's research paradigm. According to Amnesty International, at least ninety countries today torture political dissidents. Those who are recruited for the dirty work are trained, in part, through an escalating series of commitments (Haritos-Fatouros, 1988).

Administrative Obedience

Obedience to authority is a social issue of such importance that one wonders whether Milgram's results would be repeated in a different but analogous situation. In a series of experiments, Dutch social psychologists Wim Meeus and Quinten Raaijmakers (1986) constructed a moral dilemma much like Milgram's. Rather than commanding subjects to inflict physical pain, however, they engaged subjects in what they called *administrative obedience*—behavior intended to cause psychological harm.

When subjects arrived at a university laboratory, they met a man—actually a confederate—who was there to take a test as part of a job interview. If the applicant passed the test, he would get the job; if he failed, he would not. Supposedly without the applicant's knowledge, the experimenter told subjects that he was interested in the ability to work under stress. The subject's task was to read various test questions to the applicant, over a microphone from a nearby room, and to programmatically harass the applicant by making an escalating series of negative remarks. As the applicant worked on the test, then, subjects made statements such as "If you continue like this, you will fail the test," and "This job is much too difficult for you. You are more suited for lower functions."

As the events proceeded, the applicant protested the distractions. He pleaded with the subject to stop making him nervous, then angrily refused to tolerate the treatment, and eventually fell into a state of despair. Showing visible signs of tension, the applicant faltered in his test performance and, in the end, failed to get the job. As in Milgram's research, the question of obedience was straightforward: How many subjects would obey the experimenter's orders through the entire set of fifteen stress remarks, despite the apparent harm caused to a real-life applicant? In a control group that lacked a prodding experimenter, not a single subject persisted. But when the experimenter ordered subjects to go on, 92 percent of all subjects, male and female alike, exhibited complete obedience—even though they considered the task unfair and distasteful.

In a variation of their procedure, Meeus and Raaijmakers (1987) sent fifteen subjects a letter before their participation, forewarning them about what they would be asked to do. These prospective subjects were thus prepared for the possibility that their actions could make a job applicant so tense that he fails to pass the critical test. Distanced from the momentum and pressure of the experimental situation, these subjects had ample opportunity to consider the task and back out. Yet this condition produced a 100 percent rate of obedience! This result led the investigators to conclude that obedience is a compelling social phenomenon brought about by the docile manner in which people relate to figures of authority—"even in the Netherlands in the 1980's."

Defiance: When People Rebel

It is easy to despair in light of the impressive array of forces that compel people toward blind obedience. But there's good news, as illustrated by the failed coup attempt in the former Soviet Union. Just as social influence processes can breed subservience to authority, they can also breed defiance and rebellion. As suggested by the following study, the actions of an interacting group are often much harder to control than the behavior of a single individual.

Pretending to be part of a marketing research firm, William Gamson and his colleagues (1982) recruited people to participate in a supposed discussion of "community standards." Scheduled in groups of nine, subjects were told that their discussions would be videotaped for a large oil company that was suing the manager of a local service station who had spoken out against higher gas prices. After receiving a summary of the case, most subjects sided with the station manager. But there was a hitch. The oil company wanted evidence to win its case, said the experimenter—posing as the discussion coordinator. He then told each of the group members to get in front of the camera and express the company's viewpoint against the station manager. In addition, he told them to sign an affidavit giving the company permission to edit the tapes for use in court.

You can see how the obedience scenario was supposed to unfold. Actually, only one of thirty-three groups even came close to following the script. In all the others, people became incensed by the coordinator's behavior and refused to continue. Some groups were so outraged that they planned to take action. One group even threatened to blow the whistle on the firm by calling local newspapers. Faced with one emotionally charged mutiny after another, the researchers had to discontinue the experiment.

Why did this study produce such active, often passionate revolt when Milgram's had revealed such utterly passive obedience? Could the reason be the difference between the 1960s, when Milgram's research was conducted, and the 1980s? Are people more assertive or more principled than they used to be? Although many college students believe that people would conform less today than in the past, there is no relationship between the year a study was conducted and the level of obedience it produced (Blass & Krackow, 1991). So what accounts for the opposite results? One very important difference is that Milgram's subjects were all alone, whereas Gamson's were in groups. As historian Michael Walzer notes, "Disobedience, when it is not criminally but morally, religiously, or politically motivated, is always a *collective* act" (1970, cited in R. Brown, 1986, p. 17).

The earlier discussion of conformity indicated that the mere presence of one ally in an otherwise unanimous majority gives individuals the courage to dissent. Perhaps the same holds true for obedience. Notably, Milgram never had more than one subject present in the same session. But in one experiment, he did use two confederates who posed as co-teachers along with the real subject. In these sessions, one confederate refused to continue at 150 volts and the second at 210 volts. These disobedient models had a profound influence on subjects' willingness to defy the experimenter; in their presence only 10 percent of subjects delivered the maximum level of shock (see Figure 9.7). A similar result was obtained in a follow-up of the study on obedience in a hospital setting. Recall that in a study described earlier, twenty-one out of twenty-two nurses were prepared to obey an unfamiliar physician whose order violated

People are more likely to protest the command of authority in groups than on their own. In August of 1991, crowds gathered in the streets of Moscow to resist an attempted coup by hard-line communists. Despite a history of passive obedience, the Russians shown in this picture jeered the troops and blocked their tanks. Finding safety and encouragement in numbers, their efforts prevailed.

hospital policy (Hofling et al., 1966). These nurses never had a chance to consult with others. Yet in a second study, in which subjects could contact their supervisors and talk with other nurses, only two out of eighteen were willing to follow orders (Rank & Jacobson, 1977).

We should hasten to add that groups are by no means a perfect safeguard against destructive obedience. Groups often trigger aggression, as we'll see in Chapter 11. Indeed, the nine hundred followers of Jim Jones were together when they collectively followed his command to die. And lynch mobs are just that—groups, not lone individuals. Clearly, there is power in sheer numbers. That power can be destructive, or it can be used for constructive purposes. The presence and support of others often provides that extra ounce of courage that people need to resist orders they find offensive.

THE CONTINUUM OF SOCIAL INFLUENCE

As we have seen, social influence on behavior ranges from the implicit pressure of group norms, to the traps set by direct requests, to the powerful commands of authority. In each case, people choose whether to react with conformity or independence, compliance or assertiveness, obedience or defiance. At this point, let's step back and consider two important questions. First, although different kinds of pressure influence us for different reasons, is it possible to predict all the effects with a single, overarching principle? Second, what do theory and research on social influence say about human nature?

Social Impact Theory

social impact theory
The theory that social influence depends on the strength, immediacy, and number of source persons relative to target persons.

In 1981, Bibb Latané proposed that a common bond among the different processes leads people toward or away from social influence. Specifically, Latané proposed **social impact theory**, which states that social influence of any kind—that is, the total impact of others on a target person—is a function of their strength, immediacy, and number. According to Latané, social forces act on individuals in the same way that physical forces act on an object. Consider, for example, how overhead lights illuminate a surface. The total amount of light cast on a surface depends on the strength of the bulbs, their distance from the surface, and their number. As illustrated in the left portion of Figure 9.8, the same factors apply to social impact as well.

The *strength* of a source is determined by its status, ability, or relationship to a target. The stronger the source, the greater is the influence. When people view the other members of a group as highly competent, they are more likely to conform in their judgments. When it comes to compliance, sources enhance their strength by making targets feel obligated to reciprocate a small favor. To elicit obedience, authority figures gain strength by wearing uniforms or by flaunting prestigious affiliations. *Immediacy* refers to a source's proximity in time and space to the target. The closer the source, the greater is its impact. Milgram's research offers the best example. Levels of obedience were higher when the experimenter issued commands in person rather than from a remote location. When the victim suffered in close proximity to the subject, the victim acted as a contrary source of influence, and obedience levels dropped. Finally, the theory predicts that as the *number* of sources increases, so does their influence—at least up to a point. You may recall that as Asch (1956) increased the number of confederates from one to four, conformity rose. Further increases, however, had only a negligible additional effect.

Social impact theory also predicts that people sometimes resist social pressure. According to Latané, this resistance is most likely to occur when social impact is *divided* among many strong and distant *targets*, also as seen in the right part of Figure 9.8. There should be less impact on a target who is strong and far from the source than on one who is weak and close to the source; and there should be less impact on a target person who is accompanied by other targets than on one who stands alone. Thus, we have seen that conformity is reduced by the presence of an ally and that levels of obedience drop when subjects are in the presence of rebellious peers.

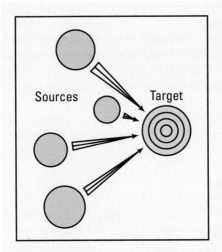 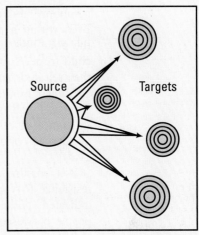

Figure 9.8   Social Impact: Source Factors and Target Factors. According to social impact theory, the total influence of other people on a target individual depends on three factors related to the source persons: their strength (size of source circles), immediacy (distance between source circles and the target), and number (number of source circles). As these factors increase, so does social influence. In addition, the total influence of other people on target individuals is diffused, or reduced, by three factors related to the target persons: their strength (size of target circles), immediacy (distance from source circle), and number (number of target circles). As these factors increase, social influence diminishes. [From Latané, 1981.]

Social impact theory has been challenged and defended on various grounds (Jackson, 1986; Mullen, 1985; Sedikides & Jackson, 1990). On the one hand, it does not enable us to explain the processes that give rise to social influence and does not answer *why* questions. On the other hand, social impact theory is extremely useful for predicting social influence—to determine *when* it will occur. Whether the topic is conformity, compliance, or obedience, social impact theory sets the stage for further research in the years to come.

Perspectives on Human Nature

From the material presented in this chapter, what general conclusions might you draw about human nature? Granted, social influence is more likely to occur in some situations than in others. But are people generally malleable or unyielding? Is there a tilt toward accepting influence or toward resistance?

There is no single, universal answer. As we saw earlier, some cultures value autonomy and independence; others emphasize conformity to one's group. Even within a given culture, values may change over time. To demonstrate the point, ask yourself: If you were a parent, what traits would you like your child to develop? When this question was put to American mothers in 1924, they selected "strict obedience" and "loyalty," key characteristics of conformity. Yet when mothers were asked the same question fifty-four years later, the emphasis had shifted noticeably in the direction of "independence" and "tolerance of others," key characteristics of autonomy. Similar trends appear in surveys conducted in West Germany, Italy, England, and Japan (Remley, 1988).

Is it possible that today's children—tomorrow's adults—will exhibit greater resistance to various forms of social influence? Were these changing values indicated, perhaps, by the surprising resistance to the coup shown by the people of Moscow and the subsequent breaking up of the Soviet Union into independent republics? Will there be other observable changes in behavior? If so, what effects will this trend have on society as a whole? Cast in a positive light, conformity, compliance, and obedience are desirable and necessary human responses. They promote unity, harmony, group solidarity, and agreement—qualities that keep groups from being torn apart by dissension. Cast in a negative light, a lack of independence, assertiveness, and defiance are undesirable behaviors that lend themselves to narrow-mindedness, cowardice, and destructive obedience—often with terrible costs. Somehow, a balance must be struck.

REVIEW

Conformity, compliance, and obedience represent three kinds of social influence, varying in the degree of pressure each brings to bear on an individual.

CONFORMITY

Conformity is the tendency for people to change their behavior to be consistent with group norms.

The Early Classics

Two classic experiments illustrate two types of conformity. Relying on the autokinetic effect, Sherif presented groups of subjects with an ambiguous task and found that their judgments gradually converged. Using a simpler line judgment task, Asch had groups of confederates make several incorrect responses and found that subjects went along about a third of the time.

Why Do People Conform?

Sherif found that people exhibit private conformity, using others for information on correct judgments in an ambiguous situation. In contrast, Asch's studies indicated that when people want to avoid appearing deviant, they conform in their public behavior.

Majority Influence

As the size of an incorrect unanimous majority increases, so does conformity—up to a point. People conform most when social norms are salient. However, the presence of a single dissenter reduces conformity dramatically, even when the dissenter disagrees with the subject and lacks competence at the task. Young adolescents are particularly vulnerable to peer pressure. Also, women conform more than men on "masculine" tasks and in face-to-face settings, but not on gender-neutral tasks or in more private settings.

Minority Influence

Sometimes minorities resist pressures to conform and are able to influence majorities. According to Moscovici, minorities exert influence by taking a consistent, unwavering position while appearing flexible in their style. Unless a dissenter is seen as biased, imbalanced, or rigid, consistency breeds influence. As an alternative, Hollander claims that to exert influence, a person should first conform to the group, earn "idiosyncrasy credits," and then dissent. Either way, it appears that majority influence is greater on direct, public measures of conformity but minorities have an impact on private, indirect measures of conformity. People gain courage to resist conformity pressures after watching others do the same.

COMPLIANCE

Perhaps the most common form of social influence occurs when we respond to direct requests.

The Discourse of Making Requests

People are more likely to comply with a request when they are taken by surprise and when the request *sounds* reasonable, even though it may offer no real reason for compliance.

The Norm of Reciprocity

We often comply when we feel indebted because the person making a request has done us a favor. People differ in the extent to which they use reciprocity for personal gain and in the extent to which they are wary of falling prey to such strategies.

Setting Traps: Sequential Request Strategies

Four compliance techniques are based on a two-step request: the first sets a trap; the second elicits compliance. In the foot-in-the-door technique, a "real" request is prefaced by first getting someone to comply with a much smaller request. People then try to be consistent with their new self-perception. In low-balling, one person gets another to agree to a request but then increases the size of that request by revealing hidden costs. Despite the increase, people feel committed to the deal and to the requester and maintain their agreement. In the door-in-the-face technique, the real request is preceded by a large request. After rejecting the first, people are likely to comply with the second because it seems small in comparison and is seen as a concession to be reciprocated. Finally, the that's-not-all technique begins with a large request, and then, before the person has a chance to respond, the apparent size of the request is reduced by the offer of a discount or bonus.

Assertiveness: When People Say No
Many people find it hard to be assertive. To do so requires that we be vigilant and recognize request traps for what they are.

OBEDIENCE
When the request is a command, and the requester is a figure of authority, the resulting influence is called obedience.

Milgram's Research: Forces of Destructive Obedience
In Milgram's research, subjects were ordered by an experimenter to deliver increasingly painful shocks to a confederate. Sixty-five percent of the subjects obeyed completely but felt tormented by the experience. Although some people are more obedient than others, Milgram's results have been repeated all over the world. Obedience levels are influenced by various situational factors, including subjects' physical proximity to both the authority and the victim. In addition, two aspects of Milgram's procedure can explain the high levels of obedience. First, subjects did not feel responsible for their actions. Second, the orders escalated gradually, so subjects were swept up in the momentum of the situation.

Administrative Obedience
In a situation that is different from but analogous to Milgram's, subjects continue to exhibit high levels of obedience when told to inflict psychological harm on another person.

Defiance: When People Rebel
Just as processes of social influence can breed obedience, they can also support acts of defiance. Research suggests that groups are more difficult to control than individuals.

THE CONTINUUM OF SOCIAL INFLUENCE

Social Impact Theory
Conformity, compliance and obedience occur for many different reasons. Nevertheless, social impact theory predicts that, in all cases, social influence depends on the strength, immediacy, and number of source persons who exert pressure relative to target persons who absorb that pressure.

Perspectives on Human Nature

There is no single answer to the question of whether people are conformists or nonconformists. There are cross-cultural differences, and even within cultures, values change over time.

Attitudes | 10

Preview

This chapter examines social influences on attitudes. We define *attitudes* and discuss how they are measured and their link to behavior. Then we consider two methods of changing attitudes. First, we look at source, message, and audience factors that elicit persuasion through the media of *communication*. Second, we consider theories and research showing that people often change their attitudes as a consequence of their own *actions*.

ollege students and professors know all too well what the term PC means. Just a few years ago, these letters stood for "personal computer." Now they describe divisive feelings about "political correctness." On one side of the debate, conservatives charge that American universities discriminate against white males in student admissions, scholarships, and faculty hiring; that they are diluting the curriculum with nontraditional course requirements; and that those who dare to criticize these policies are taunted, their freedom of speech is being infringed on, and an air of censorship and intolerance is being created (D'Souza, 1991). On the other side of the debate, campus liberals argue that affirmative action is needed to rectify past injustices and to increase diversity; that the old curriculum needs to be broadened for students to meet the challenges of life in the global community; and that the harassment of women, minorities, and homosexuals is so prevalent that sensitivity and consciousness-raising exercises are sorely needed (Stimpson, 1991).

Conservatives stand on one side, liberals on the other. This division on the college campus, as in other life settings, illustrates that people have deep-seated and passionate attitudes—not just about politics and education but about environmental issues, religion, places to live, sports teams, music, consumer products, and even themselves. Attitudes and the mechanisms of persuasion, or attitude change, are a vital part of human social life. This chapter addresses three sets of questions: (1) What is an attitude, how can it be measured, and what is its link to behavior? (2) What kinds of persuasive communications lead people to change their attitudes? (3) Why do we often change our attitudes as a result of our own actions?

THE STUDY OF ATTITUDES

attitude A positive or negative reaction to a person, object, or idea.

Do you favor or oppose gun control? What about abortion? Should smoking be banned in public places? Would you rather listen to rock music or jazz, drink Coke or Pepsi, work on an IBM computer or a Mac? As these questions suggest, everyone has positive and negative reactions to various persons, objects, and ideas. These reactions are called **attitudes**. If you think about the chapters you've read, you'll realize how pervasive attitudes are: self-esteem is an attitude each of us has about ourselves; attraction is a positive attitude toward other persons; and prejudice is a negative attitude about certain groups.

In *The Psychology of Attitudes*, Alice Eagly and Shelly Chaiken (1993) note that there are two schools of thought on how the term *attitude* should be defined. One view is that an attitude is a combination of affective, behavioral, and cognitive reactions to an object (Breckler, 1984; Rajecki, 1982). In this *tricomponent* approach, an attitude is (1) a positive, negative, or mixed *affective* reaction consisting of our feelings about an object; (2) a *behavioral* predisposition, or tendency to act in a certain manner toward an object; and (3) a *cognitive* reaction in which our evaluation of an object is based on our beliefs, images, and long-term memories (Judd et al., 1991a).

Thoughts and feelings are not always related to each other, nor do they necessarily guide our behavior. Because of this lack of consistency, many social psychologists prefer to keep the three components separate and to use the term *attitude* in primarily affective terms (Petty & Cacioppo, 1986; Pratkanis, 1989; Zanna & Rempel, 1988). In this *single-component* definition, an attitude is a positive or negative evaluation, at some level of intensity, toward an object—nothing more, nothing less. "Like," "dislike," "love," "hate," "admire," and "detest" are the kinds of words people use to describe their attitudes.

How Attitudes Are Measured

In 1928, Louis Thurstone published an article called "Attitudes Can Be Measured." What he neglected to anticipate, however, is that the measurement of attitudes is tricky business. One review of the research uncovered more than five hundred different methods of determining an individual's attitude (Fishbein & Ajzen, 1972).

Self-Report Measures   The easiest way to assess a person's attitude about something is to ask. Although *self-report* is straightforward, attitudes are sometimes too complex to be measured with a single question. As recognized by public opinion pollsters, one problem is that responses to a single question can be influenced by its wording, context, and other extraneous factors. When a sample of Americans were asked about "assistance to the poor," for example, 63 percent said too little money was spent. When asked about "welfare," however, only 19 percent gave that response (Sussman, 1988). In another poll, respondents who were asked if "People should have the freedom to express their opinions publicly" were more likely to say yes if they had earlier answered a question about the Catholic church rather than about the American Nazi Party (Ottati et al., 1989). Clearly, one's response to an attitude question can be influenced by the context in which it is asked (Tourangeau et al., 1991).

Recognizing the problems with single-question measures, researchers often use multi-item questionnaires called *attitude scales* (Dawes & Smith, 1985; J. P. Robinson et al., 1991). Attitude scales come in various forms, perhaps the most popular being the *Likert Scale,* named after its inventor, Rensis Likert (1932). In this technique, subjects are presented with a list of statements on an attitude object and are asked to indicate on a multiple-point scale how strongly they agree or disagree with each statement. The person's total attitude score is derived by summing his or her responses to all the items.

Whether attitudes are measured by one question or by a full-blown scale, the results should be taken with caution. All self-report measures assume that people will express their true attitudes. Sometimes this is a reasonable assumption to make, but sometimes it is not (see Chapter 1). Wanting to make a good impression, people do not want to admit their faults and prejudices. Indeed, that's why David Duke, a former Ku Klux Klan leader who is now an ultra-conservative legislator in Louisiana, always seems to get more votes in secret-ballot elections than public opinion polls predict he will get.

Covert Measures   There are two possible solutions to the self-report problem. The first is to increase the accuracy of self-report measures. To get respondents to answer attitude questions truthfully, some researchers use the *bogus pipeline*, an elaborate mechanical device that supposedly records one's true feelings. Not wanting to get caught in a lie, subjects tend to answer attitude questions more truthfully when they think they're wired to a lie-detection device (Arkin & Lake, 1983; Jones & Sigall, 1971).

The second solution is to use indirect, covert measures. For years, social psychologists have tried to find an accurate measure of attitudes that is not based on self-reports. One possible alternative is observable behavior—such as facial expressions, tone of voice, and body language. For example, when Gary Wells and Richard Petty (1980) unobtrusively videotaped college students listening to a speech, they noticed that when the speaker took a position subjects agreed with (that tuition costs should be lowered), most students made vertical head movements. But when the speaker took a contrary position (that tuition costs be raised), head movements were in a horizontal direction. Without realizing it, subjects signaled their attitudes by nodding and shaking their heads.

Although behavior provides clues, it is far from perfect as a measure of attitudes. Sometimes we nod our heads because we agree; at other times we nod to be polite. The problem is that people monitor their overt behavior just as they monitor self-reports. But what about internal, physiological reactions that are more difficult to control? Could the body betray how we feel? In the past, researchers tried to divine attitudes from involuntary physical reactions. They measured perspiration, monitored heart rate, and observed pupil dilation. The results, however, were always the same: measures of arousal tell us the *intensity* of one's attitude toward an object but not whether that attitude is positive or negative. On the physiological record, love and hate look the same (Petty & Cacioppo, 1983).

John Cacioppo and Richard Petty (1981), however, have discovered a physiological measurement technique that is more precise: the facial electromyograph (EMG). As illustrated in Figure 10.1, different muscles in the face contract when people are happy from when they are sad. Smiling and frowning are obvious examples. But since not all muscular changes can be seen with the naked eye, the facial EMG is used. To see if the facial EMG could be used to measure the affect associated with attitudes, Cacioppo and Petty (1979) recorded subjects' facial muscle activity while they listened to a message with which they agreed or disagreed. Subjects who listened to the agreeable message exhibited a facial muscle pattern of happiness; those who heard the disagreeable message exhibited the sadness pattern. Yet outside observers who watched subjects' faces without assistance were unable to see these subtle changes. Research shows that

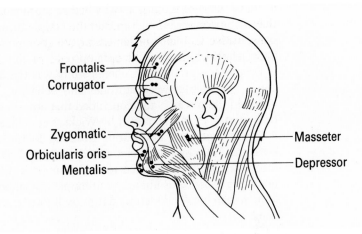

Figure 10.1   The Facial EMG: A Covert Measure of Attitudes.   The facial EMG makes it possible to detect differences between positive and negative attitudes. Notice the major facial muscles and recording sites for electrodes. When people hear a message with which they agree rather than disagree, there is a relative increase in EMG activity in the depressor and zygomatic muscles but a relative decrease in the corrugator and frontalis muscles. These changes cannot be seen with the naked eye. [From Cacioppo & Petty, 1981.]

the facial EMG can monitor the intensity as well as the direction of an attitude (Cacioppo et al., 1986).

The Link Between Attitudes and Behavior

People take for granted the statement that attitudes influence behavior. It is natural to assume that voters' opinions of opposing candidates predict their selection on election day, that consumers' attitudes toward competing products influence the purchases they make, and that feelings of prejudice give rise to discrimination. As sensible as these assumptions seem, however, the link between attitudes and behavior is far from automatic.

Sociologist Richard LaPiere (1934) was the first to notice that attitudes and behavior don't always go hand in hand. In the 1930s, LaPiere took a young Chinese couple on a three-month, 10,000-mile automobile trip, visiting 250 restaurants, hotels, and campgrounds throughout the United States. Although prejudice against Asians was widespread at the time, the couple was refused service only once. Yet when LaPiere wrote back to the places they had visited and asked if they would accept Chinese patrons, more than 90 percent of those who returned an answer said they would not. Self-reported attitudes did not correspond with behavior.

This study was provocative but seriously flawed. LaPiere measured attitudes several months after his trip, and during that time the attitudes may have changed. He also did not know whether those who responded to his letter were the same people who had greeted the couple in person. It is even possible that the Chinese couple was served wherever they went only because they were accompanied by LaPiere himself.

Despite the problems, LaPiere's study was the first of many to find a lack of correspondence between attitudes and behavior. Then in 1969, Allan Wicker reviewed the research and concluded that attitudes are correlated with behavior only weakly, if at all. Sobered by Wicker's conclusion, researchers were puzzled: Is it really possible that voting does *not* follow from political opinions, that consumer purchasing is *not* based on attitudes toward a product, or that discrimination is *not* related to underlying prejudice? Is the study of attitudes useless to those of us interested in human social behavior? No, not at all. Before long, researchers had identified the conditions under which attitudes do forecast behavior.

Putting Attitudes in Context   One key factor is the level of *correspondence,* or similarity, between attitude measures and behavior. Perhaps the reason that LaPiere (1934) did not find a correlation between self-reported prejudice and overt discrimination was that he had asked proprietors about Asians in general but then observed their behavior toward only one couple. To predict a specific act of discrimination, he should have measured people's more specific attitudes toward a young, well-dressed, attractive Chinese couple accompanied by an American professor.

Analyzing more than a hundred studies, Icek Ajzen and Martin Fishbein (1977) found that attitudes correlate with behavior only when attitude measures closely match the behavior in question. Illustrating the point, Andrew Davidson and James Jaccard (1979) tried to use attitudes to predict whether women would use birth control pills within the next two years. Attitudes were measured in a series of questions ranging from very general ("How do you feel about birth control?") to very specific ("How do you feel about using birth control pills during the next two years?"). The more specific the initial attitude question was, the better it predicted the behavior.

The link between our feelings and our actions should also be placed within a broader context. Attitudes are one determinant of social behavior, but there are many other determinants as well. This limitation formed the basis for Fishbein's (1980) *theory of reasoned action,* which Ajzen (1991) then expanded and called the **theory of planned behavior**. This theory states that attitudes influence behavior through a process of deliberate decision making and that their impact is limited in four respects (see Figure 10.2).

First, as we just described, behavior is influenced less by general attitudes than by attitudes toward a specific behavior. Second, behavior is influenced not only by attitudes but by *subjective norms*—our beliefs about what others think we should do. As we saw in Chapter 9, social pressures toward conformity, compliance, and obedience often lead us to behave in ways that are at odds with our inner convictions. Third, attitudes give rise to behavior only when we

theory of planned behavior   The theory that attitudes toward a specific behavior combine with subjective norms and perceived control to influence a person's action.

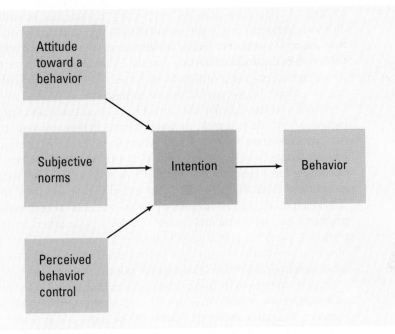

Figure 10.2 Theory of Planned Behavior. According to the theory of planned behavior, attitudes toward a specific behavior combine with subjective norms and perceived control to influence a person's intentions. These intentions, in turn, guide but do not completely determine behavior. As you can see, this theory places the link between attitudes and behavior within a broader context. [Based on Ajzen, 1991.]

perceive the behavior to be within our *control*. To the extent that people lack confidence in their ability to engage in some behavior, they are unlikely to form an intention to do so. Fourth, although attitudes—along with subjective norms and perceived control—contribute to an *intention* to behave in a particular manner, people often do not or cannot follow through on their intentions.

A good deal of research supports the theories of reasoned action and planned behavior (Ajzen & Madden, 1986; Fishbein & Stasson, 1990; Madden et al., 1992). Indeed, this general approach—that is, placing the link between attitudes and behavior into a broader context—has successfully been used to predict a wide range of behaviors such as losing weight, donating blood, exercising, smoking, attending church, shoplifting, voting, and choosing an occupation (Sheppard et al., 1988).

Strength of the Attitude According to the theory of planned behavior, specific attitudes combine with social factors to produce behavior. Sometimes attitudes have greater influence on behavior than do these other factors;

sometimes they have less. In large part, it depends on the *strength* of the attitude. Everyone has some attitudes that are nearer and dearer to the heart than others. Computer jocks, for instance, often form strong attachments to IBM, Apple, or other competing brands. Political activists have fiery passions for one political party over others. In each case, the attitude is held with confidence and is difficult to change (Schuman & Johnson, 1976).

Several factors indicate the strength of an attitude and its correlation with behavior (Petty & Krosnick, in press). One is that people tend to behave in ways that are consistent with attitudes when they are well informed. In one study, college students were asked which of two candidates they preferred in an upcoming local election for mayor. Those who knew a lot about the campaign issues were later the most likely to actually vote for their favored candidate (Davidson et al., 1985). In another study, students were questioned about their positions on environmental issues and later were asked to take action—sign petitions, participate in a recycling project, and so on. Once again, the more informed the students were, the more consistent their environmental attitudes were with their behavior (Kallgren & Wood, 1986).

Second, the strength of an attitude is indicated not only by the amount of information on which it is based but also by how that information was acquired. Research shows that attitudes are more stable and more predictive of behavior when they are formed through direct personal experience than when they are based on indirect, secondhand information. In a series of experiments, for example, Russell Fazio and Mark Zanna (1981) introduced two groups of subjects to a set of puzzles. One group actually worked on sample puzzles; the other group watched someone else work with them. Subjects then reported their interest in the puzzles (attitude) and were given an opportunity to spend time working on them (behavior). As it turned out, attitudes and behavior were more consistent among the subjects who had previously sampled the puzzles. Attitudes born of direct experience are especially hard to change (Wu & Shaffer, 1987).

A third factor related to attitude strength is that strongly held attitudes are highly *accessible* to awareness, which means they are quickly and easily brought to mind (Fazio, 1990). To return to our earlier examples, computer jocks think often about their computer preferences, and political activists think often about their party allegiances. It turns out that many of our attitudes—not just those that are passionately held—are easily brought to mind by the mere sight or mention of the attitude object (Bargh et al., 1992). Weak attitudes are usually not as accessible, though situational factors may bring them to the surface. Attitudes thus correlate with behavior when people are questioned about their attitudes over and over again (Powell & Fazio, 1984), when they become self-focused by staring into a mirror (Gibbons, 1978), or when they overhear others discussing the attitude issue (Borgida & Campbell, 1982).

To summarize, recent research on the link between attitudes and behavior leads to an important conclusion. Our feelings toward an object do not always determine our actions because other factors must be taken into account.

However, when attitudes are strong and specific to a particular behavior, their effects are beyond dispute. Under these conditions, voting *is* motivated by political opinions, consumer purchasing *is* affected by product attitudes, and racial discrimination *is* rooted in feelings of prejudice. Attitudes are important determinants of behavior. The question now is, how are these attitudes changed?

PERSUASION BY COMMUNICATION

On a day-to-day basis, we are all involved in the process of changing attitudes. Advertisers flood consumers with images and slogans in order to sell cars, soft drinks, laundry detergents, and computers. Similarly, politicians make speeches, pass out bumper stickers, kiss babies, and follow public opinion polls to win votes. Indeed, attitude change is sought whenever parents socialize children, or scientists advance theories, or religious groups seek converts, or trial lawyers argue cases in front of a jury. Some appeals work; others do not. Some are coercive; others are subtle. Some serve the public interest; others serve personal interests. The point is, there is nothing inherently virtuous or evil about changing attitudes, or **persuasion**. We do it all the time.

persuasion The process of changing attitudes.

If you wanted to change someone's attitude, you would probably try making a persuasive *communication*. Appeals made in person and through the mass media rely on the spoken word, the written word, and the picture that is worth a thousand words. What determines whether an appeal succeeds or fails? Does a speaker's physical appearance matter? Is it more effective to use logical reasoning or propaganda aimed at primitive emotions? Are some people more difficult to influence than others? To understand why certain approaches work while others do not, or why a certain technique works on one occasion but not on another, we need to know *how* and *why* persuasive communications achieve their results. For that, we need a road map of the persuasion process.

Two Routes to Persuasion

It's a familiar scene in American politics: every four years, presidential candidates launch extensive campaigns for office. In a way, if you've seen one election, you've seen them all. The names and dates may change, but over and over again opposing candidates accuse each other of ducking the issues and turning the election into a flag-waving, slogan-chanting popularity contest. Whether or not the accusations are true, they illustrate that politicians are keenly aware that they can win votes through two completely different methods. They can stick to the issues, or they can base their appeals on other grounds.

To account for these alternative approaches, Richard Petty and John Cacioppo (1986) propose a dual-process model of persuasion. This model is based on the

**central route to per-
suasion** The process
in which a person
learns and thinks
carefully about a com-
munication and is
influenced by the
strength of its argu-
ments.

**peripheral route to
persuasion** The
process in which a
person does not think
carefully about a com-
munication and is
influenced instead by
cues that are periph-
eral to the message.

assumption that we do not always process communications the same way. When
people think carefully about the contents of a message, they take a **central
route to persuasion** and are influenced by the strength and quality of the
arguments. When people do not think carefully about the contents of a message
but focus instead on other cues, they take a **peripheral route to persuasion**.
As we'll see, the route taken depends on whether people are willing and able to
think carefully about the information contained within the message itself.

The Central Route   In the first systematic attempt to study persuasion, Carl
Hovland and his colleagues (1949, 1953) started the Yale Communication and
Attitude Change Program. They proposed that for a persuasive message to have
influence, the receivers of that message must be motivated to accept it, but first
they must learn its contents. According to this view, we can be persuaded only
by arguments we attend to, comprehend, and retain in memory. Whether we
are talking about a personal appeal, a newspaper editorial, a sermon, or a TV
commercial, these basic requirements remain the same.

Several years later, William McGuire (1968, 1969) reiterated the information-processing steps necessary for persuasion and, like the Yale group before
him, distinguished between the learning or *reception* of a message, a necessary
first step, and its subsequent *acceptance*. In fact, he used this distinction to
explain the surprising finding that a receiver's self-esteem and intelligence are
unrelated to persuasion. In McGuire's scheme, these characteristics have opposite effects on reception and acceptance. People who are smart or high in
self-esteem are better able to learn a message but are less likely to accept its call
for a change in attitude. People who are less smart or low in self-esteem are
more willing to accept the message but may have trouble learning its contents.
Overall, then, neither group is necessarily more vulnerable to persuasion than
the other—a prediction supported by a good deal of research (Rhodes & Wood,
1992).

elaboration The
process of thinking
about and scrutinizing
the arguments con-
tained in a persuasive
communication.

For Anthony Greenwald (1968) and others, persuasion requires a third,
intermediate step: **elaboration**. To illustrate, imagine you are offered a job and
your prospective employer tries to convince you over lunch to accept. You listen
closely, learn the terms of the offer, and understand what it all means. But if it's
an important interview, your head will spin with questions as you weigh the
pros and cons and contemplate the implications: Would I have to move? Is there
room for advancement? Am I better off staying where I am? Confronted with
personally significant messages, we don't just listen for the sake of collecting
information. We think about that information. Thus, the message is effective
to the extent that it leads us to dwell on favorable rather than unfavorable
thoughts.

These theories of attitude change all share an assumption that recipients of
persuasive appeals are attentive, active, critical, and thoughtful. This assumption is correct—some of the time. When it is, and when people consider a
message carefully, their reaction to it depends on its contents. In these instances,
messages have greater impact when they are easily learned than when they are

more difficult and when they stimulate favorable elaboration. Ultimately, strong arguments are persuasive and weak arguments are not. On the central route to persuasion, the process is eminently thoughtful, often logical.

The Peripheral Route "The receptive ability of the masses is very limited, their understanding small; on the other hand, they have a great power of forgetting." The author of this statement was Adolf Hitler (1933, p. 77). Believing that people are poor processors of information, Hitler relied heavily in his propaganda on the use of slogans, uniforms, marching bands, flags, and other symbols. For Hitler, "Meetings were not just occasions to make speeches, they were carefully planned theatrical productions in which settings, lighting, background music, and the timing of entrances were devised to maximize the emotional fervor of an audience" (Qualter, 1962, p. 112). Do these ploys work? Can "the masses" be manipulated into persuasion? As Hitler's method suggests, audiences are not always thoughtful. Sometimes people do not follow the central route to persuasion but instead take a short cut along the peripheral route. Rather than make an effort to learn the message and think through the issues, they base their evaluations on superficial cues. Three kinds of peripheral cues are particularly compelling: heuristics, attributions, and mood.

Political candidates rely on two different routes to persuasion. On the one hand, they try to persuade voters on the central route by addressing issues in domestic and foreign policy. On the other hand, they try to win votes on the peripheral route through the use of emotional appeals, marching bands, and catchy slogans.

heuristic   A rule of thumb used to evaluate a message superficially, without careful thinking about its content.

On the peripheral route to persuasion, people often evaluate a communication by using simple-minded **heuristics**, or rules of thumb (Chaiken, 1987; Chaiken et al., 1989). If a communicator has a good reputation, speaks fluently, or writes well, we tend to assume that his or her information must be correct. Likewise, if a message contains a long litany of arguments or intimidating statistics, then again we assume that it must be correct. Rather than take the time to scrutinize all the speaker's arguments, we take the easy way out, accepting the message according to heuristics.

Another way people evaluate persuasive messages without carefully considering the content is by making quick *attributions* about the communicator's motives (Eagly et al., 1981a). Confronted with speakers who appear to argue against their own interests, for example, we attribute what they say to the evidence, not to self-serving motives. The liberal who takes a conservative position on something and the advertiser who issues a warning on the dangers of the advertised product are both likely to turn more than a few heads. Other attribution rules are also used. Consider the use of consensus information. If an entire panel of speakers agrees on a topic, we assume the evidence is valid. If an entire audience reacts favorably, then again we assume the evidence is valid.

Finally, people might automatically agree or disagree with a message because of the kind of *mood* it elicits. Common sense says that people are "soft touches" when they're in a good mood. Later in this chapter, we will find that research supports this notion. Depending on the situation, almost anything that makes us feel good—whether it's food, humor, pleasant music, or an attractive model—can increase our willingness to accept a persuasive communication (Schwarz et al., 1991a).

Route Selection   Thanks to Petty and Cacioppo's (1986) distinction between the central and peripheral routes, we can see that although people may be influenced by the soundness of a message, they may also be influenced by less relevant factors. This distinction explains how the persuasion process can seem so logical on some occasions yet so illogical on others. Voters may select their candidate according to the issues or according to slogans. Juries may base their verdicts on evidence or on a defendant's appearance. And consumers may base their purchases on marketing reports or on product images. It all depends on whether we have the *ability* and the *motivation* to take the central route or whether we rely on peripheral cues instead.

To understand the conditions that lead people to take one route or the other, it's helpful to view persuasive communication as the outcome of three factors: a *source* (who), a *message* (says what and in what context), and an *audience* (to whom). Each of these factors influences a receiver's approach to a communication. If a source speaks clearly, if the message is important, if there is a bright and captive audience that cares deeply about the issue and has time to absorb the information, then that audience will be willing and able to take the effortful central route. But if the source speaks at a rate too fast to comprehend, if the message is trivial, or if the audience is distracted, pressed for time, or uninter-

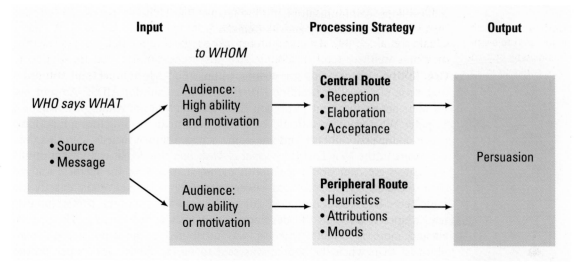

Figure 10.3   A Road Map: Two Routes to Persuasion.   Based on characteristics of the source, the message, and the audience, recipients of a communication take either a central or a peripheral route to persuasion. On the central route, message contents are learned and fully processed before they are accepted. On the peripheral route, less cognitive effort is exerted, and persuasion is based on heuristics, attributions, and moods. This two-process model helps explain how persuasion can seem logical on some occasions and illogical on others.

ested, then the less strenuous peripheral route will be taken. A key determinant in the selection of a route is one's level of personal involvement—the extent to which a message has relevance for one's values and goals (Johnson & Eagly, 1989; Petty & Cacioppo, 1990). Communicators can employ certain techniques to increase your involvement. For example, the use of rhetorical questions—a technique used in roughly 30 percent of all radio commercials (Howard, 1990b)—motivates people to think about and process a message more carefully (Burnkrant & Howard, 1984; Petty et al., 1981b).

Figure 10.3 presents a road map of persuasive communication. In the next three sections, we follow this map from input factors, through the central or peripheral routes, to the end result: persuasion.

The Source

From the moment he announced that he was infected with the virus that causes AIDS, basketball star Magic Johnson became a powerful spokesman for health organizations seeking to educate the public. Not being a medical expert or a professional speaker, why was Johnson so effective in this role? In general, what makes some communicators more effective than others? There are two key characteristics: credibility and likability.

Credibility   Imagine you are waiting in line in a supermarket, and you catch a glimpse of a swollen headline: "Doctors Report Cure for AIDS!" As your eye wanders across the front page, you discover that you are reading the *National Enquirer.* What would you think? Now imagine you are reading through periodicals in a university library, and you come across a similar article—but this time it appears in the *New England Journal of Medicine.* Now what would you think?

Chances are, you would react with more excitement to the medical journal than to the supermarket tabloid—even though both sources report exactly the same news. In a study conducted during the cold war era of the 1950s, subjects read a speech favoring the development of nuclear submarines. The speech elicited more agreement when it was attributed to an eminent American physicist than when the source was said to be the Soviet newspaper *Pravda* (Hovland & Weiss, 1951). Likewise, when subjects read a speech favoring more lenient treatment of juvenile offenders, they changed their attitudes more when they thought the speaker was a trial judge than when the speaker was supposed to be a convicted drug dealer (Kelman & Hovland, 1953).

Why are some sources more believable than others? Why are the journal, the physicist, and the judge more credible than the tabloid, *Pravda,* and the drug dealer? For communicators to be perceived as credible, they must have two characteristics: *competence* and *trustworthiness.* Competence refers to a speaker's ability. People who are knowledgeable, smart, or well spoken, or who have impressive credentials, are persuasive by virtue of their expertise (Hass, 1981). Experts can have a remarkably disarming effect on us. We tend to assume they know what they're talking about. So when they speak, we listen. And when they take a position, even one that is extreme, we yield. In short, people tend to accept what experts say without much scrutiny (Maddux & Rogers, 1980)—unless they contradict us on issues that are personally important (Heesacker et al., 1983).

Still, we are confronted by plenty of experts in the world whose opinions do not sway us. Why? The reason is that expertise is not enough. To be credible, communicators must also be trustworthy—that is, they must be willing to report what they know truthfully and without compromise. If a speaker is bought off, has an ax to grind, or is simply telling an audience what it wants to hear, that speaker will be suspected of bias. Common sense arms us with a simple rule of caution: beware of those who have something to gain from successful persuasion (Eagly et al., 1981a).

This rule has interesting implications. One is that people are easily impressed by others who take unpopular stands or argue against their own self-interests. When subjects read a political speech accusing a large company of polluting a local river, those who thought that the speechmaker was a pro-environment candidate addressing an environmentalist group perceived him to be biased. In contrast, subjects who thought he was a pro-business candidate addressing company supporters assumed he was sincere (Eagly et al., 1978). Trust is also established by presenting speakers who are not purposely trying to change our views. For that reason, people are influenced more when they think they are accidentally overhearing a persuasive communication than when they are presented with a sales pitch intended for their ears (Walster & Festinger, 1962). That's why advertisers use the "overheard communicator" trick in which the source tells a buddy about a new product that really works. Feeling as if they are eavesdropping on a personal conversation, viewers assume that what one friend says to another can be trusted.

Likability   More than anything else, Magic Johnson's power as an AIDS spokesman is based on his popularity, his personal charm, his winning smile, and his "regular guy" image that people can identify with. Do these qualities enhance a communicator's effectiveness? As Dale Carnegie (1936) implied in the title of his classic best seller, *How to Win Friends and Influence People,* being liked and being persuasive go hand in hand. So what makes a communicator likable? As described in Chapter 5, two characteristics that enhance attraction are *similarity* and *physical attractiveness.*

A study by Diane Mackie and others (1990) illustrates the importance of interpersonal similarity. Students from the University of California at Santa Barbara read a strong or a weak speech that argued against the continued use of college entrance exams. Half of the subjects were led to believe that the speech was written by a fellow UCSB student, and half thought that it was delivered by a student from the University of New Hampshire. Very few subjects changed their attitudes after reading the weak arguments. Many of those who read the strong message did change their attitudes—but only when it was delivered by a fellow UCSB student. The importance of communicator similarity in this study is depicted in Figure 10.4.

The link between similarity and persuasiveness has useful implications for those who wish to exert influence. We're all similar to one another in at least some respects. We might agree with each other's politics, share a common friend, have similar tastes in food, or enjoy spending summers on the same beach. Aware of the interpersonal benefits of similarity, the astute communicator can use common bonds to enhance his or her impact on an audience. There are limits, however. Similarity increases persuasion most when the similarities involved seem relevant to the content of the communication (Berscheid, 1966).

When it comes to physical attractiveness, advertising practices suggest that beauty is also persuasive. Billboards, magazine ads, and TV commercials are filled with glamorous "supermodels" who are tall, slender (for women), muscular (for men), with glowing complexions and radiant smiles. Sure these models can turn heads, you may think, but can they change minds?

In a study that addressed this question, male and female college students approached others on campus and introduced themselves as members of an organization that was trying to get the university to stop serving meat during breakfast and lunch. These student research assistants gave reasons for this

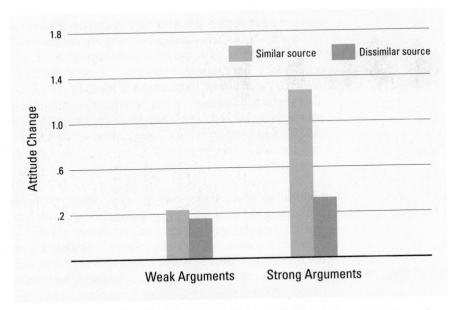

Figure 10.4   Persuasive Benefits of Communicator Similarity.   Students read a strong or a weak speech against continued use of the SATs, a speech supposedly written by a fellow student from the same school or by a student from a different university. As you can see, subjects were persuaded by the strong speech—but only when it was delivered by a communicator similar to themselves. [From Mackie et al., 1990.]

position and then asked their subjects to sign a petition. Attractive communicators were able to convince 41 percent of their subjects to sign the petition; those who were somewhat less attractive succeeded only 32 percent of the time (Chaiken, 1979). In fact, a speaker's physical attractiveness sometimes matters more than the quality of his or her presentation (Kahle & Homer, 1985; Pallak, 1983).

The Sky's Not the Limit: When What You Say Is More Important Than Who You Are   To this point, it must seem as if the source of a persuasive message is more important than the message itself. Is that true? Advertisers have debated the issue of celebrity endorsements for years. David Ogilvy (1985), a giant in advertising, believes that celebrities are not effective because viewers know they've been bought and paid for. Ogilvy is not alone in his skepticism. Still, advertisers scramble furiously to sign high-priced entertainers, athletes, and public figures. TV commercials regularly feature a parade of stars: Michael Jordan, Jamie Lee Curtis, Bo Jackson, Hammer, and Paula Abdul are just a few examples. The bigger the star, supposedly the more valuable the endorsement.

Compared to the contents of a message, does the source really make the difference that advertisers pay for? Are we so impressed by the expert and so drawn to the charming person that we embrace whatever they have to say? And are we so scornful of nonexperts and unattractive people that they don't stand a chance? In light of what we know about the central and peripheral routes to persuasion, the answer to all these questions is the same: it depends.

First, a receiver's *involvement* plays an important role. When a message has personal relevance to your life, you pay attention to it and think carefully about its arguments and implications. When a message does not have relevance, you may listen with only one ear, take the source at face value, and spend little time scrutinizing the information. For example, Richard Petty and his colleagues (1981a) had students listen to a speaker propose that seniors should be required to take comprehensive exams in order to graduate. Three aspects of the communication situation were varied. First, subjects were led to believe that the

Advertisers are so convinced that beauty sells products that they hire the most glamorous models in the world. Supermodel Cindy Crawford has a multimillion dollar contract with Revlon.

speaker was either an education professor from Princeton or a high school student. Second, subjects heard either well-reasoned arguments based on hard evidence or a weak message based on anecdotes and personal opinion. Third, subjects were told that the proposed exams were being considered for the following year (That means me!) or that the exams would not take effect for another ten years (I'll be long gone by then!).

Personal involvement determined the relative impact of source expertise and speech quality. Among subjects who would not be affected by the proposed change, attitudes were based on the speaker's credibility: the professor was persuasive; the high school student was not. Among subjects who believed that the proposed change would affect them directly, attitudes were based on the quality of the speaker's proposal: strong arguments were persuasive; weak arguments were not. As depicted in Figure 10.5, people follow the source rather than the message under low levels of involvement, taking the peripheral route to persuasion. In contrast, message factors outweigh the source under high levels of involvement, when people care enough to take the central route to persuasion. Even the tilt toward likable communicators is reduced when receivers take the central route (Chaiken, 1980).

There is a second limit to source effects. It is often said that time heals all wounds; it may also heal the effects of a bad reputation. When Hovland and Weiss (1951) varied communicator credibility (for example, the physicist versus *Pravda*), they found the change had a substantial and immediate effect on persuasion. But when they measured subjects' attitudes again four weeks later, the effect had vanished. Over time, the amount of attitude change produced by the credible source decreased, while the amount of change produced by the noncredible source increased. This latter finding—the delayed persuasive impact of a noncredible communicator—is called the **sleeper effect**.

sleeper effect A delayed increase in the persuasive impact of a noncredible source.

To explain this unforeseen result, the Hovland group proposed the *discounting cue hypothesis*. According to this hypothesis, although people immediately discount what noncredible communicators say, over time they dissociate what is said from who says it. In other words, people tend to remember the message but forget the source (Pratkanis et al., 1988). To examine the role of memory in this process, Herbert Kelman and Carl Hovland (1953) reminded a group of subjects of the source's identity before their attitudes were reassessed. If the sleeper effect was due to forgetting, they reasoned, then it could be eliminated by reinstating the link between the source and the message. As you can see in Figure 10.6, they were right. When subjects' attitudes were measured after three weeks, those who were not reminded of the source showed the usual sleeper effect. Those who were reminded of the source did not. For these subjects, the effects of high and low credibility endured.

The sleeper effect has generated a good deal of controversy (Cook et al., 1979; Greenwald et al., 1986). There is no doubt that credible communicators lose their initial impact over time. But researchers had a harder time finding evidence for delayed persuasion by a noncredible source. Exasperated by their own failures to obtain this result, Paulette Gillig and Anthony Greenwald (1974) asked, "Is it time to lay the sleeper effect to rest?" The answer, though, is no.

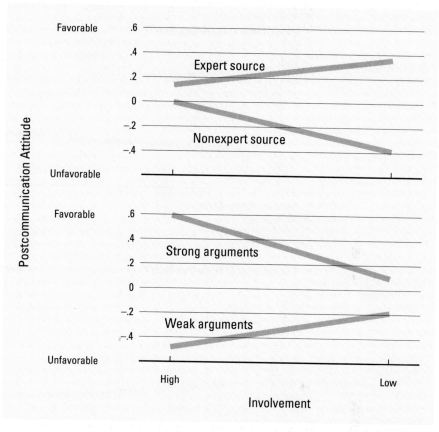

Figure 10.5   Source Versus Message: The Role of Audience Involvement.   In this study, subjects who were high or low in their personal involvement heard a strong or a weak message from an expert or a nonexpert. Notice that for high-involvement subjects, persuasion was based on the strength of arguments (bottom left), not on source expertise (top left). For low-involvement subjects, persuasion was based more on the source (top right) than on the arguments (bottom right). These results indicate that source characteristics have more impact on those who don't care enough to take the central route to persuasion. [From Petty et al., 1981a.]

More recent research shows that the sleeper effect is reliable—provided subjects don't learn who the source is until *after* they receive the original message (Greenwald et al., 1986; Gruder et al., 1978; Pratkanis et al., 1988). To appreciate the importance of timing, imagine you're flipping through a magazine and you come across what appears to be a review of a new CD. Before you begin reading, however, you notice in the fine print that this so-called review is really an advertisement paid for by the recording company. Aware that you can't trust what you read, you skim the ad and reject it. Now imagine the same

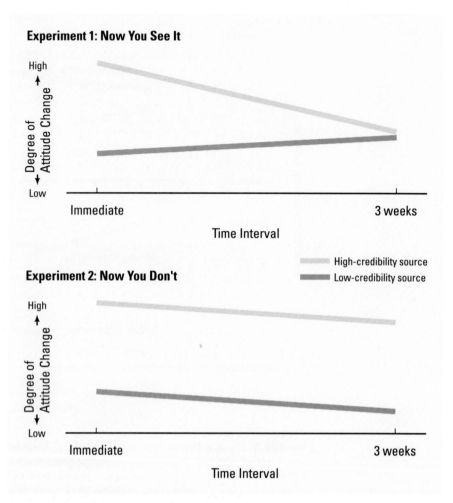

Figure 10.6   The Sleeper Effect.   In Experiment 1, subjects changed their immediate attitudes more in response to a message from a high- than from a low-credibility source. When attitudes were remeasured after three weeks, the high-credibility source lost impact and the low-credibility source gained impact—the sleeper effect. Experiment 2 shows that the sleeper effect disappeared when subjects were reminded of the source. These results suggest that over time, people tend to remember the message but forget the source. [From Kelman & Hovland, 1953.]

situation, except that you read the entire ad before realizing what it is. Again, you reject it. But notice the difference. This time, you read the message with an open mind. You may have rejected it later, but after a few weeks the information has a chance to sink in and influence your evaluation of the CD. This experience illustrates the sleeper effect.

The Message

Obviously, not all sources are created equal. Some are more credible or likable than others. On the peripheral route to persuasion, audiences are influenced heavily, maybe too heavily, by these and other source characteristics. But when we care enough about an issue to take the central route, the strength of the message determines its success. On the central route to persuasion, it matters whether a scientist's theory is supported by the data or whether a manufacturer has a sound product. Keep in mind, though, that the target of a persuasive appeal—whether it is a community of scientists or consumers—comes to know a message only through the medium of communication: *what* a person has to say and *how* that person says it.

Volume of Information   Communicators often struggle over how much information is needed to create the strongest possible impact on an audience. Should a persuasive message be long and crammed with facts or short and to the point? Is it better to present more than you need or less than you have? The

Research on the sleeper effect shows that people often forget the source of a message. [Drawing by Ed Fisher; © 1976 The New Yorker Magazine, Inc.]

"It is a superb vision of America, all right, but I can't remember which candidate projected it."

answer to these questions seems to depend on whether the audience is processing the message according to the central or peripheral route and whether the added material is novel or repetitious.

When we process a message with our eyes and ears half closed, we fall back on a simple heuristic: the longer the message, or the more arguments it contains, the more valid it must be. To those members of an audience who are unable or unmotivated to take the central route to persuasion, the length of a message gives the superficial appearance of factual support—regardless of the quality of the arguments (Petty & Cacioppo, 1984; Wood et al., 1985a). Advertisers discovered this same principle through trial and error. As David Ogilvy (1985) concludes from his years of experience, "the more facts you tell, the more you sell" (p. 88).

When people process a communication carefully, however, message length is a two-edged sword. If a message is long because it contains a good deal of supporting information, then longer does indeed mean better. The more supportive arguments you can offer, or the more sources you can find to speak on your behalf, the more persuasive will be your appeal (Harkins & Petty, 1981). But what if the added information is not all that supportive? If the added arguments are weak, or if the new sources are redundant, an alert audience will not be tricked by length alone. If increasing the length of a message means diluting its quality, your appeal might well *lose* impact (Harkins & Petty, 1987; Petty & Cacioppo, 1984).

There's one other wrinkle. Sometimes the volume of information may be increased not by adding novel arguments or sources but by repeating the same message from the same source over and over again. In Chapter 5, we noted that the more exposure people have to a stimulus, the more they like it—but only up to a point (Zajonc et al., 1972). When people are exposed to a strong message for a second, third, or fourth time, its impact increases. At some point, however, a repeated message becomes "overexposed" and its impact begins to diminish (Bornstein, 1989)—especially when presented to people who are easily bored (Bornstein et al., 1990).

Message Discrepancy Persuasion is defined as the process of changing attitudes. But just how much are people willing to change in response to a message? Before addressing an audience, all communicators confront a critical strategic question. How extreme a position should they take? How *discrepant* should a message be from the audience's position in order to achieve the greatest impact? Common sense suggests two opposite answers. One approach is to go all out on the assumption that the more change you advocate, the more you get. A second approach is to exercise caution, because if you ask for too much change, the audience will reject the message outright. Which approach seems more effective? Suppose you were trying to convert your conservative friends into political liberals, or the other way around. Would you stake out a radical position in the hope of moving them toward the center, or would you preach moderation in order to avoid being cast aside?

There are two answers to this question. First, communicators must ensure that their argument is based on premises that are acceptable, not offensive, to an audience (Holtgraves & Bailey, 1991). Second, communicators should advocate a position that is moderately discrepant from that of the audience—a compromise between the two approaches. To some extent, the more discrepant the message, the greater the change in attitudes. But there is a breaking point beyond which increased discrepancy produces less change. This relationship between discrepancy and persuasion can be pictured as an upside-down U. There is a complicating factor, however. Experts more than nonexperts can get away with taking an extreme position. In a study by Stephen Bochner and Chester Insko (1966), subjects read an essay arguing that the average adult sleeps too much and should get either 8, 7, 6, 5, 4, 3, 2, 1, or 0 hours of sleep per night. For some subjects, the author of the essay was identified as a Nobel Prize–winning physiologist. For others, the author was said to be a YMCA director. In both cases, attitude change increased with message discrepancy up to a point, then decreased. How extreme that point was, however, depended on the source. Figure 10.7 shows that when the nonexpert recommended as few as

Figure 10.7 Message Discrepancy and Attitude Change. In this study, subjects, believing that adults should get eight hours of sleep per night, read an essay that recommended varying amounts of less sleep. As you can see, attitude change increased with message discrepancy up to a point, then decreased. A high-credibility source was persuasive at higher levels of discrepancy than was a low-credibility source. [From Bochner & Insko, 1966.]

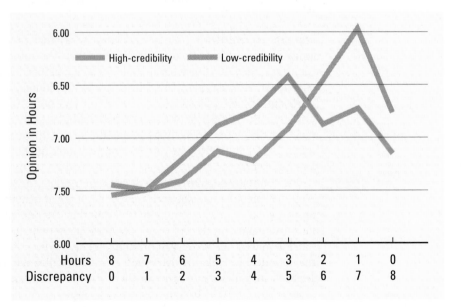

This political ad illustrates the use of fear appeals. Shown during the 1988 presidential election, the commercial warned that a vote for Dukakis was a vote for crime.

three hours of sleep, the amount of attitude change decreased. For the expert, that decrease was not evident until he recommended no sleep at all!

Appeals to Emotion   Many trial lawyers say that to win cases, they have to appeal to juries through the heart rather than the mind. Sure the evidence is important, they say. But what matters most is whether the jury views their client with anger, disgust, sympathy, or sadness. Of course, very few messages are based entirely on rational argument or on emotion. And it's possible that the best approach to take depends on whether the attitude of an audience is based more on beliefs or on feelings about the object in question (Edwards, 1990; Millar & Millar, 1990). In this section, we look at the role of emotion in the persuasion process.

One common persuasive technique is to use fear, or scare tactics. During the 1988 U.S. presidential election, George Bush relied heavily on negative advertising to defeat his opponent, Michael Dukakis. At one point, for example, the Bush campaign produced a TV commercial in which prisoners were shown cruising in and out of prison through a revolving door. The message was one of fear: if you elect Dukakis, hardened criminals will walk the streets. Presidential elections are unique in many ways, but the use of fear appeals is widespread. To indoctrinate prospective members, certain religious cults use scare tactics. So do public health organizations that graphically portray the victims of cigarette smoking, drugs, and unsafe sex. That's why magazine ads for condoms often use fear appeals—the most extreme being "I enjoy sex but I don't want to die for it" (Struckman-Johnson et al., 1990). Even commercial advertisers try to frighten consumers into buying their products. Who, after all, would want to get caught with dandruff, bad breath, body odor, or a dirty collar?

Is fear effective? Can people be frightened into persuasion? And if so, is it better to arouse just a little nervousness or a full-blown anxiety attack? To answer these questions, social psychologists compare the effects of communications that vary in their fearfulness. In the first such study, Irving Janis and Seymour Feshbach (1953) found that high levels of fear arousal did not generate increased agreement with a communication. Since then, however, research has shown that scaring people does motivate change—provided that the threatening message includes reassuring instructions on how to avoid the danger (Leventhal, 1970; Rogers, 1983a). Without specific advice on how to cope, people panic and tune out. In one study, for example, subjects who had a chronic fear of cancer were less likely than others to detect logical errors in a message that advocated regular cancer checkups (Jepson & Chaiken, 1990). But when clear instructions are included, fear works. Antismoking films that tell smokers how to quit lead to more negative attitudes about cigarettes when they show gory scenes of lung-cancer operations than do charts filled with dry statistics (Leventhal et al., 1967). Similarly, driving-safety films are more effective when they show close-ups of broken bones and bloody accident victims than controlled collisions using dummies instead of real passengers (Rogers & Mewborn, 1976).

Just as fear helps to induce persuasion, so do positive emotions. When American presidents want to sway votes on an important bill, for example, they often invite undecided members of Congress to a meal at the White House. Gregory Razran (1938) once referred to this as the "luncheon technique." It seems to work, too. In one experiment, subjects who snacked on peanuts and soda were more likely to agree with a series of controversial arguments than were those who did not (Janis et al., 1965). Of course, you don't have to feed people to make them feel good. Soft lights, tender memories, funny movies, upbeat music, and a picturesque setting can all lull people into a positive emotional state, ripe for persuasion.

According to Alice Isen (1984), people who feel good tend to view the world through rose-colored glasses. Filled with good spirits, we become more sociable, more generous, and more positive in our opinions. We also make decisions more quickly and with relatively little thought. The net effect is that unless we are faced with a message we really care about, positive feelings activate the peripheral route to persuasion, allowing superficial cues to take on added importance (Isen & Means, 1983; Worth & Mackie, 1987). For example, popular music increases the persuasiveness of TV commercials when the message is trivial to viewers but not when it is important (Park & Young, 1986).

What is it about feeling good that leads people to take short cuts rather than the more effortful central route to persuasion? There are several possible explanations (Schwarz et al., 1991a). One is that people are motivated to savor the moment, protect their happy mood, and not ruin it by concentrating on new information (Isen, 1984). A second possibility is that positive feelings are distracting, causing the mind to wander and impairing one's ability to think carefully about a persuasive message (Mackie & Worth, 1989).

Presentation Order In the summer before the 1992 presidential election, as in most recent elections, the Democrats held their national convention a month or so before the Republicans held theirs. These conventions are watched on TV by millions of voters. Do you think the order in which they are scheduled places one party at an advantage? Other things being equal, if you believe that information presented first has more impact, you would be predicting a *primacy effect* (advantage to the Democrats). If you believe that information presented last has the edge, you would be predicting a *recency effect* (advantage to the Republicans).

There are good reasons for both predictions. On the one hand, first impressions are important. On the other hand, memory fades over time, and people often remember only the last thing they heard before making a decision. Confronted with these contrasting predictions, Norman Miller and Donald Campbell (1959) searched for the "missing link" that would determine the relative effects of primacy and recency. They discovered that the missing link is *time*. In a jury simulation study, subjects (1) read a summary of the plaintiff's case, (2) read a summary of the defendant's case, and then (3) made a decision. The researchers varied how much time separated the two messages and how much time elapsed between the second message and the decisions. When subjects read the second message right after the first and then waited a whole week before reporting their opinion, a primacy effect prevailed, and the side that came first was clearly favored. Both messages faded equally from memory, so only the greater impact of first impressions was left. However, when subjects made a decision immediately after the second message but a full week after the first, a recency effect took over. The second argument was fresher in memory, thus favoring the side that presented last. Using these results as a guideline, let's return to the question raised by our example. What is the impact on election day of how the national conventions are scheduled? Think for a moment about the placement and timing of these events. The answer appears in Figure 10.8.

The Audience

Although source and message factors are important, the astute communicator should also take his or her audience into account. Presentation strategies that succeed with some people may fail with others. Audiences taking the central

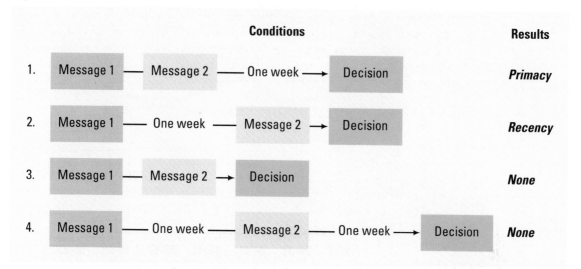

Figure 10.8 Effects of Presentation Order and Timing on Persuasion. This study demonstrated the role of presentation order and the timing of opposing arguments on persuasion. If you apply these results to our example, you will see that the Democratic and Republican conventions resemble the fourth row of this figure. From these results, it seems that the scheduling of these events is fair, promoting neither primacy nor recency.

route to persuasion, for example, bear little resemblance to those found on the peripheral route. In this section, we'll see that the impact of a persuasive message depends on two additional characteristics: the receiver's personality and his or her expectations concerning the communication.

Individual Differences: What Turns You On? Early on, social psychologists tried to identify types of people who were more or less vulnerable to persuasion. Although little has come of these efforts, one characteristic does seem to make a difference: age. It is often said that people change their views often in early adulthood, only later to settle into a stable set of attitudes and values. To see if this portrayal of the life cycle is accurate, Jon Krosnick and Duane Alwin (1989) examined political opinion data collected from 2,500 Americans. Respondents were polled three times—some between the years 1956 and 1960, others between 1972 and 1976. By dividing respondents into seven age groups and analyzing whether their views remained the same or changed over time, Krosnick and Alwin found support for an *impressionable years* hypothesis, as there was less attitude stability in the youngest, 18-to-25-year-old age group than in all the others. They then conducted their own survey before and after the 1980 presidential election and again found the same result. The full pattern is illustrated in Figure 10.9.

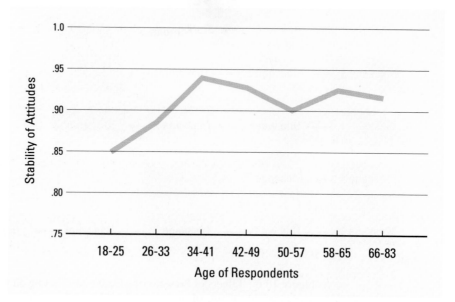

Figure 10.9   Stability of Attitudes in Adulthood: Evidence for the Impressionable Years Hypothesis.   Adults of different ages were surveyed three times within the space of four years. As predicted by the impressionable years hypothesis, there was less attitude stability (in other words, more change) among 18- to 25-year-olds than among older respondents. [From Krosnick & Alwin, 1989.]

Although people are somewhat more impressionable in their youth than later in life, we all are vulnerable to persuasive communications. Assuming that everyone has attitudes that can be changed, researchers look for the right "match" between aspects of the message and characteristics of an audience. Thus, we ask, what kinds of messages turn *you* on?

Earlier we saw that people process information more carefully when they are highly involved. Involvement can be affected by the importance of a message or situation. According to Cacioppo and Petty (1982), however, there are also individual differences in the extent to which people become involved and take the central route to persuasion. Cacioppo and Petty reasoned that individuals differ in how much they enjoy effortful cognitive activities or, as they call it, the **need for cognition (NC).** People who are high rather than low in their need for cognition like to work on difficult problems, search for clues, make fine distinctions, and analyze situations. These personality differences can be identified by items contained in the Need for Cognition Scale, some of which are shown in Table 10.1.

The need for cognition has interesting implications for changing attitudes. If people are prone to approach or avoid effortful cognitive activities, then the knowledgeable communicator could design messages unique to a particular

need for cognition (NC)   A personality variable that distinguishes people on the basis of how much they enjoy effortful cognitive activities.

1. I really enjoy a task that involves coming up with new solutions to problems.

2. Thinking is not my idea of fun.

3. The notion of thinking abstractly is appealing to me.

4. I like tasks that require little thought once I've learned them.

5. I usually end up deliberating about issues even when they do not affect me personally.

6. It's enough for me that something gets the job done; I don't care how or why it works.

Table 10.1 Need for Cognition Scale: Sample Items. Are you high or low in the need for cognition? These statements are taken from the NC Scale. If you agree with items 1, 3, and 5 and disagree with items 2, 4, and 6, you would probably be regarded as high in your NC. [From Cacioppo & Petty, 1982.]

audience. In theory, the high-NC audience should receive information-oriented appeals, and the low-NC audience should be treated to appeals based on peripheral cues such as heuristics, attribution rules, and mood. The theory is fine, but does it work? Can a message be customized according to the information-processing style of its recipients? In a test of this hypothesis, subjects read an editorial that consisted of either a strong or a weak set of arguments. As predicted, the higher subjects' NC scores were, the more they thought about the material, the better they remembered it, and the more persuaded they were by the strength of its arguments (Cacioppo et al., 1983). In contrast, people who are low in the need for cognition are persuaded by cues found along the peripheral route—such as a speaker's reputation and physical appearance (Cacioppo & Petty, 1984) and even the reactions, cheering or jeering, of others in the audience (Axsom et al., 1987).

Just as people high in the need for cognition crave information, other personality traits are associated with an attraction to other kinds of messages. Consider individual differences in *self-monitoring*. As described in earlier chapters, high self-monitors regulate their behavior from one situation to another out of concern for public self-presentation. Low self-monitors are less image conscious and behave instead according to their own beliefs and preferences. Applying this idea to persuasion, it is possible that high self-monitors are responsive to messages that promise desirable social images. This technique is common in advertising. Soft-drink ads try to attract the young at heart; commercials for beer conjure up visions of evening relief from hard work; individuality and uniqueness are the qualities used to sell blue jeans (Schudson, 1986). These ads offer no factual information about the quality of a product. Instead, the image is the message.

To test the self-monitoring hypothesis, Mark Snyder and Kenneth DeBono (1985) showed image-oriented or information-oriented magazine ads to high and low self-monitors. In an ad for Irish Mocha Mint coffee, for example, a man and woman were depicted as relaxing in a candlelit room over a cup of coffee. The image-oriented version promised to "Make a chilly night become a cozy evening." The informational version read, "A delicious blend of three great flavors—coffee, chocolate, and mint." As predicted, high self-monitors were willing to pay more for products after receiving imagery ads, while low self-monitors were influenced more by the information-oriented appeals. As shown in Figure 10.10, this study suggests that a message may be persuasive to the extent that it meets the psychological needs of its audience (DeBono, 1987; DeBono & Packer, 1992).

Just as different people are attracted to different approaches, an attitude object may lend itself to a certain type of message based on the function it serves. According to Sharon Shavitt (1990), some attitude objects (for example, products such as home appliances) serve a practical, *utilitarian* function for users, while other objects (for example, jewelry and team sweatshirts) serve a more personal, *social identity* function. Reasoning that a message is effective only

Figure 10.10 Information-Oriented Versus Image-Oriented Ads: The Role of Self-Monitoring.   High and low self-monitors estimated how much they would pay for products presented in image-oriented or informational magazine ads. As you can see, low self-monitors preferred products depicted in informational ads (left), while high self-monitors preferred those depicted in image-oriented ads (right). [Data from Snyder & DeBono, 1985.]

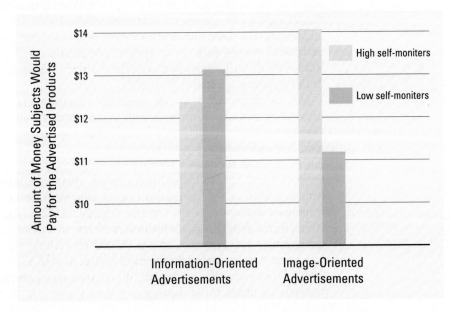

if it focuses on the main function of the attitude object, Shavitt showed subjects ads that emphasized either the utilitarian or the social identity aspects of various products. She found that the utilitarian ads were more effective for utilitarian objects such as air conditioners and brands of coffee ("The delicious, hearty aroma of Sterling Blend Coffee comes from a blend of the freshest coffee beans") but that appeals to social identity were more effective for promoting personal products such as greeting cards and perfume ("Astoria is the sophisticated scent that tells people you're *not* one of the crowd").

Forewarning: Ready or Not, Here I Come!

Probably the toughest audience to persuade is the one that knows you're coming. When people are aware that someone is trying to change their attitude, they become motivated to resist. All they need is some time to collect their thoughts and come up with a good defense. Jonathan Freedman and David Sears (1965) found this out when they told groups of high school seniors to expect a speech on why teenagers should not be allowed to drive (not a popular position, as you can imagine). The students were warned either two or ten minutes before the talk began or not at all. Those who were the victims of a sneak attack were the most likely to agree with the speaker's position. Those who had a full ten minutes' warning were the least likely to agree. Forewarning is most likely to bolster resistance when a message is important (Petty & Cacioppo, 1979). Apparently, to be forewarned is to be forearmed. But why?

At least two processes are at work. To understand these, let's take a closer look at what forewarning really does. Subjects in the Freedman and Sears (1965) study were put on notice in two ways: (1) they were told the position the speaker would take, and (2) they were told that the speaker intended to persuade them. Psychologically, these two aspects of forewarning have very different effects.

The first effect is cognitive. Knowing in advance what position a speaker will take enables us to come up with counterarguments and, as a result, to become more resistant to change. To explain this effect, William McGuire (1964) drew an analogy: protecting a person's attitudes from persuasion, he said, is like inoculating the human body against disease. In medicine, injecting a small dose of infection into a patient stimulates the body to build up a resistance to it. According to this **inoculation hypothesis**, attitudes can be immunized the same way. As with flu shots and other vaccines, our defenses can be reinforced by exposure to weak doses of the other side's position before we actually encounter the full presentation. Studies of negative political advertising show that inoculation can be used to combat the kinds of attack messages that sometimes win elections (Pfau & Burgoon, 1988; Pfau et al., 1990). It has even been suggested that parents can protect children from advertising propaganda by exposing them to small doses of TV commercials, while critically discussing the claims that are made (Pratkanis & Aronson, 1992).

Simply knowing that someone will be trying to persuade us also elicits a motivational reaction. We brace ourselves to resist the attempt—regardless of

inoculation hypothesis The idea that exposure to weak versions of a persuasive argument tends to increase later resistance to that argument.

"Before you launch in, Maynard, is this a <u>major</u> policy speech?"

An audience becomes difficult to persuade when it is poised and ready for the message.
[Drawing by H. Martin; © 1987 The New Yorker Magazine, Inc.]

what position is taken. As a TV viewer, you have no doubt heard the irritating phrase "And now, we pause for a message from our sponsor." What does this warning tell us? Not knowing yet who the sponsor is, even the grouchiest among us is in no position to object. Yet imagine how you would feel if an experimenter said to you, "In a few minutes, you will hear a message prepared according to well-established principles of persuasion and designed to induce you to change your attitudes." If you are like the subjects who actually heard this forewarning, you may be tempted to reply, "Oh yeah? Try me!" Indeed, subjects rejected that message, without counterargument and without much advance notice (Hass & Grady, 1975).

When people are told that someone is trying to change their attitudes or otherwise manipulate them, a red flag goes up. That red flag is called *reactance*, a concept introduced in Chapter 5. People want to maintain the freedom to think, feel, and act as they (not others) choose. When we sense that a specific freedom is threatened, we become motivated to maintain it; when we sense that a freedom is slipping away, we try to restore it. So when someone comes on too strong, we often exhibit *negative attitude change*, or "boomerang effect," by moving in a direction opposite to the one advocated—even when the speaker's position is consistent with our own (Heller et al., 1973). Sometimes, the motive to protect a freedom can supersede our desire to hold a specific opinion.

PERSUASION BY OUR OWN ACTIONS

Anyone who has ever acted on stage knows how easy it is to become so absorbed in a role that the experience seems real. Feigned laughter can make an actor feel happy, and crocodile tears can turn into sadness. Even in real life, the effect can be dramatic. In 1974, Patty Hearst—a sheltered college student from a wealthy family, was kidnapped. By the time she was arrested many months later, she was a gun-toting revolutionary who called herself Tania. How could someone be so totally converted? In Hearst's own words, "I had thought I was humoring [my captors] by parroting their clichés and buzzwords without believing in them. . . . In trying to convince them I convinced myself."

Role Playing: All the World's a Stage

The Patty Hearst case illustrates the powerful effects of *role playing*. Of course, you don't have to be kidnapped or terrorized to know how it feels to be coaxed or guided into behavior that is at odds with your inner convictions. People often engage in attitude-discrepant behavior, as part of a job, for example, or to please others. As commonplace as this seems, it raises a rather profound question. When we play along, saying and doing things that are discrepant with our attitudes, do we begin to change those attitudes as a result? How we feel can determine the way we act. Is it also possible that the way we act can determine how we feel?

According to Irving Janis (1968), attitude change persists more when it is inspired by our own behavior than when it stems from passive exposure to a persuasive communication. Janis conducted a study in which one group of subjects listened to a speech that challenged their positions on a topic and others were handed an outline and asked to give the speech themselves. As predicted, subjects changed their attitudes more after giving the speech than after listening to it (Janis & King, 1954). According to Janis, role playing works by making people learn the message more effectively. That is why people remember arguments they come up with on their own better than they do arguments provided by others (Slamecka & Graff, 1978). In fact, attitude change is more enduring when people who read a persuasive message merely *expect* that they will later have to communicate that message to others (Boninger et al., 1990).

There's more to role playing than improved memory. The effects of enacting a role can be staggering—in part because it is so easy to confuse what we do, or what we say, with how we really feel. Think about the times you've dished out compliments you didn't mean, or smiled at someone you didn't like, or nodded your head to a statement you disagreed with. It's a simple fact of social life that we regularly shade what we say to please a particular listener. People put on a more conservative face when they expect to confront a political conservative and a more liberal face when they talk to a political liberal (Tetlock, 1983). American presidents often change their tune before and after election day (Tetlock, 1981). And college professors write more positive letters of recommendation when students reserve the right to see their files than when confidentiality is ensured (Ceci & Peters, 1984).

What's fascinating is not that people adjust what they say to please others but the powerful effects this role playing has on private attitudes: when people say what an audience wants to hear, they soon come to believe their own statements. In one study, for example, subjects read about a man and then described him to someone who supposedly either liked or disliked him. As it turned out, subjects described the man in more positive terms when their listener was favorably disposed. In the process, however, they also convinced themselves. When subjects said good things, they recalled the description they read as more positive and came to like the person. When they said bad things, they recalled a more negative description and came to dislike him. This study suggests that, to some extent, "saying is believing" (Higgins & Rholes, 1978).

Consider the implications. We are accustomed to thinking that attitudes determine behavior. People help others whom they like and hurt those whom they dislike. Thus, to produce a lasting change in someone's behavior, we try first to change their attitudes. But research on role playing emphasizes the flip side of the coin—that behavior can determine attitudes. We come to like people because we have helped them, and we blame those whom we have hurt. To change people's inner feelings, maybe we should begin by focusing on their behavior. Why do people experience changes of attitude in response to changes in their own behavior? One answer to this question is provided by the theory of cognitive dissonance.

Cognitive Dissonance Theory: The Classic Version

Many social psychologists believe that people are motivated by a desire for cognitive consistency—a state of mind in which one's beliefs, attitudes, and behaviors are all compatible with each other (Abelson et al., 1968). Cognitive consistency theories seem to presuppose that people are generally logical. Leon Festinger (1957), however, turned this assumption on its head. Struck by the irrationality of human behavior, Festinger proposed *cognitive dissonance theory,* which held that a powerful motive to maintain cognitive consistency can give rise to irrational, often maladaptive behavior.

According to Festinger, we hold many cognitions about ourselves and the world around us. These cognitions include everything we know about our own beliefs, attitudes, and behavior. Although most of our cognitions coexist peace-

Knowing that exposure to the sun increases the risk of skin cancer doesn't prevent some people from basking in the sun's dangerous rays. Awareness of the discrepancy between our knowledge and behavior arouses cognitive dissonance.

fully, sometimes they clash. Consider some examples. You say you're on a diet, yet you just dove head first into a chocolate mousse. Or you waited on line for hours to get into a concert, and then the music was disappointing. Or you baked for hours under the hot summer sun, even though you knew of the health risks. Each of these scenarios harbors inconsistency and conflict. You have already committed yourself to one course of action, yet you realize that what you did is inconsistent with your attitude.

**cognitive disso-
nance** An unpleas-
ant psychological state
often aroused when a
person holds two con-
flicting cognitions.

Under certain specific conditions, discrepancies such as these can produce an unpleasant state of tension known as **cognitive dissonance**. But discrepancy doesn't always produce dissonance. If you were forced to break a diet for a Thanksgiving dinner, your indiscretion would not lead you to experience dissonance. Likewise, if you mistakenly thought that the mousse you ate was low in calories, only later to find out the truth, then again you would not experience much dissonance. As we will see, what really hurts is knowing that you committed yourself to an attitude-discrepant behavior freely and with some knowledge of the consequences. When that happens, dissonance is aroused,

"It's a crazy idea, but it just might work."

One way to reduce dissonance is to minimize the importance of the conflict. [From *The Wall Street Journal*. Permission, Cartoon Features Syndicate.]

and—in self-defense—you become motivated to reduce it. There are many possible ways to do so, as shown in Table 10.2. Often the easiest is to change your attitude so that it becomes consistent with your behavior.

Right from the start, cognitive dissonance theory captured the imagination. Festinger's basic proposition is simple, yet its implications are far-reaching. In this section, we examine three research areas that demonstrate the breadth of what dissonance theory has to say about attitude change.

Justifying Attitude-Discrepant Behavior: When Doing Is Believing

Imagine for a moment that you are a subject in the classic study by Leon Festinger and J. Merrill Carlsmith (1959). As soon as you arrive, you are greeted by an experimenter who says that he is interested in various measures of performance. Wondering what that means, you all too quickly find out. The experimenter hands you a wooden board containing forty-eight square pegs in square holes and asks you to turn each peg a quarter turn to the left, then a quarter turn back to the right, then back to the left, then back again to the right. The routine seems endless. After thirty minutes, the experimenter comes to your rescue. Or does he? Just when you think things are looking up, he hands you another board, another assignment. For the next half hour, you are to take twelve spools of thread off the board, put them back, take them off, and put them back again. By now, you're just about ready to tear your hair out. As you think back over better times, even the first task begins to look good.

Finally, you're done. After one of the longest hours of your life, the experimenter lets you in on a secret: there's more to this experiment than meets the eye. You were in the control group. To test the effects of motivation on

Techniques	Examples
Change your attitude.	"I don't really need to be on a diet."
Change your perception of the behavior.	"I hardly ate any chocolate mousse."
Add consonant cognitions.	"Chocolate mousse is very nutritious."
Minimize the importance of the conflict.	"I don't care if I'm overweight— life is short, mousse is great!"
Reduce perceived choice.	"I had no choice; the mousse was prepared for this special occasion."

Table 10.2   Ways to Reduce Dissonance.   "I need to be on a diet, yet I just dove head first into a chocolate mousse." If this were you, how would you reduce the dissonance aroused by the discrepancy between your attitude and behavior?

performance, other subjects are being told that the experiment will be fun and exciting. You don't realize it, but you're now being set up for a critical part of the study. Would you be willing to tell the next subject that the experiment is enjoyable? As you hem and haw, the experimenter offers to pay for your services. Some subjects are offered one dollar, others are offered twenty dollars. In either case you agree to help out. Before you know it, you find yourself in the waiting room trying to dupe an unsuspecting fellow student (who is really a confederate).

By means of this elaborate, staged presentation, subjects were goaded into an attitude-discrepant behavior, an action that was inconsistent with their private attitudes. They knew full well how dull the experiment really was, yet they raved about it. Did this conflict arouse cognitive dissonance? It depends on how much subjects were paid. Suppose you were one of the lucky ones offered twenty dollars for your assistance. By today's standards, that payment would be worth eighty dollars—surely a sufficient justification for telling a little white lie, right? Knowing they were well compensated, these subjects experienced little, if any, dissonance. But wait a minute. Suppose you were paid only one dollar. Surely your integrity is worth more than that, don't you think? In this case, you have **insufficient justification** for going along, and you need some way to cope. According to Festinger (1957), unless you can deny your overt behavior (which usually is not possible), you will feel compelled to change your attitude about the task. If you can convince yourself that the experiment wasn't all bad, then saying it was interesting was all right.

The results were just as Festinger and Carlsmith had predicted. When the experiment was presumably over, subjects were asked how they felt about the

insufficient justification   A condition in which people freely perform an attitude-discrepant behavior without receiving a large reward.

Ratings of Task Enjoyment		
No Lie	**$20 Lie**	**$1 Lie**
5.9	9.8	23.5

Table 10.3 Justifying Attitude-Discrepant Behavior: The Classic Experiment. Subjects in an experiment they found boring (attitude) were asked to say that it was enjoyable (behavior) to a fellow student. One group was paid a dollar to lie; a second group was offered twenty dollars. In a third group that did not have to lie, subjects admitted that the task was boring. So did those paid twenty dollars—an ample justification for misrepresenting their true attitude. Subjects paid only one dollar, however, rated the task as more enjoyable. Behaving in an attitude-discrepant manner without justification, the one-dollar subjects reduced their dissonance by changing their attitude. [Data from Festinger & Carlsmith, 1959.]

self-persuasion The processes by which people change their attitudes in response to their own actions.

peg-board tasks. Control group subjects, who did not mislead a confederate, admitted the tasks were pretty boring. So did those in the twenty-dollar condition, who had ample justification for what they did. Subjects who were paid only one dollar, however, said they thought the experiment was somewhat enjoyable. Having performed an attitude-discrepant behavior without sufficient justification, these subjects reduced their cognitive dissonance by changing their attitude. The results can be seen in Table 10.3. Two aspects of this study are noteworthy. First, it demonstrated the phenomenon of **self-persuasion**; that is, when people behave in ways that are discrepant with their attitudes, they often go on to change those attitudes—without exposure to a persuasive communication. Second, the findings contradicted the time-honored belief that big rewards produce great change. In fact, the more subjects were paid for their inconsistent behavior, the more justified they felt and the *less* likely they were to change their attitudes.

insufficient deterrence A condition in which people refrain from engaging in a desirable activity, even though only mild punishment is threatened.

Just as small reward is insufficient justification for attitude-discrepant behavior, mild punishment is **insufficient deterrence** for attitude-discrepant *nonbehavior*. Think about it. What happens when people refrain from doing something they really want to do? Do they devalue the activity and convince themselves that they never really wanted to do it in the first place? In one study, children were prohibited from playing with an attractive toy by being threatened with either mild or severe punishment. All subjects refrained. As cognitive dissonance theory predicts, however, only those subjects faced with mild punishment—an insufficient deterrent—showed disdain for the forbidden toy. Those who confronted the threat of severe punishment did not (Aronson & Carlsmith, 1963). Once again, cognitive dissonance theory turned common sense on its head: the less severe the threatened punishment, the more attitude change was produced.

Justifying Effort: Coming to Like What We Suffer For Have you ever spent tons of money or tried really hard to achieve something, only to discover that it wasn't worth all the effort? This kind of inconsistency between effort and outcome can arouse cognitive dissonance and motivate a change of heart toward the unsatisfying outcome. The hypothesis is simple but profound: we alter our attitudes to justify our suffering.

In a classic test of this hypothesis, Eliot Aronson and Judson Mills (1959) invited female students to take part in a series of group discussions about sex. But there was a hitch. Because sex is a sensitive topic that many people shy away from, subjects were told they would have to pass an "embarrassment test" before joining the group. The test consisted of reading sexual material aloud to a male experimenter. One group of subjects experienced what amounted to a *severe* initiation in which they had to recite obscene words and lurid passages taken from paperback novels. A second group underwent a *mild* initiation in which they read a list of more ordinary words pertaining to sex. A third group was admitted to the discussions without an initiation test.

Moments later, all subjects were given earphones and permitted to listen in on the group they would soon be joining. Actually what they heard was a tape-recorded discussion about "secondary sex behavior in the lower animals." It was dreadfully boring. When it was over, subjects were asked to rate how much they liked the group members and their discussion. Keep in mind what dissonance theory predicts: the more time or money or effort you choose to invest in something, the more anxious you will feel if the outcome is disappointing. One way to cope with this unnerving inconsistency is to alter your attitudes. That's exactly what happened. Subjects who had endured a severe initiation rated the discussion group more favorably than did those who had endured little or no initiation.

It's important to note that embarrassment is not the only kind of "effort" we feel the need to justify to ourselves. As a general rule, the more you pay for something—whether you pay in physical exertion, pain, time, or money—the more you will come to like it (Wicklund & Brehm, 1976). This principle has some provocative implications. Research suggests, for example, that the harder psychotherapy patients have to work at their own treatment, the more likely they are to feel better when that treatment is over (Axsom, 1989; Axsom & Cooper, 1985). Effort justification may also help to explain why college fraternities and sororities tend to foster lifelong loyalties, or why 58 percent of Vietnam veterans, compared to only 29 percent of other Americans, say that "The U.S. was right to get involved in the Vietnam war" (Witteman, 1990). Even today, twenty years later, those who risked their lives in that war must justify their nightmare.

Justifying Difficult Decisions: When Good Choices Get Even Better Whenever we have to make difficult decisions—whether to marry, what school to attend, what job to accept—we experience some dissonance. By definition, a decision is difficult when the alternative courses of action are about equally desirable. Marriage offers comfort and stability; staying single paves the way for discovering new relationships. One job might pay more money; the other might involve more interesting work. Once we make tough decisions like these, we are at risk. Negative aspects of the chosen alternative are at odds with our decision. So are the positive aspects of the unchosen alternative. According to dissonance theory, we will try to rationalize whatever we decide by exaggerating the positive features of our chosen alternative and the negative features of the unchosen alternative.

To examine this hypothesis, Jack Brehm (1956) recruited female subjects to evaluate a number of consumer products, presumably as part of a marketing research project. After rating a toaster, a coffee pot, a radio, a stopwatch, and other products, subjects were told they could take one home as a gift. In the high-dissonance condition, subjects were offered a difficult choice between two items they found equally attractive. In the low-dissonance group, they were offered an easier choice between a desirable and an undesirable item. After receiving their gift, subjects read a few research reports, then re-evaluated the various products. The results provided strong support for dissonance theory. In the low-dissonance group, subjects' postdecision ratings were about the same as their predecision ratings. In the high-dissonance condition, however, subjects' ratings increased for the chosen item and decreased for the nonchosen item. Subjects who were torn between two equivalent alternatives coped by reassuring themselves that they had made the right choice.

This phenomenon appears in a wide range of settings. For example, Robert Knox and James Inskter (1968) took dissonance theory to the racetrack and found that bettors who had already placed their two dollars on a horse were more optimistic about winning than were those who were standing in line waiting to take the plunge. Similarly, Dennis Regan and Martin Kilduff (1988) visited several polling stations on election day and found that voters were more likely to believe that their candidates would win when they were interviewed after submitting their ballots than before. Since bets and votes cannot be retracted, people who committed themselves to a decision were motivated to prevent postdecision dissonance. So they convinced themselves that the decision they made was right.

Cognitive Dissonance Theory: A New Look

Following in Festinger's bold footsteps, a generation of social psychologists explored the implications of cognitive dissonance theory. Through systematic research, it became evident early on that Festinger's (1957) original theory was not to be the last word. People do change their attitudes to justify attitude-

Dissonance theory predicts that this college senior will justify her selection of a graduate school by focusing on its positive features and minimizing the negative.

discrepant behavior, effort, and difficult decisions. But for dissonance to be aroused, certain conditions must be present (Brehm & Cohen, 1962; Greenwald & Ronis, 1978; Wicklund & Brehm, 1976). As summarized by Joel Cooper and Russell Fazio's (1984) "new look at dissonance theory," we now have a pretty good idea of what those conditions are, and why.

According to Cooper and Fazio, four steps are necessary for the arousal and reduction of dissonance. First, a person's attitude-discrepant behavior must produce unwanted *negative consequences*. Recall Festinger and Carlsmith's (1959) initial study. Not only did their subjects say something they knew to be false, they also had deceived a fellow student into taking part in a painfully boring experiment. Had these subjects lied without causing hardship, they would *not* have altered their attitudes to justify the action (Cooper et al., 1974). To borrow an expression from schoolyard basketball, "no harm, no foul." In fact, negative consequences may arouse dissonance even when people's actions are perfectly consistent with their attitudes—as when students who wrote against fee increases were led to believe that their essays backfired, leading a university committee to favor an increase (Scher & Cooper, 1989).

The second necessary step in the process is a feeling of *personal responsibility* for the unpleasant consequences of behavior. Personal responsibility consists of two factors. The first is the freedom of *choice*. When people believe that they had no choice but to behave as they did, there is no dissonance and no attitude change (Linder et al., 1967). If Festinger and Carlsmith had coerced their subjects into raving about the boring experiment, subjects would not have felt the need to further justify their actions by changing their attitudes. However, the experimental situation led subjects to think that their actions were voluntary and that the choice was theirs. Pressured without realizing it, subjects believed they didn't have to comply with the experimenter's request.

For people to feel personally responsible, they must also believe that the potential negative consequences of their actions were *foreseeable* at the time (Goethals et al., 1979). When the outcome could not have been anticipated, then there's no dissonance and no attitude change. Had Festinger and Carlsmith's subjects lied about the experiment in private, only later to find out that their statements had been tape-recorded for subsequent use, then again they would not have felt the need to further justify their behavior.

The third necessary step in the process is *physiological arousal.* Right from the start, Festinger viewed cognitive dissonance as a state of tension that people are motivated to reduce—much like hunger, thirst, and other basic drives. This emphasis on arousal appears to be well placed. In a study by Robert Croyle and Joel Cooper (1983), subjects wrote essays supporting or contradicting their own attitudes. Some of the subjects were ordered to do so; others were led to believe the choice was theirs. During the experiment, electrodes attached to the subjects' fingertips recorded their level of physiological arousal. As predicted by cognitive dissonance theory, those who freely wrote attitude-discrepant essays were the most aroused. Other researchers have obtained similar results (Elkin & Leippe, 1986; Losch & Cacioppo, 1990). Also, if dissonance-related arousal is inhibited by taking a tranquilizer or drinking alcohol, attitude change does not result (Cooper et al., 1978; Steele et al., 1981).

The fourth step in the dissonance process is closely related to the third. It isn't enough to feel generally aroused. The person must also make an *attribution* for that arousal to his or her own behavior. Suppose you just lied to a friend, or studied for an exam that was canceled, or made a tough decision that you might soon regret. Suppose further that even though you are upset, you believe your discomfort is caused by some external factor, not by your dissonance-producing behavior. Under these circumstances, will you exhibit attitude change as a symptom of cognitive dissonance? Probably not. When subjects are led to believe that their dissonance-related arousal is due to a drug they have supposedly taken (Zanna & Cooper, 1974), to the anticipation of painful electric shocks (Pittman, 1975), or to a pair of prism goggles they had to wear (Losch & Cacioppo, 1990), attitude change does not take place. Figure 10.11 summarizes the four steps in the production and reduction of dissonance.

Alternative Routes to Self-Persuasion

It is important to distinguish between the empirical facts as uncovered by dissonance researchers and the theory they use to explain them. The facts

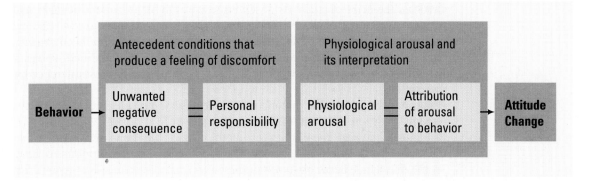

Figure 10.11 Necessary Conditions for the Arousal and Reduction of Dissonance. "A New Look at Dissonance Theory" suggests that four steps are necessary for attitude change to result from the production and reduction of dissonance.

themselves are clear: under certain conditions, people who behave in attitude-discrepant ways go on to change their attitudes. Whether this reflects a human need to reduce dissonance, however, is a matter of some controversy. As we are about to see, three alternative explanations of self-persuasion have been proposed.

Self-Perception Theory Daryl Bem's (1965) *self-perception theory,* described in Chapter 2, posed the first serious challenge to dissonance theory. Noting that people don't always have firsthand knowledge of their own attitudes, Bem proposed that we infer how we feel by observing ourselves and the circumstances of our own behavior. This sort of self-persuasion is not fueled by the need to reduce tension or justify and defend our actions. Instead, it is a cool, calm, and rational process in which people interpret ambiguous feelings by observing their own behavior. But can Bem's theory replace dissonance theory as an explanation of self-persuasion?

Bem confronted this question head-on. What if dispassionate observers who are not motivated by the need to reduce dissonance were to read a step-by-step description of a dissonance study and predict the results? This approach to the problem was ingenious. Observers, Bem reasoned, can have the same behavioral information as the subjects themselves, but they don't experience the same personal conflict. If observers could generate the same results as real subjects, it would show that dissonance arousal is not necessary for the observed changes in attitudes. To test his hypothesis, Bem (1967) described Festinger and Carlsmith's (1959) study to observers and had them guess subjects' attitudes. Some were told about the one-dollar condition, some about the twenty-dollar condition; others heard about the control group procedure. The results closely paralleled the original study. As observers saw it, subjects who said the task was interesting for twenty dollars didn't mean it; they just went along for the money. But those who made the same claim for only one dollar must have been sincere. Why else would they have gone along? As far as Bem was concerned, subjects themselves reason the same way. No conflict, and no arousal—just inference by observation.

So can we conclude that dissonance isn't necessary, just self-perception? That's a tough question. It's not easy to come up with a critical experiment to distinguish between these theories. Both predict the same results, but for different reasons. And both offer unique support for their own points of view. On the one hand, Bem's observer studies show that dissonance-like results *can* be obtained without arousal. On the other hand, the subjects of dissonance manipulations *do* experience arousal, and that arousal seems necessary for attitude change to take place. Can we say that one theory is right, and the other wrong?

Fazio and his colleagues (1977) concluded that both theories are right but apply to different situations. When people behave in ways that are strikingly at odds with their attitudes, they feel the unnerving effects of dissonance and change their attitudes to rationalize their actions. When people behave in ways that are not terribly discrepant with how they feel, however, they experience relatively little tension and form their attitudes as a matter of inference. In short, highly discrepant behavior produces attitude change through dissonance, and slightly discrepant behavior produces change through self-perception.

Impression-Management Theory   A second alternative to the dissonance view of self-persuasion is provided by *impression-management theory*, which says that what matters is not a motive to *be* consistent but a motive to *appear* consistent. None of us wants to be called fickle or to be viewed as a hypocrite. So we calibrate our attitudes and behaviors only publicly—for the sake of impression management, the desire to present ourselves to others in a particular light (Baumeister, 1982; Tedeschi et al., 1971). Or perhaps we are motivated not by a desire to appear consistent but by a desire to avoid being held responsible for any unpleasant consequences of our actions (Schlenker, 1982). Either way, this theory places the emphasis on our concern for self-presentation. According to this view, then, subjects in the Festinger and Carl-smith study did not want the experimenter to think they had sold out for a paltry sum of money.

If impression-management theory is correct, then cognitive dissonance does not produce attitude change at all—only reported change. In other words, if subjects were to state their attitudes anonymously, or if they were to think that the experimenter could determine their true feelings through physiological measures, dissonance-like effects should vanish. Sometimes the effects do vanish, but at other times they do not. In general, the research suggests that self-persuasion can be motivated by impression management, but it can also occur in situations that do not clearly arouse self-presentation concerns (Baumeister & Tice, 1984).

Self-Affirmation Theory A third competing explanation relates self-persuasion to the self. According to Elliot Aronson, situations that arouse dissonance do so because they threaten the self-concept (Aronson, 1969; Thibodeau & Aronson, 1992). This being the case, Festinger and Carlsmith's subjects were motivated to change their attitudes toward the boring task in order to repair damage to the self, not to resolve inconsistency.

Claude Steele (1988) takes the notion two steps further. First, dissonance-producing situations—engaging in attitude-discrepant behavior, exerting wasted effort, or making difficult decisions—set in motion a process of *self-affirmation* designed to revalidate the integrity of the self-concept. Second, this revalidation can be achieved in many ways, not just by resolving dissonance Steele' self-affirmation theory thus makes a unique prediction: if the active ingredient in dissonance situations is a threat to the self, then people who have an opportunity to affirm the self in other, more general ways will not suffer from the effects of dissonance. Give Festinger and Carlsmith's one-dollar subjects a chance to donate money, help a victim in distress, or solve a problem, and their self-concepts should bounce back without any further need to justify their actions.

Research supports this hypothesis. Steele (1988), for example, reports that he and his colleagues recruited college students—some were science oriented, others were not. All subjects were asked to rate ten popular music albums and were then offered a choice of keeping either their fifth- or sixth-ranked album. A few minutes after making this decision, all subjects were asked to rerate the ten albums. In the meantime, half of the subjects were told to put on a white lab coat in preparation for another experiment. The results were intriguing. As predicted by dissonance theory, most subjects coped with the difficult decision by inflating their ratings of the chosen album relative to the unchosen album. The key word, however, is "most." Among science-oriented students who dressed in white lab coats—a symbol of their personal values and professional goals—later ratings of the chosen and unchosen albums did not change. For them, wearing a lab coat was an act of self-affirmation, enough to eliminate their need to reduce dissonance.

To summarize, dissonance theory maintains that people change their attitudes to justify certain attitude-discrepant behaviors, efforts, and decisions. Self-perception theory argues that the change occurs because people infer how they feel by observing their own behavior. Impression-management theory claims that the attitude change is spurred by self-presentation concerns. Self-affirmation theory says that the change is motivated by threats to the self (see Figure 10.12).

Theories

	Cognitive Dissonance	Self-Perception	Impression Management	Self-Affirmation
Is the change of attitude motivated by a desire to reduce or prevent unpleasant feelings?	Yes	No	Yes	Yes
Does a person's private attitude really change?	Yes	Yes	No	Yes
Must the change be directly related to the attitude-discrepant behavior?	Yes	Yes	Yes	No

Figure 10.12   Theories of Self-Persuasion: Critical Comparisons.   Here we compare the major theories of self-persuasion. Notice that each alternative challenges a different aspect of dissonance theory. Self-perception theory assumes that attitudes change as a matter of inference, not motivation. Impression-management theory maintains that the change is more apparent than real, reported for the sake of public self-presentation. Self-affirmation theory contends that the motivating force is a concern for the self and that attitude change will not occur when the self-concept can be affirmed in other ways.

Attitudes and attitude change are an important part of social life. In this chapter, we have seen that persuasion can be achieved in different ways. The most common approach is through communication from *others*. Faced with newspaper editorials, junk mail, books, TV commercials, and other messages, we take one of two routes to persuasion. On the central route, attitude change is based on the merits of the communication. On the peripheral route, it is based on more superficial cues. A second, less obvious means of persuasion originates within *ourselves*. When people behave in ways that contradict their true convictions, they often go on to change their attitudes. Once again, there is not one single route to such change, but many: dissonance, self-perception, impression management, and self-affirmation are among the possible avenues.

REVIEW

THE STUDY OF ATTITUDES

An attitude is a combination of affective, behavioral, and cognitive reactions, positive or negative, toward an object.

How Attitudes Are Measured

The most common way to measure attitudes is through self-reports such as attitude scales. To get respondents to answer questions honestly, the bogus pipeline may be used. Alternatively, covert measures may be used, such as nonverbal behavior and the facial electromyograph (EMG).

The Link Between Attitudes and Behavior

Attitudes do not necessarily correlate with behavior, but under certain conditions there is a correlation. Attitudes predict behavior best when they're specific rather than general and strong rather than weak. Attitudes also compete with other influences on behavior.

PERSUASION BY COMMUNICATION

The most common approach to changing attitudes is persuasive communication. The question is, what factors make some appeals more effective than others?

Two Routes to Persuasion

When people learn and think about the contents of a message, they take the central route to persuasion and are influenced by the strength of the arguments. When people do not think carefully about a message, they take the peripheral route to persuasion and are influenced instead by other cues. The route taken depends on whether people have the ability and motivation to fully process the communication.

The Source

Attitude change is greater for messages delivered by a source that is high rather than low in credibility. Two factors enhance a source's credibility: competence and trustworthiness. Attitude change is also greater when the source is likable. Research shows that similarity and attractiveness contribute to a communicator's likability. Although the source is important, there are limits. First, when an audience has a high level of personal involvement, source factors are less important than message quality. Second, the sleeper effect shows that people often forget the source but not the message, so the effects of source credibility dissipate over time.

The Message

Obviously, the message carries great weight. Four message factors come into play. First, how much information should be presented? When an audience takes the peripheral route, lengthy messages are persuasive. On the central route, length works only if the added information does not dilute the message. Repetition is effective, but only up to a point. Second, how discrepant should a speaker's position be from an audience's? The more extreme the message, the greater the attitude change will be—again, only up to a point. Third, how persuasive are appeals to emotion? Fear messages motivate attitude change when they include instructions on how to avoid the threatened danger. Positive emotions also work, as people in a good mood are more easily persuaded by peripheral cues. Fourth, is it better to argue first or second? The most beneficial order depends on how much time elapses—between the two arguments and between the second argument and the final decision.

The Audience
People may differ in how difficult or easy they are to persuade. For example, we tend to be more impressionable as young adults than later in life. Also, different kinds of messages influence different kinds of people. For example, people who are high rather than low in the need for cognition are persuaded more by the strength of an argument. Those who are high rather than low in self-monitoring are influenced more by image-oriented appeals. Forewarning increases resistance to persuasive communication. It inoculates the audience, providing the opportunity to generate counterarguments, and it arouses reactance.

PERSUASION BY OUR OWN ACTIONS

Role Playing: All the World's a Stage
The way people act can influence how they feel, as behavior can determine attitudes.

Cognitive Dissonance Theory: The Classic Version
Under certain conditions, inconsistency between our attitudes and behavior produces an aversive state called cognitive dissonance. Motivated to reduce the tension, people will often change their attitudes to justify their behavior. Three classic experiments demonstrate the implications of dissonance theory. In these studies, subjects changed their attitudes in order to justify (1) attitude-discrepant behavior performed without sufficient justification, (2) effort that produced an undesirable outcome, and (3) difficult decisions that they had made.

Cognitive Dissonance Theory: A New Look
As research progressed, four conditions were found necessary for dissonance to be aroused. First, an attitude-discrepant behavior must produce unwanted negative consequences. Second, the person must accept personal responsibility for these outcomes. Third, the person must experience physiological arousal. Fourth, the person must attribute the cause of that arousal to the behavior in question.

Alternative Routes to Self-Persuasion
Alternative explanations of dissonance-related attitude change have been proposed. Self-perception theory maintains that people logically infer their attitudes by observing their own behavior. Impression-management theory says that people are motivated not to be consistent, only to appear consistent to others. According to

self-affirmation theory, dissonance is aroused by threats to the self-concept and can be reduced through a range of self-affirming behaviors, even without a change of attitude.

Group Processes

11

Preview

This chapter describes social influence in a group context. First, we focus on *collective processes,* the effects of the presence of others on an individual's behavior. Then we turn to *group processes* among individuals directly interacting with each other. In the final section on *cooperation, competition, and conflict,* we examine how groups and individuals intensify or reconcile their differences.

Have you ever watched the performance of a symphony orchestra? It's a magnificent spectacle: bows in the string section cocked at a precise angle; shiny French horns and trombones flashing in the spotlights; drums, gongs, and cymbals chiming in right on cue. Recently, one of us attended the American première performance of the Ulster Orchestra. It was a delightful evening of great music. But it was also a study in contrasts. On the one hand, there was the orchestra, with its members so closely attuned to one another. On the other hand, this orchestra makes its home in Northern Ireland, one of the most strife-torn and violence-ridden places on Earth. Inside Ulster Hall, Catholic and Protestant musicians make beautiful music together, while outside the hall Catholics and Protestants wage war on each other.

The paradox presented by the Ulster Orchestra is a fitting introduction to the topic of this chapter. For better or worse, groups affect all of us and the society in which we live. Here, we take a close look at how groups influence the behavior of their own members and how they behave in interactions with other groups.

COLLECTIVE PROCESSES: THE PRESENCE OF OTHERS

In one of her most memorable lines, the American writer Gertrude Stein insisted that a "rose is a rose is a rose." No such claim of uniformity has ever been made for groups. Groups vary tremendously in size, organization, and purpose. In this chapter, we distinguish between two major types. Groups in which people engage in a common activity but have little if any direct interaction with each other are called **collectives.** The audience at a concert is a collective, as is an angry crowd roaming the streets outside the concert hall. An orchestra, however, is different. Members of this kind of group have extensive interactions with each other. As described in Chapter 4, they also share a common social category (musician) and experience a common fate (the success or failure of their performance). We begin our discussion of group influence by examining collective processes. Groups in which members interact directly are considered later in the chapter.

collectives People engaged in common activities but with minimal direct interaction.

Social Facilitation: When Others Arouse Us

Social psychologists have long been fascinated by how the presence of others affects behavior. You may recall that in Chapter 1, we declared a tie for the title of "founder of social psychology." One of the winners was Norman Triplett, whose article "The Dynamogenic Factors in Pacemaking and Competition" (1897–1898) is often cited as the earliest publication in social psychology. Triplett began his research by studying the official bicycle records from the

Racing Board of the League of American Wheelmen for the 1897 season. He noticed that cyclists who competed against others performed better than those who cycled alone against the clock. After dismissing various theories of the day, he proposed his own hypothesis: the presence of another rider releases the competitive instinct, which increases nervous energy and, thereby, enhances performance. Triplett tested this hypothesis by having forty children wind up a fishing reel, alternating between performing alone and working parallel to each other. On the average, winding time was faster when the children worked side by side rather than alone.

Subsequent researchers studied the side-by-side, parallel activities used by Triplett and, also, the effects of performing in front of an audience. In both settings, their results were inconsistent. Sometimes the presence of others enhanced performance; at other times it impaired performance. Stumped by such puzzling findings, social psychologists must have felt that Triplett's lead had turned into a blind alley. But then Robert Zajonc (1965, 1980) came up with an elegant solution: the presence of others increases arousal, which affects performance in different ways depending on the specific task.

The Zajonc Solution This solution involves three basic steps. First, says Zajonc, the presence of others creates an increase in nonspecific drive. Most social psychologists define *drive* as diffuse arousal that energizes behavior. However, the exact physiological properties of drive are not well understood and the physiological effects of the presence of others may be more subtle than was originally assumed (Cacioppo et al., 1990; Geen, 1989). In the second step of Zajonc's model, increased drive enhances an individual's tendency to perform the *dominant response*. The dominant response is the reaction elicited most quickly and easily by a given stimulus. For example, if someone says "bacon," most people think "eggs." Third, Zajonc contends that the quality of a person's performance will vary according to the *task* at hand. On an easy task (one that is simple or well learned), the dominant response is usually correct. But on a difficult task (one that is complex or unfamiliar), the dominant response is often incorrect.

Now, let's put these three steps together (see Figure 11.1). Suppose you are trying to memorize some easy associations such as "bacon-eggs." Here, the presence of others will increase arousal, elicit the dominant response, and *enhance* your performance. But what if your task is more difficult? If you are trying to learn some strange associations such as "bacon-algebra," the presence of others will increase arousal, elicit the dominant response, and *impair* your performance. You'll start to say "eggs," which will interfere with your remembering "algebra." Taken together, these two effects of the presence of others—helping performance on easy tasks, but hurting performance on difficult tasks—are known as **social facilitation.** Unfortunately, this term is often confusing. As countless students have struggled to remember, the facilitation in "social facilitation" occurs only on easy tasks. On difficult ones, the social facilitation effect is performance impairment.

social facilitation
The finding that the presence of others enhances performance on easy tasks and impairs performance on difficult tasks.

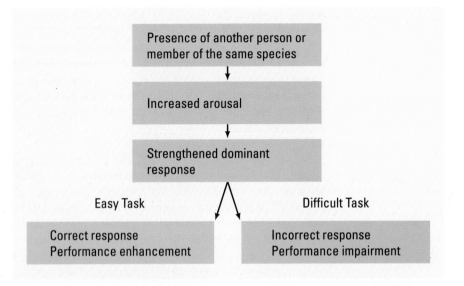

Figure 11.1   Social Facilitation: The Zajonc Solution.   According to Zajonc, the presence of others increases arousal, and arousal strengthens the dominant response to a stimulus. On an easy task, the dominant response is usually correct and thus the presence of others enhances performance. On a difficult task, the dominant response is often incorrect and thus the presence of others impairs performance.

Zajonc regards social facilitation as universal—occurring not only in human activities but also among animals and even insects. Consider, for example, cockroaches. How fast will they run? Research by Zajonc and his colleagues (1969) demonstrated that their speed is a matter of social facilitation. In this study, all the participating insects were placed in a brightly lit start box connected with a darkened goal box. When the track was a simple one, with a straight runway between the start box and the goal box, cockroaches running in pairs ran more quickly toward the goal box than those running alone. But in a more complex maze, with a right turn required to reach the goal box, solitary cockroaches outraced pairs.

Although Zajonc's theory of social facilitation emphasizes the role of task difficulty, expectations about the task can also influence performance (Sanna & Shotland, 1990). When college students who had little experience with computers played the interactive computer game Zork, those who had been led to expect a successful performance did better when another person was present than when they were alone (Robinson-Staveley & Cooper, 1990). In contrast, as you can see from Figure 11.2, those who had been led to expect a poor performance did not benefit from the presence of another person. Thus, it

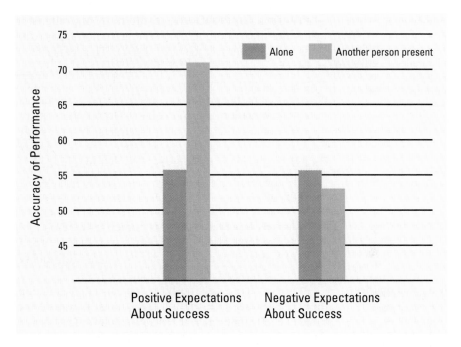

Figure 11.2   Computers and the Presence of Others.   College students who had little experience with computers were led to expect either a successful or an unsuccessful performance when they played an interactive computer game. Compared with those who worked alone, those who had positive expectations performed better when another person was present. But those who had negative expectations did not benefit from another's presence. [Data from Robinson-Staveley & Cooper, 1990].

appears that group learning situations can be helpful to those who are reasonably confident about their abilities, but are not useful for those who are worried about their performance.

Despite its elegance and predictive power, Zajonc's formulation has its critics. Two aspects of his theory have received particular attention. Zajonc maintains that social facilitation is uniquely *social*. But is it? Could nonsocial, inanimate objects produce the same effects? Zajonc is also convinced that the mere presence of others is sufficient to affect performance. Indeed, his perspective is often called the **mere presence** theory of social facilitation. But others have their doubts. Perhaps social facilitation effects will occur only when the others who are present have certain characteristics. Debating such issues, a number of alternative explanations have been proposed (Bond, 1982; Carver & Scheier, 1981b; Guerin & Innes, 1982; Mullen & Baumeister, 1987). Here, we consider two of the major variations on Zajonc's theme.

mere presence   The theory that the mere presence of others is sufficient to produce social facilitation effects.

evaluation apprehension   The theory that the presence of others will produce social facilitation effects only when those others are seen as potential evaluators.

Alternative Explanations   **Evaluation apprehension** was the first and remains the most thoroughly researched alternative (Cottrell, 1968; Henchy & Glass, 1968; Jones & Gerard, 1967). This perspective accepts the uniquely social character of social facilitation but rejects mere presence. Instead, it is argued that performance will be enhanced or impaired only in the presence of others who are in a position to evaluate that performance. Usually, presence and potential evaluation go hand in hand. To pry them apart, researchers have come up with some rather unusual procedures. In one study, for example, subjects worked on a task alone, in the presence of two other supposed subjects (actually confederates), or in the presence of two blindfolded confederates supposedly preparing for a perception study (Cottrell et al., 1968). Compared with subjects working alone, those working in the presence of seeing confederates were more likely to come up with dominant responses. In the presence of the blindfolded confederates, however, dominant responses were no more frequent than among subjects working alone. According to evaluation apprehension theorists, the mere presence of uninvolved, disinterested, and unobservant bystanders is *not* sufficient to produce social facilitation effects.

distraction-conflict theory   The theory that the presence of others will produce social facilitation effects only when those others distract from the task and create attentional conflict.

Another theoretical position on social facilitation, **distraction-conflict theory**, disputes both the uniquely social nature of social facilitation and the sufficiency of mere presence (Baron, 1986). This theory points out that being distracted while we're working on a task creates attentional conflict. We're torn between focusing on the task and inspecting the distracting stimulus. Conflicted about where to pay attention, our arousal increases and we suffer from information overload. People, of course, can be distracting, but so can flying objects, flashing lights, and loud noises. According to distraction-conflict theory, there is nothing uniquely social about "social" facilitation. Distraction-conflict theory also calls mere presence into question. People are usually distracting, but not always. When they are a familiar part of our social environment, their presence should not affect our performance.

Table 11.1 summarizes the three theories of social facilitation we have described. Is one of these theories right and the others wrong? Probably not. Comprehensive reviews of the research evidence have drawn different conclusions about which theory best accounts for the existing findings (Bond & Titus, 1983; Guerin, 1986). All of these theories are useful in pointing out the different ways in which the presence of others can affect performance: by just being there, as evaluators, and as a distraction. Our understanding of performance in the presence of others also benefits from the study of another collective phenomenon we examine in the following section.

Social Loafing: When Others Relax Us

The tasks employed in research on social facilitation involve individually *identifiable* contributions in the presence of others. What each person does is known. But on some tasks, contributions are *pooled* so that the specific performance of any one individual cannot be determined. The other founder of social

Questions	Answers		
	Mere Presence	Evaluation Apprehension	Distraction-Conflict
Is it uniquely social?	Yes	Yes	No
Is mere presence sufficient?	Yes	No	No

Table 11.1 Social Facilitation: Questions and Answers. For theories of social facilitation, the major issues in dispute are whether it is produced only by social stimuli and whether the mere presence of others is sufficient. As you can see, the three theories described in the text provide different answers to these questions.

psychology, French agricultural engineer Max Ringelmann, investigated group performance on these kinds of collective endeavors. In research conducted during the 1880s, Ringelmann discovered that compared with what people produced on their own, individual output declined when they worked together on simple tasks like pulling a rope or pushing a cart (Kravitz & Martin, 1986; Ringelmann, 1913).

social loafing A group-produced reduction in individual output on easy tasks where contributions are pooled.

Almost one hundred years later, Bibb Latané and his colleagues (1979) found that **social loafing**, group-produced reductions in individual output, still flourishes. When, for example, college students were told to cheer or clap as loudly as they could, the sound pressure generated by each individual decreased as the size of the group increased (see Figure 11.3). Social loafing is not restricted to simple motor tasks. Sharing responsibility with others also reduces the amount of effort people put into cognitive tasks (Weldon & Gargano, 1988). In short, when others are there to pick up the slack, people slack off.

Social loafing poses a threat to the productivity of group efforts throughout society, so much so that Latané and his colleagues called it a "social disease." Fortunately, this disease can be treated. Social loafing is reduced or eliminated entirely when participants believe that their individual contributions are identifiable (Williams et al., 1981). Nor do people loaf on tasks they regard as personally meaningful (Brickner et al., 1986; Williams & Karau, 1991). Anticipated evaluation of the group's performance also affects social loafing. Expecting that groups with a good performance will be rewarded provides a powerful incentive *not* to loaf (Sheppard & Wright, 1989). Indeed, simply believing that group members will have sufficient information to be able to evaluate the quality of the group product improves performance (Harkins & Szymanski, 1989).

For Stephen Harkins and Kate Szymanski, the role of evaluation in social loafing struck a familiar chord, reminding them of the evaluation apprehension theory of social facilitation. They noted that the connection between evaluation

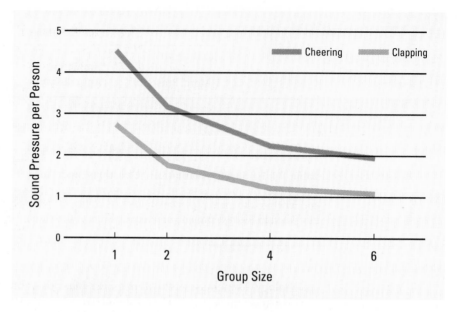

Figure 11.3 Social Loafing: When Many Produce Less.   Social loafing is a group-produced reduction in individual output on simple tasks. In this study, college students were told to cheer or clap as loudly as they could. The sound pressure produced by each of them decreased as the size of the group increased. [From Latané et al., 1979.]

of an individual's work and the presence of others depends on whether individual contributions to the group effort are identifiable or are pooled together. When individual contributions can be identified, the presence of others *increases* evaluation as everyone is aware of how everyone else has performed. When individual contributions are pooled, the presence of others *decreases* evaluation as any potentially identifying marks of an individual's performance are swallowed up in the group product.

This analysis laid the foundation for a unified paradigm encompassing both social facilitation and social loafing (Harkins, 1987; Harkins & Szymanski, 1987). The theoretical integration makes four predictions. First, when the presence of others increases evaluation of an individual's work, performance on easy tasks should be *enhanced* because we try harder. But, second, performance on difficult tasks should be *impaired* because the pressure gets to us. As we have seen, research on social facilitation confirms these two predictions. Third, when the presence of others decreases evaluation, performance on easy tasks should be *impaired* because we get bored and can slack off without being caught. This, as we have seen, is social loafing.

Now take the fourth step. What should happen to performance on a difficult task when the presence of others decreases evaluation of an individual's work?

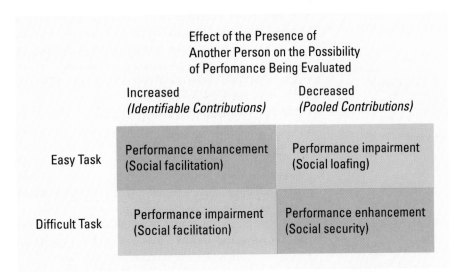

Figure 11.4   Social Facilitation and Social Loafing: A Unified Paradigm. According to the unified paradigm, social facilitation and social loafing are mirror images. Whenever the presence of others increases the possibility of being evaluated (as it does on tasks where each person's contribution is identifiable), performance will be enhanced on easy tasks and impaired on difficult ones. In contrast, whenever the presence of others decreases the possibility of being evaluated (as it does on tasks where all contributions are pooled), performance will be impaired on easy tasks and enhanced on difficult ones.

Under these circumstances, performance should be *enhanced*. The task is challenging enough to engage our best efforts, but we don't get rattled by fear of failure because individual performance can't be observed. There's no official name for this last effect, but we're inclined to call it "social security." These four predictions are summarized in Figure 11.4, and research on the unified paradigm has obtained the predicted pattern of results (Bartis et al., 1988; Jackson & Williams, 1985). By viewing social loafing as the mirror image of social facilitation, the unified paradigm reconciles the work of the two founders: Triplett and Ringelmann—together at last.

Deindividuation: When People Lose Control

Some other pioneers in social psychology regarded the presence of others as even more profound, and more troubling, than did Triplett and Ringelmann. Based on their research in France, Gabriel Tarde (1890) and Gustave Le Bon (1895) viewed collective influence as virtually mesmerizing. They believed that under the sway of the crowd, people would turn into copycat automatons or, worse still, uncontrollable mobs.

The destructive potential of collectives is amply confirmed by human history (Staub, 1989). And current events are no exception. In Northern Ireland and India, religious groups take bloody revenge against each other. In what was formerly East Germany, rampaging groups of neo-Nazis attack and murder immigrant workers from Asia and Africa. In Lebanon, warring factions have turned what used to be called the "Switzerland of the Middle East" into a bombed-out battleground. And in many American cities, racial and ethnic tensions simmer close to the boiling point. Sometimes they explode. In the spring of 1991, black motorist Rodney King was brutally beaten by a group of white Los Angeles police officers. In the spring of 1992, white truck driver Reginald Denny was brutally beaten by a group of black gang members during the "days of rage" that erupted in Los Angeles when King's assailants were acquitted of criminal charges brought against them. As the videotape of each incident was played over and over, people were stunned by the ferocity of the attacks on King and Denny. How can such things happen?

Presumably, there are many contributing causes. As described in Chapter 4, people's identification with their own group and prejudice against members of the other group can increase hostility and aggression (Reicher, 1984). In addition, factors examined in Chapter 8 are often present, including the imitation of aggressive models, intense frustration, high temperatures, alcohol

Captured on videotapes that were shown repeatedly on TV, the interracial beatings of black motorist Rodney King and white truck driver Reginald Denny shocked the nation. Deindividuation may explain, at least in part, why these attacks were so violent.

consumption, and weapons that trigger aggressive thoughts and actions. But the astonishingly high level of violence exhibited by groups in some situations suggests that another process may also be involved: the breakdown of internal controls against unacceptable behavior.

deindividuation
The loss of a person's sense of individuality and a loosening of normal constraints against deviant behavior.

Social psychologists call this breakdown **deindividuation**, the loss of a person's sense of individuality and a loosening of normal restraints against deviant behavior. At first, deindividuation was considered a purely collective phenomenon (Festinger et al., 1952). Although later research found that the presence of others is not necessary for deindividuation to occur, a collective setting is particularly conducive (Diener et al., 1976; Mullen, 1986).

Environmental Cues   According to Steven Prentice-Dunn and Ronald Rogers (1982, 1983), two types of environmental cues, accountability and attentional, influence deviant behavior. *Accountability cues* tell people how far they can go without being held responsible. For example, environmental cues indicating that people are anonymous (being part of a large crowd, wearing masks or hoods) decrease accountability. Think about it. What would you do if you knew you were perfectly anonymous—that is, invisible? In his novel *The Memoirs of an Invisible Man,* H. F. Saint gives his answer to this question: anonymity offers perfect freedom to engage in behaviors that are normally inhibited.

Saint's fiction is well grounded in real fact. When college students were asked what they would do if they could be totally invisible for twenty-four hours, most of their responses referred to criminal acts such as robbing a bank (Dodd, 1985). Even more compelling evidence of the effects of anonymity is provided by research on actual behavior. In the laboratory, anonymity has been created by refraining from mentioning subjects' names and having them dress up in enveloping clothing, sometimes complete with hoods masking their face from view. Control subjects are addressed by name and retain their regular clothing. Compared with controls, anonymous subjects are more aggressive (Zimbardo, 1970). They are also more likely to use obscene language (Singer et al., 1965). Prentice-Dunn and Rogers believe that accountability cues such as anonymity loosen restraints against deviant behavior by changing an individual's *cost-reward calculations.* Thinking they won't be caught and punished, people can deliberately choose to engage in gratifying but usually inhibited behaviors.

In one study, however, anonymous subjects wearing hoods were *less* aggressive than those in their normal attire (Zimbardo, 1970). As the Ku Klux Klan proves beyond a shadow of a doubt, people wearing hoods often engage in appalling violence. But outside the KKK, wearing a hood over one's face is considered rather weird, making an individual feel awkward and self-conscious. According to Prentice-Dunn and Rogers, wearing a bizarre costume is an example of the second type of environmental cue that can influence deviant behavior. *Attentional cues* focus a person's attention on the self or away from it. Attentional cues that increase self-awareness, such as wearing inappropriate clothing, should decrease deindividuated behavior. In contrast, attentional cues that decrease self-awareness, such as intense stimulation from the environment, should increase the potential for deindividuation. Have you ever been at a party with flashing strobe lights and music so loud that you could feel the room vibrate? If so, did it seem that you were somehow merging with the pulsating crowd around you and your individual identity was slipping away? In laboratory research, subjects whose self-awareness is reduced by environmental circumstances are more uninhibited, extreme, and aggressive in their actions (Diener, 1979; Prentice-Dunn & Rogers, 1980; Spivey & Prentice-Dunn, 1990).

Prentice-Dunn and Rogers maintain that when a person's attention is deflected away from the self because of intense environmental stimulation, a change in consciousness takes place. A person in this *deindividuated state* attends less to internal standards of conduct, reacts more to the immediate situation, and is less sensitive to long-term consequences of behavior (Diener, 1980). Behavior slips out from the bonds of cognitive control, and people act on impulse. From a legal perspective, it could be argued that the deindividuated state is a condition of diminished capacity that reduces personal responsibility for one's acts. And, indeed, such arguments have been made and sometimes accepted. A South African judge recently reduced the sentences of individuals convicted of a murder that occurred during violent clashes between Inkatha police and Xhosha-speaking residents loyal to the African National Congress. Convinced by expert testimony describing the process of deindividuation, the judge concluded that a less severe sentence was appropriate (Colman, 1991). The effects of accountability and attentional cues on deviant behavior are outlined in Figure 11.5.

Self-Awareness In their research on attentional cues, Prentice-Dunn and Rogers assume that reduced self-awareness increases the likelihood of deviant behavior. Actually, the relationship between self-awareness and such behavior is more complex, as we can see from research on aggression. Self-awareness affects aggression through two different pathways: (1) strengthening adherence to personal standards of conduct (Carver, 1975; Scheier et al., 1974) and (2) intensifying emotional experience (Gibbons, 1990).

To map out the connections created by adherence to personal standards, imagine two different people. One believes that aggression is immoral, but the other believes that aggression is permissible. The first individual fits the specifications outlined by Prentice-Dunn and Rogers. Increase this person's self-awareness, and behavior will conform to the *aggression-rejecting* standard: aggression will decrease. If, however, self-awareness is reduced in a situation conducive to violence, this normally law-abiding citizen could become part of a mob that tears places, or people, apart.

Now turn to the other individual. Increase this person's self-awareness and behavior will conform to the *aggression-accepting* standard: aggression will increase. If, however, this person's self-awareness is reduced in a benign environment, aggressive tendencies should decline. At the prom, hoodlums may come to fight but stay to dance.

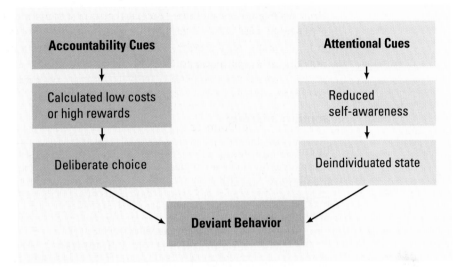

Figure 11.5 Environmental Cues and Deviant Behavior. Prentice-Dunn and Rogers propose that two types of environmental cues can produce deviant behavior. Accountability cues, such as anonymity, make deviant behavior less costly and more rewarding by indicating that the individual can get away with it. This increases the probability that the individual will deliberately choose to engage in this behavior. Attentional cues, such as intense environmental stimulation, reduce self-awareness and trigger a deindividuated state, in which cognitive controls are diminished and the individual acts impulsively.

The second pathway between self-awareness and aggression is an emotional one. Regardless of personal standards, self-awareness intensifies emotional experience. Because an angry individual becomes more angry when he or she is self-aware, aggression is likely to increase. In a burst of emotion, standards dissolve and the feeling takes over.

These dual effects of self-awareness on aggression may account for why mob violence is hard to start *and* hard to stop. Since most people presumably have principles and values that oppose brutality and violence, a drastic decrease in self-awareness may be necessary to reduce normal restraints and unleash the frenzy of the crowd. Once highly emotional behavior has begun, however, it can be self-perpetuating: fueled by the deindividuated state and intensified by a few jolts of self-awareness.

GROUP PROCESSES: INTERACTING WITH OTHERS

As we have seen, the range of collective social influence is enormous: from bicycle races to mob violence. Collective processes, however, are only minimally social. People are in the same place at the same time working on a common task or reacting to the same event, but they don't engage in extensive interaction with each other. In this section, we consider social influence in groups where interaction among members is direct and meaningful.

Joining a Group

Interactive groups come in all shapes and sizes: large and small, organized and disorganized, short-term and long lasting. Sometimes group membership is involuntary. You didn't choose your family. But membership in most interactive groups usually takes place on a voluntary basis. You decide to join an existing group or get together with others to create a brand new one. Why do people join groups? How do groups develop over time?

The major reason that people join a group is their belief that group membership will bring rewards: the companionship of people they like, a positive sense of social identity through associating with a group they value, information or skills that they desire, and cooperation on projects they want to pursue. Group membership, of course, has costs as well as rewards: having to get along with group members you dislike, being frustrated when the group spins its wheels or goes off in the wrong direction. But individuals preparing to join a group are usually optimistic about the group. They expect more rewards than costs, believe that the anticipated rewards will be more positive than the anticipated costs will be negative, and think that rewards are more likely than costs to occur (Brinthaupt et al., 1991).

Once an individual has joined a group, a process of adjustment takes place. The individual assimilates into the group, making whatever changes are necessary to fit in. The group accommodates to the newcomer, making whatever changes are necessary to include that individual. According to Richard Moreland and John Levine (1989), group socialization often relies on the relationship between newcomers and more established members. Newcomers gain acceptance by modeling their behavior on what the oldtimers do. Oldtimers may hold explicit training sessions for newcomers. And, acting as mentors, oldtimers can develop close personal relationships with newcomers in order to help them learn the ropes and be successful in the group. Having a mentor is useful to anyone joining a new group but may be especially helpful to those, such as women and people of color, joining groups from which they were previously excluded (Irons & Moore, 1985).

Roles, Norms, and Cohesiveness

Despite their variation in specific characteristics, all interactive groups can be described in terms of three essential factors: roles, norms, and cohesiveness

(Forsyth, 1983; Levine & Moreland, 1990). People's *roles* in a group, their set of expected behaviors, can be formal or informal. Formal roles are designated by titles: teacher or student in a class, vice president or account executive in a corporation. Informal roles are less obvious but still powerful. Robert Bales (1958), for example, proposed that regardless of people's titles, enduring groups give rise to two fundamental types of roles: an instrumental role to help the group achieve its tasks, and an expressive role to provide emotional support and maintain morale. The same person can fill both roles, but often different individuals assume one or the other.

Bales' view of group roles is patterned after the division of labor in the traditional family between the "breadwinner" father and the "caretaking" mother. Does this pattern still hold? Are males more likely to take an instrumental, task-oriented role and females an expressive, socially oriented role?

People join a group because they believe that group membership will bring rewards such as companionship, social identity, information or skills, and cooperation.

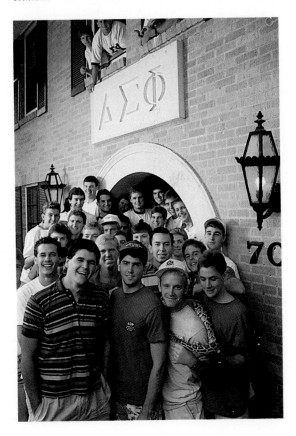

Under some circumstances, the answer is yes. In mixed-sex groups working on tasks that allow for both kinds of roles, males engage in more task-oriented activity and females in more positive social behavior. (Wood, 1987; Wood et al., 1985b).

Such gender differences, however, are not fixed and immutable. When men and women in a mixed-sex group were given feedback indicating either high or low competence, those who believed they were highly competent were more task oriented, while those who perceived themselves as lacking competence engaged more often in positive social behaviors (Wood & Karten, 1986). The same pattern of results was obtained for both genders, suggesting that the male preference for task-oriented roles and the female preference for socially oriented roles reflect underlying differences between men and women in their beliefs about their own competence. Such differences may be created and sustained by self-evaluations; women appear to be far more likely than men to underestimate the quality of their work (Beyer, 1990). Among men and women who feel equally competent about task performance, the roles they adopt and the manner in which they behave are often remarkably similar (Dovidio et al., 1988a, 1988b).

Interactive groups also establish *norms,* rules of conduct for members. Like roles, norms may be formal or informal. Fraternities and sororities, for example, usually have written rules for the behavior expected from their members. Informal norms are more subtle. People may not even be aware of a group's informal norms yet be strongly influenced by them. Have you ever spent hours trying to figure out what to wear at a party given by a group to which you belong? Dress codes don't have to be written down to affect our behavior.

The third characteristic of interactive groups is *cohesiveness.* Some groups are close knit, experiencing high cohesiveness. In other groups, the bond among group members is loose and cohesiveness low. Cohesiveness refers to the forces exerted on a group that push its members closer together (Cartwright & Zander, 1960; Festinger, 1950). Such forces can be positive (attraction to group members) or negative (costs involved in leaving the group). Cohesiveness can be based on joint involvement in the task, mutual concern about group members, or both (Zaccaro & McCoy, 1988). It can also be increased by attack from outsiders (Lanzetta, 1955). As noted in Chapter 9, there are strong pressures toward behavioral and attitudinal conformity in highly cohesive groups: members conform to prevailing group norms and reject those who deviate (Schachter, 1951; Wright et al., 1986).

Whistle blowers who refuse to keep silent about unethical or incompetent practices often experience the full weight of the cohesive group against them. Take, for example, Jerome LiCari, former head of research and development at the Beech-Nut Nutrition Corporation. When LiCari tried to convince corporate officials to stop selling fake apple juice falsely advertised as "100-percent fruit juice" for babies, he was told to be a team member or else he would be fired (Traub, 1988). Unable to change company practices, LiCari resigned. His experience illustrates how difficult it is to be the lone voice of honesty confront-

"This might not be ethical. Is that a problem for anybody?"

In highly cohesive groups, members conform to the prevailing group norm. [Drawing by Vietor; © 1987 The New Yorker Magazine, Inc.]

ing the stone wall of a cohesive group. It is much easier to speak up when you have allies, and, indeed, people are more likely to blow the whistle when there are a larger number of witnesses to the wrongdoing (Miceli et al., 1991). Fortunately, the Beech-Nut incident did not end with LiCari's resignation. Six years later, the former president and vice president who had refused to take his advice were each sentenced to a prison term of a year and a day along with a fine of $100,000. Sometimes refusing to listen to a whistle blower can be a very expensive proposition.

Group Polarization: Gaining Conviction

Once a group has formed—with roles, norms, and some degree of cohesiveness—it begins to make decisions and take actions. The issues faced by groups range from the trivial ("Where do we party?") to the profound ("Shall we go to war?"). Whatever the issue, the attitudes of group members affect what they do. How does being in a group influence people's opinions? Does it water them down—or concentrate them? Let's see.

If you have ever watched the Democratic and Republican national conventions on TV, you may have noticed that the Democrats often sound more liberal when they get together as a party than they do on an individual basis. Likewise, the Republicans frequently deliver a more conservative message as a group than they do as individuals. But why? What happens to those in each party who hold more moderate views? Common sense would suggest that when you put a group of people together, discussion of differing opinions will result in some overall compromise as everyone moves toward the group average. But that isn't what happens. Instead, individuals who start off with roughly similar views end up with more extreme positions after group discussion. Put a group of moderate liberals together and they become more liberal; put a group of moderate conservatives together and they become more conservative.

group polarization
The exaggeration through group discussion of initial tendencies in the thinking of group members.

This effect is called **group polarization**, the exaggeration through group discussion of initial tendencies in the thinking of group members (Moscovici & Zavalloni, 1969; Myers & Lamm, 1976). It is more likely to occur on important issues than on trivial ones (Kerr, 1992). Racial prejudice, for example, is a very important issue. Is it susceptible to group polarization? In one study attempting to answer this question, high school students responded to an initial questionnaire and were classified as high, medium, or low on racial prejudice (Myers & Bishop, 1970). Groups of like-minded students then met for a discussion of racial issues, with their individual attitudes on these issues assessed before and after their interaction. Group polarization was dramatic. Students low in prejudice to begin with were even *less* prejudiced after the group discussion; students moderate or high in prejudice became even *more* prejudiced.

To determine what produces group polarization, consider what takes place in a group discussion: a group member hears arguments from and learns the position of other members of his or her own group. Each of these three components—arguments, positions, and own group—plays a role in group polarization. When people hear arguments from others, they learn new information. According to **persuasive arguments theory**, group polarization is determined by the number and persuasiveness of the arguments that are presented to group members (Vinokur & Burnstein, 1974). The more persuasive arguments to which members are exposed, the more extreme their attitudes become (Hinsz & Davis, 1984).

persuasive arguments theory The theory that group polarization is produced by the number and persuasiveness of the arguments presented in group discussion.

But what if we find out what others believe without being told why they believe it? Committee deliberations, for example, often begin with a "straw poll" requiring members to indicate their opinions. Could just knowing the positions of others in the group produce group polarization? Some researchers think so (Brown, 1965; Sanders & Baron, 1977). Their reasoning is based on *social comparison theory*. As described in Chapter 2, social comparison theory holds that people construct their view of social reality by comparing themselves with others (Festinger, 1954).

The construction of social reality in like-minded groups is a two-step process. First, people discover more support for their own opinion than they had originally anticipated. Second, this discovery sets up a new, more extreme norm and motivates group members to go beyond that norm. If believing X is good, then believing Triple X is even better. By adopting a more extreme attitudinal position, people can distinguish themselves from the group in a manner approved by the group. Among Republicans, a person gains social approval and increases self-esteem through strong support of private enterprise. Among Democrats, a person gains social approval and increases self-esteem through strong support of government assistance to those in need. According to the social comparison perspective, "people are motivated to see themselves as basically similar to others, yet different—in the right direction and to the right extent" (Lamm & Myers, 1978, p. 178).

For many years, persuasive arguments theory and social comparison theory were the two dominant explanations for group polarization. Like Olympic competitors they were pitted against each other, carefully modified and refined during breaks from competition, and then sent out again in head-to-head contests. In real life, the two are often inseparable; we hear arguments and learn positions at the same time. When the two are separated in laboratory competitions, persuasive arguments theory tends overall to have the edge (Isenberg, 1986; Laughlin & Earley, 1982). But different situations can affect the balance of power (Kaplan, 1987; Kaplan & Miller, 1987). Having each scored some points, the two competitors seemed ready to rest on their laurels when suddenly a new contender showed up.

The new contender is based on a concept you may recall from Chapter 4, *social categorization:* people's tendency to categorize themselves and others in terms of social groups (Turner & Oakes, 1989). The social categorization approach to group polarization focuses on how individuals react to information from ingroups (to which they belong or want to belong) and outgroups (to which they don't belong and don't want to). According to this formulation, only persuasive arguments from an ingroup should influence members' attitudes, and social comparison should take place only in regard to ingroup opinions (Hogg et al., 1990; Mackie, 1986). Republicans should be persuaded by and compare with other Republicans, while Democrats should be persuaded by and compare with other Democrats.

Is this emphasis on the role of social categorization justified? Research by Diane Mackie and Joel Cooper (1984) indicates that it is. The undergraduates selected to participate in this study held a mildly favorable attitude toward retaining standardized tests (such as the Scholastic Aptitude Test) as a criterion for admission to their university. All subjects expected that they would be joining group A for an upcoming discussion of this issue. They then listened to a tape recording of arguments either favoring or opposing the use of standardized tests. Half of the subjects were told they were listening to a previous discussion by group A (the ingroup); the other half believed this discussion took place among members of group B (the outgroup).

As predicted, subjects' opinions were influenced only by the ingroup. Those hearing favorable arguments became even more convinced that standardized tests should be retained—the group polarization effect. Those hearing opposing arguments from the ingroup changed their initial opinions and joined the ingroup's opposition to the tests. Listening to the exact same arguments made by the outgroup had little effect. Neither favorable nor opposing arguments from the outgroup changed subjects' initial opinions. Thus, a group discussion influences our subsequent attitudes and beliefs by means of what we hear *and* from whom we hear it.

Groupthink: Losing Perspective

The persuasion, social comparison, and social categorization processes involved in group polarization may set the stage for an even greater, and perhaps more dangerous, bias in group decision making. Consider three major decisions made by American presidents and their advisers: Kennedy's approval of the Bay of Pigs invasion in Cuba, Nixon's denial of responsibility for the Watergate break-in, and Reagan's decision to provide arms to Iran in an effort to secure the release of American hostages. If any of us had been watching these groups during their decision making, we would have felt reassured by their cool, calm, and collected behavior. Yet as we now know, the decisions made by each of these groups were seriously flawed and resulted in disastrous military or political consequences. How could such seemingly intelligent discussions among such presumably intelligent individuals go so wrong?

groupthink A group decision-making style characterized by an excessive tendency among group members to seek concurrence.

According to Irving Janis (1982), the culprit is **groupthink**, an excessive tendency to seek concurrence among group members. Groupthink emerges when the need for agreement takes priority over the motivation to obtain accurate knowledge and make appropriate decisions. Janis diagnosed three major contributing factors in the development of groupthink: cohesiveness, structure, and the situational context. Since highly cohesive groups are more likely to reject members with deviant opinions, Janis believed they would be more susceptible to groupthink. Group structure was also said to be important. Groups that are composed of people from similar backgrounds, isolated from other people, directed by a strong leader, and lacking in systematic procedures for making and reviewing decisions should be particularly likely to fall prey to groupthink. Finally, Janis emphasized that stressful situations can provoke groupthink. Under stress, urgency can overrule accuracy, and the reassuring support of other group members becomes especially desirable.

Behavioral Symptoms Groupthink strikes at the heart of the group's decision-making process, interfering with the identification of problems as well as with the development of effective solutions (Moreland & Levine, 1992). Behavioral symptoms of groupthink include the following:

Overestimation of the group: Members maintain an illusion of invulnerability and an exaggerated belief in the morality of the group's positions. Did Kennedy and his advisers sufficiently question the wisdom of the invasion plan they had inherited from the Eisenhower administration? Or did they think that, as the "best and brightest," they could surely pull off a little invasion?

Closed-mindedness: Members rationalize the correctness of the group's actions and believe stereotypes about the characteristics of the targets of these actions. Did Nixon and his advisers ever think seriously about what was appropriate for political activities in a democracy? Or were they convinced that anything goes against "the enemy"?

Increased pressures toward uniformity: The pressures to sustain group cohesiveness grow increasingly strong. Group members censor their own thoughts and act as "mindguards" to discourage deviant thoughts by other group members. Those who refuse to conform are expelled from the group. Did Reagan and those who supported the exchange with Iran really listen to those who opposed it? Or were officials who wouldn't join the team and support the policy simply "cut out of the loop"?

By preventing an open consideration of possible alternatives, the behavioral symptoms of groupthink can result in the defective decision making outlined in Figure 11.6. In turn, a defective decision-making process increases the likelihood that a group will make bad decisions and perform poorly.

Research on Groupthink There have been surprisingly few experiments or correlational studies on groupthink, and the available evidence provides only mixed support for Janis' model. For example, it is not at all clear that high cohesiveness is a necessary condition (Flowers, 1977; Leana, 1985). Instead, groupthink may depend on a combination of strong attraction to the group but uncertainty about approval (Longley & Pruitt, 1980; McCauley, 1989). When people long to be fully accepted by the group but fear that expressing deviant opinions will lead to rejection, they are unlikely to speak out and may even change their real beliefs in order to become more comfortable in the group. In contrast, deviant opinions are easier to express and more likely to be genuinely considered in a well-established group whose members have strong personal relationships with each other.

Some structural factors may be particularly important in setting the stage for groupthink. Groups perceived by their members as isolated from others perform more poorly than do groups perceived as more open to outsiders (Moorhead & Montanari, 1986). In addition, groups led by highly directive leaders voicing their preference for a specific course of action are more susceptible to groupthink (Flowers, 1977; Leana, 1985). The effects of stress have also been documented. Individuals differ in how resistant to groupthink they are under stressful conditions (Callaway et al., 1985). There appears, however, to be a general tendency for groups to close ranks and reject deviant opinions when coping with stressful events such as an impending deadline (Kruglanski & Webster, 1991).

Although little controlled research on groupthink has been conducted, there are numerous case studies and historical analyses, frequently focusing on the deliberations and actions of government and military officials (McCauley, 1989; Tetlock, 1979). But the possible range of groupthink goes well beyond these kinds of groups. Groupthink tendencies have been identified in groups as diverse as a university board of trustees (Hensley & Griffin, 1986) and autonomous work groups in a battery assembly plant (Manz & Sims, 1982). Some of the major business scandals and catastrophes of recent years may also be

Figure 11.6   Groupthink: Antecedents, Symptoms, and Consequences.   According to Janis, highly cohesive groups with like-minded members working under stressful conditions run a particularly high risk of groupthink. The behavioral symptoms of groupthink emerge when agreement has a higher priority than accurate information and appropriate decisions. Groupthink creates a defective decision-making process that increases the probability of a bad decision. [Based on Janis, 1982.]

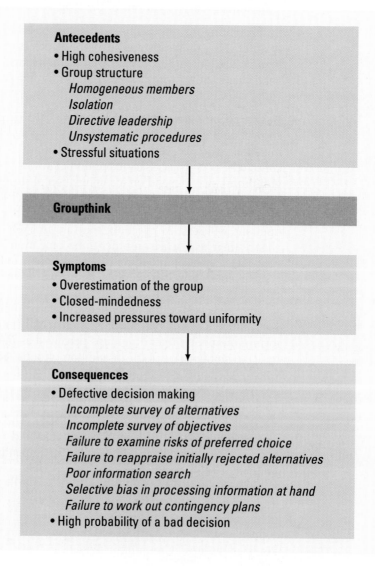

attributable, at least in part, to groupthink. In his book *Belly Up* (1985), Phillip Zweig describes how the refusal to face financial facts and to re-examine options contributed to the collapse of the Penn Square Bank in Oklahoma, the first of a series of major commercial bank failures in the United States during the 1980s.

The potential for groupthink to cause great harm to individuals, groups, and the society as a whole highlights how important it is to prevent it. Janis urged groups to guard against groupthink by taking three major steps: consult widely with outsiders, have leaders who make an active effort to encourage criticism, and establish a strong norm of critical review of all decisions. Groups adopting this preventative approach should have a much better chance of making wise choices and implementing effective actions.

Group Performance

The study of groupthink upsets popular preconceptions about groups. Aren't two heads better than one? According to Ivan Steiner (1972), it depends—on the available resources, the group process, and the type of task involved. Although a group typically has more resources than does an individual, difficulties in coordinating members' efforts can hinder the group's effectiveness. And the type of task determines what kinds of resources affect performance.

On an *additive* task, the group product is the *sum* of all the members' contributions. Donating to a charity is an additive task, as is making noise at a pep rally. As we have seen, people often indulge in social loafing during additive tasks. Even so, groups usually outperform an individual working alone. Each member's contribution may be less than it would be if that person worked alone, but the total is still greater than the amount only one member could provide.

On a *conjunctive* task, the group product is determined by the individual with the *poorest* performance. Mountain-climbing teams are engaged in a conjunctive task; the "weakest link" will determine their success or failure. Because of this vulnerability to the poor performance of any one group member, group performance tends to be worse than the performance of a single, average individual.

On a *disjunctive* task, the group product is determined by the performance of the individual with the *best* performance. Advertising personnel trying to develop a creative ad campaign are engaged in a disjunctive task. All they need is that one good idea, that one compelling way to sell their product. In terms of sheer probability, groups have an edge on individuals in the performance of disjunctive tasks. There is a greater likelihood that a group will contain at least one person with that bright idea. However, group process—particularly in large groups—can interfere with coming up with the bright idea and getting it accepted by the group (Littlepage, 1991). Let's take a look at some of the problems in coordination and communication that can reduce the effectiveness of group performance.

Just as the strength of a chain depends on its weakest link, the group product on a conjunctive task is determined by the individual with the poorest performance. In mountain climbing, for example, if one person slips or falls, the whole team is endangered.

brainstorming
A technique that attempts to increase creative ideas by encouraging group members to speak freely without criticizing their own or others' contributions.

Brainstorming: Coming Up With Ideas   During the 1950s, advertising executive Alex Osborn developed a technique called **brainstorming**. Brainstorming involves bringing together a group of individuals, presenting a problem requiring a creative solution, and setting the following ground rules:

- Express all ideas that come to mind, even if they sound crazy.
- The more ideas, the better.
- Don't worry whether the ideas are good or bad; they can be evaluated later.
- All ideas belong to the group, so members should feel free to build on each other's work.

Osborn (1953) claimed that by using these procedures, groups could generate more and better ideas than could individuals working alone. The gimmick caught on, and brainstorming was soon a popular corporate exercise. But when the research caught up with the hype, it turned out that Osborn's faith in group process was unfounded. In fact, "nominal groups" (several individuals working alone) produce a greater number of ideas than do "real groups" in which members interact with each other (Diehl & Stroebe, 1991). As for the quality of those ideas, nominal groups perform at least as well as real groups and often better. Despite their ineffectiveness on the task at hand, brainstorming groups do have one clear benefit: people enjoy them. If, then, your goal is to build team spirit, getting group members together for a brainstorming session is a reasonable approach. But if what you really want is some good ideas, it's better to let people work on their own.

A number of possible explanations have been proposed for the superiority of individuals over groups in the generation of ideas (Mullen et al., 1991). According to Michael Diehl and Wolfgang Stroebe, however, *production blocking* is the major factor (Diehl & Stroebe, 1991; Stroebe & Diehl, 1991). Alone, people produce at their own pace without any distractions. In a group, they have to listen to what others are saying while they wait their turn to speak up. Distracted by listening to others, people forget some of their ideas. But what about fighting the effects of distraction by rehearsing one's own ideas? The good news is that rehearsal does protect existing ideas. The bad news is that it interferes with generating additional ones. Overall, an uninterrupted stream of both thought and expression provides the best growing conditions for a good idea.

Recently, it has been suggested that "electronic brainstorming" can combine the best of both worlds: the freedom enjoyed by individuals working alone and the stimulation produced by the ideas of others (Gallupe et al., 1991). In electronic brainstorming, individuals work alone at a computer terminal that displays a sample of the ideas previously generated by various group members. Initial research on this intriguing possibility found that, regardless of whether they had access to others' ideas, subjects who entered their ideas in a computer were more productive than those who wrote them down on paper or stated them to other group members. Computers, then, were helpful to everyone. But even this high tech approach failed to create an advantage for groups sharing ideas compared with individuals who were aware only of their own thoughts.

Biased Sampling: Getting Ideas on the Table   In addition to coordination problems such as production blocking, group performance may also be less than optimal because of difficulties in getting ideas on the table. Garold Stasser (1992) points out that not all the information available to individual members will necessarily be brought before the group. Instead, information that is shared among group members is more likely to enter the group discussion than information that is not common knowledge. Stasser calls this effect *biased sampling*.

Biased sampling is a serious problem when there is a "hidden profile," in which the sum total of information held by all group members favors an alternative that each individual member regards as inferior. In one study, for example, university students read descriptions of hypothetical candidates for student-body president before gathering in four-person groups to decide which candidate to endorse (Stasser & Titus, 1985). Actually, candidate A was by far the best, having 8 positive and 4 negative characteristics. Candidate B also had 4 negative characteristics, but only 4 positive attributes.

However, subjects were not fully informed about all of the candidates' characteristics. For candidate A, the 8 *positive* characteristics were spread out among group members, so that each subject knew about 2 but not about the other 6. All subjects were informed about all 4 of candidate A's negative characteristics. For candidate B, the 4 *negative* characteristics were spread out among group members, so that each subject knew about 1 but not about the other 3. All subjects were informed about all 4 of candidate B's positive characteristics. Thus, each subject was aware of 2 positives and 4 negatives for candidate A, and of 4 positives and 1 negative for candidate B. Not surprisingly, candidate B was the heavy favorite over candidate A before the group discussion took place.

The important question, however, is whether group members were able to share their information and, thereby, detect the hidden profile favoring candidate A. The unfortunate answer is that A's virtues remained hidden from the group as a whole. After discussing the candidates, almost three times as many groups selected B as selected A. Unshared information remained unshared and, inadequately informed, groups made a bad decision.

Sometimes, bad decisions have tragic consequences. The commission formed to investigate the loss of the space-shuttle *Challenger,* in which all seven crew members were killed, concluded that inadequate sharing of information contributed to the disaster:

> The decision to launch the *Challenger* was flawed. Those who made the decision were unaware of the recent history of problems concerning the O rings and the joint and were unaware of the initial written recommendation of the contractor advising against the launch [under certain circumstances]. . . . If the decision-makers had known all the facts, it is highly unlikely that they would have decided to launch. (*Report of the Presidential Commission,* 1986, p. 82)

Not everyone, though, agrees that failure to get the facts on the table was the major cause of the accident. In their analysis, Barbara Romzek and Melvin Dubnick (1987) cite the political pressures put on NASA to complete the launch of the space shuttle and the transfer of decision-making authority within NASA from expert professionals to administrators. These factors changed the grounds on which the launch decision was made and made it more likely that safety would *not* come first. Although providing crucial information to decision makers is necessary for good performance, it is not sufficient. Decision makers also have to be motivated to take such information seriously.

Communication Networks: The Flow of Ideas   The flow of information within a group is determined by the group's *communication network,* which defines who can speak with whom. In a classic study, Harold Leavitt (1951) examined the effects of four different types of communication networks, shown in Figure 11.7. Two of these networks (the wheel and the Y) are highly

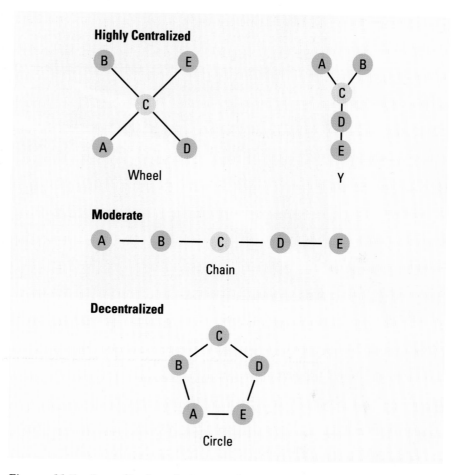

Figure 11.7 Centralized and Decentralized Communication Networks. In Leavitt's research, subjects participated in one of four communication networks. The wheel and the Y are highly centralized; in each, group member C plays the central role in the flow of information. The chain is less centralized; C has only a slightly more important role than other group members. The circle is decentralized; all members have an equal role in conveying information. [Based on Leavitt, 1951.]

centralized; in each, group member C plays a key role in the flow of information. One network (the chain) is less centralized; the importance of C's role is reduced. The fourth network (the circle) is *decentralized*; all members have an equal role in conveying information. Overall, subjects who participated in the two highly centralized communication networks (the wheel and the Y) were faster and more accurate in their performance than were those who participated in the other two networks.

On January 28, 1986, the space shuttle *Challenger* blew up shortly after liftoff, killing all seven crew members. The mechanical cause of the disaster was soon identified: faulty O-ring seals in the booster-rocket joints. But human error was also involved, as the decision-making process leading up to the launch was flawed by inadequate communication and political pressure.

But centralization does not always improve performance. In Leavitt's research, the task was relatively simple. When Marvin Shaw (1954) presented groups with a more difficult and complicated task, groups with a *less* centralized network (the chain) made fewer errors than did those with a highly centralized network (the wheel). Taken together, the research by Leavitt and Shaw indicates that the effects of communication networks on performance involve two factors: efficiency and information overload. Simple tasks benefit from the efficiency of centralized communication networks. When the group faces a more difficult situation, with a complex task or stressful working conditions, such rigid structures have serious disadvantages (Worchel & Shackelford, 1991). In centralized networks, individuals occupying crucial roles can be overwhelmed by the onslaught of information and perform poorly.

The *Challenger* disaster highlights another drawback to highly centralized communication networks. Problems with the O-ring seals had been noted in February 1984, and a meeting to discuss the rings was scheduled for May 30. But before the meeting could be held, the two officials responsible for holding it left NASA. Indeed, the May 30 meeting never took place; nor was the need for such a meeting ever communicated to those who took over the jobs of the key officials. It was, in the words of former deputy administrator Hans Mark, "a classic example of having something fall between the 'cracks'" (Romzek & Dubnick, 1987, p. 234). Centralized networks, which place heavy responsibility for communication on one person or just a few individuals, create the potential for very large cracks and deadly mistakes.

Summing Up: Groups Versus Individuals Although difficulties in coordination and communication often reduce the effectiveness of groups, the performance of a group can be superior to that of an individual (Hinsz, 1990; Laughlin et al., 1991). For example, group discussion can reduce the influence of various cognitive biases (Wright et al., 1990). And group recall of information is better than the recall of a single group member, though not as good as that of the same number of individuals working alone (Clark & Stephenson, 1989). Overall, group performance tends to be better than the performance of the average individual member, but it is often inferior to the performance of the best individual or the pooled potential of all group members (Hill, 1982). Since so many decisions in our society are made by groups—in business, government, the military, and education—we all have an investment in working to improve group performance.

COOPERATION, COMPETITION, AND CONFLICT: RESPONDING TO DIFFERENCES

The importance of group performance is dramatically evident for some of the major issues confronting our world today. What determines whether people will act responsibly to protect the environment? What factors contribute to the escalation of conflict? Are there ways to reduce conflict once it has started? The answers to these questions involve a complex interaction between individual characteristics and group processes. In Chapter 13, we examine the effectiveness of specific kinds of leadership in specific organizational circumstances. Here, we consider individual and group influences on cooperation, competition, and conflict. When there are differences between us, how do we respond?

Mixed Motives and Difficult Dilemmas

Social psychological research on cooperation and competition often focuses on situations that elicit mixed motives. In such situations, the individual can make either a cooperative or a competitive choice. Since either choice carries with it the possibility of gain and the risk of loss, individuals are torn about what to do. They have mixed motives, as some factors draw them toward cooperative behavior and other factors urge them on to competitive behavior. With this perspective in mind, let us examine a number of difficult dilemmas that people face.

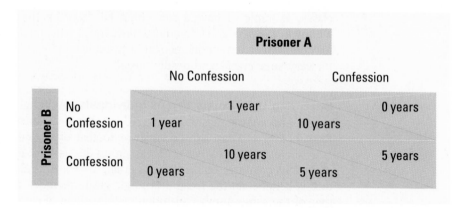

Figure 11.8   The Prisoner's Dilemma Game.   In the original prisoner's dilemma, from which the game took its name, each of two criminals is offered immunity from prosecution in exchange for a confession. If both stay silent, both get off with a light sentence on a minor charge (upper left). If both confess, both receive a moderate sentence (lower right). But if one turns state's evidence while the other stays mum, the confessing criminal goes free and the silent criminal spends a long time in jail.

The Prisoner's Dilemma Game   We begin with a detective story. Two partners in crime are picked up by the police for questioning. Although the police believe they have committed a serious crime, there is only enough evidence to convict them on a minor charge. In order to sustain a conviction for the serious crime, the police will have to convince one of them to testify against the other. Separated during questioning, the criminals weigh their options. If neither confesses, they will both get a light sentence on the minor charge. If both confess and plead guilty, they both will receive a moderate sentence. But if one confesses and the other stays silent, the confessing criminal will obtain immunity from prosecution while the silent criminal gets the maximum penalty for the serious crime. The choices available in this dilemma are diagrammed in Figure 11.8.

prisoner's dilemma game (PDG)   A research paradigm that creates mixed motives; participants are encouraged to cooperate by moderate rewards, but are tempted to compete by even larger ones.

This story formed the basis for the research paradigm known as the **prisoner's dilemma game (PDG)**. In the two-person PDG, subjects are given a series of choices in which they have two alternatives: cooperative and competitive. If both individuals make the cooperative choice, they both obtain a moderate reward. If both make the competitive choice, they both suffer a moderate loss. But if one cooperates while the other competes, the competitor obtains a large reward while the cooperator suffers a large loss. It's really a perplexing situation. You want to cooperate and take home that moderate reward. But if you cooperate and the other person doesn't, you end up with a large loss. If both of you compete, you both lose. What are you going to do?

By now, thousands of players have participated in the prisoner's dilemma game and researchers have a pretty good understanding of how people behave in this mixed-motive situation. First, they reciprocate. Tit-for-tat, cooperation is matched by cooperation in return, while competition provokes competitive reactions (Enzle et al., 1975). However, cooperation and competitiveness do not take place on a level playing-field. Competitiveness is a very strong determinant of reciprocity. Once one player makes a competitive move, the other player is highly likely to follow suit (Kelley & Stahelski, 1970). Cooperation is less constraining on the other person. People who are consistently and unconditionally cooperative can be exploited and taken advantage of (Shure et al., 1965). The judgment of history is that the cooperative policies of British prime minister Neville Chamberlain only served to convince Hitler that he could take whatever he wanted.

Second, individual differences also influence whether behavior will be cooperative or competitive. Different people have different preferences for their own and another's outcomes (Knight & Dubro, 1984; Messick & McClintock, 1968). People with a *cooperative orientation* seek to maximize joint gains. Those with an *individualistic orientation* seek to maximize their own gain and are less cooperative, as are those with a *competitive orientation,* who seek to maximize their own gain relative to that of others (Kuhlman & Marshello, 1975).

Third, groups as well as individuals can play the prisoner's dilemma game. Typically, groups are less cooperative and more competitive than individuals (Schopler et al., 1991). According to Chester Insko and his colleagues (1990), the competitiveness of groups has its roots in fear and greed: the fear that the other group will exploit ours, and the greedy desire to maximize the outcomes achieved by our group at the other group's expense. Individuals, of course, can also be driven by fear and greed, but competition between groups seems to intensify such motives. Indeed, the mere anticipation of interacting with a group sets up expectations for an abrasive interaction (Hoyle et al., 1989). And, as is so often the case, self-fulfilling prophecies have a way of coming true: what we expect turns out to be what we get.

Social Dilemmas   In the prisoner's dilemma game, all choices are public. You know who your friends, and enemies, are. There is another kind of dilemma, however, where it's harder to tell who deserves the credit or the blame. In a **social dilemma**, the most rewarding choice for an individual will, if taken by all individuals, produce the most harmful outcome for everyone. Like sins, social dilemmas come in two varieties: commission and omission. The excessive exploitation of natural resources is a social sin of *commission.* If people take as much as they desire, nothing will be left (Hardin, 1968). Ocean dumping brings short-term profits to some companies and municipalities. Long-term, it can destroy the delicate ecological balance on which everyone depends. In contrast, the failure of those who use a public service, like public TV or the blood supply, to contribute to its support is a social sin of *omission.* If no one gives, the service

social dilemma   A situation in which the most rewarding choice for an individual will, if taken by all individuals, produce the most harmful outcome for everyone.

can't continue (Olson, 1965). Thus, a social dilemma is produced by the conflict between private benefit and the public good.

No single individual can solve a social dilemma. A solution requires the cooperative efforts of many people who don't know each other and will never meet. Compounding the difficulty of solving social dilemmas is the fact that many of them develop over time. The problems caused by selfish choices may not be apparent until long after many such choices have been made (Platt, 1973). Who would ever have thought years ago that using aerosol sprays could damage the ozone layer? In a social dilemma, the choices of a stranger affect our own well-being, and what is done today determines tomorrow's quality of life.

Research on social dilemmas highlights three general circumstances that hinder their solution. First, social sins of omission are especially difficult to rectify (Brewer & Kramer, 1986). People are more willing to refrain from taking something they want (stop exploiting) than to give up something they already have (make a contribution). Second, group ownership is a problem, at least in the United States. When a resource is shared among members of a group, it is depleted more rapidly than when the resource belongs to only one person (Martichuski & Bell, 1991). And, third, uncertainty about the size of the

A social dilemma is produced by a conflict between private benefit and the public good. When individuals dump trash at their convenience, they spoil the environment for everyone.

resource pool increases selfish behavior (Budescu et al., 1990). Lacking a firm estimate about available resources, people take more for themselves and expect others to do likewise.

A variety of more specific factors also influence how people respond to a social dilemma. Consider, for example, some *personal* characteristics (Messick & Brewer, 1983). The effects of personal orientation in a social dilemma are similar to those found in the prisoner's dilemma game. People with a cooperative orientation are less likely to behave in a competitive, resource-consuming fashion than are people with individualistic or competitive orientations (Liebrand & van Run, 1985). Mood, too, affects behavior when resources are scarce. People experiencing negative moods, like anger and sadness, have difficulty delaying gratification and take what they want without sufficient regard for the long-term consequences (Knapp & Clark, 1991). In addition, prior experience has an impact on social dilemmas. Individuals given a chance to manage their own, privately controlled resource are more socially responsible in using a collectively controlled resource than are those without this preliminary opportunity (Allison & Messick, 1985a).

Information about what others are doing may be a particularly important determinant of responses to a social dilemma. Imagine that you live in an area suffering from a water shortage, and you learn that others are making a serious effort to conserve. What's your reaction? On the one hand, the socially responsible behavior of others encourages you to cooperate too (Orbell et al., 1988). On the other hand, since you know that others are trying to remedy the problem, you may be tempted to engage in social loafing and become a *free rider*: letting others sacrifice without giving up anything yourself (Kerr & Bruun, 1983; Kerr & MacCoun, 1985b).

But what if you learn that others are making selfish choices? Every night on the TV news you see people watering their lawns and washing their cars. Are you prepared to give up showers and to drink bottled water? Here, too, there are counteracting tendencies. On the one hand, the socially irresponsible behavior of others encourages you to follow suit. When you see other people take a free ride, you may feel you'd be a *sucker* to continue your own efforts to conserve (Kerr, 1983). On the other hand, you realize the resource is being rapidly depleted, and you feel the need for urgent action. Because selfish models evoke both selfish motives and societal concerns, people exposed to such models are slow to respond to a crisis (Messick et al., 1983). Interestingly, though, when a resource is endangered by purely environmental forces rather than aggravated by human actions, people are more likely to conserve (Rutte et al., 1987; Samuelson et al., 1984). The absence of selfish models allows individuals to respond in the best interests of the community.

And, indeed, a strong sense of belonging to the community modifies a person's response to a social dilemma. Individuals are more socially responsible when they share a meaningful group membership with other people involved in the dilemma (Kramer & Brewer, 1984). Unfortunately, many social dilemmas involve very large groups (a nation or the whole world) in which personal identification with the welfare of the community is difficult to establish. In general, large groups are more likely to exploit limited resources than are small groups (Allison et al., 1992; Kerr, 1989). Table 11.2 summarizes various personal factors that can contribute to a constructive solution to a social dilemma.

An alternative approach to solving social dilemmas targets the *structural* arrangements outlined in Table 11.2. For instance, making charitable contributions tax deductible is a structural tactic designed to increase such contributions by appealing to an individual's selfish interests. Unless we are willing to write every good act into the tax code, however, such egoistic solutions to social dilemmas are limited (Lynn & Oldenquist, 1986). Another option is to privatize what are now collectively owned resources. As we have seen, research conducted in the United States indicates that people take better care of a privately owned resource than of one owned by a group. But privatizing a resource means that what one gets, others lose. Who gets? Who decides who gets?

The most commonly employed structural solution to social dilemmas is what Garrett Hardin (1968) called "mutual coercion mutually agreed upon": giving up individual freedom and setting up an authority who will decide who gets

---

Table 11.2   Solving Social Dilemmas. Behavior in a social dilemma is influenced by personal factors and by structural arrangements. The characteristics listed here contribute to the solution of a social dilemma through direct effects on individuals or through deliberate modifications of social structures.

Personal Factors

- Having a cooperative personal orientation

- Being in a good mood

- Having direct, hands-on experience with managing endangered resources

- Learning about how others are behaving:
  Following the lead of unselfish models
  Responding to the crisis created by selfish models

- Having a sense of group identification with other people facing the same dilemma

- Being in a smaller group

Structural Arrangements

- Creating a payoff structure that rewards cooperative behavior and/or punishes selfish behavior

- Removing resources from the public domain and handing them over to private ownership

- Establishing a superordinate authority to control use of the resource what. When a valuable resource is threatened with extinction, people will opt for authority (Messick et al., 1983; Sato, 1987). The Environmental Protection Agency was established by the federal government to protect the quality of the environment. But maintaining a regulating authority such as the EPA is not cost free (Yamagishi, 1986). If regulatory agencies fail to work effectively, the society suffers a double loss—of the endangered resource and of the funds used to support the agency. To solve a social dilemma, people often have to decide where to place their trust: in their fellow citizens or in government authorities.

intergroup public goods paradigm (IPG) A research paradigm used to study both intragroup and intergroup behavior. Within each group, members decide whether to contribute to the group's efforts, but all group members share the outcome obtained during interactions with another group.

The Intergroup Public Goods Paradigm The **intergroup public goods paradigm (IPG)** offers another approach to the study of cooperation and competition (Rapoport et al., 1989). In this paradigm, two groups compete for a single reward. Within each group, each member makes an individual decision about whether to invest his or her own private resources in order to help the group obtain the reward. However, the reward itself is a "public good," which must be shared by all members of the winning group regardless of their individual investments. Like social dilemmas and team sports, the IPG paradigm creates the temptation to take a free ride on the efforts of others. Thus, mixed motives occur at two levels: *intra*group as members decide whether to contribute and *inter*group as groups decide whether to cooperate or compete with each other.

Research by Gary Bornstein and his colleagues (1989) examined the effects of communication at each of these levels. Subjects were given the opportunity to talk with members of their own group, talk as a group with the other group, or both. As you can see from Figure 11.9, groups who were allowed to talk only among themselves had the highest rate of member contributions. In contrast, groups who talked only to each other had the highest rate of keeping between-group cooperative agreements. Groups who allowed both within- and between-group communication were moderate in making contributions and in keeping their agreements.

It's not surprising that between-group communication reduced member contributions. Because of the way the IPG paradigm is set up, the most common between-group agreement requires members *not* to contribute. As more between-group agreements are reached and kept, member contributions inevitably decline. The more interesting question concerns within-group communication. Why did talking within one's own group reduce the number of between-group agreements that were kept? One possible explanation highlights people's motives to avoid exploitation and to obtain the maximum posssible profit. In the IPG paradigm, like the prisoner's dilemma game, the most profitable outcome is obtained by the group that competes while the other group cooperates. Perhaps talking with members of one's own group increases fear and greed, factors identified by research on the prisoner's dilemma game as increasing competition.

Another possible explanation for why intragroup communication can make it harder to achieve intergroup cooperation emphasizes cognitive processes. A

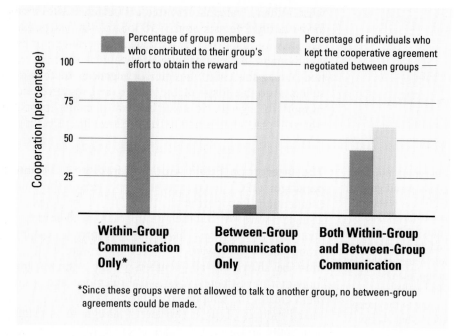

Figure 11.9   Effects of Intragroup and Intergroup Communication.   Groups of subjects were given the chance to discuss strategy among themselves (intragroup), with another group (intergroup), or both. Intragroup cooperation (contributing to the group's effort to obtain the reward) was greatest for those allowed to talk only among themselves. Intergroup cooperation (sticking with the cooperative agreement made between the groups) was greatest for those allowed to talk only with the other group. Those who were allowed to talk among themselves and with the other group exhibited moderate amounts of intragroup and intergroup cooperation. [Data from Bornstein et al., 1989.]

potentially competitive interaction with another group creates competing demands for our attention. Do we focus on members of our own group or on members of the opposing group? As it turns out, people attend carefully to information about members of their own group, especially if that information is inconsistent with their initial expectations (Ruscher et al., 1991). In response to members of the opposing group, however, people are content to concentrate on information that fits their preconceived ideas. This differential allocation of attention has important effects on interpersonal perceptions. Members of one's own group are viewed as complex individuals, but members of the other group remain oversimplified stereotypes that can more easily elicit hostile responses.

If biased attention provoked by information overload is the problem, then reducing the amount of information individuals have to cope with should correct the bias. And it does. One-on-one competitions, in which each opponent has only one person to think about, stimulates thoughtful consideration of information about the opponent (Ruscher & Fiske, 1990). Other circumstances that should reduce information overload include not having an opportunity to talk with members of one's own group and, perhaps, less intensely competitive situations. As Bornstein and his colleagues note, the IPG paradigm is perceived by participants as highly competitive. Under more benign conditions, communication and cooperation within a group can "spill over" and enhance cooperation with other groups (Keenan & Carnevale, 1989).

Conflict Escalation

Although some cultures value one more than the other, cooperation and competition are basic facts of human social life. As such, each may be beneficial or harmful. Cooperation allows people to work together more effectively than they could work by themselves, but it can also turn into passive complacency or, as we have seen, invite exploitation. Competition motivates people to perform at the highest level of their skills and talents, but it can deteriorate into ruthless disregard for others or serve as the basis for violent conflicts.

When a competition becomes a conflict, the motive changes from winning to conquering. Watching a hard-fought football game in which the players seem to go out of their way to hurt each other, we may be uncertain about whether this is a competition or a conflict. What we do know is that it's a game. Seeing the dead bodies lying in the streets of Sarajevo, the besieged city in Bosnia-Herzegovina caught in the crossfire of the civil war raging in the former Yugoslavia, we know that this is a conflict—and that it's no game. In this section, we describe various factors that contribute to the escalation of conflict.

Threat Capacity   Among advocates of capital punishment and some foreign policy experts, it is an article of faith that *threat capacity*, the ability to punish someone who engages in a prohibited behavior, acts as a deterrent. But the rule of reciprocity tells us that threats and punishments can also elicit aggression. When a person or group behaves in a threatening or punitive manner, the target person or group is likely to retaliate in kind (Youngs, 1986). Moreover, the use of coercive tactics can escalate a conflict beyond the level of aggression initially involved (Deutsch, 1973).

The extent to which threat capacity can increase conflict even at the expense of self-interest was demonstrated in a classic study by Morton Deutsch and Robert Krauss (1960). These investigators asked pairs of female subjects to imagine that each of them was in charge of a trucking company carrying merchandise over a road to a specific destination. For every completed trip, subjects would earn a flat rate minus operating expenses calculated at the rate of one cent per minute. Each subject was assigned a name, either Acme or Bolt, for her trucking company and was given a road map, shown in Figure 11.10. Subjects started from separate points and went to separate destinations. At one

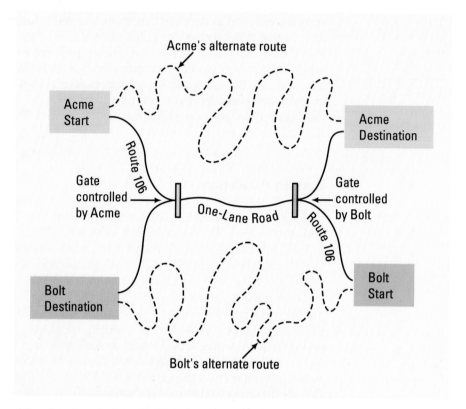

Figure 11.10   The Road Map for the Acme and Bolt Trucking Game.   In the trucking game devised by Deutsch and Krauss, subjects were assigned to either the Acme or the Bolt Trucking Company and were instructed to deliver their merchandise as quickly as possible. The quickest route is over the one-lane road. Having control over a gate blocking the other player's use of the one-lane road reduced the players' ability to cooperate with each other. [From Deutsch & Krauss, 1960.]

point, however, their paths crossed on a one-lane road. To avoid the one-lane road, subjects could take an alternative route, but the by-pass took longer to travel and therefore increased operating expenses.

At each end of the one-lane road was a gate. In the *bilateral-threat* condition, each player in the trucking game had control over one of the gates. In the *unilateral-threat* condition, only one of the players controlled a gate. In the *no-gates* condition, neither player controlled a gate, and the road was open to all traffic. Players who controlled a gate were allowed to close it—and they did. The effect of being able to block the other person's progress was clear: both players suffered. Overall, players earned more money in the no-gate condition than in the unilateral condition, and those in the bilateral condition earned least of all. These results suggest that once coercive means are available, people use them even when doing so damages their own outcomes. Subsequent research, however, provides a reassuring qualification. Subjects in the study by Deutsch and Krauss used imaginary money; it was all pretend. Subjects who played a similar game with real money were more cooperative (Gallo, 1966). When the stakes were meaningful, people were more likely to pursue the cooperative arrangements they perceived to be in their own self-interest.

Resources   In essence, threat capacity is a resource that one can use during conflict. Other kinds of resources that can contribute to conflict escalation include time, energy, money, and social power to get the support of others. All else being equal, people with adequate resources at their disposal are more likely to engage in overt conflict than are those without resources (Martin, 1986). But it isn't just a matter of possessing resources that could be used during a conflict, decisions have to be made about how to allocate those resources.

Politicians and government officials, for example, have to decide whether to allocate scarce resources to "guns" (military programs) or "butter" (economic and social programs). When Roderick Kramer and his colleagues (1990) created a laboratory simulation of the guns versus butter tradeoff, they found that subjects allocated less to military programs when two conditions were met: (1) deficits were perceived in overall economic wealth as well as in military might, and (2) the high costs of military programs were readily apparent. This same set of circumstances produced the fewest attacks on the opponent. Although peace and poverty don't always coincide, economic problems can encourage opponents to resolve their differences in order to reduce their military spending.

But what happens when the allocation of resources fails to achieve the desired outcome? Do groups or individuals cut their losses? Remarkably often, the answer is no. Faced with a disastrous military campaign, a plunge in the stock market, an abusive marriage, or a budget overrun on a construction project, people often persist in making even larger investments. This process of throwing good money after bad is called **entrapment** (Brockner & Rubin, 1985). Entrapment occurs when commitments to a failing course of action are increased to justify investments already made. A number of factors increase the likelihood that people will become entrapped: the desire to save face, institutional inertia that makes it hard to change direction, and receiving negative information after major commitments have already been made (Staw & Ross, 1989). Processes like group polarization and groupthink that promote extreme judgments and defective decision making may also increase entrapment. However it comes about, entrapment contributes to conflict escalation by motivating those on the losing side of a conflict to keep trying to prevail.

entrapment The condition in which commitments to a failing course of action are increased to justify investments already made.

Perceptions of the Other   Stereotypes and prejudice are major factors in conflict escalation, especially between groups (Pruitt & Rubin, 1986). During conflict, the opposing group and its members are often perceived as "the other"—strange, foreign, alien. Held at a psychological distance and regarded as fundamentally different, the other becomes a screen on which it is possible to project one's worst fears.

Interestingly, this projection is often a *mirror image*: what we see in our enemies tends to be what our enemies see in us. As Urie Bronfenbrenner (1961) discovered when he visited the Soviet Union during the Cold War, the Soviets saw us as aggressive, exploitative, and untrustworthy—just as we saw them. Like the partners in an unhappy intimate relationship (see Chapter 6), political and military opponents can get trapped into always believing the worst about each other and discounting any indications of more positive characteristics. Sometimes, maintaining negative assumptions requires some fancy footwork. A few years ago, when Mikhail Gorbachev embraced an arms reduction plan that had initially been proposed by Ronald Reagan, many conservatives in the United States decided that the plan must favor the Soviets and urged Reagan to reject it (Tetlock et al., 1991).

Taken to an extreme, negative perceptions of the other can result in *dehumanization,* the perception that people lack human qualities or are "subhuman." Often based on negative stereotypes about outgroups, dehumanization intensifies intergroup conflict (Struch & Schwartz, 1989) and serves both to justify past aggression and to incite further aggression (Bandura, 1990). Like other severe negative evaluations of others, dehumanization creates a vicious cycle: conflict leads to dehumanization, which leads to harm, which leads to further

In many European countries, racial attacks against Asian and African immigrants have increased. Here, skinheads in Hannover, Germany, practice the dehumanizing politics of "us" versus "them" and call for the expulsion of all foreigners.

dehumanization to justify the harm, which leads to more harm, and so on (Bar-Tal, 1990). Since dehumanization is the ultimate version of "us" versus "them," the cure for it requires seeing "them" as more like "us." George Orwell's experience during the Spanish Civil War illustrates the point. Sighting an enemy soldier holding up his trousers with both hands while running beside a nearby trench, Orwell was unable to take the easy shot:

> I had come here to shoot at "Fascists"; but a man who is holding up his trousers isn't a "Fascist," he is visibly a fellow creature, similar to yourself, and you don't feel like shooting at him. (p. 254)

Reducing Conflict

It's not difficult to understand why conflict tends to escalate once it gets started. Threat capacity, entrapment, and negative perceptions push both parties toward increasingly aggressive behavior. Group polarization and groupthink can also contribute to more belligerent opinions and actions. In light of all the social psychological pressures that encourage escalation, the surprising thing about conflict is that it doesn't always get worse. Enemy images—and the aggressive behavior they promote—can change, sometimes dramatically (Silverstein, 1989). Consider, for example, this item from the history of the Cold War. In March 1983, Ronald Reagan described the Soviet Union as an "evil empire," and further escalation of the conflict between the United States and the Soviet Union seemed inescapable. But just five years later, in May 1988, Reagan and Gorbachev stood shoulder to shoulder in Red Square proclaiming their personal friendship and pledging cooperation between their countries. The end of the Cold War shows us that it is possible to reduce long-lasting, deeply ingrained conflicts. In this section, we consider some approaches that can help give peace' a chance.

True GRIT   One of the major issues of contention between the United States and the Soviet Union during the 1980s was the continuing bloody war in Afghanistan between Soviet troops and Afghan guerrillas. In February 1988, Gorbachev took this issue off the table by announcing the withdrawal of the Soviet army from Afghanistan, contingent only on successful completion of U.N.-sponsored peace talks between Afghanistan and Pakistan. Once this accord was signed in April, the Soviets began withdrawing their forces in May—*before* Reagan and Gorbachev met in Moscow.

Although Gorbachev's decision to withdraw from Afghanistan occurred in the context of a continuing dialogue between the United States and the Soviet Union, it was essentially a unilateral action. No reciprocal concessions by the United States were required. Instead, Gorbachev seemed intent on creating a more favorable climate for subsequent negotiations (and on cutting his losses in what had been a ruinous war). The notion that unilateral concessions can

graduated and reciprocated initiatives in tension-reduction (GRIT) A strategy for unilateral, persistent efforts to establish trust and cooperation between opposing parties.

reverse an escalating conflict is central to a peacemaking strategy developed by Charles Osgood (1962): **graduated and reciprocated initiatives in tension-reduction (GRIT)**. To see how GRIT works, imagine yourself using its four basic components (Lindskold et al., 1986a, 1986b).

1. You issue a general statement of your intention to reduce conflict. You also clearly announce your peaceful intentions each time you take a tension-reducing initiative. Throughout, you invite the other party to reciprocate. By these steps, you hope to enlist public support and put pressure on the other party to respond cooperatively.
2. You carry out your tension-reducing initiatives as announced, even if there is no immediate reciprocation. These acts serve to establish your credibility. You enhance your credibility further by employing tension-reducing initiatives that can be verified by the other party or by a neutral outside observer.

The end of the Cold War dramatically demonstrates that it is possible to reduce long-lasting, deeply ingrained conflicts.

3. Once the other party makes a cooperative move, you quickly reciprocate. Your cooperative response risks at least as much as—and, if possible, more than—the other party's cooperative behavior.
4. You maintain a retaliatory capability in order to deter exploitation by the other party. If the other party attacks, you retaliate at precisely the same level. By avoiding excessive retaliation, you attempt to prevent conflict escalation. Once retaliation has taken place, you resume your unilateral tension-reducing efforts.

In essence, GRIT is reciprocity embedded within an overall push for peace. It sets out the peace agenda clearly and avoids escalation by keeping any retaliatory actions within the level established by the other party (Axelrod, 1984). Reciprocal strategies like GRIT give the other party a greater sense of control over the interaction, which reduces the perceived risk of cooperative behavior (Friedland, 1990). But GRIT is more than simply a reciprocal strategy. Although attacks by the other party are met by retaliation, the strategist using GRIT quickly resumes unilateral tension-reducing initiatives. Patiently and persistently, GRIT sends the message "We won't be exploited, but what we really want is peace."

In addition to obtaining immediate benefits for both parties, practice in GRIT can smooth the way for future bargaining efforts where GRIT is not explicitly employed. This added benefit was demonstrated in a study by Svenn Lindskold and Gyuseog Han (1988) in which male subjects participated in the prisoner's dilemma game (PDG) described earlier in this chapter. Subjects believed they were playing PDG with another subject, but actually the other player's moves were programmed by the experimenters. During the PDG, some subjects were given experience with GRIT. In this condition, the simulated player sent a note announcing, "I will be making [the cooperative choice] on the next trial." He then made that choice and continued to do so unless the subject chose the competitive response. If that happened, the simulated player retaliated by making the competitive response, but then went back to making cooperative choices. The simulated player's choice was communicated to the real subject prior to every trial. Subjects in the no-message control condition experienced the same pattern of choices from the simulated player, but did not receive any prior communications about those choices.

After the PDG was over, subjects worked on a bargaining task involving the same (simulated) other player and were told to make as much money as possible. On this task, bargaining was more effective and quicker for subjects who had been the recipients of GRIT than for those who had not received any messages. Interestingly, when subjects were asked to evaluate the other person, those in the GRIT condition were *not* more positive in their evaluations than were those in the no-message control condition. These findings suggest that it is not necessary to like an opponent to make peace. Instead, recognizing common interests and establishing at least a minimal level of trust seem the essential ingredients.

"Your mother and I still think two dollars a week is plenty, but, in an effort to avoid litigation, we're willing to go to two seventy-five."

Negotiations occur whenever there is a conflict that the parties wish to resolve without getting into an open fight or relying on an imposed legal settlement. [Drawing by Lorenz; © 1989 The New Yorker Magazine, Inc.]

Negotiations and Bargaining   GRIT is a useful and effective strategy for beginning the peace process. But once this process is set in motion, extended negotiations are usually required to reach a final agreement. Negotiations on complex issues such as nuclear arms control and international environmental protection, as well as efforts to make peace in volatile regions such as the Middle East, often go on for years or even decades. But negotiations are not restricted to political and military matters. Unions and management engage in collective bargaining to establish employee contracts. Divorcing couples negotiate the terms of their divorce, by themselves or through their lawyers. Indeed, negotiations and the bargaining they involve occur whenever there is a conflict that the parties wish to resolve without getting into an open fight or relying on an imposed legal settlement. There is an immense amount of research on negotiations and bargaining (Pruitt & Rubin, 1986; Sheppard et al., 1990). In this section, we provide a brief summary of those factors most relevant to conflict reduction.

Negotiations and bargaining are strongly influenced by the social context. Bargainers who anticipate having to interact with each other in the future are more cooperative with each other than are those not expecting such interactions (Pruitt, 1981). But what about bargainers who expect to meet the people they work for after the deal is struck? Although representative bargainers are strongly committed to obtaining the maximum gains for their constituents, they are decidedly flexible about the strategy they adopt (Enzle et al., 1992). When the other side is highly cooperative, representative bargainers are more *competitive* and exploitative than are bargainers who represent only their own interests. However, when a cooperative strategy is more profitable, representative bargainers are more *cooperative* than are nonrepresentative bargainers. Lion or lamb, representative bargainers seize whatever approach offers the best chance of satisfying the demands of their constituents.

For all bargainers, not just those who represent others, flexibility is perhaps the single most important factor in successful negotiations (Rubin et al., 1990; Thompson, 1990b). Overall, the most effective bargaining strategy combines flexibility and strength (McGillicuddy et al., 1984). For example, compromising late in a bargaining session is often a more successful approach than compromising early or not compromising at all (Nemeth & Brilmayer, 1987). A weak bargainer who compromises early invites exploitation; a rigid bargainer who refuses to compromise at all sets the stage for the breakdown of negotiations.

integrative agreement A negotiated resolution to a conflict in which all parties obtain outcomes that are superior to what they would have obtained from an equal division of the contested resources.

Flexibility is also necessary for creating **integrative agreements** in which both parties gain outcomes that are better than a 50/50 split-the-difference compromise. The problem with the "fixed-pie" assumption ("what I win, you lose") underlying such 50/50 compromises is aptly illustrated by the tale of the orange and two sisters. One sister wanted the juice to drink; the other wanted the peel for a cake. Their solution was to slice the orange in half! Both sisters could have had what they wanted from the whole orange, but neither of them was flexible enough to realize that their interests were entirely compatible. Perhaps because this sort of flexible thinking takes time to develop, experienced negotiators are more likely to reach an integrative agreement than are inexperienced ones (Thompson, 1990a).

During particularly difficult or important negotiations, outside assistance may be sought. Some negotiations involve an *arbitrator* who has the power to impose a settlement. But it is more common for conflicting parties to request the participation of a *mediator* who works with them to try to reach a voluntary agreement. Traditionally, mediators have been employed in labor-management negotiations and international conflicts (Carnevale, 1985). But, increasingly, they help resolve a wide range of other disputes, such as those involving tenants and landlords, divorcing couples, and feuding neighbors (Pruitt & Kressel, 1985). Trained in negotiation and conflict management, mediators can often play an important role in reaching a cooperative solution (Emery & Wyer, 1987).

Cyrus Vance arrives in Belgrade in the spring of 1992 and speaks to reporters. As personal envoy of the secretary-general of the United Nations, Vance was trying to negotiate a ceasefire in Yugoslavia's civil war.

Mediators, too, emphasize the importance of flexibility. In one study, questionnaires were completed by 255 professional mediators (Lim & Carnevale, 1990). Their responses indicated that no one tactic was seen as uniformly superior. Instead these mediators believed that tactics should be adjusted to fit the specific situation. Flexibility alone, however, is not sufficient for success as a mediator. Trust is also required. Mediators who are perceived as objective and neutral are more effective than those viewed as biased by the parties to the dispute (Welton & Pruitt, 1987). Recently, the role of trust in a mediator was highlighted by the selection of Cyrus Vance, age seventy-five, to represent the United Nations in efforts to negotiate an end to the hostilities in Yugoslavia. Some thought he was too old for such a difficult assignment. But mediating a complex and violent conflict is no time for amateurs. Vance's vast experience and extraordinary credibility far outweighed any concerns about his age, and Vance got the job.

superordinate identity The perception that members of different groups belong to a larger whole that encompasses both groups.

Finding Common Ground Ever since the human species first appeared on planet Earth, there have been countless conflicts between innumerable groups. Each of these conflicts is unique, as is every attempt at conflict resolution. Still, one element stands out in all successful efforts to find a constructive solution to conflict: finding common ground. Recognition of a **superordinate identity** is one way that common ground can be established between groups in conflict.

When group members perceive that they have a shared identity, belonging to something larger than and encompassing the two groups, the attractiveness of outgroup members is increased (Gaertner et al., 1989), and interactions between the groups often become more peaceful (Coombs, 1987; Turner, 1981).

But how can groups engaged in violent conflict, bashing each other both verbally and physically, identify with each other? As described in Chapter 4, Muzafer Sherif and his colleagues (1961) faced this problem when the fierce intergroup competition and rivalry they had created between two groups of boys at summer camp resisted all initial efforts to restore the peace. Propaganda about how nice the other group was didn't work, nor did having the boys get together under pleasant circumstances. Only when the Rattlers and the Eagles had to cooperate to get what both groups wanted did negative perceptions and aggressive behaviors cease. Like the integrative agreements reached in successful bargaining, *superordinate goals* elicit cooperation by appealing to people's self-interest. Because everyone stands to benefit, no one has to be altruistic or compassionate to cooperate in the pursuit of a shared goal.

Superordinate goals and a superordinate identity are closely connected. The experience of intergroup cooperation increases the sense of belonging to one, superordinate group (Gaertner et al., 1990). Even the mere expectation of a cooperative interaction increases empathy (Lanzetta & Englis, 1989). As described in previous chapters, empathy plays a constructive role in human affairs—enhancing helpfulness and reducing aggression. And empathy, the perception of similarities rather than differences, may be the first step toward the development of a superordinate identity that both groups can share.

On the road to peace, both kinds of common ground are needed. Cooperation on common goals makes similarities more visible, and a sense of a common identity makes cooperation more likely. Those who would make peace, not war, realize that it is in their own self-interest to do so and understand that the cloak of humanity is large enough to cover a multitude of lesser differences.

REVIEW

COLLECTIVE PROCESSES: THE PRESENCE OF OTHERS

In collectives, people are engaged in common activities but have minimal direct interaction.

Social Facilitation: When Others Arouse Us

In an early experiment in social psychology, Triplett found that children performed faster when they worked side by side rather than alone. Subsequent research obtained mixed results, but the concept of social facilitation solved the puzzle. The presence of others enhances performance on easy tasks but impairs performance on difficult tasks. Researchers continue to debate whether there is something uniquely social about social facilitation and whether the mere presence of others is sufficient to affect performance. Different answers to these questions are provided by the theories of mere presence, evaluation apprehension, and distraction-conflict theory.

Social Loafing: When Others Relax Us

In early research on tasks involving pooled contributions, Ringelmann found that individual output declined when people worked with others. These group-produced reductions in individual output are called social loafing. Social loafing does not occur when individual contributions are identifiable, the task is personally meaningful, or the group product can be evaluated by group members. In the unified paradigm, social loafing is the mirror image of social facilitation. When individual contributions are pooled into a joint product, the presence of others impairs performance on easy tasks but enhances performance on difficult tasks.

Deindividuation: When People Lose Control

Deindividuation diminishes a person's sense of individuality and loosens normal constraints against deviant behavior. Two types of environmental cues can loosen constraints. Accountability cues, such as anonymity, signal that an individual will not be held responsible for deviant actions. Attentional cues influence self-awareness. Intense environmental stimulation that reduces self-awareness can produce a change in consciousness—a deindividuated state—in which the individual acts impulsively. Self-awareness has two major effects on a person's behavior. It increases adherence to standards and intensifies emotional experience.

GROUP PROCESSES: INTERACTING WITH OTHERS

Joining a Group

People join groups in order to secure the rewards of group membership. The socialization of newcomers into a group often depends on the relationship they form with oldtimers who act as models, trainers, and mentors.

Roles, Norms, and Cohesiveness

Interacting groups can be characterized in terms of three major factors: the expected set of behaviors they have for their members (roles), the rules of conduct they establish for members (norms), and the degree of attraction to the group and barriers to leaving it that group members experience (cohesiveness).

Group Polarization: Gaining Conviction

When individuals who have similar, although not identical, opinions participate in a group discussion, their opinions become more extreme. Explanations for this effect, known as group polarization, emphasize different aspects of group discussion: the persuasiveness of arguments heard, social comparison with a perceived group norm, and the influence of one's own ingroup.

Groupthink: Losing Perspective

Groupthink emerges when agreement among group members becomes more important than accurate knowledge and careful decision making. The symptoms of groupthink produce defective decision making, which can lead to a bad decision. Groupthink may be most likely when people are strongly attracted to the group but uncertain that they will be accepted. Other factors that increase groupthink include isolation from others, directive leaders, and stress.

Group Performance

Groups bring the multiple resources of their members to bear on a task, but problems in group process may interfere with optimal use of these resources. Aspects of group process that can impair group performance include production blocking, which retards the production of ideas because members are distracted by hearing the ideas of others; biased sampling, in which a group fails to find out about information that is not shared among all its members; and inefficient or overloaded communication networks.

COOPERATION, COMPETITION, AND CONFLICT: RESPONDING TO DIFFERENCES

Mixed Motives and Difficult Dilemmas

In mixed-motive situations, such as the prisoner's dilemma game, people are torn between wanting to cooperate and wanting to compete. Reciprocity, personal orientation, and being in a group influence behavior in these situations. In a social dilemma, private benefit conflicts with the public good. Social dilemmas include excessive exploitation of resources and failure to contribute to public services. Behavior in a social dilemma is influenced by general circumstances, personal factors, and structural arrangements. Research using the intergroup public goods paradigm indicates that in this highly competitive situation, intragroup communication decreases intergroup cooperation. When groups compete, individuals pay more attention to members of their own group and, therefore, fail to correct their stereotyped views of members of the other group.

Conflict Escalation

Conflict is most likely to escalate when those involved have the ability to punish their opponents, possess resources to devote to the conflict, become entrapped by efforts to justify past investments, and develop rigid, negative, dehumanizing perceptions of the other.

Reducing Conflict

GRIT—an explicit strategy for the unilateral, persistent pursuit of trust and cooperation between opposing parties—is a useful strategy for beginning the peace process. However, extended negotiations and bargaining are usually required to reach a final agreement. Flexibility is the key to successful negotiations and to integrative agreements. Successful negotiations are most likely with experienced bargainers; mediators can also be helpful in the negotiation process. Superordinate goals and a superordinate identity increase the likelihood of a peaceful resolution of differences.

APPLYING SOCIAL PSYCHOLOGY

IV

Preview

In Part IV, we use the theories and research findings of social psychology to explore settings and problems in the real world. Chapter 12 applies social psychology to the *law*, including such topics as the selection of jurors, the presentation of evidence, jury deliberations, and perceptions of justice. Chapter 13 describes the social side of *business* both in the workplace and in the marketplace. Chapter 14 explores the social psychology of psychological and physical *health*, with an emphasis on stress and coping. These chapters illustrate that basic and applied social psychology are connected in an unbroken circle of mutual influence. Basic research provides the necessary foundation of knowledge, and applied research discovers unresolved issues to be addressed in the theory and research of the future.

Law   12

Preview

This chapter examines applications of social psychology to the law. First, we consider three stages in the life of a jury trial: the *selection of jurors,* an often controversial process; the *courtroom drama* in which the evidence is presented; and the deliberations of *the jury as a group.* Next, we consider *posttrial factors* such as sentencing and the prison experience, a possible result of a guilty verdict. Finally, we discuss the *perception of justice* inside and outside the courtroom.

T he judge called it "one of the most difficult cases of our time." It was also one of the most emotional. The courtroom was brimming with spectators and news reporters from all over the country, yet it was so quiet you could hear a pin drop. On June 17, 1987, after a tumultuous seven-week trial and thirty hours of deliberation, the jury reached its verdict. Bernhard Goetz, an electrical engineer, had become known as New York City's subway vigilante. For shooting four black teenagers who had approached him for money, Goetz was charged with assault, attempted murder, reckless endangerment, and carrying an illegal weapon. Public opinion was sharply divided. To some, Goetz was a victim-turned-hero who had acted reasonably in his own defense. To others, he was a villain, a cold-blooded killer who had taken the law into his own hands. Finally, two and a half years after the shooting, the jury foreman stood up and announced the verdict: except for the illegal gun charge, Goetz was *not guilty.*

As in the theater, this trial was packed with drama. At center stage were the defendant, Bernhard Goetz; his victims, two of whom testified in court; the judge; opposing lawyers; and a jury of twelve ordinary citizens. The questions were simple yet remarkably difficult to answer. Under the circumstances, was it reasonable for Goetz to fear that he was about to be mugged? If so, was it reasonable for him to react by using deadly force? The factual evidence was mixed. According to the prosecution, Goetz was looking for trouble when he chose to sit next to the boisterous teenagers while carrying a loaded gun. Although the youths carried screwdrivers in their pockets and tried to panhandle five dollars, they made no threats. Two passengers, eyewitnesses to the event, testified that one victim was shot while seated and that at least one other was shot in the back. There was even a confession from Goetz himself. But the defense lawyer painted a different picture of the event, arguing that Goetz had every reason to be afraid for his safety. He had been mugged before; his victims had a record of prior arrests; and the incident took place in a subway system rife with crime. As for the shooting itself, a medical examiner testified that in his opinion all the victims were shot while standing and facing the defendant—despite what the witnesses thought they had seen.

The jury's decision in this case was highly controversial. Regardless of how one feels about the verdict, however, the trial illustrates the profound importance of social psychology at work in the legal system. What kinds of people do lawyers select as jurors, and why? Can eyewitnesses accurately recall the details of traumatic events? How do juries manage to reach unanimous decisions, often after days of exhausting deliberation? And what factors influence the severity of the sentence imposed by judges? In this chapter, we take social psychology to the courtroom to answer these questions. But first, let's place the trial into a broader context.

In the American criminal justice system, trials are just the tip of an iceberg. Once a crime takes place, it must be detected and reported in order to come to the attention of the police. Through an investigation, the police must then find a suspect and decide whether to make an arrest. If they do, the suspect is held

The highly publicized and controversial trial of Bernhard Goetz, known as the New York City subway vigilante, offers a glimpse into social psychology at work in the courtroom.

in custody or bail is set, and either a judge or a grand jury decides if there is sufficient evidence for a formal accusation. If there is, the prosecuting and defense attorneys begin a lengthy process of discovery during which they gather evidence. At this point, many defendants plead guilty as the result of a deal negotiated by the lawyers. In cases that do go to trial, the ordeal does not end with a verdict. Following a conviction, the judge must decide on a sentence, and the defendant must decide whether to appeal to a higher court. For those serving time in prison, decisions concerning their release are made by parole boards.

As Figure 12.1 illustrates, the criminal justice apparatus is complicated, and the actors behind the scenes are numerous. Yet through it all, the trial—a relatively infrequent event—is the heart and soul of the system. The threat of trial motivates parties to gather evidence and, later, to negotiate a deal. And when it's over, the trial forms the basis for later sentencing and appeals decisions. Social psychologists have a lot to say about trials—and about the rest of the legal system as well (Kagehiro & Laufer, 1992). In the following pages, we divide the trial into three stages—the selection of jurors, the presentation of evidence, and the jury's deliberations.

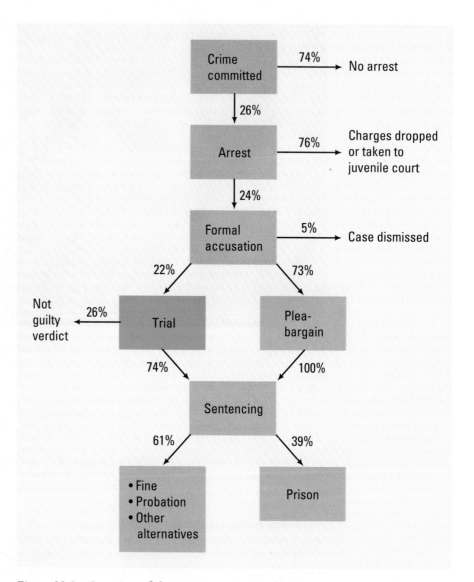

Figure 12.1   Overview of the American Criminal Justice System.   This flow chart presents the movement of cases through different branches of the criminal justice system. Percentages indicate the proportion of cases that reach a particular stage. As this chart illustrates, the trial is just one aspect of the criminal justice system. [Based on Konecni & Ebbesen, 1982. As adapted from the President's Commission on Law Enforcement and Administration of Justice (1967).]

SELECTION OF JURORS

The jury that tried Bernhard Goetz consisted of eight men and four women. Nine of the jurors were white; two were black; one was Hispanic. Three had themselves been the victims of subway crime. With ten million New Yorkers to choose from, how was this particular jury selected, and why?

Jury selection is a three-stage process. First, a court compiles a master list of eligible citizens who live in the community. Second, in an effort to obtain a representative sample from that community, a certain number of people from the list are randomly drawn and summoned for duty. If you've ever been called, you know what happens next. Before people who appear at the courthouse are selected for a jury, they are subjected to what is known as the **voir dire**, a pretrial interview in which the judge or opposing lawyers question prospective jurors for signs of bias. If someone knows one of the litigants, or has a financial interest in the outcome of the case, or has already formed an opinion, one of the lawyers will ask the judge to excuse the person. In fact, if it can be demonstrated that an entire community is biased, perhaps because of pretrial publicity, the trial might be postponed or moved to another location.

voir dire The pretrial examination of prospective jurors by the judge or opposing lawyers to uncover signs of bias.

Although the procedure seems rather straightforward, there is more to the story. In addition to excluding individuals who are obviously biased, lawyers are permitted to make **peremptory challenges**. That is, they can reject a certain limited number of prospective jurors who are not obviously biased, and they can do so without having to state reasons or obtain the judge's approval. Why would lawyers challenge someone who appears, at least on the surface, to be impartial? What guides the decision to accept some jurors and reject others? These kinds of questions make the voir dire extremely interesting to social psychologists (Hans & Vidmar, 1986; Kassin & Wrightsman, 1988).

peremptory challenges The means by which lawyers can exclude a limited number of prospective jurors without the judge's approval.

Trial Lawyers as Intuitive Psychologists

Trial lawyers have been known to use some outrageous strategies to select juries. Under pressure to make selections quickly and without much information, lawyers—like everyone else—rely on implicit personality theories and cultural stereotypes. As discussed in Chapter 3, an implicit personality theory is a set of assumptions that people make about how certain attributes are related to each other and to behavior. When people believe that all members of a group share the same attributes, these theories are called stereotypes.

As far as trial practice is concerned, numerous how-to books claim that the astute lawyer can predict a juror's verdict by simple demographics (Fulero & Penrod, 1990). Take occupation, for example. It has been suggested that athletes lack sympathy for fragile, injured victims; that engineering types are unemotional; and that cabinetmakers are so meticulous in their work that they are never fully satisfied with the evidence. Rumor has it, for example, that prosecutors exclude butchers from juries on the assumption that anyone who spends forty hours a week cutting dead animals into little pieces cannot easily be shocked by the details of a violent crime. Clarence Darrow, the most prominent trial lawyer of the twentieth century, was especially attuned to ethnic biases. He maintained that jurors of southern European descent favored the defense and those of Scandinavian and German heritage favored the prosecution (Sutherland & Cressey, 1974). Still other jury experts offer advice based on clothing, handwriting, body language, and astrology. Perhaps the most interesting rule is also the simplest: "If you don't like a juror's face, chances are he doesn't like yours either!" (Wishman, 1986, pp. 72–73).

Pretrial Attitudes and Bias

If assumptions based on appearances were correct, predicting how jurors would vote would be easy. But the folk wisdom of trial lawyers is not supported by research. Demographic factors such as sex, age, race, income, education, and occupation do not consistently predict juror decisions (Hastie et al., 1983). Personality factors are not consistently informative either (Kassin & Wrightsman, 1983). This does not mean that individual differences do not exist; it means only that simple cookbook recipes such as "women are lenient" and "authoritarian types are prone to convict" can prove hopelessly misleading. Sometimes, women are more lenient as jurors than men are; at other times it's the other way around. Sometimes, authoritarian personalities are more punitive; at other times they are less. Whether juror characteristics predict verdicts depends on the specifics of a particular case—hence, the birth of a new service industry: scientific jury selection.

Scientific Jury Selection   Rather than rely on hunches, successful financial investors, baseball managers, and gamblers play the odds whenever they can. Now, many trial lawyers do too. Recent years have seen the "art" of jury selection transformed into a "science."

It all began in the Vietnam era, when the federal government decided to prosecute a group of antiwar activists known as the Harrisburg Seven. The case against the defendants was strong, and the trial was to be held in Harrisburg, Pennsylvania. To help the defense select a jury, sociologist Jay Schulman and others (1973) surveyed the local community by interviewing 840 residents. Two kinds of information were taken from each resident: demographic characteristics (for example, sex, race, age, and education) and attitudes relevant to the trial (for example, attitudes toward the government, the war, and political dissent). By analyzing the correlations between demographics and attitudes, Schulman's team came up with a profile of the ideal juror for the defense: "a female Democrat with no religious preference and a white-collar job or a skilled blue-collar job" (p. 40). Guided by their results, the defense team selected its jury. The rest is history. Against all odds, the trial concluded with a hung jury, split 10 to 2 in favor of acquittal.

Today, that technique—known as **scientific jury selection**—is used often, especially in civil trials involving large amounts of money. The procedure is simple. Because lawyers are often not allowed to ask jurors intrusive personal questions, they try to determine jurors' attitudes from available information about their backgrounds. Through a community-wide survey, statistical relationships are sought between general demographic factors and attitudes relevant to a particular case. During the voir dire, lawyers ask prospective jurors about their backgrounds—occupation, religion, marital status, and so on—and then use peremptory challenges to exclude people whose profiles are associated in the community with attitudes unfavorable to the lawyer's case.

As you might expect, this is a controversial enterprise. It is perfectly legal as long as the prospective jurors themselves are not approached. But is it effective? Although lawyers who have used scientific jury selection boast an impressive winning percentage, it is impossible to know if these victories are attributable to the jury selection surveys (Berman & Sales, 1977). Social psychologists assume that attitudes can influence verdicts and that scientific jury selection can help lawyers identify these attitudes. As we'll see, such a linkage can be seen in cases involving rape and capital punishment.

Rape Myths In December 1991, Americans were riveted to their TV screens to watch the trial of William Kennedy Smith—live from Palm Beach, Florida. Then in February 1992, public attention shifted to Indianapolis, Indiana, where former heavyweight boxing champion Mike Tyson was being accused of rape by a contestant of the Miss Black America beauty pageant. In the first case, the woman had met Smith in a bar and then drove him at 2 A.M. to the Kennedy family's estate on the beach. In the second case, the woman had met Tyson at the pageant and joined him in his hotel room, also late at night. Tearfully, both women testified that they were physically overpowered and raped. In response, both defendants claimed that the women were fully consenting sexual partners. On the surface, these "he said, she said" trials seemed similar. In one important way, however, they were not: Smith's jury found him innocent; Tyson's found him guilty.

Few crimes test the criminal justice system as rape does. On the one hand, false accusations made by vindictive, regretful, or money-seeking lovers can put innocent men in prison. On the other hand, genuine rape victims are often humiliated by defense attorneys who try to justify their client's actions by impugning the victim's character and sexual lifestyle. A number of states have thus enacted **rape shield laws** designed to limit the kinds of embarrassing and often irrelevant personal questions that are asked of victims who testify (Borgida, 1981). Still, if it comes down to one person's word against another's, the

scientific jury selection A method of selecting juries through surveys that yield correlations between demographics and trial-relevant attitudes.

rape shield laws Statutes that restrict the kinds of personal questions lawyers can ask rape victims who take the witness stand.

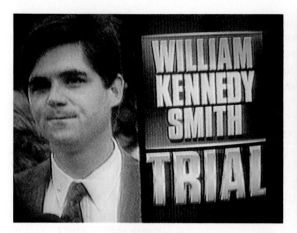

Recently, William Kennedy Smith (left) and Mike Tyson (right) were put on trial. In both cases, women testified that they were raped, and the men claimed that there was mutual consent. On the surface, these trials seemed similar. But were they? Smith was acquitted, while Tyson was convicted and sentenced to prison.

judge and jury confront the question of credibility: Who should be believed, the victim or the defendant?

Eugene Borgida and Nancy Brekke (1985) found that perceptions of the victim and the defendant depend largely on one's beliefs and attitudes about rape. In a series of studies, hundreds of men and women from the twin cities of Minneapolis and St. Paul took part in mock juries. After filling out questionnaires, subjects watched a simulated trial in which a woman said she was forcibly raped but the man claimed she had freely consented to have sex. The results showed that subjects' decisions were unrelated to their personality or demographic backgrounds, including gender. What did make a difference, however, were their attitudes about women and rape. As measured by the Rape Myth Acceptance Scale, earlier shown on page 377, subjects who agreed that "women have an unconscious wish to be raped" or that "any healthy woman can successfully resist a rapist if she really wants to," were less likely to vote guilty than were those who disagreed with these misconceptions. Other research shows that jurors who empathize with rape victims—perhaps because they personally knew someone who had once been raped—are more likely to trust the woman's side of the story than are those who do not (Wiener et al., 1989).

Death Qualification   If you had to sentence someone to die, could you do it? As you might expect, not everyone answers this question in the same way. Yet your answer could mean the difference between life and death for a defendant convicted of murder. Today, a vast majority of states in the United States permit capital punishment. Among those that do, it is often the jury that decides not only the verdict but the sentence as well: Should the convicted murderer be imprisoned for life or executed?

death qualification
A jury selection procedure used in capital cases that permits judges to exclude prospective jurors who say they would refuse to vote for the death penalty.

In cases that involve crimes punishable by death, a special jury-selection practice known as **death qualification** is used. Through death qualification, judges may exclude all prospective jurors who say they would refuse to vote for the death penalty under any conditions. These jurors are then excluded for the entire trial. To ensure that *sentencing* decisions are unbiased, it makes sense to exclude those who admit they are not open-minded. But does this selection practice tip the balance toward the prosecution when it comes to the *verdict*? Are death-qualified juries prone to convict?

Through a series of studies, Phoebe Ellsworth and her colleagues have examined this question. Their results show that compared to people who oppose the death penalty, those in favor of it are prosecution-minded on a host of criminal justice issues. They are more concerned about crime, more trustful of the police, more cynical about defense lawyers, and less tolerant of procedures that protect the accused (Fitzgerald & Ellsworth, 1984). When it comes to verdicts, the difference between jurors who are death-qualified and those who are excluded can be substantial. In one study, for example, 288 people watched a staged, videotaped murder trial and participated in mock juries. Subjects who were death-qualified, saying they were willing to impose the death penalty, were more likely to vote guilty before deliberating than were those who would have been excluded for their refusal to impose a death sentence. As illustrated in Figure 12.2, this difference among individuals persisted even after they deliberated on juries (Cowan et al., 1984). Similar results have also been found in studies of real jurors (Moran & Comfort, 1986).

As the research evidence mounted, American courts had to face a sobering prospect. Had the hundreds of prisoners on "death row" been tried by juries that were biased against them? In *Lockhart v. McCree* (1986), the U.S. Supreme Court considered the issue. To inform the Court of recent research developments, the American Psychological Association submitted an exhaustive review of the literature (Bersoff & Ogden, 1987)—but to no avail. In an opinion that disappointed many social psychologists, the Court rejected the APA's claims and ruled that death qualification does not violate a defendant's right to a fair trial. Should the Supreme Court have been persuaded by the research evidence? Some say yes (Ellsworth, 1991); others say no (Elliott, 1991). Either way, it is now important to identify alternative, nonprejudicial methods that can be used to select future capital juries. It turns out, for example, that many people who are excluded because of their *general* opposition to capital punishment say they would impose the death penalty on *specific* defendants found guilty of committing atrocious acts of violence (Cox & Tanford, 1989).

Ethical Dilemmas Before concluding our discussion of jury selection, let's consider some of the delicate ethical issues that it raises. Is justice enhanced or

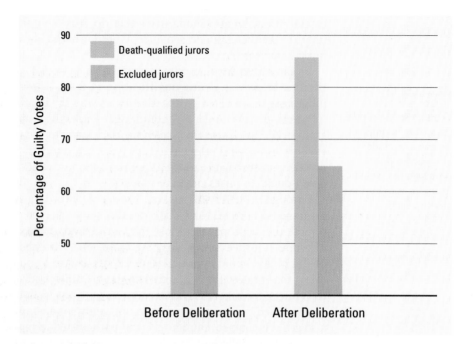

Figure 12.2 Link Between Death Qualification and Verdicts.   In this study, mock jurors who passed the death-qualification test were compared to those who would be excluded for their refusal to vote for the death penalty. As you can see, death-qualified subjects were more likely than excluded subjects to vote guilty of murder both before and after deliberations. [Data from C. L. Cowan et al., 1984.]

impaired by scientific jury selection? Should defense lawyers be allowed to conduct pretrial surveys? Is it fair for prosecutors to do the same? And is the goal for lawyers to eliminate jurors who are biased or to create a jury slanted in their direction? These are difficult questions, and the answers frequently depend on whom you ask.

Proponents of scientific jury selection argue that picking juries according to survey results is simply a more refined version of what lawyers are permitted to do by intuition. The problem, they say, is not the *science* but the *law* that permits lawyers to use peremptory challenges to exclude jurors who are not obviously biased. However, critics argue that scientific jury selection can tip the scales of justice in favor of wealthy clients who can afford to pay for the service. The implications are disturbing. In rape trials, and in trials that involve the death penalty, prosecution and defense lawyers can stack juries in their favor by conducting pretrial survey research. In other cases as well, lawyers can sometimes use science to increase the chance of winning.

"Are we to understand, then, that you would have no scruples about imposing the death penalty?"

No doubt this prospective juror would survive the death qualification test.

THE COURTROOM DRAMA

Once a jury is selected, the trial officially begins, and much of the evidence previously gathered comes to life. The trial itself is a well-orchestrated event. Lawyers make opening statements; witnesses answer questions; lawyers make closing arguments; and the judge instructs the jury. Yet there are many problems in this all-too-human enterprise. The evidence may not be accurate; jurors may be biased by extraneous factors; and judges' instructions may fall on deaf ears. In this section, we identify some of the problems and possible solutions.

The Defendant

"My intention was to murder them, to hurt them, to make them suffer as much as possible. . . . If I had more bullets, I would have shot all of them again and again." These self-incriminating words were spoken by Bernhard Goetz, video-taped by the police, and shown to Goetz's jury. As the statement indicates, people accused of crime are sometimes their own worst enemies. Whether guilty or innocent, suspects often confess—only to retract their confessions later on. The reasons for this predicament vary. Goetz's lawyer argued that his client was so exhausted when he turned himself in to the police that he had imagined much of what he said. Other defendants claim they were pressured into making false confessions.

Police Confessions   Years ago, the police used brute force and intimidation to get confessions. Today, "third degree" tactics are more psychological. In *Criminal Interrogation and Confessions,* the most popular how-to manual written for the police, Fred Inbau and John Reid (1986) present sixteen elaborate ploys that can be used to extract confessions. One approach is to minimize the offense by making excuses on behalf of the suspect. Lulled into a false sense of security and led to expect leniency, the suspect caves in. A second approach is to frighten the suspect into confessing by exaggerating the charges or pretending to have solid damaging evidence. In this scenario, the suspect is led to think that it is futile to mount a defense. A third approach is to befriend the suspect and use that friendship to offer sympathy and friendly advice. These ploys may sound as though they come from a television script, but they are often used in real life (Kassin & McNall, 1991; Wald et al., 1967; White, 1979).

Do people ever confess to crimes they did not commit? Every now and then it happens. When Charles Lindbergh's baby was kidnapped and murdered in 1932, more than two hundred people offered unsolicited confessions. Why? Getting attention, cleansing the soul, and relieving one's guilt are possible motives. It may seem hard to imagine that anyone would confess to a serious crime he or she did not commit, but there are some rather chilling examples on record (Bedau & Radelet, 1987). Consider, for example, the story of eighteen-year-old Peter Reilly, who returned home one night, found his mother's dead body, and called the police. The police immediately suspected Reilly of the murder and had him take a lie-detector test—which they said he failed. After being told that the test results were infallible, Reilly became confused and disoriented. Eventually, he confessed and pleaded guilty: "Well, it really looks like I did it." Two years later, new evidence revealed that Reilly could not have committed the murder and that his confession, which even he had come to believe, was false (Barthel, 1976).

The Reilly case never went to trial, but it raises a key question. How does the legal system treat confessions elicited by various methods of interrogation? Whenever a suspect confesses but then retracts the confession and goes to trial, the judge must determine whether the statement was voluntary or coerced. If it was clearly coerced—as when the suspect was isolated for long periods of time, deprived of food or sleep, threatened, or abused into submission—it is excluded. Otherwise, it is admitted into evidence for the jury to evaluate. As such, juries are confronted with a classic attributional dilemma: a suspect's statement to the police may reflect his or her guilt (personal attribution), or it may simply be a way to avoid the negative consequences of silence (situational attribution). According to attribution theory, jurors should reject all confessions made in response to external pressure. But wait—recall the "fundamental attribution error" encountered in Chapter 3, the tendency for observers to overattribute behavior to persons and neglect the influence of situational forces. Is it possible that jurors view the suspect who confesses as guilty, despite the pressures of interrogation? It depends.

First, it depends on the methods used to elicit the confession. Consider, for example, your reaction to two common ploys: the *threat* of harm or punishment and the *promise* of leniency or immunity from prosecution. By law, both tactics are unacceptable. Psychologically, however, there's an important difference. When mock jurors hear that a defendant confessed to the police after having been threatened, they fully discount the confession—they judge it to be coerced and vote for acquittal. When a defendant is said to have confessed in response to an offer of favorable treatment, however, people do not completely disregard

In Los Angeles, people can record a sixty-second confession for the price of a phone call. In an estimated two hundred anonymous calls per day, people confess to an array of deeds ranging from marital infidelity to murder. Some of these confessions may be true; others may be fabricated. Either way, it makes you wonder: would these callers ever "bare their souls" to the police, or confess to crimes they did not commit?

the confession. They concede that it was involuntary, but they vote guilty anyway. This pattern, called the *positive coercion bias*, suggests that people view the promise of reward as a weaker form of pressure than a threat of punishment (Kassin & Wrightsman, 1985).

The jury's interpretation of confession evidence also depends on how that evidence is presented. Today, many police departments videotape confessions for the record. But how are these events staged for the camera and introduced in court? We saw in Chapter 3 that observers who watch two people having a conversation overemphasize the impact on that interaction of the person who is visually salient. On the basis of this finding, Daniel Lassiter and Audrey Irvine (1986) taped a mock confession from three different camera angles: either the interrogator or the suspect or both were visible. Even though all subjects heard the same exchange of words, those who watched the suspect considered the interrogation to be less coercive than did those who were focused on the interrogator. The practical implications are striking. When the camera directs all eyes toward the accused, jurors are likely to underestimate the amount of pressure exerted by the "hidden" interrogator. Yet that is precisely how confessions are taped. Anyone who saw excerpts of Goetz's statement to the police would vividly recall his image on the TV screen but remember little of his interrogator.

The Lie-Detector Test   As in the case of Peter Reilly, people sometimes confess after being told that they have failed the **polygraph**, or lie-detector test (Lykken, 1981). The polygraph is an instrument that records multiple channels of physiological arousal. Rubber tubes are strapped around the suspect's torso to measure breathing; blood pressure cuffs are wrapped around the upper arm to measure pulse rate; and electrodes are placed on the fingertips to record perspiration. The instrument is used to detect deception on the assumption that when people lie, they become anxious in ways that can be measured. Here's how the test works. After convincing a suspect that the polygraph is effective and establishing his or her baseline level of arousal, the examiner asks a series of yes-no questions and compares how the suspect reacts to emotionally arousing *crime-relevant questions* ("Did you hurt your mother last night?") and *control questions* that are arousing but not relevant to the crime ("Did you hurt anybody when you were younger?"). In theory, innocent suspects—whose denials are truthful—should be more aroused by control questions, and guilty suspects—whose denials are false—should be more aroused by the crime-relevant questions (Podlesny & Raskin, 1977).

Does the lie-detector test really work? Although many people think it is foolproof, professional opinion is split. Some researchers report accuracy rates in the range of 80 to 90 percent (Horvath, 1984; Raskin, 1986). Others say that these claims are exaggerated and that there are serious problems (Lykken, 1981). One problem is that truthful persons too often "fail" the test. For example, a study of polygraph records obtained from police files revealed that

polygraph   A mechanical instrument that records physiological arousal from multiple channels; often used as a lie-detector test.

although 98 percent of suspects later known to be guilty were correctly identified as such, 45 percent of those who were eventually found innocent were judged deceptive (Patrick & Iacono, 1991). A second problem is that the test can be faked, as people are able to beat the polygraph by tensing their muscles, biting their tongues, and squeezing their toes while answering the control questions (Honts et al., 1985). What, then, are we to conclude? After carefully reviewing all the research, Leonard Saxe and his colleagues (1985) concluded that there is no simple answer. Under certain conditions—as when the suspect is naive and the examiner is competent—it is possible for the polygraph to detect truth and deception at fairly high levels of accuracy. The problems just described, however, remain hard to overcome. Thus, many states do not allow polygraph results into evidence. In those that do, the results are admitted only when both sides agree.

The Victim

One of the most electrifying moments in the Goetz trial came when James Ramseur, one of the men who was shot, took the stand after initially refusing to testify. Ushered into the courtroom by armed guards, Ramseur had an angry expression on his face and his hands deep in his pants pockets. After refusing to place his hand on the Bible to take the oath, he was gone within minutes. Ramseur reappeared days later; but after ranting and raving, cursing the judge, and uttering obscenities to the jury, he was cited for contempt of court (Johnson, 1987c). This incident is atypical. But it illustrates that victims, like defendants, can have a dramatic impact on a trial.

When victims testify, it is usually in trials involving serious crimes. The less serious the crime, the less likely a person is even to report it to the police (Greenberg & Ruback, 1982). So how do juries react to the victim who takes the witness stand? In general, the reaction is one of sympathy and understanding. But on occasion, crime victims are blamed for their misfortune—as when women who are raped are accused of being careless or too seductive. One explanation of the tendency for people to blame the victim is the hindsight bias described in Chapter 2. After an event occurs, even one that is infrequent, people look back and overestimate how predictable the event was, claiming, "I knew it all along." For crime victims needing social support, this Monday-morning quarterbacking can have harmful consequences. In one study, for example, subjects who read about the behavior of a woman who was raped later viewed the rape as foreseeable and her behavior as blameworthy. Yet subjects who read the same story without knowing she had been raped did not view her actions in negative terms (Janoff-Bulman et al., 1985). It's no wonder that so many women who are sexually assaulted report feeling as if they—not the accused—are on trial.

A second explanation for the tendency to blame victims is that people need to believe in a just world, as discussed in Chapter 3. To protect ourselves from the threatening implications of someone else's suffering—that we too are vulnerable—we delude ourselves into thinking that the victim must have done something to deserve his or her fate (Carli & Leonard, 1990). In the case of rape, victims who find fault with themselves—blaming the fact that they're too trusting or that they carelessly let a stranger into the house, left a window open, or walked alone at night—are more prone to get depressed after the initial trauma (Frazier, 1990).

The Eyewitness

"I'll never forget that face!" When these words are uttered, police officers, prosecutors, judges, and juries all listen. Sometimes, however, eyewitnesses make costly mistakes—not only in research laboratories but in real life. Consider the story of William Jackson, identified in a line-up by two witnesses. Because of that evidence alone, Jackson was convicted and sentenced to serve from fourteen to fifty years in prison. Five years into his term, it was revealed that another man was responsible for the crimes—a man who resembled Jackson. Within hours, Jackson was freed: "They took away part of my life, part of my youth," he said. "I spend five years down there, and all they said was 'we're sorry'" ("We're Sorry," 1982).

It is estimated that some 77,000 people a year are charged with crimes solely on the basis of eyewitness evidence (Goldstein et al., 1989). As eyewitnesses, people are called on to remember just about anything—a face, a car accident, a conversation. Over the years, literally hundreds of controlled studies have been conducted. From this research, three general conclusions may be drawn. First, eyewitnesses are imperfect; second, certain factors systematically affect their performance; third, judges and juries are not sufficiently informed about these factors (Wells & Loftus, 1984; Williams et al., 1992; Yarmey, 1979).

People tend to think human memory is like a video camera: if you turn on the power and focus the lens, all observations will be recorded for subsequent playback. Unfortunately, it's not that simple. Researchers find it useful to view memory as a three-stage process involving *acquisition, storage,* and *retrieval.* Acquisition refers to a witness's perceptions at the time of the event in question. Second, the witness stores the acquired information in memory to avoid forgetting. Third, when the information is needed, the witness retrieves it from storage. This model suggests that errors can occur at three different points.

Acquisition   Some kinds of persons and events are more difficult to perceive than others. As common sense tells us, brief exposure time, poor lighting, distance, physical disguise, and distraction are all factors that can severely limit a witness's perceptions. Research has uncovered other less obvious factors as well.

After the tragic assassination of President John F. Kennedy, dozens of eyewitnesses came forward to describe what they saw. Some reported one gunman in the sixth-floor window of a nearby building; others reported two or three gunmen in the building; and still others thought the shots were fired from the ground. Such are the pitfalls of eyewitness testimony.

Yerkes-Dodson law
The finding that there is a curvilinear relation between arousal and performance on complex tasks.

Consider the effects of a witness's state of mind—for example, the kind of stress that was experienced by the subway passengers who witnessed Goetz's bloody shooting. According to the time-honored **Yerkes-Dodson law**, there is a curvilinear relation between arousal and performance on reasonably complex tasks (Deffenbacher, 1983; Yerkes & Dodson, 1908). Thus, although stress has a positive effect up to a point, extremely high levels of stress—as when people witness dangerous and violent crimes—tend to impair performance (Brigham et al., 1983). Alcohol, a drug often involved in crime, also causes problems. When subjects in one study witnessed a live staged crime, those who had earlier consumed fruit juice were more accurate in their recollections than were those who had been served an alcoholic beverage (Yuille & Tollestrup, 1990).

weapon-focus effect
The tendency for weapons to draw attention and impair a witness's ability to identify the culprit.

The **weapon-focus effect** is also an important factor. People who are accosted by someone who pulls out a gun, a razor blade, or a knife are less able to identify the assailant than are people who are not threatened with a weapon. This disparity occurs for two reasons. First, people become agitated by the sight of a threatening stimulus—as when the subjects of one study were approached by an experimenter holding a syringe or threatening to administer an injection

(Maass & Kohnken, 1989). Second, even in harmless situations a witness's eyes are drawn like a magnet to a weapon—leaving less attention available for other information. To demonstrate, Elizabeth Loftus and her colleagues (1987) showed subjects slides of a customer who approached a bank teller and pulled out either a handgun or a checkbook. By recording eye movements, the researchers found that subjects spent more time looking at the gun than at the checkbook. The net result was an impairment in their ability to identify the perpetrator in a line-up.

There is still another important consideration. By varying the racial make-up of subjects and target persons in laboratory experiments and real-life interactions, researchers discovered that people find it relatively difficult to recognize members of a race other than their own—a finding known as the **cross-race identification bias** (Brigham et al., 1982; Malpass & Kravitz, 1969). To demonstrate, eighty-six convenience store clerks in El Paso, Texas, were asked to identify three male customers—one white, one black, and one Mexican-American—all experimental confederates who had stopped in and made a purchase earlier that day. Figure 12.3 shows that the white, black, and Mexican-American clerks were most likely to make accurate identifications of customers belonging to their own racial or ethnic group (Platz & Hosch, 1988). The underlying cause of the cross-racial identification bias is not yet known. It doesn't seem to indicate prejudice, nor does it seem to be caused by a lack of interracial contact (Brigham & Malpass, 1985). Whatever the cause, this bias has important implications for eyewitness testimony.

cross-race identification bias The tendency for people to be better at identifying members of their own race than members of other races.

Storage In the fall of 1991, law professor Anita Hill accused Supreme Court justice nominee Clarence Thomas of sexual harassment. She asserted that he had made certain statements ten years earlier—statements she said she could repeat word for word. That same year, TV star Roseanne Arnold said that she had vivid memories of being sexually abused as a baby by her mother. These two stories have little in common, but both raise the same important question: Can remembrances of the past be trusted (Toufexis, 1991)?

As one would expect, memory for faces and events tends to decline with the passage of time. Longer intervals between an event and its retrieval are generally associated with increased forgetting (Shapiro & Penrod, 1986). But not all memories fade, and time alone does not cause memory slippage. After witnessing an event, we often generate and receive new information about it. Consider the plight of the subway passengers trapped in their seats during Goetz's shooting spree. When it was over, they undoubtedly talked to one another, read about the incident in the papers, described it to friends, answered police questions, and looked at mug shots. By the time these witnesses appeared in court, was their original memory still "pure," uncontaminated by postevent information?

reconstructive memory The theoretical concept that eyewitness memory can be altered by exposure to postevent information.

According to Elizabeth Loftus (1979), it probably was not. Based on an extensive program of research, Loftus proposed a theory of **reconstructive**

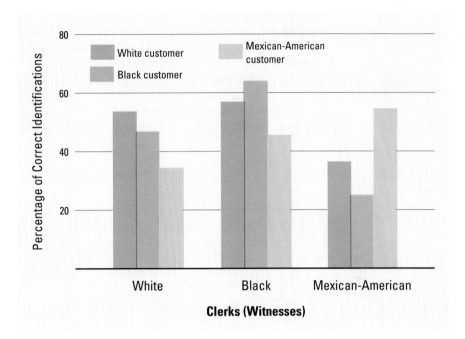

Figure 12.3   The Cross-Race Identification Bias.   In this study, convenience store clerks tried to identify three customers—one white, one black, and one Mexican-American—all of whom had stopped in during the day. As you can see, the clerks were more likely to correctly identify customers of their own racial or ethnic group. [Data from Platz & Hosch, 1988.]

memory. After we observe something, she says, additional information about the event—whether true or not—becomes integrated into the fabric of our memory. To illustrate, consider a classic experiment by Loftus and John Palmer (1974). Subjects viewed a film of a traffic accident and then answered questions, including the following: "About how fast were the cars going when they *hit* each other?" Other subjects received the same question, except the verb *hit* was replaced by either *smashed, collided, bumped,* or *contacted*. Even though all subjects saw the same accident, the wording of the question affected their reports. Figure 12.4 shows that subjects given the "smashed" question estimated the highest average speed and those responding to the "contacted" question estimated the lowest. But there's more. One week later, subjects were called back for additional probing. Had the wording of the questions caused subjects to reconstruct their memories of the accident? Yes, indeed. When asked whether they had seen broken glass at the accident site (none was actually present), 32 percent of the "smashed" subjects said they had. Consistent with

Loftus's theory, what these subjects remembered of the accident was based on two sources: the event itself and postevent information.

Loftus's provocative theory has aroused much controversy. Does postevent information actually alter or impair a witness's real memory, never to be retrieved again (Belli, 1989; Loftus et al., 1978; Tversky & Tuchin, 1989)? Or does it merely lead subjects to follow the experimenter's "suggestion," leaving their original memory intact for retrieval under the right conditions (Bekerian & Bowers, 1983; Dodson & Reisberg, 1991; McCloskey & Zaragoza, 1985)?

Figure 12.4   Biasing Eyewitness Reports with Loaded Questions.   Subjects viewed a film of a traffic accident and then answered this question: "About how fast were the cars going when they _____ (hit, smashed, collided, bumped, or contacted) each other?" As you can see, the wording of the question influenced speed estimates (top). One week later, it also caused subjects to reconstruct their memory of other aspects of the accident (bottom). [Top: data from Loftus & Palmer, 1974. Bottom: from Loftus & Loftus, 1976.]

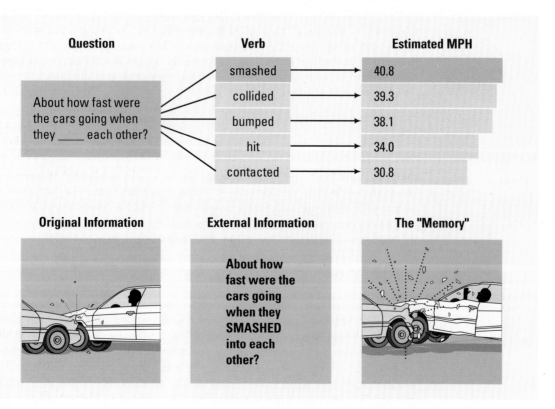

While the theoretical debate rages at a lively pace, the all-important practical lesson remains: whether memory is truly altered or not, eyewitness *reports* are hopelessly biased by postevent information.

This phenomenon raises an additional question. If adults can be misled by postevent information, what about children? In 1983, Judy Johnson complained to the police in Manhattan Beach, California, that her three-year-old son had been molested at the McMartin Pre-School by Raymond Buckey, a teacher. Before long, the police had contacted other parents and children and charged Ray and his mother, Peggy McMartin Buckey, with sexually abusing hundreds of boys and girls. In interviews with a social worker, several children said they were forced to play "naked games" and then were frightened into silence. Some even told bizarre stories of satanic rituals in which they drank blood, dug up bodies at cemeteries, jumped out of airplanes, and sacrificed animals on a church altar (Carlson, 1990; DeBenedictis, 1990).

Were the stories accurate? Were the children competent to testify in court? On the one hand, there were striking consistencies in the reports of different children. On the other hand, the social worker who conducted the interviews often prompted the children with suggestive questions, urging them to describe acts they had initially denied and scolding those who claimed ignorance. Based on the testimony of eleven children, the case went to trial. Then in 1990, after thirty-three months—the longest criminal trial in American history—the jury found the defendants not guilty. As one juror explained, "I believe that the children believed what they were saying, but I couldn't tell if they were repeating what they had been told . . . I had a hard time picking fact from fiction" (Mydans, 1990, p. A18).

Can leading questions cause children to confuse appearance and reality? Since the McMartin case, thousands of child sex-abuse cases involving preschool teachers, babysitters, family members, and strangers have inundated the courts. With each complaint, the legal system struggles to decide whether children are competent to take the witness stand or are too suggestible, too prone to confuse reality and fantasy. In some trials, juries do not trust the recollections of young children. Yet in others—for example, the recent sex abuse case against the Little Rascals Day Care Center in North Carolina—defendants are convicted solely on the basis of such testimony (Taub, 1992). To provide some guidance, researchers are studying children's eyewitness memory (Ceci et al., 1989; Doris, 1991; Perry & Wrightsman, 1991).

At this point, some tentative conclusions can be drawn. Laboratory experiments clearly indicate that preschool-age children are more likely than older children and adults to incorporate postevent suggestions into their memory. For example, subjects ranging from three to twelve years old were read an illustrated story about a girl who got a stomachache after eating her breakfast eggs too fast. The next day, half of the subjects were reminded of the girl who had a *headache* after eating her *cereal* too fast. Two days later, subjects were asked to select the pictures—eggs or cereal, a stomachache or headache—that had accompanied the original story. Among those who were not misled, children of all ages were

In the McMartin Preschool trial, Raymond and Peggy Buckey were accused of sexual abuse. Although eleven children testified, the jury concluded that their memories could not be trusted because of suggestive questions that had been asked.

accurate about 90 percent of the time in their ability to recognize the original pictures. Among subjects who were misled, however, the three- and four-year-old preschoolers were accurate only 37 percent of the time. As shown in Figure 12.5, the young children in this situation were quite suggestible (Ceci et al., 1987).

But are they too suggestible to testify in court? Maybe, maybe not. To study the process for stressful, real-life experiences, Gail Goodman and her colleagues (1991) questioned children who had received immunization shots at a health clinic. By suggesting events that did not occur ("Did the doctor take you to another room?" "Did he kiss you?"), the investigators found that although preschoolers were easily misled about relatively inconsequential aspects of the experience, they almost never reported acts of abuse that were suggested but did not occur. Additional research confirms this important point: it is not easy to induce children, even preschoolers, to falsely report that they were physically touched in sensitive places or otherwise involved in actions that are normally associated with abuse (Leippe et al., 1991; Rudy & Goodman, 1991). Young children may be vulnerable to the biasing memory effects of postevent information, but their testimony in abuse cases should be taken seriously.

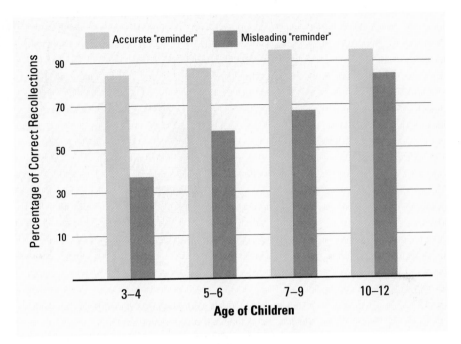

Figure 12.5   Are Child Witnesses Suggestible?   Children of varying ages heard a story followed by a "reminder" that was either accurate or misleading. When their memory was tested two days later, most subjects who received the accurate reminder correctly remembered the original story. However, many of those who received misleading information—especially the three- and four-year-olds—were mistaken in their recollections. [Data from Ceci et al., 1987.]

Retrieval   For eyewitnesses, testifying is only the last in a series of efforts to retrieve what they say from memory. Before witnesses reach the courtroom, they are questioned by police and lawyers, view a line-up or mug shots, and even assist in the construction of a facial composite or an artist's sketch of the perpetrator. Yet each of these retrieval opportunities increases the risk of error and distortion.

Clearly, nothing an eyewitness does has greater impact than a line-up identification. When the police make an arrest, they often call on witnesses to view a live or photographic line-up that includes the suspect and other individuals. The line-up may take place within days of a crime or months later. Either way, this procedure—much like a multiple-choice test—is better than the older method of presenting witnesses with just one person known to be suspected by the police. Yet tragic cases of mistaken identity continue to occur.

"Do you swear to tell your version of the truth as you perceive it, clouded perhaps by the passage of time and preconceived notions?"

[© 1989 Sidney Harris.]

Basically, three factors affect identification performance. The first is the *line-up construction* itself. A few years ago, comedian Richard Pryor was in a skit on the TV show "Saturday Night Live" in which he appeared in a line-up alongside a nun, a refrigerator, and a duck. Lo and behold, the eyewitness—having already described a male criminal—picked Pryor. It obviously doesn't take a social psychologist to see the problem with this particular situation. To be fair, a line-up should include at least three other persons, called "foils," who resemble the suspect in their general appearance (Nosworthy & Lindsay, 1990). Some psychologists have argued instead that the foils should match the witness's description of the culprit (Lüüs & Wells, 1991). Either way, anything that makes the suspect distinctive, compared to the others, increases his or her chance of being selected (Buckhout, 1974). This is what happened in the case of Steve Titus, a man mistakenly accused of rape when the police showed the victim his photograph along with pictures of five other men. Although the foils resembled Titus in their appearance, his picture stood out like a sore thumb. It was smaller than all the others and was the only one without a border. Titus was also the only man in the group with a smile on his face (Loftus & Ketcham, 1991).

Second, *line-up instructions* to the witness are important. In a study by Roy Malpass and Patricia Devine (1981), students saw a staged act of vandalism,

	Percentage of False Identifications	
	Unbiased Instructions	Biased Instructions
Culprit Present	0	25
Culprit Absent	33	78

Table 12.1 Effects of Line-up and Instructions on False Identifications. After witnessing a crime, subjects were told either that the culprit was in the line-up (biased instruction) or that he might or might not be present (unbiased instruction). Subjects then viewed a line-up in which the real culprit was present or absent. Notice the percentage of subjects in each group who identified an innocent person. Those who received the biased instruction were far more likely to make a false identification, picking an innocent person rather than no one at all—especially when the real culprit was not in the line-up. [Data from Malpass & Devine, 1981.]

after which they attended a line-up. Half of the students received "biased" instructions: they were led to believe that the culprit was in the line-up. The others were told that he might or might not be present. Line-ups were then presented either with or without the culprit. When subjects received biased instructions, they felt compelled to identify *someone*. The result was that many subjects picked an innocent person (see Table 12.1). Again, the story of Steve Titus is a case in point. The police told the victim to pick her assailant from a group of six photographs. After studying the pictures for several minutes and shaking her head in confusion, she was urged to concentrate and make a selection. "This one is the closest," she said. "It has to be this one" (Loftus & Ketcham, 1991, p. 38).

The third factor is perhaps the most subtle, as it pertains to *mug-shot-induced biases*. When witnesses view a line-up after having looked at mug shots, they are inclined to identify anyone whose photograph they have previously seen (Brigham & Cairns, 1988; Brown et al., 1977; Gorenstein & Ellsworth, 1980). Clearly, the person looks familiar—but from the crime scene or the photos? All too often, witnesses remember a face but forget the circumstances in which they originally saw it.

Courtroom Testimony Eyewitnesses are sometimes inaccurate, but that's only part of the problem. The other part is that their in-court testimony is persuasive and not easily evaluated. To understand how juries view eyewitness testimony, Gary Wells, Rod Lindsay, and their colleagues conducted an impressive series of experiments (Lindsay et al., 1981; Wells et al., 1979). They staged the theft of a calculator in front of unsuspecting research subjects who were cross-examined after trying to pick the culprit from a photo spread. Other subjects served as mock jurors, observed the questioning, and evaluated the witnesses. Not only did jurors overestimate eyewitness accuracy, but they were also unable to distinguish between witnesses who made correct identifications and those who did not.

There seem to be two problems. First, the subject of human memory is not something we know about through common sense. Brian Cutler and others (1988), for example, found that mock jurors were not sensitive to the effects of line-up instructions, weapon focus, and other key aspects of an eyewitnessing situation. The second problem is that subjects in this study—and in others as well—based their judgments on how *confident* the witness was, a factor that surprisingly does not predict accuracy (Bothwell et al., 1987; Kassin et al., 1991; Wells & Murray, 1984). Jurors, by the way, are not alone in their erroneous assumptions. Even the U.S. Supreme Court has claimed that confidence signals accuracy (*Neil v. Biggers,* 1972).

The Psychological Expert

Having identified some of the problems with information obtained from defendants, victims, and eyewitnesses, perhaps psychologists can put their knowledge to use by educating juries so they can better evaluate the evidence. Is this a goal that can and should be achieved? These days, psychologists are being asked with increasing frequency to testify as expert witnesses on coerced confessions, the polygraph, the suggestibility of children in abuse cases, and the coping behavior of rape victims and battered wives (Borgida et al., in press; Frazier & Borgida, 1992; Schuller & Vidmar, 1992).

Perhaps the most controversial form of expert testimony is on the subject of eyewitness evidence. Like physicians who testify about a patient's medical condition, and like economists who testify on antitrust matters, eyewitness experts are called by a particular party to tell the jury about relevant theory and memory research. What, specifically, do they say to the jury? What research findings do the experts present in court? Based on a survey of sixty-three eyewitness experts, Table 12.2 lists some of the eyewitness phenomena believed to be most worthy of expert testimony (Kassin et al., 1989)—many of which are not known by the average person (Kassin & Barndollar, 1992).

Psychologists disagree over whether receiving such advice from experts helps or hinders the jury (Loftus, 1983; McCloskey & Egeth, 1983). Who is right? Is the jury better off with or without help from experts? Although it's too early to draw firm conclusions, research suggests two ways in which expert testimony enables jurors to become more competent judges of an eyewitness. First, it's clear that eyewitness experts lead people to scrutinize the evidence more carefully. Since people place too much faith in eyewitness testimony, a dose of

Eyewitness Factor	Statement
Wording of questions	An eyewitness's testimony about an event can be affected by how the questions put to that witness are worded.
Line-up instructions	Police instructions can affect an eyewitness's willingness to make an identification and/or the likelihood that he or she will identify a particular person.
Postevent information	Eyewitness testimony about an event often reflects not only what the witness actually saw but also information obtained later on.
Accuracy-confidence	An eyewitness's confidence is not a good predictor of his or her identification accuracy.
Mug-shot biases	Eyewitnesses sometimes identify as a culprit someone they have seen in another situation or context.
Cross-race bias	Eyewitnesses are better at identifying others of the same race than they are at identifying members of another race.
Stress	Very high levels of stress impair the accuracy of eyewitness testimony.
Weapon focus	The presence of a weapon impairs an eyewitness's ability to accurately identify the perpetrator's face.

Table 12.2   What Eyewitness Experts Say in Court. Presented with a list of eyewitness factors, sixty-three experts were asked what research findings were strong enough to present in court. These statements are among those supported by most experts. The statements are ranked according to the amount of support they elicited. [From Kassin et al., 1989.]

skepticism is a healthy result. Second, it is possible, but not yet certain, that expert testimony can help jurors distinguish between credible and noncredible eyewitnesses (Cutler et al., 1989; Wells, 1986).

Pretrial Publicity

The Goetz case attracted enormous publicity. So did the recent drug trial of former Panamanian leader Manuel Noriega, the grisly multiple-murder trial in Milwaukee of Jeffrey Dahmer, the imprisonment of "Hotel Queen" Leona

Helmsley, the acquittal of the Los Angeles police officers who beat Rodney King, and the rape trials of William Kennedy Smith and Mike Tyson. Although few cases draw this much attention, many do find their way into the mass media long before they appear in court. As such, the system struggles with this dilemma: Does exposure to pretrial news stories corrupt prospective jurors?

Public opinion surveys consistently indicate that the more people know about a case, the more likely they are to presume the defendant guilty, even while they claim to be impartial (Moran & Cutler, 1991). There's nothing mysterious about this result. The information in news reports usually comes from the police or the district attorney's office, so it often reveals facts unfavorable to the defense. The real question, of course, is whether this information has an impact on juries that go on to receive hard evidence in court and deliberate to a verdict.

To examine the effects of pretrial publicity, Geoffrey Kramer and his colleagues (1990) played a videotaped re-enactment of an armed robbery trial to

[Drawing by Dana Fradon; © 1990 The New Yorker Magazine, Inc.]

"My client has been convicted by the media, but I am confident that his conviction will be overturned on appeal by the three major networks and the 'Times.'"

hundreds of subjects participating in 108 mock juries. Before watching the tape, subjects were exposed to TV reports and newspaper clippings about the case. Some received material that was neutral. Others received information that was incriminating—revealing, for example, that the defendant had a prior record or implicating the defendant in a hit-and-run accident in which a small child was killed. Even though subjects were instructed to base their decisions solely on the evidence, pretrial publicity had a marked effect. Among subjects exposed to neutral material, 33 percent voted guilty after deliberating in a jury. Among those exposed to prejudicial material, that figure increased to 48 percent. What's worse, judges and defense lawyers could not identify in a simulated voir dire which jurors were biased by the publicity. Indeed, 48 percent of those who were questioned and not challenged—jurors who claimed they were impartial and unaffected by the publicity—went on to vote guilty (Kerr et al., 1991). These results are presented in Figure 12.6.

Figure 12.6 Contaminating Effects of Pretrial Publicity. In this study, subjects were exposed to prejudicial or neutral news reports on a robbery defendant, watched a videotaped trial, and voted before and after participating in a mock jury deliberation. As you can see, pretrial publicity increased the conviction rate only slightly before deliberations (left). After deliberations, however, it more clearly increased the conviction rate—even, ironically, among subjects perceived as impartial by judges and lawyers (right). [Data from Kerr et al., 1991.]

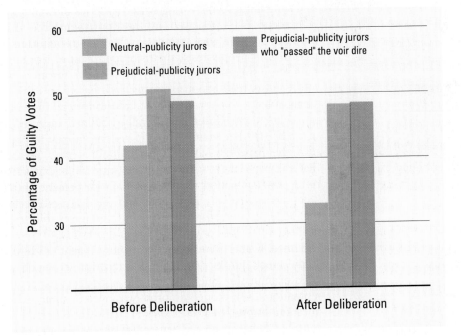

There are two ways in which pretrial publicity is potentially dangerous. First, it often divulges negative information that, for one reason or another, is not allowed into the trial record. Second, there is the matter of timing. Because many news stories precede the actual trial, jurors become informed about certain facts even before they enter the courtroom. From what we know about the power of first impressions, the implications are clear. If jurors receive prejudicial news information about a defendant *before* trial, that information will distort how they interpret the rest of the case. Is there a solution? Since this biasing effect persists despite jury selection practices and cautionary instructions from the judge, justice may demand that highly publicized cases be postponed or moved to other, less informed communities.

Inadmissible Testimony

Just as jurors are biased by news stories, on occasion they receive extralegal information from the trial itself. Consider the following example. According to the rules, lawyers are not permitted to assault the character of a witness by referring to prior arrests—unless the witness was convicted. Yet that's exactly what Goetz's lawyer did. While cross-examining one of the victims, he repeatedly referred to the victim's arrest record. With each reference, the prosecutor objected. Eventually, the judge issued a warning to Goetz's lawyer and ordered the jury to disregard the prejudicial information (Johnson, 1987b).

If something seems wrong with this series of events, you should know that it is a scene often replayed in the courtroom. But can people really strike information from their minds the way court reporters can strike it from the record? Can people resist the forbidden fruit of inadmissible testimony? Common sense suggests they cannot. So does the research. In one study, a group of mock jurors read about a murder case based on evidence so weak that not a single subject voted guilty. A second group read the same case, except that the prosecution introduced an illegally obtained tape recording of a phone call made by the defendant: "I finally got the money to pay you off . . . when you read the papers tomorrow, you'll know what I mean." The defense argued that the illegal tape should not be admissible, but the judge disagreed. As a result, the conviction rate increased to 26 percent. In a third group, as in the second, the tape was introduced and the defense objected. This time, however, the judge sustained the objection and told jurors to disregard it. Still, 35 percent of them voted for conviction (Sue et al., 1973).

Similar results were found in a more recent study of "dirty tricks." In that study, mock jurors read a trial transcript in which a lawyer implied in a cross-examination question that the opponent's expert witness had a tarnished reputation. Even though no proof was offered, subjects who were exposed to the question lowered their estimates of this witness's credibility. In fact, the witness became "damaged goods" regardless of whether the question was met with an admission, a denial, or an objection sustained by the judge. These results are depicted in Figure 12.7 (Kassin et al., 1990b).

Why are people unable or unwilling to follow a judge's plea to disregard inadmissible evidence? Imagine yourself in the jury box, and three reasons become apparent. First, the added instruction draws attention to the information in controversy. It's like being told *not* to think about white bears. Try it, and you'll see the problem. Daniel Wegner (1989) finds that when people try to suppress a particular thought, that thought intrudes on consciousness with remarkable frequency. A second reason is that instructions to disregard, like censorship, restrict a juror's decision-making freedom. As such, they can backfire by arousing reactance. Thus, when a judge emphasizes the ruling by forbidding jurors from using the information, they become even *more* likely to use it (Wolf & Montgomery, 1977). The third reason is the easiest to understand. Jurors want to reach the right decision. If they stumble onto relevant

Figure 12.7 Damaging Influence of Inadmissible Testimony. In this study, mock jurors read a trial transcript in which a lawyer asked the opponent's expert, "Isn't it true that your work is poorly regarded by your colleagues?" Compared to the rating of a control condition in which the question was not asked (left), ratings of the expert's credibility were lowered by the question—regardless of whether it was followed by an admission ("Yes, it is"), a denial ("No, it isn't"), or an objection sustained by the judge. [Data from Kassin et al., 1990b.]

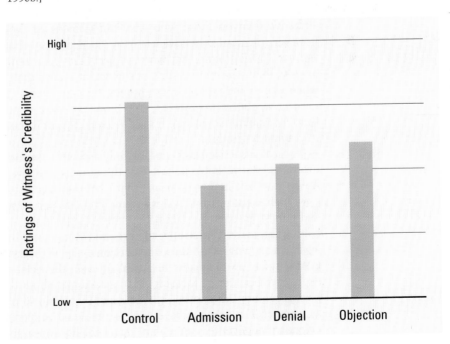

information, they want to use it—whether it satisfies the law's technical rules or not. If you were on the Goetz jury, wouldn't the arrest records of his victims lead you to suspect they had criminal intentions? If you had participated in the study described earlier, wouldn't the incriminating phone call have led you to doubt the defendant's innocence? Apparently, it's hard to ignore information that seems relevant to a case (Wissler & Saks, 1985)—especially when it vindicates the accused (Thompson et al., 1981).

Physical Appearance of the Litigants

When Troy Canty—one of the men Goetz shot—appeared in court, he was dressed in a suit and tie. No doubt he believed that his well-groomed appearance could influence the jury's opinion of his testimony. Goetz's lawyer believed it too. In front of the jury box, he mounted on easels poster-size enlargements of the four youths dressed in their street clothes (Shipp, 1987).

"You can't judge a book by its cover" is a saying often breached by social perceivers. As described in Chapter 3, numerous studies reveal that when people are asked about others they don't know, their impressions are influenced by appearance. Does this bias extend into the courtroom, or is justice truly blind? Do judges and juries evaluate defendants and victims, in part, by the images they present? Research suggests they do. In one study, Pennsylvania state judges were less likely to send convicted defendants to prison if they were physically attractive than if they were not (Stewart, 1980). In another study, Texas judges set lower bail and imposed smaller fines on suspects who were attractive than on those who were not (Downs & Lyons, 1991). Sometimes, however, physical attractiveness may be a liability. Harold Sigall and Nancy Ostrove (1975) found that when subjects judged a woman accused of stealing $2,200, they were more lenient if she was attractive than when she was not. But when she swindled the same money by charming a middle-aged man into making a phony investment, the attractive defendant was sentenced more severely. Apparently, people react negatively toward others who use their beauty to commit a crime.

Physical attractiveness is not the only aspect of appearance that can influence decisions. Many people believe that the human face reveals a person's character. As we saw in Chapter 3, people with babyish faces consisting of large round eyes, high eyebrows, and a small round chin are perceived to be youthful, naive, and honest. In contrast, faces consisting of small eyes, low brows, and a square chin are perceived as strong, mature, and dominant. To examine the possible legal consequences of these perceptions, Diane Berry and Leslie McArthur (1988) wrote two versions of a trial. In one, the defendant was charged with negligence because he forgot to warn a customer about the hazards of a product he was selling. In the other, the defendant was said to have deliberately misled a customer in order to make a sale. As predicted, subjects found the baby-faced defendant negligent, a crime that "matched" his appearance. Yet they judged the mature-faced defendant guilty of the crime involving deception. A similar bias was uncovered in the decisions made by small-claims court judges (Zebrowitz & McDonald, 1991).

Judge's Instructions

One of the most important rituals of any trial is the judge's instruction to the jury. Through these instructions, juries are educated about relevant legal concepts, informed of the verdict options, admonished to disregard extralegal factors, and advised on how to conduct their deliberations. To make verdicts adhere to the law, juries are supposed to comply with these instructions. The task seems simple enough, but there are problems.

To begin with, the jury's intellectual competence has been called into question. For years, the courts have doubted whether jurors understood their instructions. One skeptical judge put it bluntly when he said that "these words may as well be spoken in a foreign language" (Frank, 1949, p. 181). To some extent, he may have been right. When actual instructions are tested with mock jurors, the results reveal high levels of misunderstanding—a serious problem in light of the fact that jurors have many misconceptions about the law (Smith, 1991b). Fortunately, there is hope. When conventional instructions—which are esoteric, poorly written, and filled with legal jargon—are rewritten in plain English, comprehension rates increase markedly (Elwork et al., 1982). Similarly, jurors make better use of probability concepts (for example, "proof beyond a reasonable doubt") when they are presented in clear, quantitative terms (Kage-hiro, 1990).

Comprehension is a necessary first step, but presentation factors are also important. Consider, for example, the following study (Kassin & Wrightsman, 1979). Subjects watched a videotaped auto-theft trial that included, for the defense, an all-important instruction stating that the defendant is presumed innocent and that the prosecutor must prove guilt beyond a reasonable doubt. The statement itself was easy to understand. What mattered, however, was its *timing*. Among subjects who never received the instruction, 63 percent voted guilty. When the instruction followed the evidence, as is the custom in most courts, the conviction rate remained high at 59 percent. When it preceded the evidence, however, the rate dropped sharply, to 37 percent. Why did the postevidence instructions have virtually no impact? The researchers asked half of the subjects for their opinions at various points during the trial and found that these mid-trial opinions were predictive of final verdicts. In other words, it was simply too late for a presumption-of-innocence instruction because many subjects had already made up their minds. Indeed, Vicki Smith (1991a) found that pre-evidence instructions led mock jurors to defer judgment until after the trial and improved their ability to apply the law.

Incomprehension and poor timing are two reasons why a judge's instructions have little impact. But there's a third reason: juries sometimes disagree with the

jury nullification
The jury's power to disregard, or "nullify," the law when it conflicts with their personal conceptions of justice.

law. During the voir dire, Goetz's lawyer asked prospective jurors the following question: "If you find that the prosecution has proved the case beyond a doubt, and if the judge instructs you that you must convict on that basis, would you feel obligated to do so?" (McKillop, 1987). By asking this question, Goetz's lawyer raised the controversial issue of **jury nullification**. You may not realize it, but juries—because they deliberate in private—can choose to disregard, or "nullify," their judge's instructions. The pages of history are filled with poignant examples. Consider the case of someone tried for euthanasia, or "mercy killing." By law, it is murder. To the defendant, it might be a noble act performed on behalf of a loved one. Faced with this kind of conflict, over which public opinion is divided (Sugarman, 1986), juries often evaluate the issue in human terms, disregard their judge's instructions, and vote for acquittal (Horowitz, 1988; Horowitz & Willging, 1991).

THE JURY AS A GROUP

Anyone who has seen *Twelve Angry Men* can appreciate how colorful and passionate a jury's deliberation can be. As we saw in Chapter 9, this film classic opens with a jury eager to convict a young Hispanic man of murder—no ifs, ands, or buts. The group selects a foreman and takes a show-of-hands vote. The result is an 11-to-1 majority, with actor Henry Fonda the lone dissenter. After many tense moments, Fonda manages to convert his peers, and the jury votes unanimously for acquittal.

It is often said that the unique power of the jury is that individuals come together privately as a *group*. Is this assumption justified? *Twelve Angry Men* is fiction, but does it realistically portray what transpires in the jury room? And in what ways does the legal system control the group dynamics?

Leaders, Participants, and Followers

In theory, all jurors are created equal. In practice, however, dominance hierarchies develop. As in other decision-making groups, a handful of individuals control the discussion; others participate at a much lower rate; and still others watch from the sidelines, speaking only to cast their votes (Hastie et al., 1983; Saks, 1977). It's almost as if there's a jury within the jury. But what kinds of people emerge as leaders?

It's natural to assume that the foreperson is the leader. The foreperson, after all, calls for votes, acts as a liaison between the judge and jury, and announces the verdict in court. It seems like a position of importance, yet the selection process is rather casual. Sometimes the judge makes an arbitrary appointment.

At other times, the jury picks a member within the first minute or so. It's interesting that when jurors make the selection, the outcomes follow a predictable pattern (Stasser et al., 1982). People of higher occupational status or with previous experience on a jury are frequently chosen. Sex differences are also common. When Norbert Kerr and others (1982) examined the records of 179 trials held in San Diego, they found that 50 percent of the jurors were female but 90 percent of the forepersons were male. Other patterns, too, are evident. The first person who speaks is often the one chosen as foreperson (Strodtbeck et al., 1957). And when jurors deliberate around a rectangular table, those who sit at the heads of the table are more likely to be chosen than are those seated in the middle (Bray et al., 1978; Strodtbeck & Hook, 1961). To complete the picture, men are more likely than women to speak first and take the prominent seats (Nemeth et al., 1976).

If you find such inequalities bothersome, fear not: forepersons may act as nominal leaders, but they do *not* exert more than their fair share of influence over the group. In fact, although they spend more time than others talking about procedural matters, they spend less time expressing opinions on the verdict (Hastie et al., 1983). It may be most accurate to think of the foreperson not as the jury's leader but as its moderator. If you've seen *Twelve Angry Men*, you will recall that actor Martin Balsam—not Henry Fonda—was the foreperson. He was also among the least influential members of the jury.

The Deliberation Process

If the walls of the jury room could talk, they would say that the decision-making process passes through three stages (Hastie et al., 1983; Stasser et al., 1982). Like other problem-solving groups, juries begin in a relaxed, open-ended *orientation* period during which they set an agenda, raise questions, and explore the facts. Then as soon as differences of opinion are revealed—usually when the first vote is taken—factions develop and the group shifts abruptly into a period of *open conflict*. With the battle lines sharply drawn, discussion takes on a more focused, argumentative tone. Together, jurors scrutinize the evidence, construct stories to account for that evidence, and discuss the judge's instructions (Pennington & Hastie, 1992). If all jurors agree, they return a verdict. If they do not agree, the majority tries to achieve a consensus by converting the holdouts through information and social pressure. At that point, the group enters a period of *reconciliation*, during which it smooths over the conflicts and affirms its satisfaction with the outcome. If the holdouts continue to disagree, however, the jury declares itself hung. This process is diagrammed in Figure 12.8.

As interesting as the process seems, when it comes to decision-making *outcomes,* deliberations are not as important as might be assumed. This surprising result was first discovered by Harry Kalven and Hans Zeisel (1966). By interviewing the members of 225 criminal juries, they were able to reconstruct

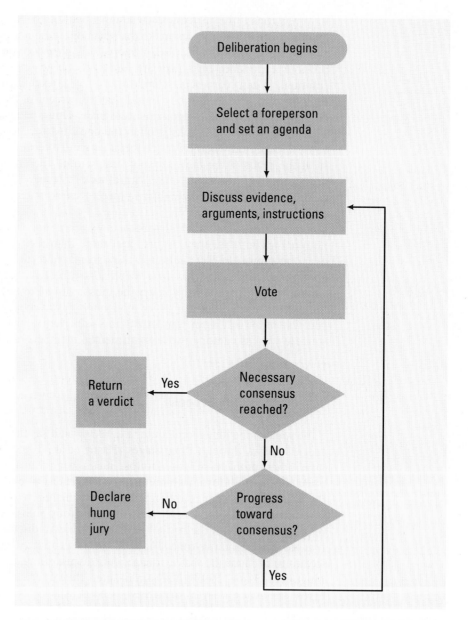

Figure 12.8   Jury Deliberations: The Process.   As indicated by this flow chart of the deliberation process, juries move through various tasks en route to a verdict. They begin by setting an agenda and reviewing the case. If all jurors agree, they return a verdict. If there is disagreement, they continue to discuss the case until they reach a consensus. If the holdouts continue to disagree with the majority, the jury declares itself hung. [Based on Hastie et al., 1983.]

how these juries split on their very first vote. Out of 215 juries that opened with an initial majority, 209 reached a final verdict that was consistent with this vote. This result is also found in mock jury research (Kerr, 1981; Stasser & Davis, 1981; Tanford & Penrod, 1986), as presented in Table 12.3. It led Kalven and Zeisel to conclude that "the deliberation process might well be likened to what the developer does for an exposed film; it brings out the picture, but the outcome is predetermined" (1966, p. 489). Henry Fonda's heroics notwithstanding, one can usually predict the final verdict by knowing what the individual jurors think as they enter the jury room.

leniency bias The tendency for jury deliberation to produce a tilt toward acquittal.

There is one reliable exception to this majority-wins rule. It is that deliberation tends to produce a **leniency bias** favoring the criminal defendant. All other things being equal, individual jurors are more likely to vote guilty on their own than in a group; they are also more prone to convict before deliberations than after (MacCoun & Kerr, 1988). As shown in Table 12.3, juries that are equally divided in their initial vote are likely to return not-guilty verdicts. Apparently, it is easier to raise a reasonable doubt in other people's minds than to remove such a doubt. It is interesting that in their classic study of *The American Jury* (1966), Kalven and Zeisel surveyed 555 judges who reported how they would have voted in some 3,500 jury trials. As it turned out, judges and juries agreed

Table 12.3 The Road to Agreement: From Individual Votes to a Group Verdict. Research has shown that these verdicts (rendered by six-person mock juries) are reached by juries that begin with different combinations of initial votes. You can see that the results support the majority-wins rule. But also notice that there is a leniency bias: when the initial vote is split, juries gravitate toward acquittal. [Data from Kerr, 1981. As cited in Stasser et al., 1982.]

Initial Votes (Guilty–Not Guilty)	Final Jury Verdicts		
	Conviction	Acquittal	Hung
6–0	100%	0%	0%
5–1	78	7	16
4–2	44	26	30
3–3	9	51	40
2–4	4	79	17
1–5	0	93	7
0–6	0	100	0

78 percent of the time. When they disagreed, it was usually because the jury acquitted a defendant thought guilty by the judge. Perhaps these disagreements are due, in part, to the fact that juries function as groups but judges function as individuals.

Knowing that the majority tends to prevail doesn't tell us *how* juries manage to resolve disagreements en route to a verdict. From the conformity studies discussed in Chapter 9, we know that there are two possibilities. Sometimes, people conform because, through a process of *informational influence,* they are genuinely persuaded by what others say. At other times, however, people yield to the pressures of *normative influence* by changing their overt behavior in the majority's direction even though, privately, they disagree. When it comes to jury deliberations, justice demands that a consensus be reached through a vigorous exchange of views and information, not by heavy-handed social pressure. But is it? Research shows that juries achieve unanimity not by one process or the other but by both (Kaplan & Schersching, 1981; Stasser & Davis, 1981; Tanford & Penrod, 1986). When we consider that jurors are urged to vote with an independent conscience and yet are prodded toward compromise and agreement, this result makes sense. The problem is that certain factors can upset the delicate balance between informational and normative influence. Social pressure is increased, for example, in juries that vote by a public roll call or show of hands (Davis et al., 1989) and in deadlocked juries that are called into the courtroom and urged by the judge to resolve their differences (Kassin et al., 1990a). In addition, the U.S. Supreme Court within the past twenty years has altered the decision-making dynamics of the jury. In the following pages, we look at two important changes and what they mean.

Jury Size: How Small Is Too Small?

In Boulder, Colorado, lawyer Melvin Tatsumi had a client who was charged with criminal mischief. Fearing the "mob mentality of 12 people," he requested a one-person jury ("It would be easy," 1985). Although the judge went along with the idea, the district attorney argued that "a jury of one is a contradiction of terms." An appeals court agreed.

How many people does it take to form a jury? In keeping with the British tradition, twelve used to be the magic number. Then in the case of *Williams v. Florida* (1970), the defendant, Williams, was convicted of armed robbery by a six-person jury. He appealed the verdict to the U.S. Supreme Court but lost. Because of this precedent, American courts are today permitted to cut their trial expenses by using six-person juries in cases that do not involve the death penalty. Juries consisting of fewer than six people are not permitted (*Ballew v. Georgia,* 1978).

The Supreme Court approached the question as a social psychologist would. It sought to determine whether the change would affect the decision-making process. Unfortunately, the Court misinterpreted the available research so badly that Michael Saks concluded it "would not win a passing grade in a high school psychology class" (1974, p. 18). Consider, for example, whether a reduction in size affects the minority's ability to resist normative pressures. The Supreme Court didn't think it would. Citing Asch's (1956) conformity studies, the Court concluded that a juror's resistance depends on the *proportional* size of the majority. But is that true? Is the lone dissenter caught in a 5-to-1 bind as insulated as the minority in a 10-to-2 split? To the Court, those 83-to-17 percent divisions are psychologically identical. Yet Asch's (1956) research showed exactly the opposite—that nothing enables dissenters to maintain their independence better than the presence of an ally.

The size of a jury can make a difference in other ways, too. The smaller the jury, the less likely it is to represent minority segments of the population, and the more likely it is to begin deliberating at or near unanimity (Roper, 1980). This reduction in diversity is not trivial. It could be the difference between having Henry Fonda on your jury or not. Indeed, when it comes to decision making, smaller juries spend less time deliberating and recall less of the evidence (Saks, 1977). They are also less likely to declare themselves hung (Kerr & MacCoun, 1985a; Zeisel, 1971). This result is undesirable, since many hung juries remain deadlocked because of legitimate disagreements over close and difficult cases (Kalven & Zeisel, 1966).

Less-Than-Unanimous Verdicts

The jury's size is not all that has changed. In 1972, the Supreme Court considered whether states may accept jury verdicts that are not unanimous. In one case, two defendants had been convicted by non-unanimous juries, one by a vote of 11 to 1, the other by 10 to 2 (*Apodaca v. Oregon*, 1972). In a second case, the verdict was determined by a 9-to-3 margin (*Johnson v. Louisiana*, 1972). In both decisions, the Supreme Court upheld the verdicts.

The Court was divided in its view of these cases. Five justices argued that a non-unanimous decision rule would not adversely affect the jury; four justices believed that it would reduce the intensity of deliberations and undermine the potential for minority influence. Table 12.4 presents these alternative points of view. Which do you find more convincing? Imagine yourself on a jury that needs only a 9-to-3 majority to return a verdict. You begin by polling the group. Lo and behold, you already have the nine votes needed. What next? According to one script, the group continues to argue vigorously and with open minds. According to the alternative scenario, the group begins to deliberate, but the dissenters are quickly cast aside—after all, their votes aren't important. Again, which scenario seems more realistic?

To answer that question, Reid Hastie and his colleagues (1983) recruited more than eight hundred people from the Boston area to take part in sixty-nine mock juries. After watching a re-enactment of a murder trial, the groups were instructed to reach a verdict by a 12-to-0, a 10-to-2, or an 8-to-4 margin. The

Mr. Justice White, for the Majority:

We have no grounds for believing that majority jurors, aware of their responsibility and power over the liberty of the defendant, would simply refuse to listen to arguments presented to them in favor of acquittal, terminate discussion, and render a verdict. On the contrary, it is far more likely that a juror presenting reasoned argument in favor of acquittal could either have his arguments answered or would carry enough other jurors with him to prevent conviction. A majority will cease discussion and outvote a minority only after reasoned discussion has ceased to have persuasive effect or to serve any other purpose—when a minority, that is, continues to insist upon acquittal without having persuasive reasons in supporrt of its position.

Mr. Justice Douglas, for the Minority:

Non-unanimous juries need not debate and deliberate as fully as most unanimous juries. As soon as the requisite majority is attained, further consideration is not required either by Oregon or by Louisiana even though the dissident jurors might, if given the chance, be able to convince the majority . . . The collective effort to piece together the puzzle of historical truth . . . is cut short as soon as the requisite majority is reached in Oregon and Louisiana . . . It is said that there is no evidence that majority jurors will refuse to listen to dissenters whose votes are unneeded for conviction. Yet human experience teaches us that polite and academic conversation is no substitute for the earnest and robust argument necessary to reach unanimity.

Table 12.4 *Johnson v. Louisiana* (1972): Contrasting Views. Notice the contrasting views in the U.S. Supreme Court's decision to permit non-unanimous jury verdicts. Justice Byron White wrote the majority opinion in support of the ruling; Justice William Douglas wrote the dissenting opinion. The decision to permit less-than-unanimous juries was reached by a vote of 5 to 4. [From *Johnson v. Louisiana* (1972).]

differences were striking. Compared to juries needing unanimous decisions, the others spent less time discussing the case and more time voting. After reaching the required number of votes, they often rejected the holdouts, terminated discussion, and returned a verdict. Afterwards, subjects in the non-unanimous juries rated their peers as more closed-minded and themselves as less informed and less confident about their final decision. What's worse, Hastie's team saw in tapes of the deliberations that majority-rule juries adopted "a more forceful, bullying, persuasive style" (1983, p. 112).

Today, a few states permit less-than-unanimous verdicts in criminal trials. A substantial number do so for civil cases. Yet it is clear that this procedure weakens jurors who are in the voting minority, breeds closed-mindedness, inhibits discussion, and leaves many jurors uncertain about their decisions. Henry Fonda, step aside. The jury has reached its verdict.

POSTTRIAL: TO PRISON AND BEYOND

As soon as Goetz's verdict was announced, a boisterous crowd gathered outside the courthouse. Some demonstrators were joyous; others were angry. One man carried a sign that read "Criminals think twice or we will Goetz you"; another held up a placard that read "Racist Rambo's gonna pay." When the jury's foreperson was spotted in a bank that week, the tellers broke into applause. Two weeks later, for reasons unknown, Goetz's lawyer was attacked in the street and beaten. The trial was over, but its impact lingered. For the defendant, there was more to come. Goetz was acquitted on the major charges. But for the possession of an illegal weapon, he awaited sentencing.

The Sentencing Process

Four months after the trial ended, Goetz received his punishment: six months in jail. Public reaction to the judge's sentence was as polarized as public reaction to the jury's verdict. Some argued that it was too lenient, others that it was too severe (Johnson, 1987a).

Sentencing decisions—usually made by judges, not juries—are often controversial. One reason for the controversy is that many Americans misperceive judges as too lenient in their sentencing (Stalans & Diamond, 1990). Another is that people disagree on the goals served by imprisonment. People who think that the purpose is to punish, incapacitate, or deter offenders from committing future crimes prefer longer sentences. Those who say that prison should reform and rehabilitate convicted felons believe shorter terms make more sense (McFatter, 1978).

Judges also disagree about sentencing-related issues. In fact, a common complaint about the legal system is that there is too much *sentencing disparity*—that punishments are inconsistent from one judge to the next. Anthony Partridge and William Eldridge (1974) compiled identical sets of files taken from twenty actual cases, sent them to fifty federal judges, and found major disparities in their sentencing decisions. In one case, for example, judges read about a man who was convicted of extortion and tax evasion. One judge recommended a three-year prison sentence, while another recommended twenty years in prison and a fine of $65,000. It is hard to believe these two judges read the same case. Other research, however, reveals similar differences. In Dade County, Florida, Judge Ellen Morphonios was known as "Maximum Morphonios" when she sentenced an offender to a prison term of 1,698 years and then reassured him that he would probably serve only half of that time! In contrast, New York State judge Bruce Wright is nicknamed "Turn 'Em Loose Bruce" for his reputation for leniency (Wrightsman, 1991).

What seems to be the problem? Ebbe Ebbesen and Vladimir Konecni (1981) analyzed the sentencing records of more than 1,200 felons convicted in San

Diego, California. As in previous research, they found a good deal of inconsistency, but not because judges used idiosyncratic strategies or based their decisions on extralegal factors. Rather, these judges tended to use the same strategy. They made decisions quickly and closely followed the presentencing advice provided by their probation officers. Sentencing disparity is a problem, in part, because judges receive conflicting recommendations from those who advise them. And like the rest of us, those who advise them differ in their beliefs about the goals of imprisonment (Carroll et al., 1987).

The Prison Experience

It is no secret that today's prisons are overcrowded and that prison life can be cruel, violent, and degrading. The setting is oppressive and highly regimented; many prison guards are abusive; and the inmates often fall into a state of despair (Paulus, 1988; Sutherland & Cressey, 1974). Thus, it is natural for social psychologists to wonder: Is there something in the situation that leads guards and prisoners to behave as they do? Would the rest of us react in the same way?

For ethical reasons, one obviously cannot place subjects inside a real prison. So a team of researchers from Stanford University did the next best thing. They constructed their own prison in the basement of their psychology department building (Haney et al., 1973; Zimbardo et al., 1973). Complete with iron-barred cells, a solitary-confinement closet, and a recreation area for guards, the facility housed twenty-one subjects—all healthy and stable men between the ages of seventeen and thirty who had answered a newspaper ad promising fifteen dollars a day for a two-week study of prison life. By the flip of a coin, half of the subjects were designated to be guards; the other half became prisoners. Neither group received specific instructions on how to fulfill its role.

On the first day, each of the subject prisoners was unexpectedly "arrested" at his home, booked, fingerprinted, and driven to the simulated prison by officers of the local police department. The prisoners were then stripped, searched, and dressed in loose-fitting smocks with an identification number, a nylon stocking to cover their hair, rubber sandals, and a chain bolted to the ankle. The guards were supplied with khaki uniforms, nightsticks, handcuffs, keys, reflector sunglasses, and whistles. The rules specified that prisoners were to be called by number, routinely lined up to be counted, fed three bland meals, and permitted three supervised toilet visits per day. The stage was set. Subjects were on their own. It remained to be seen just how seriously they would take their roles and react to one another in this novel setting.

The events of the next few days were startling. Filled with a sense of power and authority, three or four of the guards became progressively more abusive. They harassed the inmates, forced them into crowded cells, woke them up during the night, and subjected them to hard labor and solitary confinement. These guards were particularly cruel when they thought they were alone with

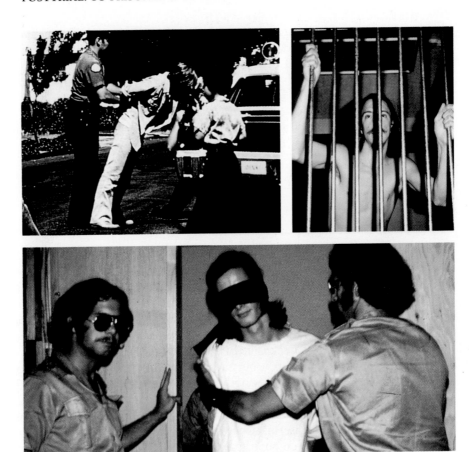

In this simulation study of prison behavior, subjects were arbitrarily assigned to be prisoners or guards. Local police officers arrested the prisoners, who were brought to a jail constructed at Stanford University. After several days, the guards took on cruel, authoritarian roles that demoralized the prisoners to such an extent that the experiment was terminated.

a prisoner. The prisoners themselves were rebellious at first, but their efforts were met with retaliation. Soon they were all passive, submissive, and demoralized. After thirty-six hours, the experimenters had to release their first prisoner, who was suffering from an acute depression. On succeeding days, other prisoners had to be released. By the sixth day, the remaining prisoners were so shaken by the experience, that—to the disappointment of some of the guards—the study was terminated. It is reassuring, if not remarkable, that after a series of debriefing sessions, subjects seemed to show no signs of lasting distress.

Although this study has been criticized for methodological and ethical reasons (Banuazizi & Movahedi, 1975; Savin, 1973b), its results are impressive. Within a brief period of time, under relatively mild conditions, and with a group of men not prone to violence, the Stanford study recreated the behaviors actually found behind prison walls. Apparently, even "normal" people can become dehumanized by their institutional roles. At this point, however, research with real inmates in real prisons is needed to examine the effects of overcrowding and other aspects of prison life (Ruback & Innes, 1988).

JUSTICE: A MATTER OF PROCEDURE?

People tend to measure the success of a legal system by its ability to achieve fair and accurate results. But is that all there is to justice? Let's step back for a moment from the problems with evidence, juries, and other specifics and ask if it is possible to define justice in a way that is unrelated to outcomes.

In a book called *Procedural Justice* (1975), John Thibaut and Laurens Walker proposed that our satisfaction with how disputes are resolved—legal or other-wise—depends not only on outcomes but on the procedures used to achieve those outcomes. Two aspects of procedure are important: *decision control*—whether a procedure affords the involved parties the power to accept, reject, or otherwise influence the final decision; and *process control*—whether it offers parties an opportunity to present their case to a third-party decision maker. In the courtroom, of course, the disputants are limited in their decision control. Thus, their satisfaction must depend on whether they feel that they had a chance to express their views.

There are two ways to look at the effects of process control on perceptions of justice. Originally, it was thought that people want an opportunity to express their opinions only because having a "voice" in the process improves their chances of achieving a favorable ruling. In this view, process control is satisfying because it increases decision control (Thibaut & Walker, 1978). Recent re-search, however, suggests that people value the chance to present their side of a story even when doing so does not influence the ultimate outcome. In other words, process control is more than just an instrumental means to an end. By making people feel that their voice is worth hearing, process control can be an end in itself (Lind et al., 1990; Lind & Tyler, 1988).

This aspect of the legal system is very important. It means, for example, that whether people agree or disagree with how the Goetz case turned out, they are likely to find solace in the fact that Goetz and his accusers all had their "day in court." Yet certain members of the legal community are openly critical of that so-called day in court. As law professor Alan Dershowitz put it, "Nobody really wants justice. Winning is the only thing to most participants in the criminal justice system, just as it is to professional athletes" (1982, p. xvi). Dershowitz's skepticism is centered on something that many of us take for granted: the **adversarial model** of justice. In the adversarial system—as practiced in North America, Great Britain, and a few other countries—the prosecution and defense oppose each other, each presenting one side of the story in an effort to win a favorable verdict. In contrast, most other countries use an **inquisitorial model**, in which a neutral investigator gathers the evidence from both sides and then presents the findings in court. With two such different methods of doing justice, social psychologists could not resist the temptation to make comparisons. Which system, they ask, do people prefer?

To make the comparison, Laurens Walker and his colleagues (1974) constructed a business simulation in which two companies competed for a cash prize. Assigned to the role of president of a company, subjects learned that someone on their staff was accused of spying on the competition. To resolve the dispute, a "trial" was held. In some cases, the trial followed an adversarial procedure in which the two sides were presented by law students who were chosen by subjects and whose payment was contingent on winning. Other cases followed an inquisitorial model in which a single law student—appointed by the experimenter and paid regardless of the outcome—presented both sides. Regardless of whether they had won or lost the verdict, subjects who took part in the adversarial trial were more satisfied than those who were involved in the inquisitorial trial. Even a group of impartial observers preferred the adversarial proceedings.

Other researchers have reported similar results, not only with American and British subjects who are used to the adversary system, but with French and West Germans as well (Lind et al., 1978). It seems that any method that offers participants a voice in the proceedings—including methods that are nonadversarial—is perceived as fair and just (Folger & Greenberg, 1985; Sheppard, 1985). Even among Chinese subjects—whose culture emphasizes interpersonal harmony and who prefer to resolve disputes in ways that minimize conflict—process control is desirable (Leung, 1987).

adversarial model
A dispute-resolution system in which the prosecution and defense oppose each other, as each presents one side of the story.

inquisitorial model
A dispute-resolution system in which a neutral investigator gathers evidence from both sides and then presents the findings in court.

CLOSING STATEMENT

This chapter focuses on the trial, events that precede it, and events that follow from it. Yet we've only scratched the surface. In recent years, more and more judges, lawyers, and policy makers have come to recognize that social psychology can make important contributions to the legal system. Thus, with increasing frequency, social psychologists are called on for expert advice in and out of court and are cited in judicial opinions. Indeed, as the case of Bernhard Goetz suggests and as research confirms, evidence—the human beings who provide it and those who evaluate it—is an imperfect human enterprise. Whether we examine police officers, eyewitnesses, crime victims, judges, juries, or prison guards, our conclusion is the same. Through an understanding of social psychology, we can identify some of the problems—and perhaps even the solutions.

REVIEW

Embedded in a large criminal justice system, relatively few cases come to trial. Yet the trial is the heart and soul of the system.

SELECTION OF JURORS

Once called for service, prospective jurors are questioned by the judge or lawyers. Those who are clearly biased are excluded. A limited number of others may also be rejected by lawyers.

Trial Lawyers as Intuitive Psychologists

Pressured to make juror selections quickly, lawyers rely on various implicit personality theories and cultural stereotypes.

Pretrial Attitudes and Bias

General demographic and personality factors do not reliably predict how jurors will vote. What matters are trial-relevant attitudes. Thus, lawyers sometimes hire psychologists to conduct surveys that identify correlations between demographics and relevant attitudes. They then use demographic information on prospective jurors to predict their verdicts. Research shows that beliefs about rape predict juror verdicts in rape cases and that jurors who favor the death penalty are more likely to find capital defendants guilty than are jurors who oppose the death penalty. Both intuitive and scientific jury selection methods raise ethical issues concerning their effects on justice.

COURTROOM DRAMA

Once the jury is selected, evidence previously gathered is presented in court.

The Defendant

Suspects often make self-incriminating statements. The police elicit confessions by using various ploys. Under such pressure, people sometimes confess to crimes they didn't commit. In court, judges and juries are supposed to reject coerced confessions, but various factors affect whether pressure tactics are perceived as coercive. By recording physiological arousal, the polygraph can be used as a lie-detector test.

Polygraphers report high rates of accuracy; but truthful persons are too often judged guilty, and the test can be faked.

The Victim
Although people are sympathetic to crime victims, victims are often blamed for their misfortune. One possible reason is the hindsight bias. Another is that people need to believe in a just world to cope with the personally threatening implications of crime.

The Eyewitness
Eyewitness memory is a three-stage process: acquisition, storage, and retrieval. During acquisition, various factors are important. Stress increases performance up to a point, but extremely high levels of arousal impair performance; alcohol impairs memory; the presence of a weapon impairs a witness's ability to identify the perpetrator; and witnesses have trouble recognizing members of a race other than their own. During storage, misleading postevent information influences eyewitness testimony. Although it is unclear if memory is truly altered, it is clear that eyewitness *reports* are biased by postevent information. Young children are even more suggestible in this regard. During retrieval, line-up identifications have great impact. They can be biased against a suspect, however, when the suspect is distinctive compared to the others, when instructions lead witnesses to believe the culprit is definitely in the line-up, and when the suspect was seen in pre-line-up photographs.

In court, eyewitness testimony is difficult to discredit. Jurors overestimate credibility, cannot distinguish between accurate and inaccurate witnesses, and are not aware of certain factors that influence eyewitness performance. People are too persuaded by a witness's level of confidence—a factor that does not reliably predict the accuracy of identification.

The Psychological Expert
Psychologists are sometimes called to testify as experts on eyewitness evidence. Research indicates that expert testimony leads people to scrutinize eyewitnesses more carefully. It is not yet clear whether it enables jurors to distinguish between accurate and inaccurate eyewitnesses.

Pretrial Publicity
Public opinion surveys show that the more knowledge people have about a case, the more likely they are to presume the defendant guilty. Research shows that this presumption can bias jury verdicts.

Inadmissible Testimony
Once inadmissible testimony leaks out in court, the jury is contaminated. A judge's cautionary instruction may make the situation worse. Such an instruction draws attention to the forbidden testimony, arouses psychological reactance, and leads jurors to believe the information is relevant.

Physical Appearance of the Litigants
Research suggests that jurors and judges favor litigants who are physically attractive, but people react negatively to those who use their attractiveness to commit a crime.

People are also more likely to view baby-faced defendants as guilty of negligence and mature-faced defendants as guilty of intentional deception.

Judge's Instructions

Despite their importance, instructions to the jury often have little impact. One problem is that jurors often do not comprehend the instructions. Another is that instructions are usually delivered after the presentation of evidence—after many jurors have formed tentative opinions. An additional issue is that jurors may not follow instructions that conflict with their personal conceptions of justice.

THE JURY AS A GROUP

Leaders, Participants, and Followers

Dominance hierarchies develop in the jury room. Forepersons tend to be males and to be seated at the head of the table. They tend to play the role of moderator rather than group leader.

The Deliberation Process

Juries begin deliberations in an inquisitive orientation period. Upon voting, factions form and the group shifts into a period of open conflict filled with informational and normative pressures. When it comes to outcomes, the initial majority typically wins, although deliberation produces a bias toward leniency.

Jury Size: How Small Is Too Small?

The U.S. Supreme Court ruled that the use of six-person juries is acceptable, although research shows that these smaller groups do not deliberate as long as twelve-person juries and are less likely to declare themselves hung.

Less-Than-Unanimous Verdicts

In some states, juries are permitted to reach verdicts by a less-than-unanimous majority. Research shows, however, that once the required majority is reached, these juries reject the holdouts, terminate discussion, and return a verdict. Such deliberations leave jurors less informed and less confident in their decisions.

POSTTRIAL: TO PRISON AND BEYOND

The Sentencing Process

Sentencing, usually decided by the judge, is controversial. Many people think judges are too lenient, and punishments for the same offense are often inconsistent from one case to another. Part of the problem is that people have different opinions on the goals of sentencing.

The Prison Experience

To determine if the prison experience is defined by situational roles, Stanford researchers built a simulated prison and recruited healthy male adults to act as guards and prisoners. Some of the guards were abusive, and prisoners became passive. Within days, prisoners were so distressed that the study had to be terminated.

JUSTICE: A MATTER OF PROCEDURE?

Satisfaction with the resolution of disputes depends not only on whether one wins or loses but on the procedures used to achieve the outcome. People value the chance to present their case. In legal settings, people of all cultures prefer models of justice that offer participants a voice in the proceedings.

Business

13

Preview

This chapter examines the *social side of business:* the role of social factors in two aspects of our lives. First, we step into *the workplace,* and look at social influences on hiring and evaluation decisions, leadership, and worker motivation. Second, we enter *the marketplace,* and examine consumer behavior and economic risk-taking activities such as gambling and investing in the stock market.

W hen Lee Iacocca took over Chrysler Corporation in 1979, the company was in deep financial trouble. The American automobile industry was suffering through a worldwide oil crisis and experiencing intense competition from Japanese imports. Chrysler was out of step. Thousands of unsold gas-guzzling cars were gathering dust in a parking lot, and the corporation was losing close to a billion dollars a year.

Iacocca went on to become something of a folk hero as he steered the "New Chrysler Corporation" into profitability after five years. There were two secrets to Iacocca's success. First, he was a flamboyant leader *in the workplace*. To make Chrysler competitive, Iacocca convinced his workers to take unprecedented pay cuts and motivated them to take pride in their work. Second, he renewed Chrysler's tarnished public image by rallying support *in the marketplace*. Desperate for money, he persuaded the federal government to help. Then he introduced a new line of cars and projected an image of American know-how and dependability as he walked through assembly lines in a series of TV commercials. All was well until the 1990s, when Chrysler and other automakers slumped, and Iacocca resorted to Japan-bashing in a desperate attempt to fire up the sale of American cars; then in 1992, he announced that he would retire.

In many ways, Iacocca's ups and downs are a lesson in the social psychology of business. In this chapter, two applications in particular are considered. First, we examine **industrial/organizational (I/O) psychology**, the study of human behavior in businesses and other organizations. This field is broad and includes in its ranks social and nonsocial psychologists who teach in business schools or universities, conduct research, and work in private industry. Whatever the setting, I/O psychology raises practical questions about job interviews, the evaluation and promotion process, leadership, motivation, and other aspects of life in the workplace. Second, we see that many social psychologists specialize in **consumer psychology**, the study of decision making and behavior in the marketplace. Employed by marketing firms and advertising agencies, consumer psychologists study some of the noneconomic factors that influence how people decide to purchase different products and services and take risks with their money through gambling and investment in the stock market.

industrial/organizational (I/O) psychology The study of human behavior in business and other organizational settings.

consumer psychology The study of decision making and behavior in the marketplace.

THE SOCIAL SIDE OF BUSINESS

True or false: Americans have more leisure time today than they had in the past. Assuming that the quality of life improves from one generation to the next, and that modern technology saves time, most people agree with this statement. In fact, nothing could be farther from the truth. In 1973, the average American worked outside the home for 40.6 hours a week. By 1985, that figure was up to 48.8 hours, an astonishing increase of 20 percent (Schor, 1991). Priorities have also changed. Americans used to be content with a job that offered good wages, reasonable hours, decent working conditions, and security. Today, they want jobs that are also meaningful, jobs that provide both a sense of accomplishment and an opportunity for advancement (see Figure 13.1). In light of the devotion people have for their work, and its link to the self-concept (as children we were asked, "What do you want to be when you grow up?"; as adults we hear, "What do you do for a living?"), it is important to identify the social factors that influence this significant human experience.

The impact of social psychological factors in the workplace was first recognized in 1924—thanks to a study of industrial lighting. That year, a team of psychologists sought to examine the effects of lighting on workers at the Hawthorne plant of Western Electric near Chicago (Roethlisburger & Dickson, 1939). Proceeding logically, the researchers turned the lights up in a test room, kept the original lighting in a control room, and compared the effects. Much to their surprise, productivity rates increased in both rooms and then increased as well when the illumination was diminished to a level so dim that workers could barely see what they were doing! Over the next five years, no matter what the researchers did—whether they varied the number of coffee breaks, the length of the workweek, location, incentive system, or method of payment—productivity always increased.

It seemed that the project had failed, as no single change in working conditions had a unique effect on productivity. Think for a moment about the results, however, and you will see why the Hawthorne studies are so important. With striking consistency, it was the presence of researchers in the factory and

Figure 13.1 What Americans Want Most from Their Work. American adults who were asked to choose the most important aspect of a job selected these features most often.ʼ [From Harris, 1987.]

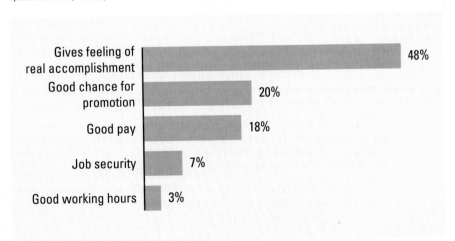

Hawthorne effect
The finding that workers who were observed increased their productivity regardless of what actual changes were made in the work setting.

the special attention they gave to employees, not the specific changes in conditions, that made a difference. As soon as workers realized they were singled out for attention, they became more motivated and worked harder. Many researchers criticized the methods used in this study and the interpretation of the results (Adair, 1984; Parsons, 1974). Still, the phenomenon that has come to be known as the **Hawthorne effect** laid a foundation for I/O psychology and the study of social influences in the workplace.

THE WORKPLACE

The two of us who wrote this book work on college campuses, surrounded by students, professors, and administrators. We spend our time in classrooms, offices, laboratories, and libraries. For women and men in other occupations—store clerks, cab drivers, doctors, construction workers, secretaries, farmers, teachers, accountants, carpenters, musicians, firefighters, and airline pilots—the workplace is different. Yet despite the diversity, certain common concerns arise: How are job applicants selected, and how is their performance evaluated? Are workers judged by objective credentials, or do first impressions and stereotypes play a role? What makes for an effective leader who can exert influence over others and mobilize their support? What motivates a person to work hard and feel satisfied with a job? In this section, we enter the workplace and address these important questions.

Personnel Selection

For all kinds of organizations, the secret to success begins with the recruitment and development of a competent staff. As such, personnel selection is the first important step.

Traditional Employment Interviews   Anyone who has ever applied for a desirable job knows that you have to climb hurdles and jump through hoops to get hired. The routine is familiar: you submit a résumé, fill out an application, and perhaps bring in samples of your work or take a standardized test of your ability or personality. You may even be put on the "hot seat" in a live face-to-face interview (Schmidt et al., 1992).

In a traditional employment interview, a representative of the organization and an applicant meet to discuss the job. The interview thus provides a two-way opportunity for the applicant and employer to evaluate each other. What a social perception dilemma these opportunities present! As an applicant, you have only a few minutes or, if you're lucky, a few hours to make a favorable impression. As an interviewer, you have the same brief moment to penetrate the

The employment interview plays an important role in the hiring process despite the difficulties it presents. The applicant must somehow convey a favorable impression, while the interviewer must try to see beyond the applicant's self-presentation.

applicant's self-presentation and learn enough about the person to make a sound hiring decision.

Very few employers would consider hiring a complete stranger for a responsible position without an interview. Would you? Like most of us, you probably trust your ability to size people up. As quoted in the *Wall Street Journal,* one head-hunter (a consultant who helps companies find qualified executives) stated, "A good interviewer can probe the candidate's basic mental and emotional patterns and determine whether he will fit not only the job but also the company" (Bauman, 1982). Do interviews promote sound hiring, or do they promote decisions that are biased by personal characteristics? Title VII of the Civil Rights Act forbids all employers from discriminating on the basis of sex, race, age, religion, or national origin. But can anyone guarantee that those factors do not influence the evaluation of job applicants? And does the interview process itself intensify or diminish those possible biases?

Research suggests that interviewing has mixed effects. On the positive side, live interviews may diminish the tendency to make stereotyped judgments.

Studies on sex differences show that when prospective employers rate applicants from résumés and other written material, they tend to evaluate men more favorably than they evaluate women (Powell, 1987)—at least for occupations that are not stereotypically feminine (Glick et al., 1988). As employers receive more information on an applicant's objective credentials, however, this bias is reduced (Tosi & Einbender, 1985). What happens in a live interview? Does gender become more salient, or do job-relevant attributes take over? To answer this question, Laura Graves and Gary Powell (1988) studied 483 interviewers who visited college campuses to recruit prospective graduates for entry-level corporate jobs. While on campus, each interviewer rated one student and answered this question: "What are the chances that this applicant will receive a job offer from your company?" Of the applicants sampled, 53 percent were male, 47 percent female. More to the point, there was no evidence at all of sex discrimination, as men and women were equally likely to get hired—a result found in other research as well (Raza & Carpenter, 1987). Apparently, face-to-face interaction brings to life the applicant's speaking ability, interest in the company, and other relevant attributes that do not show up on paper.

The bad news is that although interviews sometimes result in the right selection of employees, often they lack a high level of predictive validity (Harris, 1989). What's worse, an employer's preconceptions about an applicant can distort the whole interview process. Thus when subjects in one study were led to believe that an applicant was not suitable for a particular job, they prepared interview questions that sought negative information (Binning et al., 1988). And when white subjects questioned an applicant who was black rather than white, they sat farther away and held shorter interviews—a distant interpersonal style that causes interviewees to behave in a more nervous, awkward manner (Word et al., 1974).

In a field study that illustrates the problem, Amanda Phillips and Robert Dipboye (1989) surveyed 34 managers from different branch offices of a large corporation and 164 job applicants whom they had interviewed. They found that managers' pre-interview expectations, which were based on written application materials, influenced the kinds of interviews they conducted as well as the outcomes: the higher their expectations, the more time they spent "recruiting" rather than evaluating and the more likely they were to make a favorable hiring decision. It seems that job interviews can become part of a vicious cycle, or self-fulfilling prophecy. Without realizing it, employers use the opportunity to create realities that bolster their prior beliefs (see Figure 13.2).

"Scientific" Alternatives to the Traditional Interview Live interviews bring to life both job-relevant and -irrelevant personal characteristics. With the process being so variable, should interviews be eliminated? Should they be "computerized," leaving applicants to interact with companies through a programmed sequence of questions and answers administered on a microcomputer (Martin & Nagao, 1989)? Chances are, not too many people would feel comfortable making important decisions in such an impersonal, futuristic manner.

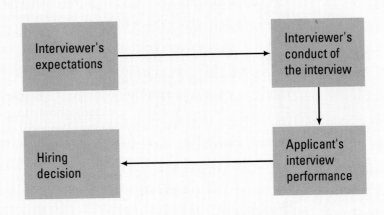

Figure 13.2   Job Interviews: A Self-Fulfilling Prophecy?   One study of interviewers and job applicants appears to indicate that interviewers' expectations influence the kinds of interviews conducted and applicants' performance. The higher the expectations, the more the interviewer tries to impress rather than evaluate the applicant and make a favorable hiring decision. Without realizing they are doing so, employers may use job interviews to create a reality that supports their prior beliefs. [Phillips & Dipboye, 1989.]

Is it possible, then, to preserve the human touch of an interview, without bias and error?

To improve the prediction of job performance, organizations have sought "scientific" methods of evaluation. It's estimated, for example, that three thousand firms in the United States and many more in Europe use *graphology*, or handwriting analysis, to predict job-relevant traits such as honesty, sales ability, and leadership potential (Rafaeli & Klimoski, 1983). Controlled research, however, does not support the claim that handwriting can be used in this way. In one study, for example, professional graphologists tried to predict various aspects of job performance by analyzing the handwriting contained in the autobiographical sketches of bank employees. From the information in those same materials, the researchers also made predictions. A comparison of predicted and actual employee performance revealed that the graphologists were no more effective than the researchers. In fact, they were no more accurate than they would have been by flipping a coin (Ben-Shakhar et al., 1986).

Many organizations use the *polygraph,* or lie-detector test, as a screening device. As described in Chapter 12, the polygraph is an instrument that records physiological arousal in different parts of the body. Based on an assumption that lying creates stress, a polygraph examiner conducts an interview and compares the subject's level of arousal in response to different kinds of questions. Those who use lie-detector tests argue that the polygraph sharpens their ability to hire employees who are capable and honest. But opponents argue that the test invades an individual's privacy, that it is often misused, and that its results are not sufficiently accurate. Research shows that there are considerable problems with the use of the polygraph (Saxe et al., 1985). That is why, in 1988, the U.S. government passed a bill limiting the use of lie-detector tests to jobs that involve security and public safety. It is also the reason many companies now require applicants to take "integrity tests," questionnaires designed to assess a person's character by asking questions about drug use, drinking, shoplifting, petty theft, and other transgressions. Research suggests that these tests are promising (Goldberg et al., 1991; Sackett et al., 1989).

structured interviews Interviews in which each job applicant is asked a standard set of questions and evaluated on the same criteria.

One legitimate way to improve human judgment without the aid of physiological recordings or lie tests is to conduct **structured interviews**. A structured interview is like a standardized test in that the same information is obtained in the same situation from all applicants, who are then compared on a common, relevant set of dimensions (Campion et al., 1988). By asking a standard set of questions or using a standard set of tasks, employers can keep themselves from unwittingly conducting interviews that are slanted to merely confirm their preconceptions. So far, research has shown that structured interviews are successful, better than conventional interviews, in the selection of insurance agents, sales clerks, and other workers (Wiesner & Cronshaw, 1988).

A second improvement is the use of *assessment centers* in which a group of applicants take part in a group of activities—written tests, role-playing exercises, and so on—that are monitored by a group of evaluators. Instead of using one method (an interview) and one evaluator (an interviewer), multiple methods and multiple evaluators are used. Assessment centers are thus more effective than traditional interviews at identifying applicants who will succeed in a particular position (Gaugler et al., 1987; Thornton & Byham, 1982). Since they are expensive to operate, however, they tend to be used only to select or promote candidates for upper-echelon positions.

Performance Appraisal

performance appraisal The process of evaluating an employee's work within the organization.

Even after a person is hired for a job, the evaluation process continues. Nobody enjoys being scrutinized by a boss, or by anyone else for that matter. Still, **performance appraisal**—the process of evaluating an employee's work and communicating the results to that person—is an inevitable fact of life in the workplace. Performance appraisals provide a basis for placement decisions, transfers, promotions, changes in salary, bonuses, and layoffs. They also give feedback to employees about their status within the organization. It's no wonder that I/O psychologists have studied this process in great detail.

It would be easy if a worker's performance could be measured according to *objective,* quantifiable criteria—if typists could be evaluated by the number of lines they type, automobile dealers by the number of cars they sell, and doctors by the number of patients they treat. Quantitative measures like these often are not available, however, nor do they take into account the quality of work. By

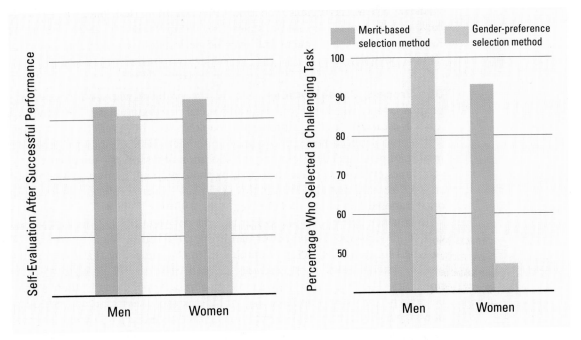

Figure 13.3   Gender Differences in Self-Evaluation: Unintended Effects of Affirmative Action?   College students were assigned to act as task leaders and were led to believe that they were selected on the basis of merit or gender. The selection method had no effect on the self-evaluations of male leaders. As you can see, however, women who thought they were selected because of gender later devalued their own job performance (left) and sought simple rather than demanding work assignments (right). [Data from Heilman et al., 1987; Heilman et al., 1991.]

One solution concerns the timing of evaluations in relation to the observation of performance. Evaluations are less prone to error when they are made right after performance than when there is a delay of days, weeks, or months. Once memory for the details begins to fade, evaluators tend to fall back on stereotypes and other biases (Heneman & Wexley, 1983; Murphy & Balzer, 1986). A second solution is to increase the number of raters used. As in assessment centers, a multiple-rater system—in which a final evaluation represents the average of ratings made by independent sources—is better than a single rater (Sackett & Wilson, 1982). Whatever bias a single individual brings to bear on his or her performance ratings can be offset, to some extent, by the ratings of others. Third, it is possible to teach people the skills necessary for accurate appraisals. Various training programs have been developed. Overall, research suggests that accuracy can be increased by alerting evaluators to the biases of social perception, focusing their attention on job-relevant behaviors, sharpening their memory skills, informing them of performance norms to use as a frame of reference within the organization, and providing them with practice and feed-back in the use of the rating scales (Bernardin & Beatty, 1984; Hedge & Kavanagh, 1988). No system will ever be perfect, but considerable improve-ment is possible.

Due Process Considerations   Part of the problem with performance ap-praisals is that evaluators exhibit various social perception biases, resulting in a loss of *accuracy*. In this all-too-human enterprise, however, there's another serious problem: *fairness*. Performance appraisals—because they are linked to important personnel decisions and the allocation of resources—are often biased, sometimes even deliberately distorted, by those who are motivated by political and self-serving agendas within the workplace. Clearly, office politics is an organizational fact of life (Longnecker et al., 1987).

To enhance fairness, Robert Folger and his colleagues (1992) have proposed a "due process model" of performance appraisal. In general, this model is designed to guard the rights of employees in the same way that the criminal justice system seeks to protect the accused. The model consists of three principles. The first is that there should be *adequate notice*; that is, there should be clear performance standards that employees can understand and ask ques-tions about. The second is that employees should receive a *fair hearing*, in which they are evaluated by supervisors who know their work, and in which they receive timely feedback as well as an opportunity to present their own case. The third principle is that appraisals should be based only on *evidence* of job performance, not on prejudice, corruption, or other external considerations. As indicated by research on reactions to pay raise decisions, procedural fairness can be just as important to workers as a favorable outcome (Folger & Konov-sky, 1989).

Leadership

Regardless of where you're employed, the work experience depends in large part on the quality of leadership within the organization. What personal and situational factors make for effective leaders? There is no single formula. Some leaders succeed by winning supporters, others by mending fences, uniting rivals, negotiating deals, building coalitions, solving problems, or stirring emotions. Either way, there is one common denominator: good leadership requires social influence (Bass, 1990; Hollander & Offermann, 1990; Shaw, 1981).

Trait Approach   One approach is to identify the traits that characterize "natural-born" leaders. According to the "great person theory," exceptional in-dividuals rise up to determine the course of human events. This approach has had some support over the years, as traits such as intelligence, ambition, a need for power, self-confidence, and an ability to adapt to change are characteristic of people who go on to become leaders (Kenny & Zaccaro, 1983; Sorrentino & Field, 1986; Winter, 1987). Even physical height may play a role—a possibility suggested by a study showing that male and female managers in a corporation were over an inch taller on average than nonmanagement employees (Egolf & Corder, 1991). In this regard, it's interesting that between the years 1900 and 1988, the tallest candidate for U.S. president won an astonishing 20 out of 22 elections (1972 and 1976 being the only exceptions).

Think about the great leaders of the twentieth century, those who could transform the status quo by making supporters believe that anything is possible. Martin Luther King, Jr., was that kind of leader. For better or worse, so were Vladimir Lenin, Adolf Hitler, Franklin D. Roosevelt, Mahatma Gandhi, John F. Kennedy, Fidel Castro, Margaret Thatcher, Mikhail Gorbachev, and Nelson Mandela. In their best seller *In Search of Excellence,* Thomas Peters and Robert Waterman (1982) studied sixty-two of America's best businesses and found that their success was due largely to the ability of the leaders to elicit extraordinary efforts from ordinary human beings.

transformational leaders Leaders who inspire followers to transcend their own needs in the interest of a common cause.

What's so special about these individuals? Based on the work of political scientist James MacGregor Burns (1978), Bernard Bass (1985) calls these great persons **transformational leaders**. Transformational leaders motivate their followers to transcend their personal needs in the interest of a common cause. Through a blend of consciousness raising and raw emotional inspiration, transformational leaders articulate a vision for the future and mobilize others to

Martin Luther King, Jr., was a transformational leader who inspired massive changes by making his supporters believe that anything was possible.

join in that vision. Bass and his colleagues asked people who work for business managers, executives, army officers, school principals, government administrators, fire chiefs, and store owners to describe the most outstanding leaders they know (Bass & Avolio, 1990; Hater & Bass, 1988). As shown in Table 13.1, the descriptions revealed four attributes: charisma, inspiration, intellectual stimulation, and individualized consideration of others.

Interactional Models   An alternative is to view leadership as an interaction between personal and situational factors. According to this approach, great leaders are, to some extent, a product of their time, place, and circumstance, as different situations call for different styles of leadership. Bass (1985) suggested that transformational leaders are most likely to emerge in times of growth, change, and crisis. It could be argued, for example, that Chrysler needed a flamboyant star like Iacocca when the corporation hit rock bottom but needed a different kind of leader during calmer periods. Indeed, Iacocca, once a knight in shining armor, lost some of his luster a few years ago when it was found that Chrysler had secretly altered odometers to sell used cars as new. Then he came under fire for accepting a salary of $4 million and whining about Japanese automakers while his company lost money and laid off workers. Iacocca himself admitted that his attention wandered after the initial crisis had passed (Gwynne, 1990).

Table 13.1   Characteristics of Transformational Leaders.   When people are asked to describe the best leaders they know, four characteristics are most often cited: charisma, an ability to inspire others, intellectual stimulation, and individualized consideration. These attributes are evident in the following descriptions. [Bass & Avolio, 1990.]

Characteristic	Description
Charisma	Has a vision; gains respect, trust, and confidence; promotes a strong identification of followers. ("Has a sense of mission which he or she communicates to me")
Inspiration	Gives pep talks, increases optimism and enthusiasm, and arouses emotion in communications. ("Uses symbols and images to focus our efforts")
Intellectual Stimulation	Actively encourages a re-examination of existing values and assumptions; fosters creativity and the use of intelligence. ("Enables me to think about old problems in new ways")
Individualized Consideration	Gives personal attention to all members, acts as adviser, and gives feedback in ways that are easy to accept, understand, and use for personal development. ("Coaches me if I need it")

contingency model of leadership The theory that leadership effectiveness is determined both by the personal characteristics of leaders and by the control afforded by the situation.

Illustrative of the interactional approach is a **contingency model of leadership,** developed by Fred Fiedler (1967), that takes both traits and situations into account. According to Fiedler, the key difference among leaders is whether they are more *task oriented* (single-mindedly focused on the job) or *relations oriented* (concerned about the feelings of employees). If you watch the TV show "L.A. Law," you may recognize these contrasting styles in the two senior partners: Douglas Brackman is a mercenary, no-nonsense advocate of the bottom line; and Leland MacKenzie is a gentle, grandfatherly figure, attentive to the personal needs of his staff. According to Fiedler, the amount of control a leader has determines which type of leadership is more effective. Leaders enjoy *high situational control* when they have good relations with their staff, a position of power, and a clearly structured task. Leaders enjoy *low situational control* when they have poor relations with their staff, limited power, and a task that is not clearly defined.

Putting the personal and situational components together, research in different work groups suggests that task-oriented leaders are the most effective in clear-cut situations that are either low *or* high in control and that relations-oriented leaders perform better in situations that afford a moderate degree of control. In low-control situations, groups need guidance, which task-oriented leaders provide by staying focused on the job. In high-control situations, when conditions are already favorable, these same leaders maintain a relaxed, low profile. Relations-oriented leaders are different. They offer too little guidance in low-control situations, and they meddle too much in high-control situations. In ambiguous situations, however, relations-oriented leaders—precisely because of their open, participative, social style—motivate workers to solve problems in creative ways. This pattern of results is illustrated in Figure 13.4.

Studies of military units, sports teams, schools, hospitals, and other organizations generally support Fiedler's contingency model (Peters et al., 1985; Strube & Garcia, 1981). Although the results are far from perfect (Vecchio, 1983), the main point is well taken: good leadership requires a "match" between personal style and the demands of a specific situation (Fiedler & Chemers, 1984). A mismatch—that is, the wrong type of person for the situation—can have negative consequences for both the leader and the organization. Martin Chemers and others (1985) surveyed college administrators to determine both their leadership style and their situational control. The result: mismatches were associated with increased job stress, stress-related illness, and absence from work—symptoms that diminish a leader's productivity and competence (Fiedler & Garcia, 1987).

Although Fiedler's model takes both persons and situations into account, it still may not be sophisticated enough. Edwin Hollander (1985) criticizes its "top-down" view of leadership in which workers are inert, passive, and faceless creatures to be soothed or aroused at management's discretion. Instead, says Hollander, leadership is a two-way street in which there is a mutual influence between a leader and follower. According to Hollander's *transactional* model, an effective leader provides tangible rewards, listens to followers, and fulfills their needs in exchange for an expected level of job performance. Perhaps that is why

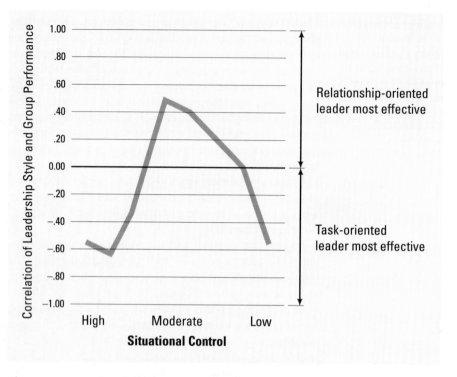

Figure 13.4   Fiedler's Contingency Model of Leadership.   Numerous studies suggest that task-oriented leaders are most effective when a situation is either low *or* high in control and that relations-oriented leaders excel in situations that afford a moderate degree of control. [From Fiedler, 1967.]

people are more likely to support leaders who allow them to express their opinions (Tyler et al., 1985).

Leadership Among Women and Minorities   Look at the top of America's Fortune 500 companies, and you'll find that only 3.6 percent of board-of-directors members are women—a percentage that is not much higher in the healthcare industry, government, or educational institutions. Look at the percentage of African-Americans, Hispanics, and Asians in the top ranks of these same organizations, and you'll find that they fare even worse. Even today, you can count on one hand the number of U.S. senators who are female or the number of major league baseball managers who are Black. Despite the recent progress that has been made in entry-level and middle-level positions, working women and minorities who seek positions of leadership still seem blocked by a "glass ceiling"—a barrier so subtle that it's transparent yet so strong that it keeps them from reaching the top of the hierarchy (Morrison & Von Glinow,

1990). Women may also encounter "glass walls" that keep them from moving laterally within an organization—from positions in public relations to those in core areas such as production, marketing, and sales (Lopez, 1992).

Clearly, there are women who are qualified for positions of power. Research shows that male and female managers have similar aspirations, abilities, values, and job-related skills. When Alice Eagly and Blair Johnson (1990) analyzed the results of 150 separate studies of sex differences in leadership, for example, they found that female leaders in the workplace are as task oriented as their male counterparts. The only difference is that women are more democratic in their approach—that is, they are more likely than men to invite subordinates to participate in the decision-making process. This result is consistent with Judy Rosener's (1990) impression, as reported in the *Harvard Business Review*, that although earlier generations of female executives felt the need to prove they were tough, many of today's leading women are drawing successfully on qualities traditionally viewed as feminine. It is also consistent with Sally Helgesen's (1990) observation that female managers interact more with their subordinates, share information and power, and spin more extensive networks, or "webs of inclusion"—a leadership style she calls the "feminine advantage."

So what's wrong? If women are competent at leadership, why have so few managed to reach the top? For women, the path to power—from their entry into the labor market, to recruitment in an organization, and up the promotion ladder—is something of an "obstacle course" (Ragins & Sundstrom, 1989). One problem is that many women are deeply conflicted about having to juggle a career and family responsibilities (Crosby, 1991). But another problem is societal. Lingering gender stereotypes portray women as followers rather than leaders, and people are uneasy about women who assume leadership roles. In one study, men and women who were seated at the head of the table in all-male or all-female groups were automatically tagged as leaders. In mixed-sex groups, however, this head-of-the-table bias applied only to men who sat in that position (Porter et al., 1985). In another study, subjects were observed from behind a one-way mirror as they took part in a discussion group with male and female confederates who were trained to behave similarly. Regardless of their sex, all confederates who played an assertive role were quite reasonably perceived as leaders. Yet subjects smiled and nodded less often, and frowned more often, in response to the female leaders than to the male leaders—a subtle but sure sign of disapproval (Butler & Geis, 1990). Combining the results of sixty-one studies, Eagly and her colleagues (1992) found that female leaders are often devalued in comparison to equivalent males—when they adopt a "masculine" style of leadership (directive and task focused) or occupy "masculine" positions (for example, business manager or athletic coach).

Statistics show that minorities also fight an uphill battle for leadership positions in the workplace. In interviews, 84 percent of black MBA graduates from five prestigious business schools said they believed that race had a negative impact on their salaries, performance appraisals, and promotions (Jones, 1986). Research does not clearly suggest that employee evaluations are biased by race (Sackett & DuBois, 1991; Waldman & Avolio, 1991). Still, in light of what social psychologists know about the subtleties of modern racism, as described in Chapter 4, business leaders should be sensitive to the indirect ways that minorities are handicapped in the pursuit of leadership. A study of blacks in the banking industry, for example, revealed that they often feel excluded socially from informal work groups, are not well "networked," and lack the kinds of sponsors, role models, and "mentors" that are so helpful for upward mobility within an organization (Irons & Moore, 1985).

Motivation

A key question that I/O psychologists ask is, what motivates individuals to work hard, and to work well? What drives *your* on-the-job performance? Are you driven by strictly economic concerns, or do you have other personal needs to fulfill? There is no single answer. At work, as in the rest of life, our behavior often stems from the convergence of many different motives.

Economic Reward Models Out of necessity, people work for money. In strictly economic terms, however, payment is more complicated than it may appear. To begin with, an employee's overall satisfaction with his or her compensation depends not only on salary (gross income, take-home pay) but on raises (upward or downward changes in pay, how these changes are determined), the method of distribution (number of checks received, differences within the company), and benefits (vacation time, sick leave, insurance, pensions, and other services). Each of these factors is part of the formula for satisfaction (Heneman & Schwab, 1985; Scarpello et al., 1988). In fact, many rewards are not monetary but symbolic—such as titles, office size and location, carpeting, furnishings, proximity to a window, and the ability to regulate access by others (Becker, 1981; Sundstrom, 1986).

Perhaps the most popular theory of worker motivation is Victor Vroom's (1964) *expectancy theory*. According to Vroom, people are rational decision makers who analyze the benefits and costs of possible courses of action and exert effort when they believe it will produce a desired outcome, monetary or symbolic. Expectancy theory has been used successfully to predict various job-related behaviors and career choices such as which college to attend or which job offer to accept (Mitchell, 1974). As an application of the theory, organizations have devised some new and innovative motivational programs. A survey of 1,600 companies revealed that many of them now use (1) individual incentive programs that provide an opportunity to earn time off or extra pay, (2) small-group incentive plans, in which members of a work unit can win bonuses for reaching specified goals, (3) profit-sharing plans, in which workers earn money from company profits, (4) recognition programs, in which "employees of the month" are singled out for gifts or trophies, and (5) pay-for-knowledge plans that raise salaries for workers who are flexible and can perform different jobs within a work unit (Horn, 1987).

People may strive for reward, but there's more to money than just economics and more to motivation than just the size of a pay check. Additional, social psychological factors must also be considered.

Intrinsic Motivation Under certain conditions, reward systems that increase *extrinsic motivation* may undermine *intrinsic motivation*. As discussed in Chapter 2, people are extrinsically motivated when they engage in an activity for money, recognition, or other tangible rewards, and they are intrinsically motivated when they perform for the sake of interest, challenge, or sheer enjoyment. Business leaders want their employees to feel intrinsically motivated and committed to their work. So where do expectancy theory and incentive programs fit in? Is tangible reward the bottom line or not?

When people start getting paid for a task they already enjoy, they sometimes lose interest in it. In the first demonstration of this effect, Edward Deci (1971) recruited college students to work for three one-hour sessions on block-building puzzles they found interesting. During the first and third sessions, all subjects were treated in the same manner. In the second session, however, half of the subjects were paid one dollar for each puzzle they completed. To measure intrinsic motivation, Deci left subjects alone during a break in the first and third sessions and recorded the amount of time they spent on the puzzles rather than on other available activities. Compared to subjects in the unrewarded group, those who had been paid in the second session later showed less interest in the puzzles when the money was no longer available (see Figure 13.5).

This finding, that rewards undermine intrinsic motivation, has been established in numerous studies (Deci & Ryan, 1985; Lepper & Greene, 1978). By making people feel controlled rather than autonomous, various extrinsic factors commonly found in the workplace—punishment, close supervision, evaluation, deadlines, and competition—also have adverse effects on motivation and on performance. Thus, Teresa Amabile (1983b) found that people who were paid for artistic activities produced less creative work than those who were not paid, a finding that extends to creative problem-solving situations as well (McGraw & McCullers, 1979). To be maximally productive, people must feel internally driven, not compelled by outside forces.

If money undermines intrinsic motivation, how can employers use monetary incentives? To answer this question, it's important to recognize that reward can serve two different functions, depending on how it is presented. On the one hand, it can be perceived as *controlling* your behavior, a function that results in the detrimental effects just described (for example, a weekly salary or sales commission). On the other hand, reward can have *informational* value if it offers positive feedback about the quality of your performance (for example, earned bonuses and scholarships). Research shows that although controlling-type rewards adversely affect intrinsic motivation, informational rewards have a positive effect (Enzle & Ross, 1978; Harackiewicz, 1979; Ryan et al., 1983). In a study of managers and subordinates in an office-machine company, Deci and his colleagues (1989) found that the less controlling the managers were, the

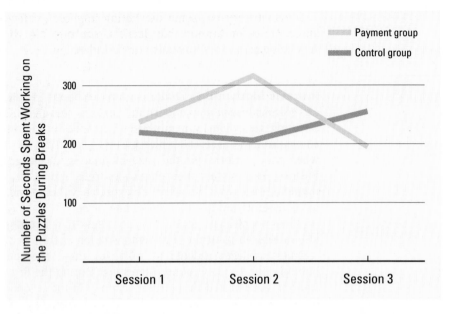

Figure 13.5   The Effect of Payment on Intrinsic Motivation: Turning Play into Work.   In this study, subjects worked three times on puzzles they found interesting. After each session the amount of free time spent on the puzzles served as a record of subjects' intrinsic motivation. During the second session, half of the subjects were paid for puzzles they completed, and half were not. Notice that those paid in the second session later showed less interest in the puzzles when the money was no longer available. [Data from Deci, 1971.]

more satisfied the workers were with the company as a whole. Indeed, when Studs Terkel (1974) interviewed secretaries, stock brokers, baseball players, garbage collectors, and other workers, over and over again he heard two complaints: being too closely watched, or "spied on," and getting too little positive feedback—in other words, too much control and not enough strokes.

Equity Motivation   A second aspect of payment that influences motivation is the perception that it is *fair.* According to *equity theory,* presented in Chapter 6, people want rewards to be equitable, which means that the ratio between inputs and outcomes should be the same for the self as for others. Relative to coworkers, then, the better your job performance is, the more money you should earn. If you feel overpaid or underpaid, however, you will experience distress—and try to relieve that distress by (1) restoring actual equity, say, by working less or getting a raise, or (2) convincing yourself that equity already exists (Greenberg, 1982).

Equity theory has some fascinating implications for behavior in the workplace. Consider, for example, Jerald Greenberg's (1988) study of employees in a large insurance firm. To allow for refurbishing, close to two hundred workers had to be moved temporarily from one office to another. Randomly, the workers were assigned to offices that usually belonged to others who were higher, lower, or equal in rank. Predictably, the higher the rank, the more spacious the office, the fewer the number of occupants, and the larger the desk. Would the random assignments influence job performance? By keeping track of the number of insurance cases processed, and by rating the complexity of the cases and the quality of the decisions made, Greenberg was able to derive a measure of job performance for each worker before, during, and after the office switch. To restore equity, he reasoned, workers assigned to higher-status offices would feel overcompensated and improve their job performance, and those sent to lower-status offices would feel undercompensated and lower their performance. That is exactly what happened. Figure 13.6 shows that the results offered sound support for equity theory.

Figure 13.6 Equity in the Workplace. Insurance company workers were moved temporarily to offices that were higher, lower, or equal in status to their own rank. Supporting equity theory, those assigned to higher-status offices increased their job performance, and those sent to lower-status offices showed a decrease. When workers were reassigned to original offices, productivity levels returned to normal. [Based on Greenberg, 1988.]

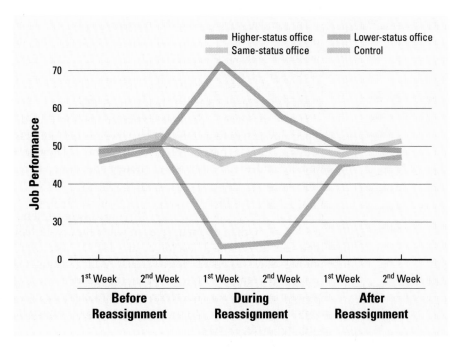

Satisfaction depends not only on equity outcomes but on the belief that the *procedures* used to determine those outcomes were fair and clearly communicated (Brockner et al., 1990; Folger, 1986; Moorman, 1991). For example, Greenberg (1990) studied workers in three manufacturing plants owned by the same parent company. Business was slow, so the company reduced its payroll through temporary pay cuts. Would the cuts make workers feel underpaid? If so, how would the workers restore equity? Concerned that the policy might trigger employee theft, Greenberg randomly varied the conditions in the three plants. In one, the employees were told, without an explanation, that they would receive a 15 percent pay cut for ten weeks. In the second, the same pay cut was accompanied by an explanation and expressions of regret. In the third plant, salaries were not cut. By keeping track of inventories for the ten weeks before, during, and after the pay cuts, Greenberg was able to estimate the employee theft rate. The result: workers whose pay was cut stole more from the company, presumably to restore equity—but only when they were not provided with an adequate explanation for their loss.

Equity in the workplace is important, perhaps more for men than for women. In studies of reward allocation, subjects are led to believe that they and a partner are working at a task for which they will be paid. They work separately, receive false feedback on their performance, and then are told that they must decide how to divide a joint reward. In this situation, women typically pay themselves less than men do and react less strongly when they are underpaid by others (Major & Deaux, 1982). Similarly, a study of male and female graduates of an Ivy League business school showed that the men were more likely than the women to negotiate starting salaries higher than the salaries initially offered (Gerhart & Rynes, 1991).

The gender wage gap has been narrowing in recent years, but at a snail's pace. In 1980, women earned 60 cents for every dollar that men were paid. By 1990, the figure was up only slightly, to 68 cents. That may be why, in a survey of career expectations among male and female college seniors, the women expected to earn $1,238 less than the men upon entering the job market and $18,659 less at the peak of their careers (Jackson et al., 1992).

There are several possible explanations for this difference. First, women expect lower pay than men do even when they are just as qualified, resulting, perhaps, from a history of discrimination (Major & Konar, 1984). Second, women tend to care less about money and more about interpersonal relationships (Crosby, 1982). Third, women may be satisfied with less money because they tend to compare themselves to other women, not to the more highly paid men (Chesler & Goodman, 1976). Fourth, women tend to evaluate themselves less favorably than do men, so even when they work harder and perform better, they feel less entitled (Major et al., 1984). Whatever the explanation, these findings have to make you wonder. Will working women of the future be content to remain underpaid? Is the gender wage gap here to stay? Not necessarily. If the sex difference in reward expectations is rooted in experience, it should diminish as successive generations of women become more established in high-paying careers.

Quality Circles   In addition to feelings of intrinsic motivation and pay equity, job satisfaction is also influenced by the extent to which people are included in important organizational decisions. In recent years, American companies have introduced *participative decision making* (PDM) by giving employees a voice in decisions that used to be made by management alone. According to its proponents, PDM boosts employee morale, increases motivation and productivity, and reduces turnover and absenteeism. Benefits such as these have been found, especially when employees want input (Vroom & Jago, 1988) and participate directly in decision making rather than indirectly, through elected representatives (Rubenowitz et al., 1983).

One form of PDM, imported from Japan, has generated some excitement in recent years. As Japanese industries soared to the top of the world market, business leaders in other countries tried to discover their secret to success. In doing so, they learned that Japanese workers exhibit high levels of commitment to their jobs, perhaps because they take part in *quality circles.* A quality circle is a small group of employees who do similar work and meet regularly to exchange ideas on how to improve their product, the production process, or the work environment. Impressed by the success of Japanese companies, many American corporations—including General Motors, Ford, Westinghouse, RCA, and General Electric—adopted the concept. Promising to increase productivity, quality circles are catching on.

Are quality circles all they're cracked up to be? To find out, Mitchell Marks and his colleagues (1986) assessed both job satisfaction and productivity among machine operators in an American corporation. Half of the operators took part in a quality circle; the other half did not. Before the program, questionnaire measures of satisfaction were administered as part of a company-wide policy to monitor changes in the workplace. Twenty months after the quality circles had begun, the same questionnaires were readministered. Organizational records were also used to measure changes in worker productivity and attendance. As you can see in Figure 13.7, the results were impressive. Compared to employees who did not participate, those who took part in the quality circle felt more content. They liked having a voice in decision making and held more positive views of the company, their own achievements, and the opportunity for advancement. On measures of performance, they exhibited both an increase in productivity and a decrease in absenteeism.

THE MARKETPLACE

Just as social psychology can be used to understand behavior in the workplace, it can shed light on the decisions we make as consumers in the marketplace. What determines the way people choose to save, spend, gamble, or invest their earnings? How do we react to the many forces that push, pull, squeeze, and

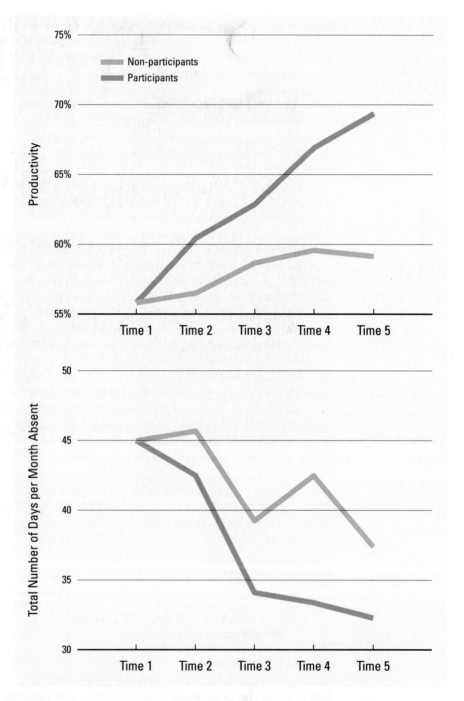

Figure 13.7 Benefits of the Quality Circle. For twenty months, machine operators who took part in quality circles were compared to those who did not. As you can see, the participants exhibited two striking improvements in their job performance: increased productivity (top) and decreased absenteeism (bottom). [From M. L. Marks et al., 1986.]

stretch us in different directions? This section examines two aspects of the marketplace: consumer behavior and economic risk-taking.

Consumer Behavior

Do you drink Coke, Pepsi, or a different soft drink? Would you rather eat at Burger King or McDonald's? Do you drive a Ford, a Chrysler, a General Motors car, or a foreign import? When you consider all the purchasing decisions people make on a day-to-day basis, it's easy to see why social psychologists are interested in applying their knowledge to the study of consumer behavior (Cohen & Chakravarti, 1990).

Product Attributes   The factors that influence consumer choices are numerous. To some extent, perceptions of a product are based on its intrinsic qualities. Thus, car buyers take into account size, safety, fuel efficiency, comfort, attractiveness, and durability. Likewise, supermarket shoppers evaluate a food by its flavor, nutritional content, cholesterol content, and the number of calories it contains. When consumers are asked to explain their purchasing decisions, these are the kinds of factors they say are important. Interestingly, however, different product brands cannot always be distinguished by their intrinsic qualities—as when people claim to prefer the taste of their beer or soft drink but then fail to pick that brand in blind taste tests (Stander, 1973).

In addition to the product itself, people are influenced by *extrinsic* factors such as price, packaging, advertising, sales promotions, availability, and information provided by outside sources. For example, we are influenced in complex ways by price and are particularly attentive to information about a product that is advertised at a relatively low cost (Gotlieb & Dubinsky, 1991). If a product is too expensive, it may become unaffordable for many buyers. If it's priced too low, however, we often assume that it lacks quality. In contrast to what you might think, price and quality are not always related. Yet studies show that for certain "prestige" products such as wine, jewelry, and perfume, a high price tag increases ratings of quality and desirability—the "you get what you pay for" assumption (McConnell, 1968; Peterson, 1977). Exploiting our tendency to link price and quality, marketing experts often introduce new brand names at higher-than-average prices or in stores that have a high-class image. In fact, they sometimes introduce "phantoms" to the market—new products that are advertised but not available. The reason: We crave objects that we cannot have, thus increasing their attractiveness and market value (Pratkanis & Farquhar, 1992).

Packaging is also important. Ideally, a package grabs attention, is easy to remember, gives information about a product, and motivates prospective buyers to take the plunge. According to Stanley Sacharow (1982), the package may also influence the perceived connection between price and quality. For example, the success of generic foods in the supermarket is based on a simple gimmick.

Faced with unadorned black-and-white boxes, cans, and labels, consumers are led to assume that discount prices are possible because of the low cost of packaging, not because of inferior quality.

Psychographics   Years ago, Lee Iacocca revitalized Chrysler by marketing its new cars to a select group of consumers: conservative, family-oriented, blue-collar traditionalists. This segmenting of the market is common. Manufacturers of consumer products often divide prospective buyers into specific groups and then target those groups in their advertisements. Typically, consumers are broken down by broad demographic factors such as sex, age, ethnic background, income, geographical region, and marital status. Baby-boomers, also known as the thirty- or forty-something generation, are a major consumer group. So are children, a vulnerable audience in need of protection. Advertising aimed at the under-18 age group is often controversial. For example, studies recently published in the *Journal of the American Medical Association* showed that "Joe Camel," the cool cartoon character used to promote Camel cigarettes in magazines, store displays, and billboards, appeals more to children than to adults. It has also increased dramatically the number of teenagers who smoke Camels (Brody, 1991).

The "Joe Camel" advertising campaign has special appeal to children. In a large-scale study of twelve-to-eighteen-year-olds and adults, 94 percent of youngsters—compared to only 58 percent of adults—correctly named the brand associated with the logo. Since the start of this campaign, Camel's share of the illegal children's cigarette market has skyrocketed—from 0.5 percent to 32.8 percent. [Brody, 1991.]

psychographic profiles Correlations between consumer characteristics and purchasing behavior; used to segment consumers for marketing purposes.

Today, many companies use **psychographic profiles** to divide people into categories according to their values and lifestyles (Mitchell, 1983; Wells, 1975). These profiles are developed by asking consumers a series of questions concerning their motives, activities, interests, and attitudes. By correlating the responses with self-report measures of purchasing behavior, researchers identify distinct groups. A widely used system called *VALS* (an acronym for "values and life-styles") divides American consumers into five groups: Belongers, Emulators, Achievers, Societally Conscious, and Need-Directed (Meyers, 1984; see Table 13.2). Another approach, the List of Values (LOV) Scale, divides consumers on the basis of their relative commitment to self-fulfillment, excitement, a sense of accomplishment, self-respect, a sense of belonging, security, being well respected, fun and enjoyment, and warm relationships with others. In one study, for example, people who placed a high value on "self-respect" were more likely than those who valued a "sense of belonging" to shop for nontraditional health foods (Homer & Kahle, 1988).

Table 13.2 Psychographic Profiles of American Consumers. By correlating various consumer characteristics and purchasing behavior, marketing researchers have identified psychologically different types of consumers. Do you fit into one of these types? [Meyers, 1984; Rice, 1988.]

Type of Consumer	Description
Belongers	Traditionalists with old-fashioned values; drive medium-sized American cars; drink Coke, Pepsi, or Budweiser; eat at family restaurants; receptive to ads that arouse patriotism, loyalty, and a feeling of togetherness; the group to whom Iacocca sold Chrysler cars
Emulators	Insecure young adults in search of an identity; purchase products thought to enhance their self-image; prefer "muscle" cars like the Chevy Camaro and are receptive to ads that promise social acceptance; the type who smoked Marlboro cigarettes in response to the rugged, masculine image of the Marlboro man
Achievers	Wealthy materialists who own a Mercedes or BMW; wear shirts with prestigious logos; like the high-powered corporate image of IBM computers; drink expensive wines; are receptive to ads that depict the trappings of personal success
The Societally Conscious	Baby-boomers and others who care more about personal health and fulfillment than about money; drink fruit juices, bottled water, and diet sodas; drive small, foreign cars; like user-friendly, counterculture Apple computers; receptive to ads that depict inner-directedness and creativity
The Need-Directed	People on low incomes, struggling to make ends meet; as far as marketers are concerned, this group of nonconsumers does not exist

Once a group of prospective buyers is singled out, products, packages, and advertisements are customized to appeal to that group. A few years ago, the Miller Brewing Company discovered that two-thirds of all beer in the United States is consumed between 4 and 8 P.M., usually at home. As a result, the company staged TV commercials showing a sunset and developed the familiar slogan "When it's time to relax, one beer stands clear; if you've got the time, we've got the beer" (Schudson, 1986). In another example, Merrill Lynch learned that its clients like to see themselves as independent and nonconforming. As a result, the investment firm dropped ads that depicted a thundering herd of bulls and instead developed new ads that portrayed one lone bull, "a breed apart" (Rice, 1988).

Personality variables can also be used to determine what approach to take with different consumers. As described in Chapter 10, Mark Snyder and Kenneth DeBono (1985) found that people who are high and low in *self-monitoring* are drawn to different kinds of advertisements. Alert to the appropriateness of their behavior, high self-monitors are attracted to products that

[Bill Whitehead.]

"I CAN'T COME RIGHT NOW, MOM...
I'M WATCHING A COMMERCIAL
SPECIFICALLY TARGETED TO
MY DEMOGRAPHIC SEGMENT
OF THE POPULATION."

promise to enhance a desired social image. In contrast, low self-monitors—those who behave according to stable dispositions—seek products according to their intrinsic quality.

Just as individuals are drawn to different approaches, certain kinds of products naturally lend themselves to image-oriented or informational advertisements (Shavitt, 1990). For selling cosmetics, jewelry, clothing, and other items designed for one's outward appearance, an image-oriented approach is best. For selling home appliances, stereo equipment, tools, and other functional items, an informational approach should be taken. Many marketing experts thus distinguish between "feeling" products and "thinking" products (Schudson, 1986).

Advertising   We all say that we hate it, don't pay attention to it, don't believe it, and are not affected by it. Yet advertising is an indispensable part of business and is a dominant force of popular culture. Like it or not, TV commercials, magazine and newspaper ads, billboards, and direct-mail flyers influence us. But what makes an advertising campaign effective? Over the years, the industry's giants and researchers have vigorously debated the value of celebrity endorsements, repetition, appeals to emotion, comparative ads that bash the competition, jingles, slogans, humor, sexual arousal, free samples, and other gimmicks (Alwitt & Mitchell, 1985; Fox, 1984; Wells et al., 1989).

In Chapter 10, we saw that an audience can be persuaded by the quality of arguments contained in a message (the central route) or by superficial cues (the peripheral route). According to Richard Petty and John Cacioppo (1986), audiences that are able to process the message content and are involved enough to do so take the central route to persuasion. Those who lack either the ability or the motivation to think carefully about the content rely instead on cues that are peripheral to the message itself. In keeping with this distinction, advertising experts drive on both routes. Sometimes they focus on the processing of "central" commercial information (Harris, 1983). At other times they focus on the role of "peripheral" factors such as music (Yalch, 1991) and the arousal of emotion (Peterson et al., 1986).

Although many advertising techniques have captured the public's attention, few have caused as much furor as the use of subliminal messages. In 1957, Vance Packard published *The Hidden Persuaders*, an exposé of Madison Avenue. As the book climbed to the top of the best-seller list, it awakened in the public a fear of being manipulated by forces that could not be seen or heard. What had Packard uncovered? In the 1950s, amid growing fears of communism and the birth of rock 'n' roll, a group of advertisers were said to have used **subliminal advertising**, the presentation of commercial messages outside of conscious awareness. It all started in a drive-in movie theater in New Jersey, where the words "Drink Coca-Cola" and "Eat popcorn" were flashed on the screen for a fraction of a second. Although the audience never noticed the message, Coke sales were said to have increased 18 percent and popcorn sales 58 percent over a six-week period of intermissions (Brean, 1958).

subliminal advertising   The presentation of commercial messages outside of conscious awareness.

Advertisers may disagree about different promotional strategies, but they all agree that the first task is to heighten consumer awareness of the product. A few years ago, the California raisin industry developed one of the most memorable ad campaigns ever. Created from clay, animated raisin figures—dressed in cool shades and white gloves—strutted across a stage to the classic tune, "I Heard It Through the Grapevine."

Can subliminal advertising really influence us without our being aware of it? At the time, research on the topic was so sketchy, and the public was so outraged by the sinister implications, that the matter was dropped like a hot potato. But today there is renewed interest, new research developments, and continued controversy. Does subliminal advertising work? In what has become a multi-million-dollar industry, companies sell self-help tapes that play soft music or nature sounds and that also contain fleeting messages designed to help listeners relax, lose weight, stop smoking, and improve their sex lives. To deter shoplifting, many department stores play canned music that contains subaudible anti-theft statements like "I am honest" and "I will not steal." In some cases, faint erotic images are embedded in visual ads to heighten the appeal of a product. Without regard for research evidence, and despite the advertising industry's firm denials, there are those who believe in the power of hidden persuaders.

Social psychologists have yet to reach a consensus on the impact of subliminal messages on attitudes and behavior. In Chapter 5, we saw that mere exposure to a stimulus—whether it's a foreign word, an object, or a face—tends to increase our liking for that stimulus even if it is flashed for only one millisecond and cannot later be recognized (Kunst-Wilson & Zajonc, 1980). In other words, subliminal presentations can influence attitudes, apparently without awareness. Can they also influence behavior?

In one study, subjects participated with two confederates in what seemed to be a group decision-making experiment. According to plan, the confederates disagreed on many judgments, leaving the subjects to cast tie-breaking votes. The judgments were about matters of opinion and the confederates were strangers, so the subjects had no *apparent* reason to take sides. But they did have a *subliminal* reason. Before the groups convened, subjects viewed a slide show in which pictures of one confederate or the other, or a blank slide, were briefly flashed. Although subjects were not aware of their exposure to the slides, they later sided in their voting with the confederate who was "familiar" as a result of the initial exposure (Bornstein et al., 1987).

Some consumer advocates charge that faint sexual images are being hidden in print ads to sell products. As shown by this sarcastic reply from the American Association of Advertising Agencies, the industry has repeatedly denied the charges.

PEOPLE HAVE BEEN TRYING TO FIND THE BREASTS IN THESE ICE CUBES SINCE 1957.

The advertising industry is sometimes charged with sneaking seductive little pictures into ads.

Supposedly, these pictures can get you to buy a product without your even seeing them.

Consider the photograph above. According to some people, there's a pair of female breasts hidden in the patterns of light refracted by the ice cubes.

Well, if you really searched you probably *could* see the breasts. For that matter, you could also see Millard Fillmore, a stuffed pork chop and a 1946 Dodge.

The point is that so-called "subliminal advertising" simply doesn't exist. Overactive imaginations, however, most certainly do.

So if anyone claims to see breasts in that drink up there, they aren't in the ice cubes.

They're in the eye of the beholder.

ADVERTISING
ANOTHER WORD FOR FREEDOM OF CHOICE.
American Association of Advertising Agencies

Fortunately, there are limits to subliminal persuasion, and people cannot be manipulated into behaving in ways that seem unnatural. Steven Neuberg (1988) found that when normally competitive people were exposed without awareness to words related to competitiveness (such as *mean, hostile,* and *cutthroat*), they behaved more aggressively in a later game-playing situation than did those who had received words that were neutral (such as *house, place,* and *water*). Among subjects who were not normally competitive, however, these same presentations had no effect on behavior. It may not be possible to subliminally induce people to behave in ways that are incompatible with their predispositions.

What about subliminal messages to drink Coke, eat popcorn, or purchase a particular product? And what about the subliminal self-help tapes for which people pay $19.95? When Timothy Moore (1982) reviewed the existing research, he concluded that "what you see is what you get"—which is nothing, "complete scams." It now appears that Moore was right. In a controlled experiment, Anthony Greenwald and his colleagues (1991) had subjects listen every day for five weeks to a subliminal self-help tape that contained a hidden message designed to improve memory or raise self-esteem. For half of the subjects, the two tapes were correctly labeled; for the others, the labels were reversed. There were two main results: (1) test scores on objective measures of memory and self-esteem were not any higher after exposure to the tapes than before, yet (2) subjects perceived an improvement in their memory or self-esteem—depending on which label was on the tape, not on which message the tape contained (see Figure 13.8). People are quick to believe in the power of the hidden message. But beware: subliminal self-help tapes do not have therapeutic value.

Economic Risk-Taking

Instead of using money to purchase products, we often choose to take risks in the hope of scoring financial gains. How are these risk-taking decisions made? Why do some people gamble away their hard-earned income, despite dreadfully low odds of winning? And how are investments in the stock market influenced by noneconomic social factors? This section examines these and related questions.

Gambling   Anyone who has played poker for money, dropped coins into a slot machine, bet on the winner of a sports event, or bought lottery tickets knows how tempting and seductive gambling can be. Every year, people from all walks of life spend unimaginable amounts of money in casinos, racetracks, off-track betting parlors, state lotteries, bingo, and numbers games. Americans spend billions of dollars a year in legal and illegal gambling activities and, predictably, lose about 20 percent of that figure. Gambling is a big business that can have a devastating impact on how people manage their personal finances.

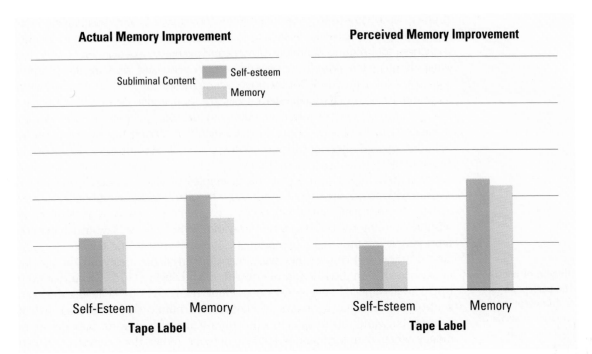

Figure 13.8 Subliminal Self-Help Tapes: Therapy or Fraud? For five weeks, subjects listened to a subliminal self-help tape that was supposed to improve memory or self-esteem. For some, the tapes were correctly labeled; for others, the labels were reversed. This graph shows the pre-to-post exposure effects on actual memory test scores (left) and responses to the question "Do you think the tape has improved your memory?" (right). Notice two results: (1) memory was *not* enhanced by the content of the subliminal message, yet (2) subjects thought their memory had improved when the label led them to expect such improvement. It appears that people are too quick to believe in the therapeutic power of the hidden message. [Greenwald et al., 1991.]

Gambling is a truly puzzling phenomenon. Ordinarily, people do not like to take large risks. That's why they invest in pension plans, purchase insurance, and seek job security. Offered a hypothetical choice between receiving a certain $1,000 or a fifty-fifty chance of obtaining $2,500, most people choose the smaller, guaranteed alternative (Kahneman & Tversky, 1984). Why, then, do so many people gamble? To be sure, certain games—such as poker and black jack—contain an element of skill that enables some players to win more than others. By and large, however, money is lost in games of chance. So why do so many people persist against the odds and engage in self-defeating economic behavior?

From a clinical perspective, "compulsive gamblers" are people who lose huge sums of money and then beg, borrow, and steal to cover debts, denying the problem and lying to their families. As in the case of former baseball star Pete Rose, compulsive gamblers suffer from a serious disorder, like drug or alcohol addiction, and require treatment (American Psychiatric Association, 1987). But what about people who like to gamble on occasion and who are not compulsive? Do they gamble out of an unconscious desire to lose, as psychoanalyst Sigmund Freud (1928) suggested? Does the occasional victory lead them to believe they are on the verge of raking in the big jackpot, as proposed by behaviorist B. F. Skinner (1953)? Or are gamblers driven not by the desire to win but by the sheer thrill and excitement that accompanies all forms of risk-taking?

Social psychologists find that the principles of social perception can help explain why people are so easily seduced into gambling, a nonrational economic activity. From a *motivational* perspective, gambling is viewed as a symptom of wishful thinking, or self-deception (Hayano, 1988). As we saw in Chapter 2, most people are unrealistically optimistic about the future and tend to exaggerate the amount of control they have over uncontrollable life events. In a series of experiments on the **illusion of control**, Ellen Langer (1975) found that even bright, well-adjusted college students delude themselves by believing they can control the outcome in games of chance that mimic skill situations. When subjects cut cards against a competitor in a game of high-card, they bet more money when their competitor seemed nervous rather than confident. When subjects played the lottery, they were more reluctant to sell their ticket after choosing a number themselves than after receiving an assigned number. These behaviors are hardly rational. But don't many of us fall prey to these same illusions? Watch people playing slot machines and you will notice that they try to influence their luck by moving from one machine to another with coins in hand. Or watch players throwing dice in a serious game of craps, backgammon, or Monopoly, you will notice that they often blow on the dice, roll hard for high numbers, and roll soft for low numbers (Henslin, 1967).

The effects on gambling are clear. To exploit our tendency to infuse games of chance with the illusion of control, many states provide an element of choice in their lotteries by having players pick number combinations themselves. Go to the racetrack, and you will find bettors sizing up the horses or studying the data contained in racing forms. In casinos, the dealers are instructed not to intimidate players by shuffling the cards in fancy ways. Why are we so easily fooled? According to Langer, people need to feel that they can control the important events in their lives. Additional research supports this hypothesis. The illusion of control and increased betting are most likely to be found among individuals who have a burning desire for control (Burger & Cooper, 1979). Thankfully, most people behave more rationally when the stakes are high (Dunn & Wilson, 1990).

From a *cognitive* perspective, gambling can be viewed as a natural outcome of the predictions people make about chance events (Wagenaar, 1988). The problem is that many people are misguided about the nature of randomness. Suppose you flipped a coin six times. Which sequence of heads (H) and tails (T)

illusion of control
The perception that chance events are more controllable than they really are.

Filled with pages of statistics, racing forms fill bettors with an exaggerated sense of control.

would you be most likely to obtain: HHHTTT, HTTHTH, or HHHHHH? When asked this question, most subjects pick the second alternative. In fact, the three patterns are equally likely. Consider another example. In the Pennsylvania Daily Number game, a number between 000 and 999 is randomly drawn every day, and the payoff is always 500 to 1—regardless of how many winners there are. In no way is it possible to strategically influence the outcome. Yet a study of number selections shows that ticket purchasers shy away from numbers that have won in the recent past (Halpern & Deveraux, 1989). Why?

According to Daniel Kahneman and Amos Tversky (1972), people falsely assume that any sequence of events, if produced by a truly random process, should appear representative of the expected long-term outcome. Since a large number of coin flips will produce an average of 50 percent heads and 50 percent tails, people erroneously assume that this ratio will emerge even in a small sample of flips. Reflecting this assumption, people often exhibit what is known as the **gambler's fallacy**—the belief that random processes are self-correcting, that temporary deviations in one direction are to be matched by subsequent deviations in the opposite direction. That's why, after a string of heads, people are likely to predict that the next coin will land tails up, or why, after a long run of red numbers on the roulette wheel, people increase their betting on black numbers. The gambler's fallacy is also the reason many slot machine addicts say that a machine is "hot" if it has not surrendered a jackpot for a long period of time.

gambler's fallacy
The false belief that random processes are self-correcting.

It's ironic that just as gamblers assume that the law of averages implies self-correction for *random* events, they make the opposite but also incorrect assumption for events determined by *skill*. The saying "When you're hot, you're hot" illustrates that in tasks involving skill rather than luck, people often expect continuity from one outcome to the next. In an interesting study of this bias, basketball fans were asked the following question: Do you think a player has a better chance of making a shot after having just made two or three shots than he does after having just missed his last two or three shots? What do *you* think? Out of one hundred fans, ninety-one answered "yes," affirming the belief that one event can be used to forecast another. This result certainly fits our intuition, but—believe it or not—an analysis of NBA shooting records casts a shadow of doubt on this assumption. At least at the professional level, the chance of hitting a basket is no greater after previous hits than after previous misses. In fact, randomly generated events produce the same number of hot and cold streaks as a basketball player's record (Gilovich et al., 1985).

That we often bet money on the basis of defective prediction strategies explains part of the gambler's dilemma. But it doesn't explain why people persist after losing over and over again. To understand this problem, it is important to focus on how gamblers interpret their outcomes. In Chapter 2, we noted that people usually take credit for success and explain away failure. Applying these findings to gambling, Thomas Gilovich (1983) questioned subjects one week after they had bet on a series of pro football games. He found that they spent more time trying to explain the games they had lost than those they had won. Although subjects accepted winning without scrutiny, they consistently cited random or fluke events to explain losses—a fumble on the goal line, an injury to a key player, or a close call by the referee—all to suggest that victory had been close at hand.

Can this attributional bias inspire persistent gambling? In basketball, the shot that circles the rim of the hoop and pops out may bolster the belief that a certain player is hot, but it may also be used to maintain the belief that another player is cold. Likewise, according to Gilovich, the gambler's ace in the hole is to recall a point in time when he or she was winning and should have quit. We have all heard those regretful last words: "I was close; I could have won if . . ." Well, maybe next time.

Investing in the Stock Market   October 19, 1987, was called Black Monday. On that day, the stock market dived even more deeply than it had in the famous crash of 1929, resulting in an estimated loss of $500 billion. Worst of all, no one really knew why. Was the economy on the verge of collapse, or were psychological factors to blame? Some Wall Street analysts sought to find rational economic reasons, citing a rising American trade deficit, a recent increase in the prime rate, and political events at home and abroad. Others said the crash was triggered by false beliefs, fear-arousing rumors, conformity pressures, and other social influences—compounded by the speed with which brokers can buy and sell stocks through computers. Forget interest rates, trade deficits, and the gross national product, they said; if you want to predict the market, talk to investors.

The odds of making money are far better on the stock market than in gambling casinos—a majority of investors come out ahead. In many ways, however, putting money into stocks is a lot like gambling. In a book entitled *A Random Walk Down Wall Street,* economist Burton Malkiel (1981) reported that over the long haul, mutual fund portfolios compiled by experts perform no better than randomly selected groups of stocks! Indeed, when *Consumer Reports* evaluated the advice of professional brokers, it concluded that "A monkey throwing darts at the stock pages . . . could probably do as well in overall investment performance, perhaps even better" (Shefrin & Statman, 1986, p. 52).

Like most people, you may be puzzled by this cynical remark. Don't some professionals turn a greater profit than others? And if stock prices rise and fall in reaction to economic conditions, can't the astute investor take advantage of these relationships? The answer to both questions is not necessarily. It's true that some brokers perform better than others for a period of time, perhaps even four or five years. But just as a basketball player is no more likely to sink a basket after four hits than after four misses, investors are no more likely to succeed after a string of wins than after a string of losses. Since many traders have access to the same information, and since prices can change on a moment's notice, movements in the market cannot be predicted with reliability. The only way to guarantee profit is to use confidential information—an illegal activity.

If stock market decisions are not made on strictly economic grounds, then what are they based on? Recent research suggests that predictions of the future on Wall Street, as in Las Vegas, are influenced by social psychological factors. Shortly after the October 1987 crash, economist Robert Shiller sent questionnaires to a group of active traders to try to determine what caused the crisis. For the nearly one thousand investors who responded, the crucial event was the news concerning the market itself, including a sharp decline that occurred on the morning of the crash. In other words, price movements in the stock market were triggered not by objective economic information but by other price movements in the market. Does this phenomenon ring a bell? Research on social comparison (Chapter 2) and conformity (Chapter 9) has shown that when people feel they cannot clearly and concretely measure their own opinion, they turn to others for information. Perhaps that is why investors are more influenced by news and stock market tips during periods of rising or falling prices than during periods of relative stability (Schachter et al., 1985).

Earlier we saw that with coin flips and other chance events, gamblers often assume that a hot streak is due to turn cold, and vice versa. When it comes to games of skill such as basketball, however, people often make the opposite assumption—that hot streaks forecast continued success and that cold spells predict failure. Both of these assumptions are incorrect. One event does not imply another. But what about the ups and downs of the stock market? Do either of these beliefs influence the decisions made by investors? How would *you* play the money game?

To see what happens, Stanley Schachter and his colleagues (1987) presented college students with recent price histories of stocks that had increased, decreased, or remained stable over a three-week period. The conventional wisdom of Wall Street is that investors should "buy low and sell high." Yet, as Figure 13.9 shows, most subjects decided to buy stocks that were on the rise and sell those that were on the decline. In a follow-up study, similar decisions were made by a more sophisticated group of students attending the business school at Columbia University.

Do people always go with the flow of the marketplace, or do they sometimes conform to the buy low–sell high rule? Paul Andreasson (1987) believes the answer may depend on attributions. According to Andreasson, investors may well follow conventional wisdom. But what about price changes for which they have an explanation? What if a rise in stock prices is attributed to certain world events? As far as the market is concerned, these attributions can produce a self-fulfilling prophecy by leading investors to believe that the changes will persist—that rising prices will continue to climb and declining prices will continue to fall. To test his hypothesis, Andreasson simulated the market on a computer and found that without news stories to explain fluctuations, subjects assumed that prices would return to previous levels, buying stocks when the price was low and selling when the price was high. However, subjects who also received *Wall Street Journal* explanations for the changes pursued the strategy observed by Schachter and his colleagues (1987): they rode with stocks that were climbing and bailed out of those that were on the decline. It doesn't stretch the imagination to see how these findings relate to Black Monday. Faced with key changes in the market, the financial news media often seize on current events for an explanation. Whether these attributions are correct or incorrect is irrelevant. Either way, they can turn an initial dip in the market into a full-fledged crash.

Stock market behavior is complicated by another social factor. Hersh Shefrin and Meir Statman (1985) believe that many investors lack the self-control necessary for sound investment decisions. When people own shares of a stock that is climbing, they often sell too early so they can enjoy the quick pleasure of making a profit. This tendency is easy to understand. But when people own stock that is falling, they often wait too long before selling in the hope that they might avoid a financial loss. Why do people continue to hang on in a failing situation? When the handwriting is on the wall, why compound the problem by throwing good money after bad?

In a book called *Too Much Invested to Quit,* Alan Teger (1980) described a dollar-auction game that illustrates part of the dilemma. Imagine yourself in the following situation. The auctioneer tells you and other participants that a one-dollar bill is about to be sold. As in a typical auction, the highest bidder will receive the dollar in exchange for the amount bid. Unlike the typical auction, however, the second highest bidder must also pay the amount bid—but will receive nothing in return. You and the other participants are asked not to communicate, and the minimum opening bid is set at five cents. Then before you know it, the bidding begins. In laboratory experiments, two subjects

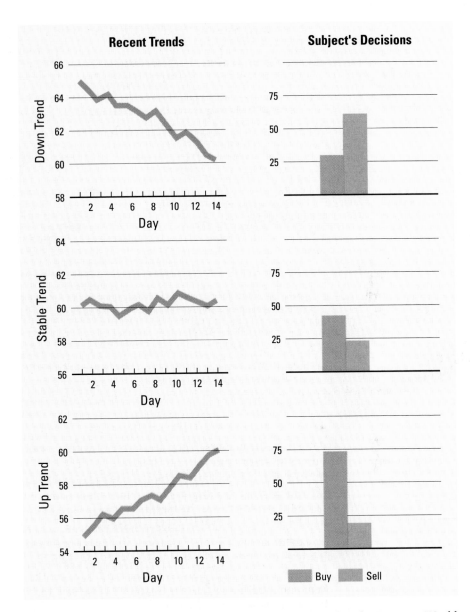

Figure 13.9 Simulated Stock Market: Using the Past to Predict the Future. Would you buy or sell a stock that has risen steadily for three weeks? What about one that drops in the same period of time? In this study, subjects learned the recent trends of stocks that increased, decreased, or remained stable. As you can see, most subjects chose to buy stocks that had risen (bottom) and to sell those that had fallen (top). [Based on Schachter et al., 1987.]

MANKOFF

"Spurred by hopes for a continued revitalization of the American short story along with expectations that rock and roll will never die, the stock market staged a brisk rally today in moderately active trading."

The financial news media often seize upon current events to explain changing stock prices. Whether or not these explanations are correct, they can influence the behavior of investors and cause initial changes to spiral. [© 1986 Robert Mankoff.]

compete in the auction. They are supplied with a small amount of money that is theirs to keep, and they are free to quit the experiment at any time. What happens next can be startling. Some pairs reasonably choose to take the money and run without making a single bid. Other pairs, however, get involved in escalating bidding wars. According to Teger, bidding for the dollar frequently climbs into the five-dollar range—more than the amount allocated for play by the experimenter. On one occasion, the auctioneer had to terminate the game after the two participants had bid $24.95 and $25.00.

The dollar auction helps us understand how people can become financially overcommitted in real life. In Chapter 11, we saw that individuals and groups often become *entrapped* by their own initial commitments as they try to justify or salvage investments already made. In business, the economic conditions under which an investment is made sometimes justify continued commitment. When there is a reasonable likelihood of success, and when potential earnings are high relative to the additional necessary costs, it pays to persist. In certain long-term investments, sizable up-front costs have to be endured before the delayed benefits materialize. As in the dollar auction, however, entrapment may also occur when economic conditions do not provide a basis for optimism. On these occasions, investors take a failing course of action to justify prior decisions, protect their self-esteem, and save face in front of others (Brockner &

Rubin, 1985; Staw & Ross, 1987). Investors who are losing money on a failing stock too often try to "hang tough" and "weather the storm"—only to sink deeper and deeper.

On a more positive note, people can be taught how to use economic rules of thumb that would keep them from throwing good money after bad. In a series of studies, Richard Larrick and his colleagues (1990) found that people often violate the *sunk cost principle*, which states that only future costs and benefits, not past commitments, or "sunk costs," should be considered in making a decision. To appreciate the implications, imagine that you bought a fifteen-dollar ticket to a basketball game weeks in advance but then, on the day of the game, you don't feel well, it's snowing, and your favorite player is injured. Do you still go to the game to make sure you use the ticket? Not wanting to "waste" the money, many of us would go—even though the money is already sunk, and even though we would have to bear the added costs of getting sick, driving in bad weather, and sitting through a boring game. To see if there is a more "rational" economic choice, ask yourself this question: Would you go to the game if someone called that day and offered you a free ticket? If you said that you would go if you had paid for the ticket but not if it were free, then, like investors who don't know when to cut their losses, you fell into the sunk cost trap and should have stayed home.

In a study of University of Michigan professors, Larrick and his colleagues found that the economists were more likely than their counterparts in other disciplines to use the sunk cost principle—not only in hypothetical problems but in their own personal decisions. More important, they found that ordinary people can be taught to apply the rule as well. Indeed, a full month after one brief training session, college students were more likely to report using the rule in their own lives. Sometimes a little knowledge can go a long way.

REVIEW

This chapter presents applications of social psychology to two aspects of business: the workplace (industrial/organizational psychology) and the marketplace (consumer psychology).

THE SOCIAL SIDE OF BUSINESS

In business, behavior is influenced not only by economic factors, but by social psychology as well. The Hawthorne studies showed that worker productivity was increased by social factors such as the attention paid to the workers.

THE WORKPLACE

Personnel Selection

Employment interviews are common practice, but they have mixed effects on hiring decisions. On the one hand, there seems to be less sex discrimination in decisions made with interviews than without. On the other hand, interviews often do not result in an accurate identification of successful employees, in part because interviewer expectations may bias the interview process and predetermine the outcome. To improve matters, many companies use handwriting analysis, lie-detector tests, and other "scientific" approaches, although there are serious questions concerning their validity. More effective is the structured interview, in which applicants are evaluated in a standardized manner.

Performance Appraisal

Once hired, workers are evaluated on a periodic basis. Sometimes objective measures of performance are available, but usually the evaluations are based on subjective judgments of supervisors, the employees themselves, or others. Supervisor ratings are biased by the halo effect, contrast effects, and the tendency for individual raters to use a restricted range on a numerical scale. When people evaluate themselves, the biases of self-perception and presentation produce inflated self-ratings of performance. There are also sex differences. Self-ratings are higher among men than among women, especially when women think they were preferentially selected. Performance appraisals are improved when ratings are made shortly after an observation, by multiple raters, and by raters who have been trained in the necessary skills. Due process is also important, to achieve procedural fairness.

Leadership

Leadership requires social influence. To understand the determinants of good leadership, two approaches have been taken. One approach is to search for personal characteristics associated with effective leaders. In particular, research has identified transformational leaders who motivate followers around a common cause. These leaders have charisma, an ability to inspire, an ability to intellectually stimulate, and a personal concern for others. A second approach assumes that leadership is determined by an interaction of personal and situational factors. According to Fiedler's contingency model, task-oriented leaders excel in high- and low-control situations, and relations-oriented leaders are effective in moderate-control situations. Despite gains made in recent years, working women and minorities are underrepresented in positions of leadership, suggesting they are blocked by a "glass ceiling." Many women are qualified, but they encounter obstacles—including gender stereotypes and uneasiness about women who assume a leadership role. Part of the problem for blacks is that they feel excluded from social networks within the workplace.

Motivation

Both economics and social psychology influence worker motivation. On the economic side, Vroom's expectancy theory says that workers behave in ways that are expected to produce a desirable outcome. Incentive programs are thus used to motivate by reward. However, social psychological factors are also important. Research on intrinsic and extrinsic motivation suggests that when people perceive a reward as controlling their behavior, they lose interest in the work itself. When reward represents positive information about the quality of performance, however, it can enhance intrinsic motivation. Equity theory says that a worker's perception of fairness is also important. People adjust their productivity levels upward when they feel overpaid and downward when they feel underpaid. For various reasons, women accept as equitable a lower level of pay than men. Finally, quality circles appear to enhance worker satisfaction and productivity.

THE MARKETPLACE

Interested in how people manage their finances, researchers study consumer behavior and economic risk-taking activities.

Consumer Behavior

The factors that influence consumer purchases are numerous and include intrinsic product qualities and extrinsic factors such as price and packaging. Marketing experts group consumers by psychographic and personality profiles and then target their marketing efforts at these specific groups. In advertising, researchers focus both on how consumers process commercial information and on the role of peripheral cues. One advertising technique that has attracted controversy is the use of subliminal messages. Research shows, however, that although subliminal presentations can influence attitudes, claims made about their commercial implications are without support.

Economic Risk-Taking

Through gambling and stock market investments, people often take financial risks. Americans spend large sums of money in gambling-related activities for various reasons. First, people fall prey to an illusion of control. Second, they exhibit the gambler's fallacy, which gives rise to the belief that chance events can be predicted. Third, they incorrectly assume that in events involving skill, hot streaks and cold spells will continue. Fourth, gamblers persist through failure because they take credit for wins and explain away losses.

The odds of making a profit are better in the stock market than in the casino. Investment decisions, however, are also subject to social influences. One study suggests that the stock market crash of 1987 was triggered in part by news of what the other investors were doing. Other experiments indicate that investors are too heavily influenced by attributions for price movements appearing in the news media—attributions that can set in motion a self-fulfilling prophecy. People also get entrapped by their initial commitments, which lead them to stick with failing courses of action rather than cut their losses. Thankfully, research shows that people can be taught the principle that only future costs and benefits are relevant to economic decisions.

Health 14

Preview

This chapter explores the social psychology of psychological and physical health. Our major focus is on the process of *stress and coping*. Three aspects of this process are examined: *stressful events*, an individual's *appraisal* of these events and of possible ways to cope with them, and *coping* strategies aimed at reducing stress. In the closing section, we discuss some approaches to *treatment and prevention*.

I n the 1991 special election in Pennsylvania for the U.S. Senate, Harris
Wofford seemed destined for defeat. His opponent, former U.S. attorney
general Richard Thornburgh, was well known and well connected. Wofford had none of these advantages. He was an obscure state official, without
personal charisma or a large campaign fund. All Wofford had was an issue:
healthcare. As it turned out, that was enough. After Wofford's upset victory,
polls indicated that voters supported him because of his advocacy of significant
changes in the healthcare system in the United States. Suddenly, healthcare was
back on the political agenda as the Washington establishment discovered what
most people already knew: Americans value their health and want to protect it.

Fortunately, social psychologists didn't wait for Wofford's election to put
health on their agenda. For over a decade, research on health-related issues has
been one of the most rapidly expanding areas in all of social psychology (Rodin
& Salovey, 1989; Snyder & Forsyth, 1991). Social psychologists focusing on
health are employed in colleges and universities, schools of medicine and of
public health, and government agencies. Their investigations examine both
psychological and physical conditions.

social-clinical inter-
face The study of
social-psychological
factors involved in
psychological health
and disturbance.

health psychology
The study of physical
health and illness by
psychologists from
various areas of spe-
cialization.

The study of social psychological factors involved in psychological health is
called the **social-clinical interface**. Here, social psychologists share similar
interests with clinical and counseling psychologists, who specialize in the study
and treatment of psychological disorders. The social-clinical interface is an
active and challenging area of theory and research (Brehm & Smith, 1986;
Leary & Maddux, 1987). Social psychology also plays an important role in
health psychology, the study of physical health and illness by psychologists
from various areas of specialization (Taylor, 1990). Health psychologists make
an important contribution to the understanding, treatment, and prevention of
disease and injury. This chapter draws on both the social-clinical interface and
health psychology to address two major health concerns: the process of stress
and coping and approaches to treatment and prevention.

STRESS AND COPING: AN OVERVIEW

What do the following people have in common?

Students studying for an important exam
People who have lost their job
Soldiers on a battlefield
Children in the inner city
Refugees
Working mothers
Survivors of natural disasters
First-year college students

The answer is stress. All of these people are coping with stress brought on by life events that range from troublesome to life threatening. Stress is a universal experience. At some time or another, everyone faces the need to cope with it. In their study of stress and coping, social psychologists emphasize psychological factors: thoughts, feelings, and behaviors prompted by life events, by personality, and by social relations. Psychological factors, however, do not exist in a vacuum. The process of stress and coping is also influenced by genetic inheritance, physiology, and cultural context. As depicted in Figure 14.1, all of these elements affect how we experience and manage stress.

There is wide variation in how people respond to threatening, potentially stressful events (Folkman & Lazarus, 1985). An individual may respond effectively in one instance but have great difficulty in another. And different individuals respond in various ways. The same event can wreak havoc on the health of some individuals while leaving others relatively untouched. To understand the reasons for this variation, consider the approach to stress and coping developed by Richard Lazarus and Susan Folkman (Lazarus, 1991; Lazarus & Folkman, 1984).

stress An unpleasant state in which people perceive the demands of an event as taxing or exceeding their ability to satisfy or alter those demands.

According to these researchers, the stress and coping process outlined in Figure 14.1 is an ongoing transaction between the environment and the person, unique for each individual at each point in time. **Stress** is an unpleasant state that arises when people perceive that the demands of an event seriously tax or exceed their ability to satisfy or alter those demands. Such perceptions, called **appraisal**, determine whether stress will be experienced. Appraisal of the threatening situation and of available resources with which to respond also influences the person's **coping** strategy: those thoughts, feelings, and behaviors by which the individual tries to reduce stress. Coping effectively with stress helps maintain good health; coping poorly can harm it. In the following pages, we examine each component of the stress and coping process: potentially stressful events, appraisal, and various coping responses.

appraisal Judgments about the demands made by a potentially stressful event and about one's ability to meet those demands.

coping Efforts to reduce stress.

STRESSFUL EVENTS

What experiences do *you* consider stressful? If you jot down a list of your prime candidates, you might find a few general categories emerging. Here, we divide potential stressors into three types: life events, major crises, and microstressors.

Life Events: Change Versus Negativity

In his pioneering work on stress, Thomas Holmes proposed that all change is stressful because it forces people to adapt to new, unfamiliar circumstances (Holmes & Masuda, 1974; Holmes & Rahe, 1967). Holmes acknowledged that

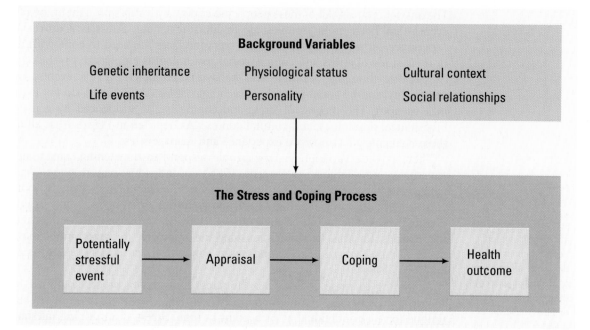

Figure 14.1   The Stress and Coping Process.   The stress and coping process involves a potentially stressful event, the appraisal of that event and of coping possibilities, and attempts to cope. Played out against a variety of background factors unique to the individual, the stress and coping process influences the individual's health outcomes.

some changes require more adjustment than do others. Nevertheless, he believed that the change produced by both positive (for example, getting married, receiving a promotion) and negative (for example, getting divorced, being fired) life events is stressful and can damage a person's health. Holmes' formulation generated a great deal of research—and a great deal of controversy. Are positive and negative events functionally equivalent because both produce changes in people's lives? Do they have similar effects on health?

Increasingly, the evidence goes against both of these propositions. Positive and negative life events have very different implications for stress and coping (Bryant, 1989; Larsen & Ketelaar, 1991). One reason for this difference lies in the nature of emotional experience. Good feelings and bad feelings are not opposite ends of a single continuum. Joy is not simply the absence of sadness, nor is sadness simply the absence of joy. Instead, positive and negative emotions are distinct, relatively independent experiences (Clark & Watson, 1988). And because they are relatively independent, they are not mutually exclusive. People can experience happiness and distress simultaneously (Carver & Scheier, 1990). For example, women appear to experience more intense happiness *and* more intense distress in response to significant life events, like marriage, than do men

(Fujita et al., 1991; Wood et al., 1989). The emotional consequences of positive and negative life events run on separate tracks.

The health consequences of positive and negative life events also differ (Taylor, 1991). Negative life events are associated with both physical illness and psychological distress (Sarason & Sarason, 1984). For the most part, the long-term results of adjusting to positive life change are either beneficial or trivial (Stewart et al., 1986; Thoits, 1983). There may, however, be some exceptions to the general rule that good events are not harmful. Among the teenage girls and college-age men studied by Jonathon Brown and Kevin McGill (1989), those who were high in self-esteem enjoyed better health after experiencing positive life events. But for subjects low in self-esteem, positive life events were associated with increased illness. Positive life events, say Brown and McGill, clash with the negative expectations of individuals with low self-esteem, producing stress and vulnerability to illness.

In order to separate positive and negative life events, researchers ask subjects to indicate whether a given event had a positive or negative effect on their life. Some items from one widely used questionnaire, the Life Experiences Survey (Sarason et al., 1978), are reprinted in Table 14.1. The number, intensity, or duration of positive events is tabulated separately from the number, intensity, or duration of negative events. Then each category is correlated with measures of subjects' health status.

negative affectivity

A pervasive tendency to experience distress, dissatisfaction, and a wide variety of negative emotions.

But this approach, too, has its problems. Consider, for example, **negative affectivity**—a pervasive tendency to experience distress, dissatisfaction, and a wide variety of negative emotions (Watson & Clark, 1984). Negative affectivity does not appear to be strongly or consistently associated with *objective* measures of actual physical illness. However, individuals high in negative affectivity do *report* more stressful experiences, physical symptoms, and psychological distress (Clark & Watson, 1991). This pattern of results raises some questions about the meaning of an association between (1) self-reports of negative life events and (2) self-reports of symptoms or distress. Does this association indicate a true relationship between stress and adjustment? Or are both types of self-reports produced by the personality trait of negative affectivity?

The best way to resolve this uncertainty is to use statistical techniques to remove the influence of negative affectivity from the relationship between life-events stress and health outcomes. Doing so is fast becoming common practice. Recent studies indicate that once negative affectivity has been taken into account, stressful life events are still associated with increased psychological distress (Aldwin et al., 1989; Headey & Wearing, 1989; Ormel & Wohlfarth, 1991). The small size of such "purified" effects, however, suggests that life-events stress has only a relatively minor influence on health.

Major Crises: Catastrophe and War

As an alternative to examining the cumulative impact of multiple life events, some researchers focus on the effects of a single major crisis (Maser & Solomon,

Listed below are some events that sometimes bring about change in the lives of those who experience them and that necessitate social readjustment. Please check those events that you have experienced in the recent past and indicate the time period during which you have experienced each event. Also, for each item checked, please indicate the extent to which you viewed the event as having either a positive or a negative impact on your life at the time the event occurred. A rating of –3 would indicate an extremely negative impact. A rating of 0 suggests no impact either positive or negative. A rating of +3 would indicate an extremely positive impact.

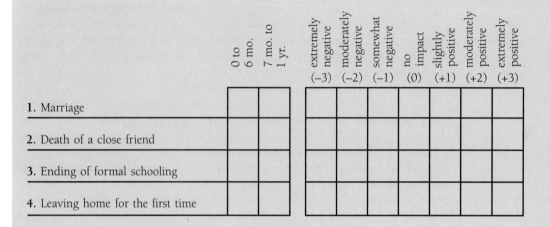

Table 14.1   The Life Experiences Survey: Instructions and Sample Items. By asking subjects to indicate whether a specific event had a positive or negative impact on their lives, the Life Experiences Survey makes it possible to examine the effects of positive and negative life events separately. These two types of life events have different health consequences. [Based on Sarason et al., 1978.]

1990). Various major stressors have been studied, including divorce (Bloom et al., 1978), widowhood (Stroebe & Stroebe, 1983), airplane crashes (Jacobs et al., 1990), adjusting to a new culture (Rogler et al., 1991; Williams & Berry, 1991), and wartime effects on civilians (Garbarino et al., 1991; Hobfoll et al., 1989). In this section, we concentrate on two major stressors that have received particular attention: environmental catastrophes and experiences during combat.

Environmental disasters have strong effects on psychological adjustment. Anxiety, somatic complaints, alcohol consumption, and phobias increase in the wake of an environmental catastrophe (Rubonis & Bickman, 1991). The 1979 accident at the Three Mile Island nuclear plant illustrates the point. Near meltdown in the core of a nuclear reactor exposed residents of surrounding communities to radioactive gases and required the evacuation of over 100,000 people. Studies conducted after the accident revealed sharply increased stress among individuals living close to the plant, with mothers of young children suffering the highest levels of psychological distress (Hartsough & Savitsky, 1984). A year later, there was renewed anxiety and apprehension when radioactive gases trapped in the damaged reactor were vented into the air (Baum et al., 1982). Most of the stress caused by the accident and the later venting procedure subsided fairly rapidly, although there were some indications of more enduring stress reactions.

The Three Mile Island disaster was caused by human error. As frightening as such accidents are, naturally caused catastrophes may be even more upsetting (Rubonis & Bickman, 1991). Do you remember where you were on October 17, 1989? If you happened to be in the San Francisco Bay area, you'll probably never forget that day. Struck by the most severe earthquake since 1906, highways and bridges collapsed, and fires raged out of control. Thousands were left homeless. Thousands were injured. And sixty-two people died.

By coincidence, Susan Nolen-Hoeksema and Jannay Morrow (1991) had administered some trauma-relevant measures to a group of Stanford University students two weeks before the earthquake. Follow-up assessments made some ten days after the quake and then again six weeks later provided these investigators with that rarest of studies: a before-and-after examination of coping with a natural disaster. This research indicated that psychological distress after the quake was greatest among three groups of students: those who were more distressed before the quake; those who reported having a brooding, self-focused response to problems before or after the quake; and those who experienced more dangers and difficulties during the quake. Thus, vulnerability to the stressful effects of having experienced a natural disaster was increased by both personal and situational factors.

Of all the major stressors, combat experience is one of the worst. Soldiers in combat face the constant threat of mutilation or death, observe the death or injury of other soldiers, and worry about what their lives will be like when they return home. Even though it has been almost twenty years since the end of the Vietnam War, a number of Vietnam veterans still suffer from **posttraumatic stress disorder**, the experience of enduring physical and psychological problems after an extremely stressful event (Davidson & Baum, 1985; Helzer et al., 1987). According to an extensive study conducted by the Centers for Disease Control (1988), more Vietnam veterans suffer from depression, anxiety, and alcohol abuse than do veterans who served outside of Vietnam during the war years. In this study, symptoms of posttraumatic stress disorder sometime during or after the war were reported by 15 percent of the Vietnam veterans surveyed. Some 2 percent were still experiencing posttraumatic stress disorder more than fifteen years after their military service was completed.

Another study of Vietnam veterans found that the severity of the men's combat experience (for example, being shot at, being ambushed, going into tunnels to capture enemy soldiers, retrieving dead bodies) was the strongest predictor of posttraumatic stress disorder (Goldberg et al., 1990). Veterans of World War II and the Korean War who participated in heavy combat also

posttraumatic stress disorder The experience of enduring physical and psychological problems after an extremely stressful event.

On October 17, 1989, the San Francisco Bay area was struck by a major earthquake. Research indicates that coping with the stress created by this natural disaster was influenced by both personal and situational factors.

reported more symptoms of stress after the war was over (Elder & Clipp, 1989). Interestingly, however, those who experienced heavy combat were also more likely to become more resilient and less helpless over time. Thus, the study of major stressors highlights both vulnerability and resistance. Although "crisis growth" may not be typical, it does occur (Holahan & Moos, 1990).

Microstressors: The Hassles of Everyday Life

Research on stress and coping examines the "microstressors" of ordinary life as well as the "macrostressors" of life change and major crises. Strained relationships, deadlines, fighting traffic, running the rat race, and struggling to make ends meet are unfortunate but inevitable aspects of the daily routine. These kinds of everyday hassles and social pressures can contribute to distress and illness (Kohn et al., 1991; Weiten, 1988). Interpersonal conflicts appear to be the most upsetting of daily stressors, with longer-lasting effects than most other microstressors (Bolger et al., 1989).

Some daily hassles and pressures are architecturally induced. Andrew Baum and Stuart Valins (1979) compared first-year college students living in two types of dormitories: a long-corridor dormitory (as shown in Figure 14.2A) and one divided into suites (Figure 14.2B). The dormitories were quite similar in furnishings and surroundings, but Baum and Valins predicted that one type of dorm would be more stressful than the other. Which dorm do *you* think would be more stressful?

If you've ever lived in a long-corridor dormitory, you probably found it easy to come up with the correct answer: compared with those living in suites, corridor residents experienced more stress. Students living in long corridors complained more about feeling crowded and about the difficulty of avoiding unwanted social contact. They also were more prone to avoid and withdraw from others, even outside the dormitory. Why was corridor residence more stressful than suite life? Baum and Valins believe that the answer lies in the way these spatial arrangements affect social control. Because corridor residents had to share more space with more people (such as in the bathroom and lounge areas), it was more difficult for them to regulate their social contacts.

Research on prison crowding reveals a similar pattern. The number of inmates sharing a space has a greater effect on stress than does the amount of space available (Paulus, 1988). In college or in prison, unpredictable and uncontrollable social interaction is stressful. It may also be dangerous. Crowded

---

Figure 14.2 Stress in the Dorms: Which Is the More Stressful Place to Live? Research on stress in different types of dormitories indicated that corridor residents experienced more stress than those living in suites. [From Baum & Valins, 1977.]

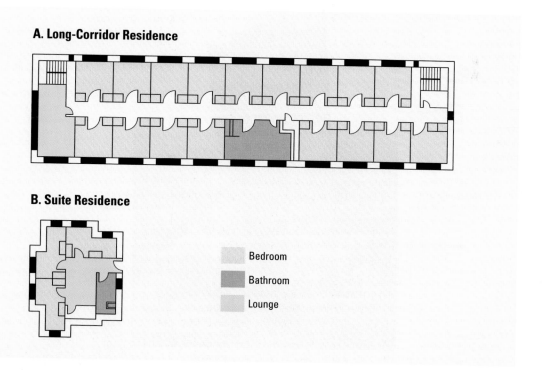

prisons and massive dormitories are often plagued with vandalism and violence. At the University of Cincinnati, the problems in Sander Hall, a 26-story tower housing 1,300 students, proved insurmountable. On June 23, 1991, university administrators pulled the plug and blew it up!

Just as architectural arrangements organize the space we live in, so do *social roles* impose a certain order on our daily lives. Social roles are established by socially shared expectations about how people in a given position should behave. Being a parent or a child is a social role, as is being a professor or a student. People can occupy a great many different roles or only a few. The nature of the relationship between having multiple roles and experiencing stress has been much debated. According to the *scarcity hypothesis,* more roles produce more stress, because time and energy will be stretched thin (Goode, 1960). In

Living in crowded conditions where privacy is in short supply is often stressful and sometimes dangerous. After repeated efforts to reduce violence and vandalism in Sander Hall had failed, officials at the University of Cincinnati decided to demolish the dormitory.

contrast, the *enhancement hypothesis* predicts that a greater number of roles will reduce stress, because disappointment in one area of life can be compensated for by success in another (Sieber, 1974). Concern about the effects of multiple roles has increased in recent years as large numbers of married women with children have entered the work force. Although a majority of married women with children are employed, they still perform much more of the housework and childcare than do their husbands (Hochschild, 1989). Many of these women feel "stressed out."

Despite these feelings, however, having multiple roles is usually associated with increased well-being (Rodin & Ickovics, 1990). Employed women experience less psychological distress and better physical health than do unemployed women (Spitze, 1988; Verbrugge, 1987). But the benefits of employment depend on the quality of those roles (Barnett & Baruch, 1985). Among married women, employment is clearly beneficial only for those who have positive attitudes toward their employment (Repetti et al., 1989). Indeed, work satisfaction appears to influence whether a woman's employment is associated with positive or negative effects on the marriage itself (Greenstein, 1990). Employment is correlated with less risk of marital disruption among women who enjoy their work but with more risk among women who are dissatisfied with their work. Exploring the various ways in which stress at work and stress at home are related is an increasingly important aspect of research on stress and coping (Eckenrode & Gore, 1990; Frankenhaeuser et al., 1991).

APPRAISAL

From the stresses and strains experienced by women today as they attempt to balance their work and family responsibilities, we turn to an anonymous author some 2,500 years ago who wrote an extraordinary poem about human suffering: the Book of Job. A pious and prosperous man as the poem begins, Job is soon beset by great calamities. He loses his property, his children, and his health. Job and his friends try to understand how these terrible things could happen. His friends argue that Job's plight must be a punishment sent by God and tell Job to repent. Because he believes that his sufferings far exceed any wrongdoing on his part, Job cannot accept this explanation. In despair, he doubts his capacity to withstand continued hardship and longs for death. Eventually, however, Job finds strength and peace through trusting in God's will.

According to the model displayed in Figure 14.1, Job and his friends were engaged in the process of appraisal. They considered *explanations* for Job's suffering and formed *expectations* about his ability to cope with his situation. These same themes are found in research on stress and coping.

Explanations: Learned Helplessness and Depression

Depression is a psychological disorder characterized by negative moods (such as feelings of sadness and despair), low self-esteem, pessimism, lack of initiative, and slowed thought processes. It can also involve disturbances in sleeping and eating patterns, as well as reduced sexual interest. Around 5 percent of the population will experience a major depression sometime during their lives (Robins et al., 1984). Many more will suffer from brief, relatively mild bouts with the "blues." Women are more likely than men to suffer from depression (Nolen-Hoeksema, 1987). Many factors influence the onset and duration of a depressive episode—including social context, physiological processes, and genetic inheritance (Paykel, 1982). Social psychologists, however, have focused on the effects of cognitive factors. Here, we examine a view of depression that emphasizes people's explanations for their unpleasant experiences.

learned helplessness
The phenomenon in which experience with an uncontrollable event creates passive behavior toward a subsequent threat to well-being.

The *original* **learned helplessness** model of depression was based on observations of animals and humans exposed to uncontrollable, aversive stimulation. In one study, for example, dogs that received a series of electric shocks over which they had no control later failed to escape from additional shocks by crossing a barrier into a compartment where no shocks were delivered (Seligman & Maier, 1967). Those that had not received uncontrollable shocks learned quickly to avoid the subsequent shocks. Similarly, human subjects exposed to inescapable bursts of noise failed to protect themselves in a later situation where the noise could be easily avoided (Hiroto, 1974).

According to Martin Seligman (1975), these findings indicate that both animals and humans exposed to an uncontrollable event learn that control is not possible and, therefore, stop trying to exert control. Moreover, nondepressed human subjects exposed to uncontrollable events in research on learned helplessness exhibit many of the characteristics of depressed individuals: feelings of discouragement, pessimism about solving problems, and lack of initiative. Thus, said Seligman, depression is a form of helplessness learned from experiencing uncontrollable outcomes.

Not everyone agreed with this conclusion and Seligman's theory soon became highly controversial (Buchwald et al., 1978; Wortman & Brehm, 1975). To address shortcomings in the original formulation, Lyn Abramson and her colleagues (1978) developed the *reformulated* model of learned helplessness. This model holds that perceiving a lack of control in one situation is *not* sufficient to produce helpless feelings and behaviors in a different situation. Instead, the person's attributions for what caused the initial lack of control are crucial. The reformulated model emphasizes three types of attributions:

Stable versus unstable: Is the cause for an uncontrollable event perceived as enduring across time (stable) or as temporary (unstable)?
Global versus specific: Is the cause for an uncontrollable event perceived as extending across many events in the person's life (global) or as limited to a particular occasion (specific)?

Internal versus external: Does the person attribute the cause of an uncontrollable event to personal characteristics and behaviors (internal) or to environmental forces (external)?

According to the reformulated model of learned helplessness, those individuals who make *stable* and *global* attributions for an uncontrollable event are more likely to expect future events to be uncontrollable. In turn, the expectation of a lack of control produces passive and helpless behavior in new situations. Those who make *internal* attributions are said to be more likely to experience low self-esteem. The combination of stable, global, and internal attributions for an uncontrollable event should produce a depressive reaction, as Figure 14.3 indicates.

Attributions that are stable, global, and internal usually refer to enduring personal characteristics. Blaming a bad exam grade on a lack of intellectual ability is an example of such an attribution. The person expects this relatively fixed characteristic of the self to produce poor performance on a variety of future intellectual tasks. Such an attributional "triple whammy" locks the person into the worst possible box: a bleak future caused by an aspect of the self that cannot be changed.

Figure 14.3 The Reformulated Model of Learned Helplessness. According to this model, attributing an uncontrollable event to a stable and global cause leads to the expectation of a lack of control over future events. This expectation then produces depressed behavior and feelings. Attributing an uncontrollable event to an internal cause is said to lead to low self-esteem, which characterizes many depressed individuals.

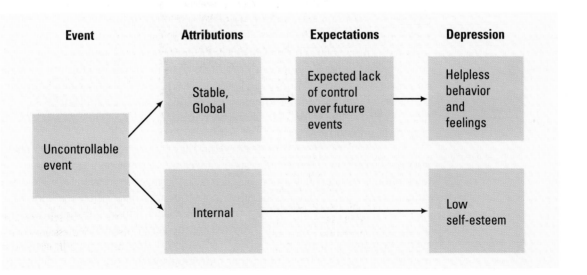

What would make someone close the attributional lock on such a depressing box? Sometimes the *situation* leaves us no choice because the explanation for a failure is obvious. Many students, for example, come to college thinking they might want to become a physician. Then they struggle through the lab in organic chemistry and discover that their lab skills are less than superlative. For some, this is a depressing situation. Their lack of skill in laboratory science creates the expectation that they will not be able to control their occupational future by going to medical school. The relationship between situation-specific attributions of self-blame and health outcomes will be discussed in a later section of this chapter.

In more ambiguous circumstances, explanations can be a matter of *personal style*. Some people habitually use stable, global, and internal attributions to explain failure and other unpleasant events in their lives. This tendency is called the **depressive explanatory style**. The reformulated model of learned helplessness maintains that these individuals are at greater risk for depression. People who tend to use unstable, specific, and external attributions to discount success and other pleasant life experiences may also be at greater risk (Peterson & Seligman, 1987). Table 14.2 displays an example from the Attributional Style Questionnaire, a frequently used measure of explanatory style (Peterson & Villanova, 1988).

depressive explanatory style A habitual tendency to attribute negative events to causes that are stable, global, and internal.

Three approaches have been taken to assessing the influence of the depressive explanatory style. First, style and depression can be measured at the same time. From their review of over one hundred studies, Paul Sweeney and his colleagues (1986) concluded that there is a clear association between the depressive explanatory style and being depressed. But correlation does not prove causation. To explore the possibility of a causal relationship, longitudinal studies investigate the relationship between initial style and later adjustment.

In one such study, the responses made by ninety-nine male college graduates in 1946 to an open-ended question about their wartime experiences were scored for depressive explanatory style (Peterson et al., 1988). Although style did not predict physical health status in young adulthood, there was a link between initial explanatory style and health at age forty-five and older. After forty-five, those men who had displayed a depressive explanatory style in their youth tended to have more health problems than those whose youthful explanatory style was more optimistic. Relying on letters and diaries written some fifty years earlier, another longitudinal study yielded mixed results (Burns & Seligman, 1989). Only initial explanatory style for *positive* events was related to current depression.

Longitudinal studies are interesting, but they do not represent the best test of whether depressive explanatory style can cause depression. According to the reformulated model of learned helplessness, depressive explanatory style is a vulnerability factor that has negative consequences *only* when the individual experiences stress. Thus, the best test of the model requires an initial measure of depressive explanatory style followed by the actual occurrence of a stressful event. Research that meets this best-test standard does not provide consistent results. Some studies have found that individuals with a pre-existing depressive

Try to vividly imagine yourself in the situation that follows. If such a situation happened to you, what would you feel had caused it? Events may have many causes, but we want you to pick only one—the *major* cause if this event happened to *you*. Please write this cause in the blank provided. Next we ask you some questions about this cause. Circle one number after each question.

Situation: You meet a friend who acts in a hostile manner toward you.

1. Write down the *one* major cause _____

2. Is this cause due to something about you or something about other people or circumstances?

   Totally due to
   other people   Totally due
   or circumstances   1 2 3 4 5 6 7   to me

3. In the future will this cause again be present?

   Will never again   Will always
   be present   1 2 3 4 5 6 7   be present

4. Is the cause something that influences just this situation, or does it also influence other areas of your life?

   Influences just   Influences
   this particular   all situations
   situation   1 2 3 4 5 6 7   in my life

Table 14.2   The Attributional Style Questionnaire: An Example. The Attributional Style Questionnaire measures attributions about imagined events—both positive and negative. In this example, you are asked to imagine a negative event and then indicate your attributions for its causes. High ratings on questions 2 through 4 indicate an internal, stable, and global attribution. [Based on Peterson & Seligman, 1987.]

---

explanatory style are more likely to become depressed after a stressful event (Metalsky et al., 1987; Riskind et al., 1987), but other studies have not replicated this effect (Follette & Jacobson, 1987; Ramírez et al., 1992).

Expectations: Agency and Outcome

The mixed results of research on the depressive explanatory style are typical of efforts to demonstrate a causal connection between cognitive factors and depression (Haaga et al., 1991; Monroe & Simons, 1991; Robins, 1988). Such inconsistent findings are not the only reason that researchers have begun to wonder about the importance of attributions in the stress and coping process. Research on naturally occurring traumatic events, such as the loss of a child from sudden infant death syndrome, suggests that attributions are more likely to be a symptom of distress rather than a cause (Downey et al., 1990).

As you can see from Figure 14.3 (page 649), attributions for why a distressing event has occurred were never the only factor considered by theories within the learned helplessness tradition. Instead, expectations about future events were viewed as the key element having a direct influence on behavior. The role of expectations is further elaborated by the most recent revision of learned helplessness: *hopelessness theory* (Abramson et al., 1989). According to this theory, expected lack of control is necessary but *not* sufficient to put an individual at risk for developing passive behavior and depressed feelings. The individual must also expect future events to be undesirable and unpleasant. Although expecting future negative outcomes does appear to serve as a connection between depressive explanatory style and depression (Hull & Mendolia, 1991), hopelessness theory has yet to be fully investigated. There is, however, a large body of research on each of the two types of expectations it describes: *agency expectations* about personal control over future events and *outcome expectations* about the quality of these events. Let's examine how these expectations relate to people's health.

Agency Expectations: Perceived Control, Hardiness, and Self-Efficacy
In general, expecting to have control over what happens to you is associated with more effective coping in stressful situations. As we saw earlier, research comparing residents of long-corridor dormitories with those who lived in suites indicates that spatial arrangements increasing people's sense of social control are associated with better psychological and social adjustment (Baum & Valins, 1979). Similarly, perceived control over physically stressful stimulation, such as unpleasant noise, has been shown to reduce the negative aftereffects produced by such stressors (Glass & Singer, 1972).

Perceptions of control may be especially meaningful among people whose lives are regulated to a large extent by others (Rodin et al., 1982). For example, elderly residents of nursing homes who were given increased control over daily events became more active and happier (Langer & Rodin, 1976; Schulz, 1976). Follow-up studies of these senior citizens suggested that continuing expectations of control had positive effects on health and longevity, while abrupt loss of perceived control was damaging to health (Rodin & Langer, 1977; Schulz & Hanusa, 1978). Negative reactions to loss of control may underlie the difficulties medical patients often experience in adjusting to a hospital routine (Taylor, 1979).

The effects of perceived control on health have also been studied in terms of differences among individuals (Lefcourt & Davidson-Katz, 1991). Among college students, those who believe that their outcomes in life are controlled by their own actions are less depressed than those who believe that their outcomes are controlled by powerful others or by chance (Ganellen & Blaney, 1984). Similarly, cancer patients who believe that they have some control over the course of their illness have a better psychological adjustment (G. Marks et al., 1986; Taylor et al., 1984). However, perceived control by others is not always associated with difficulties in coping. Among female cancer patients with a good

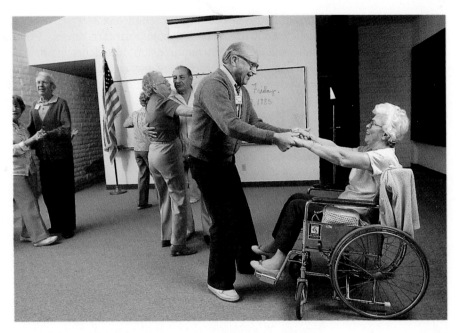

Among senior citizens living in a nursing home, those who were given increased control over daily events became more active and happier.

prognosis, believing that others had control over whether the cancer would reoccur was correlated with a favorable psychological adjustment (Taylor et al., 1991).

Hardiness is a more complex measure of individual differences in agency expectations. It combines three components:

Control: The belief that one's outcomes are controlled by one's own actions
Challenge: The perception of change as a normal part of life
Commitment: Having a sense of meaning and mastery in one's life

Management personnel in a large company who obtained high scores on the composite measure of hardiness reported less serious illnesses than those who obtained low scores (Kobasa et al., 1982). But some research indicates that high hardiness scores are associated only with fewer *self-reports* of symptoms, not with a lower incidence of *actual* illness (Allred & Smith, 1989).

Perceived control refers to expectations that we can control what happens to us. As Albert Bandura (1977a) has emphasized, however, people can exert control only by doing something. Bandura's concept of **self-efficacy** refers to a situation-specific, positive expectation that what needs to be done can be done. Consider, for example, two individuals with differing skills: one excels at athletics; the other is a superb musician. Put them both on a tennis court, and the athlete will have a greater sense of self-efficacy about performing well than will the musician. But put them both in a band, and the musician will have the

self-efficacy A person's belief that he or she is capable of the specific behavior required to produce a desired outcome in a given situation.

greater sense of self-efficacy. High levels of self-efficacy in managing pain are associated with increased pain tolerance among women in labor, individuals suffering from recurrent tension headaches, and arthritis patients (O'Leary, 1985). A sense of self-efficacy may also be associated with enhanced functioning of the immune system and long-term reductions in vulnerability to infection (Bandura et al., 1988; Wiedenfeld et al., 1990).

Outcome Expectations: Optimism   Outcome expectations are distinctly single-minded. They don't care about control or who's able to do what. For an outcome expectation, all that counts is the quality of what's to come: a good time or a bad one. The person who obtains high scores on the Life Orientation Test, a widely used measure of *optimism*, has positive expectations for life outcomes (Scheier & Carver, 1987). During a stressful period in college, students who held more optimistic expectations reported fewer symptoms (Scheier & Carver, 1985). Similarly, optimistic patients showed better adjustment after coronary by-pass surgery than did those who were pessimistic (Scheier et al., 1989).

Recent research by Timothy Elliott and his colleagues (1991) suggests that outcome expectations may be particularly important early in the recovery process. The subjects in this study, men and women who had suffered traumatic spinal-cord injuries, completed a two-factor hope scale (Snyder et al., 1991). On an outcome-oriented subscale (which includes items such as "I meet the goals that I set for myself"), being more hopeful was associated with better psychosocial adjustment for subjects who were recently injured but not for those whose injury was more long-standing. In contrast, more hopeful scores on a self-efficacy subscale (which includes items such as "I can think of many ways to get out of a jam") were associated with better adjustment only for subjects who had lived, and coped, with their injury for some time. These findings suggest that different types of positive expectations may be differentially useful depending on the type of stress faced by the individual. The hope that gets us started may not be the same as the hope that keeps us going.

Was Pollyanna Right?

Pollyanna is the name of the upbeat heroine created by American writer Eleanor Porter. Although Pollyanna used to get a bad press for her boundless belief that even the most ominous cloud has a bright and shining silver lining, the research reviewed in this section indicates that Pollyanna should have been an outstandingly healthy person. As we've seen, *not* having a depressive explanatory style is associated with good adjustment, and people who expect to be able to influence their life outcomes and to obtain the outcomes they desire also enjoy good health.

That's not all. As described in Chapter 2 on the self, people seem to have a million ways to help them feel good about themselves. They take credit for

"I'm an optimist. I'm convinced that everything is going to go to hell, but not for a while yet."

[Drawing by Weber; © 1991 The New Yorker Magazine, Inc.]

success and distance themselves from failure; find excuses for short-comings, before and after the fact; discover comparisons with others that cast a favorable light on themselves; and have unrealistic beliefs about their ability to control events and their chances of securing desirable outcomes. These self-enhancing distortions and illusions are particularly pronounced among well-adjusted individuals (Taylor & Brown, 1989). A host of pro-Pollyanna books, readily identifiable by titles like *Learned Optimism* (Seligman, 1990) and *Positive Illusions* (Taylor, 1989), convey the message: Looking at life through rose-colored glasses is good for your health.

But there are some serious problems with assuming that the positive thinking of a Pollyanna leads straight to good health (Tennen & Affleck, 1987). We need, for example, to be very careful about that word "leads." As noted earlier, the causal relationship between the depressive explanatory style and health outcomes continues to be debated. Similar controversy exists about whether positive expectations and beliefs play a causal role (Barnett & Gotlib, 1988; Segal, 1988). Whatever the outcome of this debate, no credible scientist believes that explanations and expectations are the *sole* determinants of a person's health status. Positive thinking cannot guarantee good health, and it would be a cruel mistake to blame victims of illness for a "bad attitude" (Holroy & Coyne, 1987; Krantz & Hedges, 1987).

We also need to understand precisely what measures of positive thinking are actually measuring. Recently, the role of negative affectivity—the pervasive tendency to experience distress, dissatisfaction, and a wide variety of negative emotions that was described earlier in this chapter—has been much discussed (Clark & Watson, 1991; Smith & Rhodewalt, 1991). For instance, research on hardiness (Allred & Smith, 1989; Rhodewalt & Zone, 1989) and the Life Orientation Test used to assess optimism (T. W. Smith et al., 1989b) indicates that, at least in part, these measures may assess *the absence of* negative affectivity. Such findings are troublesome for two reasons. First, they raise the possibility that there is no meaningful distinction between (the lack of) negative affectivity and various measures of positive thinking. If this is the case, then we don't need measures of perceived control, self-efficacy, hardiness, and optimism. Just one, of negative affectivity, will do.

Second, even if there is a meaningful distinction, negative affectivity is still a factor to be reckoned with. Since negative affectivity is associated with self-reports of psychological distress and physical illness, it could be the glue that bonds measures of positive thinking and reports of health status together. Researchers need to remove the glue to see if the relationship still holds. And if it does, will it last? One study suggests that the power of positive thinking may be more limited than we might expect. When Darlene Goodhart (1985) asked, "Was Pollyanna right?" she examined the separate effects of positive and negative thoughts to find the answer. Her findings demonstrated short-term benefits for positive thinking. But the absence of negative thoughts had more enduring consequences. In the long run, well-being may depend more on peaceful serenity than on euphoric happiness.

Which brings us back to Job. At the end of the Biblical account, Job recovers his health, property, and family prosperity. He does not, however, regain the sense of personal control and optimism he enjoyed prior to being struck by calamity. Instead, Job's hard-won serenity is based on his belief that life has meaning and purpose. Such beliefs may be particularly important for those who have to cope with extremely stressful experiences (Schwartzberg & Janoff-Bulman, 1991; Thompson & Janigian, 1988). Pollyanna has her charm, but Job is a hero of the human condition.

COPING

When people cope, they seek to reduce the stress produced by a threat that strains or exceeds their resources. But *how* do people cope? Although various categories of coping have been proposed, most classification schemes include three major types (Amirkhan, 1990; Endler & Parker, 1990). By means of

approach strategies
A general coping orientation in which a person confronts a threat directly and tries to reduce or eliminate it.

avoidance strategies
A general coping orientation in which a person tries to ignore or evade the potentially harmful consequences posed by a threat.

approach strategies, the individual confronts the threat directly and tries to eliminate or reduce it. By using **avoidance strategies**, the individual tries to ignore or evade the potential harmful consequences posed by the threat. The third type of coping response attempts to counter the threat by obtaining help from others. This section describes some specific examples of approach and avoidance strategies, and then considers how the support we receive from other people can affect how well we cope with stress.

Approach Strategies

We have seen that *beliefs* in personal control have a positive association with health. But what about the *actual use* of control? Is it always beneficial to confront a stressor head-on and try to control it? Perhaps surprisingly, the answer is no. There are costs to imposing control, and sometimes these costs exceed the benefits (Burger, 1989). To exert control, an individual must remain vigilant, alert, and actively engaged. Such efforts are physiologically taxing (Light & Obrist, 1980; Smith et al., 1985). Indeed, physiological arousal is greatest when control demands are highest: on difficult tasks rather than easy or impossible ones (Brehm & Self, 1989). Whenever someone is thinking hard, working fast, or trying mightily to influence other people, exerting control is effortful and arousing (T. W. Smith et al., 1989a).

And with control comes responsibility. If people aren't sure that their efforts at control will be fully successful, the responsibility of having control can be a source of emotional distress (Burger et al., 1983; Rodin et al., 1980). The first exam in a course, a new job, unfamiliar people to get to know—all of these circumstances can be highly stressful as individuals attempt to exert control without being confident of success.

Because of the costs of effort and responsibility, the benefits of exercising control will vary depending on the demands of the stressful situation and the resources of the individual (Matthews et al., 1980; Miller, 1981). Beneficial use of control involves selectivity and efficiency: selecting what can, in fact, be controlled and exercising only that level of control necessary for success (Affleck et al., 1987; Aldwin & Revenson, 1987). Indiscriminate use of maximum efforts at control runs the risk of increasing stress rather than reducing it. There are times to "mellow out" and times to "bear down." The trick is knowing when to do which.

Are there people who have failed to master this knowledge, who habitually exercise too much control? The most detailed consideration of this question has come from research on the Type A behavior pattern. Here, we examine what we know about Type A and what we are still learning.

The Type A Behavior Pattern: A Dangerous Lifestyle? In the 1950s, two cardiologists, Meyer Friedman and Ray Rosenman, began studying the relationship between cholesterol level and coronary heart disease (CHD). CHD was

The Type A behavior pattern   A pattern of behavior characterized by extremes of competitive striving for achievement, a sense of time urgency, hostility, and aggression.

then, as it is now, the leading cause of premature death in the United States. Some 45 percent of the deaths from CHD occur in individuals under sixty-five years of age (Houston, 1988). Based on their research, Friedman and Rosenman developed the concept of the **Type A behavior pattern** (Friedman & Rosenman, 1959). Individuals exhibiting this behavior pattern are characterized by extremes of competitive striving for achievement, a sense of time urgency, hostility, and aggression. Those who do not exhibit this behavior pattern are called Type B. Friedman and Rosenman classified subjects as Type A or Type B by means of a *structured interview*. During this interview, information is gathered about subjects' past experiences, and observations are made of nonverbal behaviors such as rapidity and explosiveness of speech, expressive gestures, and general restlessness. Among the over three thousand men participating in the longitudinal Western Collaborative Group Study, those initially classified as Type A developed twice the rate of CHD as those initially classified as Type B (Rosenman et al., 1975).

These dramatic results produced a dramatic response. To facilitate research on Type A, a number of self-report questionnaires were designed to measure it. The most widely used of these questionnaires is the Jenkins Activity Survey (Jenkins et al., 1979). Both the psychological and the physiological characteristics of the Type A behavior pattern were extensively studied (Feuerstein et al., 1986). Massive research generated different views of Type A, but many researchers adopted the understanding of Type A developed by David Glass.

The treadmill test is often used as part of the diagnostic workup to examine for the presence of coronary heart disease (CHD). The possible relationship between the Type A behavior pattern and CHD is a major topic of research in health psychology.

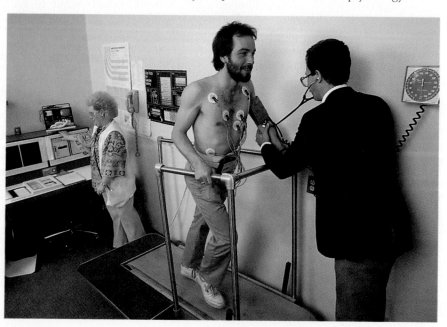

Glass (1977) proposed that the Type A behavior pattern is a coping style elicited by perceived loss of control in stressful situations. Under nonstressful, nonchallenging circumstances, Type A's and Type B's respond similarly. But when confronted with difficult, challenging situations, Type A's persist longer (Strube & Boland, 1986). They are also more physiologically aroused (Holmes et al., 1984). And they resist giving up control to others (Miller et al., 1985). Furthermore, Type A's perceive threats to their personal control more readily than do Type B's (Rhodewalt & Davison, 1983). They also challenge themselves by setting particularly difficult goals (Ward & Eisler, 1987). In short, Type A's experience stress more frequently and react to it more vigorously. The conclusion seemed quite clear: "hurry sickness" and its frequent companion "workaholism" are bad for our health.

Or are they? Recent research on Type A draws a more complicated picture. First, the use of self-report measures, such as the Jenkins Activity Survey, has been discredited. When the structured interview developed by Friedman and Rosenman was compared with the Jenkins Activity Survey, it was found that many individuals were classified differently by the two measures (Matthews et al., 1982). Unlike the structured interview, the Jenkins scale is heavily contaminated with negative affectivity (Suls & Wan, 1989) and does not correlate with physiological reactivity (Contrada, 1989). Perhaps for these reasons, the Type A pattern as defined by the Jenkins Activity Survey is a poor predictor of CHD (Booth-Kewley & Friedman, 1987).

Then concerns developed about the structured interview version of Type A. Later studies in which it was used obtained a much weaker association between the Type A pattern and CHD than had been found in earlier studies (Matthews & Haynes, 1986). Todd Miller and his colleagues (1991) think they know why. Recent studies often focus on at-risk individuals: those who smoke, have high cholesterol, or already have CHD (Matthews, 1988). Within the restricted range of health outcomes that occur in such populations, Type A has little effect. In addition, for reasons not now understood, Type A does not predict fatal heart attacks. Miller and his colleagues maintain that once these boundary conditions are established, there is a clear relationship between Type A and CHD. When Type A is assessed by the structured interview, 70 percent of middle-aged men suffering from some form of CHD are Type A, compared with only 46 percent of healthy middle-aged men. You should note that most of the middle-aged men participating in studies of Type A are white and middle class. There has been relatively little research on the association between Type A and CHD among women, people of color, and individuals from other socioeconomic classes (O'Rourke et al., 1988).

The ups and downs in the predictive fortunes of Type A have generated some new lines of inquiry about possible psychological factors contributing to CHD. One approach tries to separate the wheat from the chaff in the overall behavior pattern by isolating a single, toxic element. At present, the leading suspect identified by this approach is *hostility*. Some researchers emphasize hostile beliefs and attitudes—such as cynicism, distrust, and suspicion (Barefoot et al., 1989; Williams et al., 1980). Others highlight the overt expression of hostility and anger (Dembroski & Czajkowski, 1989). Although a relationship between hostility and CHD has been demonstrated in a number of studies, some research has failed to find evidence of such an association (Rhodewalt & Smith, 1991). Another approach is to search for more general dimensions of personality. Perhaps personality varies along an agreeable-antagonistic continuum, with those toward the extreme antagonistic end subject to repeated excessive arousal and greater risk for CHD (Costa et al., 1989). Or perhaps there is a generic "maladaptive personality" that places individuals at risk for a whole range of diseases (Friedman & Booth-Kewley, 1987).

Research on Type A has now been going on since before many of the readers of this textbook were even born. The cumulative achievement of these studies stands as the most sustained and most sophisticated effort ever undertaken to determine the relationship between psychological factors and physical illness. Yet, as we have seen, each advance raises new questions. There is good reason to continue to try to find the answers: treatments designed to modify the Type A behavior pattern have been shown to reduce the risk of CHD (Friedman et al., 1986; Gill et al., 1985). There is also good reason to view research on Type A as a cautionary tale warning us against oversimplified notions about psychol-

Is workaholism bad for your health? Yes, according to initial research on the Type A behavior pattern. But competitive striving for achievement is only one aspect of Type A. Recent research examines some possible alternative risk factors such as hostility and a broad-based "maladaptive" personality. [Drawing by Kleh; © 1991 The New Yorker Magazine, Inc.]

"I hope you don't mind. We're workaholics."

ogy and health. Enlarging our understanding of the connections between mind and body requires patient, careful research by dedicated individuals. It's not a job for the faint-hearted!

Self-Blame: Too Heavy a Price for Control?   When they hear the word *control*, most people think of active efforts to manage something: win that argument; stop that criticism; change those job requirements. But control comes in many guises. Knowledge, for instance, is a form of control. Knowing why something is happening increases the likelihood of making sure it goes your way—if not now, then the next time. But just how far will people go to find an explanation? Confronted with catastrophe, will people feel better if they believe that they are to blame for what they are suffering? One study of patients with spinal-cord injuries suggested that people might be willing to pay this heavy price for control. Those who blamed themselves for the accident that devastated their lives were better adjusted than those who did not blame themselves (Bulman & Wortman, 1977).

These startling results triggered a wave of studies on the relationship between blame and adjustment. This research indicated that one kind of blame for misfortune is often detrimental. Across a variety of negative life events, blaming *others* is usually associated with poor adjustment (Tennen & Affleck, 1990). Since blaming others is a form of giving up personal control, these findings are consistent with research we described earlier indicating the beneficial effects of perceived control.

The effects of *self*-blame, however, are highly variable: sometimes associated with better adjustment (Schulz & Decker, 1985), sometimes with poorer adjustment (Kiecolt-Glaser & Williams, 1987; Nielson & MacDonald, 1988). One approach to resolving such discrepancies relies on a distinction between types of self-blame (Janoff-Bulman, 1979):

Behavioral self-blame: People blame their behavior for producing undesirable outcomes.
Characterological self-blame: People blame their enduring personal characteristics.

These two types have different implications for control. Because behavior can be changed, behavioral self-blame is an *unstable,* internal attribution that opens the door to future control. By modifying their behavior, people might be able to reduce current stresses or avoid future ones. In contrast, enduring personal characteristics are hard to change, and characterological self-blame is a *stable,* internal attribution that does not hold out the promise of re-establishing control.

According to this analysis, behavioral self-blame should be associated with good adjustment and characterological self-blame with poor adjustment. These predictions have been tested in a number of studies examining women's adjustment after having been raped. As would be expected, characterlogical self-blame is sometimes a better predictor of psychological distress than is behavioral self-blame (Hill & Zautra, 1989). But often both types of self-blame are associated with distress (Frazier, 1990; Meyer & Taylor, 1986). Currently, there is no evidence that rape victims who blame their own behavior for their victimization cope better than those who do not.

Susan Solomon and her colleagues (1989) provide an alternative perspective. They propose that the effects of blame depend, at least in part, on the kind of negative event a person has experienced. Subjects participating in their research were rural residents of the St. Louis, Missouri, area. Some of these individuals had suffered through one or both of two natural disasters that occurred in the winter of 1982: a devastating flood and then subsequent contamination of their neighborhood by the toxic chemical dioxin. A comparison group of individuals who had not experienced either disaster was also included in the study. Among flood victims, those who blamed themselves had more psychiatric symptoms than those who did not; blaming others was not related to symptomatology. Among dioxin victims, blaming oneself had no consistent association with distress, but those who blamed others were *better* adjusted.

These results can be understood in terms of the relationship between blame and other coping strategies. Blaming oneself for a natural disaster seems too high a price to pay for an illusion of control. Flood victims who blamed themselves were more distressed and less likely to seek practical assistance from relief agencies. In contrast, the usually dysfunctional response of blaming others can be beneficial for victims of technological disasters. Such disasters are, in fact, often caused by human error. If so, blaming others is not only rational, it can also motivate successful efforts to obtain financial compensation from the responsible parties. Overall, it appears that blame contributes to effective coping to the extent that it encourages behavioral responses that meet the victim's needs.

Avoidance Strategies

You've seen it on TV. Terrorists or criminals take innocent victims hostage for political reasons or financial ransom. Police surround the airplane or building; negotiations begin. We all hold our breath, concerned about getting the hostages out alive and worried about how they are coping with their frightening situation. If you were a hostage, how would you cope? Would you adopt a problem-solving, take-charge approach and attempt to influence events? Or would you try to clear your head and manage your own anxiety so as to be better prepared for whatever lies ahead? These two reactions represent the approach strategy of *problem-focused coping* and the avoidance strategy of *emotion-focused coping* (Folkman & Lazarus, 1988). Is one more effective than the other? To help answer this question, consider an elaborate simulation examining the psychological adjustment of hostages.

In this study, fifty-seven airline employees voluntarily participated in a training exercise conducted by the Special Operations and Research Staff from the FBI Academy (Strentz & Auerbach, 1988). Some of the volunteers were

Terry Anderson, pictured here with his sister, Peggy Say, and his daughter, Sulome, greets the crowd gathered to celebrate his release from nearly seven years of captivity as a hostage in the Middle East. Research simulating the conditions of being taken hostage indicates that avoidance strategies designed to decrease anxiety are more beneficial than are efforts to exert control.

trained in problem-focused coping techniques to help each other, to interact with their captors, and to gather intelligence. Others were trained in emotion-focused coping techniques designed to decrease anxiety: deep breathing, muscle relaxation, and distraction. Volunteers in a control condition did not receive instruction in either coping technique.

After the training session, the volunteers were "abducted" by FBI agents acting as terrorists. Automatic weapons were fired (with blanks), and bloody injuries were simulated. The volunteers were "held captive" in one room and isolated by pillow cases placed over their heads. A few cooperative "hostages" were released. After four days, other FBI agents "stormed" the building and "rescued" the hostages. The exercise was conducted in a very realistic manner, and the volunteers reported that it had been an exceedingly stressful experience. Volunteers' self-reports as well as observations of their behavior revealed that subjects who had been instructed in anxiety-management techniques coped better than those given training in problem solving or no training at all. For this kind of short-term, low-control situation, emotion-focused coping was more effective in reducing psychological distress than were problem-focused efforts to exert control.

But what about stressors that endure over a longer period? Are there circumstances in which it is better to deny and avoid than to confront and control? Chronic long-term avoidance and denial may prevent a person from ever coming to terms with a stressful experience and, thereby, severely impair coping effectiveness (Lazarus, 1983; Suls & Fletcher, 1985). Still, denial and avoidance can sometimes be beneficial (Smith, 1991; Ward et al., 1988). A major trauma with long-lasting consequences—such as the death of a loved one, a life-threatening illness, job loss, or divorce—calls into question basic assumptions about personal invulnerability, the meaningfulness of life, and self-worth (Janoff-Bulman & Timko, 1987). Individuals faced with such serious threats to their understanding of themselves and the world in which they live need psychological breathing space, time to incorporate the trauma without demolishing their psychological integrity. If people are unable to avoid or deny such threats early in the coping process, they may be overwhelmed.

self-focus model of depression The hypothesis that depressive mood and cognitions are intensified and maintained by an excessive focus on the self.

Self-Focus: Brooding Versus Escape   Among those who may not deny enough are the depressed. In their **self-focus model of depression**, Tom Pyszczynski and Jeff Greenberg propose that the ability to cut one's losses and move on is an important ingredient of healthy coping (Pyszczynski & Greenberg, 1987; Pyszczynski et al., 1991). According to these researchers, experiencing an unrecoverable loss and brooding about its significance for the self produce depressed mood and a state of excessive self-focus. Self-focus then intensifies depressed feelings, lowers self-esteem, promotes self-blame, and increases pessimistic expectations—all of which work together to dig the pit of depression deeper and deeper.

The effects of self-focus on depression may contribute to a striking gender difference in stress-related disorders. Just as women greatly outnumber men in suffering from depression, so do men greatly outnumber women in suffering from alcoholism. These gender differences could reflect the different ways that women and men cope with an uncomfortable, unpleasant self-focus (Ingram et al., 1988). Stressful events for which an individual feels at least partially responsible increase self-focus. Women tend to intensify that self-focus and become depressed; men are more likely to try to escape from self-focus through alcohol. As described in Chapter 2, men who experience considerable stress and have high levels of self-awareness are especially likely to consume large amounts of alcohol (Hull et al., 1986). Longitudinal research indicates that gender differences existing as early as age seven, or perhaps even among preschoolers, are associated with later depression at age eighteen (Block et al., 1991). Depression-prone girls are self-focused and overcontrolled; depression-prone boys are aggressive and undercontrolled.

In short, excessive self-focus is a double-barreled threat to psychological health. First, it encourages brooding and ruminating about losses and problems. Not only does rumination reduce active, problem-solving coping; it also interferes with emotion-focused coping strategies such as distraction (Morrow & Nolen-Hoeksema, 1990; Wood et al., 1990). Second, even when the individual is able to break out of the grip of self-focused rumination and makes active efforts at distraction, these efforts are sometimes self-destructive (Baumeister, 1990; Baumeister & Scher, 1988). Substance abuse of all kinds (alcohol, drugs, cigarettes, and overeating), promiscuous sexual behavior, chronic aggressive behavior, self-mutilation, and suicide may all be increased by an individual's attempt to avoid a disturbing awareness of personal shortcomings. As Rick Ingram (1990) has pointed out, an enduring and inflexible self-focus appears to be involved in a wide variety of psychological problems and disorders.

Fortunately, however, constructive efforts to avoid self-focus (such as working, studying, and exercising) can produce beneficial results that increase self-esteem and improve one's mood. Furthermore, depression may sow its own seeds of recovery. In studies conducted by Brett Pelham (1991), severely depressed college students had at least one aspect of self that they evaluated reasonably favorably, even though most of their self-evaluations were quite negative. Indeed, favorable evaluations of this "best self" were *positively* correlated with degree of depression: the more depressed subjects were, the more positive were their evaluations! Pelham believes that the "best self" is a defensive reaction to depression that opens up a potential escape route. But his findings on this issue are still preliminary. Further research is needed to determine if the "best self" is a true reversal of the vicious cycle of depression or just a temporary source of relief.

Social Support: When Others Care

If the world is crashing down around you, what do you do? Do you try to hold it up by yourself? Do you try to avoid thinking about it? Or do you try to get some help from others? So far, we have described the advantages and disadvantages of approach strategies attempting to control the stressor and of avoidance strategies attempting to reduce psychological distress. Now we turn to the role of **social support**, potentially useful resources provided by others.

social support Potentially useful coping resources provided by other people.

Models of Social Support In Chapter 7 on helping, we discussed various factors that influence people's willingness to provide help to others and their reactions to receiving help. Research on social support examines how assistance from others is related to physical and mental health (Cohen & Syme, 1985; Wills, 1990). Several different models of social support have been proposed (B. R. Sarason et al., 1990).

Early studies often defined social support in terms of a person's *number of social contacts*. For example, one study of over six thousand residents of Alameda

County, California, used a measure of social support that combined (1) marital status, (2) contact with close friends and relatives, (3) church membership, and (4) formal and informal group associations (Berkman & Syme, 1979). During a nine-year follow-up of mortality rates, it was found that those with more extensive social contacts lived longer. In general, social ties are a good predictor of better health and longer life (House et al., 1988). Recent research on recovery from an initial heart attack suggests that one tie may be sufficient (Case et al., 1992). The mostly male patients in this study were less likely to experience another heart attack if they lived with someone than if they lived alone. Living with more than one person did not provide any additional health benefits.

Despite its predictive utility, however, the social contact model of social support cannot provide a full understanding of how interpersonal relationships affect health and well-being. Not all social contacts are supportive, and stressful relationships have negative effects on adjustment (Rook, 1990). Indeed, James Coyne (1991) believes that the harm created by stressful relationships outweighs the benefits received from supportive ones. From Coyne's perspective, the key to good health is *not* having bad relationships.

Even very good relationships can sometimes be a source of stress. Sharing the distress of troubled loved ones is stressful, and attempting to help them can tax our own resources (Coyne & Smith, 1991). For example, after the Three Mile Island nuclear accident, men who lived nearby showed fewer indications of stress if they had a good relationship with their wife (Solomon et al., 1987). However, women who had a good marital relationship were *more* likely to experience stress. Because of their traditional responsibilities for taking care of others, women incur higher "costs of caring" than do men (Kessler et al., 1985).

Another reason why a simple count of social contacts is not an adequate model of social support is that too many such contacts can actually reduce social support. Consider the plight of the urban poor in India, packed into overcrowded residences (up to eleven people per room) that often lack running water and indoor toilets. Just like college students living in long-corridor dorms, impoverished Indians living in overcrowded homes should experience stress from their loss of social control and cope with this stress by social withdrawal. But how would this coping strategy affect social support and health? According to Gary Evans and his colleagues (1989), social withdrawal results in a loss of social support, which in turn is associated with increased symptoms of psychological distress. Paradoxically, people with the greatest number of social contacts may end up with the least social support.

A second model of social support focuses on the *number of helpers* available to a person in need. This perspective defines social support in terms of the number of people from whom an individual has received support in the recent past (Barrera & Ainlay, 1983). Individuals with a greater number of providers should have better health. It seems reasonable. But, in fact, research has typically found that those with more providers experience *worse* health (Cohen & Hoberman, 1983). Such findings illustrate the interactive nature of social support. Social support isn't some inert substance we carry in our pocket to ensure protection against adversity. To obtain support from others, people must seek it out. Since they are more likely to seek social support when they need it, those who have more need usually have more supporters (Conn & Peterson, 1989).

A third model of social support emphasizes the quality of a person's relationships rather than their quantity. The *intimacy model* predicts that having a close, confiding relationship with a significant other will be associated with better health. And often it is. Women who have an intimate relationship with a spouse or boyfriend are less likely to become depressed than are those without such a relationship (Brown & Harris, 1978; Costello, 1982). Similarly, among gay and bisexual men infected with the human immunodeficiency virus (HIV) that causes AIDS, those with a history of close, confiding relationships have lower levels of suicidal intent (Schneider et al., 1991).

You'll notice that the intimacy model characterizes beneficial relationships as close and *confiding*. Perhaps the confiding aspect is crucial. According to James Pennebaker (1990), it's no accident that religious rituals, psychotherapy, consciousness-raising sessions, and self-help groups place a premium on "opening up." Confession, he says, is good for the body as well as the soul. But why? In his **theory of inhibition and confrontation**, Pennebaker emphasizes two reasons. First, he proposes that *not* confronting one's feelings and beliefs about

theory of inhibition and confrontation
The theory that failure to confront a traumatic event is damaging to physical health, whereas expressing one's reactions to the event is beneficial.

The intimacy model, one of several perspectives on social support, predicts that having close, confiding relationships will be associated with better health. For many people, their family ties provide this type of support and caring.

668

Chapter 14 HEALTH

a distressing event requires active inhibition, which is physiologically stressful. Second, the failure to translate the psychological consequences of a trauma into language makes it more difficult to understand the event and cope with it. Confrontation reverses these harmful effects: physiological stress is reduced and coping is facilitated. Although confrontation often involves talking with other people, the presence of others is not necessary. Pennebaker's own research typically has subjects talk into a tape recorder or write down their thoughts and feelings. Subjects who talk or write about upsetting events usually show improvement on various indicators of physical health.

As Pennebaker and his colleagues (1990) have discovered, however, confrontation is not without its drawbacks. Compared with first-semester college students who provided a written description of their day's activities, those who wrote down their "very deepest thoughts and feelings about coming to college" for twenty minutes on each of three consecutive days were less likely in subsequent months to go to the student health center for treatment of an illness. But those who confronted their thoughts and emotions about coming to college were also more homesick and more worried about college at the end of the semester. Under some circumstances at least, it appears that there is a psychological cost for the physical health benefits of confronting personal conflicts and fears.

The fourth and final model of social support that we consider defines social support in terms of its *perceived availability* (Sarason et al., 1983). Like this chapter, this approach views social support as a coping resource that can be called upon to help reduce the harmful impact of stressful events (Hobfoll & Stephens, 1990). Those individuals who have the security of believing that ample support is available to them should cope more effectively than those who doubt the adequacy of their social resources. As a coping resource, social support involves different kinds of potential assistance (Cohen & McKay, 1984; House, 1981). Supportive others can provide reassurance about our self-worth, affirmation of our involvement in a caring social network, and information about the threat we face and how we might cope with it. Social support can also include tangible assistance such as time, money, and labor. Tangible benefits help us out directly; they also demonstrate that someone cares.

As we would expect from the intimacy model, emotional support providing reassurance and affirmation appears to be the most consistently beneficial (Wills, 1991). But such warm and comforting treatment by others does not always improve an individual's health status. For example, overprotectiveness by family and friends can make it more difficult for an individual to engage in the often unpleasant behaviors (for example, dietary control, exercise, and learning to manage pain without medications) necessary for recovery (Kaplan & Toshima, 1990). Rather than regard social support as one-size-fits-all, it is more useful to think in terms of a match among the individual, the type of support needed, and the type of provider who gives it (Dakof & Taylor, 1990; Hill, 1991). Before drawing up a prescription for social support, we want to know *who* needs *what* from *whom*.

buffer effect The
effect whereby a pro-
tective factor, such as
social support, shields
a person from the
adverse effects of high
stress.

Effects of Social Support Just as there are different models of what social support is, so are there different perspectives on how it operates. Initially, affectionate assistance from others was thought to provide a buffer against stress (Cassel, 1974; Cobb, 1976). A **buffer effect** involves an interaction between stress and the protective factor of social support. Under low stress, social support is not necessary for good health and doesn't affect it. But when stress is high, high levels of social support should buffer the individual against harmful consequences. In a buffer effect, those who experience high stress *and* have little social support have the worst health.

Research by Judith Siegel (1990) illustrates that stress-buffering effects are not confined to social support from humans. In this study, over 1,000 individuals sixty-five years of age or older were asked whether they owned a pet and, if they did, what kind. The number of negative life events experienced in the previous six months was also assessed. Subjects then reported every two months over a one-year period on how many times they had contacted a physician. The results of this study, graphed in Figure 14.4, indicated that having a pet acted as a buffer against the harmful effects of negative life events. Among subjects who did not own a pet, those who had experienced many negative events reported more contacts with physicians than did those who had experienced only a few negative events. Among pet owners, however, doctor contacts were not signifi-cantly affected by the number of negative life events they had experienced. More detailed analyses revealed that dogs served to buffer the stress of their owners, but ownership of cats or birds did not. As Siegel acknowledges, we don't know whether physician contacts reflected physical illness, psychological distress, or both. It does appear, however, that the presence of one's own pet dog reduces physiological arousal under stressful conditions (Allen et al., 1991). Thanks, Fido!

Despite their prominence in theories of social support and some impressive research evidence, the stress-buffering effects of social support are controversial (Kessler et al., 1992). And, indeed, buffer effects are not always found. In the nine-year longitudinal study described at the beginning of this section, there was a *direct* relationship between social support and health (Berkman & Syme, 1979). Residents of Alameda County who had more social contacts lived longer—regardless of the level of potential stressors such as poor health, poor health practices, and limited financial resources.

Research on possible physiological correlates of social support has also found a direct relationship between social support and health. When the presence of secretory immunoglobulin A (S-IGA), a major antibody contained in bodily secretions, was measured in college students before, during, and after their final exams, those who reported more adequate social support had higher levels of S-IGA (Jemmott & Magloire, 1988). Since S-IGA defends against infection, this study connects social support with reduced susceptibility to disease. The association between social support and S-IGA was not affected by the level of stress, which was highest during the exam period. A number of other investiga-tors have also suggested that social support may have beneficial effects on the

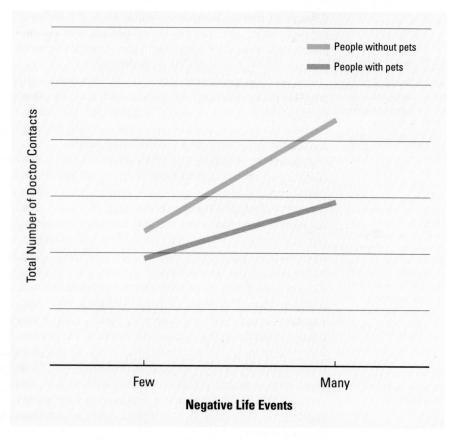

Figure 14.4   Effects of Pet Ownership on Coping with Negative Life Events: Dogs Only.   Among the elderly subjects participating in this study, those who did not own a pet reported more contacts with their physician after experiencing many negative life events than after experiencing only a few such events. Pet owners, however, did not visit their physician significantly more often when they experienced many negative life events. This buffer effect of pet ownership was found only among those who owned dogs. [Data from Siegel, 1990.]

functioning of the immune system (Baron et al., 1990; Kennedy et al., 1990; O'Leary, 1990).

What determines whether social support buffers an individual against high stress or is a health benefit regardless of the level of stress? At present, we don't really know. Some researchers maintain that it depends on the type of social support: perceived social support buffers stress, while social contacts have a direct effect on health (Cohen & Wills, 1985). Unfortunately for the sake of parsimony, exceptions to this rule abound. For example, social contacts can operate as a buffer. In one study, those premed students who typically interacted with a greater number of friends, neighbors, and members of voluntary organizations experienced less anxiety during the week before taking the Medical College Admissions Test (MCAT) than did students with fewer social contacts (Bolger & Eckenrode, 1991). Before and after that week of high stress, however, number of social contacts did not predict level of anxiety. Even more striking, the method of operation of social support can change over time. Buffer effects in a new situation can turn into direct effects as people become familiar with their social surroundings (Lepore et al., 1991).

Research by Leonard Pearlin and his colleagues (1981) on employment disruption—being fired, laid off, or downgraded—illustrates yet another type of relationship between social support and health. For these individuals, social support didn't serve as a buffer against the depressive effects of employment difficulties, nor was there a direct relationship between social support and depression. Instead, the relationship was *indirect*. High levels of social support in the face of job disruption were correlated with positive changes over time in self-esteem and feelings of mastery, which in turn were correlated with less depression.

Social support may, then, act indirectly on adjustment through its effects on feelings about the self. When others care enough to help us, we feel better about ourselves. It can also go the other way. Those who feel better about themselves will find it easier to establish supportive relationships with others (Heller, 1979). Or perhaps perceived social support and good relationships with others are both products of an optimistic, outgoing personality (Cutrona et al., 1990; I. G. Sarason et al., 1990). In any event, the rich get richer—and less depressed. The three different ways in which social support can affect health are diagrammed in Figure 14.5.

Understanding the complexities of social support is an important endeavor because so many of life's difficulties occur in a social context and so much of how we cope with stress involves other people. Even professional treatment for health problems is, to a large extent, a social event. Medical treatment is delivered by medical personnel, and psychological treatment can be considered a form of social support (Brehm, 1987; Wills, 1987). In the final section of this chapter, we examine some approaches to treatment and prevention based on theory and research in social psychology.

TREATMENT AND PREVENTION

Social psychology contributes in many different ways to the development of treatment interventions and prevention programs. Here, we focus on the role of choice in treatment effectiveness and on effective ways to inform individuals about preventive strategies.

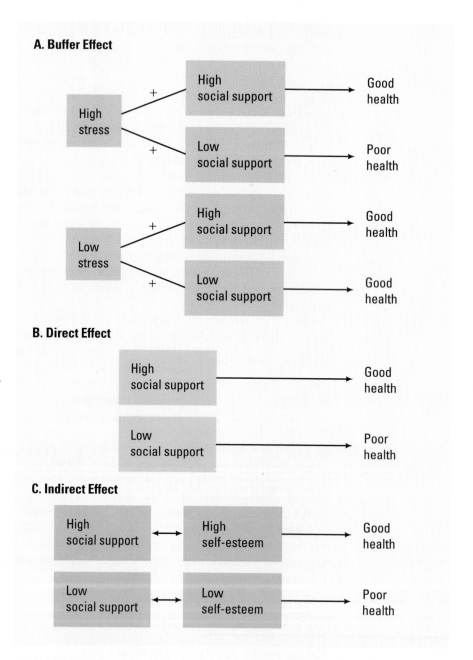

Figure 14.5 How Does Social Support Affect Health? Three Possible Paths.
Research on social support reveals three possible ways in which it can affect health. In a buffer effect, high levels of social support protect the individual from the adverse effects of high levels of stress. In a direct effect, social support promotes good health, regardless of the level of stress. In an indirect effect, social support influences health through its relationship with a person's feelings of self-worth.

Treatment: Having a Choice and Making an Effort

When you seek treatment for a psychological or physical problem, do you want to have a choice about the treatment you receive? Although the notion of patient-choice, as opposed to doctor-dictate, used to be regarded with considerable skepticism by the medical community, there is increasing evidence that choice has beneficial effects on treatment outcome. Even relatively minor choices, such as allowing a patient to decide the order in which procedures will be performed, can reduce psychological distress (Miller & Mangan, 1983). And providing more significant choices, such as deciding on the type of treatment, has been shown to increase the effectiveness of treatments for alcoholism (Miller, 1985) and of programs for weight reduction (Mendonca & Brehm, 1983).

Having some choice about the nature of a treatment one is about to receive could have a number of psychological consequences. Perceived control, for example, should be enhanced and, as we have seen, perceived control can contribute to more effective coping with stress. Choice could also increase people's feelings of self-efficacy as they are free to select the method of treatment that they believe is particularly suitable for them. It has been suggested that the stress-buffering effects of staying physically fit are produced by the increased sense of personal control and self-efficacy created by the physically fit individual's ability to maintain a self-imposed discipline (Brown, 1991).

If the people won't go to the doctor, bring the doctor to the people. Neighborhood clinics reach out to those in need of treatment and prevention programs.

Choice of an *effortful* treatment may be particularly beneficial. The individual making such a choice is confronted with the need to justify having voluntarily taken on a difficult and perhaps unpleasant activity. As described in Chapter 10, this predicament arouses cognitive dissonance. One way to reduce dissonance in this situation is to become more motivated to succeed: "Why have I chosen to do this? Because it's *very* important to me to get better." Since highly motivated individuals are careful and conscientious about carrying out treatment regimes, it's not surprising that greater motivation is usually associated with greater improvement. To examine this line of reasoning, Danny Axsom (1989) either did or did not give snake-phobic subjects an explicit choice about undertaking a treatment that was described as either requiring "*extreme* exertion" or being "so easy." Compared with subjects in the other experimental conditions, those given an explicit choice about continuing with an extremely effortful treatment reported greater motivation to change their phobic behavior and, in fact, came closer to the five-foot-long New Jersey corn snake used to measure approach behavior.

The emphasis on effortful, active coping created by providing choices is highly appropriate for treatments—such as diet and exercise regimes—that require high levels of attention and involvement from the patient. Obviously, however, total personal choice could have some serious disadvantages. Individuals who always resist the influence of others are less likely to comply with medical advice and may benefit less from some kinds of medical treatment (Burish et al., 1984; Wallston & Wallston, 1984). More generally, there are times when distraction and emotional disengagement can be more helpful than continued vigilance and feelings of personal responsibility (Langer et al., 1975; Ridgeway & Mathews, 1982). It has been found, for example, that distraction helps cancer patients undergoing chemotherapy (Carey & Burish, 1988). Similarly, distracting music reduces pain and discomfort during dental procedures (Anderson et al., 1991).

Negative effects of effortful strivings to succeed are particularly likely to occur among people coping with anxiety-based problems. Trying hard to obtain an outcome that requires a more easy-going approach, individuals suffering from insomnia or sexual difficulties (such as not having an orgasm or not getting an erection) often get caught in a vicious cycle. They try, fail, get more anxious, try harder, fail again—and so on (Tennen & Affleck, 1991). For these problems, *not* trying is often the best medicine. Earlier in this chapter, we saw that there is no magic answer about what kind of coping strategy is best. Nor is there any universally beneficial treatment approach. The art of treatment consists of weighing the alternatives and selecting what will be most helpful for the specific individual.

Prevention: Getting the Message Across

We live in what could be aptly described as the "era of prevention." Many serious threats to health are preventable (Rogers, 1983b). Just watch TV, read a newspaper, leaf through a magazine, or sit in on a health education class: there are programs for AIDS prevention, campaigns to persuade smokers to break their habit, and laws that mandate the wearing of seat belts. To a large extent, we know what to do and what not to do to promote good health and avoid trauma. The problem is convincing ourselves and others to translate that knowledge into action. Research indicates that several major factors are involved in convincing people to practice good health habits and to change bad ones (Taylor, 1990). These factors are summarized in Figure 14.6. Let's consider them one by one.

Figure 14.6 Aiming for Good Health.   Several major factors help convince people to engage in healthy practices. Recognition that a threat to health exists and a sense of personal vulnerability create the motivation to act. Healthy behaviors are also promoted by positive models and social norms. A sense of self-efficacy about being able to carry out healthy behaviors and the belief that such behaviors will be effective increase the likelihood of active efforts. Factors above the arrow can increase progress toward the goal of healthy practices; those below the arrow are roadblocks in the way.

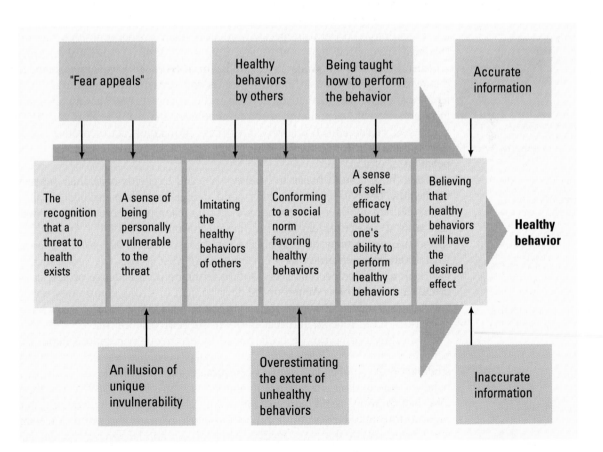

First, the person needs to believe that unhealthy practices pose a serious threat to his or her well-being. As described in Chapter 10 on attitudes, graphic displays of frightening consequences ("fear appeals") are typically used for this purpose: the gory lung-cancer operation to impress the smoker with the dangers of smoking, the bloody accident victim to persuade people to use seat belts. But fear appeals have some serious drawbacks. Instead of motivating the individual to engage in healthy behavior, they can produce helpless resignation, wishful fantasies about escape, and avoidance of thinking about the threat (Rippetoe & Rogers, 1987). Because of these possible negative effects, fear appeals are seldom used in isolation and are more effective when combined with the other factors discussed in this section.

Many health psychologists distinguish between an intellectual understanding that certain practices threaten health and a personal acceptance of that threat. Perceiving oneself to be at risk should prompt protective behavior, but those who cling to an *illusion of unique invulnerability* can engage in unhealthy practices without anxiety (Lehman & Taylor, 1987; Perloff, 1987). At first, studies on risky sexual behavior seemed to confirm the power of this dangerous illusion. Sexually active female undergraduates who saw themselves as less likely than other women to get pregnant were less likely to use effective contraception (Burger & Burns, 1988) and gay males who underestimated the risk of getting AIDS from unsafe sex were more likely to engage in high-risk sex (Bauman & Siegel, 1987).

Recently, however, both of these findings have been challenged. According to this research, perceptions of both gay males and sexually active undergraduate females are accurate rather than defensive: those who report *more* involvement in unprotected sex perceive themselves to be *more* at risk (Joseph et al., 1990; Whitley & Hern, 1991). But why don't these individuals act to protect themselves from the risk that they so accurately perceive? The answer may lie in the behavior of others.

When those around us act in healthy ways and explicitly state their support for healthy behaviors, they provide good models and help establish healthy norms. Direct modeling is useful; we are, for example, more likely to wear seat belts if we see others wearing theirs (Howell et al., 1990). And health-supportive norms may be crucial (Stasson & Fishbein, 1990). When Thomas Coates and his colleagues (1990) examined the reasons why the San Francisco gay community has been so successful in reducing the incidence of new cases of HIV infection, they pointed to the development of strong community norms encouraging safe sex. It's a lot easier to change your behavior when you know that others have done so and that they will support your efforts.

But healthy norms can be undermined by erroneous perceptions about the behaviors of others. Adolescents who smoke cigarettes as well as college students who smoke marijuana overestimate the prevalence of their own behavior among their peers (Chassin et al., 1990; Suls et al., 1988). Since these false beliefs imply social support for maintaining poor health practices, it is important to publicize accurate prevalence rates, perhaps especially to teenagers. Unfortunately, the mass media's need for sensationalism and drama may interfere with getting an accurate message across. An examination of the most popular movies from 1977 to 1988 indicates that after a decline in the mid-1980s, depictions of risky habits (such as cigarette smoking, alcohol use, and illegal drug use) began to rise toward the end of the decade (Terre et al., 1991). These shifts over time are most apparent for smoking behavior in comedy and R-rated movies. (see Figure 14.7).

Figure 14.7 Smoking in the Movies. After eliminating science fiction and fantasy films as well as those set in the distant past or future, Lisa Terre and her colleagues examined the frequency of smoking behaviors in the remaining most popular movies from 1977 to 1988. As you can see from the trends in comedy and R-rated movies, such portrayals declined in the mid-1980s, but were on the rise again by the end of the decade. Since the mass media can affect people's view of reality, the frequent depiction of risky health practices may create the impression that these practices are more common than, in fact, they are. [Adapted from Terre et al., 1991.]

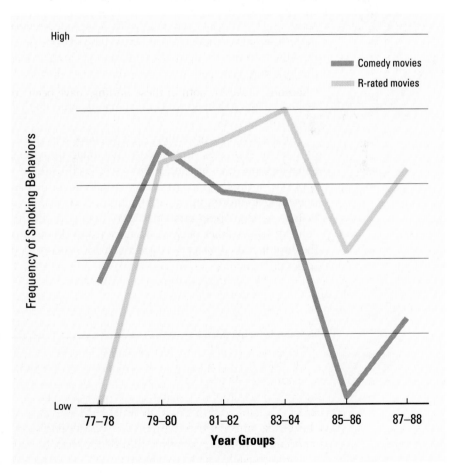

A sense of self-efficacy and self-confidence about performing healthy behaviors also plays an essential role in prevention. Self-efficacy beliefs appear to have wide utility in both the adoption and maintenance of various healthy behaviors, including nonsmoking and abstinence from alcohol (Maddux, 1991). And fear appeals work best when combined with information reassuring people that they can, in fact, perform the desired health practice (Rogers, 1983a). If people do not know how to perform the necessary behaviors, they should be taught. Smoking-prevention programs often teach young children specific techniques for resisting peer pressures and refusing the offer of a cigarette (Baum, 1984; Evans et al., 1984).

Finally, people need good, solid, accurate information about the effectiveness of the healthy behaviors they are being urged to adopt (Weinstein, 1989). When people believe that something works, they are more likely to develop positive attitudes about it and try it out. Indeed, they can sometimes be too easily convinced. After listening to a fear-arousing radio broadcast, subjects who had been reassured that a proposed prevention program was highly likely to be successful were quite positive in their evaluation of the program, regardless of the quality of the arguments that supported its probable success (Gleicher & Petty, 1992). Subjects provided with a less clear expectation of success were more discerning; they based their evaluations on the quality of the arguments presented. In the short run, fearful people can be tricked by false promises. In the long run, however, overselling the virtues of some health practices (such as eating oat bran) or underplaying the potentially harmful side-effects of others (such as jogging) can create confusion and cynicism that interfere with adopting effective behaviors.

The approach to prevention that we have described in this chapter consists of a set of strategies designed to encourage individuals to engage in healthy behaviors and give up unhealthy ones. Each of these strategies emphasizes at least one of the three major factors usually identified as essential ingredients in preventative efforts: information, motivation, and behavioral skills (Fisher & Fisher, 1992). These strategies also highlight the importance of the social context. Just as other people influence us, so do our attitudes and actions affect the health-related behaviors practiced by others. Prevention is very much a social phenomenon.

REVIEW

STRESS AND COPING: AN OVERVIEW

Stress is an unpleasant state that arises when people perceive the demands of an event as taxing or exceeding their ability to satisfy or alter those demands. The appraisal of demands and of resources to meet them determines whether stress will be experienced and affects how the person copes. The effectiveness of coping responses influences health.

STRESSFUL EVENTS

Life Events: Change Versus Negativity

Early research on life events maintained that change itself affected health outcomes. More recent research indicates that positive and negative life events have different effects on health. Individuals high in negative affectivity report both more stressful life events and more symptoms. When this tendency is taken into account, the effect of negative life events on health is small.

Major Crises: Catastrophe and War

Environmental catastrophes increase psychological distress. Both personal and situational factors affected the stress created by a severe earthquake. Individuals suffering from posttraumatic stress disorder experience enduring psychological and physical problems, even long after the event itself is over. Soldiers who experience heavy combat are more likely to suffer posttraumatic stress disorder, but they may also become more resilient and less helpless than those who have not come through such an ordeal.

Microstressors: The Hassles of Everyday Life

Everyday hassles and social pressures can contribute to the experience of stress. Sharing living space, for example, decreases control over social events and is stressful. In general, having multiple social roles is associated with increased well-being. The quality of social roles, however, is an important factor.

APPRAISAL

Explanations: Learned Helplessness and Depression

According to the original learned helplessness model of depression, experiencing an uncontrollable event creates depressive symptoms. In contrast, the reformulated model highlights the role of attributions. The depressive explanatory style is a habitual tendency to make stable, global, and internal attributions for uncontrollable events. Research has obtained mixed results on whether the depressive explanatory style can be a cause of depression.

Expectations: Agency and Outcome

Hopelessness theory, a third-generation model of learned helplessness, emphasizes two kinds of expectations that have been widely researched: agency expectations about personal control over future events and outcome expectations about the quality of future events. Perceived control, manipulated in experiments, has positive effects on coping with stress. When measured as an individual difference variable, perceived control is associated with better health, as is hardiness, which combines perceived control with other components. People who are high in self-efficacy believe that they are capable of the specific behavior required to produce the desired outcome in the specific situation. A sense of self-efficacy is associated with better health and, according to recent research, improved immune functioning. Optimism, the anticipation of positive future events, is an outcome expectation associated with better adjustment to psychologically and physically stressful events. Research on hope indicates that expecting positive outcomes may be especially beneficial in the early stages of coping, while self-efficacy beliefs may be especially beneficial for long-term coping.

Was Pollyanna Right?

A positive bias is associated with good health, but the causal relationship is unclear. Positive thinking cannot guarantee good health, and victims of illness should not be blamed for having a "bad attitude." Moreover, negative affectivity may play an important role in the relationship between positive thinking and health. When positive and negative thoughts are considered separately, the absence of negative thoughts may have the greatest long-term benefits. Have a sense of meaning and purpose can be crucial in coping with extremely stressful experiences.

COPING

By means of approach strategies, the individual confronts the threat directly and tries to eliminate or reduce it. By using avoidance strategies, the individual tries to ignore or evade the potential harmful consequences posed by the threat. Social support from others also helps the individual cope.

Approach Strategies

There are costs to exerting control: increased physiological arousal and increased responsibility under circumstances where success is not certain. Because of these costs, attempts to exert control can increase stress rather than reduce it. Early research on the Type A behavior pattern viewed it as a strong predictor of coronary heart disease. Type A individuals were found to experience stress more frequently and to react to it more vigorously than Type B individuals. Later research revealed problems in the measurement of the Type A pattern, limits to the populations in which it predicts CHD, and no association with fatal heart attacks. Alternatives to Type A include focusing on more narrow predictors of CHD (such as hostile attitudes or behavior) or on broader ones (such as antagonistic or maladaptive personalities). Although blaming oneself for misfortune can be regarded as an effort to maintain control, there is only scattered evidence that self-blame is associated with better adjustment. Blaming others for misfortunes is usually associated with poorer coping, but is correlated with a good adjustment for victims of technological disasters. In general, blame should be beneficial to the extent that it fosters behavior that meets the needs of the individual.

Avoidance Strategies

Although chronic denial and avoidance can be harmful, a person's health can sometimes benefit from avoidance tactics such as concentrating on feeling better, distracting one's attention, and initially denying the full implications of a traumatic event. The self-focus model of depression proposes that people who brood and ruminate about significant losses are at risk for depression. In general, women are more inclined to remain self-focused and become depressed; men are more likely to try to avoid self-focus, sometimes in self-destructive ways. It has been suggested that severe depression can motivate people to develop a positive evaluation of at least one aspect of self, which can open up a possible escape route from depression.

Social Support: When Others Care

Various models of social support have been proposed: the number of social contacts a person has; the number of helpers assisting a person in need; the presence of a close, confiding relationship; and the perceived availability of social support as a coping resource. Although confronting a trauma by talking or writing about it appears to improve physical health, this process may also increase psychological distress. Social support can affect health by a number of different paths. In a buffer effect, social support has no effect under unstressful conditions but enhances well-being in stressful circumstances. In a direct effect, social support enhances well-being regardless of the level of stress experienced. In an indirect effect, social support enhances well-being through its relationship with self-esteem.

TREATMENT AND PREVENTION

Treatment: Having a Choice and Making an Effort

Giving patients some choice about the treatment they will receive can enhance treatment effectiveness. Having choice should increase perceived control and self-efficacy. When an especially effortful treatment is voluntarily chosen, dissonance is aroused. When people reduce dissonance by increasing their motivation to succeed, treatment effectiveness is enhanced. Under some circumstances, distraction and emotional disengagement are more beneficial than high levels of attention and personal involvement.

Prevention: Getting the Message Across

A number of factors help convince people to practice good health habits. When combined with information reassuring people that they can perform the desired health practice, "fear appeals" can increase a person's motivation. If people do not know how to perform the desired behavior, they should be taught. Research on the relationship between perceived personal risk and health practices has obtained mixed findings. At least some individuals perceive their risk accurately yet continue to engage in unsafe behavior. Such individuals may need the support of others, who can model healthy behaviors directly and also establish a social norm. Providing the public with accurate knowledge about the effectiveness of preventive strategies is essential.

Glossary

Action identification theory The theory that our *interpretation* of our own behavior in high-level or low-level terms forms the basis for self-perception. (2)

Actor-observer effect The tendency to attribute our own behavior to situational causes and behavior of others to personal factors. (3)

Adversarial model A dispute-resolution system in which the prosecution and defense oppose each other, as each presents one side of the story. (12)

Aggression Behavior intended to injure another person. (8)

Altruistic Motivated by the desire to increase another's welfare. (7)

Altruistic personality A trait or combination of traits said to produce helping across a wide variety of situations, even where there are no external rewards for helping. (7)

Angry aggression Impulsive, emotional behavior intended solely to injure another person. (8)

Applied research Research whose goal is to increase the understanding of naturally occurring events or to find solutions to practical problems. (1)

Appraisal Judgments about the demands made by a potentially stressful event and about one's ability to meet those demands. (14)

Approach strategies A general coping orientation in which a person confronts a threat directly and tries to reduce or eliminate it. (14)

Arousal-affect model The proposal that aggression is influenced by the intensity of arousal and by the type of emotion produced by a stimulus. (8)

Arousal: cost-reward model The proposition that people react to emergency situations by acting in the most cost-effective way to reduce the arousal of shock and alarm. (7)

Attachment style The way a person typically interacts with significant others. (6)

Attitude A positive or negative reaction to a person, object, or idea. (10)

Attribute ambiguity Circumstances in which the causes of behavior are unclear. (5)

Attribution theory A generic term for a group of theories that describe how people explain the causes of behavior. (3)

Audience inhibition A person's reluctance to help for fear of making a bad impression on observers. (7)

Authoritarian personality A personality trait characterized by rigid authority, submissiveness to authority, and prejudice toward others who are different. (4)

Avoidance strategies A general coping orientation in which a person tries to ignore or evade the potentially harmful consequences posed by a threat. (14)

Balance theory The theory that people desire consistency in their thoughts, feelings, and social relationships. (5)

Base-rate fallacy The finding that people are relatively insensitive to consensus information presented in the form of numerical base rates. (3)

Basic research Research whose goal is to increase the understanding of human behavior, often by testing hypotheses based on a theory. (1)

Basking in reflected glory (BIRGing) Increasing self-esteem by associating with others who are successful. (2)

Belief in a just world The belief that individuals get what they deserve in life; used to explain why people disparage victims. (3)

Belief perseverance The tendency to maintain beliefs even after they have been discredited. (3)

Brainstorming A technique that attempts to increase creative ideas by encouraging group members to speak freely without criticizing their own or others' contributions. (11)

Buffer effect The effect whereby a protective factor, such as social support, shields a person from the adverse effects of high stress. (14)

Bystander effect The effect whereby the presence of others inhibits helping. (7)

Catharsis The reduction of the motive to aggress that is said to result from engaging in or witnessing any aggressive act. (8)

Central route to persuasion The process in which a person learns and thinks carefully about a communication and is influenced by the strength of its arguments. (10)

Central traits   Traits that exert a powerful influence on overall impressions, causing us to assume the presence of other traits as well. (3)

Cognitive dissonance   An unpleasant psychological state often aroused when a person holds two conflicting cognitions. (10)

Cognitive heuristics   Information-processing short cuts that enable us to make judgments that are quick but often in error. (3)

Cognitive-neoassociation analysis   The view that unpleasant experiences create negative affect, which in turn stimulates associations connected with anger and fear. Emotional and behavioral outcomes then depend, at least in part, on higher-order cognitive processing. (8)

Collectives   People engaged in common activities but with minimal direct interaction. (11)

Communal relationships   Relationships in which the participants expect and desire mutual responsiveness to each other's needs. (6)

Companionate love   A secure, trusting attachment. (6)

Comparison level (CL)   The average, general outcome an individual expects in a relationship. (6)

Comparison level for alternatives (CLalt)   The average, general outcome an individual expects from alternative relationships or lifestyles. (6)

Compliance   Changes in behavior that are elicited by direct requests. (9)

Confirmation bias   The tendency to seek, interpret, and create information that verifies existing beliefs. (3)

Conformity   The tendency to change perceptions, opinions, or behavior in ways that are consistent with group norms. (9)

Consumer psychology   The study of decision making and behavior in the marketplace. (13)

Contact hypothesis   The theory that direct contact between hostile groups will reduce prejudice under certain conditions. (4)

Contingency model of leadership   The theory that leadership effectiveness is determined both by the personal characteristics of leaders and by the control afforded by the situation. (13)

Contrast effect   The tendency to perceive stimuli that differ from expectations as being even more different than they really are. (4)

Coping   Efforts to reduce stress. (14)

Correlation   An association between two variables. A correlation is positive when both variables increase or decrease together. It is negative when as one variable increases the other decreases. (1)

Correspondent inference theory   The theory that we make inferences about someone whose actions are freely chosen and unexpected and result in a small number of desirable effects. (3)

Covariation principle   A principle of attribution theory that people attribute behavior to factors that are present when a behavior occurs and absent when it does not. (3)

Cross-race identification bias   The tendency for people to be better at identifying members of their own race than members of other races. (12)

Cultivation   The process by which the mass media (particularly television) construct a version of social reality for the viewing public. (8)

Cycle of family violence   The transmission of aggressive behavior across generations. (8)

Death qualification   A jury selection procedure used in capital cases that permits judges to exclude prospective jurors who say they would refuse to vote for the death penalty. (12)

Debriefing   A disclosure, made to subjects after research procedures are completed, in which the researcher explains the purpose of the research, attempts to resolve any negative feelings, and emphasizes the scientific contribution made by subjects' participation. (1)

Deception   Research methods that provide false information to subjects. (1)

Deindividuation   The loss of a person's sense of individuality and a loosening of normal constraints against deviant behavior. (11)

Dependent variables   The factors measured in an experiment to see if they are affected by the independent variable. (1)

Depressive explanatory style   A habitual tendency to attribute negative events to causes that are stable, global, and internal. (14)

Diffusion of responsibility   The belief that others will or should take the responsibility for providing assistance to a person in need. (7)

Discrimination   Any behavior directed against persons because of their identification with a particular group. (4)

Displacement   Aggressing against a substitute target because aggressive acts against the source of the frustration are inhibited by fear or lack of access. (8)

Distraction-conflict theory   The theory that the presence of others will produce social facilitation effects only when those others distract from the task and create attentional conflict. (11)

Door-in-the-face technique   A two-step compliance technique in which an influencer prefaces the real request with a request so large that it is rejected. (9)

Downward social comparison   Defensive tendency to compare ourselves to others who are worse off than we are. (2)

Egocentric bias   Bias toward perceiving and recalling oneself as a central actor in past events. (2)

Egoistic   Motivated by the desire to increase one's own welfare. (7)

Elaboration   The process of thinking about and scrutinizing the arguments contained in a persuasive communication. (10)

Empathy-altruism hypothesis   The proposition that empathic concern for a person in need produces an altruistic motive for helping. (7)

Entrapment   The condition in which commitments to a failing course of action are increased to justify investments already made. (11)

Equity theory   The theory that people are most satisfied with a relationship when the ratio between benefits and contributions is similar for both partners. (6)

Evaluation apprehension   The theory that the presence of others will produce social facilitation effects only when those others are seen as potential evaluators. (11)

Exchange relationships   Relationships in which the participants expect and desire strict reciprocity in their interactions. (6)

Excitation transfer   The process whereby arousal caused by one stimulus is added to arousal from a second stimulus and the combined arousal is attributed to the second stimulus. (6)

Experiment   A form of research that can examine cause-and-effect relationships because (1) the experimenter has control over the events that occur and (2) subjects are randomly assigned to conditions. (1)

Experimental realism   The degree to which experimental procedures are involving to subjects and lead them to behave naturally and spontaneously. (1)

Experimenter expectancy effects   The effects produced when an experimenter's expectations about the results of an experiment affect his or her behavior toward a subject and thereby influence the subject's responses. (1)

External validity   The degree to which one can be reasonably confident that the same results would be obtained for other people and in other situations. (1)

Facial feedback hypothesis   The hypothesis that changes in facial expression can lead to corresponding changes in emotion. (2)

False-consensus effect   The tendency to overestimate the consensus for our own opinions, attributes, and behavior. (3)

Foot-in-the-door technique   A two-step compliance technique in which an influencer prefaces the real request by first getting a person to comply with a much smaller request. (9)

Frustration-aggression hypothesis   The dual proposition that frustration always elicits the motive to aggress and that all aggression is caused by frustration. (8)

Fundamental attribution error   The tendency to underestimate the impact of situations on other people's behavior and to focus on the role of personal causes. (3)

Gambler's fallacy   The false belief that random processes are self-correcting. (13)

Gender-role orientation   The extent to which people report having characteristics ordinarily associated with males and females. (4)

Good mood effect   The effect whereby a good mood increases helping behavior. (7)

Graduated and reciprocated initiatives in tension-reduction (GRIT)   A strategy for unilateral, persistent efforts to establish trust and cooperation between opposing parties. (11)

Group   Two or more persons perceived as related because of their direct interactions, membership in the same social category, or common fate. (4)

Group polarization   The exaggeration through group discussion of initial tendencies in the thinking of group members. (11)

Groupthink   A group decision-making style characterized by an excessive tendency among group members to seek concurrence. (11)

Habituation   Adaptation to something familiar, so that both physiological and psychological responses are reduced. (8)

Hard-to-get effect　The tendency to prefer people who are highly selective in their social choices over those who are more readily available. (5)

Hawthorne effect　The finding that workers who were observed increased their productivity regardless of what actual changes were made in the work setting. (13)

Health psychology　The study of physical health and illness by psychologists from various areas of specialization. (14)

Heuristic　A rule of thumb used to evaluate a message superficially, without careful thinking about its content. (10)

Hindsight bias　The tendency, once an event has occurred, to overestimate one's ability to have foreseen the outcome. (2)

Hypothesis　A testable prediction about the conditions under which an event will occur. (1)

Idiosyncrasy credits　Interpersonal "credits" that a person earns by following group norms. (9)

Illusion of control　The perception that chance events are more controllable than they really are. (13)

Illusory correlations　Overestimates of the association between variables that are only slightly correlated or not correlated at all. (4)

Implicit personality theory　A network of assumptions people make about the relationships among traits and behaviors. (3)

Impression formation　The process of integrating information about a person to form a coherent impression. (3)

Incompatible responses　Responses that are mutually exclusive, so that experiencing one precludes experiencing the other. (8)

Independent variables　The factors manipulated in an experiment to see if they affect the dependent variable. (1)

Industrial/organizational (I/O) psychology　The study of human behavior in business and other organizational settings. (13)

Informational influence　Influence that produces conformity because a person believes others are correct in their judgments. (9)

Information integration theory　The theory that impressions are based on (1) perceiver dispositions and (2) a weighted average of a target person's traits. (3)

Informed consent　An individual's deliberate, voluntary decision to participate in research, based on the researcher's description of what will be required during such participation. (1)

Ingroup favoritism　The tendency to discriminate in favor of ingroups over outgroups. (4)

Inoculation hypothesis　The idea that exposure to weak versions of a persuasive argument tends to increase later resistance to that argument. (10)

Inquisitorial model　A dispute-resolution system in which a neutral investigator gathers evidence from both sides and then presents the findings in court. (12)

Instrumental aggression　Behavior intended to injure another person in order to obtain something of value. (8)

Insufficient deterrence　A condition in which people refrain from engaging in a desirable activity, even though only mild punishment is threatened. (10)

Insufficient justification　A condition in which people freely perform an attitude-discrepant behavior without receiving a large reward. (10)

Integrative agreement　A negotiated resolution to a conflict in which all parties obtain outcomes that are superior to what they would have obtained from an equal division of the contested resources. (11)

Interactionist perspective　An emphasis on the combined effects of both the person and the situation on human behavior; serves as common ground for personality and social psychologists. (1)

Intergroup public goods paradigm (IPG)　A research paradigm used to study both intragroup and intergroup behavior. Within each group, members decide whether to contribute to the group's efforts, but all group members share the outcome obtained during interactions with another group. (11)

Internal validity　The degree to which there can be reasonable certainty that the independent variable in an experiment caused the effects obtained on the dependent variable. (1)

Interpersonal attraction　A person's desire to approach another person. (5)

Interpersonal repulsion　A person's desire to avoid another person. (5)

Interrater reliability　The degree to which different observers agree on their observations. (1)

Intimate relationships　Close relationships between two adults involving at least one of the following: emotional attachment, fulfillment of psychological needs, and interdependence. (6)

Investment　Resources put into a relationship that cannot be retrieved if that relationship ends. (6)

Jealousy   The reaction to a perceived threat to an existing relationship. (6)

Jigsaw classroom   A cooperative learning method used to reduce racial prejudice through interaction in group efforts. (4)

Jury nullification   The jury's power to disregard, or "nullify," the law when it conflicts with their personal conceptions of justice. (12)

Kinship selection   Preferential helping of blood relatives, which increases the odds that genes held in common will be transmitted to subsequent generations. (7)

Learned helplessness   Used by various theories to explain the development of depression, the phenomenon in which experience with an uncontrollable event creates passive behavior toward a subsequent threat to well-being. (14)

Leniency bias   The tendency for jury deliberation to produce a tilt toward acquittal. (12)

Loneliness   A feeling of deprivation produced by dissatisfaction with existing social relations. (5)

Longitudinal research   Studying the same subjects over a period of time so that changes in behavior can be observed. (8)

Low-balling   A two-step compliance technique in which the influencer secures agreement with a request but then increases the size of that request by revealing hidden costs. (9)

Matching hypothesis   The proposition that people are attracted to and form relationships with those who are similar to them in particular characteristics, such as physical attractiveness. (5)

Mere exposure   The phenomenon in which the more often people are exposed to a stimulus, the more positively they evaluate that stimulus. (5)

Mere presence   The theory that the mere presence of others is sufficient to produce social facilitation effects. (11)

Misattribution   An inaccurate explanation that shifts the cause for arousal from the true source to another one. (5)

Mitigating information   Information about a person's situation indicating that he or she should not be held personally responsible for aggressive actions. (8)

Modern racism   A form of prejudice that surfaces in subtle ways when it is safe, socially acceptable, and easy to rationalize. (4)

Mundane realism   The degree to which the experimental situation resembles places and events that exist in the real world. (1)

Need for cognition (NC)   A personality variable that distinguishes people on the basis of how much they enjoy effortful cognitive activities. (10)

Negative affectivity   A pervasive tendency to experience distress, dissatisfaction, and a wide variety of negative emotions. (14)

Negative affect reciprocity   The quid-pro-quo exchange of behaviors, often nonverbal in nature, expressing negative feelings. (6)

Negative affect escape model   The view that increasing levels of negative affect increase aggression up to a point, beyond which the person tries to escape, becomes passive, or collapses. (8)

Negative state relief model   The proposition that people help others in order to counteract their own feelings of sadness or depression. (7)

Nonverbal behavior   Behavior that communicates a person's feelings without words—through facial expressions, body language, and vocal cues. (3)

Normative influence   Influence that produces conformity because a person fears the negative social consequences of appearing deviant. (9)

Norm of justice   A moral standard requiring people to help those who they believe deserve assistance. (7)

Norm of social responsibility   A moral standard emphasizing people's obligation and duty to help those in need. (7)

Obedience   Behavior change produced by the commands of authority. (9)

Outgroup homogeneity bias   The tendency to assume that there is greater similarity among members of outgroups than of ingroups. (4)

Overjustification   The tendency for intrinsic motivation to diminish for activities that have become associated with reward or other extrinsic factors. (2)

Passionate love   Romantic love characterized by high arousal, intense attraction, and fear of rejection. (6)

Peremptory challenges   The means by which lawyers can exclude a limited number of prospective jurors without the judge's approval. (12)

Performance appraisal   The process of evaluating an employee's work within the organization. (13)

Peripheral route to persuasion   The process in which a person does not think carefully about a communication and is influenced instead by cues that are peripheral to the message. (10)

Personal attribution   Attribution to *internal* characteristics of an actor, such as ability, personality, mood, or effort. (3)

Personal norms   An individual's feelings of moral obligation to provide help to specific others in specific situations. (7)

Personal space   The physical distance people like to maintain between themselves and others. (5)

Persuasion   The process of changing attitudes. (10)

Persuasive arguments theory   The theory that group polarization is produced by the number and persuasiveness of the arguments presented in group discussion. (11)

Pluralistic ignorance   The phenomenon in which each person in a group assumes that the reason for his or her own behavior is different from the reason other group members are acting in the same way. (7)

Polygraph   A mechanical instrument that records physiological arousal from multiple channels; often used as a lie-detector test. (12)

Pornography   Explicit sexual materials. (8)

Posttraumatic stress disorder   The experience of enduring physical and psychological problems after an extremely stressful event. (14)

Prejudice   Negative feelings toward persons based solely on their membership in certain groups. (4)

Primacy effect   The finding that information presented early in a sequence has more impact on impressions than information presented later. (3)

Priming   The tendency for recently used words or ideas to come to mind easily and influence the interpretation of new information. (3)

Prisoner's dilemma game (PDG)   A research paradigm that creates mixed motives; participants are encouraged to cooperate by moderate rewards, but are tempted to compete by larger rewards. (11)

Private conformity   The change of beliefs that occurs when a person privately accepts the position taken by others. (9)

Private self-consciousness   A personality characteristic of individuals who are introspective, often attending to their own inner states. (2)

Psychographic profiles   Correlations between consumer characteristics and purchasing behavior; used to segment consumers for marketing purposes. (13)

Psychological reactance   The theory that people react against threats to specific behavioral freedoms by perceiving a threatened freedom as more attractive and trying to re-establish it. (5)

Public conformity   A superficial change in overt behavior, without a corresponding change of opinion, produced by real or imagined group pressure. (9)

Public self-consciousness   A personality characteristic of individuals who focus on themselves as social objects, as seen by others. (2)

Racism   Discrimination based on a person's skin color or ethnic heritage. (4)

Rape shield laws   Statutes that restrict the kinds of personal questions lawyers can ask rape victims who take the witness stand. (12)

Realistic conflict theory   The theory that hostility between groups is caused by direct competition for limited resources. (4)

Reciprocity   A quid-pro-quo mutual exchange—for example, liking those who like us. (5)

Reconstructive memory   The theoretical concept that eyewitness memory can be altered by exposure to postevent information. (12)

Reinforcement-affect model   The theory that positive feelings in someone's presence increase attraction to that person, while negative feelings decrease attraction. (5)

Relative deprivation   Feelings of discontent aroused by the belief that one fares poorly compared to others. (4)

Scientific jury selection   A method of selecting juries through surveys that yield correlations between demographics and trial-relevant attitudes. (12)

Script   A preconception about a sequence of events likely to occur in a particular kind of situation. (3)

Self-awareness theory   The theory that self-focused attention leads people to notice self-discrepancies, thereby motivating either an escape from self-awareness or a change in behavior. (2)

Self-concept   The sum total of an individual's beliefs about his or her own personal attributes. (2)

Self-disclosure   Revelations about the self that a person makes to other people. (6)

Self-discrepancy theory   The theory linking the perception of discrepancies between a person's self-concept and various self-guides to specific, negative emotional states. (2)

Self-efficacy   A person's belief that he or she is capable of the specific behavior required to produce a desired outcome in a given situation. (14)

Self-esteem An affective component of the self, consisting of a person's positive and negative self-evaluations. (2)

Self-evaluation maintenance A theory predicting the conditions under which people react to the success of significant others with either pride or jealousy. (2)

Self-focus model of depression The hypothesis that depressive mood and cognitions are intensified and maintained by an excessive focus on the self. (14)

Self-fulfilling prophecy The process by which a perceiver's expectations about a person eventually lead that person to behave in ways that confirm those expectations. (3)

Self-handicapping Behaviors designed to sabotage one's own performance in order to provide a subsequent excuse for failure. (2)

Self-monitoring The tendency to change behavior in response to the self-presentation concerns of the situation. (2)

Self-perception theory The theory that when internal cues are difficult to interpret, people gain self-insight by observing their own behavior. (2)

Self-persuasion The processes by which people change their attitudes in response to their own actions. (10)

Self-presentation Strategies people use to shape what others think of them. (2)

Self-reference effect The finding that information is recalled better when it is relevant to the self than when it is not. (2)

Self-schemas Beliefs people hold about themselves that guide the processing of self-relevant information. (2)

Sexism Discrimination based on a person's gender. (4)

Sex ratio The number of men per 100 women in a given population. When men outnumber women, the sex ratio is high. When women outnumber men, the sex ratio is low. (6)

Situational attribution Attribution to factors *external* to an actor, such as the task, other people, or luck. (3)

Sleeper effect A delayed increase in the persuasive impact of a noncredible source. (10)

Social anxiety A feeling of discomfort in the presence of others, often accompanied by the social awkwardness and inhibition characteristic of shyness. (5)

Social categorization The classification of persons into groups on the basis of common attributes. (4)

Social-clinical interface The study of social psychological factors involved in psychological health and disturbance. (14)

Social cognition The study of how people perceive, remember, and interpret information about themselves and others. (1)

Social comparison theory The theory that people evaluate their own abilities and opinions by comparing themselves to others. (2)

Social dilemma A situation in which the most rewarding choice for an individual will, if taken by all individuals, produce the most harmful outcome for everyone. (11)

Social exchange A perspective that views people as motivated to maximize benefits and minimize costs in their relationships with others. (6)

Social facilitation The finding that the presence of others enhances performance on easy tasks and impairs performance on difficult tasks. (11)

Social identity theory The theory that people favor ingroups over outgroups in order to enhance their self-esteem. (4)

Social impact theory The theory that social influence depends on the strength, immediacy, and number of source persons relative to target persons. (9)

Social learning theory The view that behavior is learned through the observation of others as well as through the direct experience of rewards and punishments. (8)

Social loafing A group-produced reduction in individual output on easy tasks where contributions are pooled. (11)

Social norms General rules of conduct reflecting standards of social approval and disapproval. (7)

Social perception A general term for the processes by which people come to understand one another. (3)

Social power The ability to influence others and to resist their influence on us. (6)

Social psychology The scientific study of the way individuals think, feel, and behave in social situations. (1)

Social roles theory The theory that small gender differences are magnified in perception by the contrasting social roles occupied by men and women. (4)

Social support Potentially useful coping resources provided by other people. (14)

Sociobiology The application of the principles of evolutionary biology to the understanding of social behavior. (5)

Stage theories Theories reflecting the view that relationships develop through a specific set of stages in a specific order. (6)

Stereotypes Beliefs that associate groups of people with certain traits. (4)

Stress An unpleasant state in which people perceive the demands of an event as taxing or exceeding their ability to satisfy or alter those demands. (14)

Structured interviews Interviews in which each job applicant is asked a standard set of questions and evaluated on the same criteria. (13)

Subliminal advertising The presentation of commercial messages outside of conscious awareness. (13)

Superordinate goals Shared goals that can be achieved only through cooperation among individuals or groups. (4)

Superordinate identity The perception that members of different groups belong to a larger whole that encompasses both groups. (11)

That's-not-all technique A two-step compliance technique in which the influencer begins with an inflated request, then decreases the apparent size of that request by offering a discount or bonus. (9)

Theory An organized set of principles used to explain observed phenomena. (1)

Theory of inhibition and confrontation The theory that failure to confront a traumatic event is damaging to physical health, whereas expressing one's reactions to the event is beneficial. (14)

Theory of planned behavior The theory that attitudes toward a specific behavior combine with subjective norms and perceived control to influence a person's action. (10)

Theory of social penetration A theory about the development of close relationships that emphasizes the gradual increase in the breadth and depth of exchanges between partners. (6)

Threat-to-self-esteem model The theory that reactions to receiving assistance depend on whether help is perceived as supportive or threatening. (7)

Transformational leaders Leaders who inspire followers to transcend their own needs in the interest of a common cause. (13)

Triangular theory of love The theory that the basic components of love are intimacy, passion, and decision/commitment. (6)

Two-factor theory of emotion The theory that the experience of emotion is based on two factors: physiological arousal and a cognitive interpretation of that arousal. (2)

The Type A behavior pattern A pattern of behavior characterized by extremes of competitive striving for achievement, a sense of time urgency, hostility, and aggression. (14)

Voir dire The pretrial examination of prospective jurors by the judge or opposing lawyers to uncover signs of bias. (12)

Weapon-focus effect The tendency for weapons to draw attention and impair a witness's ability to identify the culprit. (12)

Weapons effect The tendency of weapons to increase the likelihood of aggression by their mere presence. (8)

What-is-beautiful-is-good stereotype The belief that physically attractive individuals also possess desirable personality characteristics. (5)

Yerkes-Dodson law The finding that there is a curvilinear relation between arousal and performance on complex tasks. (12)

References

Abeles, R. P. (1976). Relative deprivation, rising expectations and black militancy. *Journal of Social Issues, 32,* 119–137.

Abelson, R. P. (1981). Psychological status of the script concept. *American Psychologist, 36,* 715–729.

Abelson, R. P., Aronson, E., McGuire, W. J., Newcomb, T. M., Rosenberg, M. J., & Tannenbaum, P. H. (1968). *Theories of cognitive consistency: A sourcebook.* Chicago: Rand McNally.

Abramson, L. Y., Metalsky, G. I., & Alloy, L. B. (1989). Hopelessness depression: A theory-based subtype of depression. *Psychological Review, 96,* 358–372.

Abramson, L. Y., Seligman, M. E. P., & Teasdale, J. (1978). Learned helplessness in humans: Critique and reformulation. *Journal of Abnormal Psychology, 87,* 49–74.

Adair, J. G. (1984). The Hawthorne effect: A reconsideration of the methodological artifact. *Journal of Applied Psychology, 69,* 334–345.

Adams, J. S. (1965). Inequity in social exchange. In L. Berkowitz (Ed.), *Advances in experimental social psychology* (Vol. 2, pp. 267–299). New York: Academic Press.

Aderman, D. (1972). Elation, depression, and helping behavior. *Journal of Personality and Social Psychology, 24,* 91–101.

Aderman, D., Brehm, S. S., & Katz, B. (1974). Empathic observation of an innocent victim: The just world revisited. *Journal of Personality and Social Psychology, 29,* 342–347.

Adorno, T., Frenkel-Brunswik, E., Levinson, D., & Sanford, R. N. (1950). *The authoritarian personality.* New York: Harper.

Affleck, G., Tennen, H., Pfeiffer, C., & Fifield, J. (1987). Appraisals of control and predictability in adapting to a chronic disease. *Journal of Personality and Social Psychology, 53,* 273–279.

Aida, Y., & Falbo, T. (1991). Relationships between marital satisfaction, resources, and power strategies. *Sex Roles, 24,* 43–56.

Ainsworth, M., Blehar, M. C., Waters, E., & Wall, S. (1978). *Patterns of attachment: A psychological study of the strange situation.* Hillsdale, NJ: Erlbaum.

Ajzen, I. (1991). The theory of planned behavior. *Organizational Behavior and Human Decision Processes, 50,* 179–211.

Ajzen, I., & Fishbein, M. (1977). Attitude-behavior relations: A theoretical analysis and review of empirical research. *Psychological Bulletin, 84,* 888–918.

Ajzen, I., & Madden, T. J. (1986). Prediction of goal-directed behavior: Attitudes, intentions, and perceived behavioral control. *Journal of Experimental Social Psychology, 22,* 453–474.

Aldwin, C. M., Levenson, M. R., Spiro, A., III, & Bossé, R. (1989). Does emotionality predict stress? Findings from the normative aging study. *Journal of Personality and Social Psychology, 56,* 618–624.

Aldwin, C. M., & Revenson, T. A. (1987). Does coping help? A reexamination of the relation between coping and mental health. *Journal of Personality and Social Psychology, 53,* 337–348.

Alexander, R. D. (1974). The evolution of social behavior. *Annual Review of Ecology and Systematics, 5,* 325–383.

Alicke, M. D. (1985). Global self-evaluation as determined by the desirability and controllability of trait adjectives. *Journal of Personality and Social Psychology, 49,* 1621–1630.

Alicke, M. D., Smith, R. H., & Klotz, J. L. (1986). Judgments of physical attractiveness: The role of faces and bodies. *Personality and Social Psychology Bulletin, 12,* 381–389.

Allen, J. B., Kenrick, D. T., Linder, D. E., & McCall, M. A. (1989). Arousal and attribution: A response-facilitation alternative to misattribution and negative-reinforcement models. *Journal of Personality and Social Psychology, 57,* 261– 270.

Allen, J. L., Walker, L. D., Schroeder, D. A., & Johnson, D. E. (1987). Attributions and attribution-behavior relations: The effect of level of cognitive development. *Journal of Personality and Social Psychology, 52,* 1099–1109.

Allen, K. M., Blascovich, J., Tomaka, J., & Kelsey, R. M. (1991). Presence of human friends and pet dogs as moderators of autonomic responses to stress in women. *Journal of Personality and Social Psychology, 61,* 582–589.

Allen, V. L. (1965). Situational factors in conformity. In L. Berkowitz (Ed.), *Advances in Experimental Social Psychology, 2,* 133–175.

Allen, V. L., & Levine, J. M. (1969). Consensus and conformity. *Journal of Experimental Social Psychology, 5,* 389–399.

Allen, V. L., & Levine, J. M. (1971). Social support and conformity: The role of independent assessment of reality. *Journal of Experimental Social Psychology, 7,* 48–58.

Allen, V. L., & Wilder, D. A. (1975). Categorization, belief similarity, and intergroup discrimination. *Journal of Personality and Social Psychology, 32,* 971–977.

Alley, T. R. (1988). *Social and applied aspects of perceiving faces.* Hillsdale, NJ: Erlbaum.

Allison, S. T., McQueen, L. R., & Schaerfl, L. M. (1992). Social decision making processes and the equal partitionment of shared resources. *Journal of Experimental Social Psychology, 28,* 23–42.

Allison, S. T., & Messick, D. M. (1985a). Effects of experience on performance in a replenishable resource trap. *Journal of Personality and Social Psychology, 49,* 943–948.

Allison, S. T., & Messick, D. M. (1985b). The group attribution error. *Journal of Experimental Social Psychology, 21,* 563– 579.

Allison, S. T., Messick, D. M., & Goethals, G. R. (1989). On being better but not smarter than others: The Muhammad Ali effect. *Social Cognition, 7,* 275–295.

Allport, F. H. (1924). *Social psychology.* Boston: Houghton Mifflin.

Allport, F. H., et al. (1953). The effects of segregation and the consequences of desegregation: A social science statement. *Minneapolis Law Review, 37,* 429–440.

Allport, G. W. (1954). *The nature of prejudice*. Reading, MA: Addison-Wesley.

Allport, G. W. (1985). The historical background of social psychology. In G. Lindzey & E. Aronson (Eds.), *Handbook of social psychology* (Vol. 1, 3rd ed., pp. 1–46). New York: Random House.

Allport, G. W., & Postman, L. J. (1947). *The psychology of rumor*. New York: Holt.

Allred, K. D., & Smith, T. W. (1989). The hardy personality: Cognitive and physiological responses to evaluative threat. *Journal of Personality and Social Psychology, 56,* 257–266.

Altman, I. (1973). Reciprocity of interpersonal exchange. *Journal for Theory of Social Behavior, 3,* 249–261.

Altman, I. (1987). Centripetal and centrifugal trends in psychology. *American Psychologist, 42,* 1058–1069.

Altman, I., & Taylor, D. A. (1973). *Social penetration: The development of interpersonal relationships*. New York: Holt, Rinehart and Winston.

Alwitt, L. F., & Mitchell, A. A. (Eds.). (1985). *Psychological processes and advertising effects: Theory, research, and application*. Hillsdale, NJ: Erlbaum.

Amabile, T. M. (1983a). Brilliant but cruel: Perceptions of negative evaluators. *Journal of Experimental Social Psychology, 19,* 146–156.

Amabile, T. M. (1983b). *The social psychology of creativity*. New York: Springer-Verlag.

Amato, P. R. (1983). Helping behavior in urban and rural environments: Field studies based on a taxonomic organization of helping episodes. *Journal of Personality and Social Psychology, 45,* 571–586.

Ambady, N. & Rosenthal, R. (1992) Thin slices of expressive behavior as predictors of interpersonal consequences: A meta-analysis. *Psychological Bulletin, 111,* 256–274.

American Psychiatric Association. (1987). *Diagnostic and statistical manual of mental disorders* (3rd ed., rev.). Washington, DC: Author.

American Psychological Association. (1990). Ethical principles of psychologists. *American Psychologist, 45,* 390–395.

American Psychological Association. (1992, May). APA continues to refine its ethics code. *APA Monitor*, pp. 38–42.

Amir, Y. (1969). Contact hypothesis in ethnic relations. *Psychological Bulletin, 71,* 319–342.

Amirkhan, J. H. (1990). A factor analytically derived measure of coping: The coping strategy indicator. *Journal of Personality and Social Psychology, 59,* 1066–1074.

Andersen, S. M., & Klatzky, R. L. (1987). Traits and social stereotypes: Levels of categorization in person perception. *Journal of Personality and Social Psychology, 53,* 235–246.

Andersen, S. M., & Ross, L. (1984). Self-knowledge and social inference: I. The impact of cognitive/affective and behavioral data. *Journal of Personality and Social Psychology, 46,* 280–293.

Anderson, C. A. (1989). Temperature and aggression: Ubiquitous effects of heat on occurrence of human violence. *Psychological Bulletin, 106,* 74–96.

Anderson, C. A., & DeNeve, K. M. (1992). Temperature, aggression, and the negative affect escape model. *Psychological Bulletin, 111,* 347–351.

Anderson, C. A., & Harvey, R. J. (1988). Discriminating between problems in living: An examination of depression, loneliness, shyness, and social anxiety. *Journal of Social and Clinical Psychology, 6,* 482–491.

Anderson, C. A., Lepper, M. R., & Ross, L. (1980). Perseverance of social theories: The role of explanation in the persistence of discredited information. *Journal of Personality and Social Psychology, 39,* 1037–1049.

Anderson, C. A., & Sechler, E. S. (1986). Effects of explanation and counterexplanation on the development and use of social theories. *Journal of Personality and Social Psychology, 50,* 24–34.

Anderson, N. H. (1965). Averaging versus adding as a stimulus combination rule in impression formation. *Journal of Experimental Social Psychology, 70,* 394–400.

Anderson, N. H. (1968). Likableness ratings of 555 personality-trait words. *Journal of Personality and Social Psychology, 9,* 272–279.

Anderson, N. H. (1981). *Foundations of information integration theory*. New York: Academic Press.

Anderson, N. H., & Hubert, S. (1963). Effects of concomitant verbal recall on order effects in personality impression formation. *Journal of Verbal Learning and Verbal Behavior, 2,* 379–391.

Anderson, R. A., Baron, R. S., & Logan, H. (1991). Distraction, control, and dental stress. *Journal of Applied Social Psychology, 21,* 156–171.

Andreasson, P. B. (1987). On the social psychology of the stock market: Aggregate attributional effects and the regressiveness of prediction. *Journal of Personality and Social Psychology, 53,* 490–496.

Angelo, B. (1991, June 3). "The ultimate horror show." *Time*, p. 59.

Apodaca v. Oregon, 406 U.S. 404 (1972).

Apple, W., Streeter, L. A., & Krauss, R. M. (1979). Effects of pitch and speech rate on personal attributions. *Journal of Personality and Social Psychology, 37,* 715–727.

Applegate, M. W. (1984). Flexibility for behavioral and social research in revised HHS human subjects research. In J. E. Sieber (Ed.), *NIH readings on the protection of human subjects in behavioral and social science research* (pp. 170–173). Frederick, MD: University Publications of America.

Archer, D., & Gartner, R. (1984). *Violence and crime in cross-national perspective*. New Haven, CT: Yale University Press.

Archer, D., Iritani, B., Kimes, D. D., & Barrios, M. (1983). Five studies of sex differences in facial prominence. *Journal of Personality and Social Psychology, 45,* 725–735.

Archer, J. (1991) Human sociobiology: Basic concepts and limitations. *Journal of Social Issues, 47,* 11–26.

Arendt, H. (1963). *Eichmann in Jerusalem: A report on the banality of evil*. New York: Viking.

Arkes, H. R., Wortmann, R. L., Saville, P., & Harkness, A. R. (1981). The hindsight bias among physicians weighing the likelihood of diagnoses. *Journal of Applied Psychology, 66,* 252–254.

Arkin, R. M. (1981). Self-presentation styles. In J. T. Tedeschi (Ed.), *Impression management theory and social psychological research* (pp. 311–333). New York: Academic Press.

Arkin, R. M., & Lake, E. A. (1983). Plumbing the depths of the bogus pipeline: A reprise. *Journal of Research in Personality, 17,* 81–88.

Arling, G. (1976). The elderly widow and her family, neighbors, and friends. *Journal of Marriage and the Family, 38,* 757–768.

Aron, A. (1988). The matching hypothesis reconsidered again: Comment on Kalick and Hamilton. *Journal of Personality and Social Psychology, 54,* 441–446.

Aron, A., Aron, E. N., Tudor, M., & Nelson, G. (1991). Close relationships as including other in the self. *Journal of Personality and Social Psychology, 60,* 241–253.

Aronson, E. (1969). The theory of cognitive dissonance: A current perspective. In L. Berkowitz (Ed.), *Advances in experimental social psychology* (Vol. 4, pp. 1–34). New York: Academic Press.

Aronson, E. (1988). *The social animal.* San Francisco, CA: Freeman.

Aronson, E., Blaney, N., Stephan, C., Sikes, J., & Snapp, M. (1978). *The jigsaw classroom.* Beverly Hills, CA: Sage.

Aronson, E., Brewer, M., & Carlsmith, J. M. (1985). Experimentation in social psychology. In G. Lindzey & E. Aronson (Eds.), *Handbook of social psychology* (Vol. 1, 3rd ed., pp. 441–486). New York: Random House.

Aronson, E., & Carlsmith, J. M. (1963). Effect of severity of threat on the devaluation of forbidden behavior. *Journal of Abnormal and Social Psychology, 66,* 584–588.

Aronson, E., & Carlsmith, J. M. (1968). Experimentation in social psychology. In G. Lindzey & E. Aronson (Eds.), *Handbook of social psychology* (Vol. 2, 2nd ed., pp. 1–79). Reading, MA: Addison-Wesley.

Aronson, E., & Cope, V. (1968). My enemy's enemy is my friend. *Journal of Personality and Social Psychology, 8,* 8–12.

Aronson, E., & Linder, D. (1965). Gain and loss of esteem as determinants of interpersonal attractiveness. *Journal of Experimental Social Psychology, 1,* 156–172.

Aronson, E., & Mills, J. (1959). The effect of severity of initiation on liking for a group. *Journal of Abnormal and Social Psychology, 59,* 177–181.

Aronson, E., & Worchel, S. (1966). Similarity versus liking as determinants of interpersonal attractiveness. *Psychonomic Science, 5,* 157–158.

Asch, S. E. (1946). Forming impressions of personality. *Journal of Abnormal and Social Psychology, 41,* 258–290.

Asch, S. E. (1951). Effects of group pressure upon the modification and distortion of judgments. In H. Guetzkow (Ed.), *Groups, leadership, and men.* Pittsburgh, PA: Carnegie Press.

Asch, S. E. (1955, November). Opinions and social pressure. *Scientific American,* pp. 31–35.

Asch, S. E. (1956). Studies of independence and conformity: A minority of one against a unanimous majority. *Psychological Monographs, 70,* 416.

Asch, S. E., & Zukier, H. (1984). Thinking about persons. *Journal of Personality and Social Psychology, 46,* 1230–1240.

Ash, M. G. (1992). Cultural contexts and scientific change in psychology: Kurt Lewin in Iowa. *American Psychologist, 47,* 198–207.

Asimov, I. (1986). *Foundation and earth.* Garden City, NY: Doubleday.

Askenasy, H. (1978). *Are we all Nazis?* Secaucus, NJ: Lyle Stuart.

Associated Press. (1988, October 10). Skirting the issue? *The National Law Journal,* p. 43.

Attorney General's Commission on Pornography (1986, July). *Final report.* Washington, DC: U.S. Department of Justice.

Aukett, R., Richie, J., & Mill, K. (1988). Gender differences in friendship patterns. *Sex Roles, 19,* 57–66.

Austin, W., & Walster, E. (1974). Reactions to confirmations and disconfirmations of expectancies of equity and inequity. *Journal of Personality and Social Psychology, 30,* 208–216.

Averill, J. R. (1982). *Anger and aggression.* New York: Springer-Verlag.

Axelrod, R. (1984). *The evolution of cooperation.* New York: Basic Books.

Axsom, D. (1989). Cognitive dissonance and behavior change in psychotherapy. *Journal of Experimental Social Psychology, 25,* 234–252.

Axsom, D., & Cooper, J. (1985). Cognitive dissonance and psychotherapy: The role of effort justification in inducing weight loss. *Journal of Experimental Social Psychology, 21,* 149–160.

Axsom, D., Yates, S., & Chaiken, S. (1987). Audience response as a heuristic cue in persuasion. *Journal of Personality and Social Psychology, 53,* 30–40.

Babad, E., & Katz, Y. (1991). Wishful thinking—against all odds. *Journal of Applied Social Psychology, 21,* 1921–1938.

Backman, C. W., & Secord, P. F. (1959). The effect of perceived liking on interpersonal attraction. *Human Relations, 12,* 379–384.

Baldwin, M. W., & Holmes, J. G. (1987). Salient private audiences and awareness of the self. *Journal of Personality and Social Psychology, 52,* 1087–1098.

Bales, R. F. (1958). Task roles and social roles in problem-solving groups. In E. E. Maccoby, T. M. Newcomb, & E. L. Hartley (Eds.), *Readings in social psychology* (3rd ed., pp. 437–447). New York: Holt.

Ballew v. Georgia, 435 U.S. 223 (1978).

Banaji, M. R., & Steele, C. M. (1989). Alcohol and self-evaluation: Is a social cognition approach beneficial? *Social Cognition, 7,* 137–151.

Bandura, A. (1973). *Aggression: A social learning analysis.* Englewood Cliffs, NJ: Prentice-Hall.

Bandura, A. (1977a). Self-efficacy: Toward a unifying theory of behavioral change. *Psychological Review, 84,* 191–215.

Bandura, A. (1977b). *Social learning theory*. Englewood Cliffs, NJ: Prentice-Hall.

Bandura, A. (1983). Psychological mechanisms of aggression. In R. G. Geen & E. I. Donnerstein (Eds.), *Aggression: Theoretical and empirical reviews: Vol. l. Theoretical and methodological issues* (pp. 1–40). New York: Academic Press.

Bandura, A. (1990). Selective activation and disengagement of moral control. *Journal of Social Issues, 46,* 27–46.

Bandura, A., Cioffi, D., Taylor, C. B., & Brouillard, M. E. (1988). Perceived self-efficacy in coping with cognitive stressors and opioid activation. *Journal of Personality and Social Psychology, 55,* 479–488.

Bandura, A., Ross, R., & Ross, S. (1961). Transmission of aggression through imitation of aggressive models. *Journal of Abnormal and Social Psychology, 63,* 575–582.

Banuazizi, A., & Movahedi, S. (1975). Interpersonal dynamics in a simulated prison: A methodological analysis. *American Psychologist, 30,* 152–160.

Bard, M. (1971). The study and modification of intra-familial violence. In J. L. Singer (Ed.), *The control of aggression and violence* (pp. 149–164). New York: Academic Press.

Barefoot, J. C., Dodge, K. A., Bercedis, L. P., Dahlstrom, W. G., & Williams, R. B. (1989). The Cook-Medley Hostility Scale: Item content and ability to predict survival. *Psychosomatic Medicine, 51,* 46–57.

Bargh, J. A., Chaiken, S., Govender, R., & Pratto, F. (1992). The generality of the automatic attitude activation effect. *Journal of Personality and Social Psychology.*

Bargh, J. A., Lombardi, W. J., & Higgins, E. T. (1988). Automaticity of chronically accessible constructs in person × situation effects on person perception: It's just a matter of time. *Journal of Personality and Social Psychology, 55,* 599–605.

Bargh, J. A., & Pietromonaco, P. (1982). Automatic information processing and social perception: The influence of trait information presented outside of conscious awareness on impression formation. *Journal of Personality and Social Psychology, 43,* 437–449.

Bar-Hillel, M. (1980). The base-rate fallacy in probability judgments. *Acta Psychologica, 44,* 211–213.

Barnes, R. D., Ickes, W., & Kidd, R. F. (1979). Effects of the perceived intentionality and stability of another's dependency on helping behavior. *Personality and Social Psychology Bulletin, 5,* 367–372.

Barnett, P. A., & Gotlib, I. H. (1988). Psychosocial functioning and depression: Distinguishing among antecedents, concomitants, and consequences. *Psychological Bulletin, 104,* 97–126.

Barnett, R. C., & Baruch, G. K. (1985). Women's involvement in multiple roles and psychological distress. *Journal of Personality and Social Psychology, 49,* 135–145.

Baron, J. N., & Reiss, P. C. (1985a). Reply to Phillips & Bollen. *American Sociological Review, 50,* 372–376.

Baron, J. N., & Reiss, P. C. (1985b). Same time, next year: Aggregate analyses of the mass media and violent behavior. *American Sociological Review, 50,* 347–363.

Baron, L., & Straus, M. A. (1984). Sexual stratification, pornography, and rape in the United States. In N. M. Malamuth & E. Donnerstein (Eds.), *Pornography and sexual aggression* (pp. 185–209). New York: Academic Press.

Baron, R. A. (1977). *Human aggression*. New York: Plenum.

Baron, R. A. (1983a). The control of human aggression: An optimistic perspective. *Journal of Social and Clinical Psychology, 1,* 97–119.

Baron, R. A. (1983b). The control of human aggression: A strategy based on incompatible responses. In R. G. Geen & E. I. Donnerstein (Eds.), *Aggression: Theoretical and empirical reviews: Vol. 2. Issues in research* (pp. 173–190). New York: Academic Press.

Baron, R. A., & Ball, R. L. (1974). The aggression-inhibiting influence of nonhostile behavior. *Journal of Experimental Social Psychology, 10,* 23–33.

Baron, R. A., & Kepner, C. R. (1970). Model's behavior and attraction toward the model as determinants of adult aggressive behavior. *Journal of Personality and Social Psychology, 14,* 335–344.

Baron, R. A., & Ransberger, V. M. (1978). Ambient temperature and the occurrence of collective violence: The "long, hot summer" revisited. *Journal of Personality and Social Psychology, 36,* 351–360.

Baron, R. M. (1988). An ecological framework for establishing a dual-mode theory of social knowing. In D. Bar-Tal & A. W. Kruglanski (Eds.), *The social psychology of knowledge* (pp. 48–82). New York: Cambridge University Press.

Baron, R. S. (1986). Distraction-conflict theory: Progress and problems. In L. Berkowitz (Ed.), *Advances in experimental social psychology* (Vol. 19, pp. 1–40). Orlando, FL: Academic Press.

Baron, R. S., Cutrona, C. E., Hicklin, D., Russell, D. W., & Lubaroff, D. M. (1990). Social support and immune function among spouses of cancer patients. *Journal of Personality and Social Psychology, 59,* 344–352.

Barrera, M., Jr., & Ainlay, S. L. (1983). The structure of social support: A conceptual and empirical analysis. *Journal of Community Psychology, 11,* 133–143.

Barry, W. A. (1970). Marriage research and conflict: An integrative review. *Psychological Bulletin, 73,* 41–54.

Bar-Tal, D. (1976). *Prosocial behavior: Theory and research*. Washington, DC: Hemisphere.

Bar-Tal, D. (1990). Causes and consequences of delegitimization: Models of conflict and ethnocentrism. *Journal of Social Issues, 46,* 65–81.

Bar-Tal, D., & Saxe, L. (1976). Perceptions of similarly and dissimilarly attractive couples and individuals. *Journal of Personality and Social Psychology, 33,* 772–781.

Barthel, J. (1976). *A death in Canaan*. New York: Dutton.

Bartis, S., Szymanski, K., & Harkins, S. G. (1988). Evaluation and performance: A two-edged knife. *Personality and Social Psychology Bulletin, 14,* 242–251.

Bass, B. M. (1985). *Leadership and performance beyond expectations*. New York: Free Press.

Bass, B. M. (1990). *Bass & Stogdill's handbook of leadership: Theory, research, & managerial applications* (3rd ed.). New York: Free Press.

Bass, B. M., & Avolio, B. J. (1990). *Manual: The multifactor leadership questionnaire.* Palo Alto, CA: Consulting Psychologists Press.

Bassili, J. N., & Provencal, A. (1988). Perceiving minorities: A factor-analytic approach. *Personality and Social Psychology Bulletin, 14,* 5–15.

Bassili, J. N., & Racine, J. P. (1990). On the process relationship between person and situation judgments in attribution. *Journal of Personality and Social Psychology, 59,* 881–890.

Batson, C. D. (1983). Sociobiology and the role of religion in promoting prosocial behavior: An alternative view. *Journal of Personality and Social Psychology, 45,* 1380–1385.

Batson, C. D. (1991). *The altruism question.* Hillsdale, NJ: Erlbaum.

Batson, C. D., Batson, J. G., Griffitt, C. A., Barrientos, S., Brandt, J. R., Sprengelmeyer, P., & Bayly, M. J. (1989). Negative-state relief and the empathy-altruism hypothesis. *Journal of Personality and Social Psychology, 56,* 922–933.

Batson, C. D., Batson, J. G., Slingsby, J. K., Harrell, K. L., Peekna, H. M., & Todd, R. M. (1991). Empathic joy and the empathy-altruism hypothesis. *Journal of Personality and Social Psychology, 61,* 413–426.

Batson, C. D., Bolen, M. H., Cross, J. A., & Neuringer-Benefiel, H. E. (1986). Where is the altruism in the altruistic personality? *Journal of Personality and Social Psychology, 50,* 212–220.

Batson, C. D., Coke, J. S., Jasnoski, M. L., & Hanson, M. (1978). Buying kindness: Effect of an extrinsic incentive for helping on perceived altruism. *Personality and Social Psychology Bulletin, 4,* 86–91.

Batson, C. D., Duncan, B. D., Ackerman, P., Buckley, T., & Birch, K. (1981). Is empathic emotion a source of altruistic motivation? *Journal of Personality and Social Psychology, 40,* 290–302.

Batson, C. D., Dyck, J. L., Brandt, J. R., Batson, J. G., Powell, A. L., McMaster, M. R., & Griffitt, C. (1988). Five studies testing two new egoistic alternatives to the empathy-altruism hypothesis. *Journal of Personality and Social Psychology, 55,* 52–77.

Batson, C. D., Fultz J., Schoenrade, P. A., & Paduano, A. (1987). Critical self-reflection and self-perceived altruism: When self-reward fails. *Journal of Personality and Social Psychology, 53,* 594–602.

Batson, C. D., O'Quin, K., Fultz, J., Vanderplas, M., & Isen, A. M. (1983). Influence of self-reported distress and empathy on egoistic versus altruistic motivation to help. *Journal of Personality and Social Psychology, 45,* 706–718.

Baum, A. (Ed.). (1984). Social psychology and cigarette smoking [Special issue]. *Journal of Applied Social Psychology, 14*(3).

Baum, A., Fleming, R., & Singer, J. E. (1982). Stress at Three Mile Island: Applying psychological impact analysis. In L. Bickman (Ed.), *Applied social psychology annual.* (Vol. 3, pp. 217–248). Beverly Hills, CA: Sage.

Baum, A., & Valins, S. (1977). *Architecture and social behavior: Psychological studies of social density.* Hillsdale, NJ: Erlbaum.

Baum, A., & Valins, S. (1979). Architectural mediation of residential density and control: Crowding and the regulation of social contact. In L. Berkowitz (Ed.), *Advances in experimental social psychology* (Vol. 12, pp. 131–175). New York: Academic Press.

Bauman, L. J., & Siegel, K. (1987). Misperception among gay men of the risk for AIDS associated with their sexual behavior. *Journal of Applied Social Psychology, 17,* 329–350.

Bauman, M. H. (1982, August 16). What you can and can't learn from interviews. *The Wall Street Journal.*

Baumeister, R. F. (1982). A self-presentational view of social phenomena. *Psychological Bulletin, 91,* 3–26.

Baumeister, R. F. (1990). Suicide as escape from self. *Psychological Review, 97,* 90–113.

Baumeister, R. F. (1991). *Escaping the self.* New York: Basic Books.

Baumeister, R. F., Chesner, S. P., Sanders, P. S., & Tice, D. M. (1988). Who's in charge here? Group leaders do lend help in emergencies. *Personality and Social Psychology Bulletin, 14,* 17–22.

Baumeister, R. F., & Scher, S. J. (1988). Self-defeating behavior patterns among normal individuals: Review and analysis of common self-destructive tendencies. *Psychological Bulletin, 104,* 3–22.

Baumeister, R. F., & Showers, C. J. (1986). A review of paradoxical performance effects: Choking under pressure in sports and mental tests. *European Journal of Social Psychology, 16,* 361–383.

Baumeister, R. F., & Steinhilber, A. (1984). Paradoxical effects of supportive audiences on performance under pressure: The home field disadvantage in sports championships. *Journal of Personality and Social Psychology, 47,* 85–93.

Baumeister, R. F., & Tice, D. M. (1984). Role of self-presentation and choice in cognitive dissonance under forced compliance: Necessary or sufficient causes? *Journal of Personality and Social Psychology, 46,* 5–13.

Baumgardner, A. H. (1991). Claiming depressive symptoms as a self-handicap: A protective self-presentation strategy. *Basic and Applied Social Psychology, 12,* 97–113.

Baumrind, D. (1964). Some thoughts on ethics of research: After reading Milgram's "Behavioral Study of Obedience." *American Psychologist, 19,* 421–423.

Baumrind, D. (1985). Research using intentional deception: Ethical issues revisited. *American Psychologist, 40,* 165–174.

Baxter, L. A. (1987). Self-disclosure and disengagement. In V. J. Derleg & J. H. Berg (Eds.), *Self-disclosure: Theory, research, and therapy* (pp. 155–174). New York: Plenum.

Beaman, A. L., Barnes, P. J., Klentz, B., & McQuirk, B. (1978). Increasing helping rates through information dissemination: Teaching pays. *Personality and Social Psychology Bulletin, 4,* 406–411.

Beaman, A. L., Cole, C. M., Preston, M., Klentz, B., & Steblay, N. M. (1983). Fifteen years of foot-in-the-door research: A meta-analysis. *Personality and Social Psychology Bulletin, 9,* 181–196.

Beaman, A. L., Klentz, B., Diener, E., & Svanum, S. (1979). Objective self-awareness and transgression in children: A field study. *Journal of Personality and Social Psychology, 37,* 1835–1846.

Beck, E. M., & Tolnay, S. E. (1990). The killing fields of the deep south: The market for cotton and the lynching of blacks, 1882–1930. *American Sociological Review, 55,* 526–539.

Becker, F. D. (1981). *Workspace.* New York: Praeger.

Bedau, A., & Radelet, M. (1987). Miscarriages of justice in potentially capital cases. *Stanford Law Review, 40,* 21–179.

Beggan, J. K. (1992). On the social nature of nonsocial perception: The mere ownership effect. *Journal of Personality and Social Psychology, 62,* 229–237.

Bekerian, D. A., & Bowers, J. M. (1983). Eyewitness testimony: Were we misled? *Journal of Experimental Psychology: Learning, Memory, and Cognition, 9,* 139–145.

Bell, P. A. (1992). In defense of the negative affect escape model of heat and aggression. *Psychological Bulletin, 111,* 342–346.

Belli, R. F. (1989). Influences of misleading postevent information: Misinformation interference and acceptance. *Journal of Experimental Psychology: General, 118,* 72–85.

Belmore, S. M. (1987). Determinants of attention during impression formation. *Journal of Experimental Psychology: Learning, Memory, and Cognition, 13,* 480–489.

Bem, D. J. (1965). An experimental analysis of self-persuasion. *Journal of Experimental Social Psychology, 1,* 199–218.

Bem, D. J. (1967). Self-perception: An alternative interpretation of cognitive dissonance phenomena. *Psychological Review, 74,* 183–200.

Bem, D. J. (1972). Self-perception theory. In L. Berkowitz (Ed.), *Advances in experimental social psychology* (Vol. 6, pp. 1–62). New York: Academic Press.

Bem, S. L. (1974). The measurement of psychological androgyny. *Journal of Consulting and Clinical Psychology, 42,* 155–162.

Bem, S. L. (1981). Gender schema theory: A cognitive account of sex typing. *Psychological Review, 88,* 354–364.

Benassi, M. A. (1982). Effects of order of presentation, primacy, and physical attractiveness on attributions of ability. *Journal of Personality and Social Psychology, 43,* 48–58.

Benedict, M. E., & Levine, E. L. (1988). Delay and distortion: Tacit influences on performance appraisal effectiveness. *Journal of Applied Psychology, 73,* 507–514.

Benefit beat. (1991, June 10). *Time,* p. 15.

Benjamin, L. T., Jr. (1986). Why don't they understand us? A history of psychology's public image. *American Psychologist, 41,* 941–946.

Ben-Shakhar, G., Bar-Hillel, M., Bilu, Y., Ben-Abba, E., & Flug, A. (1986). Can graphology predict occupational success? Two empirical studies and some methodological ruminations. *Journal of Applied Psychology, 71,* 645–653.

Benson, P. L., Karabenick, S. A., & Lerner, R. M. (1976). Pretty pleases: The effects of physical attractiveness, race, and sex on receiving help. *Journal of Experimental Social Psychology, 12,* 409–415.

Berg, J. H. (1984). Development of friendship between roommates. *Journal of Personality and Social Psychology, 46,* 346–356.

Berg, J. H., & Clark, M. S. (1986). Differences in social exchange between intimate and other relationships: Gradually evolving or quickly apparent? In V. J. Derlega & B. A. Winstead (Eds.), *Friendship and social interaction* (pp. 102–128). New York: Springer-Verlag.

Berg, J. H., & McQuinn, R. D. (1986). Attraction and exchange in continuing and noncontinuing dating relationships. *Journal of Personality and Social Psychology, 50,* 942–952.

Berglas, S., & Jones, E. E. (1978). Drug choice as a self-handicapping strategy in response to noncontingent success. *Journal of Personality and Social Psychology, 36,* 405–417.

Berkman, L., & Syme, S. L. (1979). Social networks, host resistance, and mortality: A nine-year follow-up study of Alameda County residents. *American Journal of Epidemiology, 109,* 186–204.

Berkowitz, L. (1962). *Aggression: A social psychological analysis.* New York: McGraw-Hill.

Berkowitz, L. (1969). The frustration-aggression hypothesis revisited. In L. Berkowitz (Ed.), *Roots of aggression* (pp. 1–28). New York: Atherton.

Berkowitz, L. (1970). The self, selfishness, and altruism. In J. R. Macaulay & L. Berkowitz (Eds.), *Altruism and helping behavior* (pp. 143–151). New York: Academic Press.

Berkowitz, L. (1972). Social norms, feelings, and other factors affecting helping and altruism. In L. Berkowitz (Ed.), *Advances in experimental social psychology.* (Vol. 6, pp. 63–108). New York: Academic Press.

Berkowitz, L. (1986). Situational influences on reactions to observed violence. In L. R. Huesmann & N. M. Malamuth (Eds.), *Journal of Social Issues: Media Violence and Antisocial Behavior, 42*(3), 93–106.

Berkowitz, L. (1987). Mood, self-awareness, and willingness to help. *Journal of Personality and Social Psychology, 52,* 721–729.

Berkowitz, L. (1989). Frustration-aggression hypothesis: Examination and reformulation. *Psychological Bulletin, 106,* 59–73.

Berkowitz, L. (1990). On the formulation and regulation of anger and aggression: A cognitive-neoassociationistic analysis. *American Psychologist, 45,* 494–503.

Berkowitz, L., & Donnerstein, E. (1982). External validity is more than skin deep: Some answers to criticisms of laboratory experiments. *American Psychologist, 37,* 245–257.

Berkowitz, L., & Heimer, K. (1989). On the construction of the anger experience: Aversive events and negative priming in the frustration of feelings. In L. Berkowitz (Ed.), *Advances in experimental social psychology* (Vol. 22, pp. 1–37). San Diego: Academic Press.

Berkowitz, L., & Lepage, A. (1967). Weapons as aggression-eliciting stimuli. *Journal of Personality and Social Psychology, 7,* 202–207.

Berkowitz, L., & Rogers, K. H. (1986). A priming effect analysis of media influences. In J. Bryant & D. Zillmann (Eds.), *Perspectives on media effects* (pp. 57–81). Hillsdale, NJ: Erlbaum.

Berman, J., & Sales, B. (1977). A critical evaluation of the systematic approach to jury selection. *Criminal Justice and Behavior, 4,* 219–240.

Bernardin, H. J., & Beatty, R. W. (1984). *Performance appraisal: Assessing human behavior at work.* Boston: Kent.

Berndt, T. J. (1979). Developmental changes in conformity to peers and parents. *Developmental Psychology, 15,* 606–616.

Bernstein, W. M., Stephenson, B. O., Snyder, M. L., & Wicklund, R. A. (1983). Causal ambiguity and heterosexual affiliation. *Journal of Experimental Social Psychology, 19,* 78–92.

Berry, D. S. (1990). Taking people at face value: Evidence for the kernel of truth hypothesis. *Social Cognition, 8,* 343–361.

Berry, D. S., & McArthur, L. Z. (1988). What's in a face?: Facial maturity and the attribution of legal responsibility. *Personality and Social Psychology Bulletin, 14,* 23–33.

Berry, D. S., & Zebrowitz-McArthur, L. (1986). Perceiving character in faces: The impact of age-related craniofacial changes in social perception. *Psychological Bulletin, 100,* 3–18.

Berscheid, E. (1966). Opinion change and communicator-communicatee similarity and dissimilarity. *Journal of Personality and Social Psychology, 4,* 670–680.

Berscheid, E. (1983). Emotion. In H. H. Kelley, E. Berscheid, A. Christenson, J. H. Harvey, T. L. Huston, G. Levinger, E. McClintock, L. A. Peplau, & D. R. Peterson, *Close relationships* (pp. 110–168). New York: Freeman.

Berscheid, E. (1985). Interpersonal attraction. In G. Lindzey & E. Aronson (Eds.), *Handbook of social psychology* (Vol. 2, 3rd ed., pp. 413–484). New York: Random House.

Berscheid, E., Dion, K., Walster, E., & Walster, G. W. (1971). Physical attractiveness and dating choice: A test of the matching hypothesis. *Journal of Experimental Social Psychology, 7,* 173–189.

Berscheid, E., & Peplau, L. A. (1983). The emerging science of relationships. In H. H. Kelley, E. Berscheid, A. Christenson, J. H. Harvey, T. L. Huston, G. Levinger, E. McClintock, L. A. Peplan, & D. R. Peterson, *Close relationships* (pp. 1–19). New York: Freeman.

Berscheid, E., Snyder, M., & Omoto, A. M. (1989). The relationship closeness inventory: Assessing the closeness of interpersonal relationships. *Journal of Personality and Social Psychology, 57,* 792–807.

Berscheid, E., & Walster, E. (1974a). A little bit about love. In T. Huston (Ed.), *Foundations of interpersonal attraction* (pp. 355–381). New York: Academic Press.

Berscheid, E., & Walster, E. (1974b). Physical attractiveness. In L. Berkowitz (Ed.), *Advances in experimental social psychology.* (Vol. 7, pp. 157–215). New York: Academic Press.

Berscheid, E., & Walster, E. (1978). *Interpersonal attraction* (2nd ed.). Reading, MA: Addison-Wesley.

Berscheid, E., Walster, E., & Campbell, R. (1972). *Grow old along with me.* Unpublished manuscript, Department of Psychology, University of Minnesota.

Bersoff, D. N., & Ogden, D. W. (1987). In the Supreme Court of the United States: Lockhart v. McCree. *American Psychologist, 42,* 59–68.

Betancourt, H. (1990). An attribution-empathy model of helping behavior: Behavioral intentions and judgments of help-giving. *Personality and Social Psychology Bulletin, 16,* 573–591.

Bettencourt, B. A., Brewer, M. B., Croak, M. R., & Miller, N. (1992). Cooperation and the reduction of intergroup bias: The role of reward structure and social orientation. *Journal of Experimental Social Psychology, 28,* 301–319.

Beyer, S. (1990). Gender differences in the accuracy of self-evaluations of performance. *Journal of Personality and Social Psychology, 59,* 960–970.

Bickman, L. (1974). The social power of a uniform. *Journal of Applied Social Psychology, 4,* 47–61.

Biemiller, L. (1991, December 18). Campus health experts are frustrated about progress on AIDS education. *Chronicle of Higher Education,* pp. A33–A34.

Bierbrauer, G. (1979). Why did he do it? Attributions of obedience and the phenomenon of dispositional bias. *European Journal of Social Psychology, 9,* 67–84.

Bierhoff, H. W., Klein, R., & Kramp, P. (1991). Evidence for the altruistic personality from data on accident research. *Journal of Personality, 59,* 263–280.

Bierly, M. M. (1985). Prejudice toward contemporary outgroups as a generalized attitude. *Journal of Applied Social Psychology, 15,* 189–199.

Biernat, M. (1991). Gender stereotypes and the relationship between masculinity and femininity: A developmental analysis. *Journal of Personality and Social Psychology, 61,* 351–365.

Binning, J. F., Goldstein, M. A., Garcia, M. F., & Scatteregia, J. H. (1988). Effects of preinterview impressions on questioning strategies in same- and opposite-sex employment interviews. *Journal of Applied Psychology, 73,* 30–37.

Bisanz, G. L., & Rule, B. G. (1989). Gender and the persuasion schema: A search for cognitive invariants. *Personality and Social Psychology Bulletin, 15,* 4–18.

Blake, R. R., & Mouton, J. S. (1984). *Solving costly organizational conflicts.* San Francisco: Jossey–Bass.

Blanchard, D. C., & Blanchard, R. J. (1984). Affect and aggression: An animal model applied to human behavior. In R. J. Blanchard & D. C. Blanchard (Eds.), *Advances in the study of aggression* (Vol. 1, pp. 1–62). New York: Academic Press.

Blanchard, F. A., Lilly, T., & Vaughn, L. A. (1991). Reducing the expression of racial prejudice. *Psychological Science, 2,* 101–105.

Blascovich, J., & Kelsey, R. M. (1990). Using electrodermal and cardiovascular measures of arousal in social psychological research. In C. Hendrick & M. S. Clark (Eds.), *Review of personality and social psychology: Vol. 11. Research methods in personality and social psychology* (pp. 45–73). Newbury Park, CA: Sage.

Blass, T. (1984). Social psychology and personality: Toward a convergence. *Journal of Personality and Social Psychology, 47,* 1013–1027.

Blass, T. (1991). Understanding behavior in the Milgram obedience experiment: The role of personality, situations, and their interactions. *Journal of Personality and Social Psychology, 60,* 398–413.

Blass, T., & Krackow, A. (1991, June). *The Milgram obedience experiments: Students' views vs. scholarly perspectives and actual findings.* Paper presented at the annual meeting of the American Psychological Society, Washington, DC.

Block, J. H., Gjerde, P. F., & Block, H. (1991). Personality antecedents of depressive tendencies in 18-year-olds: A prospective study. *Journal of Personality and Social Psychology, 60,* 726–738.

Blood, R. O., & Wolfe, D. M. (1960). *Husbands and wives: The dynamics of married living.* New York: Free Press.

Bloom, B., Asher, S. J., & White, S. W. (1978). Marital disruption as a stressor: A review and analysis. *Psychological Bulletin, 85,* 867–894.

Bly, R. (1990). Iron men. Reading, MA: Addison-Wesley.

Bobo, L. (1988). Attitudes toward the black political movement: Trends, meaning, and effects of racial policy preferences. *Social Psychology Quarterly, 51,* 287–302.

Bochner, S., & Insko, C. A. (1966). Communicator discrepancy, source credibility, and opinion change. *Journal of Personality and Social Psychology, 4,* 614–621.

Bodenhausen, G. V. (1990). Stereotypes as judgmental heuristics: Evidence of circadian variations in discrimination. *Psychological Science, 1,* 319–322.

Bolger, N., & Eckenrode, J. (1991). Social relationships, personality, and anxiety during a major stressful event. *Journal of Personality and Social Psychology, 61,* 440–449.

Bolger, N., DeLongis, A., Kessler, R. C., & Schilling, E. A. (1989). Effects of daily stress and negative mood. *Journal of Personality and Social Psychology, 57,* 808–818. Bond, C. F., Jr. (1982). Social facilitation: A self-presentational view. *Journal of Personality and Social Psychology, 42,* 1042–1050.

Bond, C. F., Jr., & Brockett, D. R. (1987). A social context-personality index theory of memory for acquaintances. *Journal of Personality and Social Psychology, 52,* 1110–1121.

Bond, C. F., Jr., & Titus, L. T. (1983). Social facilitation: A meta-analysis of 241 studies. *Psychological Bulletin, 94,* 265–292.

Boninger, D. S., Brock, T. C., Cook, T. D., Gruder, C. L., & Romer, D. (1990). Discovery of reliable attitude change persistence resulting from a transmitter tuning set. *Psychological Science, 1,* 268–271.

Booth, A., & Johnson, D. (1988). Premarital cohabitation and marital success. *Journal of Family Issues, 9,* 255–272.

Booth-Kewley, S., & Friedman, H. S. (1987). Psychological predictors of heart disease: A quantitative review. *Psychological Bulletin, 101,* 343–362.

Borgida, E. (1981). Legal reform of rape laws: A psycholegal approach. In L. Bickman (Ed.), *Applied social psychology annual* (Vol. 2, pp. 211–241). Beverly Hills, CA: Sage.

Borgida, E., & Brekke, N. (1981). The base-rate fallacy in attribution and prediction. In J. H. Harvey, W. J. Ickes, & R. F. Kidd (Eds.), *New directions in attribution research* (Vol. 3, pp. 66–95). Hillsdale, NJ: Erlbaum.

Borgida, E., & Brekke, N. (1985). Psychological research on rape trials. In A. Burgess (Ed.), *Research handbook on rape and sexual assault* (pp. 313–324). New York: Garland.

Borgida, E., & Campbell, B. (1982). Belief relevance and attitude-behavior consistency: The moderating role of personal experience. *Journal of Personality and Social Psychology, 42,* 239–247.

Borgida, E., Gresham, A. W., Bull, M. A., & Regan, P. C. (in press). Children as witnesses in court: The influence of expert psychological testimony. In A. Burgess (Ed.), *Child trauma: Vol. 1. Issues and research.* New York: Garland.

Borgida, E., & Nisbett, R. E. (1977). The differential impact of abstract vs. concrete information on decisions. *Journal of Applied Social Psychology, 7,* 258–271.

Bornstein, G., Rapoport, A., Kerpel, L., & Katz, T. (1989). Within- and between-group communication in intergroup competition for public goods. *Journal of Experimental Social Psychology, 25,* 422–436.

Bornstein, R. F. (1989). Exposure and affect: Overview and meta-analysis of research, 1968–1987. *Psychological Bulletin, 106,* 265–289.

Bornstein, R. F., Kale, A. R., & Cornell, K. R. (1990). Boredom as a limiting condition on the mere exposure effect. *Journal of Personality and Social Psychology, 58,* 791–800.

Bornstein, R. F., Leone, D. R., & Galley, D. J. (1987). The generalizability of subliminal mere exposure effects: Influence of stimuli perceived without awareness on social behavior. *Journal of Personality and Social Psychology, 53,* 1070–1079.

Bothwell, R. K., Deffenbacher, K. A., & Brigham, J. C. (1987). Correlation of eyewitness accuracy and confidence: Optimality hypothesis revisited. *Journal of Applied Psychology, 72,* 691–695.

Bower, G., Black, J., & Turner, T. (1979). Scripts in text comprehension and memory. *Cognitive Psychology, 11,* 177–220.

Boyden, T., Carroll, J. S., & Maier, R. A. (1984). Similarity and attraction in homosexual males: The effects of age and masculinity-femininity. *Sex Roles, 10,* 939–948.

Bradbury, T. N., & Fincham, F. D. (1990). Attributions in marriage: Review and critique. *Psychological Bulletin 107,* 3–33.

Braddock, J. H., II. (1985). School desegregation and black assimilation. *Journal of Social Issues, 41,* 9–22.

Bray, R. M., Johnson, D., & Chilstrom, J. T., Jr. (1982). Social influence by group members with minority opinions: A comparison of Hollander & Moscovici. *Journal of Personality and Social Psychology, 43,* 78–88.

Bray, R. M., Struckman-Johnson, C., Osborne, M., McFarlane, J., & Scott, J. (1978). The effects of defendant status on decisions of student and community juries. *Social Psychology, 41,* 256–260.

Breakey, W. R., & Fischer, P. J. (1990). Homelessness: The extent of the problem. In M. Shinn & B. C. Weitzman (Eds.), *Journal of Social Issues: Urban Homelessness, 46,* 31–48.

Brean, H. (1958, March 31). What hidden sell is all about. *Life,* pp. 104–114.

Breckler, S. J. (1984). Empirical validation of affect, behavior, and cognition as distinct components of attitude. *Journal of Personality and Social Psychology, 47,* 1191–1205.

Brehm, J. W. (1956). Post-decision changes in desirability of alternatives. *Journal of Abnormal and Social Psychology, 52,* 384–389.

Brehm, J. W. (1966). *A theory of psychological reactance.* New York: Academic Press.

Brehm, J. W., & Cohen, A. R. (1962). *Explorations in cognitive dissonance.* New York: Wiley.

Brehm, J. W., & Self, E. A. (1989). The intensity of motivation. *Annual Review of Psychology, 40,* 109–131.

Brehm, S. S. (1987). Social support and clinical practice. In J. E. Maddux, C. D. Stoltenberg, & R. Rosenwein (Eds.), *Social processes in clinical and counseling psychology* (pp. 26–38). New York: Springer-Verlag.

Brehm, S. S. (1988). Passionate love. In R. J. Sternberg & M. L. Barnes (Eds.), *The psychology of love* (pp. 232–263). New Haven, CT: Yale University Press.

Brehm, S. S. (1992). *Intimate relationships* (2nd ed.). New York: McGraw-Hill.

Brehm, S. S., & Brehm, J. W. (1981). *Psychological reactance: A theory of freedom and control.* New York: Academic Press.

Brehm, S. S., & Smith, T. W. (1986). Social psychological approaches to psychotherapy and behavior change. In S. L. Garfield & A. E. Bergin (Eds.), *Handbook of psychotherapy and behavior change* (3rd ed., pp. 69–115). New York: Wiley.

Brewer, M. B. (1979). Ingroup bias in the minimal intergroup situation: A cognitive-motivational analysis. *Psychological Bulletin, 86,* 307–324.

Brewer, M. B. (1988). A dual process model of impression formation. In T. K. Srull & R. S. Wyer, Jr. (Eds.), *Advances in social cognition* (Vol. 1, pp. 1–36). Hillsdale, NJ: Erlbaum.

Brewer, M. B. (1991). The social self: On being the same and different at the same time. *Personality and Social Psychology Bulletin, 17,* 475–482.

Brewer, M. B., Dull, V., & Lui, L. (1981). Perceptions of the elderly: Stereotypes as prototypes. *Journal of Personality and Social Psychology, 41,* 656–670.

Brewer, M. B., & Kramer, R. M. (1986). Choice behavior in social dilemmas: Effects of social identity, group size, and decision framing. *Journal of Personality and Social Psychology, 50,* 543–549.

Brewer, M. B., & Miller, N. (1984). Beyond the contact hypothesis: Theoretical perspectives on desegregation. In N. Miller & M. B. Brewer (Eds.), *Groups in contact: The psychology of desegregation* (pp. 281–302). New York: Academic Press.

Brickner, M. A., Harkins, S. G., & Ostrom, T. M. (1986). Effects of personal involvement: Thought-provoking implications for social loafing. *Journal of Personality and Social Psychology, 51,* 763–769.

Briggs, S. R., & Cheek, J. M. (1988). On the nature of self-monitoring: Problems with assessment, problems with validity. *Journal of Personality and Social Psychology, 54,* 663–678.

Brigham, J. C., & Cairns, D. L. (1988). The effect of mugshot inspections on eyewitness identification accuracy. *Journal of Applied Social Psychology, 18,* 1394–1410.

Brigham, J. C., Maass, A., Snyder, L. S., & Spaulding, K. (1982). The accuracy of eyewitness identifications in a field setting. *Journal of Personality and Social Psychology, 42,* 673–681.

Brigham, J. C., Maass, A., Snyder, L. S., & Spaulding, K. (1983). The effect of arousal on facial recognition. *Basic and Applied Social Psychology, 4,* 279–293.

Brigham, J. C., & Malpass, R. S. (1985). The role of experience and contact in the recognition of faces of own- and other-race persons. *Journal of Social Issues, 41,* 139–155.

Brinthaupt, R. M., Moreland, R. L., & Levine, J. M. (1991). Sources of optimism among prospective group members. *Personality and Social Psychology Bulletin, 17,* 36–43.

Brock, T. C. (1968). Implications of commodity theory for value exchange. In A. G. Greenwald, T. C. Brock, & T. M. Ostrom (Eds.), *Psychological foundations of attitudes* (pp. 243–275). New York: Academic Press.

Brockner, J. (1983). Low self-esteem and behavioral plasticity: Some implications. In L. Wheeler & P. Shaver (Eds.), *Review of personality and social psychology* (Vol. 4, pp. 237–271). Beverly Hills, CA: Sage.

Brockner, J., DeWitt, R. L., Grover, S., & Reed, T. (1990). When is it important to explain why? Factors affecting the relationship between managers' explanations of a layoff and survivors' reactions to the layoff. *Journal of Experimental Social Psychology, 26,* 389–407.

Brockner, J., & Rubin, J. Z. (1985). *Entrapment in escalating conflicts: A social psychological analysis.* New York: Springer-Verlag.

Brody, J. E. (1991, December 11). Smoking among children is found linked to cartoon advertisements. *New York Times,* p. D22.

Bronfenbrenner, U. (1961). The mirror-image in Soviet-American relations. *Journal of Social Issues, 17,* 45–56.

Brown, B. B., Clasen, D. R., & Eicher, S. A. (1986). Perceptions of peer pressure, peer conformity dispositions, and self-reported behavior among adolescents. *Developmental Psychology, 22,* 521–530.

Brown, C. E., Dovidio, J. F., & Ellyson, S. L. (1990). Reducing sex differences in visual displays of dominance: Knowledge is power. *Personality and Social Psychology Bulletin, 16,* 358–368.

Brown, E., Deffenbacher, K., & Sturgill, W. (1977). Memory for faces and the circumstances of encounter. *Journal of Applied Psychology, 62,* 311–318.

Brown, G. W., & Harris, T. (1978). *Social origins of depression: A study of psychiatric disorder in women.* New York: Free Press.

Brown, J. D. (1990). Evaluating one's abilities: Shortcuts and stumbling blocks on the road to self-knowledge. *Journal of Experimental Social Psychology, 26,* 149–167.

Brown, J. D. (1991). Staying fit and staying well: Physical fitness as a moderator of life stress. *Journal of Personality and Social Psychology, 60,* 555–561.

Brown, J. D., & McGill, K. L. (1989). The cost of good fortune: When positive life events produce negative health consequences. *Journal of Personality and Social Psychology, 57,* 1103–1110.

Brown, J. D., & Smart, S. A. (1991). The self and social conduct: Linking self-representations to prosocial behavior. *Journal of Personality and Social Psychology, 60,* 368–375.

Brown, R. (1965). *Social psychology.* New York: Free Press.

Brown, R. (1986). *Social psychology* (2nd ed.). New York: Free Press.

Brown, R., & Kulik, J. (1977). Flashbulb memories. *Cognition, 5,* 73–99.

Bruch, M. A., Gorsky, J. M., Collins, T. M., & Berger, P. A. (1989). Shyness and sociability examined: A multicomponent analysis. *Journal of Personality and Social Psychology, 57,* 904–915.

Bruner, J. S., & Potter, M. C. (1964). Interference in visual recognition. *Science, 144,* 424–425.

Bruner, J. S., & Tagiuri, R. (1954). Person perception. In G. Lindzey (Ed.), *Handbook of social psychology* (Vol. 2, pp. 634–654). Reading, MA: Addison-Wesley.

Bryan, J. H., & Test, M. A. (1967). Models and helping: Naturalistic studies in aiding behavior. *Journal of Personality and Social Psychology, 6,* 400–407.

Bryant, F. B. (1989). A four-factor model of perceived control: Avoiding, coping, obtaining, and savoring. *Journal of Personality, 57,* 773–797.

Bryson, J. B. (1991). Modes of response to jealousy-evoking situations. In P. Salovey (Ed.), *The psychology of jealousy and envy* (pp. 178–207). New York: Guilford.

Buchwald, A. M., Coyne, J. C., & Cole, C. S. (1978). A critical evaluation of the learned helplessness model of depression. *Journal of Abnormal Psychology, 87,* 180–193.

Buck, R. & Ginsburg, B. (1991). Spontaneous communication and altruism: The communicative gene hypothesis. In M. S. Clark (Ed.), *Review of personality and social psychology: Vol. 12. Prosocial behavior.* (pp. 176–214). Newbury Park, CA: Sage.

Buckhout, R. (1974, December). Eyewitness testimony. *Scientific American,* pp. 23–31.

Budescu, D. V., Rapoport, A., & Suleiman, R. (1990). Resource dilemmas with environmental uncertainty and asymmetric players. *European Journal of Social Psychology, 20,* 475–487.

Bull, R., & Rumsey, N. (1988). *The social psychology of facial appearance.* New York: Springer-Verlag.

Bulman, R. J., & Wortman, C. B. (1977). Attribution of blame and coping in the "real world": Severe accident victims react to their lot. *Journal of Personality and Social Psychology, 35,* 351–363.

Bumpass, L., Sweet, J., & Castro Martin, T. (1990). Changing patterns of remarriage. *Journal of Marriage and the Family, 52,* 747–756.

Burchill, S. A. L., & Stile, W. B. (1988). Interactions of depressed college students with their roommates: Not necessarily negative. *Journal of Personality and Social Psychology, 55,* 410–419.

Burger, J. M. (1981). Motivational biases in the attribution of responsibility for an accident: A meta-analysis of the defensive-attribution hypothesis. *Psychological Bulletin, 90,* 496–512.

Burger, J. M. (1986). Increasing compliance by improving the deal: The that's-not-all technique. *Journal of Personality and Social Psychology, 51,* 277–283.

Burger, J. M. (1989). Negative reactions to increases in perceived control. *Journal of Personality and Social Psychology, 56,* 246–256.

Burger, J. M. (1991). Changes in attributions over time: The ephemeral fundamental attribution error. *Social Cognition, 9,* 182–193.

Burger, J. M., Brown, R., & Allen, C. K. (1983). Negative reactions to personal control. *Journal of Social and Clinical Psychology, 1,* 322–342.

Burger, J. M., & Burns, L. (1988). The illusion of unique invulnerability and use of effective contraception. *Personality and Social Psychology Bulletin, 14,* 264–270.

Burger, J. M., & Cooper, H. M. (1979). The desirability of control. *Motivation and Emotion, 3,* 381–393.

Burger, J. M., & Petty, R. E. (1981). The low-ball compliance technique: Task or person commitment? *Journal of Personality and Social Psychology, 40,* 492–500.

Burish, T. G., Carey, M. P., Wallston, K. A., Stein, J. J., Jamison, R. N., & Lyles, J. N. (1984). Health locus of control and chronic disease: An external orientation may be advantageous. *Journal of Social and Clinical Psychology, 2,* 326–332.

Burnkrant, R. E., & Howard, D. J. (1984). Effects of the use of introductory rhetorical questions versus statements on information processing. *Journal of Personality and Social Psychology, 47,* 1218–1230.

Burns, J. M. (1978). *Leadership.* New York: Harper & Row.

Burns, M. O., & Seligman, M. E. P. (1989). Explanatory style across the life span: Evidence for stability over 52 years. *Journal of Personality and Social Psychology, 56,* 471–477.

Burnstein, E., & Schul, Y. (1982). The informational basis of social judgments: The operations in forming an impression of another person. *Journal of Experimental Social Psychology, 18,* 217–234.

Burson, N., Carling, R., & Kramlich, D. (1986). *Composites: Computer-generated portraits.* New York: Morrow.

Burt, M. C. (1980). Cultural myths and supports for rape. *Journal of Personality and Social Psychology, 38,* 217–230.

Bushman, B. J. (1984). Perceived symbols of authority and their influence on compliance. *Journal of Applied Social Psychology, 14,* 501–508.

Bushman, B. J. (1988). The effects of apparel on compliance: A field experiment with a female authority figure. *Personality and Social Psychology Bulletin, 14,* 459–467.

Bushman, B. J., & Cooper, H. M. (1990). Effects of alcohol on human aggression: An integrative research review. *Psychological Bulletin, 107,* 341–354.

Bushman, B. J., & Geen, R. J. (1990). Role of cognitive-emotional mediators and individual differences in the effects of media violence on aggression. *Journal of Personality and Social Psychology, 58,* 156–163.

Buss, A. H. (1961). *The psychology of aggression.* New York: Wiley.

Buss, A. H. (1980). *Self-consciousness and social anxiety.* San Francisco: Freeman.

Buss, D. M. (1988a). The evolutionary biology of love. In R. J. Sternberg & M. L. Barnes (Eds.), *The psychology of love* (pp. 100–118). New Haven, CT: Yale University Press.

Buss, D. M. (1988b). The evolution of human intrasexual competition: Tactics of mate attraction. *Journal of Personality and Social Psychology, 54,* 616–628.

Buss, D. M. (1989). Sex differences in human mate preferences: Evolutionary hypotheses tested in 37 cultures. *Behavioral and Brain Sciences, 12,* 1–14.

Buss, D. M., & Barnes, M. (1986). Preferences in human mate selection, *Journal of Personality and Social Psychology, 50,* 559–570.

Buss, D. M., Gomes, M., Higgins, D. S., & Lauterbach, K. (1987). Tactics of manipulation. *Journal of Personality and Social Psychology, 52,* 1219–1229.

Butler, D., & Geis, F. L. (1990). Nonverbal affect responses to male and female leaders: Implications for leadership evaluations. *Journal of Personality and Social Psychology, 58,* 48–59.

Buunk, B. P. (1991). Jealousy in close relationships: An exchange-theoretical perspective. In P. Salovey (Ed.), *The psychology of jealousy and envy* (pp. 148–177). New York: Guilford.

Buunk, B. P., & Van Yperen, N. W. (1991). Referential comparisons, relational comparisons, and exchange orientation: Their relation to marital satisfaction. *Personality and Social Psychology Bulletin, 17,* 709–717.

Buunk, B., & Bringle, R. G. (1987). Jealousy in love relationships. In D. Perlman & S. Duck (Eds.), *Intimate relationships: Development, dynamics, and deterioration* (pp. 123–147). Newbury Park, CA: Sage.

Buunk, B., & Hupka, R. B. (1987). Cross-cultural differences in the elicitation of sexual jealousy. *Journal of Sex Research, 23,* 12–22.

Byrne, D. (1971). *The attraction paradigm.* New York: Academic Press.

Byrne, D., & Clore, G. L. (1970). A reinforcement model of evaluative processes. *Personality: An International Journal, 1,* 103–128.

Byrne, D., Clore, G. L., & Smeaton, G. (1986). The attraction hypothesis: Do similar attitudes affect anything? *Journal of Personality and Social Psychology, 51,* 1167–1170.

Byrne, D., Ervin, C. E., & Lamberth, J. (1970). Continuity between the experimental study of attraction and real-life computer dating. *Journal of Personality and Social Psychology, 16,* 157–165.

Byrne, D., & Murnen, S. K. (1988). Maintaining loving relationships. In R. J. Sternberg & M. L. Barnes (Eds.), *The psychology of love* (pp. 293–310). New Haven, CT: Yale University Press.

Cacioppo, J. T., & Petty, R. E. (1981). Electromyograms as measures of extent and affectivity of information processing. *American Psychologist, 36,* 441–456.

Cacioppo, J. T., & Petty, R. E. (1982). The need for cognition. *Journal of Personality and Social Psychology, 42,* 116–131.

Cacioppo, J. T., & Petty, R. E. (1984). The need for cognition: Relationship to attitudinal processes. In R. P. McGlynn, J. E. Maddux, C. D. Stoltenberg, & J. H. Harvey (Eds.), *Interfaces in psychology: Social perception in clinical and counseling psychology* (pp. 113–139). Lubbock, TX: Texas Tech Press.

Cacioppo, J. T., Petty, R. E., & Morris, K. (1983). Effects of need for cognition on message evaluation, recall, and persuasion. *Journal of Personality and Social Psychology, 45,* 805–818.

Cacioppo, J. T., Petty, R. E., Losch, M. E., & Kim, H. S. (1986). Electromyographic activity over facial muscle regions can differentiate the valence and intensity of affective reactions. *Journal of Personality and Social Psychology, 50,* 260–268.

Cacioppo, J. T., Rourke, P. A., Marshall-Goodell, B. S., Tassinary, L. G., & Baron, R. S. (1990). Rudimentary physiological effects of mere observations. *Psychophysiology, 27,* 177–186.

Cacioppo, J. T., & Tassinary, L. G. (1990). Inferring psychological significance from physiological signals. *American Psychologist, 45,* 16–28.

Caldwell, M. A., & Peplau, L. A. (1984). The balance of power in lesbian relationships. *Sex Roles, 10,* 587–599.

Callaway, M. R., Marriott, R. G., & Esser, J. K. (1985). Effects of dominance on group decision making: Toward a stress-reduction explanation of groupthink. *Journal of Personality and Social Psychology, 49,* 949–952.

Campbell, D. J., & Lee, C. (1988). Self-appraisal in performance evaluation: Development versus evaluation. *Academy Management Review, 13,* 302–313.

Campbell, J. D. (1990). Self-esteem and clarity of the self-concept. *Journal of Personality and Social Psychology, 59,* 538–549.

Campbell, J. D., & Fairey, P. J. (1989). Informational and normative routes to conformity. *Journal of Personality and Social Psychology, 57,* 457–468.

Campbell, J. D., Tesser, A., & Fairey, P. J. (1986). Conformity and attention to the stimulus: Some temporal and contextual dynamics. *Journal of Personality and Social Psychology, 51,* 315–324.

Campion, M. A., Pursell, E. D., & Brown, B. K. (1988). Structured interviewing: Raising the psychometric properties of the employment interview. *Personnel Psychology, 41,* 25–42.

Cantor, N., & Mischel, W. (1979). Prototypes in person perception. In L. Berkowitz (Ed.), *Advances in experimental social psychology* (Vol. 12, pp. 3–52). New York: Academic Press.

Caprara, G. V., D'Imperio, G., Gentilomo, A., Mammucari, A., Renzi, P., & Travaglia, G. (1987). The intrusive commercial: Influence of aggressive TV commercials on aggresssion. *European Journal of Social Psychology, 17,* 23–31.

Carey, M. P., & Burish, T. G. (1988). Etiology and treatment of the psychological side effects associated with cancer chemotherapy: A critical review and discussion. *Psychological Bulletin, 104,* 307–325.

Carli, L. L. (1990). Gender, language, and influence. *Journal of Personality and Social Psychology, 59,* 941–951.

Carli, L. L. (1989). Gender differences in interaction styles and influence. *Journal of Personality and Social Psychology, 56,* 565–576.

Carli, L. L., Ganley, R., & Pierce-Otay, A. (1991). Similarity and satisfaction in roommate relationships. *Personality and Social Psychology Bulletin, 17,* 419–426.

Carli, L. L., & Leonard, J. B. (1990). The effect of hindsight on victim derogation. *Journal of Social and Clinical Psychology, 9,* 331–343.

Carlo, G., Eisenberg, N., Troyer, D., Switzer, G., & Speer, A. L. (1991). The altruistic personality: In what context is it apparent? *Journal of Personality and Social Psychology, 61,* 450–458.

Carlsmith, J. M., & Anderson, C. A. (1979). Ambient temperature and the occurrence of collective violence: A new analysis. *Journal of Personality and Social Psychology, 37,* 337–344.

Carlsmith, J. M., & Gross, A. E. (1969). Some effects of guilt on compliance. *Journal of Personality and Social Psychology, 11,* 232–239.

Carlson, M. (1990, January 29). Six years of trial by torture. *Time,* pp. 26–27.

Carlson, M., Charlin, V., & Miller, N. (1988). Positive mood and helping behavior: A test of six hypotheses. *Journal of Personality and Social Psychology, 55,* 211–229.

Carlson, M., Marcus-Newhall, A., & Miller, N. (1990). Effects of situational aggressive cues: A quantitative review. *Journal of Personality and Social Psychology, 58,* 622–633.

Carlson, M., & Miller, N. (1987). Explanation of the relation between negative mood and helping. *Psychological Bulletin, 102,* 91–108.

Carlson, R. (1984). What's social about social psychology? Where's the person in personality research? *Journal of Personality and Social Psychology, 47,* 1304–1309.

Carnegie, D. (1972). *How to win friends and influence people.* New York: Pocket Books. (Original work published 1936)

Carnevale, P. J. (1985). Mediation of international conflict. *Applied Social Psychology Annual, 6,* 87–105.

Carpenter, S. L. (1988). Self-relevance and goal-directed processing in the recall and weighing of information about others. *Journal of Experimental Social Psychology, 24,* 310–332.

Carroll, J. S., Perkowitz, W. T., Lurigio, A. J., & Weaver, F. M. (1987). Sentencing goals, causal attributions, ideology, and personality. *Journal of Personality and Social Psychology, 52,* 107–118.

Cartwright, D., & Zander, A. (1960). Group cohesiveness: Introduction. In D. Cartwright & A. Zander (Eds.), *Group dynam-ics: Research and theory* (2nd ed., pp. 69–94). Evanston, IL: Row, Peterson.

Carver, C. S. (1975). Physical aggression as a function of objective self-awareness and attitudes toward punishment. *Journal of Experimental Social Psychology, 11,* 510–519.

Carver, C. S., & Scheier, M. F. (1981a). *Attention and self-regulation: A control-theory approach to human behavior.* New York: Springer-Verlag.

Carver, C. S., & Scheier, M. F. (1981b). The self-attention-induced feedback loop and social facilitation. *Journal of Experimental Social Psychology, 17,* 545–569.

Carver, C. S., & Scheier, M. F. (1987). The blind men and the elephant: Selective examination of the public-private literature gives rise to a faulty perception. *Journal of Personality, 55,* 525–541.

Carver, C. S., & Scheier, M. F. (1990). Origins and functions of positive and negative affect: A control-process view. *Psychological Review, 97,* 19–35.

Case, R. B., Moss, A. J., Case, N., McDermott, M., & Eberly, S. (1992) Living alone after myocardial infarction: Impact on prognosis. *Journal of the American Medical Association, 267,* 515–519.

Cash, T. F. (1990). Losing hair, losing points?: The effects of male pattern baldness on social impression formation. *Journal of Applied Social Psychology, 20,* 154–167.

Caspi, A., & Harbener, E. S. (1990). Continuity and change: Assortive marriage and the consistency of personality in adulthood. *Journal of Personality and Social Psychology, 58,* 250–258.

Cassel, J. (1974). Psychosocial processes and "stress": Theoretical formulation. *International Journal of Health Services, 6,* 471–482.

Castro Martin, T. C., & Bumpass, L. L. (1989). Recent trends in marital disruption. *Demography, 26,* 37–51.

Cate, R. M., & Lloyd, S. A. (1988). Courtship. In S. Duck (Ed.), *Handbook of personal relationships: Theory, research, and interventions* (pp. 409–427). New York: Wiley.

Cate, R. M., Lloyd, S. A., & Long, E. (1988). The role of rewards and fairness in developing premarital relationships. *Journal of Marriage and the Family, 50,* 443–452.

Ceci, S. J., & Peters, D. (1984). Letters of reference: A naturalistic study of the effects of confidentiality. *American Psychologist, 39,* 29–31.

Ceci, S. J., Peters, D., & Plotkin, J. (1985). Human subjects review, personal values, and the regulation of social science research. *American Psychologist, 40,* 994–1002.

Ceci, S. J., Ross, D. F., & Toglia, M. P. (1987). Suggestibility of children's memory: Psycholegal implications. *Journal of Experimental Psychology, 116,* 38–49.

Ceci, S. J., Ross, D. F., & Toglia, M. P. (1989). *Perspectives on children's testimony.* New York: Springer-Verlag.

Center to Prevent Handgun Violence. (1991, September 23). Bells ring, bullets fly: Students nationwide more prone to violence. AP release reprinted in *Press & Sun-Bulletin* (p. 3A). Binghamton, NY: Binghamton Press Company.

Centers for Disease Control. (1991). Premarital sexual experience among adolescent women—United States, 1970–1988. *Morbidity and Mortality Weekly Report, 39,* Nos. 51 & 52.

Centers for Disease Control Vietnam Experience Study. (1988). Health status of Vietnam veterans: I. Psychosocial characteristics. *Journal of the American Medical Association, 259,* 2701–2707.

Chacko, T. I. (1982). Women and equal employment opportunity: Some unintended effects. *Journal of Applied Psychology, 67,* 119–123.

Chaiken, S. (1979). Communicator physical attractiveness and persuasion. *Journal of Personality and Social Psychology, 37,* 1387–1397.

Chaiken, S. (1980). Heuristic versus systematic information processing and the use of source versus message cues in persuasion. *Journal of Personality and Social Psychology, 39,* 752–766.

Chaiken, S. (1987). The heuristic model of persuasion. In M. P. Zanna, J. M. Olson, & C. P. Herman (Eds.), *Social influence: The Ontario symposium* (Vol. 5, pp. 3–39). Hillsdale, NJ: Erlbaum.

Chaiken, S., & Baldwin, M. W. (1981). Affective-cognitive consistency and the effect of salient behavioral information on the self-perception of attitudes. *Journal of Personality and Social Psychology, 41,* 1–12.

Chaiken, S., Liberman, A., & Eagly, A. (1989). Heuristic and systematic information processing within and beyond the persuasion context. In J. Uleman and J. A. Bargh (Eds.), *Unintended thought* (pp. 212–252). New York: Guilford.

Chapman, L. J. (1967). Illusory correlation in observational report. *Journal of Verbal Learning and Verbal Behavior, 6,* 151–155.

Chassin, L., Presson, C. C., & Sherman, S. J. (1990). Social psychological contributions to the understanding and prevention of adolescent cigarette smoking. *Personality and Social Psychology Bulletin, 16,* 133–151.

Check, J. V. P., & Guloien, T. H. (1989). Reported proclivity for coercive sex following repeated exposure to sexually violent pornography, nonviolent dehumanizing pornography, and erotica. In D. Zillmann & J. Bryant (Eds.), *Pornography: Research advances and policy considerations* (pp. 159–184). Hillsdale, NJ: Erlbaum.

Chemers, M. M., Hays, R. B., Rhodewalt, F., & Wysocki, J. (1985). A person-environment analysis of job stress: A contingency model explanation. *Journal of Personality and Social Psychology, 49,* 628–635.

Cheng, P. W., & Novick, L. R. (1990). A probabilistic contrast model of causal induction. *Journal of Personality and Social Psychology, 58,* 545–567.

Chesler, P., & Goodman, E. J. (1976). *Women, money, and power.* New York: Morrow.

Chipman, S. F., Brush, L. R., & Wilson, D. M. (Eds.) (1985). *Women and mathematics.* Hillsdale, NJ: Erlbaum.

Chiriboga, D. A., Coho, A., Stein, J. A., & Roberts, J. (1979). Divorce, stress, and social support: A study in help-seeking behavior. *Journal of Divorce, 3,* 121–135.

Church, G. J. (1991, September 2). Anatomy of a Coup. *Time,* pp. 33–44.

Cialdini, R. B. (1988). *Influence: Science and practice* (2nd ed.). Glenview, IL: Scott, Foresman.

Cialdini, R. B., & Ascani, K. (1976). Test of a concession procedure for inducing verbal, behavioral, and further compliance with a request to give blood. *Journal of Applied Psychology, 61,* 295–300.

Cialdini, R. B., Borden, R. J., Thorne, A., Walker, M. R., Freeman, S., & Sloan, L. R. (1976). Basking in reflected glory: Three (football) field studies. *Journal of Personality and Social Psychology, 34,* 366–375.

Cialdini, R. B., Cacioppo, J. T., Bassett, R., & Miller, J. A. (1978). Low-ball procedure for producing compliance: Commitment then cost. *Journal of Personality and Social Psychology, 36,* 463–476.

Cialdini, R. B., Darby, B. L., & Vincent, J. E. (1973). Transgressional altruism: A case for hedonism. *Journal of Personality and Social Psychology, 9,* 502–516.

Cialdini, R. B., & De Nicholas, M. E. (1989). Self-presentation by association. *Journal of Personality and Social Psychology, 57,* 626–631.

Cialdini, R. B., & Fultz, J. (1990). Interpreting the negative mood-helping literature via "mega" analysis: A contrary view. *Psychological Bulletin, 107,* 210–214.

Cialdini, R. B., Kallgren, C. A., & Reno, R. R. (1991). A focus theory of normative conduct: A theoretical refinement and reevaluation of the role of norms in human behavior. *Advances in Experimental Social Psychology, 24,* 201–234.

Cialdini, R. B., & Kenrick, D. T. (1976). Altruism as hedonism: A social development perspective on the relationship of negative mood state and helping. *Journal of Personality and Social Psychology, 34,* 907–914.

Cialdini, R. B., Reno, R. R., & Kallgren, C. A. (1990). A focus theory of normative conduct: Recycling the concept of norms to reduce littering in public places. *Journal of Personality and Social Psychology, 58,* 1015–1026.

Cialdini, R. B., Schaller, M., Houlihan, D., Arps, K., Fultz, J., & Beaman, A. L. (1987). Empathy-based helping: Is it selflessly or selfishly motivated? *Journal of Personality and Social Psychology, 52,* 749–758.

Cialdini, R. B., Vincent, J. E., Lewis, S. K., Catalan, J., Wheeler, D., & Darby, B. L. (1975). Reciprocal concessions procedure for inducing compliance: The door-in-the-face technique. *Journal of Personality and Social Psychology, 31,* 206–215.

Clanton, G., & Smith, L. G. (Eds.). (1977). *Jealousy.* Englewood Cliffs, NJ: Prentice-Hall.

Clark, L. A., & Watson, D. (1988). Mood and the mundane: Relations between daily life events and self-reported mood. *Journal of Personality and Social Psychology, 54,* 296–308.

Clark, L. A., & Watson, D. (1991). General affective dispositions in physical and psychological health. In C. R. Snyder & D. R. Forsyth (Eds.), *Handbook of social and clinical psychology: The health perspective* (pp. 221–245). New York: Pergamon Press.

Clark, M. S. (1983a). Reactions to aid in communal and exchange relationships. In J. D. Fisher, A. Nadler, & B. DePaulo (Eds.), *New directions in helping: Vol. 1. Recipient reactions to aid* (pp. 281–304). New York: Academic Press.

Clark, M. S. (1983b). Some implications of close social bonds for help-seeking. In B. M. DePaulo, A. Nadler, & J. D. Fisher (Eds.), *New directions in helping: Vol. 2. Help-seeking* (pp. 205–229). New York: Academic Press.

Clark, M. S. (1984). Record keeping in two types of relationships. *Journal of Personality and Social Psychology, 47,* 549–557.

Clark, M. S., & Mills, J. (1979). Interpersonal attraction in exchange and communal relationships. *Journal of Personality and Social Psychology, 37,* 12–24.

Clark, M. S., Mills, J., & Powell, M. C. (1986). Keeping track of needs in communal and exchange relationships. *Journal of Personality and Social Psychology, 51,* 333–338.

Clark, M., Mills, J. R., & Corcoran, D. M. (1989). Keeping track of needs and inputs of friends and strangers. *Personality and Social Psychology Bulletin, 15,* 533–542.

Clark, M. S., Ouellette, R., Powell, M. C., & Milberg, S. (1987). Recipient's mood, relationship type, and helping. *Journal of Personality and Social Psychology, 53,* 94–103.

Clark, M. S., & Taraban, C. (1991). Reactions to and willingness to express emotion in communal and exchange relationships. *Journal of Experimental Social Psychology, 27,* 324–336.

Clark, M. S., & Waddell, B. (1985). Perceptions of exploitation in communal and exchange relationships. *Journal of Social and Personal Relations, 2,* 403–418.

Clark, N. K., & Stephenson, G. M. (1989). Group remembering. In P. B. Paulus (Ed.), *Psychology of group influence* (2nd ed., pp. 357–391). Hillsdale, NJ: Erlbaum.

Clark, R. D., & Maass, A. (1990). The effects of majority size on minority influence. *European Journal of Social Psychology, 20,* 99–117.

Clark, R. D., III, & Maass, A. (1988). Social categorization in minority influence: The case of homosexuality. *European Journal of Social Psychology, 18,* 347–364.

Clark, R. D., III, & Word, L. E. (1972). Why don't bystanders help? Because of ambiguity? *Journal of Personality and Social Psychology, 24,* 392–400.

Clark, R. D., III, & Word, L. E. (1974). What is the apathetic bystander? Situational characteristics of the emergency. *Journal of Personality and Social Psychology, 29,* 279–287.

Clary, E. G., & Orenstein, L. (1991). The amount and effectiveness of help: The relationship of motives and abilities to helping behavior. *Personality and Social Psychology Bulletin, 17,* 58–64.

Cleek, M. G., & Pearson, T. A. (1985). Perceived causes of divorce: An analysis of interrelationships. *Journal of Marriage and the Family, 47,* 179–183.

Clore, G. L., & Byrne, D. (1974). A reinforcement-affect model of attraction. In T. L. Huston (Ed.), *Foundations of interpersonal attraction* (pp. 143–170). New York: Academic Press.

Coates, D., Renzaglia, G. J., & Embree, M. C. (1983). When helping backfires: Help and helplessness. In J. D. Fisher, A. Nadler, & B. DePaulo (Eds.), *New directions in helping: Vol. 1.*

Recipient reactions to aid (pp. 251–279). New York: Academic Press.

Coates, T. J., Stall, R. D., & Hoff, C. C. (1990). Change in sexual behavior among gay and bisexual men since the beginning of the AIDS epidemic. In L. Temoshok & A. Baum (Eds.), *Psychosocial perspectives on AIDS* (pp. 103–137). Hillsdale, NJ: Erlbaum.

Cobb, S. (1976). Social support as a moderator of life stress. *Psychosomatic Medicine, 38,* 300–314.

Cochran, S. D., & Mays, V. M. (1989). Women and AIDS-related concerns: Roles for psychologists in helping the worried well. *American Psychologist, 44,* 529–535.

Cohen, E. G. (1984). The desegregated school: Problems in status power and interethnic climate. In N. Miller, & M. B. Brewer (Eds.), *Groups in contact: The psychology of desegregation* (pp. 77–96). New York: Academic Press.

Cohen, J. B., & Chakravarti, D. (1990). Consumer psychology. *Annual Review of Psychology, 41,* 243–288.

Cohen, S., & Hoberman, H. M. (1983). Positive events and social supports as buffers of life change. *Journal of Applied Social Psychology, 13,* 99–125.

Cohen, S., & McKay, G. (1984). Social support, stress and the buffering hypothesis. In A. Baum, S. E. Taylor, & J. E. Singer (Eds.), *Handbook of psychology and health: Vol. 4. Social psychological aspects of health* (pp. 253–267). Hillsdale, NJ: Erlbaum.

Cohen, S., & Syme, S. L. (Eds.). (1985). *Social support and health.* Orlando, FL: Academic Press.

Cohen, S., & Wills, T. A. (1985). Stress, social support, and the buffering hypothesis. *Psychological Bulletin, 98,* 310–357.

Collins, N. L., & Read, S. J. (1990). Adult attachment, working models, and relationshp quality in dating couples. *Journal of Personality and Social Psychology, 58,* 644–663.

Colman, A. M. (1991). Crowd psychology in South African murder trials. *American Psychologist, 46,* 1071–1079.

Colvin, C. R., & Funder, D. C. (1991). Predicting personality and behavior: A boundary on the acquaintanceship effect. *Journal of Personality and Social Psychology, 60,* 884–894.

Commission on Obscenity and Pornography. (1970). *Report of the commission on obscenity and pornography.* New York: Bantam Books.

Condon, J. W., & Crano, W. D. (1988). Inferred evalution and the relation between attitude similarity and interpersonal attraction. *Journal of Personality and Social Psychology, 54,* 789–797.

Condry, J., & Condry, S. (1976). Sex differences: A study of the eye of the beholder. *Child Development, 47,* 812–819.

Conger, J. D., Conger, A. J., & Brehm, S. S. (1976). Fear level as a moderator of false feedback effects in snake phobics. *Journal of Consulting and Clinical Psychology, 44,* 135–141.

Conn, M. K., & Peterson, C. (1989). Social support: Seek and ye shall find. *Journal of Social and Personal Relationships, 6,* 345–358.

Contrada, R. (1989). Type A behavior, personality hardiness, and cardiovascular response to stress. *Journal of Personality and Social Psychology, 57,* 895–903.

Cook, S. W. (1975). A comment on the ethical issues involved in West, Gunn, and Chernicky's "Ubiquitous Watergate: An Attributional Analysis." *Journal of Personality and Social Psychology, 32,* 66–68.

Cook, S. W. (1976). Ethical issues in the conduct of research in social relations. In C. Selltiz, L. S. Wrightsman, & S. W. Cook, *Research methods in social relations* (3rd ed., pp. 199–249). New York: Holt, Rinehart and Winston.

Cook, S. W. (1984). The 1954 social science statement and school desegregation: A reply to Gerard. *American Psychologist, 39,* 819–832.

Cook, S. W. (1985). Experimenting on social issues: The case of school desegregation. *American Psychologist, 40,* 452–460.

Cook, S. W., & Pelfrey, M. (1985). Reactions to being helped in cooperating interracial groups: A context effect. *Journal of Personality and Social Psychology, 49,* 1231–1245.

Cook, T., Armor, D., Crain, R., Miller, N., Stephan, W., Walberg, H., & Wortman, P. (Eds.) (1984). *School desegregation and black achievement.* Washington, DC: National Institute of Education.

Cook, T. D., & Campbell, D. T. (1979). *Quasi-experimentation: Design and analysis issues for field settings.* Chicago: Rand McNally.

Cook, T. D., Gruder, C. L., Hennigan, K. M., & Flay, B. R. (1979). History of the sleeper effect: Some logical pitfalls in accepting the null hypothesis. *Psychological Bulletin, 86,* 662–679.

Cook, T. D., Kendzierski, D. A., & Thomas, S. V. (1983). The implicit assumptions of television research: An analysis of the 1982 NIMH report on television and behavior. *Public Opinion Quarterly, 47,* 161–201.

Cook, T. D., Leviton, L. C., & Shadish, W. R., Jr. (1985). Program evaluation. In G. Lindzey & E. Aronson (Eds.), *Handbook of social psychology* (Vol. 1, 3rd ed., pp. 699–777). New York: Random House.

Cooley, C. H. (1964). *Human nature and the social order.* New York: Schocken Books. (Original work published 1902)

Coombs, C. H. (1987). The structure of conflict. *American Psychologist, 42,* 355–363.

Cooper, H. (1990). Meta-analysis and the integrative research review. In C. Hendrick & M. S. Clark (Eds.), *Review of personality and social psychology: Vol. 11. Research methods in personality and social psychology* (pp. 142–163). Newbury Park, CA: Sage.

Cooper, H., & Good, T. (1983). *Pygmalion grows up: Studies in the expectation communication process.* New York: Longman.

Cooper, J., & Fazio, R. H. (1984). A new look at dissonance theory. In L. Berkowitz (Ed.), *Advances in experimental social psychology* (Vol. 17, pp. 229–267). New York: Academic Press.

Cooper, J., & Mackie, D. (1986). Videogames and aggression in children. *Journal of Applied Social Psychology, 16,* 726–744.

Cooper, J., Zanna, M. P., & Goethals, G. R. (1974). Mistreatment of an esteemed other as a consequence affecting dissonance reduction. *Journal of Experimental Social Psychology, 10,* 224–233.

Cooper, J., Zanna, M. P., & Taves, P. A. (1978). Arousal as a necessary condition for attitude change following induced compliance. *Journal of Personality and Social Psychology, 36,* 1101–1106.

Cooper, W. H. (1981). Ubiquitous halo. *Psychological Bulletin, 90,* 218–224.

Coopersmith, S. (1967). *The antecedents of self-esteem.* San Francisco: Freeman.

Coovert, M. D., & Reeder, G. D. (1990). Negativity effects in impression formation: The role of unit formation and schematic expectations. *Journal of Experimental Social Psychology, 26,* 49–62.

Cornell, L. L. (1989). Gender differences in remarriage and divorce in Japan and the United States. *Journal of Marriage and the Family, 51,* 457–463.

Costa, P. T., Jr., McCrae, R. P., & Dembroski, T. M. (1989). Agreeableness versus antagonism: Explication of a potential risk factor for CHD. In A. W. Siegman & T. M. Dembroski (Eds.), *In search of coronary-prone behavior: Beyond Type A* (pp. 41–63). Hillsdale, NJ: Erlbaum.

Costello, C. G. (1982). Social factors associated with depression: A retrospective community study. *Psychological Medicine, 12,* 329–339.

Cottrell, N. B. (1968). Performance in the presence of other human beings: Mere presence, audience, and affiliation effects. In E. C. Simmel, R. A. Hoppe, & G. A. Milton (Eds.), *Social facilitation and imitative behavior* (pp. 91–110). Boston: Allyn & Bacon.

Cottrell, N. B., Wack, D. L., Sekerak, G. J., & Rittle, R. H. (1968). Social facilitation of dominant responses by the presence of an audience and the mere presence of others. *Journal of Personality and Social Psychology, 9,* 245–250.

Court, J. H. (1984). Sex and violence: A ripple effect. In N. M. Malamuth & E. I. Donnerstein (Eds.), *Pornography and sexual aggression* (pp. 143–172). New York: Academic Press.

Cowan, C. L., Thompson, W. C., & Ellsworth, P. C. (1984). The effects of death qualification on jurors' predisposition to convict and on the quality of deliberation. *Law and Human Behavior, 8,* 53–80.

Cox, M., & Tanford, S. (1989). An alternative method of capital jury selection. *Law and Human Behavior, 13,* 167–183.

Coyne, J. C. (1991). Social factors and psychopathology: Stress, social support, and coping processes. *Annual Review of Psychology, 42,* 401–425.

Coyne, J. C., & Smith, D. A. F. (1991). Couples coping with a myocardial infarction: A contextual perspective on wives' distress. *Journal of Personality and Social Psychology, 61,* 404–412.

Cozby, P. C. (1973). Self-disclosure: A literature review. *Psychological Bulletin, 79,* 73–91.

Cramer, R. E., McMaster, M. R., Bartell, P. A., & Dragna, M. (1988). Subject competence and the minimization of the bystander effect. *Journal of Applied Social Psychology, 18,* 1133–1148.

Cramer, R. E., Weiss, R. F., Steigleder, M. K., & Balling, S. S. (1985). Attraction in context: Acquisition and blocking of person-directed action. *Journal of Personality and Social Psychology, 49,* 1221–1230.

Crocker, J. C., & Major, B. (1989). Social stigma and self-esteem: The self-protective properties of stigma. *Psychological Review, 96,* 608–630.

Crocker, J., Voelkl, K., Testa, M., & Major, B. (1991). Social stigma: The affective consequences of attributional ambiguity. *Journal of Personality and Social Psychology, 60,* 218–228.

Cronbach, L. J. (1955). Processes affecting scores on "understanding of others" and "assumed similarity." *Psychological Bulletin, 52,* 177–193.

Crosby, F. (1976). A model of egoistical relative deprivation. *Psychological Review, 83,* 85–113.

Crosby, F. (1982). *Relative deprivation and working women.* New York: Oxford University Press.

Crosby, F. J. (1991). *Juggling.* New York: Free Press.

Crosby, F., Bromley, S., & Saxe, L. (1980). Recent unobtrusive studies of black and white discrimination and prejudice: A literature review. *Psychological Bulletin, 87,* 546–563.

Cross, H. A., Halcomb, C. G., & Matter, W. W. (1967). Imprinting or exposure learning in rats given early auditory stimulation. *Psychonomic Sciences, 7,* 233–234.

Croyle, R., & Cooper, J. (1983). Dissonance arousal: Physiological evidence. *Journal of Personality and Social Psychology, 45,* 782–791.

Croyle, R. T., & Ditto, P. H. (1990). Illness cognition and behavior: An experimental approach. In *Journal of Behavioral Medicine, 13,* 31–52.

Croyle, R. T., & Hunt, J. R. (1991). Coping with health threat: Social influence process in reaction to medical test results. *Journal of Personality and Social Psychology, 60,* 382–389.

Crutchfield, R. S. (1955). Conformity and character. *American Psychologist, 10,* 195–198.

Csikszentmihalyi, M., & Figurski, T. J. (1982). Self-awareness and aversive experience in everyday life. *Journal of Personality, 50,* 15–28.

Cunningham, J. A., Strassberg, D. S., & Haan, B. (1986). Effects of intimacy and sex-role congruency on self-disclosure. *Journal of Social and Clinical Psychology, 4,* 393–401.

Cunningham, M. R. (1979). Weather, mood, and helping behavior: Quasi experiments with the sunshine Samaritan. *Journal of Personality and Social Psychology, 37,* 1947–1956.

Cunningham, M. R., Barbee, A. P., & Pike, C. L. (1990a). What do women want? Facialmetric assessment of multiple motives in the perception of male physical attractiveness. *Journal of Personality and Social Psychology, 59,* 21–72.

Cunningham, M. R., Shaffer, D. R., Barbee, A. P., Wolff, P. L., & Kelley, D. J. (1990b). Separate processes in the relation of elation and depression to helping: Social versus personal concerns. *Journal of Experimental Social Psychology, 26,* 13–33.

Cunningham, M. R., Steinberg, J., & Grev, R. (1980). Wanting to and having to help: Separate motivations for positive mood

and guilt-induced helping. *Journal of Personality and Social Psychology, 38,* 181–192.

Cupach, W. R., & Comstock, J. (1990). Satisfaction with sexual communication in marriage: Links to sexual satisfaction and dyadic adjustment. *Journal of Social and Personal Relationships, 7,* 179–186.

Curtis, R. C., & Miller, K. (1986). Believing another likes or dislikes you: Behaviors making the beliefs come true. *Journal of Personality and Social Psychology, 51,* 284–290.

Cutler, B. L., Penrod, S. D., & Dexter, H. R. (1989). The eyewitness, the expert, and the the jury. *Law and Human Behavior, 13,* 311–332.

Cutler, B. L., Penrod, S. D., & Stuve, T. E. (1988). Juror decision making in eyewitness identification cases. *Law and Human Behavior, 12,* 41–55.

Cutrona, C. (1982). Transition to college: Loneliness and the process of social adjustment. In L. A. Peplau & D. Perlman (Eds.), *Loneliness: A sourcebook of current theory, research, and therapy* (pp. 291–309). New York: Wiley.

Cutrona, C. E., Suhr, J. A., & MacFarlane, R. (1990). Interpersonal transactions and the psychological sense of support. In S. Duck & R. C. Silver, (Eds.), *Personal relationships and social support* (pp. 30–45). Newbury Park, CA: Sage.

Dabbs, J. M., Jr., Frady, R. L., Carr, T. S., & Besch, N. F. (1987). Saliva testosterone and criminal violence in young adult prison inmates. *Psychosomatic Medicine, 49,* 174–181.

Dabbs, J. M., Jr., Hopper, C. H., & Jurkovic, G. J. (1990). Testosterone and personality among college students and military veterans. *Personality and Individual Differences, 11,* 1263–1269.

Dabbs, J. M., Jr., & Morris, R. (1990). Testosterone, social class, and antisocial behavior in a sample of 4,462 men. *Psychological Science, 1,* 209–211.

Dabbs, J. M., Jr., Ruback, R. B., Frady, R. L., Hopper, C. H., & Sgoutas, D. S. (1988). Saliva testosterone and criminal violence among women. *Personality and Individual Differences, 9,* 269–275.

Dakof, G. A., & Taylor, S. E. (1990). Victims' perceptions of social support: What is helpful from whom? *Journal of Personality and Social Psychology, 58,* 80–89.

Dallas, M. E., & Baron, R. S. (1985). Do psychotherapists use a confirmatory strategy during interviewing? *Journal of Social and Clinical Psychology, 3,* 106–122.

Danheiser, P. R., & Graziano, W. G. (1982). Self-monitoring and cooperation as a self-presentational strategy. *Journal of Personality and Social Psychology, 42,* 497–505.

Darley, J. M., & Batson, C. D. (1973). From Jerusalem to Jericho: A study of situational and dispositional variables in helping behavior. *Journal of Personality and Social Psychology, 27,* 100–108.

Darley, J. M., & Fazio, R. (1980). Expectancy confirmation processes arising in the social interaction sequence. *American Psychologist, 35,* 867–881.

Darley, J. M., Fleming, J. H., Hilton, J. L., & Swann, W. B., Jr. (1988). Dispelling negative expectancies: The impact of interaction goals and target characteristics on the expectancy confirmation process. *Journal of Experimental Social Psychology, 24,* 19–36.

Darley, J. M., & Gross, P. H. (1983). A hypothesis-confirming bias in labeling effects. *Journal of Personality and Social Psychology, 44,* 20–33.

Darwin, C. (1872). *The expression of the emotions in man and animals.* London: John Murray.

Davidson, A. R., & Jaccard, J. J. (1979). Variables that moderate the attitude-behavior relation: Results of a longitudinal survey. *Journal of Personality and Social Psychology, 37,* 1364–1376.

Davidson, A. R., Yantis, S., Norwood, M., & Montano, D. E. (1985). Amount of information about the attitude object and attitude-behavior consistency. *Journal of Personality and Social Psychology, 49,* 1184–1198.

Davidson, L. M., & Baum, A. (1985). Implications of post-traumatic stress for social psychology. *Applied Social Psychology Annual, 6,* 207–232.

Davis, J. H., Kameda, T., Parks, C., Stasson, M., & Zimmerman, S. (1989). Some social mechanics of group decision-making: The distribution of opinion, polling sequence, and implications for consensus. *Journal of Personality and Social Psychology, 57,* 1000–1012.

Davis, M. H. (1983). Measuring individual differences in empathy: Evidence for a multidimensional approach. *Journal of Personality and Social Psychology, 44,* 113–126.

Davis, M. H., & Oathout, H. A. (1987). Maintenance of satisfaction in romantic relationships: Empathy and relational competence. *Journal of Personality and Social Psychology, 53,* 397–410.

Davis, S. (1990). Men as success objects and women as sex objects: A study of personal advertisements. *Sex Roles, 23,* 43–50.

Dawes, R. M., & Smith, T. L. (1985). Attitude and opinion measurement. In G. Lindzey & E. Aronson (Eds.), *The handbook of social psychology* (Vol. 2, pp. 509–566). New York: Random House.

Dawkins, R. (1976). *The selfish gene.* New York: Oxford University Press.

Deaux, K., & Emswiller, T. (1974). Explanations for successful performance on sex-linked tasks: What is skill for the male is luck for the female. *Journal of Personality and Social Psychology, 29,* 80–85.

Deaux, K., & Lewis, L. L. (1984). The structure of gender stereotypes: Interrelationships among components and gender label. *Journal of Personality and Social Psychology, 46,* 991–1004.

Deaux, K., & Major, B. (1987). Putting gender into context: An interactive model of gender-related behavior. *Psychological Review, 94,* 369–389.

Deaux, K., Winton, W., Crowley, M., & Lewis, L. L. (1985). Level of categorization and content of gender stereotypes. *Social Cognition, 3,* 145–167.

DeBenedictis, D. J. (1990, April). McMartin Preschool's lessons. *ABA Journal,* pp. 28–29.

DeBono, K. G. (1987). Investigating the social-adjustive and value-expressive functions of attitudes: Implications for persuasion processes. *Journal of Personality and Social Psychology, 52,* 279–287.

DeBono, K. G., & Packer, M. (1992). The effects of advertising appeal on perceptions of product quality. *Personality and Social Psychology Bulletin.*

Deci, E. L. (1971). Effects of externally mediated rewards on intrinsic motivation. *Journal of Personality and Social Psychology, 18,* 105–115.

Deci, E. L., & Ryan, R. M. (1985). *Intrinsic motivation and self-determination in human behavior.* New York: Plenum.

Deci, E. L., Connell, J. P., & Ryan, R. M. (1989). Self-determination in a work organization. *Journal of Applied Psychology, 74,* 580–590.

Deffenbacher, K. (1983). The influence of arousal on reliability of testimony. In S. Lloyd-Bostock & B. Clifford (Eds.), *Evaluating witness evidence* (pp. 235–251). London: Wiley.

DeGree, C. E., & Snyder, C. R. (1985). Adler's psychology (of use) today: Personality history of traumatic life events as a self-handicapping strategy. *Journal of Personality and Social Psychology, 48,* 1512–1519.

DeJong, W. (1979). An examination of self-perception mediation of the foot-in-the-door effect. *Journal of Personality and Social Psychology, 37,* 2221–2239.

DeLamater, J. (1987). Gender differences in sexual scenarios. In K. Kelley (Ed.), *Females, males, and sexuality: Theories and research* (pp. 127–139). Albany, NY: State University of New York Press.

Demaré, D., Briere, J., & Lips, H. M. (1988). Violent pornography and self-reported likelihood of sexual aggression. *Journal of Research in Personality, 22,* 140–153.

DeMaris, A., & Rao, K. V. (1992). Premarital cohabitation and subsequent marital stability in the United States: A reassessment. *Journal of Marriage and the Family, 54,* 178–190.

Dembroski, T. M., & Czajkowski, S. M. (1989). Historical and current developments in coronary-prone behavior. In A. W. Siegman & T. M. Dembroski (Eds.), *In search of coronary-prone behavior: Beyond Type A* (pp. 21–39). Hillsdale, NJ: Erlbaum.

Dengerink, H. A., Schnedler, R. W., & Covey, M. K. (1978). Role of avoidance in aggressive responses to attack and no attack. *Journal of Personality and Social Psychology, 36,* 1044–1053.

DePaulo, B. M. (1992). Nonverbal behavior and self-representation. *Psychological Bulletin, 111,* 203–243.

DePaulo, B. M., Dull, W. R., Greenberg, J. M., & Swaim, G. W. (1989). Are shy people reluctant to help? *Journal of Personality and Social Psychology, 56,* 834–844.

DePaulo, B. M., Epstein, J. A., & LeMay, C. S. (1990). Responses of the socially anxious to the prospect of interpersonal evaluation. *Journal of Personality, 58,* 623–640.

DePaulo, B. M., Lanier, K., & Davis, T. (1983). Detecting the deceit of the motivated liar. *Journal of Personality and Social Psychology, 45,* 1096–1103.

DePaulo, B. M., Lassiter, G. D., & Stone, J. I. (1982). Attentional determinants of success at detecting deception and truth. *Personality and Social Psychology Bulletin, 8,* 273–279.

DePaulo, B. M., LeMay, C. S., & Epstein, J. A. (1991). Effects of importance of success and expectations for success on effectiveness at deceiving. *Personality and Social Psychology Bulletin, 17,* 14–24.

Derlega, V. J., & Berg, J. H. (1987). *self-disclosure: Theory, research, and therapy.* New York: Plenum.

Derlega, V. J., Wilson, M. & Chaikin, A. L. (1976). Friendship and disclosure reciprocity. *Journal of Personality and Social Psychology, 34,* 578–587.

Derlega, V. J., Winstead, B. A., Wong, P. T. P., & Hunter, S. (1985). Gender effects in an initial encounter: A case where men exceed women in disclosure. *Journal of Social and Personal Relations, 2,* 25–44.

Dershowitz, A. M. (1982). *The best defense.* New York: Vintage Books.

Desforges, D. M., Lord, C. G., Ramsey, S. L., Mason, J. A., Van Leeuwen, M. D., West, S. C., & Lepper, M. R. (1991). Effects of cooperative contact on changing negative attitudes toward stigmatized social groups. *Journal of Personality and Social Psychology, 60,* 531–544.

Deutsch, F. M. (1989). The false consensus effect: Is the self-justification hypothesis justified? *Basic and Applied Social Psychology, 10,* 83–99.

Deutsch, M. (1973). *The resolution of conflict.* New Haven, CT: Yale University Press.

Deutsch, M., & Gerard, H. B. (1955). A study of normative and informational social influences upon individual judgment. *Journal of Abnormal and Social Psychology, 51,* 629–636.

Deutsch, M., & Krauss, R. M. (1960). The effect of threat upon interpersonal bargaining. *Journal of Abnormal and Social Psychology, 61,* 181–189.

Devine, P. G. (1989). Stereotypes and prejudice: Their automatic and controlled components. *Journal of Personality and Social Psychology, 56,* 5–18.

Devine, P. G., & Baker, S. M. (1991). Measurement of racial stereotype subtyping. *Personality and Social Psychology Bulletin, 17,* 44–50.

Devine, P. G., Monteith, M. J., Zuwerink, J. R., & Elliot, A. J. (1991). Prejudice with and without compunction. *Journal of Personality and Social Psychology, 60,* 817–830.

Diehl, M., & Stroebe, W. (1991). Productivity loss in idea-generating groups: Tracking down the blocking effect. *Journal of Personality and Social Psychology, 61,* 392–403.

Diener, E. (1979). Deindividuation, self-awareness, and disinhibition. *Journal of Personality and Social Psychology, 37,* 1160–1171.

Diener, E. (1980). Deindividuation: The absence of self-awareness and self-regulation in group members. In P. B. Paulus (Ed.), *Psychology of group influence* (pp. 209–242). Hillsdale, NJ: Erlbaum.

Diener, E., & Crandall, R. (1978). *Ethics in social and behavioral research.* Chicago: University of Chicago Press.

Diener, E., Fraser, S. C., Beaman, A. L., & Kelem, R. T. (1976). Effects of deindividuation variables on stealing among Halloween trick-or-treaters. *Journal of Personality and Social Psychology, 33,* 178–183.

DiLalla, L. F., & Gottesman, I. I. (1991). Biological and genetic contributions to violence—Widom's untold tale. *Psychological Bulletin, 109,* 125–129.

Dillard, J. P. (1991). The current status of research on sequential-request compliance techniques. *Personality and Social Psychology Bulletin, 17,* 283–288.

Dion, K. K., Berscheid, E., & Walster, E. (1972). What is beautiful is good. *Journal of Personality and Social Psychology, 24,* 285–290.

Dion, K. L. (1987). What's in a title? The Ms. stereotype and images of women's title of address. *Psychology of Women Quarterly, 11,* 21–36.

Dion, K. L., & Cota, A. A. (1991). The Ms. stereotype: Its domain and the role of explicitness in title preference. *Psychology of Women Quarterly, 15,* 403–410.

Dion, K. L., & Dion, K. K. (1976). Love, liking and trust in heterosexual relationships. *Personality and Social Psychology Bulletin, 2,* 187–190.

Dion, K. L., & Dion, K. K. (1988). Romantic love: Individual and cultural perspectives. In R. J. Sternberg & M. L. Barnes (Eds.), *The psychology of love* (pp. 264–289). New Haven, CT: Yale University Press.

Dodd, D. K. (1985). Robbers in the classroom: A deindividuation exercise. *Teaching in Psychology, 12,* 89–91.

Dodge, K. A., & Coie, J. D. (1987). Social-information-processing factors in reactive and proactive aggression in children's peer groups. *Journal of Personality and Social Psychology, 53,* 1146–1158.

Dodge, K. A., & Crick, N. R. (1990). Social information-processing bases of aggressive behavior in children. *Personality and Social Psychology Bulletin, 16,* 8–22.

Dodson, C., & Reisberg, D. (1991). Indirect testing of eyewitness memory: The (non)effect of misinformation. *Bulletin of the Psychonomic Society, 29,* 333–336.

Dolan, B., & West, A. E. (1991, June 29). Should you worry about getting AIDS from your dentist? *Time,* pp. 50–51.

Dollard, J., Doob, L. W., Miller, N. E., Mowrer, O. H., & Sears, R. R. (1939). *Frustration and aggression.* New Haven, CT: Yale University Press.

Donne, J. (1975). Meditation, 17. In A. Raspa (Ed.), *Devotions upon emergent occasions* (p. 87). Montreal: McGill-Queen's University Press. (Original work published 1624)

Donnerstein, E. (1984). Pornography: Its effects on violence against women. In N. M. Malamuth & E. Donnerstein (Eds.), *Pornography and sexual aggression* (pp. 53–81). New York: Academic Press.

Donnerstein, E., & Barrett, G. (1978). The effects of erotic stimuli on male aggression towards females. *Journal of Personality and Social Psychology, 36,* 180–188.

Donnerstein, E., & Berkowitz, L. (1981). Victim reactions in aggressive erotic films as a factor in violence against women. *Journal of Personality and Social Psychology, 41,* 710–724.

Donnerstein, E., & Donnerstein, M. (1976). Research in the control of interracial aggression. In R. G. Geen and E. C. O'Neal (Eds.), *Perspectives on aggression* (pp. 133–168). New York: Academic Press.

Donnerstein, E., & Hallam, J. (1978). Facilitating effects of erotica on aggression against women. *Journal of Personality and Social Psychology, 36,* 1270–1277.

Donnerstein, E., Linz, D., & Penrod, S. (1987). *The question of pornography.* New York: Free Press.

Doris, J. (Ed.). (1991). *The suggestibility of children's recollections: Implications for eyewitness testimony.* Washington, DC: American Psychological Association.

Dornbusch, S. M., Hastorf, A. H., Richardson, S. A., Muzzy, R. E., & Vreeland, R. S. (1965). The perceiver and the perceived: Their relative influence on categories of interpersonal perception. *Journal of Personality and Social Psychology, 1,* 434–440.

Dovidio, J. F. (1984). Helping behavior and altruism: An empirical and conceptual overview. In L. Berkowitz (Ed.), *Advances in experimental social psychology* (Vol. 17, pp. 361–427). New York: Academic Press.

Dovidio, J. F., Allen, J. L., & Schroeder, D. A. (1990). Specificity of empathy-induced helping: Evidence for altruistic motivation. *Journal of Personality and Social Psychology, 59,* 249–260.

Dovidio, J. F., Brown, C. E., Heltman, K., Ellyson, S. L., & Keating, C. F. (1988a). Power displays between women and men in discussion of gender-linked tasks: A multichannel study. *Journal of Personality and Social Psychology, 55,* 580–587.

Dovidio, J. F., Ellyson, S. L., Keating, C. F., Heltman, K., & Brown, C. E. (1988b). The relationship of social power to visual displays of dominance between men and women. *Journal of Personality and Social Psychology, 54,* 233–242.

Dovidio, J. F., Evans, N., & Tyler, R. (1986). Racial stereotypes: The contents of their cognitive representations. *Journal of Experimental Social Psychology, 22,* 22–37.

Dovidio, J. F., & Gaertner, S. L. (1981). The effects of race, status, and ability on helping behavior. *Social Psychology Quarterly, 44,* 192–203.

Dovidio, J. F., & Gaertner, S. L. (1983). The effects of sex, status, and ability on helping behavior. *Journal of Applied Social Psychology, 13,* 191–205.

Dovidio, J. F., & Gaertner, S. L. (Eds.). (1986). *Prejudice, discrimination, and racism: Theory and research.* Orlando, FL: Academic Press.

Dovidio, J. F., Piliavin, J. A., Gaertner, S. L., Schroeder, D. A., & Clark, R. D, II. (1991). The arousal:cost-reward model and the process of intervention: A review of the evidence. In M. S. Clark (Ed.), *Review of personality and social psychology 12: Prosocial behavior* (pp. 86–118). Newbury Park, CA: Sage.

Downey, G., Silver, R. C., & Wortman, C. B. (1990). Reconsidering the attribution-adjustment relation following a major negative event: Coping with the loss of a child. *Journal of Personality and Social Psychology, 59,* 925–940.

Downs, A. C., & Lyons, P. M. (1991). Natural observations of the links between attractiveness and initial legal judgments. *Personality and Social Psychology Bulletin, 17,* 541–547.

Doyle, J. A. (1983). *The male experience.* Dubuque, IA: Brown.

Drigotas, S. M., & Rusbult, C. E. (1992). Shall I stay or should I go? A dependence model of breakups. *Journal of Personality and Social Psychology, 62,* 62–87.

Driscoll, R., Davis, K. W., & Lipetz, M. E. (1972). Parental interference and romantic love. *Journal of Personality and Social Psychology, 24,* 1–10.

D'Souza, D. (1991). *Illiberal education: The politics of race and sex on campus.* New York: Free Press.

Duck, S. (Ed.) (1988). *Handbook of personal relationships: Theory, research, and interventions.* New York: Wiley.

Duck, S. W. (1977). *The study of acquaintance.* Westmead, England: Saxon House, Teakfield.

Duclos, S. E., Laird, J. D., Schneider, E., Sexter, M., Stern, L., & Van Lighten, O. (1989). Emotion-specific effects of facial expressions and postures on emotional experience. *Journal of Personality and Social Psychology, 57,* 100–108.

Duncan, B. L. (1976). Differential social perception and attribution of intergroup violence: Testing the lower limits of stereotyping of blacks. *Journal of Personality and Social Psychology, 34,* 590–598.

Duncan, G. J., & Hoffman, S. D. (1985). A reconsideration of the economic consequences of marital dissolution. *Demography, 22,* 485–497.

Dunn, D. S., & Wilson, T. D. (1990). When the stakes are high: A limit to the illusion-of-control effect. *Social Cognition, 8,* 305–323.

Dunning, D., Griffin, D. W., Milojkovic, J. D., & Ross, L. (1990). The overconfidence effect in social prediction. *Journal of Personality and Social Psychology, 58,* 568–581.

Dunning, D., & Story, A. L. (1991). Depression, realism, and the overconfidence effect: Are the sadder wiser when predicting future actions and events? *Journal of Personality and Social Psychology, 61,* 521–532.

Dutton, D. G. (1987). Wife assault: Social psychological contributions to criminal justice policy. *Applied Social Psychology Annual, 7,* 238–261.

Dutton, D. G., & Aron, A. P. (1974). Some evidence for heightened sexual attraction under conditions of high anxiety. *Journal of Personality and Social Psychology, 30,* 510–517.

Duval, S., & Wicklund, R. A. (1972). *A theory of objective self-awareness.* New York: Academic Press.

Duval, T. S., Duval, V. H., & Mulilis, J. P. (1992). Effects of self-focus, discrepancy between self and standard, and outcome expectancy favorability on the tendency to match self to standard or to withdraw. *Journal of Personality and Social Psychology, 62,* 340–348.

Eagly, A. H. (1987). *Sex differences in social behavior: A social-role interpretation*. Hillsdale, NJ: Erlbaum.

Eagly, A. H., Ashmore, R. D., Makhijani, M. G., & Longo, L. C. (1991). What is beautiful is good, but . . . : A meta-analytic review of research on the physical attractiveness stereotype. *Psychology Bulletin, 110,* 107–128.

Eagly, A. H., & Carli, L. L. (1981). Sex of researchers and sex-typed communications as determinants of sex differences in influenceability: A meta-analysis of social influence studies. *Psychological Bulletin, 90,* 1–20.

Eagly, A. H., & Chaiken, S. (1993). *The psychology of attitudes*. Fort Worth, TX: Harcourt, Brace Jovanovich.

Eagly, A. H., & Chravala, C. (1986). Sex differences in conformity: Status and gender-role interpretations. *Psychology of Women Quarterly, 10,* 203–220.

Eagly, A. H., & Crowley, M. (1986). Gender and helping behavior: A meta-analytic review of the social psychological literature. *Psychological Bulletin, 100,* 283–308.

Eagly, A. H., & Johnson, B. T. (1990). Gender and leadership style: A meta-analysis. *Psychological Bulletin, 108,* 233–256.

Eagly, A. H., & Kite, M. E. (1987). Are stereotypes of nationalities applied to both women and men? *Journal of Personality and Social Psychology, 53,* 451–462.

Eagly, A. H., Makhijani, M. G., & Klonsky, B. G. (1992). Gender and evaluation of leaders: A meta-analysis. *Psychological Bulletin, 111,* 3–22.

Eagly, A. H., & Steffen, V. J. (1984). Gender stereotypes stem from the distribution of women and men into social roles. *Journal of Personality and Social Psychology, 46,* 735–754.

Eagly, A. H., & Steffen, V. J. (1986). Gender and aggressive behavior: A meta-analytic review of the social psychology literature. *Psychological Bulletin, 100,* 309–330.

Eagly, A. H., & Wood, W. (1982). Inferred sex differences in status as a determinant of gender stereotypes about social influence. *Journal of Personality and Social Psychology, 43,* 915–928.

Eagly, A. H., & Wood, W. (1991). Explaining sex differences in social behavior: A meta-analytic perspective. *Personality and Social Psychology Bulletin, 17,* 306–315.

Eagly, A. H., Wood, W., & Chaiken, S. (1978). Causal inferences about communicators and their effect on opinion change. *Journal of Personality and Social Psychology, 36,* 424–435.

Eagly, A. H., Wood, W., & Chaiken, S. (1981a). An attribution analysis of persuasion. In J. Harvey, W. Ickes, & R. Kidd (Eds.), *New directions in attribution research* (Vol. 3, pp. 37–62). Hillsdale, NJ: Erlbaum.

Eagly, A. H., Wood, W., & Fishbaugh, L. (1981b). Sex differences in conformity: Surveillance by the group as a determinant of male nonconformity. *Journal of Personality and Social Psychology, 40,* 384–394.

Ebbesen, E. B., Kjos, G. L., & Konecni, V. J. (1976). Spatial ecology: Its effects on the choice of friends and enemies. *Journal of Experimental Social Psychology, 12,* 505–518.

Ebbesen, E. B., & Konecni, V. J. (1981). The process of sentencing adult felons: A causal analysis of judicial decisions. In

B. D. Sales (Ed.), *The trial process* (pp. 413–458). New York: Plenum.

Eccles, J. S., Jacobs, J. E., & Harold, R. D. (1990). Gender role stereotypes, expectancy effects, and parents' socialization of gender differences. *Journal of Social Issues, 46,* 183–201.

Eckenrode, J., & Gore, S. (1990). *Stress between work and family*. New York: Plenum.

Eden, D. (1990). Pygmalion without interpersonal contrast effects: Whole groups gain from raising manager expectations. *Journal of Applied Psychology, 75,* 394–398.

Edwards, K. (1990). The interplay of affect and cognition in attitude formation and change. *Journal of Personality and Social Psychology, 59,* 202–216.

Edwards, V. J., & Spence, J. T. (1987). Gender-related traits, stereotypes, and schemata. *Journal of Personality and Social Psychology, 53,* 146–154.

Egolf, D. B., & Corder, L. E. (1991). Height differences between low and high job status female and male corporate employees. *Sex Roles, 24,* 365–373.

Eisenberg, N., Cialdini, R. B., McCreath, H., & Shell, R. (1987). Consistency-based compliance: When and why do children become vulnerable? *Journal of Personality and Social Psychology, 52,* 1174–1181.

Eisenberg, N., & Fabes, R. (1991). Prosocial behavior and empathy: A multi-method developmental perspective. In M. S. Clark (Ed.), *Review of personality and social psychology 12: Prosocial behavior* (pp. 34–61). Newbury Park, CA: Sage.

Eisenberg, N., Fabes, R. A., Miller, P. A., Fultz, J., Shell, R., Mathy, R. M., & Reno, R. R. (1989). Relation of sympathy and personal distress to prosocial behavior: A multimethod study. *Journal of Personality and Social Psychology, 57,* 55–66.

Eisenberg, N., & Miller, P. A. (1987). The relation of empathy to prosocial and related behaviors. *Psychological Bulletin, 101,* 91–119.

Eisenberger, R., Cotterell, N., & Marvel, J. (1987). Reciprocation ideology. *Journal of Personality and Social Psychology, 53,* 743–750.

Eiser, J. R., & Stroebe, W. (1972). *Categorization and social judgment*. New York: Academic Press.

Ekman, P., Davidson, R. J., & Friesen, W. V. (1990). The Duchenne smile: Emotional expression and brain physiology II. *Journal of Personality and Social Psychology, 58,* 342–353.

Ekman, P., & Friesen, W. V. (1974). Detecting deception from the body or face. *Journal of Personality and Social Psychology, 29,* 288–298.

Ekman, P., Friesen, W. V., & Ellsworth, P. (1972). *Emotion in the human face*. Elmsford, NY: Pergamon Press.

Ekman, P., Friesen, W. V., O'Sullivan, M., Chan, A., Diacoyanni-Tarlatzis, I., Heider, K., Krause, R., LeCompte, W. A., Pitcairn, T., Ricci-Bitti, P., Scherer, K., Tomita, M., & Tzavaras, A. (1987). Universals and cultural differences in the judgments of facial expressions of emotion. *Journal of Personality and Social Psychology, 53,* 712–717.

Ekman, P., & O'Sullivan, M. (1991). Who can catch a liar? *American Psychologist, 46,* 913–920.

Elder, G. H., Jr. (1969). Appearance of education in marriage mobility. *American Sociological Review, 34,* 519–533.

Elder, G. H., Jr., & Clipp, E. C. (1989). Combat experience and emotional health: Impairment and resilience in later life. *Journal of Personality, 57,* 311–341.

Elkin, R. A., & Leippe, M. R. (1986). Physiological arousal, dissonance, and attitude change: Evidence for a dissonance-arousal link and a "don't remind me" effect. *Journal of Personality and Social Psychology, 51,* 55–65.

Elliott, R. (1991). Social science data and the APA: The *Lockhart* brief as a case in point. *Law and Human Behavior, 15,* 59–76.

Elliott, T. R., Witty, T. E., Herrick, S., & Hoffman J. T. (1991). Negotiating reality after physical loss: Hope, depression, and disability. *Journal of Personality and Social Psychology, 61,* 608–613.

Ellis, D. (1992, January 13). The deadliest year yet. *Time,* p. 18.

Ellsworth, P. C. (1991). To tell what we know or wait for Godot? *Law and Human Behavior, 15,* 77–90.

Elmer-Dewitt, P. (1991, November 25). How safe is sex? *Time,* pp. 72–74.

Elms, A., & Milgram, S. (1966). Personality characteristics associated with obedience and defiance toward authoritative command. *Journal of Experimental Research in Personality, 1,* 282–289.

Elwork, A., Sales, B. D., & Alfini, J. J. (1982). *Making jury instructions understandable.* Charlottesville, VA: Miche.

Emery, R. E. (1989). Family violence. *American Psychologist, 44,* 321–328.

Emery, R. E., & Wyer, M. M. (1987). Divorce mediation. *American Psychologist, 42,* 472–480.

Endler, N. S., & Parker, J. D. A. (1990). Multidimensional assessment of coping: A critical evaluation. *Journal of Personality and Social Psychology, 58,* 844–857.

Enzle, M. E., Hansen, R. D., & Lowe, C. A. (1975). Causal attribution in the mixed-motive game: Effects of facilitory and inhibitory environmental forces. *Journal of Personality and Social Psychology, 31,* 50–54.

Enzle, M. E., Harvey, M. D., & Wright, E. F. (1992). Implicit role obligations versus social responsibility in constituency representation. *Journal of Personality and Social Psychology, 62,* 238–245.

Enzle, M. E., & Ross, J. M. (1978). Increasing and decreasing intrinsic interest with contingent rewards: A test of cognitive evaluation theory. *Journal of Experimental Social Psychology, 14,* 588–597.

Epstein, J. L. (1985). After the bus arrives: Resegregation in desegregated schools. *Journal of Social Issues, 41,* 23–43.

Epstein, S. (1983). A research paradigm for the study of personality and emotions. In M. M. Page (Ed.), *Nebraska Symposium on Motivation: 1982* (pp. 91–154). Lincoln: University of Nebraska Press.

Epstein, Y. M., Suedfeld, P., & Silverstein, S. J. (1973). The experimental contract: Subjects' expectations of and reactions to some behaviors of experimenters. *American Psychologist, 28,* 212–221.

Erdley, C. A., & D'Agostino, P. R. (1988). Cognitive and affective components of automatic priming effects. *Journal of Personality and Social Psychology, 54,* 741–747.

Eron, L. D. (1980). Prescription for reduction of aggression. *American Psychologist, 35,* 244–252.

Eron, L. D. (1986). Interventions to mitigate the psychological effects of media violence on aggressive behavior. In L. R. Huesmann & N. M. Malamuth (Eds.), *Journal of Social Issues: Media Violence and Antisocial Behavior, 42*(3), 155–169.

Eron, L. D. (1987). The development of aggressive behavior from the perspective of a developing behaviorism. *American Psychologist, 42,* 435–442.

Eron, L. D., & Huesmann, L. R. (1984). The control of aggressive behavior by changes in attitudes, values, and the conditions of learning. In R. J. Blanchard & D. C. Blanchard (Eds.), *Advances in the study of aggression* (Vol. 1, pp. 139–171). New York: Academic Press.

Eron, L. D., Huesmann, L. R., Lefkowitz, M. M., & Walder, L. O. (1972). Does television cause aggression? *American Psychologist, 27,* 253–263.

Evans, G. W., Palsane, M. N., Lepore, S. J., & Martin, J. (1989). Residential density and psychological health: The mediating effects of social support. *Journal of Personality and Social Psychology, 57,* 994–999.

Evans, R. I., Smith, C. K., & Raines, B. E. (1984). Deterring cigarette smoking in adolescents: A psychosocial-behavioral analysis of an intervention strategy. In A. Baum, S. E. Taylor, & J. E. Singer (Eds.), *Handbook of psychology and health: Vol. 4. Social psychological aspects of health* (pp. 301–318). Hillsdale, NJ: Erlbaum.

Fabes, R. A., Fultz, J., Eisenberg, N., May-Plumlee, T., & Christopher, F. S. (1989). Effects of rewards on children's prosocial motivation: A socialization study. *Developmental Psychology, 25,* 509–515.

Fagot, B. I., Leinbach, M. D., & O'Boyle, C. (1992). Gender labeling, gender stereotyping, and parenting behaviors. *Developmental Psychology, 28,* 225–230.

Farkas, A. J., & Anderson, N. H. (1979). Multidimensional input in equity theory. *Journal of Personality and Social Psychology, 37,* 879–896.

Farr, R. M. (1991). The long past and the short history of social psychology. *European Journal of Social Psychology, 21,* 371–380.

Fazio, R. H. (1987). Self-perception theory: A current perspective. In M. P. Zanna, J. M. Olson, & C. P. Herman (Eds.), *Social influence: The Ontario Symposium* (Vol. 5, pp. 129–150). Hillsdale, NJ: Erlbaum.

Fazio, R. H. (1990). Multiple processes by which attitudes guide behavior: The MODE model as an integrative framework. In M. P. Zanna (Ed.), *Advances in experimental social psychology* (Vol. 23, pp. 75–109). New York: Academic Press.

Fazio, R. H. (1990). A practical guide to the use of response latency in social psychological research. In C. Hendrick &

M. S. Clark (Eds.), *Review of personality and social psychology: Vol. 11. Research methods in personality and social psychology* (pp. 74–97). Newbury Park, CA: Sage.

Fazio, R. H., Effrein, E. A., & Falender, V. J. (1981). Self-perceptions following social interactions. *Journal of Personality and Social Psychology, 41,* 232–242.

Fazio, R. H., & Zanna, M. P. (1981). Direct experience and attitude-behavior consistency. In L. Berkowitz (Ed.), *Advances in experimental social psychology* (Vol. 14, pp. 162–202). New York: Academic Press.

Fazio, R. H., Zanna, M. P., & Cooper, J. (1977). Dissonance and self perception: An integrative view of each theory's proper domain of application. *Journal of Experimental Social Psychology, 13,* 464–479.

Federal Bureau of Investigation. (1989). *Uniform crime reports.* In *1991 World Almanac* (p. 849).

Feeney, J. A., & Noller, P. (1990). Attachment style as a predictor of adult romantic relationships. *Journal of Personality and Social Psychology, 58,* 281–291.

Fehr, B., & Russell, J. A. (1991). The concept of love viewed from a prototype perspective. *Journal of Personality and Social Psychology, 60,* 425–438.

Fein, S. (1991). The suspicious mind. Doctoral dissertation, University of Michigan.

Fein, S., Hilton, J. L., & Miller, D. T. (1990). Suspicion of ulterior motivation and the correspondence bias. *Journal of Personality and Social Psychology, 58,* 753–764.

Feingold, A. (1988). Matching for attractiveness in romantic partners and same-sex friends: A meta-analysis and theoretical critique. *Psychological Bulletin, 104,* 226–235.

Feingold, A. (1990). Gender differences in effects of physical attractiveness on romantic attraction: A comparison across five research paradigms. *Journal of Personality and Social Psychology, 59,* 981–993.

Feingold, A. (1992). Good-looking people are not what we think. *Psychological Bulletin, 111,* 304–341.

Fellner, C. H., & Marshall, J. R. (1981). Kidney donors revisited. In J. P. Rushton & R. M. Sorrentino (Eds.), *Altruism and helping behavior* (pp. 351–365). Hillsdale, NJ: Erlbaum.

Felson, R. B. (1989). Parents and the reflected appraisal process: A longitudinal analysis. *Journal of Personality and Social Psychology, 56,* 965–971.

Fenigstein, A. (1987). On the nature of public and private self-consciousness. *Journal of Personality, 55,* 543–553.

Fenigstein, A., Scheier, M. F., & Buss, A. H. (1975). Public and private self-consciousness: Assessment and theory. *Journal of Consulting and Clinical Psychology, 43,* 522–527.

Ferguson, T. J., & Rule, B. G. (1983). An attributional perspective on anger and aggression. In R. G. Geen & E. I. Donnerstein (Eds.), *Aggression: Theoretical and empirical reviews: Vol. l. Theoretical and methodological issues* (pp. 41–74). New York: Academic Press.

Festinger, L. (1950). Informal social communication. *Psychological Review, 57,* 271–282.

Festinger, L. (1951). Architecture and group membership. *Journal of Social Issues, 7,* 152–163.

Festinger, L. (1954). A theory of social comparison processes. *Human Relations, 7,* 117–140.

Festinger, L. (1957). *A theory of cognitive dissonance.* Stanford, CA: Stanford University Press.

Festinger, L., & Carlsmith, J. M. (1959). Cognitive consequences of forced compliance. *Journal of Abnormal and Social Psychology, 58,* 203–210.

Festinger, L., Pepitone, A., & Newcomb, T. (1952). Some consequences of de-individuation in a group. *Journal of Abnormal and Social Psychology, 47,* 382–389.

Festinger, L., Schachter, S., & Back, K. W. (1950). *Social pressures in informal groups: A study of human factors in housing.* New York: Harper.

Feuerstein, M., Labbé, E. E., & Kuczmierczyk, A. R. (1986). *Health psychology: A psychobiological perspective.* New York: Plenum.

Fiedler, F. E. (1967). *A theory of leadership effectiveness.* New York: McGraw-Hill.

Fiedler, F. E., & Chemers, M. M. (1984). *Improving leadership effectiveness: The leader match concept* (2nd ed.). New York: Wiley.

Fiedler, F. E., & Garcia, J. E. (1987). *Leadership: Cognitive resources and performance.* New York: Wiley.

Filsinger, E. E., & Thoma, S. J. (1988). Behavioral antecedents of relationship stability and adjustment: A five-year longitudinal study. *Journal of Marriage and the Family, 50,* 785–795.

Fincham, F. D., & Bradbury, T. N. (1987). The impact of attributions in marriage: A longitudinal analysis. *Journal of Personality and Social Psychology, 53,* 510–517.

Fincham, F. D., & Bradbury, T. N. (1989). Perceived responsibility for marital events: Egocentric or partner-centric bias? *Journal of Marriage and the Family, 51,* 27–35.

Fincham, F. D., Bradbury, T. N., & Scott, C. K. (1990). Cognition in marriage. In F. D. Fincham & T. N. Bradbury (Eds.), *The psychology of marriage: Basic issues and applications* (pp. 118–149). New York: Guilford.

Fischer, C. S. (1976). *The urban experience.* New York: Harcourt Brace Jovanovich.

Fischhoff, B. (1975). Hindsight ≠ foresight: The effect of outcome knowledge on judgment under uncertainty. *Journal of Experimental Psychology: Human Perception and Performance, 1,* 288–299.

Fishbein, M. (1980). A theory of reasoned action: Some applications and implications. In H.E. Howe & M. M. Page (Eds.), *Nebraska Symposium on Motivation* (Vol. 27, pp. 65–116). Lincoln: University of Nebraska Press.

Fishbein, M., & Ajzen, I. (1972). Attitudes and opinions. In P. H. Mussen & M. R. Rosenzweig (Eds.), *Annual Review of Psychology, 23,* 487–544.

Fishbein, M., & Stasson, M. (1990). The role of desires, self-predictions, and perceived control in the prediction of training session attendance. *Journal of Applied Social Psychology, 20,* 173–198.

Fisher, J. D., Bell, P. A., & Baum, A. (1984). *Environmental psychology* (2nd ed.). New York: Holt, Rinehart and Winston.

Fisher, J. D., & Fisher, W. A. (1992). Changing AIDS-risk behavior. Psychological Bulletin, 111, 455–474.

Fisher, J. D., Nadler, A., & Whitcher-Alagna, S. (1982). Recipient reactions to aid. *Psychological Bulletin, 91,* 27–54.

Fisher, W. A., & Barak, A. (1989). Sex education as a corrective: Immunizing against possible effects of pornography. In D. Zillmann & J. Bryant (Eds.), *Pornography: Research advances and policy considerations* (pp. 289–320). Hillsdale, NJ: Erlbaum.

Fiske, A. P. (1991). The cultural relativity of selfish individualism: Anthropological evidence that humans are inherently sociable. In M. S. Clark (Ed.), *Review of personality and social psychology: Vol. 12. Prosocial behavior* (pp. 176–214). Newbury Park, CA: Sage.

Fiske, S. T. (1980). Attention and weight in person perception: The impact of negative and extreme behavior. *Journal of Personality and Social Psychology, 38,* 889–906.

Fiske, S. T., Bersoff, D. N., Borgida, E., Deaux, K., & Heilman, M. E. (1991). Social science research on trial: Use of sex stereotyping research in *Price Waterhouse v. Hopkins. American Psychologist, 46,* 1049–1060.

Fiske, S. T., & Neuberg, S. L. (1990). A continuum of impression formation from category-based to individuating processes: Influences of information and motivation on attention and interpretation. In M. P. Zanna (Ed.), *Advances in experimental social psychology* (Vol. 23, pp. 1–74). New York: Academic Press.

Fiske, S. T., & Taylor, S. E. (1991). *Social cognition.* New York: McGraw-Hill.

Fitzgerald, F. S. (1925). *The Great Gatsby.* New York: Scribner.

Fitzgerald, R., & Ellsworth, P. C. (1984). Due process vs. crime control: Death qualification and jury attitudes. *Law and Human Behavior, 8,* 31–52.

Flannelly, K. J., Blanchard, R. J., & Blanchard, D. C. (Eds.). (1984). *Biological perspectives on aggression.* New York: Alan R. Liss.

Fleming, J. H., & Darley, J. M. (1991). Mixed messages: The multiple audience problem and strategic communication. *Social Cognition, 9,* 25–46.

Fleming, J. H., Darley, J. M., Hilton, J. L., & Kojetin, B. (1990). Multiple audience problem: A strategic communication perspective on social perception. *Journal of Personality and Social Psychology, 58,* 593–609.

Fleming, J. H., & Scott, B. A. (1991). The costs of confession: The Persian Gulf War POW tapes in historical and theoretical perspective. *Contemporary Social Psychology, 15,* 127–138.

Fleming, J. S., & Courtney, B. E. (1984). The dimensionality of self-esteem: II. Hierarchical facet model for revised measurement scales. *Journal of Personality and Social Psychology, 46,* 404–421.

Fletcher, G. J. O., Danilovics, P., Fernandez, G., Peterson, D., & Reeder, G. D. (1986). Attributional complexity: An individual differences measure. *Journal of Personality and Social Psychology, 51,* 875–884.

Fletcher, G. J. O., & Ward, C. (1988). Attribution theory and processes: A cross-cultural perspective. In *The cross-cultural challenge to social psychology* (pp. 230–244). Newbury Park, CA: Sage Publications.

Flowers, M. L. (1977). A laboratory test of some implications of Janis's groupthink hypothesis. *Journal of Personality and Social Psychology, 35,* 888–896.

Foa, E. B., & Foa, U. G. (1980). Resource theory: Interpersonal behavior as exchange. In K. J. Gergen, M. S. Greenberg, & R. H. Willis (Eds.), *Social exchange: Advances in theory and research* (pp. 77–101). New York: Plenum.

Folger, R. (1986). Rethinking equity theory: A referent cognitions model. In H.W. Bierhoff, R. L. Cohen, & J. Greenberg (Eds.), *Justice in social relations* (pp. 145–162). New York: Plenum.

Folger, R., & Greenberg, J. (1985). Procedural justice: An interpretive analysis of personnel systems. In K. Rowland & G. Ferris (Eds.), *Research in personnel and human resource management* (Vol. 3, pp. 141–183). Greenwich, CT: JAI Press.

Folger, R., & Konovsky, M. A. (1989). Effects of procedural and distributive justice on reactions to pay raise decisions. *Academy of Management Journal, 32,* 115–130.

Folger, R., Konovsky, M. A., & Cropanzano, R. (1992). A due process metaphor for performance appraisal. *Research in Organizational Behavior, 14,* 129–177.

Folkes, V. S. (1982). Forming relationships and the matching hypothesis. *Personality and Social Psychology Bulletin, 8,* 631–636.

Folkes, V. S. (1985). Mindlessness or mindfulness: A partial replication and extension of Langer, Blank, and Chanowitz. *Journal of Personality and Social Psychology, 48,* 600–604.

Folkes, V. S., & Sears, D. O. (1977). Does everybody like a liker? *Journal of Experimental Social Psychology, 13,* 505–519.

Folkman, S., & Lazarus, R. S. (1985). If it changes it must be a process: Study of emotion and coping during three stages of a college examination. *Journal of Personality and Social Psychology, 48,* 150–170.

Folkman, S., & Lazarus, R. S. (1988). Coping as a mediator of emotion. *Journal of Personality and Social Psychology, 54,* 466–475.

Follette, V. M., & Jacobson, N. S. (1987). Importance of attributions as a predictor of how people cope with failure. *Journal of Personality and Social Psychology, 52,* 1205–1211.

Fong, G. T., Krantz, D. H., & Nisbett, R. E. (1986). The effects of statistical training on thinking about everyday problems. *Cognitive Psychology, 18,* 253–292.

Fontaine, G. (1990). Cultural diversity in intimate intercultural relationships. In D. D. Cahn (Ed.), *Intimates in conflict: A communication perspective* (pp. 209–224). Hillsdale, NJ: Erlbaum.

Forgas, J. P. (1992). Mood and the perception of atypical people: Affect and prototypicality in person memory and impressions. *Journal of Personality and Social Psychology, 62.*

Forgas, J. P., & Bower, G. H. (1987). Mood effects on person-perception judgments. *Journal of Personality and Social Psychology, 53,* 53–60.

Forsterling, F. (1985). Attributional retraining: A review. *Psychological Bulletin, 98,* 495–512.

Forsyth, D. R. (1983). *An introduction to group dynamics.* Monterey, CA: Brooks/Cole.

Forsythe, S. M. (1990). Effects of applicant's clothing on interviewer's decision to hire. *Journal of Applied Social Psychology, 20,* 1579–1595.

Fosterling, F. (1989). Models of covariation and attribution: How do they relate to the analogy of analysis of variance? *Journal of Personality and Social Psychology, 57,* 615–625.

Fox, S. (1984). *The mirror makers: A history of American advertising and its creators.* New York: Morrow.

Frable, D. E. S. (1989). Sex typing and gender ideology: Two facets of the individual's gender psychology that go together. *Journal of Personality and Social Psychology, 56,* 95–108.

Frable, D. E. S., & Bem, S. L. (1985). If you're gender-schematic, all members of the opposite sex look alike. *Journal of Personality and Social Psychology, 49,* 459–468.

Franck, K. A. (1980). Friends and strangers: The social experience of living in urban and non-urban settings. *Journal of Social Issues, 36*(3), 52–71.

Frank, J. (1949). *Courts on trial.* Princeton, NJ: Princeton University Press.

Frankenhaeuser, M., Lundberg, U., & Chesney, M. (Eds.). (1991). *Women, work, and health: Stress and opportunities.* New York: Plenum.

Frazier, P. A. (1990). Victim attributions and post-rate trauma. *Journal of Personality and Social Psychology, 59,* 298–304.

Frazier, P. A., & Borgida, E. (1992). Rape trauma syndrome: A review of case law and psychological research. *Law and Human Behavior, 16,* 293–311.

Freedman, J. L. (1986). Television violence and aggression: A rejoinder. *Psychological Bulletin, 100,* 372–373.

Freedman, J. L. (1988a). Keeping pornography in perspective. *Contemporary Psychology, 33,* 858–860.

Freedman, J. L. (1988b). Television violence and aggression: What the evidence shows. *Applied Social Psychology Annual, 8,* 144–162.

Freedman, J. L., & Fraser, S. C. (1966). Compliance without pressure: The foot-in-the-door technique. *Journal of Personality and Social Psychology, 4,* 195–202.

Freedman, J. L., & Sears, D. O. (1965). Warning, distraction, and resistance to influence. *Journal of Personality and Social Psychology, 1,* 262–266.

French, J. P. R., Jr., & Raven, B. H. (1959). The bases of social power. In D. Cartwright (Ed.), *Studies in social power* (pp. 150–167). Ann Arbor: University of Michigan Press.

Freud, S. (1951). *Group psychology and the analysis of the ego.* New York: Liveright. (Original work published 1922)

Freud, S. (1959a). *Beyond the pleasure principle: A study of the death instinct in human aggression* (J. Strachey, Trans.). New York: Bantam Books. (Original work published 1920)

Freud, S. (1959b). Dostoevsky and parricide. In J. Strachey (Ed.), *Freud: The collected papers.* New York: Basic Books. (Original work published 1928)

Freud, S. (1959c). Fragments of an analysis of a case of hysteria. *Collected papers* (Vol. 3). New York: Basic Books. (Original work published 1905)

Frey, D. L., & Gaertner, S. L. (1986). Helping and the avoidance of inappropriate interracial behavior: A strategy that perpetuates a nonprejudiced self-image. *Journal of Personality and Social Psychology, 50,* 1083–1090.

Friedland, N. (1990). Attribution of control as a determinant of cooperation in exchange interactions. *Journal of Applied Social Psychology, 20,* 303–320.

Friedman, H. S., & Booth-Kewley, S. (1987). The "disease-prone personality": A meta-analytic view of the construct. *American Psychologist, 42,* 539–555.

Friedman, M., & Rosenman, R. H. (1959). Association of specific overt behavior pattern with blood and cardiovascular findings: Blood cholesterol level, blood clotting time, incidence of arcus senilis and clinical coronary artery disease. *Journal of the American Medical Association, 169,* 1286–1296.

Friedman, M., Thoresen, C. E., Gill, J. J., Ulmer, D., Powell, L. H., Price, V. A., Brown, B., Thompson, L., Rabin, D. D., Breall, W. S., Bourg, E., Levy, R., & Dixon, T. (1986). Alteration of Type A behavior and its effect on cardiac recurrences in post-myocardial infarction patients: Summary results of the recurrent coronary prevention project. *American Heart Journal, 112,* 653–665.

Friedrich-Cofer, L., & Huston, A. C. (1986). Television violence and aggression: The debate continues. *Psychological Bulletin, 100,* 364–371.

Friend, R., Rafferty, Y., & Bramel, D. (1990). A puzzling misinterpretation of the Asch "conformity" study. *European Journal of Social Psychology, 20,* 29–44.

Frost, D. E., & Stahelski, A. J. (1988). The systematic measurement of French and Raven's bases of social power in workgroups. *Journal of Applied Social Psychology, 18,* 375–389.

Fujita, F., Diener, E., & Sandvik, E. (1991). Gender differences in negative affect and well-being: The case for emotional intensity. *Journal of Personality and Social Psychology, 61,* 427–434.

Fulero, S., & Penrod, S. D. (1990). Attorney jury selection folklore: What do they think and how can psychology help? *Forensic Reports, 3,* 223–259.

Fultz, J., Batson, C. D., Fortenbach, V. A., McCarthy, P. M., & Varney, L. L. (1986). Social evaluation and the empathy-altruism hypothesis. *Journal of Personality and Social Psychology, 50,* 761–769.

Funder, D. C. (1982). On the accuracy of dispositional vs. situational attributions. *Social Cognition, 1,* 205–222.

Funder, D. C. (1987). Errors and mistakes: Evaluating the accuracy of social judgment. *Psychological Bulletin, 101,* 75–90.

Furnham, A., & Gunter, B. (1984). Just world beliefs and attitudes towards the poor. *British Journal of Social Psychology, 23,* 265–269.

Gaertner, S. L., & Dovidio, J. F. (1986). The aversive form of racism. In J. F. Dovidio & S. L. Gaertner (Eds.), *Prejudice, discrimination, and racism: Theory and research* (pp. 61–89). Orlando, FL: Academic Press.

Gaertner, S. L., Mann, J. A., Dovidio, J. F., Murrell, A. J., & Pomare, M. (1990). How does cooperation reduce intergroup bias? *Journal of Personality and Social Psychology, 59,* 692–704.

Gaertner, S. L., Mann, J. A., Murrell, A. J., & Dovidio, J. F. (1989). Reducing intergroup bias: The benefits of recategorization. *Journal of Personality and Social Psychology, 57,* 239–249.

Gaertner, S. L., & McLaughlin, J. P. (1983). Racial stereotypes: Associations and ascriptions of positive and negative characteristics. *Social Psychology Quarterly, 46,* 23–30.

Gallo, P. S., Jr. (1966). Effects of increased incentives upon the use of threat in bargaining. *Journal of Personality and Social Psychology, 4,* 14–20.

Gallup, G. G., Jr. (1977). Self-recognition in primates: A comparative approach to the bidirectional properties of consciousness. *American Psychologist, 32,* 329–337.

Gallupe, R. B., Bastianutti, L. M., & Cooper, W. H. (1991). Unblocking brainstorms. *Journal of Applied Psychology, 76,* 137–142.

Gamson, W. A., Fireman, B., & Rytina, S. (1982). *Encounters with unjust authority.* Homewood, IL: Dorsey.

Ganellen, R. J., & Blaney, P. H. (1984). Stress, externality, and depression. *Journal of Personality, 52,* 326–337.

Gangestad, S., & Snyder, M. (1985). "To carve nature at its joints": On the existence of discrete classes in personality. *Psychological Review, 92,* 317–349.

Gangestad, S., & Snyder, M. (1991). Taxonomic analysis redux: Some statistical considerations for testing a latent class model. *Journal of Personality and Social Psychology, 61,* 141–146.

Garbarino, J., Kostelny, K., & Dubrow, N. (1991). What children can tell us about living in danger. *American Psychologist, 46,* 376–383.

Garcia, S., Stinson, L., Ickes, W., Bissonnette, V., & Briggs, S. R. (1991). Shyness and physical attractiveness in mixed-sex dyads. *Journal of Personality and Social Psychology, 61,* 35–49.

Garner, D. M., Garfinkel, P. E., Schwartz, D., & Thompson, M. (1980). Cultural expectations of thinness in women. *Psychological Reports, 47,* 483–491.

Gaugler, B. B., Rosenthal, D. B., Thornton, G. C., III, & Bentson, C. (1987). Meta-analysis of assessment center validity. *Journal of Applied Psychology, 72,* 493–511.

Gavin, L., & Furman, W. (1989). Age difference in adolescents' perceptions of their peer groups. *Developmental Psychology, 25,* 827–834.

Geen, R. G. (1968). Effects of frustration, attack, and prior training in aggressiveness upon aggressive behavior. *Journal of Personality and Social Psychology, 9,* 316–321.

Geen, R. G. (1981). Behavioral and physiological reactions to observed violence: Effects of prior exposure to aggressive stimuli. *Journal of Personality and Social Psychology, 40,* 868–875.

Geen, R. G. (1989). Alternative conceptions of social facilitation. In P. B. Paulus (Ed.), *Psychology of group influence* (2nd ed., pp. 15–51). Hillsdale, NJ: Erlbaum.

Geen, R. G., & Quanty, M. B. (1977). The catharsis of aggression: An evaluation of a hypothesis. In L. Berkowitz (Ed.), *Advances in experimental social psychology* (Vol. 10, pp. 1–37). New York: Academic Press.

Geen, R. G., & Thomas, S. L. (1986). The immediate effects of media violence on behavior. In L. R. Huesmann & N. M. Malamuth (Eds.), *Journal of Social Issues, 42*(3), 7–27.

Geis, F. L., Brown, V., Jennings (Walstedt), J., & Porter, N. (1984). TV commercials as achievement scripts for women. *Sex Roles, 10,* 513–525.

Geiselman, R. E., Haight, N. A., & Kimata, L. G. (1984). Context effects in the perceived physical attractiveness of faces. *Journal of Experimental Social Psychology, 20,* 409–424.

Gelles, R. J., & Conte, J. R. (1990). Domestic violence and sexual abuse of children: A review of the research in the eighties. *Journal of Marriage and the Family, 52,* 1045–1058.

Gelles, R. J., & Cornell, C. P. (1990). *Intimate violence in families* (2nd ed.). Newbury Park, CA: Sage.

Gelles, R. J., & Straus, M. A. (1988). *Intimate violence.* New York: Simon & Schuster.

Gerard, H. B. (1983). School desegregation: The social science role. *American Psychologist, 38,* 869–877.

Gerard, H. B., Whilhelmy, R. A., & Connolley, R. S. (1968). Conformity and group size. *Journal of Personality and Social Psychology, 8,* 79–82.

Gerbner, G., Gross, L., Morgan, M., & Signorielli, N. (1980). The "mainstreaming" of American Violence: Profile no. 11. *Journal of Communications, 30*(3), 10–29.

Gerbner, G., Gross, L., Morgan, M., & Signorielli, N. (1986). Living with television: The dynamics of the cultivation process. In J. Bryant & D. Zillmann (Eds.), *Perspectives on media effects* (pp. 17–40). Hillsdale, NJ: Erlbaum.

Gerdes, E. P. (1979). College students' reactions to social psychological experiments involving deception. *Journal of Social Psychology, 107,* 98–110.

Gergen, K. J. (1973). Social psychology as history. *Journal of Personality and Social Psychology, 26,* 309–320.

Gergen, K. J. (1985). The social constructionist movement in modern psychology. *American Psychologist, 40,* 266–275.

Gergen, M. (1990). Beyond the evil empire: Horseplay and aggression. *Aggressive Behavior, 16,* 381–398.

Gerhart, B., & Rynes, S. (1991). Determinants and consequences of salary negotiations by male and female MBA graduates. *Journal of Applied Psychology, 76,* 256–262.

Gerstel, N. (1988). Divorce and kin ties: The importance of gender. *Journal of Marriage and the Family, 50,* 209–219.

Gibbons, F. X. (1978). Sexual standards and reactions to pornography: Enhancing behavioral consistency through self-focused attention. *Journal of Personality and Social Psychology, 36,* 976–987.

Gibbons, F. X. (1990). self-attention and behavior: A review and theoretical update. In M. P. Zanna (Ed.), *Advances in experimental social psychology* (Vol. 23, pp. 249–303). New York: Academic Press.

Gibbons, F. X., & Wicklund, R. A. (1982). self-focused attention and helping behavior. *Journal of Personality and Social Psychology, 43,* 462–474.

Gifford, R., & Gallagher, T. M. B. (1985). Sociability: Personality, social context, and physical setting. *Journal of Personality and Social Psychology, 48,* 1015–1023.

Gilbert, D. T. (1989). Thinking lightly about others: Automatic components of the social inference process. In J. S. Uleman & J. A. Bargh (Eds.), *Unintended thought: Limits of awareness, intention, and control* (pp. 189–211). New York: Guilford.

Gilbert, D. T., & Hixon, J. G. (1991). The trouble of thinking: Activation and application of stereotypic beliefs. *Journal of Personality and Social Psychology, 60,* 509–517.

Gilbert, D. T., & Jones, E. E. (1986). Perceiver-induced constraint: Interpretations of self-generated reality. *Journal of Personality and Social Psychology, 50,* 269–280.

Gilbert, D. T., & Krull, D. S. (1988). Seeing less and knowing more: The benefits of perceptual ignorance. *Journal of Personality and Social Psychology, 54,* 193–202.

Gilbert, D. T., Krull, D. S., & Malone, P. S. (1990). Unbelieving the unbelievable: Some problems in the rejection of false information. *Journal of Personality and Social Psychology, 59,* 601–613.

Gilbert, D. T., McNulty, S. E., Giuliano, T. A., & Benson, J. E. (1992). Blurry words and fuzzy deeds: The attribution of obscure behavior. *Journal of Personality and Social Psychology, 62,* 18–25.

Gilbert, D. T., & Osborne, R. E. (1989). Thinking backward: Some curable and incurable consequences of cognitive busyness. *Journal of Personality and Social Psychology, 57,* 940–949.

Gilbert, D. T., Pelham, B. W., & Krull, D. S. (1988). On cognitive busyness: When person perceivers meet persons perceived. *Journal of Personality and Social Psychology, 54,* 733–740.

Gilbert, S. J. (1981). Another look at the Milgram obedience studies: The role of the gradated series of shocks. *Personality and Social Psychology Bulletin, 7,* 690–695.

Gill, J. J., Price, V. A., Friedman, M., Thoresen, C. E., Powell, L. H., Ulmer, D., Brown, B., & Drews, F. R. (1985). Reduction of Type A behavior in healthy middle-aged American military officers. *American Heart Journal, 110,* 503–514.

Gillig, P. M., & Greenwald, A. G. (1974). Is it time to lay the sleeper effect to rest? *Journal of Personality and Social Psychology, 29,* 132–139.

Gilligan, C. (1982). *In a different voice: Psychological theory and women's development.* Cambridge, MA: Harvard University Press.

Gilovich, T. (1983). Biased evaluation and persistence in gambling. *Journal of Personality and Social Psychology, 40,* 797–808.

Gilovich, T. (1987). Secondhand information and social judgment. *Journal of Experimental Social Psychology, 23,* 59–74.

Gilovich, T. (1991). *How we know what isn't so: The fallibility of human reason in everyday life.* New York: Free Press.

Gilovich, T., Vallone, R., & Tversky, A. (1985). The hot hand in basketball: On the misperception of random sequences. *Cognitive Psychology, 17,* 295–314.

Gladue, B. A., & Delaney, H. J. (1990). Gender differences in perception of attractiveness of men and women in bars. *Personality and Social Psychology Bulletin, 16,* 378–391.

Glass, D. C. (1977). *Behavior patterns, stress, and coronary disease.* Hillsdale, NJ: Erlbaum.

Glass, D. C., & Singer, J. E. (1972). *Urban stress.* New York: Academic Press.

Gleicher, F., & Petty, R. E. (1992). Expectations of reassurance influence the nature of fear-stimulated attitude change. *Journal of Experimental Social Psychology, 28,* 86–100.

Glenn, N. D. (1990). Quantitative research on marital quality in the 1980s: A critical review. *Journal of Marriage and the Family, 52,* 818–831.

Glenn, N. D. (1991). The recent trend in marital success in the United States. *Journal of Marriage and the Family, 52,* 261–270.

Glenn, N. D., & Kramer, K. B. (1987). The marriages and divorces of the children of divorce. *Journal of Marriage and the Family, 49,* 811–825.

Glick, P. (1985). Orientation toward relationships: Choosing a situation in which to begin a relationship. *Journal of Experimental Social Psychology, 21,* 544–562.

Glick, P. (1991). Trait-based and sex-based discrimination in occupational prestige, occupational salary, and hiring. *Sex Roles, 25,* 351–378.

Glick, P. C. (1988). Fifty years of family demography: A record of social change. *Journal of Marriage and the Family, 50,* 861–873.

Glick, P., Zion, C., & Nelson, C. (1988). What mediates sex discrimination in hiring decisions? *Journal of Personality and Social Psychology, 55,* 178–186.

Godfrey, D. K., Jones, E. E., & Lord, C. G. (1986). Self-promotion is not ingratiating. *Journal of Personality and Social Psychology, 50,* 106–115.

Goethals, G. R. (1986). Fabricating and ignoring social reality: Self-serving estimates of consensus. In J. M. Olson, C. P. Herman, & M. P. Zanna (Eds.), *Relative deprivation and social comparison: The Ontario Symposium* (Vol. 4, pp. 135–157). Hillsdale, NJ: Erlbaum.

Goethals, G. R., Cooper, J., & Naficy, A. (1979). Role of foreseen, foreseeable, and unforeseeable behavioral consequences in the arousal of cognitive dissonance. *Journal of Personality and Social Psychology, 37,* 1179–1185.

Goethals, G. R., & Darley, J. (1977). Social comparison theory: An attributional approach. In J. M. Suls & R. L. Miller (Eds.), *Social comparison processes: Theoretical and empirical perspectives* (pp. 259–278). Washington, DC: Hemisphere.

Goffman, E. (1955). On face-work: An analysis of ritual elements in social interaction. *Psychiatry, 18,* 213–231.

Goffman, E. (1959). *The presentation of self in everyday life.* Garden City: Doubleday.

Goldberg, J., True, W. R., Eisen, S. A., & Henderson, W. G. (1990). A twin study of the effects of the Vietnam War on posttraumatic stress disorder. *Journal of the American Medical Association, 263,* 1227–1232.

Goldberg, L. R. (1978). Differential attribution of trait-descriptive terms to oneself as compared to well-liked, neutral, and disliked others: A psychometric analysis. *Journal of Personality and Social Psychology, 36,* 1012–1028.

Goldberg, L. R., Grenier, J. R., Guion, R., Sechrest, L. B., & Wing, H. (1991). *Questionnaires used in the prediction of trustworthiness in pre-employment selection decisions: An A.P.A. task force report.* Washington, DC: American Psychological Association.

Goldberg, P. (1968). Are women prejudiced against women? *Transaction, 5,* 28–30.

Goldman, M. (1986). Compliance employing a combined foot-in-the-door and door-in-the-face procedure. *Journal of Social Psychology, 126,* 111–116.

Goldstein, A. G., Chance, J. E., & Schneller, G. R. (1989). Frequency of eyewitness identification in criminal cases: A survey of prosecutors. *Bulletin of the Psychonomic Society, 27,* 71–74.

Goodall, J. (1990). *Through a Window.* Boston: Houghton Mifflin.

Goode, W. J. (1960). A theory of strain. *American Sociological Review, 25,* 483–496.

Goodhart, D. E. (1985). Some psychological effects associated with positive and negative thinking about stressful event outcomes: Was Pollyanna right? *Journal of Personality and Social Psychology, 48,* 216–232.

Goodman, G. S., Hirschman, J., Hepps, D., & Rudy, L. (1991). Children's memory for stressful events. *Merrill-Palmer Quarterly, 37,* 109–158.

Goodwin, R. (1990). Sex differences among partner preferences: Are the sexes really very similar? *Sex Roles, 23,* 501–513.

Gorenstein, G. W., & Ellsworth, P. C. (1980). Effect of choosing an incorrect photograph on a later identification by an eyewitness. *Journal of Applied Psychology, 65,* 616–622.

Gotlieb, J. B., & Dubinsky, A. J. (1991). Influence of price on aspects of consumers' cognitive process. *Journal of Applied Psychology, 76,* 541–549.

Gottlieb, J., & Carver, C. S. (1980). Anticipation of future interaction and the bystander effect. *Journal of Experimental Social Psychology, 16,* 253–260.

Gottman, J. M., & Levenson, R. L. (1988). The social psychophysiology of marriage. In P. Noller & M. A. Fitzpatrick (Eds.), *Perspectives on marital interaction* (pp. 182–200). Clevedon, England: Multilingual Matters.

Gould, S. J. (1978, November 16). Sociobiology: The art of storytelling. *New Scientist,* pp. 530–533.

Gould, S. J. (1991). Exaptation: A crucial tool for an evolutionary psychology. *Journal of Social Issues, 47,* 43–65.

Gouldner, A. W. (1960). The norm of reciprocity: A preliminary statement. *American Sociological Review, 25,* 161–178.

Granberg, D., & Brent, E. (1983). When prophecy bends: The preference-expectation link in U.S. presidential elections. *Journal of Personality and Social Psychology, 45,* 477–491.

Grauerholz, E., & Serpe, R. T. (1985). Initiation and response: The dynamics of sexual interaction. *Sex Roles, 12,* 1041–1059.

Graves, L. M., & Powell, G. N. (1988). An investigation of sex discrimination in recruiters' evaluations of actual applicants. *Journal of Applied Psychology, 73,* 20–29.

Gray, B. H. (1982). The regulatory context of social and behavioral research. In T. L. Beauchamp, R. R. Faden, R. J. Wallace, Jr., & L. Walters (Eds.), *Ethical issues in social science research* (pp. 329–355). Baltimore: Johns Hopkins University Press.

Gray-Little, B., & Burks, N. (1983). Power and satisfaction in marriage: A review and critique. *Psychological Bulletin, 93,* 513–538.

Graziano, W. G., Leone, C., Musser, L. M., & Lautenschlager, G. J. (1987). Self-monitoring in children: A differential approach to social development. *Developmental Psychology, 23,* 571–576.

Green, S. K., Buchanan, D. R., & Heuer, S. K. (1984). Winners, losers, and choosers: A field investigation of dating initiation. *Personality and Social Psychology Bulletin, 10,* 502–511.

Greenberg, J. (1982). Approaching equity and avoiding inequity in groups and organizations. In J. Greenberg & R. L. Cohen (Eds.), *Equity and justice in social behavior* (pp. 389–435). New York: Academic Press.

Greenberg, J. (1988). Equity and workplace status: A field experiment. *Journal of Applied Psychology, 73,* 606–613.

Greenberg, J. (1990). Employee theft as a reaction to underpayment inequity: The hidden costs of pay cuts. *Journal of Applied Psychology, 75,* 561–568.

Greenberg, J., & Folger, R. (1988). *Controversial issues in social research methods.* New York: Springer-Verlag.

Greenberg, J., & Pyszczynski, T. (1985). The effects of an overheard ethnic slur on evaluations of the target: How to spread a social disease. *Journal of Experimental Social Psychology, 21,* 61–72.

Greenberg, J., Pyszczynski, T., & Solomon, S. (1982). The self-serving attributional bias: Beyond self-presentation. *Journal of Experimental Social Psychology, 18,* 56–67.

Greenberg, M. S., & Ruback, R. B. (1982). *Social psychology of the criminal justice system.* Monterey, CA: Brooks/Cole.

Greenberg, M. S., & Westcott, D. R. (1983). Indebtedness as a mediator of reactions to aid. In J. D. Fisher, A. Nadler, & B. M. DePaulo (Eds.), *New directions in helping: Vol. 1. Recipient reactions to aid* (pp. 85–112). New York: Academic Press.

Greenstein, T. N. (1990). Marital disruption and the employment of married women. *Journal of Marriage and the Family, 52,* 657–676.

Greenwald, A. G. (1968). Cognitive learning, cognitive responses to persuasion, and attitude change. In A. Greenwald, T. Brock, & T. Ostrom (Eds.), *Psychological foundations of attitudes* (pp. 147–170). New York: Academic Press.

Greenwald, A. G. (1980). The totalitarian ego: Fabrication and revision of personal history. *American Psychologist, 35,* 603–618.

Greenwald, A. G., & Banaji, M. R. (1989). The self as a memory system: Powerful but ordinary. *Journal of Personality and Social Psychology, 57,* 41–54.

Greenwald, A. G., & Pratkanis, A. R. (1984). The self. In R. S. Wyer & T. K. Srull (Eds.), *Handbook of social cognition* (Vol. 3, pp. 129–178). Hillsdale, NJ: Erlbaum.

Greenwald, A. G., Pratkanis, A. R., Leippe, M. R., & Baumgardner, M. H. (1986). Under what conditions does theory obstruct research progress? *Psychological Review, 93,* 216–229.

Greenwald, A. G., & Ronis, D. L. (1978). Twenty years of cognitive dissonance: Case study of the evolution of a theory. *Psychological Review, 85,* 53–57.

Greenwald, A. G., Spangenberg, E. R., Pratkanis, A. R., & Eskenazi, J. (1991). Double-blind tests of subliminal self-help audiotapes. *Psychological Science, 2,* 119–122.

Griffitt, W. (1987). Females, males, and sexual responses. In K. Kelley (Ed.), *Females, males, and sexuality: Theories and research* (pp. 141–173). Albany, NY: State University of New York Press.

Griggs, L. (1990, July 2). A losing battle with AIDS. *Time,* pp. 42–43.

Gross, A. E., & Fleming, I. (1982). Twenty years of deception in social psychology. *Personality and Social Psychology Bulletin, 8,* 402–408.

Gross, A. E., & Latané, J. G. (1974). Receiving help, reciprocation, and interpersonal attraction. *Journal of Applied Social Psychology, 4,* 210–223.

Gruber, K. J., & White, J. W. (1986). Gender differences in the perceptions of self's and others' use of power strategies. *Sex Roles, 15,* 109–118.

Gruder, C. L., Cook, T. D., Hennigan, K. M., Flay, B. R., Alessis, C., & Halamaj, J. (1978). Empirical tests of the absolute sleeper effect predicted from the discounting cue hypothesis. *Journal of Personality and Social Psychology, 36,* 1061–1074.

Grush, J. E. (1980). Impact of candidate expenditures, regionality, and prior outcomes on the 1976 Democratic presidential primaries. *Journal of Personality and Social Psychology, 38,* 337–347.

Guerin, B. (1986). Mere presence effects in humans: A review. *Journal of Experimental Social Psychology, 22,* 38–77.

Guerin, B., & Innes, J. M. (1982). Social facilitation and social monitoring: A new look at Zajonc's mere presence hypothesis. *British Journal of Social Psychology, 21,* 7–18.

Guerrero, L. K., & Andersen, P. A. (1991). The waxing and waning of relational intimacy: Touch as a function of relational stage, gender and touch avoidance. *Journal of Social and Personal Relationships, 8,* 147–165.

Guimond, S., & Dubé-Simard, L. (1983). Relative deprivation theory and the Quebec nationalist movement: The cognition-emotion distinction and the personal-group deprivation issue. *Journal of Personality and Social Psychology, 44,* 526–535.

Guttentag, M., & Secord, P. F. (1983). *Too many women? The sex ratio question.* Beverly Hills, CA: Sage.

Gwaltney, L. (1986). *The dissenters.* New York: Random House.

Gwynne, S. C. (1990, March 5). Can Iacocca do it again? *Time,* p. 40.

Haaga, D. A. F., Dyck, M. J., & Ernst, D. (1991). Empirical status of cognitive theory of depression. *Psychological Bulletin, 110,* 215–236.

Hakmiller, K. L. (1966). Threat as a determinant of downward comparison. *Journal of Experimental Social Psychology* (Suppl. 1), 32–39.

Halford, W. K., Hahlweg, K., & Dunne, M. (1990). The cross-cultural consistency of marital communication associated with marital distress. *Journal of Marriage and the Family, 52,* 487–500.

Hall, E. T. (1966). *The hidden dimension.* Garden City, NY: Doubleday.

Hall, J. A., & Veccia, E. M. (1990). More "touching" observations: New insights on men, women, and interpersonal touch. *Journal of Personality and Social Psychology, 59,* 1155–1162.

Halpern, A. R., & Deveraux, S. D. (1989). Lucky numbers: Choice strategies in the Pennsylvania Number game. *Bulletin of the Psychonomic Society, 27,* 167–170.

Hamilton, D. L., Dugan, P. M., & Trolier, T. K. (1985). The formation of stereotypic beliefs: Further evidence for distinctiveness-based illusory correlations. *Journal of Personality and Social Psychology, 48,* 5–17.

Hamilton, D. L., & Gifford, R. K. (1976). Illusory correlation in interpersonal perception: A cognitive basis of stereotypic judgments. *Journal of Experimental Social Psychology, 12,* 392–407.

Hamilton, D. L., & Rose, T. L. (1980). Illusory correlation and the maintenance of stereotypic beliefs. *Journal of Personality and Social Psychology, 39,* 832–845.

Hamilton, D. L., & Zanna, M. P. (1974). Context effects in impression formation: Changes in connotative meaning. *Journal of Personality and Social Psychology, 29,* 649–654.

Hamilton, W. D. (1964). The genetical evolution of social behavior: I and II. *Journal of Theoretical Biology, 7,* 1–52.

Hammersla, J. F., & Frease-McMahan, L. (1990). University students' priorities: Life goals vs. relationships. *Sex Roles, 23,* 1–14.

Hampton, R. L., Gelles, R. J., & Harrop, J. W. (1989). Is violence in black families increasing? A comparison of 1975 and 1985 national survey rates. *Journal of Marriage and the Family, 51,* 969–980.

Haney, C., Banks, C., & Zimbardo, P. (1973). Interpersonal dynamics in a simulated prison. *International Journal of Criminology and Penology, 1,* 69–97.

Hans, V. P., & Vidmar, N. (1986). *Judging the jury.* New York: Plenum.

Hansen, C. H. (1989). Priming sex-role stereotypic event schemas with rock music videos: Effects on impression favorability, trait inferences, and recall of a subsequent male-female interaction. *Basic and Applied Social Psychology, 10*, 371–391.

Hansen, C. H., & Hansen, R. D. (1988). Finding the face in the crowd: An anger superiority effect. *Journal of Personality and Social Psychology, 54,* 917–924.

Hansen, C. H., & Hansen, R. D. (1990). Rock music videos and antisocial behavior. *Basic and Applied Social Psychology, 11,* 357–369.

Hansen, G. L. (1985). Dating jealousy among college students. *Sex Roles, 12,* 713–721.

Hansen, J. E., & Schuldt, W. J. (1984). Marital self-disclosure and marital satisfaction. *Journal of Marriage and the Family, 46,* 923–926.

Hansson, R. O., Stroebe, M. W., & Stroebe, W. (1988). Bereavement and widowhood. *Journal of Social Issues, 44,* 37–52.

Harackiewicz, J. M. (1979). The effects of reward contingency and performance feedback on intrinsic motivation. *Journal of Personality and Social Psychology, 37,* 1352–1363.

Hardin, G. (1968). The tragedy of the commons. *Science, 162,* 1243–1248.

Haritos-Fatouros, M. (1988). The official torturer: A learning model for obedience to the authority of violence. *Journal of Applied Social Psychology, 18,* 1107–1120.

Harkins, S. G. (1987). Social loafing and social facilitation. *Journal of Experimental Social Psychology, 23,* 1–18.

Harkins, S. G., & Petty, R. E. (1981). Effects of source magnification of cognitive effort on attitudes: An information processing view. *Journal of Personality and Social Psychology, 40,* 401–413.

Harkins, S. G., & Petty, R. E. (1987). Information utility and the multiple source effect. *Journal of Personality and Social Psychology, 52,* 260–268.

Harkins, S. G., & Szymanski, K. (1987). Social loafing and social facilitation: New wine in old bottles. In C. Hendrick (Ed.), *Review of personality and social psychology: Group processes and intergroup relations* (Vol. 9, pp. 167–188). Beverly Hills, CA: Sage.

Harkins, S. G., & Szymanski, K. (1989). Social loafing and group evaluation. *Journal of Personality and Social Psychology, 56,* 934–941.

Harris, L. (1987). *Inside America.* New York: Vintage Books.

Harris, M. J., & Rosenthal, R. (1985). Mediation of interpersonal expectancy effects. *Psychological Bulletin, 97,* 363–386.

Harris, M. M. (1989). Reconsidering the employment interview: A review of recent literature and suggestions for future research. *Personnel Psychology, 42,* 691–726.

Harris, R. J. (Ed.) (1983). *Information processing research in advertising.* Hillsdale, NJ: Erlbaum.

Harrison, A. A., & Saeed, L. (1977). Let's make a deal: An analysis of revelations and stipulations in lonely hearts advertisements. *Journal of Personality and Social Psychology, 35,* 257–264.

Hartley, E. L. (1946). *Problems in prejudice.* New York: King's Crown Press.

Hartsough, D. M., & Savitsky, J. C. (1984). Three Mile Island: Psychology and environmental policy at a crossroads. *American Psychologist, 39,* 1113–1122.

Harvey, J. H., Town, J. P., & Yarkin, K. L. (1981). How fundamental is the "fundamental attribution error"? *Journal of Personality and Social Psychology, 43,* 345–346.

Hass, R. G. (1981). Effects of source characteristics on the cognitive processing of persuasive messages and attitude change. In R. Petty, T. Ostrom, & T. Brock (Eds.), *Cognitive responses in persuasion* (pp. 141–172). Hillsdale, NJ: Erlbaum.

Hass, R. G. (1984). Perspective taking and self-awareness: Drawing an *E* on your forehead. *Journal of Personality and Social Psychology, 46,* 788–798.

Hass, R. G., & Eisenstadt, D. (1990). The effects of self-focused attention on perspective-taking and anxiety. *Anxiety Research, 2,* 165–176.

Hass, R. G., & Grady, K. (1975). Temporal delay, type of forewarning, and resistance to influence. *Journal of Experimental Social Psychology, 11,* 459–469.

Hastie, R. (1984). Causes and effects of causal attribution. *Journal of Personality and Social Psychology, 46,* 44–56.

Hastie, R., Penrod, S. D., & Pennington, N. (1983). *Inside the jury.* Cambridge, MA: Harvard University Press.

Hatch, O. G. (1982). Psychology, society, and politics. *American Psychologist, 37,* 1031–1037.

Hater, J. J., & Bass, B. M. (1988). Superiors' evaluations and subordinates' perceptions of transformational and transactional leadership. *Journal of Applied Psychology, 73,* 695–702.

Hatfield, E. (1988). Passionate and companionate love. In R. J. Sternberg & M. L. Barnes (Ed.), *The psychology of love* (pp. 191–217). New Haven, CT: Yale University Press.

Hatfield, E., Greenberger, E., Traupmann, J., & Lambert, P. (1982). Equity and sexual satisfaction in recently married couples. *Journal of Sex Research, 18,* 18–32.

Hatfield, E., & Rapson, R. L. (1987). Passionate love: New directions in research. In W. H. Jones & D. Perlman (Eds.), *Advances in personal relationships* (Vol. 1, pp. 109–139). Greenwich, CT: JAI Press.

Hatfield, E., & Sprecher, S. (1986). *Mirror, mirror . . . The importance of looks in everyday life.* Albany, NY: State University of New York Press.

Hawkins, S. A., & Hastie, R. (1990). Hindsight: Biased judgments of past events after the outcomes are known. *Psychological Bulletin, 107,* 311–327.

Hayano, D. M. (1988). Dealing with chance: self-deception and fantasy among gamblers. In J. S. Lockard & D. L. Paulhus (Eds.), *Self-deception: An adaptive mechanism?* (pp. 186–199). Englewood Cliffs, NJ: Prentice-Hall.

Hayduk, L. A. (1978). Personal space: An evaluative and orienting overview. *Psychological Bulletin, 85,* 117–143.

Hayduk, L. A. (1983). Personal space: Where we now stand. *Psychological Bulletin, 94,* 293–335.

Hays, R. B. (1985). A longitudinal study of friendship development. *Journal of Personality and Social Psychology, 48,* 909–924.

Hays, R. B. (1988). Friendship. In S. Duck (Ed.), *Handbook of personal relationships: Theory, research, and interventions* (pp. 391–408). New York: Wiley.

Hazan, C., & Shaver, P. (1987). Romantic love conceptualized as an attachment process. *Journal of Personality and Social Psychology, 52,* 511–524.

Headey, B., & Wearing, A. (1989). Personality, life-events, and subjective well-being: Toward a dynamic equilibrium model. *Journal of Personality and Social Psychology, 57,* 731–739.

Hearold, S. (1986). A synthesis of 1043 effects of television on social behavior. In G. Comstock (Ed.), *Public communication and behavior* (Vol. 1, pp. 65–133). Orlando, FL: Academic Press.

Hedge, J. W., & Kavanagh, M. J. (1988). Improving the accuracy of performance evaluations: Comparison of three methods of performance appraiser training. *Journal of Applied Psychology, 73,* 68–73.

Heesacker, M., Petty, R. E., & Cacioppo, J. T. (1983). Field dependence and attitude change: Source credibility can alter persuasion by affecting message-relevant thinking. *Journal of Personality, 51,* 653–666.

Heider, F. (1958). *The psychology of interpersonal relations.* New York: Wiley.

Heilman, M. E., Rivero, J. C., & Brett, J. F. (1991). Skirting the competence issue: Effects of sex-based preferential selection on task choices of women and men. *Journal of Applied Psychology, 76,* 99–105.

Heilman, M. E., Simon, M. C., & Repper, D. P. (1987). Intentionally favored, unintentionally harmed? Impact of sex-based preferential selection on self-perceptions and self-evaluations. *Journal of Applied Psychology, 72,* 62–68.

Helgesen, S. (1990). *The female advantage: Women's ways of leadership.* New York: Doubleday Currency.

Heller, J. F., Pallak, M. S., & Picek, J. M. (1973). The interactive effects of intent and threat on boomerang attitude change. *Journal of Personality and Social Psychology, 26,* 273–279.

Heller, K. (1979). The effects of social support: Prevention and treatment implications. In A. P. Goldstein & F. H. Kanfer (Eds.), *Maximizing treatment gains: Transfer enhancement in psychotherapy* (pp. 353–382). New York: Academic Press.

Helzer, J. E., Robins, L. N., & McEvoy, L. (1987). Post-traumatic stress disorder in the general population: Findings of the epidemiologic catchment area survey. *New England Journal of Medicine, 317,* 1630–1634.

Henchy, T., & Glass, D. C. (1968). Evaluation apprehension and the social facilitation of dominant and subordinate responses. *Journal of Personality and Social Psychology, 10,* 446–454.

Hendrick, C. (Ed.). (1989). *Review of personality and social psychology: Vol. 10. Close relationships.* Newbury Park, CA: Sage.

Hendrick, C., & Hendrick, S. (1989). Research on love: Does it measure up? *Journal of Personality and Social Psychology, 56,* 784–794.

Hendrick, S. S., Hendrick, C., & Adler, N. L. (1988). Romantic relationships: Love, satisfaction, and staying together. *Journal of Personality and Social Psychology, 54,* 980–988.

Hendrick, S. S., Hendrick, C., Slapion-Foote, M. J., & Foote, F. H. (1985). Gender differences in sexual attitudes. *Journal of Personality and Social Psychology, 48,* 1630–1642.

Heneman, H. G., & Schwab, D. P. (1985). Pay satisfaction: Its multidimensional nature and measurement. *International Journal of Psychology, 20,* 129–141.

Heneman, R. L., & Wexley, K. N. (1983). The effects of time delay in rating and amount of information observed on performance rating accuracy. *Academy of Management Journal,* 677–686.

Henley, N. M. (1977). *Body politics: Power, sex, and nonverbal communication.* Englewood Cliffs, NJ: Prentice-Hall.

Hensley, T. R., & Griffin, G. W. (1986). Victims of groupthink. *Journal of Conflict Resolution, 30,* 497–531.

Henslin, J. M. (1967). Craps and magic. *American Journal of Sociology, 73,* 316–330.

Hepworth, J. T., & West, S. G. (1988). Lynchings and the economy: A time-series reanalysis of Hovland and Sears (1940). *Journal of Personality and Social Psychology, 55,* 239–247.

Herman, C. P., Zanna, M. P., & Higgins, E. T. (1986). *Physical appearance, stigma, and social behavior: The Ontario Symposium* (Vol. 3). Hillsdale, NJ: Erlbaum.

Herr, P. M. (1986). Consequences of priming: Judgment and behavior. *Journal of Personality and Social Psychology, 51,* 1106–1115.

Herrington, L. H. (1985). Victims of crime: Their plight, our response. *American Psychologist, 40,* 99–103.

Hess, R. D., & Miura, I. T. (1985). Gender differences in enrollment in computer camps and classes. *Sex Roles, 13,* 193–203.

Hewstone, M., & Brown, R. (1986). Contact is not enough: An intergroup perspective on the "contact hypothesis." In M. Hewstone & R. Brown (Eds.), *Contact and conflict in intergroup encounters* (pp. 1–44). Oxford, England: Basil Blackwell.

Hewstone, M., & Jaspars, J. (1987). Covariation and causal attribution: A logical model of the intuitive analysis of variance. *Journal of Personality and Social Psychology, 53,* 663–672.

Higgins, E. T. (1989). Self-discrepancy theory: What patterns of self-beliefs cause people to suffer? In L. Berkowitz (Ed.), *Advances in experimental social psychology* (Vol. 22, pp. 93–136). New York: Academic Press.

Higgins, E. T., Bond, R. N., Klein, R., & Strauman, T. (1986). Self-discrepancies and emotional vulnerability: How magnitude, accessibility, and type of discrepancy influence affect. *Journal of Personality and Social Psychology, 51,* 5–15.

Higgins, E. T., King, G. A., & Mavin, G. H. (1982). Individual construct accessibility and subjective impressions and recall. *Journal of Personality and Social Psychology, 43,* 35–47.

Higgins, E. T., Rholes, C. R., & Jones, C. R. (1977). Category accessibility and impression formation. *Journal of Experimental Social Psychology, 13,* 141–154.

Higgins, E. T., & Rholes, W. S. (1978). "Saying is believing": Effects of message modification on memory and liking for the person described. *Journal of Experimental Social Psychology, 14,* 363–378.

Higgins, R. L., & Harris, R. N. (1988). Strategic "alcohol" use: Drinking to self-handicap. *Journal of Social and Clinical Psychology, 6,* 191–202.

Hill, C. A. (1991). Seeking emotional support: The influence of affiliative need and partner warmth. *Journal of Personality and Social Psychology, 60,* 112–121.

Hill, C. T., & Stul, D. E. (1987). Gender and self-disclosure. In V. J. Derlega & J. H. Berg (Eds.), *Self-disclosure: Theory, research, and therapy* (pp. 81–100). New York: Plenum

Hill, G. W. (1982). Groups versus individual performance: Are N + 1 heads better than one? *Psychological Bulletin, 91,* 517–539.

Hill, J. L., & Zautra, A. J. (1989). Self-blame attributions and unique vulnerability as predictors of post-rape demoralization. *Journal of Social and Clinical Psychology, 8,* 368–375.

Hilton, J. L., & Darley, J. M. (1985). Constructing other persons: A limit on the effect. *Journal of Experimental Social Psychology, 21,* 1–18.

Hilton, J. L., & Darley, J. M. (1991). The effects of interaction goals on person perception. *Advances in Experimental Social Psychology, 24,* 235–267.

Hilton, J. L., & Fein, S. (1989). The role of typical diagnosticity in stereotype-based judgments. *Journal of Personality and Social Psychology, 57,* 201–211.

Hindy, C. G., Schwarz, J. C., & Brodsky, A. (1989). *If this is love, why do I feel so insecure?* New York: Atlantic Monthly Press.

Hinsz, V. B. (1989). Facial resemblance in engaged and married couples. *Journal of Social and Personal Relationships, 6,* 223–229.

Hinsz, V. B. (1990). Cognitive and consensus processes in group recognition memory performance. *Journal of Personality and Social Psychology, 59,* 705–718.

Hinsz, V. B., & Davis, J. H. (1984). Persuasive arguments theory, group polarization, and choice shifts. *Personality and Social Psychology Bulletin, 10,* 260–268.

Hinsz, V. B., Tindale, R. S., Nagao, D. H., Davis, J. H., & Robertson, B. A. (1988). The influence of the accuracy of individuating information on the use of base rate information in probability judgment. *Journal of Experimental Social Psychology, 24,* 127–145.

Hiroto, D. S. (1974). Locus of control and learned helplessness. *Journal of Experimental Psychology, 102,* 187–193.

Hirt, E. R., Deppe, R. K., & Gordon, L. J. (1991). Self-reported versus behavioral self-handicapping: Empirical evidence for a theoretical distinction. *Journal of Personality and Social Psychology, 61,* 981–991.

Hitler, A. (1933). *Mein Kampf* (E. T. S. Dugdale, Trans.). Cambridge, MA: Riverside.

Hobfoll, S. E., Lomranz, J., Eyal, N., Bridges, A., & Tzemach, M. (1989). Pulse of a nation: Depressive mood reactions of Israelis to the Israel-Lebanon War. *Journal of Personality and Social Psychology, 56,* 1002–1012.

Hobfoll, S. E., & Stephens, M. A. P. (1990). Social support during extreme stress: Consequences and interventions. In B. R. Sarason, I. G. Sarason, & G. R. Pierce (Eds.), *Social support: An interactional view* (pp. 454–481). New York: Wiley.

Hochschild, A. (1989). *The second shift: Working parents and the revolution at home.* New York: Viking.

Hoffman, C., & Hurst, N. (1990). Gender stereotypes: Perception or rationalization? *Journal of Personality and Social Psychology, 58,* 197–208.

Hoffner, C., & Badzinski, D. M. (1989). Children's integration of facial and situational cues to emotion. *Child Development, 60,* 411–422.

Hofling, C. K., Brotzman, E., Dalrymple, S., Graves, N., & Pierce, C. (1966). An experimental study of nurse-physician relations. *Journal of Nervous and Mental Disease, 143,* 171–180.

Hofstede, G. (1980). *Culture's consequences.* Beverly Hills, CA: Sage.

Hogg, M. A., & Abrams, D. (1990). Social motivation, self-esteem and social identity. In D. Abrams & M. Hogg (Eds.), *Social identity theory: Constructive and critical advances* (pp. 28–47). New York: Springer-Verlag.

Hogg, M. A., Turner, J. C., & Davidson, B. (1990). Polarized norms and social frames of reference: A test of the self-categorization theory of group polarization. *Basic and Applied Social Psychology, 11,* 77–100.

Hokanson, J. E., Loewenstein, D. A., Hedeen, C., & Howes, M. J. (1986). Dysphoric college students and roommates: A study of social behaviors over a three-month period. *Personality and Social Psychology Bulletin, 12,* 311–324.

Holahan, C. J., & Moos, R. H. (1990). Life stressors, resistance factors, and improved psychological functioning: An extension of the stress resistance paradigm. *Journal of Personality and Social Psychology, 58,* 909–917.

Hollander, E. P. (1958). Conformity, status, and idiosyncrasy credit. *Psychological Review, 65,* 117–127.

Hollander, E. P. (1985). Leadership and power. In G. Lindzey & E. Aronson (Eds.), *Handbook of social psychology* (3rd ed., Vol. 2, pp. 485–537). New York: Random House.

Hollander, E. P., & Offermann, L. R. (1990). Power and leadership in organizations. *American Psychologist, 45,* 179–189.

Holmes, D. S. (1976a). Debriefing after psychological experiments I. Effectiveness of postdeception dehoaxing. *American Psychologist, 31,* 858–867.

Holmes, D. S. (1976b). Debriefing after psychological experiments II. Effectiveness of postexperimental desensitizing. *American Psychologist, 31,* 868–875.

Holmes, D. S., & Appelbaum, A. S. (1970). Nature of prior experimental experience as determinant of performance in a subsequent experiment. *Journal of Personality and Social Psychology, 14,* 195–202.

Holmes, D. S., McGilley, B. M., & Houston, B. K. (1984). Task-related arousal of Type A and Type B persons: Level of challenge and response specificity. *Journal of Personality and Social Psychology, 46,* 1322–1327.

Holmes, J. G., & Rempel, J. K. (1989). Trust in close relationships. In C. Hendrick (Ed.), *Review of personality and social psychology: Close relationships* (Vol. 10, pp. 187–220). Newbury Park, CA: Sage.

Holmes, T. H., & Masuda, M. (1974). Life change and illness susceptibility. In B. S. Dohrenwend & B. P. Dohrenwend (Eds.), *Stressful life events: Their nature and effects* (pp. 45–72). New York: Wiley.

Holmes, T. H., & Rahe, R. H. (1967). The Social Readjustment Rating Scale. *Journal of Psychosomatic Research, 11,* 213–218.

Holroy, K. A., & Coyne, J. (1987). Personality and health in the 1980s: Psychosomatic medicine revisited? *Journal of Personality, 55,* 359–375.

Holtgraves, T., & Bailey, C. (1991). Premise acceptability and message effectiveness. *Basic and Applied Social Psychology, 12,* 157–176.

Holtgraves, T., & Yang, J. N. (1992). Interpersonal underpinnings of request strategies: General principles and differences due to culture and gender. *Journal of Personality and Social Psychology, 62,* 246–256.

Holtzworth-Munroe, A., & Jacobson, N. S. (1987). An attributional approach to marital dysfunction and therapy. In J. E. Maddux, C. D. Stoltenberg, & R. Rosenwein (Eds.), *Social processes in clinical and counseling psychology* (pp. 153–170). New York: Springer-Verlag.

Homans, G. C. (1961). *Social behavior.* New York: Harcourt, Brace & World.

Homer, P. M., & Kahle, L. R. (1988). A structural equation test of the value-attitude-behavior hierarchy. *Journal of Personality and Social Psychology, 54,* 638–646.

Honts, C. R., Hodes, R. L., & Raskin, D. C. (1985). Effects of physical countermeasures on the physiological detection of deception. *Journal of Applied Psychology, 70,* 177–187.

Horn, J. C. (1987, July). Bigger pay for better work. *Psychology Today,* pp. 54–57.

Horney, K. (1939). *New ways in psychoanalysis.* New York: Norton.

Horowitz, I. A. (1988). Jury nullification: The impact of judicial instructions, arguments, and challenges on jury decision making. *Law and Human Behavior, 12,* 439–453.

Horowitz, I. A., & Willging, T. E. (1991). Changing views of jury power: The nullification debate, 1787–1988. *Law and Human Behavior, 15,* 165–182.

Hort, B. E., Fagot, B. I., & Leinbach, M. D. (1990). Are people's notions of maleness more stereotypically framed than their notions of femaleness? *Sex Roles, 23,* 197–212.

Horvath, F. (1984). Detecting deception in eyewitness cases: Problems and prospects in use of the polygraph. In G. Wells & E. Loftus (Eds.), *Eyewitness testimony: Psychological perspectives* (pp. 214–255). New York: Cambridge University Press.

House, J. S. (1981). *Work stress and social support.* Reading, MA: Addison-Wesley.

House, J. S., Landis, K. R., & Umberson, D. (1988). Social relationships and health. *Science, 241,* 540–545.

Houston, B. K. (1988). Introduction. In B. K. Houston & C. R. Snyder (Eds.), *Type A behavior pattern: Research, theory, and intervention* (pp. 1–7). New York: Wiley.

Houston, D. A. (1990). Empathy and the self: Cognitive and emotional influences on the evaluation of negative affect in others. *Journal of Personality and Social Psychology, 59,* 859–868.

Houts, A. C., Cook, T. D., & Shadish, W. R., Jr. (1986). The person-situation debate: A critical multiplist perspective. *Journal of Personality, 54,* 52–105.

Hovland, C. I., Janis, I. L., & Kelley, H. H. (1953). *Communication and persuasion: Psychological studies of opinion change.* New Haven, CT: Yale University Press.

Hovland, C. I., Lumsdaine, A. A., & Sheffield, F. D. (1949). *Experiments on mass communication.* Princeton, NJ: Princeton University Press.

Hovland, C. I., & Sears, R. R. (1940). Minor studies in aggression: VI. Correlation of lynchings with economic indices. *Journal of Psychology, 9,* 301–310.

Hovland, C. I., & Weiss, W. (1951). The influence of source credibility on communication effectiveness. *Public Opinion Quarterly, 15,* 635–650.

Howard, D. J. (1990a). The influence of verbal responses to common greetings on compliance behavior: The foot-in-the-mouth effect. *Journal of Applied Social Psychology, 20,* 1185–1196.

Howard, D. J. (1990b). Rhetorical question effects on message processing and persuasion: The role of information availability and the elicitation of judgment. *Journal of Experimental Social Psychology, 26,* 217–239.

Howard, G. S. (1985). The role of values in the science of psychology. *American Psychologist, 40,* 255–265.

Howard, J. A., Blumstein, P., & Schwartz, P. (1987). Social or evolutionary theories? Some observations on preferences in human mate selection. *Journal of Personality and Social Psychology, 53,* 194–200.

Howell, R. H., Owen, P. D., & Nocks, E. C. (1990). Increasing safety belt use: Effects of modeling and trip length. *Journal of Applied Social Psychology, 20,* 254–263.

Hoyle, R. H., Pinkley, R. L., & Insko, C. A. (1989). Perceptions of social behavior: Evidence of differing expectations for interpersonal and intergroup interactions. *Personality and Social Psychology Bulletin, 15,* 365–376.

Huesmann, L. R. (1982). Television violence and aggressive behavior. In D. Pearl, L. Bouthilet, & J. Lazar (Eds.), *Television and behavior: Vol. II. Technical reviews* (pp. 126–137). Rockville, MD: National Institutes of Mental Health.

Huesmann, L. R., & Eron, L. D. (Eds.). (1986). *Television and the aggressive child: A cross-national comparison.* Hillsdale, NJ: Erlbaum.

Huesmann, L. R., Eron, L. D., Klein, R., Brice, P., & Fischer, P. (1983). Mitigating the imitation of aggressive behaviors by changing children's attitudes about media violence. *Journal of Personality and Social Psychology, 44,* 899–910.

Huesmann, L. R., Eron, L. D., Lefkowitz, M. M., & Walder, L. O. (1984). Stability of aggression over time and generations. *Developmental Psychology, 20,* 1120–1134.

Huesmann, L. R., Eron, L. D., & Yarmel, P. W. (1987). Intellectual functioning and aggression. *Journal of Personality and Social Psychology, 52,* 232–240.

Huff, C., & Cooper, J. (1987). Sex bias in educational software: The effect of designers' stereotypes on the software they design. *Journal of Applied Social Psychology, 17,* 519–532.

Hull, J. G., & Mendolia, M. (1991). Modeling the relation of attributional style, expectancies, and depression. *Journal of Personality and Social Psychology, 61,* 85–97.

Hull, J. G., & Young, R. D. (1983). Self-consciousness, self-esteem, and success-failure as determinants of alcohol consumption in male social drinkers. *Journal of Personality and Social Psychology, 44,* 1097–1109.

Hull, J. G., Young, R. D., & Jouriles, E. (1986). Applications of the self-awareness model of alcohol consumption: Predicting patterns of use and abuse. *Journal of Personality and Social Psychology, 51,* 790–796.

Hunter, C. E., & Ross, M. W. (1991). Determinants of health-care workers' attitudes toward people with AIDS. *Journal of Applied Social Psychology, 21,* 947–956.

Huston, T. L. (1973). Ambiguity of acceptance, social desirability, and dating choice. *Journal of Experimental Social Psychology, 9,* 32–42.

Huston, T. L. (1983). Power. In H. H. Kelley, E. Berscheid, A. Christenson, J. H. Harvey, T. L. Huston, G. Levinger, E. McClintock, L. A. Peplau, & D. R. Peterson, *Close relationships* (pp. 169–219). New York: Freeman.

Ickes, W., Bissonnette, V., Garcia, S., & Stinson, L. L. (1990). Implementing and using the Dyadic Interaction Paradigm. In C. Hendrick & M. S. Clark (Eds.), *Review of personality and social psychology: Vol. 11. Research methods in personality and social psychology* (pp. 16–44). Newbury Park, CA: Sage.

Ickes, W. J., Patterson, M., Rajecki, D. W., & Tanford, S. (1982). Behavioral and cognitive consequences of reciprocal versus compensatory responses to preinteraction expectancies. *Social Cognition, 1,* 160–190.

Ickovics, J. R., & Rodin, J. (1992). Women and AIDS in the United States: Epidemiology, natural history, and mediating mechanisms. *Health Psychology, 11,* 1–16.

Inbau, F. E., & Reid, J. E. (1986). *Criminal interrogation and confessions* (3rd ed.). Baltimore: Williams & Wilkins.

Ingram, R. E. (1990). Self-focused attention in clinical disorders: Review and a conceptual model. *Psychological Bulletin, 107,* 156–176.

Ingram, R. E., Cruet, D., Johnson, B. R., & Wisnicki, K. S. (1988). Self-focused attention, gender, gender role, and vulnerability to negative affect. *Journal of Personality and Social Psychology, 55,* 967–978.

Insko, C. A., Drenan, S., Solomon, M. R., Smith, R., & Wade, T. J. (1983). Conformity as a function of the consistency of positive self-evaluation with being liked and being right. *Journal of Experimental Social Psychology, 19,* 341–358.

Insko, C. A., Schopler, J., Hoyle, R. H., Dardis, G. J., & Graetz, K. A. (1990). Individual-group discontinuity as a function of fear and greed. *Journal of Personality and Social Psychology, 58,* 68–79.

Insko, C. A., Sedlak, A. J., & Lipsitz, A. (1982). A two-valued logic or two-valued balance resolution of the challenge of agreement and attraction effects in p-o-x triads, and a theoretical perspective on conformity and hedonism. *European Journal of Social Psychology, 12,* 143–167.

Intons-Peterson, M. J., Roskos-Ewoldsen, B., Thomas, L., Shirley, M., & Blut, D. (1989). Will educational materials reduce negative effects of exposure to sexual violence? *Journal of Social and Clinical Psychology, 8,* 256–275.

Irons, E. D., & Moore, G. W. (1985). *Black managers: The case of the banking industry.* New York: Praeger.

Isen, A. M. (1970). Success, failure, attention, and reaction to others: The warm glow of success. *Journal of Personality and Social Psychology, 15,* 294–301.

Isen, A. M. (1984). Toward understanding the role of affect in cognition. In R. S. Wyer & T. K. Srull (Eds.), *Handbook of social cognition* (Vol. 3, pp. 179–236). Hillsdale, NJ: Erlbaum.

Isen, A. M., & Levin, P. A. (1972). Effect of feeling good on helping: Cookies and kindness. *Journal of Personality and Social Psychology, 21,* 384–388.

Isen, A. M., Clark, M., & Schwartz, M. H. (1976). Duration of the effect of good mood on helping: "Footprints in the sands of time." *Journal of Personality and Social Psychology, 34,* 385–393.

Isen, A. M., & Means, B. (1983). The influence of positive affect on decision-making strategy. *Social Cognition, 2,* 18–31.

Isen, A. M., Shalker, T. E., Clark, M., & Karp, L. (1978). Affect, accessibility of material in memory, and behavior: A cognitive loop? *Journal of Personality and Social Psychology, 36,* 1–12.

Isenberg, D. J. (1986). Group polarization: A critical review and meta-analysis. *Journal of Personality and Social Psychology, 50,* 1141–1151.

It would be easy to poll this jury. (1985). *National Law Journal.*

Izard, C. E. (1990). Facial expressions and the regulation of emotions. *Journal of Personality and Social Psychology, 58,* 487–498.

Jackson, J. M. (1986). In defense of social impact theory: Comment on Mullin. *Journal of Personality and Social Psychology, 50,* 511–513.

Jackson, J. M., & Williams, K. D. (1985). Social loafing on difficult tasks: Working collectively can improve performance. *Journal of Personality and Social Psychology, 49,* 937–942.

Jackson, L. A., Gardner, P. D., & Sullivan, L. A. (1992). Explaining gender differences in self-pay expectations: Social comparison standards and perceptions of fair pay. *Journal of Applied Psychology*.

Jacobs, G. A., Quevillon, R. P., & Stricherz, M. (1990). Lessons from the aftermath of Flight 232: Practical considerations for the mental health professional's response to air disasters. *American Psychologist, 45,* 1329–1335.

Jacobs, J. E. (1991). Influence of gender stereotypes on parent and child mathematics attitudes. *Journal of Educational Psychology, 83,* 518–527.

Jacobson, D. S. (1987). Family type, visiting patterns, and children's behavior in the stepfamily: A linked family system. In K. Pasley & M. Ihinger-Tallman (Eds.), *Remarriage and stepparenting* (pp. 257–272). New York: Guilford.

James, W. (1890). *Psychology.* New York: Holt.

Jamieson, D. W., Lydon, J. E., Stewart, G., & Zanna, M. P. (1987). Pygmalion revisited: New evidence for student expectancy effects in the classroom. *Journal of Educational Psychology, 79,* 461–466.

Janis, I. L. (1968). Attitude change via role playing. In R. Abelson, E. Aronson, W. McGuire, T. Newcomb, M. Rosenberg, & P. Tennenbaum (Eds.), *Theories of cognitive consistency: A sourcebook* (pp. 810–818). Chicago: Rand McNally.

Janis, I. L. (1982). *Groupthink* (2nd ed.). Boston: Houghton Mifflin.

Janis, I. L., & Feshbach, S. (1953). Effects of fear arousing communications. *Journal of Abnormal and Social Psychology, 48,* 78–92.

Janis, I. L., Kaye, D., & Kirschner, P. (1965). Facilitating effects of "eating while reading" on responsiveness to persuasive communications. *Journal of Personality and Social Psychology, 1,* 181–186.

Janis, I. L., & King, B. T. (1954). The influence of role playing on opinion change. *Journal of Abnormal and Social Psychology, 49,* 211–218.

Janoff-Bulman, R. (1979). Characterological versus behavioral self-blame: Inquiries into depression and rape. *Journal of Personality and Social Psychology, 37,* 1798–1809.

Janoff-Bulman, R., & Timko, C. (1987). Coping with traumatic life events: The role of denial in light of people's assumptive worlds. In C. R. Snyder & C. E. Ford (Eds.), *Coping with negative life events: Clinical and social psychological perspectives* (pp. 135–159). New York: Plenum.

Janoff-Bulman, R., Timko, C., & Carli, L. L. (1985). Cognitive biases in blaming the victim. *Journal of Experimental Social Psychology, 21,* 161–177.

Jemmott, J. B., III, & Magloire, K. (1988). Academic stress, social support, and secretory immunoglobulin A. *Journal of Personality and Social Psychology, 55,* 803–810.

Jemmott, J. B., III, Ashby, K. L., & Lindenfeld, K. (1989). Romantic commitment and the perceived availability of opposite-sex persons: On loving the one you're with. *Journal of Applied Social Psychology, 19,* 1198–1211.

Jenkins, C. D., Zyzanski, S. J., & Rosenman, R. H. (1979). *The Jenkins Activity Survey.* New York: Psychological Corp.

Jenkins-Hall, K., & Sacco, W. P. (1991). Effects of client race and depression on evaluations by white therapists. *Journal of Social and Clinical Psychology, 10,* 322–333.

Jennings (Walstedt), J., Geis, F. L., & Brown, V. (1980). Influence of television commercials on women's self-confidence and independent judgment. *Journal of Personality and Social Psychology, 38,* 203–210.

Jepson, C., & Chaiken, S. (1990). Chronic issue-specific fear inhibits systematic processing of persuasive communications. *Journal of Social Behavior and Personality, 5,* 61–84.

Johansson, G., von Hofsten, C., & Jansson, G. (1980). Event perception. *Annual Review of Psychology, 31,* 27–53.

Johnson v. Louisiana, 406 U. S. 356 (1972).

Johnson, B. T., & Eagly, A. H. (1989). Effects of involvement on persuasion: A meta-analysis. *Psychological Bulletin, 106,* 290–314.

Johnson, D. J., & Rusbult, C. E. (1989). Resisting temptation: Devaluation of alternative partners as a means of maintaining commitment in close relationships. *Journal of Personality and Social Psychology, 57,* 967–980.

Johnson, K. (1987a, October 20). Goetz sentenced to six months in jail on gun charge. *New York Times,* p. 15.

Johnson, K. (1987b, May 5). Victim admits changes in details at Goetz trial. *New York Times,* p. 21.

Johnson, K. (1987c, May 21). Youth Goetz shot rejects questions. *New York Times,* p. 16.

Johnson, W. O. (1991, August 5). How far have we come? *Sports Illustrated,* pp. 39–47.

Johnson-George, C., & Swap, W. (1982). Measurement of specific interpersonal trust: Construction and validation of a scale to assess trust in a specific other. *Journal of Personality and Social Psychology, 43,* 1306–1317.

Johnston, J., & Ettema, J. (1986). Using television to best advantage: Research for prosocial television. In J. Bryant & D. Zillmann (Eds.), *Perspectives on media effects* (pp. 143–164). Hillsdale, NJ: Erlbaum.

Jones, E. E. (1964). *Ingratiation: A social psychological analysis.* New York: Appleton-Century-Crofts.

Jones, E. E. (1990). *Interpersonal perception.* New York: Freeman.

Jones, E. E., & Davis, K. E. (1965). A theory of correspondent inferences: From acts to dispositions. In L. Berkowitz (Ed.), *Advances in experimental social psychology* (Vol. 2, pp. 219–266). New York: Academic Press.

Jones, E. E., Davis, K. E., & Gergen, K. (1961). Role playing variations and their informational value for person perception. *Journal of Abnormal and Social Psychology, 63,* 302–310.

Jones, E. E., & Gerard, H. B. (1967). *Foundations of social psychology.* New York: Wiley.

Jones, E. E., & Harris, V. A. (1967). The attribution of attitudes. *Journal of Experimental Social Psychology, 3,* 1–24.

Jones, E. E., & Nisbett, R. E. (1972). The actor and the observer: Divergent perceptions of causality. In E. E. Jones, D. E.

Kanouse, H. H. Kelley, R. E. Nisbett, S. Valins, & B. Weiner (Eds.), *Attribution: Perceiving the causes of behavior* (pp. 79–94). Morristown, NJ: General Learning Press.

Jones, E. E., & Pittman, T. S. (1982). Toward a general theory of strategic self presentation. In J. Suls (Ed.), *Psychological perspectives on the self*. Hillsdale, NJ: Erlbaum.

Jones, E. E., Rhodewalt, F., Berglas, S., & Skelton, J. A. (1981). Effects of strategic self-presentation on subsequent self-esteem. *Journal of Personality and Social Psychology, 41,* 407–421.

Jones, E. E., Rock, L., Shaver, K. G., Goethals, G. R., & Ward, L. M. (1968). Pattern of performance and ability attribution: An unexpected primary effect. *Journal of Personality and Social Psychology, 10,* 317–340.

Jones, E. E., & Sigall, H. (1971). The bogus pipeline: A new paradigm for measuring affect and attitude. *Psychological Bulletin, 76,* 349–364.

Jones, E. W. (1986). Black managers: The dream deferred. *Harvard Business Review, 64,* 84–93.

Jones, J. M., Levine, I. S., & Rosenberg, A. A. (Eds.). (1991). Homelessness [Special issue]. *American Psychologist, 46 (11).*

Jones, R. A. (1985). *Research methods in the social and behavioral sciences.* Sunderland, MA: Sinauer.

Jones, W. H., & Carpenter, B. N. (1986). Shyness, social behavior, and relationships. In W. H. Jones, J. M. Cheek, & S. R. Briggs (Eds.), *Shyness: Perspectives on research and treatment* (pp. 227–238). New York: Plenum.

Jones, W. H., & Carver, M. D. (1991). Adjustment and coping implications of loneliness. In C. R. Snyder & D. R. Forsyth (Eds.), *Handbook of social and clinical psychology: The health perspective* (pp. 395–415). New York: Pergamon Press.

Jones, W. H., Hobbs, S. A., & Hackenbury, D. (1982). Loneliness and social skills deficits. *Journal of Experimental Social Psychology, 42,* 682–689.

Joseph, J. G., Montgomery, S. B., Ostrow, D. G., Kirscht, J. P., Kessler, R. C., Phair, J., & Chmiel, J. (1990). Assessing the costs and benefits of an increased sense of vulnerability to AIDS in a cohort of gay men. In L. Temoshok & A. Baum (Eds.), *Psychosocial perspectives on AIDS* (pp. 65–79). Hillsdale, NJ: Erlbaum.

Josephson, W. L. (1987). Television violence and children's aggression: Testing the priming, social script, and disinhibition predictions. *Journal of Personality and Social Psychology, 53,* 882–890.

Jourard, S. M. (1964). *The transparent self.* New York: Van Nostrand.

Judd, C. M., Drake, R. A., Downing, J. W., & Krosnick, J. A. (1991a). Some dynamic properties of attitude structures: Context-induced response facilitation and polarization. *Journal of Personality and Social Psychology, 60,* 193–202.

Judd, C. M., & Park, B. (1988). Out-group homogeneity: Judgments of variability at the individual and group levels. *Journal of Personality and Social Psychology, 54,* 778–788.

Judd, C. M., Ryan, C. S., & Park, B. (1991b). Accuracy in the judgment of in-group and out-group variability. *Journal of Personality and Social Psychology, 61,* 366–379.

Jussim, L. (1989). Teacher expectations: Self-fulfilling prophecies, perceptual biases, and accuracy. *Journal of Personality and Social Psychology, 57,* 469–480.

Kagehiro, D. K. (1990). Defining the standards of proof in jury instructions. *Psychological Science, 1,* 194–200.

Kagehiro, D. K., & Laufer, W. S. (Eds.). (1992). *Handbook of psychology and law.* New York: Springer-Verlag.

Kahle, L. R., & Homer, P. M. (1985). Physical attractiveness of the celebrity endorser: A social adaptation perspective. *Journal of Consumer Research, 11,* 954–961.

Kahneman, D., Slovic, P., & Tversky, A. (Eds.). (1982). *Judgment under uncertainty: Heuristics and biases.* New York: Cambridge University Press.

Kahneman, D., & Tversky, A. (1972). Subjective probability: A judgment of representativeness. *Cognitive Psychology, 3,* 430–454.

Kahneman, D., & Tversky, A. (1973). On the psychology of prediction. *Psychological Review, 80,* 237–251.

Kahneman, D., & Tversky, A. (1984). Choices, values, and frames. *American Psychologist, 39,* 341–350.

Kalick, S. M., & Hamilton, T. E., III. (1986). The matching hypothesis revisited. *Journal of Personality and Social Psychology, 51,* 673–682.

Kalick, S. M., & Hamilton, T. E., III. (1988). Closer look at a matching simulation: Reply to Aron. *Journal of Personality and Social Psychology, 54,* 447–451.

Kallgren, C. A., & Wood, W. (1986). Access to attitude-relevant information in memory as a determinant of attitude-behavior consistency. *Journal of Experimental Social Psychology, 22,* 328–338.

Kalven, H., & Zeisel, H. (1966). *The American jury.* Boston: Little, Brown.

Kamin, L. J. (1986, February). Is there crime in the genes? The answer may depend on who chooses what evidence. *Scientific American,* pp. 22–27.

Kaplan, M. F. (1987). The influencing process in group decision making. In C. Hendrick (Ed.), *Review of personality and social psychology: Group processes* (Vol. 8, pp. 189–212). Beverly Hills, CA: Sage.

Kaplan, M. F., & Miller, C. E. (1987). Group decision making and normative versus informational influence: Effects of type of issue and assigned decision rules. *Journal of Personality and Social Psychology, 53,* 306–313.

Kaplan, M. F., & Schersching, C. (1981). Juror deliberation: An information integration analysis. In B. Sales (Ed.), *The trial process* (pp. 235–262). New York: Plenum.

Kaplan, R. M., & Toshima, M. T. (1990). The functional effects of social relationships on chronic illness and disability. In B. R. Sarason, I. G. Sarason, & G. R. Pierce (Eds.), *Social support: An interactional view* (pp. 427–453). New York: Wiley.

Karlsen, C. F. (1987). *The devil in the shape of a woman*. New York: Norton.

Kassin, S. M. (1979). Consensus information, prediction, and causal attribution: A review of the literature and issues. *Journal of Personality and Social Psychology, 37*, 1966–1981.

Kassin, S. M. (1985). *An empirical study of Rule 11 sanctions*. Washington, DC: Federal Judicial Center.

Kassin, S. M., & Barndollar, K. A. (1992). On the psychology of eyewitness testimony: A comparison of experts and prospective jurors. *Journal of Applied Social Psychology, 22.*

Kassin, S. M., Ellsworth, P. C., & Smith, V. L. (1989). The "general acceptance" of psychological research on eyewitness testimony: A survey of the experts. *American Psychologist, 44*, 1089–1098.

Kassin, S. M., & McNall, K. (1991). Police interrogations and confessions: Communicating promises and threats by pragmatic implication. *Law and Human Behavior, 15*, 233–251.

Kassin, S. M., Rigby, S., & Castillo, S. R. (1991). The accuracy-confidence correlation in eyewitness testimony: Limits and extensions of the retrospective self-awareness effect. *Journal of Personality and Social Psychology, 61*, 698–707.

Kassin, S. M., Smith, V. L., & Tulloch, W. F. (1990a). The dynamite charge: Effects on the perceptions and deliberation behavior of mock jurors. *Law and Human Behavior, 14*, 537–550.

Kassin, S. M., Williams, L. N., & Saunders, C. L. (1990b). Dirty tricks of cross-examination: The influence of conjectural evidence on the jury. *Law and Human Behavior, 14*, 373–384.

Kassin, S. M., & Wrightsman, L. S. (1979). On the requirements of proof: The timing of judicial instruction and mock juror verdicts. *Journal of Personality and Social Psychology, 37*, 1877–1887.

Kassin, S. M., & Wrightsman, L. S. (1983). The construction and validation of a Juror Bias Scale. *Journal of Research in Personality, 17*, 423–442.

Kassin, S. M., & Wrightsman, L. S. (1985). Confession evidence. In S. M. Kassin & L. S. Wrightsman (Eds.), *The psychology of evidence and trial procedure* (pp. 67–94). Beverly Hills, CA: Sage.

Kassin, S. M., & Wrightsman, L. S. (1988). *The American jury on trial: Psychological perspectives*. Washington, DC: Hemisphere.

Katz, D., & Braly, K. W. (1933). Racial stereotypes of 100 college students. *Journal of Abnormal and Social Psychology, 28*, 280–290.

Katz, I., Wackenhut, J., & Hass, G. (1986). Racial ambivalence, value duality, and behavior. In J. F. Dovidio, & S. L. Gaertner, (Eds.), *Prejudice, discrimination, and racism: Theory and research* (pp. 35–60). Orlando, FL: Academic Press.

Kazdin, A. E. (1982). Observer effects: Reactivity of direct observation. In D. P. Hartmann (Ed.), *New directions for methodology of social and behavioral science (No. 14): Using observers to study behavior* (pp. 5–19). San Francisco: Jossey-Bass.

Keen, S. (1991). *Fire in the belly*. New York: Bantam Books.

Keenan, P. A., & Carnevale, P. J. D. (1989). Positive effects of within-group cooperation on between-group negotiation. *Journal of Applied Social Psychology, 19*, 977–992.

Kelley, H. H. (1950). The warm-cold variable in first impressions of persons. *Journal of Personality, 18*, 431–439.

Kelley, H. H. (1967). Attribution theory in social psychology. In D. Levine (Ed.), *Nebraska Symposium on Motivation* (Vol. 15, pp. 192–241). Lincoln: University of Nebraska Press.

Kelley, H. H. (1983). Love and commitment. In H. H. Kelley, E. Berscheid, A. Christenson, J. H. Harvey, T. L. Huston, G. Levinger, E. McClintock, L. A. Peplau, & D. R. Peterson, *Close relationships* (pp. 265–314). New York: Freeman.

Kelley, H. H., & Stahelski, A. J. (1970). Social interaction basis of cooperators' and competitors' beliefs about others. *Journal of Personality and Social Psychology, 16*, 66–91.

Kelman, H. C. (1961). Processes of opinion change. *Public Opinion Quarterly, 25*, 57–78.

Kelman, H. C. (1967). Human use of human subjects: The problem of deception in social psychology experiments. *Psychological Bulletin, 67*, 1–11.

Kelman, H. C., & Hamilton, V. L. (1989). *Crimes of obedience: Toward a social psychology of authority and responsibility*. New Haven, CT: Yale University Press.

Kelman, H. C., & Hovland, C. I. (1953). "Reinstatement" of the communicator in delayed measurement of opinion change. *Journal of Abnormal and Social Psychology, 48*, 327–335.

Kennedy, R. (1989). *Life choices* (2nd ed.). New York: Holt, Rinehart and Winston.

Kennedy, S., Kiecolt-Glaser, J. K., & Glaser, R. (1990). Social support, stress, and the immune system. In B. R. Sarason, I. G. Sarason, & G. R. Pierce (Eds.), *Social support: An interactional view* (pp. 253–266). New York: Wiley.

Kenny, D. A., & Albright, L. (1987). Accuracy in interpersonal perception: A social relations analysis. *Psychological Bulletin, 102*, 390–402.

Kenny, D. A., Horner, C., Kashy, D. A., & Chu, L. (1992). Consensus at zero acquaintance: Replication, behavioral cues, and stability. *Journal of Personality and Social Psychology, 62*, 88–97.

Kenny, D. A., & Zaccaro, S. J. (1983). An estimate of variance due to traits in leadership. *Journal of Applied Psychology, 68*, 678–685.

Kenrick, D. T. (1986). How strong is the case against contemporary social and personality psychology? A response to Carlson. *Journal of Personality and Social Psychology, 50*, 839–844.

Kenrick, D. T., Baumann, D. J., & Cialdini, R. B. (1979). A step in the socialization of altruism as hedonism: Effects of negative mood on children's generosity under public and private conditions. *Journal of Personality and Social Psychology, 37*, 747–755.

Kenrick, D. T., & Cialdini, R. B. (1977). Romantic attraction: Misattribution versus reinforcement explanations. *Journal of Personality and Social Psychology, 35*, 381–391.

Kenrick, D. T., Gutierres, S. E., & Goldberg, L. L. (1989). Influence of popular erotica on judgments of strangers and mates. *Journal of Experimental Social Psychology, 25,* 159–167.

Kenrick, D. T., Sadalla, E. K., Groth, G., & Trost, M. R. (1990). Evolution, traits, and the stages of human courtship: Qualifying the parental investment model. *Journal of Personality, 58,* 97–116.

Kernis, M. H., Grannemann, B. D., & Barclay, L. C. (1989). Stability and level of self-esteem as predictors of anger arousal and hostility. *Journal of Personality and Social Psychology, 56,* 1013–1022.

Kernis, M. H., & Wheeler, L. (1981). Beautiful friends and ugly strangers: Radiation and contrast effects in perceptions of same-sex pairs. *Personality and Social Psychology Bulletin, 7,* 617–620.

Kerr, N. L. (1981). Social transition schemes: Charting the group's road to agreement. *Journal of Personality and Social Psychology, 41,* 684–702.

Kerr, N. L. (1983). Motivation losses in small groups: A social dilemma. *Journal of Personality and Social Psychology, 45,* 819–828.

Kerr, N. L. (1989). Illusions of efficacy: The effects of group size on perceived efficacy in social dilemmas. *Journal of Experimental Social Psychology, 25,* 287–313.

Kerr, N. L. (1992). Issue importance and group decision making. In S. Worchel, W. Wood, & J. A. Simpson (Eds.), *Group process and productivity* (pp. 68–88). Newbury Park, CA: Sage.

Kerr, N. L., & Bruun, S. E. (1983). Dispensability of member effort and group motivation losses: Free-rider effects. *Journal of Personality and Social Psychology, 44,* 78–94.

Kerr, N. L., Harmon, D. L., & Graves, J. K. (1982). Independence of multiple verdicts by jurors and juries. *Journal of Applied Social Psychology, 12,* 12–29.

Kerr, N. L., Kramer, G. P., Carroll, J. S., & Alfini, J. J. (1991). On the effectiveness of voir dire in criminal cases with prejudicial pretrial publicity: An empirical study. *American University Law Review, 40,* 665–701.

Kerr, N. L., & MacCoun, R. J. (1985a). The effects of jury size and polling method on the process and product of jury deliberation. *Journal of Personality and Social Psychology, 48,* 349–363.

Kerr, N. L., & MacCoun, R. J. (1985b). Role expectations in social dilemmas: Sex roles and task motivation in groups. *Journal of Personality and Social Psychology, 49,* 1547–1556.

Kessler, R. C., Kendler, K. S., Heath, A., Neale, M.C., & Eaves, L. J. (1992). Social support, depressed mood, and adjustment to stress: A genetic epidemiologic investigation. *Journal of Personality and Social Psychology, 62,* 257–272.

Kessler, R. C., McLeod, J. D., & Wethington, E. (1985). The costs of caring: A perspective on the relationship between sex and psychological distress. In I. G. Sarason & B. R. Sarason (Eds.), *Social support: Theory, research and applications* (pp. 491–506). Dordrecht, The Netherlands: Martinus Nkjhoff.

Kiecolt-Glaser, J. K., & Williams, D. A. (1987). Self-blame, compliance, and distress among burn patients. *Journal of Personality and Social Psychology, 53,* 187–193.

Kiesler, C. A. (1971). *The psychology of commitment.* New York: Academic Press.

Kiesler, C. A., & Kiesler, S. B. (1969). *Conformity.* Reading, MA: Addison-Wesley.

Kihlstrom, J. F. (1987). Introduction to the special issue: Integrating personality and social psychology. *Journal of Personality and Social Psychology, 53,* 989–992.

Kihlstrom, J. F., & Cantor, N. (1984). Mental representations of the self. In L. Berkowitz (Ed.), *Advances in experimental social psychology* (Vol. 17, pp. 1–47). New York: Academic Press.

Kilham, W., & Mann, L. (1974). Level of destructive obedience as a function of transmitter and executant roles in the Milgram obedience paradigm. *Journal of Personality and Social Psychology, 29,* 696–702.

Kilpatrick, D. G., Edmunds, C. N., & Seymour, A. (1992). *Rape in America.* Arlington, VA: National Victim Center.

Kinder, D. R., & Sears, D. O. (1981). Prejudice and politics: Symbolic racism versus racial threats to the good life. *Journal of Personality and Social Psychology, 40,* 414–431.

Kitson, G. C., & Morgan, L. A. (1990). The multiple consequences of divorce: A decade review. *Journal of Marriage and the Family, 52,* 913–924.

Klein, J. G. (1991). Negativity effects in impression formation: A test in the political arena. *Personality and Social Psychology Bulletin, 17,* 412–418.

Klein, S. B., & Loftus, J. (1988). The nature of self-referent encoding: The contributions of elaborative and organizational processes. *Journal of Personality and Social Psychology, 55,* 5–11.

Klein, W. M., & Kunda, Z. (1992). Motivated person perception: Constructing justifications for desired beliefs. *Journal of Experimental Social Psychology, 28,* 145–168.

Kleinke, C. L. (1986). Gaze and eye contact: A research review. *Psychological Bulletin, 100,* 78–100.

Kluegel, J. R. (1990). Trends in whites' explanations of the black-white gap in socioeconomic status, 1977–1989. *American Sociological Review, 55,* 512–525.

Knapp, A., & Clark, M. S. (1991). Some detrimental effects of negative mood on individuals' ability to solve resource dilemmas. *Personality and Social Psychology Bulletin, 17,* 678–688.

Knight, G. P., & Dubro, A. F. (1984). Cooperative, competitive, and individualistic social values: An individualized regression and clustering approach. *Journal of Personality and Social Psychology, 46,* 98–105.

Knowles, E. S. (1980). An affiliative-conflict theory of personal and group spatial behavior. In P. B. Paulus (Ed.), *Psychology of group influence* (pp. 133–188). Hillsdale, NJ: Erlbaum.

Knowles, E. S. (1983). Social physics and the effects of others: Tests of the effects of audience size and distance on social judgments and behavior. *Journal of Personality and Social Psychology, 45,* 1263–1279.

Knox, R. E., & Inskter, J. A. (1968). Postdecision dissonance at post-time. *Journal of Personality and Social Psychology, 8,* 319–323.

Kobak, R. R., & Hazan, C. (1991). Attachment in marriage: Effects of security and accuracy of working models. *Journal of Personality and Social Psychology, 60,* 861–869.

Kobasa, S. C., Maddi, S. R., & Kahn, S. (1982). Hardiness and health: A prospective study. *Journal of Personality and Social Psychology, 42,* 168–177.

Koestner, R., Franz, C., & Weinberger, J. (1990). The family origins of empathic concern: A 26-year longitudinal study. *Journal of Personality and Social Psychology, 58,* 709–717.

Koestner, R., & Wheeler, L. (1988). Self-presentations in personal advertisements: The influence of implicit motives of attraction and role expectations. *Journal of Social and Personal Relationships, 5,* 149–160.

Kohlberg, L. (1981). *The philosophy of moral development: Moral stages and the idea of justice: Vol. 1. Essays on moral development.* New York: Harper & Row.

Kohn, A. (1990). *The brighter side of human nature.* New York: Basic Books.

Kohn, P. M., Lafreniere, K., & Gurevich, M. (1991). Hassles, health, and personality. *Journal of Personality and Social Psychology, 61,* 478–482.

Kolditz, T. A., & Arkin, R. M. (1982). An impression management interpretation of the self-handicapping strategy. *Journal of Personality and Social Psychology, 43,* 492–502.

Kollock, P., Blumstein, P., & Schwartz, P. (1985). Sex and power in interaction: Conversational privileges and duties. *American Sociological Review, 50,* 34–46.

Konecni, V. J., & Ebbesen, E. B. (1982). *The criminal justice system: A social-psychological analysis.* San Francisco: Freeman.

Koop, C. E. (1987). Report of the Surgeon General's Workshop on Pornography and Public Health. *American Psychologist, 42,* 944–945.

Korte, C. (1980). Urban-nonurban differences in social behavior and social psychological models of urban impact. *Journal of Social Issues, 36*(3), 29–51.

Koss, M. P. (1989). Hidden rape: Sexual aggression and victimization in a national sample of students in higher education. In M. A. Pirog-Good & J. E. Stets (Eds.), *Violence in dating relationships: Emerging social issues* (pp. 145–168). New York: Praeger.

Kozlowski, S. W., Kirsch, M. P., & Chao, G. T. (1986). Job knowledge, ratee familiarity, conceptual similarity, and halo error: An exploration. *Journal of Applied Psychology, 71,* 45–49.

Kramer, G. P., Kerr, N. L., & Carroll, J. S. (1990). Pretrial publicity, judicial remedies, and jury bias. *Law and Human Behavior, 14,* 409–438.

Kramer, R. M., & Brewer, M. B. (1984). Effects of group identity on resource use in a simulated commons dilemma. *Journal of Personality and Social Psychology, 46,* 1044–1057.

Kramer, R. M., Meyerson, D., & Davis, G. (1990). How much is enough? Psychological components of "guns versus butter"

decisions in a security dilemma. *Journal of Personality and Social Psychology, 58,* 989–993.

Krantz, D. S., & Hedges, S. M. (1987). Some cautions for research on personality and health. *Journal of Personality, 55,* 351–357.

Kraut, R. E. (1973). Effects of social labeling on giving to charity. *Journal of Experimental Social Psychology, 9,* 551–562.

Kravitz, D. A., & Martin, B. (1986). Ringelmann rediscovered: The original article. *Journal of Personality and Social Psychology, 50,* 936–941.

Krebs, D. (1987). The challenge of altruism in biology and psychology. In C. Crawford, M. Smith, & D. Krebs (Eds.), *Sociobiology and psychology: Ideas, issues, and applications* (pp. 81–118). Hillsdale, NJ: Erlbaum.

Krosnick, J. A., & Alwin, D. F. (1989). Aging and susceptibility to attitude change. *Journal of Personality and Social Psychology, 57,* 416–425.

Krueger, J., & Rothbart, M. (1988). Use of categorical and individuating information in making inferences about personality. *Journal of Personality and Social Psychology, 55,* 187–195.

Kruglanski, A. W. (1989). The psychology of being "right": The problem of accuracy in social perception and cognition. *Psychological Bulletin, 106,* 395–409.

Kruglanski, A. W., & Freund, T. (1983). The freezing and unfreezing of lay-inferences: Effects of impressional primacy, ethnic stereotyping, and numerical anchoring. *Journal of Experimental Social Psychology, 19,* 448–468.

Kruglanski, A. W., & Mayseless, O. (1988). Contextual effects in hypothesis testing: The role of competing alternatives and epistemic motivations. *Social Cognition, 6,* 1–20.

Kruglanski, A. W., & Webster, D. M. (1991). Group members' reactions to opinion deviates and conformists at varying degrees of proximity to decision deadline and of environmental noise. *Journal of Personality and Social Psychology, 61,* 212–225.

Kuhlman, D. M., & Marshello, A. F. J. (1975). Individual differences in game motivation as moderators of pre-programmed strategy effects in prisoner's dilemma. *Journal of Personality and Social Psychology, 32,* 922–931.

Kukla, A. (1982). Logical incoherence of value-free science. *Journal of Personality and Social Psychology, 43,* 1014–1017.

Kukla, A. (1984). Objectivity revisited. *Journal of Personality and Social Psychology, 47,* 681–683.

Kulik, J. A., & Mahler, H. I. M. (1989). Stress and affiliation in a hospital setting: Preoperative roommate preferences. *Personality and Social Psychology Bulletin, 15,* 183–193.

Kunda, Z. (1987). Motivated inference: Self-serving generation and evaluation of causal theories. *Journal of Personality and Social Psychology, 53,* 636–647.

Kunda, Z. (1990). The case of motivated reasoning. *Psychological Bulletin, 108,* 480–498.

Kunda, Z., & Schwartz, S. H. (1983). Undermining intrinsic moral motivation: External reward and self-presentation. *Journal of Personality and Social Psychology, 45,* 763–771.

Kunst-Wilson, W. R., & Zajonc, R. B. (1980). Affective discrimination of stimuli that cannot be recognized. *Science, 207*, 557–558.

Kurdek, L. A. (1991a). Correlates of relationship satisfaction in cohabiting gay and lesbian couples: Interpretation of contextual, investment, and problem-solving models. *Journal of Personality and Social Psychology, 61*, 910–922.

Kurdek, L. A. (1991b). The dissolution of gay and lesbian couples. *Journal of Social and Personal Relationships, 8*, 265–278.

Kurdek, L. A. (1991c). Sexuality in homosexual and heterosexual couples. In K. McKinney & S. Sprecher (Eds.), *Sexuality in close relationships* (pp. 177–191). Hillsdale, NJ: Erlbaum.

Kurdek, L. A., & Schmitt, J. P. (1986). Relationship quality in heterosexual married, heterosexual cohabitating, and gay and lesbian relationships. *Journal of Personality and Social Psychology, 51*, 711–720.

Kutchinsky, B. (1978). Pornography in Denmark—A general survey. In R. Dhavan & C. Davies (Eds.), *Censorship and obscenity* (pp. 111–126). London: Martin Robertson.

Lacayo, R. (1991, April 1). Law and disorder. *Time*, pp. 18–21.

Lacayo, R. (1992, May 11). Anatomy of an acquittal. *Time*, pp. 30–32.

Lagerspetz, K. M. J., & Lagerspetz, K. Y. H. (1983). Genes and aggression. In E. C. Simmel, M. E. Hahn, & J. K. Walters (Eds.), *Aggressive behavior: genetic and neural approaches* (pp. 89–101). Hillsdale, NJ: Erlbaum.

Laird, J. D. (1974). Self-attribution of emotion: The effects of expressive behavior on the quality of emotional experience. *Journal of Personality and Social Psychology, 29*, 475–486.

Laird, J. D. (1984). The real role of facial response in the experience of emotion: A reply to Tourangeau and Ellsworth, and others. *Journal of Personality and Social Psychology, 47*, 909–917.

Lamm, H., & Myers, D. G. (1978). Group-induced polarization of attitudes and behavior. In L. Berkowitz (Ed.), *Advances in experimental social psychology* (Vol. 11, pp. 145–195). New York: Academic Press.

Landy, F. J., & Farr, J. L. (1983). *The measurement of work performance: Methods, theory, and applications.* New York: Academic Press.

Langer, E. J. (1975). The illusion of control. *Journal of Personality and Social Psychology, 32*, 311–328.

Langer, E. J. (1989). *Mindfulness.* Reading, MA: Addison-Wesley.

Langer, E. J., Blank, A., & Chanowitz, B. (1978). The mindlessness of ostensibly thoughtful action. *Journal of Personality and Social Psychology, 36*, 635–642.

Langer, E. J., Chanowitz, B., & Blank, A. (1985). Mindlessness-mindfulness in perspective: A reply to Valerie Folkes. *Journal of Personality and Social Psychology, 48*, 605–607.

Langer, E. J., Janis, I. L., & Wolfer, J. A. (1975). Reduction of psychological stress in surgical patients. *Journal of Experimental Social Psychology, 11*, 155–165.

Langer, E. J., & Rodin, J. (1976). The effects of choice and enhanced personal responsibility for the aged: A field experiment in an institutional setting. *Journal of Personality and Social Psychology, 34*, 191–198.

Langlois, J. H. (1986). From the eye of the beholder to behavioral reality: Development of social behaviors and social relations as a function of physical attractiveness. In C. P. Herman, M. P. Zanna, & E. T. Higgins (Eds.), *The Ontario Symposium: Vol. 3. Physical appearance, stigma, and social behavior* (pp. 23–51). Hillsdale, NJ: Erlbaum.

Langlois, J. H., & Roggman, L. A. (1990). Attractive faces are only average. *Psychological Science, 1*, 115–121.

Langston, C. A., & Cantor, N. (1989). Anxiety and social constraint: When making friends is hard. *Journal of Personality and Social Psychology, 56*, 649–661.

Lanzetta, J. T. (1955). Group behavior under stress. *Human Relations, 8*, 29–52.

Lanzetta, J. T., & Englis, B. G. (1989). Expectations of cooperation and competition and their effects on observers' vicarious emotional responses. *Journal of Personality and Social Psychology, 56*, 543–554.

Lanzetta, J. T., & Orr, S. P. (1986). Excitatory strength of expressive faces: Effects of happy and fear expressions and context on the extinction of a conditioned fear response. *Journal of Personality and Social Psychology, 50*, 190–194.

LaPiere, R. T. (1934). Attitudes vs. action. *Social Forces, 13*, 230–237.

Larrick, R. P., Morgan, J. N., & Nisbett, R. E. (1990). Teaching the use of cost-benefit reasoning in everyday life. *Psychological Science, 1*, 362–370.

Larsen, K. S. (1990). The Asch conformity experiment: Replication and transhistorical comparisons. *Journal of Social Behavior and Personality, 5*, 163–168.

Larsen, R. J., & Ketelaar, T. (1991). Personality and susceptibility to positive and negative emotional states. *Journal of Personality and Social Psychology, 61*, 132–140.

Larsen, R., & Csikszentmihalyi, M. (1983). The Experience Sampling Method. In H. T. Reis (Ed.), *New directions for naturalistic methods in the behavioral sciences* (pp. 41–56). San Francisco: Jossey-Bass.

Larson, J. R., Jr. (1986). Supervisors' performance feedback to subordinates: The impact of subordinate performance valence and outcome dependence. *Organizational Behavior and Decision Processes, 37*, 391–408.

Lassiter, G. D. (1988). Behavior perception, affect, and memory. *Social Cognition, 6*, 150–176.

Lassiter, G. D., & Irvine, A. A. (1986). Videotaped confessions: The impact of camera point of view on judgments of coercion. *Journal of Applied Social Psychology, 16*, 268–276.

Lassiter, G. D., Stone, J. I., & Rogers, S. L. (1988). Memorial consequences of variation in behavior perception. *Journal of Experimental Social Psychology, 24*, 222–239.

Latané, B. (1981). The psychology of social impact. *American Psychologist, 36*, 343–356.

Latané, B., & Darley, J. M. (1970). *The unresponsive bystander: Why doesn't he help?* New York: Appleton-Century-Crofts.

Latané, B., & Nida, S. (1981). Ten years of research on group size and helping. *Psychological Bulletin, 89,* 308–324.

Latané, B., Williams, K., & Harkins, S. (1979). Many hands make light the work: The causes and consequences of social loafing. *Journal of Personality and Social Psychology, 37,* 822–832.

Latané, B., & Wolf, S. (1981). The social impact of majorities and minorities. *Psychological Review, 88,* 438–453.

Lau, R. R. (1984). Dynamics of the attribution process. *Journal of Personality and Social Psychology, 46,* 1017–1028.

Lau, R. R. (1985). Two explanations for negativity effects in political behavior. *American Journal of Political Science, 29,* 119–138.

Laughlin, P. R., & Earley, P. C. (1982). Social combination models, persuasive arguments theory, social comparison theory, and choice shift. *Journal of Personality and Social Psychology, 42,* 273–280.

Laughlin, P. R., Vanderstoep, S. W., & Hollingshead, A. B. (1991). Collective versus individual induction: Recognition of truth, rejection of error, and collective information processing. *Journal of Personality and Social Psychology, 61,* 50–67.

Lawrence, V. W. (1991). Effect of socially ambiguous information on white and black children's behavioral and trait perceptions. *Merrill-Palmer Quarterly, 37,* 619–630.

Lazarus, R. S. (1983). The costs and benefits of denial. In S. Breznitz (Ed.), *The denial of stress* (pp. 1–30). New York: International Universities Press.

Lazarus, R. S. (1984). On the primacy of cognition. *American Psychologist, 39,* 124–129.

Lazarus, R. S. (1991). *Emotion and adaptation.* New York: Oxford University Press.

Lazarus, R. S., & Folkman, S. (1984). *Stress, appraisal, and coping.* New York: Springer.

Leana, C. R. (1985). A partial test of Janis' groupthink model: Effects of group cohesiveness and leader behavior on defective decision making. *Journal of Management, 11,* 5–17.

Leary, M. R. (1983). *Understanding social anxiety: Social, personality, and clinical perspectives.* Beverly Hills, CA: Sage.

Leary, M. R. (1987). A self-presentation model for the treatment of social anxieties. In J. E. Maddux, C. D. Stoltenberg, & R. Rosenwein (Eds.), *Social processes in clinical and counseling psychology* (pp. 126–138). New York: Springer-Verlag.

Leary, M. R., & Kowalski, R. M. (1990). Impression management: A literature review and two-component model. *Psychological Bulletin, 107,* 34–47.

Leary, M. R., & Maddux, J. E. (1987). Progress toward a viable interface between social and clinical-counseling psychology. *American Psychologist, 42,* 904–911.

Leavitt, H. J. (1951). Some effects of certain communication patterns on group performance. *Journal of Abnormal and Social Psychology, 46,* 38–50.

Le Bon, G. (1895). *Psychologie des foules.* Paris: Félix Alcan.

Lee, J. A. (1977). A typology of styles of loving. *Personality and Social Psychology Bulletin, 3,* 173–182.

Lee, J. A. (1988). Love-styles. In R. J. Sternberg & M. L. Barnes (Ed.), *The psychology of love* (pp. 38–67). New Haven, CT: Yale University Press.

Lefcourt, H. M., & Davidson-Katz, K. (1991). Locus of control and health. In C. R. Snyder & D. R. Forsyth (Eds.), *Handbook of social and clinical psychology: The health perspective* (pp. 246–266). New York: Pergamon Press.

Lefkowitz, M. M., Eron, L. D., Walder, L. O., & Huesmann, L. R. (1977). *Growing up to be violent.* New York: Pergamon Press.

Lehman, D. R., Lempert, R. O., & Nisbett, R. E. (1988). The effects of graduate training on reasoning: Formal discipline and thinking about everyday-life events. *American Psychologist, 43,* 431–442.

Lehman, D. R., & Taylor, S. E. (1987). Date with an earthquake: Coping with a probable, unpredictable disaster. *Personality and Social Psychology Bulletin, 13,* 546–555.

Leigh, G. K., Homan, T. B., & Burr, W. R. (1987). Some confusions and exclusions of the SVR theory of dyadic pairing: A response to Murstein. *Journal of Marriage and the Family, 49,* 933–937.

Leippe, M. R., Romanczyk, A., & Manion, A. P. (1991). Eyewitness memory for a touching experience: Accuracy differences between child and adult witnesses. *Journal of Applied Psychology, 76,* 367–379.

Lennox, R. D. (1988). The problem with self-monitoring: A two-sided scale and a one-sided theory. *Journal of Personality Assessment, 52,* 58–73.

Leonard, K. E. (1989). The impact of explicit aggressive and implicit nonaggressive cues on aggression in intoxicated and sober roles. *Personality and Social Psychology Bulletin, 15,* 390–400.

Lepore, S. J., Evans, G. W., & Schneider, M. L. (1991). Dynamic role of social support in the link between chronic stress and psychological distress. *Journal of Personality and Social Psychology, 61,* 899–909.

Lepper, M. R., & Greene, D. (Eds.). (1978). *The hidden costs of reward.* Hillsdale, NJ: Erlbaum.

Lepper, M. R., Greene, D., & Nisbett, R. E. (1973). Undermining children's intrinsic interest with extrinsic reward: A test of the "overjustification" hypothesis. *Journal of Personality and Social Psychology, 28,* 129–137.

Lerner, M. J. (1980). *The belief in a just world: A fundamental delusion.* New York: Plenum.

Lerner, M. J., & Meindl, J. R. (1981). Justice and altruism. In J. P. Rushton & R. M. Sorrentino (Eds.), *Altruism and helping behavior: Social, personality, and developmental perspectives* (pp. 213–232). Hillsdale, NJ: Erlbaum.

Lerner, M. J., & Simmons, C. H. (1966). Observers' reaction to the "innocent victim": Compassion or rejection? *Journal of Personality and Social Psychology, 4,* 203–210.

Leslie, L. A., Huston, T. L., & Johnson, M. P. (1986). Parental reactions to dating relationships: Do they make a difference? *Journal of Marriage and the Family, 48,* 57–66.

Leung, K. (1987). Some determinants of reactions to procedural models for conflict resolution: A cross-national study. *Journal of Personality and Social Psychology, 53,* 898–908.

Levenson, R. W., & Gottman, J. M. (1985). Physiological and affective predictors of change in relationship satisfaction. *Journal of Personality and Social Psychology, 49,* 85–94.

Leventhal, H. (1970). Findings and theory in the study of fear communications. In L. Berkowitz (Ed.), *Advances in experimental social psychology* (Vol. 5, pp. 119–186). New York: Academic Press.

Leventhal, H., Watts, J. C., & Pagano, F. (1967). Effects of fear and instructions on how to cope with danger. *Journal of Personality and Social Psychology, 6,* 313–321.

Levin, I. P., Schnittjer, S. K., & Thee, S. L. (1988). Information framing effects in social and personal decisions. *Journal of Experimental Social Psychology, 24,* 520–529.

Levin, J., & Fox, J. A. (1985). *Mass murder.* New York: Plenum.

Levine, J. M. (1989). Reaction to opinion deviance in small groups. In P. B. Paulus (Ed.), *Psychology of group influence* (2nd ed., pp. 187–231). Hillsdale, NJ: Erlbaum.

Levine, J. M., & Moreland, R. L. (1990). Progress in small group research. *Annual Review of Psychology, 41,* 585–634.

Levine, R. A., & Campbell, D. T. (1972). *Ethnocentrism: Theories of conflict, ethnic attitudes, and group behavior.* New York: Wiley.

Levinger, G. (1988). Can we picture "love"? In R. J. Sternberg & M. L. Barnes (Ed.), *The psychology of love* (pp. 139–158). New Haven, CT: Yale University Press.

Levy, M. B., & Davis, K. E. (1988). Love styles and attachment styles compared: Their relation to each other and to various relationship characteristics. *Journal of Social and Personal Relationships, 5,* 429–471.

Lewicki, P. (1983). Self-image bias in person perception. *Journal of Personality and Social Psychology, 45,* 384–393.

Lewin, K. (1935). *A dynamic theory of personality.* New York: McGraw-Hill.

Lewin, K. (1947). Group decision and social change. In T. M. Newcomb & E. L. Hartley (Eds.), *Readings in social psychology* (pp. 330–344). New York: Holt.

Lewin, K. (1951). Problems of research in social psychology. In D. Cartwright (Ed.), *Field theory in social science* (pp. 155–169). New York: Harper & Row.

Lewis, M., & Brooks-Gunn, J. (1979). *Social cognition and the acquisition of self.* New York: Plenum.

Lewontin, R. C., Rose, S., & Kamin, L. J. (1984). *Not in our genes.* New York: Pantheon Books.

Liebert, R. M., & Sprafkin, J. (1988). *The early window* (3rd ed.). New York: Pergamon Press.

Liebrand, W. B. G., & van Run, G. J. (1985). The effects of social motives on behavior in social dilemmas in two cultures. *Journal of Experimental Social Psychology, 21,* 86–102.

Lifton, R. J. (1986). *The Nazi doctors: Medical killing and the psychology of genocide.* New York: Basic Books.

Liggett, J. C. (1974). *The human face.* New York: Stein & Day.

Light, K. C., & Obrist, P. A. (1980). Cardiovascular response to stress: Effects of opportunity to avoid shock experience, and performance feedback. *Psychophysiology, 17,* 243–252.

Likert, R. (1932). A technique for the measurement of attitudes. *Archives of Psychology, 140,* 1–55.

Lim, R. G., & Carnevale, P. J. D. (1990). Contingencies in the mediation of disputes. *Journal of Personality and Social Psychology, 58,* 259–272.

Lind, E. A., Erickson, B. E., Friedland, N., & Dickenberger, M. (1978). Reactions to procedural models for adjudicative conflict resolution: A cross national study. *Journal of Conflict Resolution, 22,* 318–341.

Lind, E. A., Kanfer, R., & Farley, P. C. (1990). Voice, control, and procedural justice: Instrumental and noninstrumental concerns in fairness judgments. *Journal of Personality and Social Psychology, 59,* 952–959.

Lind, E. A., & Tyler, T. R. (1988). *The social psychology of procedural justice.* New York: Plenum.

Linder, D. E., Cooper, J., & Jones, E. E. (1967). Decision freedom as a determinant of the role of incentive magnitude in attitude change. *Journal of Personality and Social Psychology, 6,* 245–254.

Lindsay, R. C. L., Wells, G. L., & Rumpel, C. M. (1981). Can people detect eyewitness-identification accuracy within and across situations? *Journal of Applied Psychology, 66,* 79–89.

Lindskold, S., & Han, G. (1988). GRIT as a foundation for integrative bargaining. *Personality and Social Psychology Bulletin, 14,* 335–345.

Lindskold, S., Han, G., & Betz, B. (1986a). The essential elements of communication in the GRIT strategy. *Personality and Social Psychology Bulletin, 12,* 179–186.

Lindskold, S., Han, G., & Betz, B. (1986b). Repeated persuasion in interpersonal conflict. *Journal of Personality and Social Psychology, 51,* 1183–1188.

Linville, P. W., Fischer, G. W., & Salovey, P. (1989). Perceived distributions of the characteristics of in-group and out-group members: Empirical evidence and a computer simulation. *Journal of Personality and Social Psychology, 57,* 165–188.

Linville, P. W., & Jones, E. E. (1980). Polarized appraisals of out-group members. *Journal of Personality and Social Psychology, 38,* 689–703.

Linz, D., Donnerstein, E., & Penrod, S. (1984). The effects of multiple exposures to filmed violence against women. *Journal of Communication, 34*(3), 130–147.

Linz, D., Donnerstein, E., & Penrod, S. (1987). The findings and recommendations of the Attorney General's Commission on Pornography: Do the psychological "facts" fit the political fury? *American Psychologist, 42,* 946–953.

Linz, D., Donnerstein, E., & Penrod, S. (1988). Effects of long-term exposure to violent and sexually degrading depictions of women. *Journal of Personality and Social Psychology, 55,* 758–768.

Littlepage, G. E. (1991). Effects of group size and task characteristics on group performance: A test of Steiner's model. *Personality and Social Psychology Bulletin, 17,* 449–456.

Lloyd, S. A., Cate, R. M., & Henton, J. M. (1984). Predicting premarital relationship stability: A methodological refinement. *Journal of Marriage and the Family, 46,* 71–76.

Lockard, J. S., & Paulhus, D. L. (1988). *Self-deception: An adaptive mechanism?* Englewood Cliffs, NJ: Prentice-Hall.

Locke, K. D., & Horowitz, L. M. (1990). Satisfaction in interpersonal interactions as a function of similarity in level of dysphoria. *Journal of Personality and Social Psychology, 58,* 823–831.

Lockhart v. McCree, 54 U.S.L.W. 4449 (1986).

Locksley, A., Borgida, E., Brekke, N., & Hepburn, C. (1980). Sex stereotypes and social judgment. *Journal of Personality and Social Psychology, 39,* 821–831.

Loeber, R. (1982). The stability of antisocial and delinquent child behavior: A review. *Child Development, 53,* 1431–1446.

Loftus, E. F. (1979). *Eyewitness testimony.* Cambridge, MA: Harvard University Press.

Loftus, E. F. (1983). Silence is not golden. *American Psychologist, 38,* 564–572.

Loftus, E. F., & Ketcham, K. (1991). *Witness for the defense: The accused, the eyewitness, and the expert who puts memory on trial.* New York: St. Martin's Press.

Loftus, E. F., Loftus, G. R., & Messo, J. (1987). Some facts about "weapon focus." *Law and Human Behavior, 11,* 55–62.

Loftus, E. F., Miller, D. G., & Burns, H. J. (1978). Semantic integration of verbal information into visual memory. *Journal of Experimental Psychology: Human Learning and Memory, 4,* 19–31.

Loftus, E. F., & Palmer, J. C. (1974). Reconstruction of automobile destruction: An example of the interaction between language and memory. *Journal of Verbal Learning and Verbal Behavior, 13,* 585–589.

Loftus, G. R., & Loftus, E. F. (1976). *Human memory: The processing of information.* Hillsdale, NJ: Erlbaum.

London, P. (1970). The rescuers: Motivational hypotheses about Christians who saved Jews from the Nazis. In J. R. Macaulay & L. Berkowitz (Eds.), *Altruism and helping behavior* (pp. 241–250). New York: Academic Press.

Long, E. C. J., & Andrews, D. W. (1990). Perspective taking as a predictor of marital adjustment. *Journal of Personality and Social Psychology, 59,* 126–131.

Longley, J., & Pruitt, D. G. (1980). Groupthink: A critique of Janis's theory. In L. Wheeler (Ed.), *Review of personality and social psychology* (Vol. 1, pp. 74–93). Beverly Hills, CA: Sage.

Longnecker, C. O., Gioia, D. A., & Sims, H. P. (1987). Behind the mask: The politics of employee appraisal. *Academy of Management Executive, 1,* 183–193.

Lopez, J. A. (1992, March 3). Study says women face glass walls as well as ceilings. *Wall Street Journal,* pp. B1, B8.

Lord, C. G., & Saenz, D. S. (1985). Memory deficits and memory surfeits: Differential cognitive consequences of to-

kenism for tokens and observers. *Journal of Personality and Social Psychology, 49,* 918–926.

Lorenz, K. (1966). *On aggression.* New York: Harcourt, Brace & World.

Lortie-Lussier, M. (1987). Minority influence and idiosyncrasy credit: A new comparison of the Moscovici and Hollander theories of innovation. *European Journal of Social Psychology, 17,* 431–446.

Losch, M. E., & Cacioppo, J. T. (1990). Cognitive dissonance may enhance sympathetic tonus, but attitudes are changed to reduce negative affect rather than arousal. *Journal of Experimental Social Psychology, 26,* 289–304.

Lott, A. J., & Lott, B. E. (1974). The role of reward in the formation of positive interpersonal attitudes. In T. L. Huston (Ed.), *Foundations of interpersonal attraction* (pp. 171–189). New York: Academic Press.

Lott, B. (1985). The devaluation of women's competence. *Journal of Social Issues, 41,* 43–60.

Lovdal, L. T. (1989). Sex role messages in television commercials: An update. *Sex Roles, 21,* 715–724.

Lui, K., Darrow, W. W., & Rutherford, G. W., III. (1988). A model-based estimate of the mean incubation period for AIDS in homosexual men. *Science, 240,* 1333–1335.

Luks, A. (1988, October). Helper's high. *Psychology Today,* pp. 39–40.

Lundberg-Love, P., & Geffner, R. (1989). Date rate: Prevalence, risk factors, and a proposed model. In M. A. Pirog-Good & J. E. Stets (Eds.), *Violence in dating relationships: Emerging social issues* (pp. 169–184). New York: Praeger.

Lupfer, M. B., Clark, L. F., Hutcherson, H. W. (1990). Impact of context on spontaneous trait and situational attributions. *Journal of Personality and Social Psychology, 58,* 239–249.

Lüüs, C. A. E., & Wells, G. L. (1991). Eyewitness identification and the selection of distractors for lineups. *Law and Human Behavior, 15,* 43–58.

Lykken, D. T. (1981). *A tremor in the blood: Uses and abuses of the lie detector.* New York: McGraw-Hill.

Lynn, M. & Oldenquist, A. (1986). Egoistic and nonegoistic motives in social dilemmas. *American Psychologist, 41,* 529–534.

Lynn, S. J., & Bates, K. (1985). The reaction of others to enacted depression: The effects of attitude and topic valence. *Journal of Social and Clinical Psychology, 3,* 268–282.

Lytton, H., & Romney, D. M. (1991). Parents' differential socialization of boys and girls: A meta-analysis. *Psychological Bulletin, 109,* 267–296.

Maass, A., & Clark, R. D., III. (1984). Hidden impact of minorities: Fifteen years of minority influence research. *Psychological Bulletin, 95,* 428–450.

Maass, A., & Kohnken, G. (1989). Eyewitness identification: Simulating the "weapon effect." *Law and Human Behavior, 13,* 397–408.

Macaulay, J. R. (1970). A shill for charity. In J. Macaulay & L. Berkowitz (Eds.), *Altruism and helping behavior* (pp. 43–59). New York: Academic Press.

Maccoby, E. E. (1990). Gender and relationships: A developmental account. *American Psychologist, 45,* 513–520.

Maccoby, E. E., & Jacklin, C. N. (1974). *The psychology of sex differences.* Stanford, CA: Stanford University Press.

MacCoun, R. J., & Kerr, N. L. (1988). Asymmetric influence in mock jury deliberation: Jurors' bias for leniency. *Journal of Personality and Social Psychology, 54,* 21–33.

Mackie, D. M. (1986). Social identification effects in group polarization. *Journal of Personality and Social Psychology, 50,* 720–728.

Mackie, D. M., & Cooper, J. (1984). Attitude polarization: Effects of group membership. *Journal of Personality and Social Psychology, 46,* 575–585.

Mackie, D. M., & Worth, L. T. (1989). Processing deficits and the mediation of positive affect in persuasion. *Journal of Personality and Social Psychology, 57,* 27–40.

Mackie, D. M., Worth, L. T., & Asuncion, A.G. (1990). Processing of persuasive in-group messages. *Journal of Personality and Social Psychology, 58,* 812–822.

Macklin, R. (1982). The problem of adequate disclosure in social science research. In T. L. Beauchamp, R. R. Faden, R. J. Wallace Jr., & L. Walters (Eds.), *Ethical issues in social science research* (pp. 93–214). Baltimore: Johns Hopkins University Press.

Madden, T. J ., Ellen, P. S., & Ajzen, I. (1992). A comparison of the theory of planned behavior and the theory of reasoned action. *Personality and Social Psychology Bulletin, 18,* 3–9.

Maddux, J. E. (1991). Self-efficacy. In C. R. Snyder & D. R. Forsyth (Eds.), *Handbook of social and clinical psychology: The health perspective* (pp. 57–78). New York: Pergamon Press.

Maddux, J. E., Norton, L. W., & Leary, M. R. (1988). Cognitive components of social anxiety: An investigation of the integration of self-presentation theory and self-efficacy theory. *Journal of Social and Clinical Psychology, 6,* 180–190.

Maddux, J. E., & Rogers, R. W. (1980). Effects of source expertness, physical attractiveness, and supporting arguments on persuasion: A case of brains over beauty. *Journal of Personality and Social Psychology, 39,* 235–244.

Major, B., Carrington, P. I., & Carnevale, P. J. D. (1984). Physical attractiveness and self-esteem: Attributions for praise from an other-sex evaluator. *Personality and Social Psychology Bulletin, 10,* 43–50.

Major, B., & Deaux, K. (1982). Individual differences in justice behavior. In J. Greenberg & R. L. Cohen (Eds.), *Equity and justice in social behavior* (pp. 13–76). New York: Academic Press.

Major, B., & Konar, E. (1984). An investigation of sex differences in pay expectations and their possible causes. *Academy of Management Journal, 27,* 777–792.

Major, B., McFarlin, D. B., & Gagnon, D. (1984). Overworked and underpaid: On the nature of gender differences in personal entitlement. *Journal of Personality and Social Psychology, 47,* 1399–1412.

Major, B., Schmidlin, A. M., & Williams, L. (1990). Gender patterns in social touch: The impact of setting and age. *Journal of Personality and Social Psychology, 58,* 634–643.

Makepeace, J. (1989). Dating, living together, and courtship violence. In M. A. Pirog-Good & J. E. Stets (Eds.), *Violence in dating relationships: Emerging social issues* (pp. 94–107). New York: Praeger.

Malamuth, N. M. (1983). Factors associated with rape as predictors of laboratory aggression against women. *Journal of Personality and Social Psychology, 45,* 432–442.

Malamuth, N. M. (1984). Aggression against women: Cultural and individual causes. In N. M. Malamuth & E. I. Donnerstein (Eds.), *Pornography and sexual aggression* (pp. 19–52). New York: Academic Press.

Malamuth, N. M. (1986). Predictors of naturalistic sexual aggression. *Journal of Personality and Social Psychology, 50,* 953–962.

Malamuth, N. M., & Billings, V. (1986). The function and effects of pornography: Sexual communications versus the feminist model in light of research findings. In J. Bryant & D. Zillmann (Eds.), *Perspectives on media effects* (pp. 83–108). Hillsdale, NJ: Erlbaum.

Malamuth, N. M., & Briere, J. (1986). Sexual violence in the media: Indirect effects on aggression against women. In L. R. Huesmann & N. M. Malamuth (Eds.), *Journal of Social Issues: Media Violence and Antisocial Behavior, 42*(3), 75–92.

Malamuth, N. M., & Ceniti, J. (1986). Repeated exposure to violent and nonviolent pornography: Likelihood of raping ratings and laboratory aggression against women. *Aggressive Behavior, 12,* 129–137.

Malamuth, N. M., & Check, J. V. P. (1981). The effects of mass media exposure on acceptance of violence against women: A field experiment. *Journal of Research in Personality, 15,* 436–446.

Malamuth, N. M., Check, J. V. P., & Briere, J. (1986). Sexual arousal in response to aggression: Ideological, aggressive, and sexual correlates. *Journal of Personality and Social Psychology, 50,* 330–340.

Malamuth, N. M., & Donnerstein, E. I. (1982). The effects of aggressive-pornographic mass media stimuli. In L. Berkowitz (Ed.), *Advances in experimental social psychology* (Vol. 15, pp. 103–154). New York: Academic Press.

Malkiel, B. (1981). *A random walk down Wall Street* (2nd ed.). New York: Norton.

Malloy, T. E., & Albright, L. (1990). Interpersonal perception in a social context. *Journal of Personality and Social Psychology, 58,* 419–428.

Malone, J., Tyree, A., & O'Leary, K. D. (1989). Generalization and containment: Different effects of past aggression for husbands and wives. *Journal of Marriage and the Family, 51,* 687–697.

Malpass, R. S., & Devine, P. G. (1981). Eyewitness identification: Lineup instructions and the absence of the offender. *Journal of Applied Psychology, 66,* 482–489.

Malpass, R. S., & Kravitz, J. (1969). Recognition for faces of own and other race. *Journal of Personality and Social Psychology, 13,* 330–334.

Manis, M., Nelson, T. E., & Shedler, J. (1988). Stereotypes and social judgment: Extremity, assimilation, and contrast. *Journal of Personality and Social Psychology, 55,* 28–36.

Manis, M., Paskewitz, J. R., & Cotler, S. (1986). Stereotypes and social judgment. *Journal of Personality and Social Psychology, 50,* 461–473.

Manucia, G. K., Baumann, D. J., & Cialdini, R. B. (1984). Mood influences on helping: Direct effects or side effects? *Journal of Personality and Social Psychology, 46,* 357–364.

Manz, C. C., & Sims, H. P., Jr. (1982). The potential for "groupthink" in autonomous work groups. *Human Relations, 35,* 773–784.

Margolin, G., & Wampold, B. E. (1981). A sequential analysis of conflict and accord in distressed and nondistressed marital partners. *Journal of Consulting and Clinical Psychology, 49,* 554–567.

Margolin, L., & White, L. (1987). The continuing role of physical attractiveness in marriage. *Journal of Marriage and the Family, 49,* 21–28.

Marks, G., & Miller, N. (1982). Target attractiveness as a mediator of assumed attitude similarity. *Personality and Social Psychology Bulletin, 8,* 728–735.

Marks, G., & Miller, N. (1987). Ten years of research on the false-consensus effect: An empirical and theoretical review. *Psychological Bulletin, 102,* 72–90.

Marks, G., Richardson, J. L., Graham, J. W., & Levine, A. (1986). Role of health locus of control beliefs and expectations of treatment efficacy in adjustment to cancer. *Journal of Personality and Social Psychology, 51,* 243–250.

Marks, M. L., Mirvis, P. H., Hackett, E. J., & Grady, J. F., Jr. (1986). Employee participation in a quality circle program: Impact on quality of work life, productivity, and absenteeism. *Journal of Applied Psychology, 71,* 61–69.

Markus H. (1977). Self-schemata and processing information about the self. *Journal of Personality and Social Psychology, 35,* 63–78.

Markus, H. R., & Kitayama, S. (1991). Culture and the self: Implications for cognition, emotion, and motivation. *Psychological Review, 98,* 224–253.

Markus, H., Hamill, R., & Sentis, K. P. (1987). Thinking fat: Self-schemas for body weight and the processing of weight-relevant information. *Journal of Applied Social Psychology, 17,* 50–71.

Markus, H., & Nurius, P. (1986). Possible selves. *American Psychologist, 41,* 954–969.

Markus, H., Smith, J., & Moreland, R. L. (1985). Role of the self-concept in the perception of others. *Journal of Personality and Social Psychology, 49,* 1494–1512.

Marlowe, D., & Gergen, K. (1969). Personality and social interaction. In G. Lindzey & E. Aronson (Eds.), *The handbook of social psychology* (2nd ed., pp. 590–665). Reading, MA: Addison-Wesley.

Marques, J. M. (1990). The black sheep effect: Outgroup homogeneity in social comparison settings. In D. Abrams & M. Hogg (Eds.), *Social identity theory: Constructive and critical advances* (pp. 131–151). New York: Springer-Verlag.

Marsh, H. W., & Parker, J. W. (1984). Determinants of student self-concept: Is it better to be a relatively large fish in a small pond even if you don't learn to swim as well? *Journal of Personality and Social Psychology, 47,* 213–231.

Marshall, G. D., & Zimbardo, P. G. (1979). Affective consequences of inadequately explained physiological arousal. *Journal of Personality and Social Psychology, 37,* 970–988.

Marshall, W. L. (1989). Pornography and sex offenders. In D. Zillmann & J. Bryant (Eds.), *Pornography: Research advances and policy considerations* (pp. 185–214). Hillsdale, NJ: Erlbaum.

Martichuski, D. K., & Bell, P. A. (1991). Reward, punishment, privatization, and moral suasion in a commons dilemma. *Journal of Applied Social Psychology, 21,* 1356–1369.

Martin, C. L. (1987). A ratio measure of sex stereotyping. *Journal of Personality and Social Psychology, 52,* 489–499.

Martin, C. L., & Nagao, D. H. (1989). Some effects of computerized interviewing on job applicant responses. *Journal of Applied Psychology, 74,* 72–80.

Martin, C. L., Wood, C. H., & Little, J. K. (1990). The development of gender stereotype components. *Child Development, 61,* 1891–1904.

Martin, J. (1986). The tolerance of injustice. In J. M. Olson, C. P. Herman, & M. P. Zanna (Eds.), *Relative deprivation and social comparison: The Ontario Symposium* (Vol. 4, pp. 217–242). Hillsdale, NJ: Erlbaum.

Maser, J. D., & Solomon, S. (Eds.) (1990). Traumatic stress: New perspectives in theory, measurement, and research. Part II. Research findings [Special issue]. *Journal of Applied Social Psychology, 20* (21).

Maslach, C. (1979). Negative emotional biasing of unexplained arousal. *Journal of Personality and Social Psychology, 37,* 953–969.

Masters, W. H., & Johnson, V. E. (1979). *Homosexuality in perspective.* Boston: Little, Brown.

Mathes, E. W., Adams, H. E., & Davies, R. M. (1985). Jealousy: Loss of relationship rewards, loss of self-esteem, depression, anxiety, and anger. *Journal of Personality and Social Psychology, 48,* 1552–1561.

Matsumoto, D. (1987). The role of facial response in the experience of emotion: More methodological problems and a meta-analysis. *Journal of Personality and Social Psychology, 52,* 769–774.

Matthews, K. A. (1988). Coronary heart disease and Type A behaviors: Update on and alternative to the Booth-Kewley and Friedman (1987) quantitative review. *Psychological Bulletin, 104,* 373–380.

Matthews, K. A., Batson, C. D., Horn, J., & Rosenman, R. H. (1981). "Principles in his nature which interest him in the fortunes of others . . .": The heritability of empathic concern for others. *Journal of Personality, 49,* 237–247.

Matthews, K. A., & Haynes, S. G. (1986). Type A behavior pattern and coronary disease risk: Update and critical evaluation. *American Journal of Epidemiology, 123,* 923–958.

Matthews, K. A., Krantz, D. S., Dembroski, T. M., & MacDougall, J. M. (1982). Unique and common variance in structural interview and Jenkins Activity Survey measures of the Type A behavior pattern. *Journal of Personality and Social Psychology, 42,* 303–313.

Matthews, K. A., Scheier, M. F., Brunson, B. I., & Carducci, B. (1980). Attention, unpredictability, and reports of physical symptoms: Eliminating the benefits of predictability. *Journal of Personality and Social Psychology, 38,* 525–537.

Mayerson, N. H., & Rhodewalt, F. (1988). Role of self-protective attributions in the experience of pain. *Journal of Social and Clinical Psychology, 6,* 203–218.

McAdams, D. P. (1982). Intimacy motivation. In A. J. Stewart (Ed.), *Motivation and society* (pp. 133–171). San Francisco: Jossey-Bass.

McAdams, D. P. (1988). Personal needs and personal relationships. In S. Duck (Ed.), *Handbook of personal relationships: Theory, research, and interventions* (pp. 7–22). New York: Wiley.

McAdams, D. P., & Bryant, F. B. (1987). Intimacy motivation and subjective mental health in a nationwide sample. *Journal of Personality, 55,* 395–414.

McAdams, D. P., Healy, S., & Krause, S. (1984). Social motives and friendship patterns. *Journal of Personality and Social Psychology, 47,* 828–838.

McAdams, D. P., & Vaillant, G. E. (1982). Intimacy motivation and psychosocial adjustment: A longitudinal study. *Journal of Personality Assessment, 46,* 586–593.

McArthur, L. A. (1972). The how and what of why: Some determinants and consequences of causal attribution. *Journal of Personality and Social Psychology, 22,* 171–193.

McArthur, L. Z., & Post, D. L. (1977). Figural emphasis and person perception. *Journal of Experimental Social Psychology, 13,* 520–535.

McCarthy, C. R. (1981). The development of federal regulations for social science research. In A. J. Kimmel (Ed.), *New directions for methodology of social and behavioral science (No. 10): Ethics of human subject research* (pp. 31–39). San Francisco: Jossey-Bass.

McCauley, C. (1989). The nature of social influence in groupthink: Compliance and internalization. *Journal of Personality and Social Psychology, 57,* 250–260.

McClelland, D. C. (1951). *Personality.* New York: Holt, Rinehart and Winston.

McClelland, D. C. (1985). How motives, skills, and values determine what people do. *American Psychologist, 40,* 812–825.

McCloskey, M., & Egeth, H. (1983). Eyewitness identification: What can a psychologist tell a jury? *American Psychologist, 38,* 550–563.

McCloskey, M., & Zaragoza, M. (1985). Misleading postevent information and memory for events: Arguments and evidence against memory impairment hypotheses. *Journal of Experimental Psychology, 114,* 3–18.

McConahay, J. B. (1986). Modern racism, ambivalence, and the modern racism scale. In J. F. Dovidio, & S. L. Gaertner, (Eds.), *Prejudice, discrimination, and racism: Theory and research* (pp. 91–125). Orlando, FL: Academic Press.

McConnell, J. D. (1968). Effect of pricing on perception of product quality. *Journal of Applied Psychology, 52,* 331–334.

McDougall, W. (1908). *An introduction to social psychology.* London: Methuen.

McFatter, R. M. (1978). Sentencing strategies and justice: Effects of punishment philosophy on sentencing decisions. *Journal of Personality and Social Psychology, 36,* 1490–1500.

McGillicuddy, N. B., Pruitt, D. G., & Syna, H. (1984). Perceptions of fairness and strength of negotiation. *Personality and Social Psychology Bulletin, 10,* 402–409.

McGinniss, J. (1983). *Fatal vision.* New York: Signet.

McGraw, K. O., & McCullers, J. C. (1979). Evidence of a detrimental effect of extrinsic incentives on breaking a mental set. *Journal of Experimental Social Psychology, 15,* 285–294.

McGuire, W. J. (1964). Inducing resistance to persuasion. In L. Berkowitz (Ed.), *Advances in experimental social psychology* (Vol. 1, pp. 192–229). New York: Academic Press.

McGuire, W. J. (1967). Some impending reorientations in social psychology: Some thoughts provoked by Kenneth Ring. *Journal of Experimental Social Psychology, 3,* 124–139.

McGuire, W. J. (1968). Personality and susceptibility to social influence. In E. F. Borgatta & W. W. Lambert (Eds.), *Handbook of personality theory and research* (pp. 1130–1187). Chicago: Rand McNally.

McGuire, W. J. (1969). The nature of attitudes and attitude change. In G. Lindzey & E. Aronson (Eds.), *Handbook of social psychology* (2nd ed., Vol. 3, pp. 136–314). Reading, MA: Addison-Wesley.

McGuire, W. J., & McGuire, C. V. (1988). Content and process in the experience of self. In L. Berkowitz (Ed.), *Advances in experimental social psychology* (Vol. 20, pp. 97–144). New York: Academic Press.

McGuire, W. J., McGuire, C. V., & Winton, W. (1979). Effects of household sex composition on the salience of one's gender in the spontaneous self-concept. *Journal of Experimental Social Psychology, 15,* 77–90.

McHugh, M. C., Koeske, R. D., & Frieze, I. H. (1986). Issues to consider in conducting nonsexist psychological research: A guide for researchers. *American Psychologist, 41,* 879–890.

McKenzie-Mohr, D., & Zanna, M. P. (1990). Treating women as sexual objects: Look to the (gender schematic) male who has viewed pornography. *Personality and Social Psychology Bulletin, 16,* 296–308.

McKillop, Peter. (1987, May 4). Slotnik for the defense. *Newsweek,* p. 62.

McMullen, P. A., & Gross, A. E. (1983). Sex differences, sex roles, and health-related help-seeking. In B. M. DePaulo, A. Nadler, & J. D. Fisher (Eds.), *New directions in helping: Vol. 2. Help-Seeking* (pp. 233–263). New York: Academic Press.

Mead, G. H. (1934). *Mind, self, and society.* Chicago: University of Chicago Press.

Mearns, J. (1991). Coping with a breakup: Negative mood regulation expectancies and depression following the end of a romantic relationship. *Journal of Personality and Social Psychology, 60,* 327–334.

Mednick, S. A., Gabrielli, W. F., Jr., & Hutchings, B. (1984). Genetic influences in criminal convictions: Evidence from adoption court. *Science, 224,* 891–894.

Meeus, W. H. J., & Raaijmakers, Q. A. W. (1986). Administrative obedience: Carrying out orders to use psychological-administrative violence. *European Journal of Social Psychology, 16,* 311–324.

Meeus, W. H. J., & Raaijmakers, Q. A. W. (1987). Administrative obedience as a social phenomenon. In W. Doise & S. Moscovici (Eds.), *Current issues in European social psychology* (Vol. 2, pp. 183–230). Cambridge, England: Cambridge University Press.

Meindl, J. R., & Lerner, M. J. (1983). The heroic motive: Some experimental demonstrations. *Journal of Experimental Social Psychology, 19,* 1–20.

Melamed, T. (1991). Individual differences in romantic jealousy: The moderating effect of relationship characteristics. *European Journal of Social Psychology, 21,* 455–461.

Melton, G. B., & Gray, J. N. (1988). Ethical dilemmas in AIDS research: Individual privacy and public health. *American Psychologist, 43,* 60–64.

Melton, G. B., Levine, R. J., Koocher, G. P., Rosenthal, R., & Thompson, W. C. (1988). Community consultation in socially sensitive research. *American Psychologist, 43,* 573–581.

Mendonca, P. J., & Brehm, S. S. (1983). Effects of choice on behavioral treatment of overweight children. *Journal of Social and Clinical Psychology, 1,* 343–358.

Merton, R. (1948). The self-fulfilling prophecy. *Antioch Review, 8,* 193–210.

Messick, D. M., & Brewer, M. B. (1983). Solving social dilemmas: A review. In L. Wheeler & P. Shaver (Eds.), *Review of personality and social psychology* (Vol. 4, pp. 11–44). Beverly Hills, CA: Sage.

Messick, D. M., & Cook, K. S. (Ed.). (1983). *Equity theory: Psychological and sociological perspectives.* New York: Praeger.

Messick, D. M., & Mackie, D. M. (1989). Intergroup relations. *Annual Review of Psychology, 40,* 51–81.

Messick, D. M., & McClintock, C. G. (1968). Motivational bases of choice in experimental games. *Journal of Experimental Social Psychology, 4,* 1–25.

Messick, D. M., Wilke, H., Brewer, M. B., Kramer, R. M., Zemke, P. E., & Lui, L. (1983). Individual adaptation and structural change as solutions to social dilemmas. *Journal of Personality and Social Psychology, 44,* 294–309.

Metalsky, G. I., Halberstadt, L. J., & Abramson, L. Y. (1987). Vulnerability to depressive mood reactions: Toward a more powerful test of the diathesis-stress and causal mediation components of the reformulated theory of depression. *Journal of Personality and Social Psychology, 52,* 386–393.

Meyer, C. B., & Taylor, S. E. (1986). Adjustment to rape. *Journal of Personality and Social Psychology, 50,* 1226–1234.

Meyers, W. (1984). *The image-makers: Secrets of successful advertising.* London: Orbis.

Miceli, M. P., Dozier, J. B., & Near, J. P. (1991). Blowing the whistle on data fudging: A controlled field experiment. *Journal of Applied Social Psychology, 21,* 271–295.

Michaels, J. W., Edwards, J. N., & Acock, A. C. (1984). Satisfaction in intimate relationships as a function of inequality, inequity, and outcomes. *Social Psychology Quarterly, 47,* 347–357.

Middlemist, R. D., Knowles, E. S., & Matter, C. F. (1976). Personal space invasions in the lavatory: Suggestive evidence for arousal. *Journal of Personality and Social Psychology, 33,* 541–546.

Mikulincer, M., Florian, V., & Tolmacz, R. (1990). Attachment styles and fear of personal death: A case study of affect regulation. *Journal of Personality and Social Psychology, 58,* 273–280.

Milavsky, J. R., Kessler, R. C., Stipp, H. H., & Rubens, W. S. (1982). *Television and aggression: A panel study.* New York: Academic Press.

Milgram, S. (1963). Behavioral study of obedience. *Journal of Abnormal and Social Psychology, 67,* 371–378.

Milgram, S. (1964). Issues in the study of obedience: A reply to Baumrind. *American Psychologist, 19,* 848–852.

Milgram, S. (1965). Some conditions of obedience and disobedience to authority. *Human Relations, 18,* 57–76.

Milgram, S. (1970). The experience of living in cities. *Science, 167,* 1461–1468.

Milgram, S. (1974). *Obedience to authority: An experimental view.* New York: Harper & Row.

Milgram, S., Bickman, L., & Berkowitz, L. (1969). Note on the drawing power of crowds of different size. *Journal of Personality and Social Psychology, 13,* 79–82.

Milgram, S., & Sabini, J. (1978). On maintaining urban norms: A field experiment in the subway. In A. Baum, J. E. Singer, & S. Valins (Eds.), *Advances in environmental psychology* (Vol. 1). Hillsdale, NJ: Erlbaum.

Millar, M. G., & Millar, K. U. (1990). Attitude change as a function of attitude type and argument type. *Journal of Personality and Social Psychology, 59,* 217–228.

Millar, M. G., & Tesser, A. (1986). Effects of affective and cognitive focus on the attitude-behavior relation. *Journal of Personality and Social Psychology, 51,* 270–276.

Millar, M. G., & Tesser, A. (1989). The effects of affective-cognitive consistency and thought on the attitude-behavior relation. *Journal of Experimental Social Psychology, 25,* 189–202.

Miller, A. G. (1986). *The obedience experiments: A case study of controversy in social science.* New York: Praeger.

Miller, A. G., Ashton, W., & Mishal, M. (1990). Beliefs concerning the features of constrained behavior: A basis for the fundamental attribution error. *Journal of Personality and Social Psychology, 59,* 635–650.

Miller, A. G., Jones, E. E., & Hinkle, S. (1981). A robust attribution error in the personality domain. *Journal of Experimental Social Psychology, 17,* 587–600.

Miller, C. T. (1984). Self-schemas, gender, and social comparison: A clarification of the related attributes hypothesis. *Journal of Personality and Social Psychology, 46,* 1222–1229.

Miller, D. T. (1977). Altruism and threat to a belief in a just world. *Journal of Experimental Social Psychology, 13,* 113–124.

Miller, D. T., & McFarland, C. (1987). Pluralistic ignorance: When similarity is interpreted as dissimilarity. *Journal of Personality and Social Psychology, 53,* 298–305.

Miller, D. T., Taylor, B., & Buck, M. L. (1991). Gender gaps: Who needs to be explained? *Journal of Personality and Social Psychology, 61,* 5–12.

Miller, D. T., Turnbull, W. & McFarland, C. (1990). Counterfactual thinking and social perception: Thinking about what might have been. *Advances in Experimental Social Psychology, 23,* 305–331.

Miller, J. G. (1984). Culture and the development of everyday social explanation. *Journal of Personality and Social Psychology, 46,* 961–978.

Miller, J. G., & Bersoff, D. M. (1992). Culture and moral judgment: How are conflicts between justice and interpersonal responsibilities resolved? *Journal of Personality and Social Psychology, 62,* 541–554.

Miller, J. G., Bersoff, D. M., & Harwood, R. L. (1990). Perceptions of social responsibility in India and in the United States: Moral imperatives or personal decisions? *Journal of Personality and Social Psychology, 58,* 33–47.

Miller, M. L., & Thayer, J. F. (1989). On the existence of discrete classes in personality: Is self-monitoring the correct joint to carve? *Journal of Personality and Social Psychology, 57,* 143–155.

Miller, N., & Brewer, M. B. (Eds.) (1984). *Groups in contact: The psychology of desegregation.* New York: Academic Press.

Miller, N., & Campbell, D. T. (1959). Recency and primacy in persuasion as a function of the timing of speeches and measurements. *Journal of Abnormal and Social Psychology, 59,* 1–9.

Miller, N., & Carlson, M. (1990). Valid theory-testing meta-analyses further question the negative state relief model of helping. *Psychological Bulletin, 107,* 215–225.

Miller, N., & Cooper, H. (Eds.). (1991). Meta-analysis in personality and social psychology [Special issue]. *Personality and Social Psychology Bulletin, 17* (3).

Miller, N. E. (1941). The frustration-aggression hypothesis. *Psychological Review, 48,* 337–342.

Miller, P. A., & Eisenberg, N. (1988). The relation of empathy to aggressive and externalizing/antisocial behavior. *Psychological Bulletin, 103,* 324–344.

Miller, S. M. (1981). Predictability and human stress: Toward a clarification of evidence and theory. In L. Berkowitz (Ed.), *Advances in experimental social psychology* (Vol. 14, pp. 203–256). New York: Academic Press.

Miller, S. M., Lack, E. R., & Asroff, S. (1985). Preference for control and the coronary-prone behavior pattern: "I'd rather do it myself." *Journal of Personality and Social Psychology, 49,* 492–499.

Miller, S. M., & Mangan, C. E. (1983). Interacting effects of information and coping style in adapting to gynecologic stress: Should the doctor tell all? *Journal of Personality and Social Psychology, 45,* 223–236.

Miller, T. Q., Turner, C. W., Tindale, R. S., Posavac, E. J., & Dugon, B. L. (1991). Reasons for the trend toward null findings in research on Type A behavior. *Psychological Bulletin, 110,* 469–485.

Miller, W. R. (1985). Motivation for treatment: A review with special emphasis on alcoholism. *Psychological Bulletin, 98,* 84–107.

Mills, J. (1976). A procedure for explaining experiments involving deception. *Personality and Social Psychology Bulletin, 2,* 3–13.

Mita, T. H., Dermer, M., & Knight, J. (1977). Reversed facial images and the mere-exposure hypothesis. *Journal of Personality and Social Psychology, 35,* 597–601.

Mitchell, A. (1983). *The nine American lifestyles.* New York: Macmillan.

Mitchell, T. R. (1974). Expectancy models of job satisfaction, occupational preference, and effort: A theoretical, methodological, and empirical appraisal. *Psychological Bulletin, 81,* 1096–1112.

Monroe, S. M., & Simons, A. D. (1991). Diathesis-stress theories in the context of life stress research: Implications for the depressive disorders. *Psychological Bulletin, 110,* 406–425.

Montepare, J. M., & McArthur, L. Z. (1988). Impressions of people created by age-related qualities of their gaits. *Journal of Personality and Social Psychology, 55,* 547–556.

Montgomery, R. L., & Haemmerlie, F. M. (1986). Self-perception theory and the reduction of heterosexual anxiety. *Journal of Social and Clinical Psychology, 4,* 503–512.

Montgomery, R. L., & Haemmerlie, F. M. (1987). Self-perception theory and heterosocial anxiety. In J. E. Maddux, C. D. Stoltenberg, & R. Rosenwein (Eds.), *Social processes in clinical and counseling psychology* (pp. 139–152). New York: Springer-Verlag.

Moore, B. S., Underwood, B., & Rosenhan, D. L. (1973). Affect and altruism. *Developmental Psychology, 8,* 99–104.

Moore, T. E. (1982). Subliminal advertising: What you see is what you get. *Journal of Marketing, 46,* 38–47.

Moorhead, G., & Montanari, J. R. (1986). An empirical investigation of the groupthink phenomenon. *Human Relations, 39,* 399–410.

Moorman, R. H. (1991). Relationship between organizational justice and organizational citizenship behaviors: Do fairness perceptions influence employee citizenship? *Journal of Applied Psychology, 76,* 845–855.

Moran, G., & Comfort, C. (1986). Neither "tentative" nor "fragmentary": Verdict preference of impaneled felony jurors as a function of attitude toward capital punishment. *Journal of Applied Psychology, 71,* 146–155.

Moran, G., & Cutler, B. L. (1991). The prejudicial impact of pretrial publicity. *Journal of Applied Social Psychology, 21,* 345–367.

Moray, N. (1959). Attention in dichotic listening: Affective cues and the influence of instructions. *Quarterly Journal of Experimental Psychology, 11,* 56–60.

Moreland, R. L., & Levine, J. M. (1989). Newcomers and oldtimers in social groups. In P. B. Paulus (Ed.), *Psychology of group influence* (2nd ed., pp. 143–186). Hillsdale, NJ: Erlbaum.

Moreland, R. L., & Levine, J. M. (1992). Problem identification by groups. In S. Worchel, W. Wood, & J. A. Simpson (Eds.), *Group process and productivity* (pp. 17–47). Newbury Park, CA: Sage.

Mori, D., Chaiken, S., & Pliner, P. (1987). Eating lightly and the self-presentation of femininity. *Journal of Personality and Social Psychology, 53,* 693–702.

Morrison, A. M., & Von Glinow, M. A. (1990). Women and minorities in management. *American Psychologist, 45,* 200–208.

Morrow, J., & Nolen-Hoeksema, S. (1990). Effects of responses to depression on the remediation of depressive affect. *Journal of Personality and Social Psychology, 58,* 519–527.

Morton, T. U. (1978). Intimacy and reciprocity of exchange: A comparison of spouses and strangers. *Journal of Personality and Social Psychology, 36,* 72–81.

Moscovici, S. (1980). Toward a theory of conversion behavior. In L. Berkowitz (Ed.), *Advances in Experimental Social Psychology, 6,* 149–202.

Moscovici, S. (1985). Social influence and conformity. In G. Lindzey & E. Aronson (Eds.), *The handbook of social psychology* (3rd ed., pp. 347–412). New York: Random House.

Moscovici, S., & Personnaz, B. (1991). Studies in social influence VI: Is Lenin orange or red? Imagery and social influence. *European Journal of Social Psychology, 21,* 101–118.

Moscovici, S., Lage, E., & Naffrechoux, M. (1969). Influence of a consistent minority on the responses of a majority in a color perception task. *Sociometry, 32,* 365–380.

Moscovici, S., & Zavalloni, M. (1969). The group as a polarizer of attitudes. *Journal of Personality and Social Psychology, 12,* 125–135.

Mouton, J., Blake, R., & Olmstead, J. (1956). The relationship between frequency of yielding and the disclosure of personal identity. *Journal of Personality, 24,* 339–347.

Muehlenhard, C. L., Goggins, M. F., Jones, J. M., & Satterfield, A. T. (1991). Sexual violence and coercion in close relationships. In K. McKinney & S. Sprecher (Eds.), *Sexuality in close relationships* (pp. 155–175). Hillsdale, NJ: Erlbaum.

Mueller, J. H. (1982). Self-awareness and access to material rated as self-descriptive and nondescriptive. *Bulletin of the Psychonomic Society, 19,* 323–326.

Mugny, G. (1982). *The power of minorities.* London: Academic Press.

Mullen, B. (1983). Operationalizing the effect of the group on the individual: A self-attention perspective. *Journal of Experimental Social Psychology, 19,* 295–322.

Mullen, B. (1985). Strength and immediacy of sources: A meta-analytic evaluation of the forgotten elements of social impact theory. *Journal of Personality and Social Psychology, 48,* 1458–1466.

Mullen, B. (1986). Atrocity as a function of lynch mob composition: A self-attention perspective. *Personality and Social Psychology Bulletin, 12,* 187–197.

Mullen, B., Atkins, J. L., Champion, D. S., Edwards, C., Hardy, D., Story, J. E., & Vanderklok, M. (1985). The false consensus effect: A meta-analysis of 115 hypothesis tests. *Journal of Experimental Social Psychology, 21,* 262–283.

Mullen, B., & Baumeister, R. F. (1987). Group effects on self-attention and performance: Social loafing, social facilitation, and social impairment. In C. Hendrick (Ed.), *Review of personality and social psychology: Group processes and intergroup relations* (Vol. 9, pp. 189–206). Beverly Hills, CA: Sage.

Mullen, B., Johnson, C., & Salas, E. (1991). Productivity loss in brainstorming groups: A meta-analytic integration. *Basic and Applied Social Psychology, 12,* 3–23.

Mulvey, E. P., & Haugaard, J. L. (1986, August 4). *Report of the Surgeon General's Workshop on Pornography and Public Health.* Washington, DC: Office of the Surgeon General.

Mummendey, A., Simon, B., Dietze, C., Grünert, M., Haeger, G., Kessler, S., Lettgen, S., & Schäferhoff, S. (1992). Categorization is not enough: Intergroup discrimination in negative outcome allocation. *Journal of Experimental Social Psychology, 28,* 125–144.

Murphy, K. R., & Balzer, W. K. (1986). Systematic distortions in memory-based behavior ratings and performance evaluation: Consequences for rating accuracy. *Journal of Applied Psychology, 71,* 39–44.

Murphy, K. R., Balzer, W. K., Lockhart, M. C., & Eisenman, E. J. (1985). Effects of previous performance on evaluations of present performance. *Journal of Applied Psychology, 70,* 72–84.

Murphy, K. R., & Reynolds, D. H. (1988). Does true halo affect observed halo? *Journal of Applied Psychology, 73,* 235–238.

Murray, H. A. (1938). *Explorations in personality.* New York: Oxford University Press.

Murstein, B. I. (1972). Physical attractiveness and marital choice. *Journal of Personality and Social Psychology, 22,* 8–12.

Murstein, B. I. (1986). *Paths to marriage.* Beverly Hills, CA: Sage.

Murstein, B. I. (1987). A clarification and extension of the SVR theory of dyadic pairing. *Journal of Marriage and the Family, 49,* 929–933.

Murstein, B. I., Cerreto, M., & MacDonald, M. G. (1977). A theory and investigation of the effect of exchange orientation on marriage and friendship. *Journal of Marriage and the Family, 39,* 543–548.

Murstein, B. I., & Christy, P. (1976). Physical attractiveness and marital adjustment in middle-aged couples. *Journal of Personality and Social Psychology, 34,* 537–542.

Murstein, B. I., Merighi, J. R., & Vyse, S. A. (1991). Love styles in the United States and France: A cross-cultural comparison. *Journal of Social and Clinical Psychology, 10,* 37–46.

Mydans, S. (1990, January 19). For jurors, facts could not be sifted from fantasies. *New York Times*, p. A18.

Myers, D. G., & Bishop, G. D. (1970). Discussion effects on racial attitudes. *Science, 169*, 778–779.

Myers, D. G., & Lamm, H. (1976). The group polarization phenomenon. *Psychological Bulletin, 83*, 602–627.

Nadler, A. (1986). Helpseeking as a cultural phenomenon: Differences between city and kibbutz dwellers. *Journal of Personality and Social Psychology, 51*, 976–982.

Nadler, A. (1991). Help-seeking behavior: Psychological costs and instrumental benefits. In M. S. Clark (Ed.), *Review of personality and social psychology: Vol. 12. Prosocial behavior* (pp. 290–311). Newbury Park, CA: Sage.

Nadler, A., & Fisher, J. D. (1986). The role of threat to self-esteem and perceived control in recipient reactions to help: Theory development and empirical validation. In L. Berkowitz (Ed.), *Advances in experimental social psychology* (Vol. 19, pp. 81–122). New York: Academic Press.

Nathan, B. R., & Tippins, N. (1989). The consequences of halo "error" in performance ratings: A field study of the moderating effect of halo on test validation results. *Journal of Applied Psychology, 75*, 290–296.

National Center on Child Abuse and Neglect. (1988). *Study findings: Study of national incidence and prevalence of child abuse and neglect: 1988*. Washington, DC: U.S. Department of Health and Human Services.

Neil v. Biggers, 409 U.S. 188 (1972).

Neimeyer, R. A., & Neimeyer, G. J. (1983). Structural similarity in the acquaintance process. *Journal of Social and Clinical Psychology, 1*, 146–153.

Neisser, U. (1981). John Dean's memory: A case study. *Cognition, 9*, 1–22.

Nemeth, C. (1986). Differential contributions of majority and minority influence. *Psychological Review, 93*, 23–32.

Nemeth, C., & Brilmayer, A. G. (1987). Negotiation versus influence. *European Journal of Social Psychology, 17*, 45–56.

Nemeth, C., & Chiles, C. (1988). Modelling courage: The role of dissent in fostering independence. *European Journal of Social Psychology, 18*, 275–280.

Nemeth, C., Endicott, J., & Wachtler, J. (1976). From the '50s to the '70s: Women in jury deliberations. *Sociometry, 39*, 38–56.

Nemeth, C., & Kwan, J. (1987). Minority influence, divergent thinking, and detection of correct solutions. *Journal of Applied Social Psychology, 17*, 788–799.

Nemeth, C., Mayseless, O., Sherman, J., & Brown, Y. (1990). Exposure to dissent and recall of information. *Journal of Personality and Social Psychology, 58*, 429–437.

Nemeth, C., Swedlund, M., & Kanki, G. (1974). Patterning of the minority's responses and their influence on the majority. *European Journal of Social Psychology, 4*, 53–64.

Neuberg, S. L. (1988). Behavioral implications of information presented outside of conscious awareness: The effect of sub-liminal presentation of trait information on behavior in the prisoner's dilemma game. *Social Cognition, 6*, 207–230.

Neuberg, S. L. (1989). The goal of forming accurate impressions during social interactions: Attenuating the impact of negative expectancies. *Journal of Personality and Social Psychology, 56*, 374–386.

Neuberg, S. L., & Fiske, S. T. (1987). Motivational influences on impression formation: Outcome dependency, accuracy-driven attention, and individuating processes. *Journal of Personality and Social Psychology, 53*, 431–444.

Newcomb, T. M. (1961). *The acquaintance process*. New York: Holt, Rinehart and Winston.

Newman, L. S., & Uleman, J. S. (1989). Spontaneous trait inference. In J. S. Uleman & J. A. Bargh (Eds.), *Unintended thought* (pp. 155–188). New York: Guilford.

Newtson, D. (1974). Dispositional inference from effects of actions: Effects chosen and effects foregone. *Journal of Experimental Social Psychology, 10*, 487–496.

Newtson, D., Hairfield, J., Bloomingdale, J., & Cutino, S. (1987). The structure of action and interaction. *Social Cognition, 5*, 191–237.

Nielson, W. R., & MacDonald, M. R. (1988). Attributions of blame and coping following spinal cord injury: Is self-blame adaptive? *Journal of Social and Clinical Psychology, 7*, 163–175.

Nieva, V. F., & Gutek, B. A. (1981). *Women and work: A psychological perspective*. New York: Praeger.

Nigro, G. N., Hill, D. E., Gelbein, M. E., & Clark, C. L. (1988). Changes in the facial prominence of women and men over the last decade. *Psychology of Women Quarterly, 12*, 225–235

Nisbett, R. E., Fong, G. T., Lehman, D. R., & Cheng, P. W. (1987). Teaching reasoning. *Science, 238*, 625–631.

Nisbett, R. E., & Kunda, Z. (1985). Perception of social distributions. *Journal of Personality and Social Psychology, 48*, 297–311.

Nisbett, R. E., & Ross, L. (1980). *Human inference: Strategies and shortcomings of social judgment*. Englewood Cliffs, NJ: Prentice-Hall.

Nisbett, R. E., & Schachter, S. (1966). Cognitive manipulation of pain. *Journal of Experimental Social Psychology, 2*, 227–236.

Nisbett, R. E., & Wilson, T. D. (1977). Telling more than we can know: Verbal reports on mental processes. *Psychological Review, 84*, 231–259.

Nolen-Hoeksema, S. (1987). Sex differences in unipolar depression: Evidence and theory. *Psychological Bulletin, 101*, 259–282.

Nolen-Hoeksema, S., & Morrow, J. (1991). A prospective study of depression and posttraumatic stress symptoms after a natural disaster: The 1989 Loma Prieta earthquake. *Journal of Personality and Social Psychology, 61*, 115–121.

Noller, P., & Fitzpatrick, M. A. (1990). Marital communication in the eighties. *Journal of Marriage and the Family, 52*, 832–843.

Norton, A. J. (1987, July–August). Families and children in the year 2000. *Children Today*, pp. 6–9.

Norton, A. J., & Moorman, J. E. (1987). Current trends in marriage and divorce among American women. *Journal of Marriage and the Family, 49*, 3–14.

Nosworthy, G. J., & Lindsay, R. C. L. (1990). Does nominal lineup size matter? *Journal of Applied Psychology, 75,* 358–361.

Nuttin, J. M., Jr. (1987). Affective consequences of mere ownership: The name letter effect in twelve European languages. *European Journal of Social Psychology, 17,* 381–402.

Ogilvy, D. (1985). *Ogilvy on advertising.* New York: Vintage Books.

Ohbuchi, K., & Kambara, T. (1985). Attacker's intent and awareness of outcome, impression management, and retaliation. *Journal of Experimental Social Psychology, 21,* 321–330.

Ohbuchi, K., Kameda, M., & Agarie, N. (1989). Apology as aggression control: Its role in mediating appraisal of and response to harm. *Journal of Personality and Social Psychology, 56,* 219–227.

O'Leary, A. (1985). Self-efficacy and health. *Behaviour Research and Therapy, 23,* 437–451.

O'Leary, A. (1990). Stress, emotion, and human immune function. *Psychological Bulletin, 108,* 363–382.

O'Leary, K. D. (1988). Physical aggression between spouses: A social learning theory perspective. In V. B. Van Hasselt, R. L. Morrison, A. S. Bellack, & M. Hersen (Eds.), *Handbook of family violence* (pp. 31–55). New York: Plenum.

O'Leary, K. D., Barling, J., Arias, I., Rosenbaum, A., Malone, J., & Tyree, A. (1989). Prevalence and stability of physical aggression between spouses: A longitudinal analysis. *Journal of Consulting and Clinical Psychology, 57,* 263–268.

O'Leary, K. D., & Smith, D. A. (1991). Marital interaction. *Annual Review of Psychology, 42,* 191–212.

Oliner, S. P., & Oliner, P. M. (1988). *The altruistic personality: Rescuers of Jews in Nazi Europe.* New York: Free Press.

Olson, J. M. (1988). Misattribution, preparatory information, and speech anxiety. *Journal of Personality and Social Psychology, 54,* 758–767.

Olson, J. M., Herman, C. P., & Zanna, M. P. (Eds.). (1986). *Relative deprivation and social comparison: The Ontario Symposium* (Vol. 4). Hillsdale, NJ: Erlbaum.

Olson, J. M., & Ross, M. (1988). False feedback about placebo effectiveness: Consequences for the misattribution of speech anxiety. *Journal of Experimental Social Psychology, 24,* 275–281.

Olson, M. (1965). *The logic of collective action.* Cambridge, MA: Harvard University Press.

Olzak, S., & Nagel, J. (1986). *Competitive ethnic relations.* New York: Academic Press.

Orbell, J. M., Dragt, van de A. J. C., & Dawes, R. M. (1988). Explaining discussion-induced cooperation. *Journal of Personality and Social Psychology, 54,* 811–819.

Ormel, J., & Wohlfarth, T. (1991). How neuroticism, long-term difficulties, and life situation change influence psychological distress: A longitudinal model. *Journal of Personality and Social Psychology, 60,* 744–755.

Orne, M. T. (1962). On the social psychology of the psychological experiment: With particular reference to demand characteristics and their implications. *American Psychologist, 17,* 776–783.

O'Rourke, D. F., Houston, B. K., Harris, J. K., & Snyder, C. R. (1988). The Type A behavior pattern: Summary, conclusions and implications. In B. K. Houston & C. R. Snyder (Eds.), *Type A behavior pattern: Research, theory, and intervention* (pp. 1–7). New York: Wiley.

O'Rourke, D. F., Houston, B. K., Harris, J. K., & Snyder, C. R. (1988). The Type A behavior pattern: Summary, conclusions, and implications. In B. K. Houston & C. R. Snyder (Eds.), *Type A behavior pattern: Research, theory, and intervention* (pp. 312–334). New York: Wiley.

Orwell, G. (1968). Looking back on the Spanish War. In S. Orwell & I. Angus (Eds.), *The collected essays, journalism and letters of George Orwell: Vol. 2. My country right or left, 1940–1943* (pp. 249–267). New York: Harcourt, Brace & World. (Original work written in 1942)

Osborn, A. F. (1953). *Applied imagination.* New York: Scribner.

Osgood, C. E. (1962). *An alternative to war or surrender.* Urbana: University of Illinois Press.

Oskamp, S. (Ed.). (1988). *Television as a social issue: Applied social psychology annual* (Vol. 8). Newbury Park, CA: Sage.

Ottati, V. C., Riggle, E. J., Wyer, R. S., Schwarz, N., & Kuklinski, J. (1989). Cognitive and affective bases of opinion survey responses. *Journal of Personality and Social Psychology, 57,* 404–415.

Otten, C. A., Penner, L. A., & Altabe, M. N. (1991). An examination of therapists' and college students' willingness to help a psychologically distressed person. *Journal of Social and Clinical Psychology, 10,* 102–120.

Otten, C. A., Penner, L. A., & Waugh, G. (1988). That's what friends are for: The determinants of psychological helping. *Journal of Social and Clinical Psychology, 7,* 34–41.

Packard, V. (1957). *The hidden persuaders.* New York: Pocket Books.

Pallak, S. R. (1983). Salience of a communicator's physical attractiveness and persuasion: A heuristic versus systematic processing interpretation. *Social Cognition, 2,* 158–170.

Palys, T. S. (1986). Testing the common wisdom: The social content of video pornography. *Canadian Psychology, 27,* 22–35.

Papastamou, S. (1986). Psychologization and processes of minority and majority influence. *European Journal of Social Psychology, 16,* 165–180.

Park, B. (1986). A method for studying the development of impressions of real people. *Journal of Personality and Social Psychology, 51,* 907–917.

Park, C. W., & Young, S. M. (1986). Consumer response to television commercials: The impact of involvement and background music on brand attitude formation. *Journal of Marketing Research, 23,* 11–24.

Parks, M. R., Stan, C. M., & Eggert, L. L. (1983). Romantic involvement and social network involvement. *Social Psychology Quarterly, 46,* 116–131.

Parsons, H. M. (1974). What happened at Hawthorne? *Science, 183,* 922–932.

Partridge, A., & Eldridge, W. B. (1974). *The second circuit sentencing study: A report to the judges of the second circuit.* Washington, DC: Federal Judicial Center.

Patrick, C. J., & Iacono, W. G. (1991). Validity of the control question polygraph test: The problem of sampling bias. *Journal of Applied Psychology, 76,* 229–238.

Patterson, G. R. (1984). Siblings: Fellow travelers in coercive family processes. In R. J. Blanchard & D. C. Blanchard (Eds.), *Advances in the study of aggression* (Vol. 1, pp. 173–215). New York: Academic Press.

Patterson, M. L. (1983). *Nonverbal behavior: A functional perspective.* New York: Springer-Verlag.

Paulhus, D., Graf, P., & Van Selst, M. (1989). Attentional load increases the positivity of self-presentation. *Social Cognition, 7,* 389–400.

Paulhus, D. L., & Levitt, K. (1987). Desirable responding triggered by affect: Automatic egotism? *Journal of Personality and Social Psychology, 52,* 245–259.

Paulus, P. B. (1988). *Prison crowding: A psychological perspective.* New York: Springer-Verlag.

Paunonen, S. V. (1989). Consensus in personality judgments: Moderating effects of target-rater acquaintanceship and behavior observability. *Journal of Personality and Social Psychology, 56,* 823–833.

Paykel, E. S. (1982). *Handbook of affective disorders.* New York: Guilford.

Pearl, D., Bouthilet, L., & Lazar, J. (Eds.). (1982). *Television and behavior: Ten years of scientific progress and implications for the eighties* (Vols. 1 & 2). Washington, DC: U.S. Government Printing Office.

Pearlin, L. I., Menaghan, E. G., Lieberman, M. A., & Mullan, J. T. (1981). The stress process. *Journal of Health and Social Behavior, 22,* 337–356.

Peek, C. W., Fischer, J. L., & Kidwell, J. S. (1985). Teenage violence toward parents: A neglected dimension of family violence. *Journal of Marriage and the Family, 47,* 1051–1058.

Pelham, B. W. (1991). On the benefit of misery: Self-serving biases in the depressive self-concept. *Journal of Personality and Social Psychology, 61,* 670–681.

Pelham, B. W., & Swann, W. B., Jr. (1989). From self-conceptions to self-worth: The sources and structure of self-esteem. *Journal of Personality and Social Psychology, 57,* 672–680.

Pennebaker, J. W. (1989). Confession, inhibition, and disease. In L. Berkowitz (Ed.), *Advances in experimental social psychology* (Vol. 22, pp. 211–244). San Diego: Academic Press.

Pennebaker, J. W. (1990). *Opening up.* New York: Morrow.

Pennebaker, J. W., Colder, M., & Sharp, L. K. (1990). Accelerating the coping process. *Journal of Personality and Social Psychology, 58,* 528–537.

Pennebaker, J. W., Dyer, M. A., Caulkins, R. J., Litowitz, D. L., Ackreman, P. L., Anderson, D. B., & McGraw, K. M. (1979). Don't the girls get prettier at closing time: A country and western application to psychology. *Personality and Social Psychology Bulletin, 5,* 122–125.

Penner, L. A., Dertke, M. C., & Achenbach, C. J. (1973). The "flash" system: A field study of altruism. *Journal of Applied Social Psychology, 3,* 362–370.

Pennington, N., & Hastie, R. (1992). Explaining the evidence: Tests of the story model for juror decision making. *Journal of Personality and Social Psychology, 62,* 189–206.

Peplau, L. A., Bikson, T. K., Rook, K. S., & Goodchilds, J. D. (1982). Being old and living alone. In L. A. Peplau & D. Perlman (Eds.), *Loneliness: A sourcebook of current theory, research, and therapy* (pp. 327–347). New York: Wiley.

Peplau, L. A., Russell, D., & Heim, M. (1979). The experience of loneliness. In I. Frieze, D. Bar-Tal, & J. Carroll (Eds.), *New approaches to social problems: Applications of attribution theory* (pp. 53–78). San Francisco: Jossey-Bass.

Perdue, C. W., Dovidio, J. F., Gurtman, M. B., & Tyler, R. B. (1990). Us and them: Social categorization and the process of intergroup bias. *Journal of Personality and Social Psychology, 59,* 475–486.

Perdue, C. W., & Gurtman, M. B. (1990). Evidence for the automaticity of ageism. *Journal of Experimental Social Psychology, 26,* 199–216.

Perlman, D., & Oskamp, S. (1971). The effects of picture context and exposure frequency on evaluations of negroes and whites. *Journal of Experimental and Social Psychology, 7,* 503–514.

Perlman, D., & Peplau, L. A. (1981). Toward a social psychology of loneliness. In S. Duck & R. Gilmour (Eds.), *Personal relationships, 3: Personal relationships in disorder* (pp. 31–56). New York: Academic Press.

Perloff, L. S. (1987). Social comparison and illusion of invulnerability to negative life events. In C. R. Snyder & C. E. Ford (Eds.), *Coping with negative life events: Clinical and social psychological perspectives* (pp. 217–242). New York: Plenum.

Perry, D. G., Perry, L. C., & Rasmussen, P. (1986). Cognitive social learning mediators of aggression. *Child Development, 57,* 700–711.

Perry, N. W., & Wrightsman, L. S. (1991). *The child witness: Legal issues and dilemmas.* Newbury Park, CA: Sage.

Personnaz, B. (1981). Study in social influence using the spectrometer method: Dynamics of the phenomena of conversion and covertness in perceptual responses. *European Journal of Social Psychology, 11,* 431–438.

Peters, L. H., Hartke, D. D., & Pohlmann, J. T. (1985). Fiedler's contingency theory of leadership: An application of the meta-analytic procedures of Schmidt and Hunter. *Psychological Bulletin, 97,* 274–285.

Peters, T. J., & Waterman, R. H. (1982). *In search of excellence: Lessons from America's best-run companies.* New York: Warner.

Peterson, C., & Seligman, M. E. P. (1987). Explanatory style and illness. *Journal of Personality, 55,* 237–265.

Peterson, C., Seligman, M. E. P., & Vaillant, G. E. (1988). Pessimistic explanatory style is a risk factor for physical illness: A thirty-five-year longitudinal study. *Journal of Personality and Social Psychology, 55,* 23–27.

Peterson, C., & Villanova, P. (1988). An expanded Attributional Style Questionnaire. *Journal of Abnormal Psychology, 97,* 87–89.

Peterson, R. A. (1977). Consumer perceptions as a function of product, color, price, and nutritional labeling. In W. D. Perreault, Jr. (Ed.), *Advances in consumer research* (pp. 61–63). Atlanta: Association for Consumer Research.

Peterson, R. A., Hoyer, W. D., & Wilson, W. R. (Eds.). (1986). *The role of affect in consumer behavior.* Lexington, MA: Lexington Books.

Pettigrew, T. F. (1969). Racially separate or together? *Journal of Social Issues, 25,* 43–69.

Pettigrew, T. F., & Martin, J. (1987). Shaping the organizational context for black American inclusion. *Journal of Social Issues, 43,* 41–78.

Petty, R. E., & Cacioppo, J. T. (1979). Effects of forewarning of persuasive intent and involvement on cognitive responses and persuasion. *Personality and Social Psychology Bulletin, 5,* 173–176.

Petty, R. E., & Cacioppo, J. T. (1983). The role of bodily responses in attitude measurement and change. In J. Cacioppo & R. Petty (Eds.), *Social psychophysiology: A sourcebook* (pp. 51–101). New York: Guilford.

Petty, R. E., & Cacioppo, J. T. (1984). The effects of involvement on response to argument quantity and quality: Central and peripheral routes to persuasion. *Journal of Personality and Social Psychology, 46,* 69–81.

Petty, R. E., & Cacioppo, J. T. (1986). *Communication and persuasion: Central and peripheral routes to attitude change.* New York: Springer-Verlag.

Petty, R. E., & Cacioppo, J. T. (1990). Involvement and persuasion: Tradition versus integration. *Psychological Bulletin, 107,* 367–374.

Petty, R. E., Cacioppo, J. T., & Goldman, R. (1981a). Personal involvement as a determinant of argument-based persuasion. *Journal of Personality and Social Psychology, 41,* 847–855.

Petty, R. E., Cacioppo, J. T., & Heesacker, M. (1981b). Effects of rhetorical questions on persuasion: A cognitive response analysis. *Journal of Personality and Social Psychology, 40,* 432–440.

Petty, R. E., & Krosnick, J. A. (Eds.). (in press). *Attitude strength: Antecedents and consequences.* Hillsdale, NJ: Erlbaum.

Pfau, M., & Burgoon, M. (1988). Inoculation in political campaign communication. *Human Communication Research, 15,* 91–111.

Pfau, M., Kenski, H. C., Nitz, M., & Sorenson, J. (1990). Efficacy of inoculation strategies in promoting resistance to political attack messages: Application to direct mail. *Communication Monographs, 57,* 25–43.

Phillips, A. P., & Dipboye, R. L. (1989). Correlational tests of predictions from a process model of the interview. *Journal of Applied Psychology, 74,* 41–52.

Phillips, D. P. (1983). The impact of mass media violence on U.S. homicides. *American Sociological Review, 48,* 560–568.

Phillips, D. P. (1986). Natural experiments on the effects of mass media violence on fatal aggression: Strength and weaknesses of a new approach. In L. Berkowitz (Ed.), *Advances in experimental social psychology* (Vol. 19, pp. 207–250). New York: Academic Press.

Phillips, R. (1988). *Putting asunder: A history of divorce in Western society.* Cambridge, England: Cambridge University Press.

Pietromonaco, P. R., & Rook, K. S. (1987). Decision style in depression: The contribution of perceived risk versus benefits. *Journal of Personality and Social Psychology, 52,* 399–408.

Piliavin, J. A., Dovidio, J. F., Gaertner, S. S., & Clark, R. D., III. (1981). *Emergency intervention.* New York: Academic Press.

Pines, A., & Aronson, E. (1983). Antecedents, correlates, and consequences of sexual jealousy. *Journal of Personality, 51,* 108–136.

Pistole, M. C. (1989). Attachment in adult romantic relationships: Style of conflict resolution and relationship satisfaction. *Journal of Social and Personal Relationships, 6,* 505–510.

Pittman, T. S. (1975). Attribution of arousal as a mediator of dissonance reduction. *Journal of Experimental Social Psychology, 11,* 53–63.

Pittman, T. S., & Heller, J. F. (1987). Social motivation. *Annual Review of Psychology, 38,* 461–489.

Plaskin, G. (1988, September 5). Bryant Gumbel. *Us,* pp. 29–35.

Platt, J. (1973). Social traps. *American Psychologist, 28,* 641–651.

Platz, S. J., & Hosch, H. M. (1988). Cross-racial/ethnic eyewitness identification: A field study. *Journal of Applied Social Psychology, 18,* 972–984.

Pliner P., & Chaiken, S. (1990). Eating, social motives, and self-presentation in women and men. *Journal of Experimental Social Psychology, 26,* 240–254.

Pliner, P., Chaiken, S., & Flett, G. L. (1990). Gender differences in concern with body weight and physical appearance over the life span. *Personality and Social Psychology Bulletin, 16,* 263–273.

Plomin, R., & Fulker, D. W. (1987). Behavioral genetics and development in early adolescence. In R. M. Lerner & T. T. Foch (Eds.), *Biological-psychosocial interactions in early adolescence* (pp. 63–94). Hillsdale, NJ: Erlbaum.

Plous, S. (1989). Thinking the unthinkable: The effects of anchoring on likelihood estimates of nuclear war. *Journal of Applied Social Psychology, 19,* 67–91.

Plous, S. (1991). Biases in the assimilation of technological breakdowns: Do accidents make us safer? *Journal of Applied Social Psychology, 21,* 1058–1082.

Podlesny, J. A., & Raskin, D. C. (1977). Physiological measures and the detection of deception. *Psychological Bulletin, 84,* 782–799.

Polivy, J., Garner, D. M., & Garfinkel, P. E. (1986). Causes and consequences of the current preference for thin female physiques. In C. P. Herman, M. P. Zanna, & E. T. Higgins (Eds.), *The Ontario Symposium: Vol. 3. Physical appearance, stigma, and social behavior* (pp. 89–112). Hillsdale, NJ: Erlbaum.

Poppen, P. J., & Segal, N. J. (1988). The influence of sex and sex role orientation on sexual coercion. *Sex Roles, 19,* 689–701.

Porter, N., Geis, F. L., Cooper, E., & Newman, E. (1985). Androgyny and leadership in mixed-sex groups. *Journal of Personality and Social Psychology, 49,* 808–823.

Porterfield, A. L., Mayer, F. S., Dougherty, K. G., Kredich, K. E., Kronberg, M. M., Marsee, K. M., & Okazaki, Y. (1988). Private self-consciousness, canned laughter, and responses to humorous stimuli. *Journal of Research in Personality, 22,* 409–423.

Powell, G. N. (1987). The effects of sex and gender on recruitment. *Academy of Management Review, 12,* 731–743.

Powell, M. C., & Fazio, R. M. (1984). Attitude accessibility as a function of repeated attitudinal expression. *Personality and Social Psychology Bulletin, 10,* 139–148.

Pozo, C., Carver, C. S., Wellens, A. R., & Scheier, M. F. (1991). Social anxiety and social perception: Construing others' reactions to the self. *Personality and Social Psychology Bulletin, 17,* 355–362.

Pratap, A. (1990, August 13). "Romance and a little rape." *Time,* p. 69.

Pratkanis, A., & Aronson, E. (1992). *Age of propaganda: The everyday use and abuse of persuasion.* San Francisco: Freeman.

Pratkanis, A. R. (1989). The cognitive representation of attitudes. In A. R. Pratkanis, S. J. Breckler, & A. G. Greenwald (Eds.) *Attitude structure and function* (pp. 71–93). Hillsdale, NJ: Erlbaum.

Pratkanis, A. R., & Farquhar, P. H. (1992). A brief history of research on phantom alternatives: Evidence for seven empirical generalizations about phantoms. *Basic and Applied Social Psychology, 13,* 103–122.

Pratkanis, A. R., Greenwald, A. G., Leippe, M. R., & Baumgardner, M. H. (1988). In search of reliable persuasion effects: III. The sleeper effect is dead. Long live the sleeper effect. *Journal of Personality and Social Psychology, 54,* 203–218.

Pratto, F., & Bargh, J. A. (1991). Stereotyping based on apparently individuating information: Trait and global components of sex stereotypes under attention overload. *Journal of Experimental Social Psychology, 27,* 26–47.

Pratto, F., & John, O. P. (1991). Automatic vigilance: The attention-grabbing power of negative social information. *Journal of Personality and Social Psychology, 61,* 380–391.

Prentice, D. A. (1990). Familiarity and differences in self- and other-representations. *Journal of Personality and Social Psychology, 59,* 369–383.

Prentice-Dunn, S., & Rogers, R. W. (1980). Effects of deindividuating situational cues and aggressive models on subjective deindividuation and aggression. *Journal of Personality and Social Psychology, 39,* 104–113.

Prentice-Dunn, S., & Rogers, R. W. (1982). Effects of public and private self-awareness on deindividuation and aggression. *Journal of Personality and Social Psychology, 43,* 503–513.

Prentice-Dunn, S., & Rogers, R. W. (1983). Deindividuation in aggression. In R. G. Geen & E. I. Donnerstein (Eds.), *Aggression: Theoretical and empirical reviews: Vol. 2. Issues in research* (pp. 155–171). New York: Academic Press.

President's Commission on Law Enforcement and Administration of Justice (1967). *The challenge of crime in a free society.* Washington, DC: U.S. Government Printing Office.

Proctor, R. C., & Eckerd, W. M. (1976). *"Toot-Toot"* or spectator sports. Psychological and therapeutic implications. *American Journal of Sports Medicine, 4,* 78–83.

Prud'Homme, A. (1991, March 25). Police brutality! *Time,* pp. 16–18.

Pruitt, D. G. (1981). *Negotiation behavior.* New York: Academic Press.

Pruitt, D. G., & Kressel, K. (1985). The mediation of social conflict: An introduction. *Journal of Social Issues, 41*(2), 1–10.

Pruitt, D. G., & Rubin, J. Z. (1986). *Social conflict.* New York: Random House.

Pryor, J. B., & Merluzzi, T. V. (1985). The role of expertise in processing social interaction scripts. *Journal of Experimental Social Psychology, 21,* 362–379.

Purcell, P., & Stewart, L. (1990). Dick and Jane in 1989. *Sex Roles, 22,* 177–185.

Pyszczynski, T. A., & Greenberg, J. (1987). Self-regulatory perseveration and the depressive self-focusing style: A self-awareness theory of reactive depression. *Psychological Bulletin, 102,* 122–138.

Pyszczynski, T., Hamilton, J. C., Greenberg, J., & Becker, S. E. (1991). self-awareness and psychological dysfunction. In C. R. Snyder & D. R. Forsyth (Eds.), *Handbook of social and clinical psychology: The health perspective* (pp. 138–157). New York: Pergamon Press.

Qualter, T. H. (1962). *Propaganda and psychological warfare.* New York: Random House.

Quattrone, G. A. (1985). On the congruity between internal states and action. *Psychological Bulletin, 98,* 3–40.

Quattrone, G. A. (1986). On the perception of a group's variability. In S. Worchel & W. G. Austin (Eds.), *Psychology of intergroup relations* (2nd ed.). Chicago: Nelson Hall.

Quattrone, G. A., & Jones, E. E. (1980). The perception of variability within ingroups and outgroups: Implications for the law of small numbers. *Journal of Personality and Social Psychology, 38,* 141–152.

Rafaeli, A., & Klimoski, R. J. (1983). Predicting sales success through handwriting analysis: An evaluation of the effects of training and handwriting sample context. *Journal of Applied Psychology, 68,* 212–217.

Ragins, B. R., & Sundstrom, E. (1989). Gender and power in organizations: A longitudinal perspective. *Psychological Bulletin, 105,* 51–88.

Rainville, R. E., & Gallagher, J. G. (1990). Vulnerability and heterosexual attraction. *Sex Roles, 23,* 25–31.

Rajecki, D. W. (1982). *Attitudes.* Sunderland, MA: Sinauer.

Ramírez, E., Maldonado, A., & Martos, R. (1992). Attributions modulate immunization against learned helplessness in humans. *Journal of Personality and Social Psychology, 62,* 139–146.

Rank, S. G., & Jacobson, C. K. (1977). Hospital nurses' compliance with medication overdose orders: A failure to replicate. *Journal of Health and Social Behavior, 18,* 188–193.

Rapoport, A. (1991). Ideological commitments in evolutionary theories. *Journal of Social Issues, 47,* 83–99.

Rapoport, A., Bornstein, G., & Erev, I. (1989). Intergroup competition for public goods: Effects of unequal resources and relative group size. *Journal of Social and Personality Psychology, 56,* 748–756.

Raschke, H. J. (1977). The role of social participation in post-separation and postdivorce adjustment. *Journal of Divorce, 1,* 129–140.

Raskin, D. C. (1986). The polygraph in 1986: Scientific, professional, and legal issues surrounding application and acceptance of polygraph evidence. *Utah Law Review,* 29–74.

Raup, D. M. (1986). The nemesis affair: *A story of the death of dinosaurs and the ways of science.* New York: Norton.

Raza, S. M., & Carpenter, B. N. (1987). A model of hiring decisions in real employment interviews. *Journal of Applied Psychology, 72,* 596–603.

Razran, G. H. S. (1938). Conditioning away social bias by the luncheon technique. *Psychological Bulletin, 35,* 693.

Read, S. J. (1987). Constructing causal scenarios: A knowledge structure approach to causal reasoning. *Journal of Personality and Social Psychology, 52,* 288–302.

Reeder, G. D. & Brewer, M. B. (1979). A schematic model of dispositional attribution in interpersonal perception. *Psychological Review, 86,* 61–79.

Regan, D. T. (1971). Effects of a favor and liking on compliance. *Journal of Experimental Social Psychology, 7,* 627–639.

Regan, D. T., & Kilduff, M. (1988). Optimism about elections: Dissonance reduction at the ballot box. *Political Psychology, 9,* 101–107.

Regan, J. W. (1971). Guilt, perceived injustice, and altruistic behavior. *Journal of Personality and Social Psychology, 18,* 124–132.

Reicher, S. D. (1984). The St. Pauls' riot: An explanation of the limits of crowd action in terms of a social identity model. *European Journal of Social Psychology, 14,* 1–21.

Reifman, A., Klein, J. G., & Murphy, S. T. (1989). Self-monitoring and age. *Psychology and Aging, 4,* 245–246.

Reifman, A. S., Larrick, R. P., & Fein, S. (1991). Temper and temperature on the diamond: The heat-aggression relationship in major-league baseball. *Personality and Social Psychology Bulletin, 17,* 580–585.

Reik, T. (1957). A psychologist looks at love. In T. Reik (Ed.), *Of love and lust* (pp. 1–194). New York: Farrar, Straus and Cudahy. (Original work published 1944)

Reinisch, J. M., & Sanders, S. A. (1986). A test of sex differences in aggressive response to hypothetical conflict situations. *Journal of Personality and Social Psychology, 50,* 1045–1049.

Reis, H. T., & Wheeler, L. (1991). Studying social interaction with the Rochester Interaction Record. In M. P. Zanna (Ed.), *Advances in experimental social psychology* (Vol. 24, pp. 269–318). San Diego: Academic Press.

Reis, H. T., Wilson, I. M., Monestere, C., Bernstein, S., Clark, K., Seidl, E., Franco, M., Gioioso, E., Freeman, L., & Radoane, K. (1990). What is smiling is beautiful and good. *European Journal of Social Psychology, 20,* 259–267.

Reisenzein, R. (1983). The Schachter theory of emotion: Two decades later. *Psychological Bulletin, 94,* 239–264.

Reiss, I. L. (1986). A sociological journey into sexuality. *Journal of Marriage and the Family, 48,* 233–242.

Reiss, M., Rosenfeld, R., Melburg, V., & Tedeschi, J. T. (1981). Self-serving attributions: Biased private perceptions and distorted public descriptions. *Journal of Personality and Social Psychology, 41,* 224–231.

Remley, A. (1988, October). The great parental value shift: From obedience to independence. *Psychology Today,* 56–59.

Remondet, J. H., Hansson, R. O., Rule, B., & Winfrey, G. (1987). Rehearsal for widowhood. *Journal of Social and Clinical Psychology, 5,* 285–297.

Repetti, R. L., Matthews, K. A., & Waldron, I. (1989). Employment and women's health: Effects of paid employment on women's mental and physical health. *American Psychologist, 44,* 1394–1401.

Report of the Presidential Commission on the Space Shuttle Challenger Accident. (1986, June 6). Washington, D.C., U.S. Government Printing Office.

Rhodes, N., & Wood, W. (1992). Self-esteem and intelligence affect influenceability: The mediating role of message reception. *Psychological Bulletin, 111,* 156–171.

Rhodewalt, F., & Agustsdottir, S. (1986). Effects of self-presentation on the phenomenal self. *Journal of Personality and Social Psychology, 50,* 47–55.

Rhodewalt, F., & Davison, J., Jr. (1983). Reactance and the coronary-prone behavior pattern: The role of self-attribution in responses to reduced behavioral freedom. *Journal of Personality and Social Psychology, 44,* 220–228.

Rhodewalt, F., Morf, C., Hazlett, S., & Fairfield, M. (1991). Self-handicapping: The role of discounting and augmentation in the preservation of self-esteem: *Journal of Personality and Social Psychology, 61,* 122–131.

Rhodewalt, F., Saltzman, A. T., & Wittmer, J. (1984). Self-handicapping among competitive athletes: The role of practice in self-esteem protection. *Basic and Applied Social Psychology, 5,* 197–209.

Rhodewalt, F., & Smith, T. W. (1991). Current issues in Type A behavior, coronary proneness, and coronary heart disease. In C. R. Snyder & D. R. Forsyth (Eds.), *Handbook of social and clinical psychology: The health perspective* (pp. 57–78). New York: Pergamon Press.

Rhodewalt, F., & Zone, J. B. (1989). Appraisal of life change, depression, and illness in hardy and nonhardy women. *Journal of Personality and Social Psychology, 56,* 81–88.

Rice, B. (1988, March). The selling of life-styles. *Psychology Today,* pp. 46–50.

Rice, M. E., & Grusec, J. E. (1975). Saying and doing: Effects on observer performance. *Journal of Personality and Social Psychology, 32,* 584–593.

Ridgeway, V., & Mathews, A. (1982). Psychological preparation for surgery: A comparison of methods. *British Journal of Clinical Psychology, 2,* 271–280.

Ridley, M., & Dawkins, R. (1981). The natural selection of altruism. In J. P. Rushton & R. M. Sorrentino (Eds.), *Altruism and helping behavior: Social, personality, and developmental perspectives* (pp. 19–39). Hillsdale, NJ: Erlbaum.

Ringelmann, M. (1913). Recherches sur les moteurs animés: Travail de l'homme. *Annales de l'Institut National Agronomique, 2e série, tom XII,* 1–40.

Riordan, C. A., & Tedeschi, J. T. (1983). Attraction in aversive environments: Some evidence for classical conditioning and negative reinforcement. *Journal of Personality and Social Psychology, 44,* 683–692.

Rippetoe, P. A., & Rogers, R. W. (1987). Effects of components of protection-motivation theory on adaptive and maladaptive coping with a health threat. *Journal of Personality and Social Psychology, 52,* 596–604.

Riskind, J. H., Rholes, W. S., Brannon, A. M., & Burdick, C. A. (1987). Attributions and expectations: A confluence of vulnerabilities in mild depression in a college student population. *Journal of Personality and Social Psychology, 52,* 349–354.

Robins, C. J. (1988). Attributions and depression: Why is the literature so inconsistent? *Journal of Personality and Social Psychology, 54,* 880–889.

Robins, L. N., Helzer, J. E., Weissman, M. M., Orvaschel, H., Gruenberg, E., Burke, J. D., & Reigier, D. A. (1984). Lifetime prevalence of specific psychiatric disorders in three sites. *Archives of General Psychiatry, 41,* 949–958.

Robinson, I., Ziss, K., Ganza, B., Katz, S, & Robinson, E. (1991). Twenty years of the sexual revolution, 1965–1985: An update. *Journal of Marriage and the Family, 53,* 216–220.

Robinson, J. P., Shaver, P. R., & Wrightsman, L. S. (Eds.) (1991). *Measures of personality and social psychological attitudes.* San Diego: Academic Press.

Robinson-Staveley, K., & Cooper, J. (1990). Mere presence, gender, and reactions to computers: Studying human-computer interaction in the social context. *Journal of Experimental Social Psychology, 26,* 168–183.

Rodin, J. (1985). The application of social psychology. In G. Lindzey & E. Aronson (Eds.), *Handbook of social psychology* (Vol. 2, 3rd ed. pp. 805–881). New York: Random House.

Rodin, J., Bohm, L. C., & Wack, J. T. (1982). Control, coping, and aging: Models for research and intervention. In L. Bickman (Ed.), *Applied social psychology annual* (Vol. 3, pp. 153–180). Beverly Hills, CA: Sage.

Rodin, J., & Ickovics, J. R. (1990). Women's health: Review and research agenda as we approach the 21st century. *American Psychologist, 45,* 1018–1034.

Rodin, J., & Langer, E. J. (1977). Long-term effects of a control-relevant intervention with the institutionalized aged. *Journal of Personality and Social Psychology, 35,* 897–902.

Rodin, J., Rennert, K., & Solomon, S. L. (1980). Intrinsic motivation for control: Fact or fiction. In A. Baum & J. E. Singer (Eds.), *Advances in environmental psychology: Vol. 2.*

Applications of personal control (pp. 131–148). Hillsdale, NJ: Erlbaum.

Rodin, J., & Salovey, P. (1989). Health psychology. In M. R. Rosenzweig & L. W. Porter (Eds.), *Annual review of psychology, 40,* 533–579.

Rodin, M. J., Price, J. M., Bryson, J. B., & Sanchez, F. J. (1990). Asymmetry in prejudice attribution. *Journal of Experimental Social Psychology, 26,* 481–504.

Roethlisberger, F. J., & Dickson, W. J. (1939). *Management and the Worker.* Cambridge, MA: Harvard University Press.

Rofé, Y. (1984). Stress and affiliation: A utility theory. *Psychological Review, 91,* 235–250.

Rogers, M., Miller, N., Mayer, F. S., & Duval, S. (1982). Personal responsibility and salience of the request for help: Determinants of the relation between negative affect and helping behavior. *Journal of Personality and Social Psychology, 43,* 956–970.

Rogers, R. W. (1983a). Cognitive and psychological processes in fear appeals and attitude change: A revised theory of protection motivation. In J. Cacioppo & R. Petty (Eds.), *Social psychophysiology: A sourcebook* (pp. 153–176). New York: Guilford.

Rogers, R. W. (1983b). Preventative health psychology: An interface of social and clinical psychology. *Journal of Social and Clinical Psychology, 1,* 120–127.

Rogers, R. W., & Mewborn, R. C. (1976). Fear appeals and attitude change: Effects of a threat's noxiousness, probability of occurrence, and the efficacy of coping responses. *Journal of Personality and Social Psychology, 34,* 54–61.

Rogers, R. W., & Prentice-Dunn, S. (1981). Deindividuation and anger-mediated interracial aggression: Unmasking regressive racism. *Journal of Personality and Social Psychology, 41,* 63–73.

Rogers, T. B., Kuiper, N. A., & Kirker, W. S. (1977). Self-reference and the encoding of personal information. *Journal of Personality and Social Psychology, 35,* 677–688.

Rogler, L. H., Cortes, D. E., & Malgady, R. G. (1991). Acculturation and mental health status among Hispanics: Convergence and new directions for research. *American Psychologist, 46,* 585–597.

Rohrer, J. H., Baron, S. H., Hoffman, E. L., & Swander, D. V. (1954). The stability of autokinetic judgments. *Journal of Abnormal and Social Psychology, 49,* 595–597.

Romzek, B. S., & Dubnick, M. J. (1987). Accountability in the public sector: Lessons from the Challenger tragedy. *Public Administration Review, 47,* 227–238.

Rook, K. S. (1987). Reciprocity of social exchange and social satisfaction among older women. *Journal of Personality and Social Psychology, 52,* 145–154.

Rook, K. S. (1988). Toward a more differentiated view of loneliness. In S. Duck (Ed.), *Handbook of personal relationships: Theory, research, and interventions* (pp. 571–589). New York: Wiley.

Rook, K. S. (1990). Parallels in the study of social support and social strain. *Journal of Social and Clinical Psychology, 9,* 118–132.

Roper, R. T. (1980). Jury size and verdict consistency: "A line has to be drawn somewhere"? *Law and Society Review, 14,* 977–999.

Rose, S. M. (1985). Same- and cross-sex friendships and the psychology of homosociology. *Sex Roles, 12,* 63–74.

Rosen, S. (1983). Perceived inadequacy and help-seeking. In B. M. DePaulo, A. Nadler, & J. D. Fisher (Eds.), *New directions in helping: Vol. 2. Help-Seeking* (pp. 73–107). New York: Academic Press.

Rosen, S., Tomarelli, M. M., Kidda, M. L., Jr., & Medvin, N. (1986). Effects of motive for helping, recipient's inability to reciprocate, and sex on devaluation of the recipient's competence. *Journal of Personality and Social Psychology, 50,* 729–736.

Rosenbaum, A., & O'Leary, K. D. (1986). The treatment of marital violence. In N. S. Jacobson & A. S. Gurman (Eds.), *Clinical handbook of marital therapy* (pp. 385–405). New York: Guilford.

Rosenbaum, M. E. (1986). The repulsion hypothesis: On the nondevelopment of relationships. *Journal of Personality and Social Psychology, 51,* 1156–1166.

Rosenberg, M. (1965). *Society and the adolescent self-image.* Princeton, NJ: Princeton University Press.

Rosener, J. B. (1990). Ways women lead. *Harvard Business Review, 68,* 119–125.

Rosenfield, D., Folger, R., & Adelman, H. F. (1980). When rewards reflect competence: A qualification of the overjustification effect. *Journal of Personality and Social Psychology, 39,* 368–376.

Rosenhan, D. L. (1970). The natural socialization of altruistic autonomy. In J. R. Macaulay & L. Berkowitz (Eds.), *Altruism and helping behavior* (pp. 251–268). New York: Academic Press.

Rosenhan, D. L., Salovey, P., & Hargis, K. (1981). The joys of helping: Focus of attention mediates the impact of positive affect on altruism. *Journal of Personality and Social Psychology, 40,* 899–905.

Rosenman, R. H., Brand, R. J., Jenkins, C. D., Friedman, M., Strau, R., & Wurm, M. (1975). Coronary heart disease in the Western Collaborative Group Study: Final follow-up experience of 8½ years. *Journal of the American Medical Association, 233,* 872–877.

Rosenthal, R. (1966). *Experimenter effects in behavioral research.* New York: Appleton-Century-Crofts.

Rosenthal, R. (1976). *Experimenter effects in behavioral research.* New York: Irvington.

Rosenthal, R. (1985). From unconscious experimenter bias to teacher expectancy effects. In J. B. Dusek, V. C. Hall, & W. J. Meyer (Eds.), *Teacher expectancies* (pp. 37–65). Hillsdale, NJ: Erlbaum.

Rosenthal, R. (1991). *Meta-analytic procedures for social research* (2nd ed.). Newbury Park, CA: Sage.

Rosenthal, R., & Jacobson, L. (1968). *Pygmalion in the classroom: Teacher expectation and pupils' intellectual development.* New York: Holt, Rinehart and Winston.

Ross, E. A. (1908). *Social psychology: An outline and source book.* New York: Macmillan.

Ross, L. (1977). The intuitive psychologist and his shortcomings: Distortions in the attribution process. In L. Berkowitz (Ed.), *Advances in experimental social psychology* (Vol. 10, pp. 174–221). New York: Academic Press.

Ross, L., Amabile, T. M., & Steinmetz, J. L. (1977a). Social roles, social control, and biases in social-perception processes. *Journal of Personality and Social Psychology, 35,* 485–494.

Ross, L., Bierbrauer, G., & Hoffman, S. (1976). The role of attribution processes in conformity and dissent. *American Psychologist, 31,* 148–157.

Ross, L., Greene, D., & House, P. (1977b). The false consensus phenomenon: An attributional bias in self-perception and social-perception processes. *Journal of Experimental Social Psychology, 13,* 279–301.

Ross, M. (1989). The relation of implicit theories to the construction of personal histories. *Psychological Review, 96,* 341–357.

Ross, M., & Conway, M. (1985). Remembering one's own past: The construction of personal histories. In R. Sorrentino & E. T. Higgins (Eds.), *Handbook of motivation and cognition* (pp. 122–144). New York: Guilford.

Ross, M., McFarland, C., & Fletcher, G. J. O. (1981). The effect of attitude on the recall of personal histories. *Journal of Personality and Social Psychology, 40,* 627–634.

Ross, M., & Sicoly, F. (1979). Egocentric biases in availability and attribution. *Journal of Personality and Social Psychology, 37,* 322–336.

Rossi, P. H. (1990). The old homeless and the new homelessness in historical perspective. *American Psychologist, 45,* 954–959.

Rothbart, M., & Lewis, S. (1988). Inferring category attributes from exemplary attributes: Geometric shapes and social categories. *Journal of Personality and Social Psychology, 55,* 861–872.

Rotton, J., & Frey, J. (1985). Air pollution, weather, and violent crimes: Concomitant time-series analysis of archival data. *Journal of Personality and Social Psychology, 49,* 1207–1220.

Ruback, R. B., & Greenberg, M. S. (1986). Ethical and legal aspects of applied social psychological research in field settings. In M. J. Saks & L. Saxe (Eds.), *Advances in applied social psychology* (Vol. 3, pp. 207–229). Hillsdale, NJ: Erlbaum.

Ruback, R. B., & Innes, C. A. (1988). The relevance and irrelevance of psychological research: The example of prison crowding. *American Psychologist, 43,* 683–693.

Rubenowitz, S., Norrgren, F., & Tannenbaum, A. S. (1983). Some social psychological effects of direct and indirect participation in ten Swedish companies. *Organization Studies, 4,* 243–259.

Rubenstein, C. M., & Shaver, P. (1982). *In search of intimacy.* New York: Delacorte.

Rubin, D. C. (Ed.). (1986). *Autobiographical memory.* New York: Cambridge University Press.

Rubin, J. Z., Kim, S. H., & Peretz, N. M. (1990). Expectancy effects and negotiation. *Journal of Social Issues, 46,* 125–139.

Rubin, J. Z., Provenzano, F. J., & Luria, Z. (1974). The eye of the beholder: Parents' views on sex of newborns. *American Journal of Orthopsychiatry, 44,* 512–519.

Rubin, Z. (1973). *Liking and loving.* New York: Holt, Rinehart and Winston.

Rubin, Z. (1974). Lovers and other strangers: The development of intimacy in encounters and relationships. *American Scientist, 62,* 182–190.

Rubin, Z., Hill, C. T., Peplau, L. A., & Dunkel-Schetter, C. (1980). Self-disclosure in dating couples: Sex roles and the ethic of openness. *Journal of Marriage and the Family, 42,* 305–317.

Rubin, Z., & Peplau, L. A. (1975). Who believes in a just world? *Journal of Social Issues, 31*(3), 65–89.

Ruble, D. N., & Ruble, T. L. (1982). Sex stereotypes. In A. G. Miller (Ed.), *In the eye of the beholder: Contemporary issues in stereotyping* (pp. 188–252). New York: Praeger.

Rubonis, A. V., & Bickman, L. (1991). Psychological impairment in the wake of disaster: The disaster-psychopathology relationship. *Psychological Bulletin, 109,* 384–399.

Rudy, L., & Goodman, G. S. (1991). Effects of participation on children's reports: Implications for children's testimony. *Developmental Psychology, 27,* 527–538.

Runciman, W. C. (1966). *Relative deprivation and social justice: A study of attitudes to social inequality in twentieth century England.* Berkeley: University of California Press.

Rusbult, C. E. (1980a). Commitment and satisfaction in romantic associations: A test of the investment model. *Journal of Experimental Social Psychology, 16,* 172–186.

Rusbult, C. E. (1980b). Satisfaction and commitment in friendships. *Representative Research in Social Psychology, 11,* 96–105.

Rusbult, C. E. (1983). A longitudinal test of the investment model: The development (and deterioration) of satisfaction and commitment in heterosexual involvement. *Journal of Personality and Social Psychology, 45,* 101–117.

Rusbult, C. E., Johnson, D. J., & Morrow, G. D. (1986). Impact of couple patterns of problem solving on distress and nondistress in dating relationships. *Journal of Personality and Social Psychology, 50,* 744–753.

Rusbult, C. E., Verette, J., Whitney, G.A., Stovik, L. K., & Lipkus, I. (1991). Accommodation processes in close relationships: Theory and preliminary empirical evidence. *Journal of Personality and Social Psychology, 60,* 53–78.

Rusbult, C. E., Zembrodt, I. M., & Gunn, L. K. (1982). Exit, voice, loyalty, and neglect: Responses to dissatisfaction in romantic involvements. *Journal of Personality and Social Psychology, 43,* 1230–1242.

Ruscher, J. B., & Fiske, S. T. (1990). Interpersonal competition can cause individuating processes. *Journal of Personality and Social Psychology, 58,* 832–843.

Ruscher, J. B., Fiske, S. T., Miki, H., & Van Manen, S. (1991). Individuating processes in competition: Interpersonal versus intergroup. *Personality and Social Psychology Bulletin, 17,* 595–605.

Rushton, J. P. (1981). The altruistic personality. In J. P. Rushton & R. M. Sorrentino (Eds.), *Altruism and helping behavior: Social, personality, and developmental perspectives* (pp. 251–266). Hillsdale, NJ: Erlbaum.

Rushton, J. P., Fulker, D. W., Neale, M. C., Nias, D. K. B., & Eysenck, H. J. (1986). Altruism and aggression: The heritability of individual differences. *Journal of Personality and Social Psychology, 50,* 1192–1198.

Rushton, J. P., Russell, R. J. H., & Wells, P. A. (1984). Genetic similarity theory: Beyond kin selection. *Behavior Genetics, 14,* 179–193.

Russell, D. E. H. (1984). *Sexual exploitation.* Beverly Hills, CA: Sage.

Russell, D., Cutrona, C. E., Rose, J., & Yurko, K. (1984). Social and emotional loneliness: An examination of Weiss's typology of loneliness. *Journal of Personality and Social Psychology, 46,* 1313–1321.

Russell, G. W. (1983). Psychological issues in sports violence. In J. H. Goldstein (Ed.), *Sports violence* (pp. 157–181). New York: Springer-Verlag.

Rutkowski, G. K., Gruder, C. L., & Romer, D. (1983). Group cohesiveness, social norms, and bystander intervention. *Journal of Personality and Social Psychology, 44,* 545–552.

Rutte, C. G., Wilke, H. A. M., & Messick, D. M. (1987). Scarcity or abundance caused by people or the environment as determinants of behavior in the resource dilemma. *Journal of Experimental Social Psychology, 23,* 208–216.

Ruvolo, A., & Markus, H. (1992). Possible selves and performance: The power of self-relevant imagery. *Social Cognition, 9,* 95–124.

Ryan, R. M., Mims, V., & Koestner, R. (1983). Relation of reward contingency and interpersonal context to intrinsic motivation: A review and test using cognitive evaluation theory. *Journal of Personality and Social Psychology, 45,* 736–750.

Ryckman, R. M., Robbins, M. A., Kaczor, L. M., & Gold, J. A. (1989). Male and female raters' stereotyping of male and female physiques. *Personality and Social Psychology Bulletin, 15,* 244–251.

Ryff, C. D. (1991). Possible selves in adulthood and old age: A tale of shifting horizons. *Psychology and Aging, 6,* 286–295.

Sacharow, S. (1982). *The package as a marketing tool.* Radnor, PA: Chilton.

Sachs, D. H. (1976). The effects of similarity, evaluation, and self-esteem on interpersonal attraction. *Representative Research in Social Psychology, 7,* 44–50.

Sackett, P. R., Burris, L. R., & Callahan, C. (1989). Integrity testing for personnel selection: An update. *Personnel Psychology, 42,* 491–525.

Sackett, P. R., & DuBois, C. L. Z. (1991). Rater-ratee race effects on performance evaluation: Challenging meta-analytic conclusions. *Journal of Applied Psychology, 76,* 873–877.

Sackett, P. R., & Wilson, M. A. (1982). Factors affecting the consensus judgment process in managerial assessment centers. *Journal of Applied Psychology, 67,* 10–17.

Sacks, O. (1985). *The man who mistook his wife for a hat.* New York: Summit.

Sadalla, E. K., Kenrick, D. T., & Bershure, B. (1987). Dominance and heterosexual attraction. *Journal of Personality and Social Psychology, 52,* 730–738.

Saegert, S., Swap, W., & Zajonc, R. B. (1973). Exposure, context, and interpersonal attraction. *Journal of Personality and Social Psychology, 25,* 234–242.

Safer, M. (1980). Attributing evil to the subject, not the situation: Student reactions to Milgram's film on obedience. *Personality and Social Psychology Bulletin, 6,* 205–209.

Sagar, H. A., & Schofield, J. W. (1980). Racial and behavioral cues in black and white children's perceptions of ambiguously aggressive acts. *Journal of Personality and Social Psychology, 39,* 590–598.

Saint, H. F. (1987). *Memoirs of an invisible man.* New York: Atheneum.

Saks, M. J. (1974). Ignorance of science is no excuse. *Trial, 10,* 18–20.

Saks, M. J. (1977). *Jury verdicts.* Lexington, MA: Lexington Books.

Salovey, P., Mayer, J. D., & Rosenhan, D. L. (1991). Mood and helping: Mood as a motivator of helping and helping as a regulator of mood. In M. S. Clark (Ed.), *Review of personality and social psychology: Vol. 12. Prosocial behavior* (pp. 215–237). Newbury Park, CA: Sage.

Salovey, P., & Rodin, J. (1984). Some antecedents and consequences of social-comparison jealousy. *Journal of Personality and Social Psychology, 47,* 780–792.

Salovey, P., & Rodin, J. (1988). Coping with envy and jealousy. *Journal of Social and Clinical Psychology, 7,* 15–33.

Samuelson, C. D., Messick, D. M., Rutte, C. G., & Wilke, H. (1984). Individual and structural solutions to resource dilemmas in two cultures. *Journal of Personality and Social Psychology, 47,* 94–104.

Sanders, G. S., & Baron, R. S. (1977). Is social comparison irrelevant for producing choice shifts? *Journal of Experimental Social Psychology, 13,* 303–314.

Sanford, R. N. (1950). *The authoritarian personality.* New York: Harper.

Sanna, L. J., & Shotland, R. L. (1990). Valence of anticipated evaluation and social facilitation. *Journal of Experimental Social Psychology, 26,* 82–92.

Santee, R. T., & Maslach, C. (1982). To agree or not to agree: Personal dissent amid social pressure to conform. *Journal of Personality and Social Psychology, 42,* 690–700.

Sapolsky, B. S. (1984). Arousal, affect, and the aggression-moderating effect of erotica. In N. M. Malamuth & E. I. Donnerstein (Eds.), *Pornography and sexual aggression* (pp. 85–113). New York: Academic Press.

Sarason, B. R., Sarason, I. G. & Pierce, G. R. (1990). Traditional views of social support and their impact on assessment. In

B. R. Sarason, I. G., Sarason, & G. R. Pierce (Eds.), *Social support: An interactional view* (pp. 9–25). New York: Wiley.

Sarason, I. G., & Sarason, B. R. (1984). Life changes, moderators of stress, and health. In A. Baum, S. E. Taylor, & J. E. Singer (Eds.), *Handbook of psychology and health: Vol. 4. Social psychological aspects of health* (pp. 279–299). Hillsdale, NJ: Erlbaum.

Sarason, I. G., Johnson, J. H., & Siegel, J. M. (1978). Assessing the impact of life changes: Development of the Life Experiences Survey. *Journal of Consulting and Clinical Psychology, 46,* 932–946.

Sarason, I. G., Levine, H. M., Basham, R. B., & Sarason, B. R. (1983). Assessing social support: The social support questionnaire. *Journal of Personality and Social Psychology, 44,* 127–139.

Sarason, I. G., Sarason, B. R., & Pierce, G. R. (1990). Social support: The search for theory. *Journal of Social and Clinical Psychology, 9,* 133–147.

Sarason, I. G., Sarason, B. R., Pierce, G. R., Shearin, E. N., & Sayers, M. H. (1991). A social learning approach to increasing blood donations. *Journal of Applied Social Psychology, 21,* 896–918.

Sarnoff, I., & Zimbardo, P. (1961). Anxiety, fear, and social affiliation. *Journal of Abnormal and Social Psychology, 62,* 356–363.

Sato, K. (1987). Distribution of the cost of maintaining common resources. *Journal of Experimental Social Psychology, 23,* 19–31.

Saulnier, K., & Perlman, D. (1981). The actor-observer bias is alive and well in prison: A sequel to Wells. *Personality and Social Psychology Bulletin, 7,* 559–564.

Savin, H. B. (1973a). Ethics for gods and men. *Cognition, 2,* 257.

Savin, H. B. (1973b). Professors and psychological researchers: Conflicting values in conflicting roles. *Cognition, 2,* 147–149.

Saxe, L., Dougherty, D., & Cross, T. (1985). The validity of polygraph testing: Scientific analysis and public controversy. *American Psychologist, 38,* 355–366.

Scarpello, V., Huber, V., & Vandenberg, R. J. (1988). Compensation satisfaction: Its measurement and dimensionality. *Journal of Applied Psychology, 73,* 163–171.

Scarr, S. (1988). Race and gender as psychological variables: Social and ethical issues. *American Psychologist, 43,* 56–59.

Schachter, S. (1951). Deviation, rejection, and communication. *Journal of Abnormal and Social Psychology, 46,* 190–207.

Schachter, S. (1959). *The psychology of affiliation: Experimental studies of the sources of gregariousness.* Stanford, CA: Stanford University Press.

Schachter, S. (1964). The interaction of cognitive and physiological determinants of emotional state. In L. Berkowitz (Ed.), *Advances in experimental social psychology* (Vol. 1, pp. 49–80). New York: Academic Press.

Schachter, S., Hood, D., Gerin, W., Andreasson, P. B., & Rennert, M. (1985). Some causes and consequences of dependence and independence in the stock market. *Journal of Economic Behavior and Organization, 6,* 339–357.

Schachter, S., Ouellette, R., Whittle, B., & Gerin, W. (1987). Effects of trends and of profit or loss on the tendency to sell stock. *Basic and Applied Social Psychology, 8,* 259–271.

Schachter, S., & Singer, J. (1962). Cognitive, social, and physiological determinants of the emotional state. *Psychological Review, 69,* 379–399.

Schachter, S., & Singer, J. (1979). Comments on the Maslach and Marshall-Zimbardo experiments. *Journal of Personality and Social Psychology, 37,* 989–995.

Schafer, R. B., & Keith, P. M. (1980). Equity and depression among married couples. *Social Psychology Quarterly, 43,* 430–435.

Schaller, M. (1991). Social categorization and the formation of social stereotypes: Further evidence for biased information processing in the perception of group-behavior correlations. *European Journal of Social Psychology, 21,* 25–35.

Schaller, M., & Cialdini, R. B. (1988). The economics of empathic helping: Support for a mood management motive. *Journal of Experimental Social Psychology, 24,* 163–181.

Scheier, M. F., & Carver, C. S. (1983). Two sides of the self: One for you and one for me. In J. Suls and A. G. Greenwald (Eds.), *Psychological perspectives on the self* (Vol. 2, pp. 123–157). Hillsdale, NJ: Erlbaum.

Scheier, M. F., & Carver, C. S. (1985). Optimism, coping, and health: Assessment and implications of generalized outcome expectancies. *Health Psychology, 4,* 219–247.

Scheier, M. F., & Carver, C. S. (1987). Dispositional optimism and physical well-being: The influence of generalized outcome expectancies on health. *Journal of Personality, 55,* 169–210.

Scheier, M. F., Carver, C. S., & Gibbons, F. X. (1979). Self-directed attention, awareness of bodily states, and suggestibility. *Journal of Personality and Social Psychology, 37,* 1576–1588.

Scheier, M. F., Fenigstein, A., & Buss, A. H. (1974). Self-awareness and physical aggression. *Journal of Experimental Social Psychology, 10,* 264–273.

Scheier, M. F., Matthews, K. A., Owens, J. F., Magovern, G. J., Sr., Lefebrvre, R. C., Abbott, R. A., & Carver, C. S. (1989). Dispositional optimism and recovery from coronary-artery bypass surgery: The beneficial effects on physical and psychological well-being. *Journal of Personality and Social Psychology, 57,* 1024–1040.

Scher, S. J., & Cooper, J. (1989). Motivational basis of dissonance: The singular role of behavioral consequences. *Journal of Personality and Social Psychology, 56,* 899–906.

Schlenker, B. R. (1982). Translating actions into attitudes: An identity-analytic approach to the explanation of social conduct. In L. Berkowitz (Ed.), *Advances in experimental social psychology* (Vol. 15, pp. 193–247). New York: Academic Press.

Schlenker, B. R., & Leary, M. R. (1982). Social anxiety and self-presentation: A conceptualization and model. *Psychological Bulletin, 92,* 641–669.

Schlenker, B. R., & Trudeau, J. V. (1990). The impact of self-presentations on private self-beliefs: Effects of prior self-beliefs and misattribution. *Journal of Personality and Social Psychology, 58,* 22–32.

Schlenker, B. R., & Weigold, M. F. (1992) Interpersonal processes involving impression regulation and management. *Annual Review of Psychology, 43,* 133–168.

Schlenker, B. R., Weigold, M. F., & Hallam, J. R. (1990). self-serving attributions in social context: Effects of self-esteem and social pressure. *Journal of Personality and Social Psychology, 58,* 855–863.

Schmidt, F. L., Ones, D. S., & Hunter, J. E. (1992). Personnel selection. *Annual Review of Psychology, 43,* 627–670.

Schmidt, G., & Weiner, B. (1988). An attribution-affect-action theory of behavior: Replications of judgments of help-giving. *Personality and Social Psychology Bulletin, 14,* 610–621.

Schneider, D. J. (1973). Implicit personality theory: A review. *Psychological Bulletin, 79,* 294–309.

Schneider, S. G., Taylor, S. E., Hammen, C., Kemeny, M. E., & Dudley, J. (1991). Factors influencing suicide intent in gay and bisexual suicide ideators: Differing models for men with and without human immunodeficiency virus. *Journal of Personality and Social Psychology, 61,* 776–778.

Schoeneman, T. J., & Rubanowitz, D. E. (1985). Attributions in the advice columns: Actors and observers, causes and reasons. *Personality and Social Psychology Bulletin, 11,* 315–325.

Schoenrade, P. A., Batson, C. D., Brandt, J. R., & Loud, R. E., Jr. (1986). Attachment, accountability, and motivation to benefit another not in distress. *Journal of Personality and Social Psychology, 51,* 557–563.

Schofield, J. W. (1982). *Black and white in school: Trust, tension, or tolerance?* New York: Praeger.

Schofield, J. W. (1986). Causes and consequences of the color-blind perspective. In J. F. Dovidio & S. L. Gaertner (Eds.), *Prejudice, discrimination, and racism: Theory and research* (pp. 231–253). Orlando, FL: Academic Press.

Schofield, J. W., & Pavelchak, M. A. (1989). Fallout from *The Day After:* The impact of a TV film on attitudes related to nuclear war. *Journal of Applied Social Psychology, 19,* 433–448.

Schopler, J. (1970). An attribution analysis of some determinants of reciprocating a benefit. In J. R. Macaulay & L. Berkowitz (Eds.), *Altruism and helping behavior* (pp. 231–238). New York: Academic Press.

Schopler, J., Insko, C. A., Graetz, K. A., Drigotas, S. M., & Smith, V. A. (1991). The generality of the individual-group discontinuity effect: Variations in positivity-negativity of outcomes, players' relative power, and magnitude of outcomes. *Personality and Social Psychology Bulletin, 17,* 612–624.

Schor, J. B. (1991). *The overworked American: The unexpected decline of leisure.* New York: Basic Books.

Schroeder, D. A., Dovidio, J. F., Sibicky, M. E., Matthews, L. L., & Allen, J. L. (1988). Empathy concern and helping behavior: Egoism or altruism? *Journal of Experimental Social Psychology, 24,* 333–353.

Schudson, M. (1986). *Advertising, the uneasy persuasion.* New York: Basic Books.

Schuller, R. A., & Vidmar, N. (1992). Battered woman syndrome evidence in the courtroom: A review of the literature. *Law and Human Behavior, 16,* 273–291.

Schulman, J., Shaver, P., Colman, R., Emrick, B., & Christie, R. (1973, May). Recipe for a jury. *Psychology Today,* pp. 37–44, 77, 79–84.

Schultz, N. R., Jr., & Moore, D. (1984). Loneliness: Correlates, attributions, and coping among older adults. *Personality and Social Psychology Bulletin, 10,* 67–77.

Schulz, R. (1976). Effects of control and predictability on the physical and psychological well-being of the institutionalized aged. *Journal of Personality and Social Psychology, 33,* 563–573.

Schulz, R., & Decker, S. (1985). Long-term adjustment to physical disability: The role of social support, perceived control, and self-blame. *Journal of Personality and Social Psychology, 48,* 1162–1172.

Schulz, R., & Hanusa, B. H. (1978). Long-term effects of control and predictability-enhancing interventions: Findings and ethical issues. *Journal of Personality and Social Psychology, 36,* 1194–1201.

Schuman, H., & Johnson, M. P. (1976). Attitudes and behavior. *Annual Review of Sociology, 2,* 161–207.

Schuman, H., & Kalton, G. (1985). Survey methods. In G. Lindzey & E. Aronson (Eds.), *Handbook of social psychology* (Vol. 1, 3rd ed., pp. 635–697). New York: Random House.

Schuman, H., Steeh, C., & Bobo, L. (1985). *Racial attitudes in America.* Cambridge, MA: Harvard University Press.

Schutte, N. S., Malouff, J. M., Post-Gordon, J. C., & Rodasta, A. L. (1988). Effects of playing videogames on children's aggressive and other behaviors. *Journal of Applied Social Psychology, 18,* 454–460.

Schwartz, S. H. (1977). Normative influences on altruism. In L. Berkowitz (Ed.), *Advances in experimental social psychology* (Vol. 10, pp. 221–279). New York: Academic Press.

Schwartz, S. H., & Gottlieb, A. (1976). Bystander reaction to a violent theft: Crime in Jerusalem. *Journal of Personality and Social Psychology, 34,* 1188–1199.

Schwartz, S. H., & Gottlieb, A. (1980). Bystander anonymity and reaction to emergencies. *Journal of Personality and Social Psychology, 39,* 418–430.

Schwartz, S. H., & Gottlieb, A. (1981). Participants' postexperimental reactions and the ethics of bystander research. *Journal of Experimental Social Psychology, 17,* 396–407.

Schwartz, S. H., & Howard, J. A. (1982). Helping and cooperation: A self-based motivational model. In V. J. Derlega & J. Grzelak (Eds.), *Cooperation and helping behavior: Theories and research* (pp. 327–353). New York: Academic Press.

Schwartzberg, S. S., & Janoff-Bulman, R. (1991). Grief and the search for meaning: Exploring the assumptive worlds of bereaved college students. *Journal of Social and Clinical Psychology, 10,* 270–288.

Schwarz, N. (1990). Assessing frequency reports of mundane behaviors: Contribution of cognitive psychology to questionnaire construction. In C. Hendrick & M. S. Clark (Eds.), *Review of personality and social psychology: Vol. 11. Research methods in personality and social psychology* (pp. 98–119). Newbury Park, CA: Sage.

Schwarz, N., Bless, H., & Bohner, G. (1991a). Mood and persuasion: Affective states influence the processing of persuasive communications. In M. P. Zanna (Ed.), *Advances in experimental social psychology* (Vol. 24, pp. 161–199). New York: Academic Press.

Schwarz, N., Hippler, H. J., Deutsch, B., & Strack, F. (1985). Response scales: Effects of category range on reported behavior and comparative judgments. *Public Opinion Quarterly, 49,* 388–395.

Schwarz, N., & Kurz, E. (1989). What's in a picture? The impact of face-ism on trait attribution. *European Journal of Social Psychology, 19,* 311–316.

Schwarz, N., Strack, F., Hilton, D., & Naderer, G. (1991b). Base rates, representativeness, and the logic of conversation: The contextual relevance of "irrelevant" information. *Social Cognition, 9,* 67–84.

Schwarzwald, J., Raz, M., & Zvibel, M. (1979). The applicability of the door-in-the-face technique when established behavioral customs exist. *Journal of Applied Social Psychology, 9,* 576–586.

Scott, J. P. (1983). A systems approach to research on aggressive behavior. In E. C. Simmel, M. E. Hahn, & J. K. Walters (Eds.), *Aggressive behavior: genetic and neural approaches* (pp. 1–18). Hillsdale, NJ: Erlbaum.

Sears, D. O. (1983). The person-positivity bias. *Journal of Personality and Social Psychology, 44,* 233–250.

Sears, D. O. (1986). College sophomores in the laboratory: Influences of a narrow data base on social psychology's view of human nature. *Journal of Personality and Social Psychology, 51,* 515–530.

Sears, D. O., & Allen, H. M., Jr. (1984). The trajectory of local desegregation controversies and whites' opposition to busing. In N. Miller & M. B. Brewer (Eds.), *Groups in contact: The Psychology of Desegregation* (pp. 123–151). New York: Academic Press.

Sears, D. O., & Kinder, D. R. (1985). Whites' opposition to busing: On conceptualizing and operationalizing group conflict. *Journal of Personality and Social Psychology, 48,* 1141–1147.

Secord, P. F. (1983). Imbalanced sex ratios: The social conseqences. *Personality and Social Psychology Bulletin, 9,* 525–543.

Sedikides, C., & Jackson, J. M. (1990). Social impact theory: A field test of source strength, source immediacy and number of targets. *Basic and Applied Social Psychology, 11,* 273–281.

Segal, M. W. (1974). Alphabet and attraction: An unobtrusive measure of the effect of propinquity in a field setting. *Journal of Personality and Social Psychology, 30,* 654–657.

Segal, Z. V. (1988). Appraisal of the self-schema construct in cognitive models of depression. *Psychological Bulletin, 103,* 147–162.

Seligman, C., Bush, M., & Kirsch, K. (1976). Relationship between compliance in the foot-in-the-door paradigm and size of first request. *Journal of Personality and Social Psychology, 33,* 517–520.

Seligman, M. E. P. (1975). *On depression, development, and death.* San Francisco: Freeman.

Seligman, M. E. P. (1990). *Learned optimism.* New York: Alfred A. Knopf.

Seligman, M. E. P., & Maier, S. F. (1967). Failure to escape traumatic shock. *Journal of Experimental Psychology, 74,* 1–9.

Shaffer, D. R., Smith, J. E., & Tomarelli, M. (1982). Self-monitoring as a determinant of self-disclosure reciprocity during the acquaintance process. *Journal of Personality and Social Psychology, 43,* 163–175.

Shanab, M. E., & Yahya, K. A. (1977). A behavioral study of obedience in children. *Journal of Personality and Social Psychology, 35,* 530–536.

Shanab, M. E., & Yahya, K. A. (1978). A cross cultural study of obedience. *Bulletin of the Psychonomic Society, 11,* 267–269.

Shapiro, P. N., & Penrod, S. (1986). Meta-analysis of facial identification studies. *Psychological Bulletin, 100,* 139–156.

Shaver, K. G. (1970). Defensive attribution: Effects of severity and relevance on the responsibility assigned for an accident. *Journal of Personality and Social Psychology, 14,* 101–113.

Shaver, P. R., & Hazan, C. (1988). A biased overview of the study of love. *Journal of Social and Personal Relationships, 5,* 473–501.

Shaver, P., Hazan, C., & Bradshaw, D. (1988). Love as attachment: The integration of three behavioral systems. In R. J. Sternberg & M. L. Barnes (Eds.), *The psychology of love* (pp. 68–99). New Haven, CT: Yale University Press.

Shaver, P., & Rubenstein, E. (1980). Childhood attachment experience and adult loneliness. In L. Wheeler (Ed.), *Review of personality and social psychology* (Vol. 1, pp. 42–73). Beverly Hills, CA: Sage.

Shavitt, S. (1990). The role of attitude objects in attitude functions. *Journal of Experimental Social Psychology, 26,* 124–148.

Shaw, M. E. (1954). Some effects of unequal distribution of information upon group performance in various communication nets. *Journal of Abnormal and Social Psychology, 49,* 547–553.

Shaw, M. E. (1981). *Group dynamics* (3rd ed.). New York: McGraw-Hill.

Shefrin, H. M., & Statman, M. (1985). The disposition to sell winners too early and ride losers too long: Theory and evidence. *Journal of Finance, 40,* 777–790.

Shefrin, H. M., & Statman, M. (1986, February). How not to make money in the stock market. *Psychology Today,* pp. 52–57.

Sheldon, W. H. (1954). *Atlas of man: A guide for somatotyping the adult male of all ages.* New York: Harper & Row.

Sheppard, B. H. (1985). Justice is no simple matter: Case for elaborating our model of procedural fairness. *Journal of Personality and Social Psychology, 49,* 953–962.

Sheppard, B. H., Bazerman, M. H., & Lewicki, R. J. (Eds.). (1990). *Research on negotiation in organizations* (Vol. 2). Greenwich, CT: JAI Press.

Sheppard, B. H., Hartwick, J., & Warshaw, P. R. (1988). The theory of reasoned action: A meta-analysis of past research with recommendations for modifications and future research. *Journal of Consumer Research, 15,* 325–343.

Sheppard, J. A., & Wright, R. A. (1989). Individual contributions to a collective effort: An incentive analysis. *Personality and Social Psychology Bulletin, 15,* 141–149.

Sherif, M. (1936). *The psychology of social norms.* New York: Harper.

Sherif, M. (1966). *In common predicament: Social psychology of intergroup conflict and cooperation.* Boston: Houghton Mifflin.

Sherif, M., Harvey, L. J., White, B. J., Hood, W. R., & Sherif, C. W. (1988). *The Robbers Cave experiment: Intergroup conflict and cooperation.* Middletown, CT: Wesleyan University Press. (Original work published 1961)

Sherif, M., & Hovland, C. I. (1961). *Social judgment: Assimilation and contrast effects in communication and attitude change.* New Haven, CT: Yale University Press.

Sherman, S. J., Presson, C., & Chassin, L. (1984). Mechanisms underlying the false consensus effect: The special role of threats to the self. *Personality and Social Psychology Bulletin, 10,* 127–138.

Sherrod, D. (1989). The influence of gender on same-sex friendships. In C. Hendrick (Ed.), *Review of personality and social psychology: Vol. 10. Close relationships* (pp. 164–186). Newbury Park, CA: Sage.

Shipp, E. R. (1987, May 18). Goetz lawyer tenaciously faces toughest test. *New York Times,* p. 18.

Shore, T. H., Shore, L. M., & Thornton, G. C., III. (1992). Construct validity of self- and peer evaluations of performance dimensions in an assessment center. *Journal of Applied Psychology, 77,* 42–54.

Shotland, R. L. (1989). A model of the causes of date rape in developing and close relationships. In C. Hendrick (Ed.), *Review of personality and social psychology: Vol. 10. Close relationships* (pp. 247–270). Newbury Park, CA: Sage.

Shotland, R. L., & Heinold, W. D. (1985). Bystander response to arterial bleeding: Helping skills, the decision-making process, and differentiating the helping response. *Journal of Personality and Social Psychology, 49,* 347–356.

Shotland, R. L., & Straw, M. K. (1976). Bystander response to an assault: When a man attacks a woman. *Journal of Personality and Social Psychology, 34,* 990–999.

Shrauger, J. S., & Schoeneman, T. (1979). Symbolic interactionist view of the self-concept: Through the looking-glass darkly. *Psychological Bulletin, 86,* 549–573.

Shukla, A., & Kapoor, M. (1990). Sex role identity, marital power, and marital satisfaction among middle-class couples in India. *Sex Roles, 22,* 693–706.

Shure, G. H., Meeker, R. J., & Hansford, E. A. (1965). The effectiveness of pacifist strategies in bargaining games. *Journal of Conflict Resolution, 9,* 106–117.

Sieber, J. E. (1982). Ethical dilemmas in social research. In J. E. Sieber (Ed.), *The ethics of social research: Surveys and experiments* (pp. 1–38). New York: Springer-Verlag.

Sieber, J. E. (1984). Informed consent and deception. In J. E. Sieber (Ed.), *NIH readings on the protection of human subjects in behavioral and social science research* (pp. 39–77). Frederick, MD: University Publications of America.

Sieber, J. E., & Stanley, B. (1988). Ethical and professional dimensions of socially sensitive research. *American Psychologist, 43,* 49–55.

Sieber, S. D. (1974). Toward a theory of role accumulation. *American Sociological Review, 39,* 567–578.

Siegel, J. M. (1990). Stressful life events and use of physician services among the elderly: The moderating role of pet ownership. *Journal of Personality and Social Psychology, 58,* 1081–1086.

Sigall, H., & Landy, D. (1973). Radiating beauty: The effects of having a physically attractive partner on person perception. *Journal of Personality and Social Psychology, 28,* 218–224.

Sigall, H., & Ostrove, N. (1975). Beautiful but dangerous: Effects of offender attractiveness and nature of the crime on juridic judgment. *Journal of Personality and Social Psychology, 31,* 410–414.

Sigall, H., & Page, R. (1971). Current stereotypes: A little fading, a little faking. *Journal of Personality and Social Psychology, 18,* 247–255.

Sigelman, L., & Welch, S. (1991). *Black Americans' views of racial inequality: The dream deferred.* New York: Cambridge University Press.

Silka, L. (1989). *Intuitive judgments of change.* New York: Springer-Verlag.

Silverman, I., Shulman, A. D., & Wiesenthal, D. L. (1970). Effects of deceiving and debriefing psychological subjects on performance in later experiments. *Journal of Personality and Social Psychology, 14,* 203–212.

Silverstein, B. (1989). Enemy images: The psychology of U.S. attitudes and cognitions regarding the Soviet Union. *American Psychologist, 44,* 903–913.

Silverstein, B., Perdue, L., Peterson, B., & Kelly, E. (1986a). The role of the mass media in promoting a thin standard of bodily attractiveness for women. *Sex Roles, 14,* 519–532.

Silverstein, B., Perdue, L., Peterson, B., Vogel, L., & Fantini, D. A. (1986b). Possible causes of the thin standard of bodily attractiveness for women. *The International Journal of Eating Disorders, 5,* 907–916.

Simmel, E. C., Hahn, M. E., & Walters, J. K. (1983). *Aggressive behavior: Genetic and neural approaches.* Hillsdale, NJ: Erlbaum.

Simon, H. (1990). A mechanism for social selection and successful altruism. *Science, 250,* 1665–1668.

Simpson, J. A. (1987). The dissolution of romantic relationships: Factors involved in relationship stability and emotional distress. *Journal of Personality and Social Psychology, 53,* 683–692.

Simpson, J. A. (1990). Influence of attachment styles on romantic relationships. *Journal of Personality and Social Psychology, 59,* 971–980.

Simpson, J. A., Campbell, B., & Berscheid, E. (1986). The association between romantic love and marriage: Kephart (1967) twice revisited. *Personality and Social Psychology Bulletin, 12,* 363–372.

Simpson, J. A., & Gangestad, S. W. (1991). Individual differences in sociosexuality: Evidence for convergent and dis-criminant validity. *Journal of Personality and Social Psychology, 60,* 872–883.

Simpson, J. A., Gangestad, S. W., & Lerma, M. (1990). Perception of physical attractiveness: Mechanisms involved in the maintenance of romantic relationships. *Journal of Personality and Social Psychology, 59,* 1192–1201.

Singer, J. E., Brush, C. A., & Lubin, S. C. (1965). Some aspects of deindividuation: Identification and conformity. *Journal of Experimental Social Psychology, 1,* 356–378.

Singer, J. L., & Singer, D. G. (1983). Psychologists look at television: Cognitive, developmental, personality, and social policy implications. *American Psychologist, 38,* 826–834.

Sistrunk, F., & McDavid, J. W. (1971). Sex variable in conforming behavior. *Journal of Personality and Social Psychology, 17,* 200–207.

Skinner, B. F. (1953). *Science and human behavior.* New York: Macmillan.

Skov, R. B., & Sherman, S. J. (1986). Information-gathering processes: Diagnosticity, hypothesis confirmatory strategies, and perceived hypothesis confirmation. *Journal of Experimental Social Psychology, 22,* 93–121.

Skowronski, J. J., & Carlston, D. E. (1989). Negativity and extremity biases in impression formation: A review of explanations. *Psychology Bulletin, 105,* 131–142.

Slamecka, N. J., & Graff, P. (1978). The generation effect: Delineation of a phenomenon. *Journal of Experimental Psychology: Human Learning and Memory, 4,* 592–604.

Slovic, P., Fischoff, B., & Lichtenstein, S. (1982). Facts versus fears: Understanding perceived risk. In D. Kahneman, P. Slovic, & A. Tversky (Eds.), *Judgment under uncertainty: Heuristics and biases* (pp. 463–489). New York: Cambridge University Press.

Smeaton, G., Byrne, D., & Murnen, S. K. (1989). The repulsion hypothesis revisited: Similarity irrelevance or dissimilarity bias? *Journal of Personality and Social Psychology, 56,* 54–59.

Smith, C. A. (1991). The self, appraisal, and coping. In C. R. Snyder & D. R. Forsyth (Eds.), *Handbook of social and clinical psychology: The health perspective* (pp. 116–137). New York: Pergamon Press.

Smith, E. R., & Miller, F. D. (1978). Limits on perception of cognitive processes: A reply to Nisbett and Wilson. *Psychological Review, 85,* 355–362.

Smith, K. D., Keating, J. P., & Stotland, E. (1989). Altruism reconsidered: The effect of denying feedback on a victim's status to empathic witnesses. *Journal of Personality and Social Psychology, 57,* 641–650.

Smith, R., Kim, S. H., & Parrott, W. G. (1988). Envy and jealousy: Semantic problems and experiential distinctions. *Personality and Social Psychology Bulletin, 14,* 401–409.

Smith, S. S., & Richardson, D. (1983). Amelioration of deception and harm in psychological research: The important role of debriefing. *Journal of Personality and Social Psychology, 44,* 1075–1082.

Smith, T. W., Allred, K. D., Morrison, C. A., & Carlson, S. D. (1989a). Cardiovascular reactivity and interpersonal influence: Active coping in a social context. *Journal of Personality and Social Psychology, 56,* 209–218.

Smith, T. W., Houston, B. K., & Stucky, R. J. (1985). Effects of threat of shock and control over shock on finger pulse volume, pulse rate, and systolic blood pressure. *Biological Psychology, 20,* 31–38.

Smith, T. W., Pope, M. K., Rhodewalt, F., & Poulton, J. L. (1989b). Optimism, neuroticism, coping, and symptom reports: An alternative interpretation of the Life Orientation Test. *Journal of Personality and Social Psychology, 56,* 640–648.

Smith, T. W., & Rhodewalt, F. (1991). Methodological challenges at the social/clinical interface. In C. R. Snyder & D. R. Forsyth (Eds.), *Handbook of social and clinical psychology: The health perspective* (pp. 739–756). New York: Pergamon Press.

Smith, T. W., Snyder, C. R., & Perkins, S. C. (1983). The self-serving function of hypochondriacal complaints: Physical symptoms as self-handicapping strategies. *Journal of Personality and Social Psychology, 44,* 787–797.

Smith, V. L. (1991a). Impact of pretrial instructions on jurors' information processing and decision making. *Journal of Applied Psychology, 76,* 220–228.

Smith, V. L. (1991b). Prototypes in the courtroom: Lay representations of legal concepts. *Journal of Personality and Social Psychology, 61,* 857–872.

Smither, J. W., Reilly, R. R., & Buda, R. (1988). Effect of prior performance information on ratings of present performance: Contrast versus assimilation revisited. *Journal of Applied Psychology, 73,* 487–496.

Snyder, C. R., & Forsyth, D. R. (Eds.). (1991). *Handbook of social and clinical psychology: The health perspective.* New York: Pergamon Press.

Snyder, C. R., & Fromkin, H. L. (1980). *Uniqueness: The human pursuit of difference.* New York: Plenum.

Snyder, C. R., Harris, C., Anderson, J. R., Holleran, S. A., Irving, L. M., Sigmon, S. T., Yoshinobu, L., Gibb, J., Langelle, C., & Harney, P. (1991). The will and the ways: Development and validation of an individual-differences measure of hope. *Journal of Personality and Social Psychology, 60,* 570–585.

Snyder, C. R., Higgins, R. L., & Stucky, R. J. (1983). *Excuses: Masquerades in search of grace.* New York: Wiley.

Snyder, C. R., Lassegard, M. A., & Ford, C. E. (1986). Distancing after group success and failure: Basking in reflected glory and cutting off reflected failure. *Journal of Personality and Social Psychology, 51,* 382–388.

Snyder, C. R., Smith, T. W., Augelli, R. W., & Ingram, R. E. (1985). On the self-serving function of social anxiety: Shyness as a self-handicapping strategy. *Journal of Personality and Social Psychology, 48,* 970–980.

Snyder, M. (1974). The self-monitoring of expressive behavior. *Journal of Personality and Social Psychology, 30,* 526–537.

Snyder, M. (1984). When beliefs create reality. In L. Berkowitz (Ed.), *Advances in experimental social psychology* (Vol. 18, pp. 247–305). New York: Academic Press.

Snyder, M. (1987). *Public appearances private/realities: The psychology of self-monitoring.* New York: Freeman.

Snyder, M., & DeBono, K. (1985). Appeals to image and claims about quality: Understanding the psychology of advertising. *Journal of Personality and Social Psychology, 49,* 586–597.

Snyder, M., & Gangestad, S. (1986). On the nature of self-monitoring: Matters of assessment, matters of validity. *Journal of Personality and Social Psychology, 51,* 125–139.

Snyder, M., & Ickes, W. (1985). Personality and social behavior. In G. Lindzey & E. Aronson (Eds.), *Handbook of social psychology* (Vol. 2, 3rd ed., pp. 883–947). New York: Random House.

Snyder, M., & Monson, T. C. (1975). Persons, situations, and the control of social behavior. *Journal of Personality and Social Psychology, 32,* 637–644.

Snyder, M., & Simpson, J. A. (1984). Self-monitoring and dating relationships. *Journal of Personality and Social Psychology, 47,* 1281–1291.

Snyder, M., & Simpson, J. A. (1987). Orientations toward romantic relationships. In D. Perlman & S. Duck (Eds.), *Intimate relationships: Development, dynamics, and deterioration* (pp. 45–62). Newbury Park, CA: Sage.

Snyder, M., & Swann, W. B., Jr. (1978). Behavioral confirmation in social interaction: From social perception to social reality. *Journal of Personality and Social Psychology, 36,* 1202–1212.

Snyder, M., Berscheid, E., & Glick, P. (1985). Focusing on the exterior and the interior: Two investigations of the initiation of personal relationships. *Journal of Personality and Social Psychology, 48,* 1427–1439.

Snyder, M., Tanke, E. D., & Berscheid, E. (1977). Social perception and interpersonal behavior: On the self-fulfilling nature of social stereotypes. *Journal of Personality and Social Psychology, 35,* 656–666.

Snyder, M. L., & Wicklund, R. A. (1981). Attribute ambiguity. In J. H. Harvey, W. Ickes, & R. F. Kidd (Eds.), *New directions in attribution research* (Vol. 3, pp. 197–221). Hillsdale, NJ: Erlbaum.

Solano, C. H., & Koester, N. H. (1989). Loneliness and communication problems: Subject anxiety or objective skills? *Personality and Social Psychology Bulletin, 15,* 126–133.

Solomon, S. D., Regier, D. A., & Burke, J. D. (1989). Role of perceived control in coping with disaster. *Journal of Social and Clinical Psychology, 8,* 376–392.

Solomon, S. D., Smith, E. M., Robins, L. N., & Fischbach, R. L. (1987). Social involvement as a mediator of disaster-induced stress. *Journal of Applied Social Psychology, 17,* 1092–1112.

Sorrentino, R. M., & Field, N. (1986). Emergent leadership over time: The functional value of positive motivation. *Journal of Personality and Social Psychology, 50,* 1091–1099.

South, S. J. (1991). Sociodemographic differentials in mate selection preferences. *Journal of Marriage and the Family, 53,* 928–940.

Spence, J. T. (1985). Gender identity and its implications for the concepts of masculinity and femininity. In T. B. Sonderegger (Ed.), *Nebraska Symposium on Motivation: 1984. Psychology and gender* (Vol. 32, pp. 59–95). Lincoln: University of Nebraska Press.

Spence, J. T., Deaux, K., & Helmreich, R. L. (1985). Sex roles in contemporary American society. In G. Lindzey & E. Aronson (Eds.), *Handbook of social psychology* (Vol. 2, 3rd ed., pp. 149–178). New York: Random House.

Spence, J. T., & Helmreich, R. L. (1978). *Masculinity & femininity: Their psychological dimensions, correlates, and antecedents.* Austin: University of Texas Press.

Spitze, G. (1988). Women's employment and family relations: A review. *Journal of Marriage and the Family, 50,* 595–618.

Spivey, C. B., & Prentice-Dunn, S. (1990). Assessing the directionality of deindividuated behavior: Effects of deindividuation, modeling, and private self-consciousness on aggressive and prosocial responses. *Basic and Applied Social Psychology, 11,* 387–403.

Sprecher, S. (1985). Sex differences in bases of power in dating relationships. *Sex Roles, 12,* 449–462.

Sprecher, S., & Hatfield, E. (1982). Self-esteem and romantic attraction. *Recherches de Psychologie Sociale, 4,* 61–81.

Stack, S. (1990). Divorce, suicide, and the mass media: An analysis of differential identification, 1948–1980. *Journal of Marriage and the Family, 52,* 553–560.

Stalans, L. J., & Diamond, S. S. (1990). Formation and change in lay evaluations of criminal sentencing: Misperception and discontent. *Law and Human Behavior, 14,* 199–214.

Stall, R. D., Coates, T. J., & Hoff, C. (1988). Behavioral risk reduction for HIV infection among gay and bisexual men. *American Psychologist, 43,* 878–885.

Stander, D. M. (1973, November 15). Testing new product ideas in an "Archie Bunker" world. *Marketing News,* pp. 1, 4–5, 10.

Stangor, C., Lynch, L., Changming, D., & Glass, B. (1992). Categorization of individuals on the basis of multiple social features. *Journal of Personality and Social Psychology, 62,* 207–218.

Stangor, C., Sullivan, L. A., & Ford, T. E. (1991). Affective and cognitive determinants of prejudice. *Social Cognition, 9,* 359–380.

Stasser, G. (1992). Pooling of unshared information during group discussions. In S. Worchel, W. Wood, & J. A. Simpson (Eds.), *Group process and productivity* (pp. 48–67). Newbury Park, CA: Sage.

Stasser, G., & Davis, J. H. (1981). Group decision making and social influence: A social interaction sequence model. *Psychological Review, 88,* 523–551.

Stasser, G., Kerr, N. L., & Bray, R. M. (1982). The social psychology of jury deliberations: Structure, process, and product. In N. Kerr & R. Bray (Eds.), *The psychology of the courtroom* (pp. 221–256). New York: Academic Press.

Stasser, G., & Titus, W. (1985). Pooling of unshared information in group decision making: Biased information sampling during discussion. *Journal of Personality and Social Psychology, 48,* 1467–1478.

Stasson, M., & Fishbein, M. (1990). The relation between perceived risk and preventative action: A within-subject analysis of perceived driving risk and intention to wear seatbelts. *Journal of Applied Social Psychology, 20,* 1541–1557.

Staub, E. (1989). *The roots of evil.* Cambridge, England: Cambridge University Press.

Staw, B. M., & Ross, J. (1987). Behavior in escalation situations: Antecedents, prototypes, and solutions. In L. L. Cummings and B. M. Staw (Eds.), *Research in organizational behavior* (Vol. 9). Greenwich, CT: JAI Press.

Staw, B. M., & Ross, J. (1989). Understanding behavior in escalation situations. *Science, 246,* 216–220.

Steblay, N. M. (1987). Helping behavior in rural and urban environments: A meta-analysis. *Psychological Bulletin, 102,* 346–356.

Steck, L., Levitan, D., McLane, D., & Kelley, H. H. (1982). Care, need, and conceptions of love. *Journal of Personality and Social Psychology, 43,* 481–491.

Steele, C. M. (1988). The psychology of self-affirmation: Sustaining the integrity of the self. In L. Berkowitz (Ed.), *Advances in experimental social psychology* (Vol. 21, pp. 261–302). New York: Academic Press.

Steele, C. M., Critchlow, B., & Liu, T. J. (1985). Alcohol and social behavior 2: The helpful drunkard. *Journal of Personality and Social Psychology, 48,* 35–46.

Steele, C. M., & Josephs, R. A. (1990). Alcohol myopia: Its prized and dangerous effects. *American Psychologist, 45,* 921–933.

Steele, C. M., Southwick, L., & Critchlow, B. (1981). Dissonance and alcohol: Drinking your troubles away. *Journal of Personality and Social Psychology, 41,* 831–846.

Steele, S. (1990). *The content of our character.* New York: St. Martin's Press.

Steiner, I. D. (1972). *Group process and productivity.* New York: Academic Press.

Steinmetz, S. K., & Lucca, J. S. (1988). Husband battering. In V. B. Van Hasselt, R. L. Morrison, A. S. Bellack, & M. Hersen (Eds.), *Handbook of family violence* (pp. 233–246). New York: Plenum.

Stephan, W. G. (1985). Intergroup relations. In G. Lindzey & E. Aronson (Eds.), *Handbook of social psychology* (Vol. 2, pp. 599–658). New York: Random House.

Stephan, W. G. (1986). The effects of school desegregation: An evaluation 30 years after *Brown.* In M. J. Saks & L. Saxe (Eds.), *Advances in applied social psychology* (Vol. 3, pp. 181–206). Hillsdale, NJ: Erlbaum.

Stephen, T. (1987). Taking communication seriously: A reply to Murstein. *Journal of Marriage and the Family, 49,* 937–938.

Sternberg, R. J. (1986). A triangular theory of love. *Psychological Review, 93,* 119–135.

Sternberg, R. J. (1987). Liking versus loving: A comparative evaluation of theories. *Psychological Bulletin, 102,* 331–345.

Sternberg, R. J., & Beall, A. E. (1991). How can we know what love is? An epistemological analysis. In G. J. O. Fletcher & F. D. Fincham (Eds.), *Cognition in close relationships* (pp. 257–278). Hillsdale, NJ: Erlbaum.

Stets, J. E. (1991). Cohabiting and marital aggression: The role of social isolation. *Journal of Marriage and the Family, 53,* 669–680.

Stets, J. E., & Straus, M. A. (1989). The marriage license as a hitting license: A comparison of assaults in dating, cohabiting, and married couples. *Journal of Family Violence, 41,* 33–52.

Stets, J. E., & Straus, M. A. (1990). Gender differences in reporting marital violence and its medical and psychological consequences. In M. A. Straus & R. J. Gelles (Eds.), *Physical violence in American families: Risk factors and adaptations to violence in 8,145 families* (pp. 151–165). New Brunswick, NJ: Transaction Publishers.

Stewart, A. J., Sokol, M., Healy, J. M., Jr., & Chester, N. L. (1986). Longitudinal studies of psychological consequences of life changes in children and adults. *Journal of Personality and Social Psychology, 50,* 143–151.

Stewart, J. E., II. (1980). Defendant's attractiveness as a factor in the outcome of criminal trials: An observational study. *Journal of Applied Social Psychology, 10,* 348–361.

Stimpson, C. R. (1991, September 30). Big man on campus. *The Nation,* pp. 378–384.

Storms, M. D. (1973). Videotape and the attribution process: Reversing actors' and observers' points of view. *Journal of Personality and Social Psychology, 27,* 165–175.

Storms, M. D., & McCaul, K. (1976). Attribution processes and emotional exacerbation of dysfunctional behavior. In J. H. Harvey, W. J. Ickes, & R. F. Kidd (Eds.), *New directions in attribution research* (Vol. 1, pp. 143–169). Hillsdale, NJ: Erlbaum.

Storms, M. D., & Thomas, G. (1977). Reactions to physical closeness. *Journal of Personality and Social Psychology, 35,* 412–418.

Strack, F., Martin, L. L., & Stepper, S. (1988). Inhibiting and facilitating conditions of the human smile: A nonobtrusive test of the facial feedback hypothesis. *Journal of Personality and Social Psychology, 54,* 768–777.

Strauman, T. J. (1989). Self-discrepancies in clinical depression and social phobia: Cognitive structures that underlie emotional disorders? *Journal of Abnormal Psychology, 98,* 5–14.

Strauman, T. J. (1992). Self-guides, autobiographical memory, and anxiety and dysphoria: Toward a cognitive model of vulnerability to emotional distress. *Journal of Abnormal Psychology, 101,* 87–95.

Straus, M. A. (1979). Measuring intrafamily conflict and violence: The conflict tactics (CT) scales. *Journal of Marriage and the Family, 41,* 75–88.

Straus, M. A. (1990a). The Conflict Tactics Scale and its critics: An evaluation and new data on validity and reliability. In M. A. Straus & R. J. Gelles (Eds.), *Physical violence in American families: Risk factors and adaptations to violence in 8,145 families* (pp. 49–73). New Brunswick, NJ: Transaction Publishers.

Straus, M. A. (1990b, August). Presidential address delivered at the meeting of the Society for the Study of Social Problems, Durham, NH.

Straus, M. A., & Gelles, R. J. (1986). Societal change and change in family violence from 1975 to 1985 as revealed by two national surveys. *Journal of Marriage and the Family, 48,* 465–479.

Straus, M. A., Gelles, R. J., & Steinmetz, S. K. (1980). *Behind closed doors.* Garden City, NY: Anchor Books.

Streeter, L. A., Krauss, R. M., Geller, V., Olson, C., & Apple, W. (1977). Pitch changes during attempted deception. *Journal of Personality and Social Psychology, 35,* 345–350.

Strenta, A., & DeJong, W. (1981). The effect of a prosocial label on helping behavior. *Social Psychology Quarterly, 44,* 142–147.

Strentz, T., & Auerbach, S. M. (1988). Adjustment to the stress of simulated captivity: Effects of emotion-focused versus problem-focused preparation on hostages differing in locus of control. *Journal of Personality and Social Psychology, 55,* 652–660.

Striegel-Moore, R. H., Silberstein, L. R., & Rodin, J. (1986). Toward an understanding of risk factors for bulimia. *American Psychologist, 41,* 246–263.

Strodtbeck, F. L., & Hook, L. (1961). The social dimensions of a twelve-man jury table. *Sociometry, 24,* 397–415.

Strodtbeck, F. L., James, R., & Hawkins, C. (1957). Social status in jury deliberations. *American Sociological Review, 22,* 713–719.

Stroebe, M. S., & Stroebe, W. (1983). Who suffers more? Sex differences in health risks of the widowed. *Psychological Bulletin, 93,* 279–301.

Stroebe, W., & Diehl, M. (1991). You can't beat good experiments with correlational evidence: Mullen, Johnson, and Sala's meta-analytic misinterpretations. *Journal of Basic and Applied Social Psychology, 12,* 25–32.

Stroebe, W., Insko, C. A., Thompson, V. D., & Layton, B. D. (1971). Effects of physical attractiveness, attitude similarity, and sex on various aspects of interpersonal attraction. *Journal of Personality and Social Psychology, 18,* 79–91.

Stroebe, W., Lenkert, A., & Jonas, K. (1988). Familiarity may breed contempt: The impact of student exchange on national stereotypes and attitudes. In W. Stroebe, A. W. Kruglanski, D. Bar-Tal, & M. Hewstone (Eds.), *The social psychology of intergroup conflict* (pp. 167–187). New York: Springer-Verlag.

Stroebe, W., & Stroebe, M. S. (1986). Beyond marriage: The impact of partner loss on health. In R. Gilmour & S. Duck (Eds.), *The emerging field of personal relationships* (pp. 203–224). Hillsdale, NJ: Erlbaum.

Strube, M. J. (1988). The decision to leave an abusive relationship: Empirical evidence and theoretical issues. *Psychological Bulletin, 104,* 236–250.

Strube, M. J., & Barbour, L. S. (1983). The decision to leave an abusive relationship: Economic dependence and psychological commitment. *Journal of Marriage and the Family, 45,* 785–794.

Strube, M. J., & Boland, S. M. (1986). Postperformance attributions and task persistence among Type A and B individuals: A clarification. *Journal of Personality and Social Psychology, 50,* 413–420.

Strube, M. J., & Garcia, J. E. (1981). A meta-analytical investigation of Fiedler's contingency model of leadership effectiveness. *Psychological Bulletin, 90,* 307–321.

Struch, N., & Schwartz, S. H. (1989). Intergroup aggression: Its predictors and distinctness from in-group bias. *Journal of Personality and Social Psychology, 56,* 364–373.

Struckman-Johnson, C. J., Gilliland, R. G., Struckman-Johnson, D. L., & North, T. C. (1990). The effects of fear of AIDS and gender on responses to fear-arousing condom advertisements. *Journal of Applied Social Psychology, 20,* 1396–1410.

Sue, S., Smith, R. E., & Caldwell, C. (1973). Effects of inadmissible evidence on the decisions of simulated jurors: A moral dilemma. *Journal of Applied Social Psychology, 3,* 345–353.

Sugarman, D. B. (1986). Active versus passive euthanasia: An attributional analysis. *Journal of Applied Social Psychology, 16,* 60–76.

Sugarman, D. B., & Hotaling, G. T. (1989a). Dating violence: Prevalence, context, and risk markers. In M. A. Pirog-Good & J. E. Stets (Eds.), *Violence in dating relationships: Emerging social issues* (pp. 3–32). New York: Praeger.

Sugarman, D. B., & Hotaling, G. T. (1989b). Violent men in intimate relationships: An analysis of risk markers. *Journal of Applied Social Psychology, 19,* 1034–1048.

Sullivan, H. S. (1947). *Conceptions of modern psychiatry.* Washington, DC: William Allan White Psychiatric Foundation.

Suls, J., & Fletcher, B. (1985). The relative efficacy of avoidant and nonavoidant coping strategies: A meta-analysis. *Health Psychology, 4,* 249–288.

Suls, J., & Wan, C. K. (1989). The relation between Type A behavior and chronic emotional distress: A meta-analysis. *Journal of Personality and Social Psychology, 57,* 503–512.

Suls, J., & Wills, T. A. (Eds.). (1991). *Social comparison: Contemporary theory and research.* Hillsdale, NJ: Erlbaum.

Suls, J., Wan, C. K., & Sanders, G. S. (1988). False consensus and false uniqueness in estimating the prevalence of health-protective behaviors. *Journal of Applied Social Psychology, 18,* 66–79.

Summers, G., & Feldman, N. S. (1984). Blaming the victim versus blaming the perpetrator: An attributional analysis of spouse abuse. *Journal of Social and Clinical Psychology, 2,* 339–347.

Sundstrom, E. (1986). *Work places.* New York: Cambridge University Press.

Surgeon General's Scientific Advisory Committee on Television and Social Behavior. (1972). *Television and growing up: The impact of televised violence.* Washington, DC: U.S. Government Printing Office.

Surra, C. A. (1990). Research and theory on mate selection and premarital relationships in the 1980s. *Journal of Marriage and the Family, 52,* 844–865.

Surra, C. A., & Huston, T. L. (1987). Mate selection as a social transition. In D. Perlman & S. Duck (eds.), *Intimate relationships: Development, dynamics, and deterioration* (pp. 88–120). Newbury Park, CA: Sage.

Sussman, B. (1988). *What Americans really think.* New York: Pantheon Books.

Sutherland, E. H., & Cressey, D. R. (1974). *Principles of criminology* (9th ed.). New York: Lippincott.

Swann, W. B., Jr. (1984). Quest for accuracy in person perception: A matter of pragmatics. *Psychological Review, 91,* 457–477.

Swann, W. B., Jr. (1987). Identity negotiation: Where two roads meet. *Journal of Personality and Social Psychology, 53,* 1038–1051.

Swann, W. B., Jr., & Ely, R. J. (1984). A battle of wills: Self-verification versus behavioral confirmation. *Journal of Personality and Social Psychology, 46,* 1287–1302.

Swann, W. B., Jr., & Hill, C. A. (1982). When our identities are mistaken: Reaffirming self-conceptions through social interaction. *Journal of Personality and Social Psychology, 43,* 59–66.

Swann, W. B., Jr., Hixon, J. G., & De La Ronde, C. (1992a). Embracing the bitter "truth": Negative self-concepts and marital commitment. *Psychological Science, 3,* 118–121.

Swann, W. B., Jr., Stein-Seroussi, A., & Giesler, B. J. (1992b). Why people self-verify. *Journal of Personality and Social Psychology, 62,* 392–401.

Sweeney, P. D., Anderson, K., & Bailey, S. (1986). Attributional style in depression: A meta-analytic review. *Journal of Personality and Social Psychology, 50,* 974–991.

Swim, J., Borgida, E., Maruyama, G., & Myers, D. G. (1989). Joan McKay versus John McKay: Do gender stereotypes bias evaluations? *Psychological Bulletin, 105,* 409–429.

Tajfel, H. (Ed.). (1982). *Social identity and intergroup relations.* London: Cambridge University Press.

Tajfel, H., Billig, M. G., Bundy, R. P., & Flament, C. (1971). Social categorization and intergroup behavior. *European Journal of Social Psychology, 1,* 149–178.

Tanford, S., & Penrod, S. (1984). Social influence model: A formal integration of research on majority and minority influence processes. *Psychological Bulletin, 95,* 189–225.

Tanford, S., & Penrod, S. (1986). Jury deliberations: Discussion content and influence processes in jury decision-making. *Journal of Applied Social Psychology, 16,* 322–347.

Tangney, J. P. (1991). Moral affect: The good, the bad, and the ugly. *Journal of Personality and Social Psychology, 61,* 598–607.

Tangney, J. P., & Feshbach, S. (1988). Children's television viewing frequency: Individual differences and demographic correlates. *Personality and Social Psychology Bulletin, 14,* 145–158.

Tannen, D. (1990). *You just don't understand: Women and men in conversation.* New York: Morrow.

Tarde, G. (1890). *Les lois de l'imitation. Étude sociologique.* Paris: Félix Alcan.

Taub, S. (1992, May 4). Sexual abuse: Protecting underage witnesses. *National Law Journal, 28,* 32–33.

Tavris, C., & Wade, C. (1984). *The longest war: Sex differences in perspective.* San Diego: Harcourt Brace Jovanovich.

Taylor, D. M., & Moghaddam, F. M. (1987). *Theories of inter-group relations.* New York: Praeger.

Taylor, S. E. (1979). Hospital patient behavior: Reactance, help-lessness, or control? *Journal of Social Issues, 35,* 156–184.

Taylor, S. E. (1981). A categorization approach to stereotyping. In D. Hamilton (Ed.), *Cognitive processes in stereotyping and intergroup behavior.* Hillsdale, NJ: Erlbaum.

Taylor, S. E. (1989). *Positive illusions: Creative self-deceptions and the healthy mind.* New York: Basic Books.

Taylor, S. E. (1990). Health psychology: The science and the field. *American Psychologist, 45,* 40–50.

Taylor, S. E. (1991). Asymmetrical effects of positive and nega-tive events: The mobilization-minimization hypothesis. *Psy-chological Bulletin, 110,* 67–85.

Taylor, S. E., & Brown, J. D. (1988). Illusion and well-being: A social psychological perspective on mental health. *Psychologi-cal Bulletin, 103,* 193–210.

Taylor, S. E., Falke, R. L., Shoptaw, S. J., & Lichtman, R. R. (1986). Social support, support groups, and the cancer pa-tient. *Journal of Consulting and Clinical Psychology, 54,* 608–615.

Taylor, S. E., & Fiske, S. T. (1975). Point of view and percep-tions of causality. *Journal of Personality and Social Psychology, 32,* 439–445.

Taylor, S. E., Hegelson, V. S., Reed, G. M., Skokan, L. A. (1991). Self-generated feelings of control and adjustment to physical illness. *Journal of Social Issues, 47,* 91–109.

Taylor, S. E., Lichtman, R. R., & Wood, J. V. (1984). Attribu-tions, beliefs about control, and adjustment to breast cancer. *Journal of Personality and Social Psychology, 46,* 489–502.

Taylor, S. E., & Lobel, M. (1989). Social comparison activity under threat: Downward evaluation and upward contacts. *Psychological Review, 96,* 569–575.

Tedeschi, J. T. (Ed.). (1981). *Impression management theory and social psychological research.* New York: Academic Press.

Tedeschi, J. T., Schlenker, B. R., & Bonoma, T. V. (1971). Cognitive dissonance: Private ratiocination or public spec-tacle? *American Psychologist, 26,* 685–695.

Teger, A. (1980). *Too much invested to quit.* New York: Pergamon Press.

Tellegen, A., Lykken, D. T., Bouchard, T. J., Jr., Wilcox, K. J., Segal, N. L., & Rich S. (1988). Personality similarity in twins reared apart and together. *Journal of Personality and Social Psychology, 54,* 1031–1039.

Tennen, H., & Affleck, G. (1987). The costs and benefits of optimistic explanations and dispositional optimism. *Journal of Personality, 55,* 377–393.

Tennen, H., & Affleck, G. (1990). Blaming others for threaten-ing events. *Psychological Bulletin, 108,* 209–232.

Tennen, H., & Affleck, G. (1991). Paradox-based treatments. In C. R. Snyder & D. R. Forsyth (Eds.), *Handbook of social and clinical psychology: The health perspective* (pp. 624–643). New York: Pergamon Press.

Tennen, H., Suls, J., & Affleck, G. (Eds.). (1991). Personality and daily experience [Special issue]. *Journal of Personality, 59* (3).

Tennov, D. (1979). *Love and Limerence: The experience of being in love.* New York: Stein & Day.

Terkel, S. (1974). *Working.* New York: Pantheon Books.

Terre, L., Drabman, R. S., & Speer, P. (1991). Health-relevant behaviors in media. *Journal of Applied Social Psychology, 21,* 1303–1319.

Tesser, A. (1978). Self-generated attitude change. In L. Berko-witz (Ed.), *Advances in experimental social psychology* (Vol. 11, pp. 288–338). New York: Academic Press.

Tesser, A. (1980). Self-esteem maintenance in family dynamics. *Journal of Personality and Social Psychology, 39,* 77–91.

Tesser, A. (1988). Toward a self-evaluation maintenance model of social behavior. In L. Berkowitz (Ed.), *Advances in exper-imental social psychology* (Vol. 21, pp. 181–227). New York: Academic Press.

Tesser, A., & Collins, J. E. (1988). Emotion in social reflection and comparison situations: Intuitive, systematic, and explor-atory approaches. *Journal of Personality and Social Psychology, 55,* 695–709.

Tesser, A., Pilkington, C. J., & McIntosh, W. D. (1989). Self-evaluation maintenance and the mediational role of emotion: The perception of friends and strangers. *Journal of Personality and Social Psychology, 57,* 442–456.

Tesser, A., & Smith, J. (1980). Some effects of task relevance and friendship on helping: You don't always help the one you like. *Journal of Experimental Social Psychology, 16,* 582–590.

Tetlock, P. E. (1979). Identifying victims of groupthink from public statements of decision makers. *Journal of Personality and Social Psychology, 37,* 1314–1324.

Tetlock, P. E. (1981). Pre- to post-election shifts in presidential rhetoric: Impression management or cognitive adjustment? *Journal of Personality and Social Psychology, 41,* 207–212.

Tetlock, P. E. (1983). Accountability and complexity of thought. *Journal of Personality and Social Psychology, 45,* 74–83.

Tetlock, P. E., McGuire, C. B., & Mitchell, G. (1991). Psycholog-ical perspectives on nuclear deterrence. *Annual Review of Psychology, 42,* 239–276.

Thibaut, J. W., & Kelley, H. H. (1959). *The social psychology of groups.* New York: Wiley.

Thibaut, J., & Walker, L. (1975). *Procedural justice: A psychologi-cal analysis.* Hillsdale, NJ: Erlbaum.

Thibaut, J., & Walker, L. (1978). A theory of procedure. *Califor-nia Law Review, 66,* 541–566.

Thibodeau, R., & Aronson, E. (1992). Taking a closer look: Reasserting the role of the self-concept in dissonance theory. *Personality and Social Psychology Bulletin.*

Thoits, P. A. (1983). Dimensions of life events that influence psychological distress: An evaluation and synthesis of the literature. In H. B. Kaplan (Ed.), *Psychosocial stress: Trends in theory and research* (pp. 33–103). New York: Academic Press.

Thomas, M. H. (1982). Physiological arousal, exposure to a relatively lengthy aggressive film, and aggressive behavior. *Journal of Research in Personality, 16*, 72–81.

Thompson, L. (1990a). An examination of naive and experienced negotiators. *Journal of Personality and Social Psychology, 59*, 82–90.

Thompson, L. (1990b). Negotiation behavior and outcomes: Empirical evidence and theoretical issues. *Psychological Bulletin, 108*, 515–532.

Thompson, S., & Janigian, A. S. (1988). Life schemes: A framework for understanding the search for meaning. *Journal of Social and Clinical Psychology, 7*, 260–280.

Thompson, W. C., Cowan, C. L., & Rosenhan, D. L. (1980). Focus of attention mediates the impact of negative affect on altruism. *Journal of Personality and Social Psychology, 38*, 291–300.

Thompson, W. C., Fong, G. T., & Rosenhan, D. L. (1981). Inadmissible evidence and juror verdicts. *Journal of Personality and Social Psychology, 40*, 453–463.

Thompson, W. M., Dabbs, J. M., Jr., & Frady, R. L. (1990). Changes in saliva testosterone levels during a 90-day shock incarceration program. *Criminal Justice and Behavior, 17*, 246–252.

Thornton, B. (1992). Repression and its mediating influence on the defensive attribution of reponsibility. *Journal of Research in Personality, 26*, 44–57.

Thornton, B., Hogate, L., Moirs, K., Pinette, M., & Presby, W. (1986). Physiological evidence for an arousal-based motivational bias in the defensive attribution of responsibility. *Journal of Experimental Social Psychology, 22*, 148–162.

Thornton, G. C., III, & Byham, W. C. (1982). *Assessment centers and managerial performance.* New York: Academic Press.

Thurstone, L. L. (1928). Attitudes can be measured. *American Journal of Sociology, 33*, 529–544.

Tice, D. M. (1991). Esteem protection or enhancement? Self-handicapping motives and attributions differ by trait self-esteem. *Journal of Personality and Social Psychology, 60*, 711–725.

Tiggemann, M., & Rothblum, E. D. (1988). Gender differences in social consequences of perceived overweight in the United States and Australia. *Sex Roles, 18*, 75–86.

Tilker, H. A. (1970). Socially responsible behavior as a function of observer responsibility and victim feedback. *Journal of Personality and Social Psychology, 14*, 95–100.

Tittle, C. K. (1986). Gender research and education. *American Psychologist, 10*, 1161–1168.

Tolstedt, B. E., & Stokes, J. P. (1984). Self-disclosure, intimacy, and the depenetration process. *Journal of Personality and Social Psychology, 46*, 84–90.

Top, T. J. (1991). Sex bias in the evaluation of performance in the scientific, artistic, and literary professions: A review. *Sex Roles, 24*, 73–106.

Tosi, H. L., & Einbender, S. W. (1985). The effects of the type and amount of information in sex discrimination research: A meta-analysis. *Academy of Management Journal, 28*, 712–723.

Toufexis, A. (1991, October 28). When can memories be trusted? *Time*, pp. 86–88.

Tourangeau, R., Rasinksi, K. A., & D'Andrade, R. (1991). Attitude structure and belief accessibility. *Journal of Experimental Social Psychology, 27*, 48–75.

Trafimow, D., Triandis, H. C., & Goto, S. G. (1991). Some tests of the distinction between the private and collective self. *Journal of Personality and Social Psychology, 60*, 649–655.

Traub, J. (1988, July 24). Into the mouths of babes. *New York Times Magazine*, pp. 18–20, 37–38, 52–53.

Travis, C. B., & Yaeger, C. P. (1991). Sexual selection, parental investment, and sexism. *Journal of Social Issues, 47*, 117–129.

Triandis, H. C. (1989). The self and social behavior in differing cultural contexts. *Psychological Review, 96*, 506–520.

Triandis, H. C., Bontempo, R., Villareal, M. J., Asai, M., & Lucca, N. (1988). Individualism and collectivism: Cross-cultural perspectives on self-ingroup relationships. *Journal of Personality and Social Psychology, 54*, 323–338.

Tripathi, R. C., & Srivastava, R. (1981). Relative deprivation and intergroup attitudes. *European Journal of Social Psychology, 11*, 313–318.

Triplett, N. (1897–1898). The dynamogenic factors in pacemaking and competition. *American Journal of Psychology, 9*, 507–533.

Trivers, R. L. (1971). The evolution of reciprocal altruism. *Quarterly Review of Biology, 46*, 35–57.

Trope, Y. (1986). Identification and inferential processes in dispositional attribution. *Psychological Review, 93*, 239–257.

Trope, Y., Bassock, M., & Alon, E. (1984). The questions lay interviewers ask. *Journal of Personality, 52*, 90–106.

Trope, Y., Cohen, O., & Maoz, Y. (1988). The perceptual and inferential effects of situational inducements on dispositional attribution. *Journal of Personality and Social Psychology, 55*, 165–177.

Trost, M. R., Maass, A., & Kenrick, D. T. (1992). Minority influence: Personal relevance biases cognitive processes and reverses private acceptance. *Journal of Experimental Social Psychology, 28*, 234–254.

Tucker, M. B., & Mitchell-Kernan, C. (1990). New trends in black American interracial marriage: The social structure context. *Journal of Marriage and the Family, 52*, 209–218.

Turner, J. C. (1981). The experimental social psychology of intergroup behavior. In J. C. Turner & H. Giles (Eds.), *Intergroup behavior* (pp. 66–101). Oxford, England: Basil Blackwell.

Turner, J. C. (1987). *Rediscovering the social group: A self-categorization theory.* Oxford, England: Basil Blackwell.

Turner, J. C., & Oakes, P. J. (1989). Self-categorization theory and social influence. In P. B. Paulus (Ed.), *Psychology of group influence* (2nd ed., pp. 233–275). Hillsdale, NJ: Erlbaum.

Tversky, A. & Kahneman, D. (1974). Judgment under certainty: Heuristics and biases. *Science, 185,* 1124–1131.

Tversky, A., & Kahneman, D. (1973). Availability: A heuristic for judging frequency and probability. *Cognitive Psychology, 5,* 207–232.

Tversky, B., & Tuchin, M. (1989). A reconciliation of the evidence on eyewitness testimony: Comments on McCloskey and Zaragoza. *Journal of Experimental Psychology, 118,* 86–91.

Tyler, T. R., Rasinski, K. A., & Spodick, N. (1985). Influences of voice on satisfaction with leaders: Exploring the meaning of process control. *Journal of Personality and Social Psychology, 48,* 72–81.

Unger, R. K. (1979). *Female and male: Psychological perspectives.* New York: Harper & Row.

United Nations. (1989). Special topic: International migration studies. In *United Nations demographic year book.* New York: Author.

U.S. Department of Health, Education, and Welfare. (1974, May 30). Protection of human subjects. *Federal Register, 39* (105): 18914–20 (45CFR, part 46).

Utne, M. K., Hatfield, E., Traupmann, J., & Greenberger, D. (1984). Equity, marital satisfaction, and stability. *Journal of Social and Personal Relations, 1,* 323–332.

Vaillant, G. E. (1977). *Adaptation to life.* Boston: Little, Brown.

Vallacher, R. R., & Wegner, D. M. (1985). *A theory of action identification.* Hillsdale, NJ: Erlbaum.

Vallacher, R. R., & Wegner, D. M. (1989). Levels of personal agency: Individual variation in action identification. *Journal of Personality and Social Psychology, 57,* 660–671.

Vallone, R. P., Griffin, D. W., Lin, S., & Ross, L. (1990). Overconfident prediction of future actions and outcomes by self and others. *Journal of Personality and Social Psychology, 58,* 582–592.

Van Yperen, N. W., & Buunk, B. P. (1990). A longitudinal study of equity and satisfaction in intimate relationships. *European Journal of Social Psychology, 20,* 287–309.

Vaux, A. (1988a). Social and emotional loneliness: The role of social and personal characteristics. *Personality and Social Psychology Bulletin, 14,* 722–734.

Vaux, A. (1988b). Social and personal factors in loneliness. *Journal of Social and Clinical Psychology, 6,* 462–471.

Vecchio, R. P. (1983). Assessing the validity of Fiedler's contingency model of leadership effectiveness: A closer look at Strube and Garcia. *Psychological Bulletin, 93,* 404–408.

Vemer, E., Coleman, M., Ganong, L. H., & Cooper, H. (1989). Marital satisfaction in remarriage: A meta-analysis. *Journal of Marriage and the Family, 51,* 713–725.

Verbrugge, L. M. (1987). Role responsibilities, role burdens, and physical health. In F. Crosby (Ed.), *Spouse, parent, worker: On gender and multiple roles* (pp. 154–166). New Haven, CT: Yale University Press.

Veroff, J., Douvan, E., & Kukla, R. A. (1981). *The inner American: A self-portrait from 1957 to 1976.* New York: Basic Books.

Vinokur, A., & Burnstein, E. (1974). Effects of partially shared persuasive arguments on group-induced shifts: A group-problem-solving approach. *Journal of Personality and Social Psychology, 29,* 305–315.

Vogel, D. A., Lake, M. A., Evans, S., & Karraker, K. H. (1991). Children's and adults' sex-stereotyped perceptions of infants. *Sex Roles, 24,* 605–616.

Von Lang, J., & Sibyll, C. (Eds.). (1983). *Eichmann interrogated* (R. Manheim, Trans.). New York: Farrar, Straus & Giroux.

Vroom, V. H. (1964). *Work and motivation.* New York: Wiley.

Vroom, V. H., & Jago, A. G. (1988). *Managing participation in organizations.* Engelwood Cliffs, NJ: Prentice-Hall.

Wagenaar, W. A. (1988). *Paradoxes of gambling behavior.* Hillsdale, NJ: Erlbaum.

Wagner, J. (1986). *The search for signs of intelligent life in the universe.* New York: Harper & Row.

Wagner, U., Wicklund, R. A., & Shaigan, S. (1990). Open devaluation and rejection of a fellow student: The impact of threat to self-definition. *Basic and Applied Social Psychology, 11,* 61–76.

Wald, M., Ayres, R., Hess, D. W., Schantz, M., & Whitebread, C. H. (1967). Interrogations in New Haven: The impact of Miranda. *Yale Law Journal, 76,* 1519–1648.

Waldman, D. A., & Avolio, B. J. (1991). Race effects in performance evaluations: Controlling for ability, education, and experience. *Journal of Applied Psychology, 76,* 897–901.

Walker, L. E. A. (1989). Psychology and violence against women. *American Psychologist, 44,* 695–702.

Walker, L., LaTour, S., Lind, E. A., & Thibaut, J. (1974). Reactions of participants and observers to modes of adjudication. *Journal of Applied Social Psychology, 4,* 295–310.

Wallach, M. A., & Wallach, L. (1983). *Psychology's sanction for selfishness: The error of egoism in theory and therapy.* San Francisco: Freeman.

Waller, W. W., & Hill, R. (1951). *The family, a dynamic interpretation.* New York: Dryden Press.

Wallston, B. S., & Wallston, K. A. (1984). Social psychological models of health and behavior: An examination and integration. In A. Baum, S. E. Taylor, & J. E. Singer (Eds.), *Handbook of psychology and health: Vol. 4. Social psychological aspects of health* (pp. 23–53). Hillsdale, NJ: Erlbaum.

Walster, E. (1965). The effect of self-esteem on romantic liking. *Journal of Experimental Social Psychology, 1,* 184–197.

Walster, E. (1966). Assignment of responsibility for important events. *Journal of Personality and Social Psychology, 3,* 73–79.

Walster, E. (1971). Passionate love. In B. Murstein (Ed.), *Theories of attraction and love* (pp. 85–99). New York: Springer.

Walster, E., & Festinger, L. (1962). The effectiveness of "overheard" persuasive communications. *Journal of Abnormal and Social Psychology, 65,* 395–402.

Walster, E., Aronson, V., Abrahams, D., & Rottman, L. (1966). The importance of physical attractiveness in dating behavior. *Journal of Personality and Social Psychology, 4,* 508–516.

Walster, E., Walster, G. W., & Berscheid, E. (1978a). *Equity: Theory and research*. Boston: Allyn & Bacon.

Walster, E., Walster, G. W., & Traupmann, J. (1978b). Equity and premarital sex. *Journal of Personality, 36*, 82–92.

Walster, E., Walster, G. W., Piliavin, J., & Schmidt, L. (1973). "Playing hard-to-get": Understanding an elusive phenomenon. *Journal of Personality and Social Psychology, 26*, 113–121.

Ward, C. H., & Eisler, R. M. (1987). Type A behavior, achievement striving, and a dysfunctional self-evaluation system. *Journal of Personality and Social Psychology, 53*, 318–326.

Ward, S. E., Leventhal, H., & Love, R. (1988). Repression revisited: Tactics used in coping with a severe health threat. *Personality and Social Psychology Bulletin, 14*, 735–746.

Warren, B. L. (1966). A multiple variable approach to the assortive mating phenomenon. *Eugenics Quarterly, 13*, 285–298.

Watkins, J. D. (1988, June 24). *Report of the Presidential Commission on the Human Immunodeficiency Virus Epidemic*. Washington, DC: U.S. Government Printing Office.

Watkins, M. J., & Peynircioglu, Z. F. (1984). Determining perceived meaning during impression formation: Another look at the meaning change hypothesis. *Journal of Personality and Social Psychology, 46*, 1005–1016.

Watson, D. (1982). The actor and the observer: How are their perceptions of causality divergent? *Psychological Bulletin, 92*, 682–700.

Watson, D., & Clark, L. A. (1984). Negative affectivity: The disposition to experience aversive emotional states. *Psychological Bulletin, 96*, 465–490.

Webb, E. J., Campbell, D. T., Schwartz, R. D., Sechrest, L., & Grove, J. B. (1981). *Nonreactive measures in the social sciences* (2nd ed.). Boston: Houghton Mifflin.

Weber, R., & Crocker, J. C. (1983). Cognitive processes in the revision of stereotypic beliefs. *Journal of Personality and Social Psychology, 45*, 961–967.

Wedell, D. H., Parducci, A., & Geiselman, R. E. (1987). A formal analysis of ratings of physical attractiveness: Successive contrast and simultaneous association. *Journal of Experimental Social Psychology, 23*, 230–249.

Wegner, D. M. (1989). *White bears and other unwanted thoughts: Suppression, obsession, and the psychology of mental control*. New York: Viking.

Wegner, D. M., & Schaefer, D. (1978). The concentration of responsibility: An objective self-awareness analysis of group size effects in helping situations. *Journal of Personality and Social Psychology, 36*, 147–155.

Wegner, D. M., Vallacher, R. R., Kiersted, G. W., & Dizadji, D. (1986). Action identification in the emergence of social behavior. *Social Cognition, 4*, 18–38.

Weick, K. E. (1985). Systematic observational methods. In G. Lindzey & E. Aronson (Eds.), *Handbook of social psychology* (Vol. 1, 3rd ed., pp. 567–634). New York: Random House.

Weigel, R. H., & Howes, P. W. (1985). Conceptions of racial prejudice: Symbolic racism reconsidered. *Journal of Social Issues, 41*, 117–138.

Weiner, B. (1985). "Spontaneous" causal thinking. *Psychological Bulletin, 97*, 74–84.

Weiner, B. (1986). *An attributional theory of emotion and motivation*. New York: Springer-Verlag.

Weinstein, N. D. (1980). Unrealistic optimism about future life events. *Journal of Personality and Social Psychology, 39*, 806–820.

Weinstein, N. D. (1989). Effects of personal experience on self-protective behavior. *Psychological Bulletin, 105*, 31–50.

Weiss, H. M., & Knight, P. A. (1980). The utility of humility: Self-esteem, information search, and problem-solving efficiency. *Organizational Behavior and Human Performance, 25*, 216–223.

Weiss, R. S. (1969). The fund of sociability. *Transaction, 7*, 36–43.

Weiss, R. S. (1973). *Loneliness*. Cambridge, MA: MIT Press.

Weiten, W. (1988). Pressure as a form of stress and its relationship to psychological symptomatology. *Journal of Social and Clinical Psychology, 6*, 127–139.

Weldon, E., & Gargano, G. M. (1988). Cognitive loading: The effects of accountability and shared responsibility on cognitive effort. *Personality and Social Psychology Bulletin, 14*, 159–171.

Wells, G. L. (1986). Expert psychological testimony: Empirical and conceptual analyses of effects. *Law and Human Behavior, 10*, 83–95.

Wells, G. L., Lindsay, R. C. L., & Ferguson, T. J. (1979). Accuracy, confidence, and juror perceptions in eyewitness identification. *Journal of Applied Psychology, 64*, 440–448.

Wells, G. L., & Loftus, E. F. (Eds.). (1984). *Eyewitness testimony: Psychological perspectives*. New York: Cambridge University Press.

Wells, G. L., & Murray, D. M. (1984). Eyewitness confidence. In G. Wells & E. Loftus (Eds.), *Eyewitness testimony: Psychological perspectives* (pp. 155–170). New York: Cambridge University Press.

Wells, G. L., & Petty, R. E. (1980). The effects of overt head-movements on persuasion: Compatibility and incompatibility of responses. *Basic and Applied Social Psychology, 1*, 219–230.

Wells, W. D. (1975). Psychographics: A critical review. *Journal of Marketing Research, 12*, 196–213.

Wells, W., Burnett, J., & Moriarty, S. (1989). *Advertising: Principles and practice*. Englewood Cliffs, NJ: Prentice-Hall.

Welton, G. L., & Pruitt, D. G. (1987). The mediation process: The effects of mediator bias and disputed power. *Personality and Social Psychology Bulletin, 13*, 123–133.

We're sorry: A case of mistaken identity. (1982, October 4). *Time*, p. 45.

Werner, P. D., & LaRussa, G. W. (1985). Persistence and change in sex-role stereotypes. *Sex Roles, 12*, 1089–1100.

West, C., & Zimmerman, D. H. (1983). Small insults: A study of interruptions in cross-sex conversations between unacquainted persons. In B. Thorne, C. Dramarge, & N. Henley (Eds.), *Language, gender and society* (pp. 102–117). Rowley, MA: Newbury House.

West, S. G., Gunn, S. P., & Chernicky, P. (1975). Ubiquitous Watergate: An attributional analysis. *Journal of Personality and Social Psychology, 32,* 55–65.

Wetzel, C. G., & Insko, C. A. (1982). The similarity-attraction relationship: Is there an ideal one? *Journal of Experimental Social Psychology, 18,* 253–276.

Weyant, J. M. (1978). Effects of mood states, costs, and benefits on helping. *Journal of Personality and Social Psychology, 36,* 1169–1176.

Wheeler, L., Koestner, R., & Driver, R. E. (1982). Related attributes in the choice of comparison others. *Journal of Experimental Social Psychology, 18,* 489–500.

Wheeler, L., Reis, H. T., & Bond, M. H. (1989). Collectivism-individualism in everyday social life: The middle kingdom and the melting pot. *Journal of Personality and Social Psychology, 57,* 79–86.

Wheeler, L., Reis, H., & Nezlek, J. (1983). Loneliness, social interaction, and sex roles. *Journal of Personality and Social Psychology, 45,* 943–953.

White, G. L. (1980). Physical attractiveness and courtship progress. *Journal of Personality and Social Psychology, 39,* 660–668.

White, G. L. (1981a). A model of romantic jealousy. *Motivation and Emotion, 5,* 295–310.

White, G. L. (1981b). Some correlates of romantic jealousy. *Journal of Personality, 49,* 129–147.

White, G. L., & Kight, T. D. (1984). Misattribution of arousal and attraction: Effects of salience of explanation of arousal. *Journal of Experimental Social Psychology, 20,* 55–64.

White, G. L., & Mullen, P. E. (1989). *Jealousy: Theory, research, and clinical strategies.* New York: Guilford.

White, G. L., Fishbein, S., & Rutstein, J. (1981). Passionate love: The misattribution of arousal. *Journal of Personality and Social Psychology, 41,* 56–62.

White, J. E. (1991, September 16). The pain of being black. *Time,* pp. 24–27.

White, J. W. (1983). Sex and gender issues in aggression research. In R. G. Geen & E. I. Donnerstein (Eds.), *Aggression: Theoretical and empirical reviews: Vol. 2. Issues in research* (pp. 1–26). New York: Academic Press.

White, P. A., & Younger, D. P. (1988). Differences in the ascription of transient internal states to self and other. *Journal of Experimental Social Psychology, 24,* 292–309.

White, W. S. (1979). Police trickery in inducing confessions. *University of Pennsylvania Law Review, 127,* 581–629.

Whitley, B. E., Jr., & Frieze, I. H. (1985). Children's causal attributions for success and failure in achievement settings. A meta-analysis. *Journal of Educational Psychology, 77,* 608–616.

Whitley, B. E., Jr., & Hern, A. K. (1991). Perceptions of vulnerability to pregnancy and the use of effective contraception. *Personality and Social Psychology Bulletin, 17,* 104–110.

Whittaker, J. O., & Meade, R. D. (1967). Social pressure in the modification and distortion of judgment: A cross-cultural study. *International Journal of Psychology, 2,* 109–113.

Wicker, A. W. (1969). Attitudes versus actions: The relationship between verbal and overt behavioral responses to attitude objects. *Journal of Social Issues, 25*(4), 41–78.

Wicklund, R. A. (1975). Objective self-awareness. In L. Berkowitz (Ed.), *Advances in experimental social psychology* (Vol. 8, pp. 233–275). New York: Academic Press.

Wicklund, R. A., & Brehm, J. W. (1976). *Perspectives on cognitive dissonance.* Hillsdale, NJ: Erlbaum.

Wicklund, R. A., & Frey, D. (1980). Self-awareness theory: When the self makes a difference. In D. M. Wegner & R. R. Vallacher (Eds.), *The self in social psychology* (pp. 31–54). New York: Oxford University Press.

Wicklund, R. A., & Gollwitzer, P. M. (1987). The fallacy of the private-public self-focus distinction. *Journal of Personality, 55,* 491–523.

Widmeyer, W. N., & Loy, J. W. (1988). When you're hot, you're hot! Warm-cold effects in first impressions of persons and teaching effectiveness. *Journal of Educational Psychology, 80,* 118–121.

Widom, C. S. (1989). Does violence beget violence? A critical examination of the literature. *Psychological Bulletin, 106,* 3–28.

Widom, C. S. (1991). A tail on an untold tale: Response to "Biological and genetic contributions to violence—Widom's untold tale." *Psychological Bulletin, 109,* 130–132.

Wiedenfeld, S. A., O'Leary, A., Bandura, A., Brown, S., Levine, S., & Raska, K. (1990). Impact of perceived self-efficacy in coping with stressors on components of the immune system. *Journal of Personality and Social Psychology, 59,* 1082–1094.

Wiener, R. L., Weiner, A. T. F., & Grisso, T. (1989). Empathy and biased assimilation of testimonies in cases of alleged rape. *Law and Human Behavior, 13,* 343–355.

Wiesner, W. H., & Cronshaw, S. F. (1988). A meta-analytic investigation of the impact of interview format and degree of structure on the validity of the employment interview. *Journal of Occupational Psychology, 61,* 275–290.

Wilder, D. A. (1977). Perception of groups, size of opposition, and social influence. *Journal of Experimental Social Psychology, 13,* 253–268.

Wilder, D. A. (1978). Reduction of intergroup discrimination through individuation of the outgroup. *Journal of Personality and Social Psychology, 36,* 1361–1374.

Wilder, D. A. (1986). Social categorization: Implications for creation and reduction of intergroup bias. In L. Berkowitz (Ed.), *Advances in experimental social psychology* (Vol. 19, pp. 291–355). New York: Academic Press.

Wilder, D. A., & Shapiro, P. (1991). Facilitation of outgroup stereotypes by enhanced ingroup identity. *Journal of Experimental Social Psychology, 27,* 431–452.

Wiley, M. G., Crittenden, K. S., & Birg, L. D. (1979). Why a rejection? Causal attribution of a career achievement event. *Social Psychology Quarterly, 42,* 214–222.

Williams v. Florida, 399 U.S. 78 (1970).

Williams, C. L., & Berry, J. W. (1991). Primary prevention of acculturative stress among refugees: Application of psychological theory and practice. *American Psychologist, 46,* 632–641.

Williams, J. E., & Best, D. L. (1982). *Measuring sex stereotypes: A thirty nation study.* Beverly Hills, CA: Sage.

Williams, K., Harkins, S., & Latané, B. (1981). Identifiability as a deterrent to social loafing: Two cheering experiments. *Journal of Personality and Social Psychology, 40,* 303–311.

Williams, K. D., & Karau, S. J. (1991). Social loafing and social compensation: The effects of expectations of co-worker performance. *Journal of Personality and Social Psychology, 61,* 570–581.

Williams, K. D., Loftus, E. F., & Deffenbacher, K. A. (1992). Eyewitness evidence and testimony. In D. K. Kagehiro & W. S. Laufer (Eds.), *Handbook of psychology and law* (pp. 139–166). New York: Springer-Verlag.

Williams, R. B., Haney, T. L., Lee, K. L., Kong, Y., Blumenthal, J. A., & Whalen, R. E. (1980). Type A behavior, hostility, and coronary atherosclerosis. *Psychosomatic Medicine, 42,* 539–549.

Williamson, G. M., & Clark, M. S. (1989). Providing help and desired relationship type as determinants of changes in moods and self-evaluations. *Journal of Personality and Social Psychology, 56,* 722–734.

Williamson, G. M., & Clark, M. S. (1992). Impact of desired relationship type on affective reactions to choosing and being required to help. *Personality and Social Psychology Bulletin, 18,* 10–180.

Wills, T. A. (1981). Downward comparison principles in social psychology. *Psychological Bulletin, 90,* 245–271.

Wills, T. A. (1987). Help-seeking as a coping mechanism. In C. R. Snyder & C. E. Ford (Eds.), *Coping with negative life events: Clinical and social psychological perspectives* (pp. 19–50). New York: Plenum.

Wills, T. A. (1991). Social support and interpersonal relationships. In M. S. Clark (Ed.), *Review of Personality and Social Psychology, Vol. 12. Prosocial behavior* (pp. 265–289). Newbury Park, CA: Sage.

Wills, T. A. (Ed.). (1990). [Special issue]. Social support in social and clinical psychology *Journal of social and clinical psychology, 9.*

Wills, T. A., & DePaulo, B. M. (1991). Interpersonal analysis of the help-seeking process. In C. R. Snyder & D. R. Forsyth (Eds.), *Handbook of social and clinical psychology: The health perspective* (pp. 350–375). New York: Pergamon Press.

Wills, T. A., Weiss, R. L., & Patterson, G. R. (1974). A behavioral analysis of the determinants of marital satisfaction. *Journal of Consulting and Clinical Psychology, 42,* 802–811.

Wilson, D. W. (1981). Is helping a laughing matter? *Psychology, 18,* 6–9.

Wilson, E. O. (1975). *Sociobiology: The new synthesis.* Cambridge, MA: Harvard University Press.

Wilson, J. D., & Herrnstein, R. J. (1985). *Crime and human nature.* New York: Simon & Schuster.

Wilson, J. P., & Petruska, R. (1984). Motivation, model attributes, and prosocial behavior. *Journal of Personality and Social Psychology, 46,* 458–468.

Wilson, T. D. (1985). Strangers to ourselves: The origins and accuracy of beliefs about one's own mental states. In J. H. Harvey & G. Weary (Eds.), *Attribution: Basic issues and applications* (pp. 9–36). New York: Academic Press.

Wilson, T. D., & Schooler, J. W. (1991). Thinking too much: Introspection can reduce the quality of preferences and decisions. *Journal of Personality and Social Psychology, 60,* 181–192.

Winter, D. G. (1987). Leader appeal, leader performance, and the motive profiles of leaders and followers: A study of American presidents and elections. *Journal of Personality and Social Psychology, 52,* 41–46.

Winton, W. M. (1986). The role of facial response in self-reports of emotion: A critique of Laird. *Journal of Personality and Social Psychology, 50,* 808–812.

Wishman, S. (1986). *Anatomy of a jury: The system on trial.* New York: Times Books.

Wissler, R. L., & Saks, M. J. (1985). On the inefficacy of limiting instructions: When jurors use prior conviction evidence to decide on guilt. *Law and Human Behavior, 9,* 37–48.

Witteman, P. A. (1990, April 30). Vietnam: 15 years later. *Time,* pp. 19–21.

Wittenberg,, M. T., & Reis, H. T. (1986). Loneliness, social skills, and social perception. *Personality and Social Psychology Bulletin, 12,* 121–130.

Wolf, N. (1991). *The beauty myth.* New York: Morrow.

Wolf, S. (1985). Manifest and latent influence of majorities and minorities. *Journal of Personality and Social Psychology, 48,* 899–908.

Wolf, S., & Montgomery, D. A. (1977). Effects of inadmissible evidence and level of judicial admonishment to disregard on the judgments of mock jurors. *Journal of Applied Social Psychology, 7,* 205–219.

Wolfe, D. A. (1985). Child-abusive parents: An empirical review and analysis. *Psychological Bulletin, 97,* 462–482.

Wolosin, R. J., Sherman, S. J., & Cann, A. (1975). Predictions of own and other's conformity. *Journal of Personality, 43,* 357–378.

Wood, G. (1978). The knew-it-all-along effect. *Journal of Experimental Psychology: Human Perception and Performance, 4,* 345–353.

Wood, J. (1989). Theory and research concerning social comparisons of personal attributes. *Psychological Bulletin, 106,* 231–248.

Wood, J. V., Saltzberg, J. A., Neale, J. M., Stone, A. A., & Rachmiel, T. B. (1990). Self-focused attention, coping responses, and distressed mood in everyday life. *Journal of Personality and Social Psychology, 58,* 1027–1036.

Wood, J. V., Taylor, S. E., & Lichtman, R. R. (1985). Social comparison in adjustment to breast cancer. *Journal of Personality and Social Psychology, 49,* 1169–1183.

Wood, W. (1987). Meta-analytic review of sex differences in group performance. *Psychological Bulletin, 102,* 53–71.

Wood, W., Kallgren, C. A., & Preisler, R. M. (1985a). Access to attitude-relevant information in memory as a determinant of persuasion: The role of message attributes. *Journal of Experimental Social Psychology, 21,* 73–85.

Wood, W., & Karten, S. J. (1986). Sex differences in interaction style as product of perceived sex differences in competence. *Journal of Personality and Social Psychology, 50,* 341–347.

Wood, W., Polek, D., & Aiken, C. (1985b). Sex differences in group task performance. *Journal of Personality and Social Psychology, 48,* 63–71.

Wood, W., Rhodes, N., & Whelan, M. (1989). Sex differences in positive well-being: A consideration of emotional style and marital status. *Psychological Bulletin, 106,* 249–264.

Wood, W., Wong, F. Y., & Chachere, J. G. (1991). Effects of media violence on viewers' aggression in unconstrained social interaction. *Psychological Bulletin, 109,* 371–383.

Worchel, S. (1974). The effect of three types of arbitrary thwarting on the instigation to aggression. *Journal of Personality, 42,* 300–318.

Worchel, S. (1986). The role of cooperation in reducing intergroup conflict. In S. Worchel & W. G. Austin (Eds.), *Psychology of intergroup relations* (2nd ed., pp. 288–304). Chicago: Nelson Hall.

Worchel, S., Arnold, S. E., & Baker, M. (1975). The effect of censorship on attitude change: The influence of censor and communication characteristics. *Journal of Applied Social Psychology, 5,* 222–239.

Worchel, S., & Shackelford, S. L. (1991). Groups under stress: The influence of group structure and environment on process and performance. *Personality and Social Psychology Bulletin, 17,* 640–647.

Word, C. O., Zanna, M. P., & Cooper, J. (1974). The nonverbal mediation of self-fulfilling prophecies in interracial interaction. *Journal of Experimental Social Psychology, 10,* 109–120.

Worth, L. T., Allison, S. T., & Messick, D. M. (1987). Impact of a group decision on perception of one's own and others' attitudes. *Journal of Personality and Social Psychology, 53,* 673–682.

Worth, L. T., & Mackie, D. M. (1987). Cognitive mediation of positive affect in persuasion. *Social Cognition, 5,* 76–94.

Wortman, C. B., & Brehm, J. W. (1975). Responses to uncontrollable outcomes: An integration of reactance theory and the learned helplessness model. In L. Berkowitz (Ed.), *Advances in experimental social psychology* (Vol. 8, pp. 277–336). New York: Academic Press.

Wright, E. F., Lüüs, C. A. E., & Christie, S. D. (1990). Does group discussion facilitate the use of consensus information in making causal attributions? *Journal of Personality and Social Psychology, 59,* 261–269.

Wright, J. C., & Dawson, V. L. (1988). Person perception and the bounded rationality of social judgment. *Journal of Personality and Social Psychology, 55,* 780–794.

Wright, J. C., Giammarino, M., & Parad, H. W. (1986). Social status in small groups: Individual-group similarity and the social "misfit." *Journal of Personality and Social Psychology, 50,* 523–536.

Wright, M. H., Zautra, A. J., & Braver, S. L. (1985). Distortion in control attributions for real life events. *Journal of Research in Personality, 19,* 54–71.

Wright, P. H. (1982). Men's friendships, women's friendships and the alleged inferiority of the latter. *Sex Roles, 8,* 1–20.

Wright, P. H., & Keple, T. W. (1981). Friends and parents of a sample of high school juniors: An exploratory study of relationship intensity and interpersonal rewards. *Journal of Marriage and the Family, 43,* 559–570.

Wright, R. A., & Contrada, R. J. (1986). Dating selectivity and interpersonal attraction: Toward a better understanding of the "elusive phenomenon." *Journal of Social and Personal Relationships, 3,* 131–148.

Wright, R. A., Wadley, V. G., Danner, M., & Phillips, P. N. (1992). Persuasion, reactance, and judgments of interpersonal appeal. *European Journal of Social Psychology, 22,* 85–91.

Wright, T. L., Ingraham, L. J. & Blackmer, D. R. (1985). Simultaneous study of individual differences and relationship effects in attraction. *Journal of Personality and Social Psychology, 47,* 1059–1062.

Wrightsman, L. S. (1991). *Psychology and the legal system* (2nd ed.). Belmont, CA: Brooks/Cole.

Wu, C., & Shaffer, D. R. (1987). Susceptibility to persuasive appeals as a function of source credibility and prior experience with the attitude object. *Journal of Personality and Social Psychology, 52,* 677–688.

Wuthnow, R. (1991). *Acts of compassion.* Princeton, NJ: Princeton University Press.

Wyer, R. S. (1974). Changes in meaning and halo effects in personality impression formation. *Journal of Personality and Social Psychology, 29,* 829–835.

Yalch, R. F. (1991). Memory in a jingle-jungle: Music as a mnemonic device in communicating advertising slogans. *Journal of Applied Psychology, 76,* 268–2

Yamagishi, T. (1986). The provision of a sanctioning system as a public good. *Journal of Personality and Social Psychology, 51,* 110–116.

Yarmey, A. D. (1979). *The psychology of eyewitness testimony.* New York: Free Press.

Yerkes, R. M., & Dodson, J. D. (1908). The relation of strength of stimulus to rapidity of habit formation. *Journal of Comparative Neurology and Psychology, 18,* 459–482.

Youngs, G. A., Jr. (1986). Patterns of threat and punishment reciprocity in a conflict setting. *Journal of Personality and Social Psychology, 51,* 541–546.

Yuille, J. C., & Tollestrup, P. A. (1990). Some effects of alcohol on eyewitness memory. *Journal of Applied Psychology, 75,* 268–273.

Zaccaro, S. J., & McCoy, M. C. (1988). The effects of task and interpersonal cohesiveness on performance of a disjunctive group task. *Journal of Applied Social Psychology, 18,* 837–851.

Zajonc, R. B. (1965). Social facilitation. *Science, 149,* 269–274.

Zajonc, R. B. (1968). Attitudinal effects of mere exposure. *Journal of Personality and Social Psychology Monograph Supplement, 9*(2), 1–27.

Zajonc, R. B. (1980). Compresence. In P. B. Paulus (Ed.), *Psychology of group influence* (pp. 35–60). Hillsdale, NJ: Erlbaum.

Zajonc, R. B. (1984). On the primacy of affect. *American Psychologist, 39,* 117–123.

Zajonc, R. B., Adelmann, P. K., Murphy, S. T., & Niedenthal, P. M. (1987). Convergence in physical appearance of spouses. *Motivation and Emotion, 11,* 335–346.

Zajonc, R. B., Heingartner, A., & Herman, E. M. (1969). Social enhancement and impairment of performance in the cockroach. *Journal of Personality and Social Psychology, 13,* 82–92.

Zajonc, R. B., Murphy, S. T., & Inglehart, M. (1989). Feeling and facial efference: Implications of the vascular theory of emotion. *Psychological Review, 96,* 395–416.

Zajonc, R. B., Shaver, P., Tavris, C., & Kreveld, D. V. (1972). Exposure, satiation, and stimulus discriminability. *Journal of Personality and Social Psychology, 21,* 270–280.

Zanna, M. P., & Cooper, J. (1974). Dissonance and the pill: An attribution approach to studying the arousal properties of dissonance. *Journal of Personality and Social Psychology, 29,* 703–709.

Zanna, M. P., & Rempel, J. K. (1988). Attitudes: A new look at an old concept. In D. Bar-Tal & A. Kruglanski (Eds.), *The social psychology of knowledge* (pp.315–334). New York: Cambridge University Press.

Zarate, M. A., & Smith, E. R. (1990). Person categorization and stereotyping. *Social Cognition, 8,* 161–185.

Zebrowitz, L. A., Kendall-Tackett, K., & Fafel, J. (1991a). The influence of children's facial maturity on parental expectations and punishment. *Journal of Experimental Child Psychology, 52,* 221–238.

Zebrowitz, L. A., & McDonald, S. M. (1991). The impact of litigants' babyfacedness and attractiveness on adjudications in small claims courts. *Law and Human Behavior, 15,* 603–624.

Zebrowitz, L. A., Tenenbaum, D. R., & Goldstein, L. H. (1991b). The impact of job applicants' facial maturity, gender, and academic achievement on hiring recommendations. *Journal of Appled Social Psychology, 21,* 525–548.

Zeisel, H. (1971). . . . And then there were none: The diminution of the federal jury. *University of Chicago Law Review, 38,* 710–724.

Zigler, E., Rubin, N., & Kaufman, J. (1988, May). Do abused children become abusive parents? *Parents,* pp. 100–104, 106.

Zillmann, D. (1978). Attribution and misattribution of excitatory reactions. In J. H. Harvey, W. Ickes, & R. F. Kidd (Eds.), *New directions in attribution research* (Vol. 2, pp. 335–368). Hillsdale, NJ: Erlbaum.

Zillmann, D. (1979). *Hostility and aggression.* Hillsdale, NJ: Erlbaum.

Zillmann, D. (1983). Arousal and aggression. In R. G. Geen & E. I. Donnerstein (Eds.), *Aggression: Theoretical and empirical reviews: Vol. l. Theoretical and methodological issues* (pp. 75–101). New York: Academic Press.

Zillmann, D. (1984). *Connections between sex and aggression.* Hillsdale, NJ: Erlbaum.

Zillmann, D. (1989). Effects of prolonged consumption of pornography. In D. Zillmann & J. Bryant (Eds.), *Pornography: Research advances and policy considerations* (pp. 127–157). Hillsdale, NJ: Erlbaum.

Zillmann, D., Baron, R., & Tamborini, R. (1981). Social costs of smoking: Effects of tobacco smoke on hostile behavior. *Journal of Applied Social Psychology, 11,* 548–561.

Zillmann, D., & Bryant, J. (1984). Effects of massive exposure to pornography. In N. M. Malamuth & E. I. Donnerstein (Eds.), *Pornography and sexual aggression* (pp. 115–138). New York: Academic Press.

Zillmann, D., Bryant, J., Cantor, J. R., & Day, K. D. (1975). Irrelevance of mitigating circumstances in retaliatory behavior at high levels of excitation. *Journal of Research in Personality, 9,* 282–293.

Zillmann, D., & Cantor, J. R. (1976). Effect of timing of information about mitigating circumstances on emotional responses to provocation and retaliatory behavior. *Journal of Experimental Social Psychology, 12,* 38–55.

Zillmann, D., Johnson, R. C., & Day, K. D. (1974). Attribution of apparent arousal and proficiency of recovery from sympathetic activation affecting excitation transfer to aggressive behavior. *Journal of Experimental Social Psychology, 10,* 503–515.

Zillmann, D., Katcher, A. H., & Milavsky, B. (1972). Excitation transfer from physical exercise to subsequent aggressive behavior. *Journal of Experimental Social Psychology, 8,* 247–259.

Zillmann, D., & Weaver, J. B. (1989). Pornography and men's sexual callousness toward women. In D. Zillmann & J. Bryant (Eds.), *Pornography: Research advances and policy considerations* (pp. 95–125). Hillsdale: Erlbaum.

Zimbardo, P. G. (1970). The human choice: Individuation, reason, and order versus deindividuation, impulse, and chaos. In W. J. Arnold & D. Levine (Eds.), *Nebraska Symposium on Motivation: 1969* (Vol. 17, pp. 237–307). Lincoln: University of Nebraska Press.

Zimbardo, P. G. (1973). On the ethics of intervention in human psychological research: With special reference to the Stanford prison experiment. *Cognition, 2,* 243–256.

Zimbardo, P. G. (1977). *Shyness.* New York: Jove.

Zimbardo, P. G. (1985, June). Laugh where we must, be candid where we can. *Psychology Today,* pp. 43–47.

Zimbardo, P. G., Banks, W. C., Haney, C., & Jaffe, D. (1973, April 8). The mind is a formidable jailer: A Pirandellian prison. *New York Times Magazine,* pp. 38–60.

Zuckerman, M., DePaulo, B. M., & Rosenthal, R. (1981). Verbal and nonverbal communication of deception. In L. Berkowitz (Ed.), *Advances in experimental social psychology* (Vol. 14, pp. 1–59). New York: Academic Press.

Zuckerman, M., Lazzaro, M. M., & Waldgeir, D. (1979). Undermining effects of the foot-in-the-door technique with extrinsic rewards. *Journal of Applied Social Psychology, 9,* 292–296.

Zweig, P. L. (1985). *Belly up.* New York: Crown.

Associates, p. 32.

mission of the publisher and author. **p. 313**: *Table 7.1* Benefit beat (1991, June 10). *Time*, p. 15. Copyright © 1991 The Time Inc. Magazine Company. Reprinted by permission. Album covers: "For Our Children," Courtesy Pediatric Aids Foundation; "Deadicated," Courtesy of Mikio, William Giese, The Grateful Dead, and Arista Records, Inc.; "Red, Hot, and Blue," © 1992 King Cole, Inc.; and "Tame Yourself," Courtesy of PETA. **p. 316**: © Gay Block. **p. 322**: © Jan Lukas 1985/Photo Researchers, Inc. **p. 329**: *Figure 7.10* Tesser, A., and Smith, J. (1980). Some effects of task relevance and friendship on helping: You don't always help the one you like. *Journal of Experimental Social Psychology, 16,* 582–590. Reprinted with permission of Academic Press and the authors. **p. 331**: © John Rogers/Woodfin Camp and Associates. **p. 332**: *Figure 7.11* Miller, D. T. (1977). Altruism and threat to a belief in a just world. *Journal of Experimental Social Psychology, 13,* 113–124. Reprinted with permission of Academic Press and the author. **p. 335**: © Rhoda Sidney/Stock Boston. **p. 337**: *Figure 7.12* Nadler, A., and Fisher, J. D. (1986). The role of threat to self-esteem and perceived control in recipient reactions to help: Theory development and empirical validation. In L. Berkowitz, (Ed.), *Advances in Experimental Social Psychology, 19,* 81–122. Reprinted with permission of Academic Press and the authors. **p. 340**: © Peter Blakely/SABA.

Chapter 8: **p. 344 (Opener)**: © Tom Walker/Stock Boston. **p. 349**: © AP/ Wide World Photos. **p. 354**: © Mimi Forsyth/ Monkmeyer Press Photo Service. **p. 359**: © J. Berndt/Stock Boston. **p. 361**: *Figure 8.2A* Baron R. A., and Ransberger, B. M. (1978). Ambient temperature and the occurrence of collective violence: The 'Long, Hot Summer' revisited. *Journal of Personality and Social Psychology, 36,* 351–360. Copyright 1978 by the American Psychological Association. Reprinted by permission of the publisher and author. *Figure 8.2B* Carlsmith, J. M., and Anderson, C. A. (1979). Ambient temperature and the occurrence of collective violence: A new analysis. *Journal of Personality and Social Psychology, 37,* 337–344. Copyright 1979 by the American Psychological Association. Reprinted by permission of publisher and author. **p. 366**: © Benny Stumbo/SYGMA. **p. 370**: © Comstock, Inc. **p. 372**: *Figure 8.5* Adapted from Huesmann, L. R., and Eron, L. D. (Eds.) (1986). *Television and the Aggressive Child: A Cross-National Comparison.* Reprinted by permission of Lawrence Erlbaum Associates, Inc. **p. 374**: © UPI/ Bettman Photos. **p. 376**: © Bob Mahoney. **p. 377**: *Table 8.1* Burt, M. C. (1980). Cultural myths and supports for rape. *Journal of Personality and Social Psychology, 38,* 217–230. Copyright 1980 by the American Psychological Association. Reprinted by permission. **p. 379**: *Figure 8.6* Donnerstein, E., and Hallam, J. (1978). Facilitating effects of erotica on aggression against women. *Journal of Personality and Social Psychology, 36,* 1270–1277. Copyright 1978 by the American Psychological Association. Adapted by permission. **p. 382**: *Figure 8.7* Adapted with permission of The Free Press, a division of Macmillan, Inc., from *The Question of Pornography: Research Findings and Policy Implications* by Ed-

ward Donnerstein, Daniel Linz, and Steven Penrod. Copyright © 1987 by The Free Press. Data from Donnerstein, E., and Berkowitz, L. (1981). Victim reactions in aggressive erotic films as a factor in violence against women. *Journal of Personality and Social Psychology, 41,* 710–724. Copyright 1981 by the American Psychological Association. Adapted by permission of the publisher and author. **p. 383**: *Figure 8.8* Malamuth, N. M., and Check, J. V. P. (1981). The effects of mass media exposure on acceptance of violence against women. A field experiment. *Journal of Research in Personality, 15,* 436–446. Reprinted with permission of Academic Press and the authors. **p. 385**: *Figure 8.9* Straus, M. A. (1979). Measuring intrafamily conflict and violence: The conflict tactics (CT) scales. *Journal of Marriage and the Family, 48,* 465–479. Copyrighted 1987/1979 by the National Council on Family Relations, 3989 Central Ave. N.E., Suite #550, Minneapolis, MN 55421. Reprinted by permission. **p. 387**: © AP/WIDE WORLD PHOTOS, Inc.

Part III: **p. 392 (Opener)**: © Comstock.

Chapter 9: **p. 394 (Opener)**: Dan Budnik/Woodfin Camp and Associates. **p. 398**: Glasheen Graphics. **p. 400** *Figure 9.2* A classic case of suggestibility. In Sherif, M. (1936) *The Psychology of Social Norms.* Copyright 1936 by Harper & Row, Publishers, Inc. Reprinted by permission of HarperCollins Publishers. **p. 402**: © William Vandivert. **p. 405**: *Figure 9.4* Cialdini, R. B., Reno, R. R., and Kallgren, C. A. (1990). A focus theory of normative conduct: Recycling the concept of norms to reduce littering in public places. *Journal of Personality and Social Psychology, 58,* 1015–1026. Copyright 1990 by the American Psychological Association. Reprinted by permission of the publisher and author. **p. 407**: *Figure 9.5* Berndt, T. J. (1979). Developmental changes in conformity to peers and parents. *Developmental Psychology, 15,* 606–616. Copyright 1979 by the American Psychological Association. Reprinted by permission of the publisher and author. **p. 414**: *Cartoon 9.1* This cartoon by Lee Lorenz is reproduced from *Disorderly Conduct,* Verbatim Excerpts from Actual Court Cases, selected by Rodney R. Jones, Charles M. Sevilla, and Gerald F. Uelman, by permission of W. W. Norton and Company, Inc. Illustrations copyright © Lee Lorenz. **p. 417**: © 1984 Peter Menzel/Wheeler Pictures. **p. 423**: © Archiv fur Kunst und Geschichte, Berlin. **p. 425**: © 1965 by Stanley Milgram. From the film *Obedience* distributed by New York University Film Library and Pennsylvania State University, PCR. **p. 427**: *Figure 9.6* From Milgram, S. (1974). *Obedience to Authority.* Copyright © 1974 by Stanley Milgram. Reprinted by permission of HarperCollins, Publishers, Inc. **p. 428**: *Figure 9.7* From Milgram, S. (1974). *Obedience to Authority.* Copyright © 1974 by Stanley Milgram. Reprinted by permission of HarperCollins, Publishers, Inc. **p. 433**: © Alexandra Avakian/ Contact Press Images. **p. 435**: *Figure 9.8* Latané, B. (1981). The psychology of social impact. *American Psychologist, 36,*

Publisher, Consulting Psychologists Press, Inc., Palo Alto, CA 94303, from *Transformational Leadership Development: Manual for the Multifactor Leadership Questionnaire,* by Bernard M. Bass, Ph.D., and Bruce J. Avolio, Ph.D. Copyright 1990 by Consulting Psychologists Press, Inc. All rights reserved. Further reproduction is prohibited without the Publisher's written consent. **p. 608**: *Figure 13.4* Fiedler, F. E. (1967). *A Theory of Leadership Effectiveness.* New York: McGraw-Hill. Reprinted by permission of the author. **p. 612**: *Figure 13.5* Deci, E. L. (1971). Effects of externally mediated rewards on intrinsic motivation. *Journal of Psychology and Social Psychology, 18,* 105–115. Copyright 1971 by the American Psychological Association. Reprinted by permission of the publisher and author. **p. 613**: *Figure 13.6* Greenberg, J. (1988). Equity and workplace status: A field experiment. *Journal of Applied Psychology, 73,* 606–613. Copyright 1988 by the American Psychological Association. Reprinted by permission of the publisher and author. **p. 616**: *Figure 13.7* Marks, M. L., Mirvis, P. H., Hackett, E. J., and Grady, J. F., Jr. (1986). Employee participation in a quality of work life, productivity, and absenteeism. *Journal of Applied Psychology, 71,* 61–69. Copyright 1986 by the American Psychological Association. Reprinted by permission of the publisher and author. **p. 618**: Robin Bogart. **p. 622**: © California Raisin Advisory Board. **p. 623**: © American Association of Advertising Agencies. **p. 625**: *Figure 13.8* Greenwald, A. G., Spangenberg, E. R., Pratkanis, A. R., and Eskenazi, J. (1991). Double-blind tests of subliminal self-help

audiotapes. *Psychological Science, 2,* 119–122. Reprinted by permission of the publisher. **p. 627**: © Yada Claassen/Jeroboam, Inc. **p. 631**: *Figure 13.9* Schachter, S., Ouellette, R., Whittle, B., and Gerin, W. (1987). Effects of trend and of profit or loss on the tendency to sell stock. *Basic and Applied Psychology, 8,* 259-71. Hillsdale, NJ: Lawrence Erlbaum Associates, Inc. Reprinted by permission.

Chapter 14:   **p. 636 (Opener)**: © Paul Conklin/PhotoEdit. **p. 642**: *Table 14.1* Sarason, I. G., Johnson, J. H., and Siegel, J. M. (1978). Assessing the impact of life changes: Development of the life experiences survey. *Journal of Consulting and Clinical Psychology, 46,* 932–946. Copyright 1978 by the American Psychological Association. Reprinted by permission. **p. 644**: © Peter Menzel/Stock Boston. **p. 645**: *Figure 14.2* Baum, A., and Valins, S. (1977). *Architecture and Social Behavior: Psychological Studies of Social Density.* Hillsdale, NJ: Lawrence Erlbaum Associates, Inc. Reprinted by permission. **p. 646**: © David C. Baxter/University of Cincinnati. **p. 651**: *Table 14.2* Reprinted with permission from *Journal of Psychology, 55, 2.* Copyright 1987, Duke University Press. **p. 653**: © Jeffrey M. Hamilton/Stock Boston. **p. 658**: © Stacy Pick/Stock Boston. **p. 663**: © Dominique Aubert/SYGMA. **p. 667**: © Audrey Gottleib/Monkmeyer. **p. 673**: Bob Daemmrich/Stock Boston. **p. 675**: *Figure 14.6* Terre, L., Drabman, R. S., and Speer, P. Health-related behaviors in media. *Journal of Applied Social Psychology, 21,* 1303–1319. Adapted by permission.

Name Index

Subject Index